5/01

# Lesbian Histories and Cultures

Garland Refrence Library of the Social Sciences (Vol. 1008)

# Advisory Board

# Lesbian Histories and Cultures: An Encyclopedia

Bonnie Zimmerman
*Editor*

Garland Publishing, Inc.
A member of the Taylor & Francis Group
New York and London
2000

Published in 2000 by
Garland Publishing Inc.
A Member of the Taylor & Francis Group
19 Union Square West
New York, NY 10003

10  9  8  7  6  5  4  3  2  1

Library of Congress Cataloging-in-Publication Data

Lesbian histories and cultures : an encyclopedia / Bonnie Zimmerman, editor.
        p. cm.—(Encyclopedia of lesbian and gay histories and cultures ; v. 1) (Garland
    reference library of the social sciences ; vol. 1008)
    Includes bibliographical references and index.
    ISBN 0-8153-1920-7 (alk. paper)
    1. Lesbianism—Encyclopedias. 2. Lesbians—Encyclopedias.  I. Series. II. Zimmerman,
Bonnie.

HQ75.5.L4395 1999
306.76′63′03 21—dc21                                                    99-045010

Printed on acid-free, 250-year-life paper
Manufactured in the United States of America

# Contents

This book is dedicated to

# Introduction

Bonnie Zimmerman and George E. Haggerty

*The Encyclopedia of Lesbian and Gay Histories and Cultures* in two volumes is the latest, and we hope the richest, in a long line of publications that attempt to open up for contemporary readers the complex history and wide cultural diversity of lesbian and gay life. Unlike earlier endeavors, however, which tended to limit the kinds of questions that could be asked about the past, these volumes try to avoid the stigma conventionally attached to "homosexuality" and look instead at examples of same-sex desire in different cultures at different times. They are the product of an age in which self-definition is challenged by cultural urgency of various kinds and when lesbian and gay concerns have moved out from the shadows into the bright light of national and international politics. What better moment to undo the misconceptions of the past and to reclaim the histories and cultures that have been denied us? In doing so, we hope to be seen not as appropriating the past but rather as making it available for all sorts of purposes, including but not limited to an increase in present-day awareness. Too often we have been told by others who we are or where we came from. It is time not just to claim our place in history and culture but also to negotiate with the histories and cultures to which we might most closely relate.

## History

The study of homosexuality can be said to have begun in 1869, when a generation of medical doctors established the profession of sexology, the medical and supposedly scientific study of sex. Among its earliest objects of study was "inversion"—a term that signified a range of behaviors and attitudes that would later be classed under the term *homosexuality*. Inversion redefined same-sex desire as an aspect of human personality or essential being, not a sin-laden act against nature. Many of the most prominent figures of early sexology—such as Richard von Krafft-Ebing and Havelock Ellis—described the invert, or homosexual, in excruciating and, from the perspective of today, stigmatizing or, as contemporary lesbian scholar Lillian Faderman put it, morbidifying, detail. A century later, the prominent French historian and theorist Michel Foucault would point to this construction of the modern homosexual as a signal moment in the history of sexuality.

Although homosexuality became known as "the love that dare not speak its name," in fact, even in the nineteenth century there were many names used for homosexuality: some, like *bugger*, *sodomite*, and *tribade*, referring to the specific sexual behaviors that men and women performed with members of their own gender, and others, like *homosexual*, *invert*, and *Urning*, referring to the identities that were being constructed around these behaviors. The shift from behavior to identity was also to have an unexpected impact: the beginnings of a political movement based upon that identity. Among the early generations of sexologists were several individuals who themselves identified as homosexuals and directed their scholarly activity toward both the elimination of prejudice and discrimination and the demand for equal human rights. These individuals—including Karl Maria Ulrichs, Edward Carpenter, Magnus Hirschfeld, and Anna Rüling—were pioneers in uniting scholarship and activism, as their descendants would do several generations later.

The period between roughly 1900 and 1930 was one of considerable intellectual activity in the areas of sexology and literature, particularly. But economic crisis and political repression in the United States and Europe would drive nascent gay and lesbian communities, with their potential for scholarly research and creative activity, underground. Although individuals produced monumental work, in general academic institutions generally avoided and suppressed gay and lesbian scholarship. These individuals have become heroic role models: Alfred Kinsey, for example, with his groundbreaking sexological studies, and Jeannette Foster, who self-published an extraordinary study of lesbianism in literature. With the exception of Kinsey, these figures were unable to generate an ongoing academic movement or produce individual scholars to carry on their work. Before lesbian and gay studies could become a reality, something else needed to happen. That "something else" was the gay liberation movement, which burst into public consciousness in 1969 when the patrons of the Stonewall Inn in New York City's Greenwich Village fought back against a police raid. Although political activism and organizing had existed throughout the 1950s and 1960s and had accelerated at the end of the latter decade, the three nights of what has become known as the Stonewall Rebellion galvanized a new generation. Inspired by the civil rights movement in particular, and with experience in that movement as well as in the student, antiwar, and women's liberation movements, gay and lesbian activists organized and mobilized their own movement to end the social, political, and cultural oppression of homosexuals.

Many of these activists were students in universities. They sought to bring their academic work to the service of activism and to apply their political consciousness to their scholarly work. In the same way that African American studies grew out of the civil rights and black power movements, and women's studies out of the women's liberation movement, so did gay and lesbian studies have its beginnings in the gay liberation movement. At that time, very few academics had the psychological and material security to be openly gay or lesbian and to focus their scholarly work on the study of homosexuality.

Lesbian and gay professors had long lived more or less comfortably in closets within the ivory towers; however, the growing gay and lesbian movement impelled some professors and graduate students to begin to organize within professional institutions and associations.

Gay and lesbian scholars first began to organize caucuses within professional associations in the early 1970s. For example, the gay caucus of the Modern Language Association first met in 1973 and soon organized large and enthusiastic sessions at the annual MLA meetings throughout the 1970s. Caucuses were also formed in 1974 in the American Anthropological Association and the American Sociological Association. The Lesbian and Gay Caucus in the MLA and its more scholarly counterpart, the Gay Studies Division, continue to thrive, as do the caucuses of the AAA and the ASA. Similar caucuses and divisions exist within the professional associations of historians, musicologists, art historians, psychologists, and so on. These caucuses and divisions have played an important part in opening up the academic profession to new scholarship and new ways of thinking, thus being directly responsible for much of the knowledge collected in this encyclopedia.

A second important source of knowledge came from outside formal academic institutions. From the early 1970s until the present, groundbreaking work has been done by scholars and writers not affiliated with any institutions. These independent scholars worked without financial resources or public recognition, at least until their books and articles were finally published. For some, the Gay Academic Union, founded in New York City in 1974, provided solidarity and support. The GAU, while ostensibly open to both men and women, did, like many other political groups, became a primarily male organization. Lesbians turned to other venues, including lesbian feminist collectives, women's studies programs, and feminist newspapers and journals, to produce their work.

By the mid-1970s, both gay men and lesbians in the United States had produced a substantial body of important work. Jonathan Ned Katz had published *Gay American History,* a collection of primary documents that would shape a generation of scholars; Beth Hodges had produced two journal issues on lesbian writing and publishing (one in *Margins* and the other in the influential lesbian feminist journal *Sinister Wisdom*); and under the leadership of John deCecco, the *Journal of Homosexuality* had been established as the first scholarly journal in Gay and Lesbian Studies. By 1981, we would also have seen Carroll Smith-Rosenberg's paradigm-building article, "The Female World of Love and Ritual" (published in the first issue of what would become the premier feminist scholarly journal, *Signs*), John Boswell's rewriting of the history of oppression, *Christianity, Social Tolerance, and Homosexuality,* independent scholar J. R. Roberts' *Black Lesbians: A Bibliography,* and Lillian Faderman's *Surpassing the Love of Men.* Lesbian and gay scholarship was making its mark on the map.

This energy emerged in several places at once, not only in the United States. French social and cultural theorists like Michel Foucault and Guy Hocquenghem used the political urgency of the student uprisings of 1968 to retheorize gay liberation from a post-Marxist perspective, while Luce Irigaray and Monique Wittig revised Lacanian psychoanalysis in ways that offered new paradigms for discussing gender and sexuality in a cultural context. The Australian Dennis Altman published *Homosexual Liberation and Oppression,* which investigated the social and personal consequences of internalized homophobia. In England, Mary McIntosh and Kenneth Plummer considered the ways in which homosexual identities are socially constructed; at the same time, Jeffrey Weeks traced the emergence of lesbian and gay identities. All produced foundational work that helped to give direction to the early gay liberation movement as well as to academic inquiry in the area of lesbian and gay studies. At the same time, artists, writers, and filmmakers throughout North America, Europe, and beyond were producing impressive accounts of lesbian and gay experiences, as dozens of entries in these volumes will attest.

In the 1980s, lesbian and gay scholarship would become formalized as a field of study in the United States, Canada, and a number of European countries, most particularly the United Kingdom and the Netherlands. At times Europe has taken the lead: indeed, the conference "Homosexuality, Which Homosexuality?" held in Amsterdam in 1987 holds the distinction of being the first international lesbian and gay academic conference of the contemporary era. Gay and lesbian studies is thoroughly institutionalized in the Netherlands and is growing in strength throughout Europe, Australia, and New Zealand.

In the United States, at the turn of the millennium, gay and lesbian scholarship is growing in all fields of academic endeavor. It is no longer marginal but now occupies a central place in academic publishing, curricula, and conferences. Not only are lesbian and gay scholars increasingly able to identify as such in the classroom and in scholarly work, but lesbian, gay, bisexual, and queer ideas and theories are addressed with respect by heterosexual colleagues. Lesbian and gay studies programs have emerged at several prominent institutions, and students there are as likely to take a course on the "homosexual" as on the "heterosexual" past. Like ethnic studies and women's studies previously, lesbian and gay studies has left an indelible mark on what we are permitted to know.

This encyclopedia offers accounts of the most important international developments in lesbian and gay history and attempts to assess the state of lesbian and gay culture around the world. This makes it possible to see what kinds of issues and concerns lesbian and gay scholars have had in common around the world. It also suggest how deeply varied has been the experience of those who are attracted to members of their own gender at different times and in different cultures. From one perspective, these differences are so great that no term like *gay* or *queer* or even *homosexual* can encompass them. To see sexual identity as a lens through which to view an impossibly broad range of human experience is to risk obscuring specific and very important differences; but not insisting on this perspective is to be in danger of overlooking profoundly suggestive similarities that make connections across time and space.

## Methodology

For many readers of these volumes, an immediate question may be raised as to why there are separate volumes on lesbian histories and cultures and gay histories and cultures. Some encyclopedias and reference works are co-sexual, while others have focused on either one or the other, most often concentrating on lesbian issues separately from gay male. For this publication, the editors chose to develop separate volumes, edited independently but with close cooperation and communication.

Why should lesbian and gay histories and cultures be organized and written as separate volumes? We have done so first because this assures that both histories receive full and unbiased attention. Historically, lesbianism has not always been addressed equally within gay studies. It has been assumed that lesbianism is more difficult to identify historically, more hidden and silenced, less accessible to the scholar. While it is true that chroniclers and historians have addressed female lives less thoroughly in general than male lives, these assumptions may flow less from what exists than from what we have looked for and the questions we have asked. Focusing an entire volume on lesbian histories and cultures assures that full attention be paid to recovering and collecting a full range of information that currently exists.

Moreover, as these two volumes will demonstrate, the difference of gender has always been significant in the conceptualization and experiences of lesbianism and male homosexuality and in the experiences of individuals and communities. Lesbians and gay men have shared many aspects of life—those that flow from self-affirmation and those that flow from resistance to heterosexism and homophobia—but they have also developed in profoundly different ways. Lesbians are marked as female and gay men as male, no matter what the rhetoric about inversion, and in patriarchal systems, gender matters. Feminism, in particular, has been a potent force in lesbian lives from at least the nineteenth century to the present. The more public presence of male homosexuality has often led to different emphases within legal and political movements. The degree to which male lives are recorded while female lives are ignored or suppressed affects the historical record. The fields of lesbian studies and gay studies have, until very recently, developed in an independent, though related, fashion. For these reasons, and many others, we believe that at this time readers will be best served by separate volumes. In the future, editors may choose a different strategy.

## Definitions

The most difficult question, of course, is that of definition. What do we mean by "gay" and "lesbian"? Are we only documenting evidence of homosexual behavior? Are there rules of inclusion/exclusion for different kinds of sexual behavior or identity? How do we relate to the "state of alliance" that exists in many contexts, especially in North America, between "lesbian," "gay," "bisexual," and "transgender" identities, or to the reconditioned umbrella term *queer,* which has preoccupied both the academy and many outside it over the last ten years? It would be disingenuous for the editors to say that the question of sexual behavior and self-definition—that is, did she or didn't he—did not often influence inclusion or that the issue of sexual identity did not figure prominently in the entry lists suggested and reviewed by advisory editors and by specialists in certain fields. But neither editor sees "homosexuality" as a transhistorical or transcultural condition that can be analyzed in, say, classical Greece, modern Japan, and the last twenty-five years in this history of the United States in anything like similar terms. In fact, one of the intentions of the entries included is to demonstrate the range of difference within what we loosely call lesbian history and culture and gay history and culture.

At the same time, none of us can ignore that we live in a culture in which the past has been appropriated to various ends. Those of us who are lesbian and gay have participated in this appropriation as much or as little as our nonlesbian and nongay contemporaries. The effect of this appropriation is that for better or worse we have a very rich lesbian and gay heritage that itself needs to be documented in a volume such as this. In other words, while there may be no proof that Alexander the Great or Sor Juana Inés de la Cruz were what we would call "gay" or "lesbian," gay culture and lesbian culture in the twentieth century has used such figures in defining itself and it would be a mistake to ignore this rich layering of historical detail. In this sense, the encyclopedia is archaeological: a figure, a movement, or a sexual practice might be included for its own sake or an account of its own sexual practice, of course, but it might also be included because it has been central to lesbian or gay history and mythology. This is not the same dynamic as "strategic essentialism," whereby historical understanding is sacrificed for an urgent political end; rather, it is a "practical constructionism," which tries to use historical and cultural difference to tell the story of lesbian and gay culture today as well as other stories about other cultures at other times.

For a similar reason we do not call this an encyclopedia of queer culture. "Queer" has had an important recent function in challenging the notion of sexual identity and insisting on a coalition between and among lesbian, gay, bisexual, and transgendered subjects, as well as people of color, sympathetic straights, and others. At the same time, it has created political difficulties of its own. For some, it suggests that sexual identity is the only basis from which to resist hegemonic culture. For others, it seems to dismiss the possibility of those gay and lesbian identities that have produced a rich intellectual and political culture. Queer theory, which was hailed as an answer to the seeming dead end of identity politics, has had to be rethought in light of challenges from grassroots activists as well as the rigorous self-questioning of the theorists themselves. Many of these issues are discussed in entries collected herein. It seems to us, however, that as happy as we might be to "queer" the past, we have not yet reached the point at which the differences that "lesbian" and "gay" imply can be completely ignored. On the other hand, in answer to queer theorists like Michael Warner and others who argue against the minoritizing stigma of lesbian and gay identity and suggest "queer" as an alternative identity that can resist institutionalization and various separatist or assimilative moves in an aggressively generalizing attempt to challenge the ascendancy of the normal, we offer this encyclopedia. If it does anything, it shows that the "normal" is nothing more than a fiction that has been challenged in various ways in various cultures at various times with varying success. In this sense, then, it is an encyclopedia of queer histories and cultures after all.

## How to Use the Encyclopedia

This encyclopedia is intended for a wide audience, including students, scholars in all fields, and the general public, who is interested in the state of lesbian and gay research. All efforts have been made to write entries in "user-friendly" language, avoiding jargon and technical language that would place a barrier between the experts and their readers. At the same time, the authors have maintained a high level of scholarship, in-corporating both passionate engagement and scholarly objectivity. The encyclopedia addresses areas of academic and political controversy, attempting always to address multiple points of view and varied theoretical perspectives. In particular, the authors and editors have worked hard to pay close attention to the inclusivity of race, class, and ethnicity.

The editors are particularly proud of the exceptional group of authors who have contributed entries to these volumes. These include some of the most famous names in the field of lesbian and gay studies as well as junior faculty and graduate students who will carry it forth into the future, independent scholars and writers like those who initiated this field, and the political and community activists who have maintained the important connection between scholarship and activism. These authors position themselves everywhere along the continuum of sexualities: lesbian, gay, bisexual, heterosexual, transgender, and queer. Readers will find both similarities and differences in the selection and treatment of topics in the two volumes. In a minority of cases, entries may overlap. The editors suggest that in the case of general topics—for example, sexology or history or individual countries—readers turn to the entries in each volume for a full treatment. It will prove instructive to see how a topic remains similar, or changes subtly, depending on who writes the entry and from what perspective. Other topics may appear in one volume and not the other: this is not necessarily a sign that an entry is only of interest to one group or the other. The editors found that to limit certain topics to one entry allowed them to cover many more topics over the range of two volumes. In every case, the editors hope that the two volumes are complementary in ways that will benefit users of either volume.

The reader will find that in the places where topics overlap, the entries together create a quilt or web of knowledge, one entry bordering on or leading to many others. For the student who is focused on one very specific question, each entry gives a general overview; for the browser it will lead to many additional topics and questions to be addressed in other entries.

To assist the reader in seeing the connections among the various entries included here, each is followed by a list of cross-referenced entries that relate to or expand it. In addition, each entry includes a bibliography with the most important and easily accessible titles. In the case of biographies, these include secondary rather than primary texts. Complete books are listed where possible; in addition, major articles are included. It is possible to use the book to study various topics in lesbian and gay studies. To assist the reader, we include a guide to the entries by topic. We also think, however, that these are volumes in which to browse: what better way to spend a few hours than to wend a path through a past (or a present) that is both foreign and familiar.

Readers will note that the encyclopedia does not insist upon rigid consistency in the use of certain terms. Authors have been free to use lesbian, gay, homosexual, bisexual, or queer as is appropriate to the particular requirements of their topics. Entries may also use cultural designations interchangeably, either because of personal preference or historical and political context. Different entries on related topics may emphasize different aspects of the subjects; once again, the editors have insisted upon factual consistency and accuracy while permitting individuality and even a touch of idiosyncracy.

No encyclopedia can be truly comprehensive. We could not include every topic, survey every historical period and every region of the world, or include every individual whose life included same-sex relationships. Biographical entries, in particular, needed to be selective, especially since we have included living figures. There has been an explosion of prominent figures who have "come out of the closet" in recent years, and were everyone to be included, this encyclopedia would be seriously imbalanced toward the present. Moreover, it is difficult to know who will have a long-lasting influence in the future. In considering these problems, the editors have chosen those figures who were the first in their particular fields, or who have already had unquestionable influence and notoriety. The editors recognize that our choices will be controversial, that while anyone will have chosen certain figures, in other cases, different choices might have been made.

The entries as a group move across the disciplines, across historical periods, and across cultures and nations. Some are general and expansive, others limited and particular. The editors have worked hard with the members of the advisory board to make the selections comprehensive, and both the range of fields and the entries within various fields have been the product of much thought and debate. The contributors have also worked to expand fields and define areas in a way that has made our work easier. We are grateful for the tireless efforts of everyone involved with this project.

Neither the editors nor the contributors intend these volumes to codify knowledge in the fields of lesbian and gay history and culture. These are by their natures ever-changing, and there will always be debate about what constitutes them as fields and how they are best represented historically. We hope that these volumes will participate in these debates and even provoke them. Of course, we also think that the debates will be more informed as the result of the wealth of material that is included here. There will always be a certain amount of fragmentation of information and gaps in the knowledge of these fields precisely because secrecy resulting from persecution and ignorance masquerading as science have been so strong a part of their representation historically. If lesbian and gay history and culture as told by lesbian and gay subjects (or those who identify with them) has had to struggle to find its place in contemporary letters, then this encyclopedia represents a new stage, attempting as it does to open up questions that previous encyclopedias of homosexuality considered closed.

## Acknowledgments by Bonnie Zimmerman
The editor gratefully acknowledges support from research, scholarship, and creative-activity grants and a College of Arts and Letters mini-grant, both at San Diego State University. The Research Committee of the College of Arts and Letters graciously bent its rules to provide support for the entire three-year life of this project. I thank them, especially the chair, Joanne Ferraro. I also thank the Department of Women's Studies and its faculty for the support, resources, and understanding extended to me.

This work could not have been completed without the assistance of two excellent research assistants, Sue Dunlap and Anna Andrade, whose commitment and diligence were exemplary. I particularly thank Anna, who nurtured this volume as her own project and who gave selflessly of her time and intelligence.

The editor owes a debt of thanks to many individuals for their advice in constructing the entry list and identifying and locating contributors. First, thanks is due to the superb scholars who served on the advisory board: Gloria Anzaldúa, Evelyn Blackwood, Ellen Broidy, Charlotte Bunch, Carolyn Dinshaw, Oliva M. Espín, Lillian Faderman, Sally R. Munt, Vivien Ng, Ruthann Robson, Judith Schuyf, Barbara Smith, Verta Taylor, and Martha Vicinus. Their advice was invaluable in every way, from modifying the entry list to counseling me on scholarly and ethical issues.

I also thank Wayne Dynes for his work on the *Encyclopedia of Homosexuality*, which provided a starting point for the current edition.

Many individuals provided advice about different aspects of the project, from how to organize entries on the sciences or religion to how to locate writers for particularly difficult entries. Among these distinguished individuals are Judith Mayne, Martha Mockus, Karla Jay, Lepa Mladjenovich, Leila J. Rupp, Sandra Harding, Susan E. Cayleff, Elizabeth Say, Terry Castle, Estelle Freedman, and Marcia Hermansen. I am particularly grateful to those individuals who helped me locate writers for international entries. They include Robert Howes, Judith Schuyf, Kati Mustola, and Pere Cruells, as well as the editors of a number of books—including Magda Mueller, Kate Griffin, Monika Reinfelder, and Peter Drucker—who shared the names and addresses of many of their contributors.

I am fortunate to have worked with the supportive staff of Garland Publishing, beginning with my first editor, Gary Kuris (whose departure was deeply saddening but, fortunately, not disastrous), and continuing with Marianne Lown, Leo Balk, Richard Steins, and Joanne Daniels. I am also grateful for the help I received from Jason Goldfarb and from another of Garland's encyclopedia editors, Sally Mitchell.

I received valuable assistance in obtaining illustrations for this volume from many of my contributors. I also want to thank Tee A. Corinne, Morgan Gwenwald, and Lynda Koolish for their generous donations of photographs from their own collections.

Identifying and locating contributors was made considerably easier due to the existence of the *CLAGS Directory of Lesbian and Gay Studies*, compiled by the Center for Lesbian and Gay Studies of the City University of New York. Also invaluable as resources were the E-Directory of Lesbigay Scholars, maintained by Louie Crew of Rutgers University; the Lesac list, maintained by Amy T. Goodloe; and the WILD-List, maintained by Eva Isaksson. I particularly thank these Internet pioneers for their contribution to the infrastructure of lesbian and gay scholarship.

To all of the contributors, whose names appear in a separate list, I owe a special debt for sharing their expertise and goodwill. I am also grateful to a number of individuals who helped me in the editing process, including Jane Gurko, Laurie Hatfield, Anna Andrade, Edith J. Benkov, and Holly Ransom. In addition, a number of students assisted in locating missing data for various entries, including Anna Andrade, Dawn Comeau, Andrea Dottolo, Melanie Green, Jennifer Higley, Patricia R. Hoban, and Claire H. Jackson.

I also thank the translators: Holly Ransom, Jutta Bailey, Pina Sylvers, Robert García, Ann Puntch, and Roma Ciesla.

I have been particularly fortunate to have as a coeditor George Haggerty, University of California, Riverside. I am privileged to have worked with him on a previous project, and his wisdom and collegiality have been inspirational. Although we prepared our volumes separately, we consulted and commiserated with each other in ways that made the production of an encyclopedia a pleasure, as well as a responsibility.

Finally, no acknowledgment would be complete without a tribute to the thousands of unsung heroes in and out of academia and the lesbian and gay movement whose courageous and often lonely efforts to battle the prevailing taboos against research into, and open discussion of, lesbianism have at last succeeded in making this work possible.

In conclusion, I thank my life partner, Berlene Rice, for her forbearance in enduring my long hours at the office and equally long hours of obsession and anxiety. Without her support and reassurance, I would not have been able to complete this work, or any other.

# Contributors

**Jennifer Abod** has trained women in broadcasting, established feminist radio programs on community radio, and worked as a feature reporter, moderator, talk show host, and news anchor on commercial and public radio. She is the producer of "A Radio Profile of Audre Lorde" and was cofounder and singer of the New Haven Women's Liberation Rock Band (1970–1976).

**Julie Abraham**, an Australian citizen living in the United States, teaches English and women's studies at Emory University, Atlanta, Georgia. She is the author of *Are Girls Necessary? Lesbian Writing and Modern Histories* (1996), the editor of *Diana: A Strange Autobiography* (1995), and writes reviews for the *Nation* and the *Women's Review of Books*.

**Kate Adams** holds a Ph.D. in American studies from the University of Texas, Austin, where she wrote a dissertation entitled "Paper Lesbians: Feminist Publishing and the Politics of Lesbian Identity, 1950–1990." Her essays can be found in *Lesbian Texts and Contexts* (1990), *Tilting the Tower* (1994), *Listening to Silences* (1994), and the *Journal of Homosexuality*.

**Lisa Albrecht** is associate professor of writing at the General College of the University of Minnesota, Minneapolis, where she teaches underprepared students. She also teaches women's studies. She coedited (with Rose M. Brewer) *Bridges of Power: Women's Multicultural Alliances* (1990). She is vice chair of the Minneapolis Commission on Civil Rights.

**Ilene D. Alexander**, while developing essays from her dissertation in American studies at the University of Iowa, "Learning in Other Ways: A History of a Feminist Pedagogy in the US," also works on *Never Say Uncle*, a memoir of the life and search for her gay uncle, now "gone missing" for twenty-five years. She teaches college writing and literature courses at the University of Minnesota in Minneapolis.

**Christina Allan** is an assignment editor for *Outword*.

**Davida J. Alperin** is an associate professor of political science at the University of Wisconsin, River Falls. Her research interests include black-Jewish relations, coalitions building, the political significance of collective memory, and gay and lesbian politics. She lives with her life partner and their son in St. Paul, Minnesota.

**Rebecca T. Alpert** is the codirector of the Women's Studies Program and assistant professor of religion and women's studies at Temple University, Philadelphia. Her most recent book is *Like Bread on the Seder Plate: Jewish Lesbians and the Transformation of Tradition* (1997). Alpert was ordained a rabbi from the Reconstructionist Rabbinical College in 1976.

**Meryl Altman**, associate professor of English and women's studies coordinator at DePauw University, Greencastle, Indiana, was educated at Swarthmore College in Pennsylvania and also attended Columbia University, New York City. She is working on a book about sexuality and politics in the work of Simone de Beauvoir, Doris Lessing, and other pre–"second wave" women writers.

**Deborah P. Amory** received her Ph.D. in anthropology from Stanford University, Stanford, California, in 1994. Her research explores identity politics in Swahili-speaking societies; popular culture and lesbian identity in the United States, and homosexuality in Africa. She teaches at Purchase College, State University of New York.

**Irene Anderson**, M.Ed., is the director of the Oasis Center for Sexual Assault and Relationship Violence at the University of Arizona, Tucson, and serves as the cochair of the Wingspan Domestic Violence Project, which provides outreach to, and services for, the lesbian, gay, bisexual, and transgender community in Tucson.

**Harriette Andreadis** is an associate professor of English at Texas A&M University, College Station. She has published on the reception of Sappho in early modern England and is preparing an edition of the poems of Katherine Philips and completing a book-length study of same-sex female erotics in early modern England.

**Ghazala Anwar** was born in Pakistan and resides in the United States. She has a Ph.D. in comparative religion from Temple University, Philadelphia, and has taught at several colleges. She is the director of education equity at the Philadelphia Lesbian and Gay Task Force.

**Janni Aragon** is a Ph.D. candidate in political science at the University of California, Riverside. Aragon is working on her dissertation about the theoretical politics surrounding the "second wave" feminist movement. Her areas of interests are feminist theory, popular culture, women's sexuality, Chicana/Latina feminisms, and ethnic studies.

**Katherine Arnup** teaches women's studies and Canadian studies at Carleton University, Ottawa, Ontario. She is the author of *Education for Motherhood: Advice for Mothers in Twentieth Century Canada* (1994) and the editor of *Lesbian Parenting: Living with Pride and Prejudice* (1995).

**Dawn Atkins** is the editor of *Looking Queer: Body Image and Identity in Lesbian, Bisexual, Gay, and Transgender Communities* (1998), was the founder and director (1988–1994) of the Body Image Task Force (BITF), and has presented more than one hundred body-image workshops. She is a Ph.D. candidate in anthropology at the University of Iowa, Iowa City.

**Rosemary Auchmuty** is chair of the Department of Academic Legal Studies at the University of Westminster, London, England. She writes on lesbian history and lesbian law and has taught lesbian studies courses for many years. Among her publications is *A World of Girls: The Appeal of the Girls' School Story* (1992).

**Paris Awalt** received her B.A. in Italian from the University of California, Berkeley, and is in the Ph.D. program in comparative literature at the University of California, Los Angeles. She teaches English as a second language at the American Language Institute at San Diego State University.

**Margot Gayle Backus's** articles on Ann Sexton, Judy Grahn, and Radclyffe Hall have appeared in the *Journal of Homosexuality*, *Signs*, and *Tulsa Studies in Women's Literature*. Her first book is *The Gothic Family Romance: Compulsory Heterosexuality in the Anglo-Irish Settler Colonial Order* (forthcoming).

**Holly A. Baggett** is an assistant professor at Southwest Missouri State University, Springfield. She is writing a dual biography of Jane Heap and Margaret Anderson, as well as editing the letters of Jane Heap.

**Laurie J. Baker** graduated from North Dakota State University, Fargo, and works with the Fargo Youth Commission.

**Christie Balka** is an activist and scholar who directs the Bread and Roses Community Fund in Philadelphia. A Ph.D. candidate in history at Temple University, Philadelphia, she is writing her dissertation on Greenwich Village lesbians in the 1920s and 1930s. She coedited (with Andy Rose) *Twice Blessed: On Being Lesbian, Gay, and Jewish* (1989).

**Jane R. Ballinger**, assistant professor of communication at California State Polytechnic University,

Pomona, teaches journalism, public relations, and media studies. She received her Ph.D. in journalism at the University of Texas, Austin. Her research interests include analysis of the relationships between social movements and the mainstream news media.

**Ian Barnard** teaches in the Department of Rhetoric and Writing Studies and the Department of English and Comparative Literature at San Diego State University. He is completing a book, *Queer Race: Cultural Interventions in the Racial Politics of Queer Theory*. His articles have appeared in the journals *Women's Studies, Feminist Teacher, Genders,* and *Socialist Review*.

**Nan Bauer-Maglin** is academic director of the City University of New York (CUNY) Baccalaureate Program of the Graduate School and University Center, CUNY. She has written more than thirty articles on women's writing and teaching and coedited two books: (with Donna Perry) *"Bad Girls"/"Good Girls": Women, Sex, and Power in the Nineties* (1996) and *Women and Stepfamilies: Voices, Anger, and Love* (1989).

**Evelyn Torton Beck** is a professor of women's studies and an affiliate of comparative literature and Jewish studies at the University of Maryland, College Park. Among her books are *Nice Jewish Girls: A Lesbian Anthology* (1982/1989), *The Prism of Sex: Essays in the Sociology of Knowledge* (1979), and *Kafka and the Yiddish Theater* (1971). She is at work on psychoanalytic perspectives on the writings of Franz Kafka and the art of Frida Kahlo.

**Edith J. Benkov** is professor of French at San Diego State University. She has published on medieval theater, Chrétien de Troyes, women and language, cross-dressing, Christine de Pizan, and Louise Labé. She is completing a monograph on Labé and is researching lesbians and the law.

**Rhona J. Berenstein** is an associate professor and director of film studies at the University of California, Irvine. She is the author of *Attack of the Leading Ladies: Gender, Sexuality, and Spectatorship in Classic Horror Cinema* (1996) and is producing a video documentary entitled *100 to Infinity*.

**Linda A. Bernhard** is associate professor of nursing and women's studies at Ohio State University, Columbus. She teaches, conducts research, and is involved in activist work on women's health. She and her partner enjoy singing in the Columbus Women's Chorus and watching women's basketball.

**Robin Bernstein** coedited (with Seth Clark Silberman) *Generation Q* (1996), an anthology of essays by young queers. She is an editor of *Bridges*, a biannual journal of Jewish feminist culture and politics.

**Corinne E. Blackmer** teaches American and gay and lesbian literature at Southern Connecticut State University, New Haven. Coeditor with Patricia Juliana Smith of *En Travesti: Women, Opera, Gender Subversion* (1995), she recently completed her first book, *African/Mother: Cultural Origins in the Americas* (1998), and is writing a book of essays on sexuality, class, and identity politics.

**Evelyn Blackwood** is assistant professor of women's studies and anthropology at Purdue University, West Lafayette, Indiana. Her publications include work on Native American female two-spirits, tomboys in Indonesia, and essays on culture and female same-sex sexuality and transgender practices. She is the editor of *The Many Faces of Homosexuality: Anthropology and Homosexual Behavior* (1986).

**Lucy Bland** is a senior lecturer in women's studies at the University of North London. She is the author of *Banishing the Beast: English Feminism and Sexual Morality, 1885–1918* (1995) and coeditor (with Laura Doan) of *Sexology in Culture: Labelling Bodies and Desires* (1998) and *Sexology Uncensored: The Documents of Sexual Science* (1998).

**Elyse Blankley** is professor of English and women's studies at California State University, Long Beach. Her scholarly publications have included studies of modernist literature and contemporary American fiction and poetry.

**Richmod Bollinger** earned her Ph.D. in Japanese studies at Freie Universitaet Berlin in 1997. She has published on the Japanese modern girl during the 1920s and 1930s, as well as on Japanese women writers. She has also done research on the phenomenon of assumed gender in Japanese literature.

**Marie-Jo Bonnet** is the author of *Un choix sans équivoque*, a study of love between women in France, which was her Ph.D. thesis in history at the Université de Paris VII. An activist in the women's and gay liberation movements since 1971, she is extending her study of lesbians in cultural history.

**Miriam Bottassi**, born in São Paulo, Brazil, is a librarian and documentalist and has been a lesbian feminist activist since 1976. She was a member of the Center for Women's Information (CIM), the only feminist documentation center in Brazil, from its founding in 1979 until 1995.

**Angela Bowen** is an assistant professor of women's studies and English at California State University, Long Beach. She emphasizes the lives and writing of people of color in both areas of her teaching; in her research, she focuses on the lives of black lesbian feminists, past and present.

**Nan Alamilla Boyd** has a Ph.D. from Brown University, Providence, Rhode Island. She teaches queer studies, Latina studies, and U.S. women's history in the Women's Studies Program at the University of Colorado, Boulder, where she also chairs the Program in Lesbian, Gay, Bisexual, and Transgender Studies. She is the author of *Wide Open Town: San Francisco's Lesbian and Gay History* (forthcoming).

**Kathryn A. Brandt** graduated from Bennington College, Bennington, Vermont, then pursued her activist leanings in New York City. Academically, she is inclined toward postmodernism, queer and feminist theory, and civil rights work. She is a television writer and producer and takes graduate courses in American studies at the University of New Mexico, Albuquerque.

**Lyndie Brimstone** is a senior lecturer at Roehampton Institute, London, where she convenes the multidisciplinary Women's Studies Programme. Her publications include *Towards a New Cartography: Radclyffe Hall, Virginia Woolf, and the Working of Common Land* (1991) and *"Keepers of History": The Novels of Maureen Duffy* (1990).

**Christina Brinkley**, applied social scientist and demographer-sociologist, is chair of the Department of African American and African American Women's Studies at Simmons College, Boston. Her research includes feminist/womanist theory and activism, gendered racism in higher education, U.S. women of color in the military, and public policy and quantitative/qualitative research methods.

**Kendal L. Broad** has a Ph.D. in sociology from Washington State University, Pullman. She has done research on hate crimes, the lesbian and gay movement, the contemporary U.S. women's movement, and the transgender movement. She holds a joint appointment in the Center for Women's Studies and Gender Research in the Department of Sociology at the University of Florida, Gainesville.

**Ellen Broidy** is a librarian at the University of California, Irvine, and a lecturer in UCI's Program in Women's Studies. Her research and teaching focus on the impact of new information technologies on women and women's studies and the related issues of gender and the politics of information.

**Carellin Brooks** lives in Vancouver, British Columbia.

**Bernadette J. Brooten** is the Robert and Myra Kraft and Jacob Hiatt Professor of Christian Studies at Brandeis University, Waltham, Massachusetts. Her publications include *Women Leaders in the Ancient Synagogue: Inscriptional Evidence and Background Issues* (1982) and *Love Between Women: Early Christian Responses to Female Homoeroticism* (1996).

**Jayne Relaford Brown** is a poet and writer who teaches writing courses in Pennsylvania. Her work has appeared in a number of anthologies, including *Tomboys! Tales of Dyke Derring-Do* (1995).

**Victoria Bissell Brown** received her Ph.D. in American history from the University of California, San Diego, in 1985. She taught in the Women's Studies Department at San Diego State University from 1981 to 1989. She is an associate professor of history and chair of gender and women's studies at Grinnell College, Grinnell, Iowa, and is writing a biography of Jane Addams.

**Diana L. Burgin** is a professor of Russian at the University of Massachusetts, Boston, and an associate of the Russian Research Center at Harvard University, Cambridge, Massachusetts.

**Kate Burns** is a Ph.D. candidate in literature and culture studies at the University of California, San Diego. Her dissertation traces a genealogy of the woman outlaw from the early republic to the twentieth century in U.S. literature and culture. She also writes and teaches about lesbian and queer studies, 'zines, comic books, and cyberspace culture.

**Stephanie Byrd** has written reviews in the *Lesbian Review of Books*, the *Harvard Gay and Lesbian Review*, the *Lambda Book Report*, and *Sojourner* and poetry in *Whiskey Island*, *Kenyon Review*, *Common Lives/Lesbian Lives*, *Sinister Wisdom*, and *American Voice*. She is an M.A. candidate in English at Cleveland State University in Ohio.

**Karen Cadora** received her Ph.D. from Stanford University, Stanford, California. She has an M.S. in astrophysics and works as a software engineer. Her short fiction has been published in *Yellow Silk* (1993), her critical work in *Science Fiction Studies* (1995), and her first novel, *Stardust Bound* (1994), by Firebrand.

**Elizabeth Cahn** is a lesbian architect and art therapist who works with women, lesbians, and other members of the sexual-minority community.

**Luz Calvo** is a Ph.D candidate in the History of Consciousness Program at the University of California, Santa Cruz. She is working on her dissertation, "Border Fantasies: Sexual Anxieties and Political Passions in the Mexico-U.S. Border." Her academic interests include psychoanalysis, queer theory, and critical race studies.

**Francesca Canadé Sautman** is a professor at Hunter College and the Graduate School of the City University of New York, teaching in several fields. She has published on medieval and modern folk culture and on women's cultural history in France, Italy, the Maghreb, and the United States. She is completing a book on lesbian working-class culture in France, 1880–1930.

**Jane Caputi** is the author of *The Age of Sex Crime* (1987) and *Gossips, Gorgons, and Crones: The Fates of the Earth* (1993). She collaborated with Mary Daly on Webster's *First New Intergalactic Wickedary of the English Language* (1987).

**Claudia Card**, a Fully Revolting Hag with tenure in the Department of Philosophy at the University of Madison, Wisconsin, is the author of *The Unnatural Lottery: Character and Moral Luck* (1996) and *Lesbian Choices* (1995) and the editor of *Adventures in Lesbian Philosophy* (1994) and *Feminist Ethics* (1991).

**Erin Carlston** received her Ph.D. in modern thought and literature from Stanford University, Stanford, California. She teaches in Stanford's Introduction to the Humanities and Continuing Studies programs and has written on topics in comparative literature, fascist cultural studies, and the history of sexuality. She is the author of *Thinking Fascism: Sapphic Modernism and Fascist Modernity* (1998).

**Glynis Carr** is an associate professor of English at Bucknell University, Lewisburg, Pennsylvania. She has written essays on U.S. women writers and edited a volume of feminist theory, "Turning the Century" (*Bucknell Review* 36[2], 1992). She is working on a second edited volume of ecofeminist literary criticism.

**Susan E. Cayleff** is a professor and chair of the Department of Women's Studies at San Diego State University. She is the author of *Wash and Be Healed: The Water-Cure Movement and Women's Health* (1987) and *Babe: The Life and Legend of Babe Didrikson Zaharias* (1995) and coeditor (with Barbara Bair) of *Wings of Gauze: Women of Color and the Experience of Health and Illness* (1993).

**Line Chamberland** has been active in the lesbian and feminist movements since the 1970s and teaches sociology at Maisonneuve College, Montreal, Québec, where she works on lesbian history in Québec. She directed a special issue of the French periodical *Sociologie et sociétés*: "Homosexualities: Scientific and Activist Issues" (29[1], 1997).

**Wendy Chapkis** is an associate professor of sociology and women's studies at the University of Southern Maine, Portland. She is the author of two books: *Beauty Secrets: Women and the Politics of Appearance* (1986) and *Live Sex Acts: Women Performing Erotic Labor* (1997).

**Anne Charles** teaches English and women's studies at the University of New Orleans. She is completing a manuscript on Sapphic modernism and the novels of Djuna Barnes.

**Mary C. Churchill** is an assistant professor of women's studies at the University of Colorado, Boulder. She received her Ph.D. degree in religious studies from the University of California, Santa Barbara, specializing in the study of Native American religious traditions.

**Nan Cinnater** has an M.A. in American women's history from Sarah Lawrence College, Bronxsville, New York. Formerly public education coordinator of Senior Action in a Gay Environment (SAGE), she is co-owner of Now Voyager, the lesbian and gay bookstore in Provincetown, Massachusetts. She has never hopped a freight in her life.

**Bev Clark** was a part of the first lesbian support group in Harare, Zimbabwe, and was actively involved in Gays and Lesbians of Zimbabwe (GALZ) from 1989 to 1997. With her longtime partner, Brenda Burrell, she has been instrumental in the fight for gay and lesbian equality in Zimbabwe.

**Cheryl Clarke**, black lesbian feminist poet, has been a student of African American literature since 1968. She is the author of four books of poetry, *Narratives: Poems in the Tradition of Black Women* (1982), *Living as a Lesbian* (1986), *Humid Pitch* (1989), and *Experimental Love* (1993), and is completing her fifth manuscript, entitled *Corridors of Nostalgia*.

**Diana Collecott** grew up near London and teaches British and American literature at Durham University in northeast England. She has traveled widely and held research fellowships in Japan and the United States. She broadcasts on poetry for the British Broadcasting Corporation (BBC) and is the author of *H.D. and Sapphic Modernism* (1999).

**Elizabeth Colwill**, an associate professor of history at San Diego State University, specializes in the history of gender, sexuality, and colonialism. Her publications include articles on female authorship, pornography, and the political culture of the French and Haitian revolutions. She is working on a book entitled *Sex, Savagery, and Slavery in the French and Haitian Revolutions*.

**Nerida M. Cook** has undertaken several periods of research in Thailand as part of her social anthropological training. She is engaged in funded fieldwork on women's sexual subcultures in Thailand, centered in Bangkok. She will incorporate the findings in publications and in her teaching in a course on love and sexuality cross-culturally.

**Tee A. Corinne** has been involved with the visual arts all of her life but often writes for a living. She loves to review art books. Her own books include *The Cunt Coloring Book* (1975), *Yantras of Womanlove* (1982), *Dreams of the Woman Who Loved Sex* (1988), and *Mama, Rattlesnakes, and Key Lime Pi* (1995).

**'Becca Cragin** is a Ph.D. candidate at the Institute for Women's Studies at Emory University, Atlanta. She has had articles published on feminist cultural studies and on representations of lesbian feminism in academic and popular media. She is writing a dissertation on gay and lesbian viewers of daytime talk shows.

**Julie Crawford** received her Ph.D. in English literature from the University of Pennsylvania, Philadelphia. Her dissertation is on early modern popular literature. She is also interested in the history of female homosociality and lesbianism and the history of cross-dressing and other gender-subversive women. She is an assistant professor of English and comparative literature at Columbia University, New York City.

**Jason Cromwell**, Ph.D., is a cultural anthropologist and the author of numerous articles and a forthcoming book on Transmen/FTM (female to male). A longtime member of the transcommunity, he has served on the boards of several organizations and is a cofounder of the FTM Conference and Education Project/Spectrum.

**Diane Griffin Crowder** is a professor of French and women's studies at Cornell College, Mount Vernon, Iowa. She has published extensively on the works of Monique Wittig, lesbian and feminist theory, lesbian and feminist utopian literature, lesbian body presentation, and the works of Colette. She is also interested in weaving and fiber arts.

**Margaret Cruikshank** teaches women's studies at the University of Maine, Orono. She is the author of *The Gay and Lesbian Liberation Movement* (1992) and the editor of *The Lesbian Path* (1980), *New Lesbian Writing* (1984), *Lesbian Studies* (1982), and *Fierce with Reality: An Anthology of Literature About Aging* (1995).

**Cynthia Cruz** is a Ph.D. student in education at the University of California, Los Angeles. Her research interests focus on queer theory, postcolonial pedagogies, writing and autobiography, and Chicana lesbian feminism. Her published work appears in the *International Journal of Qualitative Studies in Education*.

**Paisley Currah** teaches political science at Brooklyn College of the City University of New York, and is working on a book on identity fundamentalisms and the rights of sexual minorities in the United States.

**Ann Cvetkovich** is an associate professor of English at the University of Texas, Austin. She is the author of *Mixed Feelings: Feminism, Mass Culture, and Victorian Sensationalism* (1992). She has published articles on lesbian culture in a number of collections and in the journal *GLQ*.

**Violetta Cywicka** is an activist with the Association of Lambda Groups in Kraków, Poland.

**Ann David** is a historian and lesbian activist, who knows the Belgian situation through experience and studies. She is a volunteer in an oral-history project on older lesbians in Belgium.

**Nancy D. Davis**, M.D., is a retired psychiatrist.

**Gwendolyn Alden Dean** lives in Atlanta and is an adjunct professor of liberal arts at the Atlanta College of Art and a Ph.D. student at the Graduate Institute of the Liberal Arts at Emory University, Atlanta. She completed a B.A. in drama and an M.F.A. in studio art/performance art at the University of California, Irvine.

**Juanita Díaz-Cotto**, a black, Puerto Rican, lesbian feminist socialist, is editor of *Compañeras: Latina Lesbians (An Anthology)* (1987) under the psuedonym Juanita Ramos. Author of *Gender, Ethnicity, and the State: Latina and Latino Prison Politics* (1996), she is an associate professor of sociology, women's studies, and Caribbean studies at the State University of New York, Binghamton.

**Mildred Dickemann**, who received her Ph.D. in anthropology from the University of California, Berkeley, has taught at Merritt College, the University of Kansas, and Sonoma State University. She has published on educational anthropology, biosocial anthropology, gender, and homosexuality. She is also politically active in racial justice, environmental, and gay and transgender areas.

**Judy Dlugacz** is president and founder of Olivia Cruises and Resorts. She was instrumental in the creation of the cultural phenomenon called "women's music" and later developed exclusive vacations for women. She also manages actor/comedian Suzanne Westenhoefer.

**Laura Doan**, a professor of English at the State University of New York, Geneseo, has edited *The Lesbian Postmodern* (1994), and coedited (with Lucy Bland) *Sexology Uncensored: The Documents of Sexual Science* (1998) and *Sexology in Culture: Labeling Bodies and Desires* (1998). She is working on *Fashioning Sapphism: The Origins of a Modern English Lesbian Culture*.

**Gunilla Domellöf**, D.Ph., is director of the Department of Information and Culture at Umeå

University, Sweden. Her thesis is on Karin Boye as a critic and modernist prose writer. Through her publications, she is engaged in reevaluating Karin Boye's authorship.

**Emma Donoghue** is a novelist, playwright, and historian. Her first play, *I Know My Own Heart* (1993), was based on Anne Lister's diaries. She followed up *Passions Between Women: British Lesbian Culture, 1668–1801* (1993) with the anthology *Poems Between Women: Four Centuries of Love, Romantic Friendship, and Desire* (1997) and a biography of two lesbian poets, *We Are Michael Field* (1998).

**Julie Dorf** is the founder and executive director of the International Gay and Lesbian Human Rights Commission (IGLHRC), a nonprofit, U.S.-based organization that monitors human rights violations based on sexual orientation, gender identity, and HIV status. She worked with dissident movements in the former Soviet Union for more than eight years before launching the IGLHRC.

**Christine Downing**, professor emerita of religious studies at San Diego State University, teaches in the Mythological Studies Program at Pacifica Graduate Institute in Santa Barbara, California. Her nine books include *The Goddess* (1981) and *Myths and Mysteries of Same-Sex Love* (1989).

**Jennifer Doyle** received her Ph.D. in literature from Duke University, Durham, North Carolina. She is coeditor (with Jonathan Flatley and José Esteban Muñoz) of *Pop Out: Queer Warhol* (1996).

**Kimberly Dugan** is a Ph.D. candidate in sociology at Ohio State University, Columbus, completing her dissertation on the dynamics between the Religious Right and the gay, lesbian, and bisexual movement. Her research interests include social movements, sexuality politics, gender, and race.

**Linda Dunne**, director of the Bachelor of Arts Program at the New School for Social Research, New York City, earned her Ph.D. in literature and a certificate in women's studies from the City University of New York Graduate School and taught her first women's studies course in 1972. She lives in Manhattan and the Catskills with Brenda Goodman, a painter, and their Australian shepherd.

**Cathie Dunsford**, Ph.D., teaches writing and publishing at Auckland University in New Zealand and is director of Dunsford Publishing Consultants (160 authors published, including twenty-eight Pacific lesbian authors). She is the editor of five Pacific women's anthologies, the author of three novels—*Cowrie* (1994), *The Journey Home* (1997), and *Heart Warrior* (1999)—and on the editorial board of the *Lesbian Review of Books*.

**Elana Dykewomon** has written *Riverfinger Women* (as Elana Nachman, 1974), *Nothing Will Be as Sweet as the Taste* (1995), and the Jewish lesbian historical novel *Beyond the Pale* (1997). She was an editor of *Sinister Wisdom*, a journal of arts and politics for the lesbian imagination, from 1987 to 1995.

**Vicki L. Eaklor** is a professor of history at Alfred University, Alfred, New York, where she teaches courses in American history and women's studies, including gay American history. She also is cochair of the Committee on Lesbian and Gay History, a national affiliate of the American Historical Association.

**Deborah A. Elliston** holds a Ph.D. in anthropology from New York University. Her research in the Society Islands of French Polynesia provides the ground for her analyses of female same-sex sexuality among these Polynesians, as well as for her dissertation. Her article "Erotic Anthropology: 'Ritualized Homosexuality' in Melanesia and Beyond" appeared in *American Ethnologist* (1995).

**Oliva M. Espín** is a professor of women's studies at San Diego State University. She is a past president of the Society for the Psychological Studies of Lesbian and Gay Issues, a division of the American Psychological Association. She is the author of *Latina Realities: Essays on Healing, Migration, and Sexuality* (1997) and *Women Crossing Boundaries: A Psychology of Immigration and Transformations of Sexuality* (1999).

**Kristin G. Esterberg** is an assistant professor of sociology at the University of Massachusetts, Lowell. She is the author of *Lesbian and Bisexual Identities: Constructing Communities, Constructing Selves* (1997).

**Paula L. Ettelbrick** is the legislative counsel for the Empire State Pride Agenda and cochairs a national network of lesbian and gay statewide political groups. As an adjunct professor of law, she teaches sexuality and the law at the University of Michigan Law School, Ann Arbor, and New York University Law School, New York City. She lives with her partner and son in Manhattan.

**Leyla Ezdinli** has taught French at Smith College, Northampton, Massachusetts. She works on French and Francophone women writers and is completing a manuscript, *Prefatory Transgressions: The Cultural Politics of Romantic Authorship*.

**Lillian Faderman** is the author of several publications in lesbian studies, including *Odd Girls and Twilight Lovers: A History of Lesbian Life in Twentieth-Century America* (1991) and *Surpassing the Love of Men: Romantic Friendship and Love between Women from the Renaissance to the Present* (1981). She is a professor of English at California State University, Fresno.

**Marilyn R. Farwell** is a professor of English at the University of Oregon, Eugene. Her areas of specialization are women writers, feminist and lesbian theory, and narrative theory. She has written articles on Virginia Woolf, Adrienne Rich, and John Milton and a book, *Heterosexual Plots and Lesbian Narratives* (1996). Her most recent work is on opera and lesbian writers.

**Marisa Fernandes** of São Paulo, Brazil, a historian, activist, and lesbian feminist since 1978, is coordinator of the Collective of Lesbian Feminists in São Paulo.

**Judith Fetterley**, a professor of English and women's studies at the University at Albany, State University of New York, is the author of *The Resisting Reader and Provisions: A Reader from 19th-Century American Women* (1978) and

coeditor (with Marjorie Pryse) of *American Women Regionalists, 1850–1910* (1992). She is working on a critical study of the writers included in that anthology.

**Heather Findlay** received her B.A. in women's studies from Brown University, Providence, Rhode Island, in 1986 and her Ph.D. in English from Cornell University, Ithaca, New York, in 1992. She edited *A Movement of Eros: Twenty Years of Lesbian Erotica* (1996), and her most recent academic publication is "Queer Dora," in *GLQ* (Winter 1994). She is the editor in chief of *Girlfriends* magazine.

**Mary Margaret Fonow** is an assistant professor of women's studies at Ohio State University, Columbus. Her research and teaching interests are feminist methodology, theorizing diversity, and political economy. She is coauthor (with Judith A. Cook) of *Beyond Methodology: Feminist Scholarship as Lived Research* (1991) and the editor of *Reading Women's Lives: An Introduction to Women's Studies* (1996).

**Jacqueline Francis** is a Ph.D. candidate in art history at Emory University, Atlanta, and the 1997–1999 Andrew Wyeth Fellow in American Art at the Center for Advanced Study in the Visual Arts, Washington, D.C.

**Liz Frank** is an educator by profession and a writer and photographer by passion. Her motto is to undermine patriarchy through laughter. She has lived and traveled in many countries, but her lesbian feminist heart and mind, body and soul are now firmly settled in Namibia, where she lives a fulfilled, if sometimes too full, life with her partner and her son.

**Miriam Frank** is Master Teacher of Humanities in New York University's General Studies Program. She has worked in Detroit, the Bay Area, and New York City as a labor educator. Since 1995, she has been developing "Out in the Union," an oral history of lesbian and gay union activists.

**Trisha Franzen** is the director of the Anna Howard Shaw Center for Women's Studies and Programs at Albion College, Albion, Michigan. She is the author of *Spinsters and Lesbians: Independent Womanhood in the United States*

(1996) and is working on a biography of Anna Howard Shaw. Along with other community involvements, she serves on the Albion Board of Education.

**Susan K. Freeman** is completing her Ph.D in history at Ohio State University, Columbus. She has done research on the lesbian community in Cincinnati, Ohio, and is studying how girls have been taught about their bodies and sexuality through sex education in U.S. public schools during the twentieth century.

**Constance M. Fulmer** is a professor of English at Pepperdine University, Malibu, California. She enjoys living, walking, reading, and camping on the beach. She was born in Alabama and has taught in Tennessee and Kentucky and received her Ph.D. at Vanderbilt University, Nashville, Tennessee, where her lifelong interest in George Eliot began.

**Greta Gaard** is the author of *Ecological Politics: Ecofeminists and the Greens* (1998), the editor of *Ecofeminism: Women, Animals, Nature* (1993) and coeditor (with Patrick D. Murphy) of *Ecofeminist Literary Criticism* (1998). She is a professor of humanities at Fairhaven College/Western Washington University, Bellingham.

**Carolyn Gage** is a lesbian feminist playwright, author, and activist. She toured nationally in her one-woman show, *The Second Coming of Joan of Arc*, and has written the first manual on lesbian theater, *Take Stage! How to Direct and Produce a Lesbian Play* (1997).

**Linda Garber** is the author of *Identity Poetics: Lesbian Feminism, Diversity, and the Rise of Queer Theory* (forthcoming) and *Lesbian Sources: A Bibliography of Periodical Articles, 1970–1990* (1993) and the editor of *Tilting the Tower: Lesbians/Teaching/Queer Subjects* (1994). She is an assistant professor of women's studies at California State University, Fresno.

**Nanette K. Gartrell**, M.D., the first out lesbian on the Harvard Medical School faculty, is associate clinical professor of psychiatry at the University of California, San Francisco. She has been documenting sexual abuse by physicians since 1982 and conducting a national longitudi-

nal lesbian family study since 1986. She is the editor of *Bringing Ethics Alive: Feminist Ethics for Psychotherapy Practice* (1994).

**Alicia Gaspar de Alba**, a first-generation Chicana, is an assistant professor of Chicana/o studies at the University of California, Los Angeles, and holds a Ph.D. in American studies. Her most recent publication is *Chicano Art Inside/Outside the Master's House: Cultural Politics and the CARA Exhibition* (1998), and she has completed a historical novel on Sor Juana Inés de la Cruz entitled *Sor Juana's Second Dream* (1999).

**Barbara W. Gerber** is a Distinguished Service Professor Emerita at the State University of New York, Oswego, and the 1997–1998 president of the National Women's Studies Association. She is a counselor, educator, and sometime administrator who loves to canoe, camp in the wilderness, and be exploring.

**Zsa Zsa Gershick** works as a writer and an editor for the University of Southern California, Los Angeles, and teaches writing at Pasadena City College. She is a former journalist and the author of *Gay Old Girls: Lesbians over 60 Discuss Their Lives* (1998).

**Masha Gessen**, Moscow journalist and activist, is the author of *Dead Again: The Russian Intelligentsia After Communism* (1997) and *The Rights of Lesbians and Gay Men in the Russian Federation* (1994) and the editor and translator of *Half a Revolution: Short Fiction by Contemporary Russian Women* (1995) and other books.

**Margaret Gibson** is an independent scholar in the history of medicine and sexuality. She graduated from Harvard University, Cambridge, Massachusetts, with a B.A. in the history of science and has published several works on the medical construction of lesbian bodies. She is researching a book on American medical writing about lesbianism.

**Amy Gilley** specializes in theater, dramatic literature, and popular culture.

**Margaret Rose Gladney**, a native of Homer, Louisiana, is an associate professor of American studies at the University of Alabama, Tuscaloosa, where she teaches courses on women in the South and the civil rights movement. She and her partner, Marcia Winter, cofounded the Tuscaloosa Lesbian Coalition.

**Elena Glasberg** is an assistant professor of liberal studies at California State University, Los Angeles. She has essays in *Political and Legal Anthropological Review* (1998) and the collection *The Postcolonial U.S.* (1999). She is writing a manuscript on the study of Antarctica and the geopolitical imagination.

**Judith Glassgold**, Psy.D., is a psychologist in New Jersey specializing in the psychology of women; lesbian, gay, and bisexual issues; and abuse survivors. She is a contributing faculty member at the Graduate School of Applied and Professional Psychology at Rutgers University. Glassgold is coeditor (with Suzanne Iasenza) of *Lesbians and Psychoanalysis: Revolutions in Theory and Practice* (1995).

**Barbara Godard**, teaches English and women's studies at York University, North York, Ontario. She has translated fiction by Québec feminists, including Nicole Brossard. Her books include *Talking About Ourselves: The Cultural Productions of Canadian Native Women* (1985) and *Audrey Thomas: Her Life and Work* (1989). In addition to editing several collections, she is a founding coeditor of *Tessera*, a feminist literary theory periodical.

**Susan Gonda** completed her Ph.D. in U.S. history, women's history, and the history of law and sexuality at the University of California, Los Angeles. She teaches at San Diego State University and Grossmont College, El Cajon, California. Her dissertation is entitled "Strumpets and Angels: Rape, Seduction, and the Criminal Boundaries of Sexuality in the Nineteenth-Century Northeastern U.S."

**María C. González** is an associate professor of English at the University of Houston in Texas, where she teaches Mexican American literature and feminism. She is the author of *Contemporary Mexican American Women Novelists: Toward a Feminist Identity* (1997) and is working on Chicana queer theory.

**Amy T. Goodloe** created and maintains the www.lesbian.org Web site and manages five lesbian discussion lists. She has written and spoken about lesbian visibility on the Internet in a number of venues over the past several years.

**Debbie Gould** was a member of ACT UP/ Chicago and has been involved in a number of activist groups. She is a Ph.D. student in political science at the University of Chicago and is writing her dissertation on the emergence and decline of ACT UP, focusing on the relationship between shifting understandings of the AIDS epidemic and political mobilization.

**Jaime M. Grant** is a writer-activist who has been involved in feminist, antiracist, and queer liberation work since the 1980s. She directs the Union Institute Center for Women, an academic women's center in Washington, D.C., dedicated to coalition work. She is a recovering addict who frequently writes about feminism, racism, and sex.

**Mary Jean Green** is Edward Tuck Professor of French at Dartmouth College, Hanover, New Hampshire, where she has directed the Women's Studies Program. She has written extensively on women writers of the francophone world and edited *Postcolonial Subjects* (1996) and *Écritures de femmes* (1996). She is the author of *Marie-Claire Blais* (1995) and is completing a study of women's writing in Québec.

**Beverly Greene** is a professor of psychology at St. John's University, Jamaica, New York, and a clinical psychologist in private practice. A fellow of the American Psychological Association, she is the recipient of numerous national awards for publications and pioneering contributions to the psychological literature and for distinguished professional contributions to teaching, training, and clinical practice.

**Pat Griffin** teaches in the Social Justice Education Program at the University of Massachusetts, Amherst. Her research and writing interests focus on education and athletics, with a particular interest in women's sports. She is coeditor (with Maurianne Adams and Lee Anne Bell) of *Teaching for Diversity and Social Justice: A Sourcebook for Teachers and Trainers* (1997) and the author of *Strong Women, Deep Closets: Lesbian and Homophobia in Sports,* Human Kinetics (1998).

**Hanna Hacker** lives mostly in Austria. She is a sociologist and a historian, a university lecturer, and a cofounder of the Feminist Archives in Vienna. She has published several studies on the construction of female homosexualities in fin de siècle Europe; on gender, violence, and transgression; and on Austria's women's movements.

**Judith Halberstam** is an associate professor of literature at the University of California, San Diego. She is the author of *Skin Shows: Gothic Horror and the Technology of Monsters* (1995), *Female Masculinity* (1998), and (with Monika Treut) *The Drag King Book* (1999).

**Marny Hall** is the author of *The Lavender Couch: A Consumer's Guide to Psychotherapy for Lesbians and Gay Men* (1985) and *The Lesbian Love Companion: How to Survive Everything from Heartthrob to Heartbreak* (1998). Since the 1970s, she has worked as a lesbian couples' counselor in the San Francisco Bay Area.

**Ruth Hall**, Ph.D., is a licensed psychologist and an associate professor in the Department of Psychology at The College of New Jersey, Ewing. She maintains a private practice and consults for various organizations. Her research interests include women of color and athletes. She is the author of *Friendships between African American and White Lesbians* (1996), which examines cross-racial experiences within the lesbian community.

**Harmony Hammond**, a pioneer of the feminist art movement, cofounded A.I.R., the first women's cooperative gallery, and *Heresies* magazine. Her work has been exhibited internationally and is represented in many museum collections. A professor at the University of Arizona, Tucson, Hammond is the author of *Lesbian Art in America: A Contemporary History* (1999). She lives and works in Galisteo, New Mexico.

**Ju Hui Judy Han** has done research in queer Korean American issues, labor, feminism, and activism. She serves on various boards for the Los Angeles Culture Net/Getty Information Institute, an arts-community networking initiative, and manages an e-mail list for Korean American dykes.

**Lisa Handler** is a Ph.D. candidate in sociology and women's studies at the State University of New York, Stony Brook. She is finishing her dissertation, which explores young women's friendships as a site of resistance to, and reproduction of, gender and sexuality.

**Gillian Hanscombe** has written *Figments of a Murder* (1995), which is set in the lesbian feminist community of London in the 1970s and 1980s and was recently translated into German. She is director of the Centre for Women's Studies at the University of Exeter, England.

**Nancy A. Hardesty** is an associate professor of religion at Clemson University, Clemson, South Carolina. She is the author of *Inclusive Language in the Church* (1987) and *Women Called to Witness: Evangelical Feminism in the Nineteenth Century* (1984) and coauthor (with Letha Dawson Scanzoni) of *All We're Meant to Be: Biblical Feminism for Today* (1974, 1994). She is active in the Metropolitan Community Church of Greenville, South Carolina.

**Sabine Hark** is a sociologist by training and degree and a lesbian theorist by passion. She teaches at University of Potsdam, Germany. She is widely published on issues of lesbian identity politics and on the history of German lesbian feminism. She is working on a book tentatively entitled "Contested Territories of Knowledge: Feminism Meets Queer Theory."

**Laura Alexandra Harris** is an assistant professor of English and black studies at Pitzer College, Claremont, California. She is the editor of the collection *Femme: Feminists, Lesbians, and Bad Girls* (1997) and is conducting research on literature and writers of the Harlem Renaissance.

**Nett Hart** is a former academic with a wild attention span who found her calling as a farmer who writes, publishes, designs and builds ecologically, grows sustainably, and researches and prepares medicinal plants. She founded the nonprofit Lesbian Natural Resources to promote and sustain landyke culture and Word Weavers Lesbian Publishing.

**Susan Hawthorne** is a writer, publisher, academic, and aerialist. Her recent work focuses on issues as diverse as lesbian culture, hypertext, poetry, and economics. She is the author of a novel, *The Falling Woman* (1992), and the coeditor (with Cathie Dunsford and Susan Sayer) of *Car Maintenance, Explosives and Love* (1997), and other contemporary lesbian writings.

**Shevy Healey,** Ph.D., is a retired psychologist with a clinical practice specializing in women, lesbians, and people with disabilities. She is a founding member of both the First West Coast Conference by and for old lesbians and Old Lesbians Organizing for Change (OLOC). She writes, speaks, and does workshops on ageism, aging, homophobia, and sexism.

**Eloise Klein Healy** is the author of four books of poetry and associate editor of the *Lesbian Review of Books*. Her collection *Artemis in Echo Park* (1991) is also available on CD and audiotape. She directs the low-residency M.F.A. in Creative Writing Program at Antioch University, Los Angeles.

**Michelle Heffner Hayes** is the artistic director of the Colorado Dance Festival in Boulder, Colorado. She received her Ph.D. in dance history and theory University of California, Riverside. She lectures and writes about feminist issues in flamenco history and contemporary dance performance. She danced with choreographers Susan Rose and Stephanie Gilliand, among others.

**Dana Heller** is an associate professor of English at Old Dominion University, Norfolk, Virginia. She is the author of *The Femination of Quest-Romance: Radical Departures* (1990) and *Family Plots: The De-Oedipalization of Popular Culture* (1995) and the editor of *Cross Purposes: Lesbians, Feminists, and the Limits of Alliance* (1997).

**Lois Rita Helmbold**, an intellectual, political activist, teacher, martial artist, writer, lover, historian, and quilter, coordinates the Women's Studies Program at San Jose State University. She has published in numerous journals and anthologies and is on the editorial board of the *Lesbian Review of Books*.

**Melissa S. Herbert** is an assistant professor of sociology at Hamline University, Saint Paul, Minnesota, where she teaches gender, sexuality, and social psychology. She is the author of *Camouflage Isn't Only for Combat: The Management of Gender and Sexuality Among Women in the Military* (1998).

**Carter Heyward**, a lesbian feminist theologian and Episcopal priest, is a professor of theology at the Episcopal Divinity School, Cambridge, Massachusetts. An author of numerous books on theology, ethics, and social change, Heyward is also a poet and a founding member of a writers' and activists' community in the mountains of North Carolina.

**Kathleen Hickok** is an associate professor of English and women's studies at Iowa State University, Ames. Her book *Representations of Women: Nineteenth-Century British Women's Poetry* (1984) helped revive interest in many Victorian women poets. Hickok teaches Victorian literature, women's literature, and woman-identified literature. She and her partner have two children.

**Liz Highleyman** is editor of *Cuir Underground* newspaper and associate editor of *Bisexual Politics: Theories, Queries and Visions* (1995). Her work has appeared in the anthologies *Bi Any Other Name* (1990), *The Second Coming* (1996), and *Whores and Other Feminists* (1997). She has been active in the bisexual movement since the 1980s.

**Claudia Hinojosa** is one of the first voices of the lesbian feminist movement in Mexico. Her early activism led her to many years of journalism and independent scholarship. Mother of one son, she is involved in a project of cultural translation, on the topic of women's human rights, for the Center for Women's Global Leadership at Rutgers University, New Brunswick, New Jersey.

**Lisa Maria Hogeland** is an associate professor of English at the University of Cincinnati, where she also teaches in the Women's Studies M.A. Program. She is the author of *Feminism and Its*

*Fictions: The Consciousness-Raising Novel and the Women's Liberation Movement* (1995).

**Sharon P. Holland** is a native of Washington, D.C., and an assistant professor of English at Stanford University, Stanford, California. She recently finished a book manuscript entitled *Raising the Dead: Death and (Black) Subjectivity in Twentieth Century American Literature and Culture* and is working on a novel entitled *How Bubba the Socrates Got to Be Neither.*

**Alice Y. Hom**, a Ph.D. candidate in history at Claremont Graduate School, Claremont, California, is completing her dissertation on a comparative history of activism and organizing by lesbians of color in Los Angeles and New York from 1969 to the present. She coedited (with David L. Eng) *Q & A: Queer in Asian America* (1998).

**renée c. hoogland** is an assistant professor of lesbian studies at the University of Nijmegen, the Netherlands. She is the author of *Elizabeth Bowen: A Reputation in Writing* (1994) and *Lesbian Configurations* (1997). She has published extensively on feminist theory, postmodernism, psychoanalysis, sexuality, and representation and is researching fantasy and embodiment.

**Elizabeth Rosa Horan** has published on Gabriela Mistral, Emily Dickinson, Marjorie Agosin, Carmen Lyra, and other women writers of the Americas. She is an associate professor of English and women's studies at Arizona State University, Tempe, where she directs the Comparative Studies in Literature program.

**Judith A. Howard** is a professor of sociology at the University of Washington, Seattle. She is also coeditor of *Signs: Journal of Women in Culture and Society* and of the Gender Lens book series for Sage Publications. She teaches and studies how cognitions—stereotypes, attitudes, attributions—shape and are constrained by social interactions and institutions.

**Joan W. Howarth** is a law professor at Golden Gate University, San Francisco, where she teaches constitutional law, women and the law, and sexual orientation and the law, among other courses. She has written in the areas of feminism and the death penalty, race and innocence, and lesbian legal history.

**Lynne Huffer** is an associate professor of French at Yale University, New Haven, Connecticut. She is the author of *Another Colette: The Question of Gendered Writing* (1992) and *Maternal Pasts, Feminist Futures: Nostalgia, Ethics, and the Question of Difference* (1998). She is also the editor of a special issue of *Yale French Studies* entitled "Another Look, Another Woman: Retranslations of French Feminism" (1995).

**Mary E. Hunt,** Ph.D., is a feminist theologian who teaches in the women's studies program at Georgetown University, Washington, D.C. She is codirector of the Women's Alliance for Theology, Ethics, and Ritual in Silver Spring, Maryland, and the author of *Fierce Tenderness: A Feminist Theology of Friendship* (1991).

**Karla Hyánková** is a graduate of the Faculty of Philosophy, Charles University, Prague, Czech Republic. After the November 1989 revolution, she became a cofounder and activist in the lesbian club Lambda and a member of the Czech homosexual organization, SOHO, and of the International Lesbian and Gay Association (ILGA). She works as a freelance translator of computer-related materials.

**Prue Hyman** is the only English-born Jewish lesbian feminist academic economist in Aotearoa/ New Zealand (and could drop several components and still be the only one!). She is the author of *Women and Economics: A New Zealand Feminist Perspective* (1994) and the coeditor (with Lee Badgett) of a lesbian and gay economics symposium for the journal *Feminist Economics*— as well as enjoying her beach, animals, and friends.

**Sherrie A. Inness** is the author of *Intimate Communities: Representation and Social Transformation in Women's College Fiction, 1895–1910* (1995); *The Lesbian Menace: Ideology, Identity, and the Representation of Lesbian Life* (1997); and *Tough Girls: Women, Popular Culture, and the Gendering of Toughness* (1998), as well as the editor of several collections.

**Janice M. Irvine** is on the sociology faculty at the University of Massachusetts, Amherst. She has written in various areas of sexuality studies.

**Eva Isaksson** is a Finnish writer and works as an astronomy librarian at the University of Helsinki Observatory. Her writings include a historical study (in Finnish) of women's work in the exact sciences. She has also done research in the history of physics. As a lesbian activist, she has been involved with the International Lesbian Information Service (ILIS) and lately with networking through the Internet.

**Peter Jackson**, Ph.D., is Research Fellow in Thai History at the Australian National University, Canberra, where he is writing a book on gay and lesbian history in Bangkok. His book *Dear Uncle Go: Male Homosexuality in Thailand* (1995) was the first major study of male homoeroticism in the Southeast Asian kingdom, and his novel *The Intrinsic Quality of Skin* (1994) deals with interracial gay relationships.

**Huda Jadallah** is a Palestinian lesbian, born and raised in the San Francisco Bay Area. She is a graduate student in sociology at the University of California, Santa Barbara. Her current research is tentatively titled "Hidden Families: Arab Lesbians in the U.S. Speak." She is editing an anthology of writings by and about Arab lesbian and bisexual women.

**Janet R. Jakobsen** is an assistant professor of women's studies and religious studies and co-coordinator of the Committee for Lesbian, Gay, and Bisexual Studies at the University of Arizona, Tucson. She is the author of *Working Alliances and the Politics of Difference: Diversity and Feminist Ethics* (1997) and has worked as a policy analyst, lobbyist, and organizer in Washington, D.C.

**Karla Jay** has written, edited, and translated nine books, the most recent of which are *Dyke Life* (1995) and *Lesbian Erotics* (1995). She is the editor of New York University Press's series The Cutting Edge: Lesbian Life and Literature and has written for many publications, including *Ms* magazine, the *New York Times Book Review*, and the *Village Voice*.

**Christine Jenkins** is a member of the faculty of the Graduate School of Library and Information Science, University of Illinois, Urbana-Champaign, where she teaches courses in youth services, young adult (YA) literature, and gender issues. Her research on gay and lesbian content in YA fiction has appeared in several library publications. She also was a school library media specialist with the Ann Arbor, Michigan, public schools.

**Valerie Jenness** is an assistant professor in the Department of Criminology, Law, and Society and the Department of Sociology at the University of California, Irvine. She has published books and articles on the politics of prostitution, AIDS and civil liberties, hate crimes and hate-crime law, and the gay and lesbian and women's movements in the United States.

**Karleen Pendleton Jiménez** is a Chicana lesbian writer from Rosemead, California. She was a lecturer in Chicana/o studies at San Diego State University and the director of Queer Players, a creative writing and performance group for queer youth in the San Diego community. She currently resides in Toronto, Canada.

**Mary M. Johnson** is an M.A. candidate in liberal arts emphasizing women's studies at San Diego State University, from which she received her B.A. in liberal studies. Her primary areas of research and interest are women in sports and women and HIV/AIDS.

**Sonya Jones** is professor of English at Allegheny College, Meadville, Pennsylvania. She is the author of *History and Memory: Gay and Lesbian Literature Since World War II* (1998) and is editing *A Sea of Stories: The Shaping Power of Narrative in Gay and Lesbian Cultures*. A longtime activist, she was instrumental in shaping Allegheny's lesbigay minor.

**Miranda Joseph** is an assistant professor of women's studies and comparative cultural and literary studies at the University of Arizona, Tucson. Her article "The Perfect Moment: Gays, Christians, and the National Endowment for the Arts" appears in *Socialist Review* (1998), and "The Performance of Production and Consumption" is in *Social Text* (1998).

**Tuula Juvonen** is a Ph.D. candidate in social policy at the University of Tampere, Finland. Her thesis, "Shadow Lives and Public Secrets," will study how the silence around female and male homosexuality was broken in a Finnish town during the 1950s and 1960s.

**Ruti Kadish** is an Israeli American Ph.D. student in the Department of Near Eastern Studies at the University of California, Berkeley. She is writing her dissertation on Israeli queer identity and community.

**Mary C. Kalfatovic** is a writer in the Washington, D.C., area specializing in the performing arts. She is the author of numerous articles and reviews and of the book *Montgomery Clift: A Bio-Bibliography* (1994).

**Elizabeth Kaminski** is a Ph.D. student in the Department of Sociology at Ohio State University, Columbus. Her research interests include lesbian health (the subject of her M.A. thesis), social movements, and the construction of lesbian identities.

**Venetia Kantsa** is a Ph.D. candidate in social anthropology at the London School of Economics, University of London. Her research focuses on the articulation of female homosexual discourses in contemporary Greece. She has published articles on the construction of a lesbian community in Eressos Lesvos and the expression of politicized lesbian discourse in early 1980s.

**J. Kehaulani Kauanui** is a Ph.D. candidate in the history of consciousness at the University of California, Santa Cruz. Her dissertation examines the connection between U.S. federal blood quanta policies and biometric studies on "Hawaiian hybrids" in defining Hawaiian indigeneity and the legal practices of land dispossession, race classification, and property status.

**AnaLouise Keating** is an associate professor of English at Eastern New Mexico University, Portales, where she teaches U.S./American literature and women's studies. She is author of *Women Reading Women Writing: Self-Invention in Paula Gunn Allen, Gloria Anzaldúa, and Audre Lorde* (1996) and essays on queer theory, feminist theory, canonical American writers, Latina/Chicana writers, multiculturalism, and pedagogy.

**Anne B. Keating** teaches at New York University. She holds a Ph.D. in American studies from the University of Maryland, College Park.

**Rosemary Keefe** (formerly Curb) has a Ph.D. in English from the University of Arkansas, Fayetteville. She is professor of English and has articles, reviews, and essays in books and journals. She edited *Amazon All Stars: Thirteen Lesbian Plays* (1996), a finalist for Lambda Literary Award, and coedited (with Nancy Manahan) *Lesbian Nuns: Breaking Silence* (1985), which was translated into seven languages.

**Kendall** earned her Ph.D. in drama from the University of Texas, Austin, in 1986 with a dissertation on the Queen Anne period and subsequently taught at Smith College, Northampton, Massachusetts. She was a Fulbright Scholar at the National University of Lesotho and in 1995 moved to South Africa, where she heads the Drama Department at the University of Natal, Pietermaritzburg.

**Jean E. Kennard** is a professor of English and women's studies at the University of New Hampshire, Durham. She is the author of *Number and Nightmare* (1975), *Victims of Convention* (1978), and *Vera Brittain and Winifred Holtby* (1989). She is working on a book on Virginia Woolf, sexuality, and narrative.

**Elizabeth Lapovsky Kennedy** was a founder of women's studies at the State University of New York, Buffalo, and is a professor of women's studies at the University of Arizona, Tucson. She is the coauthor (with Ellen Carol Dubois, Gail Paradise Kelly, Carolyn W. Korsmeyer, and Lillian S. Robinson) of *Feminist Scholarship: Kindling in the Groves of Academe* (1985) and (with Madeline Davis) of *Boots of Leather, Slippers of Gold: The History of a Lesbian Community* (1993), as well as the author of numerous articles.

**Didi Khayatt** is the author of *Lesbian Teachers: An Invisible Presence* (1992), in addition to a number of articles dealing with sexuality. She has been engaged for several years in research in

Egypt. She lives in Toronto and teaches at the Faculty of Education at York University, North York, Ontario.

**Celia Kitzinger** is director of women's studies and reader in lesbian and feminist psychology in the Department of Social Sciences, Loughborough University, Great Britain. She has published eight books and nearly one hundred chapters and articles on lesbian and feminist issues, including *The Social Construction of Lesbianism* (1987), *Changing Our Minds* (1993), and *Heterosexuality* (1993).

**Alisa Klinger** is an assistant professor of English at York University, North York, Ontario. She specializes in cultural and gender studies and has published pieces on lesbian-movement politics, multiethnic lesbian print culture, lesbian ethnography, and queer campus organizing. She is completing a book on North American lesbian print activism and cultural formation.

**Marcy Jane Knopf** is a Ph.D. candidate at Miami University, Oxford, Ohio. She is the editor of *The Sleeper Wakes: Harlem Renaissance Stories by Women* (1993) and Jessie Fauset's *The Chinaberry Tree* (1995).

**Judith C. Kohl**, professor emeritus of English and humanities at Dutchess Community College, Poughkeepsie, New York, and visiting professor at Vassar College, also in Poughkeepsie, has taught contemporary drama, recent American literature, international literature, and autobiographies of marginalized Americans. Her current work includes a study of Ezra Pound and Venice.

**Ilse Kokula** has worked for the lesbian and gay and women's liberation movements for more than twenty years. She has published books and articles on history and the current situation of lesbians. She received her Ph.D. at the University of Bremen in Germany and in 1985–1986 was a professor at the University of Utrecht in the Netherlands, teaching socialization and social history of lesbians.

**Gina Kozik-Rosabal** is the assistant director of the Women's Resource Center, University of Colorado, Boulder. She is a Latina lesbian mother, a social activist, and a former professor of women's studies.

**Dorelies Kraakman** is a lecturer in gay and lesbian studies with the Department of Sociology at the University of Amsterdam in the Netherlands. She has degrees in international law and in ancient history. Since 1987, she has specialized in historical and theoretical problems of sexuality. Her dissertation is on various aspects of sexual difference in eighteenth- and nineteenth-century French erotic literature.

**Karen Christel Krahulik** is a Ph.D. candidate in American history at New York University. Her dissertation, "Queering the Cape: Gender and the Politics of Race, Sex, and Class in Provincetown, Massachusetts, 1898–1998," will be finished in 1999. She lives in Boston and Provincetown.

**Victoria Krane** is an associate professor at the School of Human Movement, Sport, and Leisure Studies at Bowling Green State University, Bowling Green, Ohio. Her area of specialization is sport psychology, and her primary research focus is lesbians in sport, particularly the impact of homophobia and coping with homophobia.

**Linda A. Krikos** is the head of the Women's Studies Library and an assistant professor of library science at Ohio State University, Columbus. Her work has been published in *Reference Services Review*, *Serials Review*, and *Research Strategies*. She is coediting (with Cindy Ingold) an update of the book *Women's Studies: A Recommended Core Bibliography, 1980–1985* (1987).

**Juliana M. Kubala** received her Ph.D. from the Institute of the Liberal Arts at Emory University, Atlanta.

**Marie J. Kuda** is an independent scholar, freelance writer and reviewer, lecturer, and archivist.

**Colleen Lamos** is an associate professor of English at Rice University, Houston, Texas. Her book, *Modernism Astray: Sexual Errancy in T. S. Eliot, James Joyce, and Marcel Proust*, was published in 1998. Her articles have appeared in

*Novel*, *Signs: Journal of Women in Culture and Society*, *Contemporary Literature*, the *James Joyce Quarterly*, the *NWSA Journal*, the *Lesbian and Gay Studies Newsletter*, and in *The Lesbian Postmodern* (1994), *Lesbian Erotics* (1995), and *Quare Joyce* (1998).

**Cassandra Langer** has a Ph.D. in art history and criticism from New York University and more than twenty years' experience as a university professor. Her most recent book is *A Feminist Critique* (1996); she also founded (with her partner, Irene Javors) Private Eye: Noir Arts Ltd., New York City's only gallery dedicated to a noir aesthetic.

**Ruth Largay**, managing editor of *Signs: Journal of Women in Culture and Society*, is a Ph.D. candidate in mass communication at the University of Georgia, Athens. Prior to returning to academia, she worked as a writer and an editor in news media and public relations for more than fifteen years.

**Alison J. Laurie**, senior lecturer in women's studies at Victoria University of Wellington, Aotearoa/New Zealand, has been involved in lesbian, gay, and feminist politics as an activist, writer, and broadcaster since the 1960s. She started the first A/NZ lesbian studies courses and was a founder of the first lesbian magazine and radio program and lesbian studies conferences.

**N'Tanya R. Lee** received her B.A. from Brown University, Providence, Rhode Island, magna cum laude. As a Ph.D. student in American studies at Yale University, New Haven, Connecticut, she has focused her research primarily on the politics of black sexuality. Her publications include *Transforming the Nation: Lesbian, Gay, Bisexual, Transgendered US Histories, 1945–1995* (1998).

**Gary Lehring** is an assistant professor of political theory in the Department of Government at Smith College, Northampton, Massachusetts. His book *Officially Gay: Politics and the Public Construction of Sexuality* is forthcoming in the utopian socialist future.

**Sue Levin** is president of WWWomen Incorporated, a leading developer of content and commu-nity for women on the World Wide Web. WWWomen has been featured in publications such as *U.S. News and World Report*, the *San Francisco Chronicle,* and *Glamour* magazine as one of the top destinations for women on the Web.

**Ellen Lewin** is an associate professor of women's studies and anthropology at the University of Iowa, Iowa City. She is the author of *Recognizing Ourselves: Ceremonies of Lesbian and Gay Commitment* (1998) and *Lesbian Mothers: Accounts of Gender in American Culture* (1993), the editor of *Inventing Lesbian Cultures in America* (1996), and coeditor (with William L. Leap) of *Out in the Field: Reflections of Lesbian and Gay Anthropologists* (1996).

**Reina Lewis** is senior lecturer in the Department of Cultural Studies at the University of East London, England. She is the author of *Gendering Orientalism: Race, Femininity and Representation* (1996) and coeditor (with Peter Horne) of *Outlooks: Lesbian and Gay Sexualities and Visual Culture* (1996). She is working on Oriental women writers and on queer aesthetics.

**Yolanda Chavez Leyva** is a Chicana historian in the Division of Behavioral and Cultural Sciences at the University of Texas, San Antonio. Her research interests include the creation of ethnic identities and the ways in which ethnicity and sexuality intersect.

**Karin Lindeqvist** has been part of the feminist and lesbian movement in Sweden since the early 1980s. She has a degree in law, and she lives and works in Stockholm with her longtime lover and favorite author, Anna-Karin Granberg, and their stunningly beautiful Neapolitan mastiff.

**Anna Livia** is the author of four novels and two collections of short stories and coeditor (with Kira Hall) of *Queerly Phrased: Language, Gender, and Sexuality* (1997). Her most recent novel is *Bruised Fruit* (1999). Born in Dublin, Ireland, she moved to the United States in 1990 and makes her home in Berkeley, California.

**Christoph Lorey**, a professor of German at the University of New Brunswick, Fredericton, Canada, is the editor of the *International Fiction*

*Review* and coeditor (with John L. Plews) of *Queering the Canon: Defying Sights in German Literature and Culture* (1998). His recent book publications include *Lessings Familienbild* (1992) and *Die Ehe im klassischen Werk Goethes* (1995).

**Dana Luciano** received her Ph.D. from the Department of English at Cornell University, Ithaca, New York, in 1999. Her teaching and research interests include American literatures, public health, feminism, and queer theory. She has published work on seduction and discipline in early American fiction and is working on a study of illness and authority in the nineteenth century.

**Judy MacLean** is a writer and editor in San Francisco, freelancing with progressive non-profit organizations. Her fiction has appeared in anthologies, including *Lesbian Love Stories II* (1991), *Queer View Mirror* (1995), and *Pillow Talk* (1998). Her humor has appeared in the *San Francisco Chronicle*, the *Washington Post*, *The Best Contemporary Women's Humor* (1994), and other publications.

**Harriet Malinowitz** is an associate professor of English and director of women's studies at Long Island University, Brooklyn. She is the chief writer of standup comic Sara Cytron's shows *A Dyke Grows in Brooklyn* and *Take My Domestic Partner—Please!*, which have been performed extensively across the country.

**Nancy Manahan**, Ph.D., coedited (with Rosemary Curb) *Lesbian Nuns: Breaking Silence* (1985). Her writing has also appeared in *Mother Jones*, *Women's Studies Quarterly*, and *Common Lives/Lesbian Lives* and in the anthologies *American Notes and Queries*, *The Lesbian Path* (1980), and *Lesbian Studies* (1982). She teaches writing and literature at Minneapolis Community and Technical College in Minnesota.

**Phyllis F. Mannocchi** teaches English, women's studies, and lesbian and gay studies at Colby College, Waterville, Maine. She is preparing an edition of the letters of Vernon Lee and hopes next to write Lee's critical biography.

**Jeanne M. Marrazzo** is an assistant professor in infectious diseases at the University of Washington, Seattle. She is the medical director of the Seattle STD/HIV Prevention and Training Center and the principal investigator of a National Institutes of Health (NIH)–funded study of sexually transmitted diseases and cervical neoplasia in lesbian and bisexual women.

**Yvonne Marshall** is an archaeologist and feminist. She is engaged in a research project that investigates how the study of nonhuman primate behavior can contribute to the development of less mechanistic and more feminist models of human evolution.

**Madeleine Marti**, D.Phil., Zurich, Switzerland, wrote her dissertation about lesbians in German literature from 1945 to 1990 (*Hinterlegte Botschaften*). She is coeditor (with Marianne Ulmi) of a literary anthology about lesbians in Europe, *Sappho küsst Europa* (1997), and works as a teacher for adults.

**Elena M. Martínez** is an associate professor of Spanish at Baruch College, City University of New York. She is the author of *Lesbian Voices from Latin America: Breaking Ground* (1996). Her articles and book reviews have appeared in the United States, Latin America, and Spain.

**Jacqueline M. Martinez** is an assistant professor of communication and women's studies at Purdue University, West Lafayette, Indiana, where she teaches courses in semiotics, phenomenology, feminist theory, and intercultural communication. Her primary interests concern persons' lived experience of race, class, and sexuality as they emerge in particular social, historical, and cultural contexts.

**Elizabeth L. Massiah** has been involved in social and political action within the lesbian and gay community since the 1980s. As a clinical social worker, she has a private practice as a therapist. She is an active member of the Edmonton, Alberta, Canada, community at large, participating as a consultant to Corrections Canada, and is involved in the funding allocation process of the local United Way.

**Sidney Matrix** is a Ph.D. candidate in comparative studies in discourse and society at the University of Minnesota, Minneapolis.

**Judith Mayne** teaches French and women's studies at Ohio State University, Columbus. She is the author of several books on film, including *The Woman at the Keyhole: Feminism and Women's Cinema* (1990) and *Directed by Dorothy Arzner* (1994).

**Jodee M. McCaw** is a psychotherapist in Toronto, Canada. She received her Ph.D. in clinical psychology from the University of Windsor; her dissertation research explored the variety of means by which people of all sexual orientations become queer-positive in a queer-negative society.

**Judith McDaniel** is a poet and activist who lives in Tucson, Arizona. Her recent publications include an edited book of Barbara Deming's poetry, *I Change, I Change* (1996); a novel, *Yes I Said Yes I Will* (1996); and *The Lesbian Couples Guide* (1995). She teaches women's studies at the University of Arizona, Tucson, and is active in feminist issues connected to immigration and welfare.

**Toni A. H. McNaron** is a professor of English and women's studies at the University of Minnesota. Her publications include *Voices in the Night: Women Speaking About Incest* (1982), *I Dwell in Possibility: A Memoir* (1991), *Poisoned Ivy: Lesbian and Gay Academics Confronting Homophobia* (1997), and *The New Lesbian Studies: Into the 21st Century* (1996), coedited with Bonnie Zimmerman.

**Denise McVea** is a freelance writer living in Dallas, Texas. A graduate of Texas Woman's University, Denton, McVea has written for numerous publications, including the *Oregonian*, the *Dallas Morning News*, *Our Texas* magazine, and *ONYX* magazine. She is conducting research in the area of Texas myth.

**Deborah T. Meem** is a professor of English and women's studies at the University of Cincinnati in Ohio. Her current research interests are the rise of lesbian consciousness during the last half of the nineteenth century and contemporary lesbian popular culture.

**Lisa Merrill** is a professor of speech communication and performance studies at Hofstra University, Hempstead, New York. Her research focuses on the construction and performance of notions of gender and sexuality on the nineteenth-century stage. Her latest book is *When Romeo Was a Woman: Charlotte Cushman and Her Circle of Female Spectators* (1998).

**Melinda R. Michels** is a Ph.D. student in anthropology at American University, Washington, D.C. She is writing her dissertation on the geography of lesbian experience in Washington, D.C., during the 1970s, especially in relation to grassroots activism and race. She also coordinates the Gay, Lesbian, Bisexual, Transgender, and Ally Resource Center at American University.

**Nerina Milletti** was born in Florence, Italy, where she lives and where she received her Ph.D. in systematic botany. Active from the mid-1970s in the feminist movement, she started a bibliographic research project (and wrote papers) on lesbian Italian history. She now maintains a lesbian Web page.

**Lepa Mladjenovic**, a radical feminist lesbian living in Belgrade, Serbia, has been active in feminist groups, Women in Black Against War, and a lesbian rights group, Labris. She works as a feminist counselor and a lecturer in women's studies. In 1994, she received the Felipa De Souze Award from the International Gay and Lesbian Human Rights Commission.

**Martha Mockus** earned her Ph.D. in comparative studies in discourse and society at the University of Minnesota, Minneapolis. She is a professional pianist and has published essays and book reviews on lesbians in country music, opera, and popular music.

**Akilah Monifa** is a lesbian of African descent who is a professor of law at New College of California, San Francisco. She is also a freelance writer.

**Irene Monroe** is a Ford Foundation Fellow and Ph.D. candidate in the Religion, Gender, and Culture program at Harvard Divinity School, Cambridge, Massachusetts. She is a graduate of Wellesley College, Wellesley, Massachusetts, and Union Theological Seminary, New York City, and the author of "Louis Farrakhan's Ministry of Misogyny and Homophobia" in *The Farrakhan Factor* (1998).

**Lisa Moore**, an associate professor of English at the University of Texas, Austin, is the author of *Dangerous Intimacies: Toward a Sapphic History of the British Novel* (1997).

**Dee Mosbacher**, M.D., Ph.D., is a psychiatric consultant, lesbian activist, and filmmaker. Her award-winning films include *Out for a Change: Homophobia in Women's Sports*, *All God's Children*, and the Academy Award–nominated film *Straight from the Heart*. Her next film is on the history of lesbian/women's music.

**Manuela Mourão** is an assistant professor of English at Old Dominion University, Norfolk, Virginia. She has published essays on Anne Thackeray Ritchie, Portuguese women writers, the representation of female desire in early-modern pornography, and nuns in Gothic fiction. She has completed *Altered Habits: (Re)Figuring the Nun in Fiction*, a book-length study of the representation of nuns in European literature.

**Marie Marmo Mullaney** earned her Ph.D. in history from Rutgers University, New Brunswick, New Jersey. She is a professor of history and chair of the Department of History and Political Science at Caldwell College, Caldwell, New Jersey, and the author of *Revolutionary Women: Gender and the Socialist Revolutionary Role* (1983), as well as numerous articles in the area of women's history.

**Marcia Munson** has been a sex educator since 1987. Her articles have appeared in the anthologies *Dyke Life* (1995), *Sexualities* (1996), and *Lesbian Friendships* (1996), and she is coeditor (with Judith Stelboum) of *The Lesbian Polyamory Reader: Non-Monogamy, Open Relationships, and Casual Sex* (1999). She has a B.S. in biology and is certified as a sexological instructor/advisor of AIDS/STD prevention by the Institute for Advanced Study of Human Sexuality.

**Sally R. Munt** is a senior lecturer in media representation and analysis at the University of

Brighton, England. She is the author of *Heroic Desire: Lesbian Identity and Cultural Space* (1997), the editor of *Butch/Femme: Inside Lesbian Gender* (1997), and coeditor (with Andy Medhurst) of *Lesbian and Gay Studies: A Critical Introduction* (1997).

**Suniti Namjoshi** has written *Building Babel*, which has a building site on the Internet. She suggests that you check it out and contribute to it if you feel like it. The URL is http://www.peg.apc.org/~spinifex/babelbuildingsite.html.

**Nancy A. Naples** is an associate professor of sociology and women's studies at the University of California, Irvine. She is the author of *Grassroots Warriors: Activist Mothering, Community Work, and the War on Poverty* (1998) and the editor of *Community Activism and Feminist Politics: Organizing Across Race, Class, and Gender* (1998).

**Joan Nestle** is an essayist, editor, poet, historian, teacher, and cofounder (with Deborah Edel) of the Lesbian Herstory Archives in New York City. Her anthologized essays in *A Restricted Country* (1987) and edited collection of femme-butch writings in *The Persistent Desire* (1992) are crucial texts in lesbian history.

**Caryn E. Neumann** is a Ph.D. candidate in history at The Ohio State University, Columbus. A former managing editor of the *Journal of Women's History*, she is completing a study of the responses of traditional women's groups to the rise of feminism in the United States.

**Esther Newton** is professor of anthropology at Purchase College, State University of New York, and a founder of queer studies in the mid-1960s. She is author of *Mother Camp* (1979). Her current projects are a collection of essays (*Too Queer for College*) and a memoir (*My Butch Career*).

**Vivien Ng** is an associate professor and chair of the Department of Women's Studies at the University at Albany, State University of New York. She was president of the National Women's Studies Association in 1993–1994 and served on the board of the Center for Lesbian and Gay Studies at the City University of New York.

**Kathleen E. Nuccio**, M.S.W., Ph.D., is an associate professor and the coordinator of the Child Welfare Training Project, in the Graduate Program in Social Work at the University of Minnesota, Duluth. Nuccio received her doctorate in social work from Bryn Mawr College, Bryn Mawr, Pennsylvania, where her dissertation was awarded the Susan B. Anthony Prize.

**Jodi O'Brien** is an associate professor of sociology at Seattle University in Washington state. Her teaching and research interests include communities, inequalities, sexual politics, and social psychology. She is the coauthor (with Peter Kollock) of *Production of Reality* (1997), coeditor (with Judith Howard) of *Everyday Inequalities: Critical Inquiries* (1998), and author of *Social Prisms* (1999).

**Robyn Ochs** is a teacher, writer, activist, and speaker who has taught—at MIT, Cambridge, Massachusetts, and at Tufts University, Medford, Massachusetts—courses on bisexual identity and on the emergence of gay, lesbian, and bisexual cultures in the United States and Canada. She is the editor of the *Bisexual Resource Guide* (3rd ed., 1999) and the *International Directory of Bisexual Groups* (11th ed., 1994).

**Karen Lee Osborne** is the author of the novels *Carlyle Simpson* (1986) and *Hawkwings* (1991), the editor of *The Country of Herself: Short Fiction by Chicago Women* (1993), and coeditor (with William J. Spurlin) of *Reclaiming the Heartland: Lesbian and Gay Voices from the Midwest* (1996).

**Nancy Seale Osborne** is a librarian emerita and archivist at the State University of New York, Oswego. She was coordinator of special collections and library instruction and served as library liaison to the Department of Art and to the women's studies program minor. She is a mother, grandmother, canoeist, and fiction writer.

**Tina O'Toole**, received her M.A. in women's studies at University College, Dublin, Ireland. She is a tutor in the English Department at University College, Cork, where she is a Ph.D. student and also teaches in the women's studies program. Her research area is Irish

women's writing, and she is writing her dissertation on new women writers in Ireland and Britain.

**Dorothy (Dottie) Painter** received her Ph.D. in communication and her J.D. from The Ohio State University, Columbus. She practices law in Columbus and teaches part-time for the Department of Women's Studies at OSU.

**Connie (Concetta) Panzarino** was born in Brooklyn, New York. She is a lesbian with spinal muscular atrophy type II. She holds an M.A. in art therapy from New York University. She wrote her autobiography, *The Me in the Mirror* (1994), and has also written three children's books.

**Charlotte J. Patterson**, professor of psychology at the University of Virginia, Charlottesville, is a developmental psychologist who has conducted research with lesbian mothers and their children.

**JoAnn Pavletich** is an assistant professor of English at the University of Houston, Downtown. Her areas of research and teaching include late-nineteenth- and early-twentieth-century U.S. culture, with an emphasis on African American literature.

**Rosa María Pegueros** is an assistant professor of Latin American history at the University of Rhode Island, Kingston, with a joint appointment in women's studies. Her lesbian writings have appeared in *Common Lives/Lesbian Lives* and in the *Lesbian News* (Los Angeles).

**Ann Pellegrini** is an assistant professor of English and American literature and language at Harvard University, Cambridge, Massachusetts. She is the author of *Performance Anxieties: Staging Psychoanalysis, Staging Race* (1997) and coeditor (with Daniel Boyarin and Daniel Hzkovitz) of *Queer Theory and the Jewish Question* (2000). Once upon a time, she was a classicist.

**Julia Penelope** lives in Lubbock, Texas, and is self-employed as a freelance lexicographer and copy editor.

**Andrea L. T. Peterson** is a freelance writer based in the Virginia suburbs of Washington, D.C. Her work has appeared in *Gay and Lesbian*

*Literature* (1998), *Gay and Lesbian Biographies* (1997), vol. 2, and dozens of publications in the United States and abroad, including *Lesbian Review of Books*, *Harvard Gay and Lesbian Review*, *Update*, *Front Page*, the *Advocate*, and *Curve*.

**Shane Phelan** is director of women's studies and an associate professor of political science at the University of New Mexico, Albuquerque. Among her most recent publications are *Playing with Fire: Queer Politics, Queer Theories* (1997) and *We Are Everywhere: A Historical Sourcebook of Gay and Lesbian Politics* (1997).

**Anne Marie Pois** is an instructor in the women's studies program and the history department at the University of Colorado, Boulder. She teaches courses on the history of U.S. women's social activism and focuses on women's peace history in her research. She is working on a biography of Emily Greene Balch.

**Nancy Polikoff** is a professor of law at American University Washington College of Law, Washington, D.C. Since the 1970s, she has litigated, written about, and taught about cases involving lesbian and gay parenting.

**Christy M. Ponticelli** is an assistant professor of sociology at the University of South Florida, Tampa. She is the author of *Gateways to Improving Lesbian Health and Health Care* (1998) and articles on conducting field research and the construction of identities within religious communities.

**Marjorie Pryse** is a professor of English and women's studies at the University at Albany, State University of New York. Her recent publication on Sarah Orne Jewett, "Sex, Class, and 'Category Crisis': Reading Jewett's Transitivity," is in *American Literature* (1998). She is coeditor (with Judith Fetterley) of *American Women Regionalists* (1992), a Norton anthology.

**María Rachid** is a lesbian feminist activist in Buenos Aires, Argentina, and a member of the groups Musas de Papel, Amenaza Lésbica, and COFEM (Feminist Communication). She is the editor of the lesbian magazine *La Rara* and one of the coordinators of queer studies at the University of Buenos Aires, Argentina.

**Nicole C. Raeburn** is a Ph.D. candidate in sociology at The Ohio State University. Her dissertation is entitled "The Rise of Lesbian, Gay, and Bisexual Rights in the Workplace." Combining institutional and social-movement theories, her study of Fortune 1000 companies examines the adoption of gay-inclusive policies, such as nondiscrimination protection, diversity training that includes sexual orientation, and domestic-partner benefits.

**Jo Reger** received her Ph.D. in sociology at Ohio State University, Columbus. She is affiliated with the University of Albany, State University of New York. She is the coauthor (with Abigail Halcli) of an article on the gendered experiences of women politicians in Britain and the United States and recently completed a study examining the continuity of chapters of the National Organization for Women.

**Renate Reimann** received her Ph.D. in sociology from the Graduate School of the City University of New York and holds graduate degrees in sociology and Protestant theology from the University of Hamburg, Germany. She is visiting assistant professor of sociology at Hamilton College in Clinton, New York. Her coedited volume (with Mary Bernstein) will be published by Columbia University Press in 2000.

**Kristen A. Renn** received her Ph.D. in higher education at Boston College in Massachusetts and is an associate dean of student life at Brown University, Providence, Rhode Island, where she oversaw programs and services for lesbian, gay, bisexual, and transgender students. She received her bachelor's degree in music from Mount Holyoke College, South Hadley, Massachusetts.

**Yolanda Retter** is a lesbian history and visibility activist of Peruvian and German descent and a lifelong lesbian. She received her Ph.D. in American studies at the University of New Mexico, Albuquerque. She manages a lesbian archive in Los Angeles and compiled the Lesbian History Project Web site, URL:http://www-lib.usc.edu/~retter/main.html.

**Lisa Rhodes** is a Ph.D. candidate in American studies at the University of Texas, Austin. She is an associate professor of cultural, social, and literary studies at National University, La Jolla, California.

**Molly Rae Rhodes** received her Ph.D. from the Department of Literature at the University of California, San Diego.

**Consuelo Rivera Fuentes** is a Chilean poet, feminist lesbian, and founder and member of the Chilean lesbian group LEA. Her recent publications include "Two Stories, Three Lovers, and the Creation of Meaning in a Black Lesbian Autobiography: A Diary" in *Black British Feminism: A Reader* (1997) and *The Bra Collection*, a book of short stories about women's clothes (forthcoming).

**Jennifer E. Robertson** is a professor of anthropology at the University of Michigan, Ann Arbor. Among her publications are *Native and Newcomer: Making and Remaking a Japanese City* (1991) and *Takarazuka: Sexual Politics and Popular Culture in Modern Japan* (1998). She is writing a book on Japanese colonial cultures.

**Christine Robinson** is a Ph.D. student and graduate instructor in the Department of Sociology at the University of Kansas, Lawrence. She has published articles on social control, sexuality, and social inequality.

**Ruthann Robson** is a professor of law at the City University of New York (CUNY) School of Law, one of the very few progressive law schools in North America. She is the author of *Lesbian (Out)Law: Survival Under the Rule of Law* (1990) and *Sappho Goes to Law School* (1998), as well as two volumes of short stories and two novels.

**Catherine Roma**, D.M.A., became one of the founding mothers of the women's choral movement when she started Anna Crusis Women's Choir in her native Philadelphia in 1975. She is founder and director of MUSE Cincinnati's Women's Choir and is an assistant professor of music at Wilmington College, Wilmington, Ohio.

**Judith Roof** is the author of *Come As You Are: Sexuality and Narrative* (1996), *Reproductions of Reproductions: Imaging Symbolic Change* (1996), and *A Lure of Knowledge: Lesbian Sexuality and Theory* (1991) and coeditor (with Robyn Wiegman) of *Who Can Speak? Authority and Critical Identity* and (with Richard Feldstein) *Feminism and Psychoanalysis* (1989).

**Suzanna Rose**, Ph.D., is a professor of psychology and women's studies at the University of Missouri, St. Louis. Her research interests concern how gender, sexual orientation, and race affect friendship and romantic relationships, with a special emphasis on lesbian love scripts and how lesbians and gay men cope with hate crimes and same-sex domestic violence.

**Becki L. Ross** teaches sociology and women's studies at the University of British Columbia, Vancouver, Canada. Her recent publications include *The House That Jill Built: A Lesbian Nation in Formation* (1995) and a chapter in *Bad Attitude/s on Trial: Feminism, Pornography, and the Butler Decision* (1997). She is researching the world of sexual entertainment (burlesque, go-go, striptease) in post–World War II Vancouver.

**Sue V. Rosser** received her Ph.D. in zoology from the University of Wisconsin, Madison, in 1973. She is director of the Center for Women's Studies and Gender Research at the University of Florida, Gainesville, where she is also a professor of anthropology. She has edited collections and written more than sixty journal articles on women and science and women's health and six books.

**Rebecca Ann Rugg** is a student in the dramaturgy and dramatic criticism program at the Yale University School of Drama, New Haven, Connecticut.

**Maria Angeles Ruiz Torralba** has worked in Spain with the federation of associations known as Coordinadora Gai-Lesbiana and was a founder member of its women's group (Group Lesbos).

**Leila J. Rupp** teaches women's history and the history of same-sex sexuality at The Ohio State University, Columbus. Among her recent books are *Worlds of Women: The Making of an International Women's Movement* (1998) and *A Desired Past: Same-Sex Love and Sexuality in the United States* (1999).

**Paula C. Rust**, Ph.D. sociology, studies sexual identities and politics, with an emphasis on bisexuality. She is an associate professor at Hamilton College, Clinton, New York. She reached political consciousness during the height of 1970s lesbian feminism, identifies as a garden-variety lesbian, and lives with her partner, Lorna, and their two chidren.

**Montserrat Sagot**, a Costa Rican sociologist and anthropologist, has a Ph.D in sociology from American University, Washington, D.C. She was a founding member of the antiviolence-against-women movement in Costa Rica. She is an associate professor of sociology at the Universidad de Costa Rica, San Jose, and chair of the Regional Master's Program in Women's Studies.

**Nancy San Martín** is a Ph.D. candidate in the history of consciousness at the University of California, Santa Cruz. Her work focuses on popular cultural narratives of nationalisms and same-sex sexualities in the United States.

**Ronni L. Sanlo,** Ed.D., is the director of the University of California, Los Angeles, Lesbian Gay Bisexual Transgender (LGBT) Campus Resource Center. She is a founding member of the National Consortium of LGBT Campus Resource Center Directors and the national chair of the Gay Lesbian Bisexual Transgender Issues Network of the National Association of Student Personnel Administrators (NASPA).

**Alejandra Sarda** is an activist out of passion and a clinical pyschologist for a living. She is committed to ending binary thinking and fundamentalism in all of its manifestations, even in lesbian, gay, transgender, and bisexual circles. She is polyamorous, glad to be alive, and proudly Latin American.

**Susan Sayer** writes fiction and nonfiction. Her short stories appear in *The Exploding Frangipani* (1990), *Subversive Acts* (1991), *Me and Marilyn Monroe* (1993), and *Car Maintenance, Explo-*sives, *and Love* (1997), the latter coedited with Cathie Dunsford and Susan Hawthorne. A Ph.D. candidate in anthropology at the University of Waikato, New Zealand, she wrote her dissertation on *The Postcolonial Lesbian Text: Readings of Four Novels by Renée.*

**Claudia Schaefer** is a professor of Hispanic literature and culture at the University of Rochester in New York. She is the author of numerous studies on twentieth-century Spain and Latin America; among her recent books is *Danger Zones: Homosexuality, National Identity, and Mexican Culture* (1996).

**Susan Schibanoff** has published numerous studies of medieval and early-modern literature that use feminist and gay and lesbian approaches. She has completed articles on same-sex desire in Hildegard of Bingen and Richardis of Stade and on poetry and male sodomy in twelfth-century literature. She is working on a book on Chaucer's queer poetics. She teaches at the University of New Hampshire, Durham.

**Claudia Schoppmann**, a historian, lives in Berlin, Germany. Her dissertation on Nazi politics and female homosexuality was published in 1991. She has written and coedited several books on German women's history, including Jewish women, lesbians, and women in exile.

**Marilyn R. Schuster** received her Ph.D. from Yale University, New Haven, Connecticut. She is a professor of French and women's studies at Smith College, Northampton, Massachusetts. Her major publications are *Women's Place in the Academy: Transforming the Liberal Arts Curriculum* (1985) (with Susan Van Dyne), *Marguerite Duras Revisited* (1993), and *Passionate Communities: Reading Lesbian Resistance in Jane Rule's Fiction* (1999).

**Judith Schuyf** received her Ph.D. in history from the University of Leiden in the Netherlands. She is a founding member of the Lesbian and Gay Studies Centre of Utrecht University in the Netherlands. She has written about lesbian history, political culture, and senior gays and lesbians, and is a senior researcher at the National Dutch Institute for War Victims.

**Dana R. Shugar** is an associate professor of English and women's studies at the University of Rhode Island, Kingston. She teaches Romantic and Victorian literature, leftist women's literature, utopian fiction, lesbian studies, and studies in race, gender, class, and sexuality. Her research interests include lesbian separatism, queer theory, lesbian literature, and ecofeminism.

**Patricia Sieber** has a Ph.D. in Chinese from the University of California, Berkeley. She is an assistant professor in the Department of East Asian Languages and Literatures at Ohio State University, Columbus. Her research focuses on issues of print, performance, gender, and sexuality in Chinese drama and fiction from the sixteenth through the twentieth centuries.

**Gina M. Siesing** completed her Ph.D. in Women, Gender, and Literature in the English department at the University of Texas, Austin. Her dissertation is entitled "Fictional Democracies: The Formation of Lesbian Literary Publics."

**Maria Josefina Silva** is coeditor of the Portuguese magazine *Lilás*. She is a specialist in lesbian culture in Portugal in the twentieth century.

**Noenoe K. Silva**, a Kanaka Maoli (native Hawaiian), has a B.A. in Hawai'ian language and a master's in library and information studies. She is a Ph.D. candidate in political science at University of Hawai'i, Manoa; her dissertation, using Hawai'ian language sources, focuses on Kanaka Maoli women's forms of resistance to colonialism.

**Sharon Silverstein** graduated from Stanford University, Stanford, California, with a B.A. in feminist studies, and from Harvard Business School, Cambridge, Massachusetts, with an M.B.A. She and Annette Friskopp celebrated a ceremony of commitment in 1992 and coauthored the book *Straight Jobs, Gay Lives* (1995). Sharon gave birth to their son in 1996.

**Christina Simmons** grew up in Indiana, graduated from Radcliffe College, Cambridge, Massachusetts, became a feminist in 1970, and received a Ph.D. in American civilization from Brown University, Providence, Rhode Island, in 1982. She teaches U.S. and Canadian women's history and the history of sexuality at the University of Windsor, Windsor, Ontario, Canada, where she lives with her partner and two sons.

**Caroline Chung Simpson** received a Ph.D. in American studies from the University of Texas, Austin, and teaches courses in Asian American studies and postwar culture in the English department at the University of Washington, Seattle. She is completing a book on the relationship between popular discourses on Japanese and Japanese American culture and identity and definitions of the postwar U.S. nation.

**Patricia Juliana Smith** is visiting assistant professor of English at the University of California, Los Angeles. She is the author of *Lesbian Panic: Homoeroticism in Modern British Women's Fiction* (1997) and coeditor (with Corinne Blackmer) of *En Travesti: Women, Gender Subversion, Opera* (1995).

**Carroll Smith-Rosenberg** is the author of the essay "The Female World of Love and Ritual" (1975), one of the first efforts to historically contextualize love among women. Her *Disorderly Conduct* (1985) examines women sexual reformers, medical representations of women, and the emergence of independent women. She is exploring the interface of race, gender, and colonialism.

**Cherry Smyth** is a writer, journalist, and curator. She is an active member of the Irish diaspora, living between London and her love interest in America. She is the author of *Queer Notions* (1992) and *Damn Fine Art by New Lesbian Artists* (1996), the first international collection of its kind.

**Jane McIntosh Snyder** is professor emeritus of classics at The Ohio State University, Columbus. Her books include *The Woman and the Lyre: Women Writers in Classical Greece and Rome* (1989) and *Lesbian Desire in the Lyrics of Sappho* (1997). She is a professional violinist with the ProMusica Chamber Orchestra of Columbus and the Chamber Orchestra of Albuquerque.

**Birgitte Soland** teaches European women's history at The Ohio State University, Columbus.

She holds a cand.mag. degree from the University of Aarhus, Denmark, and a Ph.D. in history from the University of Minnesota, Minneapolis. She has conducted research on gay and lesbian history and published "A Queer Nation? The Passage of the Gay and Lesbian Partnership Legislation in Denmark, 1989" in *Social Politics* (1998).

**Alisa Solomon** is an associate professor of English at Baruch College, City University of New York (CUNY), and of English and theater at the CUNY Graduate Center. She is a staff writer at the *Village Voice* and the author of *Re-Dressing the Canon: Essays on Theater and Gender* (1997).

**Bonnie B. Spanier** received her Ph.D. in microbiology and molecular genetics from Harvard University, Cambridge, Massachusetts. Her recent publications include *Im/partial Science: Gender Ideology in Molecular Biology* (1995), and "Biological Determination of Homosexuality" in the *NWSA Journal* (1995). She is an associate professor in the women's studies department at the University at Albany, State University of New York.

**Arlene Stein** is an assistant professor of sociology at the University of Oregon, Eugene. She is the editor of *Sisters, Sexperts, Queers: Beyond the Lesbian Nation* (1993) and the author of *Sex and Sensibility: Stories of a Lesbian Nation* (1997).

**Marc Stein** received his Ph.D. from the University of Pennsylvania, Philadelphia, taught at Bryn Mawr College, Bryn Mawr, Pennsylvania, and Colby College, Waterville, Maine, and is an assistant professor of history at York University in Toronto, Canada. A former editor of *Gay Community News*, he is completing *City of Sisterly and Brotherly Loves: The Making of Lesbian and Gay Communities in Greater Philadelphia, 1945–72*.

**Judith P. Stelboum** teaches English, women's studies, and lesbian studies at the College of Staten Island, City University of New York. Her essays, fiction, and poetry have appeared in several anthologies. She is coeditor (with Marcia Munson) of *The Lesbian Polyamory Reader: Non-Monogamy, Open Relationships, and Casual Sex* (1999).

**Lisbeth Stenberg**, a Ph.D. candidate in the Department of Literature at the University of Gothenburg, Sweden, is writing a dissertation on Selma Lagerlöf's early work, focusing on the thematics of gender and creativity analyzed from a contextual perspective.

**Linnea A. Stenson** is a visiting assistant professor of women's and gender studies at Macalester College, St. Paul, Minnesota. She is working on a book-length manuscript about pulp novels.

**Christy Stevens** received an M.A. in women's studies at San Diego State University and is a Ph.D. student in English at University of California, Irvine. Her thesis constructs a lesbian intertextual analysis of Jeanette Winterson's 1992 novel, *Written on the Body*.

**Arlene M. Stiebel** earned her Ph.D. in English and comparative literature from Columbia University, New York City. Formerly an administrator at Brown University, Providence, Rhode Island, and editor of the *Huntington Library Quarterly*, she has most recently been a professor of English at California State University, Northridge. Her publications include articles in the *Gay and Lesbian Literary Heritage* (1994) and in *Homosexuality in Renaissance and Enlightenment England* (1992).

**Elizabeth Stuart** holds the chair of Christian theology at King Alfred's College, Winchester, United Kingdom. She is the editor of the academic journal *Theology and Sexuality* and the author of a number of books on Christianity and sexuality, including *Just Good Friends: Towards a Lesbian and Gay Theology of Relationships* (1995), *People of Passion* (1996), and *Religion Is a Queer Thing* (1997).

**Darlene M. Suarez** is a Ph.D. student in cultural anthropology at the University of California, Riverside. Her research interests focus on Native American political culture, concepts of colonialism and nationalism, and the politics of sovereignty, identity, and Indian nationhood.

**Susan Talburt** teaches curricular, poststructural, and feminist theories, social and cultural foundations of education, and anthropology of education in the Department of Educational Policy Studies at Georgia State University, Atlanta. She is writing a book about lesbian faculty in higher education.

**Bette S. Tallen** is a Jewish lesbian feminist working with the office of University Initiatives at the University of Central Florida, Orlando. She also develops community workshops on "Teaching Diversity as a Skill."

**Verta Taylor** is a professor of sociology at Ohio State University, Columbus. She is the coauthor (with Leila J. Rupp) of *Survival in the Doldrums: The American Women's Rights Movement, 1945 to the 1960s* (1987), the coeditor (with Laurel Richardson and Nancy Whittier) of *Feminist Frontiers* (4th ed., 1997), and the author of *Rock-a-By Baby: Feminism, Self-Help, and Postpartum Depression* (1996).

**Giti Thadani** is a founding member and coordinator of Sakhi, the Lesbian Resource Centre in New Delhi, India. She is a writer and photographer who travels extensively in India, documenting archetypes of the cosmic Feminine, and the author of *Sakhiyani: Lesbian Desire in Ancient and Modern India* (1996).

**Polly Thistlethwaite** is a reference librarian at Colorado State University, Fort Collins. She worked with the Lesbian Herstory Archives collective in New York City from 1987 to 1997, actively participating in the effort to establish the collection in its Brooklyn townhouse.

**Suzana Tratnik** is a sociologist and writer, in Ljubljana, Slovenia, where she focuses on sociological aspects of gay, lesbian, feminist, and minority movements and subcultures.

**Valerie Traub** teaches English and women's studies at the University of Michigan, Ann Arbor. She is the author of *Desire and Anxiety: Circulations of Sexuality in Shakespearean Drama* (1992) and *The Renaissance of "Lesbianism" in Early Modern England* (forthcoming).

**Anne M. Valk** is an assistant professor of historical studies at Southern Illinois University, Edwardsville. Her dissertation, completed at Duke University, Durham, North Carolina, is a study of feminism, welfare rights, civil rights, and lesbian feminism in Washington, D.C., in the 1960s and 1970s. Her scholarly and teaching interests include oral and public history, social movements, and African American communities in the segregated South.

**Annette Van Dyke** is an assistant professor of interdisciplinary studies and women's studies at the University of Illinois, Springfield, where she directs the individual option and liberal studies programs. She is the author of *The Search for a Woman-Centered Spirituality* (1992), *Hooded Murder* (1996), and essays in *SAIL* and *MELUS*, among others.

**Linda Van Leuven** is a Ph.D. candidate in sociology at the University of California, Los Angeles. She studies sexualized interactions and how people manage relational boundaries in body- and image-oriented service occupations. Her dissertation is titled "When Frames Collide: Personal Service Work and the Negotiation of Relational Boundaries."

**Marieke Van Willigen** is an assistant professor at East Carolina University, Greenville, North Carolina. Her research investigates the effect of activism and self-help activities on individuals' well-being. She is also examining the differential effects of education on well-being for men and women. Her interests cut across social movements, gender, and medical sociology.

**Paul L. Vasey** received his Ph.D. in anthropology from the University of Montreal, in 1997. He has studied female homosexual behavior in Japanese macaques since the early 1990s. His research focuses on nonreproductive sexual behavior in animals.

**Blakey Vermeule** writes on eighteenth-century British literature and moral psychology. She teaches in the English department at Yale University, New Haven, Connecticut.

**Giney Villar** is the chair of the Womyn Supporting Womyn Centre, a lesbian organization based in the Philippines. She coauthored (with Aida F. Santos) the first out Filipina lesbian book, *Woman to Woman: Essays, Poetry, and Fiction*

(1994). She was born in Manila, has a B.S. in psychology, and is an M.A. student in humanities and women's studies at St. Scholastica's College, Manila.

**Elizabeth Wahl** received her Ph.D. in comparative literature from Stanford University, Stanford, California, where she teaches literature courses. She is the author of *Invisible Relations: Idealized and Sexualized Representations of Female Intimacy in England and France, 1600–1760* (1999).

**Linda D. Wayne** is a Ph.D. candidate in comparative studies in discourse and society at the University of Minnesota, Minneapolis. She has published in *Women and Language, RFR/DRF,* and *Transforms*.

**Alice R. Wexler** is the author of three books; *Emma Goldman in America* (1984), *Emma Goldman in Exile* (1989), and *Mapping Fate: A Memoir of Family, Risk, and Genetic Research* (1995). She is a research scholar at the Center for the Study of Women at the University of California, Los Angeles.

**Vera Whisman** is an assistant professor of sociology at Hobart and William Smith Colleges, Geneva, New York. She studies the social construction of lesbian, gay, and bisexual identities and is the author of *Queer By Choice* (1996).

**Gillian Whitlock** is an associate professor of humanities at Griffith University, Nathan, Australia. She is author of *The Intimate Empire: Reading Women's Autobiography* (1999), a study of autobiography and colonialism. She has edited a number of books in Australian studies and women's writing, including *Autographs: Contemporary Australian Autobiography* (1996).

**Robyn Wiegman** teaches feminist theory, with a special emphasis on race and sexuality, at the University of California, Irvine, where she directs the Program in Women's Studies. She is the author of *American Anatomies: Theorizing Race and Gender* (1995) and the editor of three anthologies, including *AIDS and the National Body: Essays by Thomas Yingling* (1997).

**Saskia E. Wieringa** is a senior lecturer in women's studies at the Institute of Social Studies, The Hague, Netherlands. She has published a lesbian travelog and written on women's organizations in Indonesia, sustainable development, feminist politics, and women's same-sex relations. She is involved in a research project on cross-cultural gender indicators.

**Maxine Wolfe** is a coordinator at the Lesbian Herstory Archives, New York City, a cofounder of the Lesbian Avengers, a member of ACT-UP New York since 1987 and cofounder of its Women's Committee, and a professor emerita of environmental psychology at the City University of New York Graduate School.

**Susan J. Wolfe** is a professor and chair of the English department at the University of South Dakota, Vermillion. Her research and teaching interests include work in historical linguistics, stylistics, and lesbian studies. With Julia Penelope, she coedited *The Original Coming Out Stories* (1980), *Lesbian Culture: An Anthology* (1993), and *Sexual Practice/Textual Theory: Lesbian Cultural Criticism* (1993).

**Merle Woo** is a socialist feminist activist, educator, and writer. She is the education coordinator for Bay Area Radical Women (San Francisco, California), an international Trotskyist feminist organization.

**Mary E. Wood** is an associate professor of English at the University of Oregon, Eugene.

**Yvonne Yarbro-Bejarano** is a professor of Spanish and chair of Chicana/o studies in the Center for Comparative Studies in Race and Ethnicity Program at Stanford University, Stanford, California. She is the author of *Feminism and the Honor Plays of Lope de Vega* (1994) and coeditor (with Richard Griswold del Castillo and Teresa McKenna) of *Chicano Art: Resistance and Affirmation* (1991), and a forthcoming collection of essays on Cherríe Moraga.

**Willa Young** is director of Student Gender and Sexuality Services at Ohio State University, Columbus. A lecturer in the Department of Women's Studies, she teaches courses on American women's movements and feminist perspectives on women and violence. She also facilitates a course on violence in society for physicians in the College of Medicine.

**Yvonne Zipter** is the author of *Ransacking the Closet* (1995; essays), *The Patience of Metal* (1990; poems), *Diamonds Are a Dyke's Best Friend* (1988; nonfiction study), and the nationally syndicated column "Inside Out." She holds an M.F.A. in writing from Vermont College, Montpelier, and received a Sprague-Todes Literary Award in 1997.

**Jacqueline N. Zita** holds a Ph.D. in philosophy and is chair of the women's studies department at the University of Minnesota, Minneapolis. She has published widely in the areas of sexuality, gender, corporeal philosophy, and feminist epistemology and pedagogies. Her latest book is *Body Talk: Philosophical Essays on Sex and Gender* (1998), which explores social constructions of the body across race, class, gender, and sexuality.

# Subject Guide

## Anthropology
Anthropology
Balkan Sworn Virgins
Benedict, Ruth
Colonialism
Evolution and Human Origins
Harems
Indigenous Cultures
Mâhû
Oral History

## Art
Architecture
Art, Contemporary European
Art, Contemporary North American
Art, Mainstream
Austen, Alice
Bonheur, Rosa
Brooks, Romaine
Cartoons and Comic Books
Gluck (Hannah Gluckstein)
Kahlo, Frida
Lee, Vernon
Lewis, Mary Edmonia
Millett, Kate
Photography

## Associations and Organizations
Asian Lesbian Network
Associations and Organizations
Combahee River Collective
Daughters of Bilitis
Encuentros de Lesbianas
Furies, The

Girl Scouts
International Organizations
Lesbian Avengers
National Gay and Lesbian Task Force (NGLTF)
National Organization for Women (NOW)
Queer Nation
Radicalesbians

## Biography
Addams, Jane
Allan, Maud
Allen, Paula Gunn
Anderson, Margaret Carolyn
Anne, Queen of England
Anthony, Susan B.
Anzaldúa, Gloria E.
Arnold, June
Arzner, Dorothy
Austen, Alice
Bannon, Ann
Barnes, Djuna Chappell
Barney, Natalie Clifford
Bates, Katharine Lee
Beach, Sylvia
Beauvoir, Simone de
Behn, Aphra
Benedict, Ruth
Bentley, Gladys
Bishop, Elizabeth
Blais, Marie-Claire
Blaman, Anna
Bonheur, Rosa
Bowen, Elizabeth
Bowles, Jane Auer
Boye, Karin

Brittain, Vera Mary
Brooks, Romaine
Brossard, Nicole
Brown, Rita Mae
Bryher
Cather, Willa
Chambers, Jane
Charke, Charlotte
Christina of Sweden
Colette
Compton-Burnett, Ivy
Cornwell, Anita
Cruikshank, Margaret Louise
Cushman, Charlotte
Davis, Katherine Bement
Delarus-Mardrus, Lucie
Deming, Barbara
Dickinson, Emily
Didrikson, Mildred Ella "Babe" (Zaharias)
Dietrich, Marlene
Duffy, Maureen Patricia
Dunbar-Nelson, Alice
Erauso, Catalina de
Faderman, Lillian
Field, Michael
Flanner, Janet
Foster, Jeannette Howard
Fuller, Margaret
Garbo, Greta
Gidlow, Elsa
Gittings, Barbara
Gluck (Hannah Gluckstein)
Goldman, Emma
Grahn, Judy
Grier, Barbara
Grimké, Angelina Weld
Hall, Radclyffe
Hamilton, Edith
Hampton, Mabel
Hansberry, Lorraine (Vivian)
H.D. (Hilda Doolittle)
Hildegard of Bingen, Saint
Holtby, Winifred
James, Alice
Jay, Karla
Jewett, Sarah Orne
Jewsbury, Geraldine
Joan of Arc (Jeanne d'Arc)
Johnston, Jill
Juana Inés de la Cruz, Sor
Kahlo, Frida
King, Billie Jean Moffitt

Ladies of Llangollen
Lagerlöf, Selma
Landowska, Wanda
lang, k.d. (Kathryn Dawn)
Leduc, Violette
Lee, Vernon
Lewis, Mary Edmonia
Lister, Anne
Lorde, Audre
Lowell, Amy Lawrence
Mansfield, Katherine
Marie Antoinette
Martin, Del, and Lyon, Phyllis
McCullers, Carson
Mew, Charlotte
Michel, Louise
Millay, Edna St. Vincent
Millett, Kate
Mistral, Gabriela
Mitchell, Alice
Miyamoto Yuriko
Moraga, Cherríe
Navratilova, Martina
Nestle, Joan
Nin, Anais
Noble, Elaine
O'Brien, Kate
Parker, Pat
Parnok, Sophia
Parra, Teresa de la
Penelope, Julia
Philips, Katherine
Pirie, Jane, and Woods, Marianne
Rainey, Gertrude "Ma"
Raucourt, Françoise
Renault, Mary
Rich, Adrienne
Roosevelt, Anna Eleanor
Routsong, Alma
Rukeyser, Muriel
Rule, Jane Vance
Rüling, Anna
Sackville-West, Vita
Sand, George
Sappho
Sarton, May
Scudder, Vida Dutton
Shockley, Ann Allen
Simcox, Edith Jemima
Smith, Barbara
Smith, Bessie
Smith, Lillian Eugenia

Smyth, Dame Ethel Mary
Solanas, Valerie
Stein, Gertrude
Taylor, Valerie
Teresa of Avila
Thomas, M. Carey
Toklas, Alice B.
Tsvetaeva, Marina Ivanovna
Vargas, Chavela
Vivien, Renée
Walker, A'lelia
Walker, Mary Edwards
Warner, Sylvia Townsend
Weirauch, Anna Elisabet
Wilhelm, Gale
Winsloe, Christa
Wittig, Monique
Wolff, Charlotte
Woolf, Virginia
Wu Zao
Yosano Akiko
Yoshiya Nobuko
Yourcenar, Marguerite

## Cultural Identities
African Americans
Arab Americans
Asian Americans and Pacific Islanders
Balkan Sworn Virgins
Bisexuality
Butch-Femme
Disability
Drag Kings
Fat Liberation
Identity
Identity Politics
Judaism
Latinas
Leather
Mestizaje
Native Americans
Passing Women
Sadomasochism
Situational Lesbianism
Subculture
Transgender
Women of Color

## Economics
Advertising and Consumerism

Bars
Bookstores
Businesses, Lesbian
Class
Collectives
Colonialism
Demography
Domestic Partnership
Economics
Labor Movement
Land
Olivia
Sex Work
Sexual Harassment
Socialism
Tourism and Guidebooks
Work

## Geography
Argentina
Australia
Austria
Belgium
Berlin
Brazil
Buffalo, New York
Canada
Caribbean
Central America
Cherry Grove, New York
Chicago, Illinois
Chile
China
Czech Republic
Denmark
Egypt
Finland
France
Germany
Greece
Greenwich Village
Harlem
Hawaii
Immigration
India
Indonesia
Ireland
Israel
Italy
Japan
Korea, South

Lesbos, Island of
Lesotho
London
Los Angeles, California
Mexico
Namibia
Netherlands
New Zealand
Pacific Islands
Paris
Philippines
Poland
Portugal
Provincetown, Massachusetts
Québec
Russia
San Francisco, California
Slovenia
Small Towns and Rural Areas
South Africa
Spain
Sweden
Switzerland
Taiwan
Thailand
United Kingdom
United States
Washington, D.C.
Yugoslavia, Former
Zimbabwe

### Education
Anthologies
Archives and Libraries
Athletics, Collegiate
Bibliographies and Reference Works
Boarding Schools
Colleges, Women's
Computer Networks and Services
Cruikshank, Margaret Louise
Davis, Katherine Bement
Faderman, Lillian
Foster, Jeannette Howard
Gittings, Barbara
Hamilton, Edith
High Schools, Lesbian and Gay
Jay, Karla
Lesbian Herstory Archives
Lesbian Studies
Librarians
Physical Education

Scholars
Sex Education
Sororities
Students
Teachers
Thomas, M. Carey
Women's Studies

### Health
AIDS (Acquired Immune Deficiency
    Syndrome)
Alcohol and Substance Abuse
Body Image
Health
Medicine
Nursing
Recovery Movement
Safer Sex
Self-Help
Sex Education
Sexually Transmitted Diseases
Suicide
Vegetarianism
Walker, Mary Edwards

### History
Addams, Jane
Amazons
Anne, Queen of England
Anthony, Susan B.
Antiquity
Autobiography
Biography
Boston Marriage
Brittain, Vera Mary
Christina of Sweden
Colonialism
Companionate Marriage
Deming, Barbara
Diaries and Letters
Enlightenment, European
Erauso, Catalina de
Europe, Early Modern
Female Support Networks
Fuller, Margaret
Gay Liberation Movement
Goldman, Emma
History
Hoboes
Joan of Arc (Jeanne d'Arc)

Ladies of Llangollen
Lister, Anne
Marie Antoinette
Michel, Louise
Middle Ages, European
Mitchell, Alice
Nazism
New Left
New Right
New Woman
Norton Sound Incident
Oral History
Parker-Hulme Murder Case
Passing Women
Passionlessness
Peace Movement
Pirie, Jane, and Woods, Marianne
Raucourt, Françoise
Romantic Friendship
Roosevelt, Anna Eleanor
Rüling, Anna
Sapphic Tradition
Scudder, Vida Dutton
Smashes, Crushes, Spoons
Spinsters
Suffrage Movement
Walker, A'Lelia
Walker, Mary Edwards
Witches, Persecution of
Yoshiya Nobuko

## Language, Terms, and Concepts
Androgyny
Bulldagger
Butch-Femme
Class
Closet
Coming Out
Compulsory Heterosexuality
Consciousness Raising
Dyke
Essentialism
Feminism
Gender
Gossip
Heroes
Heterosexism
Heterosexuality
Homophobia
Homosexuality
Identity

Ideology
Invisibility
Labeling
Language
Lesbian
Lesbian Continuum
Lesbian Feminism
Lesbian Nation
Liberalism
Literary Images
Mestizaje
Misogyny
Oppression
Patriarchy
Performativity
Phallus
Postmodernism
Prejudice
Queer Theory
Race and Racism
Separatism
Sexism
Sexual Orientation and Preference
Sisterhood
Situational Lesbianism
Slang
Social-Construction Theory
Stereotypes
Stigma
Subculture
Symbols
Tolerance
Woman-Identified Woman
Womanist
Women of Color

## Law
Adoption
Censorship
Crime and Criminology
Custody Litigation
Discrimination
Domestic Partnership
Donor Insemination
Human Rights
Immigration
Law and Legal Institutions
Legal Theory, Lesbian
Lesbian Impunity, Myth of
Mitchell, Alice
Norton Sound Incident

Parker-Hulme Murder Case
Pirie, Jane, and Woods, Marianne
Prisons and Prisoners
Privacy
Rights
Sexual Harassment
Witches, Persecution of


## Lesbian Movement

Activism
Ageism
Amazons
Antisemitism
Anzaldúa, Gloria
Asian Lesbian Network
Bars
Bisexual Movement
Black Feminism
Butch-Femme
Class
Collectives
Combahee River Collective
Community Centers
Consciousness Raising
Cornwell, Anita
Cruikshank, Margaret Louise
Daughters of Bilitis
Deming, Barbara
Demonstrations and Actions
Disability
Encuentros de Lesbianas
Fat Liberation
Feminism
Furies, The
Gay Liberation Movement
Gittings, Barbara
Grier, Barbara
Hampton, Mabel
Identity Politics
Invisibility
Jay, Karla
Johnston, Jill
*Ladder, The*
Leather
Lesbian Avengers
Lesbian Feminism
Lesbian Nation
Lorde, Audre
Marches and Parades
Martin, Del, and Lyon, Phyllis
Moraga, Cherríe

Nestle, Joan
Penelope, Julia
Race and Racism
Radicalesbians
Rich, Adrienne
Self-Defense
Separatism
Sex Wars
Smith, Barbara
Solanas, Valerie
Transgender
Vegetarianism
Woman-Identified Woman


## Literature

African American Literature
Allen, Paula Gunn
American Literature, Nineteenth Century
American Literature, Twentieth Century
Anderson, Margaret Carolyn
Anthologies
Anzaldúa, Gloria
Arab Literature, Modern
Arnold, June
Bannon, Ann
Barnes, Djuna Chappell
Barney, Natalie Clifford
Bates, Katharine Lee
Beach, Sylvia
Behn, Aphra
Biography
Bishop, Elizabeth
Blais, Marie-Claire
Blaman, Anna
Bowen, Elizabeth
Bowles, Jane Auer
Boye, Karin
Brossard, Nicole
Brown, Rita Mae
Bryher
Cather, Willa
Chinese Literature
Classical Literature
Colette
Coming Out Stories
Compton-Burnett, Ivy
Delarue-Mardrus, Lucie
Diaries and Letters
Dickinson, Emily
Duffy, Maureen Patricia
Dunbar-Nelson, Alice

English Literature, Eighteenth Century
English Literature, Nineteenth Century
English Literature, Twentieth Century
Fiction
Field, Michael
Foster, Jeannette Howard
French Literature
German Literature
Gothic
Grahn, Judy
Grimké, Angelina Weld
Hall, Radclyffe
Hansberry, Lorraine (Vivian)
Harlem Renaissance
H.D. (Hilda Doolittle)
Holtby, Winifred
James, Alice
Jewett, Sarah Orne
Jewsbury, Geraldine
Johnston, Jill
Juana Inés de la Cruz, Sor
Lagerlöf, Selma
Latin American Literature
Latina Literature
Leduc, Violette
Literary Criticism
Literary Images
Lorde, Audre
Lowell, Amy Lawrence
Mansfield, Katherine
McCullers, Carson
Mew, Charlotte
Millay, Edna St. Vincent
Millett, Kate
Mistral, Gabriela
Miyamoto Yuriko
Modernism
Moraga, Cherríe
Mystery and Detective Fiction
Nin, Anais
O'Brien, Kate
Pacific Literature
Parker, Pat
Parnok, Sophia
Parra, Teresa de la
Philips, Katherine
Poetry
Pulp Paperbacks
Renault, Mary
Rich, Adrienne
Routsong, Alma
Rukeyser, Muriel

Rule, Jane Vance
Sackville-West, Vita
Sand, George
Sapphic Tradition
Sappho
Sarton, May
Science Fiction
Shockley, Ann Allen
Smith, Lillian Eugenia
Spanish Literature
Stein, Gertrude
Taylor, Valerie
Toklas, Alice B.
Tsvetaeva, Marina Ivanovna
Utopian Literature
Vivien, Renée
Warner, Sylvia Townsend
Weirauch, Anna Elisabet
Wilhelm, Gale
Winsloe, Christa
Wittig, Monique
Woolf, Virginia
Wu Zao
Yosano Akiko
Yourcenar, Marguerite

## Media and Popular Culture

Advertising and Consumerism
Amazons
Camp
Cartoons and Comic Books
Comedy, Standup
Cultural Studies
Drag Kings
Flanner, Janet
Furies, The
Heroes
Humor
Johnston, Jill
Journalism
Ladder, The
Lesbian Connection
Mystery and Detective Fiction
Naiad Press
Periodicals
Publishing, Lesbian
Pulp Paperbacks
Radio
Recreation
Science Fiction
Slang

Style
Television
Tourism and Guidebooks
Vampires
'Zines

**Music and Dance**
Allan, Maud
Bentley, Gladys
Blues Singers
Choruses, Women's
Composers
Dance
Hampton, Mabel
Hildegard of Bingen, Saint
Johnston, Jill
Landowska, Wanda
lang, k.d. (Kathryn Dawn)
Music, Classical
Music Festivals
Music, Popular
Music, Women's
Opera
Rainey, Gertrude "Ma"
Smith, Bessie
Smyth, Dame Ethel Mary
Vargas, Chavela

**Politics**
Activism
Anthony, Susan B.
Bisexual Movement
Black Feminism
Censorship
Class
Coalition Politics
Collectives
Colonialism
Community Organizing
Deming, Barbara
Demonstrations and Actions
Domestic Partnership
Electoral Politics
Fat Liberation
Feminism
Gay Liberation Movement
Goldman, Emma
Human Rights
Identity Politics
Ideology

Immigration
Labor Movement
Liberalism
Marches and Parades
Military
National Gay and Lesbian Task Force (NGLTF)
National Organization for Women (NOW)
New Left
New Right
Noble, Elaine
Peace Movement
Political Theory
Roosevelt, Anna Eleanor
Rüling, Anna
Scudder, Vida Dutton
Simcox, Edith Jemima
Socialism
Suffrage Movement
Women's Liberation Movement

**Psychology**
Adolescence
Androgyny
Body Image
Children
Coming Out
Friendship
Homophobia
Identity
Immigration
Incest
Invisibility
Love
Phallus
Psychiatry
Psychoanalysis
Psychology
Psychotherapy
Recovery Movement
Relationship Violence
Sexology
Sexual Orientation and Preference
Suicide
Wolff, Charlotte

**Relationships**
Boston Marriage
Butch-Femme
Children
Companionate Marriage

Couples
Domestic Partnership
Donor Insemination
Family
Female Support Networks
Friendship
Gossip
Love
Marriage Ceremonies
Monogamy and Nonmonogamy
Mothers, Lesbian
Relationship Violence
Romantic Friendship
Sadomasochism
Safer Sex
Sex Practices
Sexually Transmitted Diseases
Singles
Smashes, Crushes, Spoons

## Religion
Antisemitism
Black Church, The
Catholicism
Christianity, Early
Churches, Lesbian and Gay
Goddess Religion
Hildegard of Bingen, Saint
Islam
Juana Inés de la Cruz, Sor
Judaism
Mythology, Classical
Mythology, Nonclassical
Protestantism
Religious Communities
Saints and Mystics
Spirituality
Synagogues
Teresa of Avila
Two-Spirit
Womanist

## Science
Animal Studies
Biological Determinism
Computer Networks and Services
Ecology and Ecofeminism
Etiology
Evolution and Human Origins
Homosexuality

Kinsey Institute
Science
Sexology
Technology

## Sexuality
Bisexuality
Clitoris
Erotica and Pornography
Heterosexuality
Homosexuality
Incest
Kinsey Institute
Leather
Libertinism
Masturbation
Passionlessness
Phallus
Sadomasochism
Safer Sex
Sex Education
Sex Practices
Sex Toys
Sex Wars
Sex Work
Sexology
Sexuality
Sexually Transmitted Diseases
Tribade

## Sociology
Adolescence
Ageism
Aging
Body Image
Children
Class
Coming Out
Community
Couples
Demography
Disability
Discrimination
Family
Food
Friendship
Gender
Gossip
Heterosexism
Homophobia

Identity
Immigration
Labeling
Love
Military
Oppression
Patriarchy
Prejudice
Prisons and Prisoners
Race and Racism
Recreation
Relationship Violence
Sexism
Singles
Situational Lesbianism
Slang
Social Work
Sociology
Stereotypes
Stigma
Style
Subculture
Suicide
Symbols
Tolerance
Tomboy
Violence

**Sport**
Athletics, Collegiate
Didrikson, Mildred Ella "Babe" (Zaharias)
Gay Games
King, Billie Jean Moffitt
Navratilova, Martina
Physical Education
Recreation
Sports, Professional
Tomboy

**Theater and Film**
All-Female Reviews (Japan)
Arzner, Dorothy
Behn, Aphra
Chambers, Jane
Charke, Charlotte
Cross-Dressing
Cushman, Charlotte

Dietrich, Marlene
Documentaries
Drag Kings
Film, Alternative
Film, Mainstream
Garbo, Greta
Hansberry, Lorraine (Vivian)
Hollywood
Moraga, Cherríe
Performance Art
Raucourt, Françoise
Theater and Drama, Contemporary
Theater and Drama, History of
Video

**Theory and Philosophy**
Anzaldúa, Gloria
Beauvoir, Simone de
Black Feminism
Combahee River Collective
Critical Theory
Ecology and Ecofeminism
Enlightenment, European
Essentialism
Ethics
Feminism
Fuller, Margaret
Ideology
Legal Theory, Lesbian
Lesbian Feminism
Liberalism
Lorde, Audre
Moraga, Cherríe
Nestle, Joan
Penelope, Julia
Philosophy
Political Theory
Postmodernism
Psychoanalysis
Queer Theory
Rich, Adrienne
Separatism
Smith, Barbara
Social-Construction Theory
Solanas, Valerie
Wittig, Monique
Womanist

# A

## Activism

Participation in a wide array of political actions designed to support a social movement or a particular political cause, which may include, but is not limited to, participation in political parties (as in "political party activism"). Activism, or "doing politics," can be defined as any struggle to gain control over definitions of self and community, to augment personal and communal empowerment, to create alternative institutions and organizational processes, and to increase the power and resources of one's variously defined community.

Feminist analyses of women's political participation have expanded the definition of the term "politics" to include a diversity of activities that are frequently rendered invisible when only participation in traditional political parties is counted. For example, since women's political actions were frequently tied to their role as mothers or to their identities as community caretakers, their political participation was often seen as a normal extension of their gender identities. In addition, some women drew upon their gendered identities to justify public roles in advocating for social welfare and social justice, thereby differentiating their "civic work" or "social housekeeping" from "politics." However, as a result of feminist theorizing and analysis of women's activism, women's community-based struggles to improve their children's education or health and safety and to fight police harassment and toxic waste are now understood as significant forms of political behavior.

With this broadened view of activism, feminist social historians have also demonstrated the significance of women's central roles in diverse social movements and labor struggles. For example, Afri-

can American women drew upon their social networks and organizational skills developed through participation in churches and social clubs to promote and support the U.S. civil rights movement, among other campaigns for social justice and economic security. Women of color in the United States have a long tradition of activism designed to protect and improve the lives of their communities. Working-class women of all racial-ethnic backgrounds have played significant roles in labor organizing that only recently has received sustained attention.

Women's activism in women's movements has included reform-oriented political work to gain passage of women's right to vote, reproductive-rights legislation, protection for battered women, pay equity, and laws against sexual harassment and sex-discrimination policies, among other legal measures. Women's movement activists of the 1970s in the United States were not always in agreement about what constitutes the primary target and the most effective strategies for political action. Splits occurred over pornography legislation, sexualities, working in separate or gender-integrated organizations, and working within the existing political system.

Many women of color and working-class women did not think that the 1970s U.S. women's movement represented their interests and formed racial-, ethnic-, or class-specific feminist organizations and networks. As in other political movements, the diversity of women's activism reflects a broad spectrum of political perspectives, social experiences, and class divisions. Women's class, race, ethnicity, country of origin, sexuality, and geographic location intersect to produce a vantage point, a site from which women experience different social

**A** problems in different ways. This, in turn, creates diverse grounds for the development of women's activism.

Social-movement theorists were particularly interested in explaining what contributes to the continuity of radical political activism. This has been a central thread in the literature on lesbian feminist activism. Taylor and Rupp (1988) discuss the ways in which women's-movement activists reproduce political identities through their everyday lives and, by extension, help sustain social-movement goals and analyses when a social movement is in a period of "abeyance." Arguing against constructions of so-called cultural feminism (a political perspective that emphasizes the creation of an alternative women's culture) as apolitical, they demonstrate the political significance of "female values, separatism, the primacy of women' relationships, and feminist ritual."

Through private rituals and creation of separate social spaces and fictive kin networks, lesbians in varying regional contexts have established the sense of community and solidarity needed for collective action. Antigay violence, discrimination in employment and housing, denial of parental and adoption rights, antigay legislation, and AIDS have mobilized lesbian activists to join forces with gay men in local organizing efforts in cities and towns across the United States. From another perspective, Stein (1992) worries that the development of numerous groups and organizations, such as support groups for lesbian mothers and women facing life-threatening diseases and organizations for lesbian professionals, among other projects, fragments lesbian activism.

In keeping alive a more radical tradition of organizing, the Lesbian Avengers, established in 1992 by activists in New York City, have waged campaigns against violence against gays and lesbians, homophobia in education and housing, and heterosexism in public spaces. Contemporary lesbian activism has also been influenced by the critique of identity politics, namely, that the bipolar gay/straight or homosexual/heterosexual designation only reproduces dominant social relations both within and across identity categories. Some lesbian activists involved in radical political activism during the 1990s have adopted the term "queer" to refer to a broad array of "identities" and "sexualities." Phelan (1993) recognizes the dilemma of identity politics but argues that one can draw upon constructed identity categories in strategic ways to enhance political mobilization and build more effective coalitions "that are not based on social identities."

Lesbians in countries around the world have joined to counter homophobia and discrimination in their communities. In many countries, lesbian activists who speak out risk public censure and imprisonment. A turning point in bringing worldwide attention to the issues of concern to lesbians occurred during the 1995 Nongovernmental Organizations' (NGO) Conference on Women held in Hairou, China, alongside the United Nations Conference on Women in Beijing, China. Women from different countries marched in support of lesbian rights and against antigay violence, and the sessions on lesbian concerns were well attended by a diversity of women. Despite the concerted efforts of activists at these meetings, a resolution on lesbian and gay rights was not included in the final Platform for Action passed by the representatives at the U.N. conference.    *Nancy A. Naples*

### Bibliography

Echols, Alice. *Daring To Be Bad: Radical Feminism in America, 1967–1975*. Minneapolis: University of Minnesota Press, 1989.

Naples, Nancy A. "Activist Mothering: Cross-Generational Continuity in the Community Work of Women from Low Income Neighborhoods." *Gender and Society* 6:3 (1992), 441–463.

Phelan, Shane. "(Be) Coming Out: Lesbian Identity and Politics." *Signs: Journal of Women in Culture and Society* 18:4 (1993), 764–790.

Schulman, Sarah. *The Lesbian Avenger Handbook: A Handy Guide to Homemade Revolution*. New York: Self-Published, 1993.

Stein, Arlene. "Sisters and Queers: The Decentering of Lesbian Feminism." *Socialist Review* 22 (1992), 33–55.

Taylor, Verta, and Leila Rupp. "Women's Culture and Lesbian Feminist Activism: A Reconsideration of Cultural Feminism." *Signs: Journal of Women in Culture and Society* 19:1 (1988), 32–61.

***See also*** Coalition Politics; Electoral Politics; International Organizations; Lesbian Avengers; Women's Liberation Movement

### Addams, Jane (1860–1935)

Born Laura Jane Addams, she was the founder of Hull House Settlement in Chicago, Illinois, and the Women's International League for Peace and Freedom, and the first American woman to be awarded the Nobel Peace Prize.

*Jane Addams. Jane Addams Memorial Collection, Special Collections, The University Library, The University of Illinois at Chicago.*

As the favored, youngest daughter of a prominent Republican businessman and state senator from Cedarville, Illinois, Jane Addams was part of the elite, first generation of college women in America. Like thousands of her cohorts, Addams had the wealth and the education to live outside the bonds of Victorian matrimony. She created both a career and a home for herself when, in 1881, she joined with her close friend, Ellen Gates Starr (1859–1940), in opening Hull House, the second "settlement house" in the United States. A settlement was a house in a working-class neighborhood where middle-class residents lived and provided a variety of educational, health, recreational, and cultural programs for their neighbors. Settlement houses were often a neighborhood's locus for political, ethnic, and union activity as well. Addams quickly rose to national prominence as a leading figure in the Progressive Era's movements for economic, sexual, and racial justice and, for the next half-century, enjoyed greater influence than any other American woman of her day. One popular magazine in 1909 called Addams "the first saint America has produced."

Contrary to myth, none of this glory and prestige came easily to Addams, and she did not enjoy it in saintly solitude. From the time of her girlhood at Rockford Female Seminary until her death, Addams was the charismatic center of a circle of female friends. Though Addams's temperamental reserve made her disdainful of the sentimental "smashes" common among college girls of the day, she did form a close bond with Starr. Starr was Addams's key confidante during her twenties. Starr's vision of a future in which the two would "work well" together emboldened Addams to extricate herself from family demands and serve, instead, as the head resident of an urban settlement. Within just a few years at Hull House, Addams had created an extended family of extraordinary women whose primary bonds were to one another and to their common political purpose. They shared the daily burdens of health and family and finances as naturally as they shared their writing, lobbying, and convictions.

Addams never treated her bond with Starr as a romantic one. It was not until she met the young and beautiful Mary Rozet Smith (1868–1934) in 1890 that Addams could declare she had been visited by "delivering love." While she and Starr drifted apart emotionally and politically, Addams and Smith grew ever closer. Addams had her own room at Smith's Chicago mansion; they bought a vacation home together in Bar Harbor, Maine; and when the two women took trips together, Addams wired ahead for one room with two double beds. Smith's wealth made possible much of the physical and programmatic expansion of Hull House and funded the extensive travel that positioned Addams for leadership in the international peace movement. At the same time, Smith's unflagging emotional support was vital to Jane Addams's tireless public endeavor.

Over the course of their forty-year partnership, Smith became the fierce guardian of Addams's health and privacy. When Smith died in 1934, friends wrote poignant letters about the couple's "beautiful friendship" and worried openly about whether Addams, in frail health, could survive the loss. She could not. Addams died fifteen months later, but not before destroying more than half of her correspondence with Smith because, as she put it, the letters were "much too intimate" to be used in a biography. What remains from that correspondence, and from Addams's correspondence with her other female friends, paints a clear picture of female-centered love and devotion lived out in historic dimensions.

*Victoria Bissell Brown*

**A**

*Bibliography*
Addams, Jane. *The Second Twenty Years at Hull-House*. New York: Macmillan, 1930.
———. *Twenty Years at Hull-House with Autobiographical Notes*. New York: Macmillan, 1910.
Linn, James Weber. *Jane Addams: A Biography*. New York: Appleton-Century, 1935.
Sklar, Kathryn Kish. "Hull House in the 1890s: A Community of Women Reformers." *Signs: Journal of Women in Culture and Society* 10 (1985), 658–677.

*See also* Female Support Networks; Peace Movement; Social Work

## Adolescence

The concept of adolescence is relatively new in human history. Before the Industrial Revolution in Europe and North America in the nineteenth century, one was accorded the status of adulthood at the time of physical maturity. Individual transitions from childhood to adulthood were relatively quick and accompanied by differential behavioral expectations. Clearly, while adolescence may be concretely defined in terms of chronological age and physiology, it is of social construction and, as such, must be regarded as intimately tied to the culture, as distinguished from being a condition that exists across time and geography. This approach to understanding human behavior is known as "developmental-stage theory." Social and behavioral scientists have described a series of tasks that are appropriate to each stage, against which people are assessed as normal, delayed, or, on occasion, precocious in developmental age.

In the twentieth century, adolescence is defined by Western social scientists as the transition time during which individuals are expected to adapt the behaviors of childhood into adult ways acceptable to the culture in which they live. Often, this period is assumed to begin at puberty and end with secondary-school completion, but, because the age range at which puberty begins is between eight and eighteen, the specific age at which adolescence begins or ends for anyone remains problematic. It is safe to assert at the end of the twentieth century in North America that there is general acceptance of adolescence as corresponding roughly with grades seven through twelve, although, for some, the period extends into the college years. This is due to the dependence of young people on their families for financial support. That can, in the case of some educational experiences (medical or law school following college, for example), extend adolescence well into what has been defined as young adulthood.

There is little contentiousness among social and behavioral scientists about the fact that adolescence is a period of dramatic change. Making the transition from childhood to young adulthood involves physiological, cognitive, emotional, social, moral, and vocational experiences and issues. Individuals in the adolescent age range are typically represented as immature and incapable of making adult decisions, and these assertions are often accepted as true by the adolescents themselves. Schools and parents alike expect and tolerate the adolescent's immature behavior and raise strong proscriptions against adultlike behaviors, especially in the sexual realm. In U.S. culture sexual behavior is reserved for heterosexual, married adults; adolescents displaying such behaviors are sanctioned by the adult world up to, and including, involvement in the legal system in attempts to control such practice. Precocious sexual behavior, especially among females, has been treated harshly (resulting in institutionalization, for example), most likely because females are assumed to be under their family's control until marriage. Girls who participate in any sexual activities with males or females are looked upon as deviant, out of control, and, therefore, subject to increased behavioral supervision.

Adolescents recognize and define themselves as different from, sometimes the opposite of, adults, appearing to some parents as purposefully contrary. This extends particularly into the arena of sexual behavior, in which young people assess themselves as ready to participate long before the adult world would agree. However, proscriptions against homosexuality remain strong in the adolescent world, especially for early adolescence. Adolescent lesbians, who recognize their affectional/sexual orientation, often have intense conflicts with parents, siblings, and peers in their home and school environment; those who hide the fact from others expend enormous amounts of energy monitoring their behavior in public. In many instances of conflicts with parents, in the past, as well as now, adolescent lesbians have been summarily placed in psychiatric institutions for treatment as if they were actually psychotic, rather than simply not living up to their parents' expectations of appropriate behavior.

Research on lesbian life-span development, of which adolescence is but one area, has a relatively short history; the first reports have publication dates in the 1980s. Very few studies have been conducted on issues associated with puberty and lesbianism, and the majority of those were combined studies of both males and females. It is likely that the ethical issues associated with conducting research on children and teenagers, the need for informed consent of subjects being the major one, has steered researchers into the adult population for subjects. Informed consent in the case of minors must be given by a parent or guardian; in a homophobic society, such consent is difficult to obtain. Teenagers seldom wish to discuss sexual issues of any sort with parents, and issues of affectional/sexual orientation, due to societal and internalized homophobia, are even more likely to be avoided. Therefore, most data regarding female adolescents' sexuality, level of information, or practices are gathered retrospectively, after the age of eighteen, when one is assumed to be able to give informed consent.

Among lesbian teenagers, there may be a reluctance to participate actively in social experiences, parties, and dating in particular. Opposite-, as well as same-sex, socializing may be fraught with tension and anxiety due to heterosexist expectations and both societal and internalized homophobia. This reluctance would best be described as normal in U.S. culture, as distinguished from evidencing what mental-health practitioners as early as the 1920s labeled delayed sexual development. Some adolescent lesbians may focus their attention on sports, the arts, clubs, or community organizations for social support; others may concentrate on doing well in school or holding a part-time job and ignore peer socializing.

The issue of personal civil rights became a facet of the youth movement in the early 1990s. This movement is more clearly articulated than was either the drug or the antiwar movement, with which older people were equally strongly allied. This youth movement is focused, fueled, and run by youth, almost exclusively. For all youth, the issue of self-determination is central and includes an insistence on being free of arbitrary parental control. An example of arbitrariness is the young lesbian who has been involuntarily placed in an institution by parents who disapprove of her actions.

Adolescence is, for all, a time to give serious consideration to both educational and vocational choices for the future. While there is general consensus that career development for males and females is different, little notice has been made of the possible differences within those categories. There may have been an assumption made that the experiences and needs of lesbians are not significantly different from the general female population. At this point, the topic of lesbians and work is largely unexplored. Data are sparse and hard to obtain. Researchers must depend upon the willingness of adult lesbians to self-identify and to be receptive to participation in their study. As more data become available, making informed educational and vocational choices will be made more specific for lesbians.

*Barbara W. Gerber*

### Bibliography

Fassinger, Ruth. "Adolescence: Options and Optimization." *Counseling Psychologist* 24:3 (1996), 491–497.

Gonsiorek, John C. "Mental Health Issues of Gay and Lesbian Adolescents." In *Psychological Perspectives on Lesbian and Gay Male Experiences.* Ed. Linda D. Garnets and Douglas C. Kimmel. New York: Columbia University Press, 1993, pp. 469–485.

Morgan, Kris S., and Laura S. Brown. "Lesbian Career Development, Work Behavior, and Vocational Counseling." *Counseling Psychologist* 19:2 (1991), 273–291.

*See also* High Schools, Lesbian and Gay; Students

## Adoption

The legal procedure for creating the relationship of parent and child between the adopter and the adoptee. In the United States, adoption law and procedure are established by individual states and can vary dramatically from one state to another. Although the term "adoption" usually calls to mind the addition of a minor child to a family, adoption historically served the principal purpose of facilitating the descent of property when a man would otherwise die without an heir. In those instances, a person would adopt an adult who would carry on the family name.

### Adoption of Adults

Adult adoption remains available today and has played a distinctive role among gay men and lesbians. Because marriage has not been available to gay men or lesbians, some couples have used adult adoption to create a legally recognized relationship between them. The creation of such a relationship

A was thought especially important when one partner had sufficient assets that his or her family members would be expected to challenge a will leaving those assets to his or her surviving partner. An adoption of one partner by the other would assure not only property distribution, but also the ability to make decisions concerning such matters as health care and burial that are customarily within the authority of the next of kin. Although some courts have approved adoptions, knowing that the couple was in a gay or lesbian relationship, others have determined that such a relationship was not a proper use of adoption statutes. Attorneys have cautioned couples considering this approach that, unlike marriage, an adoption cannot be terminated or revoked if the partners later separate.

### Adoption of Children

An unmarried adult is permitted to adopt a child in every American jurisdiction. As of 1998, only two states, Florida and New Hampshire, had statutes that prohibit a lesbian or a gay man from adopting a child. An adoption decree must be signed by a judge and customarily requires an investigation by a social worker or other professional to determine the suitability of the adoptive placement. Social workers often do not ask a prospective adoptive parent about her sexual orientation. When they do, attorneys caution applicants not to lie. At least one court has revoked an adoption after discovering that the parent had lied about his sexual orientation. Because adoption records are sealed and adoption proceedings vary both from state to state and from county to county, no one knows how many lesbians have adopted children, or been denied the ability to adopt children, as single adults.

Lesbian couples who wish to jointly parent a child face distinctive adoption issues. They may wish to adopt a child as a couple, a practice commonly referred to as "joint adoption." In the alternative, one partner may give birth to a child, and the other partner may then seek to become the child's adoptive parent. This practice is commonly referred to as "second-parent adoption." The legal issue faced by lesbian couples seeking joint adoption is whether any unmarried couple may adopt a child together in that state. Second-parent adoption raises a different legal issue. Adoption customarily extinguishes the legal relationship between a child and her biological parents. Often, the only statutory exception to this rule is a stepparent adoption, in which a biological parent's husband or wife may adopt the child while leaving intact the child's relationship with the biological parent. Lesbian couples seeking second-parent adoption must convince a court to treat their request as a stepparent adoption, even though the partners are not married to each other.

Both joint adoptions and second-parent adoptions have been granted to lesbian couples in some jurisdictions. As of 1998, appellate courts had approved one or both of these types of adoptions in the District of Columbia, Illinois, Indiana, Massachusetts, New York, New Jersey, and Vermont. In more than a dozen other states, trial court judges had granted such adoptions, but no appeals court had ruled on the issue. In two states, Colorado and Wisconsin, appeals courts had ruled that such adoptions are not permissible.

Without a joint or second-parent adoption, the child being raised by a lesbian couple has only one legally recognized parent. This can have serious ramifications. If the couple separates, the legally recognized parent has the right to custody of the child and, in most states, can cut off all contact between the child and her former partner. If the legally recognized parent dies, her parents or other relatives may be able to remove the child from the surviving partner. If the legally unrecognized parent dies, the child will be denied survivors benefits or the right to inherit in the absence of a will. Thus, joint and second-parent adoptions are an important component of building secure lesbian families.        *Nancy Polikoff*

### Bibliography

Achtenberg, Roberta, and Karen Moulding, eds. "Adult Adoption." In *Sexual Orientation and the Law*. Deerfield, Ill.: Clark, Boardman, Callaghan, 1994, 1-86–1-92.8.

Martin, April. *The Lesbian and Gay Parenting Book*. New York: Harper Perennial, 1993.

Ricketts, Wendell, and Roberta Achtenberg. "Adoption and Foster Parenting for Lesbians and Gay Men: Creating New Traditions in Family." In *Homosexuality and Family Relations*. Ed. Frederick W. Bozett and Marvin B. Sussman. New York: Harrington Park, 1990, 83–118.

*See also* Custody Litigation; Law and Legal Institutions

### Advertising and Consumerism

Lesbian (and gay) community as a consumer market. In a capitalist market economy, lesbians produce and consume commodities, defined as products made to be exchanged in a marketplace for a profit. Businesses, such as bars and bookstores, catering to lesbian and gay consumers have historically been, and continue to be, the sites of gay community and social activism. A vast array of businesses, including media, merchandise catalogs, and travel, legal, medical, financial, and communications services, target lesbians as an identifiable, distinct consumer market (market, in this sense, meaning a field of potential buyers, rather than a space of exchange).

The particular attention paid to gays and lesbians as a target market has been part of a larger trend in late-twentieth-century capitalism toward target, or niche, marketing. Attention to the gay market has been described as both resulting from the gay and lesbian movement, which has given gays and lesbians visibility as a potential market segment, and producing gay and lesbian community and identity through its imaging and addressing of gays and lesbians. There is much debate in the gay and lesbian community over the political value of such market recognition; while positively valued for giving gays and lesbians a sense of social legitimacy and recognition and presenting positive images of gays and lesbians to a mainstream audience, it is criticized for erasing those segments of the community that do not have as much money to spend (women, lesbians, and gays of color) or are less appealing to the mainstream (practitioners of sadomasochism or drag queens). Peñaloza (1996) states that in the contemporary U.S. consumer culture, the marketplace is an important arena in which lesbians and other groups can struggle for social and political inclusion.

## Capitalism Enables Lesbian Community

Social space for groups of people to live as gay or lesbian was created by the development of industrial capitalism, which enabled individuals to live outside of family units. The cultural space for lesbians to exist—economic freedom from dependence on men—is, in part, the result of the war-based economy of the first half of the twentieth century, during which time women replaced men in industrial production. As a result of the freeing of labor from its familial and rural contexts, gays and lesbians were able to create communities in urban areas. These communities were often communities of consumers, in that much of the life of the community frequently took place in bars. Boyd (1975) has argued, in de-

scribing the emergence of the Tavern Guild, a self-protection and -promotion organization of gay and lesbian bar owners and bartenders in San Francisco in the 1960s, that a gay marketplace can generate, as well as result from, a social/political movement. Gays and lesbians have since expanded beyond bars to many other sorts of businesses—bookstores, travel agencies, clothing stores, arts organizations—aimed at lesbian and gay consumers, located in gay ghettos, serving primarily gay clientele, providing services or products of particular interest to gay consumers and benefiting gay and lesbian entrepreneurs. Freeman (1995) has pointed out that the development of print capitalism and, more recently, electronic media—the circulation of gay newspapers, magazines, and direct-marketing materials such as catalogs and card packs—has generated a nonlocal space with which gays and lesbians can identify.

## Advertising to Lesbians

Print media have been extremely important organs for advertising aimed at gays and lesbians. The most important recent development in advertising addressed to gays and lesbians has been the participation of mainstream corporations selling mainstream products. Gay and lesbian media, as well as Gay Pride parades, sporting events, and resorts, have deliberately tried to attract mainstream advertisers. It has been argued that, while many gay magazines, especially those aimed at men, were once filled with personal and sex ads, in order to attract mainstream advertisers some have given up both the ads and the editorial discussion of sex, especially leather and sadomasochistic sex, choosing instead to portray gays and lesbians as normal, family oriented, and politically moderate, seeking only to be treated like straights.

National gay magazines (the *Advocate* and *Out*) and some gay marketing and research firms (Overlooked Opinions, Simmons Market Research Bureau, Mulryan/Nash, Yankelovich) have done surveys showing the consuming abilities of gays and lesbians and promoting gays and lesbians as a potent market niche with higher-than-average disposable income. There is tremendous debate over the accuracy of the figures generated and the claims made by various groups. These surveys frequently generate their income and consumption statistics based on the readership of a particular magazine or on the voluntary participation of self-identified gays and lesbians. Such methods of creating the survey

**A** sample have been criticized as producing a picture of gays and lesbians as significantly more affluent and more white than a more accurate picture of a gay and lesbian population would. Those who purchase gay and lesbian magazines and those who self-identify as gay or lesbian are likely to feel able to do so because they have a degree of economic and social security not experienced by other people (poor, non-white, female) who express or experience homosexual desire in some form. The surveys describing gays and lesbians as more wealthy than straights have been used by right-wing, antigay forces to argue that gay people do not need civil rights protection such as protection, from employment discrimination, since gays and lesbians are apparently already an economically privileged group. Recent studies by academics, as well as the Yankelovich survey, tell a different story: They show that gays and lesbians earn less than their heterosexual counterparts. However, it is precisely those white, wealthy, and, to a large extent, male gay consumers who are of primary interest to advertisers, though, as women, in general, become wealthier, lesbians become a more attractive market segment. And so in advertising that features gays and lesbians, they are likely to appear to be exclusively white and wealthy, making it harder for those who are neither to feel that gay or lesbian identity and community are relevant to them.

Mainstream advertisers have taken three approaches to reaching the gay and lesbian market. First, they have placed ads that are part of their regular campaign in gay media; Absolut Vodka is a well-known example of a company that has placed similar ads in gay and nongay publications. Second, they have developed special ad campaigns for gay outlets that explicitly invite gay identification; an example of an advertisement geared to the lesbian consumer—playing on one self-stereotype current among lesbians—is a 1996 Subaru of America ad that states: "It loves camping, dogs, and long-term commitment. Too bad it's only a car." Some companies, notably, K-Mart and Ikea, have placed such gay-oriented advertisements on television. However, many companies are wary of doing this, and even of placing ads in gay publications, for fear that their products will become identified as gay or lesbian and, therefore, not be appealing to the heterosexual market or even draw a boycott from antigay forces such as the Religious Right. (A number of articles in marketing and business publications in the mid-1990s have described the ambivalence of advertisers about the gay market, seeing it as at once lucrative and dangerous.) To avoid these dangers a third approach is quite popular: Advertisers create ads that allow or encourage gay identification but do so in a coded form that straights will not recognize. For example, Clark (1991) describes a fashion layout that appeared in *Elle* magazine, a mainstream fashion magazine, featuring a short-haired model dressed in man-style attire (jacket and tie), leaning on a motorcycle. Clark points out that this image can be read by lesbians as the image of a butch lesbian; the "swaggering" recommended in the ad copy and enacted by the model can likewise be seen as the cruising dyke.

## Implications for Lesbian and Gay Rights Movements

Both the second and third approaches assume that gays and lesbians constitute a distinct culture, with its own codes, sets of meanings, and concerns. The covert use of lesbian and gay codes in mainstream ads—a style may be marketed to straights as simply the new fashion—may be experienced by gays and lesbians not as an appeal, but rather as exploitative. As Freeman and Berlant (1993) point out, while the advertisement's erotic or exotic charge depends on its unacknowledged roots in lesbian and gay culture, the lesbian and gay cultural creativity that produced such a style is erased and the lesbian- and gay-specific meaning of the style is eroded.

Advertisers also assume that those communal codes and concerns can be used to create individual consumer desires; hence, they address gays and lesbians as individual consumers. Clark argues that such an individual address may undermine the communal and political aspects of gay and lesbian identification. Oppositional political rhetoric is transformed into a slogan for a product. Chasin (1995) suggests that, in place of an identification with a lesbian and gay political movement, both the advertisements and the survey techniques invite identification with U.S. nationalism. The treatment of the lesbian and gay community as a market niche may, as Chasin argues, undermine the movement for civil rights for sexual minorities.    *Miranda Joseph*

### Bibliography
Boyd, Nan Alamilla. "Shopping for Rights: Gays, Lesbians and Visibility Politics." *Denver University Law Review* 75:4 (Fall 1998), 1361–1373.

Chasin, Alexandra. "Selling Out: The Gay/Lesbian Market and the Construction of Gender." *Sojourner* 22 (1997), 14–15.

Clark, Danae. "Commodity Lesbianism." *Camera Obscura* 25–26 (1991), 180–201. Reprinted in *The Lesbian and Gay Studies Reader*. Ed. Henry Abelove, Michèle Aina Barale, and David Halperin. New York: Routledge, 1993, 186–201.

Freeman, Elizabeth. "Queer Bonds." Paper presented at a meeting of the American Studies Association, Pittsburgh, October 1995.

Freeman, Elizabeth, and Lauren Berlant. "Queer Nationality." In *Fear of a Queer Planet*. Ed. Michael Warner. Minneapolis: University of Minnesota Press, 1993, pp. 193–229.

Lukenbill, Grant. *Untold Millions: Positioning Your Business for the Gay and Lesbian Consumer Market*. New York: Harper Collins, 1995.

Peñaloza, Lisa. "We're Here, We're Queer, and We're Going Shopping: A Critical Perspective on the Accommodation of Gays and Lesbians into the U.S. Marketplace." *Journal of Homosexuality* 31:1–2 (Summer 1996), 9–41.

*See also* Bars; Bookstores; Businesses, Lesbian; Community; Demography; Economics; Journalism

## African American Literature

Creative writing by African American lesbians, including poetry, fiction, and drama. Also referred to as Afro-American, black, and Negro literature.

In the 1960s, African American literature occupied a place of quaint honor in historically black institutions of higher learning. One course would be offered once a year, usually during summer school sessions; and that one course would survey the whole tradition, from Lucy Terry (1730–?) to Amiri Baraka (1934–). By the end of the twentieth century, African American literature has become a vibrant and contested field of study, its texts occupying whole sections of bookstores, winning major literary honors, and changing the way readers understand the world. Black male writers, scholars, and social activists—such as Malcolm X (1925–1965), Frederick Douglass (1817–1895), Martin Delany (1812–1885), W.E.B. DuBois (1868–1863), and Eldridge Cleaver (1935–1998)—became cultural icons who embodied the aspirations and passions of the whole "race," or so it was said. But in the 1970s, writing by African American women—such as Alice Walker's *The Third Life of Grange Copeland* (1970), Toni Morrison's *The Bluest Eye* (1970), and Toni Cade (Bambara)'s anthology *The Black Woman* (1970)—challenged the predominantly male canon and critical establishments, both black and white.

In "Toward a Black Feminist Criticism" (1977), black lesbian feminist Barbara Smith (1946–)—after taking white female, white male, and black male critics to task for their insensitivity to the literary strivings of black women writers—called for a black feminist criticism "embodying the daring spirit" of the literary works themselves. Smith's notion of "daring" included "the lesbian" as a category of analysis, as a subject of inquiry, as an object of desire, and as a political entity. Smith's hallmark article inspired an entire school of black feminist critics to chart new trajectories for reading the literary expression of African American women, including searching for the meaning of "lesbian" in the African American literary tradition.

## History

Prior to the 1970s, black lesbian writers had been silent since the demise of the New Negro Renaissance, which claimed Harlem, in New York City, as its home. During this period (1917–1935), African Americans were able, for the first time, to reflect upon their contributions to American life and culture. One of its leaders, Alain Leroy Locke (1886–1954), was decidedly homosexual and exercised a profound and perturbing influence on the cultural production of African Americans when the "Negro" was in vogue. Love between women—the "sapphic cult of love," as Locke termed lesbianism—was celebrated in life and poetry during the New Negro Renaissance.

Because they validated sexuality, resistance, and autonomy, performers like "Ma" Rainey (1886–1939) and Bessie Smith (1894?–1937) assumed legendary status within black poor, working-class, and bohemian and avant garde communities; both were lesbian or bisexual. Rainey's "Prove It on Me Blues," recorded in 1928, is one example of the bold lesbianism of black women in the so-called Jazz Age. Mae V. Cowdery (1909–1953) was an open lesbian, said to wear suits and ties, cut her hair short, smoke cigarettes publicly, and frequent Greenwich Village rather than Harlem. Before committing suicide at the age of forty-two, she wrote a number of poems whose love object was female. The coded lesbian lyrics of Angelina Weld Grimké (1880–1958) were not deciphered until 1979, when

**A** critic Gloria (Akasha) Hull speculated about Grimké's secret sapphic desire. Critic Deborah McDowell has also discussed the lesbian subtext of Nella Larsen's (1891–1964) *Passing* (1927).

In his eulogy to the great American writer James Baldwin (1924–1987), Amiri Baraka said Baldwin's *Blues for Mister Charlie* (1964), a stark play that reimagines the lynching of Emmet Till, "announced the Black Arts Movement." However, others claim that Baraka's own short-lived project, the Black Arts Repertory, ushered in this new era in the tradition of black letters. The Black arts movement was certainly emboldened by people like Baraka and Baldwin and was initiated in public venues, including the theater, the jazz set, and the poetry reading. More important, the Black arts movement was the angry offspring of what came to be seen as the assimilationist civil rights movement. The Black arts movement was also the cultural kin of the Black Power movement, which came into being in 1966 with the concept "Black Power," propounded by leaders of organizations such as the Student Nonviolent Coordinating Committee (SNCC) and the Congress of Racial Equality (CORE). The Black arts movement rejected Western models, reified black folk culture, and renounced, as would the Black Power movement, integrationist themes. Both movements nodded to Malcolm X as the exemplar of black integrity and resistance. Manhood, heterosexuality, and militancy characterized the Black Arts Movement, and black women played a vital role in the perpetuation of race ideology and race mythology.

## Major Figures

Although African American literary expression in the 1960s was dominated by heterosexual longing and nostalgic nationalism, in the 1970s black lesbian voices began to emerge. Philadelphian Anita Cornwell (1923–), black lesbian polemicist and writer for *The Ladder* (est. 1956), published articles in lesbian feminist journals and anthologies. Cornwell claims that racism and sexism made her a feminist, from which vantage point she critiques racism in the white lesbian community and homophobia and heterosexism in the black community.

By the late 1970s and early 1980s, Audre Lorde (1934–1992), black, lesbian, feminist poet, mother, socialist, and author of more than ten books of poetry, had written *The Black Unicorn* (1978) and her self-styled "biomythography" *Zami: A New Spelling of My Name* (1982). Both texts historicize lesbianism in an African context, explore the African sources of what is called "lesbianism" in West. In her poetry and nonfiction, Lorde draws upon mythic and historical figures like "the Coniagui Women," "the Women of Dan," "Yemanja," "the Amazon legions of Dahomey" and the "Zamis . . . [a] Carriacou name for women who work together as friends and lovers." Lorde's evocations of a black (non-European) lesbian past served to establish a lesbian or woman-loving-woman mythos of the African diaspora, linking Africa, the Caribbean, and North America.

Lorde, influenced by the Black Arts movement of the 1960s, understood writing as instrumental to liberation and the writer as agent of change. This daring established Lorde as a signal black lesbian feminist, whose poetry, fiction, journals, speeches, and essays continue to illuminate the work to be done by black lesbian feminist writers.

Pat Parker (1944–1989), a native Texan and migrant to California, spoke in a different poetic voice than the first-generation, Caribbean New Yorker Lorde. Parker's lesbian voice was decidedly "street," butch, and oral. Her first three books of poetry, *Child of Myself* (1971), *Pit Stop* (1973), and *Womanslaughter* (1978), explored a range of identity and relationship issues, including autonomy and self-definition as a black lesbian feminist. The poem "Womanslaughter," from the volume of the same name, is a raw indictment of violence against women and the systems that aid and abet it, not least of all the criminal justice system, which in its language, "manslaughter," makes women invisible victims (or perpetrators). Her performance poem "Movement in Black" is a historical excursion into the lives of African women in the New World; while "Where Will You Be" ironically addresses the questions of who will be allies of those oppressed by racist, sexist, and heterosexist systems.

Although poetry was the most influential genre of the 1970s, one novelist did emerge: Ann Allen Shockley (1927–), whose *Loving Her* (1974), *The Black and the White of It* (short stories, 1980), and *Say Jesus and Come to Me* (1981) were among the first conscious fictional ventures to place black lesbian characters at the center of the narrative, although some consider her characterizations neither artful nor credible.

## The Emergence of a Movement

In 1979, Barbara Smith and Lorraine Bethel, two prominent black lesbian feminists, guest-edited

*Conditions: Five, "The Black Women's Issue,"* which showcased the writings of contemporary black feminists. This issue was a road map for black feminists who wanted to be lesbians, just as Toni Cade (Bambara)'s *The Black Woman* was for heterosexual black women who wanted to be feminists. It was widely and favorably reviewed, by none other than Alice Walker (1944–) in one case. In keeping with the editorial practice of *Conditions* (founded in 1976) to be a "magazine of writing for women with an emphasis on writing by lesbians," this issue was the first publication in the African American tradition and in the tradition of lesbian writing to "emphasize" black lesbian writers. *Conditions: Five* also represented a new era in women's political organizing. The lesbian feminist movement was in the process of self-criticism for the evident whiteness of its leadership, its subtle and not so subtle elitism, and its social and economic privilege. Lesbian feminist organizations, as well as journals (like *Conditions*), and newspapers, magazines, and newsletters, committed themselves to producing a multiracial, multicultural leadership.

Indeed, the women-in-print movement began to capitalize on the writings and the bodies of black lesbian feminists in the United States and international communities. The literary reading took on a particular significance in lesbian communities across the country as it had during the Black Arts movement, with poets playing key roles in educating, enlightening, and politicizing the lesbian public. Older and more seasoned writers like Parker and Lorde were joined by newer voices, including Cheryl Clarke (1947–), Jewelle Gomez (1948–), and Terri Jewell (1954–1995), as well as by fiction writers Sapphire (1950–), Evelynn Hammonds (1953–), Becky Birtha (1948–), Barbara Banks (1948–), and Shay Youngblood (1959–). Their work was published in numerous literary journals and anthologies, as well as in local lesbian and feminist newspapers.

Even writers who did not identify with the politics of lesbianism were influenced by its new openness. Alexis DeVeaux (1948–), author of a cryptic 1974 novel, *Spirits in the Street*, became more explicitly woman centered, if not necessarily lesbian, in her 1981 play, *No*, a political, erotic-romantic, woman-identified poetic evocation of negritude. Despite her reticence, a reviewer for the *Amsterdam News*, a black publication in New York City, noted for its homophobic commentary, attacked DeVeaux's work for its use of lesbian themes, which, according to the review, was not a fit topic for black writers. This attitude also can be seen in several works by ostensibly heterosexual writers—Ed Bullin's *Clara's Ole Man* (1968), Gayl Jones's *Eva's Man* (1976), and Paule Marshall's *The Chosen Place, Timeless People* (1969)—which present lesbianism as having a marginal place in, and somewhat corrupting effect on, black communities. On the other hand, works such as Rosa Guy's *Ruby* (1976), Gloria Naylor's *The Women of Brewster Place* (1982), and, most celebrated of all, Alice Walker's *The Color Purple* (1982) portray lesbianism with more complexity and empathy.

## From Margin to Mainstream

The deaths from cancer of Pat Parker in 1989 and Audre Lorde in 1992 were sadly emblematic of an era capped by untimely deaths from cancer and AIDS of many in the black and queer communities. Black lesbian writers, like all whose work was embraced by radical political movements and alternative presses, faced new challenges regarding the publication of their work. The closing of alternative presses, the flagging of book sales, the corporate takeovers of publishing companies, the chain bookstores' conquests of independent women's and gay bookstores more open to stocking alternative-press publications, and the changing tastes of audiences all threatened lesbian writers with erasure.

On the other hand, Michelle Cliff (1946–) and Sapphire, both self-identified black lesbian writers and both mentored by the black lesbian literary movement, succeeded in the 1990s in reaching beyond lesbian audiences via major-press publication. Cliff, along with Adrienne Rich (1929–), was at one time an editor of *Sinister Wisdom*, a lesbian feminist journal established in 1976, and had published two books with an alternative press before Dutton published second and third novels, *No Telephone to Heaven* (1987) and *Free Enterprise* (1993). Sapphire, a performance poet and writer, published two books of poetry, one under her own imprint and the second for an alternative press, before her novel *Push* was published by Knopf in 1996. Although both writers maintained their integrity as lesbians, their later work was not directed at lesbian audiences specifically, and their former lesbian feminist affiliations not acknowledged by the promotional apparatus of their publishers.

The publication of *Does Your Mama Know? An Anthology of Coming Out Stories* (1997), edited by Lisa C. Moore, and *Afrekete: An Anthology of Black Lesbian Writings* (1995), edited by Catherine E.

McKinley and L. Joyce DeLaney, both by alternative presses, is a further sign of the continuing vitality of black lesbian writing, writers, and readership. The study of writing by lesbian feminists, black feminists, and women of color in literature and women's studies programs in colleges and universities across the United States and elsewhere is another signal of the perpetuation of black lesbian writing. On the other hand, few African American studies programs integrate the writings of black lesbians and black gay men into their curricula.

Black lesbian writers and writing continue to engage and instruct their audiences into the new millennium. As Adrienne Rich, an inveterate promoter of the work of women of color, claimed, the meaning of love between women must ever be expanded. Black lesbian writers, like black women writers throughout the literary diaspora, are expanding those boundaries. *Cheryl Clarke*

### Bibliography

Bethel, Lorraine, and Barbara Smith, eds. *Conditions: Five, "The Black Women's Issue"* 2:2 (1979) (Special Issue).

Cornwell, Anita. *Black Lesbian in White America*. Tallahassee, Fla.: Naiad, 1983.

Gates, Henry Louis Jr., and Nellie Y. McKay, eds. *The Norton Anthology of African American Literature*. New York: Norton, 1997.

Guy-Sheftall, Beverly, ed. "Introduction." *Words of Fire: An Anthology of African American Feminist Thought*. New York: New Press, 1995, pp. 1–22.

Hull, Gloria T. *Color, Sex, and Poetry: Three Women Writers of the Harlem Renaissance*. Bloomington: Indiana University Press, 1987.

Smith, Barbara. "Toward a Black Feminist Criticism." *Conditions: Two* 1:2 (1977), 25–43.

Walker, Alice. *In Search of Our Mother's Gardens: Womanist Prose*. New York: Harcourt Brace Jovanovich, 1983.

***See also*** African Americans; Black Feminism; Blues Singers; Cornwell, Anita; Grimké, Angelina Weld; Harlem Renaissance; Lorde, Audre; Parker, Pat; Rainey, Gertrude "Ma"; Shockley, Ann Allen; Smith, Barbara; Smith, Bessie; Womanist

## African Americans

While the experience of African American women who have expressed erotic interest in other women has not been monolithic or historically constant, a few generalizations can be made that place African American lesbian history in its appropriate context. Since African American women's arrival in the New World as slaves, their lives have been primarily shaped by the forces of racial and class oppression, by African American people's strategies of survival and resistance, and by the particular values and institutions of African American communities. Survival needs, gender inequality, and an ethic of collective responsibility have required almost all African American women to prioritize their economic and caregiving responsibilities within kin networks over their personal needs for the time, liberty, and private space to explore passions considered unconventional. Thus, while some African American women have identified themselves as sexually different and formed alternative lesbian communities, the majority have maintained traditional identities as married or unmarried family caregivers and providers and have loved women in ways as yet unrecognized by late-twentieth-century historians.

Historians have documented African American women's same-sex relationships since the mid-nineteenth century and urban African American lesbian communities in the North since the Great Migration (1915–1940), particularly in Jazz Age Harlem. Those communities grew in numbers and complexity in the post–World War II decades. The movement sparked by the Stonewall Rebellion (1969) followed the black liberation struggle, and, together, both fundamentally changed African American lesbian life, forging new identities and identity politics. Yet large gaps remain in our knowledge of African American lesbian history; for example, despite the fact that, until the mid-twentieth century, the center of African American culture was in the rural South, almost nothing is known of African American homosexuality there. These gaps are largely the result of persistent neglect by scholars of lesbian and gay and African American history. In addition, lack of time, literacy, or inclination has prevented most poor and working-class African American women from keeping written records of their life in diaries or letters, leading to a paucity of sources that illuminate their daily thoughts and experience; documents that explicitly record lesbian relationships are even more scarce. These difficulties are especially acute for the documentation of slave life; slave narratives, slave owners' accounts, and white Northerner's observations each pose their own interpretive problems.

## The Civil War to the Great Migration

Before the Great Migration, African American women were involved in same-sex relationships in a number of settings, although the evidence lacks broader historical context. The letters between Rebecca Primus (1836–1932) and Addie Brown (1841–?), two free women living in Connecticut (Primus was a schoolteacher, Brown was a domestic worker), between 1859 and 1869, are a rare historical record of nineteenth-century same-sex passion by African American women. According to Hansen (1996), a historian, Brown and Primus's bond surpassed that of a "romantic friendship," for their letters reveal a long-term, loving friendship and sisterhood that also involved explicitly sexual relations that Hansen termed "bosom sex." While the Brown-Primus relationship was well known within their family and social networks, the letters make clear that they were, nonetheless, expected to marry, and both eventually saw it socially and economically necessary to do so. Another nineteenth-century example is the *Wichita Tribune*'s report (September 17, 1898) of a "Queer Love Affair" between Adele Densmore and Ruth Latham, two African American women living in St. Joseph, Missouri. Due to a "lovers' quarrel," Densmore was threatening to enlist as a man in the United States Army. The two were said to be "deeply in love," and Densmore "play[ed] the part of the man." The *Tribune* found their love "strange" yet admired "the tenderness and grace with which [Densmore] imprints on the cheeks and lips of her girl sweetheart seals of affection." Finally, African American women's involvement in same-sex relationships in all-female reform schools and prisons have been documented as well. In 1913, Margaret Otis published an article in the *Journal of Abnormal Psychology* alerting readers to the "passionate" and sometimes "intensely sexual . . . homosexual relations" between young African American and white women in a Northern reform school.

## The Jazz Age, the Harlem Renaissance, and the New African American Working Class up North

African American lesbians were among the hundreds of thousands of Southern men and women who moved north during the Great Migration. In addition to powerful economic and racial motives for quitting the South, many lesbians were also fleeing sexual and physical abuse from white men and African American men and from community norms that frowned upon women who lived outside family bounds. As a new African American urban working class emerged in the North, women experienced greater personal freedom than at any other time, and a small but significant number of migrants found jobs that gave them financial independence from men and kin and the personal liberty to fashion a lesbian life. In the 1920s, urban African American lesbian networks and communities emerged out of these unique historical forces.

Along with the politics and "high culture" of the New Negro movement and the Harlem Renaissance, African American women occupied center stage in the African American entertainment industry. Women who sought sexual autonomy were especially attracted to the wages and freedom of show business life, and lesbian relationships developed among the dancers, musicians, comics, actresses, and blues singers as they traveled throughout the country performing in musicals, cabarets, speakeasies, and minstrel and vaudeville shows. Despite their marriages and heterosexual public images, some of the finest and most prominent performers had lesbian relationships, including Gertrude "Ma" Rainey (1886–1939), Bessie Smith (1894?–1937), Ethel Waters (1896–1977), Alberta Hunter (1895–1984), Gladys Bentley (1907–1960), and Jackie "Moms" Mabley (1897–1975). Mabel Hampton (1902–1989), a working-class lesbian from the South who was a dancer and an actress in New York City, recalls that Jackie Mabley was known to throw large parties to which "all the girls in the show would go" in the 1920s. Hampton also recalls meeting lesbians in the rooming house where she lived and going to African American lesbian "rent parties" and "pay parties" independent of the entertainment industry.

The degree to which a few African American lesbians self-consciously disregarded "respectable" female behavior reveals what became possible during this time, if not what came to be the norm. Gladys Bentley, for example, gained international fame in the 1920s as a "male impersonator" who cultivated an image as a "bulldagger"; she wore men's clothes on stage and on the street and had a female "wife." In a similarly bold move, "Ma" Rainey sang "Prove It on Me Blues" for a landmark 1928 recording that defiantly stated her sexual preference for women. Black lesbians were visible in the lyrics of various "BD blues" (bulldagger blues) song recordings of this period. Male impersonation and gender inversion were prominent cultural images of lesbianism during the 1920s and early 1930s; "drag

A balls" featuring hundreds of male and female "impersonators" drew thousands of spectators and extensive coverage from the African American press.

Internationally acclaimed classic blues singer Alberta Hunter was perhaps more typical of those who sought middle-class status and acceptance from the mainstream African American community—she took great care to conceal her lesbian relationships. Similarly, Angelina Weld Grimké (1880–1958) was an elite poet of the Harlem Renaissance and was presumed to be heterosexual, yet she wrote love poetry that addressed women and had at least one "clearly lesbian relationship." Literary scholar Gloria (Akasha) Hull's research on writer and community activist Alice Dunbar-Nelson (1875–1935) revealed that, along with Dunbar-Nelson's heterosexual relationships, including marriage to poet Paul Lawrence Dunbar (1872–1906), her passionate life also included affairs with several other prominent African American women.

For the most part, African Americans have been ambivalent about homosexual behavior that does not threaten family survival or kin networks, regarding that behavior as odd, "funny," or even sinful but not a basis for exclusion from community life. Yet women who have dared to establish unmarried and childless lives outside of family bounds have been harshly judged as selfish, immoral, and decadent. During the 1920s and throughout subsequent decades, one space in which homosexual behavior seems to have been tolerated was in the underground economy and subculture of sex workers, hustlers, pimps, and gamblers. This primarily heterosexual "sporting life" included all of those who resisted dominant norms and laws about sex, gender, work, and family responsibility.

How the Depression specifically affected black lesbian life is unclear; economics may have required more women to live with kin or encouraged more couples to live together. Unlike white women, very few African American women served in the military or received the temporary well-paying jobs created by World War II industrial production. By 1949, a full 40 percent of African American working women still labored in domestic-service jobs.

For African American women involved in lesbian relationships and community life, the time between World War II and the Stonewall Rebellion of 1969 was a contradictory period of significant progress and repression. Racial barriers in employment were slowly broken, and more African American women earned enough to maintain a residence alone or with a lover. In mid- to large-sized cities, African American lesbians increased the number, quality, and scope of lesbian-only settings in which they could gather. They held open-house parties, formed social clubs, organized formal dances and other social functions, joined softball leagues, and began patronizing formerly all-white bars. African American butch-femme couples ("studs," "papas," or "lady-lovers," with their "ladies," "mamas," or "wives") braved city streets together despite rampant police violence in black neighborhoods. African American lesbians fought to defend and expand their lesbian-only social territory in many ways; this sometimes involved preventing straight men from entering a party or a bar, through physical force when necessary. At the same time, considerable social pressure was placed on African American women (through the pages of *Ebony* magazine, for example) to help legitimize African American demands for equality by conforming to the "ideal" middle-class American woman: heterosexual, "feminine," committed to the nuclear family and the "American way of life." Finally, narratives of life in Buffalo, New York, San Francisco, and New York City suggest that government discrimination, police raids, and harassment of lesbians and gays increased during this period.

Most African American lesbians living in urban areas in the 1950s and 1960s preferred to socialize at house parties held in apartments or homes in African American neighborhoods and advertised by word of mouth. After paying a small cover at the door, one could socialize with friends, dance, drink, and eat plenty of home-cooked food. Because same-sex dancing was illegal in public places, dancing was especially important. Thorpe (1996) reports that Ruth Ellis and her partner's Detroit home was known as "the gay spot" throughout the 1950s; dozens of African American women and some gay men traveled from as far away as Cleveland and Dayton, Ohio, to attend. (Ellis had also attended gatherings of African American lesbians and gays in her native Springfield, Illinois, in the 1930s.) By the late 1960s, some women were able to turn hosting parties into a profitable business venture.

Public bar life was not as prominent in African American lesbian communities as it was for working-class white lesbians. In part, this was because, until the late 1960s, there were few bars or clubs that welcomed African American lesbian patronage. Most white lesbian bars were either alienating or notoriously racist. Few African American lesbians had the capital or political connections to have their own liquor licenses and establish their own bars. There were, however, some clubs that catered solely to African American lesbians at separate times or in separate spaces. In the 1950s, for example, the Wellsworth in Harlem was a straight bar in front and a lesbian bar in back. Yet bars carried the risk of legal trouble, public exposure, and harassment from straight men, so many women avoided them.

During this and later periods, African American lesbians also participated in mainstream institutions of the African American community. For example, lesbians attended church despite its condemnation of homosexuality because the church was the central social, spiritual, and political institution of African American life. Church could also provide a covert opportunity to meet women; "Debra," for example, recalls meeting her first lesbians in Buffalo at church after migrating from the South in 1938.

## The Civil Rights Movement

The sexual identity of the thousands of lesbian participants in the African American civil rights movement was invisible to that movement and remains so to most historians. In the years before gay liberation made "coming out" a conscious political act, many African American lesbians took their invisibility for granted, despite the personal discomfort and alienation they felt in their relations with movement activists and organizations. Yvonne Flowers (1932–) was one of 250,000 at the landmark 1963 March on Washington for Jobs and Freedom and was active in the struggle for African American community control of schools in Brooklyn, New York, but she refrained from greater involvement because she was not willing to pass as straight, which she saw as a requirement for a publicly visible leadership role. The noted playwright Lorraine Hansberry (1930–1965) was a prominent activist in civil rights and left-wing causes; yet the fact that Hansberry wrote a series of letters anonymously to the lesbian magazine *The Ladder* in 1957 indicates that she was concerned about public exposure.

## Gay, Lesbian, and Women's Liberation

Ernestine Eckstein (pseud.) was one of the few African American women involved in the pre-Stonewall lesbian and gay "homophile" movement. Already involved in civil rights politics, Eckstein became a leader within Daughters of Bilitis (New York chapter) and helped organize the East Coast Homophile Organization's controversial picketing of federal

buildings and the White House in 1965. The gay liberation movement that began with the Stonewall Rebellion in 1969 affected the consciousness of thousands of African American lesbians, although few formally joined organizations; Candice Boyce, for example, was attracted to New York's Gay Activist Alliance (GAA) but left because she found the daily survival needs of African American lesbians more urgent than the concerns of GAA's white male members.

Deeply affected by African American and Third World liberation politics, and committed to lesbian and feminist organizing, African American lesbians like Anita Cornwell, Margaret Sloan, Joan Gibbs, and Gwendolyn Rogers organized during the 1970s against pervasive racism in the predominantly white women's movement. At the same time, African American lesbians struggled within the emerging African American feminist movement in efforts like the National Black Feminist Organization (NBFO).

## Independent Politics

As a result of women's experiences in these movements, autonomous African American lesbian and lesbian of color organizations were founded in the 1970s and early 1980s. Elandria Henderson's 1971 statement on "The Black Lesbian" in Chicago's *Lavender Woman* was one early articulation of the frustration, disappointment, rage, and sense of betrayal that led to the formation of separate groups. The Combahee River Collective was founded by Boston-based lesbians in 1974 as a radical, African American feminist group whose multi-issue organizing included lesbian and gay politics. Salsa Soul Sisters, which began in New York City in 1976 under the leadership of the Reverend Delores Jackson, seems to have been the first independent African American or Latina lesbian organization, followed by groups in almost every major city by 1981. Several African American lesbian conferences in the early 1980s grew out of the first National Conference of Third World Lesbians and Gays in Washington, D.C., in 1979, including the "First Black Lesbian Conference of the Western Regional States" held in San Francisco in 1980.

As authors and critics, African American lesbian writers such as Cheryl Clarke (1947–), Jewelle Gomez (1948–), Audre Lorde (1934–1992), and Barbara Smith (1946–) have played a particularly central role in the development of African American feminist theory and literature and of a collective

**A** identity among African American lesbians. They established independent women of color writing collectives, conferences, publications, and publishing institutions, including *Azalea* collective and magazine (fl. 1977); Kitchen Table: Women of Color Press (fl. 1981); *Conditions: Five, "The Black Women's Issue"* (1979); the "Ain't I a Woman" issue of *off our backs* (1979); and *Home Girls: A Black Feminist Anthology* (1983). At the same time, many of these women were raising the issues of sexism and homophobia in broader African American community contexts such as the pages of *Black Scholar* and *Essence*.

**A National Movement and National Visibility**
A number of themes characterize the late 1980s and the 1990s. First, coalitions of African American lesbians and gay men emerged, including the National Coalition of Black Lesbians and Gays, the National Black Lesbian and Gay Leadership Forum, local groups like Detroit's James Baldwin and Pat Parker Society, and the 1995 "Black Nations?/Queer Nations?" conference in New York City. Second, the number of African American lesbian organizations grew, often moving away from the ideological liberation politics of the 1970s and putting greater focus on support for coming out. Third, the cultural work of African American lesbian and bisexual musicians, poets, African drummers, singers, video/filmmakers, and artists flourished, helping to strengthen local African American lesbian communities, national networks, and pride. Fourth, growing political, cultural, regional, and class differences among African American people led to a wider range of African American lesbian communities with their own traditions, institutions, and notions of lesbian identity. On the West Coast, the Bay Area's NIA collective instituted an annual African American lesbian retreat; on the East Coast, many young African American lesbians established and embraced new pro-sex public spaces for lesbian night life like the Clit Club in New York City. Finally, the growing national visibility of individual African American lesbians (and gay men) opened up space in the 1980s and 1990s for the legitimate discussion of homosexuality and homophobia in the African American community. These individuals include the poet and activist Audre Lorde, *Essence* magazine Executive Editor Linda Villarosa, musician Me'shell Ndegeocello, and Seattle City Council member Sherry Harris (the first out African American lesbian elected official). During this period, African American les-

bians also became more active in lesbian and gay and AIDS politics, which significantly heightened their visibility in local and national media. Together, these developments helped make it possible for many more young and old African American women to come out proudly as lesbians, even as they organized against antigay political forces that threatened their civil and human rights.             *N'Tanya R. Lee*

*Bibliography*
Carby, Hazel. " 'It Just Be's Dat Way Sometime': The Sexual Politics of Women's Blues." In *Unequal Sisters: A Multicultural Reader in U.S. Women's History*. 2nd ed. Ed. Vicki L. Ruiz and Ellen Carol Dubois. New York: Routledge, 1994, 330–341.
Garber, Eric. "A Spectacle in Color: The Lesbian and Gay Subculture of Jazz Age Harlem." In *Hidden from History: Reclaiming the Gay and Lesbian Past*. Eds. Martin Duberman, Martha Vicinus, and George Chauncey, Jr. New York: Meridian, 1990, pp. 318–331.
Hansen, Karen V. " 'No *Kisses* Is Like Youres': An Erotic Friendship Between Two African American Women During the Mid-Nineteenth Century." In *Lesbian Subjects: A Feminist Studies Reader*. Ed. Martha Vicinus. Bloomington: Indiana University Press, 1996, pp. 178–207.
Hine, Darlene Clark, Wilma King, and Linda Reed. *"We Specialize in the Wholly Impossible": A Reader in Black Women's History*. Brooklyn: Carlson, 1995.
Kennedy, Elizabeth Lapovsky, and Madeline D. Davis. *Boots of Leather, Slippers of Gold: The History of a Lesbian Community*. New York: Routledge, 1993; Penguin, 1994.
Lorde, Audre. *Zami: A New Spelling of My Name*. Watertown, Mass.: Persephone, 1982; Freedom, Calif.: Crossing, 1994.
Robert, J.R. *Black Lesbians: An Annotated Bibliography*. Tallahassee, Fla.: Naiad, 1981.
Thorpe, Rochella. " 'A House Where Queers Go': African American Lesbian Nightlife in Detroit, 1940–1975." In *Inventing Lesbian Culture in America*. Ed. Ellen Lewin. Boston: Beacon, 1996, pp. 40–61.

*See also* Bentley, Gladys; Black Feminism; Blues Singers; Buffalo, New York; Bulldagger; Combahee River Collective; Cornwell, Anita; Dunbar-Nelson, Alice; Grimké, Angelina Weld; Hampton, Mabel; Hansberry, Lorraine (Vivian); Harlem; Harlem

Renaissance; Lorde, Audre; Rainey, Gertrude "Ma";
Smith, Barbara; Smith, Bessie

## Ageism

Term coined by Robert Butler, M.D. (1975), a noted
geriatric psychiatrist, when referring to discrimination by younger people against older people. "Old
people are categorized as senile, rigid in thought
and manner, old fashioned in morality and
skills. . . . Ageism allows the younger generations to
see older people as different from themselves; thus
they subtly cease to identify their elders as human
beings." This sets the stage for the systematic and
institutionalized oppression of, and discrimination
against, the old, which is even more rampant at the
end of the twentieth century than thirty years before.

As the numbers of old grow larger and the perceived economic burden of their care grows, the
younger population increasingly believes that care
of the elderly is a luxury it cannot afford. With the
greatest disparity between rich and poor in history,
intergenerational conflict and scapegoating the old
have become a prime way to distract the young from
the bleak economic realities of their lives.

Negative attitudes toward the old also serve to
avoid disturbing thoughts of one's own aging and
dying. Contemporary culture seeks to nullify eventual death by refusing to look at anything connected
to death or even to use the word. People do not die;
they "pass on" or "away." The faces of the old serve
as a fearful reminder that aging is the prelude to de-
bilitation and death. Growing old is dreaded as the
bleak season of perpetual loss, sickness, and depression with only death ahead; this, despite current
medical research and personal testimonies showing
the increasing likelihood of good health and an active, even vigorous, life until shortly before death.
Both science and culture focus on the physical aspects of aging while ignoring the attributes that can
come with life experience: maturity, wisdom, spirituality, and freedom from earlier life constraints.
The fact that most old people enjoy their independent lives with loving and often sexual relationships
seems to have escaped the notice of most, or, if noticed, is seen as the exception.

In the United States, youth is revered and endowed with admired and desirable qualities, while
the old are denigrated and relegated to inferior status. While this affects all old people, men are less
affected than women because they have always been
considered more valuable in patriarchal society. After a lifetime of sexism, women receive fewer Social
Security and pension funds than men, or none at all.
They are subject to discriminatory and rationed
medical care (a cutoff age for some services) designed to "save" money. They may be abused both at
home and in institutions as government money
pours into nursing homes instead of into independent living. An old man in heterosexual circles can
be respected for his life experience and sought as a
sexual partner. An old woman, no longer useful as a
reproducer or a sexual object to men, has no further
value. Old women also threaten younger women by
showing them their future, for, as they become the
old women they so dread, they, too, face the same
ageist battering to their self-esteem.

Old women especially aren't allowed the sense
of individuality, dignity, and respect to which their
life experience and accomplishments should entitle
them. This occurs in subtle ways, from addressing
them as children to "complimenting" them on not
looking their age. The ageist slings in birthday
cards, magazine ads, and television commercials are
supposed to be borne without comment to avoid being labeled an "old witch." To "grow old graciously," women must not challenge the ageist status
quo. For lesbians, there is the additional risk of provoking homophobic reprisals by speaking out
against ageism. It is small wonder that most old
women feel invisible and powerless.

In some respects, old lesbians fare better than
old heterosexual women, who are used to depending
upon their men. Old lesbians suffer the same devaluation by the society that all women do, but, never
having relied on men in the first place and having
had to negotiate life in a homophobic world, they
have had to learn to be resourceful and self-reliant,
coping skills that have made them true survivors.
Both old and young lesbians, by their very existence, challenge the power of the patriarchy and are,
therefore, reviled, but when old lesbians experience
ageism from their own community, that is particularly painful.

Younger lesbians, subject to the same ageist
ideology as the rest of society, may share the patriarchal view about old women and collude with the patriarchy to marginalize old lesbians within feminist
and lesbian circles. Macdonald and Rich (1991)
first called attention to this phenomenon of invisibility. Macdonald tells about being ignored in her
old age by the same lesbian and feminist groups
who called her "sister" when she was younger. She
deplores the fact that social workers who are dedi-

cated to helping the old are themselves rampantly ageist. Playing the role of "expert," they frequently treat their clients as children.

Copper (1988) also addresses the shunning of the old within the society of women. She tells her personal story of how it feels to be ignored by younger women, including lesbians and feminists, and speaks to the difficulty of getting them to see the ageist nature of their words and actions. She contends that this is a result of "age passing," which promotes denial about their own ageism. The young and middle aged cannot accept that they are ageist and seek to explain it all away by saying, "I didn't mean it that way!"

Contemporary society is becoming increasingly ageist and homophobic, and this is becoming more of a problem to old lesbians. Macdonald and Copper call attention to this and call for confronting ageism in all of its subtleties as the only viable course of action for old lesbians.

Taking the lead in this struggle is Old Lesbians Organizing for Change (OLOC), a national organization of lesbians over sixty whose mission is to confront ageism wherever it exists as it strives to empower old lesbians to become a visible, vocal force.

*Nancy D. Davis*
*Shevy Healey*

## Bibliography

Butler, Robert. *Why Survive: The Old in America*. New York: Harper and Row, 1975.

Copper, Baba. *Over the Hill: Reflections on Ageism Between Women*. Freedom, Calif.: Crossing, 1988.

Friedan, Betty. *The Fountain of Age*. New York: Simon and Schuster, 1993.

Macdonald, Barbara, with Cynthia Rich. *Look Me in the Eye: Old Women Aging and Ageism*. San Francisco: Spinster Ink, 1991.

Old Lesbians Organizing for Change (OLOC), PO Box 980422, Houston, TX 77098, an organization for lesbians sixty and older.

*See also* Aging

## Aging

Biological process of maturation that affects everyone sooner or later. Aging involves many different factors, some of which are the same for everyone regardless of sexual orientation, while others are specific to lesbians. Little research has been done on the effects of aging on lesbians. Some research has been done in the United States and in the Netherlands, but samples have been small and tend not to show much social or racial variation. Results demonstrate, however, that the position of aging lesbians is, to a large extent, determined by the position of women and of homosexuality within society at large.

### Demographic Factors

The process of biological aging runs along a predetermined course, although the interval of time between different stages depends on the general level of health in the societies concerned. In many countries, the official retirement or pension age of sixty-five marks the onset of socially recognized old age. In some societies, women over fifty-five are regarded as "young old." In Western societies, serious health problems usually start at about seventy-five to eighty years, leaving pensioners, in theory, about ten years of relative good health. From seventy-five to eighty, the "old old" start to get health afflictions, such as mobility problems, that tend to affect their normal functioning adversely. Women tend to have more chronic diseases than men.

Many Western societies have experienced a dramatic increase in the number of individuals who survive to old age. In most countries, for a variety of reasons, men die a few years earlier than women, which makes for an unequal male/female ratio that can rise as high as 1:4 for the eighties age group. The result of this is that there are probably more old lesbians than old gay men, although old lesbians tend to be more invisible. Nevertheless, even populous countries may have a low density of lesbians, which makes it difficult to organize regular neighborhood meetings in many places.

Each generation of people experiences different events that greatly affect the life history. These "cohort effects" are similar for many people within that generation and different for people of other generations. Some of these events affect all people of that generation; others are peculiar to lesbians and gays only. For example, the generation of people reaching old age at the end of the twentieth century was born between 1910 and 1930. They experienced economic crises in their adolescence, World War II in their early adulthood, and the beginning of the liberation of homosexuality in their early middle age. In the 1950s, the United States went through a period dominated by the reactionary politics of Senator Joseph McCarthy, which made homosexuality an "un-American activity." In European countries, the conservative backlash after the war and its return to "traditional values" meant the forced return of women into the home under strong social pressure to marry. In countries such as the Netherlands, participation of women in the labor market was very low, leaving only low-paid part-time jobs with no pension scheme for many women.

There have been great changes in the social position of homosexuality during the life course of many people. In experiencing these changes, they differ both from the generation before them, who lived all of their lives in total invisibility about their lesbianism, and from the generation after them, who were confronted with more openness about sexuality in general and the possibility of coming out.

Early research into the position of aging lesbians portrayed them stereotypically as lonely and "pathetic freakish figures, rejected by their families and hiding out of shame" (Kehoe 1988). The emphasis on youth culture supposedly produced a process of "accelerated aging" when youth could no longer be maintained. In fact, many researchers since have stressed that life development is not affected by sexual orientation per se but by social stigma. Coping with stigma seems a good predictor for successful aging. Furthermore, most literature suggests that gender exerts a greater influence on behavior than does sexual orientation. In other words, the salient factor in the aging of lesbians may be that they are women, not that they are homosexual.

## Aging Lesbians in Contemporary Societies

Research done on aging lesbians in the United States suggests that most lesbians have been highly educated and were, therefore, employed mainly in professional jobs with concomitant incomes. This may be, in part, a research bias since those who are more highly educated tend to be more organized and outspoken in surveys. In many countries, the socioeconomic position of women throughout the twentieth century was such that, although they might have been self-supporting for most of their lives, in fact single women have a substantially lower income than men or married women. Women typically earned 30 percent less than men; pension schemes were usually not geared toward single women, who lack the husband's pension that married women have. In the Netherlands, 25 percent of aging lesbians live on or under the social minimum.

Elderly lesbians and elderly gay men tend to associate mainly with others like themselves. Closed-coupled homosexuals with a strong commitment to a dyadic relationship have been shown to be the happiest and best adjusted.

Many women of this generation have been married and have children (and grandchildren). Many have been through a divorce, while others are widows. They came in mid-life to lesbianism through feminism in the 1970s. Although many women still recognize some difference in role between partners, strict butch-femme roles seem to have gone out of fashion. Age differences between partners are common, however.

Many aging lesbians live alone or have living-apart relationships. Living alone affects their lives to a large extent: in the amount of care they might need and in their financial and mental-health situation. These women usually lived a life of serial monogamy, which has now come to an end. In contrast to gay men, lesbians tend to establish their sexuality through a love relationship and change partners every four to seven years; gay men tend to separate sex from intimacy and emotional attraction and are usually in long-term, nonmonogamous relationships.

There is not much literature available on the sexuality of aging women, and what is available is by no means unequivocal about the influence of the aging process on sexuality of women. According to some authors, sexuality increases after menopause; according to others, it diminishes. Probably some changes do occur as the result of physiological changes, but factual changes are the result of social circumstances and gender-specific life patterns. Those who always have been sexually active will probably continue to be so. The fact that many aging lesbians are not able to find a partner, however, is instrumental in them not having sex. Kehoe found that 53 percent of her research group had not had any sexual contact during the previous year—most of them unwillingly—against only 6 percent of a gay male sample.

Although many aging lesbians believe that they have lived active lives, in the Netherlands many also reported feeling restless and depressed. This reflects the fact that they have difficulty in adjusting to living alone with little money rather than not being able to cope with old age as such.

The reduction of loneliness and isolation, therefore, seems of prime concern for aging lesbians. Much importance must be attached to friendships and support networks, which usually serve as substitutes for traditional families. Many lesbians do not get on very well with their families nor with their heterosexual surroundings. They are not interested in senior programs. Although most lesbians

**A**

rely heavily on their personal networks of (lesbian) friends for emotional, social, and instrumental support, these networks can be small and one sided and are, therefore, vulnerable.

The invisibility of old lesbians also leads to problems when care is needed. In the United States, old lesbians indicated that they wanted more recognition and support from official organizations, especially medical institutions. Most women rely on care provided by their closest friends, when available. Shifts in the national care systems from institutional care to care by friends and neighbors and back again affect their ability to cope to a large extent.

When asked about their housing preferences in later life, many lesbians will suggest some form of communal housing. Experiments with this have not proved very successful. Differences in money and the effects of official regulations on housing all seem to thwart initiatives.

### Successful Aging

The term "successful aging" refers to those processes of adaptation that contribute to optimal development in later life. "Successful aging" is dependent upon acceptance of homosexuality. The more positively homosexuality is integrated into the lifestyle, the more successful aging usually is. Most researches show a general acceptance of the aging process by lesbians. Flexibility of sex roles is regarded as an asset in the process of coping with aging. In the United States, a high level of involvement in the gay community is seen as instrumental in this process.          *Judith Schuyf*

### Bibliography

Kehoe, Monika. *Lesbians over 60 Speak for Themselves.* New York and London: Harrington, 1988.

Lee, John Alan, ed. "Gay Midlife and Maturity." *Journal of Homosexuality* 20:3–4 (1990) (Special Issue).

Reid, James D. "Development in Late Life: Older Lesbian and Gay Lives." In *Lesbian, Gay, and Bisexual Identities Over the Lifespan: Psychological Perspectives.* Ed. Anthony R. d'Augelli and Charlotte J. Patterson. New York: Oxford University Press, 1995, pp. 215–240.

Rossi, Alice S., ed. *Sexuality Across the Life Course.* Chicago: University of Chicago Press, 1994.

Schuyf, J. *Oud Roze: Homoseksuele Ouderen in Nederland* (Old Rose: The Position of Aging Gays and Lesbians in Dutch Society). Utrecht: Homostudies Utrecht, 1996.

Thorp Tully, C. "What Do Midlife Lesbians View as Important?" *Journal of Gay and Lesbian Psychotherapy* 1 (1989), 87–103.

*See also* Ageism

## AIDS (Acquired Immune Deficiency Syndrome)

An incurable disease that first appeared in the United States in 1978 and killed more than 400,000 Americans during the next twenty years.

AIDS is caused by the human immunodeficiency virus (HIV), which destroys the body's defense system against bacteria, viruses, and cancers. A person infected with HIV usually develops antibodies within six months; a positive HIV test means that antibodies to HIV are present. An HIV-positive person can remain healthy for many years before developing any of the numerous opportunistic infections, tumors, or neurological diseases that lead to a diagnosis of having AIDS.

At first, Karposi's sarcoma (KS) and Pneumocystis carinii pneumonia (PCP) were the primary indicators of AIDS, but, by the late 1980s, dozens of other infections were associated with AIDS. Because AIDS first appeared in the United States in intravenous-drug users and gay and bisexual men, conditions that most commonly affected men were first recognized. Lesbian pressure led the Centers for Disease Control (CDC) in Atlanta, Georgia, to recognize infections common in HIV-positive women as indicators of AIDS.

Early in the AIDS epidemic, a positive HIV test was considered a nearly certain prediction of developing AIDS and dying within ten to fifteen years. By the late 1990s, protease-inhibiting drugs and other treatments significantly extended the life expectancy of some HIV-positive people, to the point that AIDS was no longer considered necessarily fatal. However, these drugs were very expensive, not universally available, and not always effective. Research late in the 1990s suggested that a vaccine against HIV infection might someday be developed.

### HIV Transmission

HIV is present in certain body fluids (blood, semen, and vaginal fluid) of an infected person in sufficient quantities to spread the disease if this body fluid gets into the bloodstream of another person. (Also, breast milk plays a role in transmitting HIV from an infected mother to her baby.) HIV can travel through intact mucous membranes and through cuts in the skin. It dies quickly when exposed to air or temperature changes, and immunoglobulin A in saliva has a neutralizing effect on HIV. Anal intercourse and sharing of injection-drug needles are the most common methods of spreading HIV infection. Penis-vagina intercourse also poses high risk for spreading HIV. (AIDS is more easily sexually transmitted from a man to a woman than from a woman to a man.) Other sexual activities that might get body fluid from an HIV-infected person into the body of a partner can also be risky. Some health-care workers have been infected with HIV through accidental needle pricks. A few cases of HIV transmission through cuts, scratches, and bloody fistfights have been documented, and a few cases of suspected woman-to-woman sexual transmission of HIV have also been reported but not proven.

To prevent the spread of AIDS, safe-sex campaigns in the 1980s encouraged gay men and others to use condoms, and injection-drug users were taught to use bleach to clean shared needles. By the 1990s, safer-sex messages included awareness of other sexually transmitted diseases (STDs) and various safer-sex behaviors, but latex condoms remained the most important tool for preventing the spread of AIDS.

## Lesbians and AIDS

Since early in the AIDS epidemic, many lesbians contributed strong leadership in providing services to AIDS patients, doing political organizing to secure funding for research and education, and building coalitions among gay men, injection-drug users, people of color, prisoners, and other groups heavily affected by the disease.

Noting early research that indicated that HIV was unlikely to be spread by woman-to-woman sex, other lesbians saw AIDS as primarily a gay male concern and focused their energies on issues more directly affecting women, such as breast cancer, ecofeminism, equal employment opportunity, and ending violence against women. In the 1980s and 1990s, many more women became involved in gay politics and culture, partly as a result of the gaps left by gay men who were dying from or fighting AIDS.

In the 1990s, research confirmed that woman-to-woman sex was not a common way of spreading HIV, but other research showed that certain groups of women who have sex with women (WSW) were at risk of HIV infection because of their high rates of injection-drug use, sex for money, and sex with bisexual men. (However, many lesbians were skeptical of the CDC studies on woman-to-woman HIV transmission because, in its first four studies, the CDC defined "lesbian" as a woman who had sex only with women since 1978. While this was an important distinction for scientific purposes, it did not match the common, much broader, definition of "lesbian.")

In the 1990s, AIDS was no longer tightly clustered in subgroups of the U.S. population, and increasing numbers of women had a friend, lover, co-worker, client, child, or parent infected with HIV. There was no longer division in the lesbian community between those "involved with AIDS" and those not, because the epidemic touched everyone's life. Many early AIDS activists moved on to other work, while many lesbians who had previously avoided AIDS work found that their career paths or personal lives were affected by the epidemic in the 1990s.

Some lesbians say that working with gay men on AIDS issues improved lesbians' sex lives, because men's uninhibited, playful, and abundant sexual energy was a welcome contrast to the moralistic "just say no" message that dominated the American response to STDs in the 1980s. Safer-sex education encouraged women and men to talk explicitly about sexual activity and to experiment with new sexual styles. However, fear of AIDS put a damper on many women's sex lives, particularly those confused about how transmission might occur. Sexologists note that the beginning of the AIDS epidemic marked the end of the sexual revolution of the 1960s and 1970s, that brief period in human history when all common STDs were curable, or at least treatable, with modern medicine.

AIDS activism had a unifying effect on the gay community late in the twentieth century. In the 1970s, most lesbians and gay men existed in very different political and social circles. Gay rights activism after the Stonewall Rebellion (1969) was dominated by men, while 1970s political lesbians were primarily immersed in feminist causes. By the late 1990s, many gay organizations had gender-balanced memberships and leadership. This was partly the result of gay women and men learning to work together during the first two decades of the AIDS epidemic, and the feminist consciousness that many lesbians brought to that work.          *Marcia Munson*

### Bibliography

McIlvenna, Ted, ed. *The Complete Guide to Safer Sex*. Fort Lee: Barricade, 1992.

Merrifield, Margaret, M.D. *Come Sit by Me.* Toronto, Ont.: Women's Press, 1990.

Schneider, Beth, and Nancy Stoller. *Women Resisting AIDS.* Philadelphia: Temple University Press, 1995.

Shilts, Randy. *And the Band Played On: Politics, People, and the AIDS Epidemic.* New York: St. Martin's, 1987.

Stoller, Nancy. *Lessons from the Damned.* New York: Routledge, 1998.

*See also* Activism; Community Organizing; Health; Safer Sex; Sexually Transmitted Diseases

## Alcohol and Substance Abuse

Generally understood to be a state of uncontrollable dependency on liquor. Some of the most common characteristics of an alcoholic are use of alcohol to blunt negative feelings and to heighten positive feelings; a gradual but inevitable increase in amounts drunk and frequency of use; loss of concentration; depression; inability to form intimate relationships with people (because one's intimate relationship is with one's bottle); blackouts or failures of memory for periods of time; and general loss of interest in usual social and recreational activities. The same characteristics are used to describe individuals whose dependency is on drugs rather than alcohol.

## Research on Lesbians and Alcoholism

The most common understanding about lesbians and alcoholism is that a disproportionate percentage of lesbians in the United States have histories of abusing alcohol (and other drugs). This fact often adds grist to the mills of those who disapprove of lesbianism as a way of life. They conclude either that lesbianism is so debilitating that it drives its practitioners to drink or that the high incidence of alcoholism and drug dependence within lesbian communities signals the immorality of such a life.

In an article entitled "Research on Lesbians and Alcohol: Gaps and Implications," Hughes and Wilsnack (1994) argue that such data are questionable. Not only have almost all studies focusing on women and alcoholism until very recently used male alcoholics as the basis for interpreting data, but virtually no such studies distinguish between heterosexual and lesbian women with histories of alcohol and/or drug abuse. Furthermore, women surveyed for such studies most often have been drawn from populations in drug treatment centers rather than from the population at large. This fact, together with the often very small sample used in such studies, has skewed research results in certain predictable ways.

Hughes and Wilsnack cite a 1989 study by D.J. McKirnan and P.L. Peterson in which 748 lesbians and 2,652 gay men took part. Their findings point to three possible generalizations. First, while lesbians and gay men were not overrepresented among heavy drinkers in general, they reported rates of alcohol problems that were almost twice as high as those reported by the general population. (One might speculate that at least one reason for this high level of reporting might come from the general support within lesbian and gay communities for recovery of all sorts. Such an atmosphere might well facilitate a person's self-definition of various problematic behaviors.) Second, levels of alcohol problems among homosexuals were similar across sexes. Third, alcohol problems for lesbians and gay men did not decline with age, a finding similar to the pattern described in the National Lesbian Health Care Survey conducted by Caitlin Ryan and Judith Bradford and published in 1987 by the National Gay and Lesbian Health Foundation.

Hughes and Wilsnack argue that future research on the subject of lesbians and alcoholism (or drug abuse) could be strengthened by including questions about sexual orientation in all health surveys for women to determine similarities and differences between lesbians and heterosexual women. Additionally, future studies must be based on larger, more representative samples of lesbians (for example, different age groups, income and education levels, and ethnic minorities). Finally, such studies should explore lesbians' patterns of alcohol use over time so as to detect any apparent differences in drinking patterns between older lesbians and older heterosexual women.

What this list of historically unaddressed research variables makes clear is just how little is truly known about lesbians' use and abuse of alcohol and other drugs. But, even allowing for the dubiety currently associated with pronouncements that as many as one-third of lesbians studied drink heavily or are outright alcoholics, it remains the case that the societal context within which women discover their lesbianism remains critical, if not dangerously repressive. It also remains the case that large numbers of such women hide their lesbianism from self and others out of well-grounded fears, ignorance, and uncertainties. Therefore, attention must be paid to the psychosocial and historical realities faced by women dealing with issues of lesbian identity.

## Cultural Context

Rather than take such an individualistic approach, which inevitably blames the victim, one might analyze this perception systemically, looking to the social and cultural context within which lesbians attempt to make lives and careers. Many people leading a secret life, hiding integral aspects of their emotional and/or sexual identities, resort to some kind of numbing device to manage the pain of such choices. For many lesbians, historically, this numbing process has involved an overuse of alcohol (and, more recently, other drugs as well). In U.S. culture, alcoholism in the general population has reached alarming proportions. Available at every turn, alcohol seems almost required as part of usual social contact. The dangers of this tacit sanction of drinking for women trying to handle homoerotic feelings is obvious. If the individual lesbian is out to herself but to no one else, alcohol is an easily available route to feeling less torn and frightened about her "secret." If she is not out to herself—that is, if she denies her feelings for women out of a need to behave as all of the institutions in her world expect her to—alcohol supplies the fog within which to continue her living her heterosexual charade. Alcohol also can make it easier for her to engage in heterosexual relationships, since having a few drinks can blunt feelings enough to permit the requisite interactions between her and her latest male partner.

A measure of the place of alcohol within lesbian life can be found through a study of lesbian fiction since 1940. In a majority of such novels, lesbians drink (and smoke) with regularity and frequency. The beverage of choice and the locations in which they are consumed vary according to the class and personality of the characters involved. At times, the scene is a dark, smoke-filled bar owned often by voyeuristic and prejudiced men. At other times, lesbian characters dressed in tailored slacks and open-necked silk shirts sip cocktails or mixed drinks in one another's homes. If people find role models in the literature they read, then women certainly are encouraged to take up a glass, a bottle, or a can of something alcoholic as part of becoming a lesbian.

Researchers studying battery and other forms of physical abuse within lesbian relationships find a high degree of correlation between violence and the overuse of alcohol. Once again, however, this statistic has more to do with the nature of violence itself than with whether the people involved are lesbian or heterosexual. Comparable research dealing with heterosexual battery yields similar or even higher degrees of correlation between the abuse of alcohol and other drugs and the abuse of one's partner, girlfriend, or spouse.

In the 1970s, with the emphasis on lesbian culture and pride, much emphasis began to be placed on recovery from alcoholism. Special treatment programs in which lesbian sexuality, history, and achievements were celebrated sprang up across the country; lesbian meetings of Alcoholics Anonymous (AA) began to flower in most metropolitan centers; and lesbian communities themselves sought alternative locations to the bars for social contact. A pioneering center for this recovery movement was Minneapolis, Minnesota, which in 1972 opened one of the first lesbian and gay treatment centers (Christopher Street by name) and which still operates a private agency, Pride Institute, to which lesbians from all over the United States come to sober up. Similar programs elsewhere remain viable sites within which lesbians can begin the long and painful process of detachment, first from alcohol and other addictive chemicals and, eventually, from the harmful internalized messages about themselves as human beings.

In conclusion, while it is clear that many research findings are unrealiable, it is equally clear that discovering and living out a lesbian sexuality and politics are fraught with enough social stigma and disapprobation to make numbing one's feelings through the use of alcohol a genuine option for too many women.
*Toni A.H. McNaron*

### Bibliography

Hall, Joanne M. "Lesbians and Alcohol: Patterns and Paradoxes in Medical Notions and Lesbian Beliefs." *Journal of Psychoactive Drugs* 25:2 (1993), 109–119.

Hughes, Tonda L., and Sharon C. Wilsnack. "Research on Lesbians and Alcohol: Gaps and Implications." *Alcohol Health and Research World* 18:3 (1994), 202–205.

Nicholoff, Lee K., and Eloise A. Stiglitz. "Lesbian Alcoholism: Etiology, Treatment, and Recovery." In *Lesbian Psychologies*. Urbana and Chicago: University of Illinois Press, 1987, pp. 283–293.

Schilit, Rebecca, Gwat-Yong Lie, and Marilyn Montagne. "Substance Use as a Correlate of Violence in Lesbian Relationships." *Journal of Homosexuality* 19:3 (1990), 51–65.

Underhill, Brenda L. "Recovery Needs of Lesbian Alcoholics in Treatment." In *Feminist Perspectives on Addiction*. Ed. Nan Van Den Bergh. New York: Springer, 1991, pp. 73–86.

Weathers, B. "Alcoholism and the Lesbian Community." In *Alternative Services for Women*. Ed. Naomi Gottlieb. New York: Columbia University Press, 1980, pp. 158–169.

*See also* Recovery Movement

## All-Female Revues (Japan)

Eclectic type of musical-theater performance characterized by montage, or the linkage of apparently unrelated events and phenomena. The public spectacle of all-female revues has simultaneously disturbed and reinforced the dominant sex-gender system across cultural areas since the late nineteenth century. In Japan, the all-female Takarazuka Revue has fueled the heated debate concerning the relationship among sex, gender, and sexuality since its first performance in 1914, and continues to mediate the tension between a normative (hetero)sexual text and an unconventional (homo)sexual subtext. Inspired at home by the nearly four-hundred-year-old all-male Kabuki theater and the girls' and boys' bands that entertained customers at the larger department stores, Takarazuka founder Kobayashi Ichizô (1873–1957) was also influenced by the "chorus girls" in Europe and the United States. These included the English burlesque pantomimes, with their cross-dressed cast of young women, and the Gaiety Girl, who flourished between the late 1860s and 1910 and who was joined by the Tiller Girls and the Bluebell Girls, two long-lasting troupes that specialized in vigorous, tightly coordinated line dances. The French can-can dancers and risqué performers of the Folies Bergère also influenced the Japanese impresario. They, along with the Hoffman Girls and the Blackbirds, a troupe of black artistes in France, added to the cachet of "naughtiness" attached to all-female stage shows. Kobayashi's familiarity with Western theater extended to the American Ziegfeld Follies, whose opulent revues opened in July 1907, and today comparisons are drawn between Takarazuka and the high-kicking Radio City Rockettes, formed in 1925.

Takarazuka, Japan's premier all-female revue, spawned more than a dozen copycat troupes, most notably the Shôchiku Revue, founded in 1928, which quickly became Takarazuka's main rival in every respect. Takarazuka and Shôchiku proved to be enormously popular from the beginning, with annual audiences totaling in the millions, although only the former continues to stage year-round revues. All-female revues have stimulated the organization of hundreds of fan clubs, most of which are segregated by sex. Contrary to the prevailing view, male fans make up a significant percentage of the adoring audience, although the majority of, and the most visible and "problematic," fans are females, from teenagers to senior citizens. Many all-male fan clubs double as powerful business networks. Fan clubs often stage their own revues modeled after Takarazuka and, in this capacity, provide members with an opportunity to experiment freely with different gender roles without any sexual or political "strings" attached.

Takarazuka productions include Japanese-style classical dramas and historical subjects, such as the *Tale of Genji*; European-style and Broadway-based performances, such as *Mon Paris* and *West Side Story*; and folk dances from all over the world. In their roles as men and women, the actors both uphold the dominant ideal of heterosexuality and inform a lesbian (butch-femme-like) subcultural style. The revue continues to attract the attention of the mass media, although the charges leveled at the actors of "moral depravity" and "abnormal sexual desire" are much more muted than they were in the first half of the twentieth century, reflecting not a greater acceptance of lesbianism, but the revue's stricter conditions for media coverage. Takarazuka has influenced the emergence and popularity of various all-female performing-arts groups active in Japan today, including drumming ensembles, Kabuki troupes, alternative and feminist theaters, and palanquin-shrine (*mikoshi*) bearers. Most of these groups are able to challenge the status quo more consciously than did or does the revue itself.

*Jennifer E. Robertson*

### Bibliography

Robertson, Jennifer E. *Takarazuka: Sexual Politics and Popular Culture in Modern Japan*. Berkeley: University of California Press, 1998.

*See also* Cross-Dressing; Japan

## Allan, Maud (1873–1956)

Modern dance pioneer. Born Maud Durrant in Canada, she moved with her family to California six years later. In the early twentieth century, she danced throughout Europe, Asia, Australia, and North America, but with greatest success in England. In 1908, she gave more than 250 performances in London, including her "Vision of Salome." Her fame briefly exceeded that of Isadora Duncan (1878–1927), to whom she was compared frequently. She was patronized by high society, including royalty, Prime Minister Herbert Asquith (1852–1928), and his wife, Margot (1864–1945). Margot Asquith had a close relationship with Maud Allan, paying for her expensive London apartment for many years.

In 1918, Allan brought a libel case against the independent Member of Parliament Noel Pemerton-Billing (1881–1948). In January of that year, with World War I still under way, his newspaper had announced that the Germans held a "Black Book" containing the names of 47,000 British citizens who, as "sexual perverts," were open to blackmail. In February, he printed an article headed "The Cult of the Clitoris" that suggested that many of those would be attending a forthcoming private performance of Oscar Wilde's (1854–1900) play *Salome* and that named Allan as the central performer. Allan took the reference to the "clitoris" as implying that she was a lesbian.

During the trial, Allan was discredited in a number of ways. A history of two sexual murders committed by her brother more than twenty years earlier was presented as "evidence" of hereditary sadism. Moreover, since the play involves Salome's unrequited obsession with the imprisoned John the Baptist (called Johannan in Wilde's version) and her demand for his head, it was argued that any woman acting the part of Salome would have to be a sadist.

Allan's knowledge of certain terms, in particular "clitoris" and "sadism," further discredited her, since possession of such knowledge was taken as a sure sign of sexual perversion. Although the relationship between the clitoris and lesbianism was never made explicit, one defense witness described the clitoris as "a superficial organ that, when unduly excited or overdeveloped, possessed the most dreadful influence on any woman." By implication, lesbianism or sadism could be the result.

Toward the end of the trial, Pemberton-Billing suddenly denied that he had called Allan a lesbian. He now claimed that all he had meant was that she consorted with sexual perverts. The jury voted in Pemberton-Billing's favor, and Allan was condemned not as a lesbian, but as a sadist. The trial did not advance the British public's understanding of lesbianism.

In the late 1920s, Allan became the lover of Verna Aldrich (ca. 1890s–1970), her secretary/companion, with whom she lived for at least ten years. In 1941, she returned to the United States, where the *New York Times* identified her as "the dancer whose Salome was once considered sensational."

Lucy Bland

## Bibliography

Bland, Lucy. "Trial by Sexology? Maud Allan, Salome, and the 1918 'Cult of the Clitoris' Case." In *Sexology in Culture: Labelling Bodies and Desires*. Ed. Lucy Bland and Laura Doan. London: Polity, 1998, pp. 183–198.

Cherniavsky, Felix. *The Salome Dancer: The Life and Times of Maud Allan*. Toronto: McClelland and Stewart, 1991.

Hoare, Philip. *Wilde's Last Stand: Decadence, Conspiracy, and the First World War*. London: Duckworth, 1997.

Kettle, Michael. *Salome's Last Veil: The Libel Case of the Century*. London and New York: Grenada, 1977.

Travis, Jennifer. "Clits in Court: Salome, Sodomy, and the Lesbian 'Sadist.' " In *Lesbian Erotics*. Ed. Karla Jay. New York: New York University Press, 1995, pp. 147–163.

*See also* Clitoris; Sadomasochism

## Allen, Paula Gunn (1939–)

Native American scholar, poet, and novelist. Allen is one of the most important American Indian intellectuals and writers of the twentieth century. Her scholarship on Native American understandings of "two-spirits" (American Indians who are lesbian, gay, bisexual, or transgendered) represents some of the most significant work on the subject, laying the groundwork for more accurate and culturally relevant research in this area. Her poetry and fiction occasionally feature gay and lesbian themes as well.

Born Paula Marie Francis in Cubero, New Mexico, Allen is of Laguna, Lakota, Scottish, and Lebanese heritages. At the University of Oregon, she earned a B.A. in literature in 1966 and an M.F.A. in creative writing two years later. She went on to attain a Ph.D. in American studies from the University of New Mexico, Albuquerque, in 1975. A professor of Native American studies, women's studies, and English, she has taught at several universities, most notably, the University of California at Berkeley and at Los Angeles.

**A**

*Paula Gunn Allen. Photo by Tama Rothschild. Used with permission of Paula Gunn Allen.*

As a scholar, Allen is probably most well known for two groundbreaking books: *Studies in American Indian Literature: Critical Essays and Course Designs* (1983), which she edited, and *The Sacred Hoop: Recovering the Feminine in American Indian Traditions* (1986). Her work as a creative writer includes one novel, *The Woman Who Owned the Shadows* (1983), and seven collections of poetry.

In both nonfiction and fiction, Allen has addressed Native American lesbian and gay ways of life. Her essay *"Hwame, Koshkalaka, and the Rest: Lesbians in American Indian Cultures"* published in *The Sacred Hoop* remains an important contribution to the field. She also has written several poems with lesbian and gay themes, including *"Koshkalaka*, Ceremonial Dyke" and "Never Cry Uncle," "Some Like Indians Endure," and "Beloved Women." *Raven's Road,* a novel in progress, also features a Native American lesbian character. Chapters of this novel have appeared as "Deep Purple" (*Spider Woman's Granddaughters: Traditional Tales and Contemporary Writing by Native American Women* [1989]), "Selections from Raven's Road" (*Living the Spirit: A Gay American Indian Anthology* [1989]), and "The Medicine Song of Allie Hawker" (*Intricate Passions: A Collection of Erotic Short Fiction* [1988]).

Allen is important not only because of her writing on two-spirits, but also because of her participa-

tion in gay and lesbian communities on the West Coast, where she has lived on and off for many years. That Allen has been married to both men and women is not surprising in light of the cultural understandings of many Native communities. As she herself has written, in *Intricate Passions*: "I am not especially defined by my sex life, nor complete without it."                    *Mary C. Churchill*

### Bibliography

Donovan, Kathleen M. *Feminist Readings of Native American Literature: Coming to Voice.* Tucson: University of Arizona Press, 1998.

Hansen, Elizabeth. *Paula Gunn Allen.* Boise, Idaho: Boise State University Press, 1990.

Holford, Vanessa. "Re-Membering Ephanie: A Woman's Re-Creation of Self in Paula Gunn Allen's *The Woman Who Owned the Shadows,*" *Studies in American Indian Literatures* 61 (Spring 1994), 99–113.

Keating, AnaLouise. *Women Reading Women Writing: Self-Invention in Paula Gunn Allen, Gloria Anzaldúa, and Audre Lorde.* Philadelphia: Temple University Press, 1996.

Van Dyke, Annette. "The Journey Back to Female Roots: A Laguna Pueblo Model." In *Lesbian Texts and Contexts: Radical Revisions.* Ed. Karla Jay and Joanne Glasgow. New York: New York University Press, 1990, pp. 339–354.

*See also* Native Americans; Two-Spirit

### Amazons

A matriarchal tribe of warrior women first represented in ancient Greek myth and rewritten in the contemporary era by feminists and lesbians as an identity opposed to patriarchy and an original separatist culture. The historical status of Amazons—whether they existed as real women in the ancient Greek world or were a fantastic patriarchal creation—remains a point of scholarly and feminist contention. This has not prevented strong identifications within lesbian feminist circles.

First named in Homer's *Iliad* (ca. 750–700 B.C.E.), Amazons proliferated in the official histories and geographies of the ancient Athenian city-state, as well as in its poetry, vase painting, and architecture. Feminist scholars read these myths as serving a patriarchal project of the colonial expansion of ancient Athens. They managed citizen-men's fears of potential uprisings among "their" women and slaves, by showing the Athenian male hero always killing or marrying the "barbarian," sexually deviant Amazons. Similarly motivated regenerations of Amazon myths appear throughout Western history, especially during European "discoveries" of the New World. Small (1991) writes of Amazons spotted by Christopher Columbus (1451–1506) and other Spanish explorers, and Montrose (1991) examines how and why the British Empire had explorers mapping Amazons during Queen Elizabeth I's reign (1558–1603).

Despite scholarly historical alignment of Amazons with patriarchal myth, contemporary lesbians have identified with the Amazon. Hers is a female body that suggests distinctly different qualities from the dominant culture's insistence on women's "natural" dependence on men and the heterosexual family. Seen as a strong, independent warrior, the Amazon counters the traditional, passive feminine body, often being depicted as an athletic or androgynous figure.

The tribal, nationalist aspect of classical Amazons has well suited separatist arrangements of "woman-identified" culture set apart from men. The phrase "Amazon nation" has broadly circulated since the mid-1970s to describe lesbian subculture, as the "woman-only" culture of the Amazons is seen as an original example of lesbian separatism. Johnston (1973) suggests the need for "a return to the harmony of statehood and biology through the remembered majesties of women," in her last chapter, "Archdykes and Amazons." Writers often express this separatist vision through the mythic link between Amazons and islands, mapping the necessity of separation from dominant culture. Québec author Nicole Brossard (1943–) and French novelist Monique Wittig (1935–) favor the island metaphor in their important poetic fictions. And in "This Place Named for Califia," poet Healy (1991) takes over the Spanish and American mythology that first imagined California as ruled by a black Amazonian queen, Califia: ". . . that island, floating like the legends ahead of an exploring army. / The story of the women beyond / the river, the fall, or like this / place, the island of women / living without men just beyond / the mist, beyond this weather . . . an island real enough to be necessary, a kind of woman / necessary enough to be real."          *Molly Rae Rhodes*

## Bibliography

DuBois, Page. *Centaurs and Amazons: Women and the Pre-History of the Great Chain of Being.* Ann Arbor: University of Michigan Press, 1982.

Healy, Eloise Klein. "This Place Named for Califia." In *Artemis in Echo Park.* Ithaca, N.Y.: Firebrand, 1991, p. 37.

Johnston, Jill. *Lesbian Nation: The Feminist Solution.* New York: Simon and Schuster, 1973.

Montrose, Louis. "The Work of Gender in the Discourse of Discovery." *Representations* 33 (Winter 1991), 1–41.

Salmonson, Jessica Amanda. *The Encyclopedia of Amazons: Woman Warriors from Antiquity to the Modern Era.* New York: Doubleday, 1991.

Small, Deborah with Maggie Jaffe. *1492: What's It Like to Be Discovered?* New York: Monthly Review Press, 1991.

Zeitlin, Froma. "The Dynamics of Misogyny: Myth and Myth Making in the Oresteia." In *Women in the Ancient World: The Arethusa Papers.* Ed. John Peradotto and J.P. Sullivan. Albany: State University of New York Press, 1984, pp. 159–194.

***See also*** Brossard, Nicole; Johnston, Jill; Wittig, Monique

## American Literature, Nineteenth Century

Because open expression of lesbian emotion was even less acceptable in the nineteenth century than it has been in the twentieth, affecting not only what could be published but censoring presumably private documents such as letters and diaries, questions of evidence surround any discussion of the imaginative record of its representation. While the work of sexologists such as Richard von Krafft-Ebing (1840–1902) and Havelock Ellis (1859–1939), by creating the category of the homosexual, may have produced a certain self-consciousness in the portrayal of relations between women in the last quarter of the nineteenth century, one must remember that they aimed at codifying and analyzing identities and behaviors understood to be already in existence. Thus, though the record is clearer for the second half of the century than for the first, if one invokes aggressive reading strategies as a justifiable approach to decoding the severely censored, it is possible to trace a lesbian presence throughout nineteenth-century American literature.

### Early Expressions of Attachments Between Women

Charles Brockden Brown's *Ormond* (1798) provides an early treatment of passionate attachment between women. Written in reaction to Samuel Richardson's *Clarissa* (1747–1748), *Ormond* replaces Richardson's plot of seduction, rape, and suicide with Constantia's successful, and lethal, repulse of Ormond and ends happily with her reunion with her beloved Sophia who has traveled twenty-four miles, the last three on foot, to rescue her. Brown (1771–1810) contextualizes the nature of their relationship through his portrait of the cross-dressing and androgynous Martinette, who shows that it is possible to be "imbued with a soul that was a stranger to the sexual distinction." An early feminist, Brown offers Constantia as a model for the woman of the new American republic and links her independence and self-love to her relation to Sophia.

Unfortunately, Brown's interest in the radical potential of love between women was not immediately pursued. Instead, writers such as James Fenimore Cooper (1789–1851) chose to present love between women in the context of the relationship of sisters—Cora and Alice in *The Last of the Mohicans* (1826); Judith and Hetty in *The Deerslayer* (1841). Catherine Sedgwick's *Hope Leslie* (1827) is radical in its creation of an independent, aggressive heroine who defies patriarchal efforts to imprison her in a conventional marriage, but it follows Cooper's model for presenting attachment between women. Hope's passionate search for her biological sister, from whom she has been separated since childhood, parallels her search for her Indian "sister," Magawisca, and both attachments are thus conventionally acceptable. Though *Hope Leslie* contains a cross-dressing woman whose strange encounters with Hope provide the text's sole erotic element, Sedgwick (1789–1867) presents passion of any kind as dangerous to women.

In *The Blithedale Romance* (1852), Nathaniel Hawthorne (1804–1864) adopts a similar strategy when he reveals the mysterious relationship between Priscilla and Zenobia to be that of half-sisters, though, until this revelation, he allows some speculation about the nature of Priscilla's adoration of the older, erotic Zenobia. Zenobia, whose suicide reinstates the theme of "seduced and abandoned" as preferable to any hint of deviant sexuality, has reminded many readers of Margaret Fuller (1810–1850), herself a feminist who had intense romantic relations with other women. In her brief autobiographical memoir, originally published in 1852, and subsequently reprinted as "Autobiographical Sketch" in *The Portable Margaret Fuller* (1994), Fuller provides an account of her "first feeling," a passionate attachment to an older English lady whose departure left her in a depression that she recognized to be "out of the . . . natural course." In 1842, Fuller published her translation of the *Correspondence of Fraulein Gunderode with Bettine Von Arnim* and her meditations on the significance of their passionate attachment. Later, Fuller would write about George Sand (1804–1876), flamboyant symbol of the sexually deviant woman, whom she insisted on meeting when she went to Paris in 1846. In the story of Marianna, included in *Summer on the Lakes* (1843), Fuller offers a portrait of the emotionally charged environment of the female boarding school, one of the more likely settings in American (and continental) literature for the representation of passions between women.

## Lesbian Texts and Authors

Specifically lesbian texts and authors, as well as modes of writing conducive to the representation of lesbian emotion, begin to appear in the second half of the nineteenth century. As Terry Castle has argued in *The Apparitional Lesbian* (1993), the ghost story in which the beloved is dead offered women writers a safe way to represent the hauntingly intense passion of women for women. Elizabeth Stuart Phelps (1844–1911), whose "Since I Died" (1873) is included in Susan Koppelman's *Two Friends* (1994), a collection of nineteenth-century American lesbian stories, deserves mention for constructing a significant variation of the "ghosting" of lesbian emotion. In *The Story of Avis* (1876), Phelps locates emotional intensity in the passionate attachment of narrator for character, expressed through the erotics of watching. This strategy allows her novel to serve as a public space in which it is possible for one woman to openly admire another because the eroticism is disembodied. Phelps's unabashed adoration of the extraordinarily sensual Avis has disturbed readers, as has her uncompromisingly negative treatment of Philip, the lover turned husband turned cad who dies by novel's end. If, as Castle has also suggested, the lesbian novel requires "a man who has been sacrificed," then both the narrator's attachment to Avis and her hostility to Philip mark this text as lesbian.

Another mode of writing that emerged in the second half of the nineteenth century and proved conducive to the expression of lesbian emotion is literary regionalism. *Two Friends* contains fiction by several regionalists, including Rose Terry Cooke (1827–1892), Sarah Orne Jewett (1849–1909),

Mary Wilkins Freeman (1852–1930), Kate Chopin (1851–1904), and Alice Brown (1856–1948). With its focus on the self-consciously marginal woman, odd and even deviant, frequently living in a predominantly female community, regionalism presents characters who are free to say they don't like boys and free to say they do like girls. The potential of regionalism to create a space for the odd woman can be seen as early as Catherine Sedgwick's *Redwood* (1824), in which the regional character, Deborah Lenox, is described as a six-foot Amazon who might be mistaken for a "grenadier." Possibly based on the historical figure of Deborah Sampson (1760–1827), who cross-dressed to fight in the American Revolution and had relations with other women, Sedgwick's Deborah is a self-avowed spinster who successfully rescues a younger woman from rape. Similarly, Harriet Beecher Stowe (1811–1896), in *The Pearl of Orr's Island* (1862), creates the eccentric Aunt Roxy, who, on hearing of the proposed marriage between Mara and Moses that others believe will be the "salvation" of Moses, declares that she is not "one of the sort that wants to be a-usin' up girls for the salvation of fellers."

Jewett, who traced her origins as a writer to Stowe's *Pearl*, must figure prominently in any treatment of lesbianism in nineteenth-century American literature. *Deephaven* (1877), the first text since *Ormond* to present love between women as the basis for a story, describes the experience of Helen and Kate, who spend a summer in a small town in Maine and set up housekeeping together, the region providing a space in which such choices are at least temporarily possible. Imagining such a relationship in fiction may have made it possible for Jewett to form her own "Boston Marriage" with Annie Fields (1834–1915). Jewett's stories take up such issues as cross-dressing ("An Autumn Holiday" [1880]) role reversal ("Tom's Husband" [1882]) and the love of one woman for another across class and time and space ("Martha's Lady" [1897]). "A White Heron" (1886) records a young girl's rejection of aggressive male sexuality in favor of a life with nature in which birds are not killed, stuffed, and studied but allowed, like herself, to fly free. In the context of the "bad boy" literature of the 1870s and 1880s, which idolized boys and licensed their behavior particularly as it disrupted feminine spaces (e.g., Mark Twain's *Tom Sawyer* [1876]), fiction such as "A White Heron" and Cooke's "Miss Beulah's Bonnet" (1880), whose character finally declares herself "free to say I never did like boys," may be read as an alternative argument in favor of girls and against compulsory heterosexuality.

Freeman, who lived for twenty years with her friend, Mary John Wales (d. 1916), and married only late in life, exhibits an awareness of deviance that makes her perhaps even more recognizable as a lesbian to twentieth-century readers than Jewett. In *The Long Arm* (1895), Phoebe Dole murders the man who plans to marry Maria Wood, the woman with whom she has lived for more than forty years, and she justifies her act by claiming that "there are other ties as strong as the marriage one." Phoebe's unusually long arm, the key to unraveling the mystery, signals her deviance and places her within a category recognizably lesbian to late-nineteenth-century readers, that of the masculine woman. *By The Light of the Soul* (1906) deserves particular mention among Freeman's later novels, which frequently focus on obsessive relationships between women, for its re-eroticizing of the relation between half-sisters, as well as for the explicit decision of one sister to choose life with another woman over marriage. In her earlier short fiction, Freeman treated the passionate attachment of women to each other more positively, though still acknowledging that it falls outside the norm. In "Two Friends" (1887), Sarah's love for Abby exceeds that of men for women and, as the story's conclusion makes clear, marks the lesbian choice as superior to the heterosexual alternative.

Perhaps the most open portrayal of a lesbian relationship in nineteenth-century American literature occurs in Henry James's (1843–1916) *The Bostonians* (1886). A classic treatment of one kind of lesbian triangle, *The Bostonians* records the struggle of Olive Chancellor and Basil Ransom for possession of Verena Tarrant, a struggle Basil "wins" not so much because he possesses phallic force as because Olive doubts the legitimacy of her claim on Verena. Despite the suggestion that her attraction to feminism stems from her rivalry with men over women, Olive emerges as a heroic figure. Yet Verena, whose future with Ransom James acknowledges to be grim, is no less a lesbian than Olive for, as Emma Donaghue, in *Passions Between Women* (1993), asks, "How can there be a female husband without a female husband's wife?" By acknowledging Verena's attachment to Olive as well as Olive's to Verena, James counters the idea that only the masculine woman is a true lesbian.

No account of lesbianism in nineteenth-century American literature would be complete without ref-

A erence to Louisa May Alcott's *Little Women* (1868), for Jo March has offered generations of readers a compelling model of the adolescent tomboy. Unable to get over her disappointment at not being a boy, Jo hates visits and being nice to old ladies and prefers a run in the fields or, like Fuller's Marianna, those amateur theatrics that give her a chance to dress up in doublet and hose and play suitor to the sisters she wishes she could marry. Though Alcott (1832–1888) capitulated to public pressure for a "happy" heterosexual ending, she refused to marry Jo to Laurie, insisting that the charm of the relationship for Jo lies in its lack of erotic content. By resisting this particular heterosexual plot and by marrying her to a man more a father than a lover, Alcott preserves Jo's tomboy identity into adulthood. In Alcott's *Work* (1872), Christie Devon forms her first and most lasting emotional relationship with a woman who turns out to be the sister of the man she marries just hours before he leaves for the Civil War. David's death shortly thereafter leaves Christie and Letty to make a life together that is also the center of a female and feminist community.

Though critics have searched for evidence of a failed heterosexual romance to "explain" the work of Emily Dickinson (1830–1886), her letters provide ample evidence of her passionate attachment to Sue Gilbert, the woman who would later marry her brother, Austin. While Dickinson wrote poetry that explores the psychological effect on women of heterosexual passion, according to Bennett (1990), "her most important and characteristic erotic poetry . . . is written in a homoerotic mode" and celebrates the pleasures and pains of a passion recognizably lesbian to twentieth-century readers. Additionally, one can read Dickinson's fascination with the "tiny tale," the form her poetry takes and the theme of many of her poems ("It would have starved a Gnat / To live so small as I"), as a mode of lesbian eroticism in which the ironic exaggeration of the small serves to celebrate the explosive force of a female sexuality conventionally seen as insignificant.

In any discussion of Dickinson, it is important to remember that her poetry was unpublished during her lifetime. As Bennett has noted, "Generally speaking, poetry was more conservative than fiction in the period," and, indeed, the poetry published by American women during the nineteenth century provides little record of lesbian experience. Still, Bennett has begun the work of recovering nineteenth-century American lesbian poetry, a tradition that would include Fuller's verses to Anna Barker and poetry by such writers as Celia Thaxter (1835–1894), Annie Fields, and Sophie Jewett (n.d.), part of an intimate circle at Wellesley College that included Katharine Lee Bates (1859–1929), author of "America, the Beautiful," and Florence Converse (1871–1967), whose *Diana Victrix* (1897) Faderman (1981) has labeled a lesbian novel. Faderman would add to this list Adah Isaacs Menken (1835–1868), cross-dressing friend of George Sand, although, as Foster (1975) notes, little of what might be called lesbian finds its way into the poetry collected in *Infelicia* (1868).

Among African American writers, identifiably lesbian texts and authors do not appear until the twentieth century, though Hansen (1996) has recovered the record of lesbian emotion in the nineteenth century through letters. According to Gilman (1985), by the eighteenth century the sexuality of black women (and men) was "an icon for deviant sexuality in general"; and Donoghue (1993) notes the pornography of a 1745 medical treatise "which features a hugh centrefold-style engraving of the vulva of a 'hermaphroditical' Angolan woman sold into slavery in America." The pathologizing of black women's sexuality was intensified in the nineteenth century through the figure of the "Hottentot Venus," whose "abnormal" and "deviant" genitalia and body shape provided the central image for the period. Given this history, in which racism, sexism, and homophobia reinforced and justified one another, it is not surprising that nineteenth-century African American writers sought to portray women in terms that would be recognized as unmistakably "normal." However, since there obviously were African American lesbians in the nineteenth century, it is quite likely that further research will produce literary texts that reflect their experience more directly.

*Judith Fetterley*

## Bibliography

Bennett, Paula. *Emily Dickinson, Woman Poet*. Iowa City: University of Iowa Press, 1990.

Castle, Terry. *The Apparitional Lesbian: Female Homosexuality and Modern Culture*. New York: Columbia University Press, 1993.

Donoghue, Emma. *Passions Between Women: British Lesbian Culture, 1668–1801*. London: Scarlet Press, 1993.

Faderman, Lillian. *Surpassing the Love of Men: Romantic Friendship and Love between Women from the Sixteenth Century to the Present*. New York: William Morrow, 1981.

Foster, Jeannette. *Sex Variant Women in Literature.* [n.p.]: Vantage, 1956. 2nd ed. Baltimore: Diana, 1975.

Gilman, Sander. "Black Bodies, White Bodies: Toward an Iconography of Female Sexuality in Late Nineteenth-Century Art, Medicine, and Literature." In *"Race," Writing, and Difference.* Ed. Henry Louis Gates, Jr. Chicago: University of Chicago Press, 1985, pp. 223–261.

Hansen, Karen V. "(No *Kisses* Is Like Youres): An Erotic Friendship Between Two African American Women During the Mid-Nineteenth Century." In *Lesbian Subjects.* Ed. Martha Vicinus. Bloomington: Indiana University Press, 1996, pp. 178–207.

Koppelman, Susan, ed. *Two Friends.* New York: Penguin, 1994.

*See also* Bates, Katharine Lee; Boarding Schools; Boston Marriage; Cross-Dressing; Dickinson, Emily; Fuller, Margaret; Jewett, Sarah Orne; Literary Images

## American Literature, Twentieth Century

Like the story of twentieth-century American literature generally, the story of twentieth-century lesbian American literature begins in Paris, with the salon of Natalie Barney (1876–1972), who gathered important French and expatriate writers and formed the nucleus of an unabashed lesbian community. Barney is also remembered for her many intense and "operatic" erotic activities (the word is Karla Jay's), especially her love affairs with painter Romaine Brooks (1874–1970) and English-born poet Renée Vivien (Pauline Mary Tarn [1877–1909]). Few now read the formally conservative verse (often based on fragments from Sappho) of Barney and Vivien, or Barney's epigrammatic memoirs, partly because both chose to write in French. Novelist Djuna Barnes (1892–1982) immortalized this community, and particularly Barney's larger-than-life sexual persona, in *The Ladies' Almanack* (1928).

### Expatriate Writing

While the writings of the Paris group may be forgotten, they became lesbian icons (as Sappho was for them) for later generations, based upon their elegant style and visibility, more than for anything they ever wrote. On the other hand, the richer work of three expatriates, Barnes, H.D. (1886–1961), and Gertrude Stein (1874–1946), continued to inspire lesbian and nonlesbian writing. Stein, too, may be most familiar through her public persona, especially as expressed through her most accessible work, *The Autobiography of Alice B. Toklas* (1932). Stein and Toklas (1877–1967) form an iconic lesbian couple, and Stein's relationships with such visual artists as Paul Cezanne (1839–1906), Henri Matisse (1869–1954), and Pablo Picasso (1881–1973), and her influence on younger American writers, especially Ernest Hemingway (1899–1961), are well known. But she should also be credited as a major figure in the reinvention of literary language now called "modernism." Her most serious and experimental writing presents a challenge to conventional realist narrative, a questioning of the very ability of words and sentences to represent the world. Much of her writing is highly demanding—the reader must make meaning as the viewer of a Cubist painting does. Such works as "As a Wife Has a Cow: A Love Story" and "Lifting Belly" (1915–1917) have been interpreted as "coding" lesbian sexuality, but they never do so through simple allegories or one-to-one correspondences. The term "code" can only hint at Stein's ambitious attempt to address the inadequacy of literary convention for expressing lesbian existence by exploding and reinventing language entirely. (One early realist novel, *Q.E.D.; or, Things as They Are*, about a lesbian love triangle, was written in 1903 but remained unpublished until 1950.)

Because of the hunger for clear and positive representation in an economy of scarcity, it has sometimes been hard for lesbian readers to value Stein's work. The same has been true for Djuna Barnes, whose best novel, *Nightwood* (1936), displays the devastating end of a love between two women against the nightmarish background of a Paris full of deviance, desire, and grotesque beauty. *Nightwood* is more open and direct about the sexuality of its characters than Stein's experimental work, but some readers find its torrent of images unmanageable, and some critics also find Barnes's work unacceptably "dark" or lurid or too dependent on sexological stereotypes of perversion. More recently, critics have seen her as writing in productive tension with those stereotypes and have revalued her other novel, *Ryder* (1928), and her play, *The Antiphon* (1958), which deal strongly with the sexual exploitation of women and girls. Barnes greatly influenced some later lesbian writers, such as novelist Bertha Harris, who have continued to explode the confines of narrative in search of a new language to express a lesbian world. Writers more concerned

A with reaching a broad audience and/or providing positive images have tended instead to follow the conventionally realist path of British novelist Radclyffe Hall (1880–1943), author of *The Well of Loneliness* (1928), who is credited with introducing the butch character to literature and inventing the coming out story.

Hilda Doolittle (1886–1961), who wrote under the name H.D., was a prolific and experimental writer in many genres, including poetry, fiction, drama, and autobiographical memoir, the distinction among these genres often being blurry. As a poet, she was a founding member of the Imagist group, which emphasized clarity and concreteness, hated sentimentality, and—in the words of Ezra Pound (1885–1972), to whom H.D. was at one time engaged—"broke the pentameter," establishing free verse as the literary norm and, in a sense, inventing modernism. (Amy Lowell [1874–1925], poet and wealthy patron, was also for some time a member of this group, though less formally inventive: A few of her poems have explicit lesbian content.) Unsurprisingly, the fiction that remained unpublished until after H.D.'s death in 1961 is the most explicitly lesbian, recounting her important attachments to women throughout her life. The work she chose to publish gives a much more heterosexual impression, both through the autobiographical elements and the large-scale religious symbolism of her later works.

H.D. shared with Barney and Vivien the use of classical material and a particular veneration for ancient Greece. Her gift was greater, and so her use of this material ranged from straight translation to adaptation to historical novel to the creation of a spiritual symbol system that dovetailed with Freudian analysis (she was analyzed by Sigmund Freud [1856–1939] himself in the 1930s). In the 1970s, feminist criticism rescued H.D.'s work from undeserved oblivion, and she is now recognized as a major modernist writer. Later lesbian writers, especially Adrienne Rich (1929–), honor H.D. as a forebear.

One writer of that generation who never expatriated herself was Willa Cather (1873–1947), a realist novelist with a commitment to history. Often marginalized unfairly as a "regionalist" writer (some of her work deals with her native Nebraska), she is better seen as a moralist concerned with the preservation of enduring human values in diverse local settings. Cather lived a lesbian life (though very privately); in her work, however, one must trace lesbianism more delicately and indirectly through such features as an interest in male homosocial couples and homoerotic bonds between men; decentering or refusal of heterosexual plots; and an erotic gaze directed at a female character by the author and implicitly by the female reader. Like the question of Stein's "codes," Cather's work raises interesting theoretical issues about naming and secrecy: Who *is* a lesbian writer? What does *lesbian writing* mean?

## Varieties of Lesbian Writing

As these examples show, a wide variety of style and approach characterizes early-twentieth-century lesbian writing: There was (and, indeed, still is) no one way of "writing lesbian." Lesbian literature was not isolated from the main currents of modernist writing, nor did it simply imitate or react to those innovations and trends; lesbian writing was central and formative to the mainstream tradition. Also, the history of American literature would be incomplete without mention of the portrayal of lesbianism in the fiction of nonlesbian writers, and particularly such mainstream male modernist writers as Hemingway, William Faulkner (1897–1962), John Dos Passos (1896–1970), and William Carlos Williams (1883–1963). Lesbian characters or themes could function as scapegoats to counter men's fear of women writers or simply as a daring sign of the modern. white male writers of various sexualities particularly invoked the "exotic," freer, and sexually ambiguous atmosphere of Harlem in this way. Finally, modernism generally would look quite different without the crucial contributions of such lesbians as bookseller and publisher Sylvia Beach (1887–1962), whose English-language bookshop in Paris was an important gathering place for the expatriate community, or Margaret Anderson (1886–1973) and Jane Heap (1887–1964), editors of the *Little Review*, an early little magazine in which many key texts first appeared.

Ironically, however, the experimental nature of work by Stein, Barnes, and H.D., and Cather's self-protective privacy, meant that their lesbian context was not "discovered" until the advent of feminist and lesbian criticism in the 1970s. That paradigm shift has also led to rereadings of other important and innovative American writing—such as the novels and stories of Carson McCullers (1917–1967) and Jane Bowles (1917–1973) and the poetry of Elizabeth Bishop (1911–1979) and Muriel Rukeyser (1913–1980)—with attention to the lesbian aspects of their lives and their creative visions.

The critical rewriting of the Harlem Renaissance has also enabled us to recognize and value lesbian experience in largely unpublished work by such well-respected writers as Angelina Weld Grimké (1880–1958) and Alice Dunbar-Nelson (1875–1935) and to identify lesbian themes and subtexts in important, complex works like Nella Larsen's (1891–1964) *Passing* (1929). But recognizably lesbian fiction tended to follow a more conventionally narrative path.

## The 1950s

During the 1950s, representation of lesbians was hard to come by outside of pulp paperback fiction. Often written by men to titillate a presumptively male audience, with loud and lurid covers and tortured prose, these cheap novels came with endings designed to reassure the "normal" reader (and distract the censor): the suicide of the "real" lesbian and/or the "conversion" by marriage of the more feminine lesbian. Sometimes they were packaged as medical literature, with an authenticating doctor's preface or afterword to reiterate that the deviant behavior inside was not being advocated. Still, in a time of scarcity and censorship, many lesbian readers and some lesbian writers turned to this genre for images of desire between women and female strength, reading (or writing) against the grain. The work of Valerie Taylor (1913–1997) and Ann Bannon (1937–) was reprinted by feminist presses in the 1970s (though with plain covers!). The pulps have also had an afterlife in the responses of younger lesbian writers and visual artists.

As Abraham (1996) writes, *The Price of Salt* (1952) by Patricia Highsmith (1921–1995) writing as Clare Morgan "is often referred to as a breakthrough text because of its happy ending." Another early pioneer was Canadian writer Jane Rule (1931–), best known for *Desert of the Heart* (1964). Rule's well-made realist stories and novels, which testify that lesbians are complex, real, and moral creatures, began appearing when these were brave assertions. But it took the political breakthroughs of feminism and the Stonewall Rebellion (1969) and the creation of women-owned and lesbian-owned presses and bookstores (now mostly gone) to enable a true burgeoning of overtly lesbian feminist literature in many genres and styles.

## Lesbian Feminist Literature and Beyond

Within fiction, some writers continued to push the limits of what could be said: Bertha Harris (1937–), through a rich intertextuality and different layerings of narrative in *Confessions of Cherubino* (1972) and *Lover* (1976), and June Arnold (1926–1982), through the invention of a nongendered pronoun and other suspensions of realist conventions, in *The Cook and the Carpenter* (1973) and *Sister Gin* (1975). Others seemed more concerned to find, imagine, or reinvent a safe space for lesbian community, whether through a mythologized past, a science-fiction alternative future, or political struggle in the present: *Patience and Sarah* (1972) by Isabel Miller (Alma Routsong), first self-published as *A Place for Us* in 1969; Sally Gearhart's *The Wanderground* (1978); Joanna Russ's *The Female Man* (1975); and *Riverfinger Woman* (1974) by Elana Nachmann (later Elana Dykewomon). Still others examined the complexities of lesbian identity discovered against the background of racial, ethnic, or class differences, as in Alice Bloch's *The Law of Return* (1983) (Judaism and Zionism), Paula Gunn Allen's *The Woman Who Owned the Shadows* (1983) (Native American), Ann Allen Shockley *Loving Her* (1974) and *Say Jesus and Come to Me* (1982) (African American), and Maureen Brady's *Folly* (1982) (set among workers in a Southern textile mill). Rita Mae Brown broke through to a large mainstream audience with her comic picaresque *Rubyfruit Jungle* (1973).

Much 1970s writing was inspired by a political impulse to "break silence" and "tell the truth" about lesbian existence. Even when the truth was complicated or unpretty—as, for example, in Kate Millett's free-form autobiographies, *Flying* (1974) and *Sita* (1977)—it seemed important to tell as much of it as possible. No life was too ordinary to become literature. The title of Michelle Cliff's 1980 poetic meditation, *Claiming an Identity They Taught Me To Despise*, could stand for this whole generation. No one had more to do with these developments than two poets, Adrienne Rich and Audre Lorde (1934–1992).

Rich and Lorde defined an aesthetic of honesty, openness, and commitment, and set the highest literary standards, both in their poems and in such essays as Rich's "When We Dead Awaken: Writing as Re-Vision" (1971) and "Women and Honor: Some Notes on Lying" (1975) and Lorde's *Cancer Journals* (1980) and "The Uses of the Erotic (1978)." Their writing helped inspire parallel movements in literary criticism as women and lesbians moved into the academy in greater numbers and with greater visibility. Rich's call, in her "Transcen-

A dent Etude (1978)," for "a whole new poetry beginning here," was, in a way, answered by a cohort of poets beginning in the 1970s and 1980s, including Pat Parker, Judy Grahn, Robin Morgan, June Jordan, Olga Broumas, Minnie Bruce Pratt, Irena Klepfisz, Joy Harjo, Cheryl Clarke, Cherríe Moraga, and countless others in movement journals, workshops, and anthologies. Most of these poets wrote in a free-form way—Rich saw her own breaking free from patriarchal standards going along with her liberation from traditional verse forms—but the work of Marilyn Hacker and others to transform more formal verse from within shows this connection was not inevitable. Rich's essay "Compulsory Heterosexuality and Lesbian Existence" (1980) and Lorde's "biomythography," *Zami: A New Spelling of My Name* (1982), would capture both the power and the pain of struggles over lesbian, feminist, and racial identity politics through the 1980s, and both became cornerstones of women's studies teaching.

During the 1980s, specifically sexual self-expression became an explosive issue. Some writers, including some who consciously identified as bisexual or as members of sadomasochist (S/M) subcultures, reacted against what they saw as feminist censorship, with, for example, such explicitly confrontational S/M writing as that contained in the anthology *Coming to Power* (1982) and the magazines *Bad Attitude* and *On Our Backs* and the work of Pat Califia, Artemis Oakgrove, and Susie Bright. Other writers, such as Andrea Dworkin, reaffirmed combating violence against women as a prior, and deeper, lesbian and feminist commitment. While much of this debate focused on visual images, fiction also mattered: The status of fantasy and the nature of authentic experience were put into question, as was the responsibility of the writer to herself and her community within a wider world still hostile to lesbians and still prone to stereotype. A related resurgence of interest in butch-femme lives, which 1970s lesbian feminism had downplayed, gave rise to such novels as Leslie Feinberg's *Stone Butch Blues* (1993) and the work of Lee Lynch. Important writers to whom these debates gave voice included Joan Nestle and Dorothy Allison, whose 1992 novel, *Bastard Out of Carolina*, was nominated for a National Book Award.

In sheer number, the 1990s seem dominated by several sorts of genre fiction: formulaic romances; detective stories; erotically stimulating stories, consciously crafted to evoke the reader's desire and deliberately written by lesbians for lesbians, though some of it works with conventions familiar from male pornography; science fiction and fantasy. The use of lesbian characters in fiction by women not publicly identified as lesbians, ranging from Alice Walker's *The Color Purple* (1982) to the most exploitive versions of lesbian chic, has also risen steadily. As encouraging developments, one might signal the publication of serious lesbian fiction, such as Margaret Erhart's *Unusual Company* (1987), by mainstream publishing houses; increasing study of lesbian literature within the academy, especially in women's studies classes; and a continuing interest in the 1990s in experimental fiction by such writers as Sarah Schulman and Rebecca Brown.

*Meryl Altman*

### Bibliography

Abraham, Julie. *Are Girls Necessary? Lesbian Writing and Modern Histories*. New York and London: Routledge, 1996.

Hull, Gloria T. *Color, Sex, and Poetry: Three Women Writers of the Harlem Renaissance*. Bloomington: Indiana University Press, 1987.

Jay, Karla, and Joanne Glasgow, eds. *Lesbian Texts and Contexts: Radical Revisions*. New York: New York University Press, 1990.

Munt, Sally, R. ed. *New Lesbian Criticism: Literary and Cultural Readings*. New York: Columbia University Press, 1993.

Smith, Barbara. "Toward a Black Feminist Criticism." In *The New Feminist Criticism: Women, Literature, and Theory*. Ed. Elaine Showalter. New York: Pantheon, 1985, pp. 168–185.

Stimpson, Catharine R. "Zero Degree Deviancy: The Lesbian Novel in English." In *Where the Meanings Are: Feminism and Cultural Spaces*. New York: Methuen, 1988, pp. 97–110.

Wolfe, Susan J., and Julia Penelope, eds. *Sexual Practice, Textual Theory: Lesbian Cultural Criticism*. Oxford: Blackwell, 1993.

Zimmerman, Bonnie. *The Safe Sea of Women: Lesbian Fiction, 1969–1989*. Boston: Beacon, 1990.

***See also*** African American Literature; Allen, Paula Gunn; Anderson, Margaret Carolyn; Arnold, June; Asian American Literature; Bannon, Ann; Barnes, Djuna Chappel; Barney, Natalie Clifford; Beach, Sylvia; Bishop, Elizabeth; Bowles, Jane Auer; Brown, Rita Mae; Cather, Willa; Grahn, Judy; Harlem Renaissance; H.D. (Hilda Doolittle); Latina Literature; Lorde, Audre; McCullers, Carson; Millett, Kate; Moraga, Cherríe; Parker, Pat; Pulp Paperbacks; Rich, Adrienne; Routsong, Alma; Rukeyser, Muriel; Rule, Jane Vance; Shockley, Ann Allen; Stein, Gertrude

## Anderson, Margaret Carolyn (1886–1973)

A publisher and editor, Margaret Anderson was the founder of the *Little Review* (1914–1929), one of the most prominent literary journals of the twentieth century, and was in the vanguard of artistic modernism and sexual radicalism. Born to middle-class parents in Indiana, Anderson rebelled early in life and moved to Chicago in 1909. There she supported herself as a book reviewer and an assistant on the *Dial*. Starting her own magazine, the *Little Review*, in 1914, Anderson engaged controversy by promoting anarchism, imagism, psychoanalysis, feminism, and sexual liberation. During this period, she published the early works of T.S. Eliot (1888–1965), H.D. (1886–1961), Sherwood Anderson (1876–1941), and Amy Lowell (1874–1925). Her 1915 editorial attacking intolerance toward "inversion" has been deemed the earliest defense of homosexuality by a lesbian in the United States.

In 1916, Anderson met Jane Heap (1887–1964), a cross-dressing artist who became her lover and coeditor. The following year, the two women moved to New York City, where they published Ezra Pound (1885–1972), Djuna Barnes (1892–1982), Gertrude Stein (1874–1946), Dorothy Richardson (1873–1957), and Mina Loy (1882–1966), among others. Many of the short stories and prose pieces contributed by women during this period contained homoerotic themes. By the 1920s, the *Little Review* became increasingly experimental, turning to surrealism, dada, Machine Age æsthetics, and avant-garde theater. Anderson's most daring effort was the serialization of James Joyce's *Ulysses*. She and Heap were convicted in 1921 on obscenity charges and fined.

The trial led to both financial and personal strains for Anderson. She became enthralled by the teachings of George Gurdjieff (1872–1949), a Russian mystic who had a small following among New York intellectuals and the expatriate community in Paris. She left Heap and the *Little Review* and traveled to France to study with Gurdjieff. Accompanying Anderson was her new lover, opera singer Georgette Leblanc (1869–1941), with whom she would live for the next twenty years. When LeBlanc died in 1941, Anderson returned to America, where she be-

gan a ten-year relationship with Dorothy Caruso (1893–1955), widow of Enrico. In her post–*Little Review* years, Anderson wrote three autobiographies and a lesbian novel entitled *Forbidden Fires*, which she failed to have published in her lifetime. Anderson died in France in 1973.          *Holly A. Baggett*

### Bibliography

Baggett, Holly A. "Aloof from Natural Laws: Margaret C. Anderson and the *Little Review*, 1914–1929." Ph.D. diss., University of Delaware, 1992.

Bryer, Jackson. "A Trial-Track for Racers": Margaret C. Anderson and the *Little Review*." Ph.D. diss., University of Wisconsin-Milwaukee, 1965.

***See also*** Barnes, Djuna Chappell; Stein, Gertrude

## Androgyny

A term for the union of male and female qualities—psychological, literary, or physical—that at times has been equated with homosexuality. Androgyny is a classic term that denotes the union of male (andro) and female (gyne) characteristics. This union has been described in a number of ways, usually utopian. In psychology, it may be the balance of reason and emotion or assertion and vulnerability in one person; in literature, it may be the writer or the character accessing her or his opposite-gendered side. Physical androgyny most often means cross-dressing, for, while an androgyne may display both male and female bodily characteristics, one who does so is usually termed a "hermaphrodite." The term "androgyny" is also associated with, and sometimes equated with, homosexuality because both positive and negative definitions of the homosexual have assumed that the lesbian or gay man crosses the gender norms of her or his culture.

Androgyny is an ancient, although not always a neutral, concept in both Eastern and Western cultures. The Chinese principles of yin and yang have been considered a version of androgyny. Aristophanes (448?–380? B.C.E.) in Plato's (427?–347? B.C.E.) *Symposium* defines love through a myth in which the first humans become divided parts of a whole, each seeking the other: males seeking males, females seeking females, and men and women seeking each other. Iconoclastic views of biblical creation assume that Adam was an androgyne before the fall. Although Plato's myth allows for homosexual desire, many symbolic versions of androgyny emphasize the heterosexual model of male-female union, such as the theory of creativity that idealizes the artist accessing his or her psychologically opposite-gendered side in order to "birth" a work of art (Carl Jung [1875–1961]). Because both the West's and the East's symbolic systems associate male with light and reason and female with dark and body, and because most theories presuppose the essential nature of male and female characteristics, the combination often results in a hierarchical and heterosexual model.

Androgyny is also closely bound up with homosexuality and feminism. Sexologists of the late nineteenth century, such as Richard von Krafft-Ebing (1840–1902), described homosexuality as a pathology of crossing social and physical gender boundaries. Virginia Woolf (1882–1941) used the term positively in her version of female creativity in *A Room of One's Own* (1929). Woolf's ideal artist is the person in whom neither male nor female characteristics predominate, and, if read as a code word for the homosexual, Woolf's androgyny is a happy revision of the sexologists' theories. In the 1970s, literary and psychological feminist theories idealized androgyny as a means to go beyond stereotypical gender roles. Lesbians have exhibited conflicting responses to this concept. In the 1970s, lesbian feminists Adrienne Rich (1929–) and Mary Daly (1928–) first hailed this term as utopian but, shortly after, denounced it as male dominated and heterosexual. Other feminist and lesbian writers, such as Judy Grahn (1940–) and Gloria Anzaldúa (1942–), implied androgyny in their descriptions of early Native American cultures that honored as spiritually superior cross-dressing (and, likely, homosexual) males or females. In the 1990s, postmodern queer theory redefined androgyny as an image of undecidability. In queer theory, the privileged homosexual figure, such as the butch-femme couple, enacts an androgyny that questions the naturalness and essentialism of gender categories.

Depending on its definition, then, androgyny has been a useful or a problematic concept for lesbians. *Marilyn R. Farwell*

### Bibliography

Anzaldúa, Gloria. *Borderlands/La Frontera: The New Mestiza*. San Francisco: Aunt Lute, 1987.

Bazin, Nancy. *Virginia Woolf and the Androgynous Vision*. New Brunswick, N.J.: Rutgers University Press, 1973.

Grahn, Judy. *Another Mother Tongue: Gay Words, Gay Worlds*. Boston: Beacon, 1984.

Heilbrun, Carolyn G. *Toward a Recognition of Androgyny*. New York: Harper Colophon, 1973.

Weil, Kari. *Androgyny and the Denial of Difference*. Charlottesville: University Press of Virginia, 1992.

*See also* Anzaldúa, Gloria; Butch-Femme; Cross-Dressing; Grahn, Judy; Queer Theory; Rich, Adrienne; Two-Spirit; Woolf, Virginia

## Animal Studies

It is probably incorrect to speak of lesbian animals because virtually nothing is known about the cognitive aspects of sexuality in nonhuman species (hereafter, animals). In contrast, female homosexual behavior involving courtship, pair bonding, mounting, and other forms of genital contact has been noted in many animal species. Isolated anecdotes concerning female homosexual behavior exist for numerous species, but very few studies have focused on this behavior and attempted to place it within a larger constellation of social and sexual behaviors. As of the late 1990s, the most detailed studies of female homosexual behavior in animals had been on birds, primates, and domestic livestock.

There is a long history of interest in female homosexual behavior in animals dating back to, at least, the Middle Ages, when zoologists equated "natural" sexual behavior with reproduction. Muddled notions about homosexual behavior in animals such as pigeons were used by medieval zoologists to cast lesbianism as anathema. While the logic that equates all that is "natural" with all that is socially desirable is flawed, its popular appeal is undeniable, even in the late twentieth century.

Some of the first systematic studies of female homosexual behavior in animals were conducted in the late Victorian era. The use of caged subjects was prevalent and meant that these interactions were invariably characterized as abnormal products of captivity, unlikely to be found in "nature." During the 1890s, research on pigeons argued that an absence of opposite-sex partners and artificial confinement could "force" females to choose same-sex mates. Thus, female choice of same-sex mates was seen as a Hobson's choice—that is, a choice made for want of any male alternatives. This perspective is still common.

Later studies of domestic livestock argued that "artificial" effects of domestication produced female homosexual behavior. The economic benefits associated with livestock reproduction may have further promoted the view of female homosexual behavior as an undesirable "problem." For example, a 1948 study of mounting between domestic hens (one of the first to treat this subject as worthy of investigation in its own right) concluded that the behavior was "aberrant." This study and others focusing on domestic livestock were clearly undertaken to eliminate female homosexual behavior rather than attempt to understand it as an integral part of the species' repertoire.

By the beginning of the 1960s, a link between hormonal "imbalances" and homosexual mounting was sought, using female rodents and macaques. Where previous research had focused on the environmental context in which homosexual behavior occurred, hormonal studies emphasized a biological basis for the behavior. Once again, this perspective echoed the notion of homosexual behavior as an abnormality.

With the emergence of sociobiology in the late 1970s, a paradigmatic shift occurred, which resulted in female homosexual behavior being viewed not as an abnormality, but as an adaptation that could indirectly facilitate reproductive success. For example, some researchers suggest that cows engage in homosexual behavior in order to attract bulls to copulate with them. Other researchers studying gulls, terns, and snow geese argue that, if females are "abandoned" by their male mates, they form homosexual pair-bonds and help brood and raise each other's young. It is noteworthy that the notion of female homosexual behavior as abnormal was discarded only when a paradigm emerged that indirectly linked the behavior with reproduction.

The perspective that homosexual behavior has some adaptive function may have promoted the view that it serves various social roles. For example, homosexual behavior appears to be a tension-reduction mechanism that female pygmy chimpanzees employ during feeding competition. In European rabbits, homosexual mounting seems to contribute to the establishment and maintenance of the dominance hierarchy. Social functions are often interpreted by zoologists as the primary reason for homosexual interactions, thus negating any sexual component to this behavior.

A number of observations suggest that female homosexual behavior in animals is sexual. For example, in domestic hens, bonobo chimpanzees, and pukekos (a New Zealand swamp bird), female homosexual behavior can involve genital contact and stimulation. In species such as cows and pigeons, females will remain with female mates, despite the presence of courting males. In Ugandan kobs (an African ungulate) and Japanese macaques, females engage in aggressive competition with males for female mates. Although many zoologists resort to elaborate and speculative explanations for the presence of female homosexual behavior, in numerous instances it appears that it is simply sexual stimulation that motivates animals to engage in the behavior.

*Paul L. Vasey*

### Bibliography

Boswell, J. *Christianity, Social Tolerance, and Homosexuality*. Chicago: University of Chicago Press, 1980.

Dagg, Anne I. "Homosexual Behaviour and Female-Male Mounting in Mammals: A First Survey." *Mammal Review* 14 (1984), 155–185.

Vasey, Paul L. "Homosexual Behavior in Primates: A Review of Evidence and Theory." *International Journal of Primatology* 16 (1995), 173–204.

*See also* Biological Determinism

### Anne, Queen of England (1665–1714)

Member of the house of Stuart and queen of England (1702–1714). During her lifetime, it was fashionable for upper- and upper-middle-class British, Scottish, and Irish women to form, as she did, close romantic and sometimes erotic relationships with other women. Feminism flourished in the writings of Mary Astell (1666–1731), Judith Drake (n.d.), and a host of women poets, many of whom praise Queen Anne as a model of womanly excellence, reason, and leadership. There was also a movement of women playwrights, and, in most of their plays, some dedicated to the queen and many others dedicated to "The Ladies," loving relationships between women feature centrally.

A tomboy in her youth, Anne was more interested in politics and history than in needlework. She played the guitar, was a capable horsewoman, had an unusually low speaking voice, and was indifferent to male suitors. Her mother, aunt, and grandmother had all died by the time she was six, and she detested her father, King James II (1633–1701), who separated her from her sister and moved her about through her youth in an effort to thwart her rise to leadership.

But Anne developed passionate attachments to girls. She conducted a love affair through letters

A with Frances Apsley (n.d.) before falling deeply in love at thirteen with Sarah Jennings (1660–1744), later Churchill and Marlborough. The attachment of Anne and Sarah continued into their adult lives and was disturbing to members of the royal family, who found it an "immoderate passion" and demanded it be cut off. Anne refused to end her relationship with Sarah, and once she became queen, she elevated Sarah to the post of first lady of the bedchamber, which allowed them to share adjoining bedrooms. The queen bestowed many gifts on her beloved and her beloved's husband, John Churchill, the first duke of Marlborough (1650–1722), the most extravagant being Blenheim Palace.

Catharine Trotter (1679–1749) was one of the successful women playwrights of Queen Anne's time. Trotter had a passionate relationship with Lady Sarah Piers and wrote what is arguably the first lesbian play in English, *Agnes de Castro* (1695), dedicated to Piers. Another playwright, Delarivier Manley (1671?–1724), voraciously heterosexual by her own accounts, wrote several novels that ridicule lesbianism in general and openly attack the queen's "favourite," Sarah Churchill. Manley's *Secret Memoirs . . . from the New Atalantis* (1709) includes a scurrilous account of what Manley called a "cabal" of fashionable lesbians and makes vicious fun of Catharine Trotter and a number of other prominent women for their relationships with each other. However, in some of Manley's plays written just before and during Queen Anne's reign, as in popular plays by five other women, loving relationships between women feature centrally.

After about twenty-five years of intimacy, the queen and Sarah Churchill began to disagree, especially about politics, and, by 1705–1708, their relationship had soured. The queen developed a new relationship with a young relative of Sarah's named Abigail Hill (d. 1734), later Masham. Sarah, enraged by the queen's new attachment and insecure regarding her own political power, asserted to the queen, and to the public, her belief that Anne's intimacy with Abigail amounted to an obsessive passion unbefitting a monarch. Cruel pamphlets and songs were published, accusing Queen Anne of being a female Edward II and Abigail her Gaveston. Sarah castigated Anne for "having no inclenation [*sic*] for any but of one's own sex." The scandal coincided with a decrease in production of plays by women and a sudden disappearance of female-friendship themes in women's plays that were produced. No plays by women were staged in 1707–1708, when the scandal peaked, and, though less public genres, such as poetry, the novel, and essay writing, continued among women, an age of fashionable feminism and lesbianism seems to have ended by the time the queen died in 1714.

It must be noted that despite the queen's "inclinations," one of her primary jobs as monarch was to bear an heir to the Stuart line. She was married at the appropriate time to a suitably pedigreed but dull-witted man with syphilis. Not realizing that his disease rendered the possibility of bearing a healthy child impossible, "poor Queen Anne," as she was often called, spent her entire adult life pregnant or recovering from childbirth. She bore about twenty children (counts vary, according to whether early miscarriages are included or not), only one of whom survived infancy, only to die at the age of eleven. Thus, Anne was the last of the Stuart monarchs.

*Kendall*

### Bibliography

Cotton, Nancy. *Women Playwrights in England, c. 1363–1750*. Lewisburg, Penn.: Bucknell University Press, 1980.

Green, David. *Sarah, Duchess of Marlborough*. New York: Scribner, 1967.

Gregg, Edward. *Queen Anne*. London: Routledge, 1980.

Kendall. "Finding the Good Parts: Sexuality in Women's Tragedies in the Time of Queen Anne." In *Curtain Calls: British and American Women and the Theatre, 1660–1820*. Ed. Mary Anne Schofield and Cecilia Macheski. Athens: Ohio University Press, 1991, pp. 165–176.

Morgan, Fidelis. *A Woman of No Character: An Autobiography of Mrs Manley*. London: Faber and Faber, 1986.

### Anthologies

Any compilation of writings by and about lesbians, on a more or less cohesive theme; sometimes collectively undertaken, most often edited by a few, frequently published by women's presses. In many anthologies, significant lesbian content appears under a broader "feminist," "queer," or "lesbian, gay (male), bisexual, and transgender" rubric.

### Characteristics

Since the 1960s, there has been an explosion of lesbian and feminist expression in all areas and taking myriad forms, from women's studies departments to 'zines, from film and performance art to public policy challenges and direct-action tactics. Impelled by these changes, anthologies have proliferated, becoming a staple product of mainstream and alternative publishers and finding a secure place on lesbian bookshelves. The broad spectrum of opinion to which an anthology can give voice provides a powerful lens for investigating and, indeed, defining lesbian cultural expression across changing times, politics, and cultures. Collections of short personal narratives arose, posits Zimmerman (1984), out of the consciousness-raising groups of the 1960s and early 1970s; grouping many short pieces in anthology form may have arisen to reflect a democratic impulse toward publishing nonprofessional writers, as well as the prevalence of journalistic writing in the early years of the modern women's movement. Anthologies also provide a conversational space that tends to support the idea of "coming out" as a continual process. In their foregrounding of identity issues, lesbian personal narratives wield historical and political significance, suggests Zimmerman, who notes also that, in terms of the lesbian feminist movement, they have charted individual as well as collective development. And, over the years, they have embodied the tension between claims for unity and for diversity in lesbian feminist politics, the ambivalence between conceptions of a monolithic "lesbian identity" and claims of specificity from groups marginalized even within lesbianism, such as lesbians of color or working-class lesbians.

## Early Anthologies

Before the 1970s, lesbians could publish their writing in nonspecific collective volumes, but not until 1973, with the publication of *Amazon Expedition: A Lesbian Feminist Anthology,* edited by Phyllis Birkby, was the lesbian anthology in its own right born. In 1976, *The Lesbians Home Journal: Stories from The Ladder,* edited by Barbara Grier and Coletta Reid, collected fiction written for the pioneering lesbian journal since 1956. Lesbian separatism, as well as awareness of classism and racism within the women's movement, were espoused by the Furies, who published several anthologies of articles from their newspaper of the same name, including *Class and Feminism* (1974) and *Lesbianism and the Women's Movement* (1975), all with Diana Press. Other pivotal works include *The Lesbian Reader: An Amazon Quarterly Anthology* (1975), edited by Gina Covina and Laurel Galana, and *Country Women: A Handbook for the New Farmer* (1976),

edited by Sherry Thomas, which chronicled the development of the women's land movement. Equally significant were works such *Our Right to Love: A Lesbian Resource Book* (1978, rev. 1996), edited by Ginny Vida, and *The Lesbian Path* (1980), edited by Margaret Cruikshank. In 1972, Karla Jay and Allan Young edited *Out of the Closets*, the first of several anthologies to bring together essays on lesbian and gay male life. Such writings have empowered lesbians to speak from previously silenced locations on the margins of mainstream culture, both debunking conventional wisdom and creating community and solidarity through shared experience and growing consciousness.

## Varieties of Anthologies

Among the most popular anthologies are those that collect personal narratives, often focusing on lesbian coming out stories. The earliest of these is the classic collection, *The Coming Out Stories* (1980), edited by Susan Wolfe and Julia Penelope Stanley. Through each funny, painful story, it built community one lesbian at a time and subsequently was widely emulated. The coming out genre now encompasses general collections, as well as those focused around specific identities, experiences, or cultures.

Most of the early coming out anthologies had a predominantly white, middle-class focus, reflecting the makeup of "second wave" feminism and its writings. In response, lesbians of color addressed their invisibility and the contradictions in their experience as members of diverse communities in the pivotal *This Bridge Called My Back: Writings by Radical Women of Color* (1981), edited by Cherríe Moraga and Gloria Anzaldúa. This attempt to redress a significant cultural lack through producing new texts and a new politics, and through claiming multiple marginal identities, was a transformative event in lesbian culture. *Home Girls: A Black Feminist Anthology* (1983), edited by Barbara Smith, was another important collection published by Kitchen Table: Women of Color Press. Later, Anzaldúa edited *Making Face, Making Soul / Haciendo Caras / Creative and Critical Perspectives by Feminists of Color* (1990). In addition to numerous other anthologies on African American, Latina, Asian, Native American, and Jewish lesbians, international anthologies bring together contributions from lesbians of many nationalities, ethnicities, and religious backgrounds.

In the 1980s and 1990s, the lesbian anthology as a genre gained momentum and popularity and established an important place in lesbian movements and communities. Thematic anthologies expressed the blossoming of lesbian culture in all directions, including sexuality and erotica, poetry and fiction, politics, families, and academic scholarship. The anthologies produced by the end of the 1990s are far too numerous to be listed here.

Erotica has proved to be one of the most popular anthology types, ranging from the controversial collection of writings on sadomasochism, *Coming to Power,* edited by the Samois collective (1982), to widely read collections of "soft-core" stories, poems, and graphics. As the varieties of sexual expression and experience became more public in lesbian communities, anthologies captured those realities, including bisexuality and butch-femme identities. Other anthologies provide a place for specific communities of lesbians, such as women with disabilities or survivors of violence, to collect a diverse body of personal narratives and analyses.

Literary anthologies have played a significant role in the development of lesbian culture since 1975, with the publication of a slim volume titled *Amazon Poetry,* edited by Elly Bulkin and Joan Larkin. This became the nucleus of *Lesbian Poetry* (1981), also edited by Bulkin and Larkin, which was published with a companion volume, *Lesbian Fiction,* edited by Bulkin. Subsequently, collections of lesbian short stories became a staple with alternative presses, and, by the 1990s, mainstream publishers realized the marketing potential of such anthologies. Penguin has been a leader in this field, with a series of short-story anthologies edited by Joan Nestle and Naomi Holoch under the title *Women on Women,* the first one appearing in 1990. Subsequent anthologies include *The Penguin Book of Lesbian Short Stories* (1993), edited by Margaret Reynolds, and *Chloe Plus Olivia: An Anthology of Lesbian Literature from the Seventeenth Century to the Present* (1994), edited by Lillian Faderman.

From university course offerings to conferences and journals, lesbianism became an important field of study in the academy, and scholarly anthologies played an important role in the development of lesbian studies within programs of women's studies and queer studies. The first anthology to articulate the premises of the field was *Lesbian Studies: Present and Future* (1982), edited by Margaret Cruikshank; this groundbreaking anthology was revised and expanded in 1996 as *The New Lesbian Studies: Into the 21st Century,* edited by Bonnie Zimmerman and Toni McNaron. Another collection of essays that attempted to define the parameters of lesbian studies was *Tilting the Tower* (1994), edited by Linda Garber. In addition, numerous anthologies of lesbian, gay, and queer scholarship have appeared since 1990, some providing an overview of the field, and others specific to lesbian, gay, and queer studies in history, literature, anthropology, political theory, social theory, and other fields.

In the late 1990s, anthologies engaged questions of identity and community for lesbians who are sisters, mothers, daughters, poets, rebels, Jewish, Christian, Canadian, Australian, Israeli, differently abled, transgendered, vampires, and lovers of Southern cooking. Writings on commitment ceremonies, religion, and parenting gather together various perspectives on life's milestones, while other collections help define and create the varieties of lesbian communities.

Lesbian writing and publishing efforts are as vital to the creation and recording of lesbian culture as are activism, art, and policy. In their increasingly varied scope, lesbian anthologies are uniquely able to express the sweeping range of opinion held by lesbians about the issues important to their lives and survival. And, as Zimmerman argues, collections of multiple voices can inform a politics that, rather than limit itself to either individual or collective lesbian identities, can grapple with the need for unity as well as diversity and effect concrete changes in lesbian lives.

*Kathryn A. Brandt*

### Bibliography

Zimmerman, Bonnie. "The Politics of Transliteration: Lesbian Personal Narratives." *Signs: Journal of Women in Culture and Society* 9:4 (1984), pp. 663–682.

*See also* Coming Out Stories; Lesbian Studies; Publishing, Lesbian

### Anthony, Susan B. (1820–1906)

American feminist and women's rights advocate. Born February 15, 1820, in a small rural town in Massachusetts, Susan Brownell Anthony became one of the most famous and enduring champions of equal rights for women in U.S. history. Anthony grew up in a plain, hardworking Quaker family, whose patriarch, Daniel Anthony, opposed taxes and slavery and ardently believed in the education of females.

After receiving a good education, Anthony felt compelled to teach and, in 1845, went off to teach in the Academy in Canandaigua, New York. In 1849, she gave up teaching to work in the temperance movement, at which time she became interested in the abolition of slavery and the advancement of women's rights. She fostered friendships with several prominent women's rights advocates of the time, including Elizabeth Cady Stanton (1815–1902), Lucretia Mott (1793–1880), and Lucy Stone (1818–1893). Stanton had called the first American women's rights convention in 1848 in Seneca Falls, where she had demanded the right to vote. By 1852, Anthony had joined Stanton, and the two became intimate and enduring friends. Biographer Barry (1988) called Stanton and Anthony "one of the greatest couples of the nineteenth century."

By 1869, Anthony had organized the National Women's Suffrage Association. In 1890, this group joined the American Woman Suffrage Association to form the National American Woman Suffrage Association (NAWSA). The white suffragist group, however, largely excluded black women suffragists. Anthony, who needed the support of the Southern states in pushing for woman suffrage, capitulated under the racism of her white compatriots. At one point, Anthony asked her longtime friend, black abolitionist and feminist Frederick Douglass (1817–1895), not to attend the 1895 NAWSA convention in Atlanta, Georgia, believing his presence would offend the Southerners.

When the Fourteenth and Fifteenth Amendments to the Constitution were proposed to extend the vote to African American males, Anthony demanded the same rights for women. She was unsuccessful, and, in 1872, she voted anyway, in an election for U.S. representatives. Anthony was indicted after posting the ballot. Hoping to get arrested so that she could test her tactic in the courts, she was instead fined $100. She never paid it.

One of Anthony's most passionate friendships was with fellow suffragist Anna Dickinson (1842–1932). Although recognizing her affections for Dickinson as "elderly sister" love, Anthony nonetheless invited Dickinson to share her bed and ardently urged her not to marry a man. Anthony had several similar relationships with other women. A woman sharing such a friendship with Anthony would invariably refer to herself as Anthony's "niece."

When Anthony first began her crusade, women had few legal rights. Due to her work and the efforts of her associates, women now have opportunities for higher education, property rights, the right to hold office, and the right to vote. Her campaign lasted

fifty years. In 1892, she became president of the NAWSA and held office until she was eighty years old. She died in 1906 at the age of eighty-six.

*Denise McVea*

### Bibliography

Barry, Kathleen. *Susan B. Anthony: A Biography of a Singular Feminist*. New York: New York University Press, 1988.

Harper, Ida Husted. *Life and Works of Susan B. Anthony*. New York: Arno, 1969.

Katz, Jonathan. *Gay American History*. New York: Harper and Row, 1976.

Stanton, Elizabeth Cady, and Susan B. Anthony. *History of Woman Suffrage*. New York: Fowler and Wells, 1881.

Wheeler, Marjorie Spruill. *One Woman, One Vote*. Troutdale, Oreg.: New Sage, 1995.

*See also* Suffrage Movement

## Anthropology

Social science devoted to the study of culture, or "whole ways of life" of people around the world. The discipline is defined by its central methodology, known as fieldwork, which involves living with, studying, and observing a group of people, typically in the developing world. The published result of an anthropologist's fieldwork, the ethnography, consists of a detailed account of the lives and the culture of the people so studied.

### Characteristics and Critiques

The academic discipline of anthropology has been described by many, including some anthropologists, as fundamentally masculinist and white. That is, the anthropologist's quest for knowledge is (sometimes consciously) styled after nineteenth-century Euro-American explorers' adventures of "discovery" in the "primitive" wilderness of Africa or the Pacific islands. Not surprisingly, early anthropological research often reflected only the points of view of men in other cultures. As a science, it was also often financially supported by, or useful to, colonial governments.

Since the 1960s, various critiques of anthropology have emerged, all with important consequences for the anthropology of lesbians and lesbian anthropologists. The imperialism of white Euro-American anthropology has been criticized by postcolonial scholars. With the rise of 1970s feminism in the

A United States, feminist anthropology emerged as a powerful critique of anthropology and as a source of theoretical insight. Studies of lesbians and gay men also started to emerge at that time, due partly to the growth of the post-Stonewall (1969) gay liberation movement and partly to the success of feminist anthropology. By the 1990s, lesbian studies within anthropology began to make important contributions to the discipline as a whole, notwithstanding the continued marginalization of lesbians and other women and the dismissal of community-based studies in the United States as "unimportant" and "not real anthropology."

There is a clear connection between the silencing and marginalization of women within professional anthropology, lesbian invisibility in society at large and particularly within professional settings, and the history of lesbian anthropology and lesbian anthropologists. The great irony is that the two most famous American anthropologists of the twentieth century were Margaret Mead (1901–1978) and Ruth Benedict (1887–1948), who were also sometimes lovers. This fact is still rarely recognized in the discipline and has yet to be critically explored. It also provides evidence that the problems of homophobia and discrimination plague anthropology as any other profession. But lesbians have been active (and successful) anthropologists throughout the twentieth century, although they typically have been denied important academic jobs. And, beginning in the 1980s, compelling ethnographies of lesbian communities were being written, often (and unusually for anthropology) focusing on communities in the United States. The remainder of this entry addresses both of these distinct, but related, issues: lesbian anthropology—that is, anthropological studies that focus on lesbians—and the professional lives of lesbian anthropologists.

## The Anthropology of Lesbians

Relatively little has been written about lesbians cross-culturally, as Blackwood (1986) noted in an important and early discussion of how anthropological research "constructs" lesbianism. Almost ten years later, Weston's (1993) review of lesbian and gay anthropology highlights the discrepancy between cross-cultural studies of homosexuality and anthropological research conducted in U.S. lesbian communities. As these authors note, there is an important branch of gay and lesbian studies within anthropology that specifically seeks to document the range of sexual behaviors and identities around the world. However, most of these studies focus on

men's sexuality and, largely because there is so little information available on the topic, fail to adequately theorize women's sexualities and lives.

There are several reasons for the absence of cross-cultural studies of women's sexualities. Two of the most important sources of historical information for nonliterate societies, nineteenth-century (and earlier) traveler's accounts and colonial records, rarely discuss women's lives. In literate non-Western societies (such as Japanese or Muslim societies), literacy also often remained a male prerogative. Most important, the category of "lesbian" is a historically specific, Euro-American term, which means it may not reflect categories used in non-Western societies, although women in those same societies might report important erotic and/or sexual ties with each other. Typically, they also marry and bear children, and, perhaps most important, their identities are simply not defined by their sexual behaviors in the Western sense of the term "lesbian."

An important exception to this rule of women's invisibility in lesbian and gay anthropology lies in descriptions of women who cross-dressed. Evidence of female transvestites, or cross-dressers, who also inhabited different social roles than other women, exists in several Native American societies and in the nineteenth-century Balkans, for example. The question of these cross-dressing women's sexuality is more ambiguous, for the reasons outlined above. More recently, some women in postcolonial contexts reject the label of "lesbian" precisely because of its genesis in Western, imperialist cultures. Thus, some Native American women identify as "two-spirit," emphasizing an indigenous tradition for cross-dressing women in their societies.

These difficulties of naming and interpretation also arise in several classic ethnographies that mention or address the phenomenon of woman-woman marriage in Africa. Such marriages are reported in more than thirty African ethnic groups, from Nigeria in the west, to Kenya and the Sudan in the east, and in southern Africa. Most anthropologists in the first half of the twentieth century simply assumed that, in these cases, women became "husbands"—that is, married other women—in an attempt to establish political and economic ties between groups of people; they evidently never wondered, or asked, if the marriages also might have included erotic and/or emotional dimensions. By the 1990s, scholars were only beginning to research how women in Africa describe and understand the important emotional, and sometimes sexual, ties that they share with other women.

In distinct contrast to the lack of cross-cultural studies, some important ethnographic studies of lesbians in the United States have been published, beginning in the 1980s. There are several answers to the question of why the anthropology of lesbians has been far more successful in the United States than overseas. Critiques of anthropology as a colonialist and imperialist project, and demands by marginalized communities to document their own lives, have led to a growing commitment among some anthropologists to conduct research in their "home" communities. The 1980s boom in publishing for lesbian and gay markets has also certainly provided an outlet for these studies, which otherwise would receive little formal academic validation. Finally, organizing within the discipline of anthropology—through the Society of Lesbian and Gay Anthropologists (SOLGA)—has helped provide some support for scholarship on lesbian issues and for lesbian scholars.

Anthropological studies of lesbians in the United States explore a number of different topics. For example, Weston (1991) considers the ways in which gays and lesbians in San Francisco bend the "rules" of kinship to establish their own families that include both biological and nonbiological kin or "relatives." Lewin (1993) explores how lesbians in the Bay Area negotiated meanings of motherhood during the beginnings of the lesbian baby boom in the early 1980s. Kennedy and Davis (1993) develop a detailed and compelling portrait of lesbian lives in Buffalo, New York, from the 1930s through the 1950s. Based on oral histories of women in Buffalo, this work offers a much deeper understanding of 1950s butch-femme than was previously possible and suggests that the political origins of the gay liberation movement also lie in working-class cultures. These three ethnographies, in particular, represent the promise of lesbian anthropology that is also demonstrated in Lewin's 1996 volume, *Inventing Lesbian Cultures in America*.

Although each of the studies mentioned above contains important information about the lives of lesbians of color, there is a noticeable lack of anthropological studies that focus on lesbians of color in the United States. Instead, lesbian anthropology and feminist anthropology have relied importantly on the literary and cultural work of radical women of color whose analyses center on the inextricable ties among race, class, gender, and sexuality such as demonstrated by the landmark volume *This Bridge Called My Back: Writings by Radical Women of Color* (1983), edited by Cherríe Moraga and Gloria Anzaldúa. For many radical women of color, the effects of racism and economic oppression and the centrality of their cultural, racial, and class identities make it impossible to identify primarily or solely as "lesbian." It was not until the late 1990s that anthropologists began to explore these issues in their research. Kath Weston's *Render Me, Gender Me* (1996) provides a rare example of how lesbians of color and white lesbians describe (and theorize) the complexity of their multifaceted identities.

## The Lesbian as Anthropologist
Ruth Benedict and Margaret Mead were the founding mothers of American anthropology, and, although they never explicitly wrote about lesbians, much of their work can be read as a plea for tolerance of alternative sex/gender arrangements. Benedict's pioneering work in psychological anthropology, in particular, reflects the growing dominance of psychoanalysis in the United States between the world wars, even as that discipline pathologized homosexuality. In her writings, and in lectures delivered throughout the country, Mead often tried to demonstrate that alternative gender arrangements were possible by invoking the classical anthropological rhetoric of cultural relativism.

The difficulties facing lesbian anthropologists are many. In the 1980s, anthropology students were discouraged from conducting research on lesbian topics because of the difficulty of finding a job, as an employment crisis in the academic job market intensified and particularly affected women. Sexual harassment, homophobia, racism, and antisemitism form a central part of academic life and life in the field, as anywhere else. But a few lesbian anthropologists have been out in the discipline and have written important anthropological studies. In addition to the authors and studies mentioned above, Esther Newton published the earliest full-length ethnography of a gay subculture, *Mother Camp* (1972), exploring the lives of pre-Stonewall drag queens. Newton's later work considers the historical development of the gay resort of Cherry Grove on Fire Island, including the role that lesbians played there.

Following feminist anthropology and critiques of the "objective," "neutral" stance of the anthropological observer, anthropologists have begun to examine how one's personal identity is related to the work one does. This question is particularly important because of anthropologists' experiences of fieldwork. The 1996 volume *Out in the Field: Reflections of Lesbian and Gay Anthropologists* marks an important point in the "coming out" of gays and lesbians in anthropology, as authors wrote about their experiences during fieldwork and in the discipline as a whole. This volume challenges, for the first time, the widespread invisibility of lesbians and gay men in anthropology and demonstrates the complex interactions among anthropologists' personal identities, professional lives, and choices of research topics.                    *Deborah P. Amory*

### Bibliography

Blackwood, Evelyn. "Breaking the Mirror: The Construction of Lesbianism and the Anthropological Discourse on Homosexuality." In *The Many Faces of Homosexuality.* Ed. Evelyn Blackwood. New York: Harrington Park, 1986, pp. 1–18.

Jacobs, Sue-Ellen, Wesley Thomas, and Sabine Lang, eds. *Two-Spirit People: Native American Gender Identity, Sexuality, and Spirituality.* Urbana: University of Illinois Press, 1997.

Kennedy, Elizabeth Lapovsky, and Madeline D. Davis. *Boots of Leather, Slippers of Gold: The History of a Lesbian Community.* New York: Routledge, 1993.

Lewin, Ellen. *Lesbian Mothers: Accounts of Gender in American Culture.* Ithaca, N.Y.: Cornell University Press, 1993.

———, ed. *Inventing Lesbian Cultures in America.* Boston: Beacon, 1996.

Lewin, Ellen, and William L. Leap, eds. *Out in the Field: Reflections of Lesbian and Gay Anthropologists.* Urbana: University of Illinois Press, 1996.

Weston, Kath. *Families We Choose: Lesbians, Gays, Kinship.* New York: Columbia University Press, 1991.

———. "Lesbian/Gay Studies in the House of Anthropology." *Annual Review of Anthropology* 22 (1993), 157–185.

———. *Render Me, Gender Me: Lesbians Talk Sex, Class, Color, Nation, Studmuffins.* New York: Columbia University Press, 1996.

*See also* Benedict, Ruth; Indigenous Cultures; Native Americans; Oral History; Transgender; Two-Spirit

### Antisemitism

The hating, stereotyping, or scapegoating of Jews; also, causing or perpetuating Jewish invisibility; imposing social sanctions against Jews. In the most extreme cases, antisemitism leads to acts of genocide.

Jewish lesbians experience antisemitism in all of the ways nonlesbians do; however, antisemitism particularly affects lesbians in two additional ways. First, lesbians encounter antisemitism within lesbian communities. Second, antisemitism overlaps and connects with lesbophobia.

Lesbian feminism espouses a commitment to ending all oppressions; when listing particular oppressions, however, lesbian feminists often omit antisemitism. Many lesbian feminists do not recognize antisemitism because they believe it does not exist, or no longer exists, or exists but is less important or serious than racism or homophobia. This unwillingness to acknowledge or oppose antisemitism is itself antisemitic.

As antisemitism is often rendered invisible within lesbian communities, so, too, are Jewish lesbians. Jews or Jewish issues are routinely excluded from lesbian anthologies. Margaret Cruikshank (1940–), in an attempt to excuse the lack of Jews in her anthology, *The Lesbian Path* (1980), explained that "several stories" by Jewish lesbians had been published elsewhere; therefore, she saw no need to include any. Current lesbian anthologies seldom exclude Jewish contributors; however, Jewish *content* is routinely omitted, even from anthologies with a stated multicultural stance. Jewish lesbians also may be rendered invisible or irrelevant through the scheduling of lesbian events on major Jewish holidays or by the assumption that all lesbians celebrate Christmas. As Evelyn Torton Beck writes in the introduction to *Nice Jewish Girls: A Lesbian Anthology* (3rd ed., 1989): "Jewish invisibility is a symptom of anti-Semitism as surely as lesbian invisibility is a symptom of homophobia."

Ironically, although antisemitism renders Jews invisible when lesbians plan events or anthologies, antisemitism causes Jews to become an *overly visible* target for scapegoating. This apparent contradiction is not unique to antisemitism; rather, it applies to most oppressions. Traditional antisemitism scapegoats Jews as "killers of Christ"; in a slight variation, some lesbians have scapegoated Jews as "killers of the Goddess." Similarly, rather than blame Jews for the advent of communism or capitalism, some lesbians have claimed that "Jews invented patriarchy." Rather than accuse Jews of controlling the international economy, some lesbians allege that Jews have taken over the lesbian movement.

Stereotyping simultaneously makes real Jews invisible and slanderous images overly visible. Beck's introduction to *Nice Jewish Girls* explores antisemitic stereotypes in classic lesbian literature, such as Rita Mae Brown's *Rubyfruit Jungle* (1973), in which a Jewish character is described as sexually inappropriate and foul smelling.

Trivialization of the Holocaust constitutes another form of antisemitism. For example, some lesbians play out "Nazi/Jew" scenarios during sadomasochistic (S/M) sex. Some lesbians wear swastikas—both during sex and in daily life—in an attempt to proclaim their sexual desires or to transform the symbol. As Hoagland (1982) points out, these women often claim that such practices parody rather than glorify Nazism. However, "parody still validates nazism by perpetuating the language game, the conceptual framework."

Some lesbians find the S/M practice of eroticizing differences in power to be inherently oppressive and antisemitic. Reti (1986) argues that the Holocaust was "stimulated at least partially by the Nazi's appeal to sexual sadomasochism. . . . For lesbians to re-enact [these] power dynamics . . . not for educational or dramatic impact, but for *sexual entertainment*, seems to me an incredible trivialization of the suffering and deaths of millions of human beings" (emphasis in original).

Lesbian communities are no more antisemitic than the larger world; however, because of lesbian feminism's stated goal of eliminating oppression and providing "safe space" for all lesbians, antisemitism can seem more shocking and painful in this context. Some writers have suggested that, because of the small size of lesbian communities, Jewish lesbians may be more likely than Jewish nonlesbians to form friendships and romantic relationships with gentiles; therefore, lesbians may encounter more direct antisemitism. Furthermore, lesbian feminists who already have a conceptual framework for identifying and combating oppression may be more likely to confront antisemitism and thus make it more visible.

Outside of lesbian communities, Jews and homosexuals are often persecuted in tandem, as during the Nazi Holocaust or U.S. Senator Joseph McCarthy's anti-Communist hearings in the 1950s. Antisemitism and homophobia are also conceptually linked—Jews and lesbians are often used to symbolize the "other" in similar ways.

Jews, lesbians, and gay men share accusations of "conspiratorial clannishness," political subversiveness, and wealth (bigots usually do not distinguish between gay men and lesbians, despite real socioeconomic differences between the two). For example, the Religious Right trumpets the stereotype of lesbian and gay couples as "DINKs" (double income/no kids) with enormous spending power—not unlike familiar antisemitic stereotypes. Perhaps most striking, both Jews and gays have been accused of abducting and abusing children—Jews to use children's blood to make matzoh, gay men and lesbians to brutalize them sexually. In each case, this libel has justified the bloodiest violence against the group.

The stereotype of the politically correct lesbian feminist overlaps strikingly with those of the Jewish mother and the Jewish American princess (J.A.P.). All three are maligned as loud, nagging, whiny, pushy, hostile, coarse, rude, clannish, and physically ugly. All supposedly use guilt to manipulate others. In addition, lesbian feminists and Jewish mothers are labeled oversensitive, hysterical, paranoid, and cheap. Lesbian feminists and J.A.P.s are accused, paradoxically, of both promiscuity and frigidity (for example, lesbians purportedly suffer from "bed death," while J.A.P.s supposedly withhold sex from their husbands). Lesbian feminists and J.A.P.s are also accused of poor fashion sense—lesbians are said to wear plain, "mannish" clothes and no makeup; J.A.P.s, to favor garish dress and too much makeup.

Jewish lesbians have responded to antisemitism both inside and outside lesbian communities by organizing and writing about their experiences. Lesbians first publicly discussed the issue during the 1970s, when several magazines and journals published scattered articles about antisemitic incidents within lesbian communities. The subject, however, did not reach a broad audience until the 1982 publication of the first edition of *Nice Jewish Girls*, which included numerous essays and poems documenting antisemitism among lesbians. Partly in response to the book, many Jewish lesbians formed political and social groups during the 1980s to combat antisemitism and to explore Jewish lesbian identity. By the 1990s, Jewish lesbians began deliberately to explore and depict antisemitism in fiction. Outstanding examples include Jyl Lynn Felman's "Crisis" (1990), Melanie Kaye Kantrowitz's "My Jewish Face" (1990), and S. Naomi Finkelstein's "McRunes and Mazdas" (1994–1995). As a result of this work, antisemitism both inside and outside lesbian communities has gained attention and acknowledgment, although many lesbians still believe antisemitism to be nonexistent or unimportant.

*Robin Bernstein*

## Bibliography

Beck, Evelyn Torton, ed. *Nice Jewish Girls: A Lesbian Anthology*. 3rd ed. Boston: Beacon, 1989.

Hoagland, Sarah. "Sadism, Masochism, and Lesbian-Feminism." In *Against Sadomasochism: A Radical Feminist Analysis*. Ed. Robin Ruth Linden, Darlene R. Pagano, Diana E.H. Russell, and Susan Leigh Star. San Francisco: Frog in the Well, 1982, pp. 153–163.

Reti, Irene. *Remember the Fire: Lesbian Sadomasochism in a Post Nazi-Holocaust World*. Santa Cruz, Calif.: Herbooks, 1986.

Zahava, Irene, ed. *Speaking for Ourselves: Short Stories by Jewish Lesbians*. Freedom, Calif.: Crossing, 1990.

*See also* Israel; Judaism; Race and Racism; Sadomasochism

## Antiquity

Same-sex love among women in classical and Hellenistic Greece, in Rome, and elsewhere in the ancient Mediterranean world. Except for Sappho's (ca. 600 B.C.E.) poetry, there is no direct testimony by a woman of how women in antiquity experienced love between women or of how they viewed its role in their lives. Thus, the available evidence, based on a belief that male sexuality is "naturally'" active and female sexuality "naturally" passive and on a hierarchical distinction between active and passive sexual roles, expresses male views about women and about female sexuality.

The Greek and Latin terminology used to designate female homosexuals does not include "lesbian," which, in the ancient world, refers to fellatio. In the *Symposium,* Plato (427?–347? B.C.E.) calls women sexually drawn to other women *hetairistriai,* meaning female companions of women. The more frequently used Greek term is *tribas;* it and its Latin equivalent, *fricatrix,* both probably derive from verbs meaning "to rub." Latin authors often used the Greek word *tribas,* instead of *fricatrix,* as a way of suggesting that female homosexuality is essentially a foreign phenomenon. The Latin word, *virago,* meaning a masculine woman, focuses on the way in which lesbianism represents gender-role transgression.

The tendency of much scholarship on homosexuality in antiquity either to omit female experience or to not clearly differentiate it from male experience has encouraged an assumption of a greater acceptance of lesbianism than the evidence allows.

Because the ancient world viewed lesbian women through a male lens, which identified sexuality with penile penetration, most references to female homosexuality assume that one partner (endowed with an unusually enlarged clitoris or making use of a dildo) plays the active "masculine" role. Female homoeroticism is represented as occurring between two adult women, rather than as conforming to the male model of *paiderasteia* (love of an older male, usually in his twenties, for an adolescent youth), the socially validated form of male homoeroticism. The cultural acceptance of *paiderasteia* was not extended to include female-female love, which, especially in the Hellenistic period, was almost uniformly castigated as "unnatural" and shameful. The negative judgment applies to both participants in a lesbian relationship, since the presumably "feminine" receptive partner, in not allowing herself to be penetrated by a man, is also acting "unnaturally."

The understanding of female homoeroticism in antiquity derives from a variety of sources: mythology, visual art (particularly vase paintings), erotic poetry, philosophical texts, comedy, dream books, elite Hellenistic literature, astrological texts, medical texts, and love spells. Responsible interpretation of this material requires careful distinguishing by region and period.

## Ancient Greece

Except for Homeric references to the Amazons, there are no allusions to female-female love in early archaic Greek literature (750–600 B.C.E.). The early sixth century offers not only Sappho's poetry and its evocation of a fully reciprocal, unabashedly sensual love between women, but also the poetry of her near contemporary, the Spartan poet Alcman (mid-seventh century B.C.E.), who composed choral lyrics written for performance by *parthenai* (unmarried girls). Alcman's *parthenai* express the girls' longings for intimate relations with one another and contain hints that some were involved in affairs with older married women. Indeed, there is evidence that, in ancient Sparta, where unmarried girls were given public education and trained as athletes as nowhere else, female-female relationships were given public endorsement. According to Plutarch (ca. A.D. 46–ca. 127), in Sparta respectable adult women had love affairs with unmarried girls in relationships accorded the same educational function as those attributed to male *paiderasteia.*

Some scholars believe that, elsewhere in the seventh and sixth centuries B.C.E., the Greeks accepted the involvement of young girls in homoerotic relations during a period of segregation in all-female communities called *thiasoi*, as in Sappho's "school" or Artemis's temple at Brauron. This may have included relations between teachers or priestesses and students (as in the male pattern), but also (unlike that pattern) between the girls themselves. One of Alcman's lyrics has been interpreted as describing an exclusive bonding between two such girls, validated not for its initiatory value but simply as an expression of mutual attachment.

Whereas two out of the three earliest Greek lyric poets (Sappho's contemporary Alcaeus is the third) wrote poems referring to female homosexuality, in the classical period (fifth and fourth centuries B.C.E.)—when the *thiasoi* had disappeared, and women were confined to the domestic sphere—it seems to have become a taboo subject, at least in Athens. Therefore, it is not known if wives of citizens turned to one another for the intimacy and passion they were unlikely to find in heterosexual marriages with men whose own eroticism seems mostly to have been directed into *paiderastic* relationships. Accounts of female-female lovemaking between *heterai* (courtesans) probably refer to scenes designed to titillate male customers, but these women may also have engaged in freely chosen sexual relationships with one another.

Vases dating from the late sixth and early fifth centuries B.C.E. in Corinth or Boetia depict erotic encounters between adult women, not between women and girls. One shows a kneeling woman fingering the genitals of another; some show women with dildoes, including a two-ended dildo. Visual art, particularly vase painting, tends to be more explicit in its rendition of female-female eroticism than literary texts.

There are few literary references. A Pindar (518–438 B.C.E.) fragment from the first half of the fifth century speaks of the erotic response one woman has to the beauty of another. The fifth-century philosopher Parmenides wrote that active—that is, masculine—women and passive (feminine) men result from the male and female seeds at conception not melding properly. The conditions are thus congenital, not curable, and lifelong. In the fourth century B.C.E., Plato's *Symposium* describes lesbian love originating (just as heterosexual and male homosexual love do) from the splitting of the original round people.

After Plato, there is a long silence that extends until the beginning of the Augustan age (late first century B.C.E. into the first decade A.D.). One possible exception is the third-century B.C.E. Italian woman poet Nossis of Locri, who wrote erotic poems that may have referred to lesbian relationships. Almost all extant Roman-period sources (except for Plutarch's nonjudgmental description of female-female love in archaic Sparta—and he was not talking about his own world) condemn lesbian relations, even though many condone particular forms of male homoeroticism. Women engaged in same-sex erotic relationships are viewed as trying to play male roles and claim male privilege and, thus, judged as acting against "nature"—that is, against the cultural norms. The first critical references to Sappho's homoeroticism appear at this time.

## Rome

Nothing is known of the language of affection used by Roman women nor whether same-sex eroticism occurred among unmarried girls. Much of the evidence concerning Roman women applies only to the wives of citizens who were not secluded in their homes as women in classical Greece were, although they and their sexuality were still seen as needing to be controlled by men. A married woman's sexual involvement with another woman was defined as adultery. For an elite woman to engage in lesbian sex was unpardonable, though slaves or prostitutes may have been encouraged to do so to titillate male voyeurs.

Roman-period (ca. 200 B.C.E.–A.D. 200) literature testifies to a general familiarity with the concept of female homoeroticism. The earliest extant Latin reference to female homosexuality appears in a second-century B.C.E. comedy by Plautus (ca. 254–184 B.C.E.), in which a female slave is represented as forcing sexual intercourse upon her mistress. Toward the beginning of the first century B.C.E., Seneca (55 B.C.E.–A.D. 40?) presents a fictitious legal case centering on a man who finds his wife in bed with another woman and kills them both, after first looking to see if the partner was a man with a penis of his own or a woman with an artificial one. In the first century A.D., the poet Phaedrus composed a fable about the origin of the active participants in lesbian sex and the passive partners in male homosexuality; his tale describes Prometheus, returning to the creation of humans after having too much to drink, accidentally putting female sexual organs on some male bodies and male genitals on some female bodies. During the same period, Petronius's *Satyricon* portrays two married women

**A** at a banquet getting drunk and beginning to fondle each other; that one is an ex-prostitute and that neither is really respectable is made inescapably clear. Martial (ca. A.D. 40–ca. 104) writes of a matron viewed as utterly respectable because she is reported to have never taken on any lovers, until it is discovered that, in imitation of men, she has a female beloved. The second-century A.D. Syrian Iamblichos wrote a popular novel about a marriage between an Egyptian princess and a female subject. Lucian's (ca. A.D. 115?–ca. 180) *Dialogues of the Courtesans* describes a marriage between two courtesans, one of whom, claiming to have been born just like other women but with the mind and desires of a man, takes on a man's name and dress. She boasts that she can give pleasure as well as any man—and doesn't need a penis to do so.

Astrological texts, an important source for nonelite Roman-period attitudes toward lesbianism, present female homoeroticism as the result of being born under a particular configuration (usually one in which Venus appears in what was regarded as a masculine house) and, thus, as a lifelong orientation. These texts often lump together homoerotic, adulterous, and promiscuous women because all take on an active sexual role, or lump lesbians with passive males because both refuse to conform to sanctioned gender roles. Though caused by the stars, lesbianism is viewed negatively; yet astrologers seem to aim at helping women accept their fate rather than change it.

Artemidoros's *Oneirokritika* (second century A.D.), the most influential Hellenistic book about the classification of dreams, assumes a dominating, penetrating model for female-female homoeroticism. If a woman dreams that she possesses another woman, it means she will share her secrets with that woman; if she dreams she is possessed by another woman, she will be divorced or widowed; if she dreams of making love with a female stranger, she will attempt futile projects.

Medical texts from the Roman period that deal with lesbians also take for granted the dominant phallic assumptions. Viewing healthy female sexuality as passive, they recommend either mind control or surgery to correct the pathology of the presumed active partner: surgery to remove an overlarge clitoris or psychological treatment to deal with the lack of ethical restraint on lust.

## Hellenistic Egypt

In Hellenistic Egypt (ca. 300 B.C.E.–A.D. 300), women commissioned love spells, which invoke the aid of underworld spirits to attract other women. Extant examples of such spells (probably composed by men) provide the names of the women who purchased them and of the women whose love they sought to compel. The formulaic language of these spells assumes a male model of domination and conquest and leaves unclear whether the aim is a long-term public relation or a clandestine affair.

Several different sources—some of these spells, several of the novels cited above, the writings of the Alexandrian astrologer Ptolemy (fl. A.D. 121–151)—suggest that, at least in Egypt and Syria, long-term relations between women were sometimes understood in relation to the model of heterosexual marriage. Since, in the Roman-ruled world, official matrimony was available only to citizens and marriage otherwise meant only cohabitation (perhaps sanctified in a private ceremony), two women living together might well have considered themselves married. Although the early Christian father Clement of Alexandria (ca. A.D. 150–ca. 214) speaks of women who marry other women (using both the active and the passive form of the verb "to marry") as an unspeakable practice, he nonetheless describes their relation in terms of a socially accepted institution.

## Jewish and Early Christian Texts

Postexilic (ca. 100 B.C.E.–A.D. 70) biblical texts prohibit male anal intercourse (though Roman-period rabbis permitted anal intercourse in marriage) but make no reference to female homosexuality. Hellenistic-period Jewish texts represent sexual love between women as not just a practice of foreigners, but as something that also occurs within Judaism. Talmudic rabbis disagree as to whether lesbianism is to be construed as harlotry. The school of Hillel is said to allow women who rub with each other to marry priests, while the school of Shammai does not. These discussions of lesbian sexuality make no distinction between active and receptive partners and assume that the women involved would also marry men.

Early Christian literature views homoeroticism somewhat differently from other Roman-period sources. Like his gentile contemporaries, Paul (d. A.D. 67) sees women's love of women as "unnatural" because it challenges gender boundaries, but, unlike those contemporaries, he groups female homosexuals and male homosexuals in the same category and condemns not only the receptive, but also the active, partner in male-male love. Early Christian apocalyptic writings put male and female homosexuals in the same pit in hell. *Christine Downing*

## Bibliography

Brooten, Bernadette J. *Love Between Women: Early Christian Responses to Female Homoeroticism.* Chicago: University of Chicago Press, 1996.

Cantarella, Eva. *Bisexuality in the Ancient World.* New Haven, Conn.: Yale University Press, 1992.

Dover, K.J. *Greek Homosexuality.* Cambridge, Mass.: Harvard University Press, 1978.

Perry, William Armstrong, III. *Pederasty and Pedagogy in Archaic Greece.* Chicago: University of Chicago Press, 1996.

Richlin, Amy. *The Gardens of Priapus: Sexuality and Aggression in Roman Humor.* New Haven, Conn.: Yale University Press, 1983.

Winkler, John J. *The Constraints of Desire.* New York: Routledge, 1990.

*See also* Christianity, Early; Classical Literature; Judaism; Sappho

## Anzaldúa, Gloria E. (1942–)

*Chicana-tejana* poet, fiction writer, and cultural theorist. Born in the Rio Grande Valley of south Texas to sixth-generation *mexicanos*, Anzaldúa has won numerous awards, including the Before Columbus Foundation American Book Award, the Lamda Lesbian Small Book Press Award, an NEA Fiction Award, and the Sappho Award of Distinction. As one of the first openly lesbian Chicana writers, Anzaldúa has played a major role in redefining lesbian and Chicano/a identities. And as coeditor of *This Bridge Called My Back: Writings by Radical Women of Color* (1981) and editor of *Making Face, Making Soul/Haciendo Caras: Creative and Critical Perspectives by Feminists of Color* (1990), Anzaldúa has played an equally vital role in developing an inclusionary feminist movement.

Anzaldúa's writings synthesize autobiography with political and spiritual issues to explore multiple overlapping themes, including Nahuatl mythic traditions, U.S. white supremacy, and the interlocking systems of oppression that marginalize people who—because of their sexuality, gender, ethnicity, and/or economic status—do not belong to dominant cultural groups. In essays such as "Speaking in Tongues" (1979), "La Prieta" (1981), and "En Rap-port, in Opposition" (1987), Anzaldúa draws on her own experiences as a working-class Chicana dyke to investigate the destructive effects of externally imposed labels, homophobia and sexism, and conflicts among women of all colors. She calls for multicultural feminist communities and maintains that alliance work requires the flexibility to shift between identities.

*Borderlands/La Frontera: The New Mestiza* (1987) represents Anzaldúa's most extensive attempt to mediate between diverse cultures. This collection of essays and poems defies easy classification but can perhaps be best described as cultural autobiography, for Anzaldúa blends personal experience with history and social protest with poetry and myth to (re)construct her individual and collective identities. In blurring the boundaries between apparently distinct categories, her concepts of the Borderlands and mestiza consciousness have made a significant impact on twentieth-century cultural theory.

Anzaldúa's poetry and fiction employ code switching, surrealistic description, and mythic imagery to challenge conventional literary standards. By exploring diverse issues simultaneously, including lesbian sexuality, butch-femme roles, bisexuality, homophobia and sexism, altered states of reality, and hetero-/homosexual relationships, Anzaldúa expands existing definitions of lesbian and Chicana identities. "El Paisano Is a Bird of Good Omen" (1983), for example, depicts Andrea, a Chicana dyke with heightened spiritual powers, on the eve of her wedding to Zenobio, a gay Chicano.

For Anzaldúa, sexuality cannot be separated from ethnicity, class, culture, gender, or other systems of difference. By emphasizing the cultural- and class-specific dimensions of her sexuality, Anzaldúa destabilizes monolithic definitions of homosexuality and exposes the ethnocentricity of academic "queer theory." This emphasis on multiple systems of difference enables her to go beyond definitions of homosexuality that focus primarily on gender, sexual-object choice, and sexual desire. In her work, sexuality represents a component in a constantly shifting process of identity (re)formation and political activism. As she explains in "To(o) Queer a Writer" in *InVersions* (1991), the "new *mestiza* queers" she envisions have "the ability, the flexibility, the amorphous quality of being able to stretch this way and that way. We can add new labels, names and identities as we mix with others."

*AnaLouise Keating*

## A

**Bibliography**

Keating, AnaLouise. *Women Reading Women Writing: Self-Invention in Paula Gunn Allen, Gloria Anzaldúa, and Audre Lorde.* Philadelphia: Temple University Press, 1996.

Lugones, María. "On Borderlands/La Frontera: An Interpretive Essay." *Hypatia* 7 (1992), 31–37.

Warland, Betsy, ed. *InVersions: Writing by Dykes, Queers & Lesbians.* Vancouver: Press Gang, 1991.

Zimmerman, Bonnie. *The Safe Sea of Women: Lesbian Fiction, 1969–1989.* Boston: Beacon, 1990.

*See also* Latina Literature; Mestizaje

## Arab Americans

Diverse ethnic group that includes people who have emigrated from, or whose descendants have emigrated from, Arab countries, including those in Southwest Asia and North Africa. Arab Americans also include people of mixed ethnic heritage. Because immigration is partly due to political climate in the country of origin, immigration patterns vary among Arab people from different regions. Thus, Arabs from certain countries have longer histories of immigration to the United States than Arabs from other countries. Arab Americans occupy a variety of jobs and come from diverse class backgrounds.

Arab Americans experience racism in many ways, including the perpetuation of stereotypes about submissive Arab women who are treated poorly by men. The discrimination and marginality that Arabs experience has caused Arab American families and communities to maintain strong bonds.

Arab family structure is patriarchal and based on extended kinship networks. Obligation and duty to the family are expected, subsuming individual desires. This is in direct contrast to the dominant individualistic attitude emphasized in the United States, which poses a unique set of conflicts for Arab lesbians in that country. In Arab culture, a man's honor resides in the women of the family, particularly in women's sexuality. Thus, women's sexuality is tightly controlled according to accepted cultural norms to protect men's honor. Coming out as a lesbian, then, may be seen as a negative reflection and a shame upon the family and a manifestation of a woman's lack of familial duty and concern.

For as long as there have been Arabs in America, there have been Arab American women who loved other women, although they may not have personally or publicly identified as lesbian. Although the history of Arab lesbians in the United States is undocumented, this does not mean that they do not have a long history. It merely means that it has been rendered invisible due to the necessity for secrecy in order to remain a part of the Arab community and survive.

The visible Arab lesbian community formed as part of a larger movement of people coming into their identity as lesbians of color. Lesbians from different ethnicities and races formed separate organizations. The first publicly visible Arab lesbian group, the Arab Lesbian Network, was formed in the United States in May 1989 in Berkeley, California, by Huda Jadallah, a Palestinian lesbian born and raised in the United States. The first gathering included five Arab lesbians. The group grew in size and became part of a developing international network of self-identified Arab lesbians. The Arab Lesbian Network changed its name in the course of its development to include bisexual women (Arab Lesbian and Bisexual Women's Network). There was also a group that included men called the Arab Lesbian, Gay, and Bisexual Network.

These organizations were both social and political. In 1990, the Arab Lesbian and Bisexual Women's Network marched for the first time with a banner in the San Francisco Freedom Day Parade. During the U.S. invasion of Iraq in 1991, the networks organized actively to educate the public about the war and to raise funds for survivors in Iraq. Although the Arab Lesbian and Bisexual Women's Network disbanded as a formal group in 1992, informal gatherings continued.

At the same time that the Arab Lesbian and Bisexual Women's Network was forming on the West Coast, the Gay and Lesbian Arabic Society (GLAS) was forming on the East Coast. This organization was dominated by men but did include a few women. GLAS formed several branches during the 1990s, including Washington, D.C. (the original group), Los Angeles, and New York City. The Lesbian Arab Network (LAN) held its first meeting at the Lesbian and Gay Community Services Center in New York City on June 10, 1990. LAN's main function was to serve as a social support group; it had seven members at its peak and ceased to exist formally by the end of 1991, although the informal network of Arab lesbians continued to expand.

In March 1996, the first Arab lesbian, bisexual, and transgender women's e-mail list was formed by

Katherine Sherif. Although the members of the list group were mainly from the United States, there were also members from other countries. Queer-Arabs, an e-mail list group formed by Sherif at the same time is open to men and women, Arabs and non-Arabs, queers and nonqueers. Although dominated by men, there are some Arab lesbians on the list.

Arab lesbians in the United States created a visible network of social support during the 1990s. In 1991, they had a visible presence at the First National Lesbian Conference in Atlanta, Georgia. In August 1997, the First National Queer Arab Women's Gathering took place in Marin, California, where plans were laid for ongoing activities.

*Huda Jadallah*

### Bibliography

Aswad, Barbara C., and Barbara Bilge. *Family and Gender Among American Muslims: Issues Facing Middle Eastern Immigrants and Their Descendants*. Philadelphia: Temple University Press, 1996.

Jadallah, Huda, and Pearl Saad. "A Conversation About the Arab Lesbian and Bisexual Women's Network." In *Plural Desires: Writing Bisexual Women's Realities*. Ed. The Bisexual Anthology Collective. Toronto: Sister Vision, 1995.

Kadi, Joanna. *Food for Our Grandmothers: Writings by Arab-American and Arab-Canadian Feminists*. Boston: South End, 1994.

*See also* Immigration

## Arab Literature, Modern

Twentieth-century writing, primarily produced after the various independence movements shook colonial rule across Africa and Asia after the end of World War II, and again in the 1950s and 1960s. Colonialism brought with it the widespread use of French, in particular, primarily in the Maghrib (Northwest Africa) and in Lebanon. A rich Francophone (French-language) literature thus came to life, which must be included in a discussion of Arab literature. While Arabic and French have marked stylistic differences, and different ways of encoding culturally specific situations, the themes and the cultural fabric of Arab literature in all languages remain similar.

"Lesbians" and "lesbianism" are not frequently discussed topics in critical works about Arab litera-

ture. In discussions of same-sex relations in Arab literature, one cannot assume the existence of an immutable, monolithic "Arab" or "Islamic" ahistorical reality that allows generalizations, nor that hostility to lesbianism is particularly Muslim (as opposed to Christian or Jewish). Many Arab authors, regardless of gender or sexual orientation, have represented lesbian situations and characters in their writings, particularly in works of fiction. A number of ostensibly heterosexual authors, as well as others who may have to code their sexual identity, have used "lesbianism" as a narrative or poetic tool or as an escape into the "safety" of the female. In its most superficial form, lesbianism is part of a system of transgression against an oppressive moral order. In more feminist versions, representations of lesbianism are allegorical of militant protest by women against an alienated condition and an act of ultimate defiance against a male-dominated and brutal social order.

The rise of Arab feminism in the late nineteenth and early twentieth centuries provides an important backdrop for understanding lesbian representation. It was very strong in Egypt, for instance, where the first women's demonstration took place in 1919, under the leadership of Huda Sha'rawi (1879–1949). In 1949, Durriyah Shafiq (1908–1975) led a more militant feminist movement called the Nile Daughters Party, which demanded the abolition of polygamy, the institution of European-type divorce laws, and the right to vote and be elected in Parliament. In 1951, Shafiq's party marched on Parliament, demanding equal rights for women and to present a petition, its demands written in blood, to the king.

How does one locate "lesbian" characters and situations in Arab literature, since decoding latent homosexual behavior through the homosocial does not fit the culture of the Arab world? There is, in effect, fairly little discomfort at discussing and representing male homosexuality in the literature of the Arab world, albeit not necessarily sympathetically. Naguib Mahfouz (1911–), Gamal Ghitany (1945–), Mouloud Mammeri (1917–1989), Rachid Boudjedra (1941–), and Rafik Ben-Salah (n.d.), among others, have all spoken, in different ways, of male homosexuality, and Rachid O. (n.d.) has openly written about his own homosexuality.

On the other hand, love between women is not as obvious in literary works, for a number of reasons. Gender codes vary considerably between the West and the Arab world. Assuming maleness as a preferable gendered identity is not uncommon among assertive (often heterosexual) women, fictional and real, who suffer from the very restrictive and negative expectations placed on their social and sexual roles. As a result, women have, for instance, written poetry ostensibly addressed to other women in ambiguous modes. In the modern period, Zeidan (1996) claims that the Lebanese Wardah al-Yaziji (1838–1924) addressed another woman in her love poetry purely as a covering device, although Ahmed (1992) has contested that restrictive interpretation. Al-Yaziji used the technique more aggressively when writing to cA'ishah Taymur, evoking a famous love story of the seventeenth century with the verse "You are unique among women. So how could I but / love a peerless lover?" cA'ishah Taymur (1840–1902) was an aristocratic woman poet, with strong links to the Egyptian *khedives* (royal family). After she became a widow, she actively engaged in her poetic career, interrupted by seven years of mourning for her eldest daughter. Her love poetry had many daring aspects; in her book of poems, she included poems in colloquial Arabic, something quite unorthodox at the time, and used a male persona, writing love poetry to a recipient identified by feminine grammatical forms. For the Egyptian feminist Mayy Ziyadah (1886–1941), this was merely a technique in response to the social unacceptability of female public expressions of emotions and in accord with Taymur's tendency to imitate male literature. Yet what is important in these female voices borrowing a male persona is less whether these poets truly experienced same-sex love, than the ways in which classical Arabic poetry allows publicly entertaining ambiguity about gender and the object of love. The tradition of a woman writer addressing words of love to an unidentified person, revealed to be a woman, is continued by the Lebanese Etel cAdnan (1925–). Her "Love Poems," which were written in English, are discreetly but clearly addressed to a woman.

Gender ambiguity is one way writers have broached the topic of female transgression of sexual boundaries without explicitly speaking of lesbian behavior. For instance, in Tahar Ben Jelloun's (1944–) poetic narrative *Harrouda* (1971), the mysterious woman Harrouda, witch and beggar, transgresses all taboos, religious, social, and sexual, and escapes all definition; her many disguises make her a mythical figure, and, in one of them, she is seen brandishing a gigantic plastic penis. Ben Jelloun explored the "crossing over" of a woman into a forbidden identity in greater detail in *The Sand Child* (1987), in which a girl is made to pass as a boy from childhood because her father can't abide the birth of another daughter. S/he is then married to her cousin, an ailing young girl struggling with physical challenges, with whom s/he has a strongly sadomasochistic rapport, at once complicit and hostile. Yet, in the end, Zohra's transgendered life fails, and a return to her female self results in molestation and destruction.

"Lesbians" appear in trace form in several works by well-known male authors. In Rachid Boudjedra's *La Répudiation* (1969), famous for its depiction of male homosexuality, the French slang word *gouine* (dyke, loosely) appears in a description of heterosexual fantasies and dysfunction. The Syrian Nizar Qabbani (1923–), who has been called the most popular modern poet in the Arab world, has on occasion evoked women's right to pleasure, including, according to Khairallah (1995), a "joyful and positive rendering of a love scene between two lesbians" in his "Al-Qasida al-shirrira" ("The Evil Poem," 1971). The Egyptian Majîd Tubiya's (1938–) novel *Rîm Tasbugh Sha^crahâ* (Rîm Dyes Her Hair [1982]) contains an allusion to same-sex relations. In none of these cases, however, are "lesbians" the real focus of the passage.

Love between women is, not surprisingly, most narratively developed in the works of several women writers. Nawal El Saadawi (1931–), in *Imra'a^cind Nuqtat al-Sifr* (Woman at Point Zero [1979]), parallels Firdaous's love for her teacher, Miss Iqbal, a form of extreme longing and passion that is never actualized, with the love pangs felt for the man with whom she will fall in love. While the Western-defined term "lesbian," or an Arabic equivalent, is not present in most authors' work, a noteworthy exception is found in Nawal El Saadawi's *Jannât wa-Iblîs* (Innocence of the Devil [1992]). Here, a woman with an ambiguous status with respect to gender, honor, and power confronts the patriarchal order. The woman works for the director of a facility, carries out his orders, and is treated by him like a sexual object. She finally rebels, affirms that she hates him and all men, and, in fact, loves women. The crucial element in this confrontation is the director's attempt at mustering religion against her ("You will go to Hell with the people of Lot," "Lesbianism is *haram*" [forbidden]) and her own resistance on the very plane of theology: "No, Sir! It is not mentioned in the Book of God."

In Assia Djebar's (1936–) short story "Femmes d'Alger dans leur appartement" (Women of Algiers in Their Apartment) (1980), Sahrah feels a sudden rush of desire for a woman friend who is lying ill in the hospital, but the feelings are not acted upon. Yet this attraction is built up throughout the story by allusions to her ambiguous rapport with her other women friends, and some of their improper gender behaviors—for instance, one of them practices judo. The possibility that such relationships could fully take place has been detailed in several works. The Syrian Alîfa Rifᶜat, in a short story titled "Sadîqatî" (My Girlfriend, or Female Friend [1981]), and, most notably, the Lebanese Hanân Al Shay'kh (1945–), in *Women of Sand and Myrrh* (1989), have both developed the theme of love between women. In Hanan al Shay'kh's novel, two married women living in Saudi Arabia, where they are increasingly confined and feel like prisoners who want to escape from the country, experience a passionate but short-lived affair. The novel brings together the many strands that compose recognizable themes in Arab writing by women about women in a tender and powerful depiction of the overwhelming possibilities that exist for love between women.

*Francesca Canadé Sautman*

## Bibliography

Ahmed, Leila. *Women and Gender in Islam: Historical Roots of a Modern Debate*. New Haven, Conn.: Yale University Press, 1992.

Khairallah, As'ad E. "Love and the Body in Modern Arabic Poetry." In *Love and Sexuality in Modern Arabic Literature*. Ed. Roger Allen and Hilary Kilpatrick. London: Saqi, 1995, pp. 210–223.

Malti-Douglas, Fedwa. *Men, Women, and Gods: Nawal El Saadawi and Arab Feminist Poetics*. Berkeley: University of California Press, 1995.

Zeidan, Joseph T. *Arab Women Novelists*. Albany: State University of New York, 1996.

*See also* Egypt; Islam

## Architecture

In architecture, as in many male-identified and male-dominated professions, lesbians and lesbian perspectives must be investigated indirectly. In both historic and contemporary contexts, the lesbian presence is often shadowy and can be discovered by locating woman-identified women and women's networks. While acceptance of lesbians as practitioners is beginning, there is little awareness of lesbian or bisexual female architects in history (with the possible exception of Eileen Gray), and lesbian theories on architecture are just becoming visible in the profession's public discourse.

One of the most prolific twentieth-century architects, Julia Morgan (1872–1957), was the first American woman to receive a certificate from the prestigious Ecole des Beaux-Arts in Paris. Although Morgan never married, and scholarship remains mute on her intimate relationships, she was part of a large network of wealthy and professional women of the first half of the twentieth century who were the clients for many of her architectural commissions, which included private residences, women's schools, women's clubs, and the YWCA.

Scholarship on modern architecture revived interest in another influential female architect, Eileen Gray (1878–1976). Born in Scotland, Gray produced lacquer work, furniture, and interior-design projects prior to her self-taught practice in architecture. Although only a few of the buildings that she designed were built, she was a founding member of UAM (Union des Artists Modernes), an important association of modern architects and planners. By the 1950s, Gray's most famous house, E.1027, was erroneously attributed to Le Corbusier (1887–1965), in part because he had covered the walls with murals of his own design during a visit there.

In his biography of Gray, Adam (1987) "purposely refrained from probing too deeply into the private lives of those who were at times her most intimate friends" but reported that Gray "had several affairs with men and women" and traveled in a social circle that included Natalie Barney (1876–1972), Gertrude Stein (1874–1946), and Romaine Brooks (1874–1970).

The education of women in architecture in the United States was fostered by the Cambridge School of Architecture and Landscape Architecture, which existed from 1915 to 1942 and provided professional design education for women, who were excluded from attending existing institutions. Histories of the school do not provide direct information about the sexual or affectional orientation of the female students or teachers. However, the school's existence supported the development of extensive, supportive networks of women design practitioners for many decades.

The most widely known architect associated with the Cambridge School is Eleanor Raymond (1887–1989). In 1931, her Raymond House was featured in *Architectural Forum* as the first home in the International Style to be built in New England. In 1948, Raymond and Dr. Maria Telkes received wide recognition for their Dover Sun House, heated exclusively by solar energy. Raymond's professional and personal life was inscribed within a circle of women colleagues and clients, including her friend and "companion," Ethel Power, editor of *House Beautiful*.

The "second wave" of feminism in the United States stimulated development of new perspectives on women and architecture, although most groups and publications still addressed the issue of sexual orientation indirectly. In the early 1970s, seven women architects and planners collaborated to develop the Women's School of Planning and Architecture (WSPA), which held summer sessions from 1975 until 1981. Leslie Kanes Weisman and Noel Phyllis Birkby's essay on the WSPA in *Learning Our Way* (1983) describes an implicit lesbian agenda in listing intentions and goals such as "to offer women a separatist experience" and "to explore the possibilities for designing and building new environments for an evolving women's culture"—including lesbian centers. However, a decade later, Weisman's book *Discrimination by Design: A Feminist Critique of the Man-Made Environment* (1992) mentions lesbians only once, as potential victims of housing discrimination in suburbs.

In 1987, Pauline Fowler reiterated the goal of developing spaces for women's culture in "Women Building Culture: Architecture for Feminists." This was followed by Margaret Lew's 1988 essay in the journal *Trivia,* in which she undertook "an architectural exploration of an emerging reality found in the work of lesbian poets and theorists." Her project combined a spatial analysis of Pueblo architecture with excerpts from the writings of Monique Wittig (1935–), Mary Daly (1928–), and other radical lesbian feminists. In response to Fowler's call for "a new narrative" combining new, woman-centered forms to create spaces for women's culture, Lew called attention to the difficulty of "trying to critique a material reality without questioning the cultural definition of woman embedded in it." Despite the growing body of feminist scholarship in architecture during the 1990s, lesbians and lesbian perspectives continue to be marginalized.

*Elizabeth Cahn*

## Bibliography

Adam, Peter. *Eileen Gray: Architect/Designer.* New York: Abrams, 1987.

Boutelle, Sarah Holmes. "The Women's Network." In *Julia Morgan: Architect.* New York: Abbeville, 1988, pp. 83–127.

Bunch, Charlotte, and Sandra Pollack. *Learning Our Way: Essays in Feminist Education.* Trumansburg, N.Y.: Crossing, 1983.

Cole, Doris. *Eleanor Raymond: Architect.* Philadelphia: Art Alliance and East Brunswick, N.J.: Associated University Presses, 1981.

Fowler, Pauline. "Women Building Culture: Architecture for Feminists." In *Work in Progress: Building Feminist Culture.* Ed. Rhea Tregebov. Toronto: The Women's Press, 1987, pp. 129–147.

Lew, Margaret. "Relocating the Hedge Transforms the House: Monique Wittig and Pueblo Architecture." *Trivia: A Journal of Ideas* 12 (Spring 1988), 6–35.

*See also* Barney, Natalie; Brooks, Romaine; Stein, Gertrude; Wittig, Monique

## Archives and Libraries

Since the 1970s, archives and libraries have served as critical components in efforts to preserve and document lesbian lives and experiences. Whether independently organized and staffed or functioning as a subset of a larger academic, public, or special library, these collections of books, journals, ephemera, and artifacts share the goal of collecting, protecting, and making available both the primary and secondary sources essential to an investigation and examination of lesbianism.

## Characteristics and Development

Archives and libraries are not necessarily identical in either their mission or their organization. Libraries collected, however grudgingly or in some cases unwittingly, materials by and about lesbians well before the advent of the first archive organized around and focused on lesbianism. Authors widely known as lesbian have been well represented in most library collections. With the development of women's studies and then lesbian, gay, and queer studies, libraries, particularly in the academic sector, have needed to reassess their acquisitions policies and begin consciously to build collections in support of these emerging dynamic disciplines. No longer relegated to the fiction or psychology sections or hidden away in a "protected collection," most academic and many large public libraries actively and openly collect lesbian materials, including monographs, journals, and media. With almost seven hundred different subject headings covering a broad spectrum of lesbian-related topics (everything from Lesbian Avengers to Lesbian Heroes), the ability to identify and locate library materials has improved markedly. Specialized bibliographies, until fairly recently available only in limited runs from alternative presses, now appear on the publications lists of mainstream academic and trade publishers. Beginning with such groundbreaking titles as Jeannette Foster's *Sex Variant Women in Literature* (F. Muller, [1958]) and *Black Lesbians: An Annotated Bibliography,* compiled by J.R. Roberts (Naiad, 1981), and continuing with significant additions to reference collections, such as Clare Potter's groundbreaking *Lesbian Periodicals Index* (Naiad, 1986), *Contemporary Lesbian Writers of the United States: A Bio-Bibliographical Critical Sourcebook* (Greenwood, 1993) and *Lesbian Sources: A Bibliography of Periodical Articles, 1970–1990* (Garland, 1993), library reference materials have literally come out of the closet. In addition, several respected presses, such as Routledge and Columbia University Press, have developed monographic series focusing on lesbian and gay issues.

One possibly unavoidable result of the enhanced visibility and availability of materials on lesbian topics has been a steady increase in the number of attempts to censor or remove these materials from school and community libraries. Religious conservatives have targeted the children's book *Heather Has Two Mommies* (1989) for removal both from school curricula and library shelves, and the young-adult novel *Annie on My Mind* (1982) has sustained similar attacks. Although lesbian collections in academic libraries are not free from the threat (and reality) of malicious vandalism, these materials have a relatively safe haven in college and university libraries, particularly those on campuses with active women's studies programs. The safety and the availability of lesbian materials in public and school libraries are less assured. Books and videos that speak to youth, whether providing young people with information about their own feelings and inclinations or offering the children of lesbian and gay families the opportunity to see the reality of their lives reflected in a book on a library shelf, remain an endangered species in many school and community libraries.

Some communities, however, have made major strides with respect to the visibility of lesbians in libraries. In 1994, to commemorate the twenty-fifth anniversary of the Stonewall Rebellion, the New York Public Library sponsored a major exhibit entitled *Becoming Visible: The Legacy of Stonewall* at its main branch on Forty-second Street and Fifth Avenue. With materials drawn largely from its own archival collections, including oral histories, the New York Public Library recognized and celebrated the significant contributions of lesbians and gay men to the cultural, intellectual, and political life of New York City. The opening of the San Francisco Public Library (SFPL) at the Civic Center in April 1996 marked another milestone in the relationship of lesbian and gay materials and libraries. The James C. Hormel Lesbian and Gay Center became the first dedicated space for lesbian and gay materials in a major public library in the United States. Anchored by a beautifully designed reading room and exhibit space, the Hormel Center serves as the point of entry to the SFPL's impressive collection of lesbian and gay materials, which features, among other treasures of particular interest to lesbians, the archives of Naiad Press.

The oral histories at the New York Public Library and the archival and manuscript collections at the San Francisco Public Library provide two examples of major institutions assuming responsibility for collecting, organizing, and making available lesbian materials. Other large libraries, both academic and public, have also begun the slow and often painstaking work of tracking down archival and manuscript sources. The University of California, Berkeley, and Duke University, Durham, North Carolina, are examples of major university libraries that have determined that they have a duty to collect and preserve lesbian history.

## Lesbian Archives

Individual and community-based archival initiatives remain far ahead of either academic or public libraries in the attempt to collect and make accessible materials of particular interest to lesbians. Supported by individual, as opposed to government or corporate, contributors, heavily dependent on donations of materials in lieu of acquisitions budgets, and staffed largely by volunteers, lesbian archives are often more successful in documenting and reflecting the history and needs of a particular community or locale than are more traditional library organizations. Open to a wider range of materials and less constrained by archival or bibliographic conventions, important lesbian archives have survived the vicissitudes of lesbian politics, personal and professional disagreements, and, most significant, competition for collections resources from academic and public libraries.

It is, however, difficult to get an accurate count of the number of lesbian archives operating in the United States and internationally. Many of them operate under the umbrella of a "gay and lesbian" archive, while others consist of a few cartons of precious materials stored in a community center storage cabinet or the basement of someone's home. No discussion of lesbian archives and libraries would be complete, however, without mention of two U.S.-based archives, New York's Lesbian Herstory Archives and the June L. Mazer Lesbian Collection in Los Angeles, California. Each serves as a model of how a combination of personal initiative and community involvement can establish and maintain important community-based archival collections outside the structures and strictures of formal library organizations.

The women who founded the Lesbian Herstory Archives determined from the outset to collect, preserve, and make available all forms of print material about lesbian lives. With a prescient understanding of the significance of artifacts and ephemera in the documenting and retelling of lesbian history, the archives, from the very beginning, collected photographs, buttons, T-shirts, posters, and the like, in addition to printed and manuscript materials. Although none of the original founders were librarians or professional archivists, the group discovered early on the necessity of adhering to basic guidelines of archival preservation. Collective member Judith Schwarz's 1986 pamphlet, *Preserving Your Individual and Community History*, helped spread the word about the importance of careful handling of papers, photographs, and other documents.

The June L. Mazer Lesbian Collection first came into being in 1981 in Oakland, California, as the West Coast Lesbian Collections. In 1987, Connexxus Women's Center/Center de Mujeres brought the collection to Los Angeles. After the death of Mazer, a community activist and avid supporter of the collection, the archive was renamed in her memory. In addition to such standard library fare as published materials, including monographs and feminist and lesbian periodicals, including a complete run of *Vice Versa*, an early (1947–1948) Los Angeles-based lesbian newsletter, the Mazer Collection has acquired a number of significant archival and manuscript sources tracing both personal and organizational history.

The increasing popularity and accessibility of the World Wide Web has profoundly altered how we think about, understand, and conceptualize libraries and archives. Collections are no longer bound by the four walls of a physical space called a library or an archive but can exist instead in a virtual space, facilitating access twenty-four hours a day, seven days a week. Lesbians have begun to venture into this brave new world of cyberspace, creating new forms of communication and new definitions of community. Archives and libraries play an important role in this emerging virtual community. The Mazer Collection, for example, inaugurated Mazer On-Line in the spring of 1996, with the publication of its homepage on the World Wide Web (http://www.lesbian.org/mazer), which features a listing of upcoming events of interest to the community, a description of the collection's holdings, an article on the development of the collection by Lillian Faderman, and issues of *In the Life*, the Mazer Collection newsletter.

New information technologies enhance but will not, at least in the foreseeable future, replace libraries and archives, especially those dedicated to collecting and preserving lesbian materials. As exciting as the new technology might be to some, others are far more taken with the possibility of actually visiting a collection devoted to lesbian history, culture, and community and seeing, reading, and touching materials thoughtfully acquired and lovingly preserved. Libraries and archives help foster a sense of history and community. The Internet, however, does have the potential for broadening the definition of community and ensuring that lesbian materials exist in the virtual, as well as the real, world.

*Ellen Broidy*

### Bibliography

Gough, Cal, and Ellen Greenblatt, eds. *Gay and Lesbian Library Service*. Jefferson, N.C.: McFarland, 1990.

Nestle, Joan. "The Will to Remember: The Lesbian Herstory Archives of New York." *Feminist Review* 34 (1990), 86–93.

Thistlethwaite, Polly. "The Lesbian and Gay Past: An Interpretive Battleground." *Gay Community News* 20:4 (1995), 10–13.

*See also* Bibliographies and Reference Works; Computer Networks and Services; Lesbian Herstory Archives; Librarians; Naiad Press

## Argentina

Large South American country, colonized by Spain in the sixteenth century. Established Indian cultures were exterminated to an extent that surpasses, by far, all other Latin American countries. Blacks, brought as slaves in colonial times, were also exterminated through a policy of placing them in the front lines during independence and civil wars. By the late 1880s, inmigration was open to Europeans, resulting in a predominantly white society. Once a "model" Latin American country with prestigious universities, a large middle class, and a strongly unionized working class, decades of corrupt management and military dictatorships have devastated the country's economy and political culture.

No research has been done yet on lesbians in the ancient Indian cultures, the Colonial Era, or the Independence Era. By the end of the nineteenth century, the "first wave" of the feminist movement helped teachers, doctors, and women right's advocates, most of them socialists, live independently from men similar to their European and North American counterparts. There were also militant anarchists who were union leaders and free-love advocates. Although it is still unknown whether any of those women were lesbians, they opened women's access to the workplace and a self-determined life, prerequisites for lesbian visibility.

Between 1920 and 1959, lesbians from the upper classes profited immensely from a rite of passage consisting of a European sojourn, where they discovered the lesbian communities of Paris and London. Although many were later forced into marriage by their families (some married gay men of their class, for mutual protection), others resisted and lived their lives as artists or professionals. Middle- and working-class women entered the workforce in large numbers, permitting lesbians to earn their own living and avoid marriage. Without a visible community, relationships were subject to the strain of clandestine encounters. Lesbianism was not a subject in the arts or the media; most lesbians' only mirror of their lives came through foreign works, such as Radclyffe Hall's *The Well of Loneliness* (1928). Gender codes were strictly enforced, and lesbians were very skillful in keeping a "feminine" appearance when exposed to heterosexual eyes.

In the 1960s, women entered the university in large numbers. It was a time of strong leftist presence in the cultural and everyday life of the country, with guerrilla actions and an increasing military repression. Lesbian social circles, separated by class and professional interests, were widespread. Butch-femme codes were strict in working-class circles, popular in middle-class circles, and resisted yet present in upper-class and feminist circles. Code words for butch included *bombero* (literally firefighter, equivalent to bulldyke; still in use) and *celeste* (light blue); for femmes: *mucama* (house maid) and *rosa* (pink). Nonfeminist middle- and upper-class lesbians called themselves "better" and "gay" (both in English), while feminists began to use the word *lesbianas*. Later, *torta* (dyke) and *trola* ("lezzie") would come into use.

In the early 1970s, feminism was revived with the establishment of the Feminist Union of Argentina (UFA). Most political lesbians chose to work within it on women's issues, while remaining closeted as lesbians. In 1972, the first lesbian political group, Safo, was created, and it became the only lesbian member of the FLH (Homosexual Liberation Front), established in 1971. Members of Safo and a few others took to the streets with the FLH's gay male constituency to defy the strong homophobic tendencies of the general public and the leftist parties in the years 1973–1975.

In 1976, the military took over the government by force. During its rule, an estimated thirty thousand people were kidnapped from their homes in the middle of the night, kept in concentration camps, tortured, and finally killed. None of them received a fair trial; no one ever knew how, when, or where they died. In Argentina, they are called "the disappeared." This cruelest period in contemporary Argentinean history, which also included the devastation of the country's economy, forced lesbians back into their closets. The FLH was dismembered, as was the UFA and other feminist groups; most of the members went into exile. In place of political activity, most lesbian feminists devoted themselves to study groups, with strong security measures. There are no reports of lesbians having disappeard for being such, but, given the brutal and fascistic tendencies of the military, it is possible that, if a prisoner was suspected or known as a lesbian, her hardships would only be worse (and rape was the first and most repeated torture applied to female prisioners).

The return of democracy and lesbian exiles changed the situation dramatically. In 1984, the CHA (Argentinean Homosexual Community) was created; although gay men outnumbered lesbians in the group, lesbians have served as the organization's spokespersons. In the same year, the feminist organization Lugar de Mujer sponsored lesbian-themed workshops, through which lesbian artists and thinkers produced valuable work until internal differences and homophobia ended the experience. Slowly, lesbian bars and discos started to open. National Women's Conferences and the Latin American Feminist Encuentros (Conferences) helped many lesbians come out to themselves and/or find kindred spirits. In 1987, *Cuadernos de Existencia Lesbiana,* a lesbian magazine and group, made the lesbian presence public for the first time, during an International Women's Day celebration. In 1995, Las Lunas y las Otras (The Moons and Others) opened a lesbian feminist "house," offering a bar and workshops, movies, and parties, while the lesbian action group Lesbianas a la Vista employed street-theater techniques to make lesbian existence visible in Buenos Aires and also opened their own house in 1997, shared with Escrita en el Cuerpo (archives and library). Beginning in 1996, most lesbian, gay, bisexual, and transgender Argentinean groups began to meet at yearly national conferences taking place in different provinces each year. Pride parades have taken place in Buenos Aires since 1992; lesbians were at first reluctant to participate in them, but that has changed; after 1996, lesbians were as active and visible as other groups.

In the 1990s, lesbians from Buenos Aires obtained advantages unknown to their predecessors: meeting places, political groups, libraries, magazines (one of them with mainstream circulation), pubs and discos, and visible images of themselves. The cities of Buenos Aires and Rosario include sexual orientation in their antidiscrimination statutes.

Despite these improvements, lesbians are harassed by the police in bars and in the streets, arbitrarily arrested, and sometimes fired when their lesbianism is revealed to their employers (a fact that keeps most lesbians in the closet, given the high unemployment rates in the country). Lesbian mothers are forced into unfair private agreements with their husbands to avoid the almost certain loss of their children in court. Violence against lesbians is the norm in the most conservative areas of the country. In 1992, Erica Videla was murdered in the city of Mendoza for being a lesbian; beatings, insults, and property damage by neighbors or family members are everyday affairs. Lesbian and gay organizations have begun in several parts of the country to fight those inequities, but the struggle is only beginning.

*Alejandra Sarda*

## Bibliography

Cano, Ines. "El movimiento feminista argentino en la decada del '70" (The Argentinean Feminist Movement in the 1970s). *Revista Todo es Historia* 64 (1986), 85–93.

Fuskova, Ilse, and Claudina Marek. *Mujeres que se aman* (Women Who Love Women). Buenos Aires: Sudamericana, 1995.

Henault, Mira. "Las inmigrantes" (The Immigrants). *Revista Todo es Historia* 64 (1986), 55–61.

Hernando, Sil, and Alejandra Sarda. *Better: Oral Life Stories by Argentinean Lesbians, 1930–1976.* Toronto: Women's Press, 1997.

Kohn Loncarica, Alfredo, Argentino J. Landaburu, and Elena Pennini. "Cecilia Grierson y el Primer Congreso Femenino Internacional." *Revista Todo es Historia* 64 (1986), 62–67.

***See also*** Encuentros de Lesbianas

## Arnold, June (1926–1982)

Twentieth-century American lesbian feminist novelist and publisher. June Arnold was an important figure in the lesbian feminist literary movement of the 1970s in the United States. In addition to writing four novels, two of which have been reprinted and are considered classics of lesbian literature, she was the cofounder of the feminist publishing company Daughters Inc.

Arnold was born on October 27, 1926, in Greenville, South Carolina. Her parents were members of prominent and wealthy Southern families. After her father's death, she moved with her mother and older sister back to her mother's native city, Houston, Texas. In Houston, Arnold led the privileged life of a wealthy white Southern belle, attending the best private schools and coming out as a debutante. Like most other young women of her generation and class, Arnold followed her graduation from Rice University in 1948 by marrying and having children—five altogether, one of whom died at an early age. Unlike most of her peers, she also returned to Rice to complete an M.A. in English.

When her marriage failed, Arnold moved herself and her children to New York City's Greenwich Village, where she wrote her first novel, *Applesauce,* which was published in 1967 by McGraw-Hill, and became a militant feminist. In January 1971, when the city of New York tried to evict a group of women who had converted an abandoned city-owned building on East Third Street into a women's building, Arnold was among those who refused to leave until arrested by force. According to author Bertha Harris (1937–), this was when Arnold met her future lover and business partner, Parke Bowman (1933/1934–1992), who was one of the lawyers who came to get the women out of jail. The action also formed the core event of *The Cook and the Carpenter*, Arnold's second novel, which was published in 1973 by Daughters Inc., which she and Bowman founded the same year. By this time, Arnold and Bowman were living together and spending most of their time in Arnold's house in Vermont.

Even if she had never been a writer herself, the contribution Arnold made through Daughters Inc. would have established her as a significant figure in the history of lesbian literature in the twentieth century. During the five years of its existence, Daughters Inc. published, in most cases for the first time, twenty-two books by eighteen women, including M.F. Beal (1937–), Blanche Boyd (1945–), Rita Mae Brown (1944–), Bertha Harris (1937–), Elana Nachman (Dykewomon, 1949–), Joanna Russ (1937–), and Monique Wittig (1935–). Arnold herself published three novels: *The Cook and the Carpenter* (1973), *Sister Gin* (1975), and a reprint of *Applesauce* (1977). During this period, Arnold became a public advocate of the lesbian separatist movement, speaking in 1976 at both the national Modern Language Association Convention and the separatist Women in Print Conference, which she organized. In 1977, Daughters Inc. was featured in the *New York Times* magazine in an illustrated article on the lesbian separatist movement by Lois Gould. Believing, like many of her contemporaries, in the possibility of a full-scale feminist revolution, Arnold stressed the importance of establishing an independent communications network, free from patriarchal power, and she took a strong stand against lesbians who published with male-dominated presses.

After Daughters Inc. folded in 1978, Arnold moved back to Houston, with Bowman, and began working on her final novel, based on the life of her mother. Before she was able to finish the work, she was diagnosed with brain cancer. Despite several operations and radiation treatment, she died on March 11, 1982, at the age of fifty-five. *Baby Houston* was edited after her death and published in 1987 by Texas Monthly Press.          *Linda Dunne*

## Bibliography

Dunne, Linda. "June Arnold (1926–1982)." *Contemporary Lesbian Writers of the United States: A Bio-Bibliographical Critical Sourcebook*. Ed. Sandra Pollack and Denise D. Knight. Westport, Conn.: Greenwood, 1993.

Gould, Lois. "Creating a Woman's World." *New York Times Magazine* (January 2, 1977), 10–11, 35–37.

Harris, Bertha. Introduction. *Lover*. New York: New York University Press, 1993.

Zimmerman, Bonnie. *The Safe Sea of Women: Lesbian Fiction, 1969–1989*. Boston: Beacon, 1990.

*See also* Brown, Rita Mae; Fiction; Publishing, Lesbian; Separatism; Wittig, Monique

## Art, Contemporary European

Painting, sculpture, photography, and multimedia installations by lesbian- or queer-identified artists in Europe from 1985 to the end of the twentieth century. Although lesbian art in Europe has largely followed the pattern in North America, the number of lesbian artists exhibiting in the mainstream is smaller and less cohesive. Artists in the United Kingdom tend to look to developments in the United States rather than to other Europeans. Notoriously bound by white, upper-class privilege, the art world, in the United Kingdom, at least, has shifted markedly since 1994, partly due to lesbian and gay activism, but also because younger lesbians demand to be taken seriously, without compromising their content or being closeted.

### Historical Development

Lesbian art was marginalized or simply excluded by heterosexual feminist art in the 1970s. Artists who were lesbian dealt with the silence surrounding lesbianism in three main ways. Some saw themselves as artists, competing within the male art world, and ignored their own sexuality as subject matter. Others saw their art as part of the wider feminist aims of the women's movement. Still others made their lesbianism the central focus of their work and developed a theoretical discourse around the questions of lesbian representation. It was this latter group that was responsible for the growing presence in the 1980s of documentary photographic images to assert the visibility of "ordinary" lesbians in a positive way. Increasing homophobia, censorship, and promotion of "family" values by right-wing groups culminated in Section 28 of the Local Government Act in 1988 (known as Clause 28 before the Act was passed),

**A** which prohibited any funding of material that could be seen to "promote homosexuality." This spurred artists to defy its premise and led to a burst of lesbian and gay political and cultural activity.

Photography dominated lesbian representation in the 1980s, and Della Grace's *Love Bites* (1991), a collection exploring lesbian sadomasochism, and *Stolen Glances* (1991), a theoretical anthology of images and texts, initiated a valuable discussion around lesbian photography in the United Kingdom. Meanwhile, in Amsterdam, Diana Blok and Marlo Broekmans were producing extraordinarily fine erotic photographs that explored intense relationships between women using allegory and lyrical symbolism.

It was not until 1992 in London, when *Exposing Ourselves,* an exhibition of more than 150 works by fifty-four lesbian artists, introduced painters, such as Sue McMorran, and sculptors, such as Svar Simpson, and confronted the invisibility of out lesbians in the art world.

## Queer Influences

While figurative art (art that depicts human figures) remains the common denominator in the late 1990s, the influence of queer theory and politics, camp practices, and new technologies has made the expression of the new lesbian subject diverse. Queer has been one of the most influential and hotly contested political strategies and theorizations of the decade. Its antihomophobic, media-savvy strategies speeded up the demand for parliamentary reform in the United Kingdom with staged provocative actions, such as a mass queer wedding ceremony and a "kiss-in" in the heart of London. It aims to render redundant the binary terms of hetero- and homosexuality and to establish "queer" as a term inclusive of any sexual practice that would make the heterosexual norm strange. It claims to be free of the dominant prejudices around race and gender in imagining a queer world in which the category of "normal" would no longer have dominance. Many urban lesbian activists and artists rallied under the queer banner in the United Kingdom, in the hope of moving beyond the sexism rife among gay men and the perceived antisex prescriptiveness of some lesbian feminism. It brought an urgency and confidence to lesbian representation and a defiant "in-your-face" attitude. Just as ACT UP (AIDS Coalition to Unleash Power) has been dubbed a university for AIDS activists who graduated into all branches of health advocacy, so queer theory and politics fired up a generation of lesbian artists who could no longer accept the complacency and homophobia of the art world. If sexism and racism were no longer tolerated, why were homophobia and heterosexism?

While feminism located gender oppression as the primary category for understanding the world, queer defined sexual oppression as the primary site from which to contest inequality. However, by asserting that gender or sexuality alone constitutes identity, each risked erasing the importance of class, ethnicity, race, age, and ability.

In the United Kingdom in the late 1990s, queer has largely been derided as a crass marketing device for commodifying white gay male culture—in London, for example, a gay male club was named Call Yourself Queer. Nonetheless, queer did and continues to inspire work, from the frank, outrageous photography of Del LaGrace Volcano (formerly Della Grace) the grotesque cat-skin sculptures of Christina Berry, and the camp, ironic paintings of Sadie Lee and Dawn Mellor (all United Kingdom) to the adventurous CD-ROM art of Linda Dement and Venus Matrix in Australia.

One of the most significant aspects of queer culture is address: Art, performance, music, and text are addressed to the potential queer audience as opposed to the assumed heterosexual audience. This work is not designed to tell the straights how queers live and love to gain their acceptance, but speaks to queers themselves with their own self-referential irony and humor, regardless of whether the heterosexuals "get it" or not. It is not coming out to "them," it is coming on to themselves. Queer lesbian artists revel in their alienation, creating works that testify to their sense of disenfranchisement from mainstream, heterosexual culture. While lesbian feminist artists tried to cohere around a fixed notion of sexual identity in the 1970s and 1980s, many contemporary queer artists are located around an agreed sense of the mutability of identity and gender, a questioning of what "dyke" is, was, and will become. If lesbian feminist art was characterized by being serious, affirmational, straightforward, confessional, and didactic, queer dyke art is conspiratorial, lying, allusive, and ironic.

## Developments at the End of the 1990s

The emergence of a younger generation of black and asian artists in the United Kingdom encouraged black and Asian lesbians to create work, but, as of 1998 only two, Ingrid Pollard and Lola Flash, had had solo representation. While Flash is known for her distinc-

*The Dodge Brothers by Del LaGrace, 1997. Courtesy of Del LaGrace.*

tive reverse color style (printing the "negative" rather than the positive image) and prosex content, Pollard is reluctant to be viewed as a "lesbian" artist, since her work prioritizes race, rather than gender and sexuality, in a white, dominant culture.

The politics of race also informs the work of British Asian photographer Perminder Sekhon. When she situated *Four Asian Butches* (of the 1997 photograph of that name) outside a "Cash and Carry" grocery store, she was referencing the socioeconomic realities for many Asians in Britain, whose livelihood relies on wholesale merchandizing, as well as commenting on the exclusion of these women from the male-run family business, despite their sharp suits and ties. In a culture in which gender is heavily encoded in traditional clothing—suits and saris—the butches' transgression is more marked.

While queer may have lost its radical potential, the energy that sparked its provenance is still evident in much art by lesbians in the late 1990s, which ranges from genderfuck (playing with gender expectations) to genrefuck (parodying traditional art genres), stealing heterosexual icons, pillaging the art-historical canon, challenging the established

concepts of what constitutes "art" and what constitutes "lesbian art." Artists have used materials considered unsuitable for art, such as rubber and latex, and have reconstructed as art some objects that were formerly seen as pornographic or obscene. British conceptual sculptor Andy Cohen created pure silicon buttplugs, colored by nontoxic pigment or with high-minimalist blocks of color, to aestheticize what is normally seen as functional and highly private. Blurring the line between art and product, Cohen also makes a wry comment on the way sex toys have been cast as too low to be worthy of critical attention.

In the mid-1990s, lesbian codes gained a wider currency, and irony flourished in the energy of a knowing humor, which engaged a more popular audience beyond the queer ghettos. When painter Sadie Lee took the classic *Mona Lisa* and repainted it, inserting an exquisitely dressed butch as the central figure, and called it *Bona Lisa* (1992), this was dyke camp. All viewers got the joke, but lesbians laughed loudest. As gay male camp became increasingly sanitized and televized, dyke camp (for want of a better word) provided a sharper subversive edge

**A** since women remain culturally denigrated. Turning straight culture's artifacts into double entendres and pitting self-deprecation against glorious abjection can be significantly more radical. Frustrated by endless gay parodies of female stars, painter Dawn Mellor sought to reclaim camp and become part of it on her own terms. Her portraits of Judy Garland, Bette Davis, and Marilyn Monroe, among others, seriously disrupt the iconic image of the untouchable female star. Several of these explore motherhood, showing the star replicating her thoughtless, unseeing collusion with passive stardom in her child. One shows a woman with a child up her skirt, in a direct paralleling of the work of New York artist Carrie Moyer. Another shows the baby incorporated into the mother's breast as though the artist envies its proximity to the female star's body.

Themes around gender bending, gender blending, and transgender, evident in North American art, have been just as prominent in art in Europe and have exerted a huge influence on how lesbian art and the gender continuum are discussed. Greek artists Katerina Thomadaki and Maria Klonaris, living in Paris, have been working since 1985 on *The Angel Cycle,* which started from a medical photograph of a case in intersexuality, a subject whose sex cannot be defined within the male/female dichotomy and whose body becomes a powerful metaphor for the collapse of gender. It includes up to twenty works that have been shown internationally, consisting of multimedia performances, photo-sculptures, sound pieces, radio broadcasts, computer animations, and videos, which layer and reinvoke the image, drawing out its erotic and shape-shifting possibilities. They, too, are skeptical about the use of the label "lesbian art" about their work, which destabilizes stereotypes, including lesbian.

Del LaGrace Volcano (formerly Della Grace), an American photographer living in London, has documented the city's drag king scene since 1992 and increasingly considers the term "lesbian" a misnomer. Having identified as lesbian for more than twenty years, Grace prefers to be described as transgender or as, her/his invented term, "hermaphrodyke"—intersexual as opposed to transsexual.

Some artists have refuted the queer rubric. The work of working-class painter Mandy McCartin, who has been portraying London's urban nightlife since the mid-1980s, has not been radically affected by the queer aesthetic. Her gritty, graffiti-laden images of mean-mouthed skinheads and tough sex workers were uncompromising from the outset and

*"Feeding Time" by Dawn Mellor, 1997. Courtesy Dawn Mellor.*

could be called queer before their time. McCartin's work could also be dubbed "outsider" art, since her socialist satire is out of line with the neoconceptual and ironic figuration in contemporary gallery vogue.

Most artists who are lesbians showing in major galleries in Europe, such as Natascha Kassner in Berlin, Jaya Schurch in Italy and Switzerland, Patricia Hurl and Therry Rudin in Dublin, Ange et Damnation in Paris, and Sadie Lee and Dawn Mellor in London and Manchester, are aware of treading a thin line between success and co-option. They are all concerned about the danger of becoming invisible as lesbians the moment they gain visibility as artists. Sadie Lee faced rumors of censorship when her (1997) solo show in London's National Portrait Gallery exhibited a series of scantily clad, former burlesque dancers, despite a tradition of female nudes on those venerable walls.

At the end of the millennium, some argue that there is no such thing as lesbian or gay art—or transgendered or queer art. There is art made by lesbians, gay men, transgendered, and queer-identified artists, and there is work that represents texts or figures that can be said to operate within these identities. An exhibition of works by lesbians seeks to expose the heterocentricity of the mainstream art world, most visible at its margins, and to continue to assert the existence of lesbian artists and celebrate their diversity. But for many, it is no longer enough. Given the choice, most European lesbian artists desire that their work also be positioned within a mainstream context to challenge its confines and determine critical recognition and financial success.

*Cherry Smyth*

## Bibliography

Ashburn, Elizabeth. *Lesbian Art: An Encounter with Power*. An Art and Australia Book. Sydney: Craftsman House, 1996.

Boffin, Tessa, and Jean Fraser. *Stolen Glances: Lesbians Take Photographs*. London: Pandora, 1991.

Cooper, Emmanuel. *The Sexual Perspective: Homosexuality and Art in the Last 100 Years in the West*. London: Routledge, 1986. 2nd ed. London: Routledge, 1994.

Grace, Della. *Love Bites*. London: Gay Men's Press, 1991.

McCartin, Mandy. *From the Street: Paintings and Drawings by Mandy McCartin*. London: Gay Men's Press, 1996.

Smyth, Cherry. *Damn Fine Art by New Lesbian Artists*. London: Cassell, 1996.

*See also* Art, Contemporary North American; Camp; Photography; Queer Theory; Video

## Art, Contemporary North American

Visual representations by self-identified feminist artists after 1970. There have always been lesbians who made art and artists who were lesbian, but the category lesbian art did not exist until 1970. In the United States, the gay and women's liberation movements, based respectively on sexual orientation and gender, led to the newly formed identity lesbian feminist and her cultural counterpart, the lesbian artist, who was assumed to be feminist.

## Definitions of Lesbian Art

While there is no agreement as to what constitutes lesbian art, it is generally thought to reflect lesbian identity and to contribute to the development of that identity. However, just as there is not one lesbian identity, there is no single lesbian aesthetic. Both vary with class, race, age, and geography. Both change with the times. For instance, as lesbian identity shifted from a gender-based definition of lesbianism rooted in radical lesbian feminism of the 1970s to a more sexually based definition in the 1980s and 1990s, imagery in lesbian art shifted from an abstraction based on organic forms that symbolically suggested women's genitalia and lesbian sexuality to realistic paintings of cunts or women engaged in explicit lesbian sexual activities. The art moved from a celebration of "sameness" to a flaunting of "difference."

Is the quality "lesbian" embodied in the art object, the sexuality of the artist, the sexuality of the viewer, or the viewing context? This question, which assumes and proposes difference from art by men or straight feminists, circulates around all discussions of lesbian art and refuses an easy answer. It can be any or all of the above. Lesbian art is not a stylistic movement, but rather art that comes out of a feminist consciousness and represents the experience of being a lesbian in patriarchal culture. This consciousness may be implicitly or explicitly articulated. It may vary in style, imagery, materials used, concept, or content and can be figurative, symbolic, abstract, or conceptual.

## Art of the 1970s

As lesbian feminism was considered an extension of feminism ("feminism is the theory; lesbianism, the practice"), lesbian art was considered an extension of feminist art. Because lesbian definitions were broadened to include any woman-identified woman, female space depicted symbolically, through landscape, fruit, and flower imagery, was, by extension, considered lesbian, especially if the artist was lesbian identified. Themes that reoccurred frequently were anger, concealment, secrecy, guilt, coming out, celebrating the female body, referencing historical lesbian writers and artists, and picturing lesbians in the workplace or domestic environment. Portraits were common but decontextualized and avoided representing lesbians in subcultural spaces, such as bars. With the feminist position of not representing or objectifying women's bodies and downplaying sexuality, there were abstract images of cunts, clitorises, breasts, and vaginas or two women being warm and affectionate with each other (the second woman being the lesbian signifier), but the work almost never displayed them "doing it." Lesbian sexuality was hinted at, but rarely shown, or was humorously related to food.

With the proliferation of movement publications, there was a demand for images of lesbians by lesbians. It was not long before art was found on the

**A** walls of women's centers, bars, coffee shops, restaurants, and bookstores. Additionally, there was a strong and growing lesbian presence in feminist art projects that ranged from small consciousness-raising art groups to women's cooperative art galleries and art programs. Occasionally, lesbians exhibited with gay men. By the mid-1970s, there were a number of exclusively lesbian art exhibitions, publications, and projects. However, due to homophobia in ethnic communities and racism within feminist communities and the fact that most early feminist and lesbian art projects were organized by collectives composed almost entirely of white women, lesbian artists of color were absent from most early lesbian art projects. In the 1970s, the focus was on the shared experiences of women. Differences due to race, class, and sexuality were not easily dealt with or reflected in art. While lesbians in the United States were aware of art by lesbians in other countries, such as Canada, Mexico, England, Ireland, France, Italy, Germany, Australia, and New Zealand, there was not much exchange or influence except through feminist magazines.

In New York City, *Heresies: A Feminist Publication on Art and Politics* published "Lesbian Art and Artists" (1977). Focusing exclusively on lesbian creative work, "Lesbian Art and Artists" was the first step in filling the historical and theoretical silence around lesbian art and artists and placed contemporary art in a continuum of lesbian culture. *A Lesbian Show* (1978), curated by Harmony Hammond at the 112 Greene Street Workshop, was the first exhibition of lesbian art in New York. While no lesbian aesthetic or sensibility emerged from the art, the exhibition, which presented work by eighteen artists willing to be out in this context, was important in that it created a lesbian presence and stimulated dialogue in the mainstream and feminist art worlds and generated an art consciousness in lesbian communities.

In California, Arlene Raven, one of the founders of the Los Angeles Woman's Building, initiated a series of lesbian-based projects within the structure of the Feminist Studio Workshop (FSW): the Los Angeles League for the Advancement of Lesbianism in the Arts (LALALA) exhibition and celebration in 1975; the Natalie Barney collective that focused on historical research and documentation of lesbian artists; and the Lesbian Art Project (LAP), a three-year program of workshops, salons, and art presentations started in 1977 and continued with Terry Wolverton.

The lion-headed Barbara Urselin, born in 1641 in Augsburg, from Aldrovandus' *Opera Omnia Monstrum Historia*, 1668 *Poster for the issue "Lesbian Art and Artists" (Fall 1977) of* Heresies: A Feminist Publication of Art & Politics. *Courtesy of Harmony Hammond.*

Lesbian artists of the 1970s include Judith F. Baca, Joan E. Biren (Jeb), Janet Cooling, Tee A. Corinne, Betsy Damon, Maxine Fine, Louise Fishman, Nancy Fried, Harmony Hammond, Debbie Jones, Lili Lakich, Bettye Lane, Kate Millet, Hollis Sigler, Joan Snyder, and Fran Winant.

### Art of the 1980s

The 1980s started off with numerous projects and exhibitions of lesbian art that continued the momentum generated by the gay and women's liberation movements of the previous decade and culminated in two major exhibitions: the *Great American Lesbian Art Show* (GALAS) at the Woman's Building in Los Angeles (1980), and *Extended Sensibilities: Homosexual Presence in Contemporary Art* at the New Museum in Manhattan (1982). GALAS, organized by a collective of artists from the FSW, was noteworthy for its innovative curatorial structure: a national exhibition honoring the work of ten "out" artists who were role models for other lesbian artists, a network of more than two hundred regional "sister" exhibitions, and archives that documented the whole project. GALAS also marked the first time that lesbians of color participated in a major exhibition of lesbian art. *Extended Sensibilities,* the first museum exhibition in the United States to address the subject of homosexuality in contemporary art, included work by eight lesbian artists who had been out in the 1970s. The work in both of these exhibitions, like that in *Heresies* and *A Lesbian Show,* was diverse and nonsexual.

After *Extended Sensibilities,* there was an eight-year hiatus of projects in the art world that focused on lesbian art or artists. Lesbians continued to make and exhibit all kinds of art during this period, but there were no highly publicized exhibitions. This was primarily due to the media-generated backlash against feminism that combined with the postmodern criticism and dismissal of 1970s essentialist feminism and any art that came out of it. Postmodern feminism positioned heterosexual feminism as the norm from which to discuss the construction and representation of all women, thereby denying the potential of lesbian subjectivity. While the so-called sex wars reestablished lesbians as sexual beings, the sexual lesbian was not visually represented in fine art until the end of the decade, when lesbian artists asserted their sexuality in response to the AIDS crisis and right-wing censorship of the National Endowment for the Arts' funding of projects by artists of color and those of a "different" sexuality. This burst of creative activity signaled a growing lesbian, gay, and queer renaissance in the art world.

Favored over painting and sculpture for its supposed authenticating properties, photography became the medium of choice for self-representing difference or negotiating multiple identities. Most of the work relied on mechanical reproduction and was cool, detached, and disembodied. Reoccurring themes included deconstructing scientific, pathological, and medical definitions and representations of lesbians and the resulting stereotypes; appropriating fine-art and media images for lesbian purposes; abstract references to the lesbian body as a sexual and gendered social site; scrambling or queering signifiers of gender and sexuality; deconstructing masculinity; and reconstructing lesbian sexual identities. Lesbian queer activism combined with sex-radical imagery that had been developing separately throughout the 1980s in lesbian sex journals and 'zines. Gone was the good girl, politically correct lesbian of the 1970s. The new lesbian artist was interested in exploring and representing sexually charged spaces, activities, and identities that were previously taboo, such as butch-femme and S/M exchange.

Lesbian artists of the 1980s include Laura Aguilar, Catherine Allport, Virginia Benavidez, Deborah Bright, Kaucyila Brooke, Gaye Chan, Lenore Chinn, Heide Fasnacht, Del LaGrace, Carole Hepper, Deborah Kass, Ester Hernandez, Caroline Hinkley, Ann Meredith, Mary Patten, Marcia Salo, Connie Samaras, Susan Silton, Margaret Stratton, and Millie Wilson; Canadian artists G.B. Jones, Lyne Lapointe; Martha Fleming, and the Kiss and Tell Collective, who have exhibited extensively in the United States.

## Art of the 1990s

While the privileging of theoretically oriented feminism contributed to the dearth of visible art by lesbians throughout much of the 1980s, it also profoundly affected the work that did emerge at the end of the decade and developed in the 1990s. Informed by postmodern theory, the work dealt with the self-representation of lesbian sexual and sexualized activities; the development of a lesbian erotic art; family values; the occupation of sites of masculinity; the destruction of binary constructions of gender by way of drag, cross-dressing, performance, and surgically or hormonally altering the body; and the invasion of male-dominated fields, such as painting, cultural displacement, and activist art.

Despite the supposed gender-free territory of queer theory that many lesbians embraced, the lesbian artist was not welcome when it came to occupying queer exhibition spaces. To paraphrase historian Cassandra Langer, lesbians, caught between straight feminists and the gay male agenda, often did not exist at all or were deprived of a political existence by their inclusion as female versions of male homosexuality. Being lesbian is being marginal in an already marginal network.

It was not until the all-lesbian exhibition *All But the Obvious* (ABO), curated by Pam Gregg for the Los Angeles Center of Exhibitions (LACE) in 1990, that a strong lesbian presence was asserted within the queer visual field. ABO identified a new group of lesbian artists and influenced the direction that lesbian art would take throughout the 1990s. Intended as a challenge to the reductive and asexual aesthetics advanced by many lesbian artists of the 1970s, ABO raised questions about the relationship of representation to the construction of sexual identity. Most of the work was either photography or photo based—a reflection of its roots in postmodern feminism of the 1980s. The major difference between ABO and earlier exhibitions was its inclusion of sexually explicit lesbian images.

The 1990s witnessed a number of significant events for lesbian artists. In 1990, Lesbian Visual Artists (LVA), an organization that sponsors exhibitions and symposiums, was founded in San Francisco. There were important exhibitions in Boulder, Colorado; Chicago, Illinois; Houston and San Antonio, Texas; Irvine, California; Atlanta, Georgia; Seattle, Washington; and other places, in addition to New York City, Los Angeles, and San Francisco. Lesbian artists were well represented in the many 1994 exhibitions celebrating the twenty-fifth anniversary of the Stonewall Rebellion. *In A Different Light* (1995), a survey of queer sensibility at the University of California, Berkeley, was a historical attempt to situate lesbian, gay, and queer art making in twentieth-century art.

Lesbians artists of the 1990s include Kim Anno, Judie Bamber, Tammy Rae Carland, Patricia Cronin, Deborah Edmeades, Nicole Eisenman, Joy Episalla, Donna Evans, Maria Elena Gonzalez, Mary Klein, Julia Kunin, Zoe Leonard, Monica Majoli, Linda Matalon, Marlene McCarty, Carrie Moyer, Catherine Opie, Hanh Thi Pham, Sarah Rapson, Elizabeth Stephens, Nicola Tyson, Fan Warren, Carrie Yamaoka, and activist art by Dyke Action Machine (DAM), Fierce Pussy, Lesbian Avengers, and Oral Majority. Most lesbian artists who emerged in the 1970s and 1980s are also artists of the 1990s.

In the 1990s, lesbian art was produced and circulated primarily within lesbian communities and feminist art spaces, although the art world bestowed momentary visibility on a few lesbian artists, and lesbian work was included in exhibitions at commercial galleries and museums. Once discovered, lesbian artists had to step carefully to get the attention due their work without being co-opted in the process. Ultimately, it has been, and remains, the insistence on self-identification, self-representation, and the unruly diverse nature of lesbian art itself, both the production and the surrounding discourse, that has the power to resist cultural commodification while combating the invisibility and erasure of lesbians and lesbian content in fine art.

*Harmony Hammond*

### Bibliography

Blake, Nayland, Lawrence Rinder, and Amy Scholder, eds. *In a Different Light: Visual Culture, Sexual Identity, Queer Practice*. San Francisco: City Lights Books, 1995.

Cotter, Holland. "Art After Stonewall: 12 Artists Interviewed." *Art in America* 82 (June 1994), 56–65.

Cronin, Patricia, ed. "Representing Lesbian Subjectivities." *Art Papers* 18:6 (November/December 1994) (Special Issue).

Hammond, Harmony. "A Space of Infinite and Pleasurable Possibilities: Lesbian Self-Representation in Visual Art." In *New Feminist Criticism: Art, Identity, Action*. Ed. Joanna Frueh, Cassandra Langer, and Arlene Raven. New York: Icon Editions, 1994, pp. 97–131.

Rando, Flavia, and Jonathan Weinberg, eds. "We're Here: Gay and Lesbian Presence in Art." *Art Journal* 55:4 (Winter 1996) (Special Issue).

"Lesbian Art and Artists." *Heresies: A Feminist Publication on Art and Politics* 3 (Fall 1977) (Special Issue).

*See also* Art, Contemporary European; Photography; Video

## Art, Mainstream

"Mainstream" art generally refers to art considered important by the society in question. Historically, it is a confusing designation because art that was considered "mainstream" in the era of its creation may not be the artwork of the period studied or taught currently. For example, twentieth-century art history emphasizes the art of the Renaissance that was important during that period. However, regarding the nineteenth century, art-historical interest focuses on formal innovation, prioritizing the impressionists, the pointillists, and the postimpressionists. In that time period, such work was considered relatively marginal, while academic or salon painting, which is now considered of little importance, held the highest status. Further, media and subject matter are designated as "higher" or "lower" art forms in various eras. Classical Greek vase painting is considered "art," while most ceramics of later periods are considered "crafts" or possibly "decorative arts." Photography continues to occupy a contested space somewhere between art and craft. From the Renaissance on, easel painting and freestanding sculpture have been the media most generally considered "mainstream art" in European-American cultures.

### Representation of Lesbians

The representation of lesbians is a complex issue. The first complication arises from the difficulty of identifying the subject matter of a representation as a lesbian. Basically, the subject matter of a representation is identified as a lesbian in one of four ways.

First, the representation is of two or more unclothed female figures. The figures need not be engaged in explicitly sexual interaction, as the state of nakedness generally signifies eroticism in a Western cultural context. Second, the representation is of a female couple somehow breaking the social norms for acceptable behavior between women. Third, the representation participates in a stereotypical view of lesbian appearance, such as the "butch," the crossdresser, the 1970s flannel-shirted androgyne, or the 1990s shaved-head, tattooed, pierced urban dyke. Fourth, the representation is defined as that of a lesbian by extrapictorial information, either in the title (for example, *The Lovers*) or in the viewer's knowledge that the figure represented, historical or fictional, had same-sex relationships, such as Sappho (ca. 600 B.C.E.) or Gertrude Stein (1874–1946).

Clearly, there are limitations to all of these defining factors. The first reduces the lesbian to sexual behavior; the second recognizes the lesbian only as a dyad, not as an individual. The third participates in very limited social assumptions about style choices as identifiers of the lesbian, and the fourth requires specialized information to recognize the lesbian. All four are culturally specific to European-American cultures, as is the contemporary definition of "lesbian." Further, it is not terribly difficult to imagine representations that fit one or more of the above criteria and are not, in fact, representations of lesbians. However, discussions of representations of lesbians in art invariably use these criteria, even when addressing representations produced in non-European-American cultures.

Further complications in the discussion of representations of lesbians in art are found in issues of reception and interpretation. Lesbian studies as a field is divided on the interpretation of representations of lesbians. Some scholars argue that representations of lesbians produced by male artists or male-oriented female artists are strictly male-oriented fantasies, controlled by stereotypical assumptions, and laden with negative implications and have nothing to do with "real" lesbians. Others maintain that any representations of lesbians contribute to greater visibility and promote diverse understandings of lesbians and that even "negative" representations can have transgressive effects.

## History
Sexually explicit representation is often seen in artifacts of ancient Greek and Roman culture, including some depictions of female same-sex activity, though depictions of heterosexual and male same-sex activity are found more frequently. It is unclear whether these ancient cultures produced few representations of female same-sex activity or whether such depictions were destroyed in later periods. Much of the work of Sappho of Lesbos, the famous female poet of the Greek classical period whose poems often described love between women, was destroyed in the early Christian era, and it seems probable that sexually explicit visual representations would have been equally, or more, likely to be destroyed. Portraits of Sappho also exist, although they were created several centuries later; no contemporary portraits have been found.

Possible female homoerotic subtexts exist in some popular themes of Renaissance art, particularly depictions of witches and the three Graces. Witches were frequently portrayed nude and in all-female groups, which is sexually suggestive, given that witches were often described as participating in sexual debauchery. Hans Baldung Grien's (1484/1485–1545) *The Three Witches* (1514) depicts the women in spread-legged positions, focusing on the buttocks and genitals while touching themselves and one another. Albrecht Durer's (1471–1528) *The Four Witches* (1497) portrays the women in much more conventionally demure, standing positions, and the spatial relations and positioning make it difficult to tell whether the figures are in physical contact. In addition, although the figures are unclothed, two of them wear head coverings that suggest they are servants or working-class women, while the headdresses of the other two suggest that they are upper class. This contrast may have been suggestive of inappropriate crossings of class boundaries that support a homoerotic subtext. Since Durer also produced work with explicit male homoerotic themes and there is biographical information to suggest that he was involved in same-sex activities and relationships, it is likely that the female homoeroticism of his *Witches* was deliberate.

The positioning of the figures of the three Graces in Sandro Botticelli's (1444/1445–1510) *Primavera* (1478) is similar to Durer's positioning of his witches. Whether Renaissance culture equated the paganism of the ancient Greek Graces with the contemporary notion of pagan witches is unclear. Though Durer's witches are far more restrained and conventionally feminine than Grien's, they are far less romanticized than Botticelli's Graces. Like Durer, Botticelli also produced male homoerotic representation and was probably involved in same-sex relationships. *The*

A
*Three Graces* (1636–1640) of Peter Paul Rubens (1577–1640) is less ambiguous than either Durer's witches or Botticelli's Graces. In Rubens's version, the unclothed female figures are clearly touching and embracing one another. Rubens's interest in the depiction of nude female figures in affectionate and intimate contact extended beyond his repetition of the popular theme of the three Graces. In both *The Arrival of Marie de Medici in Marseilles* and *The Education of Marie de Medici* of the Medici series (1622–1625), there are groupings of nude female figures touching and caressing one another. It is possible that these representations are connected thematically to the paganism of the witches and the Graces, since rumors circulated that Marie de Medici was involved in witchcraft.

In the eighteenth century, explicit depictions of female same-sex activities and female autoeroticism became more common. Representations of both behaviors sometimes included the use of dildos. Primarily, these were illustrations for erotic novels such as *Therese Philosophe* (1780), attributed to Denis Diderot (1713–1784) among others, the Marquis de Sade's (1740–1814) various works, *The Memoirs of Casanova* (1826–1838), and numerous anonymously published epistles. Such depictions also occurred in political propaganda around the French Revolution, particularly in reference to Marie Antoinette (1755–1793) and her alleged sexual relationship with the Princesse de Lamballe (1749–1792). Although illustrations and political pamphlets are not usually considered to be part of mainstream art, the proliferation of such images is worth noting. Given the marginalization of same-sex activities in many historical periods, it is not surprising that more representations are available in forms meant for private viewing rather than for public, mainstream display.

## The Nineteenth Century

By the nineteenth century, representations of lesbians proliferate, particularly in France. Well-established conventions dictated representations of lesbians, and similar conventions persisted into the twentieth century. These conventions substitute other markers of difference for the heterosexual male/female dyad. Differences in coloring, race, age, or status substitute for gender difference. Lesbians were also placed in specific environments; in French painting, for example, the lesbian appears most often in the context of the harem or the brothel, both all-female living arrangements explic-

itly organized for the sexual service of men. Paintings did not represent lesbians in boarding schools or convents, though such locales were common contexts for the representation of lesbians in literature and erotica.

The harem representations were situated within the genre of painting known as Orientalism. Orientalism describes the European fascination with studying and representing the "Orient," which described South Asia, North Africa, Turkey, and the Persian Gulf countries. Although purported to be objective scholarship, Orientalism viewed the non-Western cultures in question through assumptions of European dominance and superiority and was conceptually tied to imperialism and colonialism. Orientalist depictions usually represent lesbians through sexualized nudity, sometimes with explicit physical contact, such as Jules-Robert Auguste's (1789–1850) *The Lovers* (1820s) or Jean-Auguste-Dominique Ingres's (1780–1867) *The Turkish Bath* (1863), and sometimes without, such as the bathing scenes of Jean-Léon Gérôme (1824–1904) and Edouard Debat-Ponsan (1847–1913).

Some scholars have asserted that harems and mixed-race female couples were so closely associated with lesbianism that all representations of a black woman and a white woman would have been read as lesbian. Similarly, scholars have asserted that nudity was so closely associated with prostitution that all female nudes in European contexts would have been read as prostitutes. Clearly, these connections among the harem, the brothel, and "the lesbian" indicate that French nineteenth-century culture had shared concerns around the three that probably related to race, class, and the role of women as sites of social disorder. British and some American representations of lesbians in the nineteenth century share similar conventions, but, since the British and American representations occur predominantly at the end of the century, it is uncertain whether they shared similar cultural concerns with the French or were simply influenced by the visual conventions. Portraits of Sappho were produced in France and Britain in the eighteenth and nineteenth centuries, but her relations with women were deemphasized or ignored in order to depict her as an acceptable literary icon, and it is not certain that most viewers would have identified her as a lesbian historical figure.

Gustave Courbet (1819–1879) produced two of the most striking images of lesbians in the nineteenth century, *The Awakening* or *Venus and Psyche*

(1864) and *Sleep* (1866). Although both paintings participate in some of the conventions of lesbian representation, they lack the more overt substitutions of heterosexual difference. In the *Awakening*, a dark-haired woman is leaning over a sleeping fair-haired woman, holding a flower over her face. In the later version of the painting, the figures are half-length and nude to the waist. An earlier version, now lost and assumed destroyed, is believed to have had full-length life-size figures. In the smaller version, the cropping of the frame emphasizes the passionate intensity of the gaze of the dark-haired figure. *Sleep* portrays two entwined, full-length, nude, female figures, one blonde and the other brunette. Both are asleep; the blonde's head is resting on the brunette's shoulder, with her lips near the other's breast. The brunette figure's leg is thrown over the blonde figure's waist, and the blonde figure rests her hand on the calf of the leg. While the eroticized portrayal of Courbet's images certainly participates in the depiction of lesbians for consumption by male viewers, the intensity and the sensuality of the representations appeal to many twentieth-century lesbian viewers. Courbet's lesbians are the subject of much scholarly debate.

Except for the portraits of Sappho, which may not definitely have been interpreted as lesbian, the representations discussed above fall into the first category of lesbian subject matter: the sexualized nude. It is not until the last decade of the nineteenth century that other categories of lesbian representation appear. Henri de Toulouse-Lautrec's (1864–1901) series of depictions of lesbians is remarkably free of the established conventions. Although many are part of his brothel series of the 1890s, which depicted the lives of prostitutes and, thus, participate in the conventional location of the lesbian in a sexual milieu designed for male use, these representations are much less sexualized than those of earlier artists, and physical difference between the women is not exaggerated to substitute for gender difference. Toulouse-Lautrec's portrayals utilize the second category of identifiable lesbians: a female couple whose interactions contravene social norms for same-sex interactions. His lesbian couples embrace, recline, lay a head on the other's shoulder, and are not unclothed. Other pictures in the series, depicting nightlife in Montmartre, rupture the conventions even more radically by portraying lesbian couples at the theater and dancing in nightclubs. These are the first representations of lesbians in mainstream art—Toulouse-Lautrec was a popular painter in his own era—that move lesbians out of private, sexualized contexts and into public life.

## Lesbian Artists

It is also in the last decades of the nineteenth century that lesbian artists began to create representations of lesbians. American painter Anna Klumpke's (1856–1942) 1898 portrait of her lover, the French artist Rosa Bonheur (1822–1899), is probably the best known and most mainstream of these images; it hangs in the Metropolitan Museum of Art in New York City. Another French artist, Louise Abbéma (1858–1927), conducted a long, passionate relationship with the flamboyant actress Sarah Bernhardt (1844–1923), producing her first portrait of her in 1875 and her last in 1922. The turn-of-the-century American photographer Alice Austen (1866–1952), who specialized in documenting the lives of the working classes, also documented the lives of her lovers and friends, including humorous images of them three to a bed at a "slumber party" and cross-dressed as men, complete with mustaches.

By the 1920s, lesbian social circles flourished in a number of cities. Romaine Brooks (1874–1870) was a member of the Paris group that included writer Natalie Barney (1876–1972), Brooks's lover of many years, and Radclyffe Hall (1880–1943), author of *The Well of Loneliness* (1928). Brooks painted portraits of Barney and Hall's lover, Una Troubridge (1887–1963). Troubridge wears men's clothing in her portrait, as does Brooks in her self-portrait. Along with her portraits of well-known lesbians, Brooks produced numerous paintings of pale, ethereal, androgynous women. Hannah Gluckstein (1895–1978), known as Gluck, was an English painter who shared Brooks's interest in themes of androgyny. She also cropped her hair, wore men's clothes, and painted her self-portrait in this attire but avoided the chic social circles of the Paris lesbians, although she also came from a wealthy family. Brooks painted a portrait of Gluck, but Gluck's portrait of Brooks was never completed because Brooks so disliked the image after the initial sitting that she refused to sit for another session, and the portrait was never completed. Coincidently, Hall and Troubridge had also disliked Brooks's portrait of Troubridge.

Another member of the Paris circle was the American writer and artist Djuna Barnes (1892–1982), who included caricatures of her lesbian friends and acquaintances in her illustrated books

The Book of Repulsive Women (1915), Ladies' Almanac (1928), and Ryder (1928). She and her lover, the American sculptor Thelma Wood (1901–1970), were both photographed in 1922 by Berenice Abbot (1898–1991), an American photographer who photographed many of the lesbian and gay artistic figures of New York City.

Both the Polish painter Tamara de Lempicka (1898–1980) and the Argentinean-born Leonor Fini (1908–1996), who began painting in the 1920s and 1930s, respectively, included images of lesbians among their many paintings of women. Unlike their contemporaries, their images are explicitly sexual and depict female same-sex desire as passionate and powerful. Probably the most prolific lesbian producer of lesbian images in the 1920s and the early 1930s was the German artist Jeanne Mammen (1910–1976). Under the relative freedom of the Weimar government, a diverse lesbian subculture flourished in Berlin. Mammen illustrated lesbian- and gay-oriented publications, pamphlets, and brochures, in addition to producing her own drawings and paintings that depicted many aspects of lesbian culture.

As more scholarship focused on the representation of women and of lesbians is produced, a more nuanced understanding of the historical conventions regarding the representation of lesbians will probably develop. Feminist art scholarship remains a fairly new field, and research specifically focused on lesbian themes has an even shorter history. Since feminist art historians often display discomfort and unease when discussing lesbian content, it is unsurprising that mainstream-art historians have more or less ignored the subject. Even given this lack of attention, late-twentieth-century scholarship already demonstrates that female same-sex activities, orientations, and relationships between women have been represented since the Renaissance in Western mainstream art.                    *Gwendolyn Alden Dean*

### Bibliography

Bernheimer, Charles. *Figures of Ill-Repute: Representing Prostitution in Nineteenth-Century France*. Cambridge, Mass.: Harvard University Press, 1989.

Chadwick, Whitney. *Women, Art, and Power*. London: Thames and Hudson, 1996.

Cooper, Emmanuel. *The Sexual Perspective: Homosexuality and Art in the Last 100 Years in the West*. New York: Routledge, 1986. 2nd ed. London: Routledge, 1994.

Dijkstra, Bram. *Idols of Perversity: Fantasies of Feminine Evil in Turn-of-the-Century Culture*. New York: Oxford University Press, 1986.

Faunce, Sarah, and Linda Nochlin, eds. *Courbet Reconsidered*. New Haven, Conn.: Yale University Press, 1988.

Néret, Gilles. *Erotica Universalis*. Köln, Germany: Benedikt Taschen, 1994.

Webb, Peter. *The Erotic Arts*. New York: Farrar, Straus, and Giroux, 1983.

***See also*** Antiquity; Austen, Alice; Barnes, Djuna Chappell; Barney, Natalie; Bonheur, Rosa; Brooks, Romaine; Gluck (Hannah Gluckstein); Harems; Marie Antoinette; Sappho

## Arzner, Dorothy (1900–1979)

U.S. film director. The most successful woman director in Hollywood during the 1930s, she had a career that spanned three decades. Dorothy Arzner was the great exception in Hollywood—a woman director who endured and whose career bridged the transition from silent to sound film. Arzner was born in San Francisco and moved to Los Angeles at a young age. She began her career in motion pictures after disillusionment with her planned career of medicine. Determined to learn all there was to know about motion-picture production, she started as a script typist, then moved on to become a cutter, an editor, and a screenplay writer. Arzner directed her first film, *Fashions for Women*, for Paramount Studios, in 1927. She remained at Paramount until 1932, then continued to work as an independent director until 1943, when she directed her last film, *First Comes Courage*. Throughout her career, Arzner was known as a "starmaker," as a director particularly adept at fashioning careers for her stars, especially her female stars. Paramount's most valuable and successful star in the 1920s was Clara Bow (1905–1965), and the fact that Paramount entrusted Arzner with Bow's first sound film (*The Wild Party* [1929]) indicates the respect Arzner commanded. Among those actresses who completed early (and, in some cases, their first) starring roles with Arzner were Katharine Hepburn (1907–), Ruth Chatterton (1893–1961), and Rosalind Russell (1911–1976). After leaving Hollywood, Arzner worked on a number of projects—she had a radio show, directed television commercials, and taught filmmaking.

Like most gay men and lesbians in Hollywood, Arzner was officially in the closet. But Arzner's style (tailored suits, short hair, thick eyebrows) suggested what was "officially" hidden, and her butch appearance was often noted by writers and commentators of her time. Her lifelong companion was Marion Morgan, with whom she lived from 1930 until Morgan's death in 1971. Morgan was a choreographer and a dancer, and the two met when Morgan choreographed dance sequences in early silent films directed by Arzner. The importance of dance in several of Arzner's films (especially *Dance, Girl, Dance* [1940]) reflects Morgan's continuing influence on Arzner's career.

Arzner's most successful films explored women's friendships and women's communities, from the women's college and the close bond between schoolmates in *The Wild Party* to the rivalry between two women performers in *Dance, Girl, Dance*. Lesbian themes appear indirectly in her work, from the critique of marriage (in *Christopher Strong* [1933] and *Craig's Wife* [1936]) to the independent woman, often a character who bears a resemblance to Arzner herself (Maria Ouspenskaya [1876–1949] as Madame Basilova in *Dance, Girl, Dance*). Arzner's career was largely forgotten until feminist critics and filmmakers in the 1970s rediscovered her films. *The Wild Party*, *Christopher Strong*, *Craig's Wife*, and *Dance, Girl, Dance* continue to be film-festival and classroom favorites.

*Judith Mayne*

## Bibliography

Johnston, Claire, ed. *The Work of Dorothy Arzner: Towards a Feminist Cinema*. London: British Film Institute, 1975.

Mayne, Judith. *Directed by Dorothy Arzner*. Bloomington: Indiana University Press, 1994.

———. *The Woman at the Keyhole: Feminism and Women's Cinema*. Bloomington: Indiana University Press, 1990.

*See also* Film, Mainstream; Hollywood

## Asian American Literature

Written works of persons of Asian ancestry living in North America. Only since the 1970s has Asian American literature included lesbian themes and works by openly lesbian authors. The absence of lesbian voices in Asian American literature is related to the historical struggle of Asian Americans to gain literary acceptance. The appearance of Asian American women writers and the development of Asian American feminism were important influences on the emergence of literary work by and about Asian American lesbians.

Asian Americans did not begin to settle in the United States until the mid-nineteenth century. Yet they were producing literary work as early as the late nineteenth century, when the Eurasian journalist Edith Maud Eaton (1865–1914) began publishing under the pseudonym Sui Sin Far. Although Eaton's work languished in obscurity for many years, she was rediscovered in 1976, and her work was later republished in *Mrs. Spring Fragrance and Other Writings* (1995) by Asian American feminists Amy Ling and Annette White-Parks. As Sui Sin Far, Eaton championed the cause of Chinese Americans against prejudice and often adopted the point of view of female characters who rebelled against marital and domestic expectations. This perspective derived from Eaton's personal experience as a child of interracial marriage and later from her own choice to forgo marriage in favor of a literary career. She believed that her own experience as "a serious and sober-minded spinster" of multiracial origins gave her insights into the foibles of her society. Eaton used this perspective to enlighten others about the problems and complexities of Asian American life. As the first Asian American to be published, Edith Maud Eaton provided a model for later Asian American writers, particularly women, who have generally followed her practice of using literature to comment on and correct social and cultural ignorance.

Asian American literature did not begin to gain a substantial national audience until after World War II, when writers such as Carlos Bulosan (1911–1956), Toshio Mori (1910–), Louis Chu (1915–), and Hisaye Yamamoto (1921–) attracted critical attention. Hisaye Yamamoto's work during this period is noteworthy for exploring the effects of racism and sexism on Japanese American women's lives. In short stories from the 1950s, such as "Seventeen Syllables," "Yoneko's Earthquake," and "The High-Heeled Shoes: A Memoir," Yamamoto reveals the problems that occur when women's personal desires conflict with social expectations. Her work pays particular attention to the fierce intimacies of mother-daughter relationships as an important grounds for working through those expectations. Yamamoto's focus on Asian American women's lives was later taken up by work in the 1970s, including Maxine Hong Kingston's landmark book, *The Woman Warrior: Memoirs of a Girlhood Among Ghosts* (1976).

Part autobiography, part biography, and part fiction, *The Woman Warrior* tells the story of one second-generation Chinese American girl trying to sort out the legacy of Chinese American culture for herself. Kingston emphasizes the contradictions of the stories her mother told her, which celebrate swordswomen and "female avengers" even as they admonish girls to be submissive and avoid danger: "She said I would grow up a wife and slave, but she taught me the song of the warrior woman, Fa Mu Lan. I would have to grow up a woman warrior." *The Woman Warrior* is the story of a young Asian American girl struggling to assert her own power in a world of restrictions for Asian Americans and women alike. It was received with both critical and commercial success and has since become a part of the curriculum at many colleges and universities. The success and acceptance of Kingston's book as an articulation of Asian American women's alienation in U.S. culture helped encourage the development of work by Asian American lesbians.

In the 1970s, a number of Asian American feminists and lesbians began to publish in small magazines and journals dedicated to feminist or lesbian work. This group included poets such as Janice Mirikitani, Nellie Wong, Willyce Kim, Kitty Tsui, and Merle Woo, as well as the playwright Canyon Sam. Lesbian poets such as Kim, Tsui, and Woo adhered to feminism's belief that the personal is political in order to articulate the political meaning of their lives as lesbians. They connected their efforts as lesbians to earlier Asian American efforts to overcome the effects of anti-Asian prejudice or racism. In doing so, they not only challenged white feminists, but also called on Asian Americans to recognize the connections between lesbian and Asian American struggles. Among this group of writers, Kitty Tsui and Willyce Kim emerged as the most influential Asian American lesbian writers.

The appearance of Tsui's *The Words of a Woman Who Breathes Fire* (1983) is generally considered a pivotal event in Asian American lesbian literature, establishing Tsui as a leading figure among Asian American lesbian writers. Like Kingston's book, Tsui's work is a combination of literary genres, including prose and poetry. It draws on the formative themes of both Kingston and Eaton to express the necessity, as well as the danger, of Asian American women's presence in a culture that finds "orientals so hard to tell apart." Tsui promotes the significance of "telling our experiences as Asian American women, / workers and poets, / cutting the ropes / that bind us, / breaking from / centuries of silence." Her project was shared by Kim, whose early poetry reflected many of the same concerns. In time, though, Kim began to develop as a novelist and became known for a series of lesbian adventure novels, *Dancer Dawkins and the California Kid* (1985) and the sequel *Dead Heat* (1988).

Younger writers whose work continues to explore the lesbian issues first addressed by Tsui and Kim are Chea Villanueva in *China Girls* (1991) and Tamai Kobayashi and Mona Oikawa in *All Names Spoken* (1993). Although Sky Lee's first novel, *Disappearing Moon Cafe* (1990), was well received, it did not include any lesbian characters or themes. It remains to be seen whether the 1980s flowering of Asian American lesbian writing will result in further success for the next generation.

*Caroline Chung Simpson*

### Bibliography

Aguilar-San Juan, Karen. "Landmarks in Literature by Asian American Lesbians." *Signs: Journal of Women in Culture and Society* 18 (Summer 1993), 936–943.

Leong, Russell, ed. *Asian American Sexualities: Dimensions of the Gay and Lesbian Experience.* New York: Routledge, 1996.

*See also* Asian Americans and Pacific Islanders

## Asian Americans and Pacific Islanders

Asian American lesbians identify themselves in terms of both their racial/ethnic background and their sexuality. "Asian American" is a political term that was coined in the early 1970s in the context of the Asian American movement's desire for self-definition and self-determination. The term expresses the collective consciousness of a uniquely hybrid culture that is Asian American. The Asian American movement called for racial equality, social justice, and political empowerment.

Other terms used in the 1980s and 1990s include "Asian Pacific Islander (API)," "Asian Pacific American," and "Asian American and Pacific Islander." "Asian and Pacific Islander" is originally a United States Census category that describes more than thirty diverse ethnic groups from South Asia, Southeast Asia, Central Asia, the Pacific Rim, and the Pacific Basin. These terms are often used interchangeably, but there is much disagreement within Asian American and Pacific Islander communities about their appropriateness.

The terms have their critics. After the change of immigration laws with the Immigration Act of 1964, the population of foreign-born Asians now constitutes the majority of Asians in America, and many immigrants who feel less identified with American culture do not accept the term "Asian American." The categories are also criticized for their potential to be taken as a homogenizing and monolithic category that erases the specificity of each ethnic group. Additionally, some question the inclusion of Pacific Islanders in "Asian Pacific Islander" and the "Asian Pacific American" categories, pointing out that Pacific Islanders are often underrepresented and marginalized.

These dynamics play an important role for many Asian American individuals and organizations who use these labels to name themselves and mobilize around the politics of identity. For instance, women from East Asian backgrounds usually dominate "Asian Pacific Islander" groups and can marginalize Pacific Islander and South Asian women and their issues. Some community activists and theorists have called for destablization of these terms and a fundamental change in the way we think about identity and practice.

## Cultural Activism

There is little dispute that Asian American and Pacific Islander lesbians and bisexual women face a combination of discrimination based on sexism, racism, homophobia, heterosexism, and classism. These interlocking oppressions have kept the voices and experiences of Asian American and Pacific Islander lesbian and bisexual women on the margins of history. Recovering and reconstructing Asian American and Pacific Islander women's histories remains a challenging project.

With the rise of the civil rights, women's liberation, and gay and lesbian liberation movements and the concomitant rise in the academic studies of these groups, Asian American and Pacific Islander lesbian and bisexual women's writings have been published in anthologies and other volumes. Major publications include: Willyce Kim, *Curtains of Light* (1971), *Eating Artichokes* (1972), and *Dancer Dawkins and the California Kid* (1985); Barbara Noda, *Strawberries* (1979); Kitty Tsui, *The Words of a Woman Who Breathes Fire* (1983); C. Chung, A. Kim, and A.K. Lemeshewsky, eds., *Between the Lines: An Anthology by Pacific/Asian Lesbians of Santa Cruz* (1987); and Sharon Lim-Hing, ed., *The Very Inside: An Anthology of Writing by Asian and Pacific Islander Lesbian and Bisexual Women* (1994). Writers, poets, artists, and critics since the 1970s include Lisa Asagi, Mi Ok Bruining, Connie Chan, Karin Aguilar-San Juan, Gayatri Gopinath, Alice Y. Hom, Willyce Kim, Larissa Lai, Shani Mootoo, Barbara Noda, Trinity Ordona, Jasbir Puar, Nina Revoyr, Nice Rodriguez, Canyon Sam, Indigo Som, Kitty Tsui, Merle Woo, Denise Uyehara, and Chea Villanueva. In addition, Eileen Lee and Marilyn Abbink (*Women of Gold* [1990]); Hima B. (*Straight for the Money* [1994] and *Coming Out, Coming Home: Asian and Pacific Islander Family Stories* [1995]), Shu Lea Cheang (*Fresh Kill* [1993] and *Fingers and Kisses* [1995]), Kris Lee (now Christopher Lee) (*APLBN* [1996]), and Pratibha Parmar (*Khush* [1991], *Sari Red* [1988], and *Double Trouble* [1992]) have produced films and videos that have played in both Asian American and gay and lesbian film festivals. These publications, performances, and other cultural works have contributed to the increased visibility of Asian American and Pacific Islander lesbian and bisexual women.

## Historical Background

Many Asian American and Pacific Islander lesbian and bisexual women have participated in activist groups and lesbian communities since the 1960s, and probably earlier as well, but it will be only through oral histories and careful reconstruction of primary and secondary historical sources that one will be able to definitively name these women. Based on some extant sources, one can identify a number of early activists who made an impact on Asian American lesbian and gay rights. One of them, Michiyo Fukaya (1953–1987), also known as Michiyo Cornell, attended the First National Third World Lesbian and Gay Conference that coincided with the first March on Washington for Gay and Lesbian Rights in 1979. Fukaya, as the representative of the Lesbian and Gay Asian Collective that formed during that conference, gave a speech titled "Living in Asian America: An Asian American Lesbian's Address Before the Washington Monument." She identified the difficulty of living in America as a poor woman of color who has to deal on the many fronts of racism, classism, and heterosexism, and she called for a recognition of the shared and different oppressions that divide Third World gays, lesbians, and straight people. Fukaya pointedly remarked on the racism in the predominantly white lesbian and gay movement.

A The issues that Fukaya spoke eloquently about were the same issues that led a small number of Asian American and Pacific Islander lesbians and bisexual women in various cities to form groups such as Asian Lesbians of the East Coast (ALOEC) in New York City, Asian Pacifica Sisters (APS) in San Francisco, California, Asian Pacific Lesbians and Friends (APLF) in Los Angeles, California, and D.C. Asian Lesbians (D-CALS) in Washington, D.C., in the early 1980s. Many of the women who founded these organizations had worked in other Asian American organizations or lesbian organizations and groups and thought that Asian American and Pacific Islander women's issues were not being adequately addressed. They believed that they needed a space where they could come for social gatherings, cultural support, and political action.

The late 1980s saw conferences that encouraged Asian American and Pacific Islander lesbians, bisexuals, and gay men to meet with one another: In 1987, "Breaking Silence, Beginning the Dialogue," the first meeting for Asian American and Pacific Islander lesbians and gay men in Southern California, met in Los Angeles; in 1988, "Unity Among Asians," the first North American conference for Asian lesbians and gay men, gathered in Toronto, Ontario, Canada. Two other gatherings in 1987 also helped increase networking between Asian American and Pacific Islander lesbian and bisexual women's groups around the Unites States. One such event was the first West Coast retreat for Asian American and Pacific Islander lesbian and bisexual women, in Sonoma, California, in May 1987. More than eighty women attended the retreat and contributed to organizing Asian American and Pacific Islander lesbian and bisexual women beyond small and regional social gatherings.

The second was the March on Washington for Lesbian and Gay Rights on October 11, 1987, in which more than 150,000 gay men, lesbians, bisexuals, and supporters marched to affirm and to promote the visibility of people with same-sex orientation. Groups such as ALOEC and the Boston Asian Gay Males and Lesbians (BAGMAL) helped make the Asian American and Pacific Islander presence felt. Included were two hundred or more Asian American and Pacific Islander gay men and lesbians who marched together under the banners of "Gay, Asian, and Proud." There, Asian American and Pacific Islander lesbian and bisexual women began to talk of forming an official national group, recognizing that there were enough numbers, energy, and need for such an organization. They determined that it was time to consolidate and systematically organize the already-existing personal and informal networks of friends and newsletter exchanges.

After these two historical events in 1987, in conjunction with the previous decade of organizing, a few women on the West Coast and the East Coast believed that it was possible to implement their hope for a national network, which they named the Asian Pacific Lesbian Network (APLN). In the beginning, the network consisted of an ad hoc steering committee of representatives in different parts of the country. With seed money from the National March on Washington office, they were able to sponsor the first national Asian Pacific Lesbian retreat, "Coming Together, Moving Forward," in Santa Cruz, California, September 1–4, 1989. The retreat heralded the historic attempt to organize and bring together Asian American and Pacific Islander lesbian and bisexual women from across the United States. The retreat gave Asian American and Pacific Islander lesbian and bisexual women the opportunity to discuss experiences and concerns that are rarely represented in mainstream gay and lesbian communities, and it provided a forum to define their own history.

## Activism at the End of the Twentieth Century

In a West Coast regional APLN retreat in 1993, the steering committee renamed the group as Asian Pacific Lesbian and Bisexual Network (APLBN) to address the participation of bisexual women in the organization. In 1995, a group of women in the Midwest sponsored a regional APLBN retreat in Minneapolis, Minnesota. The second national conference was held in 1998 in Los Angeles.

In addition to a number of groups that have restructured or disbanded in the 1990s, a steady stream of new groups have also organized with an ethnic-specific focus. Among them are the Asian Lesbian Bisexual Alliance (ALBA) in Seattle, Washington; the Asian Pacific Lesbian Bisexual Transgendered Network (APLBTN), in Atlanta, Georgia; the Los Angeles Asian Pacific Islander Sisters (LAAPIS) in Los Angeles; the South Asian Lesbian and Gay Association in New York City (SALGA); Chingusai, a Korean American gay, lesbian, and bisexual group in Los Angeles; Kilawin Kolektibo, a Pilipina group in New York City; O Moi, a Vietnamese group in Los Angeles and Orange County, California; KoALA, a Korean American lesbian and bisexual group in Chicago, Illinois; a Malaysian women's group in the San Francisco Bay Area; and Older Asian Sisters in Solidarity (OASIS) in San Francisco.

There is also an increasing number of Asian American and Pacific Islander lesbian and bisexual women who traverse national and geographical boundaries, making significant connections and alliances among women in the United States and other nations. Information technology, such as electronic mailing lists, Web sites, and virtual chat rooms, has been used widely to disseminate and gather information for such purposes. Electronic media offer additional opportunities and challenges for Asian American and Pacific Islander lesbian and bisexual women, who continue to express their diversity, engage in politics, and organize across ethnic and geographic boundaries.                    *Alice Y. Hom*

## Bibliography

Eng, David L., and Alice Y. Hom, eds. *Q & A: Queer in Asian America*. Philadelphia: Temple University Press, 1998.

Leong, Russell, ed. *Asian American Sexualities: Dimensions of the Gay and Lesbian Experience*. New York: Routledge, 1996.

Lim-hing, Sharon, ed. *The Very Inside: An Anthology of Writing by Asian and Pacific Islander Lesbian and Bisexual Women*. Toronto: Sister Vision, 1994.

Ratti, Rakesh, ed. *A Lotus of Another Color: An Unfolding of the South Asian Gay and Lesbian Experience*. Boston: Alyson, 1993.

Shervington, Gwendolyn L., ed. *A Fire Is Burning, It Is in Me: The Life and Writings of Michiyo Fukaya*. Norwich, Vt.: New Victoria, 1996.

*See also* Asian American Literature

## Asian Lesbian Network

Organization begun during the International Lesbian Information Service (ILIS) Conference in Geneva, Switzerland, in March 1986. Asian lesbians from Bangladesh, India, the United States, Japan, and Thailand organized an Asian lesbian workshop during the conference, noting the necessity to strengthen and expand the Asian lesbian network of support.

Three conferences have been held by the Asian Lesbian Network (ALN) since 1990. The first conference was held in Bangkok, Thailand, in December 1990. Organized by Anjaree, a Bangkok lesbian organization, the conference was attended by fifty-four lesbians, nine of whom were non-Asian.

The second conference was held in Tokyo, Japan, in May 1992. With an attendance of more than 170 lesbians from thirteen countries, the four-day conference was the largest ALN gathering to date. ALN-Nippon, the organizers of the conference, included a broad range of activities, such as workshops, concerts, cultural activities, and video presentations.

The third conference was held in Wulai, Taiwan, in August 1995. This conference was significant because the First Constitution Conference was also held at this time. More than 140 lesbians from eight countries attended the four-day conference.

Based on the ALN working constitution, the ALN structure has three components: the Secretariat, primarily responsible for financial matters, membership, and the production of the newsletter; the Working Group, which decides on policy and practices, acceptance of members, organizational representation, and disbursement of funds; and the general membership. The working constitution was presented for ratification during the fourth ALN conference, held in Quezon City, Philippines, in 1998.

Issues that have been raised in the ALN can be divided into two categories: structure and governance, and identity and politics. The fluid structure and lack of clear policies regarding membership and participation became a cause of concern during the second ALN conference. While the first ALN conference did not include non-Asians, during the second conference a parallel gathering of non-Asians, called "Lesbians Affirming Lesbians in Asia" (LALA), was held. Following several discussions, it was decided that the host country would have to make a policy regarding the participation of non-Asians. In December 1993, ALN-Taiwan hosted a preconference meeting to discuss the structure of the ALN and to settle policies before the third conference. Due to financial constraints, only lesbians from Japan were able to participate in the meeting. Together, the Japanese and Taiwanese lesbians drafted a constitution for the ALN. However, it was not resolved as to how this constitution could be ratified. Thus, ALN-Taiwan, then incoming conference host, deemed it better to leave the organization's structure loose until the constitution conference could be held. A new working constitution was thus drafted during the third conference in Taiwan.

A  The second category of issues includes those that deal with the participation of non-Asians, the definition of lesbian, the definition of Asian, the ALN vision, local and regional concerns, and the philosophy and substantive issues that bind the organization.

The main accomplishment of the ALN has been the creation of a space wherein Asian lesbians could come together to learn from one another and establish links. It has also contributed to an increased awareness and discussion of Asian lesbian issues in both local and international forums and has served as an impetus for Asian lesbian organizing. The diverse cultural, economic, and political backgrounds of ALN's membership provide the organization with its challenges, dynamism, and strength.

*Giney Villar*

### Bibliography

Asian Lesbian Network. "The Third ALN Conference Taiwan, 1995," ALN-Taiwan, P.O. Box 7–760, Taipei, Taiwan.

ALN-Nippon. "The Report of the Second ALN Conference," July 1995. Regumi Studio Tokyo, JOKI, Nakazawa Bldg. 3F 23, Araki-cho, Shinjuku, Tokyo 160, Japan.

*See also* International Organizations

### Associations and Organizations

Lesbians have joined together in a number of formal and informal groups and organizations. Some organizations are primarily social in purpose; others, political. Although relatively few lesbian organizations existed prior to the 1960s in the United States, since the 1970s a wide variety of lesbian organizations and associations have flourished.

### Early Organizations

Prior to the late 1960s, there were relatively few formal organizations or associations that lesbians could join. Although secret social groups and friendship circles have been documented as early as the 1920s and 1930s, in places such as Salt Lake City, Utah, it was not until long after the establishment of Daughters of Bilitis in San Francisco, California, in 1955 that formal organizations for lesbians in the United States began to arise in any number. In the late 1960s and 1970s, lesbians created a diverse array of formal organizations and associations at both the local and the national level. Although long lasting, exclusively lesbian, national organizations have been relatively unsuccessful, local and regional lesbian organizations have flourished. National feminist groups that include both lesbians and heterosexual women (such as the National Organization for Women, which began welcoming open lesbians after much conflict in the early 1970s) and mixed-sex gay and lesbian groups (such as the National Gay and Lesbian Task Force, founded in the early 1970s) have been relatively more enduring.

The Nucleus Club was one early secret social club. Organized in New York City in the 1930s, it held weekly parties in private homes for lesbians and gay men. Another early women's organization that included lesbians among its members was Heterodoxy, a group of radicals and feminists in Greenwich Village in New York City. Founded in 1912, the "club for unorthodox women" included a number of lesbians among its members during its thirty-year existence. More common during the first half of the twentieth century, lesbians met informally at private parties or, after World War II, in bars rather than in formal organizations or associations.

Daughters of Bilitis (DOB) was the first national lesbian organization in the United States. Founded in San Francisco in 1955, it was established originally as a private social club and an alternative to the bar scene, though it quickly became a social and political organization for lesbians. When the DOB joined the early gay rights movement with Mattachine Society and One, Inc.—two predominantly male groups in the homophile movement—one of its founders left to form two other secret social clubs for lesbians, Quatrefoil and Hale Aikane. At its height, the DOB had chapters in a number of cities and countries, including Chicago, Illinois; San Diego, California; Boston, Massachusetts; Denver, Colorado; and Melbourne, Australia. By the 1970s, when many embraced a more radical lesbian politics, most chapters had folded; in the 1990s, one chapter, in Boston, remained.

### Gay Liberation and Feminism

It was not until the late 1960s and early 1970s, with the growth of the gay liberation and feminist movements, that a variety of other lesbian organizations began to flourish. Many early lesbian organizations had a political focus. Radicalesbians, which put forth the influential position paper "The Woman-Identified Woman," was formed (1970) in New York City by lesbians from a number of existing women's and gay male groups in 1969 and the early 1970s. Members included Rita Mae Brown, Lois Hart, Ellen Bedoz, and others. Although Radicalesbians was not a long-lasting group, its position paper on lesbian feminism, which proclaimed, "A lesbian is the rage of all women condensed to the point of explosion," has been widely circulated and very influential.

The Washington, D.C.–based Furies Collective, founded in 1971 by Charlotte Bunch, Rita Mae Brown, Ginny Berson, Joan E. Biren, and others, was another short-lived but influential radical lesbian feminist collective that published a newspaper called *The Furies*. Other lesbian feminist groups of the 1970s included Lesbian Feminist Liberation (New York City), Gutter Dykes Collective (Berkeley, California), and the C.L.I.T. (Collective Lesbian International Terrors) Collective (New York City).

Throughout the 1970s and 1980s, lesbian organizations flourished across the United States. Many lesbians sought to create groups that would be specific to their own needs and activities, apart from either mixed gay and lesbian organizations or feminist organizations that also included heterosexual women. Regional groups such as the Atlanta Lesbian Feminist Alliance (Atlanta, Georgia) and the Central Ohio Lesbians (Columbus) served a variety of purposes, including social support and participation in political activities. Many lesbians attempted to work collectively and in cooperative organizations. Although not all lesbian organizations have done so, many have pioneered the use of consensus-based decision making and nonhierarchical organizational forms. Consensus decision making is often slow and tedious; still, lesbian organizations that use it believe that the process is more democratic and allows for greater participation by all group members.

Some lesbian organizations have formed around specific activities or interests. Early lesbian mothers' groups, such as Dykes and Tykes in New York City and the Lesbian Mothers Union in San Francisco, formed in the 1970s. The Lesbian Rights Project (later renamed the National Center for Lesbian Rights) was founded by attorney Donna Hitchens in 1977 in San Francisco, California, and has worked to protect the rights of lesbian mothers, in addition to assisting lesbians on other legal issues. The 1980s saw an explosion of local lesbian mothers' groups in many cities and towns, including Parents and Gonna Be Parents (Kansas City, Missouri), Lesmos (West Hempstead, New York), Lesbians Choosing Children Network (Arlington, Maryland), Our Family (San Francisco Bay Area, California), Custody Action for Lesbian Mothers (Narberth, Pennsylvania), and Gay and Lesbian Parents Coalition International (based in Washington, D.C.). The Lesbian Mothers National Defense Fund, based in Seattle, Washington, publishes information about custody cases and similar concerns.

Organizations devoted to the production of lesbian culture also proliferated in the 1970s. Nationally, Olivia Music was formed by a group of lesbian feminists in 1973 to provide women with a chance to create and disseminate music. For years, the best-known producer of "women's" (lesbian) music, Olivia artists toured the United States, and local women's music production companies, such as Allegra in Boston, formed to produce local concerts. Other organizations created coffeehouses, restaurants, bookstores, food cooperatives, and a panoply of other lesbian enterprises.

In the late 1980s and into the 1990s, many lesbians participated in mixed gay and lesbian AIDS education and service organizations, as well as direct-action groups such as ACT UP (AIDS Coalition to Unleash Power) and Queer Nation. Chapters of Lesbian Avengers, known for their creative protests, mushroomed in the mid-1990s.

Many lesbians of color have also organized in autonomous groups. In the 1970s, black women formed groups such as the Combahee River Collective, a black feminist collective in Boston, Massachusetts, that included many lesbians, and Sapphire Sapphos, a black lesbian group in Washington, D.C. Lesbians were active participants in the 1974 founding of the National Black Feminist Organization and the 1978 formation of the National Coalition of Black Lesbians and Gay Men. The National Black Lesbian and Gay Leadership Forum was established one decade later, in 1988. Salsa Soul Sisters Third World Womyn, Inc., formed an umbrella organization for women of color in New York City, and Latina lesbians have been active in Llego, the Latino/a Lesbian and Gay Organization, formed at the 1987 March for Lesbian and Gay Rights in Washington, D.C. In the 1980s, a number of Asian lesbian organizations were formed. Trikone, one of the longest-standing groups for lesbian and gay South Asians, was founded in the San Francisco Bay Area in 1986; other groups have included the New York City–based Asian Lesbians of the East Coast and Chicago Asian Lesbians Moving.

## National Organizations

Although there have been a number of attempts to form enduring national lesbian organizations, these have not been entirely successful. In 1978, following the National Women's Conference of 1977 in Houston, Texas, a group of lesbians in Los Angeles attempted to form a National Lesbian Feminist Organization (NLFO). Although a steering committee and several chapters were formed, the NLFO never became a national organization. In 1988, the National Organization for Women (NOW) sponsored a National Lesbian Rights Conference to develop a national lesbian agenda, and in 1991 Atlanta hosted the National Lesbian Conference. Still, no national lesbian organization came out of these conferences.

Many lesbians have taken leadership roles in national lesbian and gay organizations, such as the National Lesbian and Gay Task Force and the Gay and Lesbian Alliance Against Defamation, and in feminist groups such as the National Organization for Women NOW. On an international level, the International Gay and Lesbian Alliance, based in Stockholm, Sweden, represents gay and lesbian and AIDS activist groups in fifty countries on all continents. Although lesbians have been less visible than gay men in international organizations, lesbian and gay national organizations have formed in countries such as Finland, Iceland, Austria, and Greece. Lesbians have long been active in organizations in Canada, England, and the Netherlands and, since the 1970s and 1980s, in a number of Latin American countries as well.　　　*Kristin G. Esterberg*

### Bibliography

Abdulahad, Tania, Gwendolyn Rogers, Barbara Smith, and Jameelah Waheed. "Black Lesbian/Feminist Organizing: A Conversation." In *Home Girls: A Black Feminist Anthology*. Ed. Barbara Smith. New York: Kitchen Table, 1983, pp. 293–319.

Adam, Barry. *The Rise of a Gay and Lesbian Movement*. Boston: Twayne, 1987.

Echols, Alice. *Daring To Be Bad: Radical Feminism in America, 1967–1975*. Minneapolis: University of Minnesota Press, 1989.

Faderman, Lilian. *Odd Girls and Twilight Lovers: A History of Lesbian Life in Twentieth-Century America*. New York: Columbia University Press, 1991.

Martin, Del, and Phyllis Lyon. *Lesbian/Woman*. Twentieth Anniversary Edition. Volcano, Calif.: Volcano, 1991.

Radicalesbians. "The Woman Identified Woman." In *Notes from the Third Year*. Ed. Anne Koedt and Shulamith Firestone, 1971, pp. 81–84.

*See also* Combahee River Collective; Daughters of Bilitis; Furies, The; International Organizations; Lesbian Avengers; National Gay and Lesbian Task Force (NGLTF); National Organization for Women (NOW); Olivia; Queer Nation; Radicalesbians

## Athletics, Collegiate

Women have participated in intercollegiate athletics since the beginning, of the twentieth century. From the beginning, women athletes faced strong cultural opposition to the notion of athletic females. Athletics was defined as a masculine activity, and male physicians, social commentators, and college presidents expressed concern over the "masculinizing effects" of women's participation in competitive athletics and damage to the "frail" female constitution. Women physical educators, who controlled college women's sports, responded to critics by developing separate "women's rules" and stressing the health benefits of sport participation and the importance of feminine appearance and behavior among women athletes. Varsity competition was deemphasized in favor of "playdays" focused on participation and socializing.

By the 1950s, most women physical education professional groups strongly discouraged intercollegiate and high school athletic competition for women. This philosophy dominated women's athletics well into the 1960s. The 1972, passage of Title IX, however, ushered in a new era for women's intercollegiate athletics. Title IX is a federal law prohibiting sex discrimination in education programs. Capitalizing on this new legislative tool and the increasing strength of the feminist movement, women's sport advocates have pushed for augmented resources and development of women's intercollegiate athletic programs. Though not yet on equal footing with men's intercollegiate athletics, the success of Amercan women athletes in the 1996 Summer Olympics attests to the change in social attitudes toward women's athletics and to the development of world-class athletes in a variety of sports.

## Lesbians in Collegiate Athletics

For the better part of the twentieth century, lesbians have played an integral role in the development of, and advocacy for, women's collegiate athletics. Since the early 1970s, lesbian coaches, athletes, and sport administrators have been among the women who lobbied for passage of Title IX and have resisted legislative attempts to scale back the effects of this important sex-discrimination law. In addition, lesbian athletes and coaches are part of many national championship teams and represent the United States in international competitions such as the Olympic Games. Moreover, athletics serve as important support and social networks for many lesbians, who, in the face of hostility from family or friends, find their first community among other lesbian teammates and coaches. Lesbians whose gender expression challenges boundaries of traditional femininity find in athletics a place to explore and enjoy their passions for competition and the development of physical competence.

Despite growing societal acceptance of women as athletes, this acceptance is contingent on their ability and willingness to present a heterosexual and feminine appearance. The early-twentieth-century association between sports and masculinity and between masculinity and lesbians continued to haunt women athletes at the close of the century. These associations serve an important function in a sexist society. Societal hostility to lesbians and the association of lesbians with athletics are deterrents to women's participation in sports and warn women athletes and coaches that they are stepping out of "appropriate" gender boundaries. As long as lesbians are stigmatized, the lesbian label can be used to intimidate and control the development of women's sports and the participation of women in sports. Fear and intolerance of lesbians in a heterosexist and sexist society act as boundary markers to warn women who stray from expected norms of feminine heterosexuality and who challenge male privilege. For men, sports are an important arena for the development of dominant masculinist values. Women's participation in sports challenges the exclusivity of sports and their role in socializing men and boys into their dominant social roles in a sexist society. As a result, most lesbians in college athletics attempt to keep their identities hidden rather than jeopardize their opportunity to compete or coach.

## Climates for Lesbians

The climate for lesbians in college athletics can range from hostile to conditionally tolerant to open and affirming. Generally, the more public attention focused on the sport and the bigger the school, the more hostile the athletic environment tends to be. Also, team sports are often more hostile than individual sports.

In a hostile environment, lesbian presence is identified as a problem. Lesbian coaches and athletes in a hostile environment are careful to protect their identities from anyone who might be in a position to discriminate against or harass them. In a hostile environment lesbians who are discovered experience blatant and direct discrimination. Coaches are fired, and athletes are dismissed from teams or have their playing time severely diminished. Sometimes, athletes are ostracized by teammates or pressured to leave the team. The performance of lesbian coaches is often carefully scrutinized to identify other, less controversial justifications for firing: a losing season or team complaints, for example. Occasionally, a team in a losing season will complain to administrators about a lesbian coach. Some coaches engage in "negative recruiting" by telling parents of prospective athletes that there are lesbians on rival teams or that their coach is a lesbian in an effort to steer an athlete away from that program. Some coaches also tell recruits and their parents that lesbians are not allowed on the team, tapping into fears about lesbians. Young athletes struggling with their own sexual identities can be the most hostile to lesbian teammates or coaches as they try to distance themselves from an identity they fear. In a hostile environment, lesbian athletes and coaches, by necessity, mask their identities by lying or maintaining a strict silence about their identities.

The most publicized example of this hostility to lesbian athletes occurred in 1991, when it was revealed in a newspaper article that Rene Portland, the Pennsylvania State University women's basketball coach, had a "no lesbian" policy. The public outcry and barrage of negative publicity directed at Penn State resulted in passage of an amendment to its nondiscrimination policy to include sexual orientation. Portland, after several months, agreed to abide by the new policy.

In a conditionally tolerant environment, lesbian visibility is identified as a problem, but lesbian coaches and athletes are tolerated as long as they maintain a public silence about their identities. In such an environment, lesbian athletes are admonished by their teammates (and sometimes their coaches) to avoid association with campus lesbian-identified groups and stay away from places associated with lesbians, such as bars, clubs, or community sport teams. Heterosexual athletes sometimes warn lesbian teammates to keep their hair long and not to talk about their partners or make their identity visible in any way. Often, whole teams "know" that the coach is a lesbian, but, as long as she never makes her identity explicit, she is tolerated. Lesbian coaches

**A** and athletes in a conditionally tolerant environment must monitor their behavior carefully to avoid overstepping the zone of tolerance implicitly agreed to.

In an open and affirming environment, discrimination and harassment of lesbians are identified problems. Lesbian athletes and coaches disclose their identities with reasonable expectations that they will not be penalized for their openness. Coaches can bring partners to games, introduce them to athletes and parents, and talk about their personal lives. Lesbian athletes can talk with teammates about homophobia and their relationships and bring dates to team social events. Heterosexual teammates speak out against antilesbian prejudice and help "socialize" younger teammates into the open and affirming environment. Athletes who are questioning their sexual identity can count on coaches to support them in this process.

Unfortunately, as the twentieth century draws to a close, most athletic climates in the United States are either hostile or conditionally tolerant. Few lesbian athletes, coaches, or athletic administrators publicly identify themselves. To the contrary, many coaches and athletes in the public eye go to great lengths to highlight their feminine heterosexuality in their appearance (long hair, makeup, high heels, and dresses) and in the visibility of their husbands or boyfriends and children. The media focus on women athletes who are able to provide such "evidence" of their feminine heterosexuality reinforces the perception that lesbians and heterosexual women who do not conform to traditional notions of femininity must be hidden.

A number of pressures work against the development of an open and affirming environment. In general, coaches and administrators in collegiate athletics are not interested in placing themselves on the cutting edge of social change on any issue. In collegiate athletics, much of the fear of association with lesbians is due to the pressure to recruit talented athletes. Many collegiate coaches assume that most high school athletes and their parents will avoid programs that publicly acknowledge the presence of lesbian coaches or athletes. Few coaches are willing to risk losing recruits to test this assumption. Also, as sports such as basketball and volleyball receive more media attention and public spectator interest increases, administrators and coaches become more image conscious. Moreover, as commercial sponsorship of women's collegiate athletics increases, the traditional conservatism of corporate executives also exerts an influence on women's athletics to present a noncontroversial feminine, heterosexual image to the public in association with their products.

## Changing the Climate

A professional dialogue about homophobia and heterosexism in collegiate athletics has begun in some collegiate coaches' associations and among some college athletic depatments. Moreover, academic disciplines, including women's studies, sport psychology, sport history, and sport sociology, are now addressing heterosexism and homophobia in athletics in research and professional writing, thereby increasing understanding of these issues. Women's sports advocacy organizations, such as the Women's Sports Foundation, are taking a public stand against discrimination against lesbians in athletics and providing education resources for coaches and administrators. In addition, an educational video, *Out for a Change: Addressing Homophobia in Women's Sports,* and an accompanying study guide are available from Woman Vision (San Francisco, California) for coaches and teachers.

Though the day when most collegiate athletic environments will be described as open and affirming for lesbian athletes and coaches is perhaps in the distant future, it is possible to imagine that time. The process of change in the larger culture is also at work in collegiate athletics. Perhaps the next generation of lesbian athletes and coaches will be free to make their important contributions to women's athletics openly and honestly, without feeling the need to mask and protect their sexual identities out of fear of discrimination or harassment. This future day will be a big step forward for all women in sports to be able to pursue athletic goals without the constraints imposed by restrictive boundaries of acceptable feminine heterosexuality.          *Pat Griffin*

### *Bibliography*

Blinde, Elaine, and Diane Taub. "Homophobia and Women's Sports: The Disempowerment of Athletes." *Sociological Focus* 25 (1992), 151–166.

Bryson, Lois. "Sport and the Maintenance of Male Hegemony." *Women's Studies International Forum* 10 (1987), 349–360.

Cahn, Susan. *Coming on Strong: Gender and Sexuality in Twentieth Century Women's Sport.* New York: Free Press, 1994.

Griffin, Pat. *Strong Women, Deep Closets: Lesbians and Homophobia in Sport.* Champaign, Ill.: Human Kinetics, 1998.

Krane, Vikki. "Lesbians in Sport: Toward Acknowledgement, Understanding, and Theory." *Journal of Sport and Exercise Psychology* 18 (1996), 237–246.

Lenskyj, Helen. "Power at Play: Gender and Sexuality Issues in Sport and Physical Activity." *International Review for the Sociology of Sport* 25 (1990), 235–245.

*See also* Physical Education; Sports, Professional

## Austen, Alice (1866–1952)

American photographer. Alice Austen spent most of her life in her family's comfortable, upper-middle-class home on Staten Island, New York, across the bay from Manhattan, although she traveled around the northeastern United States and to Europe. Her uncle taught her to use a large-format camera when she was ten years old, and she used herself, family, friends, and neighbors as primary subjects.

Most active as a photographer between the 1880s and the 1920s, Austen used a clear, unclut-tered style to show her contemporaries playing tennis, bicycling, swimming, and picnicking. She photographed commuters on the Staten Island Ferry, laborers, and immigrants newly arrived from Europe. Austen's photographs are unique among art images made by lesbians of her era in that she conveyed her involvement with women in very graphic terms, such as showing herself and her friends embracing, in bed, or cross-dressing as men. Around 1917, Gertrude Amelia Tate (ca. 1871–1962), already her lover for eighteen years, moved in with Austen.

An independent income allowed Austen to pursue her photographic interests without the need to sell her work. This changed when the stock market crashed in 1929, taking with it much of her capital. Thinking the crisis would soon pass, Austen mortgaged her house and traveled in Europe with Tate. On their return, they ran a tea room on the front lawn during summer months and struggled to live on money Tate earned teaching ballroom dancing and deportment, but in 1945 the house was lost. After a few years in a small apartment, Tate went to live with family members, who disapproved of her

*"The Darned Club" from* Alice's World: The Life and Photography of an American Original: Alice Austen, 1866–1952 *by Ann Novotny (Old Greenwich, Conn.: The Chatham Press, 1976). Courtesy The Chatham Press.*

**A**

relationship with Austen. Austen moved from one nursing home to another, then into the Staten Island Farm colony, a home for paupers, in 1950.

Many of Austen's negatives were purchased by the Staten Island Historical Society. Ultimately, they came to the attention of a publisher who arranged for the exhibition and sale of prints. The money thus earned allowed Austin to move to a comfortable residence for the last year of her life.     *Tee A. Corinne*

### Bibliography

Grubler, Mitchell. *Alice Austen: A Commemorative Journal*. New York: Alice Austen House, 1986.
———. *The Larky Life*. New York: Alice Austen House, 1991.
Kaplan, Gaile. *Fine Day*. Exhibition Catalog. Staten Island: Alice Austen House, 1988.
Novotny, Ann. *Alice's World: The Life and Photography of an American Original: Alice Austen, 1866–1952*. Old Greenwich, Conn.: Chatham, 1976.

*See also* Photography

## Australia

Island continent located in the Southern and Eastern hemispheres, but culturally dominated by the Northern and Western hemispheres. The oldest continent, whose indigenous peoples—the Aboriginals—have the oldest continuous culture in the world, it is yet one of the newest nations in the world. From these contradictory elements, Australia's small population of eighteen million has produced a diversity of cultures, among them lesbian culture.

### Context

White Australian culture has a short history, a little over two hundred years in contrast to more than one hundred thousand years of Aboriginal culture. Evidence of lesbian culture in either of these settings is still rare prior to the emergence of radical and women's movements in the late 1960s.

There is a small representation of women who broke with tradition—cross-dressers, women with lifelong companions, and outlaws—but there has been no sustained book-length work in this area, although a small traveling exhibition exploring the lives of lesbians from 1900 to the 1990s opened in Melbourne in 1996. Margaret Catchpole, a horse thief and convict; Mary Reibey, one of Australia's earliest business women (depicted on the twenty

dollar note); Alice Anderson, who opened a garage in Melbourne in 1919; Freda Du Faur (1882–1935), mountain climber (two of New Zealand's South Island peaks are named for her and her lover, Muriel Cardogan); Joan Hammond (1912–1996), opera singer; and "Montie" (who lived to be one hundred and six years old) are among the most famous. Marion/Bill Edwards, who lived "as a man" for fifty years after his female identity became known (s/he was arrested for burglary in 1906 and died in 1956), has also drawn significant attention from scholars. It was only in the 1980s that famous women who were lesbians began to be acknowledged in historical accounts of their lives. There are many more names to unearth.

Since the late 1960s, there has been an explosion of organizations and events established by, and run for, lesbians. In 1970, the Australian chapter of Daughters of Bilitis, Australia's first openly homosexual organization, was formed. Other organizations were soon to follow throughout the 1970s and onward.

### The Formal Political Culture

Australia in the 1950s and 1960s was extremely conservative, with institutionalized racist policies, such as the White Australia Policy, and the removal of Aboriginal children from their mothers. With the granting of citizenship to Aboriginal people in 1967, the Viet Nam War (1965–1972), and the emergence of progressive social movements came a period of widespread change. The changes that have taken place in Australian culture since then have also changed the nature of lesbian identity and visibility. The changes are largely due to feminists, progressive politicians, and that peculiarly Australian invention, the "femocrat" (a feminist who works in governmental positions).

Although Australian culture is heavily influenced by U.S. culture, it is by no means an exact replica. Australians, on the whole, are irreverent, informal, and inventive. Women, Aboriginals, and migrants first became part of the mainstream political agenda in 1972, when the Labor Party (left-to-center political party) leader, Gough Whitlam, was elected prime minister on a wave of political enthusiasm. In many ways, he set the political agenda of Australia for the following decades. He was ousted in 1975 in what many commentators have described as a coup. A Liberal Party (center-to-Right political party) government ran the country for the next seven years, and, from 1983, a returned Labor government held power for thirteen years. In 1996, the Liberal Party won back power and reintroduced conservative political and social policies.

The governmental structures put in place between 1972 and 1975 were critical in giving women, including lesbians, a voice; making it possible for them to rise up the public-service ladder, thereby affecting subsequent governmental policy; and including on the political agenda issues such as child care, maternity leave, equal pay, antiracist legislation, affirmative action, and antinuclear, peace, and environmental policies. The Labor government formalized many important issues that lesbians have fought for and introduced some legislation that protects lesbians.

## Lesbian Feminist Culture

In 1973, the first national lesbian conference was held at Sorrento, a seaside suburb about fifty miles from central Melbourne, run by a group calling itself Radicalesbians. It produced badges, debated theory, and published a pirated edition of U.S. writer Robin Morgan's collection of poems, *Monster* (1972). Lesbian cultural life in Australia was quickly enriched by the work of feminists from other countries, mostly the United States and the United Kingdom. But Australian lesbians also developed a rich culture of their own, including literature, theater, music, visual arts, and film. Also important has been the development of feminist and lesbian radio and, more recently, video, circus, and home pages on the Internet.

Poetry and music very quickly became important, including the works of U.S. writers and musicians. Local songwriters sometimes adapted the words of Australian folk songs to their own needs. The flowering of poetry was reflected in the first national anthology of women's writing, *Mother I'm Rooted* (1975), edited by Kate Jennings, one of the first widely available books with a substantial contribution from lesbian writers.

The Women's Theatre Group (mostly lesbians throughout its life) put on its first performance, *The Love Show*, in 1973, with others to follow over the next four years, ending with *Edges* in 1977. Songs, poetry, and women's bands played a large part in the development of a lesbian culture. Theater flourished through the combined energies of playwrights, comedians, directors, actors, technicians, publicists, and reviewers.

In the mid-1970s, the Women's Electric Band (known as WEB) played in Melbourne; in Sydney,

Clitoris (pronounced with the emphasis on the second syllable) was popular; and the Shameless Hussies came out of Adelaide. These bands, like a considerable portion of the feminist artistic and political movement, were predominately composed of lesbians. After that period, a number of lesbian singer/songwriters became well known, in particular, Robin Archer and Judy Small, as well as numerous bands that formed and reformed.

Festivals are as important to the gay and lesbian community as to the rest of the population. Mardi Gras is Australia's best-known gay and lesbian event. Held in Sydney during February and March, Mardi Gras highlights the diversity of gay and lesbian culture, from readings to theater to the huge street parade and party that brings it to a close. This event attracts more overseas visitors to Australia than any heterosexual event. Melbourne holds its Midsumma Festival during February with a similar range of events. The Lesbian Festival has become an annual national event, held in a different state each year.

An institution that appears to be peculiarly Australian are women's and lesbian circuses. Melbourne boasts the Women's Circus, with a membership of approximately one hundred women (many of them lesbians), as well as the POW (Performing Older Women's) Circus, an entirely lesbian circus made up of performers and musicians between the ages of forty and sixty-seven. The women in these circuses play music, do acrobatics and aerials, juggle, direct, teach, and train novices. The 1996 International Women's Day March included performances by both circuses before and after the march.

In literature, Elizabeth Riley's *All That False Instruction* (1975) was one of the first novels published in Australia to focus on the lives of lesbians in a positive way. The author, Kerryn Higgs, published under a pseudonym due to legal pressure from her family. Finola Moorhead's *Remember the Tarantella* (1987) depicts lesbian lives of the 1970s and 1980s, in Australia. In the 1990s, lesbian fiction and poetry were widely published, circulated, and reviewed, and many Australian lesbian writers have been recipients of mainstream awards or have been published to acclaim and widespread popularity overseas.

The Australian literary scene has been boosted by a number of festivals that focus specifically on writing, including the Australian Feminist Book Fortnights, held across the nation in 1989 and 1991. These culminated in the Sixth International Feminist

**A**

*Women's Circus, Melbourne, Australia, 1995. Photo by Susan Hawthorne.*

Book Fair in Melbourne in 1994. It is lesbians, by and large, who run the women's bookshops that make these books available. Similarly, most feminist and lesbian publishing in Australia has been generated by lesbians, including Sybylla Feminist Cooperative, Redress Women's Press, Tantrum, and Spinifex. In the 1990s, a number of joint gay and lesbian anthologies were published; this appears to be a more financially viable format for mainstream publishers.

In the visual arts, many lesbians are breaking new ground. Among them, photographer Destiny Deacon produces irreverent, confrontational, and startling pictures, many of which use small black dolls to represent the place of Aboriginal people in Australian culture. Her work, widely exhibited in Australia and overseas, is a significant contribution to contemporary Koori (Aboriginal) culture. Suzanne Bellamy's porcelain sculpture landscapes are held in many private collections around the country and have appeared on covers of books and journals. Megeara, a painter, has developed a series of works that depict women, ranging from Amazons to old women and big women. Among young painters, the surreal work of Jackie Stockdale draws on images of imagined historical women.

The Australian continent is relatively benign, with beaches, mountains, deserts, rain forests, and many wild and solitary places. In recent years, a number of women-run travel companies have been established to provide women-only tours to some of these inaccessible places. Many individuals, partners, or small groups travel on weekends and holidays into the Australian bush. In addition, there are a number of lesbian-run holiday houses in country locations.

Communication is an important issue in a country as geographically and demographically scattered as Australia. *Lesbian Network*, with a readership of near five hundred, has kept lesbians around Australia informed since 1984. Similar magazines exist in most states. They focus on news, events, and profiles of lesbians in their communities and advertise lesbian health, legal, entertainment, and business services. Programs on community radio around Australia serve the same purpose. Bent TV, an arm of community television, produces programs that focus on lesbian endeavors in the arts, sports, and politics.

Sports, too, play an important part in the lives of many women, and some of Australia's greatest sportswomen have been lesbians. Their ranks include swimmers, runners, and individuals and team players in cricket, netball, hockey, tennis, and golf. Some all-lesbian teams have been established, such as the Radclyffe Runners (a softball team) and the Fairfield Falcons (a football—Australian rules—team). Lesbian dances and balls have been a regular occurrence since the early 1970s, with as many as two thousand women attending. Some, like the Silk and Satin Ball held annually to raise money for Matrix Guild (a project to establish a home for old lesbians), provide a program with comedy or a circus performance in addition to bands.

## Lesbian and Feminist Political Action

Lesbians are at the forefront of political action and are always visible when mainstream politics takes a conservative turn. A few openly gay and lesbian candidates have stood for parliament on explicit gay and lesbian platforms. Some have been successful, among them Clover Moore in Sydney. The Australian government recognizes gay and lesbian relationships, which are considered on an equal footing with heterosexual married and common-law relationships. However, same-sex couples without wills cannot automatically leave their property to their partners.

Lesbians have also been important agitators—as activists, public servants, and femocrats—for sweeping political changes. They have been active in campaigning for such issues as child care, abortion, racism, maternity and paternity leave, ecology, land rights for Aboriginals, violence against women, and expanded services and equal treatment for poor women, women from non-English-speaking backgrounds, and Aboriginal women.

The lesbian community in Australia is as diverse as in any other large, industrialized country. Lesbians may not agree on everything, but the community also tends not to fragment easily, perhaps because its sheer numbers are still not large enough to be able to do so. The Australian lesbian community includes radical lesbian feminists, career-oriented lesbians, sadomasochist lesbians, businesswomen, artists, rural lesbians, and lesbians who do not join lesbian communities at all.

*Susan Hawthorne*

### Bibliography

Chesser, Lucy. "Australasian Lesbian Movement, 'Claudia's Group,' and Lynx: 'Non-Political' Lesbian Organisation in Melbourne, 1969–1980." *Hecate* 22:1 (1996), 69–91.

Ford, Ruth, Lyn Isaacs, and Rebecca Jones. *Forbidden Love: Bold Passion, Lesbian Stories, 1900s–1990s.* Exhibition Catalog. Melbourne: History Inverted, 1996.

Hawthorne, Susan. "The History of the Contemporary Australian Women's Movement." *Journal of Australian Lesbian Feminist Studies* 2:1 (1992), 71–79.

Hurley, Michael, ed. *A Guide to Gay and Lesbian Writing in Australia.* Sydney: Allen and Unwin, 1996.

Reekie, Gail. "She Was a Loveable Man." *Journal of Australian Lesbian Feminist Studies* 4 (June 1994), 43–50.

*See also* Pacific Literature

## Austria

Small country located in middle Europe. Until 1918, Austria was a great and multinational monarchy; in the years 1938–1945, it was part of Nazi Germany. During the nineteenth and twentieth centuries, the social and cultural history of lesbians in Austria resembled, in many aspects, that of other Western industrial countries. Especially remarkable, however, is the difficult penal situation of lesbian love and politics.

The last decades of the monarchy are one possible starting point for Austrian lesbian history and culture. Around 1900, many women in public life cultivated romantic friendships, and many combined their women-oriented eroticism with feminist politics. Irma von Troll (1847–1912), one of the first Austrian women to write about prostitution, lived in Salzburg with her female friend, and Auguste Fickert (1855–1910), the prominent cofounder of the radical women's movement in Vienna, also shared her life with a woman. The bourgeois feminist Marie von Najmájer (1844–1904), of Hungarian descent, expressed the wish that the "daughters of the twentieth century" could experience the "tender woman love" that she called "my life's most beautiful content." In a 1905 pamphlet, the Austrian philosopher Helene von Druskowitz (1856–1918), who received her doctoral degree in Switzerland, declared man to be the "curse of the world" and urged women consistently and militantly to the "preference for their own sex." Even the Empress Elisabeth (1837–1898) was allegedly highly susceptible to female erotic beauty.

Physicians practicing in Austria played an active and, for many Western countries, a determining role in defining female homosexuality. The psychiatrist Richard von Krafft-Ebing (1840–1902) systematized "cases" that he had treated under the designa-

**A**tion "female contrary sexuality" (or "inversion") in his main work, *Psychopathia Sexualis*, which appeared in more than a dozen editions after 1886. The psychoanalytic paradigm was formulated by Sigmund Freud (1856–1939) in his study "Psychogenesis of a Case of Homosexuality in a Woman" (1920).

After World War I (1914–1918), larger or more strongly visible lesbian (sub)cultures came into being. The androgynous, sexually ambiguous figures of the New Woman, the "Flapper," and its European version, the boyish "Garçonne," entered the social imaginary, including texts by Austrian authors such as Stefan Zweig (1881–1942) and Joseph Roth (1894–1939). Women of the "Third Gender" (a commonly used phrase) organized themselves in the Austrian branches of the two large German homosexual organizations, Deutscher Freundschaftsverband (German Friendship Association) and Bund für Menschenrecht (Union for Human Rights). Employed women of the lower middle class in the capital Vienna, as well as in the country subscribed to the German magazines *Frauenliebe* (Woman Love) and *Die Freundin* (The Woman-Friend), and so became part of a lesbian communication network. They composed short stories, poems, and letters for the magazines and discussed best-sellers like the German lesbian novel *The Scorpion* by Anna Weirauch (1887–1970) and the translation of *The Well of Loneliness* by Radclyffe Hall (1880–1943) that was published in 1929.

For many years, the restrictive legal situation influenced the scope of action of lesbian women. Unlike in most European countries, same-sex sexual activities were forbidden between women, as well as between men, and were punished with incarceration up to five years. This law, originating in the middle of the nineteenth century, was repealed only in 1972; one striking argument for its abolition was that, in regard to women, it was supposedly difficult to distinguish between sex and "assistance with personal hygiene." Under National Socialist rule, the Austrian legal code was assimilated into that of Germany. Paradoxically, that meant that female homosexuality in Austria had less significance in criminal law than before. Lesbian women were, however, sent to National Socialist concentration camps with the verdict "antisocial," wearing the black triangle that came with it. Exile and deportation further disrupted lesbian sub- and countercultural organization.

Only in the course of the feminist movements after 1968 did lesbian groups once again gain a public presence and become politically active. The autonomous women's movement in the 1970s swirled with controversies over lesbians defining themselves as the radical avant-garde. The 1980s then saw a broad and consistant increase of various initiatives by lesbians. Austrian lesbian meetings took place on a regular basis, and the *Lesbenrundbrief* (Lesbian Circular Letter) was published as a medium of its own. Women became involved with mixed lesbian and gay projects, such as the residential building Rosa Lila Villa (Pink-Lavender Villa) and Homosexuelle Initiative (Homosexual Initiative), the largest mixed organization, which published the magazine *Lambda-Nachrichten* (Lambda-News) and established groups in several Austrian towns. A lesbian and gay research group organized symposiums and lecture series, and Stichwort (Keyword), a large feminist archive, began to take explicit care of the documentation of lesbian politics. Other projects important to the development of lesbian culture(s) included the bookstore and café Frauenzimmer (Women's Room), the feminist magazine *An.Schläge* (Keystrokes), and the women's centers and gay and lesbian centers in the cities of Graz, Innsbruck, and Linz.

In the 1990s, the international discussions about identity politics also spread across large parts of the Austrian lesbian scene. Media and popular culture eventually discovered lesbians as a popular commercial topic; there were also widespread debates over controversial questions such as homosexual marriages and the "outing" of prominent homosexual persons. In 1996, the Austrian parliament abolished the criminal law banning positive publicity about same-sex love that had existed since 1972 and the ban against homosexual organizations.

*Hanna Hacker*

### Bibliography

Geber, Eva, Sonja Rotter, and Marietta Schneider eds. *Die Frauen Wiens: Ein Stadtbuch für Fanny, Frances, und Francesca* (The Women of Vienna: A City Book for Fanny, Frances, and Francesca). Vienna: Apfel, 1992.

Geiger, Brigitte, and Hanna Hacker. *Donauwalzer Damenwahl: Frauenbewegte Zusammenhänge in Österreich* (Blue Danube Waltz Ladies' Choice: Feminist Contexts in Austria). Vienna: Promedia, 1989.

Hacker, Hanna. *Frauen und Freundinnen: Studien zur "weiblichen Homosexualität" am Beispiel Österreich, 1870–1938* (Women and Women-

Friends: Studies in "Female Homosexuality" and the Example of Austria, 1870–1938). Weinheim-Baswel: Beltz, 1987.

Handl, Michael, Gudrun Hauer, Kurt Krickler, Friedrich Nussbaumer, and Dieter Schmutzler, eds. *Homosexualität in Österreich* (Homosexuality in Austria). Vienna: Junius, 1989.

Hauer, Gudrun, and Schmutzer, Dieter, eds. *Lambdalesebuch: Journalismus andersrum* (Lambdareader: Journalism the Other Way Round). Vienna: Regenbogen, 1996.

*See also* Nazism; Sexology

## Autobiography

Twentieth-century literary genre. Autobiographies by lesbian authors have played an important role in defining and changing lesbian identity, providing a way for lesbians to rewrite the stories of their lives and, in doing so, to change those lives themselves. However, as important as autobiography has been in constructing lesbian identity, it is a complex and problematic genre, one that has changed over the decades as it has reflected the social and intellectual world in which it is written.

## Characteristics

It is commonly thought that a key characteristic of autobiography is an understanding between the author and the reader that the author sincerely believes that what she says about herself is the truth. In other words, the reader of an autobiography assumes that the author will be as open and honest about her life as she is able to be. This expectation does not always hold up in autobiographical writings by lesbians. Because of the often hidden nature of lesbianism, the acts of writing and reading autobiography require a complex set of negotiations between author and reader, both heterosexual and lesbian. In place of an assumption that the author will tell the truth, there is often the expectation, when the author is a lesbian, that she will, and should, distort the truth through omission, half-truths, and the use of language that is coded so that only those who are "in the know" will understand what her words really mean.

One of the things that makes lesbian autobiography different from autobiographies by other kinds of writers is that a lesbian author must make a choice to either reveal, hide, or distort the nature of her sexuality. This is not just a matter of an author deciding whether or not to include intimate details about her sexual practices—it is common for heterosexual authors to choose not to reveal information about the sexual aspects of their lives. However, in a society in which heterosexuality is assumed to be normal, the effect of omitting or obscuring information about the author's sexuality is that the reader is allowed to assume that the author is heterosexual. When the author is not, the expectation of truthfulness has been clearly violated. In other words, a closeted autobiographer lies as much through omission as through outright denial.

Omission or distortion of the author's sexual identity was especially prevalent in autobiographies written by lesbians prior to the 1970s. With the exception of a few pockets of artists and intellectuals, most lesbians prior to the 1970s were caught in a social and psychological environment that bred internalized guilt and shame. For all but the most flamboyant, lesbian life was marked by silence and secrecy. Many well-known lesbians published memoirs and autobiographies, but few were completely honest about their private lives, and fewer still wrote about their sexuality. Some writers were able to create an illusion of intimacy with their readers while managing to omit any details about their private lives that might reveal characteristics that would subject them to suspicion of being lesbian. Others, who were able or willing to take greater risks, expressed their sexuality by using codes and signs that would be understood only by those familiar with gay and lesbian culture. This approach was designed to keep the hostile straight world in the dark while revealing the "truth" to those who would be less likely to condemn. Coded language and oblique references to gay and lesbian culture were used in most of the autobiographies and memoirs written during the twentieth century as ways of protecting not only the writer, but also those being written about, for, even if the author of an autobiography was willing to be identified as a lesbian, she could not assume that her friends and family members were as willing to be open. In a homophobic environment, it was necessary for lesbians to protect each other as well as themselves. Discretion, in such a society, could have more social value than truth.

### Lesbian Autobiographies

To varying degrees, lesbian writers such as Margaret Anderson (1886–1973), Sylvia Beach (1887–1962), Ethel Smyth (1858–1944), and Janet Flanner (1892–1978), each of whom published essays and

A books with autobiographical content, described their relationships with women in ways that made it possible for straight readers to ignore or overlook the true nature of those relationships and, consequently, to maintain the illusion of the author's heterosexuality. Authors such as these were assumed by both academic critics and the popular media to have been sexually frustrated unmarried spinsters, despite the fact that they had important, and often public, relationships with women.

There were, of course, exceptions. Even during the first half of the twentieth century, a few autobiographies were published by women otherwise unknown to the general public that focused attention on their sexual deviance in sensationalistic ways. *The Story of Mary MacLane* (1902) and *I, Mary MacLane* (1917) were written by an unknown young woman from Montana whose eccentric life story, with its suggestions of lesbianism, was her only claim to fame. Another autobiographical book that created a sensation because of the explicit self-identification of the author as a lesbian was *Diana: A Strange Autobiography* (1939), supposedly written by a college professor named Diana Frederics. While both MacLane and Frederics claimed to be writing their life stories to provide a model of honesty and openness, both autobiographies suggested that lesbianism was a tragic condition that was likely to lead to misery and alienation.

*The Autobiography of Alice B. Toklas* (1933) by Gertrude Stein (1874–1946) is a very different kind of autobiography. Purposefully disconnecting the autobiographical author, narrator, and subject by playing with the most fundamental premise of autobiographical writing—that the author and the subject are identical—Stein pretends to disguise her own autobiography as the autobiography of her lover, Alice B. Toklas (1877–1967). By using Toklas's voice to focus on the real subject, herself, Stein forces the reader to implicitly accept the nature of her relationship to Toklas. Yet her approach is so subtle that even the otherwise perceptive feminist critic Carolyn Heilbrun admitted to having read *The Autobiography of Alice B. Toklas* without understanding that Stein and Toklas were lesbians.

As the feminist movement of the 1970s gained strength, there was a reaction against the silence that preceded it. In 1976, at the annual meeting of the Modern Language Association, the American poet Adrienne Rich (1929–) called for an end to the erasure of lesbianism. In a talk that has become one of the benchmarks of the lesbian feminist movement of the twentieth century, Rich called upon lesbian writers and scholars to stop hiding their sexual identities and colluding in maintaining the invisibility of lesbians of the past. Rich argued that, instead of being a way to ensure safety, silence was a way to perpetuate oppression, because, she pointed out, whatever remains unspoken will eventually become unspeakable.

Rich's speech reflected the thoughts of many lesbians during the 1970s, who encouraged other lesbian writers and scholars to publicly speak the truth about their own lives and to reveal the lesbianism of earlier generations of writers in critical analyses and biographies. A rallying cry was sounded that preceded an outburst of autobiographical writings by lesbians that formed an important literary subgenre during the final quarter of the twentieth century. Autobiography provided one of the most immediate and apparently unmediated vehicles for revealing and redefining lesbian identity. During the 1970s and 1980s, a steady stream of autobiographical works by lesbians became available. The range of these works was wide, from the often shocking personal essays of Jill Johnston (1929–) that appeared weekly in the *Village Voice* and in her books, *Lesbian Nation* (1973) and *Gullible's Travels* (1974), to the quiet and contemplative journals of the novelist May Sarton (1912–1996), who was at first as reticent about her sexuality as early autobiographers had been, but who gradually became more open until, at her death, she was one of the most widely recognized lesbians in the world. Another major change during this period was the appearance of published writings by a broader range of lesbians, including women of color, such as Audre Lorde (1934–1992), whose "biomythography," *Zami: A New Spelling of My Name* (1982), has become a classic in the genre, and the women who contributed to important anthologies like *This Bridge Called My Back: Writings by Radical Women of Color* (1981), edited by Cherríe Moraga and Gloria Anzaldúa.

## The Coming Out Story

As lesbians began to speak out more, a new type of lesbian autobiography developed, the "coming out story," in which the author, who was most commonly not a well-known figure, told the story of how she discovered her lesbianism and how she made her identity known to others. Unlike in earlier autobiographies by lesbians, in which intimate relationships were hidden by omission and coding, the authors of these new personal narratives proudly declared their sexuality. The coming out story was an extremely popular and useful subgenre, with seven anthologies published between 1977 and 1982 alone. In many ways, the coming out stories of the 1970s and 1980s were an ideal response to the problem of the unspeakability of lesbianism. One of the most important things needed by the newly emerging lesbian community was a positive self-image to counter the years of demonization that had defined and silenced lesbians, and these autobiographies provided an accumulation of successful life stories from which such an image could be drawn. In very immediate and direct ways, the coming out story rewrote the lesbian story for the entire community. In an important review essay of anthologies of coming out stories, Zimmerman (1984) wrote that "speaking, especially naming one's self 'lesbian,' is an act of empowerment . . . [that] not only empowers the speaker but also, when communicated through the text, provides alternative role models for lesbians still speechless and powerless."

However, this new emphasis on speaking out as a way to build the lesbian community had an inhibiting effect as well as a liberating one. For the lesbian author to be empowered and to empower others, she had to appear to be powerful and confident about her lesbian identity. In the context of the 1970s and 1980s, a lesbian writer had to be seen as woman identified and unflaggingly positive about her sexuality if she were to be accepted as authentic. She could not be victimized by internalized homophobia that manifested itself in feelings of shame and self-hatred, nor could she admit to feeling identification with men or masculinity. The new autobiographical pact between the lesbian author and the lesbian reader seemed to require something other than complete honesty, at least when the actual experience of the author did not conform to the need for a positive lesbian image. A writer such as Kate Millett (1934–), for example, whose autobiographical works *Flying* (1974) and *Sita* (1977) were painful in their description of the author's mental illness and unhappy love affairs, was met with harsh criticism from lesbian and feminist critics, not for having been written poorly or for being dishonest, but for being negative.

During the 1990s, the nature and function of lesbian autobiography changed again under the influence of poststructuralist and queer theory, which challenged the notion that there can be any objective truth or fixed personal identity. According to queer (a term often preferred to lesbian, gay, or homosexual) theorists, all forms of gender are constructed within a social context rather than being a fixed or essential aspect of the self. Along with this new theoretical model has come a new appreciation for those members of the gay and lesbian community, such as drag queens and butch dykes, who insist on expressing and acting out their gender identities, no matter how extremely they deviate from the norm. This "gender bending," as it is called, is seen as being as authentic as identities that conform with society's view of what it means to be male and female. In this environment, autobiographical writing could no longer be judged on the basis of its adherence to truth or the degree of an author's honesty, because it is assumed that every writer of autobiography is engaged in a process of creating identity rather than either revealing or hiding it. The lines between fiction and truth are blurred when both are seen as performances.

*Linda Dunne*

### Bibliography

Benstock, Shari, ed. *The Private Self: Theory and Practice of Women's Autobiographical Writings*. Chapel Hill: University of North Carolina Press, 1988.

Brokzki, Bella, and Celeste Schenck, eds. *Life/Lines: Theorizing Women's Autobiography*. Ithaca, N.Y.: Cornell University Press, 1988.

Gilmore, Leigh. *Autobiographics: A Feminist Theory of Women's Self-Representation*. Ithaca, N.Y.: Cornell University Press, 1994.

Rich, Adrienne. "It Is the Lesbian in Us. . . ." In *On Lies, Secrets, and Silence: Selected Prose, 1966–1978*. New York: Norton, 1979, pp. 199–202.

Stanton, Domna C., ed. *The Female Autograph*. Chicago: University of Chicago Press, 1984.

Zimmerman, Bonnie. "The Politics of Transliteration: Lesbian Personal Narratives." In *Signs: Journal of Women in Culture and Society* 9:4 (1984), 663–682.

***See also*** Biography; Coming Out Stories; Rich, Adrienne; Stein, Gertrude; Toklas, Alice B.

# B

## Balkan Sworn Virgin

Traditional European female-to-male transgender. The Balkan sworn virgin is a traditional status, role, and identity by which genetic females become social men, the only such socially recognized transgendered status in modern Europe. Clover (1986) proposed that this may be a survival of a more widespread pre-Christian European status. Reported in travel accounts since the early 1800s, in mountain areas of South Serbia (including Montenegro), Macedonia, and Albania, sworn virgins still existed, primarily in northern Albania, in the 1990s. Traditionally, the status was formally assumed at puberty (the time of marriage for women) by the ratification of lineage elders before whom the young woman swore never to marry. Thereafter, he assumed masculine dress and social privileges, such as smoking and drinking, could carry a gun, participated in men's labor and intertribal feuding, and associated with men, in these sex-segregated societies. Referred to by a variety of local and regional terms (for example, Albanian *vergineshe*, Serbo-Croatian *harambasa* [woman-man]), most of these transgendered females assumed a masculine cognomen and were addressed and referred to with masculine-gendered terms, though there was individual variation. Similarly, some sworn virgins were buried in masculine dress with male rites, but others were denied such privileges. The status was almost always held for life.

Common rationales for assumption of this status were to avoid an unwanted arranged marriage or to assume the family patrimony in the absence of a male heir. However, it is clear from personal accounts (see especially Durham [1987] and Grémaux [1994]) that personal choice and childhood cross-gender identity played roles in some cases. In addition, the gain in status may have been a factor, as women held very low status in these groups. Lacking heirs, the sworn virgin could not continue the family line by direct descent; however, there are cases in which he assumed leadership of an extended family through accretion of relatives or through the marriage and procreation of a later-born male sibling. In some cases, sworn virgins acceded to a seat in the all-male village or lineage council, though this opportunity varied, depending on local custom. In general, they seem to be and to have been respected by male associates and society at large.

Although much of the descriptive literature ignores the sexuality of these men-women, most were probably chaste. There are reports of occasional heterosexual activity, but tradition prescribed burning or stoning to death as punishment for such relations. The first researcher to directly address sexuality, Grémaux, reports some sworn virgins expressing sexual attraction to women without consummating their desires, and two recent cases of liaisons with women, termed "lesbian" by neighbors. Many shared the misogynist views customary among men in these extremely male-dominant, patrilineal societies. It appears possible that females living as men in the 1990s were gradually being redefined as lesbians as traditional tribal groups were absorbed into modern industrial society and exposed to pan-European norms.                                     *Mildred Dickemann*

### Bibliography

Bullough, Bonnie, Vern Bullough, and James Elias, eds. *Gender Blending*. Amherst, N.Y.: Prometheus, 1997.

*Sokol on horseback. Photo by Antonia Young.*

Clover, Carol J. "Maiden Warriors and Other Sons." *Journal of English and Germanic Philology* 85 (1986), 35–49.

Dickemann, Mildred. "The Balkan Sworn Virgin: A Traditional European Transperson." In *Gender and Transgender Issues*. Ed. Bonnie Bullough, Vern Bullough, and James Elias. Amherst, N.Y.: Prometheus, 1997, pp. 248–255.

Durham, Mary Edith. *High Albania*. Boston: Beacon, 1987.

Grémaux, René. "Woman Becomes Man in the Balkans." In *Third Sex, Third Gender: Beyond Sexual Dimorphism in Culture and History*. Ed. Gilbert Herdt. New York: Zone, 1994, pp. 241–281.

*See also* Amazons; Transgender

## Bannon, Ann (1937–)

American novelist. Ann Bannon (a pseudonym) wrote the Beebo Brinker series, now considered a classic collection of lesbian pulp paperbacks. What distinguishes Bannon's work from the literally thousands of pulps published in the 1950s and early 1960s is her insistence on empathetic lesbian characters who rebel against social prejudice and stereotypes of perversion. This gained Bannon a devoted lesbian audience, who relished her more positive portrayals of lesbian life.

Bannon was married at the time she began to write the novels; her experience at the University of Illinois provided the fodder for her first novel, *Odd Girl Out* (1957). Set at a college, the book introduces sorority sisters Laura and Beth, two central characters of Bannon's six-novel series. While their relationship does not last, the series follows Laura to Greenwich Village in New York City in *I Am a Woman* (1959). There, with the help of Jack Mann, a gay male friend, Laura learns to negotiate the "gay world" and falls in love with Beebo Brinker. In *Women in the Shadows* (1959), Laura ends her burdensome relationship with Beebo and makes a successful go of a companionate, nonsexual relationship with Jack and becomes pregnant with his child through artificial insemination. In *The Marriage* (1960), Laura and Jack reappear as minor characters in a basically heterosexual story. *Journey to a Woman* (1960) brings the storyline back to Beth, who has left her husband to search for her long-lost love, Laura. Laura and Beth become friends, and Beth falls in love with Beebo. The final novel of the series, *Beebo Brinker* (1962), chronologically predates the other five's narratives and tells the story of its eponymous hero and how she came to Greenwich Village. All (with the exception of *The Marriage*, which is tangentially lesbian themed) were reissued by Naiad Press in the early 1980s. Bannon's novels continue to captivate lesbian readers with characters who feel familiar and navigate through a prejudiced world with grit and determination.                    *Linnea A. Stenson*

### Bibliography

Tilchen, Maida. "Ann Bannon: The Mystery Solved!" *Gay Community News* (January 8, 1983), 8–12.

Walters, Suzanna Danuta. "As Her Hand Crept Slowly up Her Thigh: Ann Bannon and the Politics of Pulp." *Social Text: Theory/Culture/Ideology* 23 (Fall/Winter 1989), 83–101.

Weinstein, Jeff. "In Praise of Pulp: Bannon's Lusty Lesbians." *Voice Literary Supplement* (October 1983), 8–9.

*See also* Naiad Press; Pulp Paperbacks

### Barnes, Djuna Chappell (1892–1982)

U.S. writer. Born in Cornwall-on-Hudson, New York, Djuna Barnes was the second of five children in the household of a British mother and a bohemian U.S. father. When Djuna was five, her father's mistress moved in with her family and began also to have children with Barnes's father. Both families lived together with Barnes's paternal grandmother, Zadel Barnes, for fifteen years until Barnes's parents divorced in 1912. Evidence points to a violent sexual experience when Barnes was sixteen with a friend of her father, with the older brother of Barnes's father's mistress, or with Barnes's father himself. Correspondence may indicate an incestuous relationship between the writer and her grandmother as well.

After a brief marriage and a short enrollment at the Pratt Institute, Barnes moved to Greenwich Village in 1915 and began a career in freelance journalism. She also began acting in and writing plays for the newly established Provincetown Playhouse. Though involved with men and women during this period, Barnes brought out *The Book of Repulsive Women* (1915), eight poems and five drawings featuring lesbian themes and including the writer's illustrations.

Barnes's journalistic work sent her, in 1921, to Paris, where she met Thelma Wood (1901–1970), a silverpoint artist from St. Louis, Missouri, who, by all accounts, was to become the most intense love interest of Barnes's life. After the pair settled together in Paris, Barnes brought out two novels, *Ryder* (1928), a novelistic account of her unconventional childhood, and *Ladies Almanack* (1928), a humorous depiction of the circle of lesbians surrounding the wealthy expatriate Natalie Barney (1876–1972). *Ryder* appeared briefly on best-seller lists; *Ladies Almanack*, written as a lark, was privately printed. Both novels appeared during the height of the artistic movement known as literary modernism. Virginia Woolf's (1882–1941) playful tale of gender transformation, *Orlando,* was published in the same year, as was Radclyffe Hall's (1880–1943) lesbian classic, *The Well of Loneliness.* In fact, a character modeled on Hall appears in *Ladies Almanack.*

After eight tempestuous years marked by infidelity and alcohol abuse, Barnes and Wood separated in 1929. Some of their difficulties are depicted seven years later in Barnes's most celebrated novel, *Nightwood* (1936), which also expresses the spirit of alienation and loss often characteristic of literary modernism. Presenting a cross-section of the disenfranchised wandering through its pages seeking various illusory goals, the novel became an underground classic for several decades after publication. T.S. Eliot's (1888–1965) introduction to the U.S edition highlights *Nightwood*'s poetic qualities.

In 1940, Barnes returned from Europe to spend the last half of her life in a Greenwich Village studio apartment in increasing ill health and reclusiveness. The year 1958 marked the publication of Barnes's last major work, *The Antiphon*, a verse drama depicting autobiographical and familial themes. Barnes's three novels and many short stories, drawings, poems, plays, and journalistic pieces have been reissued to increased critical recognition in the late twentieth century. She died in her New York City apartment at the age of ninety.    *Anne Charles*

### Bibliography

Broe, Mary Lynn, ed. *Silence and Power: A Reevaluation of Djuna Barnes*. Carbondale: Southern Illinois University Press, 1991.

Field, Andrew. *Djuna: The Formidable Miss Barnes*. Austin: University of Texas Press, 1983.

Herring, Phillip. *Djuna: The Life and Work of Djuna Barnes*. New York: Viking, 1995.

Levine, Nancy J., and Marian Urquilla, eds. "Djuna Barnes Centennial Issue." *Review of Contemporary Fiction* 13:3 (Fall 1993) (Special Issue).

O'Neal, Hank. *Life Is Painful, Nasty & Short . . . In My Case It Has Only Been Painful and Nasty: Djuna Barnes, 1978–1981, An Informal Memoir.* New York: Paragon House, 1990.

*See also* American Literature, Twentieth Century; Barney, Natalie; Greenwich Village; Hall, Radclyffe; Modernism; Woolf, Virginia

## Barney, Natalie (1876–1972)

American writer, salon hostess, and renowned lover. Born in Dayton, Ohio, Barney moved to Paris at the age of twenty-four, making it her principal residence until her death. As heiress to a railroad fortune valued at more than a billion dollars and the daughter of liberal parents, Barney was free to follow her passion for women in prose, in verse, and in bed.

Barney is perhaps best known for her theatrical love affairs with the famous women of her day, including Liane de Pougy (1869–1953), the Parisian courtesan; Renée Vivien (1877–1909), the English poet; Lucie Delarue-Mardrus (1874–1945), the French novelist; and Romaine Brooks (1874–1970), the American painter. Her methods of courtship were imaginative, to say the least. On one occasion, she had herself delivered to her lover's bedroom stark naked and surrounded by white lilies lying in a glass coffin made by Lalique. At another time, she hired a famous opera soprano to sing under the balcony of a lover who had recently left her for someone less dramatic and more faithful. Barney was also renowned as a society hostess and held a weekly salon in her home at 20 rue Jacob that continued for more than fifty years. This salon was attended by major literary and artistic figures, including Colette (1873–1954), André Gide (1869–1951), Gertrude Stein (1874–1946), Djuna Barnes (1892–1982), Oscar Wilde (1854–1900), Auguste Rodin (1840–1917), Paul Valéry (1871–1945), and Mata Hari (1876–1917).

Philosophically committed to nonmonogamy and the pursuit of pleasure, Barney inspired a large number of literary portraits, such as that of Flossie in de Pougy's *Idylle Sapphique* (Sapphic Idyll [1901]); Miss Flossie in Colette's *Claudine s'en va* (Claudine and Annie [1903]); Valerie Seymour in Radclyffe Hall's (1880–1943) *The Well of Loneli-*

ness (1928); and Laurette Wells in Delarue-Mardrus's *L'Ange et les pervers* (The Angel and the Perverts, [1930]). Although each portrait shows a rather different side of Barney's multifaceted personality, these characters share an indomitable spirit, an imperious way with words, and a profound commitment to lesbianism.

Barney's participation in the artistic milieu of Paris was active as well as contemplative. At the age of twenty-four, she published her first collection of poetry, *Quelques portraits sonnets de femmes* (Some Sonnet Portraits of Women [1900]), followed by two collections of plays. Although this early work is unremarkable, her memoirs and literary portraits, which include *Aventures de l'esprit* (Adventures of the Mind [1929]) and *Souvenirs indiscrets* (Indiscreet Memories [1960]), are lively, sometimes gossipy, insightful accounts of the people she knew and a commentary on many of the social questions of the day. She argues with characteristic humor and elegance that homosexuality is a godsend in a century facing overpopulation. Her defense of breasts is unsurpassed in its originality and passion: "Breasts: passion's accelerator, electric lead, guide to femininity wherein the first signs of arousal dwell." It is, however, in her epigrams in *Eparpillements* (Scatterings [1910]), *Pensées d'une amazone* (Thoughts of an Amazon [1920]), and *Nouvelles pensées de l'amazone* (Further Thoughts of the Amazon [1939]) that she shows a real and original talent for summing up a social situation or acquaintance in a brief, pithy turn of phrase.

Because of her outspoken commitment to lesbianism and her passionate affairs, Barney has become something of a heroine to many lesbians in Europe and North America since the 1970s. A less well-known aspect of Barney's life is her intellectual flirtation with fascism and antisemitism during World War II, which she spent with Romaine Brooks in Italy, in a villa just outside Florence. Before the war, Barney had entertained many Jewish friends and boasted of her own Jewish ancestry (her maternal grandfather was Jewish). After Benito Mussolini's (1883–1945) rise to power, however, Barney became a sympathizer of the Italian Fascist Party. She and Brooks were close friends of the poet Ezra Pound (1885–1972)—he who gave Mussolini the name of "Il Duce," the leader. Barney bought Pound his first radio, from which he was to make pro-fascist broadcasts during the war. Since Barney's house in the rue Jacob was searched by the Gestapo who asked for her by name, it is possible that Barney was acting preemptively to stop any questions being asked about herself.

Barney returned to Paris after the war and, since her personal fortune had not been adversely affected by events in Europe, was able to continue her affairs much as before. She made her last amorous conquest on a park bench in Nice at the age of eighty-two.                                    *Anna Livia*

## Bibliography

Barney, Natalie. *A Perilous Advantage*. Trans. Anna Livia. Norwich, Vt.: New Victoria, 1992.

Jay, Karla. *The Amazon and the Page*. Bloomington and Indianapolis: Indiana University Press, 1988.

Wickes, George. *The Amazon of Letters: The Life and Loves of Natalie Barney*. New York: Putnam's, 1976.

*See also* Barnes, Djuna Chappell; Brooks, Romaine; Colette; France; French Literature; Hall, Radclyffe; Paris; Stein, Gertrude; Vivien, Renée

## Bars

One of the first and, worldwide, the most prevalent and often only "public" gathering places for lesbians. In most areas, bars are also the only places, outside of private homes, where lesbians can be who they are socially and sexually. Most lesbians, especially working-class lesbians, "come out" in bars.

Evidence of lesbians using bars raided by police dates to the early 1800s in France. In the United States, accounts appear in 1890, when antivice reformers saw "mannish women" in "degenerate" working-class "fairy resorts" on the Bowery, a center of New York City's "vice" district. Since women were considered asexual, lesbians were publicly scorned as "inverts" and "sexual perverts"—women who were masculine and had male sexual desire. But women couples, only one in "male evening attire," danced together at "fairy balls" held in rented halls attached to saloons. Antivice campaigns, focused first on prostitution and later on homosexuality, closed most of these venues by 1920.

In 1920, poor and working-class "never married" women accounted for 20 percent of the urban paid-labor force. They lived in furnished-room districts, on the South and Near North Sides of Chicago, Illinois; in Greenwich Village and Harlem in New York City; and in other cities. Between 1900 and 1920, a lesbian bar culture emerged in these areas. Although small, this bar culture flourished after World War I and solidified during Prohibition (1920–1933). It grew despite public attacks against women pacifists as "lesbians" and "Bolsheviks," and despite the fact that the "heterosexual revolution" (symbolized by the flapper and sexual fulfillment within marriage) defined "feminists," "female friends," "spinsters," and "lesbians" as sick and pathetic.

Nevertheless, as women's sexual desire was acknowledged, lesbians could exist more freely in speakeasies (illegal drinking places) along with heterosexuals, who were also breaking the law and moral convention. In Greenwich Village, at Eve's Hangout, a sign up front said: "Men admitted but not welcome." Opened in 1925 by Eva Kotchever, a lesbian Jewish immigrant, it was raided by police in 1926. In Harlem, the butch-femme lesbian couple was highly visible. Black lesbians and gay men met in cabarets and clubs, like the Hot Cha, which also attracted white lesbians and gay men and heterosexuals. Lesbians also patronized "buffet/party flats" (apartment speakeasies), which, although safer, were also raided.

The Depression of the 1930s had an economic impact on lesbians, but bar culture was likely affected more by the antihomosexual backlash brought on by the end of Prohibition in 1933. Bars where lesbians and gay men openly gathered were denied licenses, raided, and closed. For several years in the 1930s, there were no gay bars in Buffalo, New York; the Roselle and Twelve-Thirty, clubs in Chicago, were closed because women dressed in male clothing. Bars had a short life, and owners monitored patrons' behaviors, relegating socializing and dancing to the back rooms. As police payoffs and crime-syndicate protection, holdovers from Prohibition, became features of lesbian bar life in the late 1930s, bars began opening again throughout the United States.

The military and war-related work of World War II brought isolated lesbians to cities with bar communities. Outside the military, there was greater freedom for working-class lesbians. Many women were on the streets, even at night because of shift-work, and were wearing pants for wartime work. More lesbian-only bars opened. In Los Angeles, California, lesbians went to the IF Club; in Harlem, lesbians went to Archer's, a women's buffet flat. In Buffalo, lesbians created bars (most short lived) by going in groups to heterosexual bars with few customers. Bar hopping became a weekend activity, and friendship groups formed. Buffalo lesbians even picketed a bar when a patron was treated negatively by the owner. From the end of the war through

**B** the 1960s, the number of lesbian bars grew in different parts of the United States. The Lighthouse opened in Lynn, Massachusetts; the BRA House, in Kalamazoo, Michigan. A cohesive bar life and culture developed, predominantly working class and young, and became a nightly phenomenon. At its center was butch-femme, a way of living and loving, as well as dressing. A much smaller and discreet affluent lesbian bar culture developed as well.

In 1948, the Kinsey Report made sexuality, including lesbianism, a daily news topic and helped unleash a government-sanctioned reign of terror. With the push for family normalcy and the anti-Communist McCarthy hearings in Congress, lesbians and gay men were vilified as perils to national security because of their supposed emotional instability. Police all over the country declared war on bars. In 1958, in New Orleans, Louisiana, one bar was raided seventy-eight times. Everywhere, large numbers of lesbians were arrested, charged with "impersonating a man" if they did not have on three pieces of women's clothing, for "lewd and lascivious acts" if holding hands or dancing, or for "no visible means of support" if unemployed. Lesbians' names were published in newspapers; many lost jobs; families threw them out or sent them, involuntarily, to psychiatric hospitals. Bar owners humiliated women by, for example, allowing only one woman at a time into the bathroom. Bar raids were unpredictable, orchestrated in collusion with owners for political gain or intimidation. The stress of a hostile society, the constant pressure to buy drinks, the men who entered bars just to provoke fights, pushed many lesbians to suicide, alcoholism, or out of public life. Yet others publicly identified as "gay" and fought back physically in the bars and when taunted on the streets. Finally, in 1969, in the context of the civil rights and Black Power movements, a reporter credited a bar "dyke" with resisting arrest during a raid on the Stonewall Inn in Greenwich Village, thus sparking the rebellion considered the beginning of the modern lesbian and gay movement.

During the 1970s, lesbian activists promoted other venues as "an alternative to the bars." The androgyny of lesbian feminism excluded and alienated many butch-femme lesbians, just as the butch-femme bar culture of the 1950s and 1960s alienated many lesbians who, nevertheless, found in it their only community. Lesbian bar raids would disappear in the United States (although not in other countries) during the next twenty years, but violent attacks against bars and their culture remained. For example, Mor or Les, a bar in St. Louis, Missouri, was firebombed in 1979 during the nationwide "Save Our Children" antigay campaign. In the early 1980s, bars became the site of the pro-sex lesbian movement, and some activist lesbians began to identify as butch-femme. In the 1980s, in larger cities, bar cultures diversified. However, as Greenwich Village attracted more affluent residents, two bars used by working-class lesbians and lesbians of color had their licenses revoked for excluding men, although gay male bars exclude women with impunity. Smaller cities often have only mixed-sex bars, although bars have been largely racially segregated everywhere. There have always been more gay male than lesbian bars, reflecting gender inequities in owning businesses, income, and safety at night on public streets.

From the mid-1980s to the early 1990s, as an outgrowth of AIDS and lesbian and gay political organizing, mixed-sex activist groups socialized together in male venues. In the Castro and Mission districts of San Francisco, California, older and exclusively lesbian bars closed. In the mixed-sex, young, cosmopolitan "queer" culture, lesbians frequent mixed lesbian, gay male, and heterosexual dance bars. "Women's nights" may be held at gay male or heterosexual bars.

Around the United States in the late 1990s, most bars still catered largely to working-class lesbians and were still located on the edges of towns or in industrial or commercial areas unpeopled at night, shared with heterosexual sex clubs and other "adult" entertainment. In the context of right-wing attacks on lesbians and gay men, it is possible that there will again be strong moves to push bar culture out of sight even in large cities, as "sex-zoning" legislation attempts to do. However, lesbian bar culture has proven to be incredibly resilient. That more lesbians go to bars than to any other lesbian venue emphasizes the major role they continue to play in lesbian life. In a homophobic world, their continued existence speaks to the needs and desires for lesbians to have places that validate the reality of lesbians' social and sexual existence. *Maxine Wolfe*

### Bibliography

Bulkin, Ellie. "An Old Dyke's Tale: An Interview with Doris Lunden." *Conditions: Six,* 2:3 (Summer 1980), 26–44.

Chauncey, George. *Gay New York: Gender, Urban Culture, and the Making of the Gay Male World, 1890–1940.* New York: Basic Books, 1944.

Garber, Eric. "A Spectacle in Color: The Lesbian and Gay Subculture of Jazz Age Harlem." In *Hidden from History: Reclaiming the Gay and Lesbian Past*. Ed. Martin Duberman, Martha Vicinus, and George Chauncey, Jr. New York: New American Library, 1989.

Kennedy, Elizabeth Lapovsky, and Madeline D. Davis. *Boots of Leather, Slippers of Gold: The History of a Lesbian Community*. New York: Routledge, 1993.

Wolfe, Maxine. "Invisible Women in Invisible Places: The Production of Social Space in Lesbian Bars." In *Queers in Space: Communities/Public Places/Sites of Resistance*. Ed. Gordon Brent Ingram, Anne-Marie Bouthillette, and Yolanda Retter. Seattle, Wash.: Bay Press, 1997, pp. 301–324.

**See also** Butch-Femme; Buffalo, New York; Chicago, Illinois; Greenwich Village; Harlem; Law and Legal Institutions; Recreation; San Francisco, California

## Bates, Katharine Lee (1859–1929)

American author, poet, and educator. She earned national acclaim in 1895 as the author of the patriotic and idealistic poem "America the Beautiful." It was later set to music and, in the twentieth century, has become the unofficial national anthem. Bates was a prolific author, publishing prose, poetry, travel books, children's stories, and scholarly texts, many of which earned awards. For more than thirty years she was chair of the English literature department of Wellesley College.

Bates was born in Falmouth, Massachusetts, the fifth and last child of the Reverend William and Cornelia Frances (Lee) Bates. Her father died three weeks after her birth, leaving the family in economic need.

Bates received the best education available to middle-class women in the late nineteenth century, attending both the Wellesley and the more advanced Newton High Schools. She received her B.A. from Wellesley College in 1880, having studied English and Greek. In 1878, while Bates was still a sophomore in college, renowned American poet Henry Wadsworth Longfellow (1807–1882) singled out her published poem "Sleep" for praise.

In 1885, she joined the English literature department at Wellesley College as an instructor. After studying at Oxford University in England, she returned to Wellesley and received her M.A. for her work in English literature. She became professor and permanent head of the Wellesley English literature department in 1891. Under her guidance, the department developed into a well-balanced program with highly respected and distinguished instructors.

Bates enjoyed a nearly twenty-five-year relationship, beginning in 1890, with fellow Wellesley professor and administrator Katharine Coman (1857–1915). In the nineteenth century, "romantic friendships," or "Boston marriages" as they were termed, were respected social institutions, and it was widely accepted for women to have close, passionate, and romantic relationships. The two women most likely would not have termed themselves "lesbian," since that term didn't come into use until the twentieth century. Nonetheless, they were a devoted couple and held each other as the emotional, spiritual, and passionate centers of their inner lives.

Coman appears frequently throughout Bates's poetry and other writings. Bates's final volume of poetry, *Yellow Clover* (1922), was written in honor of her longtime companion, friend, and lover. Its pages are filled with romantic and passionate devotion celebrating their lives together. *Paris Awalt*

### Bibliography

Burgess, Dorothy. *Dream and Deed*. Norman: University of Oklahoma Press, 1952.

Schwarz, Judith. "*Yellow Clover*: Katharine Lee Bates and Katharine Coman." *Frontiers: A Journal of Women Studies,* 4:1 (1979), 59–67.

**See also** Boston Marriage; Colleges, Women's; Romantic Friendship

## Beach, Sylvia (1887–1962)

American expatriate bookshop owner and publisher. Born in Baltimore, Maryland, Nancy Woodbridge Beach (or Sylvia, a name she adopted in her teens) was the daughter of an orthodox Presbyterian minister and his free-spirited wife, Eleanor, who taught her three daughters to love Europe, to seek pleasure and individual freedom, to admire bold and creative artists, and to shun sexual contact with men. Sylvia was a frail and unhealthy child, who often stayed home from school and church. Alone, she sought the company of books, an escape that yielded an education and a vocation.

**B**

As a young woman, Beach lived in France, Italy, and Spain for periods, working as a translator, a farmhand, and a freelance writer and serving as a secretary with the American Red Cross in war-ravaged Serbia before settling in Paris in 1919. There she discovered the three loves of her life: Adrienne Monnier (1892–1956), James Joyce (1882–1941), and the bookshop Shakespeare and Company.

Monnier, a young writer and publisher, encouraged Beach's dream of starting her own modest bookstore, and, in November 1919, Shakespeare and Company opened its doors on the Left Bank. For Monnier and Beach, it was the opening chapter of a literary life together that, for thirty-eight years, would nurture two generations of American, French, and English writers.

From 1919 to 1941, when the Nazis forced its closing and sent Beach into hiding, Shakespeare and Company was a meeting place, a clubhouse, a post office, a money exchange, and a reading room for the famous and the soon-to-be famous of the avant-garde: Joyce, Ernest Hemingway (1899–1961), Ezra Pound (1885–1972), Paul Valéry (1871–1945), André Gide (1869–1951), T.S. Eliot (1888–1965), John Dos Passos (1896–1970), and Thornton Wilder (1897–1975) among them.

A love of books, a tough, enthusiastic spirit, and an interest in people were Beach's assets, and, in 1922 she devoted her considerable energies to the publication, sale, and distribution of Joyce's *Ulysses*—considered obscene by some—soliciting subscriptions, writing letters, hiring typists, correcting endless proofs, and underwriting the financial needs of the author's family.

Beach, however, emerged from World War II a changed woman. The frugality and hardship of Shakespeare and Company's start-up years, combined with the war's privations, including a sixth-month internment by the Gestapo, had taken their toll. She was never to reopen her beloved bookshop. During her remaining years, Beach devoted her time to charity work, personal writing, and translating, and, in 1959, published her autobiography, *Shakespeare and Company*. In 1962, at age seventy-five, she suffered a fatal heart attack.    *Zsa Zsa Gershick*

### Bibliography

Fitch, Noel Riley. *Sylvia Beach and the Lost Generation: A History of Literary Paris in the Twenties and Thirties.* New York: Norton, 1983.

*See also* Paris

## Beauvoir, Simone de (1908–1986)

French existential philosopher, socialist, and writer. Beauvoir was most noted for her book *The Second Sex*, which was published in France in 1949 and translated into English in 1952.

Born January 9, 1908, Beauvoir had the opportunity to attend elite educational institutions, including the Sorbonne in Paris, from which she received her Ph.D. in philosophy in 1929. She was the daughter of Georges Bertrand de Beauvoir, a dictatorial and overbearing father, and Francoise Brasseur de Beauvoir, a cold and detached mother. Observing her parents' marriage, Beauvoir noted the juxtaposition between men and culture, and women and nature, and developed her description of women as "the Other." She became aware at an early age that men had more control over their destinies than women did. She, therefore, decided to place prime importance on acquiring male qualities, such as intellectual order, logic, and rationality. Because of this, some feminist theorists have criticized her work and style of feminism as being shaped by patriarchal values and habits and, in particular, by her lifelong relationship with the philosopher Jean-Paul Sartre (1905–1980), the leader of the existential movement in post–World War II France. Beauvoir herself claimed that her work always reflected her own vision, one she had long before she met Sartre.

Her relationship with Sartre was conflicted. While it involved mutual trust and respect, she disavowed feelings of jealousy against the other women with whom he had been actively involved. A number of her own relationships, mentioned in her journals and letters dating back to 1938, have led to questions concerning Beauvoir's ambiguous gender identity and her connection with lesbianism. Most notable is the love of her youth, Elizabeth Le Coin, and her long-term adult relationship with Sylvie le Bon, whom she later adopted to carry her name and to legally have authority over her care. In addition, Bianca Lamblin stated in her *Mémoires d'une jeune fille dérangée* (Memoirs of a Crazed Young Girl [1993]) that Beauvoir hid affairs with women. Beauvoir was also a strong supporter of the lesbian writer Violette Leduc (1907–1972), who, in turn, idolized her. Beauvoir herself refused a lesbian identity and in no way wanted to be involved in the practices of identity politics. Nevertheless, she included "the lesbian" in her monumental study, *The Second Sex* (1949).

According to Beauvoir, female homosexuals are not "undeveloped" women, and lesbianism, or, as she coins it, "invert sexuality," is not determined by any anatomical "fate"; rather, it is a decision arrived at in a total, complex situation, an attitude that is authentically motivated and freely chosen. A lesbian is an autonomous subject, not an object, and to classify her "virility" as an imitation of the male is to mark her as inauthentic. Between women, there is no notion of possession, but a re-creation of the self through each other, and, through reciprocity, each becomes at once subject and object.

Beauvoir's work continues to be widely studied and debated in an attempt to refine feminist theory and politics. She died of pulmonary edema on April 14, 1986, with Sylvie le Bon by her side, and was buried next to Sartre.          *Darlene M. Suarez*

## Bibliography

Ascher, Carol. *Simone de Beauvoir: A Life of Freedom*. Boston: Beacon, 1981.

Bair, Deirdre. *Simone de Beauvoir: A Biography*. New York: Summit Books, 1990.

Moi, Toril. *Simone de Beauvoir: The Making of an Intellectual Woman*. Oxford: Blackwell, 1994.

Simons, Margaret A. "Lesbian Connections: Simone de Beauvoir and Feminism." *Signs: Journal of Women in Culture and Society* 18:1 (Autumn 1992), 136–161.

*See also* France; Leduc, Violette

## Behn, Aphra (1640?–1689)

Seventeenth-century English poet, novelist, and playwright. Probably born in Wye, in 1640; her exact parentage is unknown. At a young age, she went to the West Indies, where she had the experiences on which her best-known novel, *Oronooko; or, The Royal Slave* (1688), is based. She returned to England in 1664 and established a liaison with a Dutch merchant, whose name she took. He died a year later, leaving her without money, and she became a spy abroad for King Charles II (1630–1685). Forced to borrow money for her passage home and unable to repay the loan, she was thrown into debtors' prison. Determined to be self-supporting, upon her release she became one of the period's foremost writers, with more than twenty published plays produced on the London stage.

Frequently cited as the first woman in England to earn her living by writing, and known as the "English Sappho" for her poems, Behn was a major dramatist when there was no other woman play-wright. She also wrote the first real novel in English, *Love Letters Between a Nobleman and His Sister* (1682–1685). Considered a scandal in her life and her writings, Behn was known for her close friendship with the king's mistress, Nell Gwyn (1650–1687), and for her long-standing liaison with John Hoyle (d. 1692), himself notorious for his gay affairs. Most of her poetry, originally published in two collections, deals with her own lesbian relationships, as well as heterosexual romances and such taboo subjects as rape, impotence, and male homosexuality.

Relationships among women are sometimes presented in Behn's verse in terms of the standard conventions of heterosexual courtship. Behn's explicitly lesbian love poem, "To the fair Clarinda, who made Love to me, imagin'd more than Woman," portrays a sexual attraction based on androgynous desire in which the speaker is the wooer. To obscure her passion, the female speaker presents herself as loving the "masculine" part of Clarinda and offering friendship to the "feminine" half. She maintains, therefore, that their love is innocent and should not be resisted. Further, she asserts, since women do not have the physical feature necessary to complete what society defines as the sex act, they are not to be condemned for their love since, by definition, it must be pure. Clarinda, to whom the poem is addressed, is presented as a hermaphrodite, a "beauteous Wonder of a different kind, / Soft Cloris with the dear Alexis join'd." But she is also an initiator of their lovemaking, as the title states. So the poem's eroticism is the reciprocal attraction of two women with clear gender-transgressing qualities.

Behn also writes in her own voice about her physical attraction to another woman in "Verses design'd by Mrs. A. Behn to be sent to a fair Lady, that desir'd she would absent herself to cure her Love. Left Unfinished." The content and the title of the poem indicate that the love is erotic and unrequited: "The more I strugl'd to my Grief I found / My self in Cupid's chains more surely bound."

As a champion of women openly allied against men in the war between the sexes, Behn writes autobiographically to Carola, "Lady Morland at Tunbridge," warning her about an unfaithful lover and advising her friend that only a sexually inexperienced and, therefore, uncompromised man would be an appropriate partner for her.

Women coming together after betrayal by faithless male lovers is the theme of Behn's entertainment "Selinda and Cloris." The two praise each other in terms of both physical and intellectual at-

**B** traction, friendship, and sexuality. Their joy together is presented as a wedding celebration that emphasizes the eroticism of their relationship.

Behn's poems depict a variety of sexual pairings, some of which are shown to be physically satisfying. But, in her work, spiritual "friendship" is reserved for same-sex couples, among which the lesbian relationships are presented as the most complete and rewarding.                    *Arlene M. Stiebel*

### Bibliography

Duffy, Maureen. *The Passionate Shepherdess*. London: Cape, 1977.

Goreau, Angeline. *Reconstructing Aphra*. New York: Dial, 1980.

Sackville-West, Vita. *Aphra Behn: The Incomparable Astrea*. New York: Viking, 1928.

Stiebel, Arlene. "Aphra Behn." In *Dictionary of Literary Biography,* vol. 131, 3rd series. Detroit, Washington, D.C., and London: Bruccoli Clark Layman, 1993, pp. 7–16.

———. "Aphra Behn." In *Gay and Lesbian Literary Heritage*. Ed. Claude J. Summers. New York: Henry Holt, 1995, pp. 53–56.

———. "Not Since Sappho." In *Homosexuality in Renaissance and Enlightenment England*. Ed. Claude J. Summers. Binghamton, N.Y.: Haworth, 1992, pp. 153–171.

*See also* Poetry

## Belgium

Small country between France, Germany, the Netherlands, and the North Sea that gained independence in 1830. Throughout history, the territory was a battlefield and an occupied land. There is a strong Catholic influence. Belgian women have voted only since 1948 and are not well represented in political life. Many women are employed in Belgium, but here, too, women are badly represented in the higher positions, and lesbians who have succeeded are mostly in the closet. In the 1990s, Belgium became a federal state: Flemish speaking in the north, French speaking in the south, and German speaking in the southeast, while its capital, Brussels, is bilingual (Flemish and French). Tourists come to visit war graves, medieval towns, the sea, and the Ardennes and to enjoy Belgian cuisine and more than one hundred kinds of good Belgian beer.

In the 1990s, the lesbian and gay movement was situated in the north and in Brussels. The south had no groups with members and activities, making a small country even smaller.

The lesbian movement consists of groups in different cities that organize social activities and set up structures to welcome new members, such as women who are taking their first steps in the lesbian world. Although these groups are political through their existence and the work they do, they emphasize social issues, and only some of the most active members have explicitly political goals. In addition, the Artemys Bookshop in Brussels stresses its lesbian character, and the group Lesbies Doe-Front (Lesbian Action Group) organizes a national lesbian day. In 1997, the Lesbian Table, a monthly gathering of all lesbian groups in Belgium, was formed. In addition to their political goals, the members want to make communication between the groups better.

In the 1980s, many lesbians had connections with the feminist movement, but this declined in the 1990s because of the heterosexism of the Belgian feminist movement. There is also a difficult relationship with the gay male movement, although many lesbian groups are members of the mixed Federatie Werkgroepen Homoseksualiteit (Federation of Workgroups on Homosexuality [FWH]), an umbrella organization founded in the 1970s that lobbies politicians and the press.

Lesbians and gays are not prosecuted by law, although in 1996 a woman lost custody of her children in a divorce case because of her lesbianism. The law is particularly discriminatory in the areas of partnership and/or marriage legislation and lesbian and gay parenthood. Many lesbians argue that it is better to work together with gay men on these matters, despite the problems of working together with men who have a very different position in society. Some lesbian groups work independently and want to work only for lesbians. They put their energy into building up a lesbian movement and community that is fully occupied with lesbian politics and women-oriented goals. The 1990s saw a growing movement of young lesbians and gays who are very open and continue to reach more, and ever younger, people.

There is no organized program of lesbian studies, and what does exist is sustained by volunteer work. Very little historical information has been discovered, although the 1618 trial records in the city of Bruges of two working-class women, Mayken and Leene, who loved each other and other women, suggest areas of potential research.

A few students have written master's theses on specific aspects of lesbianism, while some women are studying the groups that existed since the 1970s (Sappho in Ghent was the first, in 1974), and an oral-history project has begun on older lesbians. The year 1996 saw the birth of a gay and lesbian archives, the Suzan Daniel Fonds, named after the pseudonym of a woman who was the first-known activist in the 1950s. In the 1990s, research began in the fields of health, therapy, and law, although these projects are neither organized nor funded.

*Ann David*

## Bibliography

Debeuckelaere, Geert. "Mayken en Leene, een lesbische geschiedenis in Brugge uit 1618" (Mayken and Leene: a Lesbian Couple in Bruges in 1618). *Homokrant* (May 1983), 3–5.

De Gendt, Lies. "Lesbiennegroepen in Vlaanderen tussen 1974 en 1994" (Lesbian Groups in Flanders Between 1974 and 1994). Master's thesis, University of Leuven, 1995.

Meyntjens, Mips, and Ann David, Project Oudere Lesbiennes, c/o Impuls, Leuvensesteenweg 47, 3200 Aarschot, Belgium.

*See also* Early Modern Europe

## Benedict, Ruth (1887–1948)

American poet, educator, anthropologist. Graduated from Vassar College (1909) and dissatisfied as a housewife, in 1918 Benedict enrolled at Columbia University to study anthropology under Franz Boas (1858–1942). She remained affiliated with Columbia until her death, chairing the Department of Anthropology and becoming the first woman to hold the rank of full professor in the Faculty of Political Science. In 1922, while assisting Boaz, Benedict met Margaret Mead (1901–1978), then a student at Barnard College. Mead became Benedict's first graduate student at Columbia. Meanwhile, Benedict was publishing poetry under the pseudonym Anne Singleton.

Benedict and Mead were briefly lovers in the mid-1920s, and their early professional field research led to intense discussions and theories about deviancy in cultures; in their writings, they deliberately tried to change society's homophobic attitudes. Mead's *Coming of Age in Samoa* (1928) includes their defense of unconventional behavior; Benedict's "Anthropology and the Abnormal" (1934) and, especially, *Patterns of Culture* (1934) carried their "alternative standard" theory to a wide international audience. Believing that cultures could change, Benedict argued in *Patterns of Culture* that a society's narrow definitions "penalize or give preference to certain innate capacities," and, thus, those who do not fit in do not suffer from "abnormal traits" but rather from society's lack of support for their "native responses." Benedict's emphasis on culture anticipated late-twentieth-century cultural studies.

Mead married three times. She continued her study of race, sex, and aggression. In 1935, she published *Sex and Temperament in Three Primitive Societies,* and, in the years 1926–1969, she moved through the curatorial ranks at the American Museum of Natural History in New York City. For Benedict, her intimacy with Mead was "a revelation," and she remained a "woman-loving woman" the rest of her life, according to Caffrey (1989). Divorced, Benedict lived happily with Natalie Raymond for nearly a decade and then, from the early 1940s, with the clinical psychologist Ruth Valentine.

Recognized by professional journals as one of the country's leading scientists, Benedict worked hard for racial equality, speaking out and writing about race and racism, particularly while engaged in the war effort. She believed that cultural understanding was the key to peace. Her 1943 pamphlet *The Races of Mankind* sold nearly a million copies. In 1944, as an analyst in the Office of War Information, she began the research that led to her influential work *The Chrysanthemum and the Sword: Patterns of Japanese Culture* (1946), an explanation of Japanese behavior that helped shape national policy. In the late 1940s, Benedict and Mead collaborated again, heading up the Columbia University Research in Contemporary Cultures, a federally funded study of national character and foreign-origin groups in the United States. In 1947, Benedict served as the first woman president of the American Anthropological Association.

Benedict and Mead's lifelong "mutual dependency" changed the study of anthropology; their now classic writings reshaped society's general attitudes toward culture. Benedict herself shattered stereotypical images of the woman academic.

*Judith C. Kohl*

## Bibliography

Benedict, Ruth. *Patterns of Culture.* New Preface by Margaret Mead. Sentry Edition. Boston: Houghton Mifflin, 1959.

Caffrey, Margaret M. *Ruth Benedict: Stranger in This Land.* Austin: University of Austin Press, 1989.

**B**

Mead, Margaret. *An Anthropologist at Work: Writings of Ruth Benedict*. Boston: Houghton Mifflin, 1959.

Modell, Judith Schactner. *Ruth Benedict: Patterns of a Life*. Philadelphia: University of Pennsylvania Press, 1983.

*See also* Anthropology

## Bentley, Gladys (1907–1960)

U.S. entertainer. Gladys Bentley's career bridges classic blues and lesbian history during the 1920s Harlem Renaissance. Bentley's first success was as a singer and piano player in the underground sporting life of Harlem parties. In this underground milieu, she was acclaimed for her mannish appearance and homosexual renditions of popular lyrics. In August 1928, Bentley embarked on a recording career with Okeh Recording Company. Accompanying herself on the piano, she recorded blues songs such as "How Long, How Long Blues." More than a recording blues artist, Bentley's success as a performer was to be found in Harlem nightclubs, such as the Clam House and Cotton Club. Bentley's forthright and outrageous public lesbian persona was used for fictional portrayals by such writers as Carl Van Vechten (1880–1964) and Clement Wood (1925–1994). Sybil, a Black lesbian singer in Blair Nile's gay novel *Strange Brother* (1931), was inspired by Bentley. In the final stages of her career, she lived on the West Coast, performing often at Hollywood's Rose Room.

Headlining at the Clam House for several years brought Bentley success as a special event in Harlem nightlife. In his memoir, *The Big Sea*, Langston Hughes (1902–1967) describes Bentley's fascinating performances:

> But for two or three amazing years, Miss Bentley sat, and played a big piano all night long, literally all night, without stopping. . . . Miss Bentley was an amazing exhibition of musical energy—a large, dark, masculine lady, whose feet pounded the floor while her fingers pounded the keyoard—a perfect piece of African sculpture, animated by her own rhythm.

Like "Ma" Rainey (1886–1939) and Bessie Smith (1894?–1937), Bentley broke new ground for black women as artists in the 1920s Jazz Age. Bent-

ley's success was unique as a blues singer with a public lesbian persona as part of her attraction. In daily life and performance, Bentley proudly displayed her bulldagger image; her gender performance was well received by the gay and lesbian subculture of the Harlem Renaissance period. In later life, Bentley struggled with discrimination against her image as a black lesbian blues artist. In her own right, Bentley was a gender warrior in the battles over black female/lesbian sexuality.

*Laura Alexandra Harris*

### Bibliography

Bentley, Gladys. "I Am a Woman Again." *Ebony* 7 (August 1952), 92–98.

Carby, Hazel. "It Jus Be's Dat Way Sometimes: The Sexual Politics of Women's Blues." In *Unequal Sisters: A Multicultural Reader in U.S. Women's History*. 2nd ed. Ed. Vicki L. Ruiz and Ellen Carol DuBois. New York: Routledge, 1994, pp. 330–341.

Garber, Eric. "Gladys Bentley: The Bulldagger Who Sang the Blues." *Outlook* 1 (Spring 1988), 52–61.

———. "A Spectacle in Color: The Lesbian and Gay Subculture of Jazz Age Harlem." In *Hidden from History: Reclaiming the Gay and Lesbian Past*. Ed. Martin Duberman, Martha Vicinus, and George Chauncey, Jr. New York: Penguin, 1989, pp. 318–331.

*See also* African Americans; Blues Singers; Bulldagger; Harlem

## Berlin

Largest city and current capital of the reunited Germany. Since the late nineteenth century, Berlin has been an "Eldorado" for lesbian women, and not only German ones. The first testimonies to the existence of lesbians in this city, however, were written by men. In the *Archiven für Psychiatrie und Nervenkrankheiten* (Archive for Psychiatry and Mental Diseases) (1869), the well-known Berlin professor Carl Westphal (1839–1890) documented the story of a young woman, Miss N., who suffered "since her eighth year from a rage to love women and, besides kissing and joking, to engage in masturbation with them." Westphal interpreted this as an innate inversion of sexual orientation, a symptom of a neuropathic (psychopathic) condition rather than a vice or an otherwise acquired characteristic. The liberation of lesbian love from religious judgment began with this establishment of psychiatric categories, a process that has continued throughout the twentieth century. In the foundational manifesto of the lesbian and gay movement, *Sappho und Sokrates* (1896), the Berlin doctor Magnus Hirschfeld (1868–1935) argued that homosexuality was a natural and innate behavior, a mistake by Mother Nature, so to speak, akin to a harelip. What causes sickness is the secrecy, not the homosexuality itself.

At the turn of the twentieth century, Berlin had a pronounced and distinct lesbian subculture with numerous bars, cafés, parties, balls, events, and organizations. The association of Berlin female artists organized a dance on the night of New Year's Eve 1899, at which 2,500 women showed up as couples in men's and women's clothes and flirted. Also well known was a bowling club for lesbian women, which undertook trips into the environs around Berlin. The press reported on police raids in bars and on divorces caused by intimate contacts in the clubs. In personal testimonies, reports about the subculture, and writings about women-loving women before and after the turn of the century, "sexually inverted women" were not portrayed as unhappy, sick creatures but as women proclaiming the positive values of their lives.

Women also were able to practice a lesbian lifestyle in the associations, living collectives, and communication projects of the women's movement that flourished at the turn of the century. In 1904, Anna Rüling (n.d.) pointed to the merits of the homosexual women active in the women's movement but complained, nonetheless, "that the great and influential organizations of this movement have not moved a finger until today to create for the not insignificant number of its uranian members their rightful standing in state and society."

The collapse of the German Empire in 1918 brought with it a new freedom of press and assembly and an atmosphere of joyful, enthusiastic art and culture. Within this, the lesbian subculture flourished in a manner unprecedented in history. Despite mass poverty, lesbian life pulsated in bars and at dances. The favorable exchange rate for international currencies also motivated many female foreigners to live in Berlin for a while. Magazines for lesbian women frequently reported events and festivities in the approximately fifty bars and clubs. The women organized or met in many "ladies' clubs" with up to four hundred members and, together with homosexual men, in human rights organizations, such as the German Friendship Association and the Alliance for Human Rights. The latter, with 48,000 members, had its seat in Berlin. Novels were published, plays were performed, and movies, such as *Mädchen in Uniform* [Girls in Uniform] (1933), based on a play by Christa Winsloe (1888–1944), were produced. The Institute for Sexual Science, founded in 1919, offered lectures and opportunities for counseling.

In 1933, the National Socialists (Nazis) seized power and immediately closed down all lesbian and gay bars. New guidelines and ordinances stifled the existing lesbian subculture. Homosexual and feminist organizations were forbidden, and the Institute for Sexual Science was looted in May 1933. Lesbians became invisible, either moving to other parts of town where they were unknown, leaving Berlin entirely, or, in some cases, marrying for protection. The time of masquerade did not end even after the defeat of the Nazi dictatorship in 1945. The Cold War divided Berlin, resulting in distinct, but secret, subcultures in the western and eastern parts of the city.

In 1971, following the eruption of the student movement, the first group of lesbian women to advocate openly in (West) Germany for social emancipation came into being. These women founded in West Berlin the first German women's center, women's bookstore, and women's publishing house. The German women's movement was, thus, from its beginning, strongly influenced by lesbians. With the unification of Germany in 1989, a unified Berlin continued to have a diverse range of groups, political initiatives, networks, bars, counseling, and communication centers, as well as magazines from and for lesbian women in both western and eastern sections of the city.

*Ilse Kokula*

## Bibliography

Hirschfeld, Magnus. *Berlin's Third Gender*. Berlin and Leipzig: Oswald, Verlag von Hermann Nachfolger, 1905.

Kokula, Ilse. *Forms of Lesbian Subculture*. Berlin: Publishing House Rosa Winkel, 1983.

———. *Weibliche Homosexualitat um 1900 inzeitgenossischen Dokumenten* (Female Homosexuality Around 1900 in Contemporary Documents). Munich: Publishing House Women's Offensive, 1981.

Rüling, Anna. "What Interest Does the Women's Movement Have in the Homosexual Question?" In *Lesbians in Germany: 1890's–1920's*. Ed. Lillian Fuderman and Brigitte Eriksson. Tallahassee, Fla: Naiad, 1980, pp. 83–94.

# B

*See also* Germany; Nazism; Rüling, Anna; Winsloe, Christa

## Bibliographies and Reference Works

Texts that provide background information and lead researchers to more specific or in-depth materials on their topics. Book-length bibliographies, a distinct class of reference work, list books, journal articles, dissertations, chapters, and other sources on a subject, time period, or person, often with descriptive or critical notes for each source. Other kinds of reference works include encyclopedias, dictionaries, directories, indexes, handbooks, almanacs, chronologies, and other sources that contain facts, definitions, and other useful information. Researchers usually consult such sources at the beginning of their projects to help refine, focus, or narrow them or to find specific information. In short, most reference sources are designed to be consulted rather than read from cover to cover.

## Background

Until the last few decades of the twentieth century, lesbianism had not received the same amount of attention given to male homosexuality. Though the work of many researchers documents the cross-cultural, historical existence of women who loved women, often the phenomenon went unrecognized or was inconsistently defined or named. The term "lesbianism" in the modern sense did not enter the popular vocabulary until the late nineteenth century and did not appear in American library catalogs until 1954. The term "lesbians" to specify a class of persons did not appear until 1976.

As of 1998, a comprehensive bibliography on lesbianism has not been published. With few exceptions, bibliographies and reference works relating exclusively to lesbians other than medical or psychological did not appear until the 1950s. The first publication by a woman to treat lesbianism as a general phenomenon may be Anna von den Eken's *Mannweiber-Weibmanner und der Para. 175: Ein Schrift fur denkende Frauen* (Masculine Women-Feminine Men Under Paragraph 175: A Booklet for Thinking Women [1906]).

## The 1950s and Early 1960s

Jeannette Foster made the pioneering effort in lesbian bibliography with her *Sex Variant Women in Literature* (1956). Foster attempts to document lesbian history, beginning with Sappho, by analyzing literature through the ages, particularly in English, German, and French. She also includes an extensive bibliography of primary, secondary, and scientific/psychiatric materials. Reissues of the work by Diana Press (1975) and Naiad Press (1985) provide some updated material and attest to the importance of this work.

Other early efforts were made by Marion Zimmer Bradley, who compiled two "unofficial supplements" to Foster entitled "Astra's Tower Special Leaflets" in 1958, and Barbara Grier (pseud. Gene Damon), a book review editor for *The Ladder*. Together they produced a mimeographed bibliography called "The Checklist" in 1960 and issued supplements in 1961 and 1962. The San Francisco Daughters of Bilitis (DOB) published the first edition of *The Lesbian in Literature* (1967), compiled by Gene Damon and Lee Stuart, which listed approximately three thousand mostly literary titles published through 1965. The book uses a coding system to indicate the amount of lesbian content and the quality of writing for each title. The second edition (1975) drops entries deemed "trash" and includes many more biographical and autobiographical titles and a substantial number of nonfiction titles. Naiad published a third edition in 1981 that lists approximately seven thousand titles through 1980.

## The Late 1960s and the 1970s

Lesbian publishing on contemporary lesbian issues, politics, and awareness exploded, but the era still produced only a few reference titles. An example is the short pamphlet entitled *Women Loving Women: A Select and Annotated Bibliography of Women Loving Women in Literature* (1974), edited by Marie J. Kuda, published by Lavender Press to coincide with the 1974 Lesbian Writers Conference. This title focuses on fiction, poetry, biography, and autobiography and also includes a brief list of useful reference sources.

One of the first nonbibliographic reference titles on lesbianism is *Our Right to Love: A Lesbian Resource Book* (1978), edited by Ginny Vida. A collective effort, this book celebrates the spectrum of lesbian existence and contains forty essays that cover identity, relationships, health, law, activism, theory, sexuality, the media, culture, research, age, class, race, and religion. The long-awaited revision, *The New Our Right to Love: A Lesbian Resource Book* (1996), again edited by Vida, presents more than sixty new essays, many reflecting developments and changes in emphasis that took place since the first edition. These include safe sex and HIV/AIDS, the military, sports, and many more contributions by lesbians with disabilities and lesbians from various racial and ethnic communities.

In *Lesbian Peoples: Material for a Dictionary* (1979), published originally as *Brouillon pour un Dictionnaire des Amantes* (1976), Monique Wittig and Sande Zeig mix fact, fiction, and myth in dictionarylike entries to create an exclusively lesbian world. Though not a dictionary in the formal sense, this title is a fine example of the reinvention of traditional formats for innovative purposes.

With the growth of feelings of identity, many women recognized the need to preserve lesbian culture. Joan Nestle and Deborah Edel founded the Lesbian Herstory Archives in 1973, and the DOB issued all sixteen volumes of *The Ladder* on microfilm in 1975 with a print index. Additionally, Naiad and Diana released compilations from *The Ladder* and *The Furies*.

## The 1980s

Naiad published the groundbreaking title *Black Lesbians: An Annotated Bibliography* (1981), compiled by J.R. Roberts (pseud. of Barbara Rae Henry), to counteract the "overwhelming whiteness" of lesbian and women's studies research. The bibliography gathers materials about black lesbians in the United States beginning with early legends and continuing through the black and Third World gay rights movements of the 1970s. The book includes primary and secondary sources; covers lifestyles, oppression, literature and criticism, music and musicians, and periodicals; and provides an appendix relating to a "lesbian witch-hunt" in 1980 aboard the Navy ship USS *Norton Sound*. Though bibliographies on black lesbians and other lesbians of color can be found in books, journals, and anthologies, a stand-alone update has yet to be published.

The Lesbian Rights Project published two editions of *Lesbian Mothers and Their Children: An Annotated Bibliography of Legal and Psychological Materials* (1980 and 1983) to help lesbians with custody issues. This group, renamed the National Center for Lesbian Rights in 1989, also published two editions of *Lesbians Choosing Motherhood: Legal Implications of Donor Insemination and Co-Parenting* (1984 and 1991), which highlight the potential problems faced by lesbians contemplating pregnancy and motherhood. A third edition appeared in 1996 with the subtitle *Legal Implica-*

*tions of Alternative Insemination and Reproductive Technologies*.

Dolores Maggiore's *Lesbianism: An Annotated Bibliography and Guide to the Literature, 1976–1986* (1988) focuses on books, chapters, articles in scholarly journals, and dissertations and arranges them into six broad sections: the individual lesbian, minorities within a minority, lesbian families, oppression, health, and resources. Each section contains several subsections covering such topics as identity throughout history, lifestyles, couples, heterosexism in theory and practice, alcoholism, counseling and mental health, lesbians of color/Third World lesbians, aging, youth, and the differently abled. Maggiore compiled a second edition (1992) of this title that updates coverage through 1991.

Claire Potter's *Lesbian Periodicals Index* (1986) provides wide-scale access to the unique information published during the 1960s and 1970s in activist lesbian periodicals that "created community with every word put on paper." The first section of the index provides an author-subject guide to forty-two publications that represent geographic, racial, political, class, and cultural differences within lesbian communities. Potter recognized the importance of creative works and includes sections in the index for diary and journal entries, poetry, stories, humor and satire, book reviews, and visual art.

Finally, historians and other researchers, many of them self-identified lesbians, turned efforts to their own history beginning in the 1970s. Such authors as Caroll Smith-Rosenberg, Blanche Wiesen Cook, Martha Vicinus, Judith Schwarz, Lillian Faderman, and Susan Cavin have produced articles and books in English that contain extensive notes and lists of sources, which arguably can be viewed as important contributions to Western lesbian historical bibliography. Similar titles from Europe include Ilsa Kokula's *Weibliche Homosexualitat um 1900 inzeitgenossischen Dokumenten* (Female Homosexuality Around 1900 in Contemporary Documents [1981]) and Marie-Jo Bonnet's *Un Choix sans equivoque: recherches historiques sur les relations amoureuses entre les femmes, XVIe–XXe siecle* (An Unequivocal Choice: Historical Research on Love Relationships Between Women, Sixteenth–Twentieth Centuries [1981]). A new edition of Bonnet's work was published in 1995 with the title *Les Relations amoureuses entre les femmes, du XVIe au XXe siècles: essai historique* (Love Relationships Between Women, from the Sixteenth to the Twentieth Centuries: A Historical Essay).

# B

## The 1990s

Dell Richards's *Lesbian Lists: A Look at Lesbian Culture, History, and Personalities* (1990) appears at first glance to fall in the "fun" category. In reality, it gathers scattered information from a variety of scholarly sources and serves as a quick reference to pre-Stonewall (1969) lesbian history. *The Lesbian Almanac* (1996), compiled by The National Museum & Archive of Lesbian and Gay History in New York City, provides comparatively more in-depth information on both historical and contemporary lesbian life, using chronologies, quotes, and brief biographies. It includes profiles of important individuals, organizations, and programs, as well as statistics, lists of resources, and Internet sites.

Shelley Anderson's directory *Out in the World: International Lesbian Organizing* (1991) provides brief background information about lesbian rights movements throughout the world. Arranged by continent and subdivided by country, this directory lists contemporary lesbian organizations with addresses and phone and fax numbers. Not since the magazine *Connexions* published its two "Global Lesbianism" issues (no. 3 [1982] and no. 10 [1983]) has so much international information been available in one source.

Where Potter's index focused on ceased lesbian activist periodicals, Linda Garber's *Lesbian Sources: A Bibliography of Periodical Articles, 1970–1990* (1993) concentrates on sixty-four widely distributed women's studies, lesbian, gay, and feminist journals. Garber uses 162 subject headings to access literature covering the myriad aspects of lesbian life and culture. This contrasts sharply with many library catalogs and standard indexes, which tend to lump lesbian materials into a few categories. Most welcome are the sections on women of color, lesbians around the world (subdivided by region and country), African Americans, and other racial and ethnic groups.

Sandra Pollack and Denise D. Knight fill a gap in the literature with their *Contemporary Lesbian Writers of the United States: A Bio-Bibliographical Critical Sourcebook* (1993). It covers one hundred writers of fiction, poetry, and drama active from 1970 to 1992. Each essay uses the same format, consisting of five parts: biographical information, a discussion of major works and themes, the critical reception, a list of works by the author, and a list of works about the author. The book also includes lists of publishers and periodicals and a nine-page bibliography of nonfiction titles.

Another subject-oriented title, *Lesbian Health Bibliography* (1994), edited by Lisa Rankow, covers breast cancer, mental health, HIV/AIDS, and several other topics. A second edition, published in 1995, increases the number of citations to almost eight hundred and adds several new sections, including transgender/transsexuals and bisexuality.

In *Lesbians in Print: A Bibliography of 1,500 Books with Synopses* (1995), Margaret Gillon compiles titles that reflect the variety of lesbian-positive ideas and perspectives. It lists books alphabetically by title and provides the publisher, subject category, price, and other information, in addition to a brief description. Gillon also provides useful indexes and a list of feminist and lesbian and gay bookstores in the United States.

## Electronic Sources

By the mid-1990s, publishers had begun to develop CD-ROM (compact disk-read only memory) and other electronic versions of print sources, most notably indexes, encyclopedias, and dictionaries. Electronic versions add the flexibility of keyword searches, allow the combination of a number of concepts, and enable multiple-year searches. The *Women's Resources International, Women's Studies on Disc,* and the *Alternative Press Index* all provide access to substantial information by lesbians. The development of the Internet revolutionizes communications and publishing even more. Listservs, newsgroups, gophers, Web pages, and other resources facilitate networking among many lesbians around the world, and several journals are now available in full-text electronic format.

Obviously, the proliferation of materials produced by lesbians, in all formats, warrants increased efforts toward bibliographic control. Anthologies by Jewish, Latina, African American, American Indian, and Asian American lesbians exist, but more reference titles pertaining to lesbians of color need to be compiled and disseminated. The same is true for materials produced by or about lesbians in Africa, Asia, and the Middle East. Titles need to be translated whenever feasible (and safe for the authors), and information about lesbian organizations needs to be collected on a regular basis. Hopefully, the Internet and electronic publishing will, in time, make this easier. Though lesbianism goes through "hot" cycles in mainstream publishing, history shows that lesbians themselves must be the ones to make continuing efforts to produce, collect, and preserve their own culture.

*Linda A. Krikos*

## Bibliography

Allen, Jane, Linda Kerr, Avril Rolph, and Marion Chadwick, comps. *Out on the Shelves: Lesbian Books into Libraries*. Newcastle-Under-Lyme, U.K.: Association of Assistant Librarians, 1989.

Arnup, Katherine, Gloria Geller, Amy Gottlieb, and Jeri Wire, guest eds. "Etre Lesbienne" (The Lesbian Issue). *Documentation sur la Recherche Feministe* 12, 1 (1983) (Special Issue).

Bullough, Vern, W. Dorr Legg, Barrett W. Elcano, and James Kepner, eds. *An Annotated Bibliography of Homosexuality*. 2 vols. New York: Garland, 1976.

Dynes, Wayne R. *Homosexuality: A Research Guide*. New York: Garland, 1987.

Freedman, Estelle B., Barbara Charlesworth Gelpi, Susan L. Johnson, and Kathleen M. Weston, eds. "The Lesbian Issue." *Signs: Journal of Women in Culture and Society* 9:4 (Summer 1984) (Special Issue).

"The Lesbian History Issue." *Frontiers: A Journal of Women's Studies* 4:3 (1979) (Special Issue).

Gough, Cal, and Ellen Greenblatt, eds. *Gay and Lesbian Library Service*. Jefferson, N.C.: McFarland, 1990.

Lesbian History Group. *Not a Passing Phase: Reclaiming Lesbians in History, 1840–1985*. London: Women's Press, 1985; reprinted and updated, London: Women's Press, 1993.

*See also* Anthologies; Archives and Libraries; Computer Networks and Services; Foster, Jeannette Howard; Grier, Barbara; Naiad Press; Periodicals; Publishing, Lesbian

## Biography

Modern (A.D. 1600 ff.) literary genre that narrates the story of an individual life. Biographers of women who were and are lesbian face numerous difficult tasks. Their subject, if deceased, may have gone to great effort to conceal her lesbianism during her lifetime, or she may have shunned the label "lesbian" despite her lived life. This forces the biographer to assign an identity to her that may contradict the subject's own self-definition. It also raises ethical issues of disclosure if the subject consciously strove to mask or deny her lesbianism. Yet the biographer's "power to name" sexual orientation in another's life can be a posthumous source of empowerment for the subject, whose own era necessitated the denial of lesbianism for survival.

### Defining a Lesbian Life

Historians of women's lives have contributed to rendering invisible lesbian lives and identity. Carroll Smith-Rosenberg's (1975) path-breaking essay centered intimacy among women as a mainstay of nineteenth-century middle-class Anglo-American culture. Yet it also denied the sexual aspects of women's bonds and sheltered same-sex partners under the veil of actual or possible concurrent heterosexuality. These sensual, emotionally intimate bonds among women were characterized by Smith-Rosenberg as "romantic friendships" only. While this posited a woman-centered model, it also denied the lesbian behavior of these women because they lacked lesbian self-identity. Smith-Rosenberg's argument framed the debate about what is a lesbian life for years. By arguing that it is "important to place the discussion of homosexuality within its historical perspective," she denied the possibility of lesbian behavior *before* the term was constructed by European sexologists and medical writers in the 1880s.

Many biographers since then have struggled with the question of what is/was a lesbian life. Blanche Wiesen Cook, in her review of the homophobic and distorted biography of Mary Woolley (1863–1947), president of Mt. Holyoke College, and her life partner, Jeannette Marks (1875–1964), professor of English at the same school, argued that their biographer, Anna Mary Wells, "obscured and trivialized" their intimacy, despite ample evidence attesting to their devotion. Specifically, because Wells denied the possibility of sexuality shared between them, she diminished the quality of their life together. Another scholar, Lillian Faderman, contributed to this debate on what constitutes a lesbian life. Faderman defined lesbianism as a relationship wherein "two women's strongest emotions and affections are directed toward each other. Sexual contact may be part of the relationship to a greater or lesser degree, or it may be entirely absent." Heterosexual couples, Faderman points out, are not asked to provide "genital proofs" of their intimacy, and neither should lesbians.

Several other scholars contributed to the early debate on these issues. Frances Doughty described how lesbian history is unique in that, unlike black or women's history, the very existence of lesbianism must first be proven. Since there are no accepted criteria, historiography focuses more often on the *legitimacy* of narrating a lesbian existence than on the actual life and events of the subject at hand.

**B** Adrienne Rich has argued that biographies would be more accurate and powerful if the biographers handled lesbian existence as a reality. She suggested that heterosexuality be viewed as a political institution that a lesbian life challenges.

## Class, Race, and Sexuality

The implications of a biographer "naming" a subject lesbian are compounded by issues of race, social class, region, and era. Lesbian biographers, in particular, learn "to read" coded messages and subtexts in order to determine the sexual orientation of their subject.

Yet demographic markers may mislead the biographer if she insists on "reading" through a predominantly middle-class, Anglo lens. For example, in crafting a biography of the working-class ethnic southeast Texan athlete "Babe" Didrikson Zaharias (1911–1956), it was vital not to misinterpret social-class behaviors or her ethnic community's appreciation for female athletes too broadly. These factors were compounded by a six-year live-in relationship with a woman whose oral history illuminated her personal life with Didrikson. Together, these can be taken as proof of lesbian life, if not lesbian self-identity.

## Closeting Lesbian Identities

For women who sought fame, acceptance, or economic reward from a critical American public, it is painful at times to see them construct "appropriate heterosexual pasts" to blur their adult lesbian lives. Sometimes, closeted autobiographers create fictitious memories of themselves. In so doing, they sacrifice authenticity and avoid disruptive truths in favor of a harmonious, "normal," and consistent life history. Through oral histories, the subject's friends and surviving family members often help in creating this facade. Oral histories from those who knew the subject, as well as printed source materials, can either corroborate or contradict the facts of a life.

Yet oral histories can also echo the legend and fabricated version of a life; respondents can choose to create a representation of the subject's life that is in keeping with their own set of truths or silences. They may also be unwilling to reveal a subject's lesbianism from a position of loyalty to the image *she* crafted and fostered. This necessitates constant "filtering" on the biographer's part. The legend-building aspects of oral histories need to be constantly weighted and analyzed for continuities, choices, pain, silences, voices, and the articulation of legitimate identity. Numerous feminist scholars under-

score these difficulties. Also, as Cook learned when researching same-sex intimacies in the life of Eleanor Roosevelt (1884–1962), documents have been intentionally destroyed by a subject's lovers and friends—rather than reveal a lesbian bond. After Roosevelt's death, Lorena Hickok (1892–1968) and Esther Lape (1881–1981) spent hours burning letters between themselves and Roosevelt. This obliterated the documentary record and forced the biographer to realize that it was "a calculated denial of Roosevelt's passionate friendships."

Given these intentional omissions, denials, and fabricated pasts, biographers of lesbian subjects must rely on deciphering coded language, poignant innuendoes, and other veiled signals. A helpful suggestion was made by historian Susan Ware (1987). She suggested "reading" photographs as historical sources that might illuminate lesbian lives. Yet this, too, may be deceptive if the subject has devoted herself to leaving little or no visual record of her same-sex intimacy.

Postmodern interpretations have stressed the notion of multiple identities that may, in fact, shift over time; other authors stress the "cultural positioning" of a subject in relationship to her historical context. Yet even these provisos were not precise enough for Nell Irvin Painter as she reviewed three texts on the writing of biography. Painter urged that biographers include and center the individual consciousness that makes each person unique—to transcend identity politics in defining their subjects and instead work at illuminating the personal meaning of their subjects' experiences.

As Rupp (1980) argued, the biographer of a lesbian life has the demanding tasks of differentiating between intimate and supportive friendships, couple relationships, and the in-love feelings expressed by others—all without denying their significance or fixing them into rigid categories. Whether these women embraced or shunned self-identification as lesbians, she concluded, the biographer must not blur the distinctions among these different types of relationships. The biographer's ability to name is quite powerful: The assignation of "lesbian" to a woman's life at once centers her in intimacy with women and casts her outside the heterosexual norm. This placement forms the very way in which we interpret her life, relationships, relationship to the public, and self-perceptions. It is a profound step toward (re)constructing a nonhomophobic identity for women who chose to devote themselves to other women.                                        *Susan E. Cayleff*

## Bibliography

Cook, Blanche Wiesen. "Female Support Networks amd Political Activism: Lillian Wald, Crystal Eastman, Emma Goldman." *Chrysalis* 3 (1977), 43–61.

———. "The Historical Denial of Lesbianism." *Radical History Review* 20 (Spring/Summer 1979), 60–65.

Doughty, Frances. "Lesbian Biography, Biography of Lesbians." *Frontiers: A Journal of Women Studies* 4:3 (Fall 1979), 76–79.

Faderman, Lillian. *Surpassing the Love of Men: Romantic Friendship and Love Between Women from the Renaissance to the Present.* New York: William Morrow, 1981.

———. "Who Hid Lesbian History?" *Frontiers: A Journal of Women Studies* 4:3 (Fall 1979), 74–76.

Rupp, Leila J. " 'Imagine My Surprise': Women's Relationships in Historical Perspective." *Frontiers: A Journal of Women Studies* 5:3 (Fall 1980), 61–70.

Smith-Rosenberg, Carroll. "The Female World of Love and Ritual: Relations Between Women in Nineteenth-Century America." *Signs: Journal of Women in Culture and Society* 1:1 (Autumn 1975), 1–30.

Ware, Susan. *Partner and I: Molly Dewson, Feminism, and the New Deal Politics.* New Haven, Conn.: Yale University Press, 1987.

*See also* Autobiography; Didrikson, Mildred Ella "Babe" (Zaharias); Faderman, Lillian; History; Oral History; Romantic Friendship; Rich, Adrienne; Roosevelt, Anna Eleanor

## Biological Determinism

Belief that human behavior is explained and determined by our biology, in terms of our genetics, hormone levels, or brain structures. Since the mid-1980s, the United States has witnessed a set of claims that male (and perhaps female) homosexuality derives from particular brain structures and one or more gay genes. While most of the research about biology and human homosexuality has been done with male subjects, attention turned, in the 1990s, to female homosexuality, with studies based on the same assumptions, and with the same methodological flaws built into them, as studies of males. To account for sex differences in the percentage deemed "truly" homosexual and for the apparently wider range of interest in same-sex activities shown by late-twentieth-century heterosexual women, compared to heterosexual men, some scientists propose different gay genes for women and for men; since organisms evolve as a species, that idea runs counter to evolutionary theory.

## Historical Context

With political concern (both for and against) about gay and lesbian civil rights in the United States and around the world running high, scientific claims about inherent and, thus, unavoidable homosexuality are embraced by some lesbian and gay activists and attacked by most antigay religious conservatives. Published studies of genetics and sexual identity of twins and siblings, as well as of differences in size or shape of certain parts of the brains of homosexual as compared to heterosexual (mostly) men, are compelling and can be convincing to scientist and nonscientist alike. However, historical and scientific analyses of such claims reveal significant flaws in the assumptions, logic, and methods of the studies, and many of the conclusions are not supported by the data in the studies themselves.

First, history shows that claims of "biology" determining female and male homosexual behavior and/or identity are part of a long heritage of Western (white male–dominated) scientific assertions that human biology determines human behavior, characteristics, and, consequently, one's "natural" status in society. The long history of scientific claims, often by reputable scientists, about differences of concern to society (mainly class, race, and sex) includes nineteenth-century assertions that blacks and whites were separate races and so could be treated differently under the law; that women's brains were smaller than men's, accounting for women's inferior rationality, for which citizenship rights could be denied; that women's reproductive physiology (but not men's) would be impaired by higher education, and, so, for the sake of future generations, young women should not be allowed to go to college; and that non-English-speaking immigrants to the United States were inherently retarded because they could not pass intelligence tests given in English.

Healthy scientific and political skepticism has arisen, therefore, from a consistent history of political claims that are based on then-current biological theories, claims that are subsequently either disproven or abandoned due to inconsistent logic, exposure of outright fraud, lack of confirming evidence, or political shifts.

**B**

History also shows that Western culture has changed from viewing homosexuality as a behavior by individuals to believing that homosexual identity is embodied in the physical being of the individual. Biological studies of sexual preference preserve sexist and heterosexist assumptions from the nineteenth century (and earlier) that sexuality is about reproduction and that femaleness and maleness exist in human nature as primary, dichotomous, and opposed states of being that form the basis for gender differences.

Contrary to most of the scientific claims about sex and race differences, research in the late twentieth century suggesting that brain differences and gay genes account for inherent homosexuality comes from pro-gay scientists (the majority of whom are male, such as Simon LeVay, Richard Pillard, J. Michael Bailey, and Dean Hamer) who argue, much as sexologists at the end of the nineteenth century did, that homosexuality is inborn, and, therefore, homosexuals cannot be blamed for it. While many gay rights advocates welcomed those recent "scientific" claims, particularly in the face of vocal antigay religious conservatives, who assert that homosexuality is an immoral choice that must and can be eliminated by a commitment to what is moral (heterosexuality), legal scholars such as Halley (1994) argue that immutability is not a sufficient condition for civil rights in the U.S. legal tradition. The history of the struggle for citizenship and rights for Americans of African heritage, where skin color and heritage are used to trace lineage, illustrates the latter argument well.

## Feminist Interpretations

Feminist attention to women and to the social elements of "gender" has been nearly absent from most studies seeking to identify biological determinants of sexuality. The studies have originated with male scientists who are either themselves gay or openly for gay rights and who evince little familiarity with feminist perspectives that point to the influence of "culture," rather than biology (often cast as "nature versus nurture"), on human sexual relations.

"Second wave" feminists have analyzed their sexual experiences, desires, and social arrangements with an understanding of the constraints of sexism and have pointed to the political, social, and economic influences on being a lesbian, bisexual, or heterosexual woman, often at different times in the same life. Adrienne Rich wrote in 1980 of "compulsory heterosexuality" as a cornerstone of sexism, part of a system of social control over women. In this view, heterosexuality is not a conscious choice in our culture for either women or men.

However, the women's, lesbian feminist, and gay liberation movements from the 1960s onward, as well as the gay activism in response to the AIDS epidemic, have brought lesbian and gay rights issues to the public eye at the same time that society has increasingly accepted previously male-associated behaviors (smoking, promiscuity) and clothing (pants rather than skirts or dresses) for all women. However, it is still not "normal" for men to wear skirts and dresses (they are considered cross-dressing tranvestites); boys are still called sissies and faggots for playing with dolls or acting in female-associated ways; and the greatest put-down among supposedly heterosexual males is to call a male a girl or a woman. Thus, social factors impact differently on males and females when the meaning of homosexuality is considered for each sex, so that feminist theorizing can account for observed sex differences in rates and descriptions of homosexual identity without resorting to biological explanations. In contrast, one of the twin-studies researchers (J. Michael Bailey) is reported by Wheeler (1993) to have said: "In talking to women who call themselves straight, it strikes me that many of them will admit to being attracted to women even if they have no desire to act on it. You can hardly ever get [straight] men to admit to that."

## Scientific Research and Its Critique

At the end of the twentieth century, theories of biological determination or influence on sex (male-female) and sexual preference propose that androgens (certain "male" hormones) "masculinize" the brain of the human fetus to produce male-typical behaviors and desires (including heterosexual desires for females) as compared to the nonandrogenized, "feminized" brain and its female-typical behaviors and desires (heterosexual desires for males), while a gay gene or genes determines or influences the degree of masculinization or feminization of male or female, resulting in (feminized) males who desire males and (masculinized) females who desire females.

Critics of biological-determinist claims for sexual preference point to serious methodological flaws in the scientific studies themselves. Like most of the earlier studies of sex and race differences, research on biology and sexuality is frequently inadequate by strict scientific standards: The size of the sample is too small; the sample is not representative of the population at large; the samples lack proper controls; contradictions among the studies are not accounted for sufficiently; and identification of sexual orientation of the individuals studied is not clear. For example, the research looking for genetic evidence for being lesbian (or gay—the studies on males were done first) is now focused on twin and sibling studies. Bailey and Pillard have said that they find a much higher incidence of an identical twin also being lesbian or gay as compared to lower "concordance" for a fraternal twin, a nontwin biological sibling, or an adoptive sibling. Without even exposing the serious limitations of their actual data, the studies are questionable scientifically because the samples are not random. Rather, the researchers place ads in lesbian and gay newspapers asking for lesbian and gay volunteers who were cotwins or had adoptive siblings. With the media coverage about the biology of being gay, it is not a surprise that many more lesbians and gay males with lesbian or gay cotwins and siblings come forward to be part of these studies. Indeed, the one consistent result is that the studies show higher proportions of lesbian or gay siblings than in the general population. Despite the skewed samples on which their studies are based, the researchers do not consider alternative explanations for a (possibly) high concordance of identical twins being lesbian or gay—that is, the well-documented unique closeness of identical twins brought up together.

In another example, in some studies if a person did not self-identify as gay, he was classified as heterosexual. In some studies persons engaged in both homosexual and heterosexual activities were classified as homosexual, while in other studies only "truly" homosexual individuals (those who never engaged in, or desired, sexual activity with the other sex) were considered homosexual. The pronoun "he" is appropriate here, because most of the studies have been on males. As more attention is given to women, the "problem" noted above by Bailey—that women seem (or are more willing to say they are) more fluid in their sexual interest with regard to gender—has generated the conclusion by some researchers that only 1 percent of women are "truly homosexual" as compared to at least 3 percent of men; further, female homosexuality is somehow different biologically. The concept of the "true homosexual" reproduces the fallacious belief that biology is true human identity, while culture is merely layered over biology. Thus, unless questions are raised about the presuppositions on which studies are based, researchers will simply assert that the studies

are promising and that only more and better research is needed to confirm the theories.

## Research Assumptions

The following are presuppositions of the research, assumptions that critics of biological determinism of sexuality say are at least questionable and at most incorrect. First, sexual behavior is viewed as mechanically driven by a physical entity and involving genital manipulation and copulatory activity, rather than unconsciously acquired behavior learned from the socializing environments of family, culture, and society. "Sexual preference" is rejected for "sexual orientation," a biological condition that inheres in the body to steer sexual behavior toward one sex or away from the other. Evidence countering this assumption is cross-cultural and historical, showing a wide range and combination of human sexual behaviors that are taken as "normal" in different cultures at different times. Dramatic changes in sexual behavior have occurred with social and political changes, such as the "second wave" (post-1969) of feminism.

A second key and questionable assumption of the studies is that homosexuality and heterosexuality are mutually exclusive conditions, such that certain biological characteristics (the size of shape of certain brain structures or the information in certain genes) of homosexuals are different from those of heterosexuals. Countering this assumption is historical evidence that the concept of *the* homosexual—an individual with a set identity, rather than an individual who engages in homosexual *behaviors* at different times or in different circumstances in his or her life—emerged in Western culture only in the eighteenth century and was institutionalized in nineteenth-century medicine, and is, thus, a cultural creation rather than a biological given. At different times in history and in different cultures, homosexual activity did not in any way preclude the possibility of heterosexual activity at the same moment in time or in the future.

A third key presupposition to be questioned is that "true" homosexuality is associated with feminine behavior and appearance in men and the reverse in women, linking assumed attributes of maleness and femaleness with sexual orientation or preference. In the 1950s, Money and Ehrhardt (1972) studied girls who had been exposed *in utero* to high levels of androgens ("male" hormones). The researchers claimed that the "masculinization" of the female fetuses' brains produced the following

**B**

results (remember this was the 1950s): wearing pants rather than dresses, wanting careers more and babies less, higher IQs, and (subsequently) lesbian identity. The claim for higher IQs as a result of being masculinized was dropped when the higher socioeconomic class of the families, and, thus, higher measured IQs generally, was taken into account. The researchers did not factor in, however, the effects on the girls of genital surgery several times or the attention given them for their "problem" (which might include infertility) by their parents and doctors, influences that surely could have turned a girl away from traditionally feminine activities. A new version of that stereotype that confounds male-female gender with sexual orientation is found in the association of male gayness with the female-associated X chromosome. Geneticist Dean Hamer claims to have found a "gay gene" in males, located on the X chromosome, which, in males, must come from the mother since males are XY and females are XX.

A common assumption of pro-gay researchers is that studies showing the biological basis of homosexuality will lead to full civil rights for lesbians and gays because society will understand that it is not an issue of choice. Countering this is the history of Jews and gays in Nazi Germany and that of Americans of African descent. Furthermore, this argument apparently would allow discrimination against those who admit to choosing lesbian experiences and relationships over heterosexual ones for political, social, or other reasons.

As more female researchers engage in biological studies and more studies are done with women, and as U.S. society continues to look to genetics to explain human behavior, more claims will emerge. To evaluate them fully, they must be understood in the context of the long history of subsequently rejected assertions about the biological basis of sexuality—and other culturally shaped behaviors.

*Bonnie B. Spanier*

### Bibliography

Burr, Chandler. *A Separate Creation: The Search for the Biological Origins of Sexual Orientation.* New York: Hyperion, 1996.

De Cecco, John P., and David Allen Parker, eds. *Sex, Cells, and Same-Sex Desire: The Biology of Sexual Preference.* New York: Haworth, 1995.

Halley, Janet E. "Sexual Orientation and the Politics of Biology: A Critique of the Argument from Immutability." *Stanford Law Review* 46 (February 1994), 503–568.

Money, John, and Anke A. Ehrhardt. *Man and Woman, Boy and Girl.* Baltimore: Johns Hopkins University Press, 1972.

Spanier, Bonnie. "Biological Determinism and Homosexuality." *NWSA Journal* 7:1 (Spring 1995), 54–71.

———. *Im/Partial Science: Gender Ideology in Molecular Biology.* Bloomington: Indiana University Press, 1995.

Terry, Jennifer. "Lesbians Under the Medical Gaze: Scientists Search for Remarkable Differences." *Journal of Sex Research* 27 (1990), 317–340.

Wheeler, David L. "Studies of Lesbians Rekindles Debate Over Biological Basis for Homosexuality." *Chronicle of Higher Education* (March 17, 1993).

*See also* Animal Studies; Compulsory Heterosexuality; New Right; Sexology; Sexual Orientation and Preference

## Bisexual Movement

Though there have been in the past communities and individuals who were known to have lived a bisexual lifestyle (for example, the Bloomsbury artists' community, the Harlem Renaissance community, and Frida Kahlo [1907–1954] and her circle), the 1970s marked the beginning of the modern bisexual movement. The bi movement today consists of social, support, and political groups throughout the United States and other parts of the world.

### The Early Years

The earliest bisexual organizations in the United States grew out of the sexual liberation movement, or "sexual revolution," which was, in turn, fueled by the women's liberation movement, the gay liberation movement, and the legalization of, and increased access to, birth control. A number of bisexuals were active in the formation of various chapters of the Sexual Freedom League. The National Bisexual Liberation Group was founded in 1972 in New York City. The Bi Forum, also in New York City, began in 1975. The Bisexual Center in San Francisco, California, formed in 1976, and Bi Ways in Chicago, Illinois, began in 1978.

These years spanned the era of "bisexual chic," in which popular media publicized the bisexuality of rock stars and artists. The earliest bisexual groups were primarily social in focus, although some included a political element as well. The 1970s also saw the publication of several books about bisexuality. Janet Bode's *View from Another Closet* (1976) was perhaps the first, followed by Charlotte Wolff's *Bisexuality: A Study* (1977), and Fritz Klein's *The Bisexual Option: A Concept of One Hundred Percent Intimacy* (1978).

## The Second Wave

Many bisexuals were active within the gay liberation, and later the lesbian and gay, movement. However, several factors, including an increased focus on identity politics and hostility and rejection by some lesbians and gay men, led some bisexuals to create separate bisexual organizations.

The "second wave" of bisexual organizing, beginning in the early 1980s, was largely women led, and was strongly influenced by feminism. Many of the women involved in bisexual organizing in the 1980s had been, and were still, active in the gay, lesbian feminist, and women's movements. Feminist bisexual women's organizations were formed in Boston, Massachusetts (1983); Chicago (1984); New York City (1983); and Seattle, Washington (1986). While in the 1970s most bi groups were of mixed gender, in the 1980s a number of women-only bi groups and a smaller number of bisexual men's groups formed.

The bisexual groups of the 1980s focused on providing support and social opportunities, and a number became increasingly involved in political organizing as well, especially in the wake of the AIDS epidemic in the early 1980s. The number of bi groups continued to grow throughout the 1980s in the United States, the United Kingdom, the Netherlands, Germany, Scandinavia, Canada, Australia, and New Zealand. The mid-1980s saw the first bisexual groups devoted to political activism (San Francisco's BiPoL, and Boston's Bisexual Committee Engaging in Politics [BiCEP]), and the first regional bisexual networks (the East Coast Bisexual Network and the Bay Area Bisexual Network).

While some bisexuals focused on the creation of organizations for and by bisexual people, others were organizing within lesbian and gay communities. A major focus of the bi movement in the 1980s was to seek inclusion and recognition for bisexuals within lesbian and gay groups. Some formerly "lesbian and gay" organizations changed their titles or their statements of purpose to include bisexual people, while others chose not to. This was especially evident on college campuses, as many campus groups, which in the 1970s had changed their names

to add "lesbian," did the same in the 1980s with "bisexual" (and, increasingly, in the 1990s with "transgender"). In some areas of the country, intercommunity relationships, particularly between some lesbians and bisexual women, were tense; in other areas, bisexuals were more readily welcomed.

## Bis Organize More Widely

In 1987, in conjunction with the March on Washington for Lesbian and Gay Rights, two women from Boston distributed a flyer entitled "Are We Ready for a National Bisexual Network Yet?" The result of this flyer was the first national bisexual contingent at the march and the birth of a national bisexual organization. The first International Directory of Bisexual Groups was produced the same year in an attempt to facilitate national and international organizing.

In June 1990, San Francisco's BiPol organized the first national conference on bisexuality, with a focus on consolidating a nationwide bi organization, then known as the North American Multicultural Bisexual Network. In 1991, at a meeting in Seattle, the organization was renamed BiNet (Bisexual Network of the USA). The second U.S. national conference took place in 1993 in conjunction with the March on Washington for Lesbian, Gay, and Bi Equal Rights and Liberation, the first national march to mention bisexuals by name.

The first U.S. regional conference on bisexuality was held in Hartford, Connecticut, in 1984. By the early 1990s, there were regional conferences taking place annually in the Northwest, the Southwest, Southern California, the Midwest, and the Northeast. The first International Conference on Bisexuality was held in Amsterdam in 1991. Other international conferences have been held in London (1992), New York City (1994), Berlin (1996), and Boston (1998).

## Bisexuality in Literature and Academia

The 1990s saw an increase in the participation of college students in the bi movement and greater bisexual visibility in literature and academia. There was another wave of books about bisexuality, this time including many anthologies that focused on personal experiences, such as the influential *Bi Any Other Name: Bisexual People Speak Out* (1990).

The record-setting year was 1995, which saw the publication of numerous studies and anthologies by both mainstream and alternative presses, including the *Bisexual Resource Guide* (Bisexual Resource Center). The first national bisexual maga-

**B** zine, *Anything That Moves: Beyond the Myths of Bisexuality*, had begun publication in 1991. Computer newsgroups, electronic mailing lists, and chat lines helped connect bisexuals across geographic lines. The first college course focusing on bisexuality was taught at the University of California, Berkeley, in 1990, followed by a course the next year at the Massachusetts Institute of Technology, and several more in subsequent years at Tufts University.

## Conclusion

Not unlike lesbian and gay organizations, bisexual organizations in the 1990s developed in a number of different directions. Some bisexual people focused on organizing for, and with, other bisexual people. Others focused on working within "lesbian and gay," "lesbian, gay and bisexual," "lesbian, gay, bisexual, and transgendered," or "queer" organizations to educate heterosexuals, fight homophobia, advocate for civil rights legislation, and build community. Still others were interested in creating a broad sex and gender liberation movement that is not focused on identity politics. And, like many lesbians and gay men, many bisexual people were not involved in any organizations or movements at all, choosing instead to focus their energies on their individual lives.

*Robyn Ochs*
*Liz Highleyman*

### Bibliography

Bisexual Anthology Collective, ed. *Plural Desires: Writing Bisexual Women's Realities*. Toronto: Sister Vision, 1995.

Hutchins, Loraine, and Lani Ka'ahumanu, eds. *Bi Any Other Name: Bisexual People Speak Out*. Boston: Alyson, 1990.

Off Pink Collective. *Bisexual Lives*. London: Off Pink Publishing, 1988.

Rose, Sharon, et al., eds. *Bisexual Horizons: Politics, Histories, Lives*. London: Lawrence and Wishart, 1996.

Tucker, Naomi, eds. *Bisexual Politics: Theories, Queries, and Visions*. New York: Haworth, 1995.

*See also* Bisexuality; Kahlo, Frida; Identity; Identity Politics; Wolff, Charlotte

## Bisexuality

The capacity to be romantically and/or sexually attracted to individuals of more than one sex. Part of the confusion surrounding the term "bisexual" is that it has many different meanings. It may describe a person's historic behavior or attractions: someone who, in her or his past, has been attracted to, and/or involved with, at least one man and one woman. It may describe one's current behavior and/or attraction: someone who is currently attracted to, and/or involved with, at least one man and one woman. It may describe an individual's potential range of romantic and/or sexual attraction, or it may refer to a person's self-definition. It is not necessary for a person to meet all of the above criteria to be considered bisexual. To understand bisexuality, it is important to distinguish between identity and behavior. Like her heterosexual or lesbian counterpart, a bisexual woman may be monogamous, nonmonogamous, or celibate. She may never have had sex with men, with women, or with anyone at all. And, conversely, many, if not most, people whose historical or current behavior and/or attractions are bisexual do not identify as such.

## Characteristics

This reluctance may be a result of the negative stereotypes attached to the word; of the strong societal pressures to choose either a heterosexual or a homosexual identity (usually in correspondence with the sex of one's current romantic partner); of the pressures of homophobic culture, which make it difficult for anyone to proudly claim her same-sex attractions; and of tendencies to write life histories backward from the present, omitting or discounting facts that do not fit the writer's current understanding of herself.

Some attempts have been made to identify types of bisexuality. A few of these are self-identified bisexuality (any woman who calls herself bisexual); experimental bisexuality (a woman who is basically lesbian or heterosexual but who has experimented heterosexually or homosexually); situational bisexuality (someone who is usually heterosexual but who has homosexual relationships while in a sex-segregated environment, such as a girls' school, a prison, or the military); historical bisexuality (someone who in the past has had attractions and/or experiences with people of more than one sex, regardless of their current behavior or self-identification); defense bisexuality (someone who is homosexual but continues other-sex relationships as a cover for their homosexuality); and technical bisexuality (for example, a sex worker who is attracted to people of one sex but sleeps with people of another for money).

While bisexuality has received far less attention than heterosexuality and homosexuality, sexologists and other scientists and scholars have taken some notice. Sigmund Freud (1856–1939), for example, believed that all human beings are born bisexual—that is, without gendered-object choice. He wrote in the 1915 edition of *Three Essays on the Theory of Sexuality* that "psychoanalysis considers that a choice of an object independently of its sex—freedom to range equally over male and female objects—as it is found in childhood, in primitive states of society and early periods of history, is the original basis from which, as a result of restriction in one direction or the other, both the normal and the inverted [homosexual] types develop." Alfred Kinsey (1894–1956) put forth the idea that human sexuality does not consist of two mutually exclusive categories, heterosexual and homosexual, but rather is best understood as existing on a continuum. He argued that it is the human mind that forces sexual behavior into separate pigeonholes. He rejected the widely held idea of "homosexual" and "heterosexual" types of individuals, and argued for the conceptualization of people as individuals with certain amounts of homosexual and heterosexual experience. Anthropologist Margaret Mead (1901–1978), who was herself bisexual, believed that bisexuality was far more widespread than we realize. She (1975) wrote: "We shall not really succeed in discarding the straight jacket of our own cultural beliefs about sexual choice if we fail to come to terms with the well-documented, normal human capacity to love members of both sexes."

## Bisexuality and Lesbians

Bisexuality has been a controversial subject within lesbian circles, and the place of bisexual women within "women's communities" has often generated heated debates. Some lesbians believe that all women who have the potential to love other women have an obligation to do so and a political obligation to identify as lesbian and cease interacting with men. Others believe that the compulsory nature of heterosexuality in our cultures precludes the possibility of a woman freely "choosing" a heterosexual relationship, some going so far as to believe that, due to the negative pressures on people in same-sex relationships and the positive benefits attached to opposite-sex relationships, a bisexual woman will inevitably end up leaving a woman partner for one of the other sex. As a result of these lines of thought, bisexually identified women have often had their integrity and their commitment to feminism questioned. A study conducted in the late 1980s by sociologist Paula Rust found that most lesbian respondents held far more negative than positive views of bisexuality, though she emphasizes that lesbians are by no means unanimous in their views, with some holding positive opinions about bisexual women. Political shifts in the 1990s have doubtless shifted the landscape of opinion toward a greater acceptance of bisexuality.

In the 1990s, increasing numbers of women began to identify as bisexual. On college campuses, it was not uncommon for bisexually identified women to make up the majority of women active in a campus's lesbian, gay, and bisexual student group. (Interestingly, this does not hold true for male students). Bisexual groups, including a number of women-only groups, have increased in numbers in the United States and other countries since the early 1980s. In addition, many lesbian and gay and queer groups recognized that bisexuals were included in their membership, and some changed their names to be more welcoming to bisexuals. The term "lesbi-gay" became commonplace throughout the United States.

To understand bisexuality, one has to remember that human lives are not unidimensional, fixed objects, but rather exist on many planes: past, present, future; in action and in imagination. Thus bisexuality, like life, is complex.           *Robyn Ochs*

### Bibliography

Bi Academic Intervention. *The Bisexual Imaginary.* London: Cassell, 1996.

Bode, Janet. *View from Another Closet.* New York: Hawthorn, 1976.

Garber, Marjorie. *Vice Versa: Bisexuality and the Eroticism of Everyday Life.* New York: Simon and Schuster, 1995.

George, Sue. *Women and Bisexuality.* London: Scarlet, 1993.

Klein, Fritz. *The Bisexual Option: A Concept of One Hundred Percent Intimacy.* 2nd ed. New York: Haworth, 1993.

Mead, Margaret. "Bisexuality: What's It All About?" *Redbook* 144:3 (January 1975), 29–31.

Rust, Paula. *Bisexuality and the Challenge to Lesbian Politics.* New York: New York University Press, 1996.

Wolff, Charlotte. *Bisexuality: A Study.* Revised and expanded edition. New York: Quartet Books, 1979.

**B**

*See also* Bisexual Movement; Identity; Situational Lesbianism

### Bishop, Elizabeth (1911–1979)

American poet and memoirist, born in Worcester, Massachusetts. Bishop's father died when she was eight months old, and her mother was permanently institutionalized four years later. The orphaned child was raised by relatives in Boston, Massachusetts, and Nova Scotia. She attended Walnut Hill School and later Vassar College, where she met the poet Marianne Moore (1887–1972), who became her mentor.

Bishop traveled widely and lived in the tropics for most of her adult life; first in Key West, Florida, with Louise Crane (1909?–) and later in Brazil with her lover Lota de Macedo Soares (1910–1967), with whom Bishop enjoyed her happiest years. Her sense of outsiderhood as a lesbian, her impatience with the confinement of women's experience, and her concern with how abstract symbols distort human experience inspired her to write poems that contemplate the nature of travel, intimacy, and cross-cultural vision, and that are characterized by precise observation, conversational voice, uncanny mysteriousness, and the transition from one realm of experience to another.

Lesbian themes and modes of vision infuse most of the poems in Bishop's four published volumes. Notable in this respect are "The Gentleman of Shalott," "The Weed," and "Roosters" from *North and South* (1946); "A Cold Spring," "Insomnia," "Four Poems," and "The Shampoo" from *A Cold Spring* (1955); "Song for the Rainy Season" from *Questions of Travel* (1965); and "In the Waiting Room," "Crusoe in England," and "One Art" from *Geography III* (1976), her last and most autobiographical collection. In recent years, scholars have unearthed unpublished poems, particularly "It is marvelous to wake up together," which deal with lesbian erotic experience with great sensuous depth and psychological insight. Bishop's closeted existence, her sense of homelessness, and her battles with alcoholism contributed to several tragedies in her life, including De Macedo's suicide in 1967 and the subsequent loss of her homes in Brazil. Yet Bishop, always resilient, enjoyed a stable relationship late in life with Alice Methfessel (1944–), whom she met while teaching poetry at Harvard University. "Sonnet," one of Bishop's last poems, speaks of a "creature divided" that finally breaks free to fly "wherever it feels like, gay!" and is a fitting tribute to her lifelong struggles with censorship and self-disclosure. Bishop takes her place as a lyric poet alongside Emily Dickinson and has proven an inspiration to lesbian poets from various cultural backgrounds.

*Corinne E. Blackmer*

### Bibliography

Fountain, Gary, and Peter Brazeau. *Remembering Elizabeth Bishop: An Oral Biography*. Amherst: University of Massachusetts Press, 1994.

Giroux, Robert, ed. *One Art: Selected Letters of Elizabeth Bishop*. New York: Farrar, Straus, and Giroux, 1994.

Harrison, Victoria. *Elizabeth Bishop's Poetics of Intimacy*. Cambridge: Cambridge University Press, 1993.

Kalstone, David. *Becoming a Poet: Elizabeth Bishop with Marianne Moore and Robert Lowell*. Ed. Robert Hemenway. New York: Farrar, Straus, and Giroux, 1989.

Millier, Brett C. *Elizabeth Bishop: Life and the Memory of It*. Berkeley: University of California Press, 1993.

*See also* Brazil; Poetry

### Black Church

In general usage, the variety of black Christian churches in the United States. These congregations, which are often called "storefront churches," are not offically affiliated with the historical black denominations but are made up of African American Christians who worship in the traditional black Church style. The formal usage "The Black Church" refers to those historical and independent black Protestant denominations that were founded after the Free African Society in 1787, including the African Methodist Episcopal (A.M.E) Church; the African Methodist Episcopal Zion (A.M.E.Z) Church; the Christian Methodist Episcopal (C.M.E.) Church; the National Baptist Convention, U.S.A., Incorporated (NBC); The National Baptist Convention of America, Unincorporated (NBCA); the Progressive National Baptist Convention (PNBC); and the Church of God in Christ (COGIC).

The Black Church is a complex institution that operates as a social, political, and religious institution. It has taken both accommodating and resisting stances on civil rights issues. Whereas the Black Church has taken a resisting stance on racism, it has taken an accommodating stance on sexism, heterosexism, and homophobia. Its evangelical-conservative theology and biblical fundamentalism establish a sexual orthodoxy that promotes heterosexuality. Therefore, the Black Church, like most Christian churches in the United States, opposes homosexuality. However, heterosexuality is condoned only within the constraints of marriage and for the purpose of procreation. Homosexuality is viewed as a perversity that defiles the flesh, desecrates the sanctity of marriage, and destroys the traditional composition of the nuclear family. Because AIDS was first associated with homosexual behavior, and is now, in conservative circles, associated with both homosexual and heterosexual perversity, most black churches do not have outreach ministries in their communities to address this epidemic.

Aside from the Black Church's evangelical-conservative theology and biblical fundamentalism, its antihomosexual stance is also reflected in its ecclesiastical positions. Embedded in the ecclesiastical positions, which are sometimes called "committees," are prescribed gender roles for males and females. For example, the kitchen ministry is run by women, whereas the ordination is run by men. These ecclesiastical positions assume a heterosexual orientation, thus keeping heterosexism in place.

The homophobia in the Black Church is also linked to misogyny and is based on antifemale sentiment rather than an antihomosexual one. For example, an ecclesiastical position for a gay male in the Black Church is the choirmaster or the minister of music. Although it seems paradoxical for the Black Church to have an acknowledged "gay-friendly" position, the choirmaster is a nonthreatening position within its ecclesiastical structures. Choirmaster, or "choirmistress" or "choirqueen" as gay male choir leaders are sometimes called, is a nongendered position that may also be filled by women. Although an important leadership position within the church, and central in the church's liturgy, it is not within the church's governing and administrative hierarchy and, therefore, does not endanger the sexual integrity of the church. Heterosexual men hold most positions of authority and power. Although the choirmaster position is a visible entry point into the fold of the church, gay men assume this role at a tremendous cost to their personhood.

African American women outnumber their men by three to one in most black churches. These numbers give the impression that the Black Church is run by women. However, the Black Church's institutional sexism gives African American heterosexual women high visibility and prestige but only nominal, if any, power within the governing and administrative hierarchy of the church. In some instances, their high visibility, such as "Mother of the Church" and/or wife of the pastor, are fixed female-gender positions whose prestige is gleaned from their titles and whose power is gleaned from their association with the pastor's social circle. African American women's depiction as the "backbone" of the Black Church is meant as a compliment for their dedication to the church. However, this adulation also highlights the limited roles and duties allotted to African American women and their low, but necessary, status and function in the Black Church for its survival and stability.

On the other hand, African American lesbians are not represented in any of the church's ecclesiastical positions, which contributes to their low attendance in the Black Church. Those lesbians who enter the Black Church are closeted, and those lesbians who engage in the life of the church take "backbone" positions along with their heterosexual sisters.

The gay black churches, which are springing up mainly in large urban cities, serve as an alternative worship space to the traditional Black Church. Although these churches do not discriminate on the basis of sexual orientation, they do discriminate on the basis of gender, thus replicating the patriarchal structure found in the traditional Black Church. In these alternative gay black churches, replacing heterosexual patriarchy with homosexual patriarchy relegates lesbians once again to "backbone" positions in the church for the church's survival and stability.

*Irene Monroe*

## Bibliography

Frazier, E. Franklin. *The Negro Church in America*. New York: Schocken, 1964.

Lincoln, E. Eric. *The Black Church Since Frazier*. New York: Schocken, 1974.

Lincoln, E. Eric, and Lawrence H. Mamiya. *The Black Church in the African American Experience*. Durham, N.C., and London: Duke University Press, 1990.

*See also* Protestantism

## Black Feminism

The active engagement of black women in liberating themselves from all forms of hegemony and patri-

**B** archy, public and private, including personal interactions and internalized oppression; the recognition of the simultaneity of black women's oppression by racism, sexism, classism, and heterosexism; the use of theory, political action, education, writing, visual and performing arts, speechmaking, and other means to initiate change in black women's position and condition.

## "First Wave" History

The long history of black feminism began with the "first wave" of feminism in the nineteenth century when black women were sounding the same themes as they did during the "second wave" of women's movements, beginning in the middle 1960s. "First wave" black feminists include Maria Stewart (1803–1879), the first woman of any race to speak publicly in the United States; educator Anna Julia Cooper (1758?–1864); and the most renowned black feminist of all time, Sojourner Truth (1797–1883), whose "Ain't I a Woman" (1851) speech is legendary.

"First wave" black feminists challenged white feminists to understand that black women's oppression extended beyond sex to race and class, and black men to understand that black women were oppressed by sex, as well as by race and class. However, it was "second wave" feminists, among them lesbian activist writers Audre Lorde (1934–1992), Pat Parker (1944–1989), and Barbara Smith (1946–), who brought sexual orientation equal validation. Although the latter category has yet to be accorded the same importance by all black women who call themselves feminists, consciousness of the importance of support for lesbianism (not merely tolerance of, and/or support for, one's lesbian friends) continues to grow.

Although "first wave" black feminists expressed in various ways the idea of simultaneous oppression by race, sex, and class, it was the Combahee River Collective, a group of predominantly lesbian black feminists in Boston, Massachusetts, who first *theorized* the *concept*, after expanding it to include sexual orientation. The "Combahee River Collective Statement" (1977) has become a bedrock foundation of black feminist theory.

## "Second Wave" History

The "Combahee" began as a chapter of the National Black Feminist Organization (NBFO), which held a regional meeting in 1973 and its first national conference in New York City in 1974. Although the short-lived NBFO held few meetings, the organization was hugely important in establishing lasting networks among early black feminists.

As the Combahee collective did, black and Latina New York feminists also began meeting in 1974; by November, they formally incorporated as Third World Women Inc., later changing the name to Salsa Soul Sisters (SSS). Emphasizing black and Latin culture, they formed a drumming group and a writers' group, published a magazine, the *Gayzette*, and, in 1977, began holding annual women's Kwanzaa celebrations. After Latina lesbians left the group, SSS changed names twice, finally becoming Ancestral Lesbians United for Societal Change. They have met every Thursday since their inception and are housed at New York City's Lesbian and Gay Community Center.

Black lesbian publishing ventures of "second wave" feminism include the radical lesbian collective Azalea, which began in the late 1970s with a mission to publish unedited works by women of color and ended in the early 1980s. Consistent contributors were Anita Cornwell (1923–) and Audre Lorde. *Ache*, a magazine produced in Oakland, California, by black lesbian feminists, began in the late 1980s and lasted for approximately four years. *Conditions: Five, The Black Women's Issue* (1979), edited by Lorraine Bethel and Barbara Smith, was one of the most popular editions of the long-lived feminist magazine, which emphasized writing by lesbians. Included in the edition was Gloria Hull's "Under the Days: The Buried Life and Poetry of Angelina Weld Grimké." The tragic story of Grimké (1880–1958), a hidden black lesbian who lived in isolation well into the twentieth century, inspires black lesbians to speak out. Smith used *Conditions Five* as the foundation of her *Home Girls: A Black Feminist Anthology* (1983), which was published by Kitchen Table: Women of Color Press. The press was launched in 1980 by Audre Lorde and Barbara Smith.

Lorde and Smith expanded their lesbian political work into gay politics by serving together on the board of the National Coalition of Black Lesbians and Gays, an organization that grew out of the first Third World Conference for Lesbians and Gays in Washington, D.C., in 1979, for which Lorde was the keynote speaker. Black lesbians, sharing with black gay men oppressions specific to their blackness, chose to work together politically; in that process, and, through reading and hearing Lorde, many black gay men embraced and pass along to younger men the concept of black feminism. *Angela Bowen*

## Bibliography

Guy-Sheftall, Beverly. *Words of Fire*. New York: New Press, 1995.

Hull, Gloria. "Under the Days: The Buried Life of Angelina Weld Grimké." In *Conditions: Five, The Black Women's Issue* 2:2 (1979), 17–25.

*See also* African Americans; Combahee River Collective; Cornwell, Anita; Grimké, Angelina Weld; Latinas; Lesbian Feminism; Lorde, Audre; Parker, Pat; Race and Racism; Smith, Barbara; Women of Color

## Blais, Marie-Claire (1939–)

Québec novelist and playwright. When she was barely twenty, Marie-Claire Blais gained critical recognition for her first novel, *La Belle bête* (Mad Shadows). She was soon discovered by American literary critic Edmund Wilson (1895–1972), who helped her come to the United States on a Guggenheim Fellowship and introduced her to the artist Mary Meigs (1917–), who would become Blais's lover and lifelong friend. She soon joined Meigs and her partner, writer Barbara Deming (1917–1984), in their home on Cape Cod, Massachusetts, entering into a life that was both a liberation and an education after a Québec Catholic childhood shaped by poverty and sexual repression. Under the tutelage of Meigs, Blais explored literature, art, and music; through Deming's militant activism, she was introduced to the American protest movements of the 1960s, these new images of violence and oppression deeply affecting a sensitivity already painfully attuned to the suffering of others. In 1965, Blais published a satiric analysis of oppression in her own Québec society in her novel *Une Saison dans la vie d'Emmanuel* (A Season in the Life of Emmanuel), immediately hailed as a classic because of its dark parody of the long-idealized rural family.

Although Blais was able to live openly as a lesbian after leaving Québec, to which she returned only in the late 1970s, it was not until 1976 that lesbian experience made its first appearance in her writing, in a monologue she contributed to *La Nef des sorcières* (Ship of Witches), a collective feminist dramatic production. The lesbian community evoked in the monologue becomes the subject and the central character of Blais's 1978 *Les Nuits de l'Underground* (Nights in the Underground), her first novel grounded in lesbian experience. In all of Blais's work, relationships within the couple, lesbian or heterosexual, are fraught with difficulty, but in *Les Nuits de l'Underground* there appears, for the first time, the countervailing vision of a community of mutual caring among women, a vision that, extended beyond the lesbian community, comes to dominate Blais's later writings. However, in a 1989 novel set in a lesbian commune, *L'Ange de la solitude* (The Angel of Solitude), Blais shows greater pessimism about the future of a younger generation in a world infected with AIDS.

While lesbian characters are foregrounded in only two of Blais's novels, much of her work testifies to the power of relationships among women.

*Mary Jean Green*

## Bibliography

Green, Mary Jean. *Marie-Claire Blais*. New York: Twayne, 1995.

Meigs, Mary. *Lily Briscoe: A Self-Portrait*. Vancouver: Talonbooks, 1981.

*See also* Deming, Barbara; Québec

## Blaman, Anna (1905–1960)

Pen name of Dutch novelist Johanna Petronella Vrugt. Born in Rotterdam, the Netherlands, the daughter of a bicycle repairer and dealer, Anna Blaman suffered from frail health and lived with her mother all of her life. Although she trained to be a teacher, she never was able to work for any extended period. When she was about sixteen, she became aware of her homosexuality but "did not think a big deal about it." At twenty-eight and already suffering from the strain of her temporary teaching jobs—she could not get tenure because she never was able to fulfill the needlework qualification—she began a career as a writer. In 1936, she became so seriously ill that people feared for her life. She miraculously recovered with the help of what turned out to be the great love of her life, Alie Bosch (known as Nurse B.). Bosch did not return her love in the way she wanted, so Blaman (who around that time adopted the pseudonym, the exact meaning of which has remained a mystery) turned to a number of sexual relationships with other women, including lesbian writer Marie-Louise Doudart de la Grée (1907–1981).

*Vrouw en Vriend* (Woman and Friend), Blaman's first novel, was published in 1941. Her first literary success came with *Eenzaam Avontuur* (Lonely Adventure) in 1948. It received a prestigious literary prize from the city of Amsterdam but was condemned by the general public for its "amorality" and emphasis on sexuality as the basis for relationships. Rumors of Blaman's lesbianism, as well as the inclusion of a lesbian character, precipitated a scandal around the book. It finally was condemned by a well-publicized literary "tribunal" conducted in Rotterdam in 1949. Blaman never fully recovered from this, although she kept on writing well-received books, such as *De Kruisvaarder* (The Crusader) (1950) and *Op leven en dood* (To the Death) (1951). In 1956, she became the first woman to receive the prestigious P.C. Hooftprize for literature. She died, age fifty-five, of a cerebral embolism. Her unfinished posthumous novel, *De Verliezers* (The Losers), published in 1961, was the first to include two lesbian characters, instead of a heterosexual couple.

Blaman's work was influenced by French existentialism, and it was its "modernity" that shocked most of her critics. The "failure of romantic love" and its replacement by sexuality are its main themes, with subthemes of illness and health. The publication of many of her letters in 1988 and 1990 revealed how much of her own life was reflected in her work. Blaman's perception of her homosexuality as innate and "masculine" is projected into the male character, who usually suffers from frustrated love for a woman representing Anna's lovers, primarily Alie Bosch.                              *Judith Schuyf*

## Bibliography

Struyker Boudier, Henk. *Speurtocht naar een Onbekende. Anna Blaman en haar Eenzaam Avontuur* (Quest for an Unknown: Anna Blaman and Her Lonely Adventure). Amsterdam: Meulenhoff, 1973.

*See also* Netherlands

## Blues Singers

Musical genre that developed in the late nineteenth century and was rooted in African American spirituals and field hollers. Davis (1995) argues that, during the Reconstruction period, the personal status of African Americans transformed in three signficant ways: individual travel, education, and sexuality that "could be explored freely by individuals who now could enter into autonomously chosen personal relationships." African American women were central figures in creating and refining the "classic blues" (distinct from "country blues," a predominantly male genre), which laid the foundation for every form of popular music to follow. Of the blues singers who performed as professional artists and commanded large-scale audiences in revival-like gatherings (at the same time as male ministers were becoming a professional caste), Gertrude "Ma" Rainey (1886–1939) and Bessie Smith (1894?–1937) were the most widely known. When they preached about sexual love, they were articulating a collective experience of freedom, which, for many African American people, was the most powerful evidence that slavery no longer existed. Sexuality in the blues sounded dramatically different from the highly idealized versions of romantic love in turn-of-the-century white popular music. The prevailing ideology of domestic bliss within the confines of marriage and motherhood was largely irrelevant to African American women. The blueswomen were intensely critical of marriage in their songs, and they adopted rhetorical stances that were independent, unorthodox, challenging, and sexually adventurous.

Musically, the blues relied on a twelve-bar harmonic pattern that facilitated the delivery of each verse in a song; the twelve-bar cycle was repeated several times throughout, depending on the number of verses or instrumental solos. Many blues songs vary this structure, and others depart from it altogether. Most blues songs also followed an AAB text format, in which the B line resolved the issue addressed in the A lines. Accompaniments ranged from a simple piano or guitar to a full-blown jazz-band arrangement. In performance, the accompaniment would play off the vocalist at the end of each line, forming an internal call and response between singer and instrumentalists and adding to the meaning of the texts, laced with double entendres.

## Blues Queens

Many of the "blues queens" were lesbian or bisexual. "Ma" Rainey and Bessie Smith had affairs with the women who performed in their shows, and it is quite possible they were lovers with each other. Gladys Bentley (1907–1960) was an openly lesbian performer who sported a bulldagger image. Alberta Hunter (1895–1984) was successful in the more glamorous cabaret circuit and among European audiences. In the mid-1950s, she "retired" and worked as a nurse for twenty years in New York City. She made a celebrated comeback in 1977 at the age of eighty-two. Hunter took great pains to conceal her lesbianism. After a brief marriage, she was lovers with Carrie Mae Ward (n.d.), and she had a long-term relationship with Lottie Tyler (n.d., the niece of Bert Williams

[1874–1922]), with whom she shared her apartment. Hunter's biographer, Taylor (1987), writes that "Alberta recoiled every time a lesbian performer like Ethel Waters fought with her girlfriends in public." Waters (1896–1977), known as "Sweet Mama Stringbean," popularized the songs "Stormy Weather" and "Dinah." Taylor claims she was lovers and longtime friends with Ethel Williams (1909–?), who occasionally danced in Waters's shows. Waters raised Algretta, Williams's daughter, until the girl was twelve.

Several blues songs address lesbianism. "Ma" Rainey's "Prove It on Me Blues" (1928) is the most direct expression of lesbian sexuality and defiance. Carby (1994) observes that this song "vacillates between the subversive hidden activity of women loving women [and] a public declaration of lesbianism. The words express a contempt for a society that rejected lesbians. . . . But at the same time the song is a reclamation of lesbianism as long as the woman publicly names her sexual preference for herself." In the Paramount advertisement for this song, Rainey wears men's clothing and flirts with two feminine women on a street corner while a policeman looks on. Rainey states the possibility that some prostitutes may be lesbians, in her "Shave 'Em Dry Blues" (1924). Lucille Bogan's (also known as Bessie Jackson [1897–1948]) recording of "B.D. Women's Blues" (1935) proudly asserts that bulldaggers "can lay their jive just like a natural man / B.D. women sure is rough; they drink up many a whiskey and sure can strut their stuff." There were several variants of this lesbian song, recorded as "B.D.'s Dream" or "B.D. Women." Bertha Idaho's "Down on Pennsylvania Avenue" depicts the sexual variety found in Baltimore, where "Some freakish sights you'll surely see, / You can't tell the he's from the she's." A few men's songs also mention lesbianism. In "Bad Girl Blues," Memphis Willie B. Borum sings: "Women loving each other and they don't think about no man / They ain't playing no secret no more, these women playing it a wide open hand"; in "Boy in the Boat" (1930), George Hanna muses: "When you see two women walking hand in hand, just shake your head and try to understand."

Long before the "second wave" of women's and lesbian and gay liberation in the 1960s, these blues singers and their songs cleared an important space for lesbian sexuality within a relatively tolerant social context of African American urban culture.

Finally, the phenomenon of the lesbian or bisexual blues queen is immortalized in at least two novels. The characters of Sybil in *Strange Brother* (1931) by Blair Niles and Shug in Alice Walker's *The Color Purple* (1982) are both based on the figure of the worldly blues singer.     *Martha Mockus*

### Bibliography
Carby, Hazel. "It Jus Be's Dat Way Sometimes: The Sexual Politics of Women's Blues." In *Unequal Sisters: A Multicultural Reader in U.S. Women's History*. Second Edition eds. Vicki L. Ruiz and Ellen Carol DuBois. New York: Routledge, 1994, pp. 330–341.

Davis, Angela Y. "I Used To Be Your Sweet Mama: Ideology, Sexuality and Domesticity in the Blues of Gertrude 'Ma' Rainey and Bessie Smith." In *Sexy Bodies: The Strange Carnalities of Feminism*. Ed. Elizabeth Grosz and Elspeth Probyn. New York: Routledge, 1995, pp. 231–265.

Garber, Eric. "A Spectacle in Color: The Lesbian and Gay Subculture of Jazz Age Harlem." In *Hidden from History: Reclaiming the Gay and Lesbian Past*. Ed. Martin Duberman, Martha Vicinus, and George Chauncey, Jr. New York: Penguin, 1989, pp. 318–331.

Harrison, Daphne Duval. *Black Pearls: Blues Queens of the 1920s*. New Brunswick, N.J.: Rutgers University Press, 1988.

Taylor, Frank C. *Alberta Hunter: A Celebration in Blues*. New York: McGraw-Hill, 1987.

### Recordings
*AC/DC Blues: Gay Jazz Reissues* (Stash ST–106).

*See also* African Americans; Bentley, Gladys; Bisexuality; Harlem; Harlem Renaissance; Rainey, Gertrude "Ma"; Smith, Bessie

## Boarding Schools
English girls' boarding schools have been associated with lesbianism since Havelock Ellis (1859–1939) warned (in *Studies in the Psychology of Sex* [1901]) that places where women lived and slept together, and men were absent, were breeding grounds for lesbian seduction. Prior to the sexologists, close friendships between girls and women had been smiled upon. But, by the end of the nineteenth century, girls' schools were moving away from the earlier kind of small, family-style institution, which aimed to turn out accomplished ladies, and increasingly modeled themselves upon boys' public (i.e., private) schools, which were widely known to be places where homosexual experimentation flour-

**B** ished. Fear that girls' schools might adopt this along with the academic curriculum, competitive games, and codes of honor was accompanied by suspicion of the all-women worlds of the girls' schools and colleges and, particularly, of the strong-minded, independent women who had risen to positions of considerable power and influence as schoolmistresses. Clemence Dane's (1888–1965) repellent novel *Regiment of Women* (1919) depicts the predatory lesbian schoolmistress who was to typify antilesbian imagery in the years between the world wars. Schoolgirl "crushes," hitherto considered innocent and even character building, became the subject of warning addresses by headmistresses at such institutions as Cheltenham, Downe House, and Roedean. Antilesbianism fed into the campaign against single-sex schools that gathered pace after World War II. Lamb and Pickthorn's study of girls' schools, *Locked-Up Daughters* (1968), refers several times to the dangers of lesbianism in boarding schools ("emotional involvement and Lesbianism have always been a latent streak in the single sex school. We like to think that . . . these unhappy aspects of community life occur today much less").

There is truth in Ellis's statement that, where women are gathered together, there lesbians will be found. And, though only a small proportion of girls have ever attended a boarding school, those who have often recall lesbian teachers or lesbian affairs; some date their lesbian initiation to their school days. Historians Vicinus (1991) and Edwards (1995) have uncovered clear evidence of lesbian relationships among school and college mistresses, while novelists have depicted early experiences of lesbian love in fictionalized accounts of their own school days: love for a teacher (Dorothy Bussy [1866–1960], *Olivia* [1949]) or for a fellow student (Lucy Kinlock [1899?–1995], *A World Within a School* [1937]). Adult novels about boarding-school lesbianism, such as Rosemary Manning's *The Chinese Garden* (1962) or the unpleasant *No Talking After Lights* (1990) by Angela Lambert, (c. 1940s–) tend to be negative in tone. But Nancy Spain (1917–1964), well-known British broadcaster and writer who, like Manning (1911–1988), was herself a lesbian, wrote an amusing spoof detective novel, *Poison for Teacher* (1949), which she set in a school she called Radcliff Hall, modeled on Roedean, the school she had attended.

Novels for girls about boarding-school life, which formed a significant body of British juvenile fiction between 1880 and about 1970, are good sources for "lesbian" content. While rarely consciously engaging with lesbian feelings, girls'-school stories often tackled the "crush" and presented quite positive views of love between girls (for example, Elsie J. Oxenham's [1880–1959] Abbey books). Even in the 1950s and 1960s, widely read writers for children, such as Enid Blyton (1897–1968) and Elinor M. Brent-Dyer (1894–1969), were depicting schoolmistresses who seem obvious lesbians to the adult reader, either because of their "masculine" presentation (Miss Peters in Blyton's Malory Towers series) or because they are in accepted couple relationships with another mistress (Nancy Wilmot and Kathie Ferrars in Brent-Dyer's Chalet School series).

The girls' boarding-school story, like the girls' boarding school itself, fell victim to the prevailing heterosexism of the 1960s: Reprints of earlier novels were drastically edited, with references to kisses and shared beds expunged. Publishers closed their school-story lists, replacing them with mixed-sex adventure tales and "career" novels (nurse, secretary, air hostess, each with obligatory boyfriend). A rare feminist-era example of a lesbian novel set in a boarding school is Elana Nachman's (1949–) *Riverfinger Women* (1974). While there was a revival of critical interest in girls'-school stories in the 1980s, largely thanks to the feminist revaluing of women's experience, both boarding-school stories and boarding schools themselves are in decline: Social realism and coeducational day schools are considered more "natural" and "healthy." Those women who attended boarding schools rarely remember them with much pleasure, but many readers of boarding-school stories found in the all-girl settings a rich fantasy world whose influence extended into adulthood.

*Rosemary Auchmuty*

### Bibliography

Auchmuty, Rosemary. *A World of Girls: The Appeal of the Girls' School Story*. London: Women's Press, 1992.

Avery, Gillian. *The Best Type of School: A History of Girls' Independent Schools*. London: Andre Deutsch, 1991.

Edwards, Elizabeth. "Homoerotic Friendship and College Principals, 1880–1960." *Women's History Review* 4:2 (1995), 149–163.

Lamb, Felicia, and Helen Pickthorn. *Locked-Up Daughters: A Parents' Look at Girls' Education and Schools*. London: Hodder and Stoughton, 1968.

Vicinus, Martha. "Distance and Desire: English Boarding-School Friendships, 1870–1920." In *Hidden from History: Reclaiming the Gay and Lesbian Past*. Ed. Martin Duberman, Martha Vicinus, and George Chauncey, Jr. London: Penguin, 1991, pp. 212–229.

*See also* Colleges, Women's; Smashes, Crushes, Spoons

## Body Image

A person's experiences of, and attitudes toward, the body. This has included such areas as attitudes toward physical appearance, eating disorders, weight obsession, size, and other forms of appearance discriminations. For many years, clinicians assumed that body-image difficulties among women primarily involved, or were a result of, their reaction to the "male gaze"—the result of seeking to attract men. In this view, lesbian body-image concerns were not even considered by academic and clinical experts. Yet body image has been an important issue from an early point in the "second wave" of the women's movement and lesbian feminism.

Some feminists, especially lesbian and bisexual women, initially identified women's appearance norms (and resulting body-image problems) as a function of patriarchal control and sought quite explicitly to challenge beauty norms. The earliest publications on lesbian experience of body image came out of the fat women's liberation movement in the early 1970s. According to Vivian Mayer, in the introduction to Schoenfielder and Wieser (1983), the movement was a blending of radical feminism and radical therapy. Early writings spoke to the issues of weight discrimination in general, but also within the lesbian feminist communities.

In an early theoretical work in *Lesbian Psychologies* (1987), therapist Laura S. Brown indicated that lesbians appeared less likely to have eating disorders than straight women. She speculated that, since lesbians were very involved in fat liberation, the community seemed more accepting of a diversity of sizes. She outlined the parallels between attitudes toward fat women and lesbians and suggested that patriarchy forbids women "to love other women because it would lead them to love and value themselves." She further speculated the a lesbian's own internalized homophobia would play a part in her body image.

One would expect that, since lesbians do not think of themselves as objects defined by male subjects, they should be able to escape the negative body image heterosexual women suffer. Yet some argue that lesbians, too, accept patriarchal standards of beauty or institute their own standards that are equally restrictive, such as clothes, short hair styles, mannerisms, and physical strength.

As surveyed in the introduction to *Looking Queer* (Atkins, 1998), the first quantitative studies on lesbian body image were not published until 1990. Six studies done between 1990 and 1997 compared the body image of lesbians and heterosexual women (some comparing with gay and straight men as well) and indicate a complex interaction between gender and sexual orientation. For example, four studies found significant differences between lesbian and heterosexual women that seem to confirm the assertion that lesbians have fewer body-image difficulties. The other two found no significant differences. All of those that involved men found that heterosexual men had the fewest body-image concerns. Yet, they differed on whether gay men had fewer or more body-image concerns than women of any sexual orientation.

Many problems exist with these studies. One damaging bias is that the researchers collapsed sexual *orientation* and sexual *behavior,* assuming that women who identify as lesbians are not affected by relations with men. Any woman who identified as bisexual was excluded from the studies; yet, some lesbians who indicated they may be attracted to men as well were included. This would make it difficult to tell what, if any, impact attraction to men might have. And even though some of the studies mention the importance of lesbian culture, they do not take age or length of time in the community into consideration. For instance, if adoption of lesbian cultural values were more important than gender attraction, lesbian and bisexual women who are part of that value system might differ from women who are new to the community or do not share the appearance values.

In trying to understand these complex and sometimes contradictory results, Rothblum (1994) took a cultural approach when she analyzed the ways in which appearance affects lesbians, including the influences of traditional attitudes and institutions, the effect of homophobic stereotypes, the process of identifying with lesbian culture, the invisibility of lesbians who are also part of other oppressed groups, and the changing physical-appearance norms within the lesbian community.

To combat lesbian invisibility within the dominant society, lesbians may need to adopt specific appearance norms to be able to recognize and be recognized by other lesbians. These lesbian norms can become markers of identity, but they also can be restrictive and exclusionary, leaving out those who cannot or do not wish to conform. Yet they also provide a measure of support in recovering from, and resisting, the dominant culture ideals that have resulted in widespread eating disorders.

In *A Hunger So Wide and So Deep* (1995), feminist sociologist Becky W. Thompson was the first to directly address eating disorders and other body-image issues among both women of color and lesbians. She shows how internalized racism and homophobia play directly into the body-image problems of the women in her work, and she notes that "lessons about heterosexuality often went hand in hand with lessons about weight and dieting." Most lesbians found coming out as a beginning, not an end, to the healing process.

Newer work collected in Atkins (1998) suggests that lesbian and bisexual women may be at greater risk of eating disorders than heterosexual women unless they have the support of a feminist community. In addition, racism, ageism, and ableism within both the dominant culture and lesbian communities may lessen the protective effects. More work needs to be done that explores the complex ways early childhood, family pressures, lesbian values and norms, and feminism all compete in the body-image conceptions of lesbian and bisexual women.

What these earlier and newer works combined indicate is that lesbian culture may provide a place for women to resist sexist and heterosexist appearance norms—but that sexual orientation alone is not protective. And as lesbian and bisexual women become more assimilated into mainstream culture, they may be more at risk of conforming to dominant appearance ideals for women. If a feminist "culture of resistance" has been central to the development of positive body image among lesbians and bisexual women, it is important to change the dominant cultural norms, as well as fight for acceptance of diverse sexual orientations.                    *Dawn Atkins*

### Bibliography

Atkins, Dawn, ed. *Looking Queer: Body Image and Identity in Lesbian, Bisexual, Gay and Transgender Communities.* New York: Harrington Park, 1998.

Brown, Laura S. "Lesbians, Weight, and Eating: New Analyses and Perspectives." In *Lesbian Psychologies.* Ed. Boston Lesbian Psychologies Collective. Chicago: University of Illinois Press, 1987, pp. 294–310.

Dworkin, Sari H. "Not in Man's Image: Lesbians and the Cultural Oppression of Body Image." *Women and Therapy* 8 (1989), 27–39.

Rothblum, Esther D. "Lesbians and Physical Appearance: Which Model Applies?" *Psychological Perspectives on Lesbian and Gay Issues* 1 (1994), 84–97.

Schoenfielder, Lisa, and Barb Wieser, eds. *Shadow on a Tightrope: Writings by Women on Fat Oppression.* Introduction by Vivian Mayer. Iowa City: Aunt Lute, 1983.

Thompson, Becky W. *A Hunger So Wide and So Deep.* Minneapolis: University of Minnesota Press, 1995.

*See also* Fat Liberation

### Bonheur, Rosa (1822–1899)

French painter. Born Marie-Rosalie Bonheur on March 16, 1822, in Bordeaux, France, to Sophie Marquis and Raimond Oscar-Marie Bonheur, Rosa Bonheur became one of the most successful and honored artists of her era. After receiving her initial training from her father, she refined her skills by copying famous paintings in the Louvre. Her most

*Rosa Bonheur, by Anna Elizabeth Klumpke. The Metropolitan Museum of Art, gift of the artists in memory of Rosa Bonheur, 1922 (22.222).*

common subjects were animals, initially domestic livestock, particularly horses, then, later, panthers, lions, and tigers. Her works also included portraits and scenes of rural life.

In 1841, at the age of nineteen, she saw her first works accepted by the jury of the Paris Salon, where she exhibited regularly for the next fifteen years, collecting awards and critical acclaim. As her success at the Salon indicated, Bonheur was not an avant-garde painter; her animal paintings and genre scenes were consistent with, and considered exemplary of, the mainstream academic standards of the period. She was elected to fine-arts societies in England, the United States, and various European countries and principalities; received honors from the heads of state of Belgium, Spain, Mexico, and France; and was the first woman to achieve the rank of Officier de la Légion d'Honneur. With her sister, Juliette, she directed the School of Drawing for Young Girls in Paris from 1849 to 1860.

Bonheur flouted convention by wearing male clothing like her famous literary contemporary, George Sand (1804–1876). She received official permits from the Paris police to wear male attire and maintained that her trousers and jackets were necessary because she studied animal anatomy in slaughterhouses. Bonheur ridiculed women who donned such attire in social settings, saying, "If you see me dressed as I am, it is not for originality's sake, as too many women do, but simply to facilitate my work." It is surprising, given the hostility engendered by Sand and feminists such as Flora Tristan (1803–1844), that neither Bonheur's dress nor her public relationships with female partners interfered with her popularity.

Bonheur had known her first partner, Nathalie Micas (1824–1889), since childhood. After her father's death, when she was twenty-seven, Bonheur moved in with the Micas family. In 1853, Bonheur and Micas moved in together in Paris. Seven years later, they purchased the Château de By near the Forest of Fontainebleau and lived there with Micas's mother.

Micas, whose health was always delicate, died in 1889. In 1898, Anna Elizabeth Klumpke (1856–1945), an artist from the United States whom Bonheur first met the year Micas died, moved in with her. Bonheur commissioned Klumpke to write her biography and made a will leaving her entire estate to her new partner. (Bonheur and Micas had both had wills designating each other sole beneficiary.) Bonheur died the following year, on May 25, 1899. She was buried in Père Lachaise cemetery in the same crypt as Nathalie Micas. In 1945, Klumpke's ashes were also interred there. The epitaph reads: "Friendship is divine affection."

Bonheur never publicly identified as lesbian and made somewhat ambiguous comments regarding her sexual and romantic interests and her relationships with Micas and Klumpke. Although she said, "My private life is nobody's concern" and described Micas as her "friend" and their relationship as "sisterly," in a few letters to very close friends she described Klumpke as her wife. An oft-quoted remark—"The fact is, in the way of males, I like only the bulls I paint"—indicates a rather distinct disinterest in men that she seemed comfortable expressing. Regardless of self-identification, the circumstances of Bonheur's life have led many late-twentieth-century biographers and art historians to identify her as oriented toward her own sex.

*Gwendolyn Alden Dean*

## Bibliography

Ashton, Dore. *Rosa Bonheur: A Life and a Legend.* New York: Viking, 1981.

Collis, Rose. *Portraits to the Wall: Historic Lesbian Lives Unveiled.* London: Cassell, 1994.

Stanton, Theodore, ed. *Reminiscences of Rosa Bonheur.* New York: Hacker Art Books, 1976.

*See also* Art, Mainstream; France; Sand, George

## Bookstores

Even though feminist and lesbian and gay bookstores emerged at different times, they share the same goal of providing information to communities often ignored by the mainstream.

### Emergence of Bookstores

In the late 1960s, there were no feminist bookstores in existence in the United States and only one gay and lesbian bookstore, the Oscar Wilde Memorial Bookshop in New York City. The rebirth of the women's movement in the 1970s brought with it an increased need for literature, music, and information on women's lives. Emerging from the radical women's movement, bookstores began to appear in communities after the 1976 Women in Print Conference that brought together women interested in publishing, selling, and printing information about lesbianism and feminism. Many bookstores grew out of community organizations, such as the Women's Action Collective of Columbus, Ohio. Reflecting their

**B** activist roots, bookstores were run by collectives of women, with no distinct owners or managers and operated on a nonprofit basis. By the 1990s, 140 feminist bookstores existed in the United States.

Gay-, lesbian-, and bisexual-oriented bookstores also have their origins in the movement, and, as gay rights gained momentum in the 1980s and 1990s, bookstores appeared across the country. At the time of the Stonewall Inn Riot in 1969, the Oscar Wilde Memorial Bookshop in New York City was the only gay bookstore in the United States. By 1994, there were forty-five lesbian and gay bookstores.

Celebrating lesbian lives and culture is an important element for both types of bookstores. By carrying "classic" literature, such as Radclyffe Hall's *The Well of Loneliness* (1928), contemporary fiction, or nonfiction works on such topics as lesbian commitment ceremonies or legal rights, these bookstores provide valuable information as well as affirm a lesbian lifestyle. Bookstores support lesbian identity by selling historical symbols of lesbianism, such as black triangle pins, selling music by lesbian musicians, and celebrating Lesbian and Gay Pride events. They also provide lesbian artists, craftswomen, and writers a space to display and sell their work.

**Bookstores and Communities**

Because of these roles, bookstores are an essential part of the "ecosystem" supporting lesbian communities. This ecosystem is a connected network of activists, organizations, and institutions. By doubling as community centers, bookstores offer meeting places for activist and support groups and gathering places for lesbians seeking information on community events. Stores also offer referrals for social services, provide bulletin boards for a variety of needs, such as roommates wanted, car repair, and child care. They may also serve as safe places for women to explore what it means to be lesbian or bisexual.

Booksellers take an active role in their communities by participating in area organizations and activities, such as providing sensitivity training on gay, lesbian, and bisexual issues in corporations or speaking on activist issues at area high schools. Because of their connections to the lesbian community, many bookstores use volunteers to staff the store or attend special events.

As a part of these ecosystems, bookstores have helped lesbian communities survive and thrive during times of political backlash. A case study in Columbus, Ohio, found that, during an antifeminist backlash, many community organizations folded, but the women's bookstore remained a haven connecting and rejuvenating activists.

While lesbian, gay, and feminist movements are in different stages of development across the globe, bookstores with lesbian or feminist sections are evident in many countries. In Johannesburg, South Africa, for example, four bookstores advertise lesbian and gay offerings. Two women's bookstores are also established in Kyoto and Osaka, Japan. Bookstores catering to women, gays, or lesbians can be found in parts of Asia, Europe, the Middle East, Australia and New Zealand, Canada, and Latin America.                    *Jo Reger*

*Bibliography*

Corrigan, Theresa. "Feminist Bookstores: Part of an Ecosystem." *Sojourner: The Women's Forum* 19:3 (1993), 1–4.

Summer, Bob. "Bookselling as Cultural Politics." *Publishers Weekly* (June 27, 1994), 29–31.

Taylor, Verta, and Leila J. Rupp. "Women's Culture and Lesbian Feminist Activism: A Reconsideration of Cultural Feminism." *Signs: Journal of Women in Culture and Society* 19:1 (1993), 32–61.

Whittier, Nancy. *Feminist Generations: The Persistence of the Radical Women's Movement.* Philadelphia: Temple University Press, 1995.

Wolf, Deborah Goleman. *The Lesbian Community.* Berkeley: University of California Press, 1980.

*See also* Businesses, Lesbian; Collectives; Community; Publishing, Lesbian

**Boston Marriage**

The term "Boston marriage" was used in late-nineteenth-century New England to describe a long-term monogamous relationship between two otherwise unmarried women. The women were generally financially independent of men, either through inheritance or because of a career. They were usually feminists, New Women, often pioneers in a profession. They were also very involved in culture and social betterment, and these female values formed a strong basis for their life together. As described by Bostonian Mark DeWolfe Howe, a nineteenth-century *Atlantic Monthly* editor who had social contact with a number of these women, including Sarah Orne Jewett (1849–1909), who had a Boston marriage with Annie Fields (1834–1915), their relationships were, in every sense, "a union—there is no truer word for it." Whether these unions sometimes or often included a sexual relationship cannot be known, but it is clear that these women spent their lives primarily with other women; they gave to other women the bulk of their energy and attention; and they formed powerful emotional ties with other women. If their personalities could be projected to contemporary times, it is probable that they would see themselves as "women-identified women"— what would be called lesbians—regardless of the level of their sexual interests.

Henry James (1843–1916) intended his novel *The Bostonians* (1885), which he characterized as "a very *American* tale" (the italics are James's), to be a study of just such a relationship—"one of those friendships between women which are so common in New England," he wrote in his *Notebook*. James's sister Alice (1848–1892) had a Boston marriage with Katharine Loring (1849–1949) in the years before Alice James's death.

The term "Boston marriage" was reintroduced by Rothblum and Brehony (1993) to describe romantic but asexual relationships among lesbians of the contemporary era. These women, the authors noted, considered themselves couples in every way except that they were not currently involved sexually with each other and may never have been. Their research was presented as a challenge to the idea that sex is what constitutes a lesbian relationship. Questions do remain, however, about how useful the notion or term "Boston marriage" is in the contemporary era and to what extent internalized homophobia may account for the lack of sexuality in these relationships.                    *Lillian Faderman*

## Bibliography

Faderman, Lillian. *Surpassing the Love of Men: Romantic Friendship and Love Between Women from the Renaissance to the Present*. New York: William Morrow, 1981.

Rothblum, Esther D., and Kathleen A. Brehony. *Boston Marriages*. Amherst: University of Massachusetts Press, 1993.

**See also** Couples; James, Alice; Romantic Friendship

## Bowen, Elizabeth (1899–1972)

Anglo-Irish novelist and short story writer. Born in Dublin, Ireland, and partly educated in England, Elizabeth Bowen lived most of her life in self-imposed exile from her native Ireland. In her early twenties, she moved semipermanently to England, where she established herself as an influential literary figure in the artistic circles of Oxford and London.

Having married Alan Cameron in 1923, Bowen entertained intense relationships with both men and women, including Carson McCullers (1917–1967) and May Sarton (1912–1996). It is in this context that she found an appropriate outlet for what she regarded as her "farouche" (irascible) temperament, a trait she traced back to her Irish heritage but that can be equally attributed to her most memorable characters, regardless of nationality. Beginning with her first novel, *The Hotel* (1927), Bowen focused on female pre-adulthood, with her characters often connected to the figure of a powerful older woman, set against the background of stultifying English middle-class life.

Although Bowen was often regarded as a writer of "sensibility," her sharply satirical wit and her interest in unpredictable characters make themselves felt in each of her ten novels and in the majority of her almost eighty short stories. Developing a prose style that was highly wrought and elusive, while simultaneously sharply-edged and funny, Bowen earned an international reputation with *The Last September* (1929) and *To the North* (1932); her best-known work, *The Death of the Heart*, was published in 1938.

Bowen's influence waned in the postwar years. Throughout the 1950s, she spent considerable time teaching in the United States, where she maintained an ardent friendship with Eudora Welty (1909–). Her last two novels, *The Little Girls* (1964) and *Eva Trout* (1969), represent radical departures from earlier stylistic and narrative methods. These texts also explicitly address what hitherto had lingered under the surface, the disruptive operations of female same-sex desire. Presenting what she called "life with the lid off," Bowen abandoned the ostensibly "straight" narratives that had formerly served as a "proper" backdrop for her disconcerting fantasies. Not surprisingly, these novels alienated both the literary establishment and conventional readers. Rediscovered by lesbian feminists in the early 1990s, Bowen can be regarded as not only a prominent figure on the scene of English letters, but also as one of the most outstanding contributors to twentieth-century lesbian literature.          *renée c. hoogland*

## Bibliography

Glendinning, Victoria. *Elizabeth Bowen: Portrait of a Writer*. Harmondsworth: Penguin, 1977, 1985.

**B** hoogland, renée c. *Elizabeth Bowen: A Reputation in Writing*. New York: New York University Press, 1994.

*See also* English Literature, Twentieth Century

## Bowles, Jane Auer (1917–1973)

American writer. Born in Woodmere, Long Island, New York, on February 22, 1917, in a community and a family made up of first- and second-generation white middle-class Jewish Americans, Jane Auer Bowles was primarily known as the wife of expatriate writer Paul Bowles (1910–), and his writing largely overshadows hers.

As a young schoolgirl, Bowles developed smashes on older women, particularly torch singers. At eighteen, she frequented Greenwich Village in New York City to meet other lesbians. Bowles carried on love relationships with young women in her late teen years; she also developed similar relationships with men. In a letter, Bowles writes about her burgeoning sexuality in response to her mother's accusation that being a lesbian was just an adolescent phase: "If I really were a Lesbian they'd get up a fund for me and send me down to the village in my own private bus. . . . But I really wasn't one, so they couldn't let me go to my ruin!"

When she met Paul Bowles in 1937, they both openly discussed their equally bisexual desires. She became conscious about the pressures of making a choice about her sexuality. Before marrying on February 21, 1938, Paul and Jane mapped out a nonmonogamous relationship so that they would both be able to continue carrying on relationships with men and women.

After the wedding, Bowles began work on her novel, *Two Serious Ladies*, which was finally published in 1943 and typically categorized as a "lesbian" novel. During the course of writing this autobiographical narrative, Bowles met Helvetia Perkins (1895?–1965), who would become her first extramarital lover, in Taxco, Central America. Piecing together the predicament of simultaneous relationships with Perkins and her husband, Bowles worked through bisexual desire in her writing.

The Bowles marriage was largely characterized by frequent trips abroad, until the couple finally settled as expatriates in Tangier, Morocco, in 1948.

Bowles published several short stories after relocating to Tangier and it was there that she became involved with her second long-term lover, Cherifa (c. 1928–?), a Moroccan working-class lesbian. In the 1950s, Bowles concentrated on writing and seeing her first play, *In the Summer House* (1951, 1953), into production. It was her last "finished" piece of literature. In 1955, two collections of Bowles's fiction were compiled in the United Kingdom and in the United States, *Plain Pleasures* and *The Collected Works of Jane Bowles*.

During the last few years of her life, Bowles moved out of her home with Paul and into an apartment with Cherifa, who cared for her as she became increasingly ill. Off and on between 1967 and 1973, she was admitted to a psychiatric institution for women in Málaga, Spain, where she eventually died and is buried.

*Marcy Jane Knopf*

### Bibliography

Dillon, Millicent. *A Little Original Sin: The Life and Work of Jane Bowles*. New York: Anchor, 1990.

Dillon, Millicent, ed. *Out in the World: Selected Letters of Jane Bowles, 1935–1970*. Santa Rosa, Calif.: Black Sparrow, 1990.

Knopf, Marcy Jane. "Bi-nary Bi-sexuality: Jane Bowles' *Two Serious Ladies*." In *Representing Bisexualities: Subjects and Cultures of Fluid Desire*. New York: New York University Press, 1996.

*See also* American Literature, Twentieth Century; Bisexuality; Greenwich Village

## Boye, Karin (1900–1941)

Swedish poet, prose writer, critic, teacher, and translator. Born to an upper-middle-class family, Karin Boye grew up in Stockholm, where she graduated and trained herself to become an elementary-school teacher. After a crisis during which she replaced her Christian faith with a secular trust in life, she took up academic studies in languages, literature, and history. As a student, she joined the socialist Clarté Society.

Boye published three collections of poetry in the 1920s and started an avant-garde journal, *Spectrum*, for which she wrote influential essays. In the early 1930s, she was the leading cultural critic and introducer of European modernism in a country that, at the time, was dominated by a conservative cultural tradition. She opposed the German Nazi ideology and took part in the international struggle to create a new social ethics and a democratic alternative to fascism. Under the influence of psychoanalytic theory, she developed her early poetry, based on already-existing ideas, into a modernistic writing directed toward a revision of the fundamental values of her contemporary society. Boye combined a fight against totalitarian claims in politics and in aesthetics with an ethos in which a new understanding of humanity was central. She strongly criticized a polarized and rigid gender-identified sexuality and pointed out the necessity of substituting new forms of social life for the traditional family institution and the morals associated with it. Swedish literary historians reduced the importance of Boye's authorship by seeing it as a testimony to personal, private inner struggles, which she could not solve and which eventually led to her suicide. Only since the 1980s has this picture been supplemented by a feminist and lesbian approach to her life and work.

Boye's 1934 novel, *Kris* (Crisis), is an autobiographical fiction, a revision of her youthful crisis when the death of God also meant the loss of the language she had known. She wrote several other novels including *Astarte* (1931), *Merit Vaknar* (Merit's Awakening, 1933), *För lite* (Too Little, 1936), and *Kallocain* (1940), but *Kris* is her only novel with a lesbian theme. Celebrating her love for a young woman, the protagonist finds an ideal that helps her partake in the creation of a new view of life and reality. At the same time, the novel describes the social and ideological crises and the redefinition of values that were occurring in Europe at the time.

Boye broke the law by living openly in a lesbian relationship, and she broke with literary tradition and conventions in her writing. She managed to connect her deepest quest for a new understanding of humanity and for a society based on responsibility for oneself and others with the cultural reorientation between the two world wars. With each new generation, she finds new readers.

*Gunilla Domellöf*

### Bibliography

Domellöf, Gunilla. "Den erotiska frigörelsen i Karin Boyes roman Kris" (Erotic Emancipation in Karin Boye's Novel *Crisis*). *Kvinnovetenskaplig tidskrift* (Journal of Women's Studies) 4 (1995), 37–47.

———. " 'I oss är en mångfald levande': Karin Boye som kritiker och prosamodernist" (" 'Within Us a Multiplicity Is Living': Karin Boye as a Critic and a Modernist Prose Writer"). Ph.D. diss., University of Umeå, 1986.

———. "Karin Boye och den revolutionära humanismen" (Karin Boye and the Revolutionary Humanism). In *Kulturradikalismen: Det moderna genombrottets andra fas* (Cultural Radicalism: The Second Phase of the Modern Breakthrough). Ed. Bertil Nolin. Stockholm: Brutus Östlings Förlag, Symposion, 1993, pp. 171–203.

*See also* Modernism

# Brazil

Largest country in South America, with more than 8,000 square kilometers and, according to the 1995 census, approximately 150 million people. Its original and immigrant peoples have, through intermarriage, intermingled their different cultures, resulting in a population that, to an unusual degree, assimilates new ideas and behaviors. Brazil has maintained its traditions of cultural and sexual liberality despite its standing as the world's largest Catholic country. It preserves conservative and punitive attitudes against lesbians at the same time that lesbians survive and retain a strong identity as women.

## History

The Portuguese chronicler Pero de Magalhães tells of Indian women at the time of Francisco Orellana's sixteenth-century expedition down the Amazon River. He describes women who decided to remain chaste and to have no interaction with men, refusing to consent even when refusal meant death. They abandoned women's traditional duties and followed male pursuits: cutting their hair like men, making war with bows and arrows, and pursuing game. Each woman had another woman to whom she considered herself married.

Following the Portuguese conquest, sixteenth-century Brazil was swept by the tribunals of the Inquisition, which, between 1591 and 1595 in the northeast region, interrogated twenty-nine women accused of having lesbian relationships.

## Political Organizations

Lesbian organization in the late twentieth century began in the struggle against the rightist military dictatorship that took over in 1964 and lasted nearly thirty years. After a period of repression, imprisonment, and death, new politically active groups began to arise. At first, they fought the dictatorship in general, beginning with women who struggled for political amnesty; later, in the mid-1970s, specific

**B**

groups of women and homosexuals began to assert their rights.

In 1979, the first homosexual newspaper, *Lampião de Esquina* (Light at the Corner), was published by the gay and lesbian SOMOS group of São Paulo and Rio de Janeiro. That same year, the women's group of SOMOS separated and founded its own paper, *Chanacomchana*. Its editorial stated: "It was the first leap out of conformity and into participation. Our newspaper is our bridge. The word *chana* cannot be summarily defined as 'a female sexual organ.' It is something so much broader—as big as the counterpoints of existence."

In 1980, the First Conference of Organized Homosexuals took place in São Paulo, and thirty-three lesbians were among the 166 persons who attended. The national homosexual conferences, later called the National Conference of Lesbians and Homosexuals, continued into the late 1990s, and caucuses of lesbians and gay men exist within several political parties.

In the late 1990s, the lesbian groups active in Brazil included Coletivo de Feministas Lésbicas (Collective of Lesbian Feminists), Rede Informação um Outro Olhar (Information Network Another View), Grupo Sapho (Sappho Group), and AFINS in São Paulo; Coletivo de Lésbicas (Lesbian Collective) in Rio de Janeiro; and Grupo Lésbico (Lesbian Group) in Bahia. Publications included the bulletin *Rede Outro Olhar* and the magazine *Femme*.

## Contemporary Conditions

In late-twentieth-century Brazilian legislation, homosexuality was not criminalized, although an express prohibition against discrimination due to sexual orientation existed only in the municipal legislation of three states. Legislative proposals to ban discrimination on the basis of sexual preference were introduced at the city, state, and federal levels in the late 1990s. In 1997, a federal proposal to allow registered civil partnership between couples of the same sex was considered by the Congress.

Beginning in the 1980s, interest in lesbian themes intensified, resulting in an increase in literary and academic publications. In literature, Conceição Couto Neto organized a collection of personal narratives and letters, *Pele de Gaia* (Skin of Gaia) (1994); Bebeti do Amaral Gurgel published two novels, *A quem interessar possa* (To Whom It May Concern [1993]) and *Pecados Safados* (Sapphist Sins [1995]); Myriam Campello authored the novel *São Sebastião Blues* (1993); and Sandra

Mara Herzer produced a collection of poems and depositions, *Uma queda para o alto* (An Upward Fall [1992]). The contribution of Cassandra Rios to lesbian literature cannot be overlooked; from the 1960s onward she has authored more than twenty titles.

Noteworthy among the research projects undertaken are Denise Portinari's *O discurso da homossexualidade feminina* (Discourse on Female Homosexuality [1989]) and Carmen L. Oliveira's *Flores Raras e Banalíssimas* (Rare and Very Banal Flowers [1995]), a novelized re-creation of the romance between American poet Elizabeth Bishop (1911–1979) and her Brazilian lover, Lota de Macedo Soares (1910–1967), during the 1950s and 1960s in Rio de Janeiro.

In the 1990s, Norma Benguel, Renata Sorrah, and Florinda Bolkan were publicly identified lesbians who worked in theater, television, and motion pictures. Lesbian singers had a marked presence in music, including such well-known figures as Leci Brandão, Ángela Rorô, Cássia Eller, Zélia Duncan, Marina Lima, Maria Bethânia, and Gal Costa.

During the International Lesbian and Gay Association (ILGA) meeting in Rio de Janeiro in 1995, lesbians organized an Exposition of Lesbian Visibility, which displayed some of the cultural and artistic productions of lesbians and their activism. Activities such as seminars and conferences were organized in the late 1990s in Rio de Janeiro, São Paulo, and Salvador, Bahia.

*Miriam Bottassi*
*Marisa Fernandes*

### Bibliography

Bottassi, Miriam. "Die Räume der Amazonen: Lesben in Südamerika" (The Space of the Amazons: Lesbians in South America). In *Südamerika der Frauen* (Women of South America). Ed. Danda Prado. Munich: frauenoffensive, 1993, pp. 51–63.

Cavin, Susan. *Lesbian Origins*. San Francisco: ISM, 1985.

Fernandes, Marisa, coord. *Lésbicas no Brasil: contribuição para avaliação da década da mulher, 1985/1995* (Lesbians in Brazil: A Contribution to the Evaluation of the Decade for Women, 1985–1995). São Paulo: Coletivo de Feministas Lésbicas, 1994.

Vainfas, Ronaldo. "Homoerotismo Feminino e o Santo Officio" (Female Homoeroticism and the Holy Office). In *História das Mulheres no Brasil* (History of Women in Brazil). Ed. Mary

Del Priore, São Paulo: Editora Contexto, 1997, pp. 115–140.

*See also* Bishop, Elizabeth

## Brittain, Vera Mary (1893–1970)

British novelist, journalist, and poet. Born into a middle-class Midlands industrial family, Vera Brittain is best known for her autobiography of World War I, *Testament of Youth* (1933), which recounts her resistance to her provincial upbringing in Buxton, her successful campaign to go to Oxford University, her war work as a nurse, and the deaths at the front of her fiance, Roland Leighton, her brother Edward, and two of their close friends. It also describes Brittain's struggle to survive the horrors she had endured and the beginning of her relationship with Winifred Holtby (1898–1935), a fellow student who helped her recover.

Hoping to forge careers as writers, Brittain and Holtby shared an apartment together in London. Despite Brittain's subsequent "semidetached" marriage to political scientist George Catlin (1896–1979), her relationship with Holtby, who lived with them until her death in 1935, was considered lesbian by many. To some, the two women were virtually interchangeable; Brittain was once introduced to an audience as Miss Vera Holtby. The gossip about them elicited Brittain's vigorous denials, particularly in her book about Holtby, *Testament of Friendship* (1940). Her biographers Berry and Bostridge (1995) also insist that the relationship was not lesbian, quoting a scribbled note Berry found among her papers: "I loved Winifred but I was not in love with her."

Despite the lack of evidence of any physical intimacy between Brittain and Holtby, it is difficult, as Faderman (1981) says, not to see this relationship as lesbian. The intensity of their commitment, the endearments in the correspondance—"darling," "sweetieheart," and "beloved" are common though edited out at publication—and Brittain's frequent comparison of her partnership with Holtby to her marriage ("I am sure I love you best") all suggest a relationship that is more than friendship.

The primary bond between the two women was their support for each other's work. Both earned money as journalists, and Brittain did her best work while they lived together. In addition to *Testament of Youth,* she wrote three novels during this period: *The Dark Tide* (1923), *Not Without Honour* (1924), and *Honourable Estate* (1936). Her finest novel, *Honourable Estate,* contains the only lesbian relationship in her fiction, that between dramatist Gertrude Campbell and Janet Rutherston, a character based on her husband's mother.

In the latter years of her life, Brittain wrote two other novels; a sequel to *Testament of Youth* titled *Testament of Experience* (1957); a discussion of the trial of Radclyffe Hall's (1880–1943) lesbian novel, *The Well of Loneliness* (1928); and much pacifist and feminist nonfiction. She worked tirelessly for pacifist causes, even during World War II when it was unpopular to do so.          *Jean E. Kennard*

### Bibliography

Bailey, Hilary. *Vera Brittain*. London: Penguin, 1987.

Berry, Paul, and Mark Bostridge. *Vera Brittain: A Life*. London: Chatto and Windus, 1995.

Faderman, Lillian. *Surpassing the Love of Men: Romantic Friendship and Love Between Women from the Sixteenth Century to the Present*. New York: William Morrow, 1981.

Gorham, Deborah. *Vera Brittain: A Feminist Life*. Oxford: Blackwell, 1996.

Kennard, Jean E. *Vera Brittain and Winifred Holtby: A Working Partnership*. Hanover: University Press of New England, 1989.

*See also* Hall, Radclyffe; Holtby, Winifred

## Brooks, Romaine (1874–1970)

American artist. Romaine Brooks was born Beatrice Romaine Goddard, the youngest of three children, to Major Henry Goddard and Ella Mary Waterman. She experienced a difficult childhood due to rejection by her mother. Later, Brooks would write that her mother, even in death, was an obstacle between herself and life.

After making an initial break with her family in 1896, she studied at Le Scuola Nazionale in Rome and later at Academie Colarossi in Paris. In the summer of 1899 she, like many artists and writers of the period, went to live in Capri and began experimenting with vivid colors and light. Despite this relaxing and liberating influence on her life and art, which Brooks would later recall as her happiest time, she felt that this use of color failed to express her nature as an artist. In 1904, she moved to London and rented a studio on Tite Street, as artist James Whistler (1834–1903) had done years before her, at-

**B**

*Romaine Brooks, Self-Portrait. National Museum of American Art, Smithsonian Institution, gift of the artist.*

testing to his influence on her work despite his prior demise. However, it was not until her move to the Cornish coast, later the same year, that she experimented with subtle color and shades of gray, which would become characteristic of her art.

Her relationship with John Ellingham Brooks, whom she divorced after a year of marriage, was typical of her liaisons with other men, such as Gabriele d'Annunzio (1863–1938), with whom she wished to maintain a friendship without the objectification of desire. Disillusioned with their inability to do so, she concluded that her most significant relationships would be with women. Shortly before World War I, after several romantic liaisons with women, such as Ida Rubinstein (1885–1960), she met Natalie Barney (1876–1972), beginning a fifty-year relationship. Brooks died on December 7, 1970, in Nice, France.

From their first showings in 1910 at Galeries Durand-Ruel in Paris to her posthumous exhibitions

at the National Museum of American Art, and in France in the 1970s and 1980s, Brooks's portraits of isolated women have generated a great deal of controversy. For example, the style of her *Self-Portrait* (1923)—with its limited palette of grays, black, and white and precise outlining and atmospheric background—deliberately resurrected the visual language of symbolist decadence with its fascination for eroticism, decay, and death. Since the trials of Oscar Wilde (1854–1900), this style had been considered passé and quiet unfashionable. Yet Brooks continued to work in this genre.

Brooks grew up in the World War I period, and her style matured in the 1920s, a period of sexual experimentation and self-expression. She and her lover, Barney, grasped the profoundly complex nature of the two sexes, becoming deeply interested in the concept of androgyny and its application to modern life. Being female meant that there was a female body with female genitalia, breasts, and the potential to become pregnant. These were considered biological imperatives. Barney and Brooks disagreed with the theory that "biology is destiny," as well as the notion that it is "natural" for men to dominate and control women's life choices.

Brooks presents the self as a series of often contradictory roles and identities coexisting within an individual, rather than some fixed entity. In this respect, it is valuable to consider the ways she challenges gender stereotypes in her imagery, using costume, for example, to free the sitter, the viewer, and herself from the tyranny of categorization and stereotyping.

Brooks deliberately invoked the cultural markers of marginal, deviant, and illegal sexuality. She wanted to break out of the prison of conformity and demonstrate the sexual multidimensionality of women and men. She dared to present the lesbian body openly and, in so doing, challenge modernism's representation of women as subjects for art rather than producers of art.          *Cassandra Langer*

### Bibliography

Breeskin, Adelyn D. *Romaine Brooks*. Washington, D.C.: National Museum of American Art, Smithsonian Institution, 1986.

Langer, Cassandra. "Transgressing Le Droit Du Seigneur: The Lesbian Feminist Defining Herself in Art History." In *New Feminist Criticism: Art-Identity-Action*. Ed. Joanna Frueh, Cassandra Langer, and Arlene Raven. New York: HarperCollins, 1994, pp. 306–326.

Secrest. Meryle. *Between Me and Life: A Biography of Romaine Brooks*. New York: Doubleday, 1974.

*See also* Art, Mainstream; Barney, Natalie; Modernism

## Brossard, Nicole (1943–)

Québec poet, novelist, and theorist. Born in Montréal and educated at the Université de Montréal, Nicole Brossard has been a leading figure in postmodern writing since 1965, making issues of gender and language central to Québec poetics. She is the recipient of prestigious awards, including the Governor-General's Award (1974, 1984) and the Prix Athanase-David du Québec (1991). Internationally, her reputation as a lesbian theorist has grown with translation of her work.

Brossard's early focus on (hetero)sexuality as consciousness, and then on language-centered poetry, changed to a lesbian feminist critique of patriarchy for its appropriation of women's desire. In *French Kiss* (1974, 1986), the first of her lesbian texts, a lesbian kiss constitutes a "sapphic semantic chain" that makes the erotic body central to creative production and the public sphere.

"If it weren't lesbian, this text would make no sense," Brossard wrote in *L'Amèr ou le chapitre effrité* (1977; *Theseourmothers*, 1983). In more than twenty texts, she displaces the patriarchal structures of meaning-making and inserts the lesbian subject into the body politic, and into history, by reworking rules of syntax and genre. Her "fiction-theory" oscillates between poetry and manifesto and spirals around images or sounds in plotless, layered forms. A woman subject emerges in a utopian and erotic moment when another woman's desire as she reads makes this subject real within a lesbian community. Reinventing the forms and rituals of language, literature, and culture is highly political, Brossard writes in *La lettre aérienne* (1985; *Aerial Letter*, 1988): "A lesbian is radical or she is not a lesbian. A lesbian who does not reinvent the [wor(l)d] is a lesbian in the process of disappearing." Brossard uses fiction as "virtual reality" to image the unthinkable—the pleasure of lesbian sexuality—and so change everyday reality in *Picture Theory* (1982, 1991), *Le désert mauve* (1987; *Mauve Desert*, 1990), and *Baroque d'aube* (1995; *Baroque at Dawn*, 1997).

Brossard eroticizes the text's body and the body's text in her poetry—some of the finest lesbian erotica—especially in *Sous la langue/Under Tongue* (1987), in which the soundplay and wordplay call attention to the material surface (skin) of the text and the sensual excitation of the tongue. An erotic relation is also established through lesbian intertextuality, "the spiral of books written by women." For example, *Amantes* (1980; *Lovhers*, 1986) quotes key erotic passages from Adrienne Rich's *Twenty-One Love Poems* (1978) and Djuna Barnes's *Nightwood* (1928). "My Continent," as Brossard calls the list of lesbian writers in the final poem, is both a historical monument to lesbian creativity and an "aerien" (no-space) in which to invent new forms of loving and living. Brossard has also worked with Québec lesbian and feminist writers on many collective projects. She lives with her lover of many years in Montréal.                    *Barbara Godard*

### Bibliography

Dupré, Louise. *Stratégies du vertige: Trois poètes, Nicole Brossard, Madeleine Gagnon, France Théoret* (Vertiginous Strategies). Montréal: Les Editions remue-ménage, 1989.

Godard, Barbara. "Producing Visibility for Lesbians: Nicole Brossard's Quantum Poetics." *English Studies in Canada* 21:2 (1995), 125–137.

Huffer, Lynne. "Interview with Nicole Brossard." *Yale French Studies* 87 (1995), 115–121.

Parker, Alice. "Nicole Brossard: A Differential Equation of Lesbian Love." In *Lesbian Texts and Contexts: Radical Revisions*. Ed. Karla Jay, Joanne Glasgow, and Catherine R. Stimpson. New York: New York Univerisy Press, 1990, pp. 304–329.

*See also* Barnes, Djuna Chappell; Québec; Rich, Adrienne

## Brown, Rita Mae (1944–)

American author. Rita Mae Brown was raised in Hanover, Pennsylvania ("just north of the Mason-Dixon line"), and Fort Lauderdale, Florida. Expelled from the University of Florida for civil rights activities, she moved in 1963 to New York City, where she attended New York University and Columbia University and joined the embryonic gay rights movement. However, she was soon disillusioned with male sexism within gay rights organizations and transferred her energies to women's liberation. She joined the National Organization for Women (NOW) and be-

**B** came editor of NOW's New York newsletter. But, in 1969, NOW President Betty Friedan (1921–) referred to growing lesbian visibility as a "lavender menace," and Brown was relieved of her duties as newsletter editor. Stung, she resigned from NOW and cofounded the lesbian feminist activist group Lavender Menace. With its daughter organization, Radicalesbians, Brown helped write and publish the influential position paper entitled "The Woman-Identified Woman" (1970). She also cofounded the short-lived Furies collective, a revolutionary lesbian feminist cell in Washington, D.C. The Furies were influential because they succeeded in positioning lesbianism as the locus of meaningful change for women. They also published *Class and Feminism* (1974), the first penetrating critique of class dynamics within the feminist movement; Brown's essay "The Last Straw" represented an important part of that critique.

The Furies disbanded in 1972, and, since that time, Brown has focused primarily on writing poetry, essays, screenplays, but mostly novels. Her first and most famous novel was *Rubyfruit Jungle* (1973), a semiautobiographical *Bildungsroman* featuring young lesbian Molly Bolt. *Rubyfruit Jungle* was originally published by Daughters Inc., a feminist press, and it achieved considerable notoriety among alternative readers. Then, in 1977, it was reissued by Bantam as a mass-market paperback, with immediate and overwhelming results: It sold over a million copies and catapulted Rita Mae Brown into overnight fame and the unofficial position of spokeswoman for American lesbians.

*Rubyfruit Jungle* is a novel in the tradition of British novelist Henry Fielding (1707–1754); Molly Bolt is a kind of female Tom Jones, romping through a series of humorous sexual escapades with never a self-doubt. *Rubyfruit Jungle* represented an astonishing validation of lesbian existence. For lesbian readers, especially, Molly Bolt was a tonic. Her boundless self-confidence contrasted mightily with the angst of Stephen Gordon, heroine of Radclyffe Hall's (1880–1943) *The Well of Loneliness* (1928), the only earlier lesbian novel to gain a wide mainstream readership. *Rubyfruit Jungle* awakened the general public to the existence of lesbianism and also painted a portrait of a well-adjusted, empowered lesbian woman.

In addition to *Rubyfruit Jungle*, Rita Mae Brown has written eight novels, four mystery stories (coauthored by her cat, Sneaky Pie Brown), two books of essays, a book of poetry, and a fiction writer's manual. Her earlier essays and novels—and her life—profoundly inspired a generation of women who sought validation for their lesbian identity. Her later writing has deemphasized lesbian consciousness in favor of historical romance, mystery, and Southern regionalism. Refusing labels, Brown has consistently insisted on her right to set her own literary, political, and personal agenda.

*Deborah T. Meem*

### Bibliography

Abel, E., M. Hirsch, and E. Langland, eds. *The Voyage In: Fictions of Female Development.* Hanover, N.H., and London: Dartmouth College and the University Press of New England, 1983.

Boyle, Sharon D. "Rita Mae Brown." In *Contemporary Lesbian Writers of the United States: A Bio-Bibliographical Critical Sourcebook.* Ed. S. Pollack and D. Knight. Stamford, Conn.: Greenwood, 1993, pp. 94–105.

Mandrell, James. "Questions of Genre and Gender: Contemporary American Versions of the Feminine Picaresque." *Novel: A Forum on Fiction* 20:2 (Winter 1987), 149–170.

Zimmerman, Bonnie. *The Safe Sea of Women: Lesbian Fiction, 1969–1989.* Boston: Beacon, 1990.

*See also* American Literature, Twentieth Century; Furies, The; National Organization for Women (NOW); Radicalesbians; Woman-Identified Woman; Women's Liberation Movement

### Bryher (1894–1983)

British novelist, poet, publisher, and patron. Better known for her relationship with H.D. than for her own writing, Bryher was a benefactor of film education, hellenism, literature, and psychoanalysis. Available material on Bryher does scant justice to her lesbianism or her role as a facilitator of modernism.

The elder child of financier Sir John Ellerman, she was named Winifred Ellerman but later legalized her pseudonym Bryher. Her autobiographical novels, *Development* (1920) and *Two Selves* (1923), depict her frustration with femininity and her need for masculine freedoms. She consulted Havelock Ellis (1859–1939) about her sexual identity and later wrote her desire "to be a boy" into a series of historical novels with young male protagonists, notably *The Fourteenth of October* (1952) and *The Player's Boy* (1953). This fiction avoids heterosexual romance and foregrounds same-sex relationships.

Bryher's meeting with Hilda Doolittle Aldington (1886–1961) was vital to her survival; she expressed her devotion in "Hellenics" (*Poetry*, [1920]), *Gate to the Sea* (1958), and *The Heart to Artemis* (1962). H.D. reciprocated with such poems as "Halcyon," "Hyacinth" and "To Bryher" (*Palimpsest* [1926]), while "At Baia" implies a profound platonic bond: "Lover to lover, no kiss, / no touch, but forever and ever this."

Bryher gave H.D. financial security and brought up her only daughter. As a friend of Natalie Barney (1876–1972), Sylvia Beach (1887–1962), and Gertrude Stein (1874–1946), Bryher was also H.D.'s link with lesbian Paris and Berlin. During the 1920s, she made two marriages of convenience: with the American writer Robert McAlmon (1896–1956), funding his Contact Editions; then with British filmmaker Kenneth Macpherson (1902–1971), with whom she created Pool Productions and the magazine *Close-Up*.

With the fortune she inherited in 1933, Bryher acquired *Life and Letters To-Day*, publishing new work by H.D., Dorothy Richardson (1873–1957), and Edith Sitwell (1887–1964). During World War II, she shared H.D.'s London flat, instigating a literary circle. She also aided refugees from the Nazis, including psychoanalyst Hanns Sachs (1881–1947). After the war, she established a Foundation for Hellenic Studies and a travel fund for young writers like Laurie Lee (1914–1997) and promoted H.D.'s reputation with the help of Yale Professor Norman Pearson (1909–1976).                    *Diana Collecott*

## Bibliography

Collecott, Diana. "Bryher's Two Selves as Lesbian Romance." *Romance Revisited*. Ed. Lynne Pearce and Jackie Stacey. London: Lawrence and Wishart, 1995, pp. 128–42.

Guest, Barbara. *Herself Defined: The Poet H.D. and Her World*. New York: Doubleday, 1984.

Hanscombe, Gillian, and Virginia Smyers. *Writing for Their Lives: The Modernist Women, 1910–1940*. London: Women's Press, 1987.

Taylor, James. *Ellermans: A Wealth of Shipping*. London: Wilton House Gentry, 1976.

*See also* H.D. (Hilda Doolittle); London; Modernism; Paris

## Buffalo, New York

Mid-size industrial city with a well-documented working-class lesbian bar culture. Buffalo presents a vivid example of lesbian life outside the coastal cosmopolitan cities and suggests the importance of the industrial heartland in shaping twentieth-century gay and lesbian movements.

At the turn of the twentieth century, "Boston marriages" were fairly common in Buffalo, as evidenced by obituaries that name lifelong female partners and stories in the publications of women's clubs. In 1903, Harry Gorman, a Buffalo resident who worked as a railroad cook, was discovered to be a female; Gorman socialized with a group of similar friends, all of whom successfully worked as men on the railroad. Mabel Dodge Luhan's (1879–1962) memoirs suggest that, during this same time period, some Buffalo women were willing to explore erotic interests in women, as well as with men. In the 1920s, several groups of woman-identified women played a prominent part in the city's cultural life, founding such organizations as the Buffalo Musical Arts Society and the Buffalo Music Foundation.

As early as the 1930s, oral histories reveal that a few gay and lesbian bars existed in Buffalo. Working-class lesbians searched for and found them in order to be with others like themselves. Some lesbians also felt comfortable in the entertainment clubs in the black section of the city; these clubs were not lesbian but were lesbian friendly. By the 1940s, bars were more concentrated in the downtown section of the city and easier to find. The important bars for lesbians were Ralph Martin's, a gay male and lesbian bar, and Winter's, an all-women's bar, both of which were open for the majority of the decade. Some Native American women socialized regularly in these predominantly white bars. African American women, however, were rare visitors, feeling more comfortable at their own house parties. In bars and house parties during the 1940s, Buffalo working-class lesbians began to forge a culture of resistance built around butch-femme roles. They supported one another to keep jobs, to find partners, to build relationships, and to take the risks of going out every weekend.

The witch-hunting of gays and lesbians in the 1950s did not destroy the incipient communities of the 1940s; rather, they expanded and became more defiant, manifesting a pride that presaged lesbian and gay liberation. Butches wore their masculine clothing as much as possible and engaged in physical fights to defend their space. In some contexts,

**B**

this process led to greater unity among lesbians; in others, to greater division. The Buffalo bar communities were desegregated by African American butches and femmes in the 1950s, even though they maintained their tradition of open house parties. It is as if the growing lesbian consciousness of kind overrode the divisions of race. At the same time, the bars became class stratified. Upwardly mobile lesbians did not want to associate with the brazen masculine attire and mannerism of the rough-and-tough butches. This put them at too much risk for exposure to their families and work.

In 1958, Nelson Rockefeller (1908–1979) ran for governor on a strong antivice platform, and his election led to a grim period in Buffalo lesbian social life. Although the governor's concerns were not specifically related to lesbian life, Buffalo lesbian and gay bars, like most other bars in the city, were under constant surveillance by the State Liquor Authority. By 1962, most of the hangouts for butches and femmes during the 1950s had been raided regularly and closed, and no lesbian or gay bar remained open for more than several years. While the most common cause of harassment was a citation for serving alcohol to a minor, some bars were cited for having lesbian and gay patrons, the mere presence of whom was interpreted by the State Liquor Authority as permitting disorderly conduct.

The pressure on gay bars was so great during the 1960s that there were periods without any gay bars at all. In late 1969, during one such period, the Mattachine Society of the Niagara Frontier was formed, with many members coming from the fragmented bar communities. At about the same time, Buffalo Radical Lesbians formed as an outgrowth of the women's liberation movement. Together, these organizations marked a new era in Buffalo lesbian life. From that point on, there were public spaces for socializing outside the bars. In the 1970s, 1980s, and 1990s, Buffalo developed an active lesbian community supporting poets, writers, educators, and performers, as well as a variety of community organizations.     *Elizabeth Lapovsky Kennedy*

### Bibliography

Feinberg, Leslie. *Stone Butch Blues: A Novel.* Ithaca, N.Y.: Firebrand, 1993.

Kanes, Candace A. "Swornest Chums: Buffalo Women in Business and the Arts, 1900–1935." Master's thesis, University of Buffalo, 1992.

Katz, Johnathan, ed. "1903: Edward I. Prime Stevenson (Xavier Mayne, pseud.); Harry Gorman, A 'curious confraternity—or sorosis.'" In *Gay American History: Lesbians and Gay Men in the U.S.A.* New York: Crowell, 1976, pp. 249–250.

Kennedy, Elizabeth Lapovsky, and Madeline D. Davis. *Boots of Leather, Slippers of Gold: The History of a Lesbian Community.* New York: Routledge, 1996.

Luhan, Mabel Dodge. *Intimate Memories, vol. 1: Background.* New York: Harcourt Brace, 1933.

***See also*** Bars; Boston Marriage; Butch-Femme; Oral History

## Bulldagger

Also bulldyke, bulldiker, bulldyker, bull bitch, bull dicker, and diesel dyke. A tough, extremely butch lesbian, usually a lower-class woman who lives publicly in the masculine role, expressed through clothing, gesture, and attitude, openly resisting heterosexist definition and confinement; one who assumes the male sexual prerogative and conventionally plays the male role in lovemaking. Bulldagger has been in use at least throughout the twentieth century in the United States and almost always refers to African Americans, while bulldyke and other variations are not race specific. When used derogatorily by homophobes, bulldagger implies an unnatural woman, a castrator, and a manhater, connotations sometimes shared by lesbians as well. However, bulldagger has been reclaimed as an honorific term through the twentieth century, by blues singer Bessie Jackson (1897–1948) in her 1935 song, "B-D Woman," and by SDiane A. Bogus and Judy Grahn, who celebrate her as a courageous and proud resister of oppression and an essential connection, as Bogus (1994) avers, to the "ancient and recent black woman-loving past." She is an avatar of black female sovereignty, linked mythically to Dahomean Amazons and Queen Califia, namesake of California.

The origin of the term "bulldagger" is unclear, although it is related to dike and bulldyker. The San Francisco Lesbian and Gay History Project (1989) writes that, in the 1870s, the word "dike" was used for a man who was all dressed up for a night on the town and that, by 1900, the word "bulldyker" was being used in the prostitution district of Philadelphia, Pennsylvania, to refer to lesbian lovers. Historically, many prostitutes have had lovers who were bulldaggers.

Grahn (1984) speculates that the word "bulldagger" is related to Boadicea, a first-century A.D.

Celtic queen who led a revolt against the Roman invasion of Britain and who might have participated in ceremonial bull-slaying. Bogus (1994) traces bull mythos from ancient Egypt to Bill Pickett, cowboy extraordinaire who introduced "bulldogging" (subduing bulls) as a rodeo event and was featured in the 1923 movie *The Bulldogger*. Bogus deems it likely that it was Pickett's reputation that brought the word "bulldogger" into black culture, which, in time, mutated into bulldagger.

Famous bulldaggers include Gladys Bentley (1907–1960), a cross-dressing blues singer who attained high fame in the Harlem cabaret scene in the 1920s and 1930s. Langston Hughes (1902–1967) described Bentley as "a large, masculine lady." She performed in flashy men's attire and wore her hair short and slicked back. Gertrude "Ma" Rainey (1886–1939) sang "Prove It on Me Blues" (1928) dressed in the character of a coat-and-tie-wearing, man-disdaining bulldagger. Bessie Jackson's song "B-D Woman" honors the bulldagger and warns straight men that they had better stop using and abusing women, for they are dispensable: "Comin a time, B-D women ain't gonna need no men" and "B-D women, they can lay their claim."

Fictional representations of bulldaggers, or Queen B's, based upon Bentley, Rainey, and Bessie Smith (1894?–1937), appear in the novels of Claude McKay (1889–1948) and Carl Van Vechten (1880–1964). Ann Allen Shockley (1927–) presents a number of fictional portraits of bulldaggers, frequently musicians, in her contemporary novels.

Both Bogus and Grahn call for a reclamation of the history of the bulldagger and recognition of her archetypal powers and presence, signifying Amazonian, warriorlike, dangerous, proud, independent, matriarchal, rebellious, and sovereign lesbian resistance.                                *Jane Caputi*

### Bibliography

Bogus, SDiane A. "The Myth and Tradition of the Black Bulldagger." In *Dagger: On Butch Women*. Ed. Lily Burana Roxxie, and Linnea Due. San Francisco, Calif.: Cleis, 1994, pp. 29–36.

———. "The 'Queen B' Figure in Black Literature." In *Lesbian Texts and Contexts: Radical Revisions*. Ed. Karla Jay and Joanne Glasgow. New York: New York University Press, 1990, pp. 275–290.

Grahn, Judy. *Another Mother Tongue: Gay Words, Gay Worlds*. Boston: Beacon, 1984.

Katz, Jonathan, ed. *Gay/Lesbian Almanac: A New Documentary*. New York: Harper and Row, 1983.

San Francisco Lesbian and Gay History Project. " 'She Even Chewed Tobacce' ": A Pictorial Narrative of Passing Women in America." In *Hidden from History: Reclaiming the Gay and Lesbian Past*. Ed. Martin Duberman, Martha Vicinus, and George Chauncey, Jr. New York: Penguin, 1989, pp. 183–194.

*See also* Bentley, Gladys; Butch-Femme; Dyke; Rainey, Gertrude "Ma"; Shockley, Ann Ellen; Smith, Bessie

## Businesses, Lesbian

Those businesses that market exclusively to lesbians. Businesses owned by lesbians that do not exclusively target lesbians as their market are not included in this category.

As late as 1995, there were no studies on gay or lesbian businesses. In 1995, a survey of approximately 650 gay and lesbian businesses was conducted for *In The Pink: The Making of Successful Gay and Lesbian Businesses*. The number of lesbian businesses in the study was seventeen, approximately 2.5 percent of the total sample. Lesbian businesses in the study operated in the following U.S. states: California, Colorado, Florida, Oregon, New Jersey, New York, North Carolina, Massachusetts, Vermont, and Virginia.

All of the lesbian businesses were service businesses. Half were in the publishing industry, producing, printing, or selling lesbian-oriented printed material. The largest business in the sample was Olivia Records and Travel, with thirteen employees and 1995 annual revenues in excess of $5 million. The oldest lesbian businesses in the sample, Olivia Records and Travel and Naiad Press, were both founded in 1973.

### Marketing to Lesbians

The self-identified lesbian market in the United States was estimated to be 6.2 million by the mid-1990s. This estimate was derived from the Yankelovich MONITOR study described in *Untold Millions* (1995), which stated that the total number of self-identified gays and lesbians in the United States sixteen years of age or older was 6 percent of the population, somewhere between the percentages reported in other studies. The 6 percent figure was then applied to the latest U.S. Census Bureau data to derive the total number of self-identified lesbians in the United States. The reasons for using this study's estimate are twofold. First, the Yankelovich MONITOR study was conducted with minimal bias so that its results can be generalized to total populations. Second, unlike other studies that test solely for individuals who engage, or have engaged, in homosexual sexual activities, the Yankelovich MONITOR study tested for individuals who self-identify with a gay or lesbian lifestyle.

Lesbian businesses have used a variety of techniques successfully in communicating with the lesbian market. Those in the *In the Pink* study stated that word of mouth—referrals from lesbians to other lesbians to their company—was the most effective method of getting lesbians to do business with them. Additionally, some businesses sponsored women's sports teams, such as softball or soccer, as a way of promoting their products to the lesbian market. Mailing to lesbians on a list that the company developed itself or to a list of names from an outside organization was also used. Finally, lesbian businesses advertised in national and local gay and lesbian publications.

### Lesbian-Market Challenges

Those interviewed for the *In the Pink* study said the lesbian market was an extremely difficult one to target, for a variety of reasons. Lesbians, relative to gay men, were said to go out socially to bars and clubs less often and to be more closeted, making communication to the group as a whole more difficult. Additionally, lesbians, relative to heterosexual couples, and gay male couples, tend to make less money; the 1995 Yankelovich MONITOR study found lesbians' mean personal income to be $13,300 versus $22,500 for gay men.

Finally, creating a product or a service that appeals to all lesbians is a challenge because, as a group, lesbians are extremely diverse. There are older lesbians, rich and poor lesbians, lesbians of color, lesbians of different nationalities and religions. Generally, businesses segment their markets relative to these traits. For those who have lesbian businesses, it is necessary to find the commonalties in the group rather than stratify it.          *Sue Levin*

### Bibliography

Levin, Sue. *In The Pink: The Making of Successful Gay and Lesbian Businesses*. Binghamton, N.Y.: Haworth, 1998.

Lukenbill, Grant. *Untold Millions*. New York: HarperBusiness, 1995.

*See also* Advertising and Consumerism; Economics; Naiad Press; Olivia

## Butch-Femme

Also spelled butch-fem. Butch-femme relationships are a style of lesbian loving and self-presentation that, in the United States, can be traced back to the beginning of the twentieth century; historical counterparts can be found even earlier. Butches and femmes have separate sexual, emotional, and social identities outside of the relationship. Some butches believe that they were born different from other women; others view their identity as socially constructed.

While no exact date has been established for the start of the use of the terms "butch" and "femme" or "fem," oral histories do show their prevalence from the 1930s on. The butch-femme couple was particularly dominant in the United States, in both black and white lesbian communities, from the 1920s through the 1950s and early 1960s.

### Basic Features

Because the complementarity of butch and femme is perceived differently by different women, no simple definition can be offered. When seen through outsiders' eyes, the butch appears simplistically "masculine," and the femme, "feminine," paralleling heterosexual categories. But butches and femmes transformed heterosexual elements, such as gender attitude and dress, into a unique lesbian language of sexuality and emotional bonding. Butch-femme relationships are based on an intense erotic attraction with its own rituals of courtship, seduction, and offers of mutual protection. While the erotic connection is the basis for the relationship, and while butches often see themselves as the more aggressive partner, butch-femme relationships, when they work well, develop a nurturing balance between two different kinds of women, each encouraging the other's sexual-emotional identity. Couples often settle into long-term domestic relationships or engage in serial monogamy, a practice Elizabeth Kennedy and Madeline Davis (1993), in a study of a working-class black and white butch-femme community in Buffalo, New York, from 1940 to 1960, trace back to the 1930s, and one they view as a major lesbian contribution to an alternative for hetero-sexual marriage. In the streets of Buffalo in the 1950s, butch-femme couples were a symbol of women's erotic autonomy, a visual statement of a sexual and emotional accomplishment that did not include men.

Butch-femme relationships are complex erotic and social statements, filled with a language of stance, dress, gesture, and comradeship. Both butches and femmes carry with them their own erotic and emotional identities, announced in differ-ent ways. In the 1950s, butch women, dressed in slacks and shirts and flashing pinky rings, an-nounced their sexual expertise in a public style that often opened their lives to ridicule and assault. Many adopted men's clothes and wore short "DA" hair cuts so that they would be comfortable and their sexual identity and preference would be clearly visi-ble. As Kennedy and Davis have pointed out, the butch woman took as her main goal in lovemaking the pleasure she could give her femme partner. This sense of dedication to her lover, rather than to her own sexual fulfillment, is one of the ways a butch is clearly distinct from the men she is assumed to be imitating.

The femme woman, who can often pass as a straight woman when not with her lover, actively sought to share her life with a woman others labeled a freak. Before androgynous fashions became popu-lar, many femmes were the breadwinners in their homes because they could get jobs open to tradi-tional-looking women, but they confronted the same public scorn when appearing in public with their butch lovers. Contrary to gender stereotyping, many femmes were and are aggressive, strong women who take responsibity for actively seeking the sex-ual and social partner they desire.

## Community Aspects

Particularly in the 1950s and 1960s, the butch-femme community became the public face of les-bianism when its members formed bar communities across the country and, thus, became targets of street and police violence.

In earlier decades, butch-femme communities were tightly knit, made up of couples who, in some cases, had long-standing relationships. Exhibiting traits of feminism before the 1970s, butch-femme working-class women lived without the financial and social securities of the heterosexual world, car-ing for each other in illness and death, in times of economic depression, and in the face of the rampant homophobia of the 1950s. Younger butches were of-ten initiated into the community by older, more ex-perienced women who passed on the rituals of ex-pected dress, attitude, and erotic behavior. This sense of responsibility to each other stood the women in good stead when police raided their bars or when groups of men threatened them on the streets.

Bars were the social background for many working-class butch-femme communities, and it was in their dimly lit interiors that butches and femmes could perfect their styles and find each other. In the 1950s, sexual and social tension often erupted into fights, and many butches thought that they had to be tough to protect themselves and their women, not just in the bars but on the streets as well.

Butch-femme is not a monolithic social-sexual category. Within its general outline, class, race, and region give rise to style variations. In the black les-bian community of New York City, for instance, the terms "bulldagger" and "stud" were more com-monly used than "butch." A fem would be "my lady" or "my family." Many women of the lesbian literary world and of the upper classes also adopted this style of self-presentation. In the 1920s, Rad-clyffe Hall (1880–1943), the author of *The Well of Loneliness* (1928), called herself John in her mar-riage to Lady Una Troubridge (1887–1963). Butch-femme style also shows the impact of changing so-cial models and politics. Feminism, for instance, as well as open relationships and nonmonogamy, were incorporated into butch-femme life of the 1970s and 1980s.

With the surge of lesbian feminism in the early 1970s, butch-femme women were often ridiculed and ostracized because of their seeming adherence to heterosexual role playing. In the 1980s, however, a new understanding of the historical and sexual-social importance of butch-femme women and communities began to emerge. Controversy still ex-ists about the value of this lesbian way of loving and living, however. Members of such groups as Women Against Pornography depict butch-femme as a patriarchal, oppressive, hierarchical way of relating.

In the 1990s, queer theory turned its eyes on butches and femmes, seeing "performance" where once was seen "identity."' Writings by authors such as Judith Butler, Judith Halberstam, and Sue-Ellen Case explore butch-femme in the light of con-structed gender, parody, and play. What is clear from these shifting perspectives is that "butch and

**B** femme" is a persistently intriguing sexual, histori-cal, and theoretical subject.

The American lesbian community is now marked by a wide range of relational styles; butch-femme is just one of the ways to love, but the butch-femme community does carry with it the heritage of being the first publicly visible lesbian community.

## Related Terms

"Stone butch": a butch woman who does not allow herself to be touched during lovemaking, but who often experiences orgasm while making love to her partner. This was a sexual style prevalent in the 1940s and 1950s.

"Baby butch": a young-looking butch woman with a naive face who brings out the maternal, as well as the sexual, longings of femme women.

"Kiki": a term used from the 1940s through the 1960s for a lesbian who could be either butch or femme. A publicly kiki woman in the 1940s and 1950s was often looked upon with suspicion, though, in the privacy of butch-femme homes, dif-ferent sexual positions were often explored.

"Passing woman": a woman who works and dresses like a man; this style of self-presentation was often used in the past to transcend the gender limitations placed on women. Many working-class women "passed" in order to hold down the jobs they wanted without harassment; in earlier decades, passing women often married other women. Passing women have their own sexual identity.

[The author wishes to extend special thanks to Deborah Edel, Lee Hudson, and the New York Butch Support Group for help in preparing this entry.]                                     *Joan Nestle*

## Bibliography

Bulkin, Elly. "An Old Dyke's Tale: An Interview with Doris Lunden." *Conditions: Six* 2:3 (1980), 26–44.

Case, Sue-Ellen. "Toward a Butch-Femme Aes-thetic." *Discourse* 11:1 (Fall/Winter 1988), 55–73.

Jeffreys, Sheila. *The Lesbian Heresy: A Feminist Perspective on the Lesbian Sexual Revolution*. North Melbourne: Spinifex, 1993.

Kennedy, Elizabeth Lapovsky, and Madeline D. Davis. *Boots of Leather, Slippers of Gold: The History of a Lesbian Community*. New York: Routledge, 1993.

Lorde, Audre. *Zami: A New Spelling of My Name*. Trumansburg, N.Y.: Crossing, 1982.

Nestle, Joan, ed. *The Persistent Desire: A Femme-Butch Reader*. Boston: Alyson, 1992.

———. *A Restricted Country*. Ithaca, N.Y.: Fire-brand, 1987.

Newman, Leslea, ed. *The Femme Mystique*. Boston: Alyson, 1995.

Newton, Esther. "The Mythic Mannish Lesbian: Radclyffe Hall and the New Woman." *Signs: Journal of Women in Culture and Society* 9:4 (Summer 1984), 557–575.

***See also*** Androgyny; Bars; Buffalo, New York; Bulldagger; Hall, Radclyffe; Passing Women; Queer Theory

# C

## Camp

A cultural style or taste associated with theatricality, humor, artifice, and appropriation, often understood to be a covert way of expressing gay male identity. The question of whether there are specifically lesbian forms of camp has been the subject of complex debate. Camp itself has been notoriously difficult to define because, understood as a style or sensibility, it cannot simply be located within a specific class of object or practice. Instead, camp is in the eye of the beholder, a means by which, through strategies of reception and appropriation, straight culture can be rendered queer. Furthermore, although camp has strong, even foundational, ties to gay male culture, including fan cultures and the drag theatrical traditions of men cross-dressing as women, its relations to lesbian culture have been less evident.

Histories of gay and lesbian culture suggest that, within pre-Stonewall (1969) cultures, camp provided a mechanism for the oblique expression of sexual identities, appearing in such guises as the aristocratic and arcane tastes of Oscar Wilde (1854–1900) and other aesthetes, fan cultures around Hollywood stars and opera divas, and traditions of drag performance. With the development of social movements in the 1970s, camp was often seen as a culture of the closet that gay liberation would render obsolete. In the 1990s, new accounts, such as those published in David Bergmann's collection *Camp Grounds: Style and Homosexuality* (1993), embraced camp's pre-gay-liberation forms as a significant cultural creation and as a resource for contemporary queer cultural practices ranging from lesbian drag kings to fan cultures and AIDS activism.

The enthusiasm for camp as a boldly queer aesthetic has inspired new ways of conceptualizing lesbian camp. Such approaches have had to respond to a strong feminist resistance to drag on the grounds that it is misogynist, as well as to accounts of the historical differences between gay male and lesbian cultures. For example, in *Boots of Leather, Slippers of Gold: The History of a Lesbian Community*, which looks at Buffalo's butch-femme bar culture in the 1940s and 1950s, Elizabeth Lapovsky Kennedy and Madeline Davis argue that butch-femme roles are not a form of camp performance because they do not display the humor and playfulness of gay male drag traditions. In contrast, theorists influenced by poststructuralism, such as Sue-Ellen Case and Judith Butler, have argued that butch-femme exemplifies a camp cultural practice that undermines traditional gender roles. For example, Butler (1990) counters the charge that butch-femme is an imitation of heterosexuality by deconstructing the opposition between heterosexuality as origin and homosexuality as copy. Butler's conception of gender and sexual identity as performative and Case's (1988) analysis of theatrical uses of butch-femme link the artifice of camp to the denaturalization of categories of social identity and, thus, widen camp's embrace to encompass a range of cultural practices, including lesbian ones, that expose norms of gender and sexuality.

In addition to being integral to histories of sexual identity, camp has important connections to the history of mass culture. Andrew Ross's *No Respect: Intellectuals and Popular Culture* (1989) shows how camp played a role in the dialogue between marginal and mainstream cultures in the 1960s. This was the period during which Susan Sontag's "Notes on 'Camp' " (1966) popularized the concept for mainstream audiences (at the price of effacing its ties to

**C**

specifically gay culture). For Ross and other critics of popular culture, camp is a mechanism by which consumers express their identities and tastes through the recirculation of popular styles and idioms, appropriating older styles as they become available for new meanings. Camp thus serves as an important register of the intersections of consumer cultures and sexual cultures and provides further evidence of ties between capitalism and gay identity.

Understood in this broad sense, camp becomes relevant to lesbian cultures, especially responses to mass culture. Lesbian camp is articulated through the vicissitudes of fashion and style, including high-modernist practices, working-class bar cultures, and drag king performances. The cultures of fandom are central to lesbian camp, including the worship of mainstream stars such as Bette Davis (1908–1989) and Madonna (1958–), lesbian celebrities such as k.d. lang (1961–) and Martina Navratilova (1956–), and more obscure character actresses and cult figures. Especially visible in performance, camp is a useful category for analyzing the butch-femme dynamics of Lois Weaver's and Peggy Shaw's performances with Split Britches Theater (beginning in 1981); the Five Lesbian Brothers' play *Brave Smiles . . . another lesbian tragedy* (1992), which restages the tragic endings of Christa Winslow's *Mädchen in Uniform* (Girls in Uniform) (1933) and Lillian Hellman's (1905–1984) *The Children's Hour* (1934) as a source of humor rather than the regrettable sign of homophobia; and Sandra Bernhard's (1955–) recycling of a vast array of popular idioms in *Without You I'm Nothing* (1988). The recovery of 1950s and 1960s lesbian pulp fiction, including its lurid covers, as queer artifact is a camp gesture. The activist group the Lesbian Avengers (founded in 1992) has borrowed images of Superman and 1970s blaxploitation film star Pam Grier (1949–) for its flyers, and the band Two Nice Girls borrowed from country music in the song "I Spent My Last $10 on Birth Control and Beer" (1984).

Camp is by no means an exclusively Euro-American phenomenon, although the complex intersections of gender and race in popular culture, and especially of cross-racial appropriation and identification, demand further analysis. In the 1980s and 1990s, Chicana artists such as Ester Hernandez and Yolanda Lopez reworked the image of the Virgin of Guadalupe; in the 1990s, Cuban American performance artist Carmelita Tropicana camped on the image of 1940s film star Carmen Miranda (1913–1955), and Cheryl Dunye explored the Hollywood stereotypes of the maid and mammy in her film *Watermelon Woman* (1996). Lesbian camp reclaims rather than rejects the stereotyped images of women that are so pervasive in mass culture.

Debates about whether camp is subversive are ongoing, but it may not be possible to determine the politics of camp in general since its specific instances are so varied. That the appropriation of mass culture is a creative possibility for lesbians has, however, itself been a productive insight for fans, critics, and producers of culture.     *Ann Cvetkovich*

### Bibliography

Bergman, David, ed. *Camp Grounds: Style and Homosexuality*. Amherst: University of Massachusetts Press, 1993.

Butler, Judith. *Gender Trouble: Feminism and the Subversion of Identity*. New York: Routledge, 1990.

Case, Sue-Ellen. "Toward a Butch-Femme Aesthetic." *Discourse* 11:1 (Fall/Winter 1988), 55–73.

Kennedy, Elizabeth Lapovsky, and Madeline D. Davis. *Boots of Leather, Slippers of Gold: The History of a Lesbian Community*. New York: Routledge, 1993.

Ross, Andrew. *No Respect: Intellectuals and Popular Culture*. New York: Routledge, 1989.

Sontag, Susan. "Notes on 'Camp.' " In *Against Interpretation*. New York: Farrar, Straus, and Giroux, 1966.

*See also* Butch-Femme; Cross-Dressing; Drag Kings; Humor; Performance Art; Performativity; Pulp Paperbacks; Winsloe, Christa

## Canada

An officially bilingual, multicultural, liberal democratic nation of thirty million people, made up of ten provinces and two territories. It is the country with the largest physical land mass in the world; it sits directly north of the United States; and each region sports a minimum of four distinct seasons.

### Pre-Stonewall (1969) Histories

Knowledge of female homoerotic relations and experiences in the Canadian past is sketchy and incomplete. Before European colonization, two-spirited peoples of the First Nations in Canada had same-sex lovers and were the visionaries and the medicine people or healers of their nation. From the early 1900s on, "lesbian" culture and communities seem to have emerged gradually, unevenly, and yet steadfastly across Canada. "Romantic friends" Victoria Hayward (1876–1956), a journalist, and Edith Watson (1861–1943), a photographer, lived and worked together in numerous Canadian cities from 1912 to 1943, the year of Watson's death. American-born sculptors Frances Loring (1887–1968) and Florence Wyle (1881–1968) happily shared their craft, their income, and their converted church/ home in Toronto for fifty years, from 1917 to 1967. Canadian Writer Mazo de la Roche (1879–1961), who gained fame through her Jalna novels, was involved in an intimate relationship for more than seventy years with her adopted sister, Caroline Clement. British-born Elsa Gidlow (1898–1986), who grew up in Montreal, had her book of homo-erotic love poems, *On a Grey Thread*, published in 1923.

As subterranean gay networks began to flourish in the 1920s, Canadian gay women found each other by frequenting downtown bars in major urban centers, by placing personal ads in the pulp tabloids *Flirt* and *Frivolo* (Montréal) and *Tab*, *Flash*, and *Hush* (Toronto), and by joining competitive baseball, basketball, ice hockey, and curling leagues. Canadian women made up approximately 10 percent of the players in the All-American Girls Professional Baseball League (1943–1954), and a number were known to be lesbians. In the post–World War II period, gay women met in hostels for street women, such as Toronto's Street Haven; in training schools; in the Kingston Prison for Women; in nurses' residences; at teachers' colleges; and at suburban house parties. They socialized where they found small queer colonies: on the islands of the Gulf Stream off the west coast of British Columbia, at summer resorts on the shore of Lake Erie, on the islands in the Toronto harbor, in Hogen's Alley (a turn-of-the-century African Canadian settlement in Vancouver), and in the farming hamlets of Nova Scotia's Annapolis Valley.

Often introduced to the "demimonde" via the notorious lesbian pulp novels of the 1950s, adventurous gay women who had money traveled across the Canada-U.S. border to Provincetown, Massachusetts; Martha's Vineyard; New York City, Syracuse, Rochester, and Buffalo, New York; Detroit, Michigan; and Seattle, Washington. Many left small, remote towns and villages, agricultural communities, and mining outposts in search of employment and sexual partners from St. John's, New-foundland, to Victoria, British Columbia. Butches, femmes, and nick-nacks (bisexuals) in the 1940s, 1950s, and 1960s defied gender and heterosexual prescriptions by defending queer spaces, sporting tattoos, and raising children together while embattled with Children's Aid Societies. Some of the butches assumed male identities and sought out gender-reassignment operations at Toronto's Clarke Institute of Psychiatry.

Whether as working-class women in offices and factories, or middle-class teachers, secretaries, and nurses, gay women in Canada lived with the fear of losing friends, jobs, families, and housing—they faced enormous risks and no political movement within which to agitate for social change. They were haunted by Canadian psychiatrist Daniel Cappon's contribution to the medicomoral discourse of homosexual pathology in 1965, which constructed homosexuality as a destructive disorder that could be cured. Between 1958 and 1964, some gay women were purged from their jobs in the federal civil service, including the National Film Board, because they were suspected or confirmed homosexuals and were classified as "national security threats."

## 1960s Uprisings

In the late 1960s, a constellation of social movements in Canada seeded the ground for the emergence of feminist and lesbian political action and consciousness. The province of Québec's nationalist emphasis on French culture and language in the 1960s, heightened by the FLQ (Front de Libération du Québec) crisis in 1970, raised awareness among Anglophone activists, including lesbians, of the historic struggles waged by Francophones (inside and outside Québec) against Anglophone domination. Some Canadian feminists, both straight and lesbian, sharpened their political teeth in the course of Third World solidarity work with Latin American, Chinese, and Cuban Canadian organizations. At the same time, members of Canada's First Nations intensified their protests against the historic racism and sexism of the federal government's Indian Act (1869) and their fight for economic, spiritual, and cultural self-determination. The New Left—in particular, the Student Union for Peace Action (SUPA), the Canadian Union of Students, and the militant left of the New Democratic Party (NDP)—provided training for largely white, middle-class women who catalyzed the "second wave" women's liberation movement in English Canada with abortion rights, sex stereotyping, equal pay, birth control, and day care atop the agenda.

## Lesbian Cultural and Political Independence

Canadian lesbians were active in all of these radical initiatives, and they were prominent members, alongside gay men, of the first gay homophile/liberation groups: the Association for Social Knowledge (Vancouver), the University of Toronto Homophile Association, Gay McGill (Montréal), the Community Homophile Association of Toronto, and the Vancouver Gay Liberation Front. However, they did not begin to organize as lesbian feminists until the mid-1970s, almost five years after the start of American lesbian movement. Mostly white, middle-class lesbians across Canada defended their desire to form lesbian groups based on the double critique of gay men's sexism and the heterosexism of straight feminists. Across English Canada, American lesbian feminist writing and cultural-production magazines, book publishing, record companies, and large-scale music festivals had an intense, immediate influence. American ideas and plans were read in publications purchased at women's bookstores across the country, reprinted, and tested by Canadian lesbians in their own milieux. The Canadian nationalists among them were openly leery of American imperialism, yet they were inspired by the first lesbian-authored tracts. Lesbians across Canada launched their own newsletters and periodicals, including *Long Time Coming* (Montreal), *LOOT Newsletter* (Toronto), *Pedestal* (Vancouver), and *Web of Crones* (Hornby Island, British Columbia), and later, in the 1980s and 1990s, *Pink Ink* (Toronto), *Rites* (Toronto), *Diversity* (Vancouver), *Swerve* (Winnipeg), *Gayzette* (Halifax), *Angles* (Vancouver), *Dimensions* (Saskatoon), *Da Juice!* (Toronto), *Sami Yoni* (Toronto), *Lezzie Smut* (Vancouver), *Lickerish* (Toronto), and *X-tra!* (Ottawa, Vancouver, and Toronto).

Lesbians in Canada formed their own musical groups in the 1970s: Mama Quilla I and II, Beverly Glenn Copeland, Ferron, Heather Bishop, Equis, Sherry Shute, Carol Pope and her band Rough Trade. The tradition continued in the 1980s and 1990s with k.d. lang and members of the bands Heretix, the Red Berets, Demi-Monde, Seven Cent Posse, Women With Horns, Mother Tongue, Bratty and the Babysitters, Parachute Club, Two Penny Opera, and Mother of Pearl. Internationally exhibited lesbian visual artists made their mark, among them Shonagh Adelman, Kiss & Tell, Stephanie Martin, Midi Onodera, Marusia Bociurkiw, Jennifer Gillmor, Aerlyn Weissman, Lynne Fernie, Patricia Rozema, Sara Diamond, Shawna Dempsey, and Lorna Boschman. Lesbian writers of notable repute in the 1980s and 1990s heeded the example of Jane Rule (1931– ), an expatriate American whose *Desert of the Heart* was published in Canada in 1964. These writers include Dionne Brand, Beth Brant, Anne Marie MacDonald, Marie-Clarie Blais, Eve Zaremba, Betsy Warland, Nicole Brossard, Daphne Marlatt, Vinita Srivastava, Mary Meigs, and Julia Creet.

## Grass-Roots Politics

In terms of conventional political action, Canadian lesbian organizing did not manifest itself in identical ways from coast to coast. In small communities—such as Brandon, Manitoba; Grand Prairie, Alberta; Stephenville, Newfoundland; and London, Ontario—regular dances, coffeehouses, potluck dinners, and socials were gradually put in place as strategies of survival. In Vancouver in the 1970s, the ideology and program of "lesbian nationalism" did not take root officially and practically in the ways it did in large American cities. It seems that the sheer physical distance from New York City, the strong presence of working-class lesbians, and a powerful provincial organization—the British Columbia Federation of Women—worked to engender the collaboration of lesbian and straight feminists.

Toronto-based lesbian feminists in the 1970s seemed more attuned to developments in the United States; however, a kind of radical lesbian praxis—collective and vegetarian living, zaps in public (quick, small-scale political actions), nonmonogamous sexual relations, and concerted distrust of "the man" and the male Left—coexisted with competing ideological currents. Anarchism, gay liberation, and various versions of socialism weakened the desire for, and the commitment to, full-fledged lesbian separatism. It is conceivable that lesbian activists north of the forty-ninth parallel had heard tales of acrimony and lesbian separatist burnout south of the border and had elected to proceed, Canadian style, with caution and moderation. Moreover, in most Canadian locales, the number of out, activist lesbians was too small to support vibrant, self-sustaining splinter groups. In rural regions, lesbians worked shoulder to shoulder with gay men and other likeminded progressives. Even in Toronto, where a radical feminist agenda held sway among the majority of political dykes in the 1970s, debates erupted constantly about what such a program meant, how it could be achieved, and whom it excluded.

In the late 1970s and into the 1980s, lesbian activist energy shifted to introducing an antiheterosexist perspective to coalition building. Socialist feminist lesbians in Toronto, Saskatoon, Vancouver, Halifax, and Winnipeg strove to build links with labor unions and members of anti-imperialist liberation struggles, antinuclear activism, the sex trade, reproductive rights, antipoverty, and anti–free trade groups. Efforts were made at "binational" lesbian conferences in Montreal, Toronto, and Vancouver to provide "simultaneous translation" as a way of bridging the English/French linguistic divide. It was the Ontario Coalition for Abortion Clinics, with a large lesbian membership, that played a major role in the Canadian Supreme Court's 1988 decision to strike down the federal abortion law as an indefensible barrier to a woman's right to control her body.

In the 1990s, lesbians continued to work for social change in the context of feminist, antiracist, labor, environmental, and antipoverty politics, as well as in lesbian-centered initiatives. Challenges to the legacy of white, middle-class lesbian leadership yielded to groups that held on to the value of identity-based organizing but that abandoned the dream of a unified lesbian subject and all illusions of a coherent lesbian movement. Bisexual women in groups such as BiFace (Vancouver) and lesbian- and bi-identified transgenders and transsexuals furthered the need to deconstruct the constrictive binaries of homo/hetero and male/female on the road to gender and sexual pluralism.

## State Policing and Regulation

From the early 1970s on, brutal collisions with police forces made lesbian feminists aware of the power of state repression and contributed to the distinctiveness of lesbian and gay politics in Canada. In 1974, four lesbians were arrested at a Toronto bar for "causing a public disturbance" and were later roughed up in police custody. In 1977 in Toronto, the office of the *Body Politic*, a gay news journal with an international readership of ten thousand, was raided by Project P, an antipornography morality squad, and charged with distributing scurrilous materials. Lesbian journalists at the *Body Politic* and lesbian activists across Canada were part of a defense campaign that persevered until the paper's eventual acquittal in 1983. Antigay and antilesbian policies at the *Vancouver Sun*, the *Toronto Star*, and Vancouver's YWCA and the high-profile firings of lesbian and gay workers and soldiers in the mid-1970s further exposed the depth of discrimination and societal hostility. Mass protests against the injustices galvanized forces, politicized thousands,

and brought gay men and lesbians together to form alliances that would later spawn gender-mixed AIDS activism.

In the mid-1980s, anticensorship activity was reignited in response to charges leveled against lesbian and gay bookstores for importing and selling obscene material, including the American lesbian magazine *Bad Attitude*. (The *Bad Attitude* trial marked the second lesbian pornography trial in Canada, the first being in Ottawa in 1952.) The trial resulted in the 1992 conviction of the owner and manager of Glad Day Bookshop (Toronto) for the possession and sale of obscenity. Glad Day, L'Androgyne (Montréal), and Little Sister's Book and Art Emporium (Vancouver) have all weathered the escalation of detentions and seizures of books at the Canada-U.S. border. Little Sister's argued against the homophobic practices of Customs officers during a month-long trial in the British Columbia Supreme Court in 1994. Two years later, the bookstore was awarded 75 percent of its legal costs; the judge recognized the discriminatory targeting of lesbian and gay materials by Customs agents. However, because he did not declare the obscenity guidelines unconstitutional and a violation of the Canadian Charter of Rights and Freedoms, the bookstore turned to the British Columbia Court of Appeal in an effort to abolish Customs' harassment altogether. In 1998, the bookstore lost the appeal decision, 2–1, and was in the process of taking the case to the Supreme Court of Canada.

## Legislative Reform

One arm of lesbian and gay activism has sought to redress legal inequalities through inclusion of sexual orientation within antidiscriminatory statutes and extension of social benefits (medical, health, survivor, inheritance, and pensions) to lesbian and gay couples. Since the 1970s, civil rights strategies have been mobilized by strong provincial coalitions, such as the Ontario Coalition for Lesbian and Gay Rights, the Saskatchewan Gay Coalition, and the national body EGALE (Equality for Gays and Lesbians Everywhere). By 1998 the majority of provinces and territories included antidiscrimination protection in their Human Rights Codes—the exceptions were Prince Edward Island and the Northwest Territories. Other legal victories include a 1992 Supreme Court decision to ban discrimination against homosexuals in the Canadian Armed Forces and the Supreme Court's 1993 decision to grant refugee status to those immigrants who fear homosexual-based persecution in their home countries. In 1995, an Ontario judge ruled that nonbiological lesbian parents have the legal right to adopt the child/ren they coparent; in 1996, British Columbia followed suit. In 1995, in *R. v. Egan,* the Canadian Supreme Court ruled that same-sex couples did not have the right to spousal pension benefits under the Old Age Security Act. Lesbian and gay marriage is not legal, nor does Revenue Canada recognize lesbian and gay couples for income tax purposes, although the Ontario Court ruled in 1998 that the heterosexist definition of "spouse" in the Income Tax Act is unconstitutional. The Immigration Act does not specify the inclusion of non-Canadian partners of lesbians and gay men; however, citizenship has been awarded to queer immigrants on a case-by-case basis. In May 1996, Bill C-33—an amendment to the Canadian Human Rights Act designed to prohibit discrimination on the basis of sexual orientation—was passed by the House of Commons. In 1998, both Nova Scotia and British Columbia introduced legislation extending pension benefits to the same-sex partners of public employees—the first provinces in Canada to take this step.

Though decisions overall have been contradictory, and some queers have criticized the assimilationist thrust of the lesbian and gay movement's "we are family" campaign (i.e., the campaign for recognition of their families as equivalent in value to those of heterosexuals), there is agreement among Canadian activists that legal gains have been more numerous and substantial than those in the United States. In part, they point to a much less powerful Christian fundamentalist right wing in Canada, the pro-gay efforts of the left-leaning New Democratic Party to redefine "family" and "spouse" both provincially and federally, the cross-provincial coordination of lesbian and gay lobbying via EGALE, and a long, socialist-inspired tradition of welfare-state provisions.

## Culture and Politics

In 1998, Toronto's Lesbian and Gay Pride Day Parade attracted over 700,000 people, the second largest of its kind worldwide after San Francisco's. Cities from coast to coast host Pride days, film and video festivals, and are home to queer theater companies, art collectives, and counseling centers. The Canadian Lesbian and Gay Studies Association was formally constituted as a "learned society" in 1994, when it began meeting alongside all other academic disciplines. The Toronto Centre for Lesbian, Gay, Bisexual, and Transgender Studies sponsors numerous events, awards, and community-based courses and operates as a countrywide clearinghouse, *Centre/Fold,* for queer research and scholarship. The wealth of cultural, political, and intellectual resources would have been unimaginable in the 1950s. In the late 1990s, struggles for lesbian visibility, support for women-only spaces, and the dismantlement of institutionalized heterosexism and homophobia remained relevant and pressing in Canada, though the definition of a determinate "lesbian politics" was unclear. A Canadian contingent contributed to international negotiations concerning sexual orientation and women's sexuality at the 1995 Women's Conference in Beijing, China—an indication of one direction of mature, robust lesbian feminist energy at work both inside and outside Canada's borders. *Becki L. Ross*

## Bibliography

Bannerji, Kaushalya, Margot Francis, Denyse Hayoun, Didi Khayatt, Susanne Lubmann, Kathleen Rockhill, Caridad Silva, Mary Lou Soutar-Hynes, and Eve Zaremba, eds. "Lesbians and Politics." *Canadian Woman Studies* 16:2 (Spring 1996) (Special Issue).

Chenier, Elise. "Tough Ladies and Troublemakers: Toronto's Public Lesbian Community, 1955–1965." Master's thesis, Queen's University, 1995.

Fuller, Janine, and Stuart Blackley. *Restricted Entry: Censorship on Trial.* Vancouver: Press Gang, 1995.

Herman, Didi. *Rites of Passage: Struggles for Lesbian and Gay Legal Equality.* Toronto: University of Toronto Press, 1994.

Kinsman, Gary. *The Regulation of Desire: Homo and Hetero Sexualities in Canada.* 2nd ed. Montreal: Black Rose Books, 1996.

Ross, Becki. *The House That Jill Built: A Lesbian Nation in Formation.* Toronto: University of Toronto Press, 1995.

Stone, Sharon Dale, ed. *Lesbians in Canada.* Toronto: Between the Lines, 1990.

***See also*** Blais, Marie-Claire; Brossard, Nicole; Gidlow, Elsa; Québec; Rule, Jane Vance; Two-Spirit; United States

## Caribbean

Sea that gives its name to the region located east of the Central American isthmus and between the North and South American continents. The Caribbean is home to many islands, including the Greater Antilles—Cuba, Hispañola, and Puerto Rico. Cuba, often called "the Pearl of the Antilles," is the largest island in the Caribbean Sea and is surrounded by fifteen hundred tiny islands. It is a mere ninety miles from Miami, Florida. Other major islands of the Caribbean include Puerto Rico and Jamaica.

## Cuba

Cuba's treatment of gays, lesbians, bisexuals, and transgendered people shifted dramatically during the twentieth century. The last colony to win its independence (1898) from Spain, after a decade-long struggle, Cuba maintained the conservative attitudes of its Spanish-Catholic colonial legacy toward queer people throughout the first years of independence, which were marked by U.S. domination of the nation. Cuba's Catholic culture had little tolerance for gay and lesbian sexual or gender-bending behavior. However, even though the Catholic Church exercised considerable influence in the years before the revolution by the forces of Fidel Castro, it did not have the power to control public mores that it had in other Latin American countries. Prerevolutionary Havana, the capital of Cuba, was the playground of the Western world. Much of its economy depended on tourism from the United States and on the "sin industry"—gaming, prostitution, and nightclubs, including a vast network of gay bars. During its domination by the United States, Havana's nightlife provided middle-class and wealthy Americans with a welcome release from Prohibition and the general misery of the Great Depression. But homosexuality was not confined to these sectors of society. Gay men were present throughout Cuban society, on the farms as well as in the urban areas. A man with effeminate mannerisms or cross-dressing tendencies could become a *loca* (queen); the word literally means a "crazy one." While there was no gay community documented in that era of Cuba's history, the existence of gay men was acknowledged; they had a place, albeit a marginal one, in the social structure. Lesbians, however, were virtually invisible. The relationship of Cuban anthropologist Lydia Cabrera (1899–1991) with Venezuelan writer Teresa de la Parra (1888/1890–1936), for example, has consistently been described as a friendship, but Parra's published letters suggest that it was a lesbian relationship.

In 1959, Fidel Castro (1926/1927–) and his ruling junta overthrew the government of Fulgencio Batista, an event that changed many of the conditions of life in Cuba. Gays and lesbians had been active on the Left and in the anti-Batista movements, but they would not enjoy recognition in the new order. To their surprise and dismay, their aspirations for liberation were lost as the government turned toward a Marxist communist model. Within a short time after the revolution in Cuba, the Castro regime cracked down on gay men and, to a lesser extent, on lesbians, arresting them and sending them off to "reeducation" camps, where they were coerced into conforming to rigid gender stereotypes, or imprisoning them.

Castro himself has said little about his early treatment of gays and lesbians. In a rare interview in which he discussed the subject (excerpted in *Improper Conduct*, a 1984 documentary film directed by Nestor Almendros and Orlando Jimenez Leal), he said he believed that homosexuality was a matter to be studied (no such study was ever conducted) and that it weakened men. He also asserted that homosexuals should not be in positions in which they could influence young people. He made no mention of lesbians, but they, too, were arrested for what he characterized as "improper conduct." In fact, for most of the era following his coming to power, gays and lesbians have been systematically persecuted. *Improper Conduct* also includes interviews with an array of intellectuals and homosexuals who have suffered under the Castro regime.

In 1980, when the United States and Cuba negotiated the Mariel Boatlift for political prisoners from Cuba, Castro emptied his prisons, sending hundreds of convicted felons, including a large number of gays and lesbians, to the United States. The resettlement of those refugees, the Marielitos, was delayed for years, due, in part, to U.S. policies of exclusion of gay immigrants.

When the Soviet bloc collapsed in the 1990s, Cuba lost the subsidy that the Soviets provided its economy. Forced by that loss, and the continuing trade embargo imposed by the United States, to consider alternative funding sources, Castro relaxed the iron hold he once had on Cuban culture. A new wind of openness swept through the island as Castro permitted foreign investment and the revival of the tourist industry. Improvements in the lives of lesbians and gay men, however, have been slow to come—even slower than for heterosexual women.

While the Castro regime's maltreatment of gay men has been well documented, little has been written about lesbians in Cuba. Saddled with the traditions of machismo (an exaggerated belief that men are physically and intellectually superior to women)

**C** and marianismo (which relegates women to the diametrically opposed roles of virgins or whores), women were particularly constrained by the rigid gender roles. Even access to education was denied to them. Schools for women did not open until the 1870s, scarcely two decades before independence. Yet the continuing ideology of marianismo, which privileges the traditional heterosexual roles of motherhood and marriage for women, makes lesbian gender transgression particularly suspect and egregious. Thus, lesbian invisibility remains very problematic for Cuban women.

Still, in the new atmosphere of openness, gays and lesbians have begun to emerge from the shadows, and a nascent film industry has begun to make its presence felt. The 1994 film *Strawberry and Chocolate*, directed by Tomas Gutierrez Alea, chronicled the warm friendship between a gay man and a young leftist activist. While it was controversial in Cuba, it did not incur the censure that an earlier effort might have. Furthermore, it gained the distinction of being the first Cuban film to be nominated for a Best Foreign Film Oscar.

## Puerto Rico

While the Spanish-speaking Caribbean countries tend to share the ideologies of machismo and marianismo with Cuba—and, with them, the attendant pressures on lesbians—other countries more closely reflect the ideologies of their colonizing forces. While Puerto Rico and Cuba both were taken from Spain in the Spanish-American War, Puerto Rico became a territory of the United States. It adopted some tendencies, such as the criminalization of lesbian and gay sexuality, that more closely resemble U.S. rather than Central or South American policies. In fact, Puerto Rico's antihomosexual laws, instituted in 1902, were based almost exclusively on California state laws. No other Caribbean country carries such statutes on its books. While the laws are rarely enforced, the ideological lines are drawn between those who believe that they should be kept on the books to send a message that the state does not encourage homosexual conduct, and the lesbian activist groups who, like their gay, lesbian, and transgendered counterparts in the United States, are aligning themselves with other sexual minorities to combat these repressive policies.

## Other Islands

Despite their strong influence on Puerto Rico and Cuba, the United States and Spain were and are not the only foreign influences on Caribbean culture. England, France, and the Netherlands all had established presences in the Caribbean during the colonial era; Caribbean culture today tends to reflect the legal and social policies of a diversity of European powers, as well as forces unique to slavery and the African diaspora.

Silvera (1996) writes that words like "man royal" and "sodomite" were used in Jamaica to describe women who had sex with other women. These words implied that women in such relationships were imitating men, as no "authentic" woman-woman relationship could be recognized. The use of "sodomite" to refer to women, she argues, is unique to Jamaica, indicating the legacy of missionaries and the importance of the Judeo-Christian Bible in Afro-Caribbean culture. Audre Lorde, in *Zami: A New Spelling of My Name* (1982), refers to the "legendary" relationships between women on Carriacou, an island near Grenada, identified by the words "Madavine. Friending. Zami." For Lorde and other English-speaking Afro-Caribbean lesbians, "Zami," in particular, has come to signify a particular Afro-Caribbean lesbian history and identity.

*Rosa María Pegueros*

## Bibliography

Braulio, Mildred. "Challenging the Sodomy Law in Puerto Rico." *NACLA* 31:4 (January/February 1998), 33–34.

Dore, Elizabeth, ed. *Gender Politics in Latin America: Debates in Theory and Practice.* New York: Monthly Review Press, 1998.

Melhuus, Marit, and Kristi Anne Stolen, eds. *Machos, Mistresses, Madonnas: Contesting the Power of Latin American Gender Imagery.* New York: Verso, 1998.

Molloy, Sylvia. "Disappearing Acts: Reading Lesbian in Teresa de la Parra." In *¿Entiendes? Queer Readings, Hispanic Writings.* Ed. Emilie L. Bergmann and Paul Julian Smith. Durham, N.C.: Duke University Press, 1995.

Silvera, Makeda. "Man Royals and Sodomites: Some Thoughts on the Invisibility of Afro-Caribbean Lesbians." In *Lesbian Subjects.* Ed. Martha Vicinus. Bloomington and Indianapolis: Indiana University Press, 1996, pp. 230–256.

Stoner, K. Lynn. *From the House to the Streets: The Cuban Woman's Movement for Reform, 1898–1940.* Durham, N.C.: Duke University Press, 1991.

Young, Allen. *Gays Under the Cuban Revolution.* San Francisco: Grey Fox, 1981.

*See also* Central America; Lorde, Audre; Mexico; Parra, Teresa de la

## Cartoons and Comic Books

Drawings intended as humor, caricature, or satire. Comic strips and books often feature consistent characters involved in continuous stories. From the emergence of the comic strip industry in the late nineteenth century, through the comic-book boom era in the United States (1940s–1950s), and up to the 1990s, women rarely were employed by major publishers except as occasional inkers or colorists unless their work conformed to the popular superhero genre. As Sabin (1993) notes in his study of women and adult comics: "The first adult comics of the nineteenth century set the tone for the industry ever since—they were produced primarily by men, for men, and were about 'male subjects.'" Therefore, getting published has been difficult for women cartoon and comic-book artists, more so for women who draw lesbian characters.

*"No guilt" from Hothead Paisan Homicidal Lesbian Terrorist. Illustration by Diane DiMassa. Courtesy Stacy A. Sheehan.*

A crusade that claimed that comic books contributed to child delinquency culminated in 1954 in the institution of a restrictive code that embodied a rigorously conservative political position. Since then, most comic books involving sex, violence, and attacks on authority have been denied access to major distribution networks in the United States. Underground and independent publishers that developed in the 1960s and 1970s in reaction to such restrictions provided a space for artists who embraced political and sexual issues and/or drew outside the superhero formula. Yet most of these presses did not welcome work by women any more than the major publishers did. Therefore, by the mid-1970s, women were publishing their own work independently or through collective efforts.

The first such comic book, dedicated to "women's liberation" as its front page declared, was *It Aint Me, Babe* (1970), compiled by women on the staff of California's first feminist newspaper by the same name. While this collection of work by women did not address lesbianism specifically, it did present a vision of female collective action by portraying a sort of consciousness-raising gathering of girl and women comic-book characters such as Betty and Veronica from Archie comics, Petunia Pig, and Wonder Woman. More "women's comix" followed, and some, such as *Dyke Shorts*, *Come Out Comics*, and the ongoing *Tits 'n' Clits* and *Wimmen's Comix* (renamed *Wimmin's Comix* in 1992), have included lesbian strips.

Some readers and critics have located lesbian elements in issues of *Wonder Woman* (1940–) that trace her origins to Paradise Isle, an exclusive community of women. More explicitly lesbian cartoons and comic strips created before the early 1970s likely were distributed informally and passed around among friends. Roberta Gregory is credited as the first published artist to deal directly with lesbian themes in a comic book. Her strip, "A Modern Romance," narrates the story of Anne, a young woman starting college who feels alienated from most of her peers and eventually acknowledges her love for women. Although Gregory's work initiated a respectable history of lesbian comic-book art, it is significant that "A Modern Romance" did not appear until 1974 in *Wimmen's Comix*. Gregory also created *Dynamite Damsels* in 1976, the first single-handedly self-published comic book by a woman that addressed lesbianism.

Although many publications of the first phase of women's comix faded by the end of the 1970s, lesbian cartoons and comic strips found a venue in the many feminist, lesbian, and gay newspapers and magazines; anthologies that welcomed women cartoonists; and the emerging lesbian and queer 'zine culture. Humor collections and comic books of the 1980s and 1990s, such as *Women's Glibber*, *Gay Comix*, *Strip AIDS USA*, *What Is This Thing Called Sex?*, *Real Girl*, *Weenietoons*, *Artistic Licentiousness*, *The Best Contemporary Women's Humor*, *Strange-Looking Exile*, and *Dyke Strippers,* featured lesbian work. The increase in artists and their audiences generated the Lesbian Cartoonists Network, an organization headquartered in Santa Cruz, California. Outside the United States, contemporary lesbian cartoonists have included Leanne Franson and Cath Jackson of London, England; Rona Chadwick of Perth, Beck Main of Kings Cross, and Barbary O'Brien of Middleton, Australia; Wendy Eastwood of Serbia (former Yugoslavia); Jo Nesbitt of Amsterdam, Holland; and Noreen Stevens of Winnipeg, Manitoba, Canada.

Alison Bechdel and Diane DiMassa are two of the better-known artists of the 1980s and 1990s. New York City's feminist newspaper *Womanews* began running Bechdel's now famous "Dykes to Watch Out For" in 1983. The strip's popularity skyrocketed, and the familiar characters of Mo, Lois, Sparrow, Ginger, and others appeared on calendars, postcards, and T-shirts, as well as in more than forty newspapers throughout the United States, Canada, and the United Kingdom by 1995. DiMassa formed Giant Ass Publishing in 1991 with partner Stacy Sheehan to create the comic 'zine *HotHead Paisan, Homicidal Lesbian Terrorist*. As was true of Bechdel's experience with "Dykes," DiMassa's HotHead audience soon dramatically expanded, and Giant Ass released more than twenty issues and two book-length collections by the late-1990s, along with its share of T-shirts, coffee mugs, hats, and posters.

While Bechdel draws characters of many races and ethnicities and DiMassa gave HotHead an Italian American identity, many lesbian strips focus on white characters and their viewpoints. Cartoons and comics addressing specific lesbian constituencies have been published in 'zines such as *Girljock* for sports enthusiasts and *Brat Attack: The 'Zine for Leatherdykes and Other Bad Girls*. Lesbian cartoons and comic books likely will continue to flourish and expand their scope as long as avenues for publication continue to proliferate.     *Kate Burns*

## Bibliography

Rhodes, Molly. "Wonder Woman and Her Disciplinary Powers: The Intersection of Scientific Authority and Mass Culture in the 20th Century." In *Doing Cultural Studies of Science, Technology, and Medicine*. Ed. Roddey Reid and Sharon Traweek. New York: Routledge, 1999.

Robbins, Trina. *A Century of Women Cartoonists.* Northhampton, Mass.: Kitchen Sink, 1993.

Robbins, Trina, and Catherine Yronwode. *Women and the Comics*. Forestville, Calif.: Eclipse, 1985.

Sabin, Roger. *Adult Comics: An Introduction*. New York: Routledge, 1993.

Warren, Roz. *Dyke Strippers: Lesbian Cartoonists A to Z*. Pittsburgh: Cleis, 1995.

*See also* 'zines

## Cather, Willa (1873–1947)

American writer. Although she was born in Back Creek, Virginia, Willa Cather is most frequently associated with the Great Plains of Nebraska. Her family moved there in 1883, and two of her best-known novels are set there. Cather's career as a writer was both long and distinguished. Her first novel, *Alexander's Bridge*, was published in 1912, and her last novel, *Sapphira and the Slave Girl*, appeared in 1940. She received considerable popular and scholarly acclaim for novels such as *O Pioneers!* (1913), *My Ántonia* (1918), *The Song of the Lark* (1915), and *Death Comes for the Archbishop* (1927). Among her many awards and honorary degrees is a 1923 Pulitzer Prize for *One of Ours* (1922).

As an adult, Cather was not a social rebel. In her later years, she embraced a conservative Roman Catholicism. As an adolescent, however, the young Cather created a stir in her hometown of Red Cloud, Nebraska, when, at the age of fourteen, she began to dress as a young man. For four years, Cather played with a masculine persona. She gave herself a crew cut, dressed in male attire, and named herself "William Cather Jr." Her refusal to accept feminine norms became legendary in Red Cloud. As a student at the University of Nebraska from 1890 to 1895, Cather greatly modified, but did not entirely abandon, her male attire.

Cather never explicitly named herself a lesbian and went to considerable lengths to protect her personal privacy. However, it is clear that she lived in a world of intimate female relations, some of which were deeply passionate, if not sexual. At the University of Nebraska, Cather met and fell in love with

Louise Pound (1872–1958). She complained to Pound that it was unfair that "feminine friendship" should be "unnatural," even while she agreed that it was. They parted company in 1894.

Two other important women in Cather's life were Isabelle McClung (d. 1938) and Edith Lewis (1882–1972). McClung seems to have been the great inspiration of Cather's life. Cather once told a friend that all of her books were dedicated to McClung. For five years, Cather lived with her in the McClung family home in Pittsburgh while she worked on a women's magazine and her own fiction. After Cather moved to New York City and made it her permanent home in 1906, the two women visited often and took long vacations together. When McClung married in 1916, Cather was devastated; however, they remained close until McClung's death in 1938.

For almost forty years, Cather shared her life with Edith Lewis, whom she met in 1903. The two set up house together in 1908 and remained together until Cather's death in 1947. Cather never dedicated a book to Lewis, who devoted herself to Cather's life and work. However, it was Cather's wish that the two be buried together in Jaffrey, New Jersey, the town where they frequently spent long summer vacations.

Cather's fiction does not contain clear and unambiguous "lesbian" narratives. Nevertheless, both her writing and her life are richly suggestive of a complex homoerotic and homosocial world. She remains an important figure in lesbian history, as well as in twentieth-century fiction.    *JoAnn Pavletich*

### Bibliography

Bennet, Mildred. *The World of Willa Cather*. Rev. ed. Lincoln: University of Nebraska Press, 1961.

Lewis, Edith. *Willa Cather Living*. New York: Knopf, 1953.

O'Brien, Sharon. *Willa Cather: The Emerging Voice*. New York: Oxford University Press, 1987.

Woodress, James. *Willa Cather: Her Life and Art*. Lincoln: University of Nebraska Press, 1970.

***See also*** American Literature, Twentieth Century

## Catholicism

A major Christian religious tradition and denomination that reaches across the globe. Catholicism is widely regarded as opposed to homosexuality and unjust in its treatment of women. Thus, it is often regarded as being especially unjust to lesbians, even though some of its "best and brightest" members identify as such. Since women cannot be ordained, and since ordination is necessary to participate in most decision making, the leadership of the Roman Catholic Church is necessarily devoid of lesbians. However, lesbian women are thought to have been part of the Catholic Church from its beginnings and are among the most vocal and effective of its feminist challengers.

The tradition can be divided into its kyriarchal expression, the Roman Catholic Church as an institution, and its progressive members, who seek to transform that pyramidal structure into an egalitarian community. These two groups have divergent positions on homosexuality. Kyriarchy is opposed, although it is widely believed that many of its clergy members are gay. The progressive sector ranges from tolerant to enthusiastic.

The institutional, kyriarchal form of church made its contemporary position clearest in a "Letter to the Bishops of the Roman Catholic Church on the Pastoral Care of Homosexual Persons," issued by the Vatican Congregation for the Doctrine of the Faith in 1986. It stated that an inclination to homosexual activity is a tendency toward an intrinsic moral evil and that actual homosexual activity is immoral.

Such a pronouncement leaves little room for discussion, even less for inclusion. Catholic theology is patriarchal, meaning that men's experiences hold sway. Thus, when it comes to homosexuality, this position assumes that gay men's, and not lesbian women's, experiences are normative. Blanket condemnations in church documents apply equally to women, despite the fact that their experiences, while different, are erased. Pastoral practice is sometimes friendly, at least covertly. But some bishops encourage secular legislation such as that prohibiting adoption of children by lesbian, gay, bisexual, and transgendered people.

Progressive sectors of Catholicism, especially in the United States and Western Europe, include many persons and groups that support civil and religious rights for lesbian, gay, bisexual, and transgendered people. Dignity is the largest such organization, with dozens of chapters and thousands of members who are "out" and Catholic. The Conference for Catholic Lesbians is a group of several hundred members who meet in small base communities for prayer and sisterhood. Some Catholic les-

**C** bians also belong to Christian Lesbians Out Together (CLOUT), an ecumenical group including many ordained lesbian pastors. New Ways Ministry provides services for parents and friends of Catholic lesbian and gay people; Communications Ministry focuses specifically on nuns and priests who are lesbian and gay. Many religious orders have informal lesbian or gay caucuses.

Catholic lesbians are unearthing their history as part of feminist studies in religion. Bernadette Brooten's (1996) work on female homoeroticism in Christian scripture begins the revisionist work on women in the early church. Judith C. Brown (1986) documents seventeenth-century nuns Benedetta Carlini and Bartolomea Crivelli, whose relationship caused a scandal in their convent. Current and former nuns tell stories of their "particular friendships" and the deeply ingrained prohibition against them. Despite this, Catholic lesbians abound both in and out of convents.

The patriarchal nature of Catholicism means that all women are marginalized. Since sexuality is seen as an integral dimension of spirituality and ethics, women are prohibited from acting freely on the basis of their own insights. Rather, roles and behaviors are prescribed by the kyriarchal church. Lesbian women experience this in slightly different ways from heterosexual women, who, for example, are prohibited from using most effective forms of birth control and having abortions. Lesbian women, far from being praised for the "naturalness" of their birth control and the fact that their sexual expression does not usually "tempt" them to abort, are either ignored entirely or lumped with gay men. Catholic lesbian mothers are looked down upon. Marriage remains a sacrament reserved to heterosexuals.

Catholic lesbian women are in the leadership of many of the church reform efforts, including the movement for the ordination of women to the priesthood. Many are involved in the development of egalitarian models of church, the "women-church movement." Likewise, Catholic lesbian women are well represented among secular social activists and are leading human rights organizations, writing for lesbian and gay publications, running for elective office, and in virtually every other role for which they prepared so well in Catholic schools. Central to their training is the Catholic emphasis on love and justice, despite the efforts of church officials to place gender-specific restrictions on same. Far from being a contradiction in terms, Catholic lesbians live out the core values of their faith tradition in a thoroughly inclusive way. *Mary E. Hunt*

### Bibliography

Brooten, Bernadette. *Love Between Women: Early Christian Responses to Female Homoeroticism.* Chicago: University of Chicago Press, 1996.

Brown, Judith C. *Immodest Acts: The Life of a Lesbian Nun in Renaissance Italy.* New York: Oxford University Press, 1986.

Curb, Rosemary, and Nancy Manahan, eds. *Lesbian Nuns: Breaking Silence.* Tallahassee, Fla.: Naiad, 1985.

Hunt, Mary E. "Lovingly Lesbian: Toward a Feminist Theology of Friendship." In *A Challenge To Love: Gay and Lesbian Catholics in the Church.* Ed. Robert Nugent. New York: Crossroad, 1987, pp. 135–155.

Zanotti, Barbara, ed. *A Faith of One's Own: Explorations by Catholic Lesbians.* Trumansburg, N.Y.: Crossing, 1986.

***See also*** Christianity, Early; Religious Communities

## Censorship

As defined in this entry, censorship refers to the supervision and assessment of the actions, practices, and ethics of women for the purposes of controlling their social-sexual relations, self-representation, and, ultimately, self-determination. Sociopolitical control of lesbianism dates from early religious writings that sought to regulate the sexuality of women. In most countries, assessment and censorship of women's sexual activities in the service of institutionally endorsed male sexual privilege continue through a combination of state legislation and religious edicts. Importantly, the word "lesbian" is rarely explicitly stated within legislation or moral decrees but, instead, is implied through the use of code terms such as "sexual deviance," "perversion," "indecency," and "immoral conduct." Dominant social and political bodies interpret and judge the applicability of these terms to lesbians through the lenses of institutionalized heterosexism. The assessment and control of lesbian practices and representation occur as an unspecified aftereffect of regulatory systems within which lesbians are, in every other way, completely absent.

In the Western world, for example, the surveillance of prostitutes—initiated by legislation mandating examinations for venereal disease (1802, Paris)—was a critical step in institutionally regulating the sexual practices of single women, including lesbians. State and religious authorities rationalized increased policing through their stated concern for public safety while creating public suspicion of clandestine vice and female sexual deviance. The social organization and legislation of prostitution, deviance, and eroticism left lesbians, who were usually also poor, unwed, and/or racially or ethnically identified, vulnerable to molestation and police persecution, even as it protected the male-produced pornographic images of lesbian sex that circulated within middle-to-upper-class male circles.

In England, "first wave" feminists (late 1800s) identified the misogyny behind the officially sanctioned sexual hierarchy that stigmatized women. However, this concern was eclipsed by the growing movement for the protection of women, resulting in the reinscription of deviance in laws that criminalized same-sex acts between consenting adults. This oppressive situation became more complex when "second wave" feminists (1968–1980) reclaimed the category of sexual deviance to attack pornographic representation without reconsidering that this category had been used historically to criminalize lesbians, prostitutes, poor, and non-white women.

Administrated censorship—supported by state bodies such as the Meese Commission on Pornography (1985, United States) and extrastate bodies such as the Vatican and the World Health Organization—increased throughout the 1970s and 1980s and has authorized police raids on gay and lesbian bookstores and bars and the seizing of lesbian books, magazines, and videos in Canada, the United States, and the United Kingdom. Oppressive legislation and court rulings, such as Section 28 of the Local Government Act of 1988 (known as Clause 28 before the act was passed) in England and the Butler decision (*R. v. Butler,* 1992) in Canada have facilitated attacks on educational and health institutions distributing nondiscriminatory information on reproductive choice, safe sex, and sexual orientation, thus proving Pratibha Parmar's (1988) observation that "censorship of any kind has always had disastrous and repressive effects for communities without access to power." This repression has been challenged by gay and lesbian liberation movements and anticensorship organizations, such as Feminists for Free Expression (United States) and CENSORSTOP (Canada).                              *Linda D. Wayne*

## Bibliography

Assiter, Alison, and Carol Avedon, eds. *Bad Girls and Dirty Pictures: The Challenge to Reclaim Feminism.* London: Pluto, 1993.

Burstyn, Varda, ed. *Women Against Censorship.* Toronto: Douglas and McIntyre, 1985.

"Censorship." *Fuse* 16:2 (Winter 1992) (Special Issue).

Chester, Gail, and Julienne Dickey, eds. *Feminism and Censorship: The Current Debate.* Bridport, Dorset: Prism, 1988.

Duggan, Lisa, and Nan D. Hunter, eds. *Sex Wars: Sexual Dissent and Political Culture.* New York: Routledge, 1995.

Kinsman, Gary. *The Regulation of Desire: Sexuality in Canada.* Montreal: Black Rose, 1987.

Parmar, Pratibha. "Rage and Desire: Confronting Pornography. In *Out the Other Side: Contemporary Lesbian Writing.* Ed. Christian McEwen and Sue O'Sullivan. London: Virago, 1988, pp. 276–287.

*See also* Sex Work

## Central America

Territory bridging North and South America and comprising seven countries (Guatemala, Honduras, El Salvador, Nicaragua, Costa Rica, Panama, and Belize) that have unique, although related, histories and cultures. One of the main characteristics of these nations is the mixture of peoples derived from a variety of cultures: Spanish, as well as several Indian cultures, Afro-Caribbean cultures, and Anglo-Saxon culture.

## History

Prior to the Spanish Conquest in the sixteenth century, Central America was inhabited by Indian societies, from both the Mesoamerican and South American traditions. Although there are no studies that fully document the practice of lesbianism in Precolumbian times, a few references from the compilation of texts written to document the Conquest (known as the *Spanish Chronicles*) seem to suggest the existence of homosexual females among the Indian cultures of the region. Moreover, the presence of the goddess Xochi-quetzal in the Mesoamerican pantheon suggests that lesbianism and male homosexuality were actually part of the ideological meanings of some of these Indian groups. This goddess, embodying both female and male features, was the representation of nonprocreative sexuality and love.

The reality of woman-to-woman love during the colonial period (1540–1821) in Central America is revealed by some references found in the National Archives of Costa Rica to women publicly accused by husbands or male partners of "unnatural" conduct with other women. Due to the lack of research on the subject, the existing information is insufficient to draw conclusions about the fate of these women; however, considering the rigid Catholic values and morals that prevailed in the region, most likely those accusations had severe social consequences for them.

During the first decades of the twentieth century, the intellectual classes in Central America opened up for the first time to lesbian expressions in the arts and literature. In the 1920s and 1930s, even the well-reputed journal *Repertorio Americano* (American Repertoire)—published in Costa Rica but widely distributed in all Latin America—featured essays and poems with very open lesbian content. Thus, in this so-far unique historical period, lesbian artists and intellectuals found a space to discuss their lifestyle and express their love for other women.

This situation did not last very long, however. For most of the twentieth century, Central America experienced a severe political and economic crisis, and the vast majority of the population—with the exception of that of Costa Rica—has been denied minimal civil and democratic rights. During the 1970s and 1980s, countries such as Nicaragua, El Salvador, and Guatemala were torn by war and violence. Honduras was occupied by three nonnational armies; Panama was invaded by the United States Army; and the Costa Rican economy drastically deteriorated as a result of the political conditions in the region. The conflicts and widespread violation of human rights in much of Central America persisted well into the 1990s. Yet, by the mid-1990s, a wave of democratic elections and the signing of peace accords in countries such as El Salvador and Guatemala restored a climate of political calm in the area.

## Contemporary Conditions

In spite of the harsh political environment, lesbian life and lesbian communities exist in every country. The size and complexity of these communities are closely related to the size and complexity of the society itself. In that sense, Costa Rica has a larger and more complex lesbian community than the other countries. The economic and political climate has, nevertheless, made it very difficult for lesbians in every country to create and develop their communities and to have an independent life. In Central America, privacy is largely unknown, except for the members of the very small upper classes. The high levels of unemployment, resulting from the critical social conditions, make it almost impossible for many lesbians, particularly young ones, to find jobs that would allow them to live independently. Furthermore, the lack of adequate housing, which in some countries affects up to 70 percent of the population, makes it very difficult for lesbians to find or afford housing of their own. Often lesbians must remain embedded in family life and, therefore, practically unable to avoid supervision.

As a result of the lack of privacy, on occasion the family and even the neighbors are aware of someone's lesbianism, and she might be allowed to bring female friends to the house. Yet, in the majority of these cases, the situation is unofficial and unspeakable, and open expressions of affection are overtly censored. Very often, revelation of lesbianism is the basis for expulsion from the home. This is a critical and contradictory issue. On the one hand, the family is one of the primary sources of oppression for lesbians in Central America, but, on the other, in these societies the family is a central economic unit and relevant for the survival of its members, particularly in times of economic and political crisis. Thus, while expulsion from the home provides lesbians with more freedom to live their lives openly, it also implies the loss of the social security that the family offers.

Other important sources of oppression for lesbians in this region are the Catholic Church and traditional gender roles that operate very strongly in the local culture. Furthermore, in spite of modern psychology, lesbians must still face the myth that their sexual orientation and lifestyle are pathological. The intolerance and prejudice that prevail in Central America might be reinforced by the fact that, until the 1990s, the issue of lesbian rights was not part of the local political culture, not even among feminists, in most cases. Even more, some political parties, including leftist ones, openly prohibit lesbian and homosexual participation in their organizations. Other "progressive" parties and revolutionary movements tolerate the presence of lesbians as long as they keep their sexual orientation a private matter. While some lesbians have occupied high-ranking positions in public office in Central America, their sexual identity is never disclosed, which makes them invisible as lesbians to the general public.

Lesbian life is, therefore, mostly contained within small circles, whose boundaries are clearly defined by class and ethnicity. But despite their social-class or ethnic backgrounds, lesbians in Central America lack open social spaces to meet. The few predominantly lesbian bars that exist in the region are concentrated in San Jose, Costa Rica. Outside San Jose, there is only one lesbian-friendly bar in Tegucigalpa, Honduras, but it is a closed-door place, located in a dangerous area, and opens only during the weekends. In general, lesbian bars cannot be considered completely secure places in Central America. Even in Costa Rica, where lesbian bars have existed since the 1980s, they are still the constant targets of police harassment. In a single night, uniformed and nonuniformed police officers may come into a bar up to three or four times. Even if they do not do anything, their presence in the bar is threatening. As a result of the lack of open and safe social spaces, informal networks sustain most lesbian life and constitute the primary basis of support and affirmation for lesbians. Many lesbians rely mainly on those networks to establish their relationships and to meet with their friends.

In the 1980s, as a result of the growing feminist movement in the region and the influence of foreigners or nationals who had lived abroad, lesbians began to form the first organized groups. In general, these groups were small and took the form of consciousness-raising or support groups. That is, they did not develop into a social movement for lesbian rights. As stated before, the conditions in Central America are difficult for lesbians and even more difficult for such a movement to arise. Even in Costa Rica, the most advanced democracy in the area, lesbians' attempts to organize politically have been shattered. In 1990, the only local lesbian group at the time, Las Entendidas (Those Who Understand), directly experienced the negative consequences of hosting a regional meeting of lesbian feminists in Costa Rica. Confident in the country's democratic discourse, Las Entendidas agreed to organize the Second Latin American and the Caribbean Lesbian-Feminist Encuentro (meeting). When the news about the meeting came out, public outrage—orchestrated by the Catholic Church and right-wing groups—prompted the government to prohibit the conference and to ban lesbians from entering the country. The meeting was not canceled, but the government's discriminatory and antidemocratic stand obliged the organizers to change the meeting's dates and to move it to a secret location.

Although the meeting was held, it ended chaotically a day early when the place was attacked by men in the middle of the night. Thus, not only were the lesbians denied the right to meet—a right that is granted in the Costa Rican Constitution—but they also suffered overt repression. Nobody was injured in the attack, but the intimidation produced such levels of fear and insecurity among the members of Las Entendidas that the group disintegrated shortly after the conference.

Despite the adverse conditions, lesbians continue to form groups in practically every country. For the most part, these groups remain small and outside the public arena. Nonetheless, showing a new development in the process of building organization, the first network of gays and lesbians of Central America was created in 1996 in a meeting held in Guatemala City. The main goals of this network (Asociacion Regional Centroamericana de Gays y Lesbianas: ARCEGAL) are the promotion of lesbian and gay rights in the region and the construction of a better social and political environment for gays and lesbians.            *Montserrat Sagot*

### Bibliography

Cruz, Paquita. "The Lesbian Feminist Group 'Las Entendidas.'" In *The Costa Rican Women's Movement: A Reader*. Ed. Ilse Leitinger. Pittsburgh: University of Pittsburgh Press, 1997, pp. 147–152.

Las Entendidas. *Memoria de un Encuentro Inolvidable: Segundo Encuentro Lesbico-Feminista de America Latina y el Caribe* (Memoirs of an Unforgettable Meeting: Second Latin American and Caribbean Lesbian Feminist Meeting). San Jose, Costa Rica: Imprenta Carcemo, 1991.

Quesada, Noemi. "Erotismo en la Religion Azteca" (Eroticism in the Aztec Religion). *Revista Universidad de Mexico* 28 (1974), 16–19.

***See also*** Encuentros de Lesbianas

### Chambers, Jane (1937–1983)

American playwright and pioneer in writing theatrical works with openly lesbian characters. Born Carolyn Jane Chambers in Columbia, South Carolina, she was brought up in Orlando, Florida, attended Rollins College in Winter Park, Florida, for two years, and studied acting for one year at the Pasadena Playhouse in California. In 1956, she moved to New York City, where she landed roles in off-Broadway productions and worked as a reporter for theatrical trade papers. From 1964 to 1966, Chambers was employed as a writer and on-air personality at WMTW-TV in Poland Spring, Maine. She stayed in Maine for two more years as the director of avocation at the Poland Spring Job Corps Center. Returning to the New York area in 1969, Chambers continued working for the Job Corps and enrolled in an independent study program run by Vermont's Goddard College, from which she received a bachelor's degree in 1971. While in the Goddard program, she met Beth Allen, who became her lifelong companion and manager.

Chambers's writing began attracting attention in the early 1970s. Her civil rights play *Christ in a Treehouse* was broadcast on Connecticut Educational Television in 1971. The following year, her play *Tales of the Revolution and Other American Fables* was produced at the Eugene O'Neill Theatre in New London, Connecticut. Chambers was a founding member of the Women's Interart Center in New York City, where her plays *Random Violence* (1973), *Mine!* (1974), and *The Wife* (1974) were first presented. Another Chambers play, *A Late Snow* (1974), a comedy about five women snowbound in a mountain cabin, was produced at Playwrights Horizons in New York City. Generally considered Chambers's best play is *Last Summer at Bluefish Cove* (West Side Mainstage, New York City, 1980), a portrait of a tightly knit summer community of lesbian friends. Though suffering from a brain tumor that would eventually take her life, Chambers wrote and directed the comedy *My Blue Heaven* (Shandol Theatre, New York City, 1981). Her play *The Quintessential Image* was produced posthumously on a double bill with *In Her Own Words*, a biographical portrait compiled from her writings (Courtyard Playhouse, New York City, 1989).

Chambers wrote for a general audience and thought that the use of homosexual characters did not diminish the universal applicability or emotional truth of her plays. She was also the author of two novels (*Burning* [1978], and *Chasin' Jason* [1987]) and a collection of poetry (*Warrior at Rest* [1984]) and was a staff writer for the television daytime drama *Search for Tomorrow* (1973–1974).    *Mary C. Kalfatovic*

**Bibliography**

Hoffman, William, ed. *Gay Plays: The First Collection*. New York: Avon, 1979.

Landau, Penny M. "Jane Chambers." In *Notable Women in the American Theatre*. Ed. Alice M. Robinson. Westport, Conn.: Greenwood, 1989, pp. 117–119.

———. "Jane Chambers: In Memoriam." *Women and Performance* 1:2 (Winter 1984), 55–57.

Sisley, Emily L. "Notes on Lesbian Theatre." *Drama Review* 25:1 (March 1981), 47–56.

***See also*** Theater and Drama, Contemporary

## Charke, Charlotte (1713–1760)

English author. Charlotte Charke was also famous for performing male roles onstage and frequently cross-dressed in private life. Estranged from her father, Colley Cibber (1671–1757), Charke supported herself as an actress but also worked in male guise as a valet, a waiter, and a pastry cook. She is best known for *A Narrative of the Life of Mrs. Charlotte Charke* (1755), *Henry Dumont* (1756), and *The Art of Management* (1735).

Charke wrote in her *Narrative*: "I confess myself an odd mortal . . . and I am certain there is no one in the world more fit than myself to be laughed at." Her "oddity," her rejection of conventional feminine behavior, and her delight in jokes, such as aping her father's mannerisms upon the stage, got her into trouble throughout her life. At seventeen, she married Richard Charke, who deserted her and her infant daughter to immigrate to Jamaica. Charke was hard pressed to support her child, although she enjoyed success on the stage until the Licensing Act of 1737 made it difficult for actors to find work.

Faced with mounting debts, Charke called herself "Mr. Brown," explaining that she was "then, for some substantial reasons, en Cavalier." She married John Sacheverell in 1746 but makes no mention of living with him. Around 1747, she began to travel with another woman. They appeared together as "Mr. and Mrs. Brown," and Charke referred to her "sincere Friendship" for her companion. It is not clear how long this relationship lasted, but Charke seems to have died alone and in extreme poverty.

Scholars have disputed the reasons for Charke's cross-dressing. Charke considered becoming a female husband, explaining how a young heiress would have married her, but she claimed that conscience determined her not to go through with the hoax. When another female employer fell for her as "Mr. Brown," Charke treated it as a joke. Faderman (1981) questions her for taking this stance only a few years after a real female husband, Mary Hamilton, was whipped and imprisoned for fraud. Straub (1991) argues that Charke is " 'somewhere else' on the field of sexual possibility, but cannot or will not specify where." Yet Moore (1991) argues that, for Charke, the "pleasures and powers of cross-dressing become more explicitly sexualized" and that her "impoverished representation" of the relationship with "Mrs. Brown" "invites—or coerces—us to read between the lines" to discern a lesbian sensibility. Maureen Duffy (1933–) cites Charke's *Narrative* in her lesbian novel, *The Microcosm* (1966).

*Elizabeth Wahl*

## Bibliography

Donoghue, Emma. *Passions Between Women: British Lesbian Culture, 1668–1801*. London: Scarlet, 1993, 97–100, 164–167.

Faderman, Lillian. *Surpassing the Love of Men: Romantic Friendship and Love Between Women from the Renaissance to the Present*. New York: Morrow, 1981.

Mackie, Erin. "Desperate Measures: The Narratives of the Life of Mrs. Charlotte Charke." *English Literary History* 58 (1991), 841–865.

Moore, Lisa. " 'She Was Too Fond of Her Mistaken Bargain': The Scandalous Relations of Gender and Sexuality in Feminist Theory." *Diacritics* 21 (1991), 89–101.

Morgan, Fidelis, with Charlotte Charke. *The Well-Known Troublemaker: A Life of Charlotte Charke*. London: Faber and Faber, 1988.

Straub, Kristina. "The Guilty Pleasures of Female Theatrical Cross-Dressing and the Autobiography of Charlotte Charke." In *Body Guards: The Cultural Politics of Gender Ambiguity*. Ed. Julia Epstein and Kristina Straub. New York and London: Routledge, 1991, pp. 142–166.

*See also* Cross-Dressing; Passing Women

## Cherry Grove, New York

Summer community in the New York metropolitan area that is different from every other resort in the world in that gay men and lesbians are the majority. Located on an Atlantic barrier beach called Fire Island, the "Grove" consists of about 275 houses, a small commercial center, and a ruggedly beautiful ocean beach.

Lesbian numbers and power in the gay male–dominated Grove have fluctuated. From the 1930s to the 1960s, a distinguished and well-off group of lesbians known as "ladies" were outnumbered by men of similar upper-middle-class backgrounds by at least five to one yet still played important roles as hostesses and in the community theater. Both genders shared a common identification with the theater, but women were jokingly referred to (and referred to themselves) as "Lithuanians," suggesting an exotic group from some faraway land.

As capital and infrastructure made the Grove a more accessible resort, a diverse population of gay men flooded in. The "ladies" retreated, and a new group of working-class "dykes" and their femmes constituted a small and rather beleaguered minority from 1960 to about 1973. During this period of growing gay nationalism, promiscuous and ubiquitous male-male sexual desire was increasingly seen as the common bond between gays, a formulation that excluded lesbians far more than their being "Lithuanians" had done. Yet, during the 1970s and 1980s, lesbians gained footholds, and, by 1987, in a gritty, gradual, and individual process, they had become business and home owners, theater technicians and actors, and leaders in the volunteer fire department.

As queens (in-group slang with connotations of both effeminacy and grandeur), gay men assumed the subject position in a coherent camp sensibility that acted to marginalize, or even obliterate, lesbians symbolically: Lesbians were rarely allowed any representation as a group within the community *and* were virtually never allowed to represent the community as a whole. This exclusion was effected by gay men's far greater numbers and power, by social pressure, and by outright discrimination. Given the overwhelming hostility of the surrounding straight world and, during the 1970s and 1980s, of lesbian feminism toward the butch-femme system, which predominated in the Grove, lesbians were glad to be tolerated in a physically safe space that supported the existence of same-gender love, and they accepted playing second fiddle.

Around 1988, as gay male predominance was being undermined by illnesses and deaths from aging and from AIDS, lesbians began coming in very large numbers. In general, these newer arrivals were younger and had a more aggressive attitude toward gender equality. By the mid-1990s, lesbians had become at least half of all renters, prompting tensions between women and men that culminated in the election of Joan Van Ness, a homeowner prominent in community affairs, as Homecoming Queen, a post that had always been held by a gay man in drag. At the end of the century, the Grove seemed to be moving toward greater inclusion of women and people of color, within a free-market framework.

*Esther Newton*

## Bibliography

Newton, Esther. *Cherry Grove, Fire Island: Sixty Years in America's First Gay and Lesbian Town*. Boston: Beacon, 1993.

———. "Dick(less) Tracy and the Homecoming Queen: Lesbian Power and Representation in Gay Male Cherry Grove." In *Inventing Lesbian Cultures in America*. Ed. Ellen Lewin. Boston: Beacon, 1996, pp. 161–193.

———. "Just One of the Boys: Lesbians in Cherry Grove, 1960–1989." In *The Lesbian and Gay Studies Reader.* Ed. Henry Abelove, Michèle Aina Barale, and David M. Halperin. New York: Routledge, 1993, pp. 528–541.

*See also* Camp; Recreation; Tourism and Guidebooks

## Chicago, Illinois

Major midwestern metropolis with a long and distinguished lesbian and gay history, including the first homosexual rights organization in the United States (1924).

Chicago's documented history of women-loving-women dates to within twenty years of its incorporation as a city in 1832. Passing women served in the government and in the military, and some married other women. Nineteenth-century police records, sporting-life journals, and court documents note lesbians among the madams and working girls in the bordellos and parlor houses of the wide-open red-light districts of the Levee, the Patch, and Custom House Place, which flourished until prostitution was made illegal in 1910. Private papers of doctors and medical journals record society matrons, servants, and young women of higher education involved in passionate physical relationships.

The World's Columbian Exhibition of 1893 made Chicago a cultural capital. Lesbian artists, writers, and inventors exhibited at the fair, including the world's foremost woman sculptor, Harriet Hosmer (1830–1908). Her statue of Isabella, Columbus's queen, was at the center of a storm created by suffragists, who refused to exhibit women's work separately from their male counterparts in the Women's Building.

Many prominent women are associated with Chicago's lesbian past. The national settlement-house movement would be patterned on Hull House, the pioneer efforts of social reformer and Nobel laureate Jane Addams (1860–1935). Willa Cather (1873–1947) lived in Chicago long enough to be able to write of the city in two novels, including *The Song of the Lark.* Margaret Anderson (1886–1973) became a leader of the modernist movement during the waning years of the Chicago Renaissance as she and her lover, Jane Heap (1887–1964), made the *Little Review* the magazine of anarchy, art, and free verse. In 1915, Edith Lees Ellis (1861–1916) gave a lecture at Orchestra Hall that is likely the first public defense of homosexuality in the United States. Loie Fuller (1862–1928), called "the Electric Fairy," danced at Louis Sullivan's (1856–1924) magnificent Auditorium Theater, where decades later lesbians in the military would swing together when it was converted to a USO in World War II. Oak Park resident Jeannette Foster (1895–1981) came to study and get her Ph.D. from the University of Chicago before writing her magnum opus, *Sex Variant Women in Literature* (1956).

In the 1920s, African American lesbians mostly partied in private homes; passing women would take their partners to the African American neighborhood, Bronzeville, and "Black Belt" jazz clubs. Trumpeter Tiny Davis (n.d.) and her lover would open The Gay Spot, where hot music thrived until the club was demolished to make room for the crosstown expressway. Later, women such as Pat McCombs (n.d.) would host floating parties at private clubs, bars, or hotels for "women of color and their friends." In the 1950s, Lorraine Hansberry's (1930–1965) father challenged Chicago's racially restrictive housing covenants, providing her with material for her play, *A Raisin in the Sun* (1959).

By the 1930s, white "women who preferred men's attire" partied at private clubs, bars (sometimes raided), and predominately male drag balls. Some even were reported to have been married by a Bronzeville minister. Their more conservatively clad counterparts opened galleries, bookstores, and tea shops in the bohemian Towertown area. The Depression Era saw a proliferation of "rent parties," which would continue into the 1960s as private gatherings among friendship groups. Couples who came to the city in the 1930s and 1940s to attend universities or work in defense plants tell of partying with close gay male friends rather than expose their relationships to the challenges of all-women soirees.

Civil rights attorney and law Professor Pearl Hart (1890–1978) and lesbian novelist Valerie Taylor (1913–1997) were among the founding members of Mattachine Midwest, incorporated in 1965. A small suburban Daughters of Bilitis chapter met briefly, but Mattachine Midwest was the only functioning, proactive rights group in the Midwest until the emergence of the gay liberation movement in the late 1960s. Attorney Renee Hanover (1926–), Hart's student and later law partner, fought and won dozens of gay and lesbian rights cases beginning in the 1960s.

By the time the civil rights movement and women's liberation took hold in the city, in the second half of the 1960s, an active lesbian bar culture had developed. Lesbians in the Women's Caucus of Chicago Gay Liberation challenged the racism and antiactivist stance of most bars with boycotts and legal action. In 1971, a wholly independent group, Chicago Lesbian Liberation, was drawing seventy or more women to each meeting. In that year, the newspaper *Lavender Woman* began, later gaining national circulation until its demise in 1976.

The 1970s was Chicago's lesbian decade. The Lesbian Feminist Center housed a bookstore, a counseling and referral service, and the New Alexandria Library for Lesbian Wimmin (founded by librarian and bibliographer J.R. Roberts). From 1974 through 1978, the annual Lesbian Writers Conference drew participants and presenters from all over the country and Canada. The first annotated bibliography on lesbian literature, *Women Loving Women*, was an outgrowth of the conference. Colleen Monahan and Elaine Jacobs produced the first nationally distributed lesbian documentary film, Lavender, in 1971. Mountain Moving Coffeehouse brought every major lesbian musician, comic, and storyteller to the community from the mid-1970s throughout the 1990s. Restaurants, presses, a theater group, newspapers, and a dozen lesbian-owned businesses all thrived during this decade.

The growing distance between the principally separatist lesbian community and the older, mostly male groups working on city and state gay rights initiatives came to a head when two suburban women applied for a marriage license and were arrested after staging a sit-in at the County Clerk's Office in October 1975. Considering the action deleterious and ill timed, the old-line groups denounced it in the mainstream press. The resulting discourse between men's and women's groups, political activists and separatists, resulted in the formation of the Chicago Coalition, an inclusive, broad-based representation of businesses and organizations with a clear agenda aimed at gay rights legislation.

In 1991, the City of Chicago inaugurated the country's first Gay and Lesbian Hall of Fame, into which the mayor inducts yearly an average of five women and five men who have made a "significant contribution with far reaching effects on the quality of life for Chicago's lesbian and gay community and the City of Chicago."

In the 1990s, women's health issues were taken on by lesbians in the Howard Brown Memorial Clinic; the Lesbian Community Cancer Project was formed; and more than one hundred leaders of the lesbian community met to create the Lesbian Agenda, pushing for visibility in political, health, and rights organizations.

In October 1997, Chicago neighbor Oak Park became Illinois's first municipality to enact a domestic partnership registry; this followed the April election of longtime Illinois, Cook County, and Chicago activist Joanne Trapani (1949–) to the Village Board of Managers—the first open lesbian to win municipal office in the state. In 1994 Oak Park, and in 1997 the City of Chicago, granted domestic partnership benefits to their municipal employees.

*Marie J. Kuda*

### Bibliography

Brody, Michal, ed. *Are We There Yet? A Continuing History of Lavender Woman, a Chicago Lesbian Newspaper, 1971–1976*. Iowa City: Aunt Lute, 1985.

Darnell, Don. "Martie." *Chicago Tribune Magazine* (June 20, 1991), 20–22.

Katz, Jonathan. *Gay American History*. New York: Crowell, 1976.

Kuda, Marie J. "Chicago Gay and Lesbian History: From Prairie Settlement to WWII." *Outlines* 8:1 (1964), 25–32.

———. "Chicago Gay and Lesbian History: Special Pull-Out Section. *Outlines* 9:2 (1995), 27–30.

Sutton, Roger. "Renee Hanover." In *Hearing Us Out: Voices from the Gay/Lesbian Community*. Boston: Little, Brown, 1994, pp. 93–101.

**See also** Addams, Jane; Anderson, Margaret Carolyn; Bars; Cather, Willa; Daughters of Bilitis; Female Support Networks; Foster, Jeannette Howard; Hansberry, Lorraine (Vivian); Taylor, Valerie

## Children

Although prevalent stereotypes suggest that lesbians do not become mothers, there are almost certainly

C millions of lesbian mothers in the United States today. Most became parents in the context of heterosexual marriages before coming out as lesbians, but increasing numbers are also believed to be becoming parents after having come out. Though other routes to parenthood, such as adoption and foster care, are also involved, the largest increases in numbers of lesbians who are becoming parents have occurred through donor insemination. This trend has been seen as significant enough by some observers that it has been termed a "lesbian baby boom." In contrast to the stereotype, then, the numbers of lesbian mothers, already substantial, seem to be on the rise.

## Issues in Child Custody
Judicial and legislative bodies both in the United States and abroad have often denied child custody and visitation rights on the basis of parental sexual orientation. Courts, in particular, have sometimes assumed that lesbians are mentally ill and, hence, not fit to be parents, that lesbians are less maternal than heterosexual women and, hence, do not make good mothers, and that lesbians' relationships with sexual partners leave little time for parenting behavior.

Findings from systematic research have failed to confirm any of these judicial concerns. The idea that homosexuality constitutes a mental illness or disorder has long been repudiated by every major psychological and psychiatric professional organization. Lesbian and heterosexual women have been found not to differ markedly either in their overall mental health or in their approaches to child rearing, nor have lesbians' romantic relationships been found to detract from their ability to care for children. Thus, empirical studies have revealed no association between sexual orientation and psychological characteristics relevant to parenting.

Judicial decision making and public policies in many jurisdictions have also sometimes reflected various concerns about the well-being of children raised by lesbian mothers. Judges have voiced fears about the development of children's sexual identity, about other aspects of children's personal and social development, and about the relationships of children reared by lesbian mothers. Reflecting common prejudices, judges have sometimes even expressed concern that children living with lesbian mothers would be at heightened risk of sexual abuse or be more likely to grow up to be gay or lesbian themselves (an outcome that such judges apparently view as negative).

There is a substantial body of social-science research relevant to these concerns, but it has produced no evidence that the development of children with lesbian mothers is impaired in any signficant way relative to that among children of heterosexual parents in otherwise comparable circumstances. Indeed, the available evidence suggests that home environments provided by lesbian mothers are as likely as those provided by heterosexual parents to support and enable children's social and psychological growth.

## Children in Lesbian Families
There is tremendous diversity among families headed by lesbian mothers. Sources of diversity include economic circumstances and the racial, ethnic, religious, and cultural identities of lesbian mothers and their children. Other significant sources of diversity may include the circumstances of a child's conception, the social and legal climate of the environment in which a child grows up, and the degree to which the family configuration into which a child was born or adopted has remained intact or undergone change throughout the child's lifetime. Thus, factors such as parents' psychological well-being, parents' involvement in stable romantic relationships, and the degree of conflict among important adults in a child's life might all be expected to be important predictors of children's adjustment in homes that are headed by lesbian mothers.

The scant social-science literature devoted to diversity among children with lesbian mothers suggests that children of lesbian mothers, like other children, are better off when their parents are in good mental health, when they live in a supportive milieu, and when they are in regular contact with grandparents and other adults outside their immediate household. Among children with two lesbian mothers, available evidence suggests that those whose parents have a harmonious and satisfying couple relationship, little interparental conflict, and a relatively even division of child-care responsibilities are likely to show the most favorable development.

From the standpoint of social-science research, much remains to be done to understand similarities among, as well as differences between, families headed by lesbian and heterosexual parents and to comprehend the impact of such factors on child development. Information is needed about the many forms of diversity among families headed by lesbian mothers and about the ways in which mothers and children manage the multiple identities available to them. Information is also needed about the nature of stresses and supports encountered by children of lesbian mothers—in the parents' families of origin (with grandparents and other relatives), among parents' and children's friends, at school, and in their larger communities. Research is needed to explore the pains and pleasures of growing up in a lesbian-headed home and to identify the costs and benefits of court-ordered separations between children and their lesbian mothers. In addition, it would be useful to learn more about the ways in which effects of heterosexism and homophobia are felt by lesbian mothers and their children, and about the ways in which they cope with ignorance and prejudice that they encounter. Although many of these topics have been discussed in first-person narratives about life in families headed by lesbian mothers, they had not, as of the late 1990s, been the subject of much systematic research.

Research on children of lesbian mothers can be seen as having come to a significant turning point. Having begun to address heterosexist and homophobic concerns represented in psychological theory, judicial opinion, and popular prejudice, researchers are now in a position also to explore a broader range of issues raised by lesbian-mother families. Results of future work in this area have the potential to increase our knowledge about children growing up in nontraditional families, stimulate innovations in theoretical understanding of human development, and inform legal rulings and public policies relevant to children of lesbian mothers.

*Charlotte J. Patterson*

## Bibliography

Patterson, Charlotte J. "Children of Lesbian and Gay Parents." *Child Development* 63 (1992), 1025–1042.

———. "Children of the Lesbian Baby Boom: Behavioral Adjustment, Self-Concepts, and Sex-Role Identity." In *Contemporary Perspectives on Gay and Lesbian Psychology: Theory, Research, and Applications*. Ed. Beverly Greene and Gregory Herek. Beverly Hills, Calif.: Sage, 1994, pp. 156–175.

———. "Families of the Lesbian Baby Boom: Parents' Division of Labor and Children's Adjustment." *Developmental Psychology* 31 (1995), 115–123.

Rafkin, Louise, ed. *Different Mothers: Sons and Daughters of Lesbians Talk About Their Lives*. Pittsburgh: Cleis, 1990.

Tasker, Fiona, and Susan Golombok. "Adults Raised as Children in Lesbian Families." *American Journal of Orthopsychiatry* 65 (1995), 203–215.

*See also* Adopton; Custody Litigation; Donor Insemination; Law and Legal Institutions; Mothers, Lesbian

## Chile

Country in the southwest of South America with a population of about twelve million. A large majority of lesbians and gay men are closeted somewhere in the thick fabric of heterosexual expectations still present in Chilean society. However, this has not meant silence or passivity on the part of many gay men and lesbians who have decided to "come out," challenging in this way the public panic over moral issues created not only by religious institutions, but also by the state, formal education, and the media.

It was in this context of defiance and resistance that the first publicly known Chilean lesbian organization, Colectiva Lesbica Feminista *Ayuquelen* (Lesbian Feminist Collective *Ayuquelen:* a Mapuche [indigenous] name meaning, roughly, to be happy), was born in 1980 in the capital, Santiago. It started in reaction to the homophobic attitudes and public indifference that had led to the killing of a *tortillera* (a derogatory label for lesbian women in Chile but adopted by some as a challenge to homophobic language) by a man who had kicked her to death with total impunity.

The fact that a handful of women created a lesbian feminist group would probably be considered an ordinary event by other similar groups around the world were it not that this happened in the 1980s, during political and social riots against the military dictatorship that had come to power in 1973. *Ayuquelen* was advertised nationally, in part through the controversy created by the public coming out of their two leaders on television. For some time, *Ayuquelen* contributed to the Chilean women's movement by sponsoring workshops and generally helping create awareness of issues of gender and sexuality within feminist and other politically active women's groups. The presence of *Ayuquelen* added another dimension to these organizations. However, differences in political beliefs and strategies between *Ayuquelen* and the more powerful feminist organization La Morada (The Shelter or Home) resulted in the gradual marginalization of the former. This marginalization happened not only within explicitly feminist groups, but also within other women's organizations. As a result, *Ayuquelen* finally stopped its public actions, although two members maintained an address for

**C**

other lesbians to contact them from different parts of Chile.

The fact that their postal box continued to be advertised helped other lesbians realize that they were not alone and, although in the closet at first, a second group was created in 1990, this time in Concepción, an industrial and university city south of Santiago, where *Ayuquelen* had been born. This new group, called LEA (Lesbianas En Accion: Lesbians in Action), attracted women from different educational, class, and cultural backgrounds. Their initial purpose was not only to break out of their isolation, but also to discuss violence between lesbian couples. These initial aims expanded to other topics of interest to lesbians within a society badly damaged by the physical and ideological enforcement of military rule. LEA shared its political growth with a group of young gay men, Taller Ser (Workshop on Selfhood), who had been meeting for some time within the safe confines of a nongovernmental agency (NGO) that had as a primary aim the prevention of sexually transmitted diseases such as AIDS. This organization, CEPSS (Centro de Educacion y Salud Social y Sida: Center for Education, Social Health, and AIDS), along with LEA and Taller Ser, organized the first Encuentro Nacional de Homosexuales (National Homosexual Conference) in 1991 in Coronel, a mining town near Concepción. Two groups of gay men from Santiago were also among the people who attended this Encuentro, at the same time that a national Feminist Encuentro was being held in the seaside city of Valparaiso.

In June 1992, LEA and Colectiva *Ayuquelen* (which at that point had reorganized itself and was active once more) held their first Encuentro Nacional de Mujeres Lesbianas (National Lesbian Conference) in the suburbs of Santiago. This highly successful Encuentro was attended by women from all over the country and marked an important point in lesbian history. Since then, both LEA and Colectiva *Ayuquelen,* in conjunction with gay men's organizations and groups, have been active in the promotion and defense of gay and lesbian rights in Chile.                    *Consuelo Rivera Fuentes*

### Bibliography

Gaviola, Edda, Eliana Largo, and Sandra Palestro. *Una Historia Necesaria: Mujeres en Chile, 1973–1990* (A Necessary History: Women in Chile, 1973–1990). Santiago: Aki and Aora, 1994.

Rivera Fuentes, Consuelo. "They Do Not Dance Alone: The Women's Movements in Latin America." In *Women, Power, and Resistance: An Introduction to Women's Studies.* Ed. Tess Cosslett, Alison Easton, and Penny Summerfield. London: Open University Press, 1996, pp. 250–262.

———. "Todas Locas, Todas Vivas, Todas Libres: Chilean Lesbians, 1980–1995." In *Amazon to Zami: Towards a Global Lesbian Feminism.* Ed. Monika Reinfelder. London: Cassell, 1996, pp. 138–151.

*See also* International Organizations

## China

Largest country in Asia, and most populous in the world, with a cultural tradition thousands of years old. Until the late nineteenthth century, when the threat of cultural extinction at the hands of Western imperialist powers motivated Chinese reformers to advocate formal education for women for the sake of national salvation, literacy for women was not considered a virtue in China—whereas filial piety, absolute devotion to family, and chastity were given full state and societal support and promotion. Thus, in China's long history as a center of civilization in East Asia, with a few notable exceptions Chinese women did not (and were not able to) leave behind written records of their lives and thought.

### History

Writing a history of lesbian existence in China before the twentieth century is, therefore, difficult. There is no lesbian counterpart to the richly documented male homosexual tradition in China; however, Ko's (1994) study of erotically evocative poems about female bodies written by several seventeenth-century women poets suggests the existence of a female homoerotic sensibility. The poets were married women of the gentry class, and many of their objects of desire were courtesans and entertainers. This tradition continued into the nineteenth century, as evidenced by the poetry of Wu Zao (ca. 1800s).

Shen Fu (1763–?), an eighteenth-century scholar, recorded in his autobiographical work, *Six Chapters of a Floating Life* (1983), the strong affectional bond between his late wife and a singsong girl with whom he had also become infatuated. When he teased his wife with "Are you trying to imitate Liweng's *Pitying the Fragrant Companion*?" he was alluding to a play of the same name by maverick seventeenth-century writer Li Yu. It is a story about two women (one of whom was married) who love each other so much that they perform a wedding ceremony for themselves. The married woman conspires successfully to have her husband accept her lover as a concubine, and the two women live together happily ever after. Shen's reference strongly suggests that, at least among the gentry class, the play had become closely identified with lesbian desire.

Looking for lesbians in Chinese history, one promising area of investigation is the nature of friendships that bonded together many of the early Chinese feminists. One notable example is that between anti-Manchu revolutionary Qiu Jin (1875?–1907) and Wu Zhiying (active ca. 1900–1910), who was a poet, renowned calligrapher, and reformer in her own right. In 1904, on the seventh day of the Chinese New Year, Qiu Jin and Wu Zhiying exchanged a formal pledge of eternal friendship, an occasion that Qiu marked with a poem called "Orchid Verse." The enterprising historian might want to consider the meaning of "Orchid Verse," asking if the title was inspired by the Golden Orchid sworn sisterhood of marriage resisters in South China.

## Marriage Resisters

As a social phenomenon, marriage resistance arose from the mid-nineteenth century through the 1930s in three districts of the Pearl River Delta, a region in South China, near the city of Guangdong (Canton). Anthropologist Topley (1975) has characterized it as a "movement." It has been estimated that, at its height in the early twentieth century, the number of marriage resisters neared one hundred thousand. The origin of marriage resistance is unclear, but Stockard's research (1986) suggests that it might have evolved from the custom of "delayed transfer marriage" that permits brides to continue to reside in their natal homes for a period of time after the wedding ceremony. This custom was also peculiar to the Pearl River Delta area.

An entry in the 1853 edition of *Shunde County Gazetteer* reveals the length to which Golden Orchid members resisted living with their husbands or marriage altogether:

> Girls in the county form very close sisterhood with others in the same village. They do not want to marry, and if forced to

marry, they stay in their own families, where they enjoy few restrictions. They do not want to return to the husband's family, and some, if forced to return, commit suicide by drowning or hanging.

Their defiance of traditional roles incurred the wrath of conservative moralists. The 1904 antireform tract *Canon for Women* included a denunciation of the women of Golden Orchid (the compiler's commentary is indicated here by the use of brackets):

> Recently, there has developed a custom [this custom is deplorable] that is passed on from woman to woman. [Imitating and learning every step; forming Golden Orchid bonded sisterhood.] These women practice celibacy, vowing never to marry. [Blasphemous!] They refer to the husband's family as "cocoons." [They believe that father-in-law, mother-in-law, husband, children, etc. bind their bodies and deprive them of their freedom. The analogy "cocoon" therefore signifies suffocating bondage until death!]

It was female bonding that made marriage resistance deplorable to its critics. And it was lesbian sexuality and the possibility of an alternative family construction that frightened the moralists. The 1933 edition of the *Gazetteer of Chinese Customs* included the following in the entry on "Shunde women's Golden Orchid Sworn Sisterhood":

> Although the two women living together cannot be said to have the form/equipment of a man and a woman, they nonetheless enjoy the pleasure of male-female [intercourse]. Some say that they use friction or rubbing force, others say they use "mechanical devices.". . . They adopt a daughter to inherit their property. When the adopted daughter also forms Golden Orchid sworn sisterhood with another woman, the woman is treated like a daughter-in-law.

It is important to point out that the vow of celibacy was not intended to last a lifetime, nor was the

**C** vow necessarily taken in favor of lesbian sex. Sankar's (1985) research shows that some of the women yearned to join their husbands but feared their sworn sisters' wrath, as seen in a song sung by many of her informants, titled "The Lament of a Mh Lohk Ga Woman from Shun-te." Nonetheless, sexual relationships did develop among some of the sisters, and larger sisterhoods might have several couples.

Although marriage resistance as a movement dissipated in the 1930s in China, Golden Orchid sisters worked as domestic servants and nannies in Hong Kong and other Southeast Asian Chinese communities into the 1960s and even the 1970s. Often, upon retirement, they would live with other sisters in group homes that functioned like lay convents.

Golden Orchid sworn sisterhood continues to occupy a place in popular imagination. "Twin Bracelets" (1986?), a much-touted "Chinese lesbian story," is set in Wei'an County in Fujian Province. It describes a particular relationship between two women that is based partly on the marriage custom that, according to the author, is peculiar to the area. However, "Twin Bracelets," in spite of the enthusiastic response to it from lesbians of Chinese ancestry in the United States, is not a lesbian-positive story: Not only did one of the women commit suicide at the end of the story, but the postscript also reveals the author's own homophobic position.

## Contemporary Conditions

It is perhaps not surprising that, even in the late 1990s, there had yet to emerge a lesbian-positive literature in contemporary China. One notable exception is Anchee Min's *Red Azalea* (1994), in which she recalls with great poignancy her relationship with Yan, her company leader at a labor collective during the Cultural Revolution in the 1970s. Ruan Fang-fu, a sexologist who has done research on sexuality in China, characterizes the situation in the late twentieth century as "the dark age of homosexuality in modern China." He finds that lesbians in China are even more closeted than gay men and concludes: "It is clear that many Chinese lesbians do live painful lives, marred by fear and jealousy. But it is impossible to develop a complete and balanced picture of their lives under current conditions."

There are signs that conditions may be changing for the better at the end of the 1990s for lesbians and gay men in China. Faison (1997) of the *New York Times* reports a nascent, but increasingly open, gay life in major urban centers in China, where pa-

trons of places that cater to gay men do not seem to fear harassment by the police. Although Faison mentions lesbians here and there in the news story, the report focuses primarily on gay men. It remains uncertain whether and when a thriving lesbian subculture, like the one that exists in Taiwan, will come into its own in China.                                     *Vivien Ng*

### Bibliography

Faison, Seth. "Door to Tolerance Opens Partway as Gay Life Is Emerging in China." *New York Times,* September 2, 1997.

Ko, Dorothy. *Teachers of the Inner Chamber: Women and Culture in Seventeenth Century China*. Stanford, Calif.: Stanford University Press, 1994.

Ruan, Fang-fu. *Sex in China: Studies in Sexology in Chinese Culture*. New York: Plenum, 1991.

Sankar, Andrea. "Sisters and Brothers, Lovers and Enemies: Marriage Resistance in Southern Kwangtung." *Journal of Homosexuality* 11:3–4 (1985), 69–81.

Shen, Fu. *Six Chapters in a Floating Life*. New York: Penguin, 1983.

Stockard, Janice. *Daughters of the Canton Delta: Marriage Patterns and Economic Strategies in South China, 1860–1930*. Stanford, Calif.: Stanford University Press, 1986.

Topley, Marjorie. "Marriage Resistance in Rural Kwangtung." In *Women in Chinese Society*. Ed. Margery Wolf and Roxanne Witke. Stanford, Calif.: Stanford University Press, 1975, pp. 67–88.

*See also* Chinese Literature; Taiwan; Wu Zao

## Chinese Literature

While less conspicuous than the extensive literature on male homosexuality, writings on same-sex love between women have, nonetheless, formed part of the Chinese literary tradition from at least the seventeenth century onward. In surveying these varied writings, one can distinguish between three different periods, roughly 1600–1900 (early modern), 1900–1980 (modern), and 1980 onward (contemporary). At the beginning of each period, profound socioeconomic changes reconfigured discourses on power, gender, and sexuality, which, in turn, affected the literary representation of female homoeroticism.

Seventeenth-century China, especially the increasingly urbanized area around the lower reaches of the Yangtze, witnessed the increase in the number of affluent, educated, and leisured people. As it became a fashion among gentry families to educate their daughters, the number of women among the ranks of these sophisticated urbanites rose, with some women pioneering new careers, including itinerant teaching and commercial painting. A vibrant publishing industry catered to an expanding readership, supplying everything from sexually explicit fiction to collections of women's poetry. However, as sexuality continued to be phallocentrically structured, female homoeroticism remained invisible: It was neither "named" through a proper noun nor symbolized through reference to a classical figure (as was male homosexuality). The literary tradition conventionally portrayed women as mutual antagonists or fixated on mostly absent males; however, some innovative male-authored fiction did allow for the possibility of mutual fondness among women. In such fictional portrayals, same-sex love between women could be figured in various ways: as harmless physical play between women in anticipation of relations with a man, as a celebration of polygamous harmony among mutually infatuated female members of the same household, or as a fantasy of an all-female kingdom reproducing itself through magical dildos.

By contrast, the vast majority of early-modern Chinese women writers wrote in the classically respectable genre of autobiographical poetry. Among such female-authored poems, letters, and inscribed paintings (by, for example, Xu Yuan, Lu Qingzi, and Xue Susu [all late sixteenth–early seventeenth century]), passionate avowals of friendship among gentry women and, occasionally, between gentry women and courtesans outline another aspect of same-sex love. These writings appropriated the language derived from heterosexual romance to describe emotional and aesthetic appreciation of female friends.

In the period after 1900, China was profoundly transformed through a variety of political developments. In 1911, the emperor was dethroned and a republic declared. However, beset by internal divisions and colonial exploitation, China faced a profound identity crisis. The status of women became the subject of intense debate, as women's subordination and gender segregation in pre-1911 China came to be understood as one of the causes for China's weakness as a nation-state. Accordingly, the implementation of heterosexual relations informed by love and intimacy was thought to invigorate China politically and culturally. Such idealization of heterosexual love was buttressed by the concurrent pathologization of same-sex intimacy. In the 1910s and 1920s, Western sexological discourse was translated and embraced as scientific truth among the urban intelligentsia. In this context, female homosexuality was not only invented as a Chinese linguistic category, but was also constituted as a psychological or sexual perversion. Such a negative appraisal in popular and scientific venues also affected literary representations. Women authors, including Ding Ling (1904–1986) and Ling Shuhua (1904–1990), explored romantic friendships among "New Women" (urban, middle-class intellectuals), particularly in the context of newly founded women's schools, even as they carefully distanced their protagonists from intimations of physical passion. By contrast, male authors primarily represented lesbian sex as a form of titillating depravation, thus delineating the sanctioned limits of "New Womanhood."

In the period following the anti-Japanese and civil wars, post-1949 governments in both the Peoples Republic of China and Taiwan exerted tight control over the publication of anything that smacked of disloyalty to state and family. Only after political and economic liberalization in the 1980s and 1990s transformed the material and mental landscape of Chinese cities did representations of lesbianism resurface. While conservative sexology and family-centered values continued to dominate popular conceptions of lesbianism, feminist and lesbian activists began to circulate alternative perspectives, especially in Taiwan. There, a generation of self-avowedly lesbian writers, such as Hong Ling (1971–) and Chen Xue (1970–), began to experiment with new representations of lesbian existence. Their short stories, novellas, and novels are stylistically diverse, ranging from avant-garde "cyberpunk," to magic realism, to everyday documentation. While extremely varied in their approaches, these writers nonetheless seem intent on testing the limits of the collective imagination. While their writings are commodified through a mass market intent on sensational novelty, these literary texts appear to have succeeded in writing a complex, sympathetic, and material Chinese lesbian subject into existence.

*Patricia Sieber*

### Bibliography

Ko, Dorothy. *Teachers of the Inner Chambers: Women and Culture in Seventeenth Century*

China. Stanford, Calif.: Stanford University Press, 1994.

Sang, Tze-lang D. "The Emerging Lesbian: Female Same-Sex Desire in Modern Chinese Literature and Culture." Ph.D. diss., University of California, Berkeley, 1996.

Sieber, Patricia, ed. *Red Is Not the Only Color: Contemporary Chinese Writing on Love Between Women*. San Francisco: Cleis, 1998.

Vitiello, Giovanni. "The Fantastic Journey of an Ugly Boy: Homosexuality and Salvation in Late Ming Pornography." *Positions: East Asia Cultures Critique* 4:2 (1996), 291–320.

*See also* China; Taiwan; Wu Zao

## Choruses, Women's

In the mid-1970s, grass-roots women's choruses began to form, influenced by the "second wave" of feminism, the women's music movement, the folk revival of the 1960s, and gay and lesbian liberation. Motivated by a strong desire to sing, coupled with an urgency to create community and become politically active on the local level, these choruses attracted both lesbian and heterosexual women. In North America, Europe, and Australia, more than seventy such choirs are active.

All of the early women's choirs were created under the nurture and guidance of lesbians. Today, the choruses differ widely in makeup and diversity, and leadership and direction are shared by heterosexual and lesbian women. Some choirs have started and dissolved; many more are part of a loosely organized group called the Sister Singers Network. Some of the choruses are also a part of the GALA (Gay and Lesbian Association) Choruses network, an organization of men's, women's, and mixed choruses in North America that formed in the early 1980s.

The first women's choirs were started on the coasts. Roberta Kosse's Women Like Me (New York City) performed music exclusively by the young composer. Anna Crusis Women's Choir (Philadelphia, Pennsylvania), still active in the late 1990s, was started in fall of 1975 by Catherine Roma, and the LA Community Women's Chorus (Los Angeles, California) was started in early 1976 by Sue Fink.

There are all kinds of choirs in the women's choral movement, and the impulse that starts and sustains them varies from place to place. Some begin when a group of women gather to sing; others are founded by a single woman director or by a group of planners; in still other cases, a men's chorus in the area proves eager to have a partner chorus. Women's choruses vary in structure: Some use clear democratic majority rule, while others operate by consensus. Some choruses choose to stay a certain size, while others put no limit on how many may join. Some hold auditions; others are open to any woman who wants to sing. Some sing a popular-style repertoire, while others sing a wide variety of music. Some have no trouble deciding what to wear for concert garb; others have their most heated debates over dress.

In the mid-1970s, when many of these choirs began, their members were involved in reproductive-health issues, abortion rights, equal pay and workplace issues, the Equal Rights Amendment, the post-Stonewall movement for gay and lesbian civil rights, and/or the international peace movement. Thus, the choirs became the musical arm of the political activism of the singers. Their multifaceted mission statements speak of musical excellence and social change as complementary goals and objectives.

The repertoire of women's choruses is one of the most unusual characteristics of the whole movement. Music by women composers, ignored for many years, began to be unearthed by directors and musicologists. Some works were easily discarded because the texts proved to be inappropriate; others were meant for "unchanged voices" (boys) or for children. There has been a dearth of dramatic, moving, feminist texts set to music for the mature women's chorus. The women's choral movement has begun to change this situation: Suitable works have been discovered and performed, and many choruses have commissioned contemporary women composers to write for them.

Women's choruses also demonstate a commitment to the music of varied cultural traditions, including those of African Americans, South and West Africa, Central and South America, and Eastern Europe. The full-voice sound of these traditional musics moves choral singers into a new vocal and political stance. Bernice Johnson Reagon and Ysaye Barnwell, both of the African American vocal ensemble Sweet Honey in the Rock, have offered workshops to teach techniques, style, and performance practices of spirituals, gospel, and some South and West African music. Both women have published dynamic original choral compositions and arrangements that make women's voices sound strong by the way they are set for the voice.

Another striking feature of women's choir programs is the way stylistically disparate pieces are juxtaposed with one another. Sometimes, concerts have themes that weave vastly different pieces into a coherent whole and provide clues to the meanings of the pieces programmed. Groups of pieces may be introduced by individual choir members; texts are read aloud; material related to the work at hand may be offered; or, sometimes, extensive program notes can be read by the audience. Concerts may be interpreted in sign language for the benefit of deaf and hearing-impaired audience members.

The women's choral communities share a vision that encourages women to find and use their own voices and to honor and understand the voices of varied musical cultures. *Catherine Roma*

### Bibliography

Vukovich, Dyana. "The Anna Crusis Women's Choir." *Women and Performance: A Journal of Feminist Theory* 47:1, 50–63.

*See also* Composers; Music, Classical; Music, Women's

## Christianity, Early

Term generally referring to the churches of the ancient Mediterranean from the first through the fifth centuries A.D. Those early Christian writers who commented on sexual love between women opposed it. They argued variously that it was unnatural, impure, dishonorable, shameful, sinful, and rendered the participants deserving of punishment in hell. Early Christian condemnations of female homoeroticism resemble those of their pagan counterparts both in terminology and in their understandings of femaleness and maleness. The apostle Paul's (A.D.?–ca. 67) condemnation of female homoeroticism provided the foundation for early church teachings on the subject and remains influential in the twentieth century.

While this entry focuses on erotic relations between women, Mary Rose D'Angelo (1990) has applied Adrienne Rich's (1929–) concept of a "lesbian continuum" to early Christianity to denote bonding between female partners, regardless of erotic involvement (for example, Romans 16:12; Philippians 4:11). The Jewish Bible prohibits sexual relations between males (Leviticus 18:22; 20:13) but not be-

tween females. Some have argued that Ruth had a lesbian relationship with her mother-in-law, Naomi (see Ruth 1:14, "Ruth clung to her" [i.e., Naomi]), but this is speculation, and Ruth did marry a man, Boaz (Ruth 4:13).

### The New Testament

Within the New Testament, the gospels do not present Jesus as addressing the question of same-sex sexual expression, but the apostle Paul does condemn relations between both females and males. In his Letter to the Romans, Chapter 1, Paul states that idol worshipers could have known God through observing God's created works. He argues that God punished idol worshipers by giving "them up to the lusts of their hearts to impurity, to the degrading of their bodies among themselves" (Romans 1:24), and that "God gave them up to degrading passions. Their women exchanged natural intercourse for unnatural, and in the same way also the men, giving up natural intercourse with women, were consumed with passion for one another" (Romans 1:26–27). Such persons "deserve to die" (Romans 1:32).

Some have argued that Romans 1:26 refers to (1) intercourse between a woman and an animal (prohibited in Leviticus 18:23; 20:16); (2) intercourse during a woman's menstrual period (prohibited in Leviticus 18:19); or (3) anal intercourse between a woman and a man (not prohibited in the Jewish Bible and allowed by the majority of ancient Jewish rabbis). Romans 1:27, however, introduces sexual relations between males with the term "in the same way," thereby specifying that the females' unnatural intercourse was of the same type as that of the males. Further, other ancient sources also depicted sexual relations between women as unnatural (Plato [427?–347? B.C.E.], Seneca the Elder [55 B.C.E.–A.D. ?40], Martial [A.D. ca. 40–ca. 104], Ovid [43 B.C.E.–A.D. 17 or 18], Ptolemy [fl. A.D. 121–151], Artemidoros [second century A.D.], and probably Dorotheos of Sidon [first century A.D.]).

The best context for understanding Paul's condemnation of sexual relations between women is his own culture and its assumptions about sexual relations. While Roman-period pagan writers disagree on whether to condone sexual relations between males, nearly all of them condemn sexual relations between women. Against the background of the common cultural assumption that sexual relations should naturally occur between two unequal parties (a man and his wife, a male slave owner and his male or female slave, a man and his mistress, a man and a prostitute), such writers as Seneca the Elder, Martial, Soranos (first–second century A.D.), and Lucian (A.D. ca. 115?–ca. 180) depicted women who had sexual relations with other women as having become like men. They applied the term "tribades" (cf. the later term "tribadism") to such women and represented them as trying to transcend the passive, subordinate role accorded to them by nature and to take on a dominating, penetrating role. Ancient medical writers went as far as to prescribe a selective clitoridectomy, apparently for women whose clitorises were ostensibly capable of penetration (Soranos, as excerpted in Caelius Aurelianus [fifth century A.D.], Mustio [perhaps fifth or sixth century A.D.], and Paulus of Aegina [seventh century A.D.]). Paul's condemnation fits in well with the greater awareness of sexual love between women documented in the Roman world. Paul's earliest readers, the early church fathers, read Paul as a man of his time; they saw him as condemning homoeroticism for the same reasons that others of their culture did. Paul used the terms "impurity," "to degrade," "to exchange," "natural," and "unnatural" in the ways that others in the ancient world employed these terms.

In ancient Mediterranean culture, "impurity" meant a blurring of boundaries, in this case, of the boundaries between femaleness and maleness. Just as, according to the Book of Leviticus, impure animals were those that did not conform to delineated categories, the people about whom Paul was speaking were not maintaining the clear gender polarity and complementarity necessary for a specific social order. Thus, taking seriously Paul's description of homoeroticism as "impurity" shows it to be a societal, rather than a private, concern.

The term Paul uses for "degrade" can also be rendered "dishonor." For Paul, treatment of female and male bodies should differ, especially with respect to honor. Paul asks in his First Letter to the Corinthians 11:14: "Does not nature itself teach you that if a man wears long hair, it is degrading to him?" This required gender differentiation in hair length points to bodily appearance as a primary basis for distinguishing between women and men. According to 1 Corinthians 11:3, the man is head of woman. Short hair and the lack of a veil signify the male body, as God's image and glory (1 Corinthians 11:7); the opposite conditions, long hair and a veil, apply to the female body, marking the woman's subordinate status as the glory of man (1 Corinthians 11:7). In this hierarchical framework, a noncompliant woman brings shame upon her husband. Against

the background of the gendered cultures of the Roman world, Paul's earliest readers saw him as condemning men who had relinquished the honor due to the male sex and had become effeminate and women who did not conform to Paul's model of the man as head of woman.

Paul used the word "exchanged" to indicate that people knew the natural sexual order of the universe and left it behind. Some interpreters today argue that Paul was referring to heterosexual persons committing homosexual acts, rather than to lesbian and gay persons (for example, Boswell [1980]) or that he did not have a concept of sexual orientation at all (for example, Goss [1993]). While ancient constructions of the erotic differed from contemporary ones, both ancient astrological and medical texts attest to the concept of lifelong erotic orientations, caused, for example, by the constellation under which one was born, by the male and female seed not mingling well at conception, or by inheritance. Thus, Paul could well have been familiar with the concept of erotic orientation, without accepting that as a valid reason for homoerotic expression. Similarly, astrologers saw female homoerotic orientation as astrally determined but, nevertheless, "unnatural" (for example, Ptolemy).

If one reads Romans 1:26–27 against the backdrop of a broad range of ancient sources, "natural" intercourse means penetration of a subordinate person by a dominant one. Other Pauline texts show that Paul shared common cultural assumptions of the Roman world: Romans 7:2, in which Paul speaks of a married woman as "under a man," and 1 Corinthians 11:2–3, in which Paul calls man "head of woman." The shapers of Paul's culture saw any type of vaginal intercourse, whether consensual or coerced, as natural (including, for example, between a man and his slave). The "natural intercourse" that the females of Romans 1:26 gave up thus includes such forms of vaginal intercourse as marital relations, adultery, rape, incest, prostitution, and sexual relations between an adult male and a minor girl.

These understandings of "natural intercourse" derive from ancient understandings of nature generally. Two principal ways of conceptualizing nature were available to Paul: (1) nature as the order of creation, which would refer to the naturalness of marriage between women and men, based on Genesis 2, according to which God created woman from man (see Paul's use of Genesis 2 in 1 Corinthians 11:2–16); or (2) the ancient concept that women have a nature different from men. Either concept entails a gender hierarchy. According to either concept, sexual relations between women are "unnatural," because a sexual encounter necessarily includes an active and a passive partner, and women cannot naturally assume the active role, thus rendering natural sexual relations between women impossible.

Early Christian apocalyptic visions of hell echo Paul's teaching that these women "deserve to die" (Romans 1:32). These include images of homoerotic women suffering torture in hell for their sin: being forced to cast themselves off a cliff (*Apocalypse of Peter* [second century A.D.]), burning in hell (*Acts of Thomas* [third century A.D.]), and running in a river of fire (*Apocalypse of Paul* [third century A.D.]).

Tertullian of Carthage (A.D. ca. 160–ca. 225) derides homoerotic women as outsiders to polite society, associating them with prostitutes, and states that one would not want even to take a sip from such a woman's cup (*On the Pallium; On the Resurrection of the Flesh*).

## Homoeroticism in Early Christianity

In spite of tremendous opposition by Christians and others, women in this period engaged in the practice of woman-woman marriage. Clement of Alexandria (A.D. ca. 150–ca. 214) responds to women who had long-term relationships with other women that they defined as marriage (*Instructor*). Ptolemy, Lucian, the rabbinical commentary known as the *Sifra* (before A.D. ca. 220), Hephaistion of Thebes (fourth–fifth centuries A.D.), and possibly Iamblichos (second century A.D.) also refer to woman-woman marriage. Further, in a papyrus letter from Egypt (probably third century A.D.), a mother refers to her daughter's wife (Papyrus Oxyrhynchos 4340). Clement argues that such marriages are unnatural because (1) they defy God, who created woman from man in order for her to receive man's seed and to help him; (2) they prevent the male seed from finding a proper field; (3) the uteri of the two women are calling out to be filled with the male seed; (4) humans should not imitate such lascivious animals as the hare; and (5) Paul called female homoeroticism unnatural in Romans 1:26–27.

Hippolytos of Rome (second–third centuries A.D.) reports on a group of Gnostic Christians, called the Naassenes (defined by Hippolytos as heretical), who rejected "natural intercourse" between women and men in the belief that androgyny characterized the world above. It is not known whether they promoted same-sex love, but they did interpret Paul in Romans 1:20–27 as speaking about

an "unspeakable mystery of blessed pleasure" (*The Refutation of All Heresies*).

John Chrysostom (d. A.D. 407) argues that female homoeroticism is "far more disgraceful" than male homoeroticism, "since they ought to feel more shame than men." Chrysostom, arguing that women have a nature different from men and that, by nature, woman is commanded to be man's helper, sees homoeroticism as overturning the social order, which is protected by nature: "Nature knows her own boundaries." Chrysostom attacks homoeroticism with such invectives as "Whatever transgression you speak of, you will name none equal to this lawlessness"; "There is nothing more irrational and grievous than this outrage"; and "How many hells will suffice for such people?" (*Homilies on Romans*).

Early Christians vehemently opposed homoeroticism at the same time that they created homosocial environments in which it could occur. Shenute of Atripe in Egypt (fourth–fifth centuries A.D.) warns nuns against same-sex sexual contact (*On the Monastic Life*), as does Augustine of Hippo (A.D. 354–430), who instructs nuns to go out in groups of three (*Epistles*).

These early Christian teachings have had great influence in history. For example, an American Colonial statute in New Haven, Connecticut, placed sexual love between women under the death penalty, explicitly quoting Romans 1:26 as support (*New Haven's Settling in New England: And Some Lawes for Government*). These teachings also remain foundational for Christianity in the twentieth century. Thus, conservative Christians often quote Romans 1:26–27 in opposition to lesbian, gay, and bisexual civil rights or to same-sex marriage.

*Bernadette J. Brooten*

### Bibliography

Boswell, John. *Christianity, Social Tolerance, and Homosexuality: Gay People in Western Europe from the Beginning of the Christian Era to the Fourteenth Century.* Chicago: University of Chicago Press, 1980.

Brooten, Bernadette J. *Love Between Women: Early Christian Responses to Female Homoeroticism.* Chicago: University of Chicago Press, 1996.

D'Angelo, Mary Rose. "Women Partners in the New Testament." *Journal of Feminist Studies in Religion* 6:1 (1990), 65–86.

Goss, Robert. *Jesus Acted Up: A Gay and Lesbian Manifesto.* San Francisco: HarperSanFrancisco, 1993.

Hallett, Judith P. "Female Homoeroticism and the Denial of Roman Reality in Latin Literature." *Yale Journal of Criticism* 3 (1989), 209–227.

*See also* Antiquity; Classical Literature; Clitoris; Lesbian Continuum; Tribade

## Christina of Sweden (1626–1689)

Queen of Sweden. At the age of six, when her father, King Gustav II Adolf, died, Christina—the only child born to the king and his wife, Eleonora, to survive her first year—ascended to the throne. She was said to have been especially masculine, and she was rumored to have had affairs with young women, as well as young men.

Both her parents had hoped for a male heir to Sweden's throne, and, upon her birth, Christina was thought to be a boy. But she was not—a fact that she believed gave her mother cause to hate her. Her father bestowed on young Christina all of the honors due a prince, in spite of her gender, and, in 1630, when she was just four years old, he made her his heiress. Two years later, she became queen, although she did not actually rule until she was eighteen.

Her intellect was thought to be "unusual" for a girl, but she was not dissuaded from her number-one interest: studying. This, together with her mannish gait, her "booming voice," and her lack of interest in fine clothing, made her a bit of an anomaly. Rumors abounded about affairs between Christina and courtiers, as well as women in her court. It did not help that, to the dismay of many in her court, the queen referred to her maid in waiting, Countess Ebba Sparre, as her "bedfellow."

During her reign, Sweden prospered culturally. She brought impressive libraries to her country and was, throughout her life, a patron of the arts. Long after leaving Sweden, she founded the Accademia Reale in Rome (in 1674). Politically, she also had her successes. In particular, under her rule the Treaty of Westphalia was signed, ending the Thirty Years' War.

Christina withstood rumors of affairs and of lesbianism and even allegations that she was a hermaphrodite. It was her strong desire to travel and her desire to convert from Lutheranism to the then-illegal (in Sweden) Catholicism that led Christina to leave her throne and her homeland after twenty-two years as its ruling monarch.

After abdicating the throne at age twenty-eight, she traveled throughout Europe—often dressed as a man—making her mark in France and in Rome. In November 1655, she made a formal profession of her new faith, Catholicism. Her interest in politics, however never waned. She sought the throne of Naples a year or so later but did not succeed. She had the man she held responsible for that failure murdered, an act that would ruin her later attempt to gain the throne of Poland and earn her the reputation of being "bloodthirsty."

Her travels and political ambitions ended in 1668 in Rome, where she spent the final decades of her life. She suffered a stroke in 1689 and died shortly after.

She was portrayed by Greta Garbo (1905–1990)—another of Sweden's androgynous figures who was subject of much rumor and speculation—in the film version of her life, *Queen Christina* (1933).

*Andrea L.T. Peterson*

### Bibliography

*The Alyson Almanac.* 1994–1995 ed. Boston: Alyson, 1993.

Magill, Frank N., ed. *Great Lives from History: Renaissance to 1900 Series*, vol. 1: *A-Cov.* Pasadena, Calif.: Salem, 1989.

*See also* Androgyny; Garbo, Greta; Sweden

## Churches, Lesbian and Gay

Organized bodies of openly lesbian and gay Christian believers. The concept of lesbian and gay churches is foreign to some because, traditionally, religions have viewed homosexuality as an abomination. The first gay church, an Anglican-derived Liberal Catholic Church, was founded in Sydney, Australia, by Charles Webster Leadbeater in 1916. Thirty years later, in 1946, George Hyde, a youth minister in the independent Catholic movement, formed a church in Atlanta, Georgia, that is believed to have been the first North American church organized primarily for homosexuals. The Church of ONE Brotherhood was founded in 1956–1957 in Los Angeles, California, by Chuck Rowland. However, it was in 1968 in Los Angeles, California, that the contemporary gay church movement really began, when the Rev. Troy Perry (1940–), a Pentecostal minister who had been ousted from his church when his homosexuality became known, founded the Universal Fellowship of Metropolitan Community Church (UFMCC), a nondenominational Christian church for lesbian and gay people.

UFMCC is a Christian body, adhering to the historic Nicene Creed, although it also welcomes Unitarians, Jews, and those of other faiths and creeds into its membership. Although it has a special ministry to lesbians and gay men, all people are welcome. By the late 1990s, the fellowship had more than three hundred churches in eighteen countries, with a membership of more than 32,000. Slightly more than half of all UFMCC clergy are women, almost all of them lesbians. Indeed, UFMCC offers more opportunities than any other Christian body for lesbians to exercise a full range of ministries, including full ordination. Of the seven ruling elders in 1998, two were women. Most prominent is Nancy Wilson (1950–), pastor of the "mother church" in Los Angeles, who has worked tirelessly as the fellowship's liaison with the National Council of Churches and the World Council of Churches. In 1998, half of the district coordinators, who oversee regional groups of churches, were women.

In 1972, a few people from Los Angeles MCC who were Jewish held their first service at Beth Chayim Chadashim. The synagogue was chartered in 1974 by the Union of American Hebrew Congregations and was the first gay religious organization of any kind to be officially recognized by a national body.

In addition to exclusively and primarily separate lesbian and gay churches and synagogues such as MCC and Beth Chayim Chadashim, in the 1990s there were numerous other gay and lesbian religious groups, including Roman Catholic Dignity, Julian Fellowship (for Catholic Women), New Ways Ministry (for lesbian and gay Catholics), Episcopalian Integrity, Kinship for Seventh Day Adventists, United Methodist Affirmation, Affirmation—Gay and Lesbian Mormons, American Baptists Concerned, Brethren/Mennonite Council for Lesbian and Gay Concerns, Friends for Lesbian and Gay Concerns (Quaker), Odinshof (heathen religious and educational charity), Presbyterians for Lesbian and Gay Concerns, Unitarian/Universalists for Lesbian and Gay Concerns, United Church Coalition for Lesbian and Gay Concerns, Lesbian and Gay Christian Movement, and Hineinu (a Jewish organization)—all of which eschew the implicit or explicit condemnation of lesbians and gays found in some traditional religions.

[The author thanks Nancy Hardesty for information about the role of lesbians in UFMCC.]

*Akilah Monifa*

## Bibliography

Blumenfeld, Warren J., and Diane Raymond. *Looking at Gay and Lesbian Life*. Boston: Beacon, 1993.

Cruikshank, Margaret. *The Gay and Lesbian Liberation Movement*. New York: Routledge, 1992.

Perry, Troy D., and Thomas L. Swicegood. *Don't Be Afraid Anymore: The Story of Revered Troy Perry and the Metropolitan Community Churches*. New York: St. Martin's Press, 1990.

*See also* Protestantism; Synagogues

## Class

Traditionally defined as a social stratum sharing economic, political, and cultural characteristics. Denial of class permeates American culture. The belief that everyone is middle class constitutes a major obstacle to class consciousness. When class is acknowledged, usually race is equated with class, and the lowest rungs of the economic and status ladders are assigned to people of color, archetypally black single mother welfare recipients. Despite the assumption of classlessness, people do talk about class. Common parlance and academic sociological analysis alike concentrate on social and economic status. Marxist analysis, never popular or even adequately taught in the United States, discusses relationship to the means of production. But if blue-collar/white-collar dichotomies between manual and mental labor are less than useful for understanding women (who mostly are often pink-collar workers, segregated into so-called female jobs in service, clerical, and professional fields), the dramatic changes caused by deindustrialization and the possibility of upward mobility further complicate the issue. While discussing class as wealth and material possessions yields an inadequate analysis, understanding the structures of capitalism and locations on the class spectrum is essential. Hence, the traditional definitions must be expanded to include analysis of dominance and subordination.

The topic of class is fraught with emotional and political complexity for many lesbians, particularly feminists and/or political activists. Lesbians come from every class background, share the dominant culture, and have absorbed its misunderstandings and obstacles to class consciousness. To these, some have added guilt for class privilege. Lesbians also analyze class, write about it, and take political action to remedy class inequalities and economic injustice.

Class differences and antagonisms characterize lesbian communities. Economically and socially privileged lesbians (such as the Natalie Barney circle in Paris in the 1920s and tennis star Martina Navratilova in the 1990s) are not only the most well known, but often set the tone and lead the lesbian community. Yet working-class lesbians, struggling to create public lesbian space in the bar cultures of the 1930s–1960s, were leaders in politicizing and opening up new space for lesbians. In the 1970s, the "second wave" of feminists harshly judged butch-femme working-class lesbians. Women's liberation activists challenged such roles as male-identified and antiwoman and enshrined a new androgynous standard. While feminists framed this critique in terms of gender, it was also a covert attempt to rid feminist culture of embarrassing working-class elements. When lesbians began to champion butch-femme roles in the 1980s, they explicitly recognized and redefined lesbian eroticism, but far less frequently acknowledged the class implications of roles. Thus, the rise, fall, and resurrection of butch-femme style can serve as a template for understanding the complexities of class for lesbians. When class is acknowledged, it is often masked under other issues—in this case, erotic styles.

An institution that has facilitated lesbian lives, albeit deeply closeted, is the military. Historically and contemporarily, the military has offered working-class people a source for steady work, adventure, travel, and the ability to escape their hometown. The military has also persecuted lesbians and has been criticized by lesbians of all classes for its oppressive role in war and propping up capitalism.

Class has also played a major role in lesbians' ability to be "out." Class privilege insulates some lesbians from harsh consequences for visibility, but many working-class women have been more out than middle-class women. In the late twentieth century, organizations of corporate lesbians take a very low profile, while countercultural lesbian activists of all classes are more physically visible.

Despite official ideologies of classlessness, lesbian writers have been leaders in the contemporary exploration of class. In the early 1970s, the Furies, a Washington, D.C., area collective, published class analyses, but the topic later disappeared from lesbian publishing for the most part. In the late twentieth century, most explicitly class-conscious lesbian writing took the form of storytelling or memoir. Novelists such as Dorothy Allison and Leslie Feinberg, poets such as Judy Grahn and Pat Parker, scholars such as Madeline Davis and Elizabeth Lapovsky Kennedy, and writers of essays and journalism in the proliferation of lesbian publishing also added their voices. The literary journal *Common Lives/Lesbian Lives* explicitly gave voice to "ordinary" lesbians in its commitment to publishing diverse voices, including those of poor and working-class lesbians. Most lesbians who have brought attention to class issues come from poor or working class backgrounds, although frequently it is their upward mobility via college education that enables their voices to be heard and their ideas published. Writers of color consistently interweave race and class issues, but their ideas are often categorized as racial/ethnic issues. Consequently, class analysis is sometimes seen as the arena of white working-class women whose race is assumed and, thus, invisible. Likewise, when lesbians of color discuss race and class, race takes center stage and class becomes invisible. Thus, the publication of numerous anthologies about class by lesbians and nonlesbians alike in the 1990s was encouraging because it demonstrates that the work of developing class consciousness is expanding.

Politically active lesbians have recognized class differences, tried to defuse their power, and have also resisted class consciousness. One source of reluctance to examine class stems from the fact that the male-dominated Left has, for the most part, looked at neither women nor culture in its class analysis, but only at economic relations at the point of production. Lesbian and feminist class analysis most often examines culture. Consequently, some separatists have derided class as a useless male construct. On the other hand, lesbian activism usually does not target production, but rather tries to change systems of distribution. Sliding-scale fees for cultural events, services, and conferences are common. Some lesbians have organized funds to financially aid destitute or disaster-stricken lesbians, and a few lesbians with inheritances work together to figure how to use their resources responsibly. When lesbians have organized around production, unions and community groups have been the most common venues, rather than lesbian organizations.

*Lois Rita Helmbold*

### Bibliography

Kadi, Joanna. *Thinking Class: Sketches from a Cultural Worker*. Boston: South End, 1996.

Kennedy, Elizabeth Lapovsky, and Madeline D. Davis. *Boots of Leather, Slippers of Gold: The*

*History of a Lesbian Community*. New York: Routledge, 1993.

Moraga, Cherríe, and Gloria Anzaldúa, eds. *This Bridge Called My Back: Writings by Radical Women of Color*. Watertown, Mass.: Persephone, 1981.

Penelope, Julia, ed. *Out of the Class Closet: Lesbians Speak*. Freedom, Calif.: Crossing, 1994.

Raffo, Susan, ed. *Queerly Classed: Gay Men and Lesbians Write About Class*. Boston: South End, 1997.

Rose, Stephen J. *Social Stratification in the US: The American Profile Poster Revised and Expanded*. New York: New Press, 1992.

Zandy, Janet, ed. *Calling Home: Working-Class Women's Writings*. New Brunswick, N.J.: Rutgers University Press, 1990.

*See also* Androgyny; Barney, Natalie; Bars; Butch-Femme; Economics; Furies, The; Grahn, Judy; Hoboes; Labor Movement; Military; Navratilova, Martina; New Left; Parker, Pat; Socialism; Work

## Classical Literature

Literature of ancient Greece and Rome. This literature contains few references to same-sex sexual relations between women. Moreover, with the exception of Sappho (ca. 600 B.C.E.), whose poetry dates to the archaic period and survives in fragments only, and perhaps also of the Hellenistic poet Nossis of Locri (ca. 300 B.C.E.), literary representations of female homoeroticism from antiquity are all male authored. The extant evidence for desire or love between women, then, does not offer a window onto the experiences of ancient women so much as the satiric jests, insults, fantasies, or hostile moral judgments of ancient male authors. By contrast, the literature of classical Greece and late-republican and imperial Rome offers copious references to sexual relations between men.

## Identities and Orientations

If the asymmetry of the ancient sources represents one difficulty for assessing the meaning of female homoeroticism in classical antiquity, a further interpretive difficulty is presented by the wide gulf between ancient Mediterranean conceptions of sexual practices, gender, and their relation to categories of person, and nineteenth- and twentieth-century conceptions of homosexual and heterosexual persons. Whether or to what extent ancient Mediterranean societies had a category for lifelong erotic orientations remains a source of great dispute among twentieth-century historians of sexuality.

Although the ancients certainly recognized the phenomenon of sexual activity between persons of the same sex, they did not categorize the participants as particular kinds of persons on that basis alone. Ancient Mediterranean societies tended to sort out sexual acts—and sexual actors—not on the basis of the anatomical sex of the participants but on the degree to which the sexual acts did or did not correspond to each participant's gender identity and social status. In brief, the fundamental operative distinction for proper sexual relations was not male/female, but active/passive, not the anatomical sex of the sexual partners, but the social genders (the degree to which their sexual roles did or did not correspond to their respective positions in a rigid social hierarchy). Gender was not a matter of anatomical sex so much as an issue of social status. One achieved proper gender by assuming or asserting the proper role. This was a social universe in which citizenship was limited to males—and to a very small subset of males—and in which sex was not imagined as an activity of mutuality or reciprocity between persons but was something one person did to another.

Sexual encounters required a polarization of the participants into penetrator and penetrated, and the sexual roles assumed into "active" and "passive." These distinctions, in turn, articulated some other social distinctions: of sex (male/female), gender (masculine/feminine), age (older male/adolescent of either sex), and class (social superior/social inferior).

*Paiderastia* (pederasty) was the idealized cultural form for sexual relations between males; in it, the acts the older male was permitted to perform on or with the younger male were very carefully scripted, although what people actually did may have differed from what they were supposed to be doing. With rare exceptions, female homoeroticism is not represented as taking a pederastic form. There are intimations of a female *paiderastia* in Sappho, when the "I" (cf. fragment 102), for example, refers to a desire for a beautiful *pais* (boy), or in the sensuous depictions of comely young maidens elsewhere in Sappho's lyrics, as well as in the lyric poetry of her near-contemporary Alcman. Moreover, in Sappho 1, the poem's "I"—who is directly addressed in the poem as "Sappho"—beseeches the goddess Aphrodite to make the woman of her dreams think

"Sappho" is the woman of hers. The poem is striking in at least two regards. First, the poem anticipates, in tone and wished-for effect, magical papyri, found in Egypt and dating to the second century A.D., that record erotic spells commissioned by women and intended to make one woman fall in love with the spell's female initiator. Second, the poem's protagonist may be positioning herself as an *erastes* (lover) in pursuit of an unwilling *eroumene* (to use the feminine noun for beloved). To be sure, such depictions may be conventional; the Greeks idealized youth. Or they may indicate, as some scholars have argued, that Sappho's school for girls (on the isle of Lesbos) may have offered a structured site for the expression of female-female desire. Later, in his *Life of Lycurgus*, Plutarch (A.D. ca. 46–ca. 127) describes what may be institutionalized female pederasty in ancient Sparta.

## Female Same-Sex Relations

The available literary evidence offers no reason to suppose that the qualified social approval granted some forms of same-sex sexual relations between males extended to same-sex sexual relations between females. An exception is a passage from Plato's (427?–347? B.C.E.) *Symposium* (191e), which was composed early in the fourth century B.C.E. In that passage, the figure of Aristophanes tells his drunken male companions that humans initially came in three sexes—male, female, and androgyne—and that each of these original sexes had eight limbs and two heads. Zeus split these creatures in two, and from these half-selves are descended women who desire women, men who desire men, and women and men who desire each other. Plato's Aristophanes refers to women in search of their missing female half as *hetairistriai*, a word that implies both "comrade" and "courtesan." At minimum, it seems wise to resist taking this passage from the *Symposium* as evidence that the Greeks recognized lifelong erotic dispositions roughly equivalent to modern categories of heterosexual, homosexual, and lesbian. As Halperin (1998) argues, Plato's Aristophanes was making mischief with his myth of origins.

Despite the best efforts of scholars, however, the meaning of *hetairistriai*—and the force of Plato's joke—cannot be fully retrieved. The *Symposium* represents the first attested usage of this term, which disappears from Greek literature for five hundred years, reappearing only once, in *Dialogues of the Courtesans*, a satire by Lucian of Samosata (A.D.

ca. 115?–ca. 180). The only other classical-period reference to female homoeroticism also occurs in Plato, in this case his *Nomoi*, or *Laws*. In a passage rare for its condemnation of male pederasty, Plato also condemns female homoeroticism as unnatural (636b–c).

Thus, the nonjudgmental tone Plutarch strikes in the *Life of Lycurgus*, describing sexual liaisons between married women and unmarried adolescent girls in Sparta, is unusual. But the customs he is narrating are kept safely at a distance, both chronologically and culturally. This distancing technique is an example of a larger trend in Roman-period representations of women who desire or love other women, namely, a tendency to depict such women as either belonging to the past—preferably the Greek past—or originating somewhere else. Seneca the Elder (ca. 55 B.C.E.–A.D. 40?) literalizes this preference in one of his fictitious legal cases (*Controversiae* 1.2.23); at the moment he introduces the tale of a husband catching his wife *in flagrante* with another woman, he switches from Latin into Greek. This passage is also significant for being one of only two instances in which the literary source may refer to both women—and not simply the masculinized and, presumptively, active partner—as tribades, or tribads (cf. Asclepiades 7).

## Tribades

Of the terms used to name women who desired other women, *tribas* (and its less frequent but still serviceable Latin equivalent, *frictrix*) had the longest life; other words that encode female homoeroticism are *virago* and, possibly, *meretrix* (prostitute). The first attestation of *tribas*, which is derived from the Greek verb "to rub," occurs as a loan word in Latin texts of the first century A.D. (Seneca's *Controversiae* and a jesting fable by Phaedrus). Its first appearance in a Greek text occurs a century later.

Because classical-period Greeks and Romans conceptualized sex as occurring between a superordinate, "phallic" actor and his subordinate (socially inferior, whether in terms of gender or civic status) object of desire, the male-authored sources could not see and represent female same-sex eroticism except by making female-female eroticism fit the bill of active/passive, penetrator/penetrated. Thus, sexual activity between women, to the extent that it was even conceivable, was almost invariably represented as involving a masculinized partner, who penetrated her female beloved with a phallus substitute of some sort, either an *olisbos* (dildo) or an unusually large clitoris, which might penetrate females or even males. Thus, Martial (first century A.D.) describes Philaenis as a *tribas* who both fucks boys (*pedicat pueros*) and eats out the middles of girls. Figured as a swaggering gym dyke before the name (or the category), Philaenis pursues masculine activities with a vengeance, seeking to outlift, outdrink, and outdo manliness itself. The masculinizing turn is also seen in Lucian's *Dialogues of the Courtesans*, in which the *hetairistria*, Megilla, transgenders her name to Megillos, crops her hair, and seduces Leaina. In all other respects, Leaina is represented as an ordinary girl; indeed, she may just be an ordinary girl. It is Megilla/os, the mannish seducer, at whom Lucian takes aim.

Even in those texts that treat tribadism as a medically problematic deviation, such as the second-century A.D. astrological study of Ptolemy or Caelius Aurelianus's fifth-century A.D. medical text *On Chronic Diseases*, the diagnosis passes over the woman the *tribas* desires and focuses its attention on the masculine woman only, the tribad. Moreover, the texts concentrate not on the same-sex sexual orientation of the tribad so much as on her gender inversion. Among other things, this suggests that what the ancients stigmatized when they stigmatized women who desired other women was not same-sex sexual contact, or even the wish for such contact, per se, but the gender inversion or deviance the "masculinity" of the "active" partner represented. The diagnosis cum accusation *tribas* seemed to have been reserved for the "active," masculinized partner; the ancient sources do not stop to problematize or categorize the "passive" woman desired by the *tribas*. Either she did not represent a problem to the binary scheme of sex and gender, because she remained in place—passive, sexually receptive—or she was not fully thinkable as a possibility. The passive partner's desire for another woman did not appear to signify at all. What distinguished the tribad from other women—from "real" women—was less her desire for other women than her departure from norms of femininity (in other words, her gender trouble).

[The author wishes to thank David M. Halperin and Bernadette Brooten for conversations and challenges.]                     *Ann Pellegrini*

## Bibliography

Brooten, Bernadette. *Love Between Women: Early Christian Responses to Female Homoeroticism*. Chicago: University of Chicago Press, 1997.
Dover, Kenneth. *Greek Homosexuality*. Cambridge, Mass.: Harvard University Press, 1978.
Hallet, Judith P. "Female Homoeroticism and the Denial of Roman Reality in Latin Literature." *Yale Journal of Criticism* 3 (1989), 209–227.
Halperin, David M. *One Hundred Years of Homosexuality*. New York: Routledge, 1990.
———. "Response to Bernadette Brooten's Love Between Women." *GLQ: A Journal of Lesbian and Gay Studies* 4:4 (1998), 559–578.
Skinner, Marilyn B. "Sapphic Nossis." *Arethusa* 22 (1989), 5–18.
Winkler, John J. *Constraints of Desire*. New York: Routledge, 1990.

*See also* Antiquity; Clitoris; Lesbos, Island of; Sappho; Tribade

## Clitoris

An organ or area of the female genitalia frequently linked to sexual excitement. The clitoris has been intimately connected to historical images of lesbians and lesbianism. As long ago as ancient Greece, "tribades" were thought to use their enlarged clitorises to sexually stimulate or even penetrate their female partners. This sexual technique, called "tribadism," was associated with woman-to-woman sex through the pornography, anthropology, and marital manuals from early-modern Europe through the nineteenth century, as was the image of an oversized lesbian clitoris. When European and American doctors started to classify "female inversion" (a terminological precursor of homosexuality) in the late nineteenth century, they incorporated accounts of inverts' "hypertrophied" or enlarged clitorises, a connection that persisted well into the twentieth century.

The clitoris has been described as analogous or homologous to the penis at least since the early-modern period, up to the late twentieth century. The image of the clitoris as a "female penis" has been essential in connecting the "hypertrophied" and, consequently, hermaphroditic lesbian clitoris of pornographic and medical repute to lesbians' supposed excess masculinity, as well as to their assumed hypersexuality. Other marginalized groups, such as women of color, prostitutes, and working-class women, have also traditionally been associated with enlarged clitorises and hypersexuality.

Freudian psychoanalytic theory identified the clitoris as a contributing cause of lesbianism. While

Sigmund Freud (1856–1939) claimed that all people were bisexual in early development, persistent female homosexuality resulted from a failure to transfer the center of sexual excitement from the infantile, "masculine" clitoris to the adult, "feminine" vagina, a transition that should coincide with the transfer of affection from a mother figure to a father figure. Therefore, a lesbian was attracted to women because she maintained the primacy of her "male" organ of the clitoris and never developed beyond infantile homosexuality and mother attachment.

In the wake of the Kinsey report on female sexuality in 1953 and the feminist movements of the 1970s, the Freudian model of the clitoris fell into disrepute, especially within lesbian feminist circles. As feminist revisionists reclaimed the clitoris as the central source of sexual excitement, they emphasized the organ's complexity, dividing it into labeled parts. Feminist sex manuals of the 1970s through the 1990s also used the similarities of the clitoris and the penis in their arguments for the legitimacy of female sexuality. As a result of this "reclamation" of the clitoris, some lesbians of the 1970s and 1980s believed that penetration and vaginal sex were more "heterosexist" than clitoral stimulation. While clitoral sexuality represented the separateness of a supposedly less phallocentric lesbian sexuality to some, this position was by no means universal. For example, while lesbian sex manuals of the 1980s generally described the clitoris as a central sexual location, they began to include the "G-spot," or Grafenberg spot, as an additional, vaginal site of sexual arousal and orgasm. The controversies surrounding clitoral or vaginal sexuality frequently focused on the legitimacy or illegitimacy of dildos and formed part of broader debates about sex in the 1980s lesbian community.    *Margaret Gibson*

### Bibliography

Bennett, Paula. "Critical Clitoridectomy: Female Sexual Imagery and Feminist Psychoanalytic Theory." *Signs: Journal of Women in Culture and Society* 18 (1993), 235–259.

Gibson, Margaret. "Clitoral Corruption: Body Metaphors and American Doctors' Constructions of Female Homosexuality, 1880–1900." In *Science and Homosexualities*. Ed. Vernon Rosario II. New York: Routledge, 1996, pp. 108–132.

Laqueur, Thomas. "Amor Veneris, Vel Dulcedo Appeletur." In *Zone: Fragments for a History of the Human Body: Part Three*. Ed. Michael Feher. New York: Urzone, 1989, pp. 90–131.

Moore, Lisa Jean, and Adele E. Clarke. "Clitoral Conventions and Transgressions: Graphic Representations in Anatomy Texts, c1900–1991." *Feminist Studies* 21 (1995), 255–301.

Park, Katherine. "The Rediscovery of the Clitoris: French Medicine and the *Tribade*, 1570–1620." In *The Body in Parts: Discourses and Anatomies in Early Modern Europe*. Ed. Carla Mazzio and David Hillman. New York: Routledge, 1997, pp. 170–193.

Traub, Valerie. "The Psychomorphology of the Clitoris." *GLQ: A Journal of Lesbian and Gay Studies* 2 (1995), 81–113.

***See also*** Kinsey Institute; Phallus; Psychoanalysis; Sex Practices; Sexology; Tribade

## Closet

Mythical place where one's sexual identity was concealed in response to society's homophobia and persecution. Until recently, lesbians were compelled by society to cloak particular mannerisms, cross-dressing preferences, and their most intimate relationships from the vengeful gaze of disapproving parents, employers, and other authority figures. The consequences of failing to do so ranged from exclusion from employment, housing, or opportunities for education, to gay-bashing (being beaten solely because one is perceived to be queer), forced psychoanalytic treatment, electroshock therapy, and imprisonment.

The notion of "the closet" combines conventional definitions of privacy, seclusion, claustrophobia, and retirement with those of hiding, secrecy, and concealed troubles that, according to the Oxford English Dictionary, are "ever present, and ever liable to come into view." From these various definitions, theorists such as D.A. Miller (1988) and Eve Kosofsky Sedgwick (1990) have developed the notion of the "open secret" and the "epistemology of the closet." In other words, the closet represents the secret of homosexuality, which always threatens to be exposed and must be constantly and vigilantly silenced and rendered invisible. A lesbian or a gay man must repeatedly decide whether or not to "come out of the closet," or, in other words, reveal the secret of homosexual identity. Any lesbian or gay individual will be simultaneously in and out of the closet, if only because heterosexuality is almost always presumed unless and until the secret is revealed, and the closet door opened.

Sedgwick points out that, as a metaphor, "the closet" has been used since roughly the 1970s to refer to the open communication of any previously suppressed information or public revelation of a stigmatized identity (for example, coming out as black or as a fat woman). She goes on to say, however, that the closet has been the defining structure for gay oppression in the twentieth century. This is because lesbian and gay oppression is based upon a stigma that is typically not visible, unlike the stigmas based on race, sex, or size. Because lesbians and gay men can pass as heterosexual, being in or out of the closet is always a salient issue. Even those identities that also are not immediately recognizable—such as Jewish or Gypsy, to use Sedgwick's examples—differ from lesbian and gay identity, since they rest, to some degree, in ancestral lineage and cultural identity. One can certainly "come out" as a Jew or a Gypsy (in a manner that makes more sense than "coming out" as black or female), but "the closet" has a unique relevance for the particular ambiguity of lesbian and gay identity.

Among the most interesting ideas about the closet is that it is a way of knowing and being known—hence, the *epistemology* of the closet—that is crucial to all of Western culture at least since the Enlightenment. Sedgwick suggests that oppositions such as between secrecy and disclosure, private and public, ignorance and knowledge have become permeated by the opposition between homosexuality and heterosexuality and that this is captured in the concept and image of the closet.

Since lesbigay people so often have been forced by society to conceal their true identities, acknowledging it, even to oneself, has been fraught with anxiety. Coming out of the closet has taken many shapes and strategies across time. Because lesbigay oppresson is caught up in issues of invisibility, some of these have aimed explicitly at rendering lesbianism visible. During the 1940s and 1950s, for example, lesbians made the first forays outside of the closet by cross-dressing (wearing items of clothing usually worn by members of the opposite sex). This was not without its dangers, however. Women found to be wearing less than three articles of woman's clothing could be jailed. In the 1990s, women are far less likely to be jailed for cross-dressing, yet leaving the closet is no less fraught with emotional, physical, and economic turmoil.

In the mid-1990s, a number of highly publicized events opened the closet door wider than ever before. Lesbian surgeon Susan Love and her partner, Helen Cooksey, sued the state of Massachusetts for, and won, the legal right to coparent their daughter. In Hawai'i, a lesbian couple demanded, and won, the right to marry, only to have the courts impose an injunction against the marriage until the legal issues could be resolved. Comedian Ellen DeGeneres threw open the doors in the television industry when she came out on her television sitcom, *Ellen*. Chastity Bono, daughter of singers Sonny Bono and Cher, came out of the closet and emerged as a leader in the lesbian movement. Candace Gingrich, sister of Newt Gingrich, the Republican Speaker of the United States House of Representatives, openly protested her brother's antigay and antilesbian policies and thus reluctantly took her place on the front lines. But the closet also was used by gays and lesbians against each other in the 1990s, as the controversial practice of "outing" attests.

While the opportunities for living openly as a lesbian have increased dramatically since the 1960s in most urban areas of the United States, the backlash against lesbian and gay rights bills, the reversals in state legislatures, and the upsurge in bashing ensure that, even though the door is open, the closet is still occupied.                *Rosa María Pegueros*

### Bibliography

Miller, D.A. *The Novel and the Police*. Berkeley: University of California Press, 1988.

Sedgwick, Eve Kosofsky. *Epistemology of the Closet*. Berkeley: University of California Press, 1990.

*See also* Coming Out; Homophobia; Invisibility; Stigma

## Coalition Politics

Method of political organizing, also called "alliance politics," that has not been used regularly or with great success in lesbian social movements of the twentieth century.

Coalitions are often viewed as short-term solutions by which autonomous organizations or individuals work together on a single issue. Alliances feature longer-standing and deeper connections, in which organizations or individuals work on multiple fronts and develop more trusting political relations over long periods of time. Both coalitions and alliances involve developing alternative conceptions of feminist leadership and power.

Lesbian political social movements of the late twentieth century have been characterized primarily by single-issue organizing. Lesbians have created autonomous groups in which gender and sexual orientation have been the key areas of focus. The first lesbian political organization formed in the United States, the Daughters of Bilitis (DOB), which started in San Francisco, California, in 1955, was built upon that model. In the mid-1980s, the Lesbian Avengers, a direct-action political group, continued the tradition of lesbians organizing outside of coalitions.

There is a history of individual lesbians working in other social movements in coalition; however, as a group, lesbians tend not to work easily in coalition. Lesbian separatism, a social politic of the 1970s, emerged primarily among white lesbians who were challenging straight women's leadership in the women's movement. By the late 1970s, white lesbian separatists were criticized by lesbians of color for racist exclusion.

Racism and sexism have often been the main obstacles to coalition building among lesbians. The gay and lesbian liberation movement of the late twentieth century has been dominated by white people, and men in particular. This has led to internal division within the movement and to the rise of visibility of gay and lesbian people of color and progressive whites willing to challenge racism and sexism. Alliances within the gay and lesbian movement have been problematic, as have alliances between gays and lesbians and other social-justice movements. By the 1980s, lesbians were in leadership positions in U.S. mainstream gay and lesbian organizations; however, sexism continued to be a point of contention between lesbians and gay men. Racism has been a more divisive issue; a good example has been the emergence throughout the 1980s of many race-specific AIDS organizations that specifically served people with AIDS in communities of color. These groups are proof that the gay and lesbian movement has yet to adequately address racism internally. Lesbians have been active in AIDS political organizing with men but often work within specific racial groups.

Examples of lesbians working in coalition with other social-justice movements are few. Briefly in the mid-1980s, gay and lesbian groups and civil rights groups worked together to pass the federal Hate Crimes Statistics Act, which included adding sexual orientation to its categories of hate crimes. However, after its passing in 1987, gays and lesbians did not continue alliance work with any civil rights organizations. Another example of cross-movement organizing in the 1980s was the brief coalition between lesbians and the disability rights movement. In 1983, Sharon Kowalski, a closeted lesbian in rural Minnesota, was involved in a car accident and left with severe physical injuries. Kowalski's family did not allow her lover any access to her. A lengthy, but ultimately successful, legal battle ensued, built upon a coalition between disabled and lesbian activists. Again, after the victory, there was no continued work between lesbians and disabled activists.

In the late 1990s, lesbians continued to organize into smaller and smaller identity-based groups, by race, by class, by ability, by age, by religion, by culture, by sexual desire, and so forth. These groups help lesbians understand themselves based on a shared common identity; however, it is a limited political strategy for larger social change. Lesbians, like all people, have multiple identities; therefore, there is not a singular or universal lesbian identity. If coalition and alliance are to be viable social-change strategies for lesbians into the twenty-first century, lesbians need to develop better ways to bridge differences.

*Lisa Albrecht*

### Bibliography

Albrecht, Lisa, and Rose. M. Brewer, eds. *Bridges of Power: Women's Multicultural Alliances*. Philadelphia and Gabriola Island, B.C.: New Society, 1990.

Pharr, Suzanne. *In the Time of the Right: Reflections on Liberation*. Berkeley, Calif.: Chardon, 1996.

Reagon, Bernice Johnson. "Coalition Politics: Turning the Century." In *Home Girls: A Black Feminist Anthology*. Ed. Barbara Smith. New York: Kitchen Table: Women of Color Press, 1983, pp. 356–368.

Thompson, Karen, and Julie Andrzejewski. *Why Can't Sharon Kowalski Come Home?* San Francisco: Spinsters/Aunt Lute, 1988.

Vaid, Urvashi. *Virtual Equality: The Mainstreaming of Gay and Lesbian Liberation*. New York: Anchor, 1995.

*See also* Activism; Daughters of Bilitis; Disability; Lesbian Avengers; National Gay and Lesbian Task Force (NGLTF)

### Colette (1873–1954)

French writer. Born in Saint-Sauveur-en-Puisaye, a small Burgundian village 120 miles south of Paris, Colette moved to Paris at the age of twenty after marrying Willy (Henri Gauthier-Villars [1859–1931]), a leading figure in the social and literary salons of the period. Primarily a journalist, editor, and critic, Willy built his reputation as an impresario for other writers, signing and claiming their work as his own. Colette was exploited as one of Willy's ghostwriters as well, and she insists in her memoirs that, were it not for Willy, she never would have become a writer at all.

Colette's first book, signed "Willy," was published in 1900 as *Claudine à l'école* (Claudine at School). Much of the novel's stupefying success was due to its implicitly lesbian content in the guise of erotic relationships between adolescent girls at a provincial boarding school. Capitalizing on the allure of the novel's heroine, Claudine, Willy helped orchestrate a "Claudine" vogue: Lotions, soaps, cigarettes, perfumes, and collars bore the name of Claudine, and Claudine haircuts and outfits suddenly came into style. One of Willy's best-known gestures was that of dressing his wife and another actress in twin outfits and parading them around Paris, thereby constructing lesbianism as a public spectacle through which he might promote his own scandalous reputation. Colette wrote three more Claudine novels while married to Willy and continued the tradition of titillating sexual scenes, many of which were reportedly included at Willy's behest.

Colette's clearest association with lesbianism dates from the time of her divorce from Willy in 1906 and her growing financial, emotional, and physical attachment to Missy, née Mathilde de Morny, the Marquise de Belbeuf (also Belboeuf [1863–1944]). Missy, a well-known figure of the Parisian lesbian milieu with an aristocratic heritage and considerable wealth, became Colette's lover and protector until Colette's second marriage in 1912. During this period, Colette continued to write, but also became a dancer, an actor, and a mime artist. Colette and Missy performed together, theatrically displaying themselves as a couple, with Missy crossdressing and playing the masculine role opposite Colette. The tabloids and magazines of the period often responded with malice and shock to the couple's public displays of affection; a scene from the 1907 premiere of a mimodrama called *Rêve d'Egypte* (Dream of Egypt), in which Missy and Colette exchanged a long kiss, became particularly notorious. During her years with Missy, Colette also befriended the lesbian poet Renée Vivien (1877–1909) and her lover, the American patron Natalie Barney

(1876–1972), and she sometimes performed as a dancer in the garden on the rue Jacob where Barney held soirees celebrating the mythic cult of Lesbos.

After Colette left Missy, she married Henri de Jouvenel (1876–1935), with whom she had a daughter, Colette de Jouvenel, in 1913, and then Maurice Goudeket (1889–1977), with whom she lived until her death in 1954. The relatively brief and theatrical nature of Colette's forays into erotic relationships with women has led many biographers and critics to question the authenticity of her lesbianism, and there is much disagreement as to whether Colette can rightly be considered a lesbian writer. While a number of Colette's books, such as *Les Vrilles de la vigne* (The Tendrils of the Vine [1908]) and *La Vagabonde* (The Vagabond, [1911]), contain descriptions of lesbian eroticism, Colette's most important lesbian work is undoubtedly *Le Pur et l'impur* (The Pure and the Impure, [1941]), a book that she herself thought might one day be recognized as her best.

*Lynne Huffer*

### Bibliography

Huffer, Lynne. *Another Colette: The Question of Gendered Writing*. Ann Arbor: University of Michigan Press, 1992.

Jouve, Nicole Ward. *Colette*. Bloomington: Indiana University Press, 1987.

Marks, Elaine. *Colette*. New Brunswick, N.J.: Rutgers University Press, 1960.

Sarde, Michèle. *Colette, libre et entravée*. Paris: Stock, 1978. *Colette Free and Fettered*. Trans. Richard Miller. New York: William Morrow, 1980.

***See also*** Barney, Natalie Clifford; French Literature; Vivien, Renée

## Collectives

Developed as the creation of women's communities for the purpose of living together and/or operating a business. In practice, women's collectives have existed in the United States since at least the mid-nineteenth century, when the Woman's Commonwealth was founded in Belton, Texas. The desire for women's community can be seen as early as 1762 in English author Sarah Scott's fantasy novel, *Millenium Hall*; these dreams were not unique to European women, as the publication of Rokeya Hossain's utopian novel *Sultana's Dream* (1902) about an Indian women's community illustrates.

# C

## Characteristics

Women's interest in collectives in the United States and abroad heightened considerably during the 1960s and 1970s with the advent of contemporary feminism. Although the origins of these collectives varied (from women's participation in "hippie" communes, to the development of lesbian separatist politics, to women's desire to train for traditionally male-dominated professions, for example), women usually joined them as a way to put their politics into practice. Collectives centered on four basic goals: (1) to create a safe space for women; (2) to develop a viable feminist economy; (3) to re-create female identity free from patriarchal influence; and (4) to dismantle the patriarchy through separatism.

While features of collectives varied from community to community, two basic forms emerged during the mid-to-late 1970s. Business collectives, often located in cities, organized to produce and market women's products and material culture. They were partly responsible for the development of women's music and periodicals as large, alternative industries. Residential collectives, in contrast, generally were rurally located and often formed to provide part- or full-time living arrangements for women. While residential collectives also developed ways for women to make a living, these usually were only one focus of the collective's existence.

## Issues and Controversies

Collective experience encompassed both the best and the worst effects of lesbian politics. Collectives were often the center of exciting, effective feminist activism and certainly fostered much of contemporary lesbian theory and literature. It is difficult to overstate the feelings of excitement and power women found in their commitments to collective action. Yet, because most collectives either developed from, or took up, separatist politics, problems within separatist theory carried into collective experience. Basically, separatism's reliance on sexism as the primary oppression in human society left women with an inadequate theoretical framework to address the mechanisms of difference (ethnicity, class, sexuality, physical ability, and the like) among women themselves. Little prepared for the divisions that developed because of women's own oppressive behaviors, collectives often dissolved or moved into private ownership. Occasionally, collectives separated along further lines of identity differences: Some existed for women of color only; others developed specifically for disabled women. But even these collectives did not necessarily escape division over differences, as Juana Maria Paz's autobiography, *La Luz Journal* (1980), attests.

Participation in collectives thus waned in the late 1970s and early 1980s. By the mid-1990s, however, some indication of a renewed interest in collective formation appeared, evident in inquiries and calls for discussion posted in periodicals such as *Lesbian Connection* and on numerous electronic mailing lists.

*Dana R. Shugar*

### *Bibliography*

Andreadis, A. Harriette. "The Woman's Commonwealth: Utopia in Nineteenth-Century Texas." In *Women in Search of Utopia: Mavericks and Mythmakers*. Ed. Ruby Rohrlich and Elaine H. Baruch. New York: Shocken, 1984, pp. 86–98.

Bloodroot Collective. "Bloodroot: Brewing Visions." *Lesbian Ethics* 3:1 (Spring 1988), 3–22.

Brody, Michal, ed. *Are We There Yet? A Continuing History of Lavender Woman: A Chicago Lesbian Newspaper, 1971–1976*. Iowa City: Aunt Lute, 1985.

Cheney, Joyce, ed. *Lesbian Land*. Minneapolis: Word Weavers, 1985.

Paz, Juana Maria. *La Luz Journal*. Fayetteville, Ark.: Paz, 1980.

Shugar, Dana R. *Separatism and Women's Community*. Lincoln: University of Nebraska Press, 1995.

*See also* Businesses, Lesbian; Community; Furies, The; *Lesbian Connection;* Lesbian Nation; Separatism; Utopian Literature

## Colleges, Women's

Intimate relationships between women have existed throughout the history of women's colleges in the United States. Early leaders in women's higher education lived publicly with other academic women until the 1920s, when the stigma surrounding lesbianism increased. Lesbian relationships persisted on campuses throughout the twentieth century and remain visible at many of the remaining women's colleges. Some campuses have institutionalized lesbian studies programs and support services for lesbian students and faculty.

Before Mary Lyon (1797–1849) founded Mount Holyoke Female Seminary in 1837 as the first postsecondary institution for women, she had established an intimate friendship with another woman educator. Later in the nineteenth century, women's colleges were seen as more wholesome environments than coeducational schools, since a woman was less likely to develop an unwise friendship with a college man. A college education enabled some white, middle-class women to move outside the domestic setting and to establish relationships of their own choosing, thus paving the way for the establishment of women's communities in the women's colleges and settlement houses of the Progressive Era.

The academic New Women of the late nineteenth century created a network of relationships among teachers and students at the women's colleges. Katharine Lee Bates (1859–1929) and Katherine Coman (1857–1915) were a well-known Wellesley College faculty pair from the 1880s on. M. Carey Thomas (1857–1935) assumed the presidency of Bryn Mawr in 1894, living first in a passionate relationship with Mamie Gwinn (1861–?) and later with Mary Garrett (1839–1915). Mary E. Woolley (1863–1947) was president of Mount Holyoke College from 1901 to 1936 and lived in the president's house with former student and Mount Holyoke faculty member Jeannette Marks (1875–1964). Biographers disagree about how to describe these women's relationships, but they concur that romantic friendships were not considered uncommon or unseemly among women academics until after the turn of the twentieth century.

The prevalence of student "smashes," or crushes, at women's colleges provides further evidence of women's passion for one another on campus. Students who engaged in smashes courted the object of their emotions, usually an older student or a young teacher, with flowers, poems, and candy. Documented as early as the 1870s at Vassar, smashes were considered normative behavior, innocuous to the participants except in their tendency to disrupt campus life.

The pathologizing of lesbians early in the twentieth century interrupted the pattern of women's relationships in academe. Women's colleges and girls' boarding schools in the United States and Britain were specifically cited as environments likely to interfere with heterosexual development. In 1911, Jeannette Marks wrote that "sentimental friendships" were a detriment to a student's health and education. The YWCA visited women's colleges to give talks on "problems" such as homosexuality, and, in an attempt to prevent intimacy among women, several colleges redesigned student residences to provide single bedrooms for all.

Despite growing antilesbian sentiment, there is evidence that intimate friendships continued on several campuses into the 1920s and that there remained on some campuses significant ignorance of the stigma surrounding lesbianism. A 1920 Oberlin yearbook features the Oberlin Lesbian Society, a group devoted to writing poetry, and a senior essay from Bryn Mawr in 1921 describes the passion that students had for one another. Mary McCarthy's (1912–1989) novel *The Group* (1963), told the story of a group of Vassar women in the 1930s who discover that their leader is a lesbian.

After World War II, when many women in the United States returned to their prewar roles of wife and mother, a college education gained renewed importance as a means for women to live independently or in relationships with other women. At the same time, women's colleges were easy targets for McCarthyite accusations of harboring lesbians. Through the 1950s and 1960s, women were sometimes expelled from college for being too intensely involved with one another, but women's liberation and the growing gay rights movement eventually gave rise to organized communities of lesbians on campuses.

When elite men's colleges began accepting women in the 1970s, women's colleges came under attack again for being havens for lesbians. Economic pressure and declining enrollments required many women's colleges to close or become coeducational in the last quarter of the twentieth century: In 1969, there were 228 women's colleges; in 1997, there were eighty-four. Many of these campuses have organized groups for lesbian, bisexual, or queer-identified women, and some have specialized groups for women of color or other self-identified communities. Very few women's colleges offer administrative support services specifically for lesbian and bisexual women, though several offer domestic-partner benefits to lesbian and gay employees. Lesbian, lesbian and gay, or queer studies curricula appear at women's colleges at about the same rate as they do at coeducational liberal-arts institutions.

*Kristen A. Renn*

### Bibliography

Horowitz, Helen Lefkowitz. *Alma Mater: Design and Experience in the Women's Colleges from Their Nineteenth-Century Beginnings to the 1930s*. New York: Knopf, 1984.

——. *The Power and the Passion of M. Carey Thomas*. New York: Knopf, 1994.

MacKay, A., ed. *Wolf Girls at Vassar: Lesbian and Gay Experiences*. New York: St. Martin's, 1992.

*See also* Bates, Katharine Lee; Boarding Schools; New Woman; Romantic Friendship; Smashes, Crushes, Spoons; Thomas, M. Carey

## Colonialism

Process by which people settle in a new country—often remaining subject to their country of origin—by way of appropriating land and incorporating indigenous people as part of a new nation or society through force and/or violence, such as conquering, enslaving, and otherwise pressuring them into movement.

Westerners, through various forms of colonization, distorted the sexuality and gender constructions of colonized peoples. Lesbianism, as the modern West defines it, is not the only way same-sex experience has been understood. The profound impact of Western sexual ideology on colonized peoples has helped create a complex spectrum of identities. For many peoples, the discrete analytical category of sexuality itself is a colonial imposition that addresses the realities of only a small part of the spectrum of women who have sexual and love relationships with other women. Many worldviews entail cosmologies in which sexuality is an integral force of life and not a separate category of existence or identity.

A preoccupation with "sexual deviance" is a recurrent theme in colonial writings; from first contact, Western concepts of indigenous sexualities have consistently distorted, misrepresented, and degraded the experiences they attempted to describe. M. Jacqui Alexander has argued that the racialization and sexualization of morality provided the foundation upon which the identity and authority of colonialism rested. For these reasons, sex as a category of colonial control is a fundamental consideration when exploring lesbianism in a historical context.

Stoler (1991) asserts that colonial and imperial authority and racial distinctions were fundamentally structured in terms of gender difference. In other words, gender and sexuality were racialized, and racialization was both gendered and sexualized within the larger processes of colonialism and impe-rialist expansion. For example, in the Pacific Islands, "promiscuous" and "savage" were the earliest labels applied within colonial contexts. Promiscuity, in this example, was marked as a characterization of Pacific female gender and sexuality as specifically different from the gender and sexuality of European women. In turn, policies of regulation, spacial separation, and access were shaped by such notions. Pacific women's gender and sexuality were racialized, marked as different from those of European colonials by virtue of their "difference," and their racialization was gendered and sexualized as different from Pacific men, who were, more often than not, described as "savage," whether noble or bestial. Stoler notes that, even while sexual domination has been carefully considered on a symbolic level as part of colonialism, it has rarely been treated as the substance of imperial policy. She further argues that sexual control was more than a metaphor for colonial domination—it fundamentally worked to mark class and racial differences and was implicated in a wider set of relations of power. For example, the governing and ordering of sexual relations was central to the development of particular kinds of colonial settlements and to the assigned economic activity within them.

Lesbian identity, in contrast to sexual behavior between women, is a modern phenomenon that is often predicated on the ability of women to break from kinship ties and autonomously support themselves. In many cultures, there may be no concept of lesbianism as a separate lifestyle even though there may be same-sex intimacy, because people may not define themselves outside of kinship or have the means or desire to be economically autonomous. This link between individualism and lesbian identity has led many women who struggle with the persistence of colonial legacies to resist the contemporary categorization of "lesbian," a resistance that is often presumed by dominant lesbian communities to be a desire to hide same-sex sexual behavior. Lesbians reckoning with legacies of both colonialism and anticolonial nationalist struggles, which often turned Western constructions back on themselves and restigmatized lesbianism, are redefining their identities and practices in their own terms and constructions within postcolonial formations.

A number of theorists have developed the relationship between colonialism and lesbianism in specific cultural contexts. In relation to American Indian women, Paula Gunn Allen (1986) has written about Native lesbianism as distinct from modern

American identities because it exists within a "larger and spiritual tribal context." She suggests that one connection between the conquest of Native America and the influence of Christianity lies in the brutal suppression of medicine peoples and women's authority and in redefining notions of "proper sexual behavior" according to European practices and regulations of sexual access and reproduction. Other Native American Indian writers, such as Jaimes and Halsey (1992), counter that Allen's approach aids in the reinforcement of cultural appropriation and distortion of indigenous traditions concerning homosexuality by the dominant mainstream in a context of continued neocolonialism. For example, the invocation of Native religions by "white shamans" is often a business in which individuals profit at the expense of American Indian peoples, whose traditions are still unprotected and largely threatened.

Writing about Chicanos within the United States, Moraga (1993) theorizes the cultural and sexual colonization of an occupation that continues today. She critiques the forms of sexism and homophobia that persist in Chicano nationalist politics and argues that, "because women's bodies and those of men and women who transgress gender roles have been regarded as territories to be conquered, they are also territories to be liberated." Moraga maps the possibilities in a "Queer Aztlan," the spiritual-geographical Mexican territory where sexual freedom and agency are part of expressing fuller self-determination as a people.

As Lisa Kahaleole Chang Hall and J. Kehaulani Kauanui (1996) describe, outsiders formed a legacy of control and commodification of Pacific sexuality—from the explorers who decided the women were whores and the men weak in their lack of control over "their" women to missionaries who recorded with appalled horror their views of native sexuality—that endures in the modern world. Because Pacific cultures had oral rather than written historical traditions, the written history that survives was filtered through the censorship of those literate and horrified missionaries. The contemporary context of same-sex love for Pacific women grows out of a deliberate colonial destruction of indigenous languages and traditions; its potential for resistance is influenced by feminist, lesbian, and decolonization movements and ideologies. A prime example of this activism is the liberatory organizing of Na Mamo o Hawai'i, an indigenous group of lesbian, gay, bisexual, and/or transgender Hawai'ins

concerned connecting struggles for Hawai'in sovereignty with civil rights, including same-sex marriage.

Evelynn M. Hammonds (1995) has described the "problematic of silence" in her delineation of "a genealogy of black female sexuality" within the United States, which begins with the colonizing of black women's bodies. Within systems of American enslavement, whites' domination over, and ownership of, African peoples entailed, among other brutal realities, the common practice of rape, as well as enforced and controlled sexual reproduction. This lineage has complicated black women's attempts at claiming sexual agency. Silvera (1991) notes that many Afro-Caribbean lesbians are in a position of continued imagining and discovery of their existence in both the past and the present. In that search, Silvera notes, the Bible plays an important part in Afro-Caribbean culture, and she argues for its recognition in order to understand the historical and political contexts for the invisibility of Afro-Caribbean lesbians. She also discusses the varied effects of Christian values in slave colonies as a force in resistance and hope, as well as racism and misogyny. Alexander (1991, 1997) has documented the criminalization of lesbianism by the postcolonial state governments of the Bahamas and Trinidad and Tobago. She theorizes the "redrafting of morality" as a continued legacy of British colonialism in the role of developing legislation that targets lesbians as a "contemporary politics of recolonization" by the now independent nations. Alexander argues that "erotic autonomy" can enable a "politics of decolonization" in a fuller sense.

Writing about South Asian identities, Shah (1993) has pointed out that, in attempts to resolve the common conflict between national and racial identity and sexual identity, some South Asian queers have searched for their "very own gay tradition," including the rigorous study of past cultural forms and relics to locate lesbian activity in many Hindu texts and manuals and the linking of British colonialism with the destruction of same-sex images and homosexual expression. Shah critically argues that the past is not a "thing" waiting to be discovered and recovered, that a past regained or saved cannot secure or fix an identity for eternity. Rather than rigid, the relationships between identities and histories are fluid and constantly shifting. Shah argues that gay South Asians "use the past" by employing ancient texts and sculptures to shade contemporary meanings of sexual practices.

These are just few examples of attempts to maintain control over the meaning and interpretation of same-sex desires and relationships between women, given the various histories of colonialism, the politics of anticolonial nationalism, and the struggle for decriminalization and civil rights.

*J. Kehaulani Kauanui*

### Bibliography

Alexander, M. Jacqui. "Erotic Autonomy as a Politics of Decolonization: An Anatomy of Feminist and State Practice in the Bahamas Tourist Economy." In *Feminist Genealogies, Colonial Legacies, Democratic Futures*. Ed. M. Jacqui Alexander and Chandra Tapalde Mohanty. New York and London: Routledge, 1997, pp. 63–100.

———. "Redrafting Morality: The Postcolonial State and the Sexual Offences Bill of Trinidad and Tobago." In *Third World Women and the Politics of Feminism*. Ed. Chandra Tapalde Mohanty, Ann Russo, and Lourdes Torres. Bloomington: Indiana University Press, 1991, pp. 133–152.

Allen, Paula Gunn. *The Sacred Hoop: Recovering the Feminine in American Indian Traditions*. Boston: Beacon, 1986.

Hall, Lisa Kahaleole Chang, and J. Kehaulani Kauanui. "Same-Sex Sexuality in Pacific Literature." In *Asian American Sexualities*. Ed. Russell Leong. New York and London: Routledge, 1996, pp. 113–118.

Hammonds, Evelynn M. "Toward a Genealogy of Black Female Sexuality: The Problematic of Silence." In *Feminist Genealogies, Colonial Legacies, Democratic Futures*. Ed. M. Jacqui Alexander and Chandra Mohanty. New York: Routledge, 1997, pp. 170–182.

Jaimes, M. Annette, with Theresa Halsey. "American Indian Women at the Center of Indigenous Resistance in Contemporary North America." In *The State of Native America: Genocide, Colonization, and Resistance*. Ed. M. Annette Jaimes. Boston: South End, 1992, pp. 311–344.

Moraga, Cherríe. *The Last Generation*. Boston: South End, 1993.

Shah, Nayan. "Sexuality, Identity, and the Uses of History." In *A Lotus of Another Color: An Unfolding of the South Asian Gay and Lesbian Experience*. Ed. Rakesh Ratti. Boston: Alyson, 1993, pp. 113–132.

Silvera, Makeda. "Man Royals and Sodomites: Some Thoughts of the Invisibility of Afro-Caribbean Lesbians." In *Piece of My Heart: A Lesbian of Colour Anthology*. Ed. Makeda Silvera. Toronto: Sister Vision, 1991, pp. 14–26.

Stoler, Ann Laura. "Carnal Knowledges and Imperial Power: Gender, Race, and Morality in Colonial Asia." In *Gender at the Crossroads of Knowledge: Feminist Anthropology in the Postmodern Era*. Ed. Micaela di Leonardo. Berkeley: University of California Press, 1991, pp. 51–101.

*See also* Hawai'i; Indigenous Cultures; Native Americans

## Combahee River Collective

One of the earliest black feminist direct-action groups in the nation, formed in 1974 by a small group of Boston-based black lesbians following the eastern regional National Black Feminist Organization conference in 1973. Named for the river along which Harriet Tubman (1823–1913) led hundreds of slaves to freedom, the collective came together at a time when many of its members were struggling to define a liberating feminist practice alongside the ascendance of a predominantly white feminist movement, and a Black Nationalist vision of women deferring to black male leadership.

Early collective members included renowned black feminist writer and activist Barbara Smith, then in her late twenties and teaching at Emerson College and the University of Massachusetts, Boston; her twin sister, Beverly, a master's candidate at the Yale School of Public Health; Demita Frazier, also in her twenties and a social worker for juveniles in Boston; and Sharon Burke, an experienced writer and activist in her mid-forties. All four women identified as black lesbian feminists.

Throughout the mid-1970s, the collective met weekly at the Cambridge Women's Center. The group encouraged any black woman interested in raising her consciousness around women's issues to attend. Together, collective members engaged one another on definitive questions for a black feminist movement: What are black women's issues? What perspectives do black women bring to broader issues within and beyond the black community? Who can be identified as allies? Out of this work, in 1977 the collective first published "The Combahee River Collective Statement," which has become one of the strongest, earliest, and most often reprinted manifestos of feminist identity politics in the United States:

We are actively committed to struggling against racial, sexual, heterosexual, and class oppression and see our particular task the development of integrated analysis and practice based upon the fact that the major systems of oppression are interlocking. The synthesis of these oppressions creates the conditions of our lives. As Black women, we see Black feminism as the logical political movement to combat the manifold and simultaneous oppressions that all women of color face.

In addition to developing early black feminist politics and theory, Combahee River Collective members took these new perspectives into their activism across the city. Into the late 1970s, collective members were active in the struggle for desegregation of the Boston public schools, in community campaigns against police brutality in black neighborhoods, and on picket lines demanding construction jobs for black workers. They supported Kenneth Edelin, a black doctor at Boston City Hospital who was charged with manslaughter in the performance of an abortion, and Ella Ellison, who was arrested for murder for simply being seen in the area in which a homicide had been committed.

Finally, in 1979, when a series of murders against black women were committed in Boston's black neighborhoods, Combahee played a pivotal role in bringing together mainstream black community forces, white feminists, and progressive Left activists in Boston to combat the violence. This kind of collaborative work was made possible by the long-standing relationships the collective had cultivated over years of activist work in black, feminist, and progressive communities.

The emergence of coalition politics in the late 1970s and early 1980s can be directly attributed to the work of the Combahee River Collective (as well as other important grass-roots feminist collectives), which demonstrated the key roles that progressive feminists of color can play in acting as bridges between diverse constituencies while also creating new possibilities for change within deeply divided communities such as Boston.     *Jaime M. Grant*

## Bibliography

Barbara Smith, ed. "Combahee River Collective Statement." In *Home Girls: A Black Feminist Anthology,* pp. 272–282. New York: Kitchen Table: Women of Color Press, 1983.

*See also* Black Feminism; Coalition Politics; Smith, Barbara

## Comedy, Standup

Lesbian standup comedy first flourished in the 1980s due to the confluence of two factors: the increased visibility of the lesbian and gay rights movement and the emergence of standup comedy as a cultural phenomenon in the United States. However, it had its origins in the 1970s, most notably through the work of Robin Tyler and Maxine Feldman. Tyler, often with her partner, Patty Harrison, cut albums, made television appearances, played the college circuit, and appeared in a USO tour of Vietnam (they were thrown out of the show for kissing onstage). Though lesbian comic Lea Delaria's 1993 appearance on *Arsenio* has been widely cited as the first "out" lesbian (or gay) performance on national television, that credit, in fact, belongs to Tyler's 1979 spot on *The Phyllis Diller Show.*

While gatherings such as the National Women's Music Festival and the Michigan Womyn's Music Festival became, in the 1980s and 1990s, well-known venues for lesbian comedic acts, they were devoted strictly to music when they began operating in the early and mid-1970s. By the late 1970s, however, festival organizers found the idea of "women's music" too restrictive, and the broader concept of "women's culture" invited the participation of writers and other sorts of artists. Lesbian standups both performed their own acts and were frequently used as emcees.

Kate Clinton, for many years the preeminent lesbian standup, began her career in 1981, building a national reputation from a grass-roots base of women's clubs and coffeehouses. By the mid-1980s, standup generally exploded on the American scene via the growth of cable television and the proliferation of comedy clubs. While "out" performances in mainstream sites were rare, the popularity of standup as an entertainment form, combined with the existence of numerous organizations, clubs, and events spawned by a rapidly expanding lesbian and gay movement, created a huge demand for lesbian and gay performers and emcees. Inspired by the example of their predecessors, more lesbians embarked on standup careers in the mid-to-late 1980s; many of these combined lesbian with ethnic humor, as in the cases of Lea Delaria (Italian American), Karen Williams (African American), Sara Cytron (Jewish), and Marga Gomez (Latina). This genera-

C tion of comics could rely on regular work in urban "gay ghettos" and vacation meccas and soon became familiar faces in Provincetown, Massachusetts, clubs; establishments such as Josie's Cabaret and Juice Joint in San Francisco, California; Club Med–type resorts; and on cruises at sea.

Whereas 1970s lesbian feminists had been reputed to lack humor, the 1990s lesbian was conceived of as "chic" and playful. Lesbian comics were heard by the nation as they emceed the 1993 National March on Washington (covered live on C-SPAN), appeared on network talk shows and *Comedy Central*'s "Out There" specials, and were featured in news segments. Suzanne Westenhoeffer, a younger comic who appeared in the early 1990s, was in 1994 the first out lesbian to be featured in an hour-long HBO Comedy Special. A lesbian and gay variety show, *In the Life*, was aired on public television stations around the country and included several lesbian standups. Annually recurring events, such as the National Women's Comedy Conference in Ohio and "All Women, All Comedy" on the West Coast, showcased lesbian comedic talent for sellout audiences. As previously unimaginable levels of recognition became possible, lesbian performers strove for ever-greater visibility through sitcoms, films, and comedy-writing contracts. As of the mid-1990s, with the exception of Delaria, mainstream media appear to have courted the less "ethnic" and more "straight-appearing" lesbian and gay talent—a practice that contrasts sharply with the traditions of "women's community" events and festivals, where diversity is valued and homophobic stereotypes lack currency in programming.

Many lesbian comics believe that, even before lesbian humor was "out," covert forms of it appeared in the wider culture—the work of Lily Tomlin (1939–) and Jane Wagner (1935–) and the character of Miss Jane Hathaway on the television show *The Beverly Hillbillies* are often cited. Self-defined lesbian humor, when it appeared, punctured the myth of lesbian nonexistence; it was largely about society's elision (or adamant nonrecognition) of lesbians in the psychosexual human landscape. Heterosexual society's naive act of "not seeing" lesbians was itself the humorous subject. Within that context, it was funny for lesbians to hear the details of their own lives—generally consigned to the "private" realm—discussed publicly. Later, "out" lesbian experience came to occupy much broader public space, and "out" lesbian humor came to assume a wider audience that could laugh with the comic.

There is no consensus regarding exactly what constitutes "lesbian standup comedy." Some of the comics of the 1990s include pointed political commentary in their acts, while others focus mainly on sex, relationships, and coming out. Most agree that their humor is connected to, and derives from, painful feelings and experiences. At least two general subjects constitute the majority of lesbian standups' material: (1) the absurdity of a homophobic world that cannot fathom or adapt to lesbian existence; and (2) the nature of the lesbian subculture, including its behaviors, rituals, beliefs, desires, fears, and representations of itself in art and everyday life.

*Harriet Malinowitz*

### Bibliography

Flowers, Charles, ed. *Out, Loud, and Laughing: A Collection of Gay and Lesbian Humor*. New York: Anchor/Doubleday, 1995.

Geduldig, Lisa. "Laughing Themselves into the Mainstream." *Advocate* 592 (December 17, 1991), 78–81.

Jones, Anderson. "Standup Comics Ride the Wave of Lesbian Chic." *New York Newsday* (January 23, 1994), Sunday edition.

Martin, Linda, and Kerry Segrave. *Women in Comedy*. Secaucus, N.J.: Citadel, 1986.

Walker, Nancy A. *A Very Serious Thing: Women's Humor and American Culture*. Minneapolis: University of Minnesota Press, 1988.

Warren, Roz, ed. *Revolutionary Laughter: The World of Women Comics*. Freedom, Calif.: Crossing, 1995.

*See also* Camp; Humor; Music Festivals

### Coming Out

One of the most widely used terms among lesbians and gay men in the contemporary United States. Its meanings are various: One can come out (or be brought out) *through* one's first sexual experience with another woman, come out *into* a lesbian community, come out *of* the closet, or come out *to* a range of audiences, including oneself, as well as friends, family, employers, and "the public."

### History

Over the course of the twentieth century, use of the last two meanings (coming out *of* and *to*) has overtaken the first two (coming out *through* and *into*). Gay use of the term seems to have originally re-

*National Coming Out Day logo. Design by Keith Haring. Courtesy Human Rights Campaign.*

ferred to the practice whereby a young woman (often, though not necessarily, an upper-class debutante) was introduced to a community of her peers at a "coming out party." As gay men used the term in the early twentieth century, one could come out into the gay world, underworld, or demimonde, in a parallel fashion. Lesbians were using the term in this same sense at least by mid-century, when a woman could come out into the (largely white) bar scene or into the (mostly black) house-party circuit. This process might precede or follow one's sexual coming out, generally helped along by a more experienced (though not necessarily older) woman.

Post-Stonewall (1969) generations, however, have emphasized a new trajectory of coming out; rather than coming out *into* a new social world, one comes out *of* the isolation and invisibility of "the closet." This newer concept implicitly makes the claim that it is not only healthier and more satisfying to step out of the closet, it is also more responsible. To hide one's homosexuality, by this reasoning, is to contribute to one's own stigmatization—and, by extension, to the continued stigmatization of other lesbians and gay men. Marchers at the early Gay Pride parades chanted "Come out, come out," simultaneously imploring sidewalk observers to come out of hiding and gay bar habitués to come out onto the streets. In its late-twentieth-century usage, "coming out" is a core concept of identity politics.

Nonetheless, older meanings of the term coexist with new ones, particularly in working-class communities of color, where lesbians and gay men may come out into "the life."

## Lesbian and Gay Culture

Coming out has continued to enjoy an important place in lesbian and gay politics and cultures. The late 1980s saw the establishment of National Coming Out Day (NCOD), a nationwide holiday for lesbians, gays, bisexuals, and transgendered people. Originally an outcome of the "War Conference," a gathering of activists that followed on the heels of the 1987 March on Washington, NCOD is now part of the National Coming Out Project, sponsored by the Human Rights Campaign. NCOD, October 11, is observed by lesbian and gay groups across the United States, particularly on college campuses. Its official logo—a Keith Haring drawing of a person kicking open a closet door—is a widely recognized symbol of coming out, and one that explicitly refers to the post-Stonewall meanings of the term.

In the early 1990s, nonconsensual coming out—"outing"—was debated in queer communities and media. This practice of bringing someone else—generally a celebrity or politician—out of her or his closet, was seen by some as vital political strategy and by others as an implicitly homophobic tactic (relying for impact on the continued stigmatization of homosexuality). Queer newsmedia, notably New York City's *OutWeek*, practiced outing enthusiastically for a short time, as did poster-pasting members of Queer Nation. Among the women targeted were actresses Sandra Bernhard (1955–) and Jodie Foster (1962–), singers k.d. lang (1961–) and Michelle Shocked (1962–), and gossip columnist Liz Smith (1923–). Specifically lesbian publications and groups rarely took a positive stance toward outing, and lesbians operating within mixed lesbian, gay, and bi institutions and organizations held a range of opinions of the practice.

Most lesbians, of course, are not celebrities or public figures and relate to coming out in more personal terms. Of particular importance to many is the act of coming out to one's parents and other family members. Here again, the phenomenon is much more common among younger lesbians than among those who came out before Stonewall. The latter more often see themselves as living simultaneously in two worlds, gay and straight, and often feel no need to "mix" the two by telling their straight families about their gay lives. Weston (1991) points out

**C** that coming out to one's parents, siblings, and other family members is part of the process of creating one's own "chosen family." By revealing oneself, to a parent, for example, one also causes the true nature of the parent-child relationship to reveal itself. ("Does my parent love me truly or only on condition than I be heterosexual?") Complete rejection by parents is relatively uncommon, but the fear of it structures the experience for many lesbians as they come out to their parents. Some evidence suggests that lesbians may encounter more negative responses from parents, particularly from mothers, than do gay men.

A public coming out, whether precipitated by oneself or others, presupposes that the individual has come out to herself. Individual experiences of coming out at this level continue to be extremely important, and widely varied, processes. Many observers have suggested that the average age of coming out has dropped, as more lesbians and gay men began coming out in their teens in the late 1980s and early 1990s. Statistics are impossible to come by, but burgeoning, and increasingly younger, membership in lesbian, gay, and bisexual youth organizations suggests the presence of such a trend. And college campuses, often a location where one may come out for the first time, are seeing more students who have already come out to themselves when they arrive on campus for their first year.

## Coming Out Process

Scholars and therapists have attempted to identify a common coming out process, or trajectory, with mixed success. Such stage-sequential models identify as few as four or as many as eight stages, or change points, and generally describe a process that moves from discovery to acceptance to announcement—that is, through a series of "comings out." Troiden's (1988) summary points out that such models are "ideal types" and that individuals may order the steps differently or skip some steps entirely. Perhaps the best known of these models is that of Vivienne Cass (1979). Her six-stage sequence predicts that individuals will move from identity confusion, through identity comparison, tolerance, acceptance, and pride, to the ultimate goal of identity synthesis. Many attempts to develop models that are applicable to both lesbians and gay men (models that treat bisexuality identity formation are exceedingly rare) are problematic, as they tend to treat experiences common to gay men as

normative and experiences common to lesbians as departures from the norm. One frequently reads, therefore, that lesbians tend to first recognize their homoerotic feelings and participate in their first sexual experience with a same-gender partner at later ages than gay men, but rarely sees gay men's experiences compared to a lesbian norm. More recent work on lesbian coming out processes recognizes that, while an initial process of self-labeling is a crucial milestone, coming out in some sense continues throughout one's life, so that a lesbian identity is never entirely a finished product.

Nonetheless, the early process of recognition and naming tends to become one's "coming out story." These stories are told and retold, in what has been identified as a common ritual of lesbian and gay community life, particularly as a way of getting to know an acquaintance. Fictional treatments have been extraordinarily popular in lesbian literature, and nonfiction collections, such as *The Coming Out Stories* (Penelope and Wolfe 1980), remain widely read. The appeal of these narratives is apparently not limited to a lesbian and gay audience: On April 30, 1996, more than forty million television viewers watched Ellen Morgan, the lead character in the ABC sitcom *Ellen* come out to herself, her therapist, and her closest friends (becoming then the first lesbian or gay lead character on a continuing network program, although the show was canceled in 1998).

*Vera Whisman*

## Bibliography

Cass, Vivienne. "Homosexual Identity Formation: A Theoretical Model." *Journal of Homosexuality* 4 (1979), 219–235.

Eliason, Michele. "An Inclusive Model of Lesbian Identity Assumption." *Journal of Gay, Lesbian, and Bisexual Identity* 1 (1996), 3–19.

Muller, Ann. *Parents Matter: Parents' Relationships with Lesbian Daughters and Gay Sons*. Tallahassee, Fla.: Naiad, 1987.

Penelope, Julia, and Susan Wolfe. *The Coming Out Stories*. Freedom, Calif.: Crossing, 1980.

Troiden, Richard. *Gay and Lesbian Identity: A Sociological Analysis*. Dix Hills, N.Y.: General Hall, 1988.

Weston, Kath. *Families We Choose: Lesbians, Gays, Kinship*. New York: Columbia University Press, 1991.

*See also* Closet; Coming Out Stories; Family; History; Identity; Identity Politics; Psychology

## Coming Out Stories

Personal narratives or life histories, both written and spoken, that recount the process of self-realization, acceptance, and articulation of same-sex desire. There are as many versions of coming out stories as there are lesbians, since coming out is at once a personal coming-to-consciousness, an oral narrative, and, for many, an autobiography set into writing. Some women define what it means to come out around their first sexual experience with another woman, or when they first realized that desire, or when they voiced that desire and claimed a lesbian identity. Certain lesbians consider their sexual identity essential to their self, something innate, while others explain their lesbianism as a choice, perhaps even a political one. Many women experience a heightened sensitivity to oppression once they leave their privileged affiliation with socially sanctioned straight culture.

The coming out story as a literary narrative and an event in contemporary lesbian history can be traced specifically to the publication of *The Coming Out Stories* (1980), edited by Julia Penelope and Susan Wolfe, and *The Lesbian Path* (1980), edited by Margaret Cruikshank. Previously, collections of interviews had been published—*The New Lesbians* (1977), edited by Laurel Galana and Gina Covina, and *We're Here* (1977), edited by Angela Stewart-Park and Jules Cassidy—but *The Coming Out Stories* and *The Lesbian Path* were the first to foreground life histories written by lesbians themselves. As various theorists have noted, by bringing together in one place the personal narratives of women who did not know that there was a group to belong to, these books gave form to a moment in lesbian history when certain previously scattered individuals became a group. Although written in isolation, these personal narratives of primarily white and middle-class women have a striking similarity of theme, experience, and language. This similarity struck some reviewers as repetitive and boring. But to others, the significance of the repetition was to produce a sense of lesbian group identity. In this way, coming out stories have been related to the rituals or rites of passage that establish cohesive values and identities for a particular culture.

Of crucial importance to the coming out story is the availability of language to aid the initial coming out process, in order for women to adequately understand and articulate their desires. Hence, it is significant that many coming out stories are raw, unedited, awkward pieces of prose. While some reviewers criticize them for this lack of professionalism, others praise them as authentic, moving testimonies of real women. Many coming out narratives describe the effect of the silencing and continuous sociopolitical erasure of lesbian history and experience and the struggle to break the silence imposed on same-sex love. As one woman writes in *The Coming Out Stories:* "I did not have the word for lesbian when I was nine years old. . . . I did not know that I was coming out." Due to the censorship of lesbian expression, coming out stories are valuable insofar as they offer representations of the rich diversity of lesbian experiences and, as such, are an important resource for constructing and explaining lesbian identification. They are also useful as models for coming out in different social and interpersonal contexts.

Part of the coming out process, as expressed in the coming out story, is a reevaluation of the events of one's past in light of one's new group identity. Events that heterosexual socialization overlooks as irrelevant to the development of a "healthy" desire for the opposite sex, such as early crushes on other women, achieve newfound importance in light of the discovery of lesbianism and the construction of an alternative life story. For some critics, such as Marilyn Frye (1980), the stories do threaten to falsify the past, eliminating experiences and feelings that do not conform to the newly adopted lesbian identity. In other words, coming out stories have a narrative structure and political role that shapes lesbian identity in strictly limited ways.

Hence, the most potent critique of the first generation of coming out stories was that they identified only a narrow range of lesbian experiences: specifically, those of white, middle-class, able-bodied lesbians. They did not necessarily recognize that, added to the pressure of coming out as lesbian, many women face the pressure to conform to heterosexist norms from their ethnic and religious community and fear being ostracized and isolated from their families if they "choose" to affiliate with a lesbian community over the familial one. The groundbreaking anthology *This Bridge Called My Back* (1981), edited by Cherríe Moraga and Gloria Anzaldúa, included a number of personal narratives by lesbians of color. Following its publication, new collections of lesbian life narratives, such as *Nice Jewish Girls* (1989), edited by Evelyn Torton Beck; *Compañeras: Latina Lesbians* (1994), edited by Juanita Ramos; *Out of the Class Closet* (1994), edited by Julia Penelope; and *Afrekete* (1995), edited by Catherine E. McKinley and L. Joyce De-Laney added to the narrative model considerations in coming out for women who identify their selves ethnically and racially as well as sexually. In the 1990s, some women began to adopt the term "queer" instead of "lesbian," since it allows for the articulation of multiple and shifting identifications across lines of race, gender, ethnicity, class, and sexuality, refusing to prioritize any one aspect of the self.

Many lesbian coming out narratives are partly fictionalized or theorized and written through novels, poetry, and essays. Michelle Cliff's *Claiming an Identity They Taught Me To Despise* (1980), Audre Lorde's *Zami* (1983), Cherríe Moraga's *Loving in the War Years* (1983), Mab Segrest's *My Mama's Dead Squirrel* (1985), Gloria Anzaldúa's *Borderlands/La Frontera* (1987), Joan Nestle's *A Restricted Country* (1987), Nicole Brossard's *The Aerial Letter* (1988), Leslie Feinberg's *Stone Butch Blues* (1993), and Dionne Brand's *Bread Out of Stone* (1994) are just a few of the many texts based on lesbian life narratives and coming out stories.

Through coming out and self-naming, lesbians gain empowerment and visibility. The next step in the validation, legitimation, and celebration of lesbian lives, according to Bonnie Zimmerman (1985), is "to inscribe personal experience onto a body politic that can then take part in reconstructing the public and private institutions that presently control our lives." To preserve and pass on the myriad experiences of what it means to come out and live as a lesbian, dyke, or queer, autobiographical stories and life narratives are an integral resource for theory, politics, history, and future generations of women.

*sidney matrix*

**Bibliography**

Frye, Marilyn. "Review of *The Coming Out Stories*." *Sinister Wisdom* 14 (1980), 97–98.

Martin, Biddy. "Lesbian Identity and Autobiographical Difference(s)." In *Life/Lines: Theorizing Women's Autobiography*. Ed. Bella Brodzki and Celeste Schenck. Ithaca, N.Y.: Cornell University Press, 1988, pp. 77–103.

Zimmerman, Bonnie. "The Politics of Transliteration: Lesbian Personal Narratives." *Signs: Journal of Women in Culture and Society* 9:4 (1984), 663–682.

**See also** Anzaldúa, Gloria E.; Autobiography; Brossard, Nicole; Coming Out; Cruikshank, Margaret Louise; Identity; Lorde, Audre; Moraga, Cherríe; Nestle, Joan; Penelope, Julia

## Community

Social network providing solidarity and companionship. Lesbian community refers to a group of persons and/or spaces that affirm same-sex sexuality and love between women. Immersed in a homophobic and heterosexist society, a lesbian community is a subset of the larger society, premised on a collective resistance to societal expectations and cultural norms of gender and sexuality. Communities based on neighborhoods, race, ethnicity, age, intellectual or artistic interests, and political movements play important roles in some lesbians' lives, but the more common connotation of "lesbian community" is an affinity that has been forged around gender and sexual identities.

## Characteristics

A lesbian community fundamentally consists of women who similarly claim the identity "lesbian." Sociologists, drawing on new social-movement theory of the late twentieth century, have noted the importance of a "collective identity" in organizing movements for social change. Yet scholars and activists have demonstrated how the concept of a common lesbian identity is problematic, in that lesbians' identities differ across time, nationality, region, race, age, class, sexual practice, and political perspective.

Disagreement regarding whom community includes and what community represents to lesbians persists. While some understand community as a union of those who are similar, others point out the radical diversity among women identified as lesbians. Another viewpoint on lesbian community is that it validates a select group of lesbians—in the United States, white, middle-class lesbian feminists—while excluding those who do not fit a certain mold. Femmes, butches, lesbians of color, and poor and working-class lesbians have challenged a model of community that assumes sameness, commonality, and unity. There are few, if any, agreed upon criteria for establishing who belongs or does not belong to a lesbian community, and standards and ideals vary from person to person.

The nuances between "a lesbian community" and "the lesbian community" are significant; the former suggests that multiple communities exist, while the latter generally indicates a single, encompassing entity. In a particular city or town, "the lesbian community" often refers to lesbians in that location rather than globally. When not qualified as a bar community, a "jock" community, or otherwise, "the lesbian community" usually corresponds to a politicized lesbian feminist community. Lesbians and feminists since the 1970s have referred to "the women's community" as synonymous with the lesbian feminist community. In some instances, a lesbian or women's community refers more specifically to a communal-living arrangement or environment.

One sense of community prevalent in the twentieth century emerges from the supposition that there are lesbians, gay men, and bisexuals everywhere, united in theory because of their sexual orientation. There is some overlap between the lives and experiences of lesbians and gay men; however, lesbian communities have developed apart from male-dominated gay communities.

## Institutions

Institutional bases for lesbian communities include feminist bookstores, coffeehouses, dance clubs, women's centers and women's studies departments, and activist and support groups. Bookstores owned and run by lesbians are resources for books, magazines, music, and gifts, as well as announcements, book readings, and meetings. Likewise, coffeehouses and dance clubs provide venues for lesbians to socialize. Lesbian feminists have been instrumental in the establishment of women's studies programs and women's centers at universities throughout the world, attracting lesbian students and faculty. Finally, lesbian communities comprise a variety of groups, including ones that are generally for lesbians of a particular locale, such as Lesbianas a la Vista in Argentina, and those formed around more specific identities and interests, such as lesbian mothers, lesbian Alcoholics Anonymous, and lesbians of color in the United States.

Lesbian communities tend to thrive in particular geographical locations in countries throughout the world. Lesbians migrating from rural areas and small towns to larger cities are likely to find an environment less hostile to same-sex sexuality, although not all urban areas sustain visible lesbian communities. Cities known for their high concentration of out lesbians include ones whose histories have been documented—for instance, San Francisco, California, and New York City in the United States and Toronto in Canada. But lesbian communities are

emerging in a variety of locations. In Southeast Asia, lesbian organizations have established a public presence in the late twentieth century. Slang, Kitty Kitty, and Queer Sisters invite lesbians to join in social and group activities in Singapore, Korea, and Hong Kong, respectively. Informal groups are common in areas where lesbians suffer greater social or economic marginalization. For example, Swahili lesbians in Mombasa, Kenya, gather in groups in the Old Town and in the suburbs.

Outside large cities in the United States, festivals and conferences temporarily attract lesbians to rural campgrounds and college campuses. Since 1975, the Michigan Womyn's Music Festival has offered lesbians a yearly week-long community built entirely by women. Socializing, workshops, and entertainment allow for networking internationally and learning skills in an environment in which lesbians are the norm. Lesbian feminists make festivals, conferences, and women's events more accessible by establishing sliding-scale admission costs, providing child care, and recognizing the needs of women with disabilities. Barriers, nonetheless, remain, so that many lesbians choose not to participate in lesbian feminist or women's culture.

## Historical Communities

Published evidence of lesbian communities most often represents the experiences of women in industrialized Western countries. The preconditions for forming lesbian identities and communities may, in fact, correspond to certain trends of industrialization and urbanization, taking place in the West at an earlier date than elsewhere in the world. The best-known historical lesbian communities have arisen around bars and social-movement activity, peopled by lesbians who seek the companionship of other lesbians. While "community" was not always the word used to describe these historical networks, the concept of finding and joining with "my people" resembles what was later described as creating community.

The first recorded glimpses of lesbians visibly occupying public space include a Parisian lesbian restaurant and lesbians dancing in New York City in the late 1800s. Some lesbians found a place in the sexual underworld, mixing with prostitutes and homosexual men in the red-light districts of urban areas. However, few nineteenth-century models of lesbian community existed in a time period when "lesbian" was newly articulated as an identity.

Women in romantic friendships loved women and were surrounded by women and, therefore, did form a type of community. Because these women also maintained their positions in the heterosexual order, their bonds have not been described by their contemporaries or historians as lesbian communities.

During the twentieth century, lesbian communities became more prevalent in industrial and urban locales, though much of this history is yet to be written. For instance, historians have noted the existence of large numbers of lesbian bars and clubs in Germany in the 1920s. In Paris, the literary and artistic salons, notably those of Natalie Barney (1876–1972), attracted affluent French and expatriate lesbians in the early twentieth century. In the era of Prohibition and the Harlem Renaissance in the United States, African American lesbians convened at "buffet flats," house parties taking place in the black neighborhoods of Chicago, Illinois; Detroit, Michigan; and Harlem in New York City. The environment filled with liquor, gambling, and explicit sexuality incorporated homoeroticism was best captured by the lyrics of lesbian and bisexual blues singers.

In the early twentieth century, bars and house parties were the predominant locations in which lesbians made acquaintants with other lesbians. In the Northern, urban United States, the number of lesbian bars increased following World War II, commonly segregated in terms of race and class and invariably consisting of butches and femmes. Buffalo, New York, for instance, sustained at least three public, working-class lesbian communities by the 1950s, each revolving around bars and parties; they were divided into upwardly mobile, tough black, and tough, primarily white communities. It is assumed that working-class bar communities emerged and flourished in large and middle-size Western cities during the twentieth century, while local and national attitudes and laws produced variation across space and time.

With the emergence of feminist and gay liberation movements in the late 1960s, social-movement-oriented communities began to attract numbers of lesbians comparable to the bars. From this period, there remains abundant written and recorded evidence chronicling the existence of public lesbian communities. A central tenet of the late-twentieth-century lesbian and gay movement has been the importance of "coming out," facilitating middle-class lesbians' ability to recognize and find one another. Beginning in the late 1960s, lesbians advertised all-women dances, hosted lesbian and women's radio shows, published newsletters, circulated books and music, and made appearances in classrooms and on television, attempting to end isolation and to demystify lesbian experiences for the general public. What was historically distinct about these acts was that they were done by women who spoke as, and spoke for, lesbians, naming themselves "the lesbian community." Lesbians have continued this tradition of claiming space and sponsoring events for the benefit of lesbian communities into the final decades of the twentieth century. *Susan K. Freeman*

### Bibliography

Adam, Barry. *The Rise of a Gay and Lesbian Movement.* Boston: Twayne, 1987. Rev. ed. New York: Twayne, 1995.

D'Emilio, John. *Sexual Politics, Sexual Communities: The Making of a Homosexual Minority in the United States, 1940–1970.* Chicago: University of Chicago Press, 1983.

Kennedy, Elizabeth Lapovsky, and Madeline D. Davis. *Boots of Leather, Slippers of Gold: The History of a Lesbian Community.* New York: Routledge, 1993.

Phelan, Shane. *Getting Specific: Postmodern Lesbian Politics.* Minneapolis and London: University of Minnesota Press, 1994.

Ross, Becki. *The House That Jill Built: A Lesbian Nation in Formation.* Toronto: University of Toronto Press, 1995.

Weiss, Penny A., and Marilyn Friedman, eds. *Feminism and Community.* Philadelphia: Temple University Press, 1995.

*See also* Bars; Blues Singers; Buffalo, New York; Chicago, Illinois; Collectives; Coming Out; Community Centers; Harlem; Harlem Renaissance; Identity; Identity Politics; Lesbian Feminism; Separatism

## Community Centers

Community-based public places used for social, cultural, and political activities, sometimes providing social services and health care.

### History

The first self-described "gay community center" was opened by the Society for Individual Rights in 1966 in San Francisco, California. Approximately 10 percent of its members were lesbians. The women's liberation and gay liberation movements in

1968 and 1969 spurred the widespread creation of, first, "women's centers," then centers initially dscribed as "gay women's" and "gay." These were open for use by nonmembers and publicized their events. Lesbians participated as founders, administrators, and users of each type. The term "lesbian center" was first used in 1971. In 1972, some began describing themselves as "lesbian feminist." Most "gay" centers eventually added "lesbian" to their names during the 1980s; in the 1990s, a few added "bisexual" or "transgendered." Also in the 1990s, some centers were created by and for lesbians and gay men of color.

Between 1971 and 1996, forty-three centers in twenty-two states identified specifically as "gay women's," "lesbian," or "lesbian feminist." Approximately 30 percent of these opened between 1971 and 1974, reflecting and creating increased lesbian visibility and organizing within the women's and gay movements. They were formed in response to lesbians' experiences of homophobia in the former and sexism in the latter and lesbians' desires for places focused on their issues and needs.

The Gay Women's Services Center, which opened in March 1971 in Los Angeles, California, was described as the first social-services center for lesbians. That spring, the Daughters of Bilitis Center in New York City was renamed the Lesbian Center, reflecting a broadened constituency and governance. The Gay Women's Resource Center, founded in Seattle, Washington, in March 1971, opened in October. It was renamed the Lesbian Resource Center (LRC) in 1974 and is the oldest continuing lesbian center in the United States. In 1972, Karen Browne founded the LRC in Minneapolis, Minnesota, and, in Georgia, the Atlanta Lesbian Feminist Alliance (ALFA) opened ALFA House. In 1973, lesbian centers were also located in Denver, Colorado; Iowa City, Iowa; Eugene, Oregon; and Philadelphia, Pennsylvania. In 1974, the Chicago Women's Center renamed itself the Lesbian Feminist Center; other lesbian centers formed in Baltimore, Maryland, and East Lansing, Michigan.

New centers continued to open between 1975 and 1979, but by 1980 only nine of thirty centers formed since 1971 were still functioning, and more closed between 1980 and 1985. This was a period of renewed right-wing attacks on lesbians and gay men, people of color, and women; one lesbian center was firebombed. These attacks exacerbated political differences among lesbians. Volunteer bases eroded over arguments about maintaining women-only and lesbian-only spaces and about how to deal with issues of racism, sexual practices, and pornography. In this context, the economic situation of centers, reliant on donations and always tenuous, worsened. The elimination of federal funding for community groups in 1981, which had kept some centers economically viable, also took its toll. By 1985, there were only four lesbian centers in the United States. Then, slowly, new lesbian centers began opening.

## Characteristics

Most lesbian centers have served as space resources, depending upon users to organize activities and work as staff. They have been located in houses, offices, storefronts, industrial buildings, and churches. Only a few have owned their own spaces. In addition to public social space, they have provided emergency food and housing, job and legal referrals, classes, libraries, crisis and information telephone lines, and coming out, recovery, and youth groups. Political groups, video collectives, speakers bureaus, archives, health clinics, publishers, and theater companies were founded in their spaces, often becoming independent entities. Their coffeehouses offered venues for writers and musicians. Center newsletters have provided local, national, and international forums for discussion of political and personal issues and information about lesbian activities worldwide. One early newsletter, *Lesbian Connection,* is still mailed to more than 18,000 households. It outlives the center that housed it for twenty years—the East Lansing Lesbian Center–which closed in 1994, as did ALFA House in Atlanta. Both attributed their closings to waning interest due to new, diverse venues for the social and political activities they had offered.

After 1990, several new lesbian centers opened, including the Central Minnesota Lesbian Center in St. Cloud and Shades of Lavender in Brooklyn, New York, which began as a center for HIV-infected lesbians but subsequently opened to all lesbians. Lesbian-only centers exist in other countries as well, including the Camden Lesbian Center and Black Lesbian Group in London, England; Lesbenzentrum in Hanover, Germany; Cafe Biblio Labyris in Montréal, Québec; and the Vancouver Lesbian Center in British Columbia. The continued existence of lesbian-only centers even in cities that also have a women's center and a lesbian and gay center, as well as the designation of lesbian-

C only space within these, indicates that some lesbians still have a desire for a space of their own. And, although most lesbian and gay centers have always served as venues for activities and services for bisexual and transgendered people, the addition of these terms to the names of a few centers cannot yet be called a trend. Many new centers still use only "lesbian and gay" in their names; however, their literature is more likely to refer explicitly to bisexual and transgendered people as well.       *Maxine Wolfe*

### Bibliography

Gay and Lesbian Historical Society, P.O. Box 1258, San Francisco, California 94142. Organizations, subject and newsletter files; newspapers.

June L. Mazer Lesbian Collection, 626 N. Robertson Blvd., West Hollywood, California 90069. Organizations, subject, and newsletter files; newspapers.

Lesbian Herstory Archives, P.O. Box 1258, New York, New York 10116. Organizations, subject, centers, and newsletter files; newspapers; unpublished papers.

*See also* Community

## Community Organizing

The mobilization of "everyday" individuals at the grass-roots level to build a power base and engage in collective action toward a common goal. Local community actions often serve as a springboard for other forms of national and international activism. Community organizing is diverse in scope, tactics, and composition, may be proactive or reactive, and may seek inclusion in existing institutions or the building of alternative ones. Key principles of community organizing include personal empowerment, consciousness raising, participation of community members at all levels of planning, attention to both task completion and process, and leadership development.

Historically, lesbian community organizing has focused on issues of place and counterculture, as well as on broader and more visibly "political" issues. Two central debates concern inseparable questions: whether or not lesbians actually constitute a "community," and what role identity politics plays in organizing struggles. When identity politics gives birth to strong coalitions, lesbian community organizing is at its best. An excellent example can be seen in the coalition approach to two protests against benefit performances of the Broadway play *Miss Saigon* in 1991. The coalition, forged by lesbian and gay Asians and Pacific Islanders to protest the play because it perpetuated racist and sexist stereotypes, crossed lines of gender, class, race, and sexual orientation, grew to include more than twenty-two groups, and finally succeeded in having one fund-raiser canceled.

In the first half of the twentieth century, lesbian community organizing focused on creating a counterculture and building safe gathering places. For example, the Harlem Renaissance of the 1920s and 1930s provided a safe haven not only for writers and artists, but also for lesbian patrons seeking a place to be themselves. Lesbian and gay communities were formed in private parties, social clubs, racially integrated softball leagues, and in the emerging lesbian bars. By the early 1940s, the lesbian bar culture had become a central component in lesbian identity and community, with strict codes of confidentiality, behavior, and dress, and making clear contributions to the liberation movement that followed.

By the 1950s, lesbian community organizing expanded to include a more overtly political agenda. Paradoxically, the emergence of a homophile movement that lay the foundation for the liberationist perspective of the late 1960s and into the 1970s coexisted with internalized homophobia, apologetic pleas for acceptance, and efforts to prove to heterosexuals that lesbians were "just like them." Daughters of Bilitis (DOB) urged its members to dress "neatly and appropriately" for meetings and published articles about how to organize without alienating heterosexuals. Fear of charges of child molestation led the DOB to forbid minors from joining. At the same time, DOB's publication *The Ladder* proved an invaluable tool in extending the lesbian community to those who dared not attend a meeting in person, and it often took on discussions of controversial issues.

In the 1960s, there was a shift to a more radical and self-embracing ideology of gay liberation. Lesbian and gay newspapers proliferated, and, in April 1966, the first Gay Community Center in the United States opened in San Francisco, California. Lesbian organizers discussed the need to contest police practices and halt raids. Many lesbians were politicized by the 1969 Stonewall Rebellion and by the emerging philosophy of lesbian feminism, shifting their focus to fighting for political and economic power, inclusion in women's organizations as visible lesbians, and challenging sexism in gay male organizations.

Lesbian community organizing flourished in the 1970s with the building of lesbian separatist communities and spaces, the growth of the women's music (and festival) industry, lesbian leadership in the women's health movement, the growth of lesbian feminism, and the establishment of archives to preserve lesbian history and culture. Lesbians fought to gain civil rights protections, losing the battle to keep Dade County, Florida, from repealing its gay rights ordinance in 1977, for example, but winning the defeat of the Briggs Initiative in California in 1978, which would have banned gay teachers. Lesbians, active behind the scenes in the National Organization for Women (NOW), were referred to as the "lavender menace" by founder and then president Betty Friedan (1921–). A group of lesbians split from the Gay Liberation Front (GLF), took the name Radicalesbians, and began organizing on their own. In a dramatic stage takeover at the 1970 second Congress to Unite Women, they forced NOW to address its homophobia, and the organization changed its official position the following year. Lesbian separatists began organizing on their own as well. While some people simplistically dismiss lesbian separatists as utopian and extremist, their organizing and community building lay the foundation for many of the gains now enjoyed by all women.

In the 1980s, the growth of the New Right in voice, membership, and power mobilized lesbian and gay activists around issues of discrimination in housing, employment, tax equity, public services and accommodations, immigration, military discrimination, hate crimes, and the repeal of sodomy laws. Lesbians of color began organizing separately—both as a group and as specific identity groups within that larger rubric. Jewish lesbians gained visibility, as did lesbian mothers. But the most visible form of community organizing in the 1980s was around the issue of Acquired Immune Deficiency Syndrome (AIDS), initially known as Gay Related Immune Disorder (GRID).

Despite disagreement in the lesbian community about their role in the AIDS crisis, many lesbians responded by creating gay men's (and later lesbians') health organizations and centers, fundraising, donating blood, and providing direct care to men who were living with AIDS. Lesbians also worked to increase visibility, improve educational opportunities for lesbian and gay youth, and gain statewide civil rights protection.

In the 1990s, AIDS activism and efforts to gain statewide civil rights continued. Lesbians organized a national conference in Atlanta, Georgia, in 1991 and in 1992, formed a radical, confrontational, activist group, the Lesbian Avengers International. Definitions of "community" were stretched further than ever before with the use of the World Wide Web as an organizing tool. Three central areas of lesbian organizing were gaining family rights, fighting antigay initiatives, and including sexual orientation in the multicultural curriculum in the schools. A common element in these three struggles was the growing success of the New Right in framing public debates in the rhetoric of "family values" and "special rights."

In the arena of family rights, central goals included domestic-partnership benefits, same-sex marriage, adoption, and custody. The most far-reaching antigay initiatives of the decade were both in 1992: Colorado's Amendment 2 (invalidating any civil rights protection based on sexual orientation and forbidding the passage of any new protection) and Oregon's Proposition 9 (much broader in scope than Amendment 2). The former was passed, kept from going into effect by injunction, and later declared unconstitutional by the United States Supreme Court. The latter failed to pass. However, in 1993, antigay ballot measures were passed in three other U.S. cities. Finally, on the issue of curriculum in schools, efforts ranged from introducing "rainbow curricula" to fighting off initiatives that keep counselors from providing queer-positive referrals for queer or questioning youth.

Lesbian community organizing has made remarkable strides and created a number of institutions and national groups from which future organizers can gain resources, strategies, and historical perspective even as they maintain local autonomy. Some of the biggest challenges that lie ahead are improved coalition building and inclusive organizing, framing lesbian issues rather than allowing the religious right to frame them, and linking local struggles with national and global ones.

*Gina Kozik-Rosabal*

### Bibliography

Abbott, Sidney, and Barbara Love. *Sappho Was a Right-On Woman: A Liberated View of Lesbianism.* New York: Day, 1978.

Blasius, Mark, and Shane Phelan, eds. *We Are Everywhere: A Historical Sourcebook of Gay and Lesbian Politics.* New York: Routledge, 1997.

Shugar, Dana. *Separatism and Women's Community.* Lincoln: University of Nebraska Press, 1995.

Vaid, Urvashi. *Virtual Equality: The Mainstreaming of Gay and Lesbian Liberation.* New York: Anchor, 1995.

Yoshikawa, Yoko. "The Heat Is On Miss Saigon Coalition: Organizing Across Race and Sexuality." In *The State of Asian America: Activism and Resistance in the 1990's.* Ed. Karen Aguilar-San Juan. Boston: South End, 1994.

*See also* Activism; Coalition Politics; Daughters of Bilitis; Harlem Renaissance; Identity Politics; Lesbian Avengers; National Organization for Women (NOW); Radicalesbians

## Companionate Marriage

A term used by historians and sociologists for marriage that emphasizes companionship of spouses, especially sexual companionship, over the functions of economic partnership, childbearing, or passing on of family property, and whose promotion as an ideal in the early-twentieth-century United States involved intensification of heterosocial and heterosexual prescriptions and the stigmatization of homosocial and lesbian relations.

Historian Lawrence Stone (1979) uses the term "companionate" for marriages among English propertied families from the seventeenth century on in which love, as opposed to economic gain for the partners' families, formed a central value. He argues that such marriages represented a decline in parents' and husbands' patriarchal authority over women.

The more common use of "companionate marriage" refers to an emerging model of American marriage among the dominant White Anglo-Saxon Protestant groups in the late nineteenth and early twentieth centuries. This version also carries the connotation of increased power for women but emphasizes the sexual component of marital companionship.

As a practice and a code, companionate marriage stemmed from the emergence of the New Woman and from a cultural and economic shift from frugality and production to pleasure and consumption. Women's wage earning, education, and activism in reform and suffrage movements boosted their sense of social power and entitlement in marriage and eroded the Victorian sense of sacrifice on behalf of men and children as the essence of marriage for women. In the context of a growing consumer economy, a "sexual revolution," in which sexual knowledge and pleasure gained value, began in the 1910s. First radicals, then others, claimed women's right to birth control and sexual pleasure.

In his book *The Companionate Marriage* (1927), Denver Judge Ben B. Lindsey applied the term to the early period of a marriage, during which he proposed that a couple educated about sex should employ birth control and test the solidity of their relationship before having children. Should the partners prove incompatible, Lindsey argued, divorce by mutual consent should be possible. Social conservatives accused Lindsey of advocating free love—that is, of opposing traditional marriage—but he saw himself as saving marriage by altering its rigidities, allowing people to marry younger, and ending unhealthy sexual repression.

Following Lindsey, in the 1920s and 1930s a group of reformers and social-scientific and medical professionals began defensively to promote companionate marriage as the cultural ideal in opposition to threats perceived to be coming from Victorian prudery and bohemian or radical free love. Prudery and free love contained the danger of female independence from, and resistance to, the intense heterosexuality and/or continued male dominance of companionate marriage. By the late 1920s, as public discussion made lesbianism a more acknowledged concept, companionate-marriage reformers began to identify it as the real cause of female resistance to marriage or marital "maladjustment." Same-sex institutions and women's friendships were attacked as detrimental to the formation of "normal" heterosexual attachments. The renewed valuation of sexual activity in the new companionate marriage helped make lesbianism a sexualized symbol for female autonomy or assertiveness in any form—feminism, careers, not marrying, or resistance to male sexual dominance. Sexual-advice literature, the marriage-education movement, and popular medical writings in the 1930s propagated the companionate model and demonized lesbianism. By the 1940s, companionate marriage had become the dominant national discourse about marriage in the United States.

*Christina Simmons*

### Bibliography

Bailey, Beth L. *From Front Porch to Back Seat: Courtship in Twentieth-Century America.* Baltimore: Johns Hopkins University Press, 1988.

Ditzion, Sidney. *Marriage, Morals, and Sex in America: A History of Ideas.* New York: Bookman, 1953.

May, Elaine Tyler. *Great Expectations: Marriage and Divorce in Post-Victorian America.* Chicago: University of Chicago Press, 1980.

Rothman, Ellen K. *Hands and Hearts: A History of Courtship in America.* New York: Basic Books, 1984.

Simmons, Christina. "Companionate Marriage and the Lesbian Threat." *Frontiers: A Journal of Women Studies* 4:3 (1979), 54–59.

Stone, Lawrence. *The Family, Sex, and Marriage in England, 1500–1800.* Abr. and rev. ed. Toronto: Penguin, 1979.

*See also* New Woman

## Composers

Lesbians who have composed classical music, or music in the Western art tradition, have risked erasure from "official" histories of music. The world of composition classes, commissions, performances, recordings, and reviews is fiercely male dominated and daunting for women composers, but especially so for lesbians.

### Pre-Stonewall Composers

For research on women composers of the nineteenth century and the twentieth century prior to the Stonewall Rebellion (1969) who may have been lesbians, several important biographical factors require consideration. The absence of marriage, a troubled marriage, or devoted friendships with women while married may all indicate lesbian inclinations, as might virulent homophobia or friendships with gay men. The turn of the twentieth century in Europe and North America is an especially significant period for the investigation of lesbian composers (although use of the term "lesbian" at that time would have been unlikely), as women from diverse backgrounds challenged social prejudice and pursued successful careers as composers. Sophie Fuller (1994) states that women composers such as Rosalind Ellicott (1857–1924), Margaret Ruthven Lang (1867–1972), Oliveria Prescott (1842–1919), and Emma Steiner (1852–1929) never married, which suggests the possibility of lesbianism. Furthermore, in her work on Adela Maddison (1866–1929), Fuller (1996) notes that, although this composer married Frederick Brunning Maddison at age sixteen, she formed a close friendship with Mabel Veronica Batten (1857?–1916), the first lover of Radclyffe Hall (1880–1943) and a sometime composer and impor-tant music patron to whom Maddison dedicated her *Deux Melodies* in 1893. After Frederick Maddison's death in 1909, Adela Maddison maintained a life-long friendship with Marta Gertrud Mundt of Berlin, who worked as secretary to the Princess de Polignac (1865–1943) and was the beneficiary and coexecutor of Maddison's will; Maddison and Mundt may very well have been lovers. Dame Ethel Smyth (1858–1944) is perhaps the most famous pre-Stonewall lesbian composer. She wrote six operas, all of which were performed in her lifetime, and nine volumes of autobiography. A committed feminist and activist in the British suffrage movement, Smyth fought with great vigor and panache against sexist prejudice in the music world.

### Post-Stonewall Composers

In the post-Stonewall era, several lesbian composers have managed to stand up and be counted, although some are reluctant to be so identified. The following composers hold wide-ranging views on the intersections of feminism, lesbianism, identity, and creative work. While some do not perceive a direct connection between sexuality and music, others cultivate a compositional aesthetic based on their worldview as lesbians.

Pauline Oliveros (1932–) earned international recognition for her pioneering work with improvisation, electronic music (digital delay and the expanded accordion), audience participation, and music theater. From 1967 to 1981, she was professor of music at the University of California, San Diego. She resigned in 1981 to pursue independent work as a composer, and in 1985 she founded the Pauline Oliveros Foundation, based in Kingston, New York. Oliveros is a committed feminist and came out publicly in 1971 upon publishing her *Sonic Meditations* in *Source*, an avant-garde music journal. The *Sonic Meditations* are a collection of twenty-five short "recipes" for guided improvisation in individual or group settings that Oliveros created in 1970–1972 as a women-only project with The [Women's] Ensemble. These pieces require no formal training in music and involve making sounds, actively imagining sounds, listening to present sounds, and remembering sounds. Oliveros enjoys collaborative projects in a theatrical setting and has often worked with other lesbian and bisexual artists, such as Linda Montano (performance art), Deborah Hay and Paula Josa-Jones (dance), and Ione (theater). She has recorded a number of accordion works on compact discs, including *The Roots of the Moment*

(1988), *Deep Listening* (1989), *Crone Music* (1989), *Troglodyte's Delight* (1990), and *The Ready Made Boomerang* (1991).

Sorrel Hays (1941–) won recognition in the early 1970s for her interpretations of Henry Cowell's (1897–1965) piano works and then focused on composing her own music while producing a series of concerts and lectures on women composers for the New School for Social Research in New York City. Her most ambitious work is her opera, *Mapping Venus*, commissioned by West German Radio Cologne in 1995. Inspired by the NASA (National Aeronautics and Space Administration) Magellan Project to map Venus with women's names and by her own feminist ideas about linguistic possession of the world, Hays's libretto draws from texts by Hildegard von Bingen (1098–1179), Gertrude Stein (1874–1946), Simone de Beauvoir (1908–1986), Bella Akhmadulina (1937–), Sojourner Truth (1797–1883), Rosalía de Castro (1837–1885), and others and includes twelve languages. The work is scored for women's and girls' choruses, eight female soloists, tape, strings, brass, synthesizer, and percussion ensemble. *Dream in Her Mind* forms the basis of the one-act stage version, *Mapping Venus*, still awaiting production as of 1998. Hays works closely with her partner, Marilyn Ries, one of the first women audio engineers in the recording industry.

Jane Frasier (1951–), based in Colorado, taught music in its public school system. She runs her own music copying company, the MusicPrinter, and was chosen as an Associate of the Rocky Mountain Women's Institute for 1984–1985. Frasier writes primarily for acoustic instruments and voices, and her *Joy, Peace, and Singing* (1981) and *Seabird* (1993) for women's chorus were premiered by the Anna Crusis Women's Choir (Philadelphia, Pennsylvania) and the Atlanta Feminist Women's Chorus, respectively.

Linda Dusman (1956–), a professor of music at Clark University (Worcester, Massachusetts), has won numerous prizes and grants for her work with electroacoustic media, computer music, and sonic installation and has published her theoretical work in *Interface* (1988) and *Perspectives of New Music* (1994). In addition to setting texts by Adrienne Rich (1929–), Sappho (ca. 600 B.C.E.), and Gertrude Stein, Dusman connects her lesbianism and her work as a composer by creating forms that embody marginality and seek a reality that frees the listener from stereotypical patterns of audition. The "music" in her highly unusual sonic installation, *The Voice in Rama* (1996), is created as members of the audience pass by motion detectors and thus reflect their movement through sonic space.

Sheila Waller (1951–), a largely self-taught composer living in Colorado, initially enjoyed success in the 1960s and 1970s as a professional folk musician with nearly three hundred original songs to her credit. After formal lessons in classical theory and composition, she went on to write chamber pieces and large-scale works for traditional Celtic instruments, orchestra, and voices. Themes of fantasy and enchantment run throughout her compositions, such as her two-act opera, *The Faery's Daughter* (1992), which is based on an Irish fairy tale. Waller believes that lesbian composers, herself included, are uniquely positioned to pursue their creativity with purpose and determination.

Naomi Stephan (1938–) is a vocalist, composer, choral conductor, and director of the Asheville Women's Ensemble in North Carolina. The recipient of many awards and grants, she composes choral music almost exclusively. Her musical style is lyrical, neomedieval, and neoromantic. As a lesbian composer, she prefers to set texts by lesbian and women poets and compose for female voices. For example, "Na Maria" for soprano soloist or soprano choir, viola, bell, and percussion uses a text by the thirteenth-century *trobairitz* (female troubadours) Bieris de Romans, and "Hodie" and "Ideo" for women's chorus both use poems by Hildegard von Bingen.

The music of Kay Gardner (1941–) has crossed over between classical and women's music. In the classical realm, she has worked as a professional flautist, composer, conductor, and cofounder of the New England Women's Symphony. Her musical style is highly melodic and relies on modal scales for its shifts in color. In the 1970s, she researched the notion of a "woman's form in music" and theorized that cyclical and circular forms (rounds, palindromes), climax at the center (rather than near the end), use of treble instruments, and natural imagery all constitute a feminine aesthetic employed by women musicians in Western culture. Among her numerous recordings of original compositions are *A Rainbow Path* (1984), *Mooncircles* (1990), and *Ouroboros: Seasons of Life—Women's Passages* (1994); the latter recording is New Age healing and meditation music. Gardner is also the author of *Sounding the Inner Landscape: Music as Medicine* (1990) with accompanying tape. In 1971, she came out as a lesbian and became active in the newly emerging genre of women's music. She played in Alix Dobkin's band, Lavender Jane, and formed Wise Women Enterprises record company with Marilyn Ries. Gardner is a regular contributor to *Hot Wire: The Journal of Women's Music and Culture*.

Laura Karpman (1959–) is one of the few lesbian composers who works exclusively in film and television. Based in Los Angeles, California, she has composed scores for the NBC miniseries *A Woman of Independent Means*, the TBS documentary *A Century of Women*, the Showtime documentary *Sex, Censorship, and the Silver Screen*, and the Fox gay-themed *Doing Time on Maple Drive*.

[The author is extremely indebted to Sophie Fuller for sharing her work. Thanks also to Linda Dusman, Jane Frasier, Sorrel Hays, Naomi Stephan, and Sheila Waller for generously sending their biographical and musical materials.]    *Martha Mockus*

## Bibliography

Fuller, Sophie. " 'I Have Too Much Music & Really Have Nothing Else . . .': Reconstructing the Worlds of Adela Maddison (1866–1929)." Paper presented at the British Musicology Conference, King's College London, April 1996.

————. *The Pandora Guide to Women Composers: Britain and the United States, 1629–Present*. London: Pandora, 1994.

Kimball, Gayle. "Female Composition: Interview with Kay Gardner." In *Women's Culture: The Women's Renaissance of the 70s*. Ed. Gayle Kimball. Metuchen, N.J.: Scarecrow, 1981, pp. 163-176.

Morton, Brian, and Pamela Collins, eds. *Contemporary Composers*. Chicago and London: St. James, 1992.

Oliveros, Pauline. *Software for People: Collected Writings 1963–80*. Baltimore: Smith, 1984.

Sadie, Julie Anne, and Rhian Samuel, eds. *The Norton/Grove Dictionary of Women Composers*. London: Macmillan, 1995.

*See also* Choruses; Women's Music, Classical; Music, Women's; Smyth, Dame Ethel Mary

## Compton-Burnett, Ivy (1884–1969)

British novelist. Described as "novelists' novels," Compton-Burnett's works record the oppressive, isolated Victorian household in which she was raised, the eldest of her father's second family. After home tutoring, she attended Addiscombe Day School in Hove and then read classics at Royal Holloway College (1902–1907). Family difficulties marked much of her early life, beginning with her father's death in 1901; her mother's fatal illness in 1911 precipitated Compton-Burnett's becoming the harsh head of household; in 1917, two sisters committed suicide. The deaths of her beloved brothers—Guy in 1905 and younger Noel at the Somme in 1915—"quite smashed my life up," she lamented.

Biographer Spurling (1984) credits Margaret Jourdain (1876–1951) with restoring Compton-Burnett's emotional balance; they met in 1916. Described as a New Woman, Jourdain, a writer and an expert on English furniture and interiors (as Francis Lenygon), decorated the series of apartments they shared for more than three decades, while affectionately pampering and protecting Ivy, often explaining, "She's like a child," or noting, "Ivy lives in the past, and nothing after 1914 has any reality for her."

Indeed, the 1890–1910 milieu dominates Compton-Burnett's fiction. Her immature *Dolores* (1911) describes village relations and school settings resembling Royal Holloway; fourteen years later, Compton-Burnett published what she considered her first novel, *Pastors and Masters* (1925), developed through her technique of scant description and copious dialogue. *Brothers and Sisters* (1929), a minor sensation with its theme of incest and resulting comic complexities, contains disguised family portraits and signature Compton-Burnett characteristics: the Victorian drawing room, the distanced father, a female tyrant amidst family upheaval and crime. *More Men Than Women* (1933) and *A House and Its Head* (1935) complete this "family" group. Later novels acutely portray desperate children and usually juxtapose groups. For instance, in *Manservant and Maidservant* (1947) (United States, *Bullivant and the Lambs* [1948]), the domineering Horace Lamb, his wife, and children balance the downstairs servants headed by the butler Bullivant. *Two Worlds and Their Ways* (1949), a favorite of Compton-Burnett's, pairs the manor house against the schoolroom.

In 1951, Jourdain's death overshadowed the honor of the Order of the British Empire. Profoundly lonely and dependent on her maid, Mary, in the years following, Compton-Burnett published eight additional novels, tended her balcony garden, and, never losing her taste for sweets, entertained at tea, a custom since Holloway days, until her death following a bout of bronchitis. Paradoxically, Compton-Burnett maintained a lifelong Victorian persona, yet critics hail her novels as modern and subversive.

*Judith C. Kohl*

### Bibliography

Baldanza, Frank. *Ivy Compton-Burnett*. New York: Twayne, 1964.

Greig, Cicely. *Ivy Compton-Burnett: A Memoir*. London: Garnstone, 1972.

Liddell, Robert. *The Novels of Ivy Compton-Burnett*. London: Gollancz, 1955.

Spurling, Hilary. *The Life of Ivy Compton-Burnett*. New York: Knopf, 1984.

*See also* English Literature, Twentieth Century

## Compulsory Heterosexuality

The enforcement of male-female relationships as a social norm. In the influential essay "Compulsory Heterosexuality and Lesbian Existence" (1980), Adrienne Rich (1929–) suggests that heterosexuality is not simply the result of a natural attraction between men and women but is, in fact, an institution that is forced upon people, through various forms of psychological, physical, legal, economic, and cultural coercion.

In societies in which same-sex relationships are taboo, there are many penalties that gay and bisexual people face. Similarly, there are many pressures put on all people to form heterosexual relationships. Compulsory heterosexuality can be seen in laws forbidding same-sex sexual contact, in films and television programs that fail to represent gay and bisexual people or that represent them negatively, in antigay violence, even in the way children are often taught to imagine their futures as containing heterosexual partnerships. That some people face severe sanctions for not being heterosexual suggests that heterosexuality is enforced as a norm for all, which raises questions about the naturalness of any individual's sexual orientation. Feelings of attraction and affection toward men that are not simply the result of fear or coercion do exist in many women. It becomes almost impossible to know, however, what part of these feelings is genuine and self-generated and what part is a response to the social conditioning into heterosexuality.

This aspect of Rich's argument has been controversial. Because she was writing as a lesbian feminist about the ramifications of compulsory heterosexuality for women and for feminism, many have assumed that Rich was claiming that no heterosexual relationship can ever be authentic. She addresses this issue at the end of her essay by explaining that it is not her intention to judge individuals on their personal lives, but rather to examine heterosexuality on a structural level, as an institution that reinforces male supremacy. If feminists assume that heterosexuality is simply a natural orientation that some women share, they will miss the opportunity to analyze one of the central ways that women's freedom is limited, through the imperative that they form relationships with men.

In this essay, Rich was the first to articulate the coercive aspects of heterosexism. Before this, radical feminists explained that the reason women stayed in unequal relationships with men was because of the (primarily economic) privilege they received. That explanation probably grants too much agency to women, overestimating the degree of conscious thought put into heterosexuality. By highlighting the intensity of the cultural conditioning, the erasure of lesbian history, and the psychological and economic penalties lesbian women face, Rich challenged feminists to reconceptualize the degree to which heterosexuality is simply a "natural" sexual orientation or a calculated, "free" choice.

*'Becca Cragin*

### Bibliography

Keohane, Nannerl, Michelle Rosaldo, and Barbara Gelpi, eds. *Feminist Theory: A Critique of Ideology*. Chicago: University of Chicago Press, 1982.

Rich, Adrienne. "Compulsory Heterosexuality and Lesbian Existence." *Signs: Journal of Women in Culture and Society* 5:4 (1980), 631–660.

Thompson, Martha. "Comments on Rich's 'Compulsory Heterosexuality and Lesbian Existence.'" *Signs: Journal of Women in Culture and Society* 6:4 (1981), 790–794.

*See also* Heterosexuality; Rich, Adrienne

## Computer Networks and Services

Lesbians on the Internet. As long as computer networks have been in operation, lesbians have been using them to connect with one another. Starting with the Bulletin Board Systems (BBSs) of the 1980s and continuing through the phenomenal popularity of e-mail and the Web in the 1990s, lesbians have used the Internet to share their stories, build community, find partners and friends, agitate for political reform, and discover what it means to be lesbian.

## Newsgroups

One of the oldest forms of group communication on the Internet is the newsgroup, which functions much like an interactive bulletin board on which users can post messages for other users to see and respond to. The first newsgroup to attract lesbian participation was net.motss, later known as soc.motss, which was founded by Steve Dyer in 1983. The group's name was chosen to be deliberately obscure, to protect it from the attention of those whose intentions toward gays and lesbians would be less than friendly, but the use of the acronym MOTSS (members of the same sex) continues through the 1990s, even when new groups have emerged with the words "gay" and "lesbian" spelled out in the name. Among the most popular and active lesbian newsgroups are (the semicolons at the end are not part of the address) alt.shoe.lesbians; alt.lesbian.feminist.poetry; and soc.women.lesbian-and-bi. Most of the commercial online services, such as America Online (AOL), also have message-board areas for lesbians that function much like newsgroups.

## E-mail Discussion Lists

The most popular form of online networking is the e-mail discussion list, which operates in a manner similar to newsgroups; the main difference is that messages are sent via e-mail rather than posted to a publicly accessible space, thus providing a greater degree of privacy and making it possible for even those with the barest of Internet connections to participate. Discussion lists are typically "members only" spaces, with specific sets of criteria for joining, ranging from simply being female to more detailed requirements like being a scholar of lesbian studies or a practitioner of women-on-women S/M sex.

One of the first lesbian discussion lists was Sappho, which was founded by Jean Marie Diaz (also known online as AMBAR) in 1987 and continued in operation through the 1990s. From its inception, Sappho has been a place for all women to gather online and discuss issues of interest to lesbians and bisexual women, such as coming out to family members, safer sex between women, online dating, and lesbian life in general.

Sappho has also spawned a number of smaller lists, including those focused on geographic regions, such as the San Francisco–based ba-sappho, which was founded in 1991 by Ann Mei Chang and

has been run by Colleen Hawk since 1994, as well as those that address a specific area of interest, such as the moms list, which Dorsie Hathaway founded in 1992 as a resource and discussion network for lesbian mothers.

The real boom in lesbian lists happened in 1994, when nearly a dozen new lists appeared on the scene, focusing on a variety of topics and issues, many evident in the list's name: ba-cyberdykes, kinky-girls, boychicks, dykenet-l, lesbian-studies, lesac-net, and cleis, named after Sappho's daughter. Many of these lists were founded by Amy Goodloe or Dorsie Hathaway in response to the growing need for online spaces that matched the diversity of the lesbians using them, and both women have continued to create and maintain a variety of lesbian networks. Eva Isaksson of Finland has also been instrumental in creating lesbian networks for women outside the United States, including the sapfo-list for Finnish lesbians, founded in 1993, and euro-sappho, founded in 1994.

## Chat Rooms

The history of lesbian chat is perhaps the most difficult to trace, as the medium itself consists of fleeting conversations, very few of which are archived or made publicly accessible. The word "chat" is used to describe a real-time text-based conversation between two or more users, which typically takes place in temporary "rooms" or "channels" set up on commercial online services, such as AOL, or on a wider Internet network known as IRC (Internet Relay Chat). Most of these channels are active only when there are participants involved, but some have developed a persistent identity beyond planned periods of use, becoming permanent channels with their own set of customs, personalities, and rules of conduct.

One of the first lesbian chat spaces to evolve on AOL was an invitation-only room called "clitchat," which was active in the early 1990s. In 1992, the Gay and Lesbian Community Forum on AOL established a persistent chat space for women called Womenspace. By 1993, lesbians were also active and visible on IRC and had established a persistent channel called #sappho, which existed in conjunction with the list by that name; by the late 1990s, dozens of lesbian-themed chat rooms were regularly available to IRC users.

## Web Sites

While tools like newsgroups, mailing lists, and chat rooms facilitate the immediate exchange of news, ideas, and resources, only the Web offers the ability to publish information in a relatively permanent form, so that users can access it easily and on demand.

The Web has long been used by academics and computer professionals to exchange information, but it didn't really capture the imagination of the general public until 1994, when graphical applications for viewing the Web became popular. In early 1995, only a handful of Web sites contained information of interest to lesbians, but, by the summer of that year, more than a hundred new lesbian Web sites had emerged, including a metasite of links and information called lesbian.org, which has grown to become the most comprehensive source for lesbian information on the Internet.

While many of the new lesbian Web sites were simply small collections of links or personal bios, a few stand out as making original contributions to lesbian life and visibility online, such as Alix North's "The Isle of Lesbos," Indina Beuche's "A Dyke's World," and lesbian.org's "Sapphic Ink," a lesbian literary journal on the Web.

## Problems and Issues

Maintaining lesbian spaces on the Internet is no easy task, given the faceless, nameless aspect of online identity. Anyone who claims to be both female and dyke-identified can get into almost any lesbian on-line space, although the gatekeepers for many of these spaces are beginning to devise more complicated means of entry, such as asking the potential newcomer a series of questions supposedly designed to "verify" both her gender and her sexual identity. While the results are questionable—honest women just coming to terms with their lesbian identities can be left out, while men who have glanced through a couple of lesbian magazines can pass the test—the evidence of such tests points to both the ongoing importance of lesbian-only spaces and the difficulty of constructing a lesbian identity in cyberspace, where the textual production and performance of identities takes on a whole new dimension.

For additional information on the resources mentioned here, see http://www.lesbian.org. [The author wishes to thank Dorsie Hathaway, Eva Isaksson, Dana Bergen, Lisa Marshall Bashert, Colleen Hawk, Ann Mei Chang, and countless others for communicating the tales of early lesbian life on the Net.]      *Amy T. Goodloe*

## Bibliography

Broidy, Ellen. "Cyberdykes, or Lesbian Studies in the Information Age." In *The New Lesbian Studies*. Ed. Bonnie Zimmerman and Toni A.H. McNaron. New York: Feminist Press, 1996, pp. 203–207.

Correll, Shelley. "Ethnography of an Electronic Bar: The Lesbian Cafe." *Journal of Contemporary Ethnography* 24:3 (October 1995), 270–298.

Hall, Kira. "Cyberfeminism." In *Computer-Mediated Communication: Linguistic, Social, and Cross-Cultural Perspectives*. Ed. Susan Herring. Amsterdam: John Benjamins, 1996, pp. 147–170.

Haskel, Lisa. "Cyberdykes: Tales from the Internet." In *Assaults on Convention: Essays on Lesbian Transgressors*. Ed. Nicola Godwin, Belinda Hollows, and Sheridan Nye. London: Cassell, 1996, pp. 50–61.

Wakeford, Nina. "Sexualised Bodies in Cyberspace." In *Beyond the Book: Theory, Text, and the Politics of Cyberspace*. Ed. Warren Chernaik, Marilyn Deegan, and Andrew Gibson. London: University of London Press, 1995, pp. 93–104.

*See also* Technology

## Consciousness Raising

Feminist practice of collecting and analyzing personal experiences and narratives to uncover their political meanings. Historians of "second wave" feminism point to a variety of sources from which radical feminists developed the practice of consciousness raising (CR), including the U.S. civil rights movement, the Chinese revolution, peasant rebellions in Guatemala, the New Left, and women's own conversational style. The practice itself consisted of meeting in small groups in which women shared and analyzed stories about their lives, searching out the commonalities and connections that enabled them to see their experiences as political rather than merely personal—that is, women's individual experiences were identified as socially conditioned, as taking shape in relations of power, and as potentially subject to political intervention.

One of the most powerful issues for members of CR groups was sexuality. As Shulman (1980) has argued, women used their sexual discontents to understand how the power relations between women and men operated, how sexuality itself was constructed and practiced to women's disadvantage, and how alternatives might be envisioned. CR often had particular importance for lesbian women. Critiques of sexual practices and ideas begun in CR could open out to larger critiques of heterosexuality as an institution, while the valuing of truth and trust in the groups could make them relatively safe places for lesbians to come out.

CR had dual intentions from the start: It was a practice designed both to assemble knowledge about women's lives as a basis for feminist theory and to redress the isolation, alienation, and self-doubt that women experienced because of the mixed messages about them from patriarchal culture. As CR filtered out of the small groups of radical feminism, such as Redstockings and New York Radical Women, into more mainstream organizations like the National Organization for Women (NOW), it tended to emphasize the latter intention, most obviously when therapists were enlisted to facilitate CR groups.

By the early 1980s, CR was widely understood to be the central method of feminist analysis, as theorists such as MacKinnon (1981) argued that CR provides feminism with its politics, its epistemology, and its mode of social transformation. At the same time, however, the formal group practice of CR itself was on the decline, so that the term increasingly figured as a metaphor for all of the various ways that women might learn about women's oppression or about feminism. Formal CR was also reconfigured in the early 1980s as an antiracist teaching tool and has been similarly used to teach against homophobia. CR techniques were used in unlearning-racism workshops in the 1980s, to assemble and interrogate stories and experiences about racial difference, racial oppression, and the sources of racist beliefs. These latter developments demonstrate CR's flexibility: Whereas in the late 1960s CR emphasized women's commonality, in the 1980s it emphasized women's diversity.

*Lisa Maria Hogeland*

### Bibliography

Cross, Tia, Freada Klein, Barbara Smith, and Beverly Smith. "Face-to-Face, Day-to-Day–Racism CR." In *All the Women Are White, All the Blacks Are Men, but Some of Us Are Brave: Black Women's Studies*. Ed. Gloria T. Hull, Patricia Bell Scott, and Barbara Smith. Old Westbury, N.Y.: Feminist Press, 1982, pp. 52–56.

Koedt, Anne, Ellen Levine, and Anita Rapone, eds. *Radical Feminism*. New York: Quadrangle, 1973.

MacKinnon, Catherine A. "Feminism, Marxism, Method, and the State: An Agenda for Theory." *Signs: Journal of Women in Culture and Society* 7:3 (1982), 515–544.

Shulman, Alix Kates. "Sex and Power: Sexual Bases of Radical Feminism," *Signs: Journal of Women in Culture and Society* 5:4 (1980), 590–604.

*See also* Feminism; Women's Liberation Movement

## Cornwell, Anita (1923–)

U.S. Black lesbian feminist writer. Anita Cornwell was born in Greenwood, South Carolina, on September 23, 1923. In August 1939, she accompanied her grandmother to the New York World's Fair, after which they went to Yeadon, Pennsylvania, a suburb of Philadelphia, to visit her mother's older sister, who urged her to stay. Cornwell's mother soon joined her, and, two years later, she and her mother moved permanently to Philadelphia.

After graduating from Temple University in 1948 with a B.S. in journalism and the social sciences, Cornwell worked for local weekly newspapers and did clerical work for city, state, and federal government agencies for several years. In 1958, after participating in a summer Ford Foundation training program, she tried teaching in a minority school but resigned after two weeks, frustrated with the behavior of her adolescent students.

*Anita Cornwell. Photo by Tee A. Corinne.*

After 1961, with financial assistance from her mother, she supported herself as a freelance writer of short stories, essays, articles, interviews, book reviews, prose poems and plays, and two books: *The Girls of Summer* (1989), a young-adult novel, and *Black Lesbian in White America* (1983), a book of essays that contains an interview with Audre Lorde.

Her work has been published in journals, including *Liberator*, *Los Angeles Free Press*, *Hera*, *Essence*, *Sinister Wisdom*, *Azalea*, *Feminist Review*, *Motheroot*, *Feminary*, *National Leader*, *Labrynth*, *New York Native*, *Welcomat*, *New Directions for Women*, *Philadelphia Gay News*, *Griot*, *Black Maria*, *Phylon*, and *Elegant Teen*.

It has also appeared in anthologies, including *The Romantic* (1993), *For Lesbians Only* (1988), *Top Ranking: An Anthology on Racism and Classism in the Lesbian Community* (1980), *Lavender Culture* (1979), and *The Lavender Herring* (1976).

Her short story "A Sound of Crying," originally published in *Negro Digest* in 1964, was reissued in a 1995 anthology, *Revolutionary Tales: African American Women's Short Stories from the First Story to the Present.*                    Angela Bowen

**See also** African Americans; Black Feminism; Lorde, Audre

*Dee and Nancette in Colorado, 1984. Photo by JEB (Joan E. Biren).*

## Couples

Primary relationship between two women that blends social, psychological, sexual, and emotional elements. Though couple bonds between women were invisible, unnoticed, and unnamed through most of recorded history, such unions became salient enough in the eighteenth and nineteenth centuries to acquire a range of special labels. For example, "romantic friendship" was the preferred label for same-sex intimacies in eighteenth-century England. Some women "passed" as men, in part because that allowed female working-class lovers to cohabit without scrutiny; in addition, one member of the couple was then able to gain access to the male-only world of work. In pre-Maoist China (before 1950), female intimates unrelated by blood ties were known as sworn sisters. Anthropologists, encountering female pair bonds in certain parts of Africa, dubbed them woman-woman marriages. And, following the 1885 publication of *The Bostonians*, Henry James's (1843–1916) novel about two cohabiting spinsters, such relationships became known as Boston marriages in the United States.

### The Twentieth Century

By the end of the nineteenth century in Europe and the United States, the writings of medical doctors and sexologists caused same-sex bonds increasingly to be perceived as aberrations of nature. Exemplifying this new form of perversion was the doomed relationship between Stephen, the tormented, mannish invert, and Mary, the wavering heterosexual, depicted in Radclyffe Hall's classic novel *The Well of Loneliness* (1928). Personal accounts from the first half of the twentieth century suggest that lesbians were not deterred from establishing emotional and sexual ties with each other despite the widespread perception that same-sex bonds were abnormal. Such woman-woman unions were labeled lesbian couples, and the process of forming and maintaining such a couple was often closely linked with, and sometimes synonymous with, partners' individual lesbian identities. Because of the hostility and rejection they would face if their orientation came to light, however, prior to gay liberation lesbians took great pains to hide their relationships. As a result, their partnerships were usually visible only to the members of an underground network of like-minded friends, to the other patrons of lesbian bars they frequented, or, in many cases, only to the partners themselves.

In the second half of the twentieth century, the status of lesbian couples depended largely on their place of residence. In many countries, particularly where religious fundamentalism was firmly entrenched, lesbian partners continued to be subject to ostracism, physical abuse, and, in some instances, imprisonment or death. In Europe and North America, however, the overall status of lesbian couples gradually improved.

In the 1960s and 1970s, the new awareness of social injustice that sparked the civil rights struggle also kindled the battle for gay rights. Despite the new gay liberation message that same-sex couples were entitled to legal and social parity with heterosexual couples, many lesbian couples remained secretive, resigned to their marginal status. Others, however, experienced a new sense of pride in their partnerships. As a result, announcing their unions to family and friends, and even public, ceremonial affirmations of commitment, became common practices.

The feminist movement of the 1960s and 1970s also left an indelible stamp on lesbian relationships. Determined not to replicate the unequal power relations that characterized many heterosexual relationships, lesbians made a conscious effort to maintain egalitarian partnerships. Partners often shared chores, pooled resources, and tried to correct imbalances based on differences in race, class, income, or sex-role conditioning.

In the 1980s and 1990s, the push for parity continued on other fronts. Lesbian partners who resided in certain regions or worked for particular companies began to lobby for and receive some of the recognition and benefits typically accorded legally married spouses. Same-sex couples also gained access to many of the services available to their heterosexual counterparts. Lesbian partners who lived in or near urban areas, for example, could consult with lesbian-and-gay-friendly attorneys, physicians, therapists, and, if lesbian couples decided they wanted to start a family, they could even use the services of gay-friendly sperm banks. Full-length feature films, books, and plays depicted the triumphs and tribulations of women partners. And advertisements that appeared in gay and lesbian periodicals promoted everything from couples-only cruises to real-estate agents "who understand."

By the end of the twentieth century, however, the mainstreaming of lesbian couples was by no means complete. Despite their new level of visibility, or perhaps because of it, many lesbian partners continued to experience hostility and discrimination. Still other couples, because of their minority ethnic status, queer politics, or radical sex practices, felt doubly marginalized—outside both the dominant culture and the new lesbian mainstream.

## Psychological Profiles

According to surveys conducted in the 1970s, lesbian couples tended to be closer, more egalitarian, and, after the second year together, significantly less sexual than either gay male or heterosexual married couples. Survey data also showed that women's partnerships did not last as long as those of other couples. In *American Couples* (1983), a study of more than 1,500 lesbian couples, for example, the average length of time the respondents had cohabited was 3.7 years. In a follow-up to the study two years later, almost half of these lesbian partnerships had dissolved. In an attempt to explain the relatively rapid emotional and sexual burnout rates among lesbian couples, psychologists theorized that the need to unite against an often-hostile outside world reinforced women's socialization to bond closely. As a result of too much psychological and physical togetherness, lesbians tended to become emotionally fused with each other. Once enmeshed, sex might seem redundant, or even incestuous. As a result, partners were more likely to be receptive to new love interests.

In the last decade of the twentieth century, the merger theory of lesbian coupling was challenged by theorists from several disciplines. Feminist psychologists pointed out that the criticism of lesbians' fused relationships was based on an overvaluation of the individuality and autonomy often exhibited by male partners in heterosexual and homosexual relationships. These theorists argued that the mutuality and rapport so often displayed by women partners indicated a positive, rather than a negative, form of closeness. In fact, subsequent research studies showed that many lesbian couples enjoyed high levels of relationship satisfaction.

The research methodology used in the early surveys also came under attack. Psychologists noted that standard yes/no questions about sex were based

**C** on the model of heterosexual intercourse and, therefore, could not accurately measure sexuality between females. Finally, sociologists found that the surveys focused overwhelmingly on white, middle-class respondents. Later studies on different ethnic groups did, in fact, turn up different psychological profiles and problems. In contrast to their white counterparts, for example, African American lesbians were more likely to have children and more likely to depend on their families of origin for support. Because African American families tended to be more conservative in their attitudes toward homosexuality, many black couples could not risk disclosing the nature of their partnerships. Because, however, African American communities were accepting of homosocial relationships between women, black lesbian couples often chose to masquerade as "girlfriends" or "sisters." Consequently, these couples felt yet more invisible than their white counterparts.

By the end of the century, new studies began to reflect these critiques of earlier surveys. Rather than gathering data that reduced lesbian couples to one generic profile, new research began to measure the ways in which differences in economic status, ethnicity, age, sex-role conditioning, exposure to homophobia, and access to support contributed to the enormous diversity among lesbian couples.

*Marny Hall*

### Bibliography

Blumstein, Philip, and Pepper Schwartz. *American Couples*. New York: William Morrow, 1983.

Laird, Joan, and Robert-Jay Green. *Lesbians and Gays in Couples and Families*. San Francisco: Jossey Bass, 1996.

Mays, Vickie, Susan Cochran, and Sylvia Rhue. "The Impact of Perceived Discrimination on the Intimate Relationships of Black Lesbians." *Journal of Homosexuality* 25:4 (1993), 1–14.

Peplau, L.A. "Lesbian and Gay Relationships." In *Homosexuality Research Implications for Public Policy*. Ed. J.C. Gonsiorek and J.D. Weinrich. Newbury Park, Calif.: Sage, 1991, pp. 177–196.

Raymond, Janice. *A Passion for Friends: Toward a Philosophy of Female Affection*. Boston: Beacon, 1986.

*See also* Boston Marriage; Friendship; Monogamy and Nonmonogamy; Romantic Friendship; Sex Practices; Sexology

## Crime and Criminology

Lesbian relationships with crime, criminology, and criminal justice systems are multiple and complex. First, lesbian sexual expression itself has been, and continues to be, criminalized, thus rendering lesbians who are sexually active "criminals." Second, lesbians can be the victims of crimes, often because of bias against lesbians, women, or any of the other groups to which individual lesbians may belong. Third, lesbians may be the perpetrators of crimes, a stereotype that is prevalent in popular culture and that engenders bias in the criminal justice system.

### History

The criminalization of lesbian sexuality is ancient and long standing. The historical criminalization of lesbian sexuality is difficult to uncover because the crime itself was considered unmentionable—a sixteenth-century Swiss jurist advised that only the death sentence be read aloud and that the customary reading of the crime be omitted in cases of sex between women. While it was once believed that lesbian sexuality, especially as contrasted with gay male sexuality, was not criminalized, historians, such as Louis Crompton in his groundbreaking article, "The Myth of Lesbian Impunity" (1980), have demonstrated otherwise. Throughout Western history, women suspected of engaging in sexual relations with other women have been burned, hanged, and banished, sometimes publicly and sometimes privately by their male relatives. Many scholars connect the witch crazes in medieval Europe with lesbian sexual activity, and "femina cum feminus" (woman with woman) was a commonplace accusation in witch trials. Records discovered of a 1721 German trial show jurists pondering the legal effect of evidence concerning a "leather instrument" that the defendant Catharina Margaretha Linck apparently used when having sexual relations with a woman. The use of the instrument implicated the degree of sodomy, which, in turn, would determine the execution of the death sentence: being hung and the body burned afterward, or being burned alive, or being put to death by the sword.

The myth of lesbian impunity is largely attributable to nineteenth- and early-twentieth-century notions of female sexual purity. In 1921, for example, the British Parliament specifically chose not to include "gross indecency between women" as a crime because the parliamentary ministers believed that mentioning lesbianism in the criminal code would alert otherwise sexually innocent women to lesbian possibility. In a famous nineteenth-century British libel case, two Scottish schoolteachers argued that the charge against them for being involved in the "infamous crime of venus nefada, unnatural lust," was untrue. The judges agreed that the two Scottish, Christian schoolteachers could not physically or morally be sexually intimate, reserving such possibilities for women of other classes or continents. Thus, the notion of female sexual purity could protect women of higher classes who would otherwise be suspected of lesbianism. Nevertheless, as many scholars have demonstrated, in Europe, as well as in the United States, women of lower classes, women of color, and immigrant women suspected of lesbianism would be charged with vagrancy or prostitution and often sentenced to prison.

## United States

In the United States, the Supreme Court has upheld state statutes regulating lesbian sexual practices against constitutional challenges. As recently as 1968, every state in the United States had a statute that would render lesbian sexual expression criminal. In 1998, a little less than half the states had criminal statutes. These criminal statutes fell into three general categories: those that criminalize "unnatural" acts; those that are anatomically specific, including prohibiting oral-genital contact; and those that are gender specific, prohibiting sexual contact between persons of the same gender. Additionally, most states criminalize public sex, which not only includes sexual contact in public places, such as parks, but also has been applied to closed stalls in restrooms and even private homes if the persons can be viewed by a passerby on the street through an open window. While these statutes are not routinely enforced against lesbians, their enforcement does pose a danger to many lesbians. For example, in late 1996 a military woman was charged with violating the military's criminal-sex statute based upon the testimony of her former lover. Additionally, sex statutes can be the linchpin that supports other types of discrimination, most notoriously in lesbian child-custody cases.

The criminalization of lesbian sexuality is often linked to another type of crime—crimes against lesbians because of their sexuality. Such crimes, consisting of assault, battery, sexual assault, and murder, are generally known as hate, or bias, crimes. In some states in the United States, hate crimes merit enhanced sentencing. To prove a hate crime, the prosecution must prove that the defendant's crime was motivated by hate or bias toward the victim because of the victim's group identity, including sexual orientation, race, national origin, religion, and sometimes gender. In many other states, as well as the federal system, hate crimes do not merit enhanced sentencing but only require the collection of statistics. Since the 1970s, many nongovernmental antiviolence groups have documented the level of hate crimes against lesbians and gay men.

Many well-known cases in the United States have demonstrated that lesbians can be the targets of hate crimes. For example, in 1988 Rebecca Wight was murdered and her lover, Claudia Brenner, injured while the couple were camping on the Appalachian Trail. The man charged with shooting at the women with his rifle attempted to argue that he was provoked by witnessing their lesbian lovemaking. The judge rejected such a defense, and this rejection was upheld upon appeal. Many other well-known cases of violence against lesbians because of their lesbianism have occurred, including assaults on other campers, assaults against the women and property at Camp Sister Spirit in Mississippi, and various rapes. In a few cases, prosecutors have sought to introduce evidence that a rape victim is a lesbian to counter a defendant's claim that the victim consented to have sex with him, but such attempts can be problematic under rape-shield statutes, which prohibit use of a victim's sexual history.

Most crimes against lesbians, however, seem to occur in private. Statistics demonstrate that lesbians, similar to other women and contrasted with gay men, are more likely to experience violence from family and household members than from strangers. Younger lesbians are most at risk, experiencing violence from male relatives who disapprove of their sexual choices.

Lesbians are also the victims of crimes perpetrated by other lesbians. The issue of lesbian domestic violence has begun to receive legal recognition. In many states, statutes that provide for orders of protection in cases of domestic violence now extend to same-sex partners, although this remains the exception rather than the rule. Even in states that allow such orders of protection, however, judges trained about male-female domestic violence often have a difficult time in cases involving two women. Deciding which woman is the batterer and which woman is the victim deserving of an order of protection without reference to gender stereotypes can be diffi-

**C** cult, and judges often impose stereotypical views of gender on the women (thus deciding that the more "male"-appearing partner is the aggressor) or simply abandon the task (thus declining to enter an order of protection or entering a mutual order of protection).

In situations in which domestic violence escalates into a fatality, a lesbian accused of killing her lover may have a "battered woman defense." In 1989, a Florida court held that the battered-woman defense, previously held to be applicable only in cases in which a woman had murdered her husband, would be available to Annette Greene, accused of murdering her lover, Ivonne Julio. Despite the evidence that Greene had been battered by Julio, resulting in a broken nose and broken ribs, and had been shot at by Julio, the jury took only a short time to reject the defense and return a verdict finding Greene guilty of murder. While certainly not always successful in traditional wife-husband cases, the battered-woman defense appears to be even less successful when two women are involved.

Lesbians as perpetrators of crimes do not necessarily target lesbian victims. Like other persons, lesbians can participate in a wide array of criminal activity, including issuing checks for insufficient funds, public assistance fraud, possessing or selling drugs, shoplifting, assault, burglary, and murder. Although there is little documentation, Brownworth (1992) and Robson (1992, 1998) tend to support the thesis that lesbians are discriminated against in the criminal-justice system. Thus, being a lesbian would be a factor, similar to racial and economic factors, that would make it more likely that a woman would be prosecuted, convicted, sentenced to a jail term, and, once in jail, serve a longer sentence.

The situation of lesbians on death row is illustrative. According to lesbian journalist Brownworth (1992), of the forty-one women then on death row, seventeen, or roughly 40 percent, were implicated as lesbians during their trials and sentencings. In many cases, the prosecutors used the defendant's lesbianism to dehumanize her; the dehumanization process is generally believed to be an essential strategy to enable members of a jury to convict and recommend a sentence of death. For example, in the notorious 1992 Florida case of Aileen Wuornos, often known incorrectly as the first female serial killer, her status as a lesbian and a prostitute combined to dehumanize her. Her lesbianism, introduced into evidence by the state's star witness, her former lover, also enabled the prosecutors to subtly "explain" their ver-

sion of her crimes: her multiple murders of men who sought to use her sexual services. Similarly, in the 1992 case of Anna Cardona, the prosecution also subtly used the defendant's lesbianism, also introduced by the state's star witness and the defendant's lesbian lover, to dehumanize her and explain her crime. In 1998, Anna Cardona was on death row for the child-abuse murder of her son, and many scholars note that the only mother given the death penalty for child abuse is a lesbian.

## Global Cases

The United States has not been the only location of notorious cases in which the implication of lesbianism is inextricably bound with the legal (and media) treatment of the crime. In 1991, a twenty-five-year-old Australian woman quickly became known as the "lesbian vampire killer," based upon an accusation that she and her lover, as well as another lesbian couple, had picked up a man and lured him to his death by stabbing. Although it appeared that all four women had participated, three of them testified in their own trials of their beliefs that Tracey Wigginton had drunk the victim's blood and had cast a vampiric spell on them. Wigginton, diagnosed with multiple personality disorder, pleaded guilty, received a nine-minute trial, and was convicted. In 1955 in New Zealand, two adolescent girls, Pauline Parker and Juliet Hulme, presumed to be involved in a lesbian relationship based upon one of the girl's diaries, were convicted of murdering Pauline Parker's mother. Upon conviction, the girls were sent to separate prisons; when subsequently released, they had as a condition of their parole that they have no contact with each other. And in 1933 in France, the supposedly incestuously involved Papin sisters, employed as maids, were convicted of murdering and mutilating their female employer and her adult daughter.

## Conclusion

The real cases of lesbian criminal defendants, especially those charged with murder, occur in the shadow of cultural and media representations of lesbians as aggressors. Scholars such as Lynda Hart have explored the cultural representations of lesbians as killers in such popular movies as *Single White Female* (1992) and *Basic Instinct* (1992), demonstrating how these cultural representations positing lesbians as threats to man and family ultimately infect the trials of real women such as Wuornos. Further, media representations draw upon "true stories," including the 1990s films *Sister My Sister* (based upon the Papin sisters) and *Heavenly Creatures* (based upon Parker and Hulme), to authenticate the cultural stereotype of lesbians as pathological and violent, recycling back to the trials of contemporary lesbians accused of murder or other crimes.

Given the various ways in which lesbians are affected by criminal-justice systems—as sexual outlaws, as victims of violent crimes, and as perpetrators of actual and imaginary crimes—a simple approach to the relationships between lesbians and criminal justice is impossible. Although there is some theoretical work that attempts to integrate these complexities, by the late 1990s there was no comprehensive lesbian theory of criminal justice.

*Ruthann Robson*

### Bibliography

Brownworth, Victoria. "Dykes on Death Row." *Advocate* (June 15, 1992), 62–64.

Crompton, Louis. "The Myth of Lesbian Impunity." *Journal of Homosexuality* 6 (1980), 27–48.

Hart, Lynda. *Fatal Women: Lesbian Sexuality and the Mark of Aggression*. Princeton, N.J.: Princeton University Press, 1994.

Robson, Ruthann. *Lesbian (Out)Law: Survival Under the Rule of Law*. Ithaca, N.Y.: Firebrand, 1992.

———. *Sappho Goes to Law School: Fragments in Lesbian Legal Theory*. New York: Columbia University Press, 1998.

**See also** Law and Legal Institutions; Lesbian Impunity, Myth of; Parker-Hulme Murder Case

## Critical Theory

Term used broadly by American academics to describe criticism (particularly in literature, history, anthropology, and interdisciplinary studies, including lesbian and gay studies) that contributes to, is informed by, or is positioned as a serious critique of "theory." The latter is a highly contested term but generally refers to structuralist and poststructuralist theories (most significantly, deconstruction, Marxism, psychoanalysis, and Michel Foucault's "geneologies"), all of which proved influential to American thinkers during the decades following the political upheavals of the 1960s. Although lesbian authors and topics have never been absent from the continental tradition, American lesbian scholars have tended to regard it with hostility or indifference, opting to invoke "theory" more informally as the political critique of the naturalness of certain cultural institutions—especially heterosexuality, femininity, and the family—and to borrow from more domestic intellectual sources.

### History

Originally, the appeal of structuralism to an increasingly politicized academic audience lay in its aim to examine not the meaning of texts—understood very broadly as anything articulated through language, including film or ritual—but the structures that produce meaning itself. This so-called structuralist insight proved valuable to lesbian critics who were trying to articulate how, for instance, the meaning of "woman" is not a given but a construct, a product of various, and variable, social structures, such as patriarchy, economic class, or colonialism.

The attraction, however, was neither mutual nor free of conflict, even for early French feminist theoreticians. After Luce Irigaray (1930–), for example, was expelled in 1974 from Jacques Lacan's (1901–1981) École Freudienne, she went on to write *This Sex Which Is Not One* (1985), influential among lesbians both for its attack on Lacan and its Sapphic overtones. For her part, author and activist Monique Wittig (1935–) drew on anthropologist Claude Lévi-Strauss's (1908–) work to claim in "The Straight Mind" (1992) that, because lesbians are exempt from the marital exchanges so basic to kinship structures, "lesbians are not women." Nevertheless, the same essay includes a devastating critique of the heterocentrism of French theory.

In post-1960s Britain, meanwhile, the works of Karl Marx (1818–1883) and Michel Foucault (1926–1984) were inspiring theoretically informed research into lesbian and gay history. At the center of this research were Foucault's claims that sexual practices and identities are produced and regulated by "regimes of power-knowledge-pleasure" and that sodomy changed (mainly due to the impact of late-nineteenth-century sexological discourses) from a random, sinful practice into a new, unique species, "the homosexual." Most of these contributions to critical theory dealt with male homosexuality, but historian Judith Walkowitz's work (1980) would have an impact on future analyses of "deviant" female sexuality in Western history.

Rather than look to France, U.S. lesbian critics in the 1960s and 1970s derived their theoretical perspectives from their experiences in and out of the

American women's movement. Jill Johnston's *Lesbian Nation* (1973) was typical of the era to the extent that it defined lesbianism not as a sexual practice per se, but as a political resistance to patriarchy, encapsulated in Johnston's conviction that, potentially, "every woman is a lesbian." Other common tenets of American lesbian theory were separatism from men, nonmonogamy, and antiracism. The latter topic was thoroughly investigated by such classics as *This Bridge Called My Back* (1981), edited by Gloria Anzaldúa and Cherríe Moraga.

Feminism's dominance over lesbian theory was challenged in significant ways in the 1980s when some lesbian thinkers began to question whether homosexuality could be adequately described by a set of theories about gender. Gayle Rubin's "Thinking Sex: Notes Toward a Radical Theory of Sexual Politics" (1984) called for the development of a theory that could explain oppression on the basis, specifically, of sexuality and insisted that the subjects of such a theory must be lesbians, gay men, and other "sexual outlaws." Meanwhile, other critics were turning toward psychoanalysis, which—despite Sigmund Freud's (1856–1939) reputation among American feminists as a sexist—struck some critics as a powerful theory of sexuality and sexual repression. Generally, the advent in the 1990s of "queer theory" was accompanied by a greater affinity between lesbian scholars and continental theory.

## Major Paradigms

*Compulsory Heterosexuality.* The most influential essay to come out of American lesbian feminism is undoubtedly Adrienne Rich's "Compulsory Heterosexuality and Lesbian Existence" (1980). Rich's commitment to a specifically, if not explicitly, structural account is evident in her claim that feminist theory has been weakened by its undertheorization of heterosexuality—that is, by its persistence in seeing heterosexuality as a mere "orientation." By describing heterosexuality as an institution imposed on all women, "Compulsory Heterosexuality" effectively describes not what women are, but the system that has produced them as what they are. Rich also elaborates on the lesbian feminist claim that any woman is potentially a lesbian by placing all women on a "lesbian continuum" stretching from close female bonds to sexual relationships.

*Essentialism Versus Social Constructionism.* This debate has been staged between those who see les-

bian identity as an unchanging "essence" that can be detected across cultural and historical divides, and those who insist that identity is "socially constructed"—that is, produced in different ways by social structures that are historically shifting and subject to change. "Constructionist" historians have raised questions, for example, as to the viability of describing premodern women and texts as "lesbian" when premodern societies were characterized by radically different conceptions about, and practices of, female homosexuality.

A helpful twist on the essentialism debate was provided by Eve Sedgwick's *Epistemology of the Closet* (1990), which recasts the divide to span "minoritizing" versus "universalizing" discourses about homosexuality. For Sedgwick, the first camp bases its agenda on the idea that gays constitute a discrete grouping, a minority that, like a racial minority, is marked by certain transhistorical and cross-cultural features. In contrast, a universalizing discourse of homosexuality is "based on the supposed protean mobility of sexual desire and the potential bisexuality of every human creature."

*Critique of Identity Politics.* Critical theory is also the origin of widespread attacks on "the personal is political"—the emphasis in lesbian feminism on a politics of identity. The notion of an "authentic" or "unified" self was, in stark contrast, reconceived as the ideological centerpiece of heterocentrism. Most influential in this shift is Judith Butler's *Gender Trouble: Feminism and the Subversion of Identity* (1990), which understands all gender and sexual identities as unstable, shifting, and produced by various "hegemonic regimes," including "the heterosexual matrix." Borrowing from structuralist linguistics, Butler argues further that lesbian politics should be reconceived as "performative"—that is, based on the subject's subversive repetition of heterosexual norms. Meanwhile, other lesbian theorists have suggested that the most powerful critique of identity politics lies in lesbian antiracist discourse, which assumes a radical subjectivity multiply constituted by racial and class differences.

## Objections to Critical Theory

Throughout its rise, many scholars have objected both to the style and the content of critical theory. Some criticize the institutional power and allure held by critical theorists, as well as the inability of the genre to distinguish itself from academic Eurocentrism at large. Others simply find the discourse unnecessarily obfuscating and "male." Perhaps the most spectacular attack has been by lesbian art critic Camille Paglia's *Sex, Art, and American Culture* (1992), in which lesbian feminism is decried for its "Puritanism," poststructuralism for its "Francobabble," and critical theorists themselves for their privilege and vapidity.                    *Heather Findlay*

## Bibliography

Anzaldúa, Gloria, and Cherríe Moraga. *This Bridge Called My Back: Writings by Radical Women of Color*. Watertown, Mass.: Persephone, 1981.

Butler, Judith. *Gender Trouble: Feminism and the Subversion of Identity*. New York: Routledge, 1990.

Irigaray, Luce. *This Sex Which Is Not One*. Ithaca, N.Y.: Cornell University Press, 1985.

Johnston, Jill. *Lesbian Nation: The Feminist Solution*. New York: Touchstone, 1973.

Paglia, Camille. *Sex, Art, and American Culture*. New York: Vintage, 1992.

Rich, Adrienne. "Compulsory Heterosexuality and Lesbian Existence." *Signs: Journal of Women in Culture and Society* 5:4 (1980), 631–660.

Rubin, Gayle. "Thinking Sex: Notes for a Radical Theory of the Politics of Sexuality." In *Pleasure and Danger: Exploring Female Sexuality.* Ed. Carole S. Vance. Boston, London, Melbourne, and Henley, U.K.: Routledge and Kegan Paul, 1984, pp. 267–319.

Sedgwick, Eve. *Epistemology of the Closet*. Berkeley: University of California Press, 1990.

Walkowitz, Judith R. *Prostitution and Victorian Society: Women, Class, and the State*. Cambridge and New York: Cambridge University Press, 1980.

Wittig, Monique. *The Straight Mind and Other Essays*. Boston: Beacon Press, 1992.

*See also* Compulsory Heterosexuality; Cultural Studies; Essentialism; Identity Politics; Ideology; Johnston, Jill; Lesbian Continuum; Philosophy; Political Theory; Psychoanalysis; Queer Theory; Rich, Adrienne; Wittig, Monique

## Cross-Dressing

Women who impersonate men onstage, who wear men's clothing, and who appear as male characters are engaging in the performance practice of cross-dressing, known in earlier eras as performing "breeches roles." Evidence exists of women playing male parts for as long as women have performed in public.

## History

To some extent, objection to, and discomfort with, the theatrical enterprise has always reflected both anxieties about cross-dressing and questions about the "stability" of gender roles. Since at least the time of Tertullian (ca. A.D. 200), religious injunctions against acting as a form of deception or falsification of an individual's "identity" cited the prohibition in Deuteronomy 22:5: "Woman shall not wear that which pertaineth unto a man, neither shall a man put on a woman's garment." While all actors portray persons other than themselves, because women were banned from appearing on the professional stage for hundreds of years, female characters were necessarily depicted by cross-dressed men. Thus, objections to the "immorality" of the English-speaking theater dating from before the Renaissance through the Puritans often drew upon the presumed "unnaturalness" of the predominantly male audience's potential homoerotic response to "effeminate" boy actors portraying women, and the dangers of calling into question what were thought to be the "natural" and mutually exclusive provinces of gender.

Despite the absence of actual female performers on the professional stage in England, there was a tradition of women who cross-dressed offstage, whether female saints who dressed as men to enter monasteries or other "Englishe gentle-women," according to Puritan William Prynne, who were "soe farr past shame, past modesty, grace and nature, as to clipp their hayre like men" and "weare the breeches." Playwrights Thomas Middleton and Thomas Dekker depicted this practice in their 1610 play, *The Roaring Girl*, based on the life of Moll Frith, who had passed as a man. However, as with William Shakespeare's (1564–1616) cross-dressed female characters in *As You Like It* and *Twelfth Night*, for example, early portrayals of "women" who were passing as men were originally played by male actors.

After the Restoration in England, the first actresses appeared on the professional stage as a result of a decree from Charles II (1630–1685) in 1660. Unlike the all-male homoerotic court and theater of his grandfather James I (1566–1625), Charles felt that women performers were necessary for "useful and instructive representations of human life" to be seen onstage. Yet the widespread popularity of female characters disguised as men continued and grew once these parts were played by women. Several of the earliest English women playwrights, Aphra Behn (1640?–1689), Susanna Centlivre (1667–1723), and Catherine Trotter (1679–1749), wrote plays in which female characters cross-dress. Behn's *The Widow Ranter* (1689), Trotter's *The Revolution of Sweden* (1706), and Centlivre's *The Perjur'd Husband* (1700) contained female characters who masquerade as men, often to escape repression or to gain some freedom or power denied them as women. Centlivre was herself an actress who, in her youth, "passed" as a man to gain an education. Nearly one-third of all new plays written between 1660 and 1700 contained parts in which women dress as men.

But the earliest English-speaking women on the stage did not limit their male portrayals to the depiction of female characters who assumed male disguise for some pragmatic reason and then revealed themselves to be women, thereby providing a heterosexual "resolution" to the erotic tension they had created. Actresses such as Nell Gwyn (1650–1687) and Nance Oldfield (1683–1730) performed some of the leading male dramatic roles as well, thus inaugurating the theatrical convention referred to as playing a "breeches part." Gwyn's most successful breeches character was Florimel in John Dryden's *Secret Love* (1667); Charles II was said to have been so taken by Gwyn's cross-dressed performances that she became his mistress.

The eroticism of women playing leading male roles resonated at several different levels with different audiences. Heterosexual male spectators frequently responded favorably to performances in which women clothed in men's tight breeches displayed more of their female bodies, particularly their legs and buttocks, to their audience than women's dress would reveal. Further, the supposed "independence" of a woman wearing male clothes could be read as a sign of her sexual availability. Some viewers were intrigued by the androgynous erotic energy of an active, assertive woman dressed like a "virile" young man and found the incongruity appealing. Inevitably, some female spectators who witnessed cross-dressed female performers wooing other women onstage recognized these female suitors as potential objects of their own desire, wanting either the freedom to be like such women or to be desired by them.

Since at least the time of Henry VIII (1491–1547), popular entertainments such as the carnivals, "masques," costumed balls, and pantomimes also offered women the opportunity to cross-dress. The possibility that women in male attire might appeal to, or be drawn to, other women haunted the fringes of such masquerades, just as it did the professional theater. In 1719, the *Freethinker* warned readers about the "danger" of seduction at masquerades when "a Countess listens to the Gallantry of a Chamber-Maid." Since female cross-dressers convincingly performed social roles for which they were considered "naturally" unsuited, costumed festivities at which women cross-dressed threatened to undermine social class as well as gender, distinctions.

## The Eighteenth-Nineteenth Centuries

Eighteenth-century theater audiences flocked to see Peg Woffington (ca. 1718–1760), who first appeared in London as Macheath in John Gay's *The Beggar's Opera* (first performed 1728). Woffington was so successful in her cross-dressed roles, most notably as Sir Harry Wildair in George Farquhar's *The Constant Couple* (first performed 1699), that no male actor attempted the part for years. Certain male characters such as Macheath, Wildair, and Lothario in Nicholas Rowe's *The Fair Penitent* (first performed 1703), which Woffington also played, became part of a corpus of male roles frequently performed by other women who specialized in breeches parts. Charlotte Charke (1713–1760), for example, depicted many of these same male characters and was known to cross-dress in her offstage life as well.

Throughout the eighteenth and nineteenth centuries, *Hamlet* became part of the standard repertoire of female performers. Some claimed the character was inherently androgynous and best played by a woman. Sarah Kemble Siddons (1755–1831), the most highly acclaimed actress of her time, first played Hamlet in 1776 and continued playing the part, along with other female roles, for the next twenty-five years. Another Hamlet, actress and writer Elizabeth Inchbald (1735–1821), was highly regarded in a range of breeches roles and known to attend masquerades cross-dressed as well.

By the early nineteenth century, popular actress/manager Eliza Vestris (1797–1856) became so renowned for her breeches performances that she is credited with furthering the practice of women appearing cross-dressed as the "principal boy" character in pantomime and music hall performances. For all the eroticism of her performances, Vestris's male characterizations, rather than threatening to upset the social order, served to reinforce it, as many male spectators associated her masculine clothes and independence with heterosexual licentiousness.

In the United States in the nineteenth century, the preeminent breeches actress was Charlotte Cushman (1816–1876), who appeared as Romeo and as scores of other male characters, including Hamlet and Wolsey. Unlike Vestris, whose followers were mostly adoring male spectators, Cushman, who lived with women offstage, neither excited the passions of men nor wished to be seen as desirable by them. She presented audiences with an embodiment of male romantic characters whose public performance of desire for their female costars excited the fervent responses of some of her female spectators. Ironically, the eroticism lesbian performers such as Cushman manifested when cross-dressed—while legible to those spectators who recognized the possibility of lesbian desire—was generally acceptable only because a woman acting opposite another woman was considered by many other spectators as incapable of experiencing the emotions she performed. Yet some could see the transgressive possibilities in a woman playing a male role. Contemporary costar George Vandenhoff criticized Cushman's male performances as "epicene," and, according to actor John Coleman, Cushman's desire "to disport herself in masculine attire" led to "indecorous speculations."

Later in the nineteenth century, Sarah Bernhardt (1844–1923) performed at least twenty-five male roles, the best known of which were Hamlet and Duc de Reichstadt in Edmond Rostand's *L'Aiglon* (1900). Both women and men responded to Bernhardt's male portrayals, and, offstage, Bernhardt had long-term passionate relationships with women and men.

In the nineteenth century, cross-dressing expanded from the mainstream theater to the music halls, where popular female performers such as Annie Hindle (ca. 1847) and Vesta Tilley (1864–1952) sang comic songs in the persona of male characters costumed in military uniforms or as various male types, such as the "dandy." Hindle came to New York City from England in 1867 and was billed as the "first out-and-out male impersonator New York's stage had ever seen." In 1886, passing as "Charles" Hindle, she "married" another woman, Annie Ryan, retired, and lived with Ryan for the remainder of her life. While cross-dressing is not a signifier of the wearer's sexuality, some lesbian performers have adopted "male" clothing or undertaken the depiction of male characters to indicate their resistance to being seen according to heterosexual norms for women's appearance.

## The Twentieth Century

Women's cross-dressing has been sporadic on the mainstream twentieth-century stage. A few "male" or boyish roles, such as James Barrie's (1860–1937) Peter Pan, have been routinely performed by women, such as Eva La Gallienne (1899–1991) and Mary Martin (1913–1990). Shakespearean productions, such as Le Gallienne's *Hamlet*, are still occasionally the sites of cross-dressing. Contemporary feminist and lesbian plays, such as Eve Merriam's *The Club* (1976) and Split Britches's *Belle Reprieve* (1991), have intentionally deployed cross-dressing to reveal the artifices of clothing, gesture, and demeanor through which gender is constructed and performed.

*Lisa Merrill*

## Bibliography

Case, Sue-Ellen. *Feminism and Theatre*. New York: Methuen, 1988.

Castle, Terry. *The Female Thermometer*. New York: Oxford University Press, 1995.

Ferris, Lesley, ed. *Crossing the Stage: Controversies on Cross-Dressing*. London: Routledge, 1993.

Garber, Marjorie. *Vested Interests: Cross Dressing and Cultural Anxiety*. New York: HarperCollins, 1993.

Merrill, Lisa. *When Romeo Was a Woman: Charlotte Cushman and Her Circle of Female Spectators*. Ann Arbor: University of Michigan Press. 1998.

Senelick, Laurence. "The Evolution of the Male Impersonator on the Nineteenth-Century Popular Stage." *Essays in Theatre* 1:1 (1982), 30–44.

*See also* Behn, Aphra; Charke, Charlotte; Cushman, Charlotte; Passing Women; Theater and Drama, History of

## Cruikshank, Margaret Louise (1940–)

American educator and writer. Cruikshank played a central role in establishing the importance of lesbian studies within both women's studies and the academy through the publication of her edited anthologies *The Lesbian Path* (1980), *Lesbian Studies: Present and Future* (1982), and *New Lesbian Writing* (1984).

*Margaret Cruikshank. Photo by Barbara Giles.*

Approximately a decade after Stonewall (1969), lesbian culture and lesbian studies developed an identity connected to, yet distinct from, both the gay movement and the women's movement. As "the first book made up entirely of short personal narratives by lesbians," *The Lesbian Path* depicted that culture by offering autobiographical articles on romance, coming out, combating lesbophobia, discovering and preserving lesbian literature, teaching, publishing, aging, and other concerns by well-known lesbian writers. As Cruikshank's preface explains: "announcing our existence is still a political act."

*Lesbian Studies* describes the experiences of lesbians in the academy and explores the implications of articulating a lesbian perspective in teaching and research. It asserts the importance of studying lesbians in history, literature, and culture and offers both course syllabi and bibliographies. A testimony to the enduring significance of Cruikshank's work, *Lesbian Studies* was updated and reissued in 1996. Cruikshank's third anthology, *New Lesbian Writing*, combines fiction and nonfiction from lesbian writers around the world, exemplifying both the diversity and the coherence of lesbian literature.

As part of the Routledge series Revolutionary Thought/Radical Movements, Cruikshank's *The Gay and Lesbian Liberation Movement* (1992) provides an overview of the movement from various perspectives—as a sexual freedom movement, a political

movement, and a movement of ideas. In addition, Cruikshank describes the characteristics of gay and lesbian culture and community, the shaping role of lesbian feminism and lesbian separatism, and the debates and conflicts experienced within gay communities.

Cruikshank's recent *Fierce with Reality* (1995) focuses on aging and includes essays by several lesbian authors. Founding director of women's studies at Mankato State University in Minnesota, affiliate scholar at the Center for Research on Women at Stanford University, and visiting teacher of lesbian studies at the University of Maine, Cruikshank taught English and gay and lesbian studies at City College of San Francisco from 1981 to 1997, after which she moved permanently to Maine.

*Greta Gaard*

### Bibliography

Cruikshank, Margaret. "A Slice of My Life." In *The Lesbian Path*. San Francisco: Grey Fox, 1980, 1985, pp. 58–63.

Jurgens, Jane. "Margaret Cruikshank." In *Gay and Lesbian Literature*. Ed. Sharon Malinowski. Detroit: St. James, 1994, p. 101.

*See also* Gay Liberation Movement; Lesbian Studies

### Cultural Studies

An interdisciplinary approach to the study of humans in their social environments. As practiced in the late twentieth century, cultural studies pays a great deal of attention to mass-mediated technologies and their impact on a range of issues, including representation, economics, gender, race, politics, communication, global wealth, and ideology. And yet, because the terms "culture" and "study" might describe just about any intellectual project in or out of the academy, even practitioners of cultural studies disagree on its fundamental characteristics. Not a traditional discipline with an institutional history, nor a method of securing evidence and truth, nor a field of study attached to a particular archive, cultural studies has been most usefully understood in relation to broad historical and intellectual trends: the decentering of European geopolitical power after World War II; the rise of myriad social movements in the 1950s and 1960s in Europe and the United States, including the gay and lesbian liberation movement; the attendant focus on Marxist social criticism in the academy and, with it, the legitimation of the study of popular culture; and the emergence of identity politics as a means of repairing structural inequalities, including heterosexism, white supremacy, and male domination, in democratic social systems. While the lesbian as such is not always central in each of these arenas, her critical sojourn as an object of study in the academy has been widely influenced by the transformations wrought by cultural studies as an interdisciplinary field.

## Theoretical Basis

At its most general, cultural studies draws its theoretical perspective from Marxist analysis, inquiring into power relations and the social operations that produce consent and resistance. Because much of its scholarship originated from researchers interested in British working-class life, cultural studies takes seriously the everyday experience of individuals and has helped break down the class assumptions that associate culture with "high" cultural products of sanctioned art and literature, instead generating important work on mass culture, media, and other cultural products of the immediate moment. In its orientation toward the everyday life of individuals, cultural studies tacitly critiques social-scientific inquiry based on quantitative methods and so-called objective knowledge, and it does so by paying attention to the specific historical and local circumstances within which both individuals and knowledges are produced. Cultural studies can thus be characterized by its refusal to treat any object of study independently from the economic (or, in Marxist terminology, "material") conditions that produce it or from the questions that have been brought to bear by scholars, who are themselves socially created actors.

In its critique of the academic focus on high culture, cultural studies challenges the disciplines of English, comparative literature, philosophy, and all of the European language and culture programs (German, French, Italian, Spanish, and Portugese) to rethink their structural support of the ruling classes. Rejecting the idea that the literature and arts produced by the elite classes are examples of civilization, founding scholars in the field at the Birmingham, England, Center for Contemporary Cultural Studies reinvigorated Marx's attention to the ideological spheres of social life. Under the directorship of sociologist Stuart Hall, Birmingham School scholars posited the working class not simply as duped, but as active players in the social world. This perspective meant studying the way that working-class people not only used and interpreted, but also derived pleasure from, mass-produced entertainment forms (romance novels, popular film, or television). By emphasizing all forms of culture, cultural studies linked telecommunications, film studies, literary studies, media studies, and journalism to anthropological and sociological analysis, thereby securing its interdisciplinary agenda.

But even as the foundational texts of British cultural studies (Raymond Williams, *Culture and Society* [1963], Richard Hoggart, *The Uses of Literacy* [1969], and E.P. Thomson, *The Making of the British Working Class* [1968]) focused equally on issues concerning the working class and the relationship between high culture and ruling-class power, it was primarily the latter that became central to cultural studies scholarship as it was exported to other Western locations. The U.S. brand of cultural studies that has subsequently developed is marked by a less rigorous attention to Marxist foundations, which has no doubt facilitated its popularization in U.S. English departments, where it has provided a necessary defense of the study of popular culture, nonprint text technologies, and non-literature-based literacies.

## Feminist and Lesbian Cultural Studies

In its ability to provide more adequate methods for thinking through lived experience, resistance, and popular culture, cultural studies as practiced in the United States became especially useful to feminist scholars, many of them lesbians, in the 1980s. Influenced by postmodernist critiques of the stability of all identity categories, including that of "woman" and of "lesbian," feminist cultural studies has contributed to the ongoing conversation about the promise and the limits of experience as a basis for social knowledge and for epistemological truth. While it would be imprecise and misleading to discuss lesbian cultural studies as a field, the historical intersection of a cultural studies approach and the development of a body of knowledge constructed around the lesbian has produced some key texts. The cultural studies tradition of analyzing popular culture such as advertisements not only for the "preferred" or dominant reading, but also for "negotiated" and "resistant" readings lends itself to the thesis of a widely reprinted article by Danae Clark, "Commodity Lesbianism" (1991). In this essay, Clark argues that advertising images that do not mark themselves as "lesbian" in so many words are, nevertheless, open to be read as such by lesbian subjects, in negotiated readings. Further, Clark maps the lesbian as a subject constructed through the commodity form, one that is neither historically unchanging nor a heroic or separate identity able to transcend her situatedness in capitalist economic structures. Such a reading promotes the antiessentialist practice of cultural studies and avoids an overly simplistic insistence on the lesbian's self-produced agency, which, Clark asserts, mars much contemporary analysis of lesbian and popular culture.

Perhaps the most important recent text that demonstrates the influence of cultural studies on lesbian feminist scholarship is Sue-Ellen Case's *The Domain-Matrix: Performing Lesbian at the End of Print Culture* (1996). Case "hooks up" the lesbian—as material-historical subject, body, representation, and technology—to the matrix of culture in ways that defy distinctions between the material and the theoretical, flesh and image, science fiction and social science, and the category of "the lesbian" and other social identities. While it does not directly address the theoretical link to cultural studies, *The Domain-Matrix* nonetheless evinces in its intellectual and political obsessions a specifically lesbian contribution to cultural studies as an interdisciplinary analysis of social power, mass-mediated technologies, and the material realities of late capitalism.

While Case culls her texts from the archive of performance and popular culture, Canadian sociologist Elspeth Probyn, in *Outside Belongings* (1997), directly engages cultural studies as a discourse within the academy that she uses to articulate the lesbian into bodily, national, and philosophical meanings, or what she calls "belongings." For Probyn, belonging is a critical term aimed at understanding the way traditional disciplines and forms of government, as well as identity categories themselves, create "insiders," those who have internalized the codes, definitions, and boundary distinctions of a group, discipline, or nation in order to claim membership within it. Probyn rigorously resists the lure of insider status, even for identities such as "the lesbian" that elsewhere are "outside" circles of power. Rather, she theorizes the position of hyperconsciousness offered by "outside belonging" to argue against a neo-Marxist economic determinism that refuses to examine the complexities of pleasure or the mobility of sexuality and desire. In fruitful ways, Probyn demonstrates the promise of cultural studies for realigning the often distinct and even contentious social investments of queers, gay

men, and lesbians by forging analytical links that go beyond the easy dismissal of popular culture as the commodified realm of late-twentieth-century oppression.

Two other texts in the late 1990s develop the queer cultural studies project defined by Probyn, each with its own degree of specificity about the lesbian. Camilla Griggers' *Becoming-Woman* (1997) adds to the growing body of postmodern and queer scholarship that sees the lesbian as an ensemble of images proliferating within technologies of femininity, advertising, capitalism, and the state. Griggers rehearses the familiar double bind of a lesbian consciousness produced under specific historical conditions that must somehow struggle to critique the very conditions of her creation. *Becoming-Woman* hinges its political hopes on making productive the lesbian body's contemporary "dis-organization," what Griggers thinks of as the lesbian's being everywhere and nowhere at once.

In a different kind of theoretical text, Lauren Berlant's *The Queen of America Goes to Washington City* (1997) assembles a series of essays on sex and citizenship to think through the contemporary crisis in political activism in the United States. Frankly longing for a return to the revolutionary possibilities of the social movements of the 1960s, Berlant reviews the "conservative revolution" of Ronald Reagan's regime in the 1980s. Employing an archive of determinately ephemeral, popular, and even marginal texts (pro-life videos, sitcoms, even lesbian 'zines), Berlant takes up the sociological notion of "sexual citizenship," or the ways that sexual identities underwrite the category of the citizen to produce both deeply alienating forms of national identity and their necessary resistant counterpossibilities. In its broadest scope a reading of the American nation as increasingly privatized, even injured, *The Queen of America* offers a compelling example of the intellectual possibilities of cultural studies thought through the political lens of queer analysis.

*Elena Glasberg*

## Bibliography

Berlant, Lauren. *The Queen of America Goes to Washington City: Essays on Sex and Citizenship*. Durham and London: Duke University Press, 1997.

Blundell, Valda, John Shepherd, and Ian Taylor, eds. *Relocating Cultural Studies: Developments in Theory and Research*. New York and London: Routledge, 1993.

Case, Sue-Ellen. *The Domain-Matrix: Performing Lesbian at the End of Print Culture.* Bloomington and Indianapolis: Indiana University Press, 1996.

Clark, Danae. "Commodity Lesbianism." *Camera Obscura* 25–26 (1991), 180–210.

During, Simon, ed. *The Cultural Studies Reader.* London and New York: Routledge, 1993.

Griggers, Camilla. *Becoming-Woman.* Minneapolis and London: University of Minnesota Press, 1997.

Grossberg, Lawrence, Cary Nelson, and Paula Triechler, eds. *Cultural Studies.* New York and London: Routledge, 1992.

Probyn, Elspeth. *Outside Belongings.* New York and London: Routledge, 1996.

Warner, Michael, ed. *Fear of a Queer Planet: Queer Politics and Social Theory.* Minneapolis: University of Minnesota Press, 1993.

*See also* Critical Theory; Feminism; Identity; Liberalism; Postmodernism; Queer Theory; Social-Construction Theory; Subculture

## Cushman, Charlotte (1816–1876)

U.S. actress. Born in Boston, Massachusetts, Charlotte Cushman, "a tomboy" according to her briefly kept diary, began acting at eighteen. Famous for such roles as Meg Merrilies in Scott's *Guy Mannering*, Lady Gay Spanker in Boucicault's *London Assurance*, and Lady Macbeth (which she played opposite Edwin Forrest [1806–1872], Edwin Booth [1833–1893], and, in 1863, John Wilkes Booth [1838–1865]), Cushman is most famous for playing "breeches," or men's, parts, including roles in *Ladies At Home, or Gentlemen We Can Do Without You,* and Orlando in *As You Like It,* both all-female productions. She also played Hamlet and, notoriously, Romeo to her sister Susan's Juliet. Although reviewers sometimes criticized Cushman's acting as "hybrid," "Amazonian," and even as "amphibious" in point of sex, she was also hailed by a British reviewer in 1843 as "undoubtedly the best breeches figure in America."

Cushman also challenged gender roles through her masculine dress, which earned her nicknames like "Charley de Boots"; her associations with women, such as the party of "jolly female bachelors" she formed in Rome with Matilda Hays (1820–1897), sculptor Harriet Hosmer (1830–1908), and journalist Sara Jane Clarke (pseud.

Grace Greenwood; [1823–1904]); and her intimate relationships with women, including Hays, the poet Eliza Cook (1818–1889), and, from 1856 on, the sculptor Emma Stebbins (1815–1882). Elizabeth Barrett Browning (1806–1861) called Cushman's relationship with Hays a "female marriage." When Cushman died, Stebbins edited her letters and papers, recording that, throughout Cushman's life, "her friendships were of the nature of passions."

Among Cushman's American friends and admirers were Nathaniel Hawthorne (1804–1864), Henry Wadsworth Longfellow (1807–1882), Julia Ward Howe (1819–1910), Harriet Beecher Stowe (1811–1896), and Walt Whitman (1819–1892), who asserted that "Charlotte Cushman is probably the greatest performer on the stage in any hemisphere." Cushman became manager of Philadelphia's Walnut Street Theatre in 1843 and set out for the English stage in 1844. She was a success, earning the esteem and friendship of Thomas (1795–1881) and Jane Carlyle (1801–1866), Robert (1812–1889) and Elizabeth Barrett Browning, and Geraldine Jewsbury (1812–1880), who based a character in her feminist novel *The Half Sisters* (1848) on Cushman.

Cushman spent the rest of her life in England and in Rome, where she championed the work of women sculptors such as Hosmer, Stebbins, and Edmonia Lewis (ca. 1843–after 1911), returning occasionally to perform in America. She formally and grandly retired from the stage in New York City in 1874 and died of cancer in 1876.     *Julie Crawford*

## Bibliography

Cushman, Charlotte. *Charlotte Cushman: Her Letters and Memories of Her Life.* Ed. Emma Stebbins. Boston and New York: Houghton Mifflin, 1900.

Merrill, Lisa. *When Romeo Was a Woman: Charlotte Cushman and Her Circle of Female Spectators.* Ann Arbor: University of Michigan Press, 1998.

Puknat, Elisabeth M. "Romeo Was a Lady: Charlotte Cushman's London Triumph." *New York Theatre Annual* 9 (1951), 59–69.

Shafer, Yvonne. "Women in Male Roles: Charlotte Cushman and Others." In *Women in American Theatre.* Ed. Helen Krich Chinoy and Linda Walsh Jenkins. New York: Theatre Communications Group, 1987, pp. 74–80.

*See also* Cross-Dressing; Jewsbury, Geraldine; Lewis, Edmonia

# C

## Custody Litigation

The dispute, in court, over the control and care of children. The dispute may be between a child's mother and father upon divorce or between a child's mother and father if they were never married to each other. It may also arise between a child's parent and a third party, such as a grandparent. Of recent concern to lesbians, custody litigation may develop between a child's biological mother and the nonbiological comother upon the dissolution of the couple's relationship.

## Early Legal Literature

The legal literature began addressing lesbian-mother custody disputes in the early 1970s. At that time, it was necessary to explain that "lesbian mother" was not an oxymoron. Lesbian mothers during that period were almost entirely women who had given birth to children in the context of heterosexual marriages; they were either unaware of their lesbianism at the time they married or they suppressed their lesbian feelings, hoping that they would adapt to more socially accepted lives as married women and mothers. When such women later divorced, their ability to raise their children could be challenged either by their former husbands or by other relatives. The legal hurdles faced by lesbian mothers became the first distinctively lesbian legal issue of the 1970s. Although the climate for coming out at an earlier age has improved since the 1970s, and although, since the early 1980s, lesbians have been openly raising children without first bearing them within a marriage, many women who are unaware of their lesbian feelings or who hope that those feelings will pass still get married expecting to raise children within those marriages. Thus, custody disputes between a lesbian mother and the child's heterosexual father when those marriages dissolve remain the principal category of custody litigation facing lesbians.

Because the legal standards for resolving custody disputes are established on a state-by-state basis, the fate of a lesbian mother and her children often depends on the state in which she lives. As early as the 1970s, some states considered lesbian mothers to be acceptable custodial parents; in those states, a judge would be required to find a specific adverse impact on the child of the mother's lesbianism before her sexual orientation could be a basis for denying her custody. In 1976, the District of Columbia became the only jurisdiction to enact a statute prohibiting judges from determining custody on the basis of a parent's sexual orientation, in and of itself. In other jurisdictions, however, myths and prejudice have been, and continue to be, used to deny lesbian mothers custody of their children. Thus, in some states a mother's lesbianism, by itself, can be a basis for denying custody, while in others the court will claim that it is looking at the impact of the mother's lesbianism on the child but will actually base the denial of custody on speculation rather than on evidence presented in court. Court decisions have reflected concerns that lesbians are emotionally unhealthy or immoral and that children will be harmed in a variety of ways, including by becoming lesbian themselves, if they live with their lesbian mothers.

## Advocacy for Lesbian Mothers

Advocates for lesbian mothers have recognized from the beginning that evidence of the well-being of children raised by lesbian mothers would be a critical component of educating judges in custody litigation. Research beginning in the mid-1970s has consistently demonstrated that lesbians are as emotionally healthy and socially well adjusted as their heterosexual counterparts; that no causal connection exists between the sexual orientation of parents and that of their children; that little difference exists in the overall mental health of children raised in lesbian-mother households and those raised in heterosexual-mother households; and that the quality of parenting, not the parent's sexual orientation, is the most crucial factor for a child's healthy growth and development. Judges who accept this body of literature are more likely to rule in favor of a lesbian mother. For example, the Alaska Supreme Court in 1985 overturned a trial-court decision to award custody to a heterosexual father over a lesbian mother because the decision was based upon the trial judge's unsupported conjecture that lesbian relationships were unstable.

Lesbian mothers have also been tainted by the myth that gay men prey on children, either because a judge will group lesbians and gay men together or because a lesbian might be expected to have gay male friends who would be in the presence of her children. Therefore, advocates must often present to judges the research literature demonstrating that heterosexual males commit the vast preponderance of sexual assaults on children.

## Conditions for Custody

In custody disputes between two parents, courts primarily apply a "best interests of the child" standard, in which neither parent is favored over the other. When a parent's custody is challenged by a third party, however, the parent is customarily presumed to be the appropriate custodian. Often, the third party must show unfitness in order to prevail over the parent. Since the 1970s, there have been many custody disputes in which a third party, usually one of the child's grandparents, has challenged a lesbian mother's right to raise her child. One of the most highly publicized cases of this nature took place in the mid-1990s in Virginia between Sharon Bottoms, a divorced lesbian mother, and Sharon's mother, Kay Bottoms, who sought custody of Sharon's son, Tyler. The trial judge placed Tyler with his grandmother, ruling that Sharon was unfit because she lived with her partner, April Wade, and because her sexual conduct was illegal in Virginia and immoral in the opinion of the judge. Although a Virginia appeals court reversed the custody order, it was later reinstated by the Virginia Supreme Court.

In many cases, trial judges have granted custody to a lesbian mother, but only if she adheres to certain conditions. These conditions have included living separately from her partner, not permitting her partner to spend the night in her home when her children are present, and not taking her children to any gatherings where there are other gay men and lesbians, including predominantly gay churches. When a lesbian mother loses custody of her child and is awarded visitation rights, those rights may also be restricted by the above conditions. For example, in the Bottoms case, Sharon Bottoms was denied overnight visitation with her son; she was also prohibited from having her son in the home she shares with her partner and from having her partner present during visitation. Some appeals courts have lifted such restrictions, while others have upheld them.

It is impossible to overstate the range of judicial decisions concerning lesbian custody throughout the fifty states. At one end of the spectrum, a New Jersey appeals court articulated the benefits that children may enjoy being raised by a lesbian mother, including the ability to better perceive that the majority is not always correct, to better search out their own standards of right and wrong, and to better understand how to form beliefs based on reason and tested knowledge rather than popular sentiment and prejudice. On the other hand, a South Dakota appeals judge reasoned that a lesbian mother should be denied even visitation with her children until, after years of demonstrated conduct

and therapy, she could show that she was no longer living a life of abomination. Lesbian mothers concerned about their legal rights must always seek the opinion of an attorney within their state, although the National Center for Lesbian Rights, the only organization in the country devoted to the legal issues affecting lesbians, maintains materials on lesbian custody litigation throughout the country.

## Contemporary Issues

In recent years, a new type of lesbian custody litigation has developed. In the late twentieth century, lesbians were choosing to have children through adoption or through conception by donor insemination. These planned lesbian families have raised novel legal issues when a dispute arises either within the lesbian couple when they separate or between the couple and a known semen donor if he initiates litigation to determine his parental rights. Although many such families have written agreements concerning their child-rearing intentions, courts have, for the most part, refused to enforce such agreements, falling back upon a traditional definition of parenthood in which biology (or legal adoption) is both necessary and sufficient to confer parental status.

When a lesbian couple decides to raise a child together, usually only one can legally adopt, and, in the case of donor insemination, only one can be the biological mother. If the couple separates, the child is at serious risk of losing one of his or her parents, as the court system will not consider the nonbiological or nonadoptive mother to be a legal parent. The one legal parent will then have complete control over the extent of contact, if any, between the child and the other parent. Appellate courts in both New York and California have rejected the ability of a nonbiological or nonadoptive mother to obtain either custody or visitation rights over children jointly planned for and raised by the couple. Such a result can be avoided only if the couple completes a joint or second-parent adoption.

Just as courts have been unwilling to confer parental status in the absence of biology or adoption, they have been, for the most part, unwilling to deny parental rights to known semen donors, even when the donor has agreed before conception and birth never to assert parental rights. Although some states have statutes that deny parental rights to semen donors, most states apply these statutes only when the recipient is married to another man. Thus, a lesbian mother is always vulnerable to the claim

**C**

by a known semen donor that he should receive parental rights, which would entitle him to request visitation or even custody. The only complete protection against such a claim would be the legal termination of the donor's parental rights, something that can usually be accomplished only in the context of a second-parent adoption of the child by the biological mother's partner, and that would customarily require the consent of the donor. In states that permit such adoptions, this is the suggested course of action to prevent future custody and visitation disputes.                    *Nancy Polikoff*

### Bibliography

Benkov, Laura. *Reinventing the Family: The Emerging Story of Lesbian and Gay Parents*. New York: Crown, 1994.

Kendell, Kate, ed. *Lesbians Choosing Motherhood: Legal Implications of Alternative Insemination and Reproductive Technologies*. San Francisco: National Center for Lesbian Rights, 1996. (Available for purchase from NCLR, 870 Market Street, Suite 570, San Francisco, CA 94102.)

*Lesbian Mother Litigation Manual*. 3rd ed. San Francisco: National Center for Lesbian Rights, 1996. (Available as above.)

Rubenstein, William B. *Cases and Materials on Sexual Orientation and the Law*. St. Paul, Minn.: West, 1997.

Shapiro, Julie. "Custody and Conduct: How the Law Fails Lesbian and Gay Parents and Their Children." *Indiana Law Journal* 71 (1996), 623.

*See also* Adoption; Children; Donor Insemination; Law and Legal Institutions; Mothers, Lesbian

## Czech Republic

Republic situated in central Europe; formerly part of Czechoslovakia. After the Communist takeover in 1948, the policy was to present the country to the outer world as an ideal place to live, lacking any "deviant" groups, such as handicapped people, prostitutes, or homosexuals. In 1993, the country split into two independent states, the Czech Republic and the Slovak Republic.

Homosexuality as such was decriminalized in 1961. The last explicitly discriminating clause in the penal code was abolished in 1991. However, the almost total silence around this topic in the past has made it difficult for individuals to come to terms with their orientation.

In the former Czechoslovakia, organized groups were formed as late as 1989 and formally registered at the beginning of 1990. Lambda Union, originally operating in the Czech Republic, later split into regional groups in larger cities. In 1991, individual organizations came together as SOHO (Sdruzení organizací homosexuálních obcanù, the Association of Organizations of Homosexual Citizens). It resembles a democratic parliament that evaluates and accepts proposals, coordinates activities of individual groups, and represents them to society and its authorities. Among its members are two lesbian-only groups in the capital, Prague; in other cities, women organize within the local mixed (gay and lesbian) groups. SOHO is a member of the worldwide organization ILGA (International Lesbian and Gay Association).

SOHO's activies include a campaign for creating a positive image of lesbians and gay men as committed and responsible citizens, a lobbying effort for a domestic-partnership law, and a contribution to AIDS prevention that has been recognized by the World Health Organization, as well as Czech health-care authorities. It also works to create clubs, social events, and meeting places for lesbians and gay men.

The situation of lesbian women and the extent of their commitment to the movement reflects the situation of Czech women in general. When President Václav Havel presented his first political program, the third item was protection of the disadvantaged: "children, old people, *women*, the sick, manual workers, and ethnic minorities" (emphasis added).

In the former Czechoslovakia, lesbian women "did not exist." Until the revolution in 1989, nobody knew, spoke, or wrote about them. The only books concerning the topic were Radclyffe Hall's novel *The Well of Loneliness* (1928; translated into Czech before World War II) and Gertrude Stein's *The Autobiography of Alice Toklas* (1933; translated in the 1970s). Women who were not able to cope with their "problem" and had the courage to visit a psychiatrist or a sexologist were, with few exceptions, seen as transsexuals and offered the alternative of changing their sex surgically.

With the end of Communist rule, the situation changed significantly. Lesbian women began to have the opportunity to meet one another and to see professionally successful women and stable couples, as well as women, who, with little success, had tried to find their real identity in marriage. Prior to this, they had no name for their identity nor role models to provide support. Slowly, it became possible to find meeting places, although, just as new pubs and bars emerged, they disappeared for economic reasons. As late as 1997, there was no exclusively lesbian bar in Prague; women mostly met in a gay bar where one night was reserved for them. Other lesbian groups, such as in the city of Brno, successfully organized social events, mostly disco nights, exclusively for women.

In Prague, there are two independent lesbian groups, both of which are members of SOHO. L-klub Lambda, which split from the mixed G/L Lambda, is a voluntary community of women with homosexual orientation and their sympathizers. Its activities include consciousness raising, cultural events, and sports.

L-klub Lambda publishes a magazine, *ALIA* ("other" or "different"), for lesbian women, especially those who cannot meet in bars, married women who discovered their real orientation later in life, and young women who have problems coming out. The magazine contains legal and psychological consulting, reviews of books and films, short stories, poetry, advertisements, and news from the lesbian and gay community. In 1997, four books were published by *ALIA*, including a study of the social status of lesbian women in the Czech Republic.

The association Promluv (Speak Out) was founded at the beginning of 1994. It sponsors activities to support the rights and culture of women, primarily lesbian and bisexual, and fights against social discrimination; it publishes a bimonthly magazine, *Promluv*, with each issue devoted to a specific topic. The association organizes a national weekend for lesbian mothers and a lesbian cultural festival. It is also engaged in developing a women's center, NORA, to be located on its own premises in Prague, which will provide information and space for women's activities.          *Karla Hyánková*

***See also*** International Organizations

# D

## Dance

Despite the past contributions by, and continuing presence of, innumerable gays and lesbians in the history of ballet and modern dance from Western Europe and the United States, scholarly discussions surrounding the articulation of homosexual desire are few. Since the 1980s, dance historians have made public speculations on the private lives of gay male figures such as Vaslav Nijinsky (1890–1950), Ted Shawn (1891–1972), and Jerome Robbins (1918–), while choreographers of the 1980s and 1990s like Bill T. Jones, Mark Morris, Michael Clark, and Stephen Petronio, to name only a few, have treated the subject of male homosexuality as a central theme in their works. However, a lesbian presence in the history of dance is considerably more difficult to trace, and the articulation of a lesbian sensibility in contemporary choreography is still more challenging to define.

While a gay male choreographer can strike a threatening undercurrent of homoerotic desire by simply creating an opportunity for two men to touch on the stage, the image of two women dancing together does not necessarily create the same result. This curious double standard has its historical precedents. In the mid-to-late-nineteenth century, cross-dressed female dancers politely partnered ballerinas on the stages of the Paris Opera and provided their male spectators with a humorous and voyeuristic thrill as they danced. During the first half of the twentieth century, large ensembles of women moving in unison dominated the stage in the master works of the early moderns, such as Doris Humphrey (1895–1958) and Martha Graham (1894–1991), but their most threatening possibility lay in their rebellion against the accepted standards of female beauty

and artistic authority established in ballet. While modern dance, unlike ballet, allowed some women to assume the artistic directorship of major companies and produced female characters of great depth, the aesthetic focused on the shared experience of "humanity," and one of its best-loved metaphors was the model of heterosexual romantic courtship.

The Romantic spectacle of ballet and the narrative conventions of modern dance determined the limited possibilities for the female form on the proscenium stage as either the unattainable object of the heterosexual male viewer's desire or the necessarily heterosexual embodiment of the "human condition" for the "liberal" modern dance audience. It wasn't until the late 1960s, when avant-garde postmodern choreographers questioned the dance performance as a theatrical and political event, that the codes of sexual difference and the chain of underlying assumptions that support them were disputed and divorced from one another. Perhaps most important, male and female dancers performed roles interchangeably, and these bodies touched, supported, and were supported outside of the model of heterosexual romantic courtship. These characteristics developed further during the 1970s and 1980s in the context of contact improvisation. "Untrained" bodies from a group of participants who were both spectators and performers temporarily merged in unplanned shapes to share weight and support one another.

Young choreographers entering the world of concert dance in the 1980s had all of these tools at their disposal: leggy pyrotechnics and presentational silhouettes from ballet; epic narrative structures and the rebounding qualities of weight and momentum that characterized early modern dance; pedestrian movements and the abstract structures of

**D**

*Jill Togawa, "Prayer for My Brother." Photo by Marion Gray.*

postmodern dance; and the nonnarrative, nongendered couplings of various body types featured in contact improvisation. The 1980s also bore witness to the inclusion of artistic voices from different ethnic backgrounds. While distinguished choreographers like Katherine Dunham (1910–), Arthur Mitchell (1934–), and Alvin Ailey (1931–1989) incorporated African and black vernacular dance forms into traditional ballet and modern vocabularies from the late 1930s onward, their contributions to the mainstream stage were categorized as "Black Dance," separate from mainstream trends in concert dance. In the mid-1980s, Jawole Willa Jo Zollar, artistic director of the Urban Bush Women, borrowed from various traditions in dance and theater to create works that riveted American dance audiences with their eclectic movement vocabulary and often overtly political content. Interestingly, it was Zollar, who identifies as a straight woman, who created *Bones and Ash,* a work based on *The Gilda Stories* by novelist Jewelle Gomez (1948–), for the

1996 season at the Joyce Theater in New York City. The premiere of this work represented one of the first unabashedly lesbian portrayals of desire in a mainstream concert dance venue.

For the most part, though, lesbian choreographers working within the genre of contemporary concert dance present their work in more experimental venues, and they do not enjoy the kind of national recognition that straight female or male choreographers, gay and straight, do. "Out" lesbian performers who address sexuality in their work often find more success in obtaining an audience in dance/theater or performance art circles. However, in September 1996, San Francisco, California's, first Gay and Lesbian Dance Festival premiered at the Brady Street Dance Centre. Krissy Keefer, artistic director the Bay Area's Dance Brigade, and choreographer Anne Bluethenthal presented works of their own and those of other lesbian choreographers, such as Jill Togawa of the Purple Moon Dance Project, for this festival.

The difficulty of a lesbian artist attaining mainstream acceptance of her politicized and/or homoerotic dances reflects the enduring legacy of established concert forms. The signifying capacity for the dancing female body as heterosexualized erotic object and the decidedly straight conventions of traditional narrative force the lesbian choreographer to contend with the limits of structure and content in mainstream dance. Those who manage to obtain a kind of transgressive, self-conscious play within these limitations must then face the almost insurmountable costs of presenting their work in mainstream venues. As a result, though, the lesbian presence in dance resists a singular definition of what it is to live and love as a woman-identified woman. It may be that these artists are in a unique position to provide choreographic models in which gender is embodied across a large spectrum of qualities and the possibilities for narrative and desire fit any number of configurations. *Michelle Heffner*

### Bibliography

Banes, Sally. *Terpsichore in Sneakers*. Middletown, Conn.: Wesleyan University Press and Scranton, Penn.: Harper and Row, 1987.

Daly, Ann. "Of Hummingbirds and Channel Swimmers." *Drama Review* 31 (Spring 1987), 8–21.

Foster, Susan. "The Ballerina's Phallic Pointe." In *Corporealities: Knowledge, Culture, and Power*. Ed. Susan Foster. London and New York: Routledge, 1996, pp. 1–24.

Koegler, Horst. "Dancing in the Closet: The Coming Out of Ballet." *Dance Chronicle* 18 (1995), 231–239.

Novak, Cynthia. *Sharing the Dance: Contact Improvisation and American Culture*. Madison: University of Wisconsin Press, 1990.

Siegel, Marcia B. *The Shapes of Change: Images of American Dance*. Berkeley and Los Angeles: University of California Press, 1985.

*See also* Cross-dressing

## Daughters of Bilitis

First national lesbian organization in the United States. Daughters of Bilitis (DOB) was founded in San Francisco, California, in 1955 by four lesbian couples, including Del Martin (1921–) and Phyllis Lyon (1924–), who went on to become lifelong activists. Originally intended as a social organization and an alternative to the bar scene, DOB was named after the lesbian-themed poems of Pierre Louÿs (1870–1925), "Songs of Bilitis."

Shortly after DOB's founding, several of its members came into contact with the early homophile movement and organizations such as Mattachine and One, Inc., whose members were attempting to improve conditions for homosexuals and wanted DOB to work toward improving social acceptance for lesbians. Within the first year, DOB split into two organizations, roughly along class lines. Working-class women formed a secret social club (Quatrefoil), and middle-class women developed DOB into a public social and political organization. Del Martin became the first president, and Phyllis Lyon became the first editor of *The Ladder*, published from 1956 to 1972.

Daughters of Bilitis was incorporated as a women's social club by the state of California in 1957; the following year, two additional chapters, in Los Angeles, California, and New York City, were formed. At DOB's height, chapters emerged in a number of cities and countries, including Chicago, Illinois; San Diego, California; Boston, Massachusetts; Denver, Colorado; and Melbourne, Australia. By the 1970s, most chapters had folded; in the 1990s, one chapter, in Boston, remained.

Typical activities included "Gab 'n 'Java" discussion sessions held at members' homes, social activities such as bowling and parties, and public panels and forums. DOB sought professional speakers, including psychiatrists, lawyers, and clergy, who would address the group; its members also sought to participate in academic research on lesbians. As the organization became larger, it held national conferences and participated in other national homophile activities. For many years, DOB was the only organization that provided a voice for lesbians.

In its early years, Daughters of Bilitis emphasized the integration of lesbians into the larger heterosexual society. The group's mission included education of the female homophile to enable her to "make her adjustment to society"; public education, which DOB members hoped would lead eventually to a breakdown of taboos and prejudices; participation in research projects by psychologists and other recognized experts; and investigation of the penal code. One DOB strategy was to encourage "appropriate" dress and appearance in order to minimize the boundaries between lesbians and heterosexual women. Members also believed that lesbians would feel better about themselves if they conformed to

**D** dominant ideals for dress and behavior. By improving individual lesbians' appearance and self-esteem, the Daughters thought that society would eventually become more accepting.

Because of the severe stigma attached to homosexuality in the 1950s and women's real fears of losing their jobs simply for being suspected of lesbianism, recruitment to the organization was difficult, and numbers remained small. Despite reassurances that members' names were safe, that both homosexuals and heterosexuals were included as members, and that women could not lose their jobs simply for belonging, many of the middle-class lesbians who were DOB's primary audience feared joining. Given the police harassment, arrests, and loss of jobs homosexuals in the 1950s and 1960s faced, these fears were not ungrounded. And, in fact, DOB came under police and FBI surveillance.

In the mid-1960s, DOB flirted with an alliance with the more militant segments of the homophile movement. *The Ladder* published editorials sympathetic to tactics then considered radical, such as picketing, and debated the contentious notion that homosexuality was not an illness but instead a simple human variation.

By the late 1960s and early 1970s, many DOB members and leaders sought an alliance with the women's liberation movement. Although DOB had always been sympathetic to what would later be called a "feminist" point of view, by the late 1960s this view became even more prominent. Some even suggested that gay men might be "more adamant foes of women's rights" than heterosexual men once the goals of the male homophile movement had been achieved. But the shift to an alliance with the women's movement also proved divisive. By this time, many younger lesbians were attracted to the more radical social-change movements of the decade, and many of the older members were split about the direction of the organization. By the early 1970s, DOB was no longer a national organization. All chapters became autonomous, and *The Ladder* became an independent women's liberation paper.

*Kristin G. Esterberg*

### Bibliography

D'Emilio, John. *Sexual Politics, Sexual Communities: The Making of a Homosexual Minority in the United States 1940–1970.* Chicago: University of Chicago Press, 1983.
Esterberg, Kristin. "From Accommodation to Liberation: A Social Movement Analysis of Lesbians in the Homophile Movement." *Gender and Society* 8 (1994), 424–443.
Faderman, Lillian. *Odd Girls and Twilight Lovers: A History of Lesbian Life in Twentieth-Century America.* New York: Columbia University Press, 1991.
Martin, Del, and Phyllis Lyon. *Lesbian/Woman.* Twentieth Anniversary Edition. Volcano, Calif.: Volcano, 1991.

*See also* Ladder, The; Martin, Del, and Lyon, Phyllis; Women's Liberation Movement

### Davis, Katherine Bement (1860–1935)

American social reformer and scholar. Katherine Bement Davis's contribution to lesbian history and culture is her 1929 study, *Factors in the Sex Life of Twenty-Two Hundred Women.* Twelve hundred of the women included in her study were unmarried. She asked women not only about their sexual activities with men, but also about their sexual desires for, and activities with, women. This work, supported by the Rockefeller Foundation, capped a long career in social reform. It should be seen as heroic because it cost Davis her professional life. Cut off from her funding as a result of the study, she was forced into retirement when it was completed.

Davis was born into an old, middle-class family in Buffalo, New York, in 1860. She taught school before entering Vassar College at the age of thirty. At the age of thirty-seven, after working in reform and settlement work in New York City and Philadelphia, Pennsylvania, she entered the graduate program at the University of Chicago. In 1900, she received her Ph.D. in political economy cum laude.

Davis became the superintendent of the new Bedford Hills, New York, Reformatory for Women in 1901. Her tenure there lasted until 1913, during which time she instituted progressive and innovative programs addressing the women's educational and vocational needs. Her work was recognized and supported by John D. Rockefeller (1839–1937). In 1914, with an outstanding reputation in the field of criminology, she became commissioner of corrections for New York City, the first woman to hold a cabinet-level post in that municipality.

Davis was a supporter of women's rights and an active suffragist. In the 1920s, through work on issues of prostitution and deviance, she recognized the need for research on "normal" women's sexual attitudes and behaviors. Her findings, especially those on masturbation and homosexuality, challenged popular and academic beliefs about women's sexuality.

*Trisha Franzen*

## Bibliography

Davis, Katherine Bement. *Factors in the Sex Life of Twenty-Two Hundred Women.* New York: Harper, 1929.

Fitzpatrick, Ellen. *Endless Crusade: Women Social Scientists and Progressive Reform.* New York: Oxford University Press, 1990.

———. *Katherine Bement Davis, Early Twentieth-Century American Women, and the Study of Sex Behavior.* New York: Garland, 1987.

*See also* Sexology

## Delarue-Mardrus, Lucie (1874–1945)

French novelist and poet. Lucie Delarue-Mardrus was a prolific writer, publishing more than forty-seven novels and twelve collections of poetry. She was one of the most popular authors of the 1920s, and many of her novels began as serials in such widely read newspapers as the *Journal* and *Revue de Paris.*

Delarue married Joseph-Charles Mardrus (1868–1949), the Franco-Egyptian translator of the *Arabian Nights,* and it was he who introduced her to the literary and artistic opinion-makers of the day, including Auguste Rodin (1840–1917), Sarah Bernhardt (1844–1923), André Gide (1869–1951), and Colette (1873–1954). Despite this high-profile marriage, Delarue-Mardrus reserved her passion for women. Natalie Barney (1876–1972) introduced her to the lesbian aristocracy of Paris, and she was a frequent visitor at Barney's salon.

Although most of Delarue-Mardrus's fiction revolves around popular heterosexual themes such as unwed mothers, Norman fishermen, and war-torn romance, *L'Ange et les Pervers* (The Angel and the Perverts [1930]) tells the story of the hermaphrodite Mario/n and his/her forays into the gay and lesbian milieu of the 1920s. Elsewhere, love between women is veiled behind a heterosexual front. *Une Femme mûre et l'amour* (Love and the Mature Woman) (1935), otherwise closely based on Delarue-Mardrus's relationship with the Jewish opera singer Germaine de Castro, centers on the love of the singer for her Catholic brother-in-law. Delarue-Mardrus's poetry records the longings, desires, joys, and despairs she experienced for the women she loved. At first reading, they are not apparently lesbian, for they speak more of the emotions involved than of the women who enflamed them. Her earliest poems, "Occident" (1901) and "Ferveur" (1902), were written just after her marriage, but the passion they describe was for Impéria de Heredia, as Delarue-Mardrus's memoirs make clear.

Although the young Delarue-Mardrus was honored by kings, sultans, painters, and poets, in her seventies she was unable to get her work published due to Nazi censorship. Her lover, Germaine de Castro, was sought by the Gestapo, who, discovering that de Castro had fled, threatened to take Delarue-Mardrus in her place. The Société des Gens des Lettres provided her with a pension and sold the film rights to one of her novels, but Delarue-Mardrus died at the end of the war in near penury.

*Anna Livia*

## Bibliography

Engelking, Tama Lea. "'L'Ange et les Pervers': Lucie Delarue-Mardrus's Ambivalent Poetic Identity." *Romance Quarterly* 39:4 (November 1992), 451–466.

Livia, Anna. "Lucie Delarue-Mardrus and the Phrenetic Harlequinade." In Introduction to *The Angel and the Perverts* by Lucie Delarue-Mardrus. New York: New York University Press, 1995.

Waelti-Walters, Jennifer. *Feminist Novelists of the Belle Epoque: Love as a Life Style.* Bloomington: Indiana University Press, 1990.

*See also* Barney, Natalie; Colette; France; French Literature

## Deming, Barbara (1917–1984)

American writer and activist. Born in New York City, Barbara Deming was the second of four children, the only girl. During her teenage years, the family owned a home across the river from New York in a country neighborhood where friends included Norma Millay and her sister, poet Edna St. Vincent Millay (1892–1950). In this free and somewhat bohemian setting, Deming began to write poetry and, at the age of seventeen, had a passionate and formative love affair with Norma Millay (1893–1986).

Deming received her bachelor's degree from Bennington College in Bennington, Vermont, in 1938 and a master's degree from Case Western Re-

# D

*Barbara Deming at Seneca Women's Peace Encampment, July 1983. Photo by Judith McDaniel.*

serve in Cleveland, Ohio, in 1940. During her time at Bennington, Deming met Vida Ginsberg (1920–), with whom she was lovers for seven years and who was the first of three significant partner relationships during Deming's lifetime.

During World War II, Deming worked for the Library of Congress national-film-library project based at New York City's Museum of Modern Art. Her film reviews led to the writing of her first book, *Running Away from Myself: A Dream Portrait of America Drawn from the Films of the '40s* (1969). A bequest in the early 1950s allowed Deming to travel in Europe, where she began writing the stories collected in *Wash Us and Comb Us* (1974) and also began a novel, *A Humming Under My Feet: A Book of Travail* (1985).

In 1954, Deming met artist Mary Meigs (1917–); the two became companions almost immediately, settling in a house in Wellfleet, Massachusetts, where Mary painted and Barbara wrote poems, stories, and essays which she published occasionally in the *New Yorker* and the *Partisan Review*. In 1959, Deming and Meigs traveled to India,

where Deming became interested in the work of Gandhi (1869–1948) on nonviolence. She realized "that I was in the deepest part of myself a pacifist," and her life began to move from a personal search for truth to a political commitment to truth and justice. A spontaneous interview with Fidel Castro (1926/1927–) during a trip to Cuba in March 1960 put her in touch with the Committee for Nonviolent Action and the Peacemakers. "Meeting them," she said, "felt like finding a long-lost family." Subsequently, she joined some of the first protests against nuclear-weapons testing. On an integrated peace walk in the U.S. South, Deming was jailed for civil rights protests in Birmingham, Alabama, and Macon and Albany, Georgia, during 1963–1964. *Prison Notes* (1966) is an account of these imprisonments. Her following book, *Revolution and Equilibrium* (1971), detailed the anti–Vietnam War movement, particularly Deming's travels to North Vietnam, where she witnessed and experienced the U.S. bombing of Hanoi.

Deming's commitment to human freedom and individual dignity eventually brought her to struggles that touched her own life most directly: feminism and gay and lesbian rights. After years of suppressing her "secret" life, in 1971 Deming faced her fear of being known as a homosexual, "facing always the threat of being despised for that." Since 1969, Barbara Deming had been living with her third lover and companion, Jane Gapen (1919–1992), whose ex-husband had threatened to never let her see her two children again. It took them several years to resolve the custody issue.

Books from her lesbian feminist period include *We Cannot Live Without Our Lives* (1974) and *Remembering Who We Are* (1981). In 1983, Deming was part of a Women's Encampment for a Future of Peace and Justice demonstration near the Seneca Army Depot, near Seneca Falls, New York, during which she was arrested. Her essay about this last protest is included in a reprinting of *Prison Notes*.

*Judith McDaniel*

### Bibliography

Deming, Barbara. *A Humming Under My Feet: A Book of Travail*. London: Women's Press, 1985.
———. *Prisons That Could Not Hold*. Athens: University of Georgia Press, 1995.
McDaniel, Judith. "Introduction: The Women She Loved." In *I Change, I Change: The Poetry of Barbara Deming*. Norwich, Vt.: New Victoria, 1996.

Meyerding, Jane, ed. *We Are All Part of One Another: A Barbara Deming Reader*. Philadelphia: New Society, 1984.

*Silent Pioneers.* Interviews with Gay and Lesbian Elders. Produced by Pat Snyder, Harvey Marks, and Lucy Winer; originally shown on PBS in Fall 1984.

*See also* Peace Movement

## Demography

Study of the size, structure, and spatial distribution of a population that is time and geographic specific. "Size" refers to the number of persons in a country, city, organization, occupation, or local community. "Structure" refers to the composition of a group that has been divided according to one or more its characteristics, such as age, ethnicity, or religion. "Spatial distribution" refers to the geographic locations and movement of a population of individuals, services, and/or businesses. Lesbian identity is not typically considered a relevant factor in demographic studies. Yet all conventional demographic questions are affected when sexual identity is taken into consideration; similarly, demography is necessary for a full understanding of lesbian and gay communities.

The movement of persons both within and between countries may affect the population size and the structure of the geographic areas of origin and destination. Population size, structure, or spatial distribution are primarily affected by the number of births (fertility), deaths (mortality), and "movers" (migration). The study of these relationships constitutes a "demographic perspective" on the nature of societal organization and change. Births, deaths, and "movers" are demographic events, and processes. In San Francisco, California, for example, the proportion of lesbians in the population can generate changes in the structure and forms of relationships, partnership- and family-formation processes, and birth rates. The size of San Francisco's lesbian and gay population is dependent upon its birth, death, *and* migration rates.

Each demographic process—migration, fertility, and mortality—includes numerous concepts. "Emigration" and "immigration" refer, respectively, to movement *from* one's country of birth *to* another country. "Internal migration" refers to movement from one geographic area to another *within* the same country. The San Francisco lesbian population, and generally lesbian populations in cities with one million or more persons, are significantly affected by internal migration. "Mortality" is concerned with health, death rates, and causes of death. And "fertility" is concerned with behaviors of sexuality, contraception, and the number of persons born. For lesbian history and culture, the demographic perspective is critical in addressing questions of growth, organization, continuity, and much more. In one way or another, each question is affected by demographic factors.

Demography is a "way of knowing" and a perspective. It is interdisciplinary and quantitative. For example, whether or not a lesbian community exists *visibly* is dependent, in part, upon the size of its population. Whether or not shops, schools, or health services are sensitive to lesbian needs is related to the size and structure of the population. Both internal organization and external sensitivities may increase with the recognition of increased numbers and empowerment. In this hypothetical scenario, it is the demographic factor of size that produces greater visibility, potentially affecting economic needs, services, and lesbian-community initiatives. The scenario has included demographic factors that affect, or were affected by, nondemographic factors. Factors such as ethnicity, education, and income are not demographic factors per se but certainly are affected by, and affect, births, deaths, and "movers." Such reciprocal relationships are examined in demographic analysis.

Each demographic area of study includes numerous concepts and terms, usually with corresponding measures, such as rates, proportions, and other measures, that are specific to one or more calendar years and geographic areas. Such rates enable a reader to judge potential sources of change in their community and beyond. Similarly, demographic rates are used by market researchers to target advertising toward lesbian communities and can be used by lesbians for community planning and design.

Demography depends for its information primarily upon population censuses and large-scale surveys. Often it uses its census or survey results in the calculation of various rates, such as projections about the future population and its structure. As a research method, it transcends gender categories— that is, it is a method appropriate to researching populations who have multiple and different labels, locations, and mobility.

Demography is a key component of public-policy analysis and the assessment of program services. It provides a basis for action and decision making in education, housing construction, market analysis, tax issues, election campaigns, and community building. In an information age, one must constantly assess what is factual and what is less than true. Demography is one of several analytical lenses, or, ways of knowing, through which history and culture may be studied. Sometimes it produces fanciful results, but, most often, it is a valid lens.

*Christina Brinkley*

## Bibliography

Pressat, Roland. *Demographic Analysis: Methods, Results, Applications.* Paris: Presses Universitaires de France, 1961. Trans. Judah Matras. Chicago: Aldine Atherton, 1972.

*See also* Advertising and Consumerism; Economics; Immigration

## Demonstrations and Actions

Public, confrontational, collective political activism, including marches, zaps, disruptions, sit-ins, guerrilla street theater, strikes, and civil disobedience. Scholars and activists often contrast demonstrations and actions with more individualized forms of resistance and with activism that occurs within more "legitimate" political channels, such as lobbying, letter writing, and political-party work.

As social-movement theorists have argued, demonstrations and other contentious political actions reveal participants' dissatisfaction with the status quo and willingness to challenge existing power relations. People involved in such activism have recognized the systemic nature of what they might have previously viewed as individual problems and have acted on the conviction that they have a common purpose and must engage in collective oppositional politics to change their situation. Rather than complacent victims of social forces, collective action shows people to be agents of change.

Homosexuals in the United States may have engaged in public confrontational actions prior to 1965, but the earliest documented demonstrations occurred that year. Inspired by earlier actions of the civil rights movement, small groups of lesbians and gay men marched in front of the United Nations, the White House, the Civil Service Commission, Independence Hall, the Pentagon, and the State Department, targeting the government's discriminatory treatment.

Demonstrations and actions have different meanings in different contexts. An action that deeply challenges the status quo in one geographic location or at a particular historical moment might not be as challenging if done someplace else or at another time. Similarly, an organization's position in the extant race, class, gender, sexuality, and nationality hierarchies may influence the degree to which it is willing, or able, to take risks or challenge the established order. Breaking with the more accommodationist and discrete approaches advocated by other members of the Daughters of Bilitis (DOB) and the Mattachine Society, these first collective actions by homosexuals were, on the one hand, relatively risky (participants risked losing jobs, friends, and family) and confrontational (they focused on changing society rather than helping individual homosexuals adjust to society). Their actions provoked clashes in their homophile organizations over tactics and goals. On the other hand, in contrast to the civil disobedience, freedom rides, and large demonstrations engaged in by civil rights activists prior to, and during, the same period, these early homophile actions were tame. Ernestine Eckstein (pseud.), a veteran of the black civil rights movement and a member of DOB, believed in 1965 that picketing was almost a conservative activity.

Just four years later, the Stonewall Rebellion in New York City and subsequent emergence of the Gay Liberation Front (GLF) made these earlier, orderly pickets seem even more timid and staid. When the police conducted a raid of the Stonewall Inn on June 27, 1969, drag queens, butch dykes, street hustlers, and street youth—many of them black or Latino and working class—refused to quietly comply and instead threw coins, bottles, garbage, and bricks at the police. Nights of riots and invocations of "Gay Power!" were followed by the formation of GLF in New York City and later around the United States. Ultimately, gay liberation groups emerged in Canada, Australia, and Western Europe.

U.S. lesbian and gay liberationists argued for sexual liberation in the context of broader societal transformation. As gay liberationists, they participated in antiwar demonstrations, rallies in support of imprisoned Black Panthers, and women's-movement actions. Inspired by the confrontational tactics of other movements, liberationists engaged in militant actions that focused specifically on the oppression of lesbians and gays. Among other actions, activists marched against bar raids and police harassment; occupied the offices of the *Village Voice* and *Harper's* to protest antigay coverage; invaded the American Medical Association's 1970 convention in Chicago, Illinois; and the American Psychiatric Association's annual meeting in San Francisco, California; and held a dance-in at a straight bar in Minneapolis, Minnesota, after two lesbians were evicted for dancing together.

Actions by lesbian and gay liberationists were not only directed externally at society's homophobic institutions. GLF lesbians in T-shirts emblazoned with "Lavender Menace" disrupted the National Organization for Women's Congress to Unite Women (New York City) in 1970 to protest the homophobia of the women's movement. That same year, when a lesbian bar in Oakland, California, refused to let women post a flier about a gay women's liberation meeting, lesbians who frequented the bar organized a protest and boycott.

D'Emilio (1992) has pointed out that, as other movements from the 1960s declined, the U.S. gay liberation movement was eclipsed by a movement focused solely on lesbian and gay rights rather than overall societal transformation. Simultaneous with this shift in vision and agenda, and perhaps partly as a result of it, white lesbians and lesbians and gay men of color who were alienated by the racism and sexism of the movement began to organize autonomously. New groups that formed included Radicalesbians, Third World Gay Revolution, Salsa Soul Sisters, the Furies, Gay Women's Liberation, and the National Coalition of Black Lesbians and Gay Men.

In the late 1970s, proliferating lesbian and gay activist organizations (as well as hundreds of unaffiliated individuals) in the United States participated in many actions, including demonstrations against the antigay Save Our Children campaign (1977), the Briggs initiative to ban lesbian and gay teachers from California's schools (1978), and the light sentence given to Dan White, murderer of San Francisco City Commissioner Harvey Milk (1930–1978).

Throughout the 1980s, lesbians and gay men around the world protested their oppression. For example, in 1980 in Brazil, more than one thousand lesbians and gay men protested police roundups. The group Comunidad Homosexual Argentina participated in a massive demonstration for justice in 1984 after the end of the military dictatorship in Argentina. In 1988, ten thousand lesbians and gay men demonstrated in London against Section 28 of the Local Government Act (known as Clause 28 before the act was passed), a bill prohibiting the teaching of homosexuality. Three lesbians used a rope ladder to invade the House of Lords in protest of the clause.

Initially spurred by the AIDS crisis, beginning in the late 1980s lesbians and gay men in the United States again participated in radical activism. Lesbians, many of whom had experience in leftist and feminist organizations, played a prominent role in ACT UP (AIDS Coalition To Unleash Power), a direct-action organization famous for die-ins, disruptions, street theater, and demonstrations targeting the scientific-medical establishment and the government. Lesbians initiated numerous actions focusing on the issues faced by women with AIDS. Some lesbians in ACT UP/New York, wanting to do more activism about women's health, formed Women's Health Action Mobilization (WHAM!). ACT UP/NY and WHAM! joined in a militant demonstration in New York City against the Catholic Church's opposition to safe sex, homosexuality, and abortion. In the early 1990s, Queer Nation groups emerged in the United States, Canada, and Australia. They sponsored kiss-ins at suburban malls and large marches protesting violence against gays and lesbians. OutRage formed in London in 1990 and also engaged in direct action to protest homophobia. The Lesbian Avengers emerged in the United States in 1992, holding "zaps" (quick, small-scale political actions), demonstrations, and annual Dyke Marches to increase lesbian visibility and fight lesbian oppression. Groups in Oregon, Colorado, Maine, Iowa, and elsewhere formed to fight the Religious Right's antigay referenda.

By the mid-1990s in the United States, many of these direct-action groups had disappeared, and lesbian and gay activism inclined toward more conventional politics to secure access to the U.S. military and the right to marry.

Identities are commonly perceived to exist prior to collective action, but demonstrations and actions themselves play a large role in deconstructing, reconstructing, and transforming the identities of participants and the communities from which they come. The actions of DOB, GLF, Radicalesbians, Salsa Soul Sisters, and OutRage, among others, have all affected the meaning of "lesbian." *Debbie Gould*

### Bibliography

Adam, Barry D. *The Rise of a Gay and Lesbian Movement*. Rev. ed. New York: Twayne, 1995.

D'Emilio, John. *Making Trouble: Essays on Gay History, Politics, and the University*. New York: Routledge, 1992.

———. *Sexual Politics, Sexual Communities: The Making of a Homosexual Minority in the*

*United States, 1940–1970.* Chicago: University of Chicago Press, 1983.

Faderman, Lillian. *Odd Girls and Twilight Lovers: A History of Lesbian Life in Twentieth-Century America.* New York: Columbia University Press, 1991.

Gomez, Jewelle. "Out of the Past." In *The Question of Equality: Lesbian and Gay Politics in America Since Stonewall.* Ed. David Deitcher. New York: Simon and Schuster, 1995, pp. 18–65.

*See also* Activism; AIDS (Acquired Immune Deficiency Syndrome); Daughters of Bilitis; Furies, The; Gay Liberation Movement; Lesbian Avengers; National Organization for Women (NOW); Queer Nation; Radicalesbians; Women's Liberation Movement

## Denmark

Scandanavian nation with an international reputation for exceptional tolerance of gay men and lesbians. In 1989, Denmark became the first country in the world to legally recognize homosexual relationships; this legislation, combined with laws barring discrimination based on sexual orientation, has made Denmark a world leader in granting equal rights to gay and straight citizens. Moreover, the tone of public discourse on homosexuality is generally cordial rather than strident, and popular sentiments are more frequently characterized by acceptance and a laissez-faire attitude than overt hostility. Still, Denmark cannot claim a particularly long-standing liberal tradition in its view or treatment of homosexual citizens, and research on the lives and history of Danish lesbians suggests many similarities with patterns found in other Western nations.

### History

As was the case in many other European countries, the earliest efforts to control sexual behavior and contain it within reproductive family units resulted in the prohibition of sodomy with the Danish Law Code of 1683. Until 1930, when sexual acts between consenting adult men were finally decriminalized, male homosexuality was, therefore, punishable by law. Because sodomy was defined as nonprocreative, penetrative sex, same-sex sexuality between women was never encompassed by any form of regulation.

On the contrary, at least in the nineteenth century, the kind of loving relationships between women that feminist historians have dubbed "romantic friendships" were understood also in Denmark as natural expressions of women's tender, emotional nature, and for two unmarried women to live together was a perfectly legitimate, even respectable, choice. Especially in the second half of the nineteenth century, when new employment opportunities paved the way for female economic independence, a number of urban middle-class women chose to share their private lives with a female companion. Natalie Zahle (1827–1913), for example, the founder of the highly successful Miss Zahle's School for girls, built a home with Ingeborg Vinderen (1850–1924) from 1879 until her death in 1913. Other pioneers of female education, including Augusta Fenger (1844–1931) and Marie Topsøe (d. 1894), and Thusnelda Moltke (1843–1928) and Elise Bay (1842–1916), formed similar long-term domestic partnerships.

It was only from the end of the nineteenth century that changing understandings of sexuality threw into question the respectability of such female couples. In the 1890s, the prominent physician Christian Geill (1860–1938), inspired by German sexual science, first introduced the notion of the homosexual individual in Danish medical circles. By identifying those people whose sexual desires were aimed at persons of the same sex as "inverts" or homosexuals, he and other medical experts contributed to creating a new understanding of homosexuality as an innate condition rather than a particular form of immoral or sinful behavior. Although most attention was paid to male homosexuality, experts frequently suggested that women who violated gender norms by acting or appearing "masculine" possibly possessed sexual instincts similar to those of men and, therefore, merited inclusion in the newly developed category of sexual abnormality.

### The Twentieth Century

In the early years of the twentieth century, this new belief in homosexuality as a congenital disposition prompted the leading Danish psychiatrist, Professor Alexander Friedenreich (1849–1932), to argue for the decriminalization of sodomy between consenting adults. Ultimately, the scientific reconceptualization of homosexuality that informed Friedenreich's arguments contributed to a revision of the penal code, freeing homosexual men from the risk of legal prosecution. The impact on women's relationships was more ambiguous: While acknowledging the possibility of sexual desire between women, it slowly began to erode the moral propriety of same-sex couples.

In 1906–1907, a series of highly publicized sexual scandals involving male prostitution functioned to spread public knowledge of male homosexuality. In comparison, awareness of same-sex sexuality among women was much slower to seep into popular consciousness. Even in the 1920s and 1930s, when private networks contributed to the creation of a lesbian subculture in Copenhagen, the continued acceptance of cohabitating female couples suggests that notions of sexual deviance had not yet rendered emotional and physical intimacy between women entirely suspect. As Ina Holm, a lifelong lesbian and feminist, told Jensen (1989): "It was not as difficult to be a lesbian in the 1930s as it got to be later. Because at that time, not many people knew the concept of homosexuality."

World War II marks a turning point in lesbian history in many Western nations, but its impact on Danish lesbians remains unclear. However, the fact that the first official homosexual organization, discreetly named the Association of 1948, was formed in its immediate aftermath suggests the existence of a sizable, self-conscious gay and lesbian community. From its founding, the organization was intended as a national interest group promoting tolerance, understanding, and equality for gay men and lesbians. In addition, it was envisioned as a forum for community building and mutual support and as a social club offering entertainment for its mixed-gender membership. Though headquartered in Copenhagen, the organization sought to reach gay men and lesbians across the country through its membership publication, originally entitled *Vennen* (The Friend), but since 1954 published as *PAN*.

Promoting tolerance and equal rights for homosexuals proved a difficult task in the 1940s and 1950s. Media-generated images of homosexuals as lurking seducers of innocent youths vilified gay men and lesbians, and rigorously enforced police regulations against disturbance of public order and violations of public decency kept them the constant targets of harassment and persecution. Such pressures led to a dramatic decline in organizational membership: In 1950, the Association of 1948 counted 1,600 members; only five years later, that number had plummeted to sixty-two. It was not until the mid-1960s that public fears of homosexuality waned, and only then that the organization was able more successfully to pursue its political goal of assimilation and equal rights.

Over the years, many lesbians found companionship and community in the Association of 1948 (since 1978 known by the more candid name, the National Organization of Gay Men and Lesbians). Yet, in spite of its mixed-gender membership, both the rank and file and the elected leadership of the organization were consistently dominated by men. There is little evidence that this was a bone of contention in the 1950s and 1960s, but, in retrospect, many female members recall experiences of marginality and second-class status in the organization. As elsewhere in society, women were often assigned only tedious tasks and trivial responsibilities, while men determined organizational priorities and political strategies. It is hardly surprising, then, that the Association of 1948 seemed a less than attractive organizational home to those women who were not only lesbians, but also part of the new women's movement that emerged in the early 1970s.

## The Lesbian Movement (1970–)

Bent on changing social and sexual structures in society, lesbian feminists quickly disassociated themselves from what were perceived as pathetic and politically misguided attempts at social acceptance. Instead, the loosely organized group Lesbian Movement, founded in Copenhagen in 1974, was based on a critique of capitalism, patriarchy, and compulsory heterosexuality, and, rather than partake in a male-dominated hierarchical organization striving for legal reform, the movement created its own spaces and institutions, such as the folk high school Kvindehøjskolen, the conference center Skrækkenborg, and annual summer camps on the island of Femø, open to women only.

After flourishing in the 1970s and the early 1980s, the lesbian movement all but vanished from the political scene. While some women shifted their energies toward other forms of women-centered activism, such as rape prevention and crisis centers, and others withdrew into private networks, the renamed National Organization of Gay Men and Lesbians once again became the center for political organizing among homosexuals from the mid-1980s. Though the membership never grew to more than 3,500, the organization nevertheless won its greatest political victories in the 1980s. Beginning with the removal of homosexuality from the official list of psychological disturbances in 1980, the following years were characterized by considerable improvements in the legal status of gay men and lesbians. In 1986, homosexual couples were granted the right to

**D** inherit from each other on the same conditions as married, heterosexual couples. The following year, sexual orientation was added to the existing antidiscrimination law. Finally, in 1989, after years of intense lobbying, the Danish Parliament passed, with a considerable majority of votes, the Law on Registered Partnership Between Two Persons of the Same Sex, thereby offering homosexual couples the option of legal recognition of their private unions.

Lesbian responses to the legislation were mixed. While most applauded its symbolic significance, radical lesbians questioned whether the right of homosexuals to enter into the socially conservative institution of marriage was an objective worth pursuing. Others found that the legislation did not go far enough. The fact that registered couples were specifically excluded from adopting children, including those of a partner, certainly put a damper on the enthusiasm among many lesbians. Others regretted that the legislation precluded the option of having a religious wedding ceremony in the Lutheran state church, and that registered lesbian couples, unlike straight married couples, were denied the right to artificial insemination through the public healthcare system. Given this range of reservations about the legislation, it is symptomatic that, even five years after its passage, lesbians constituted a minority (25 percent) of those couples who had taken advantage of the legislation.

While the 1980s significantly improved the civil and legal rights of homosexuals, the 1990s were, in many ways, difficult years for the National Organization of Gay Men and Lesbians. Financial difficulties and membership decline all but decimated the organization. New political goals were difficult to define. Invisibility, belittling, and marginalization continued to be common experiences of gay men and lesbians, but determining strategies to counteract normative heterosexuality and create a truly diverse and inclusive society remained a daunting, and still unaccomplished, task. *Birgitte Soland*

### Bibliography

Bech, Henning. "Report from a Rotten State: 'Marriage' and 'Homosexuality' in 'Denmark.'" In *Modern Homosexualities: Fragments of Lesbian and Gay Experience*. Ed. Kenneth Plummer. London and New York: Routledge, 1992, pp. 134–147.

Jensen, Mona Bager. "Je ne Regrette Rien" (No Regrets). Interview with Ina Holm. *PAN* 5 (1989), 16–17.

Lützen, Karin. *At prøve lykken. 25 lesbiske livshistorier* (Trying Your Luck: 25 Lesbian Life Stories). Copenhagen: Tiderne Skifter, 1988.

———. *Hvad hjertet begærer. Kvinders kærlighed til kvinder, 1825–1985* (What the Heart Desires: Women's Love for Women, 1825–1985). Copenhagen: Tiderne Skifter, 1986.

Rosenbeck, Bente. *Kvindekøn. Den moderne kvindeligheds historie, 1880–1980* (The Female Gender: The History of Modern Womanhood, 1880–1980). Copenhagen: Gyldendal, 1987.

*See also* Domestic Partnership; Romantic Friendship

## Diaries and Letters

The letters women wrote to one another, the diaries they kept for themselves or to share with friends, almost never with any thought of publication or public exposure, constitute one of women's principal sources of information about women's lives, thoughts, language, and, especially, their feelings for one another.

Letters and diaries are cultural artifacts that communicate as much about the culture that produced them as about the individual women who wrote them. They exist especially in literate cultures that emphasize the importance of the written, rather than the spoken, word and in cultures that conceive of an individual's sense of self as a private, introspective experience, rather than a public and performative act. Letters, in particular, mark a society that both valorizes the individual voice and separates the individual from kin, friends, and associates, requiring the exchange of letters in order to maintain relations and communicate information. Who writes letters, and to whom, and who keeps diaries—this information about the common facts of everyday life—reveal a great deal about that culture, as does the content of those letters and diaries. The feelings expressed, the words used, and the meanings given those words (words such as "love," "sex," "desire") are equally products of the national culture to which the women belong and the specific female culture women themselves construct. Indeed, they mark a key point where those two cultures interact.

## History and Development

Women's letters and diaries emerged as a major female cultural endeavor in early-modern Europe (sixteenth and seventeenth centuries) and its North American colonies. Literacy and individualism were valued, separation was frequent, and communicative skills were essential. Aristocratic women, women from ruling elites and commercial families, frequently assumed the role of family secretary, communicating critical political and economic information to distant husbands, fathers, and other kin. Women recorded daily events, domestic and community rituals, the birth and nurturing of children, spiritual concerns. During the nineteenth century, well-to-do women, especially urban women, continued their extensive correspondences. Middle-class girls wrote frequent letters on leaving home to attend boarding school or, later in the nineteenth century (1870s and onward), women's colleges. The letters written by women teachers and professors describe the life of the woman intellectual and educator. The letters and diaries of women reformers and suffragists (for example, Elizabeth Cady Stanton [1815–1902], Susan B. Anthony [1820–1906], Anna Howard Shaw [1847–1919], and Florence Nightingale [1820–1910]) reveal lives filled with rich personal, professional, and political commitments.

During these years, literacy began to spread across class, ethnic, and racial divides. The rich or famous were no longer the only women to keep diaries and write letters. On the pages of their diaries and letters, poor farming women from the Great Plains or Mormon Utah expressed their most secret fears and fought the dread sense of isolation and loss of all they had known and held dear. One woman's diary, kept in the 1850s during her overland trip to California, contained but two types of notation: the number of water holes the wagon train passed and the number of graves it passed. Young girls' diaries were usually more lively. One teenage girl, just moved to Oregon, detailed the country dances she attended, remarking that she and her sisters always walked barefoot to the dances, carrying their stockings and shoes to save them from wear and tear. Another reported that keeping a diary permitted her intimacies with other young girls: "I esteem it [exchanging diaries] a very great privilege indeed . . . as we lay our hearts open to each other, it heightens our love & helps to cherish & keep alive that sweet soothing friendship and endears us to each other by that soft attraction" (Smith-Rosenberg 1986). The letters immigrant women wrote home to female kin—be that home in Ireland, Scandinavia, Poland, or Germany—form one of the most important sources of information on the immigrant experience.

It is unusual to find correspondence among African American women in the nineteenth century.

Most Southern states made literacy among enslaved African Americans a crime; educational opportunities in the North were poor. However, the correspondence of Addie Brown and Rebecca Primus, two African American women who grew up together in Hartford, Connecticut, in the mid-nineteenth century, does exist (Hansen 1996). These letters quite openly expressed the deep love the women felt for each other and their commitment to their relationship. They also offer insights into the pressures family and economic need placed on working-class women to marry men and grow apart.

## Characteristics

What women's letters and diaries demonstrate more than anything else is the central role women played in one another's lives and the frequency with which women expressed love and devotion to one another. The letters and diaries of eighteenth- and nineteenth-century women reveal the existence of a female world of great emotional strength and complexity. It was a world of intimacy, love, and erotic passion. Uniquely female rituals drew women together during every stage of their lives, from adolescence through courtship, marriage, childbirth, child rearing, death, and mourning. Women revealed their deepest feelings to one another, helped one another with the burdens of housewifery and motherhood, nursed one another's sick, and mourned for one another's dead. It was a world in which men made only a shadowy appearance. Living in the same society, nominally part of the same culture (bourgeois, farming, or working class), certainly members of the same family, women and men experienced their worlds in radically different ways. Female rituals rigorously excluded male relatives, rituals so secret that men had little knowledge of them and so pervasive that they patterned women's lives from birth to death.

Women's diaries, such as those of Lady Eleanor Butler (1739–1829) and Sarah Ponsonby (1755–1831)—the Ladies of Llangollen—or Anne Lister (1791–1840), reveal the emotional and sexual intimacies of women's lives together. Women's letters frequently convey erotic, sensual feelings; they also speak of physical pleasures. Women wrote to each other about exchanging bittersweet kisses and passionate embraces, of nights spent in each other's arms, of dancing together, of swimming naked together in the moonlight, of burning jealousies. They dreaded separation and reveled in each other's company. One young woman, in her mid-twenties in the

**D** 1840s, wrote a friend, dear since their teenage years together: "Dear darling Sarah! How I love you & how happy I have been! You are the joy of my life. . . . I cannot tell you how much happiness you gave me, nor how constantly it is all in my thoughts. . . . My darling how I long for the time when I shall see you . . ." (Smith-Rosenberg 1986). Another confessed her love after a minor tiff: "I wanted so to put my arms round my girl of all the girls in the world and tell her . . . I love her as wives do love their husbands, as *friends* who have taken each other for life—and believe in her as I believe in my God. . . . You can't get away from [my] love." Later, when the other woman married, the first wrote: "You know my dear Helena, I really was in love with you. It was a passion such as I had never known until I saw you. I don't think it was the noblest way to love you." She addressed the groom in a far different tone: "Do you know sir, that until you came along I believe that she loved me almost as girls love their lovers. *I know I loved her so.* Don't you wonder that I can stand the sight of you." Thirty years later, this same woman wrote Helena: "It isn't because you are good that I love you—but for the essence of you which is like perfume" (Smith-Rosenberg 1986).

Historians have found similar letters in the correspondence of women college presidents M. Carey Thomas (1857–1935) and Mary Wooley (1863–1947), reformers Francis Willard (1839–1898) and Eleanor Roosevelt (1884–1962), and writers and journalists Virginia Woolf (1882–1941), Natalie Barney (1876–1972), and Lorena Hickok (1893–1963). What is most striking to historians today is that the women who wrote so lovingly to and about other women frequently shared these letters with husbands (if married), other friends, and relatives. There is every indication that these women and their families considered such love both socially acceptable and compatible with heterosexual marriage.

**Historical Interpretations**

Historians debate how to interpret these letters. Some, such as Lillian Faderman in her detailed study *Surpassing the Love of Men: Romantic Friendship and Love Between Women From the Renaissance to the Present* (1981), or Marjorie Dobkin in her introduction to M. Carey Thomas's (1857–1935) teenage diary, argue that these women's letters do not, in fact, suggest sexual involvement, that their passions were platonic. Other lesbian commentators claim that women can only be considered lesbians if they self-consciously chose to define themselves as les-

bians—that is after the category "lesbian," or "sexual invert," was developed in the late nineteenth and early twentieth centuries. It appears that, for these critics, lesbianism is more an identity than a behavioral category, more a political than a sexual choice. Still others focus on the passion women expressed in their letters, the physically explicit nature of many of their activities. These scholars conclude that erotic, passionate relationships between women were common, certainly in the nineteenth century and undoubtedly before. That women related passionately to one another surprises these critics far less than the apparent acceptance heterosexual society accorded their relationships—before the twentieth century, that is. They focus on two aspects of the phenomenon of women's loving letters: the issues it raises concerning the nature of women's eroticism and the ways women have of expressing eroticism, and what sociopolitical factors might have contributed to the effacement of the female world of love and ritual.

*Carroll Smith-Rosenberg*

***Bibliography***

Davis, Natalie Zemon. *Women on the Margins: Three Seventeenth-Century Lives*. Cambridge, Mass.: Harvard University Press, 1995.

Hansen, Karen V. " 'No *Kisses* Is Like Youres': An Erotic Friendship between Two African-American Women during the Mid-Nineteenth Century." In *Lesbian Subjects*. Ed. Martha Vicinus. Bloomington and Indianapolis: Indiana University Press, 1996, pp. 178–207.

Mavor, Elizabeth. *A Year With the Ladies of Llangollen*. New York: Viking Penguin, 1984.

Smith-Rosenberg, Carroll. *Disorderly Conduct: Visions of Gender in Victorian America*. New York: Knopf, 1986.

Stanton, Elizabeth Cady. *Elizabeth Cady Stanton, Susan B. Anthony: Correspondence, Writings, Speeches*. Ed. Ellen DuBois. New York: Schocken, 1981.

Thomas, M. Carey. *The Making of a Feminist: Early Journals and Letters of M. Carey Thomas*. Ed. Marjorie Dobkin. Kent, Ohio: Kent State University Press, 1979.

Vicinus, Martha. *Independent Women: Work and Community for Single Women, 1850–1890*. Chicago: University of Chicago Press, 1985.

***See also*** Anthony, Susan B.; Autobiography; Barney, Natalie; Ladies of Llangollen; Lister, Anne; Roosevelt, Eleanor; Thomas, M. Carey; Woolf, Virginia

## Dickinson, Emily (1830–1886)

American poet. After brief periods at Amherst Academy and Holyoke Female Seminary, she settled into an outwardly uneventful life keeping house for her family. Dickinson never married. The real events in her life are her writings, which have assumed classic status in American literature.

Dickinson's letters to several of her female acquaintances are evidence that, throughout her life, she had strong emotional attachments, which may be described as love relationships, with other women. A comparison of such love letters with letters she wrote at about the same time to women who were merely good friends indicates that her impassioned language was not simply sentimental rhetoric of the period and that these involvements, while probably nongenital, were clearly homoerotic. Those letters help explain the forty or fifty poems in the Dickinson canon that cannot be understood unless recognized as love poems from one woman to another.

Certainly, Dickinson had heterosexual interests as well—the letters addressed to an unidentified Master, those to Judge Otis Lord (1812–1884), and many of her poems are irrefutable proof. But it is impossible to doubt the intensity of her involvement with women when one reads letters, especially those to the woman who became her sister-in-law, Susan Gilbert (1830–1913), with whom, if her letters and notes are any proof, she ostensibly had the most intense and enduring emotional relationship of her life.

Several biographers, most notably Rebecca Patterson, John Cody, and Richard Sewall, have dealt with Emily Dickinson's lesbianism. Patterson, in fact, suggests as a major thesis in her book, *The Riddle of Emily Dickinson* (1951), that Dickinson had a love affair with Kate Scott Anthon, which, at its conclusion in the 1860s, crushed Dickinson and accounted for her "peculiarities" during the remaining twenty-odd years of her life.

Cody (1971) adopts a Freudian approach and argues that, while Dickinson's Puritan heritage would not have permitted her to indulge in homosexual lovemaking, she had no wish to fulfill a female role since she despised her weak mother and feared her tyrannical father; thus, well into adulthood she experienced "pre-pubescent" crushes on other women, particularly Gilbert, who served as a mother-surrogate to Dickinson.

Sewall (1974), while seeming at first to reject Cody's suggestion that Dickinson was in love with Gilbert and hurt and upset when she lost her to Austin Dickinson (1829–1895), later refers to Dickinson's letters to Gilbert as "nothing less than love letters."

All of these writers cite ostensibly lesbian poems to support their biographical narrative. Dickinson's homoerotic poetry seems to span the entire length of her literary career, from one of her first poems, written in 1854 ("I have a Bird in spring") to one of her very late poems, written in 1883 ("To see her is a picture" in the third variant). While the subject of these poems is sometimes identifiable (it is frequently Gilbert), most often she is not. This is not surprising, since, as several scholars have observed, only about one-tenth of the letters Dickinson wrote and less than one-thousandth of those written to her are extant. But, while there is no way to know who the persons were who evoked some of Dickinson's most moving love lyrics, one thing is certain: Many of them were women.

The speaker in Dickinson's homoerotic poems is usually the lover and pursuer in the relationship. Such a relationship is often represented by the symbol of a nest in which the speaker finds (or at least expects to find) comfort and "home" with the other. But she recognizes that she cannot expect permanence in her love, not because it is an inherently flawed kind of love but generally because the beloved other woman will eventually marry, as it was assumed most women would in the nineteenth century, since they were without an independent source of income or a profession that would make them self-sufficient. The speaker accepts the reality of this situation but not without difficulty. What is much more difficult for her to accept, of course, is a beloved woman's cruelty that has no basis in custom or pragmatism. In such a situation, the speaker usually cries out bitterly against the other woman, but she is willing to return to her and, apparently, to be hurt again. She is frequently self-pitying. Only occasionally does she perceive herself victorious in love, and then it is a poor victory, having conquered the other woman by arousing her pity. These homoerotic poems are never joyous, but that is to be expected in a society in which heterosexual marriage was believed virtually inevitable and in which there was little possibility of two unrelated women establishing a life together if they were not wealthy through independent inheritance. *Lillian Faderman*

### Bibliography

Cody, John. *After Great Pain: The Inner Life of Emily Dickinson*. Cambridge, Mass.: Harvard University Press, 1971.

Patterson, Rebecca. *The Riddle of Emily Dickinson*. Boston: Houghton Mifflin, 1951.

Sewall, Richard. *The Life of Emily Dickinson*. New York: Farrar, Straus, and Giroux, 1974.

Smith, Martha Neil. *Rowing in Eden: Rereading Emily Dickinson*. Austin: University of Texas Press, 1992.

*See also* Diaries and Letters; Poetry; Romantic Friendship

## Didrikson, Mildred Ella "Babe" (Zaharias) (1911–1956)

Norwegian-American athlete and medical humanitarian. Born the sixth of seven children to poor immigrant parents in Port Arthur, Texas, who soon moved to Beaumont, Texas, she was nicknamed "Babe" for *baden* (baby) in Norwegian. She later claimed it was an analogy to slugger Babe Ruth (1895–1948). The toughest ruffian in her working-class neighborhood, Babe excelled at all boys' competitive games from marbles to racing; she ridiculed and shunned all "girls'" pursuits. Her parents encouraged her athleticism in a backyard rustic gymnasium. As a teen, Babe elicited confusion and condemnation from peers and the press for her appearance and mannerisms, which blurred gender boundaries.

*Babe Didrikson Zaharias. John Gray Library, Lamar University Special Collections, Beaumont, Texas. Courtesy of Susan E. Cayleff.*

Before completing high school, Babe played semiprofessional basketball for Employer's Casualty Insurance Company (ECC) in Dallas, Texas, within an all-women's company-sponsored league. She vexed her teammates, excelled on the court, and, as a two-time All-American star, led her team to a national title (1930–1931). She dominated the 1930–1931 Amateur Athletic Union (AAU) meets with U.S. and world records in the eighty-meter hurdles, the broad jump, the baseball throw, and the javelin. Self-promotion and lack of "team play" values estranged her from the larger female athletic community.

As a one-woman *team* representing ECC, she single-handedly won the AAU meet and qualified for the Los Angeles Olympics (1932). There she won two golds (hurdles and javelin) and one half-gold, half-silver medal due to her controversial style in the high jump. Media attention exploded. She spoke rowdily and postured aggressively. This period, 1932–1937, brought the cruelest scrutiny. The public's tolerance for Babe's tomboyishness evaporated as she eschewed heterosexual liaisons and prescribed femininity. National sportswriter Paul Gallico dubbed her a "Muscle Moll" and member of the "Third Sex" in *Vanity Fair* (1932), which solidified her oddity status.

After a series of stunt exhibitions, Babe transformed her image into that of a ladylike, genteel golfer. She purposefully flaunted female clothing and makeup, flirted with men, and constructed a fictitious heterosocial youth. In 1938, Babe married George Zaharias (1908–1983), professional wrestler, and tried to retreat into normalcy. There was genuine affection between them at first. In the 1940s, they helped cofound the Ladies Professional Golf Association (LPGA)—largely to increase Babe's opportunities.

In 1950, Babe met twenty-year-old Betty Dodd (1930–1993), a golf protégée from San Antonio, Texas, beginning a six-year intimate relationship. Never admittedly lesbian, it was clearly physical and emotionally sustaining. Dodd cohabitated with the Zahariases from 1950 to 1956, while Babe's intimacy with George apparently ceased. Dodd cared for Babe during a recurring bout with cancer in 1953 and 1955–1956. Their bond was made invisible by them, the press, and sports peers. Babe's own fear of public condemnation caused her disavowal of her love of Dodd. She died at age forty-five of colon cancer turned systemic.

Babe Didrikson was the most decorated athlete of her century, winning Female Athlete of the Year six times, Female Athlete of the Half-Century (1950), and more than four hundred trophies and medals. She was LPGA president, top LPGA money winner, and winner of thirteen consecutive amateur golf tournaments.

*Susan E. Cayleff*

## Bibliography

Cayleff, Susan E. *Babe: The Life and Legend of Babe Didrikson Zaharias*. Urbana: University of Illinois Press, 1995.

Didrikson, Babe Zaharias, as told to Harry Paxton. *This Life I've Led: My Autobiography*. New York: A.S. Barnes, 1955.

Johnson, Oscar, and Nancy Williamson. *"Whatta-Gal": The Babe Didrikson Story*. Boston: Little, Brown, 1975.

*See also* Sports, Professional

## Dietrich, Marlene (1901–1992)

Film actress, singer, and performer. Marlene Dietrich was born and grew up in Germany. After several years of working in films and cabarets in the 1920s, she landed her breakthrough role in *The Blue Angel* (1930), directed by Josef von Sternberg (1894–1969). Dietrich played the role of Lola Lola, a cabaret singer and femme fatale who is irresistible to men. Dietrich was seductive in the role of Lola Lola, but she also possessed another quality: She seemed to be watching herself as if studying a performance, slyly winking to the audience, contemptuously observing the men who were drawn to her like moths to a flame. After the international success of *The Blue Angel*, Dietrich and Von Sternberg came to Hollywood, where their collaboration continued with five more films: *Morocco* (1930), *Dishonored* (1931), *Shanghai Express* (1932), *Blonde Venus* (1932), and *The Devil Is a Woman* (1935). Dietrich's ironic, knowing performance style developed throughout her collaboration with von Sternberg and beyond. When their collaboration ended, Dietrich continued a successful acting career until her final film, *Just a Gigolo* (1978). In addition, Dietrich was a singer and a stage performer; during World War II, she entertained the U.S. troops abroad, and she had a very successful one-woman show in the 1970s. Dietrich had a remarkable ability to reinvent herself, and, even when she was no longer one of the top stars in Hollywood, her persona—as the cooly detached, self-mocking, always seductive performer—endured. In 1983, Maximil-ian Schell (1930–) made a documentary about Dietrich (*Marlene*) that explores the legendary persona.

Dietrich has had long-standing popularity among lesbian audiences. She often cross-dressed in her films; in *Blonde Venus* and *Morocco,* she appears on stage in the famous costume (top hat and tuxedo) that has been immortalized in the photograph collections of many lesbians. Dietrich's seductive appeal may have been directed primarily at the men in her films, but her appeal to women was often suggested as well. The air of detachment vis-à-vis heterosexual romance surrounding the Dietrich persona contributed to her lesbian appeal. The most famous example of Dietrich's cross-gender appeal occurs in *Morocco*, in which, as Amy Jolly, she appears on stage in a tux and proceeds to kiss a female member of the audience on the mouth. To be sure, the scene is framed by Dietrich's relationship to male lead Gary Cooper (1901–1961), but this moment exemplifies Dietrich's lesbian appeal throughout her career.

Rumors about Dietrich's bisexuality circulated throughout her life. In 1955, the gossip magazine *Confidential* published a story about Dietrich's "secret life," detailing relationships with several women. Biographies of Dietrich published after her death have confirmed the rumors. Dietrich was married, but she and her husband lived apart during most of their marriage, and Dietrich engaged in affairs with women, including Mercedes de Acosta (1893–1968), who was also Greta Garbo's (1905–1990) lover.

*Judith Mayne*

## Bibliography

Martin, W.K. *Marlene Dietrich*. New York and Philadelphia: Chelsea House, 1995.

Riva, Maria. *Marlene Dietrich*. New York: Knopf, 1993.

Spoto, Donald. *Blue Angel: The Life of Marlene Dietrich*. New York: Doubleday, 1992.

Weiss, Andrea. *Vampires and Violets: Lesbians in the Cinema*. London: Jonathan Cape, 1992.

*See also* Cross-Dressing; Film, Mainstream; Garbo, Greta

## Disability

One of many terms used to describe people with physical or mental limitations. The lesbian community often uses the term "differently abled," first coined in 1976 at the Michigan Womyn's Music Fes-

**D** tival in an attempt to make disability more accepted. However, no matter what term one uses to define a person with physical limitation, handicap, or disability, the fact is that difference is viewed negatively. The modern world has been altered forever by the Industrial Revolution and the resulting change in emphasis from unique handcrafted items that were functional, yet not all the same, to items that were mass-produced and identical. This change affects how people view themselves and others; there is a cultural expectation that people should look and act the same. In addition, the prejudice against difference is variable. A person who is totally paralyzed and in a wheelchair may experience less oppression than a person with severe facial disfigurement, even though the disfigured person might not be "handicapped" at all.

In conjunction with the term "differently abled," "ableism" was initially coined to define the particular methodology of oppression used traditionally against people with disabilities. In its broadest sense, ableism was seen as a system of assigning value in which people are measured against an inflexible, standardized definition for the purpose of dismissing those who could be perceived as having "lesser abilities." This model of "disability" definition is a cornerstone of patriarchy. To be branded "disabled" is to be precluded from full, validated participation in a society. Disabilities can be physical or emotional or can be based on class, sex, or race. Traditionally, men have defined women as less able and created a system that essentially determines that their efforts will be less effective in the public arena. People can be economically oppressed by their size; for example, a fat woman may not be hired for a job, a short person is seen as ineffective, or a tall person may be seen as threatening. The mutations are seemingly endless.

Women with disabilities are statistically more disadvantaged than men with disabilities, and lesbians with disabilities are the most disadvantaged of all. While women are often seen as weaker than men, they also are seen as caretakers. If a woman has a disability, she is considered to be unable to take care of others, bear children, or look physically pleasing to enhance the image of "her man." As the feminist movement encouraged women to be stronger, go to the gym, build their bodies, and eat healthier, it created a different kind of oppression for women with disabilities. These women could not compete with women who could build their bodies and, thus, had no way to incorporate this emerging

aspect of feminism into their lives. While many women were working to redefine the image of their sexuality, women with disabilities were still longing just to be seen as sexual. Traditionally, women with disabilities have been regarded as asexual, and, since "lesbian" defines one's sexuality or sexual preference, lesbians with disabilities were regarded as an impossibility.

Lesbians with disabilities have been raped and beaten because they cannot be as easily closeted, are more helpless, and are, therefore, more targeted for abuse. From 1980 to 1989, the Disabled Lesbian Alliance—a network of three hundred to four hundred lesbians with disabilities across the United States—supported one another and worked on accessibility issues in the lesbian community. Hundreds of calls were received from anonymous lesbians living at home or with homophobic caretakers. Blind lesbians were forced to rely on readers who reacted against the gay and lesbian literature they were hired to read. The difficulty of homphobia for a lesbian in a wheelchair who hires caregivers is similarly intense. More easily trapped and isolated, for many years they were prevented from participating in lesbian community events because of physical inaccessibility.

As difficult as it is to find places to hold lesbian events, it is even more difficult to find places that are physically accessible to the disabled. While the lesbian community would never think of holding a concert in a building that lacked a bathroom, it would use one without a ramp. But this robs the entire community of rich experiences. Women with disabilities bring not only a wealth of knowledge and information with them, but also an acceptance of themselves that is rare in any oppressed group. Women, especially lesbians, with disabilities have had to work very hard on their self-image and on their internalized self-hatred. This provides a model for all women and lesbians.

Fear is a great divider. Some lesbians who have broken from traditional roles such as mothering or caregiving may avoid becoming involved with women with disabilities, for fear that they will have to take care of them. Others feel that something mights happen to them, and that they, too, might become disabled.

At the disabled lesbian conference in 1981 held on the grounds of the Michigan Womyn's Music Festival, the term "temporarily able bodied" was used to define women who had no disabilities. As most people grow older, they lose various bodily functions. Eventually, everyone becomes disabled in some way or other, just as every woman is disabled by patriarchy.

Lesbians with disabilities want the same rights and privileges as their sisters, including the ability to attend a potluck, a bar, a march, or a festival. Increasing numbers of lesbians are affected with environmental illness, which require an even deeper level of awareness of disabled women's needs. Some progress has been made so that many lesbians are willing to put in a ramp so women in wheelchairs can come to an event, or hire sign-language interpreters, or provide braille programs and sighted guides so that blind women can find the bathroom. But it is more difficult to ask women who attend events to refrain from wearing perfume, sprays, or newly dry-cleaned clothing so that women with environmental illness can attend. Some temporarily able-bodied lesbians resist exercising this kind of restraint. Nevertheless, with the increase in asthma and environmental illness in the late twentieth century, more people will have these problems.

It is important to note that although some women with disabilities normally attend most large, accessible events, 20 percent of the general population has some form of disability—a number not seen at lesbian events. Most women with disabilities—mental disabilities, for example—are warehoused in institutions, and the fact that they are lesbians is held against them. Most lesbians have shared, at one point or another in the coming out process, the fear of being crazy or being labeled as such by their families. It is the responsibility of the lesbian community to reach out to those women who have suffered this fate in reality.

Being lesbian may mean rejecting some societal values, but not one another in the name of independence. Being truly independent is being interdependent and making choices that are right for oneself in the context of community. Women with disabilities highlight that issue for the lesbian community.                    *Connie Panzarino*

### Bibliography

Browne, Susan E., Debra Connors, and Nanci Stern, eds. *With the Power of Each Breath*. Pittsburgh and San Francisco: Cleis, 1985.

Keith, Lois. *What Happened to You? Writing by Disabled Women*. New York: New Press, 1996.

Panzarino, Connie. *The Me in the Mirror*. Seattle: Seal, 1994.

Saxton, Marsha, and Florence Howe, eds. *With Wings: An Anthology of Literature by and about Women with Disabilities*. New York: Feminist Press, 1987.

Tremain, Shelley, ed. *Pushing the Limits: Disabled Dykes Produce Culture*. Toronto: Women's Press, 1996.

***See also*** Music Festivals

## Discrimination

Legal term that refers to making a distinction between groups of people that is unjustified, unreasonable, or irrelevant. Governments have a long history of discriminating against lesbians on the basis of their lesbianism, as do religions and other organized groups and individuals. As the explicit laws against lesbians and lesbianism are slowly being repealed, or enforced less often, discrimination by individuals has come to be more important in policing lesbians' lives.

### Laws and Rules About Sexual Behavior

Perhaps the most blatant example of discrimination against lesbians and bisexual women are statutes that define as crimes common consensual lesbian sexual behaviors. In the United States in the mid-1990s, approximately half of the states defined as criminal some consensual lesbian sexual behavior, most often oral sex. (These statutes are typically called "sodomy statues" because they are most widely known for criminalizing sodomy, or anal intercourse.) Some states have criminalized sexual behaviors between two persons of the same sex that are not crimes if performed by a man and a woman. Robson (1992) gives an entertaining discussion of various lesbian sexual behaviors and precisely where these would and would not be crimes.

In Canada, lesbian sex was decriminalized in 1967. In the United Kingdom, consensual lesbian sex is not a crime, although there is a gross-indecency statute that applies only to gay men. Criminalizing of lesbian and gay sex was often adopted in non-Western countries as a part of colonialization; some of these statutes were still being enforced at the end of the twentieth century.

Less formal rules about sexual behavior also have a significant impact on lesbians' lives. Public displays of affection that are encouraged for heterosexual couples are most often actively discouraged for lesbians—by uncomfortable glances, hostile stares, negative comments, verbal abuse, and overt violence.

# D

## Areas of Discrimination

Lesbians have reported, and continue to report, extensive discrimination in employment. In the United States, the most notoriously discriminatory employer is the military, from which women are frequently discharged for lesbian sexual activity or for being lesbian. Women seem to be targeted more for this persecution than are gay men, and women of color are targeted disproportionately often.

Lesbians and bisexual women also report being fired from employment or otherwise punished for their sexual orientation by private employers and other governmental agencies. As a result, many do not acknowledge their sexual orientation at work, and some feel forced to make up elaborate heterosexual identities to "pass" on the job.

Gaybashing (physical violence directed against lesbians and gay men because of their sexual orientation) became increasingly acknowledged in the 1990s as a form of discrimination. Lesbians also experience the sexual violence directed against women, which is so common. Moreover, men are less likely to be held responsible for rape or other sexual assaults if their victim is seen as in some way "provoking" the attack, as lesbians have sometimes been assumed to do, solely on the basis of their sexual orientation.

One of the most important areas in which lesbians experience discrimination is with respect to their partner relationships and any children they might have. In the United Kingdom, these relationships have been called "pretended family relationships" by conservative governments, which apparently believed that only heterosexuals can have "real" families.

Lesbian couples are routinely denied the benefits that are given to married heterosexual couples and, increasingly, to unmarried heterosexual couples—immigration rights, medical and other employment benefits, pension benefits, inheritance rights, preferential status within the taxation system, and next-of-kin status. If a lesbian is critically injured in an accident, her life partner has no automatic right to visit her in the hospital or to make any choices on behalf of the injured lesbian, including with regard to treatment. In the absence of a legal power of attorney which states otherwise, the law decrees that a member of the woman's "real" family, her biological family, should act as her guardian.

Many lesbians who have children have been denied custody of their children because of their lesbianism or have been required to limit their participation in lesbian relationships and/or communities to keep custody. For example, some judges have told lesbians who want custody of their children that, if they choose to live with a lover, their custody would be revoked.

This prejudice against lesbian relationships as real relationships, equal in importance to heterosexual relationships, is widely shared. Families routinely expect their members to get married and incorporate the new husband or wife into the family, but lesbian family members are often pressured not to upset others by including their partner in "family" gatherings.

## Protection from Discrimination

In 1998 in Canada, eleven of thirteen jurisdictions provided some legal protection against discrimination for lesbians in their human rights legislation (the exceptions being Prince Edward Island and Newfoundland), although, in some instances, this protection was read in by the courts rather than explicitly legislated. This protection was greatly limited by laws that restricted family and/or sexual-partner benefits to heterosexual couples (see above). In the United States, the Constitution guarantees "equal protection of the laws" but does not extend this protection to lesbians who are discriminated against on the basis of their lesbianism. In 1998, ten states (California, Connecticut, Hawai'i, Massachusetts, Minnesota, New Hampshire, New Jersey, Rhode Island, Vermont, and Wisconsin) and many cities and towns (about 165 in 1998) also outlawed discrimination on the basis of sexual orientation. New in the 1990s were so-called family values campaigners, who saw lesbians, gay men, and bisexuals as a threat to the American family. They worked to enshrine in law an explicit right to discriminate on the basis of sexual orientation in order to preserve the (heterosexual) family.

## Future Directions

Arguing that lesbians are discriminated against on the basis of their sexual orientation became a widely used tactic in the 1990s for pressing for the expansion of lesbians' right to live how they choose. In April 1993, 300,000 lesbians, gay men, bisexuals, and heterosexuals marched on Washington, D.C., to demonstrate for an end to oppression on the basis of sexual orientation, arguing that it is a simple matter of justice to end such discrimination. Some theorists have cautioned that a reliance on antidiscrimination as a political strategy may not be the best option for gays and lesbians, prompting an extensive debate about the merits and risks of such a strategy.

*Jodee M. McCaw*

## Bibliography

Dynes, W.R., and S. Donaldson, eds. *Homosexuality: Discrimination, Criminology, and the Law.* New York: Garland, 1992.

Hunter, Nan D., Sharryl E. Michaelson, and Tom B. Stoddard. *The Rights of Lesbians and Gay Men: The Basic ACLU Guide to a Gay Person's Rights.* 3rd ed. Carbondale, Ill.: American Civil Liberties Union, 1992.

Majury, Diana. "Refashioning the Unfashionable: Claiming Lesbian Identities in the Legal Context." *Canadian Journal of Women and the Law* 7 (1994), 286–311.

Robson, Ruthann. *Lesbian (Out)law: Survival Under the Rule of Law.* Ithaca, N.Y.: Firebrand, 1992.

Wilson, Angelia, ed. *A Simple Matter of Justice? Theorizing Lesbian and Gay Politics.* London: Cassell, 1995.

**See also** Custody Litigation; Electoral Politics; Human Rights; Law and Legal Institutions; Legal Theory, Lesbian; Prejudice; Rights; Tolerance; Violence

## Documentaries

Typically defined as a film portraying actual events or histories in a factual way, in contrast to narrative films that tell an imaginative story. A precise definition, however, is both controversial and elusive, raising a number of questions. Can aspects of documentaries be staged? Can they openly promote or advocate a viewpoint or an ideology, or should they merely observe? Must all documentary films be issue oriented? Can a documentary film be poetic, artistic, or personal? Although an agreed-upon definition is hard to pinpoint, the history of lesbian documentary film can be recounted.

Lesbian documentary filmmaking can be considered from different perspectives: lesbians making films about lesbians, lesbians making films about other subjects, and nonlesbians making films about lesbians. These three classifications broadly define lesbian documentary film.

## Historical Development

Lesbian documentary filmmaking developed in conjunction with the feminist movement of the 1970s and the rise of gay men's and co-gender film productions. Feminists were attempting consciousness raising through self-exploratory documentaries, while feminist film theory was questioning the nature of the "male gaze," or point of view, in filmmaking.

Jan Oxenberg's 1972 film *Home Movie* can be considered the germinal lesbian documentary, providing a point of departure for future filmmakers. The gay and lesbian co-gender productions of this period, exemplified by the film *Word Is Out* (1978), were also greatly influential during the early years of the lesbian and gay movement. Three of the filmmakers—Barbara Hammer, Frances Reid, and Greta Schiller—who began in this early period of independent social-change documentaries, have had prodigious careers.

Barbara Hammer is not considered a traditional documentary filmmaker; however, her films have a self-revelatory aesthetic to them. Among the topics Hammer explored in the series of eight films she made between 1974 and 1979 were the sexual nature of lesbians in *Dyketactics* (1974); the taboo of menstruation in *Menses* (1974); and lesbians, mothers, and goddesses in *Moon Goddesses* (1976). Also among this series of productions was *Home* (1978), a film that documented her childhood, and *Double Strength* (1978) and *Available Space* (1978), two films documenting the stages of her romantic relationship. *Nitrate Kisses* (1992), a very accessible and successful narrative history of lesbian and gay life from the 1920s through the 1990s, maintains Hammer's experimental nature by using clips of overt lesbian sexual activity.

Unlike Hammer, Greta Schiller pursued a more traditional form of documentary filmmaking and has produced a body of work that attempts to document the past. *Greta's Girls* (1976), a short film exploring an interracial lesbian relationship, is generally acknowledged as one of the very first lesbian documentaries. A few years later, Schiller joined Lucy Winer, Frances Reid, and Robert Epstein to make *Greetings from Washington, D.C.* (1981), the co-gender production that documented the first major gay and lesbian march on Washington, D.C., in 1979. Schiller's 1985 film, *Before Stonewall*, codirected with Robert Rosenberg and researched by her partner in many productions, Andrea Weiss, is one of the most significant film portraits of homosexual history. Schiller and Weiss teamed up to make *International Sweethearts of Rhythm* (1986), a film that documents the world of black women musicians during the 1930s and 1940s, and the love story *Tiny & Ruby: Hell Drivin' Women* (1988). Their *Paris Was a Woman* (1996) details the world of lesbian artists, writers, editors, and stylesetters of Paris of the 1920s.

Frances Reid is another pioneer filmmaker whose career has spanned the course of feminist and gay and lesbian documentary making. Her 1977 film, *In the Best Interest of the Children*, was the first American documentary to address the subject of lesbian mothers and child custody. This film was significant due to its length, fifty-three minutes, and its use of the traditional narrative form to enhance viewer accessibility. Reid was the cinematographer on the Academy Award–winning documentary *The Life and Times of Harvey Milk* (1984) and produced and directed *The Changer: A Record of the Times* (1991), a biography of singer Cris Williamson and the history of women's music. She also coproduced two films with Dee Mosbacher's production company, Woman Vision. *Straight from the Heart* (1994) received a 1995 Academy Award nomination. *All God's Children* (1996), made in collaboration with Sylvia Rhue, has received multiple awards, including Best Documentary at the 1996 National Black Arts Festival and Best Film on Matters Relating to the "Black Experience" at the 1996 Black International Cinema Competition.

In the 1980s, two events had a profound impact on lesbian documentary making: the AIDS epidemic and the advent of video technology. Reid was the cinematographer on several AIDS-related productions, including *Living with AIDS* (1986) and *The Face of AIDS* (1991). The latter is one of the few documentaries to look at the AIDS epidemic in Africa.

## The 1990s

Among the young filmmakers whose careers began while documenting the course of the epidemic are Jean Carlomusto and Ellen Spiro. Spiro's *ACT UP at the FDA* (1988) captured one of the important battles for AIDS drug-treatment access. She also made the well-received *Greetings from Out Here* (1993), an autobiographical journey exploring the lesbian community of the southern United States. Carlomusto produced the lesbian safe-sex video *Current Flow* (1990) and *L Is for the Way You Look* (1991), an irreverent look at lesbian history and images.

Educational videos have also been part of this new wave of feminist filmmaking, spawned, in part, by the cost effectiveness of video production. This, in part, enabled more women, among them Sherry Freelowe, Mosbacher, and Cheryl Dunye, to become filmmakers.

Freelowe produced one of the first videos to explore the African American gay and lesbian experience in *Black Nations/Queer Nations* (1996). Mosbacher, another representative of this generation of lesbian filmmakers, began her filmmaking career when she produced the video documentaries *Closets Are Health Hazards* (1984) and, with Joan Biren, *Lesbian Physicians on Practice, Patients, and Power* (1991). Both deal with the issue of homophobia in a medical setting. In addition to *Straight from the Heart* and *All God's Children*, Mosbacher produced and directed *Out for a Change: Addressing Homophobia in Women's Sports* (1995), a film that exposes the devastating emotional impact of homophobia on all women athletes.

Dunye, not unlike Hammer, has produced films that challenge conventional definitions by interweaving narrative fiction with personal reflection. *Watermelon Woman* (1996) further extended this format when it convinced audiences that a fictional Negro film star of the 1930s known as the "Watermelon Woman" really existed.

Among internationally acclaimed lesbian filmmakers, Pratibha Parmar, a British filmmaker of South Asian heritage, is perhaps the best known. Her works include *Memory Pictures* (1989), *Flesh and Paper* (1990), and *Khush* (1991), all of which explore lesbian-of-color identities. Parmar also joined U.S. author Alice Walker to make *Warrior Marks* (1993), a controversial film that addressed the issue of ritual female genital mutilation in some African tribal cultures.

Parmar, like many other British filmmakers, has received significant governmental support for her work through Britain's Channel Four. Channel Four also funded *A Bit of Scarlet* (1996) by American Andrea Weiss, a film that explores the history of homosexuality in British films from the 1920s onward.

German filmmaker Monika Treut, better known for her narrative films, produced *Female Misbehavior* (1983–1993), a series of four short films that deal with U.S. pornography and performance artist Annie Sprinkle, lesbian female-to-male transsexualism, U.S. author Camille Paglia, and sadomasochistic breast torture.

One of the largest obstacles faced by female filmmakers has been distribution—getting their woman-centered films to their intended audiences. In 1972, Women Make Movies was founded with a mission of promoting a positive and accurate image of women in media. This nonprofit distribution company provides not only distribution services for more than 350 films by and about women, but also production assistance, workshops on grantwriting, and fund-raising.                    *Dee Mosbacher*

## Bibliography

Hammer, Barbara. "Lesbian Filmmaking: Self-Birthing." *Film Reader* 5 (1982), 60–66.

*Jump Cut* 24–25 (1981). (Special Section), 17–55. "Lesbians and Film."

Lebow, Alisa. "Lesbians Make Movies." *Cinéaste* 20:2 (1983), 18–23.

Lesage, Julia. "The Political Aesthetics of the Feminist Documentary Film." *Quarterly Review of Film Studies* 3:4 (1978), 507–523.

Olson, Jenni, ed. *The Ultimate Guide to Lesbian and Gay Film and Video*. New York: Serpent's Tale, 1996.

*See also* Film, Alternative; Video

## Domestic Partnership

Relationship of two people who share a long-term personal commitment to each other but are not related by blood, marriage, or adoption. Generally, lesbian and gay couples, who cannot legally formalize their relationships through marriage or other means, and straight couples who choose not to marry may refer to themselves or be recognized as domestic partners. In addition, under some circumstances, people who do not share a romantic relationship but who share other attributes of a familial relationship may be recognized as domestic partners. For example, some municipal domestic-partnership policies would include two elderly women who live together for economic, companionship, or other purposes indicative of their commitment of mutual caretaking even if they do not share a romantic relationship.

The term "domestic partner" was coined originally in the early 1980s by advocates who sought to challenge employment-benefits policies that routinely provided costly benefits and significant privileges, such as health insurance, family medical, parenting, and bereavement leave, and tuition reimbursement to married employees and their families but not to unmarried employees with families. Because health care, for instance, was available only to employees and their legal spouses, the policies discriminated against unmarried employees who have long-term partners. Since employment benefits constitute approximately 36 percent of a full-time employee's compensation, and since health-care costs are a major portion of that, unmarried employees were denied equal compensation for the work they performed. Thus, the genesis of domestic-partnership advocacy was to challenge an employer's rationale for paying married employees more than unmarried employees.

The *Village Voice* newspaper in New York City and the City of Berkeley, California, were among the first employers to extend health-insurance benefits to the partners of unmarried employees. By the late 1990s, hundreds of municipalities, universities, private employers, and at least two state governments (Vermont and New York) extended some, if not all, benefits to domestic partners. Some of the larger employers who extend some form of partner benefits are Levi Strauss, Disney, IBM, New York City, the cities of San Francisco, California, and Seattle, Washington, the University of Iowa, and Stanford University, Stanford, California.

While the definitions of domestic partner vary widely, the most basic requirements of two people who claim they are domestic partners is that they reside together and that they attest to the fact that they share a long-term, committed relationship. Some employers, such as the University of Chicago, use exceedingly onerous requirements by demanding, for example, that the couple produce mutual wills or other legal documents leaving each other as prime beneficiaries as proof of their partnership—standards that deprive domestic partners of freedom to take into account their entire family in their estate planning. Most private employers limit domestic-partner benefits only to the partners of lesbian and gay employees, on the theory that the discrimination they face is more burdensome because they have no option to legally marry. Public employers and many universities, on the other hand, have been much more open to the diversity of families and relationships their employees share and have extended benefits to unmarried gay and straight partners and their families.

While domestic-partnership advocacy was initiated as a means of challenging discrimination in the workplace, the term has been incorporated into the vernacular of the United States. As a policy matter, the concept of domestic partnership has extended beyond its role in distinguishing long-term committed relationships from roommate relationships for purposes of benefits. For instance, some cities, including San Francisco, Albany, New York, and Ann Arbor, Michigan, have established domestic-partnership registries that allow couples to publicly certify their relationships. While few benefits beyond the guarantee of hospital and jail visitation in city facilities are attached, it is significant that a growing number of municipal governing bodies are extending formal recognition and respect to nonmarital family relationships. For example, in 1998 New York City passed a law requiring the city to provide the same benefits, privileges, access, and acknowledgment to citizens and employees in domestic partner relationships that it does to those in marital relationships. As such, New York City is the first governmental entity to extend equal treatment to domestic partners beyond the employment context.

Likewise, beyond their role as employers, businesses have begun to treat domestic partners as spousal equivalents. Where once an unmarried couple had to pay two individual premiums to insure the contents of their home, many property insurers now charge the single family premium extended to married couples. Family has been redefined to include domestic partners in areas as diverse as frequent-flyer companion awards, museum memberships, and reduced car rental charges for an extra driver. By extension, courts, legislatures, and employers have also begun to recognize that parent-child relationships within nontraditional family structures are not so easily defined simply by biology or the marital status of the parents. Thus, the child of a lesbian couple, having one biological mother and one non-biological mother, is increasingly considered the legally recognized child of both.

There also has been movement on the concept of domestic partnership internationally, most notably in Scandinavian countries. The concept, however, is entirely different in Europe, where most employees have state-provided health benefits. In the United States, the primary motivation for domestic-partnership advocacy is to achieve "equal pay for equal work." But in countries such as Norway, Sweden, and Denmark, "domestic partnership" is more akin to discussions about marriage than about equalizing employment benefits.

The purpose of domestic-partnership advocacy has always been to recognize nonmarital family relationships. It has never been intended as a secondary substitute for, or stepping stone to, marriage for lesbian and gay couples. Its value has been in the acknowledgment that certain family relationships exist in U.S. culture that have not traditionally received legal attribution or the support of benefits or privileges extended to formally recognized families. Through domestic-partnership and family-relationship advocacy, prompted primarily by the experiences of lesbian and gay families, the concept that family status turns more on love and commitment than on formalistic relationships defined by the state appeared to be gaining ground in the last decade of the twentieth century.      *Paula L. Ettelbrick*

### Bibliography

Ettelbrick, Paula L. "Wedlock Alert: A Comment on Lesbian and Gay Family Recognition." *Journal of Law and Policy* 5:1 (1996), 107.

Leonard, Arthur S. "Mayor Giuliani Proposes His Domestic Partnership Policy." *NYLS City Law* 4:3 (1998), 49.

*See also* Couples; Economics; Marriage Ceremonies

### Donor Insemination

Medical procedure to inject semen into the uterus for the purpose of becoming pregnant. It is also known as "alternative insemination" or "artificial insemination." In the past, donor insemination was viewed as a medical procedure to respond exclusively to male infertility in heterosexual married couples. Starting in the late 1970s, as a result of the women's health movement, lesbians and heterosexual single women began to appropriate this method to conceive outside the confines of heterosexual relationships.

Although regularly discussed under the umbrella of reproductive technology, donor insemination is surprisingly easy and does not require much knowledge or equipment. Women without fertility problems simply need sperm and some type of syringe to inject the semen into the vagina. Nowadays, many women perform this procedure in the comfort of their own homes, while others continue to prefer professional medical assistance.

With the advent of AIDS in the 1980s, thorough screening of donated sperm became critical, increasing the importance of sperm banks, which test donors for HIV antibodies and other sexually transmitted diseases.

Many sperm banks and doctors in the United States offer their services to lesbians. However, others continue to assist only married couples. In countries such as Germany, sperm banks are legally prohibited from providing sperm to unmarried women. The routine shipment of frozen sperm, however, has dramatically increased access to safer donor insemination.

If using fresh sperm, it is imperative to know about the donor's sexual history and to test for sexually transmitted diseases. In addition, information about the donor's medical history and genetic heritage can prove important. Unfortunately, with increased awareness of health risks, donor insemination has become more costly, and its safe use less accessible to low-income women.

In addition to health considerations, legal, social, and psychological issues require attention. Two principal concerns govern the debate: What is the role of a donor in the life of the child? How does donor insemination affect the well-being of children?

Determining the role of the donor in the child's life is one of the most consequential decisions when using donor insemination. For fear of legal intervention, many women decide to use sperm banks or doctors' offices that provide services to lesbians and/or single women. In most states, donors legally relinquish their paternal rights and duties when providing their sperm to a bank or a doctor. Typically, such a donor would remain anonymous forever. A few sperm banks, however, have instituted programs that, with the consent of the donor, allow children to contact their genetic father at age of majority.

Little is known about the impact of donor insemination with sperm from unknown sources on children's psychological and social adjustment. The widely publicized efforts of adult adoptive children and those conceived by donor insemination to find their genetic parents have sensitized the public to the importance of knowing one's genetic heritage. However, traditionally advocated secrecy in these cases might account for much of the distress in adults who find out about their origins later in life.

Unlike heterosexual couples, lesbian mothers using this method rarely have the option of secrecy. Rather, donor insemination provides an opportunity to explain why there is no traditional father in their lives. Little is known about the specific impact of donor insemination on children in lesbian families. However, in general, studies of the psychological and social adjustment of children growing up in lesbian families do not show any significant differences between them and children growing up in heterosexual families.

The potential negative impact of donor anonymity on the child prompts many prospective mothers to opt for known donors. Choosing a known donor, however, creates a different set of concerns. Prospective birth mothers, coparents, and donors need to negotiate the extent of the donor's involvement in the child's life. It can range from having no contact to taking on a parental role. In cases of legal conflict over parental rights, however, these nuances in the degree of donor involvement become irrelevant. A sperm provider is defined as either a donor or a father, the donor having no legal claims, and the father assuming all paternal rights and responsibilities. It is vital to the family unit to be absolutely clear about the potential legal and personal consequences of choosing a known donor.

Donor insemination has become a viable option for many lesbians to conceive a child without direct contact with a man. Unfortunately, the legal approach to donor insemination still reflects its early restricted medical use within the context of heterosexual marriage. Thus, a twofold strategy of creating laws that reflect the new realities and increasing public awareness of diverse family forms is needed.

*Renate Reimann*

### Bibliography

Clunis, D. Merilee, and G. Dorsey Green. *The Lesbian Parenting Book: A Guide to Creating Families and Raising Children.* Seattle: Seal, 1995.

Patterson, Charlotte. "Children of Lesbian and Gay Parents." *Child Development* 63 (1992), 1025–1042.

Rafkin, Louise, ed. *Different Mothers: Sons and Daughters of Lesbians Talk About Their Lives.* Pittsburgh: Cleis, 1990.

Rubenstein, William B., ed. *Lesbians, Gay Men, and the Law.* New York: New Press, 1993.

*See also* Adoption; Children; Couples

### Drag Kings

Females (usually) who dress up in recognizably male costume and perform theatrically in that costume. Historical and categorical distinctions exist between the drag king and the male impersonator. Male impersonation has been a theatrical genre for at least two hundred years, while the drag king is a recent phenomenon. While the male impersonator

**D** attempts to produce a plausible performance of maleness as the whole of her act, the drag king performs masculinity (often parodically) and makes the exposure of the theatricality of masculinity into the mainstay of her act. Both the male impersonator and the drag king are different from the drag butch, a masculine woman who wears male attire as part of her daily gender expression. Furthermore, while the male impersonator and the drag king are not necessarily lesbian roles, the drag butch most definitely is.

In the 1990s, drag king culture became a subcultural phenomenon. Queer clubs in most major American cities featured drag king acts; for example, the regular weekly drag king club in New York City, Club Casanova, has as its motto "the club where everyone is treated like a king!" Other examples include a monthly club in London called Club Geezer and a quarterly club in San Francisco, California, called Club Confidential.

Some scholars have traced the use of the word "drag" in relation to men in women's costume back to the 1850s, when it was used for both stage actors playing female roles and young men who liked to wear skirts. Male impersonation as a theatrical tradition extends back to the seventeenth-century Restoration stage, but, more often than not, the trouser role was used to emphasize femininity rather than to mimic maleness. The theatrical tradition of male impersonation flourished for the first two decades of the twentieth century and then declined in popularity. Some critics have traced the careers of one or two male impersonators, such as Storme DeLaverie, to show that pockets of male impersonation still existed within subcultural gay male drag culture between the 1930s and the 1960s. However, there is general agreement that no extensive drag king culture developed within lesbian bar culture to fill the void left by the disappearance of male impersonators from the mainstream theater. Indeed, Elizabeth Lapovsky Kennedy and Madeline D. Davis comment in their oral history of the lesbian community in Buffalo, New York, that the masculinity constructed by butches in the 1940s and 1950s was accompanied by a "puzzling lack of camp"—that is, it lacked the element of parody characteristic of drag king culture.

While it seems likely that the lack of a lesbian drag tradition has much to do with the need for butches to pass in the world as men, the fact that male impersonation did not achieve any general currency within lesbian bar culture must also be attributed to mainstream definitions of white male masculinity as "nonperformative"—that is, totally untheatrical and, indeed, "real." white men derive enormous power from assuming and confirming the nonperformative nature of masculinity. For one thing, if masculinity adheres "naturally" and inevitably to men, then masculinity cannot be impersonated. For another, if the nonperformance is part of what defines white male masculinity, then all performed, theatrical masculinities stand out as suspect and open to question. For example, gay male "macho clones" so strongly exaggerate masculinity (through the use of leather and denim) that, in them, masculinity tips into feminine performance. And the black gangsta rapper who bombastically proclaims his masculinity also displays what appears to be an overstated form of maleness. These clear differences between majority and minority masculinities make the drag king act different for different women. For the white drag king whose stage act consists of performing conventional heterosexual maleness, masculinity has first to be made thoroughly theatrical before it can be performed because so many white male icons (Paul Newman [1925–] or Clint Eastwood [1930–], for example) are defined by an understated form of cool. Thus, white drag kings tend to pick on icons like Elvis Presley (1935–1977) rather than male movie stars like Tom Cruise (1962–) and Bruce Willis (1955–). But, since masculinities of color and gay masculinities have already been rendered visible and theatrical in their various relations to dominant white masculinities, the performance of these masculinities presents a somewhat easier theatrical task. A black drag king might take on a rapper persona like Ice Cube (1969–) or a soul persona like Marvin Gaye (1939–1984). A drag king who wants to perform as a gay man could take on any number of gay masculine roles like the "leather daddy" or the "biker boy." Furthermore, while white masculinity seems to be readily available for parody by the drag kings, black masculinities or queer masculinities are often performed by drag kings in the spirit of homage or tribute rather than humor.

At the end of the twentieth century, drag kings like Mo B. Dick, Dred, and Murray Hill in New York City, Elvis Herselvis and the Dodge brothers in San Francisco, California, and Del LaGrace Volcano and Jewels in London were transforming masculinity and exposing its theatricality with profound results.

*Judith Halberstam*

## Bibliography

Davy, Kate. "Fe/Male Impersonation: The Discourse of Camp." In *The Politics and Poetics of Camp*. Ed. Moe Meyer. New York: Routledge, 1994, pp. 130–148.

Drorbaugh, Elizabeth. "Sliding Scales: Notes on Storme DeLaverie and the Jewel Box Revue, the Cross-Dressed Woman on the Contemporary Stage, and the Invert." In *Crossing the Stage: Controversies on Cross-Dressing*. Ed. Lesley Ferris. London and New York: Routledge, 1993, pp. 120–143.

Halberstam, Judith. "Drag Kings: Masculinity and Performance." In *Female Masculinity*. Durham, N.C.: Duke University Press, 1998.

Murray, Sarah. "Dragon Ladies, Draggin' Men: Some Reflections on Gender, Drag, and Homosexual Communities." *Public Culture* 6:2 (Winter 1994), 343–363.

Newton, Esther. "Dick(less) Tracy and the Homecoming Queen: Lesbian Power and Representation in Gay Male Cherry Grove." In *Inventing Lesbian Cultures in America*. Ed. Ellen Lewin. Boston: Beacon, 1996, pp. 161–193.

*See also* Butch-Femme; Camp; Cross-Dressing

## Duffy, Maureen Patricia (1933–)

English poet, novelist, playwright, critic, and Fellow of the Royal Society of Literature. Maureen Duffy was the first contemporary British author to write openly about her lesbianism in her novels, poetry, and plays.

Born in Worthing, Sussex, she was the only child of Grace Rose Wright, who died of tuberculosis when Duffy was fourteen years old. Her first novel, *That's How It Was* (1962), represents a factually accurate account of the author's childhood and adolescence and pays tribute to the mother who, with little more than her indomitable will to assist her, was determined that her daughter would do more than survive the poverty of her origins and the deprivations of war. Awarded a degree in English at King's College, London, Duffy was among the first generation of British working-class children to gain access to higher education through the scholarship system.

Her output is prolific and markedly wide ranging in both form and content. Concern for unnecessary human and animal suffering, so often rooted in the ideological imposition of divisions, labels, and classifications, is a constant feature of her work and underpins many of the stylistic devices she employs. Most of her novels include characters who are lesbian, homosexual, or, as with Al in *Londoners: An Elegy* (1983) and Kit and Ajax in *Love Child* (1971), characters whose gender remains ambiguous. In addition to her poetry, her most explicit treatments of lesbian sexuality and social identity are *Rites* (1969), a play set in a public lavatory, and *The Microcosm* (1966), a novel developed from a series of interviews with lesbians living in London in the early 1960s. While the former focuses on a single, acutely condensed example of society's irrational and frequently violent reaction to women who don't fit into accepted sex/gender categories, the latter uses heterogeneous lesbian voices to create a kaleidoscopic impression of the subculture that revolved around the only bar for gay women in the city at that time.

Duffy has written more than a dozen novels, including *The Single Eye* (1964), *The Paradox Players* (1967), *Wounds* (1969), *I Want to Go to Moscow: A Lay* (1973), *Capital* (1975), *Housespy* (1978), *Gor Saga* (1981), *Change* (1987), *Illuminations* (1991), and *Occam's Razor* (1993). Her plays include *The Lay Off* (1962), *The Silk Room* (1966), *A Nightingale in Bloomsbury Square (1974), and Henry Purcell* (1995). She has published poetry collections titled *Lyrics For the Dog Hour* (1968), *The Venus Touch* (1971), *Evesong* (1975), *Memorials of the Quick and the Dead* (1979), and *Collected Poems* (1985).

Duffy is also the author of a number of nonfiction works, including two biographies—*The Passionate Shepherdess* (1977), about Aphra Behn, and *Henry Purcell* (1994)—*The Erotic World of Faery* (1972), a critical study; *Inherit the Earth* (1980), a social history; and *Men and Beasts: An Animal Rights Handbook* (1984).

A leading figure in numerous human and animal rights campaigns in Europe, Duffy was appointed honorary president of the Gay and Lesbian Humanists Society in 1989.       *Lyndie Brimstone*

## Bibliography

Brimstone, Lyndie. " 'Keepers of History': The Novels of Maureen Duffy." In *Twentieth Century Lesbian and Gay Writing*. Ed. Mark Lilly. London: Macmillan, pp. 23–46.

Rule, Jane. *Lesbian Images*. New York: Crossing Press, 1982, 1975.

*See also* English Literature, Twentieth Century

# D

## Dunbar-Nelson, Alice (1875–1935)

African American writer, educator, and activist. Born in New Orleans, Louisiana, on July 19, 1875, into a middle-class family of white, black, American Indian, and Creole ancestry, Alice Dunbar studied at Straight College in 1892 and taught in New Orleans; she continued her scholarship at Cornell University, Columbia University, and the University of Pennsylvania. Her first published work, *Violets and Other Tales* (1895), is a collection of sketches and poetry. Her second book, a collection of short stories, *The Goodness of St. Rocque* (1898), was published the year she married Paul Laurence Dunbar (1872–1906). Their marriage was short lived; they separated in 1902.

Dunbar-Nelson taught English in Wilmington, Delaware, at the all-black Howard High School, where she became head of its English Department. She was also active in a network of African American club women. Her activism led her, in 1920, to become the first African American woman elected to the Delaware Republican State Committee. Dunbar-Nelson married her second husband, black journalist Robert Nelson (1873–1949), in 1916. Together they published the *Wilmington Advocate*, a newspaper dedicated to African American advancement. During this marriage, Dunbar-Nelson wrote in her diary about her lesbian relationships with Fay Jackson Robinson and Helene London; although she veiled what she wrote, her husband read her diary and was uncomfortable with her lesbianism. Dunbar-Nelson's novellas and several poems contained evidence of her lesbianism, though she destroyed most of this literature before her death. In her diary, spanning 1921–1931, she wrote about her various affairs with women and included lines from lesbian poems later destroyed.

In Dunbar-Nelson's writings, there are three lesbian relationships that can be accounted for—with Edwina B. Kruse, London, and Robinson, all during her second marriage. There is evidence of both the physical and the emotional aspects of these relationships, as well as of her own attempt to find a space for herself in, and between, these two communities: the network of black, married club women and her marriage to Nelson. In her marriage, Dunbar-Nelson received support from Nelson both emotionally and politically, in the sense that they wrote political articles and attended political activities together. She eventually died of a heart ailment in Philadelphia in 1935.          *Marcy Jane Knopf*

### Bibliography

Hull, Gloria T. *Color, Sex, and Poetry: Three Women Writers of the Harlem Renaissance.* Bloomington: Indiana University Press, 1987.

*See also* African American Literature; American Literature, Twentieth Century; Bisexuality; Harlem Renaissance

## Dyke

American English slang term signifying a female homosexual. Throughout much of the twentieth century, the word "dyke" (also spelled dike) has been used primarily as a pejorative, signifying a "masculine" woman, a definition that has traditionally been conflated with lesbianism. The first references to this usage date back to the 1920s and 1930s. In the 1940s, dyke first appeared in slang dictionaries and was defined as a "masculine woman," a definition that persisted throughout the 1950s and 1960s. When used in African American slang, dyke was usually preceded by bull; bulldyke signified an aggressive female homosexual. Variations of this term, such as bulldagger, boondagger, and bulldiker, were also commonly used within African American slang.

Although the definition of dyke as a masculine lesbian is similar to the definition of butch, dyke was more frequently used as a derogatory epithet employed to ridicule lesbians, whereas butch appears to have been the preferred term of self-identification within the lesbian working-class bar culture of the 1940s, 1950s, and 1960s, which tended to be characterized by butch-femme roles. Some women may have worn the term "dyke" with pride, but, for the most part, it was not until the 1970s that dyke began to be widely used within lesbian feminist communities as a positive term signifying gay pride and political resistance to compulsory heterosexuality. Lesbian feminists' attempts to resignify dyke sparked critical interest in its etymological origins, resulting in searches for more affirming usages of the term. Some speculate that the word "dyke" may have originated from the Greek word *dike,* identified with Athena, the "man-woman," while others theorize that dyke evolved from hermaphrodite through a linguistic process in which the initial part of the word was dropped, and the remaining syllable, dite, was mispronounced, becoming dike. Another theory traces dyke back to the late-nineteenth- and early-twentieth-century

American usage of dike as denoting "a man in full dress, or the set of male clothing." This definition may have evolved from the Old English *dight*, meaning "to dress, clothe; to adorn, deck oneself." Through time, the definition of dike slowly shifted from a neutral male word to a derogatory slang term used to deride women who dressed in male attire.

Since the 1970s, the definition of dyke within lesbian communities has begun shifting away from the notion of the masculine lesbian. Some simply consider it to be synonymous with lesbian, regardless of gender identification, while others view dyke as signifying a woman who blurs the boundaries between masculinity and femininity. Although dyke remains a derogatory term within dominant-culture discourses, functioning as a threat that compels women to perform prescribed feminine roles and behaviors, many lesbians consider dyke a positive appellation describing a strong and independent lesbian, a definition that poses a challenge to the regulatory regimes of gender and sexuality.

*Christy Stevens*

### Bibliography

Butler, Judith. *Bodies That Matter*. New York and London: Routledge, 1993.

Dever, Carolyn. "Obstructive Behavior." In *Cross Purposes: Lesbians, Feminists, and the Limits of Alliance*. Ed. Dana Heller. Bloomington: Indiana University Press, 1997, pp. 19–41.

Grahn, Judy. *Another Mother Tongue: Gay Words, Gay Worlds*. Boston: Beacon, 1984.

Roberts, J.R. "In America They Call Us Dykes: Notes on the Etymology and Usage of " 'Dyke.' " *Sinister Wisdom* 9 (1979): 3–11.

**See also** Bulldagger; Butch-Femme; Slang

# E

## Ecology and Ecofeminism

Branch of biology dedicated to exploring not individual species, but rather the relationships of plants and animals to each other and to the environment. Ecology has attracted many lesbians; however, what began as a lesbian delight in ecology and women's seeming closeness to nature grew into an ecofeminist political engagement as lesbians reconceived the woman-nature connection in the 1980s. Ecofeminists believe that the subordination of women is fundamental to militarism and capitalism and intimately connected to the subordination of nature, people of color, animals, and the erotic.

Radical feminist critiques of patriarchal thought reveal that women have long been associated with nature, emotion, nurturance, and fertility, just as men have been associated with culture, reason, violence, and militarism. Whereas patriarchy values the properties associated with men, radical feminists offered an alternative view by valuing the properties associated with women. Thus, popular texts of radical cultural feminism, such as Sally Gearhart's lesbian utopia *The Wanderground* (1978), Mary Daly's manifesto *Gyn/Ecology: The Metaethics of Radical Feminism* (1978), and Susan Griffin's *Woman and Nature: The Roaring Inside Her* (1978), document patriarchy's assault on both women and nature and locate lesbian feminist culture as thriving particularly in relationship with nature, often in rural or wild surroundings. Both Gearhart and Griffin depict a sympathetic connection between women and nature that has the potential to transcend physical boundaries and merge their identities in ecstatic union and telepathic communication. Lesbian poet Mary Oliver (1935–) has explored the erotics of woman loving a feminized nature in poems such as "Music," "The Honey Tree," and "The Gardens."

This celebration of the woman-nature relationship may provide the conceptual foundations for both the lesbian back-to-the-land movement and the lesbian association with wilderness. In the 1970s, lesbians left the cities in droves, seeking rural spaces for building lesbian communities free from male domination. The lesbian land movement generated such journals as *Maize: A Lesbian Country Magazine* and *Country Woman*, and the book *Lesbian Land* (1985).

Whether they were planning to settle in wild spaces or just to visit there, lesbians have been leaders in restoring women's relationship with wild nature. Ann Bancroft, leader of the 1992 American Women's Antarctic Expedition (AWE), became the first woman and the first lesbian to bring an all-woman team to the Antarctic, and she accomplished this feat in an ecologically respectful manner, packing out all trash generated from the trip, as well as trash left by male explorers. Judith Niemi, coeditor of *Rivers Running Free: Stories of Adventurous Women* (1987), founded both Woodswomen and Women in the Wilderness, two of many lesbian-led organizations dedicated to teaching women how to travel safely and sustainably in wild nature. Lesbian outdoorswomen often articulate ecological theories connecting the liberation of women, lesbians, and nature through their actions.

Along with the lesbian land movement, gardening—and, more recently, organic gardening—has also been a theme in lesbian popular culture, though, as the editors of *Garden Variety Dykes* (1994) assert, lesbian gardeners have been largely unphotographed, untheorized, and unacknowledged

E in both gardening literature and lesbian literature. Yet gardening has been a vehicle for art, erotic expression, self-healing, lesbian livelihoods, and reestablishing or strengthening bonds with the earth and with the cycles of nature. Through gardening and its related concerns with pest control, soil fertility, local seeds, and crop rotation, lesbians work out the ethical dilemmas of their relationship with the earth and with other animals. As Norwood (1993) suggests, women's historic work as gardeners has laid the pathway to more aggressive involvement in the environmental movements of the late twentieth century.

The ecological, utopian vision of lesbian separatism was soon challenged both by experiences of women within those communities and by larger events, such as the near meltdown of the nuclear reactor at Three Mile Island in Pennsylvania (1979) and the discoveries of toxic exposure at Love Canal in New York State (1978). In April 1980, a conference called "Women and Life on Earth: Eco-Feminism in the 1980s" drew attention to the connections between the structures of male violence against women and violence against the earth, and activists from the conference organized a Women's Pentagon Action that drew roughly three thousand women (the majority of whom were lesbian) to encircle the Pentagon that November. A key organizer of both events, and coauthor of the Unity Statement of the Women's Pentagon Action, lesbian theorist and activist Ynestra King reframed the woman-nature connection in an essay published in 1982. According to King, there were three possible responses to the alleged woman-nature connection created by patriarchal thought: (1) it could be embraced and valued, as radical cultural feminists had done; (2) it could be rejected as a source of women's oppression, a view taken by both radical rationalist feminists and socialist feminists; or (3) it could be used strategically. The first two responses do not challenge the authenticity of the woman-nature connection, King argued, but only differ on whether to accept or reject it. The third response, which views women as part of both culture and nature and argues that any alleged woman-nature connection can be used as a strategic vantage point, marks the beginnings of ecofeminism.

The conceptual connection between lesbianism and ecofeminism can be seen by returning to the association of man/human/culture/reason as defined in opposition to woman/animal/nature/emotion—dualisms of patriarchal thought originally recognized by radical feminists. Ecofeminists point out that the oppression of lesbians is based on the patriarchal definition of sexuality and the erotic as both opposed to reason and associated with the body, animals, and nature. Lesbian ecofeminists suggest that, just as women and people of color are animalized, eroticized, and naturalized, so, too, has nature been feminized, raced, and eroticized. Through these conceptual associations, all of these forms of oppression are linked and rationalized in patriarchal thought.

With this insight, lesbian ecofeminists have examined the rhetoric of European colonialism in the Americas and found the same logic at work: By describing the indigenous people as feminine, homosexual, animalistic, and closer to nature, white Western colonizers rationalized the invasion of the Americas. Lesbian and Laguna Pueblo poet Paula Gunn Allen (1939–) has compared the white heteropatriarchal colonization of women, lesbians, indigenous people, and the earth in her poem "Some Like Indians Endure."

Lesbians who developed ecofeminist critiques in the 1980s and 1990s include Lynda Birke, Christine Cuomo, Greta Gaard, Lori Gruen, Chaia Heller, Marti Kheel, and Linda Vance. They and other lesbians have contributed significantly to the understanding of ecofeminism as a movement committed to the liberation of women, people of color, queers, animals, and the earth. *Greta Gaard*

### Bibliography

Cheney, Joyce, ed. *Lesbian Land.* Minneapolis: Word Weavers, 1985.

Collard, Andrée, and Joyce Contrucci. *Rape of the Wild: Man's Violence Against Animals and the Earth*. Bloomington: Indiana University Press, 1989.

Gaard, Greta. "Toward a Queer Ecofeminism." *Hypatia* 12:1 (Winter 1997), 114–137.

King, Ynestra. "Feminism and the Revolt of Nature." *Heresies* 13 (Fall 1982), 12–16.

Norwood, Vera. "Designing Nature: Gardeners and Their Gardens." In *Made from This Earth: American Women and Nature*. Chapel Hill: University of North Carolina Press, 1993, pp. 98–142.

Reti, Irene, and Valerie Jean Chase, eds. *Garden Variety Dykes: Lesbian Traditions in Gardening*. Santa Cruz, Calif.: HerBooks, 1994.

**See also** Ethics; Land; Peace Movement; Utopian Literature; Vegetarianism

## Economics

Lesbian and gay economics emerged during the 1980s and 1990s as an identifiable area, particularly in the United States. Lesbian critiques of the heterosexist biases in feminist economic analysis have also grown during this time period. However, this significant lesbian writing on economics has proceeded without any clearly agreed understanding of the term "lesbian economics."

Gender, race, class, and sexuality are all largely economic issues. The control of power and resources and the ability to exclude groups defined as "other" support attitudinal prejudice in perpetuating "lesbophobia" (fear of lesbianism) and heterosexism, as well as patriarchy and capitalism. Hence, lesbian economics consists of documenting discrimination, pointing out its economic, social, and psychological costs to individuals and to society and working for change, as well as developing lesbian communities, organizations, and economies and creating lesbian theory, ethics, values, and philosophy.

## Feminist Economic Analyses

Feminist economists have analyzed problems arising from orthodox (neoclassical) economic arguments and errors perpetuated by splitting the public and private spheres. They have exposed models of gender divisions of labor that perpetuate economic dependence for many women and have questioned the supposed value freedom and objectivity of these models. However, most of these feminist critics have attempted to improve neoclassical analysis and policy within the context of nuclear, sole-parent, or extended families, with an unstated assumption that heterosexuality is the norm or only pattern. Hence, feminist economics seeks to reduce women's economic dependence on men, while lesbian economics attempts more radically to cut that dependence.

Patriarchy and capitalism are based on gender, class, and race divisions of labor in both heterosexual households and the paid labor force, with male White heterosexual capitalist power reproducing itself on the backs of women. The restriction of women to low-paid jobs promotes and even necessitates heterosexuality. The framework of heterosexually based gender specialization between, and within, paid and unpaid work reinforces and justifies the status quo. In 1978, the Lesbians Ignite Fire Brigade, a New Zealand group, argued that lesbianism is an important challenge to patriarchy, with the threat of even nonpolitical lesbianism lying in its demonstration that women don't need men, personally at least. Once the romanticism and emotional mythology of heterosexuality is challenged, they argued, women would become free to see the oppression that it obscures.

The increasing opportunities for education, entry to the job market, and economic independence were essential to the emergence of separate lesbian cultures and identity in Western societies. Cultural and ethnic differences in the social construction of gender and sexuality mean that lesbian identities and economics will differ across societies. Prior to the opportunities for economic independence, only some women from the upper classes with personal wealth could establish comfortable lives separate from men. Some working-class and ethnic-minority women with fewer options cross-dressed and/or passed as men, at work and, in some cases, in relationships with women. However, feminist economists frequently ignore the fact that the emergence of lesbian politics and community, by demonstrating the possibility of independence from men, in turn strengthened the attempt of heterosexual feminists to change both their individual roles in relationships with men and the overall gender-biased structures in society.

## Lesbian Economic Analyses

Lesbians engage in documenting and analyzing economic situations, the extent and impact of discrimination, and, generally, the varieties of lesbian lives. Whether lesbians want to be visible in official statistics is a complex issue. Any official census or survey will considerably undercount lesbians and gay men, which could provide protection from those seeking to increase repressive treatment or deny equal rights. On the other hand, without visibility, the realities of discrimination can be dismissed and the need for policies to reduce it discounted.

A review by Larson (1994) of survey-based studies on lesbian life suggests that lesbians may have different economic profiles than heterosexual women in terms of labor-force participation, level of education, level of household income, demand for children, and division of labor on household tasks. Higher average levels have been found among lesbians on each of the first three variables, although caution is necessary, with white economically advantaged lesbians likely to be overrepresented in the samples and with many lesbian mothers in severe poverty. More egalitarian distribution of household tasks than among heterosexual couples has also been reported.

**E** Badgett (1995) has used the U.S. General Social Survey (which asks questions about "same-sex sexual experiences") to examine whether earnings discrimination exists against lesbian, gay, and bisexual workers. She found that, standardizing for age, education, occupation, marital status, and region, self-identified gay and bisexual men earn from 11 to 27 percent less than their straight counterparts, while lesbian and bisexual women earn 5 to 14 percent less. For women, the difference is not statistically significant, but lesbians are inclined to be in lower-paid occupations than gay men and heterosexual women.

The issue of equality versus difference, which has been important in theoretical and policy debates on gender, arises also with respect to lesbian and gay identity and rights. For example, important issues in the lesbian community include the differences and similarities between lesbian and heterosexual couple relationships and the degree of similarity with which they are to be treated by society. Many argue that lesbian relationships are different from, and have the potential to be better than, heterosexual ones, particularly in terms of power dynamics. There may be greater variety of household types, more flexibility in lesbian family structure, and less specialization of roles. Lesbians with these political perspectives find unappealing the strategy of stressing the similarity with heterosexuals, often allied in campaigns for equality with the view that sexual orientation is a genetic feature neither chosen nor able to be changed.

For other lesbians, however, expressing commitment to a partner and having this acknowledged and celebrated, for example through a ceremony, is of importance. Acceptance by society in general may also be valued. In pragmatic terms, many would argue that lesbian partner relationships should be treated as favorably as those of heterosexual couples in such areas as domestic protection, partner benefits at work, retirement benefits, honoring of wills, and next-of-kin treatment by the medical system. This might imply legalizing lesbian and gay marriage, as a few jurisdictions worldwide have done. Such a change would not appeal to all lesbians: Some would prefer abolition of the institution. On legal issues, some prefer that disputes within the community are kept away from the (patriarchal, heterosexist) judicial system, while others see the need for residual protection, with cases cited in which financial unfairness has arisen after breakups.

Access to partner benefits may seem an obvious demand, but it has a negative side. Full recognition of lesbian relationships would presumably mean that, where the benefit system is based on couples, the rules would apply equally, meaning loss of income for some lesbians. On the other hand, it can be argued that all adult benefits should be based on the individual, removing the expectation of dependence on a "spouse."

## Lesbian Markets and Economies

The resurgence of a more market-based, libertarian, individualist orthodoxy in many Western countries has affected lesbian communities. Rampant consumerism and an emphasis on the individual at the expense of the collective have led to exploitation of the emerging lesbian and, in particular, gay male markets, both by gay and straight entrepreneurs. Libertarian trends also sit well with some interpretations of postmodernism, which, in some formulations, can lead to the absence of real challenges to current power structures.

Separatist lesbian communities, which include businesses, volunteer services, and land, are all aspects of an independent lesbian economy. So, too, are household types, financial arrangements, and the sharing of tasks. Lesbian culture, including music, books, magazines, and crafts, maintained through independent publishing houses, bookshops, printers, clubs, and entertainment, has been crucial in creating communities and providing paid work for some lesbians. Fund-raising activities and entertainment have supported community activities such as lesbian telephone lines, coming out groups, and media. In Australia, as reported by Young (1991), an Adelaide lesbian community green-dollar scheme (LESY), in which credits can be deposited and drawn on based on doing or using various types of work, is an example of an organization providing for the sharing of individual skill. Gift and free-exchange systems are seen by some lesbians and feminists as an important alternative or supplement to the market economy and an acknowledgment of lesbians' different needs and resources. Sliding scales or other ways of paying for facilities and events according to financial means also highlight the underlying class issues involved.

Important issues for lesbian business and other activities include conflicts in attempting to run a business on lesbian feminist lines, the mixing of voluntary and paid labor, class and race issues, and the balance among separatism, coalition politics, and work on lesbian and other structural oppression issues. As lesbian and feminist activity has become more "acceptable" or, more cynically, as the market has noticed that it can profit from it, successful artists face the issue of staying within in the community or shifting to the mainstream. For the future, feminist environmentalists, many of whom call for a major rethinking and even repudiation of standard economics, offer useful insights into the relationship between economic and technical systems and value systems. Continuing the creation of lesbian economy and value systems and influencing those of the straight world are ongoing, difficult tasks. Many of the economic and ethical issues touched on here, including discussion of racism and classism in the economy, are developed further in the collection *Homo Economics: Capitalism, Community, and Lesbian and Gay Life,* edited by Gluckman and Reed (1997).                    *Prue Hyman*

### Bibliography

Allen, Jeffner. "Lesbian Economics." *Trivia* (1986), 37–53.

Badgett, Lee. "The Wage Effects of Sexual Orientation Discrimination." *Industrial and Labor Relations Review* 48:4 (July 1995), 726–739.

Badgett, M.V. Lee, and Rhonda M. Williams. "The Economics of Sexual Orientation: Establishing a Research Agenda." *Feminist Studies* 18:3 (1992), 649–657.

Edwalds, Loraine, and Midge Stocker, eds. *The Woman-Centered Economy: Ideals, Reality, and the Space in Between.* Chicago: Third Side, 1995.

Gluckman, Amy, and Betsy Reed, eds. *Homo Economics: Capitalism, Community, and Lesbian and Gay Life.* New York and London: Routledge, 1997.

Larson, Kathleen H. "The Economics of Lesbian Households." In *Exploring the Quincentennial: The Policy Challenges of Gender, Diversity, and International Exchange* (1994). Ed. Roberta Spalter-Roth, Debbie Clearwaters, Melinda Gish, and Susan A. Markham. Washington, D.C.: Institute of Women's Policy Research and Department of Sociology, American University, pp. 251–257.

Matthaei, Julie. "The Sexual Division of Labour, Sexuality, and Lesbian/Gay Liberation: Towards a Marxist-Feminist Analysis of Sexuality in U.S. Capitalism." *Review of Radical Political Economics* 27:2 (1995), 1–37.

Young, Carole. "LESY-Adelaide: An Example of a Lesbian Economy." *Lesbian Ethics* 4:2 (1991), 62–66.

*See also* Advertising and Consumerism; Businesses, Lesbian; Demography; Domestic Partnership

## Egypt

Country situated in the northeastern corner of the African continent, stretching almost across into Asia. Its location on the threshold of continents, along with its dependence on its lifeline, the Nile River, has defined its peoples throughout time. The ancient Egyptians, whose history extends more than four thousand years, left behind them an overwhelming and detailed record of their achievements in life and in death but very little regarding their sexual practices. Modern Egyptologists have speculated about homoerotic desires between women, but little is known beyond assumptions based on modern conceptualizations of sexual practices. For instance, Queen Hatchepsut (eighteenth dynasty, ruled 1490–1468 B.C.E.) wore a beard to establish her position as pharaoh, led armies to war, and generally challenged gender rules of her day, but nothing is known about her sexual practices.

Egyptian history spans many millennia, during which Egypt succumbed to innumerable conquests and, hence, cultural influences. Among these conquests were the Greeks, the Romans, and, finally, the Arabs in the seventh century. Arab rule of Egypt varied across centuries, bringing with it influences from other conquered cultures within its sovereignty and establishing Arab culture and language as dominant, with Islam as the religion of the majority, alongside a small minority of Coptic Christians.

Although there are no distinct words for "homosexuality" nor "heterosexuality" in Arabic, there is no doubt that homoerotic pleasures are prohibited in the *Quar'an* (Koran), as these are denounced under such ambiguous terms as "abominations" and "sodomy." Furthermore, same-sex relations are specifically forbidden by the Prophet Mohammad in the *Hadith.* Religious law, the *Shari'ah,* is practiced side by side with secular law in Egypt, each consulted according to the issue at stake. Islam accepts erotic pleasures as a fundamental right for both men and women and acknowledges that eroticism includes a range of sexual practices; it also, however, recognizes human frailty in the face of temptation and, consequently, has in place a system

**E** of sanctions that regulate the lives of the faithful. Homoerotic practices are prohibited under these sanctions.

References to female homoerotic desires and practices surface regularly in Egyptian and Arabic literary and historical texts. Once again, however, because these texts were written mostly by men, who were prohibited entry into women's quarters in this sexually segregated society, not much is actually known beyond speculation of what may have occurred in the harems and the *hammams* (baths) and the sexual fantasies of the writers. Likewise, European visitors to Egypt record incidents of "unspeakable" acts betweeen women within the locations of the harems and the *hammams*, but little is known regarding the extent or prevalence of these homoerotic desires. Still less is known about how the women thought about these acts, if they were recognized as discreet practices or if they were perceived as an extension of sensual, rather than sexual, inclinations.

Egyptian class structure continues to reproduce significant differences in access to education and resources among people, which makes generalizations about sexual practices complex. For instance, such terms as "lesbian" or "gay," as these are used in North America and Western Europe, do not render intelligible experiences outside the cultural contexts for which they were created. Therefore, although the Egyptian upper classes who are educated in Western cultures use terms like "lesbian" and "gay" to describe same-gender sexual practices, they themselves cannot be indentified as "lesbian" or "gay" since the social and political identities often associated with these terms do not have similar currencies in Egypt. Among Westernized upper-class women, "lesbian" desire is, therefore, recognized, and some women of that class are involved in intimate sexual relations with other women. Unlike "gay" men of that class, however, there are no organized meeting places, although these women manage to recognize one another and congregate within the privacy of their homes. Since women in Egypt are expected to live under the guardianship of a male, almost all are married and seem to lead normative heterosexual lives while having women lovers.

Middle- and working-class women in Egypt, whose language is primarily Arabic, do not have access to an equivalent term for "lesbian." Implications of same-gender paractices, however, are present in modern literary texts by women, which leaves no doubt as to their existence. There has been little research into this area, however, and knowledge regarding how these women conceptualize such practices is, at best, sketchy.            *Didi Khayatt*

### Bibliography

Ahmed, Leila. "Arab Culture and Writing Women's Bodies." *Feminist Issues* 9:1 (Spring 1989), 41–56.

———. *Women and Gender in Islam*. New Haven, Conn.: Yale University Press, 1992.

Hatem, Mervat. "The Politics of Sexuality and Gender in Segragated Patriarchal Systems: The Case of Eighteenth- and Nineteenth-Century Egypt." *Feminist Studies* 12:2 (Summer 1986), 250–274.

Murray, Stephen O. "Woman-Woman Love in Islamic Societies." In *Islamic Sexualities: Culture, History, and Literature*. eds. Stephen O. Murray and Will Roscoe. New York: New York University Press, 1997, p. 97.

***See also*** Arab Literature, Modern; Harems; Islam

## Electoral Politics

Processes of voting, working for candidates and elected officials, and working with elected officials to affect policy, as well as running for office.

Lesbians have been involved in electoral politics as candidates, as voters, and as activists and organizers. Most of the candidate activity to date has been in the United States, although gay men have been successful office seekers in Canada and the United Kingdom, and lesbians have been elected to office in Australia. The United States has almost 500,000 elected offices, so the chances for entry are greatest there.

### Lesbians as Candidates

Although it is impossible to know how many women candidates have been lesbians, much is known about the open lesbians who have run for office. Elaine Noble, a state representative in Massachusetts from 1974 to 1978, was the first openly lesbian candidate and legislator. Since then, many lesbians have served at the state and local levels across the country. In 1991, Sherry Harris's city council victory in Seattle, Washington, made her the first African American lesbian to be elected.

Lesbians, like gay men, have been successful in their campaigns when they were able to build coalitions beyond lesbian and gay communities. Noble's success was largely due to her attention to issues of children's welfare and women's rights as well as lesbian rights. The many lesbian officials elected in the 1980s and 1990s have had similarly broad platforms and community experience.

The Gay and Lesbian Victory Fund, which supports the candidacies of openly lesbian and gay political aspirants through fund-raising, was formed in 1991. To receive support, candidates must endorse the federal gay and lesbian civil rights bill, support AIDS funding and abortion rights, and be viable candidates. Between the 1992 and 1996 elections, more than 50 percent of the endorsed candidates have won office.

Although candidates have been finding some success, they have had to endure often intensely antigay campaigns, from both Democrats and Republicans. Very few districts are so favorable to lesbians and gays that they are exempt from this pressure.

## Lesbian Voting Behavior

Like the silence surrounding lesbian candidates, no research was conducted into lesbian or gay voting until the late 1980s. Although little is known for certain about lesbian voting patterns, the research that has been done suggests that lesbians are largely left-liberal in their political orientation. Voting surveys from the 1992 presidential campaign suggest that lesbians are significantly to the left not only of heterosexual voters, but of gay men as well. Much of this is explained by the greater feminism of lesbians; Hertzog's (1996) work on voting behavior suggests that "strong feminism" accounts for much of the difference between lesbian attitudes and voting and those of other groups. Lesbians who did not identify as "strong feminists" do not seem to vote all that differently than gay men, and gay men who identify as strong feminists voted like most of the lesbians. It is clear, however, that in "high-salience" elections, such as presidential, congressional, and gubernatorial elections, lesbians and gays vote in distinct patterns that transcend particulars such as feminism, demographics, or party affiliation. Whether this will continue over time is unclear.

The year 1992 was a watershed year for lesbians in electoral politics. After Democratic presidential candidate Bill Clinton pledged to eliminate the ban against lesbians and gays in the military, lesbians across the country came out to work for Clinton's campaign and supported it financially. The upsurge of enthusiasm and optimism about gay and lesbian citizens' inclusion in American political life was followed by cries of outrage and despair as Clinton not only did not end the ban, but in 1996 signed the Defense of Marriage Act, which denies federal recognition of same-sex marriages should they be allowed by the states. Lesbians and gays have faced another common experience of racial minorities in the United States, that of being used for electoral purposes by people with no real commitment to their rights or welfare. The Republicans' active hostility toward equality for gays means that there are precious few alternatives to the lukewarm support of the Democratic Party.

## Political Activism at the State Level

As Clinton's promises faded, gay and lesbian activists realized that the new battleground for rights was within the states, for two reasons. First, most of the laws that govern citizens' daily lives are state rather than federal, and concerns for equality and nondiscrimination can be addressed through state legislatures. Second, the antigay religious extremists have begun to launch a series of attacks at the state and local levels. These attacks take the form of ballot initiatives and referenda. In 1992, for example, Colorado and Oregon faced such measures. Both aimed to deny the possibility of equal protection to homosexual citizens. Colorado's Amendment 2 sought to ban "any statute, regulation, ordinance or policy whereby homosexual, lesbian, or bisexual orientation, conduct, practices or relationships shall constitute or otherwise be the basis of, or entitle any person or class of persons to have or claim any minority status, quota preferences, protected status or claim of discrimination." The effect of this amendment was to override existing antidiscrimination ordinances in Denver and Boulder and to preclude the possibility of passing any laws in Colorado that banned discrimination on the basis of sexual orientation. In Oregon, Measure 9 not only banned anti-discrimination legislation but mandated that schools teach that homosexuality, among other things, was morally wrong. Although Measure 9 was defeated at the polls, and the Colorado and United States Supreme Courts declared Amendment 2 unconstitutional (1994; 1996), state drives to roll back rights continued. For example, an Amendment 2-like measure was defeated in Idaho in 1994.

Electoral politics is, thus, a place for the self-assertion of both lesbians and their opponents. Battles over civil rights laws, marriage and family pol-

**E** icy, and other areas are waged in the voting booth, as well as the street. As social stigma declines, one can expect to see more lesbians visible in politics at all levels. *Shane Phelan*

### Bibliography

Button, James W., Barbara A. Rienzo, and Kenneth D. Wald. *Private Lives, Public Conflicts: Battles over Gay Rights in American Communities*. Washington, D.C.: Congressional Quarterly Press, 1997.

Herzog, Mark. *The Lavender Vote: Lesbians, Gay Men, and Bisexuals in American Electoral Politics*. New York: New York University Press, 1996.

Lachman, Linda. "Electoral Politics: An Interview with Elaine Noble." In *Our Right to Love*. Ed. Ginny Vida. Englewood Cliffs, N.J.: Prentice-Hall, 1978, pp. 128–134.

Rayside, David. *On the Fringe: Gays and Lesbians in Politics*. Ithaca, N.Y.: Cornell University Press, 1998.

Shilts, Randy. *The Mayor of Castro Street*. New York: St. Martin's Press, 1982.

*See also* Activism; Coalition Politics; Discrimination; Noble, Elaine; Political Theory

## Encuentros de Lesbianas

Encuentros de Lesbianas Feministas de Latinoamerica y el Caribe (Latin American and Caribbean Lesbian Feminist Gatherings) have been held in Latin America and the Caribbean since 1987. They constitute a regional space for exchange and interaction mainly between activists and lesbian groups from the region and Latina lesbians living in other countries.

The idea of this political space was born in the lesbian workshop at the Third Feminist Gathering of Latin America and the Caribbean (Brazil, 1985), but the organization was finally decided at the Eighth Conference of ILIS (International Lesbian Information Service) in Switzerland in 1986. The First Latin American and Caribbean Lesbian Feminist Gathering took place in Mexico in 1987.

The main goals of this first gathering were (1) to explore alternative ways of communication, work, and investigation; (2) to change the situation of lesbians in Latin America; (3) to modify oppressive legal, social, political, and work spaces; (4) to discuss daily life and question standards imposed by society; (5) to create an atmosphere of solidarity and respect; and (6) to revise prejudices and myths that society has about lesbians.

One hundred women were expected at the first gathering, but approximately 250 arrived eager to meet and share their experiences with their sisters: lesbians from all over Latin America and the Caribbean, as well as Latinas living in the United States, Canada, and Europe. Some of the topics of the workshops were sexuality, myths and gender roles; lesbianism and repression; lesbianism and politics; and lesbian mothers. At this first gathering, it was decided to strengthen the Latin American and the Caribbean Lesbian Feminist Network that was also created at the ILIS conference, celebrate the first day of full moon in March as Lesbian International Day, and continue with the organization of biannual gatherings, the next one planned for Peru.

Because of internal political problems and repression against homosexuals, the women of Peru asked to change the place of the gathering to Costa Rica. But it was not easy to organize the second gathering in Costa Rica (1989), nor the third gathering in Puerto Rico (1992). The organization of these two gatherings came "out of the closet" and produced a national debate with sometimes violent manifestations against their realization. For that reason, in Argentina, venue for the Fourth Latin American and Caribbean Lesbian Feminist Gathering (1995), the organization was done in almost complete secrecy. This situation made the dissemination of information about the gathering among lesbian women very difficult and prompted much lower participation by local women, who are afraid to be outed and/or harassed because of their participation.

The inconveniences and difficulties encountered in organizing the Lesbian Feminist Gathering in Latin America and the Caribbean shows the great need of this space for lesbians, as women, as activists, as feminists, and as Latinas. The interchange of experiences and knowledge in this "sisters meeting" encourages the exchange of ideas for the construction of a new society that improves the situation for lesbians in Latin America and the Caribbean. *María Rachid*

### Bibliography

Las Entendidas. *Memoria de un Encuentro Inolvidable: Segundo Encuentro Lesbico-Feminista de America Latina y el Caribe* (Memoirs of an Unforgettable Meeting: Second Latin American and Caribbean Lesbian Feminist Meeting). San Jose, Costa Rica: Imprenta Carcemo, 1991.

Yarbro-Bejarano, Yvonne. "Primer encuentro de lesbianas feministas latinoamericanas y caribenas" (First Latin American and Caribbean Lesbian Feminist Gathering). In *Third Woman: The Sexuality of Latinas*. Ed. Norma Alarcón, Ana Castillo and Cherríe Moraga. Berkeley: Third Woman, 1989, pp. 143–146.

*See also* International Organizations; Latinas

## English Literature, Eighteenth Century

Representations of love between women in eighteenth-century English literature fall on a continuum between two apparently contradictory images: that of the paradigmatically chaste and virtuous "romantic friendship" on the one hand, and the freakishly sexualized "sapphic" relationship on the other. Romantic friendship is perhaps best exemplified by the characters in Sarah Scott's 1762 novel, *Millenium Hall*. Scott (1723–1795), herself the lifelong companion of Lady Barbara Montagu (d. 1765), depicts love and marriage between men and women as, at worst, violent and abusive and, at best, an impious distraction from attending to life in the hereafter. In the novel, several women characters live together in a communal household (some in affectionate pairs) and improve the lives of the neighboring villagers through their good works. According to Faderman (1981), this novel was "the *vade mecum* of romantic friends" throughout the century. At the other end of the spectrum is the lascivious Phoebe of John Cleland's pornographic novel, *Memoirs of a Woman of Pleasure* (1748–1749). Cleland (1710–1789) was viewed by at least one eighteenth-century observer as a "sodomite," and his novel is infamous for its depictions of almost every kind of sexual act, including lesbianism. The novel's protagonist, Fanny, has her first sexual experience when she is "broken in" by an older prostitute to induct her into the same trade. Cleland makes a distinction between Fanny, whose "desires . . . all pointed strongly to their pole, man," and Phoebe, who may have possessed a "secret byass" toward women.

Famous literary examples of romantic friendship include that between Clarissa and Anna in Samuel Richardson's *Clarissa* (1747–1748). They wish to live together rather than marry, a model that was actually followed by two Irish noblewomen, Lady Eleanor Butler (1739–1829) and Sarah Ponsonby (1755–1831). Best known as the Ladies of Llangollen, the women twice ran away from their families together and finally settled in Wales, where they lived from 1778 until Butler's death in 1829. The ladies were well known in literary circles; they corresponded with William Wordsworth (1770–1850), Edmund Burke (1729–1797), Anna Seward (1747–1809), and others. Among the English literary elite, they were considered exemplars of chaste devotion, although their Welsh neighbors satirized their masculine dress in local newspapers. Literary representations of cross-dressing women who pursue other women romantically include the significantly named Harriot Freke, an advocate for "the Rights of Woman," in Maria Edgeworth's (1767–1849) 1801 novel *Belinda*. In poetry, the anonymous 1720 sonnet "Cloe to Artemisia" critiques heterosexual relationships as degrading to women and celebrates intimacy between women as "pleasures for their gross senses too refined," concluding: "We'll scorn the monster and his mistress too, / And show the world what women ought to do."

The eighteenth-century tradition of anonymous, often bawdy, lyric makes room for this explicit lesbian manifesto, in large part because of the poet's anonymity. References to sexual relationships between women in eighteenth-century writing tend to cluster in low-culture genres, such as the ballad, pamphlet, and pornography, or in private sources, such as memoirs, diaries, and letters. The actress Charlotte Charke (1713–1760) describes her life as "Mr. Brown," who passed for a married man for many years, in her 1755 *A Narrative of the Life of Mrs. Charlotte Charke*. In *Satan's Harvest Home*, a pamphlet satirizing metropolitan vice published in 1749, a chapter describing sex between women as "the Game at Flatts" tells the story of a Turkish noblewoman who falls in love with a "young virgin" whom she sees at a bathhouse. As in this story, lesbianism in eighteenth-century literature is frequently associated with foreign locales, customs, and even bodies—especially those of the "darker races" of the Mediterranean, Africa, and the Indian subcontinent.

The impact of travel literature and Oriental erotica on the English sexual imagination of the eighteenth century is significant. Indeed, in an 1811 libel suit, a panel of Scottish judges concluded that two women schoolteachers, accused of lesbianism by one of their pupils, could not have conducted such a relationship because the "vice" was "hitherto unknown in Britain." One judge opined that there could be "no sort of doubt," however, that in India some women's enlarged clitorises made it possible for them to sexually penetrate other women. Such representations were important precursors to nineteenth-century discourses of racial eugenics and sexual "degeneracy."

Scholarship on lesbianism in eighteenth-century England has exploded since 1990, a phenomenon well summarized by Emma Donoghue in *Passions Between Women: British Lesbian Culture, 1668–1801* (1995). Historian Trumbach (1994) has carefully described the emergence of "a role for women which was parallel to that of the molly for men" after 1770 in London. A slang term for these "women attracted to women" was "tommies," according to Trumbach, but he notes that "the more usual term was sapphist—with sapphist and tommy being the high and low terms for women, as sodomite and molly were for men." Literary historian Vicinus (1992) draws links between modern lesbian identity and what she calls "four dominant ways" in which "lesbian desire appears to have been defined" in the seventeenth and eighteenth centuries. Vicinus's four categories—the transvestite, the cross-dressed actress, the occasional lover of women, and the romantic friend—are all visible in eighteenth-century imaginative writing. Terry Castle turns to specifically literary questions in *The Apparitional Lesbian* (1993). Calling Daniel Defoe's *The Apparition of Mrs. Veal* (1706) "that first (and strangest) of lesbian love stories," Castle establishes eighteenth-century fiction as the inaugural moment and mode of lesbian representation. Woodward (1993) also examines the conjunction of the rise of the novel and the representation of female same-sex desire. The variety of scholarly approaches to, and literary representations of, love between women in the English eighteenth century bears out Vicinus's conclusion: "Many lesbian histories, contradictory, complicated, and perhaps uncomfortable, can be told."        *Lisa Moore*

## Bibliography

Castle, Terry. *The Apparitional Lesbian: Female Homosexuality and Modern Culture.* New York: Columbia University Press, 1993.

Donoghue, Emma. *Passions Between Women: British Lesbian Culture, 1668–1801.* Reprint. New York: HarperCollins, 1995. London: Scarlet, 1993.

Faderman, Lillian. *Surpassing the Love of Men: Romantic Friendship and Love Between Women from the Renaissance to the Present.* New York: William Morrow, 1981.

Moore, Lisa. *Dangerous Intimacies: Toward a Sapphic History of the British Novel.* Durham, N.C.: Duke University Press, 1997.

Trumbach, Randolph. "The Origin and Development of the Modern Lesbian Role in the Western Gender System: Northwestern Europe and the United States, 1750–1990." *Historical Reflections/Reflexions Historiques* 20:2 (Summer 1994), 285–300.

Vicinus, Martha. "'They Wonder to Which Sex I Belong': The Historical Roots of the Modern Lesbian Identity." *Feminist Studies* 18:3 (Fall 1992), 467–497.

Woodward, Carolyn. " 'My Heart Is So Wrapt': Lesbian Disruptions in Eighteenth-Century British Fiction." *Signs: Journal of Women in Culture and Society* 18:4 (Summer 1993), 838–865.

***See also*** Charke, Charlotte; Cross-Dressing; Ladies of Llangollen; Pirie, Jane and Woods, Marianne; Romantic Friendship

## English Literature, Nineteenth Century

For most of the nineteenth century in England, the word "lesbian" was virtually unknown; if used at all, it referred specifically to the island of Lesbos and its famous poet Sappho (ca. 600 B.C.E.). Love between women was not then considered sexual, since sexuality was commonly understood as requiring the presence of a penis. Nevertheless, English literature of the nineteenth century reflects the presence of what one would today define as lesbian desire. Although times overlap considerably, lesbians in nineteenth-century English literature fall into three periods. Early in the century (1800–1830), lesbianism was figured as romantic friendship or extreme eccentricity. At midcentury (1830–1870), the vampire lesbian appeared, preying on innocent girls and linking the portrayal of lesbians to the Romantic/gothic ghost tale. Yet, even while the vampire prowled among her sisters, a new lesbian was becoming visible in the literature (1860–1900)—the unconventional "odd woman," whose insistence on appropriating the style and privileges of men provoked admiration, scorn, curiosity, psychoanalysis, and ridicule as the century wore on.

Among middle-class Britons at the turn of the nineteenth century, intense romantic friendship between women (and men) was not assumed to include a sexual component. In fact, such friendships were accepted as normal, even admirable. In her semiautobiographical novel *Mary: A Fiction* (1788), Mary Wollstonecraft (1759–1797) describes a passionate loving friendship between the eponymous heroine Mary and her friend Ann, much like the actual lifelong relationship between Lady Eleanor Butler (1739–1829) and Sarah Ponsonby (1755–1831), called by the doting public the Ladies of Llangollen. One of their devotees was Anna Seward (1747–1809), who visited them at home and much of whose poetry (published in 1810) praised the life and lamented the early death of one Honora Sneyd.

The literature of romantic friendship was relentlessly conventional, reflecting widespread approval of a certain type of passionate same-sex attachment among middle-class Englishwomen. However, when women departed from accepted gender roles, they were understood as anomalous and described as such in the literature. In *Belinda* (1801), for instance, Maria Edgeworth (1767–1849) introduces the woman's rights advocate Mrs. Freke, whose mannish behavior (she strides across the room like a man and swears) is held up as "buffoonery." Sir Walter Scott (1771–1832), in *Guy Mannering* (1829), describes the gypsy Meg Merrilies as a giant in a man's greatcoat, who seems more masculine than feminine. There is never any indication that either Mrs. Freke (despite her name) or Meg engages in sexual behavior with other women; they are objectionable, rather, for their blatant usurpation of male attire and habits. Such irreverence, it was implied, could lead to blurring of class and gender boundaries and dangerous destabilizing of the architectonic English social hierarchy. Anne Lister (1791–1840), whose journal describing her life from 1824 to 1826 left no doubt about her sexuality, could live and write as she did because she was financially independent. Lister, a kind of protobutch woman, would no doubt have recognized herself in the descriptions of "mannish lesbians" in the sexological writing of the late nineteenth century.

The figure of the vampire lesbian, sucking the innocence from virginal girls, seems to have begun with Samuel Taylor Coleridge's (1772–1834) poem "Christabel" (written, though never completed, between 1797 and 1801 and published in 1816). The evil Geraldine, who gains access to the home and the bed of young Christabel by false pretenses, represents an early example of the conflation of two images: blood vampirism and lesbian sexuality. The popularity of Charles Baudelaire's (1821–1867) *Les Fleurs du Mal* (1857) cemented this dual image in the British literary mind. Charles Dickens' (1812–1870) novel *Little Dorrit* (also 1857) introduces Miss Wade, a tormented and apparently sexually frustrated woman who "seduces" (though the seduc-

tion is not explicitly sexual) a young woman of lower social class. Algernon Swinburne (1837–1909), in his poem "Anactoria" (1866) and in his unfinished novel *Lesbia Brandon* (1867?), also features the melancholy, seductive lesbian. Joseph Sheridan LeFanu (1814–1873), in his 1872 ghost story "Carmilla," revisits the Christabel story, this time imposing an unmistakably sexual meaning upon it. In LeFanu's telling of the tale, the young ingenue even wonders if the sexy Carmilla might be a boy in disguise, so intense is her desire. Finally, in the last decade of the nineteenth century, the lesbian vampire theme still flourishes, in the lush *Songs of Bilitis* (1894) by Pierre Louys (1870–1925), and even in Anglo-American Henry James's (1843–1916) story "The Turn of the Screw" (1898). As might be expected, these lesbian vampire tales are all male creations, reflecting men's simultaneous fear of, and fascination with, lesbian sexuality. Only Christina Rossetti's (1830–1894) "Goblin Market" (1859), which implies a kind of reverse vampirism (the quasi-sexual "sucking" of the two sisters saves one from parasitic male sexuality), defies this trend.

In the year 1869, two events occurred that set the stage for the articulation of lesbian identity during the last third of the nineteenth century: the publication of Karl Heinrich Ulrichs's *The Riddle of "Man-Manly" Love* and the founding of Girton College for women at Cambridge University. Ulrichs (1825–1895) described (male) homosexuality as the soul of a woman trapped in a man's body; soon his definition would be extended to include lesbianism (the soul of a man trapped in a woman's body). His book introduced the idea of homosexuality to the newly developing field of sexology (later psychology). Ulrichs positioned homosexuality as illness rather than sin; thus, his early work promoted a kind of acceptance for homosexuals and initiated the process whereby homosexual men and women could develop whole identities around their gayness. His definitions center on gender-role reversal (as opposed to modern definitions, which focus on choice of sexual partner) as indicators of homosexuality, and, during the last third of the century, women who usurp male dress and behavior might, for the first time, be suspected of "sexual inversion."

The establishment of Girton College represented the first time women were admitted to Cambridge and was considered by many an exceedingly dangerous move. It not only validated women's efforts to break into the all-male professions, but also defied reactionary wisdom concerning women's intellect (the more powerful the brain, the weaker the reproductive capacity) and provided opportunities for a few of the many "odd women" living unmarried in England at that time. Girton women reveled in their rare privilege, dressing in starched shirtfronts, smoking, and flirting with each other. The juxtaposition of Ulrichs's theories with visibly transgressive Girton collegians was an important factor in how lesbians were portrayed in literature.

The figure of Miss Sally Brass in Dickens's *The Old Curiosity Shop* (1840) prefigures the "feminist" lesbian of the late century. Brass is an attorney who dresses, talks, and walks like a man; Dickens, of course, holds her up for ridicule. But Charlotte Brontë (1816–1855) refuses to ridicule her gender-reversing characters, such as *Shirley* (1849) and Lucy Snowe in *Villette* (1853). By contrast, Wilkie Collins, in *The Woman in White* (1860), finds the dark-complected, mannish Marian Halcombe weird and anomalous. But in *Sowing the Wind* (1867), Eliza Lynn Linton (1822–1898) creates a thoroughly male-identified "odd woman" named Jane Osborn, who is eccentric and, in some ways, unattractive, but who functions as the moral center of the novel. These characters predate Ulrichs and Girton and are not specifically shown to be lesbian.

But, within a few years of 1869, the proliferation of British "New Women" found its way into fiction. Linton's 1880 novel, *The Rebel of the Family*, introduces Bell Blount, whose lesbianism is overt; she lives with a compliant "little wife" and spends most of the book trying to seduce the ingenue heroine. *Rebel* was written in the same year as Emile Zola's (1840–1902) *Nana*, and, while French literature by men had evinced a fascination with lesbian characters for a century at least, Linton's book was the first English novel to describe the lesbian as an aggressively (homo)sexual member of a feminist community. Henry James (1843–1916) apparently patterned *The Bostonians* (1886) after it, and the British New Woman fiction of the 1890s owes it a debt as well.

The 1890s represented a contentious decade in England, particularly around the issue of homosexuality. In 1895, Oscar Wilde's (1854–1900) sensational trial and conviction for sodomy coincided with the publication of Havelock Ellis's (1859–1939) *Studies in the Psychology of Sex* including a chapter, "Sexual Inversion in Women." Suddenly, the literature of the New Woman contained descriptions of lesbian relationships, romance, and community; it also referred to Ellis's assumptions about lesbians, such as that the "mannish lesbian" wished to appro-

priate the privileges of men in any way she could, including sexual desire. Many novels appeared in the 1890s that brought lesbianism into public consciousness for the first time, among them *The Odd Women* (1892) and *Born in Exile* (1893) by George Gissing (1857–1903); *The One Too Many* (1894) and *The New Woman in Haste and at Leisure* (1895) by Linton; *The Celibates* (1895) by George Moore (1852–1933); and *The Heavenly Twins* (1895) by Sarah Grand (1854–1943). In addition to novels, the poetry of Michael Field (pseudonym of niece and aunt Katharine Bradley [1846–1914] and Edith Cooper [1862–1913]) and Charlotte Mew (1869–1928) celebrated love between women in the 1890s.

In short, British literary portrayals of lesbianism underwent drastic change during the nineteenth century, as the idea "lesbian" was defined, refined, and accessible to popular understanding. In 1800, romantic friendships were not understood as sexual in any way; in 1850, lesbian sexuality could be expressed only through the image of the vampire; in 1900, the literature reflected an identifiable lesbian style and community.

*Deborah T. Meem*

## Bibliography

Chauncey, George, Jr. "From Sexual Inversion to Homosexuality: Medicine and the Changing Conceptualization of Female Deviance." *Salmagundi* 58–59 (1982–1983), 78–146.

Clark, Anna. "Anne Lister's Construction of Lesbian Identity." *Journal of the History of Sexuality* 7:1 (July 1996), 23–50.

DeJean, Joan E. *Fictions of Sappho, 1546–1937*. Chicago: University of Chicago Press, 1989.

Donoghue, Emma. *Passions Between Women: British Lesbian Culture, 1668–1801*. London: Scarlet, 1993.

Faderman, Lillian. *Surpassing the Love of Men: Romantic Friendship and Love Between Women from the Renaissance to the Present*. New York: William Morrow, 1981.

Jeffreys, Sheila. *The Spinster and Her Enemies: Feminism and Sexuality, 1880–1930*. London: Pandora, 1985.

Lesbian History Group. *Not a Passing Phase: Reclaiming Lesbians in History, 1840–1985*. London: Women's Press, 1989.

***See also*** Diaries and Letters; English Literature, Eighteenth Century; Field, Michael; Ladies of Llangollen; Lister, Anne; New Woman; Romantic Friendship; Sapphic Tradition; Sexology; Vampires

## English Literature, Twentieth Century

The twentieth century has been a particularly fruitful period for lesbianism as a theme in English literature; indeed, many of the most noteworthy British works of fiction produced in the century were either written by lesbian authors or address the issue of lesbianism in some manner. One of the earliest twentieth-century works to represent passionate affection between female characters is *The Getting of Wisdom* (1910) by the Australian émigré Henry Handel (Florence) Richardson (1870–1946), who sympathetically examined various aspects of what was then termed "deviance" in a number of her works. In this semiautobiographical novel, Richardson delineates the education of a rebellious young woman, already considered "different" by her peers, through a series of schoolgirl "crushes," a theme that would become increasingly common over the decades in what might be considered a separate subgenre of lesbian fiction, namely the girls'-school novel. Clemence Dane's (1888–1965) now forgotten *Regiment of Women* (1917), another girls'-school novel, was, according to Foster (1985), the first English-language novel "devoted wholly to [female sexual] variance." In this case, however, lesbianism is represented as psychologically morbid, as medical sexology then held it to be.

As a general rule, if lesbianism were to be represented in literature at all during the first decades of the century, it was only as a romantic friendship between adolescents or as pathological, as in the two above examples. Even in the latter instance, it could not be treated explicitly. This became evident in 1915, when D.H. Lawrence's (1885–1930) *The Rainbow* was withdrawn after a British court found indecent its relatively detailed description of a sexual encounter between Ursula Brangwen, the youthful protagonist, and her teacher. Lawrence did not treat lesbianism sympathetically in this work; the chapter in question is entitled "Shame," and Ursula eventually repudiates both her teacher and feminism, yet remains an unsatisfactory participant in heterosexual relationships, conceivably as a result of her earlier experience. As a result of the charge of indecency, however, the more explicit passage were, for many years, expurgated from subsequent editions.

Even as judicial intervention barred direct depiction of sexual activity between women, writers nevertheless found alternative means to narrate lesbianism and, thus, subvert censorship. In her first novel, *The Voyage Out* (1915), Virginia Woolf (1882–1941) uses the exotic setting of the Amazon rain forest in the fictional nation of Santa Marina as a backdrop for the erotic tensions that develop between Rachel Vinrace, an unsocialized young woman making her first venture into the larger world, and her aunt, Helen Ambrose. Published in the same year as *The Rainbow*, Woolf's novel, particularly when compared to her earlier unpublished drafts, evinces considerable self-censorship and, as a result, the novel, narrated in a traditional linear and discursive style, is generally considered beautiful but somewhat incoherent. Woolf's protagonist, after indirect and uncomfortable experiences with both heterosexuality and homosexuality, withdraws and dies of a fever, thus evading these conflicting demands.

Subsequently, Woolf found a more effective mode of representing lesbianism, by means of the stream-of-consciousness technique pioneered by James Joyce (1882–1941) and Dorothy Richardson (1873–1957). This nonlinear and free-flowing style, which emulates the fragmentary and circular patterns of human thought and is presented from numerous characters' points of view, enabled Joyce and Richardson to represent sexual matters considered improper or immoral in a manner that is semi-indirect and not entirely accessible to all readers. While this mode could, to some extent, evade censorship, Joyce's *Ulysses* (1922) was banned because of its supposedly indecent language. Both Joyce and Richardson, however, employed stream-of-consciousness—in *Finnegans Wake* (1939) and *Dawn's Left Hand* (1931), the tenth segment of the multivolumed *Pilgrimage*, respectively—to present gay and lesbian characters and situations. Woolf's first attempt at stream-of-consciousness narrative was *Jacob's Room* (1921), which includes a discreet subplot of male homosexuality. This was followed by *Mrs. Dalloway* (1926), in which the lives and desires of the closeted protagonist and her homosexual male and lesbian alter-egos (Septimus Warren Smith and Doris Kilman) are revealed in the course of a given day through the memories and reflections of the various characters. In *To the Lighthouse* (1927), Woolf presents the struggle of Lily Briscoe to reject traditional gender roles for the sake of her art and her love for other women, a conflict heightened by her love for Mrs. Ramsay, the personification of the Victorian ideal domestic woman.

Following the success of these novels, in which lesbianism, however circumspectly, becomes the central "story," Woolf, emboldened by her affair with the aristocratic Vita Sackville-West (1892–1962), made her lover the hero/heroine of *Orlando* (1928), a work of comic fantasy that satirizes English society and history through the adventures of Orlando, a character originally male but later female, who lives over five centuries without aging. Sackville-West, though not as accomplished an artist as Woolf, was a novelist, poet, and essayist in her own right. Her novel *Challenge* (1923), originally surpressed at the insistence of her family, is, on the surface, a heterosexual romance but is, in actuality, a semiautobiographical narrative based on the author's notorious affair with Violet Trefusis (1894–1972)—for which both women temporarily left their respective husbands—only Sackville-West's character is, for the sake of public mores, rendered male.

While Woolf could celebrate her love for another woman in a decidedly nonrealistic text, in the same year that *Orlando* was published another lesbian novel, Radclyffe Hall's (1880–1943) *The Well of Loneliness* (1928), was the center of legal and literary controversy. Written in a realistic, direct, unambiguous, and unhumorous style, Hall's work is a polemic for the rights of "inverts" such as her heroine Stephen Gordon, a woman who, like Hall, eschews "feminine" pursuits and dresses in men's attire. Because of its sympathetic (if not terribly explicit) handling of a sexual relationship between two women, the novel was declared obscene by a British court and remained banned until 1949. As a result, relatively few British works of fiction published in the 1930s or 1940s directly or openly deal with lesbianism.

Lesbianism did not completely disappear as a literary theme; however, in some instances, as with Compton Mackenzie's (1883–1972) *Extraordinary Women* (1928), lesbians—in this case, Hall and other literary lesbians—were treated satirically. Otherwise, writers addressing the issue generally did so in an ambiguous, often subversive, manner, primarily through the mode of the novel of manners, which, by means of characters' urbane wit and the use of double entendres, permits alternative readings for knowing (that is, gay or lesbian) readers. For example, Ivy Compton-Burnett (1884–1969), in *More Women Than Men* (1933), presents discreet gay and lesbian relationships among the faculty of a girls' school, yet, because these relationships are presented in such a matter-of-fact way, they do not draw attention to themselves and, therefore, might

go unnoticed by the unsuspecting. Also in this period, Sylvia Townsend Warner's (1893–1978) *Summer Will Show* (1936) and *The Corner That Held Them* (1949) feature unobtrusive lesbian subplots, while Mary Renault's (1905–1983) *The Friendly Young Ladies* (1994), published in the United States as *The Middle Mist* (1945), subverts its lesbian theme with an ostensibly heterosexual ending, and Dorothy Strachey's (1866–1960) *Olivia* (1949) presents a more sophisticated variation on the girls'-school novel.

The reliance on the novel of manners to present alternative sexualities persisted into the 1950s and 1960s, as can be seen in the novels of Brigid Brophy (1929–1995), particularly *King of a Rainy Country* (1956). By the early 1960s, however, as the basics of Freudian psychology gained relatively widespread acceptance and women's self-consciousness became a more frequent topic in literature, female homoerotic desire, repressed or otherwise, began to appear more often as a subtext in works by women authors, whether lesbian or not. Some notable examples of such works are Muriel Spark's (1918–) *The Prime of Miss Jean Brodie* (1961), Doris Lessing's (1919–) *The Golden Notebook* (1962), Iris Murdoch's (1919–) *An Unofficial Rose* (1962), and Elizabeth Bowen's (1899–1972) *The Little Girls* (1963) and *Eva Trout* (1968). During the greater part of the 1960s, the ruling Labour government promoted the idea that a "permissive society" is the most civilized one. To this end, the period saw a remarkable liberalization of British laws concerning censorship, marriage, divorce, contraception, abortion, and male homosexuality (which was decriminalized in 1967).

Inasmuch as these legislative changes were an indicator of sweeping changes in contemporary social and sexual mores, so were these changes reflected in the literature of the decade. And, while sexual acts between women had never been prohibited by British law (and, thus, were not directly affected legal reform), lesbianism became a topic of cultural interest. Perhaps the most noteworthy examples are the novels of lesbian author Maureen Duffy (1933–), particularly her autobiographical narrative of lesbian childhood and adolescence, *That's How It Was* (1962), and the highly experimental *The Microcosm* (1966), which presents a cross-section of lesbian subculture through the multiple points of view of the denizens of women's bar. Just as an experimental multivoiced narrative proved an apt means for Duffy to present a tapestry of stories about lives outside the mainstream, so also, for a number of authors, did bisexual experimentation became an almost fashionable topic for experimental women's fiction, regardless of the writer's own sexuality. Some significant examples from this period include Brophy's parodic girls'-school novella, *The Finishing Touch* (1963), and her transsexual fantasy, *In Transit* (1969); Ann Quin's (1936–1973) *Three* (1966); Shena Mackay's (1944–) *Music Upstairs* (1965); Sybille Bedford's (1911–) *A Favourite of the Gods* (1963) and *A Compass Error* (1969); and Elizabeth Jane Howard's (1923–) *Odd Girl Out* (1972).

Because of the gains made by both feminist and gay activism in the 1970s, lesbianism became a relatively frequent topic in fiction by lesbian and heterosexual women authors alike, the latter often configuring the idea of lesbianism (rather than lesbian individuals, in many cases) as an emblem of the ultimate insult to, or rebellion against, male authority and dominance. Although often problematic to many lesbian readers—and to radical lesbian critics, such as Palmer (1989)—such novels nevertheless indicate that lesbianism, which most critics hold to have been invisible if nonetheless existent throughout history, was now much more out in the open and, for many women, a viable alternative to a male-centered lifestyle. This trend can be seen in many of Fay Weldon's (1933–) early novels, including *Remember Me* (1976), *Little Sisters* (U.S. title, *Words of Advice* [1978]), *The Life and Loves of a She-Devil* (1983), and *The Heart of the Country* (1987); in Emma Tennant's (1937–) *The Bad Sister* (1989) and *Sisters and Strangers* (1991); and Angela Carter's (1940–1992) *Nights at the Circus* (1984), among many others. The 1980s and 1990s also produced a number of contemporary British lesbian authors of note, including Michelene Wandor, Anna Livia, Christine Crow, Emma Donahue, and mystery writer Mary Wings, most of whom tend to employ a ludic (playful or whimsical) tone in their narrative styles, a trait that is characteristic of the works of many prominent postmodern British women writers. Most prominent among these contemporary British lesbian authors is Jeanette Winterson (1959–). Her works, which have been awarded some of the more distinguished prizes in British literary circles, have reached a vast mainstream audience and include the droll "coming out" novel *Oranges Are Not the Only Fruit* (1985), the magic realist *The Passion* (1987) and *Sexing the Cherry* (1989), and the romance narrative *Written on the Body* (1992). Her more recent and increasingly complex works include *Art and Lies* (1995), which might be seen as a postmodern reenvisioning of Gertrude Stein's (1874–1946) playful, if somewhat obscure, erotic works, and *Gut Symmetries* (1997), in which she uses quantum physics to symbolize personal relationships.

British women writers have contributed amply to the creation of what might be called the lesbian novel or, at any rate, the narrative of lesbianism. Unlike their American counterparts, however, British women writers have, as a whole, produced relatively little in terms of lesbian poetry. Some of the more prominent British women poets of the twentieth century, including Charlotte Mew (1869–1928), Edith Sitwell (1887–1964), and Stevie Smith (1902–1971), have been lesbian or bisexual, yet their poetry reflects little about desire between women. Conversely, while Vita Sackville-West, Sylvia Townsend Warner, and Maureen Duffy have published homoerotic poetry, they are better known for their fiction. Also, there has been little in terms of lesbian drama in Britain historically, although numerous lesbian improvisational theater groups have arisen in the late twentieth century.

*Patricia Juliana Smith*

**Bibliography**

Abraham, Julie. *Are Girls Necessary?: Lesbian Writing and Modern Histories*. New York: Routledge, 1996.

Castle, Terry. *The Apparitional Lesbian: Female Homosexuality and Modern Culture*. New York: Columbia University Press, 1993.

DuPlessis, Rachel Blau. *Writing Beyond the Ending: Narrative Strategies of Twentieth-Century Women Writers*. Bloomington: Indiana University Press, 1985.

Faderman, Lillian. *Surpassing the Love of Men: Romantic Friendship and Love Between Women from the Renaissance to the Present*. New York: William Morrow, 1981.

Foster, Jeannette H. *Sex Variant Women in Literature*. Tallahassee, Fla.: Naiad, 1985.

Palmer, Paulina. *Contemporary Women's Fiction: Narrative Practice and Feminist Theory*. Jackson: University Press of Mississippi, 1989.

Smith, Patricia Juliana. *Lesbian Panic: Homoeroticism in Modern British Women's Fictions*. New York: Columbia University Press, 1997.

***See also*** Boarding Schools; Bowen, Elizabeth; Compton-Burnett, Ivy; Duffy, Maureen; Hall, Rad-

**E** clyffe; Mew, Charlotte; Renault, Mary; Sackville-West, Vita; Stein, Gertrude; Warner, Sylvia Townsend; Woolf, Virginia

## Enlightenment, European

Intellectual movement spanning the seventeenth to the nineteenth centuries. It included thinkers from Europe and what was to become the United States, including John Locke (1632–1704), David Hume (1711–1776), Jean-Jacques Rousseau (1712–1778), Immanuel Kant (1724–1804), Thomas Paine (1737–1809), and Jeremy Bentham (1748–1832). The European Enlightenment encompassed several movements for social and political reform of medieval hierarchical social, economic, and political systems. Human emancipation was justified by the notion that reason and empirical knowledge can become the basis for political authority, rather than the relations set in place by medieval notions of prejudice, superstition, social immobility, or ascribed status.

Although the Enlightenment thinkers differed widely, modern notions of progress, humanism, secularism, rationality, and universalism can all be traced back to aspects of Enlightenment thought; moreover, nineteenth-century radicals, liberals, and reformers as diverse as Karl Marx (1818–1883), John Stuart Mill (1806–1873), and T.H. Green (1836–1882) can also be construed as heirs of the Enlightenment. Early feminist theorists, such as Mary Wollstonecraft (1759–1797), drew on the Enlightenment's emphasis on reason in making their argument for women's equality.

The concepts of equality and freedom marked the central philosophical contribution of the European Enlightenment. But the centuries-long delay in extending these ideals to nonpropertied European men, to European women, and to non-European peoples indicate to some critics that the Enlightenment notions of progress, universalism, and freedom operated merely as ideological justifications for European capitalism, imperialism, and genocide. Frantz Fanon (1925–1961), an anticolonialist writer and revolutionary, appears to be referring to the ideals of the European Enlightenment, enunciated in documents such as the French National Assembly's Declaration of the Rights of Man and of the Citizen (1791), when he writes in *Wretched of the Earth* (1963): "Leave this Europe where they are never done talking of Man, yet murder men everywhere they find them, at the corner of every one of their own streets, in all the corners of the globe."

Many historians of sexuality have posited a link between the Enlightenment's emphasis on the individual and the appearance in the eighteenth and nineteenth centuries of new sexual and gendered identities attached to individuals in themselves (homosexuals, lesbians) rather than to those who engage in certain practices (sodomites).

Some understand the liberatory quest of sexual minorities for equality and liberty in the twentieth century as an attempt to extend the principles of the European Enlightenment to those whose social identities and practices have, through most of history, existed at the margins of hegemonic culture. On this view, a state's denial of equal rights to sexual minorities, including the right to same-sex marriage and other rights emanating from the legal recognition of same-sex relationships, constitutes a repudiation of the promises of the Enlightenment. Other social theorists view gay and lesbian rights claims as falling prey to the ideology of liberal individualism celebrated in much European Enlightenment thought. According to these critiques, liberal individualism provides a rationale for inherently unequal social and economic structures and practices by focusing solely on the individual's political rights in relation to the state, rather than on larger issues of social and economic justice.      *Paisley Currah*

### *Bibliography*

Blasius, Mark, and Shane Phelan, eds. *We Are Everywhere: A Historical Sourcebook of Gay and Lesbian Politics*. New York: Routledge, 1997.

Cassirer, Ernest. *The Philosophy of the Enlightenment*. Trans. Fritz Koelln and James Pettegrove. Princeton, N.J.: Princeton University Press, 1951.

D'Emilio, John. "Capitalism and Gay Identity." In *Powers of Desire*. Ed. Ann Snitow, Christine Stansell, and Sharon Thompson. New York: Monthly Review Press, 1983, pp. 100–113.

Hampson, Norman. *The Enlightenment*. New York: Penguin, 1968.

McIntosh, Mary. "Queer Theory and the War of the Sexes." In *Activating Theory*. Ed. Joseph Bristow and Angelia R. Wilson. London: Lawrence and Wishart, 1993, pp. 30–52.

Young, Iris. *Justice and the Politics of Difference*. Princeton, N.J.: Princeton University Press, 1990.

***See also*** Human Rights; Legal Theory, Lesbian; Liberalism; Rights

## Erauso, Catalina de (ca. 1585–1650)

Spanish adventurer who passed much of her life as a man. Born in Basque Spain, Catalina de Erauso became known in her lifetime as the "Lieutenant Nun" due to her exploits in Latin America as a soldier discovered to be a woman. According to her own testimony, at age fifteen she escaped from the Spanish convent in which she had been placed at age four, stealing from it money, needle, and scissors to disguise herself as a boy. She served as a court page in Spain, a ship's boy en route to New Spain, and, from 1603 to ca. 1620, alternately a soldier and a merchant's clerk in what is now Chile, Peru, and Argentina. About 1620, she was arrested after killing a man in a fight and, in the course of a lengthy confession, revealed herself as a woman to the bishop of Guamanga; upon inspection, she was declared a virgin, which would add to her fame. She temporarily entered a convent again and returned to Spain in 1624. Ultimately, she was granted a pension from the king of Spain, papal permission to continue cross-dressing, and honorary Roman citizenship. De Erauso returned to New Spain in 1630 and probably lived as a merchant and a mule driver until her death around 1650.

Clearly she was a passing woman, but her sexuality, due to her time and circumstances, defies easy categorization. Mutual attraction to other women (who think she is a man) appears as a theme in her memoir, with her usually in the role of rescuer who initially enjoys, but later rejects, the advances of her female admirers. In the larger context of her story, her sexuality becomes part of a picture of a person who embodied the ideal of *machismo* (masculinity) of her time and place: Her story is replete with the gambling, fighting, and killing—of both Europeans and Natives—typical of the tales of adventure and conquest of her era and after. Catalina de Erauso is significant as an early-modern example of the many women who have disguised themselves as men to live as males, an act that, in her case, seems a result of being completely male identified.

*Vicki L. Eaklor*

### Bibliography

Perry, Mary Elizabeth. "The Manly Woman: A Historical Case Study." *American Behavioral Scientist* 31 (September/October 1987), 86–100.

Stepto, Michele, and Gabriel Stepto, trans. *Lieutenant Nun: Memoir of a Basque Transvestite in the New World, Catalina de Erauso*. Foreword by Marjorie Garber. Introduction by Michele Stepto. Boston: Beacon, 1996.

*See also* Passing Women; Spain

*Doña Catalina de Erauso.* © British Museum.

DOÑA CATALINA DE ERAUSO.

## Erotica and Pornography

Explicit visual, written, and verbal representations of sexual acts and organs, capable of eliciting sensuous responses.

### Definitions

As terminology, "erotica" and "pornography" both derive from nineteenth-century moral and legal discourses. The many names used for erotic literature and art that were in use before the nineteenth century—such as licentious, bawdy, libertine, galant, and obscene—point to more varied origins.

The distinction between erotica and pornography is not definite, although it is commonly held that the former refers to art and the latter to commerce. This distinction is the outcome of nineteenth-century debates over the amorality of the arts, as reflected in the motto Art for Art's Sake. In the twentieth century, judicial authorities determined that, if any artistic value could be detected or claimed, it would safeguard a work of art from the accusation of obscenity. Norms about "good" and "bad" sex are often the markers of the distinction.

Erotica and pornography should not be confused with obscene satires or lampoons because the latter do not aim at sexual titillation. According to the Russian linguist Mikhail Bakhtin (1895–1975), sexual or scatological humorous insults are intrusions of the profane, "the low," into the realm of the sacred, "the high." Sexually charged attacks on public figures or institutions are a related form. The targets are accused of sexual behavior that is grotesque or incompatible with the norms belonging to their status, gender, or age.

Historically, lesbianism was an infrequent accusation in obscene satirical literature, except in a few epigrams by the Latin poets Catullus (ca. 84–ca. 54 B.C.E.) and Martial (A.D. ca. 40–ca. 104). Its appearance in obscene political pamphlets of the French revolutionary epoch is, therefore, significant. In these, Marie Antoinette (1755–1793) and her aristocratic friends, as well as actresses and famous courtesans, were all the butt of jokes about tribadism. Questioning why tribadism was chosen to attack these women, contemporary historians point to the fact that the political influence wielded by these women before the French Revolution (1789) was perceived as a threat to the new body politic. The tribades were portrayed either as corrupted by their insatiable lust, which symbolized the degeneracy of the aristocracy, or as would-be men who defy the exclusion of women from the public sphere. In a similar manner, imputations of lesbianism were fundamental to attacks on feminists during the last decades of the twentieth century. In contrast to the eighteenth-century political satire, however, the accusations were not humorous, nor did they portray feminists as sexually insatiable. On the contrary, they were stereotyped as women too ugly to attract a man and too ill equipped to satisfy another woman.

## History

Written or graphic representations of sexual acts between women do not appear in European culture on a large scale before the eighteenth century. The oldest examples come from fifth-century B.C.E. Greek vase paintings. Like other sexual imagery on vases and drinking cups of men and boys or men and women together, they may have served to heighten the spirits during drinking bouts. Apart from these early instances, there is no proof that the Greeks used lesbian sex as erotica.

Written representations of lesbian sex that may have aimed at titillation date from the third-century A.D. Lucian's (A.D. ca. 115?–ca. 180) *Dialogues of Prostitutes* portrays a courtesan and her female friend engaged in sexual encounters. Although medieval European culture was rich with sexual tales and songs, sexual acts between women were not part of the erotic repertory. Even early Renaissance literary eroticism, such as Giovanni Bocaccio's (1313–1375) *Decameron* or Geoffrey Chaucer's (ca. 1340–1400) *The Canterbury Tales*, do not tell lesbian tales. The Italian Pietro d'Aretino reintroduced the motif of the lesbian courtesan in his *Raggionamenti* (1534), which was republished countless times in Europe, especially in France. Its dialogic form and brothel location, both reminiscent of Lucian's *Dialogues*, were copied repeatedly by pornographers through the twentieth century.

The lesbian motif began to be explored on a large scale only in the second part of eighteenth century. Half of the titles of eighteenth-century French pornography contain lesbian sex scenes, sometimes embellished with explicit engravings. These scenes are situated in brothels, harems, convent schools, and the homes of bourgeois families. They occur between older and younger women, nuns and novices, girlfriends, whores and their female clients. The frequent representations in erotica of sex between women are signs of yet another pleasure, curiosity. Sex between women, "tribadism" as it is often called, was not new to the European tradition, which had by now embraced the major texts of antiquity. In the eighteenth century, however, it became an object of sexual curiosity to be satisfied primarily by erotic literature.

The eighteenth century produced a large amount of erotic literature, as well as innovations in form and content. A distinct feature of eighteenth-century literary eroticism is its multiplicity in form. Unlike most twentieth-century pornography, eighteenth-century erotic fiction could aim at various purposes besides arousing sexual responses. Many an erotic novel was also a philosophical treatise on enlightened ideas, a commentary on society, and a source of knowledge on sexual difference. Michel Foucault (1926–1984) designated this epoch as the time when western European society "invented" sex, by making it discursive and developing a *scientia sexualis*. By this he meant that the concept of sexuality by which we give meaning to behavior, acts, thoughts, fantasies, and identities did not exist before this era. Others have described the literature of the Enlightenment as "encyclopedic," meaning that it reproduces all sorts of available knowledge and cultural discourses. The erotic novel of the eighteenth century was a discourse of sexuality, the novelistic form allowing the author to insert bits of knowledge and to create fictional characters, such as the lesbian, to embody this knowledge.

Famous examples of erotic fiction on lesbianism are *La religieuse* (The Nun; written in 1760, published in 1796) by Denis Diderot (1713–1784), and *La nouvelle Sappho* (anonymous, 1791), the story of a young country girl who becomes the pet lover of the high priestess of the sect of Anandrines ("those without men"). Tribadism, as it was called, was rarely presented as an exclusive desire or taste for women and was seldom associated with masculine behavior. It could form part of the initiation into sexual knowledge and pleasure of young girls, in which case it was followed by a heterosexual finale. It could also be a sign of the insatiable lust of women, in which case men were not excluded from the scene. Or a woman might reject the male sex because she had been abused or betrayed by a man. Sex between women could generate solidarity and friendship, but it could also be a passing thing.

Eighteenth-century erotica produced more diverse lesbian images than ever and set the model for modern pornography. Tribadism continued to figure in most nineteenth-century and twentieth-century erotic fiction. In the nineteenth century, the number of new works decreased in France and other European countries, but the (clandestine) market for reprints of the classics grew in the last half of the century. As in the previous century, sex between women was not represented as exclusive, but as one form of sexual practice among others. The only novel in which lesbianism is the central motif is *Gamiani, ou Deux nuits d'exces* (Gamiani, or Two Nights of Excess) (1833), attributed to Alfred de Musset (1810–1857). This novel stands out among its contemporaries because the lesbian character is portrayed as pathological, a view later held by sexologists. Gamiani's inability to enjoy sex with a man is seen both as a monstrosity and as the result of sexual abuse and corruption in her youth.

At the end of the nineteenth century, lesbianism figured in decadent art and in Belle Epoque eroticism. The turn-of-the-century lesbian character was labeled with the features that sexology and psychiatry had given to the "unnatural." The focus on lesbianism coincided with a general cultural interest in degeneracy and perversions and with a revival of libertinism. Female erotic authors who wrote in this mode included Liane de Pougy (*Idylle sapphique*, [1901]) and the Viscountess de Coeur-Brûlant (*Le Roman de Violette*, [1882]). In their effort to refute this pathological model, Renée Vivien (1877–1909) and Natalie Barney (1876–1972) coined the word "lesbian" for sapphic lovers.

In the twentieth century—the age of visual culture—erotica and pornography expanded beyond its primarily written manifestations. With the advent of film, the elaboration of photographic techniques, the arrival of the glossy magazine and video, the means by which to distribute erotic imagery multiplied. Even if the diffusion of written erotica among the popular classes of the eighteenth and nineteenth centuries has been underestimated, it was twentieth-century mass-media culture that made access to a variety of pornographic products possible for a large public. Sex between women became a regular item on the wish list of consumers of pornography, of whom men were the largest group.

## Women as Consumers and Producers

Although as early as the seventeenth century individual women had been involved as authors, readers, peddlers, smugglers, and financiers in the production of pornography and erotica, the commercial production of pornography for and by women did not occur until the 1980s. When it did, state censorship was largely a thing of the past. The legal distinction between the artistic and the obscene, which previously determined whether a literary or a visual work could be distributed above ground, had gradually been phased out. In the case of lesbianism, it was replaced by a form of self-censorship.

Due to the emancipatory search for a homosexual identity, which took shape against, and through, the medical-psychiatric discourse, representations of lesbian eroticism by female authors were far from lighthearted, let alone salacious. The classic example is Radclyffe Hall's (1880–1943) *The Well of Loneliness* (1928), which was widely published and read through the 1950s, although it did not even offer its readers anything beyond a kiss. Novels like *The Well*, in which lesbian desire and sex were heavily coded in loneliness, guilt, and shame, were published in different languages on the Continent as well. In the same vein, lesbian characters appeared in films, in Germany (*Die Büchse der Pandora* [Pandora's Box], [1929]; *Mädchen in Uniform* [Girls in Uniform] [1931]), in France (*Les biches* [The Does] [1968]), and in the United States

E (*The Fox* [1968]; *The Killing of Sister George* [1968]).

For those who wanted explicit lesbian eroticism, American companies such as Fawcett-Crest published hundreds of lesbian pulp paperbacks in the 1950s and 1960s. These novels were primarily destined for a male public, but women were avid readers, too.

In the 1970s, lesbian feminist publishing collectives started to produce lesbian erotica, intended to be exempt from sexism or self-hatred. Photographer Tee Corinne (1943–) and novelist Rita Mae Brown (1944–) were very popular in the United States. Representations of sexual acts between women that aimed at arousal were still rare events in lesbian feminist erotica, however. At the same time, there was a renewed interest in lesbian novels and movies from the past, in spite of their homophobia. Their sultry atmosphere and oppressive silence were turned into a cult and even imitated by some lesbians.

Many lesbian feminists of the 1970s rejected all pornography for its objectification and degradation of women. Lesbian sex scenes were seen as solely catering to male voyeurism, intended to keep control over women's sexual pleasure.

In the 1980s, the sex-radical movement, headed by lesbian sadomasochistic groups, such as Samois in California, initiated written and visual pornography for lesbians aimed at sexual excitement. Well-known authors of lesbian pornography include Pat Califia and Susie Bright, both Americans. Krista Beinstein and Monika Treut from Germany gained reputations as, respectively, a lesbian erotic photographer and a video- and filmmaker. The American magazine *On Our Backs* and the British *Quim* catered to a lesbian public, with women in control of production and distribution. The lesbian sex scenes are often set in a sadomasochistic idiom and feature butch and femme roles. This and the already existing mistrust of pornography have led to violent confrontations between feminist antipornography lobbyists and feminist sex radicals.

The sex radicals claimed that women need to liberate their fantasies through scenarios of power, including violent ones and that explorations of polymorphous sexuality and celebrations of perversions can erase the boundaries between the erotic and the pornographic and subvert fixed gender and sexual identities. The other position insisted that the violence and exploitation is an intrinsic feature of pornography.

While lesbian pornography produced by and for male spectators still existed in the 1990s, lesbian eroticism became part of mainstream culture, in such films as *Basic Instinct* (1994) and *Bound* (1996). The representations of lesbian sexuality in the mainstream media created opportunities for political-activist debates, as well as cultural criticism. Feminists scholars have contributed to more diverse approaches to lesbian erotica and to pornography in general. Literary and film critics have developed new ways of thinking about the processes through which readers and viewers constitute themselves as desiring and gendered subjects and opened have up the prospect of the female reader and spectator of pornography. The view that pornography is, in itself, a male genre has become untenable.

*Dorelies Kraakman*

## Bibliography

Brécourt-Villars, Claudine. *Écrire d'amour. Anthologie de textes érotiques féminins, 1799–1984* (Love Writing: Anthology of Women's Erotic Texts, 1799–1984). Paris: Ramsay, 1985.

Healy, Emma. *Lesbian Sex Wars*. London: Virago, 1996.

Hughes, Alex, and Kate Ince, eds. *French Erotic Fiction: Women's Desiring Writing, 1880–1990*. Oxford: Berg, 1996.

Hunt, Lynn, ed. *The Invention of Pornography: Obscenity and the Origins of Modernity, 1500–1800*. New York: Zone, 1993.

Jay, Karla. *Lesbian Erotics*. New York: New York University Press, 1995.

Perthold, Sabine, ed. *Rote Küsse. Frauen-Film-Schaubuch* (Red Kisses: Women's Film Book). Tübingen: Claudia Gehrke, 1990.

***See also*** Barney, Natalie; Brown, Rita Mae; Hall, Radclyffe; Marie Antoinette; Sexology; Tribade; Vivien, Renée

## Essentialism

Belief that people or other beings are what they are because of some "essence" or unchanging characteristic. Essentialism is usually contrasted with social constructionism, the belief that the ways that people understand themselves and the sorts of people they can be are produced by particular historical and cultural formations. Thus, for example, in answer to the question of male dominance, essentialists might say that men are not only stronger and larger than women, they are also incapable of being gentle or cooperative; men just are aggressors, regardless of place or time. A constructionist view, in contrast, would seek to explain male dominance and aggression by referring to cultural standards of masculinity that tell men that being a man means dominating women. In this view, male size and hormone levels do not automatically translate into male aggression.

Essentialism is often confused with other theoretical issues. Overgeneralization, the problem of making excessively broad claims about a group, such as "all lesbians are gentle," is not the same as essentialism. To be essentialist, the claim that lesbians are gentle must not only be generalized, but also must be explained by referring to lesbians' inherent gentleness. To state that all lesbians are gentle because they live in communities that validate gentleness and condemn violence would be overgeneralizing but not essentialist. Essentialists would claim that lesbians just are gentle because gentleness is in lesbian natures. Lesbians might be warped by their upbringing in nonlesbian society, one might say, but among lesbians their basic nature will assert itself.

Among lesbians, the debates about essentialism have taken several shapes. Some early lesbian feminist claims about lesbians were, indeed, essentialist, as writers argued that lesbians were innately feminist rebels against patriarchy. This led to the problem of understanding exceptions: If lesbians are innately feminist, how does one explain lesbians who abuse other women, who dislike women, who don't identify with the feminist movement? One answer is to suggest that, while all lesbians are potentially or latently feminist, this potential can be blocked by living in patriarchy. This answer is inadequate for several reasons. First, the default explanation of patriarchy makes the theory invulnerable to disproof. Any exceptions to the rule can be ignored as products of patriarchy. Second, the idea that lesbians are innately feminist invites lesbians to police themselves and one another, to measure themselves against some mythical lesbian. Rather than ask questions about whether their behavior is just or loving, lesbians can get drawn into debates about whether they are "really" lesbians.

Another form of debates about essentialism concerns lesbian ancestors. Can one say that Queen Christina of Sweden (1626–1689) was a lesbian, even though the social category of lesbian did not exist in the seventeenth century? Can one claim, as Grahn (1983) does, a line of cultural descent with the first-century A.D. Celtic Queen Boudica? Social constructionists point to a history of the concept of "lesbian," which stretches back only 150 years, and argue that calling earlier women who loved women "lesbians" falsifies their history. They would detach the issue of whether women loved women from the contemporary idea of lesbianism, both for historical accuracy and because such "invented traditions" can work as part of the self-policing of lesbians.

Yet another debate about essentialism concerns the question of biology. While biological explanations for behavior need not be essentialist, many are. They suggest that a certain percentage of people "just are" lesbian or gay, and that this is not susceptible to social influences. To those who want to demand tolerance, this may be an appealing argument, as they can point out the bigotry of hating people for characteristics beyond their control. However, biological claims have proven problematic. It is just as likely that genetic discoveries would be used to "cure" homosexuality as that they would raise awareness or tolerance. Many lesbians, furthermore, do not experience their sexuality as inborn and beyond choice. Lesbian feminists, especially, often report coming out as a response to their experience of women's communities and feminist activism. Biological explanations actively distort such experiences and, thus, limit the range of lesbian politics, shifting discussions from matters of social structures such as patriarchy to questions of acceptance within existing society. *Shane Phelan*

### Bibliography

Ferguson, Kathy E. *The Man Question: Visions of Subjectivity in Feminist Theory*. Berkeley: University of California Press, 1993.

Fuss, Diana. *Essentially Speaking: Feminism, Nature, and Difference*. New York: Routledge, 1989.

Grahn, Judy. *Another Mother Tongue: Gay Worlds, Gay Words*. Boston: Beacon, 1983.

Stein, Edward, ed. *Forms of Desire: Sexual Orientation and the Social Constructionist Controversy*. New York: Garland, 1990.

Whisman, Vera. *Queer by Choice*. New York: Routledge, 1996.

*See also* Biological Determinism; Christina of Sweden; Etiology; Sexual Orientation and Preference; Social Construction Theory

# E

## Ethics

The search for wisdom in the conduct of life. Also known as moral philosophy, ethics traditionally studies the fundamental distinctions of right and wrong, good and bad, and being deserving of praise or blame that are used to evaluate choices, practices, experiences, states of affairs, agents, motives, and goals. Arising from reflection on everyday perplexities, its objective is to deepen one's understanding of normative and evaluative issues and to develop critical skills requisite to reaching a considered view of where wisdom lies. In this endeavor, lesbian ethics centers lesbian lives and the lesbian experiences (hopes, desires, relationships) of women generally. Lesbian ethics arises from contexts of woman hating, antilesbian violence, and lesbian resistance in struggles to form viable relationships and communities. Hostile environments have suppressed views from within lesbian communities of lesbian life, enforced female economic dependence on men, and made lesbians nearly inaccessible to one another. Against such histories, a major goal of lesbian ethics is to discover (or create) and affirm ways of life conducive to establishing and maintaining thriving lesbian connections.

Since the late 1970s, a substantial body of literature has developed in lesbian ethics, both abstract and concrete. Much of it is highly original, articulating alternatives to the ethics of heteropatriarchal sexual politics. The 1980s produced two journals of lesbian ethics (*Lesbian Ethics* [United States] and *Gossip: Journal of Lesbian Feminist Ethics* [United Kingdom]); feminist periodicals include articles in the area; anthologies and treatises have appeared increasingly since the late 1980s; and lesbian ethics has entered university curricula by way of feminist philosophy, gay studies, and women's studies courses in lesbian culture. Nor is lesbian ethics restricted to the printed word. Temporary lesbian communities, such as summer-camp festivals, and more enduring ones, such as land cooperatives, have been experiments in lesbian ethics, as have workshops and projects within them.

Lesbian ethics is not a particular theory or set of beliefs or practices, but a family of approaches to ethics. What makes these approaches lesbian are their paradigms and the lesbian experience that forms their starting points for reflection. This naturally gives lesbian ethics potential for great diversity. One way to understand some of that diversity is by way of the historical paradigms of amazons, sapphists, and passionate friends, which offer overlap-ping, but also divergent, conceptions of lesbian vitality. Amazon paradigms embrace the values of physical skill, mobility, self-government, and self-defense and are apt to be skeptical of commitments to nonviolence. Sapphic paradigms center the values of creativity, especially in the arts, and the erotic, which often inspires creativity. Passionate-friendship paradigms have a partnership focus, with long-range economic concerns and adjustments that domesticity entails. From sapphic standpoints, some lesbian ethics has been criticized as insufficiently attentive to sexuality. This criticism has produced interesting explorations of sexuality and the nature of lesbian bonding.

The meaning of "lesbian" is contested, as is what belongs in lesbian ethics. Some understand lesbian experience as that of those who identify as lesbians. Others count as relevant the lesbian experiences of women who do not identify as lesbian or even as bisexual. The latter tend to understand lesbian ethics as focusing on sexuality or erotic interaction, personal relationships, and social-policy questions pertaining to lesbian visibility. The former tend to have a wider view of lesbian ethics, understanding it as comprehensively as patriarchal ethics, as about all kinds of choices that lesbians face—for example, economic, educational, and dietary, as well as sexual. Regardless of how lesbian experience is defined, for ethics to *center* that experience and take it as a starting point for reflection on the conduct of life is both radical and revolutionary. Lesbian ethics as a new way of reflecting on norms and values is radical in that it goes to the roots of ethics and starts over. It is revolutionary in that basing ethical reflection on affirmed lesbian experience overturns heteropatriarchal norms and values.

Although not a theory, doctrine, or specific set of practices, lesbian ethics has been characterized by recurrent themes and topics. Topics include separatism, monogamy, sadomasochism, attitudes toward money, the significance of social class, the ethics of diet, intersections of racism with sexism and heterosexism, disability and being differently abled, fat oppression, butch and femme identities, horizontal violence in relationships, psychotherapy, and spirituality. Recurring themes include suspicion of rules, institutions, coercion, governments, hierarchies and competitions, and curiosity about the possibilities of friendship, anarchy, community, agency, empowerment, eroticism, and creativity. Like feminist ethics, lesbian ethics has been critical of traditions devaluing what is physical, emotional, material, transitory, the concrete particular—all identified in patriarchy with female-ness. Like environmental ethics, feminist and lesbian ethics have been characterized by tendencies toward holism, understanding individuals through their relationships as members of larger wholes.

Although most lesbian ethics is also feminist, much feminist ethics is not lesbian. Much feminist ethics takes heterosexual relationships as its paradigms of caring, embodying major power imbalances. Lesbian paradigms of caring tend to be of adult lovers, who are more balanced in power than parents and young children. Much feminist ethics has also tended more toward nonviolence than lesbian ethics, which draws on experiences of resisting antilesbian hostility.

Some lesbian ethics is also gay or queer, although most gay ethics is less theoretical and more concrete than lesbian ethics, as well as less revolutionary regarding established institutions such as law and the state, aiming more to integrate gays into the mainstream than to create alternatives. Queer ethics is more revolutionary and theoretical than gay ethics, but its paradigms are more diverse than those of either lesbian or gay ethics. Like gay ethics, queer ethics is less likely than lesbian ethics to give major weight to feminist concerns.      *Claudia Card*

## Bibliography

Allen, Jeffner, ed. *Lesbian Philosophies and Cultures*. Albany: State University of New York Press, 1990.

Calhoun, Cheshire. "Separating Lesbian Theory from Feminist Theory." *Ethics* 104 (1994), 558–581.

Card, Claudia. *Lesbian Choices*. New York: Columbia University Press, 1995.

Daly, Mary. *Gyn/Ecology: The Metaethics of Radical Feminism*. Boston: Beacon, 1978.

Hoagland, Sarah Lucia. *Lesbian Ethics: Toward New Value*. Palo Alto, Calif.: Institute for Lesbian Studies, 1988.

*Lesbian Ethics* (periodical), ed. Fox (pseud. of Jeanette Silveira). Albuquerque: LE Publications, 1984–.

**See also** Lesbian Feminism; Philosophy

## Etiology

Term referring both to the root cause of something (in this case, lesbianism) and to the scientific search for that cause. The dual meaning of the word points to a crucial recognition: Theories about the causes of lesbianism can be understood only by contextualizing them in a critical understanding of the sciences that have produced them. Far from neutral observers, these sciences have actively stigmatized lesbianism (and male homosexuality as well), treating it as a pathology at worst, a harmless deviance at best. They have, almost without exception, reinforced the dominance of heterosexuality by treating it as the normal pattern, therefore needing no explanation. As such, a history of the various etiologies of lesbianism is a history of the stigmatization of lesbianism and the various forms that stigmatization has taken in different historical contexts.

### History

The effort to locate the causes of lesbianism began in the late nineteenth century, perhaps as an adjunct to the larger effort to explain male homosexuality. At that time, the term "homosexuality" was used much less frequently than the term "invert." Inversion (also "the third sex") was understood as reversal of what would today be called one's gender role. The whole of a female invert's person was masculine, and a male invert's feminine, according to sexologists such as Havelock Ellis (1859–1939) and Richard von Krafft-Ebing (1840–1902). The female invert's attraction to women was merely one effect of her masculine nature. The ultimate cause of her masculinity was said by most to be congenital, whether characterized as a dangerous defect or an unfortunate variation. The key was located in the invert's body, most sexologists believed, and case studies generally included nude photographs and various physical measurements. Inversion theory could not account for the love of women among conventionally feminine women, who often were referred to as "the invert's partners" and portrayed as women passed over by men and then seduced by inverts.

Sigmund Freud's (1856–1939) theory, on the other hand, better accounted for feminine lesbians. Although he also used the term "invert," his understanding of the concept came much closer to what one would today call "homosexuality," because he distinguished between sexual preference and gender role (in his terms, "sexual object" and "sexual aim"). All persons, he believed, are capable of making a homosexual object choice, and, indeed, most have at some point in their development, meaning that the distinction between "normality" and "perversion" is a matter of degree. All aspects of adult sexuality, then, are acquired through the process of psychosexual development; even exclusive heterosexuality must be explained. Although he understood homosexuality as acquired, he firmly opposed psychoanalytic efforts to "cure" it, at least in men, believing these efforts to be both useless and unnecessary. His followers, however, particularly in the United States, would equate "acquired" with "changeable" by mid-century.

Clearly, the homosexuality concept accounted for a wider range of behaviors and identities than did the inversion concept. As such, sexologists abandoned inversion in the early twentieth century—in their studies of men. Studies of women continued to utilize the concept, because science was unable to see females as sexual subjects. Feminine sexuality was, by its nature, passive and receptive, they believed, and, as such, awakened only by the power of masculine sexuality. Two women, therefore, could not be sexual together unless one of them was essentially a man trapped in a woman's body. (This belief has been remarkably long lived; a popular sex advice book from 1969 stated: "One vagina plus another vagina equals zero.") In part for this reason, official explanations of lesbianism have continued to portray lesbianism as less common, less dangerous, and, at the same time, less comprehensible than male homosexuality.

By the mid-twentieth century, the accepted etiology of male homosexuality was psychoanalytic, minus Freud's own tolerant stance. Male homosexuality was understood to be the outcome of boyhood experience with a strong, overbearing mother and a weak, absent father. Most theories of this type ignored lesbianism; women appeared as the generators of deviance in their male children, not as deviants themselves. When psychoanalysts did attend to the etiology of lesbianism, they looked for its roots in the young girl's resolution of the oedipal complex, a process begun by her discovery that she lacks a penis—a shortchanging for which she blames her mother. Psychoanalysis predicted that a loving mother-daughter relationship would lead the girl to identify with her mother and transfer her desire for affection to her father and other males, while a lack of warmth in the mother-daughter relationship might consign the grown daughter to life as a lesbian, attempting to win the mother love she never had. Psychoanalysis, fresh from its successes in teaching the armed forces to detect homosexuality in its ranks, claimed to be able to cure lesbianism and male homosexuality.

## Contemporary Research and Theories

This link between theories of etiology and treatment regimes was severed in 1973 by the removal of homosexuality from the DSM III (third edition of the *Diagnostic and Statistical Manual* of the American Psychiatric Association). Beginning in the late 1960s and early 1970s, the behavioral and social sciences increasingly turned their backs on questions of etiology, producing instead more gay-positive, often gay-produced, research on issues of identity, community, history, and politics. The question most frequently asked about homosexuality throughout the twentieth century—What causes it?—was itself subjected to critical scrutiny, effectively for the first time. And lesbian feminist theorists, notably Adrienne Rich (1929–), broke with convention by examining the etiology of heterosexuality, seeing its institutionalization as a major force in the subordination of women (Rich 1980).

The question of homosexual etiology returned in the early 1980s with a Kinsey Institute study (Bell et al. 1981) that compared data collected from nearly 1,500 men and women and demonstrated that the psychoanalytic theories generated in the 1950s and 1960s did not match the evidence, striking perhaps the final blow against once widespread beliefs about the etiology of homosexuality. The Kinsey study, however, did not conclude that etiological questions were irrelevant or unanswerable, but it pointed prophetically toward biology as the most fertile ground for future research. Biological studies of the origins of homosexuality increased in number over the course of the 1980s; by the early 1990s, the search for the physical source of homosexuality had returned with force.

The biological research of the 1990s, however, differed from its early-twentieth-century precursors in that much, if not most, of the more recent research is the work of openly gay-identified men, and the results are widely hailed as gay affirmative. Like the earlier research, however, it is focused almost entirely on gay men. Only one of the widely reported research projects of the early 1990s focused on lesbians (Bailey et al. 1993). That small study of lesbians and their sisters found that lesbians' identical twin sisters were three times more likely also to be lesbians than lesbians' fraternal twin sisters. This study, a replication of an earlier study of gay men and their brothers, attracted relatively little media attention compared to the numerous reports of "the gay brain" and "the gay gene" that announced the work claiming to find a biological source for male homosexuality. A later study (McFadden and Pasanen, 1998) reported that a portion of the auditory systems of lesbian and bisexual women produced measurements at levels between those of heterosexual women and heterosexual men, echoing the inversion model of the early twentieth century. The researchers theorized that the inner ear, and other parts of the brain, were "masculinized" in these women by prenatal exposure to high levels of androgens.

The research remains controversial, and its authors have often been accused of making very large claims based on very modest results; Bailey et al.'s lesbian twin study, for example, found that, of identical twin sisters of lesbians, just over half were not lesbians themselves, despite sharing identical genetic blueprints. Such research may also be flawed in the same manner as most research on homosexual etiology, by treating homosexuality as a unitary phenomenon, with a single root cause.

Whatever the scientific pros and cons of this body of research, it is clear that its social and political meanings are complex. Many claim that the identification of a biological etiology for homosexuality will set the stage for true equality for lesbians and gay men. Adherents to this view cite a March 1993 *New York Times*/CBS opinion poll that found a correlation between gay-positive attitudes and the belief that one is "born gay." Critics point out that such attitudinal correlations may be fleeting, especially given the widespread desire to develop "cures" for socially unacceptable behaviors and identities; these critics hold that, since the etiological question is itself profoundly heterosexist, no answer to it can be truly liberatory. Clearly, questions of the etiology of lesbianism are not part of some value-free search for pure knowledge but, rather, socially and politically significant discourses that go to the heart of heterosexism and homophobia in the modern West.                              *Vera Whisman*

## Bibliography

Abelove, Henry. "Freud, Male Homosexuality, and the Americans." *Dissent* (Winter 1985–1986), 59–69.

Bailey, J. Michael, Richard C. Pillard, Michael C. Neale, and Yvonne Agyei. "Heritable Factors Influencing Sexual Orientation in Women." *Ar-chives of General Psychiatry* 50:3 (1993), 217–223.

Bell, Alan P., Martin S. Weinberg, and Sue Kiefer Hammersmith. *Sexual Preference: Its Development in Men and Women*. Bloomington: Indiana University Press, 1981.

Chauncey, George, J. "From Sexual Inversion to Homosexuality: Medicine and the Changing Conceptualization of Female Deviance." *Salmagundi* 58–59 (Fall/Winter 1982–1983), 114–146.

Freud, Sigmund. *Three Essays on the Theory of Sexuality*. New York: Basic Books, 1962.

McFadden, Dennis, and Edward G. Pasanen. "Comparisons of the Auditory Systems of Heterosexuals and Homosexuals: Click-Evoked Otoacoustic Emissions." *Proceedings of the National Academy of Sciences* 95 (1998), 2709–2713.

Rich, Adrienne. "Compulsory Heterosexuality and Lesbian Existence." *Signs: Journal of Women in Culture and Society* 5:4 (1980), 631–660.

*See also* Biological Determinism; Heterosexuality; Homosexuality; Kinsey Institute; Psychoanalysis; Sexology; Sexual Orientation and Preference

## Europe, Early Modern

A period (ca. A.D. 1500–1700) and an area including those countries from England and Ireland in the west to Russia in the east, and Norway and Denmark in the north to Spain and Italy in the south. Throughout Europe, this period was characterized, on the one hand, by harsh denunciation and punishment for "lesbian" activity and, on the other hand, by the official invisibility, and hence the possibility, of many forms of female emotional and erotic attachment. During this era, erotic life was not organized around an essential and exclusive division of homo- and heterosexual; neither male nor female homosexuality existed as separate categories of self-identification. Other social categories—one's position in the household, marital status, age, relation to work, lineage, and property—located people within their culture. This does not mean that women did not experience homoerotic desire or engage in a variety of same-gender erotic activities. A sparse, if conceptually rich and varied, history of same-gender erotic representations is evident in a range of discourses. Authorities in most European societies were concerned about the threat certain activities—particularly those that involved cross-gendered behaviors—

*Parmigianino, Francesco Mazzola. Nymphs, and Diana as a Stag. Vault, detail from* The Fable of Diana and Acteon. *Villa del Sanvitale, Fontanellato, Italy. Alinari/Art Resource, NY.*

might pose to patriarchal authority. At the same time, other behaviors that seem manifestly "lesbian" to twentieth-century minds did not cause social concern and were compatible with the heterosexual, patriarchal family. The early-modern period presents a heterogeneous social situation in which a cultural imperative not to acknowledge female-female eroticism increasingly conflicted with emerging disciplines dedicated to constituting and governing morality and knowledge.

Scholars of the early-modern period confront a crucial question: how to recognize and articulate women's homoerotic desires in a culture in which women's recorded voices are largely silent about sexuality. The small percentage of women who could read and write were in a position neither to define the scope of legitimate erotic activity nor to explicitly record their experiences. Consequently, most representations of women's desires and behaviors are male authored and reveal a great deal about masculine ignorance of female sexuality and fears of female erotic autonomy. However, information gleaned from historical sources, including the existence of terms such as "rubster," "frigging," *ribaude, tribade, fricatrice,* and *donna con*

*donna* and allusions to Sappho of Lesbos (ca. 600 B.C.E.), provides clues to the ways in which same-gender female desires were understood. It remains impossible, however, and perhaps unwise, to delineate a firm line between fact and fiction, representation and reality. What one can access are cultural discourses, not the "truth" of early-modern lesbianism.

## Legal Discourses

Two discourses usually deemed authoritative regarding the status of nonnormative erotic activity, the law and church doctrine, were interdependent in the early-modern period, although, in many countries, authority was beginning to be transferred from ecclesiastic to secular bodies. In general, both secular and church statutes proscribed nonreproductive erotic acts, the purpose of sex understood to be the propagation of humankind. Romans 1:26–27 provided biblical authority for condemning sodomy, a catchall category for nonprocreative sex. Under the category of sodomy, a multiplicity of erotic acts and positions were criminalized, including anal penetration and masturbation, as well as bestiality, rape, and child molestation.

Whereas, in most European states, sodomy garnered the death penalty for those convicted, not every state's sodomy statute mentioned same-gender female erotic activity. In addition, when women were brought before secular or religious authorities, it often was because they had gained local notoriety through cross-dressing, prostitution, vagrancy, or dissenting religious beliefs. Inconsistent use of the accusation of sodomy and selective sentencing rendered the status of female-female eroticism indeterminate. Christian doctrine generally viewed women as oversexed—inherently promiscuous, fallible, and unable to control their erotic urges. Yet, in contrast to the high incidence of prosecution for prostitution, adultery, bastardy, and witchcraft, few women were prosecuted for sodomy in this period.

In 1532, the Constitution of the Holy Roman Empire made sex between women a capital crime. The 1533 English Act of Parliament that made buggery (anal penetration) punishable by death did not mention women, and Sir Edward Coke (1552–1634), a prominent English jurist, opined a century later that, if women committed buggery, it was by having sex with an animal. In Scotland in 1625 the Glasgow Presbytery charged two women with sodomy and demanded that they separate from each other upon pain of excommunication. A handful of French women were prosecuted: The jurist Jean Papon documented the arrest of two women in Toulouse but implied that inadequate evidence prevented them from being put to death; Henri Estienne (1531–1598) recounted the burning of a woman in the 1530s for cross-dressing and marrying; and, in 1580, Michel de Montaigne (1533–1592) recorded the execution of another cross-dressed female "husband." In Augsburg, the Discipline Ordinance of 1537 condemned "damned, forbidden copulation" (referring to the provision of imperial law), but only one woman is thought to have been prosecuted. Likewise, only one Swiss woman was brought to trial for sodomy in Geneva between 1440 and 1789. In the Netherlands, several cross-dressers accused of "carnal conversation" with other women were whipped and exiled, although a sodomy bill was not passed in the province of Holland until 1730—and it did not mention women. In Spain, the thirteenth-century legal code known as *las siete partidas* (the seven laws) made "sins against nature" a capital crime, but it wasn't until the mid-sixteenth century that a legal gloss proposed extending the death penalty to women, and two Spanish nuns accused of using genital "instruments" were burned at the stake. Whereas sodomy often was referred to as the "Florentine vice," and throughout Italy the punishment for sodomy was burning at the stake, no documented executions of Italian women took place, although a Pescian nun, Benedetta Carlini (1590–1661), was imprisoned for thirty-five years for a variety of evil deeds, including physical intimacy with another nun.

Uniquely in Europe, Russia during the Muscovite period (fourteenth–eighteenth centuries) enacted no secular legislation prohibiting same-gender erotic activity. Of concern to Eastern Orthodox ecclesiastical authorities was the relative position of sexual partners: Two women together (or two men) were no more sinful than a woman on top of a man. With same-gender contact a sin rather than a crime, the recommended penance was confession, prostrations, exclusion from communion, and dietary abstentions. When, in 1706, Russian laws penalized male sodomy, no mention was made of women.

Although Jewish women were subject to the laws of the Christian states in which they resided, rabbinical commentary on the Old Testament possessed considerable authority in observant communities. The few rabbinic sources that discuss women's same-gender erotic practices imply that the primary concern was the transgression involved in a woman "taking the part" of a man in sexual acts or "taking the part" of the husband in marrying; both gender transgressions are proscribed.

Selective enforcement of sodomy laws, when read in the context of court testimony, suggests that the primary concern of authorities was women's usurpation of masculine prerogatives, whether in the form of cross-dressing and passing as a man, the use of instruments of genital penetration, or other challenges to patriarchal authority. When women were prosecuted, the woman who cross-dressed or used penetrative devices invariably received harsher punishment than her more "feminine" partner. The near-inconceivability of eroticism without a phallus meant that a range of female erotic activities often escaped official censure.

## Medical Discourses

In 1700, the Italian theologian Lodovico Maria Sinistrari, counselor to the Holy Inquisition, offered the most extended discussion of female sodomy to date. Defining sodomy as the insertion of a body part into the wrong vessel, he argued that only women with

**E** enlarged clitorises could commit sodomy; in fact, the presence of clitoral hypertrophy implied a presumption of guilt. Genital rubbing and the insertion of fingers or dildos he defined as mere acts of pollution, sins for which one could be absolved. Sinistrari's definition of sodomy drew from emerging medical theories about the female body. The early-modern period saw the emergence of two new discourses that were preoccupied with the construction of normative bodies: anatomies and midwiferies, and travel narratives. In particular, the "rediscovery" of the clitoris in 1559 by two Italian anatomists, Realdo Colombo (1516?–1559) and Gabriele Fallopius (1523–1562), led to the dissemination of pseudomedical ideas that linked the presence of an enlarged clitoris with "tribadism." The *tribade* (a French term derived from the Greek *tribas* and *tribein* [to rub]—hence the Latin *fricatrix*, the French *ribaude*, and the English "rubster") referred to a woman who derived pleasure from genital rubbing (frigging) and/or penetration.

The ancient Greeks viewed the tribade as a hypermasculine woman who penetrated women or *men* by means of a dildo or an enlarged clitoris; it was not until late antiquity that the tribade was associated exclusively with same-gender erotic practices. The accessibility of classical views on this subject, however, was limited until the sixteenth century, when classical texts not only became more available, but also were translated into the vernacular. Although medieval medicine was largely unconcerned with female erotic deviancy, this attitude changed as anatomists drew from Greek and Arab texts, augmenting classical knowledge with information culled from anatomical dissection. With the publication of anatomies and midwiferies, as well as narratives written by European travelers to the east and the south, the concept of tribadism was reintroduced to western Europe. At first, these works attributed tribadism to non-Christian women residing in Turkey and Africa, describing the erotic misdeeds of women in the Sultan's seraglio, the Turkish baths, and the Moroccan marketplace. By the mid-seventeenth century, in response to the promulgation of sensationalistic accounts, writers expressed fears about the existence of tribades in their own countries. The dissemination of these discourses had a contradictory effect: On the one hand, women's same-gender erotic activity was harshly stigmatized; on the other hand, more and more varied descriptions of female deviance were made culturally available. It is at this time that the term "lesbian"

first began to circulate as a marker of same-gender erotic practices. (Previously, references to "lesbian" located Sappho as a native of the island Lesbos; Sappho was known primarily as a prostitute, and lesbian sex referred to fellatio.) These discourses came close to constructing a specific bodily morphology for deviant behavior and, with it, competing models of causality, as authors debated: Did an enlarged clitoris incite unnatural lust, or did sexual "abuse" of a clitoris cause it to grow monstrously large?

As these medical discourses make clear, the history of women's same-gender eroticism is closely related to, though not identical with, the phenomena of gender transformation, hermaphroditism, and gender transitivity. Medical texts debated whether anatomical transformations from female to male were possible, with many writers arguing that such cases were actually instances of tribadism: Rather than the spontaneous eruption of a penis due to sudden motion or increased body heat, the problematic "member" was a prolapsed vagina or an enlarged clitoris. Hermaphrodites were also linked to tribadism in legal practice, with true hermaphroditism legally and socially tolerated. When accused of tribadism or sodomy, the defendant might undergo a medical examination; if the probing of a midwife or a physician revealed the presence of both penis and vagina, the hermaphrodite usually was allowed to choose a gender identity. As long as she/he did not switch back and forth, and gender appropriate clothing was worn, she/he was allowed to marry. Rabbis permitted marriage between an *androgunos* (one who possesses both penis and vagina) and a woman but prohibited such marriages with a man: Two penises, apparently, were considered too many in one marriage.

**Cross-Dressing**

Whatever the actual numbers of hermaphrodites or women with clitoral hypertrophy, cross-dressed women on the streets of European cities, ships, and the New World were numerous enough to elicit both celebration and censure. Popular street ballads, broadsheets, and prose narratives—and at least one autobiographical memoir, written by a cross-dressing Basque conquistador—extolled the successful exploits of female soldiers and sailors, although some also resorted to scorn and bawdy hilarity when sexual irregularities were suspected. James I of England and Scotland (1566–1625) instructed clergymen to preach against female transvestism (despite the fact that sumptuary legislation referred only to class infractions), and, in many continental countries, cross-dressing, often considered a form of fraud, was a serious offense. Whereas many cross-dressers adopted masculine clothing and/or identities for economic gain or adventure, some were motivated by their attachments to other women. Indeed, there are several anecdotal accounts of French cross-dressers marrying, and one English court document details the annulment of a marriage between a woman and her "female husband."

While there is no sure corollary between occasional cross-dressing, a lifetime of passing as a man, and the theatrical stage, the high incidence of transvestism as a plot device in Spanish Golden Age and English Renaissance and Restoration drama and pastoral romance allowed for the exploration of homoerotic desires in popular venues. Although English authorities who denounced the Renaissance stage often did so by emphasizing the abomination of boy actors playing the parts of women, writers throughout Europe (William Shakespeare [1564–1616], Edmund Spenser [1552–1599], Sir Philip Sidney [1554–1586], John Lyly [1554?–1606], Margaret Cavendish [1623–1673], Ludovico Ariosto [1474–1533], Lope de Vega [1562–1635], and Jorge de Montemayor [ca. 1520–1561]) included cross-dressed heroines in their plots, often exploring the varieties of attraction such characters elicited and experienced, even as they concluded their narratives with heterosexual marriage.

## Single Women

Cross-dressing, or passing, allowed some women to marry the women they loved; it also allowed some to remain unmarried in a culture that mandated the transfer of daughters directly from the governance of a father to the protection of a husband. In spite of this dictate, approximately 20 percent of adult women in northwestern Europe never married; in addition, in those states in which it was a legal option, many women filed for separation from husbands, and a large percentage of widows never remarried. Single women, particularly those in urban centers, often worked outside the home, sometimes in all-female guilds. Although many of these women lived in their father's or brother's households, others lived together, often under the auspices of charitable communities (Beguinages, widows hospices, houses for reformed prostitutes, hospitals for poor and immigrant women). Just as many of these women experienced strong affective, and possibly erotic, rela-

tionships, so, too, does evidence of material and emotional support networks among prostitutes suggest that brothels may have been an important locale for female-female bonds.

When early-modern women stepped too far outside patriarchal control, they were vulnerable to the accusation of witchcraft. Insofar as witchcraft in women was seen as stemming from lust, allegations of a variety of diabolic sexual acts peppered church writings and legal testimonies. Whereas the concern of ecclesiastical authorities was primarily intercourse with the devil, occasionally they accused suspected witches of "vices against nature." Russian churchmen connected same-gender eroticism to pagan rites in which women prayed to a female spirit. Stories about witches in Fez who seduced innocent wives first circulated in travel narratives and were reprinted in various venues.

Perhaps the most amenable site for single women's mutual affection was the convent. Nunneries offered women a refuge from marriage, as well as opportunities for political, emotional, and erotic independence. The Catholic Church's valorization of chastity, which caused women to be sequestered from men, unwittingly created conditions enabling female attachments; and, insofar as chastity referred explicitly to the protection of one's hymen from phallic penetration, a variety of pleasurable activities may have been "innocently" pursued. In recognition of the possibility of same-gender contact, monastic rules prohibited nuns from sleeping together and mandated that a lamp burn in sleeping quarters. One of the most complete documents detailing same-gender erotic activity, from a series of ecclesiastical investigations (1619–1623) of an Italian abbess, Benedetta Carlini, suggests that erotic contact among nuns could be considered by them to be compatible with religious expression. Certainly, the allegation of erotic deviance among nuns was a staple of anti-Catholic satire; and the lust of an older nun for a novice crops up frequently in Renaissance pornography.

## Literary Representations

The ideology of chastity is also implicated in the intense emotional and erotic friendships depicted in Renaissance drama. In countless stage plays, friendships between two "feminine" girls are depicted as technically chaste, yet emotionally and erotically charged. The unity, mutuality, and affection of such friends is idealized and portrayed as a foil to heterosexual antagonism; at the same time, such bonds are represented as temporary, inevitably giving way to patriarchal marriage. Often located in the past, these relations are not threatening precisely because, in the social scheme of heterosexual reproduction and affiliation, they are deemed insignificant. These literary representations correspond to certain material conditions: Throughout Europe, girls of premarital age "innocently" shared beds with friends and servants; girls in schools and convents developed intense affections; and popular mock wedding games among adolescent Russian and Italian girls were tolerated.

The popularity of classical mythology in the early-modern period also allowed for the representation of same-gender female desire, particularly in retellings and artistic renderings of the stories of Iphis and Ianthe and the goddess Diana and her female followers. Francesco Cavalli (1602–1676), for instance, centered his 1651 opera *La Calisto* on a handmaid's love for Diana, exploiting homoerotic sensuality in order to condemn it. Particularly in Italy, where women's erotic affairs were termed *donna con donna*, paintings of nude goddesses and their attendants visually registered the possibility of women's erotic self-sufficiency. These images, like expressions of intense female friendship in stage plays, were widely available to female spectators.

By the late seventeenth century, women's literacy had substantially increased. Some of the poetry women penned celebrated female friendship in terms that are emotionally and erotically charged. Katherine Philips (1632–1664), known as "the English Sappho," and the Dutch Catharina Questiers (1630–1669) and Cornelia van der Veer (1639–1702) appropriated neo-Platonic and Petrarchan conventions to express the strength of their affections, to argue for the superiority of female friendship over that of men, and to lament interruptions in relationships caused by marriage. An earlier anonymous Middle Scots poem, known only as Poem XLIX in *The Maitland Quarto Manuscript* (1586), similarly articulates a conflict between intense female bonds and marriage and may have been written by a woman. Margaret Cavendish and Aphra Behn (ca. 1640?–1689) flirted with female homoeroticism in many plays and poems.

Not all literary images of same-gender love were so idealized. The older female procuress, a staple figure of comic and satiric literature, often is represented as providing hands-on instruction of sexual technique to novice prostitutes. Satire about same-gender activities among prostitutes frequently crossed over into the pornographic, with salacious descriptions of activities ostensibly being denounced. Pornographic titillation is also evident in medical dictionaries and marital-advice books, which included explicit descriptions of female anatomy and women's erotic activities. Such texts were available in the vernacular by the end of the seventeenth century and circulated among an increasingly large reading population.

Also satirized, or at least a subject of gossip, were the erotic liaisons of aristocratic, and sometimes royal, women. The attachments of Queen Christina of Sweden (1626–1689), who abdicated rather than marry, and the English Queen Anne (1665–1714), as well as of the ladies at the French court of Henri II (1547–1559) and the English court of Charles II (1660–1685), were notorious in their day. Although these women's erotic proclivities were satirized by those critical of the monarch's reign, aristocratic libertinage often was crucial to the deployment of power, patronage, and influence.

The morality of the middle classes, however, was not so permissive. Throughout the seventeenth century, changes in religious ideologies contributed to more overt censure of same-gender attachments. In Protestant countries, a developing bourgeois ideology of "companionate marriage," which advocated the spiritual union, mutual comfort, and emotional dependence of husband and wife, idealized the marital bond as the unique site of erotic desire. While the success of this ideology was probably never as great as was advocated, its popularity contributed to a clearer distinction between female homoeroticism and heterosexuality. Conversely, in Catholic countries the Counterreformation Church took an increasingly strict line on nonprocreative sexuality, with much the same result as its Protestant counterparts: a more precise articulation of marital heterosexuality as the only proper mode of eroticism.

### Conclusion

The sum of these representations reveals that early-modern culture recognized a range of erotic activities in which women may have engaged: kissing, caressing, clitoral rubbing, mutual masturbation, penetration (with dildo, finger, or enlarged clitoris). In addition to this taxonomy of practices, a catalog of persons and relations includes the single woman, the transvestite, the *tribade*, the intimate female friend, the aristocratic libertine, and *donna con donna*. Locales consistently associated with same-gender erotic activity are nunneries, brothels, and the Turkish harem and bath. Most early-modern writers posited women's illicit erotic behaviors as a disturbance in gender—whether such a disturbance be anatomical (the presence of an enlarged clitoris or the presence of a penis and a vagina) or social (wearing male clothing, using a dildo). Two dominant theories of causality intermingled in the early-modern period: While theologians, jurists, and moralists typically viewed women's deviant sexual behavior as one of a host of possible moral failings (prostitution, vagrancy, witchcraft, resistance to patriarchal authority), medical and popular knowledge tended to ascribe to at least some women an anatomical aberration that caused them to engage in unnatural acts. Debates about innate propensity versus the effect of social conditions occasionally were punctuated with astrological theories. In the case of the tribade, the supposition was not that she was a woman with male genitals nor a male trapped inside a female body, but a woman whose bodily morphology incited a usurpation of masculine prerogatives.

Conventional historical periods often do not correspond to the realities of women's lives. A case in point is the Renaissance, an era that is lauded as a high point of creativity and progress but that also saw the tightening of patriarchal controls upon women. If, however, one marks the beginning of the early-modern period with the gradual increase in the early sixteenth century of vernacular discourses about, and inconsistent prosecution of, female sodomy, one registers the conceptual incoherence that attended same-gender female eroticism throughout the sixteenth and seventeenth centuries. Likewise, one might mark the period's end with Sinistrari's attempt, at the beginning of the eighteenth century, to codify and correlate specific erotic practices with precise punishments. The amplification and cross-fertilization of legal, theological, medical, and literary discourses; the dissemination of images of tribades to an increasingly literate populace through pornography, sexual-advice books, travel narratives, anatomies, midwiferies, and classical texts; the greater inclusion of women in artistic, literary, and scientific production—all of these were in play by the end of the seventeenth century. It is not until the rise of Enlightenment discourses of selfhood in the eigh-

teenth century, however, that new ways of conceptualizing the individual would create the conditions for the emergence of modern categories of erotic identity.                                    *Valerie Traub*

## Bibliography

Ballaster, Ros. " 'The Vices of Old Rome Revived': Representations of Same-Sex Desire in Seventeenth- and Eighteenth-Century England." In *Volcanoes and Pearl Divers: Essays in Lesbian Feminist Studies*. Ed. Suzanne Raitt. London: Onlywomen, 1994, pp. 3–36.

Brown, Judith. *Immodest Acts: The Life of a Lesbian Nun in Renaissance Italy*. Oxford: Oxford University Press, 1986.

Donoghue, Emma. *Passions Between Women: British Lesbian Culture, 1668–1801*. New York: HarperCollins, 1993.

Faderman, Lillian. *Surpassing the Love of Men: Romantic Friendship and Love Between Women, from the Renaissance to the Present*. New York: William Morrow, 1981.

Park, Katharine. "The Rediscovery of the Clitoris: French Medicine and the Tribade, 1570–1620." In *The Body in Parts: Discourses and Anatomies in Early Modern Europe,* Ed. Carla Mazzio and David Hillman. New York: Routledge, 1997, pp. 170–193.

Simons, Patricia. "Lesbian (In)Visibility in Italian Renaissance Culture: Diana and Other Cases of Donna con Donna." *Journal of Homosexuality* 27 (1994), 81–122.

Traub, Valerie. "The (In)Significance of 'Lesbian' Desire in Early Modern England." In *Erotic Politics: Desire on the Renaissance Stage*. Ed. Susan Zimmerman. London and New York: Routledge, 1994, pp. 150–169.

———. "The Psychomorphology of the Clitoris." *GLQ: A Journal of Lesbian and Gay Studies* 2 (Winter 1995), 81–113.

Vicinus, Martha. " 'They Wonder to Which Sex I Belong': The Historical Roots of the Modern Lesbian Identity." In *The Lesbian and Gay Studies Reader*. Ed. Henry Abelove, Michele Aina Barale, and David M. Halperin. New York and London: Routledge, 1993, pp. 432–452.

***See also*** Anne, Queen of England; Behn, Aphra; Christina of Sweden; Clitoris; Cross-Dressing; Law and Legal Institutions; Passing Women; Religious Communities; Sappho; Tribade

## E Evolution and Human Origins

Female-female bonding and sexual behavior in human evolution. Narratives of human evolution are powerful statements about what will and what will not count as human. The emergence of a distinctively human society has been argued to reside in the development of male-male social bonding and male-female sexual pair bonding. Relationships between females have been regarded as inconsequential to the course of human evolution. In this context, female sexuality has been regarded as a response to male behavior, so assertive female sexual behaviors such as lesbianism could exist only as unnatural, unhuman aberrations.

This orthodoxy is beginning to crumble. Since the 1970s, the visibility of women in narratives of human evolution has been increasing. Some authors now credit women with having influenced the course of evolution in their capacities as economic providers, inventors of tools, mothers, and assertive sexual beings actively seeking out and selecting preferred male partners. However, the idea that female sexual interest in other females could have affected human evolution remains unconsidered. This omission is not, however, due to a lack of potential information. There is an ever-expanding body of data documenting the widespread occurrence of female-female sexual practices in both past and present human communities and in nonhuman primate societies. The real problem lies in the unquestioned assumption that, in order to count in evolution, sex must be reproductive and, therefore, heterosexual.

Once art appears at around 100,000 years ago, direct archaeological evidence for lesbianism in the form of artistic depictions becomes a possibility. There are, for example, one-thousand-to-two-thousand-year-old Moche pots from Peru that depict women engaging in sexual acts with other women. But for the approximately five million years of human evolution taking place prior to the appearance of art, the material consists of fossilized bones and stone tools. Such remains offer few insights into the social and sexual behavior of our earliest ancestors, so indirect forms of evidence are sought. The most important sources are anthropology and primatology. Anthropology, the study of human societies past and present, has documented the enormous variety of forms that human social and sexual behavior can take. Primatology, the study of nonhuman primates, has documented the amazing diversity of social and sexual behaviors exhibited in present-day

primate societies. It is in the similarities and differences between modern human and nonhuman primate behaviors that we now seek to define the social and sexual parameters of human evolution.

## Nineteenth-Century Foundations

During the nineteenth century, speculation about the origins of humanity became intense. People looked to the Bible, classical myths, and ancient law for clues to their distant past. The most influential theorists of the time, the social evolutionists, argued that all societies progressed through universal stages of development, culminating in the nuclear family and Western civil society. Progression in sexual behavior involved the gradual abandonment of promiscuous sexual mating in favor of pair bonding, or monogamy, an arrangement that assured men control over woman's sexual and reproductive capacities. Already implicit here is the assumption that the only purpose of sex is reproduction and that it is, therefore, exclusively heterosexual.

Charles Darwin (1809–1882), founder of biological evolution and contemporary of the social evolutionists, argued that all organisms, including humans, evolved by natural selection, a process regulated by competition rather than progress. Later, Darwin added sexual selection to account for the development of different characteristics in males and females. Males, he argued, invested in sex and competed for access to females, while females invested in parenting and selected mates from among available males. Thus, males and females had different reproductive strategies and pursued different sexual interests. Sexual selection allowed, for the first time, the possibility that female sexuality had its own agenda.

## Anthropological Challenges

The twentieth century saw the rise of anthropology and the publication of detailed ethnographic accounts of human societies from all over the world. The widespread occurrence of all kinds of nonreproductive sex, including lesbianism, was recorded. However, neither anthropological theory nor narratives of human evolution made any attempt to account for them.

Kinship theory, for example, argued that the invention of incest taboos enabled men to give up their sisters for the promise of future wives, thus explaining the evolution of both male-male bonding and male-female sexual pair bonds. The relentlessly patriarchal and heterosexist nature of this theory was fruitlessly pointed out by Rubin (1975). Another line of argument promoted hunting as the key invention that led to a uniquely human society. In this scenario, male bonding developed in the cooperative context of hunting and led to the sharing of meat with dependent females and, hence, to heterosexual monogamy. Even though the ethnographic accounts of nonagricultural societies on which this theory was based showed that women gathered more than their fair share of food and supported not only their children but commonly also their menfolk, the hunting theory remained popular in the 1990s.

## Primatological Challenges

During the 1970s, results from long-term studies of nonhuman primates living in wild habitats began to demonstrate just how diverse and complex nonhuman primate societies are. Contrary to expectations, the most important and enduring relationships, aside from mother-offspring bonds, form between female kin. Enduring bonds between males are extremely rare, while enduring male-female bonds are neither common nor necessarily based on sex. These discoveries transformed appreciation of the importance of female-female bonding in nonhuman primate societies. Around the same time, the development of sociobiology from Darwin's theories of natural and sexual selection kindled new interest in the evolutionary implications of assertive female sexualities. However, sociobiologists foreclosed on the radical potential of these implications by entrenching their investigations within the sex-equals-reproduction equation. They allow females their own sexuality, but it must be reproductive and heterosexual. For a lesbian perspective on human evolution to emerge, new ideas on female-female bonding and assertive female sexuality need to come together in the absence of this reproductive imperative.

## Developments in the 1990s

The geographical and historical diversity of sexual practices and gender arrangements in human societies is a major area of research. It is striking, however, that literature on male homosexuality is far more extensive than on lesbianism (see Herdt 1996). Nevertheless, acknowledgment of the cross-cultural extent of same-sex practices has still not engendered interest in how such behaviors might have influenced human evolution. The assumption remains: If it made no contribution to reproduction, it made no contribution to directing the past.

As with human societies, the diversity of non-reproductive sexual behaviors in nonhuman primate societies is the most striking pattern to emerge. However, female-female sexuality has received the most attention. For example, among common chimpanzees sex occurs only at irregular intervals and nonreproductive sex is rare, while among Bonobo chimpanzees sex of every imaginable kind takes place almost continually. Female-female sex between nonkin partners is the most common form. These sexual exchanges enable Bonobo females to dominate males—an inconceivable occurrence among common chimpanzees. The macaque monkeys are just as diverse. Japanese macaque females engage in sex with nonkin female partners simply because they like the sex. Furthermore, they will aggressively defend these relationships against male competitors. Stumptail macaques similarly like the sex but do not hesitate to use female-female sexual interactions for social purposes, such as peacemaking and reconciliation and to improve their social prospects.

It seems likely that female-female sexual behaviors evolved as part of the pleasurable potentialities of sex. No further function needs to be invoked to explain their occurrence. That does not mean, however, that such behaviors were never co-opted to serve social or reproductive ends. In some contexts and at some times, female-female sexual behaviors no doubt contributed to some females' reproductive success either directly through parenting or indirectly through improving an individual's social position. But the contribution of female-female sexuality to evolution cannot be reduced to these instances. No human society is reducible to its means of physical reproduction; neither, then, is the course of human evolution.     *Yvonnne M. Marshall*

## Bibliography

Arboleda, Manuel. "Representations Artisticas de Actividades Homoeroticas en la Ceramica Moche" (Artistic Representations of Homoerotic Activities in Moche Pottery). *Boletin de Lima* 16 (1981), 98–107.

Hager, Lori D., ed. *Women in Human Evolution.* London: Routledge, 1997.

Herdt, Gilbert, ed. *Third Sex, Third Gender: Beyond Sexual Dimorphism in Culture and History.* New York: Zone, 1996.

Rubin, Gayle. "The Traffic in Women: Notes on the Political Economy of Sex." In *Towards an Anthropology of Women.* Ed. Rayna Reuter.

New York: Monthly Review Press, 1975, pp. 157–210.

Taylor, T. *The Prehistory of Sex*. New York: Bantam, 1996.

Vasey, Paul. "Intimate Sexual Relations in Prehistory: Lessons from the Japanese Macaques." *World Archaeology* 29 (1998), 3.

Wolfe, Linda D. "Human Evolution and the Sexual Behaviour of Female Primates." In *Understanding Behaviour*. Ed. James D. Loy and Calvin B. Peters. Oxford: Oxford University Press, 1991, pp. 121–189.

***See also*** Animal Studies; Anthropology

# F

## Faderman, Lillian (1940–)

Historian, literary critic, and educator. Born in New York City to a Latvian-Jewish mother, Faderman never knew her father. She was raised by her mother and aunt in the working-class neighborhoods of the Bronx, New York, and East Los Angeles, California, where they moved in 1948. Faderman's first language was Yiddish. In her first major book, *Surpassing the Love of Men: Romantic Friendship and Love Between Women from the Renaissance to the Present* (1981), Faderman defines "lesbian" as a relationship that is not necessarily sexual, "in which two women's strongest emotions and affections are directed toward each other." In the years since its publication, *Surpassing* has been cited widely, interpreted variously, and sometimes misrepresented and attacked as "antisex." The book is roughly contemporary with Adrienne Rich's similarly controversial conception of a "lesbian continuum." In *Odd Girls and Twilight Lovers* (1991), Faderman reiterates the themes of *Surpassing* before moving on to a decade-by-decade account of U.S. lesbian culture in the twentieth century.

Both *Odd Girls* and *Surpassing* received many accolades, including appearing on the *New York Times Book Review* list of Notable Books for 1992 and 1981, respectively. Faderman's other lesbian-themed books include *Scotch Verdict* (1983), a reconstruction of the scandal on which Lillian Hellman (1905–1984) based *The Children's Hour* (1934), and the anthologies *Lesbian Feminism in Turn-of-the-Century Germany* (with Brigitte Ericksson [1980]), reprinted in 1990 as *Lesbians in Germany, 1890s–1920s,* and *Chloe Plus Olivia: Lesbian Literature from the Seventeenth Century to the Present* (1994). Faderman lectures widely and has served on the boards of several lesbian and gay organizations and publications.

After receiving her B.A. in English from the University of California, Berkeley in 1962, Faderman earned her M.A. in 1964 and Ph.D. in 1967 in English at the University of California, Los Angeles. In 1967, she joined the English faculty of California State University, Fresno, where she has continued to teach. She was among the group that founded the CSU Fresno Women's Studies Program in 1971, as was her life partner, Phyllis Irwin

*Lillian Faderman. Photo by Phyllis Irwin.*

**F** (1929–), a classical pianist and professor of music; they met in Fresno in 1971. Faderman gave birth to their son, Avrom Faderman, in 1975.

*Linda Garber*

### Bibliography

Wiley, Catherine A. "Lillian Faderman." In *Gay and Lesbian Biography*. Ed. Michael J. Tyrkus. Detroit: St. James, 1997, pp. 160–163.

*See also* Lesbian Continuum; Rich, Adrienne; Romantic Friendship

## Family

In both traditional scholarship and popular ideology, family membership is defined by biology (parent/child, aunt, sibling, and so on) and/or by legal relationship (marriage and adoption). Within that framework, lesbians and gay men are portrayed as being outside of family, leading lives devoid of permanent attachments. Yet lesbians and gay men are involved in a myriad of relationships that exist both within and outside biology and the law. Despite the risks of rejection, they continue to come out and to find support and love, both within and beyond their families of origin. As well, despite the legal and historical denial of their intimate relationships, many choose to define these connections as family.

In contemporary Western society, the family has become contested terrain. Groups ranging from political parties on the Left and the Right to a host of religious denominations claim ownership of the "traditional" family. Such claims rest on the reification and universalization of the male breadwinner/female homemaker family. This particular family form was, in fact, a demographic anomaly of the 1950s and early 1960s. Indeed, even in that narrow time period, vast portions of the population did not mirror the image of family projected on popular television programs like *Leave It to Beaver*. Single-parent families, working mothers, and extended families were widespread throughout the postwar period.

Many organizations and institutions in contemporary society actively create and promote a myth of the heterosexual nuclear family as a "haven in a heartless world," a refuge from the brutal world outside the home. Since the late 1960s, feminists, among others, have exposed the lies beneath that image, as they have demonstrated that the family is also the place of brutal violence against women and children, of incest, and of other forms of abuse.

While many feminists, both heterosexual and lesbian, have pointed out the patriarchal, heterosexist, and oppressive character of the nuclear family, many have also argued that the family is an institution that can be reclaimed and transformed. Through political and personal struggle, they have tried to re-create relationships within their families of origin and to establish their own families of choice.

### Families of Origin

Despite the portrayal of lesbians as living outside families, the reality is that each lesbian was born into a family. That nexus can be quickly and sometimes irreparably shattered, however, as parents and siblings respond in anger, hurt, and denial to the revelation of a family member's sexual orientation. Fear of joining the ranks of what anthropologist Weston (1991) has termed "exiles from kinship," many lesbians have sought to keep their sexual orientation hidden from family members. The effort to keep such a significant part of one's life a secret can extract an enormous psychological and emotional toll. Furthermore, the difficulties of navigating a dual life are immense, and the dreaded secret is often unwittingly revealed, sometimes with painful, and even tragic, results. Nevertheless, many lesbians choose to come out, often testing the waters with a sibling before broaching the topic with other family members.

It is important to remember that there is no unitary experience of family for lesbians. On the contrary, lesbians enjoy a huge diversity of experiences. Age, ability, race, ethnicity, class, country of origin, and location—all of these variables and many others affect lesbians' lives and experiences of family. Even within the same "family of origin," reactions to a family member's coming out can range from silence and rejection to benign resignation and even celebration. Through the process of "coming out," some lesbians are forced to sever all ties with their family of origin. Others encounter love and support and are able to maintain close and enriched connections.

### Lesbian and Gay Youth

Because of their financial and legal dependence, the issue of families of origin is particularly problematic for lesbian and gay youth. Youth often need their family for food, shelter, and other forms of support. For them, the cost of revelation can be high. Statistics on street youth indicate that a high percentage of homeless teens are lesbian and gay youth who have been disowned by their families of origin. Many other young people are forced to submit to psychiatric treatment in an attempt to "cure" their sexual disorder. Fearing such outcomes, young lesbians often deny their lesbianism in order to survive within their family.

In the face of these facts, however, gay and lesbian youth are also resisting, forming youth groups, and gaining support from lesbian and gay communities. Increasingly, parents are learning to accept and even celebrate their children's sexual orientation. Parents, Families, and Friends of Lesbians and Gays (PFLAG), an organization formed in 1981, has been instrumental in helping family members understand and accept their lesbian and gay children. PFLAG provides public education and advocacy, support groups, and youth programs. By 1997, there were more than four hundred affiliated chapters of PFLAG in the United States, Canada, and ten other countries.

A 1997 American poll suggested that groups like PFLAG may be having a positive effect on parental homophobia. A survey of 1,123 adults conducted by the Mason-Dixon Political/Media Research Group in August 1997 found that 67 percent of parents said that, if a child told them he or she was gay, they would either provide support or be "OK" with it. In addition, 60 percent indicated that the child should feel free to "tell whomever they want to tell; there's nothing wrong with it." Only 7 percent indicated they would suggest that the child get psychiatric help "to change to heterosexual," and 1 percent said they would ask them to leave the house. Those results are promising for the future of lesbian and gay youth and their relationships with their families.

### Adult Lesbians and Their Families of Origin

It is not only youth for whom relationships with their families of origin can be difficult. Even as adults, living apart from their parents, lesbians can experience rejection and recriminations if their sexual orientation is revealed. Many women find themselves disowned, unwelcome in the family home. Others are welcomed only if their partner does not attend.

Lesbians' chosen families (partners, children) and their families of origin often come into conflict, sometimes with brutal results. One such example is the case of Sharon Kowalski. In 1983, Kowalski was seriously injured in a car accident. Her family of origin sought to deny the family she had formed with her partner, Karen Thompson. Kowalski's father used the law to prevent Thompson from even seeing Kowalski for a time. Only after a nine-year legal and political battle was Thompson successful in bringing Kowalski home to live with her.

In other cases, grandparents of the children of lesbian mothers have successfully prevented the nonbiological mother from gaining custody of, and in some instances access to, their children upon the death of the children's biological mother. Parents have made medical plans and funeral arrangements against a dying woman's wishes, excluding a partner from any role in caregiving and planning. Such actions are supported by the lack of legal recognition for lesbians' relationships with each other and with their children.

### Families of Choice

Within lesbian communities, the issue of family is hotly debated. Some lesbians argue that, because of the patriarchal and oppressive nature of the nuclear family, choosing to form a family serves to reinforce the heterosexual nuclear family. Rather than attempt to assimilate into mainstream society by bearing and raising children within coupled relationships, lesbians should be attempting to dismantle the institution of the family. Others within lesbian communities maintain that creating lesbian families can provide both personal support and love and serve as a vehicle for change. As heterosexual families encounter lesbian families in their workplaces, schools, and communities, they are challenged to revise and expand their notion of what constitutes a family. While the road to acceptance can be a rocky one, lesbians forming families of choice maintain that the gains they make in the struggle against heterosexism and the joy their children bring them far outweigh the pain of occasional rejection.

Despite the growing number of lesbian families, both with and without children, legislation has been slow to reflect this changing social phenomenon. In many jurisdictions, statutes explicitly exclude lesbian and gay relationships from the protection and support afforded to heterosexual relationships. In many instances, the law not only fails to recognize lesbian and gay relationships, but also actively works to undermine their existence. In most jurisdictions, lesbians are prevented from adopting or fostering children. Despite favorable rulings in some locations, in many others lesbian mothers are routinely denied custody of, and even access to, their children. They are denied access to reproductive technologies, in-

**F**cluding donor insemination. Partners of lesbian mothers are, for the most part, denied the right to adopt their partner's biological children.

Political and legal opposition to the extension of rights and benefits to lesbian and gay families is often posed in terms of the alleged danger they pose to "the family." Indeed, lesbian and gay families, and, in particular, families with children, appear to crystallize many fears about the demise of the "traditional" family. In 1992, for example, the caucus formed within the Progressive Conservative Party in Canada to oppose inclusion of sexual orientation in the Human Rights Code adopted the name Family Caucus. Other such organizations include Focus on the Family and the Coalition for Family Values. Such organizations have formed in virtually every country where lesbians and gay men have fought for legislation to protect their families. As early as 1978, the Briggs Initiative (Proposition 6) in California affirmed the "fundamental" interest of the state in preserving the family unit. While that (unsuccessful) initiative barred lesbians and gay men from teaching school or holding other positions of responsibility with children, more recent initiatives have attacked lesbian and gay families more directly. The United States Defense of Marriage Act (1995) defines marriage as an institution restricted to the union of one man and one woman. The legislation was intended to strike a blow at the ongoing struggle for gay and lesbian marriage. Section 28 of the Local Government Act 1988 (known as Clause 28 before the act was passed) in the United Kingdom characterizes lesbian and gay relationships as "pretended family relationships" and explicitly banned local schools from promoting the "acceptability of homosexuality."

Yet, in the face of such legislative and political opposition, lesbians and gay men have continued to fight for human rights protection, workplace medical and dental benefits, adoption and custodial rights, and many other reforms. In the process, they have stubbornly affirmed that "we are family."

## Community as Family

Like members of the feminist movement, the commune movement, and other social movements, some lesbians have adopted the term "family" to apply to the communities of support, solidarity, and love within which they live and work. For these women, the love that the term "family" connotes is provided by their friendship networks and geographic communities, not solely by their families of origin or their coupled relationships. Other commentators view this political stance as a dangerous one. In their view, designating every relationship that involves love and support "family" renders the concept of family so broad that it becomes meaningless. As well, it robs everything designated "nonfamily" of any emotional or social content.

Despite heated debates within the lesbian and gay movements and in the face of vigorous political and religious opposition, lesbians continue to form familial relationships with their partners and children, to renew deep and abiding connections with their families of origin, and to fight for the legal and political recognition of their families.

*Katherine Arnup*

## Bibliography

Allen, Katherine R., and David H. Demo. "The Families of Lesbians and Gay Men: A New Frontier in Family Research." *Journal of Marriage and the Family* 57 (February 1995), 111–127.

Arnup, Katherine. *Lesbian Parenting: Living with Pride and Prejudice*. Charlottetown, Prince Edward Island: gynergy, 1997.

Benkov, Laura. *Reinventing the Family: The Emerging Story of Lesbian and Gay Parents*. New York: Crown, 1994.

Demo, David H., and Katherine R. Allen. "Diversity Within Lesbian and Gay Families: Challenges and Implications for Family Theory and Research." *Journal of Social and Personal Relationships* 13:3 (1996), 415–434.

Laird, Joan. "Lesbian and Gay Families." In *Normal Family Processes*, 2nd ed. Ed. Froma Walsh. New York: Guilford, 1993, pp. 282–328.

O'Brien, Carol-Anne, and Lorna Weir. "Lesbians and Gay Men Inside and Outside Families." In *Canadian Families: Diversity, Conflict, and Change*. Ed. Nancy Mandell and Ann Duffy. Toronto: Harcourt Brace, 1995, pp. 111–139.

Weston, Kath. *Families We Choose: Lesbians, Gays, and Kinship*. New York: Columbia University Press, 1991.

*See also* Adolescence; Adoption; Children; Coming Out; Custody Litigation; Donor Insemination; Law and Legal Institutions; Mothers, Lesbian

## Fat Liberation

The movement to eradicate oppression on the basis of weight, the radical branch of which has been formed primarily by lesbians and feminists. In the 1970s, fat activists, sparked by lesbian feminist energy and radical therapy principles, uncovered these facts about dieting: The vast majority of diets fail, resulting in regaining any weight lost (and often more); many diseases attributed to "overweight" are caused by the social stress of fat hatred and the physical effects of repeated dieting (which depletes muscle before fat, including heart muscle); fat people have the same caloric intake and eat the same foods as thin people; fatness is hereditary and a physical characteristic of the same order as height. Medical studies supporting these conclusions are cited by Vivian Mayer in "The Fat Illusion" and "The Questions People Ask" (in Schoenfielder and Wieser [1983]), William Bennet and Joel Gurn (*The Dieters' Dilemma* [1982]) and *Size Acceptance and Self-Acceptance*, the NAAFA workbook (1994).

In the 1973 "Fat Liberation Manifesto," published in Schoenfielder and Wieser (1983), Judy Freespirit and Vivian Mayer (Aldebaran), of the radical feminist Fat Underground, stated: "We repudiate the mystified 'science' which falsely claims that we are unfit. It has both caused and upheld discrimination against us, in collusion with the financial interests of insurance companies, the fashion and garment industries, reducing industries, the food and drug industries, and the medical and psychiatric establishments."

Fat liberation has two basic approaches. The first, embodied by the National Association to Advance Fat Acceptance (NAAFA), founded in 1969, is the size-acceptance movement. NAAFA fights weight-based discrimination and promotes self-esteem by publishing, organizing social events, and supporting civil rights legal action.

The second, more radical, analysis of fat oppression, formulated by lesbians and feminists, insists that fat hatred is directly linked to sexism, racism, and classism. When women are obsessed about the size of their bodies, their power and resources are wasted. Many women now argue that dieting and weight-loss surgery are forms of mutilation, parallel to foot-binding and clitoridectomy—practices that women force on one another and their daughters to become acceptable to men, thereby acquiring class privilege and mobility. Mayer in Schoenfielder and Wieser (1983) cites studies showing that fat directly affects economic status (a fat woman is more likely to be poor due to social constraints and not because of negative qualities stereotypically attached to fatness, such as lack of motivation, laziness, or stupidity). For dark-skinned peoples, in whose cultures of origin fatness may be prized or considered a neutral quality, the stigmatization of size in North America reinforces racist ideas about what makes bodies acceptable or unacceptable.

Beginning with the Fat Underground in Los Angeles in 1973, fat organizations—among them, the Fat Avengers (Seattle, Washington), Life in the Fat Lane (San Francisco, California), Fat Is a Lesbian Issue (New York City), Fat Chance (San Francisco), Largesse, the Network for Size Esteem (New Haven, Connecticut), Lesbians of Size (Portland, Oregon), Sisters of Size (Seattle), Big Beautiful Lesbians (Washington, D.C.), the Lesbian Fat Activists Network (Woodstock, N.Y.), Sisters Are Fighting Fat Oppression (Minneapolis, Minnesota), and Let It All Hang Out Day (San Francisco)—have created demonstrations, Gay Pride floats, theater, pamphlets, street actions, dances, and exercise and social groups. Organizations also exist in Atlanta, Georgia; Boston and Northampton, Massachusetts; Canada; the United Kingdom; Australia; and Holland. NAAFA has had a feminist caucus since 1983; a lesbian group, since 1990. Fat-positive sexuality has always been part of fat lesbians' agenda. *FaT GiRL*, a dyke 'zine started in 1994 in San Francisco by Max Airborne, gives voice to radical fat sexual "outlaws." The longest-lived group is Fat Lip Readers' Theater (San Francisco), which first performed in 1982.

While many lesbians have developed analyses about, and organized around, fat oppression since 1973, lesbian communities, mirroring the straight world, are often resistant to their messages about health, beauty, and the effects of dieting. Fat activists attribute this to media-perpetrated illusions. In a world in which it often seems as if individuals have little or no control over their lives, women are constantly encouraged to believe that controlling their weight is a measure of their personal effectiveness. When the Fat Underground compiled its original statistics in 1973, Americans spent $10 billion a year on the diet industry (including books, doctors, medications, surgery, weight loss programs, camps and spas, and special foods and gadgets); in 1994, $33 billion. Fat activists argue that some of the increase comes from the fact that almost all diets fail, and so dieters become dependent on the diet industry, while new dieters are constantly recruited by advertising and social pressure. Women in particular continue to be economic, physical, and psychological targets of fat hatred. *Elana Dykewomon*

# F

**Bibliography**

Brown, Laura S., and Esther Rothblum, eds. *Overcoming Fear of Fat.* New York: Harrington Park, 1989.

Bruno, Barbara Altman. *Worth Your Weight.* New York: Routledge, 1996.

Dykewomon, Elana. "The Real Fat Woman Poems." *Nothing Will Be as Sweet as the Taste.* London: Onlywomen, 1995.

Fraser, Laura. *Losing It.* New York: Dutton, 1997.

Schoenfielder, Lisa, and Barb Wieser, eds. *Shadow on a Tightrope: Writings by Women on Fat Oppression.* Introduction by Vivian Mayer. San Francisco: Aunt Lute, 1983.

*See also* Advertising and Consumerism; Body Image; Discrimination; Health; Stereotypes; Stigma

## Female Support Networks

Term coined by Blanche Weisen Cook in "Female Support Networks and Political Activism: Lillian Wald, Crystal Eastman, and Emma Goldman" (1977). In it, she argued that these activist women of the Progressive Era turned to other women for emotional sustenance even though, in some cases, their sexual partners were men.

Cook's essay contributed to the developing scholarship on the importance of women's communities that first gained broad notice with Carroll Smith-Rosenberg's "The Female World of Love and Ritual: Relations Between Women in Nineteenth-Century America" (1975). While Smith-Rosenberg's work in the inaugural issue of the feminist scholarly journal *Signs: Journal of Women in Culture and Society*, noted middle-class and elite women's bonds with each other in their private lives, "Female Support Networks and Political Activism" applied this idea to prominent women and their public lives. Cook challenged the idea that women's emotional relationships had no relevance to their public work and activism.

These works signaled the growing importance of studies of worlds of women for feminist scholarship. Cook's work, along with that of others, such as Freedman (1970), acknowledged that women-centered networks existed throughout American society and were perhaps strongest when and where women gained least through existing or potential heterosexual connections. Studies of these networks demonstrated how many of women's private and public needs were satisfied within the communities and networks of women that emerged especially during the late nineteenth century in the United States. Additionally, they argued that such support was crucial politically and emotionally for women as they moved into male-dominated public arenas. According to Cook, this support from other women was "not an emotional choice but political necessity."

Feminist scholars have developed this idea that women build and are sustained by kinlike networks in a number of ways. In 1985, *Signs* devoted a special issue to examinations of women's communities in a variety of eras and places. In it Sklar examined the community within Hull House, a settlement house in Chicago, Illinois, founded in the late nineteenth century by Jane Addams, focusing on the numerous ways that institution met its residents needs. In the 1990s studies on the role of women (and men) in the civil rights movement noted that far more than material needs must be provided for people to construct and sustain political activism.

Cook's essay was important not only because of its contribution to the literature on women's communities but also because it contributed to the debate over the definition of "lesbian" in the 1970s and 1980s. Reacting in part to narrow definitions of lesbianism as exclusively sexual behavior, Cook defined lesbians as women "who love women, who choose women to nurture and support and to create a living environment in which to work creatively and independently." Other historians and theorists saw this emphasis on emotional bonds as possibly erasing or minimizing lesbians' erotic and sexual attractions and activities and reinforcing stereotypes of women as sexually passive and less sexually desiring than men. In the 1990s these debates over the importance and meaning of affectional and sexual relationships in women's lives continued.

*Trisha Franzen*

**Bibliography**

"Communities of Women." *Signs: Journal of Women in Culture and Society* 10:4 (Summer (1985) (Special Issue).

Cook, Blanche Weisen. "Female Support Networks and Political Activism: Lillian Wald, Crystal Eastman, and Emma Goldman." *Chrysalis* 3 (1977), 43–61.

Freedman, Estelle. "Separatism as Strategy: Female Institution Building and American Feminism, 1870–1930." *Feminist Studies* 5:3 (Fall 1970), 512–529.

Smith-Rosenberg, Carroll. "The Female World of Love and Ritual: Relations Between Women in Nineteenth-Century America." *Signs: Journal of Women in Culture and Society* 1:1 (Autumn 1975), 1–30.

*See also* Addams, Jane; Community

## Feminism

A diverse sociopolitical movement with a long history. Feminism denotes conscious advocacy for women's civil, social, and human rights. However, historical change and cultural variation make feminism impossible to define in any monolithic sense. Feminism includes a wide range of collective and individual beliefs and expressions concerning the situation of women in society; it may be embraced as a political strategy, a philosophical orientation, a mode of theoretical analysis, a personal commitment to a set of organic beliefs and practices, a revolutionary struggle for human freedom, a model for an ideal social state, and an entire *gestalt* (worldview) that encompasses everything from labor and economics, to language and psychology, to religion and spirituality.

Feminism opposes hierarchy based on sex and, therefore, challenges the categorical assumption of one sex's superiority and authority over the other. Feminism seeks to expose and eradicate the debasement, mistreatment, and oppression of women. It calls into question distortions of women's human capacities and limitations of their opportunities. Central to feminist thought is the belief that the sexes are not wholly predestined by God, biology, or a transcendent natural order but are socially constructed by cultural beliefs and practices that become naturalized so as to seem beyond question. Feminism confronts these ideological patterns in thought and behavior in order to reevaluate them and impel change. For example, feminist thinkers have distinguished between sex (as a biological and physiological condition) and gender (as the culturally specific ways in which human subjects are socially induced to express the properties of their sex). This distinction suggests that differences in sex or reproductive function do not inevitably produce gender dimorphism or stereotypes of femininity and masculinity. Feminism entwines personal experience and political analysis in complex ways as it works to undo the historical trivialization and isolation of women's labor, social roles, and functions.

The politicization of issues typically dismissed as private and idiosyncratic, such as body image, sexuality, intimate and familial relationships, emotional states, and religious experiences, is a key component of feminism, so much so that "the personal is the political" became a major slogan for the resurgence of feminist activity that took place in the United States in the late 1960s and early 1970s.

### History

The term "feminism" entered the common vocabulary in the early twentieth century. However, no exact date has been established for the dawn of a feminist sensibility, and there are different opinions as to how far back in history feminism extends. Some trace feminism back to ancient myths—of Amazon warriors, for example—or to pre-Christian artifacts suggesting the dominance of matrifocal social organization and goddess worship. Others trace feminism back to early European writers such as Christine de Pisan (1364–1430?), who defended women's moral and intellectual nature. The widespread persecution and murder of witches in the sixteenth and seventeenth centuries may also be seen as indicative of early feminist resistance.

Modern Western feminism developed alongside rapid industrialization, economic shifts, and changes in family structure and social organization. A major philosophical influence was the Enlightenment conception of the subject as a free-standing individual possessed of certain inalienable rights. This notion is apparent in eighteenth-century feminist writings, such as Mary Wollstonecraft's (1759–1797) *Vindication of the Rights of Women* (1789), which argued for women's education. In the United States, women's political activism for human rights was centered in the early-nineteenth-century movement to abolish slavery. Many of the women who participated in the abolitionist struggle later joined the suffrage movement, which evolved out of the 1848 Seneca Falls Convention in New York state, where women gathered to discuss their own civil rights agenda.

Feminism in the United States is often described in terms of two historical flourishings, or "waves." "First wave" feminism was chiefly mobilized around the vote, although activists also focused on standards of moral purity, education and occupations for women, and critiques of marriage and motherhood. "Second wave" feminism developed out of post–World War II economic and social changes and drew inspiration from the American

**F** civil rights movement. Activities and issues associated with the "second wave" include group consciousness raising, reproductive and sexual freedom, the formation of the National Organization for Women (NOW), passage of the Equal Rights Amendment, and the establishment of women's studies in higher education.

While these issues are far reaching, mainstream movement organizers, like their nineteenth-century predecessors, tended to concentrate on matters pertaining to white, heterosexual, middle-class women. In the 1970s and 1980s, feminism was marked by debates over its responsiveness to the concerns of African American women, Latinas, Third World women, working-class women, and lesbians. The lesbian issue erupted in controversy as "lesbian-baiting" became a favored tactic of feminism's detractors, and as some movement organizers responded defensively. While not all feminists are lesbian, nor all lesbians feminists, feminism has historically defended women's right to define their own identities and desires and to make their own choices, including the choice to live outside traditional heterosexual relationships with men. In the nineteenth century, nontraditional couplings, called "Boston marriages," made it possible for women to live and work together, although there is little evidence that these relationships were sexual. In the late twentieth century, many lesbians sought an egalitarian "sisterhood" within the feminist movement. While some feminists idealized lesbians as the "vanguard of the movement," others vilified them as the movement's greatest liability. This latter tendency prompted many lesbians to break away and form their own separatist communities.

## Contemporary Feminist Politics

In the late twentieth century, feminism became increasingly attentive to the differences and contradictions that make women, as a group, irreducible to any singular identity. Contemporary feminist politics is understood to encompass many different identities, traditions, nationalities, and objectives. In the 1990s, the term "feminism" often appeared in the plural, as "feminisms," and some feminists categorized their beliefs as liberal, radical, cultural, socialist, or lesbian feminist. While this fragmentation has suggested to some a loss of common vision, others have applauded feminism's ability to continually readapt itself, calling up new questions and drawing on new resources and international perspectives.

*Dana Heller*

### Bibliography

Cott, Nancy. *The Grounding of Modern Feminism.* New Haven, Conn.: Yale University Press, 1987.

Echols, Alice. *Daring To Be Bad: Radical Feminism in America, 1967–1975.* Minneapolis: University of Minnesota Press, 1989.

Heller, Dana. *Cross Purposes: Lesbians, Feminists, and the Limits of Alliance.* Bloomington and Indianapolis: Indiana University Press, 1997.

hooks, bell. *Ain't I a Woman: Black Women and Feminism.* Boston: South End, 1981.

Mitchell, Juliet. *Women: The Longest Revolution.* London: Virago, 1984.

Moraga, Cherríe, and Gloria Anzaldúa. *This Bridge Called My Back: Writings by Radical Women of Color.* New York: Kitchen Table: Women of Color Press, 1981, 1983.

Morgan, Robin, ed. *Sisterhood Is Powerful: An Anthology of Writings from the Women's Liberation Movement.* New York: Vintage, 1970.

*See also* Enlightenment, European; Suffrage Movement; Women's Liberation Movement

## Fiction

Certain forms of imaginative literature—most commonly, prose narratives such as novels, novellas, and short stories—the contents of which are ordinarily understood to be invented.

Fiction has been a central factor in the development of modern understandings of lesbianism within Western culture. From the mid-nineteenth century to the last decades of the twentieth century, novels have served as a primary source of accounts of lesbianism for readers of all sexual identities. Literary work has been easier to produce—because it is cheaper to write and to publish—and harder to censor than theater or, as the decades passed, than radio, film, or television. Books might be free in public libraries or for sale cheaply on drugstore racks. They could be easily hidden and read without observation. As a form of writing, fiction has been more influential than poetry, in Western culture, because of the importance of narrative, of story, as the means by which one can simultaneously describe and explain social, emotional, and sexual experience.

The novel has been the literary form dedicated to a detailed accounting of the social order and, consequently, of social deviance. It has been the literary and, more broadly, the cultural arena in which women have been most often represented, of which women are most likely to be the producers, and of which the majority of readers have historically been women. Moreover, the novel has been the literary form in which personal relationships generally, and sexual relationships specifically—especially when the focus is on women—are central subjects. Finally, novels have historically been presented as true stories, if not true in the sense of describing actual people, then true in the sense of describing the world as it is.

## Fiction as Information

The novel has shared its role as a source of information about lesbianism with scientific texts and with newspapers, to the degree to which scientists and journalists share the novelist's ability to tell stories and claim that they are true. Novels, scientific texts, and newspapers have also influenced each others' accounts of lesbianism: Novelists have relied on the theories of doctors; journalists have turned to novels for models of writing about homosexuality; and journalists' reports have been incorporated into doctors' accounts of lesbian lives. Fiction prevailed over scientific texts because novels are more accessible—easier to get hold of and to read—than medical studies. Newspapers have not generally had the space to develop their stories or the independence from public opinion that some novelists have been able to claim.

The novel's role as a source of information diminished over the last decades of the twentieth century, as a result of changes in the social situation of lesbians and, consequently, changes in mainstream cultural representations of lesbianism, as well as the generally declining influence of the printed word. The gay liberation and women's liberation movements of the late 1960s and the 1970s challenged social hostility to lesbianism and also produced new lesbian-identified presses, newspapers, and journals, which began to publish essays, poems, anthologies of personal testimonies, and political writings, as well as novels. This new cultural production also included gay and lesbian theater, music, and, eventually, film and video. Since then, the representation of lesbianism has gradually increased in mainstream publishing, newspapers, theater, music, film, and video. At the same time, television, film, and video have become more culturally influential, more widely available, and more engaging to a broad audience than the novel. But at the end of the twentieth century, print remained the chief medium for lesbians' representations of lesbianism, because publishing and circulating written materials were still comparatively inexpensive. The novel continued to be central to lesbian print culture for the reasons it has always been influential.

Identifying lesbian fiction, whether or not a novel is understood to be about lesbianism, has depended almost as much on the historical moment at which it is being read and the reader as on the novel's content or form or the life of its author. Because of the social stigma attached to lesbianism and the broad cultural hostility that that stigma reflects, critics and writers across the twentieth century (sometimes even lesbian critics and writers) have been reluctant to identify literary work as lesbian, either to spare the work and/or its author from stigma or to ensure that lesbianism continue to seem as ugly and inconsequential as possible, and so remain stigmatized. However, particularly in the second half of the twentieth century, and especially after the inception of the women's and gay liberation movements, other writers and critics (particularly, but not exclusively, self-identified lesbians) have been committed to identifying and discussing a range of literary work as lesbian, in order to develop more complex understandings of lesbianism and so defy and, ultimately, defuse the stigma.

The type of novel that has been, and still is, most consistently read as lesbian consists of a central narrative focused on a sexual relationship between two women. Other factors have added to the likelihood of a given work being interpreted as lesbian, the most important being the presence of a masculine woman. She is the character type most likely to be read as a lesbian, as a result of a combination of late-nineteenth-century scientific studies of sexuality and popular perceptions of lesbians as women who should have been, or want to be, men. The most widely known lesbian novel, Radclyffe Hall's (1880–1943) *The Well of Loneliness* (1928), which combines both a narrative about sexual relationships between women and the figure of a masculine woman, Hall's heroine, Stephen Gordon, served for decades as the model for popular and academic understandings of what a lesbian novel should be. This novel also incorporates a third element common to fiction read as lesbian: that lesbianism itself is the problem of the narrative.

From the 1970s to the 1990s, lesbian critics tried to broaden the pattern of the kind of fiction read as lesbian. One tactic was to emphasize the subversion of gender norms as a subject of lesbian

**F** novels, so that, for example, Virginia Woolf's (1882–1941) *Orlando* (1928), in which the protagonist changes from a man to a woman mid-novel, can be read as a lesbian work. Another strategy was to focus on transgression. The most radical formulation of this approach, by lesbian novelist Bertha Harris (1937–) in the 1970s, was that the lesbian should be read as she is socially perceived, as a monster, and, therefore, novels about monsters should be read as lesbian novels. Some critics have argued that lesbian fiction—and lesbian writing more broadly—is distinguished by experimental forms that replicate the disruption of conventions and the experimental forms of lesbian lives. Other critics have argued that all of the work of lesbian writers—as, for example, all of the art produced by lesbian artists—should be read as lesbian. In other words, "lesbian literature" should be constructed in the way that national literatures are constructed from the work of authors seen as belonging to the nation; women's literature is understood as literature by women, African American literature as literature by African Americans, and so forth. But others have pushed much more stringently for narrowing the range of writing considered as lesbian, arguing, for example, that many novels about female couples, which might be read as lesbian novels, were not written by lesbians and were intended as parody or pornography. A combination of factors should be required, these critics imply, so that only novels (or stories) by lesbians and "about" lesbians would be considered as lesbian fiction.

These debates mirrors general debates over definitions of lesbianism in lesbian studies, which are finally shaped by the hostility of heterosexual culture. Those arguing for a narrower definition of lesbian fiction see sexual relationships between women rarely acknowledged by the dominant culture and want more acknowledgment of this aspect of lesbian lives. Those interested in more expansive definitions of lesbian fiction also want more acknowledgment, but of a broader understanding of lesbian lives and work. Some critics fear, however, that the sexual content of lesbianism might be lost in the pursuit of a more expansive understanding of lesbianism.

## Publication History

Discussions of lesbianism and fiction often emphasize censorship, usually referring back to the obscenity trial that followed the publication of Hall's *The Well of Loneliness*, which is viewed as evidence that lesbian novels were prohibited or as a sign of subtler pressures against writing about lesbianism. Lesbian writers of Hall's and subsequent generations were certainly aware of hostility. However, the publication history of Hall's novel, which has been continuously in print around the world (and in many languages) since it was banned in Britain in 1928, suggests that censorship is not always what it seems. In the United States, in the 1950s and 1960s, publishers of the cheap paperbacks known as "pulps," seeing economic opportunity in a combination of sex and taboo, solicited writers to produce lesbian romances. They also sought out and reprinted lesbian fiction from the 1920s, 1930s, and 1940s that originally had been published by mainstream presses, from *The Well* to Gale Wilhelm's (1908–1991) *We Too Are Drifting* (1935), to Mary Renault's (1905–1983) *The Friendly Young Ladies* (1944). Through the 1970s, 1980s, and 1990s, lesbian, feminist, and university presses in the United States and Britain continued to keep in print lesbian novels from the 1920s through the 1970s, including the work first reprinted as pulps; novels that were written for the pulp market, such as Ann Bannon's (1937–) Beebo Brinker series from the late 1950s and early 1960s; and novels first published in the 1970s, such as June Arnold's (1926–1982) *Sister Gin* (1975) and Bertha Harris's *Lover* (1976), by lesbian presses that subsequently folded.

Moreover, because literary work popularly identified as lesbian was narrowly defined, lesbians who did not produce narratives focused on female couples in sexual relationships had a great deal of freedom. It was even possible to write about lesbian sexuality or female couples without social condemnation. Clarissa Dalloway's sexual responses to other women, presented through her memories in Virginia Woolf's *Mrs. Dalloway* (1925), were ignored in contemporary comment on the novel, which focused on Woolf's stylistic innovation. Gertrude Stein's (1874–1946) *The Autobiography of Alice B. Toklas* (1933) is premised on her partnership with Toklas (1877–1967), but does not include any discussion of sex or social difficulty; the book became Stein's great popular success. In Nella Larsen's (1891–1964) *Passing* (1928), the question of racial passing was so charged as to account for all of the tensions between Irene Redfield and Clare Kendry for the novel's contemporary readers.

## Conventions

In the novels that were read as about lesbianism (as often still in mainstream fiction, film, and television), female couples are usually represented in relation to heterosexuality. The lesbian lovers are shown in contrast to a heterosexual couple, in contrast to the heterosexual experience of one or both of the women in the lesbian couple, or as redeemed by the return of one of those women to heterosexuality at the end of the story. In many lesbian novels, one woman leaves her male suitor for another woman; in many others, a female couple is disrupted by a man. The endings of narratives about female couples have been, until the last decades of the twentieth century, almost always grim: Like many stories about heterosexual women, lesbian novels have ended in either (heterosexual) marriage or death. The women who did not turn to heterosexuality in the end often instead fell out of windows or fell into psychiatric breakdowns. To establish a difference within lesbian couples understood by the dominant culture as undifferentiated because of the absence of a man, the lovers in lesbian novels were invariably represented as divided by gender—masculine/feminine—and/or older/younger, richer/poorer, brunette/blonde, teacher/student. Class distinctions were usually absorbed into age differences. All-female environments—girls' schools, sororities, women's prisons—in which lesbianism could be understood as the result of the absence of men, were favored settings. Until the publication of Ann Allen Shockley's (1927–) *Loving Her* (1974), whiteness was assumed, even promoted in conjunction with the frequently upper-class status of fictional lesbians, who could then be dismissed as apart from ordinary life.

## Post-Stonewall (1969) Writing

Shockley's first novel was followed by a collection of stories, *The Black and the White of It* (1980), and another novel, *Say Jesus and Come to Me* (1982), as well as the work of other African American novelists and short-story writers, such as Alice Walker (1944–), Becky Birtha (1948–), and Jewelle Gomez (1948–). In the 1980s and 1990s, critics looked beyond the novel for the history of African American lesbian writing to the diaries of Alice Dunbar-Nelson (1875–1935) and the poetry of Angelina Weld Grimké (1880–1958). Most lesbian writing about racial difference in the post-Stonewall decades has not been in novels but in short fiction, poetry, the essay, and a range of forms of memoir and autobiography, such as Audre Lorde's (1934–1992) "biomythography," *Zami: A New Spelling of My Name* (1982), Cherríe Moraga's (1952–) *Loving in the War Years: Lo que nunca pasó por sus labios* (1983), or

anthologies such as Moraga and Gloria Anzaldúa's (1942) *This Bridge Called My Back: Writings of Radical Women of Color* (1981), which combine all of these forms of writing.

This movement away from the novel in writing about race reflects a general pattern whereby the most innovative lesbian writing of the post-Stonewall period has usually taken forms other than that of fiction, or, if fiction, it has been predominantly experimental fiction or short stories. That development underlines the limits of the lesbian novel as it has been generally recognized—as did the increasing emphasis among lesbian novelists of the 1980s and 1990s on genre fiction, such as detective fiction, science fiction, or fantasy, in which whether the girl gets the girl does not have to be the focus of the narrative.

Gay men and male couples have appeared in novels by and about lesbians from the work of high modernist Virginia Woolf to popular historical novelists such as Mary Renault, raising questions about the history of lesbians' relation to gay men and gay culture. Gay men have served in lesbian novels as guides to gay life, from Jonathan Brockett in *The Well of Loneliness* to Jack Mann in Bannon's Beebo Brinker series, suggesting the degree to which gay men represent homosexuality. Absent from the lesbian fiction of the 1970s and 1980s, gay men returned in the 1990s, often in fiction about the AIDS epidemic, by writers such Sarah Schulman (1958–) and Rebecca Brown (1956–). This reintegration of gay men into lesbian fiction was matched by the growing presence of lesbians in gay fiction in the 1980s and 1990s, in novels by Edmund White (1940–), for example, David Leavitt (1961–), and E. Lynn Harris (n.d.).

## Conclusion

Which fiction will be read as lesbian matters because of the novel's role in the development of mainstream and subcultural understandings of lesbianism. Novels read as lesbian have been consistently treated as true stories: endorsed by real and bogus medical authorities (when sufficiently attentive to scientific theories or so titillating as to need cover); praised by mainstream reviewers for their honesty (when sufficiently grim); read by hostile and friendly critics and readers alike as their authors' autobiographies; and sought out by generations of lesbian readers needing accounts of lives like their own. Readers have looked to fiction for the truth about lesbianism not only because novels

**F** represent themselves as true, but also because lesbianism has had to be justified. If the story were true, it had educational value; readers of all perspectives could tell themselves they were just looking for information, and lesbian readers, in particular, could see the novel as confirmation of their own existence. Lesbian fiction can be treated as fiction only insofar as lesbianism itself no longer needs justification.                                      *Julie Abraham*

### Bibliography

Abraham, Julie. *Are Girls Necessary? Lesbian Writing and Modern Histories*. New York: Routledge, 1996.

Castle, Terry. *The Apparitional Lesbian: Female Homosexuality and Modern Culture*. New York: Columbia University Press, 1993.

Jay, Karla, and Joanne Glasgow, eds. *Lesbian Texts and Contexts: Radical Revisions*. New York: New York University Press, 1990.

Martin, Biddy. *Femininity Played Straight: The Significance of Being Lesbian*. New York: Routledge, 1996.

Munt, Sally, ed. *New Lesbian Criticism: Literary and Cultural Readings*. New York: Columbia University Press, 1992.

Roof, Judith. *Come as You Are: Sexuality and Narrative*. New York: Columbia University Press, 1996.

Zimmerman, Bonnie. *The Safe Sea of Women: Lesbian Fiction, 1969–1979*. Boston: Beacon, 1990.

***See also*** Anzaldúa, Gloria; Arnold, June; Bannon, Ann; Dunbar-Nelson, Alice; Grimké, Angelina Weld; Hall, Radclyffe; Lorde, Audre; Moraga, Cherríe; Mystery and Detective Fiction; Pulp Paperbacks; Renault, Mary; Science Fiction; Shockley, Ann Allen; Stein, Gertrude; Wilhelm, Gale; Woolf, Virginia

### Fiction, Young Adult

Fiction written and told from a young adult perspective about a youthful protagonist facing problems and issues associated with adolescence. While coming-of-age stories have a long history and a wide readership, books began being marketed specifically to a young adult (YA) audience in the 1940s and 1950s, with the rise in visibility of a distinct teenage market. This, plus the burgeoning numbers of baby-boom adolescents, produced an upsurge of YA publishing in the United States in the 1960s. Then, as now, however, it must be noted that teen readers read widely and do not confine themselves to YA literature. Some of this literary output was dismissed by critics as "problem novels"—didactic and simplistic accounts of teenage angst in the context of current social issues. The best of them, however, were heralded as refreshing examples of a "new realism" in YA literature: books narrated by a young adult protagonist and characterized by candor, unidealized characters and settings, colloquial language, and the portrayal of realistic problems faced by contemporary adolescents that did not necessarily find resolution in a happy ending. Among these were novels that explored homosexuality and social prejudice against lesbians and gay men. The first YA novel to address these issues was John Donovan's *I'll Get There. It Better Be Worth the Trip* (1969), the story of an ambiguous relationship between two teenage boys. More recently, novels in this genre have been appearing at a rate of three to seven per year.

In contrast to the central role that smaller presses have played in gay and lesbian publishing, most gay and lesbian YA titles are from mainstream publishers. Although adolescents read gay and lesbian novels from small presses, these titles are not usually aimed solely and specifically at the YA market. As with most of YA literature, YA novels with gay and lesbian content generally feature white middle-class teens, urban or suburban settings, and gay and lesbian characters who are basically indistinguishable from their heterosexual peers. The two most common plot elements are gay and lesbian romances and the coming out story, in which young adult protagonists who are not gay or lesbian themselves come to terms with the gay or lesbian identity of parents, siblings, uncles, teachers, or friends. A few of the more recent books contain characters who "happen to be" gay or lesbian in a plot that does not revolve around sexual-orientation issues. Genre fiction aimed at YAs, such as Alyson Press' Pride Pack mystery adventure series (1995–), has also begun to appear. While the proportion of male and female narrators are approximately equal, YA books with gay male content have consistently outnumbered books with lesbian content by a ratio of nearly three to one. In addition, the vast majority of books with gay male content do not include lesbians, and vice versa.

Rosa Guy's coming-of-age romance *Ruby*, published in 1976, was the first YA novel with lesbian content and the first gay and lesbian YA novel by and about people of color. Since that time, YA books with lesbian content have appeared at a rate of roughly one to two per year, with most reflecting patterns of setting, plot, and character similar to those found in YA novels with gay male content. Lesbians in YA novels rarely reflect the social stereotypes associated with them: Few have short hair, excel at sports, play pool, drive trucks, or work in nontraditional jobs. Most of these novels feature an adolescent female protagonist in her first romantic relationship with another woman. The outcome of the romance depends very much on the age of the book. Many of the earlier novels were predictable stories of painful relationships between naive protagonists and fickle teenage temptresses. In others, teenage lesbian couples were tested with exceptional difficulties (in Sandra Scoppettone's *Happy Endings Are All Alike* [1978], for example, a young lesbian is assaulted and raped). Few adult lesbians were pictured, but they also faced misfortunes, including terminal illness, job loss, and child-custody battles. Thus, from the mid-1970s to the mid-1980s, most YA novels with lesbian content fell into the category of "problem novel," presenting lesbianism as a problem to be resolved rather than an attraction to be explored or a relationship to be created. Since the mid-1980s, however, the trend has been to treat lesbianism as simply one aspect of the conflicts and complications that any romantic relationship might create in a young adult's life. The source of the tension has shifted away from the same-sex relationship itself and toward the responses it elicits from family, friends, and community. Most late-twentieth-century novels portray teen and adult lesbians either as central characters who persevere in the face of various difficulties—including, but not limited to, homophobia and heterosexism—or as secondary characters who are part of the social milieu inhabited by the teenage protagonist.

Aside from the early prevalence of tragic teen romances and adult losses, one of the most intriguing patterns in these books is the consistent portrayal of lesbians as existing only in long-term coupled relationships. This cozy image is problematic in its ubiquity, as it frames females as entirely dependent upon connections with others for their self-definition. Fictional gay men frequently come to a realization of their sexual orientation independent of any actual relationship. Fictional lesbians, however, do not exist unless they have someone to be a lesbian *with*: Autonomous teenage lesbians are rare; autonomous adult lesbians are nonexistent. Furthermore, there is seldom any larger community outside the dyad; most fictional lesbian couples live in apparent isolation from other lesbians or gay men.

Perhaps the best-known YA novel with lesbian content is Nancy Garden's *Annie on My Mind* (1982), a realistic portrayal of the falling-in-love process of two high school girls. Other outstanding novels in this genre include M.E. Kerr's *Deliver Us from Evie* (1994), a romance between a handsome young butch and the banker's beautiful daughter, and Jacqueline Woodson's *From the Notebooks of Melanin Sun* (1995), narrated by an African American teen whose world is shaken when his long-single mother enters a relationship with a white woman. *Am I Blue? Coming Out From the Silence* (1994), edited by Marion Dane Bauer, is a notable anthology of sixteen short stories exploring gay and lesbian issues in the lives of teenagers; half of the stories feature lesbians.

Not surprisingly, YA fiction with lesbian or gay content has come under persistent attack from individuals and groups (chiefly religious fundamentalists) who object to any inclusion of homosexuality in materials for younger audiences. However, in a 1995 case involving the presence of *Annie on My Mind* in the high school libraries of Olathe, Kansas, a federal judge ruled that the school board's removal of the book was a violation of students' First Amendment rights and, thus, unconstitutional.

*Christine Jenkins*

### Bibliography

Clyde, Lauren A., and Marjorie Lobban. *Out of the Closet and into the Classroom: Homosexuality in Books for Young People.* Port Melbourne, Australia: ALIA Thorpe, 1992.

Cuseo, Allan A. *Homosexual Characters in Young Adult Novels: A Literary Analysis, 1969–1982.* Metuchen, N.J.: Scarecrow, 1992.

Jenkins, Christine. "From Queer to Gay and Back Again: Young Adult Novels with Gay/Lesbian/Queer Content, 1969–1997." *Library Quarterly* 69 (July 1998), 298–334.

*See also* Adolescence; Fiction

## Field, Michael

Pen name for Katherine Harris Bradley (1846–1914) and Edith Emma Cooper (1862–1913), an

English couple who collaboratively wrote poetry and plays. In 1865, Bradley assumed care for three-year-old Edith, when Edith's mother, Bradley's aunt, became an invalid. Bradley and Cooper were seldom separated thereafter, although Bradley attended Newnham College of Cambridge University, College de France, England, Paris. In 1878, Cooper accompanied Bradley to University College in Bristol, where they participated in suffrage organizations, debate societies, and antivivisectionist activities. By the time Cooper was twenty, she and Bradley had sworn "Against the world, to be / Poets and lovers evermore." From then on, they lived together, traveled abroad together, and collaborated on two dozen tragic dramas on classical and historical themes and eight volumes of neopagan lyric poetry. In private life, Bradley called herself "Michael," and Cooper was "Field" or, more often, "Henry"; friends referred to them as "the Fields." Comparing themselves to Elizabeth (1806–1861) and Robert Browning (1812–1889), the two women declared: "We are closer married." Their relationship may have contributed to the theories of their friend Havelock Ellis (1859–1939), the British sexologist.

In 1884, "Michael Field" was welcomed as a promising new writer, but when he was revealed as a spinster aunt and niece, public interest quickly faded. Nonetheless, praise from fellow poets, including Robert Browning, George Meredith (1828–1909), Arthur Symons (1865–1945), W.B. Yeats (1865–1939), Vernon Lee (1856–1935), and George Moore (1852–1933), encouraged the women to continue writing. Their plays are well researched and often at least mildly feminist. Bradley and Cooper's close friends, the couple Charles Ricketts (1866–1931) and Charles Shannon (1863–1937), privately printed elegant illustrated editions of four of their tragedies at the Vale Press.

Michael Field's poetry compares with the late-century aesthetic lyrics of Oscar Wilde (1854–1900), whom they knew. *Long Ago* (1889) is a collection of intense, sensuous verses based on Sappho (ca. 600 B.C.E.); it contains the transsexual poem "Tiresias," extolling the joys and pleasures of female sexuality. *Underneath the Bough* (1893) includes "A Girl," often considered Bradley's enraptured tribute to her partner. When Cooper developed cancer, Bradley nursed her until her death, then died of cancer herself within a year. Their collaborative journal, *Works and Days* (1933), published after their deaths, seems to confirm the sexuality implied in their poetry.                    *Kathleen Hickok*

### Bibliography

Laird, Holly. "Contradictory Legacies: Michael Field and Feminist Restoration." *Victorian Poetry* 33:1 (Spring 1995), 111–128.

Leighton, Angela. *Victorian Women Poets: Writing Against the Heart*. Hemel Hempstead, England: Harvester Wheatsheaf, 1992; Charlottesville, Va.: University Press of Virginia, 1992, pp. 202–243.

Prins, Yopie. "A Metaphorical Field: Katherine Bradley and Edith Cooper." *Victorian Poetry* 33:1 (Spring 1995), 129–148.

White, Chris. "'Poets and Lovers Evermore': Interpreting Female Love in the Poetry and Journals of Michael Field." *Textual Practice* 4:2 (Summer 1990), 197–212. Reprinted in *Sexual Sameness: Textual Differences in Lesbian and Gay Writing*. Ed. Joseph Bristow. New York: Routledge, 1992, pp. 26–43.

*See also* Poetry

## Film, Alternative

Film produced and distributed outside established, commercial channels. Alternative film provides forms of expression and creative opportunities for marginalized filmmakers and audiences; it includes the majority of lesbian films with explicit lesbian content.

The phrase "alternative film" began to be used in the 1970s, the result of debates among filmmakers and critics concerning the possibilities of a new and different kind of cinema that would challenge both the form and the production/distribution models of Hollywood cinema. The "alternative" in alternative film is thus an alternative to the classical Hollywood cinema: produced by large studios with equally large budgets, featuring well-known stars, and appealing to the largest possible audiences. Alternative film was characterized not just by its different means of production, but also by a different style, for one of the concerns of the creators of alternative film was to provide an aesthetic alternative to Hollywood. If Hollywood cinema provided a seamless form of entertainment based on a realist aesthetic, then alternative film sought to engage spectators more actively by providing different forms of identification.

Lesbian alternative film traces its origins to feminism and the women's movement, which, in the 1960s and 1970s, defined women's "images" as crucial to an understanding of both women's oppression and women's liberation and to new ways of understanding film that emerged in the 1970s. To be sure, there had been alternative cinema long before the 1970s. But something changed during that decade: Film became a more accessible medium for potential filmmakers, and the generation of filmmakers who came of age had been exposed to an image culture throughout their lives. Lesbian alternative film shared with feminist alternative film an attempt to use film both as consciousness raising and as the means to create new and challenging portraits of (lesbian) women's lives. At the same time, lesbian alternative film was influenced by the emergence of new ways of thinking about the medium of film.

Alternative film refers not only to individual films, but also to the ways in which films are seen. In the 1970s, alternative films were viewed in film festivals, at colleges and universities, and in museums. Alternative viewing sites thus constituted a challenge to commercial cinema. The development of home-viewing systems and of a wide range of independent production and distribution practices in the 1980s and 1990s have meant that alternative film has a much wider potential audience than was possible in the 1970s.

## Lesbian Alternative Filmmaking

Lesbian alternative film emerged in the 1970s through the work of directors such as Barbara Hammer, Jan Oxenberg, and Chantal Akerman. Three strains of alternative filmmaking developed, and they have continued to characterize trends through the 1980s and 1990s.

First, in the autobiographical and personal-essay format, film is used as a means of tracing the emergence of lesbian identity and of exploring the various ways in which film can function as a first-person form of narration. Virtually all of Hammer's 1970s films fall into this category, from the lyrical evocation of lesbian sexuality in *Women I Love* (1979), which shows a variety of women, including Hammer herself, to the exploration of the highs and lows (literally) of lesbian relationships in *Double Strength* (1978), which represents Hammer's relationship (and its demise) with a trapeze artist. Oxenberg's *Home Movie* (1973) was the first of many films to use childhood home movies as a device to explore coming out as a lesbian. In the 1990s, the New York City–based cable television series *Dyke TV* (several episodes of which are available on home video) developed a regular segment on this theme, entitled "I Was a Lesbian Child," in which adult lesbians examine childhood images and their own lesbian formations.

Autobiographical and personal-essay films typically use voice-over narration (often that of the filmmaker herself) and lyrical imagery to explore the imagery of lesbian identity. The autobiographical film is not unique to lesbian filmmaking, and, in fact, there was, and continues to be, a strong link between lesbian alternative film and feminist alternative film. Michelle Citron's *Daughter Rite* (1978), for example, interweaves staged interviews with two sisters and the filmmaker's own home movies (which are slowed down, repeated, and reexamined in a variety of ways). The film's meditation on the strong bonds between women and on the reconsideration of the past suggests how the preoccupations of feminist and lesbian alternative film have shared strong similarities.

The second category is the revisionist film, in which various genres and/or (mis)representations of lesbians and lesbianism are read critically. The medium of film is used self-critically to create both a critical look at the past and an appropriation of popular forms to lesbian ends. This category includes self-reflexive films, as well as films that attempt to take established genres and "lesbianize" them. While this "revisionist" approach has been more characteristic of lesbian alternative film (and video) in the late 1980s and 1990s, its bases were present in the emergent 1970s. Oxenberg's *Comedy in Six Unnatural Acts* (1975) looks at popular conceptions of lesbianism, both from without (the lesbian Girl Scout leader who lures young girls with cookies) and from within (the mating rituals of the lesbian community, in which two women's first date is quite literally a community event). By grouping the stereotypes together, the film mocks them and defuses their power simultaneously.

Hammer's *Nitrate Kisses* (1993) examines the ways in which lesbianism has been both represented and elided in a variety of contexts, from early cinema to Nazi Germany. Su Friedrich's *Damned If You Don't* (1987) explores the lesbian sexual awakening of a nun at the same time that the film *Black Narcissus*, Michael Powell's 1947 film with Deborah Kerr in the role of a nun in a convent, is quoted, paraphrased, and reread. In other words, the evocation of lesbian sexuality occurs in the film through a double process of a lyrical evocation of love between two women and the simultaneous deconstruction of a

**F** classical film in which sexual repression is evident throughout. Lesbianism may be repressed in the Powell film, but the very project of Friedrich's film is to tease it out. Friedrich's film is not content simply to "read" *Black Narcissus*; rather, the deconstruction of that film becomes the stimulus for the creation of another film, another story.

The third category of lesbian alternative film involves the rewriting of the cinema. This category is the most amorphous, for it includes those films in which lesbianism is evoked, less to provide a portrait of lesbian identity or a representation of sexuality, as to rewrite the very language of cinema. The "lesbian" in this category of alternative film is less evident than in the previous two categories, and the films in this category have been quite controversial in lesbian communities, particularly when they are projected in gay and lesbian film festivals. In the 1970s, this category is best defined by Chantal Akerman's *Je tu il elle* (I you he she) (1974), a film divided into three parts and connected by the voyage of the protagonist, played by Akerman herself, as she moves from a room, to a truck ride with a man, to an encounter with her female lover in an apartment. The film concludes with a scene of lovemaking between the two women, after which the protagonist leaves. This is hardly a film that proclaims the joys of lesbian love or the affirmation of lesbian identity; nonetheless, it uses lesbianism as a point of interrogation about the very nature of cinematic pleasure, voyeurism, and narrative. The film is controversial not only because it does not fit neatly into the category of "lesbian alternative film," but also, and especially, because Akerman herself has resisted the identity of "lesbian filmmaker"—and once refused to let a gay and lesbian film festival show the film.

Still, it is important to include such films as *Je tu il elle* in the category of lesbian alternative film, not so much to appropriate them as to keep in mind that the very definition of "lesbian cinema" is not necessarily clear-cut, straightforward, or obvious. Such flexibility in definition encourages a consideration of how lesbianism informs the notion of "alternative film" in different ways. Midi Onodera's *Ten Cents a Dance* (1985), for instance, has also been controversial, particularly in the context of gay and lesbian film festivals, because the film (like Akerman's) situates its lesbian scene as only one of three in the film. But *Ten Cents a Dance* is also an original exploration of the aesthetics of desire and communication. It has provoked controversy and

discussion about what lesbian film is and should be—and that is exactly one of the important functions of alternative film.

These three categories should be understood as fluid, for a striking characteristic of lesbian alternative film is its hybridity—its crossing of established boundaries and its mixing of genres. *Ten Cents a Dance* may fit most appropriately into the category of rewriting the cinema, but it also draws from the autobiographical film (in its first section, Onodera plays the role of the experienced lesbian on a date) and the revisionist film (a split screen is used throughout, recalling how in wide-screen films of the 1950s, such as *Pillow Talk* [1959], similar devices portrayed sexuality in a very different way). Additionally, many lesbian filmmakers work across different categories.

Because of its commitment to stylistic and aesthetic innovation, lesbian alternative film is often defined in opposition to the narrative feature (for example, *Desert Hearts* [1985], directed by Donna Deitch) and the documentary film (for example, *In the Best Interests of the Children* [1977], directed by Liz Stevens, Frances Reid, and Cathy Zheutlin). However, the impact of alternative filmmaking has been such that the hybrid quality of lesbian cinema challenges those divisions. *Forbidden Love* (1993), directed by Lynne Fernie and Aerlyn Weissman, is both a documentary and a narrative feature *and* draws from the categories of alternative film described—it includes autobiographical coming out stories, a rewriting of lesbian pulp fiction of the 1950s and 1960s, and, in the juxtaposition of the love story and the interviews with lesbians, it, too, attempts to create a new kind of cinematic language. Onodera's *A Displaced View* (1988) is an experimental documentary that draws upon the different modes of alternative film. Onodera explores her own identity and her relationship to her mother and grandmother, with particular attention to the ways in which hybrid identities are forged. Rose Troche's *Go Fish* (1994) was one of the most commercially successful lesbian features since *Desert Hearts*, and it, too, draws upon virtually all of the techniques associated with lesbian alternative film.

Alternative modes of distribution and exhibition are central to the success of lesbian alternative film. Some lesbian films have become widely available in commercial outlets; the video versions of *Forbidden Love* and *Go Fish* can be found in large video rental stores, and cable television has offered some screenings of lesbian film. While these successes are important, there would be no such thing as lesbian alternative cinema without groups like Women Make Movies, the New York City–based distributor committed to a wide range of women's filmmaking, including lesbian alternative film. Nor would lesbian alternative cinema be a reality without both gay and lesbian and women's film festivals, which continue to provide opportunities to see films and videos that challenge viewers' notions of what images can be.

*Judith Mayne*

## Bibliography

Dyer, Richard. *Now You See It: Studies on Lesbian and Gay Film.* New York: Routledge, 1990.

Weiss, Andrea. *Vampires and Violets: Lesbians in the Cinema.* London: Jonathan Cape, 1992.

**See also** Documentaries; Film, Mainstream; Video

## Film, Mainstream

Lesbians in mainstream cinema have been alternately visible and invisible since the 1910s. Yet, even in those instances when lesbian characters or women who exhibit lesbian traits (such as sexually desiring or having an intense emotional bond with another woman) can be discerned, they are often white and middle-class. In fact, the majority of lesbian portrayals have been produced by Western filmmakers who depict white heterosexuality as the norm. Thus, in many films, the characters who seem to be lesbians *also* express sexual interest in men, or their passions for women are implied but rarely shown directly. In Sidney Drew's 1914 U.S. comedy, *A Florida Enchantment*, for example, a lesbian attraction is hinted at when Lillian Travers (Edith Storey) swallows magical seeds and becomes a man. Her sex-change leads her to court a number of women. The lesbian implications come less from the story line, though, than from the viewer's knowledge that the hero is played by an actress.

As *A Florida Enchantment* suggests, describing images of lesbians in mainstream film is often less about locating characters and more about pinpointing allusions to lesbianism. In Hollywood movies, images of lesbians or lesbian-associated conduct include stereotypes of the predator (Barbara Stanwyck as the lecherous madam in Edward Dmytryk's *Walk on the Wild Side* [1962]) and the prison warden (Evelyn Harper as the sadistic matron in John Cromwell's *Caged* [1950]). The most popular predatory image of lesbians, whether produced

in Hollywood or elsewhere, remains the vampire. In some instances the lesbian vampire is depicted in metaphorical terms, while in others she finds literal representation. In both cases, however, the appellation "lesbian" is an approximation. The lesbian vampires of the cinema are not solely female identified, nor do they always pursue their victims in explicitly sexual ways. What renders them lesbian is their preference for females and their association with enduring stereotypes: They are usually aggressive, nonreproductive, sexually and socially aberrant, and conventionally masculine in behavior. Metaphorical lesbian vampires can be found in Roberto Rossellini's *Rome, Open City* (1944–1945) and Claude Chabrol's *Les Biches* (1967). Literal representations appear in Lambert Hillyer's *Dracula's Daughter* (1936), Roy Baker's *The Vampire Lovers* (1970), Harry Kumel's *Daughters of Darkness* (1971), and Tony Scott's *The Hunger* (1983).

It is difficult to locate the first cinematic representation of a lesbian, given that female-identified desire is often depicted in veiled terms. In spite of this limitation, Countess Geschwitz (Alice Roberts) in G.W. Pabst's *Die Büchse des Pandora* (Pandora's Box [1929]) seems to be the premier lesbian of cinema. Although Geschwitz pursues a heterosexual affair as the narrative progresses, she does so to protect the woman she loves, Lulu (Louise Brooks). As with other lesbian representations, the countess's desires are heavily implied—especially in a waltz scene when Lulu and Geschwitz dance together—but do not take explicit shape. In the few instances of explicit portrayals in the 1920s, lesbians often exemplify the evils of unrestrained desire, as in the images of embracing women in the orgy sequence in Cecil B. De Mille's *Manslaughter* (1922).

While the 1930s did not bring a radical revision of prior depictions, Leontine Sagan's *Mädchen in Uniform* (Girls in Uniform 1931) remains a sensitive portrayal of adolescent female desire and a compelling anti-Fascist narrative. In Sagan's movie, Manuela (Hertha Thiele), a student at a boarding school, falls in love with one of her teachers, Fraulein von Bernburg (Dorothea Wieck). After boldly declaring her love for von Bernburg late in the film, Manuela is rejected by the school's headmistress and prepares to leap to her death from a stairwell. In one version, her schoolmates save her, but, in most of the prints that circulated internationally in the early 1930s, Manuela commits suicide. Lesbian love is punished in yet another production from the 1930s. In Jacques Deval's *Club des Femmes*

**F** (The Girls' Club [1936]), the action takes place in a women's dormitory. In this all-female environment, Alice (Else Argal) becomes enamored of Juliette (Josette Day) and exhibits jealousy when Juliette returns the affections of a man. By the narrative's end, Alice is banished to a leper colony.

The on-screen death of lesbian desire is nowhere more evident than in William Wyler's *These Three* (1936). Unlike *Mädchen in Uniform*, however, death results not by suicide but from revisions to the film's source material: Lillian Hellman's play, *The Children's Hour* (1934). Hellman's work tells the story of two women who run a girls' school. One of their students starts a rumor that they are lesbians. The girl's grandmother begins a campaign to close the school. In the original play, and in Wyler's second adaptation, *The Children's Hour* (1962), the lie becomes a trigger for one of the women to recognize that she is, indeed, a lesbian. In the 1962 adaptation, Martha (Shirley MacLaine) realizes that she is in love with her friend, Karen (Audrey Hepburn) and commits suicide. In the 1936 film, however, both the rumor and the revelation of lesbianism are removed and replaced with hints of heterosexual promiscuity.

While portrayals of lesbians in the 1930s were few and far between, some movie stars cultivated an ambiguous sexuality both on and off screen. Marlene Dietrich (1901–1992) and Greta Garbo (1905–1990) were often marketed as stars who appealed to women, and both played roles that could be interpreted as lesbian. Paramount publicized Josef von Sternberg's *Morocco* (1930) with the following slogan: "Dietrich—the woman all women want to see." In one scene in particular, Dietrich wears a man's tuxedo and kisses another woman. Garbo, too, wears male drag in the 1930s and embraces an actress. In Rouben Mamoulian's *Queen Christina* (1933), Garbo rules Sweden in male attire and passionately kisses her lady-in-waiting, Countess Ebba Sparre (Elizabeth Young). Despite the erotic charge of these scenes, Dietrich and Garbo play lesbians in only the most allusive of terms.

Allusion and implication remain popular representational strategies to depict lesbians and are especially evident in Hollywood movies made between the 1930s and the 1960s. For example, Sandra Shaw portrays a woman who likes to wear men's clothing in Rowland Brown's 1933 movie, *Blood Money*. While she is shown with a boyfriend in a number of scenes, she also appears wearing a double-breasted man's suit and in the company of a woman late in the film. While a lesbian relationship is implied in this sequence, it is never explicitly shown. Allusion is even more apparent in Alfred Hitchcock's *Rebecca* (1940), since the eponymous character, who is independent, aggressive, and rejects her husband, is already dead before the movie begins. The strongest clue to suggest Rebecca's departure from heterosexual norms is provided by Mrs. Danvers (Judith Anderson), a spinster who tends the mansion in which Rebecca once lived and who not only adores her previous employer, but also hints at an illicit relationship with her.

This practice of allusion may have had something to do with Hollywood's Production Code, a set of guidelines intended to ensure that motion pictures adhered to moral standards of the day. The code's strictures were imposed on studios by their own professional organization, the Motion Picture Producers and Distributors of America (MPPDA), from the early 1930s until the late 1960s. Failure to meet the standards of the code could result in a $25,000 fine and the threat that a movie would not be widely released in the United States. One of the prohibitions detailed in the Production Code is "sex perversion," a phrase meant to refer to practices unacceptable to normative heterosexuality, such as bestiality, bisexuality, transvestitism, and homosexuality. The prohibition against sex perversion ensured that representations of lesbians were either nonexistent or elusive.

The Production Code files for the MPPDA contain evidence of efforts designed to censor lesbianism. Thus, for example, censors required revisions for a scene in the original script of *Dracula's Daughter* (1936), in which a beautiful female vampire asks a young woman to undress and pose in the nude. In the final version, the model disrobes behind a screen, and only her bare neck and shoulders are shown to the audience. This alteration was designed to remove female sex perversion from the movie. Yet, such efforts were not always successful, since the vampire's attraction to her model is quite palpable in the final cut of *Dracula's Daughter*.

Suggestions of lesbian desire persisted in the 1950s, 1960s, and 1970s, as in Orson Welles's *Touch of Evil* (1958), in which Mercedes McCambridge plays a Chicana butch who watches Janet Leigh get attacked. In Robert Wise's *The Haunting* (1963), Claire Bloom portrays a neurotic woman who seductively torments Julie Harris. Lesbianism remains implied in both films and is collapsed with sadism.

The failure on the part of mainstream filmmakers to directly depict lesbians continued into numerous films that, like their predecessors in earlier decades, imply the existence of lesbians but do not portray them in straightforward ways. Diane Kurys's *Entre Nous* (1983) is a good example of this continuing practice, as are Steven Spielberg's *The Color Purple* (1985) and Jon Avnet's *Fried Green Tomatoes* (1991). In the first instance, Kurys tells the story of her mother's intense friendship with another woman just after World War II. While both women have significant ties to men, their friendship with each other is the most satisfying and emotionally intimate. Despite the passion that the women exhibit for each other, Kurys keeps their relationship platonic. Spielberg's *The Color Purple* is slightly more explicit than *Entre Nous* in its depiction of lesbian love. Based on Alice Walker's 1982 novel, *The Color Purple* traces the story of Celie (Whoopi Goldberg), an African American woman living in the U.S. South, who must endure her husband's physical and mental abuse and who falls in love with a singer named Shug (Margaret Avery). The novel's exploration of the women's affair is not only explicit but also lengthy. The film adaptation, however, streamlines their romance and reduces its importance. Noteworthy, however, is that *The Color Purple* remains one of the few mainstream films to depict lesbian love between women of color.

Like *Entre Nous* and *The Color Purple*, *Fried Green Tomatoes* portrays a close friendship between two women. (Actually, the movie traces the friendships between two pairs of women, but the characters played by Mary Stuart Masterson [Idgie] and Mary Louise Parker [Ruth] suggest lesbian desire.) Although Fannie Flagg's novel, *Fried Green Tomatoes at the Whistle Stop Cafe* (1987), depicts the rapport between Idgie and Ruth in explicitly lesbian terms, Jon Avnet portrays them as friends. Yet spectator responses to the movie indicate that, while some viewers choose to read the protagonists as heterosexual, others, especially lesbians, remain convinced that the women are gay.

The practice of reading against the grain of mainstream images of lesbians has become common among gay women. Spectators have become adept at reading the allusions and implications that have been coded into cinematic images. Only rarely do viewers get the opportunity to enjoy mainstream films with openly lesbian characters. Those rare instances include the interracial relationship between a white, Québecois woman and a black, anglophone lesbian in Patricia Rozema's Canadian film *When Night Is Falling* (1995) and

the role of Jane (Whoopi Goldberg), an African American lesbian, in Herbert Ross's *Boys on the Side* (1995). While the Canadian film depicts the women's romance in sexual terms, Ross's Hollywood movie shies away from lesbian romance and traces, instead, the relationship between a lesbian and a straight woman.

As this summary of lesbian representations in the history of mainstream cinema indicates, images of lesbians are rarely straightforward. They have to be teased out of the allusions that are built into many movies. Despite the effort demanded to locate cinematic lesbians, though, there is pleasure to be had in searching for them. Hopefully, there will be more mainstream portrayals of lesbians in future films so that the search will not be in vain.

*Rhona J. Berenstein*

## Bibliography

Creekmur, Corey, and Alexander Doty, eds. *Out in Culture: Gay, Lesbian, and Queer Essays on Popular Culture*. Durham, N.C.: Duke University Press, 1995.

Russo, Vito. *The Celluloid Closet: Homosexuality in the Movies*. New York: Harper and Row, 1985.

Weiss, Andrea. *Vampires and Violets: Lesbians in Film*. New York: Penguin, 1993.

White, Patricia. "Female Spectator, Lesbian Specter: *The Haunting*." In *Inside/Out: Lesbian Theories, Gay Theories*. Ed. Diana Fuss. New York: Routledge, 1991, pp. 142–172.

Wilton, Tamsin, ed. *Immortal Invisible: Lesbians and the Moving Image*. London: Routledge, 1995.

Zimmerman, Bonnie. "Daughters of Darkness: Lesbian Vampires." *Jump Cut* 24–25 (Fall 1980), 23–24.

***See also*** Dietrich, Marlene; Film, Alternative; Garbo, Greta; Hollywood

## Finland

Scandinavian republic located in northern Europe between Sweden and Russia and containing five million citizens. Once part of Sweden, Finland was an autonomous grand principality of Russia from 1809 to 1917 while maintaining its Lutheran Christianity.

The earliest record of a Finnish woman who married another woman dates to a court case in

1713. Anna Jöransdotter had been acting as a soldier until her lance corporal was informed that "Johan Jöransson" was a woman. Rather than believe this, he assumed her to be a hermaphrodite until a physical search revealed her to be a woman. Most likely because of her fully developed female body, she was not assumed to have been guilty of sodomy and was punished only by imprisonment with hard labor.

The first case of female sexual inversion was published in a Finnish medical journal in 1882. "Fruntimmer XYZ" had been repeatedly treated in a mental hospital because she had erotic feelings toward women and wanted to act accordingly. However, the treatment did not cure her.

The legal reform of 1889 incorporated female homosexual acts into the penal code by changing the formulation from "man" to "person": One "who fornicates with another person of the same sex" could be sentenced to jail for a maximum of two years. The inclusion of women was a direct recommendation of the penal-code comittee.

The Finnish Women's Association, founded in 1884 and inspired by Christian and nationalistic ideals, did not oppose the law. Nevertheless, in a letter to German sexologist Magnus Hirschfeld (1868–1935) published in 1914, a Finnish lawyer made a connection between "the bearded leaders of the Finnish women's rights organizations with their broad shoulders and young female companions" and a certain type of homosexual woman.

In 1906, these suffragists celebrated the passage of legislation giving women the right to vote and to be elected into the Parliament. The posthumous edited letters and diaries of one of the first women members of Parliament, Hilda Käkikoski (1864–1912), made her an icon for women who wanted to achieve an independent life and who, like her, were attracted to other women. Another example of such a woman was the modernist poet and writer Hagar Olsson (1893–1978), who formed a close relationship with another Swedish-speaking poet, Edith Södergran (1892–1923).

The period between the civil war in 1918 and the beginning of World War II in 1939 witnessed both a backlash against independent women and the rise of the flapper in the mixed literary circles of Helsinki. Discussions about sexuality and gender nonconformity began to recast public awareness of earlier instances of female bonding in erotic terms. The poems written by Isa Asp (1853–1872), for example, were seen in the 1930s to portray erotic sentiments resembling those of the Greek poet Sappho.

The fear of denunciation, court cases, and socially ruined lives made women-loving women keep a low profile, even though women were charged with homosexual acts in only a few cases. Due to strict alcohol laws, women could not frequent bars without male escort even after the wars, thus restricting their ability to meet and build a community around shared lesbianism. This continued until the late 1960s, when the mixed gay organization Psyke started to organize dance evenings.

Homosexual behavior ceased being illegal in 1971; three years later, SETA (Sexual Equality) split from Psyke and began making gay politics more visible and focused on emancipation. Due to their efforts, homosexuality was removed from the list of medical disorders in 1981.

In the 1980s, the lesbian feminist group Akanat began to gather around well-established Unioni, the League of Finnish Feminists. Among other activities, Akanat published a lesbian magazine, Torajyvä (1982–1988). Increased international contacts also influenced the lesbian sadomasochistic group Ekstaasi, which ran a café and staged performances in Helsinki. At the same time, the mixed gay clubs run by SETA continued to attract lesbians on women's evenings.

The visibility and activity of lesbians continued into the 1990s. The Lesbian Studies Network, active from 1990 to 1995, supported students and advanced lesbian studies in academe as a part of women's studies. The first lesbian publishing company, Meikänainen, was founded in 1992. The 1990s also saw the coming out of prominent lesbians and bisexuals, such as the writer Pirkko Saisio (1949–) and the theater director Vivica Bandler (1917–). Lesbians and gay men continued to work together in SETA, winning a ban against discrimination in 1995 and working for the legal acknowledgment of homosexual partnerships, including reproductive rights and the right to adopt children.

*Tuula Juvonen*

### Bibliography

Bandler, Vivica, with Carita Backström. *Adressaten okänd* (Addressee Unknown). Helsingfors: Schildts, 1992.

Holmström, Roger. *Hagar Olsson och den öppna horisonten. Liv och diktning, 1920–1945* (Hagar Olsson and the Open Horizon: Life and Poetry, 1920–1945). Esbo: Schildts, 1993.

Löfström, Jan. "A Premodern Legacy: The 'Easy' Criminalization of Homosexual Acts Between Women in the Finnish Penal Code of 1889."

*Journal of Homosexuality* 34:3–4 (1998), 532–79.

Saarinen, Terhi. *Alussa oli kellari. Viisi helsinkiläistä lesbotarinaa* (In the Beginning There Was a Cellar: Five Lesbian Stories from Helsinki). Helsinki: Seta julkaisut, 1994.

*See also* Russia; Sweden

## Flanner, Janet (1892–1978)

U.S. journalist. Janet Flanner was the second of three daughters born into a middle-class family in Indianapolis, Indiana; her undertaker father committed suicide in his mortuary in 1912. Eight years later, Flanner married and moved to Greenwich Village in New York City. After the marriage dissolved, Flanner met Solita Solano (1888–1975), the drama editor of the *New York Tribune*, who became her first woman lover. Intent on escaping what they perceived to be U.S. provincialism, the pair sailed for Europe in 1921 and settled in Paris shortly thereafter. There Flanner finished an autobiographical first novel, *The Cubical City* (1926), and began writing one-thousand-word dispatches for the newly founded *New Yorker* magazine. These "Letters from Paris," published fortnightly under the byline "Genêt" (a French version of "Janet" coined by Flanner's editor), featured accounts of European events of interest to the *New Yorker*'s U.S.-based readership. News of notable lesbian expatriates, such as Gertrude Stein (1874–1946) and Sylvia Beach (1887–1962), appeared in her columns, along with references to more conventional subjects.

Flanner figured importantly in the circle of lesbians frequenting the salon of Natalie Barney (1876–1972) and is the model for a character in *Ladies Almanack* (1928), Djuna Barnes's (1892–1982) humorous send-up of the group. While still living with Solano, who reputedly also had taken another lover at the time, Flanner became sexually and emotionally involved with Noel Haskins Murphy (1894–?), a U.S. expatriate widow who had settled in France. Years later, back in the United States during World War II, Flanner entered a third "passionate friendship," with Italian journalist Natalia Danesi Murray (1901–?), who published their correspondence after Flanner's death. Flanner, with varying success, seems to have juggled relationships with these three women in the last decades of her life. What is certain is that she maintained abiding emotional ties with each woman well into old age

and, indeed, until the connections were severed by death.

Most famous for the *New Yorker* "Letters," Flanner also published a series of profiles and monographs portraying such figures as Adolf Hitler (1889–1945) and Marshal Pétain (1856–1951), the premier of Vichy France (1940–1944). *Paris Journal, 1944–1965,* one of several collections of her Paris correspondence, won the National Book Award in 1966.
*Anne Charles*

*Bibliography*

Castle, Terry. "The Gaiety of Janet Flanner." In *The Apparitional Lesbian: Female Homosexuality and Modern Culture.* New York: Columbia University Press, 1993, pp. 186–199.

Flanner, Janet. *Darlinghissima: Letters to a Friend.* Ed. Natalia Danesi Murray. New York: Harvest, 1985.

Wineapple, Brenda. *Genêt: A Biography of Janet Flanner.* New York: Ticknor and Fields, 1989.

*See also* Barnes, Djuna Chappell; Barney, Natalie; Beach, Sylvia; Journalism; Paris; Stein, Gertrude

## Food

The sustenance of life, source of one of life's greatest pleasures, and the most common expression of hospitality. Every culture and society has food that distinguishes it from its neighbors. While lesbians may not have particular foods that attach to lesbian culture, certain traditions have been taken up so as to be expected of at least segments of the community.

Potluck dinners, or the practice of sharing a feast by having each household contribute a particular dish, have become common among lesbians, at least in the United States, and can be said to be elevated to an art form. While allowing a community to come together for a meal, such meals relieve a particular individual from the traditional womanly chore of producing and hosting an entire, coordinated meal without being able to sit and enjoy it. Potluck dinners or other occasions involving the serving of food offered lesbians the opportunity to gather together in an informal social setting that cost little and did not have the perils associated with bar life.

Another food custom adopted by many lesbians, particularly lesbian separatists, is vegetarianism. Growing out of the concerns of the ecofeminists for the health of the planet, several lesbian-feminist collectives, notably Bloodroot (in Connecticut), held vegetarianism as a prime tenet of their institutional philosophy. Vegetarianism also reflects the separatists' concern with the hierarchy of power in modern life. In a traditional patriarchy, males are at the head of the hierarchy, followed by women, children, people of lower classes, and, at the bottom, animals. Vegetarian lesbian separatists, in breaking with traditional forms of patriarchy, discourage the eating of animal flesh. They seek, in the name of women and sometimes in worship of the goddess, to bring about the healing of the age-old rift from nature that resulted from men asserting dominion over the earth. Essential to this re-creation of womanspirit is the distancing from all destructive energy. Thus, vegetarianism goes hand in hand with back-to-the-earth movements and the goal of self-sufficiency. Women in ancient times were the gatherers of the produce of the earth and healers who used herbs and flowers in their treatments. Thus, many of those who worship the goddess do not eat meat.

The "food conspiracy" (buying food in bulk at cost for distribution within a cooperative) also has been a feature of more highly developed lesbian communities, such as those in Iowa City, Iowa, and Berkeley, California. These practices were developed, again, as a response to the perceived monopoly of patriarchal, environmentally destructive food conglomerates; lesbians hoped to make wholesome food widely available at low cost to women throughout their communities.          *Rosa María Pegueros*

### Bibliography

Faderman, Lillian. *Odd Girls and Twilight Lovers: A History of Lesbian Life in Twentieth-Century America*. New York: Columbia University Press, 1991.

Gearheart, Sally Miller. "The Spiritual Dimension: Death and Resurrection of a Hallelujah Dyke." In *Our Right to Love*. Ed. Ginny Vida. Englewood Cliffs, N.J.: Prentice-Hall, 1978.

Shugar, Dana. *Separatism and Women's Community*. Nebraska: University of Nebraska Press, 1995.

**See also** Collectives; Goddess Religion; Separatism; Vegetarianism

### Foster, Jeannette Howard (1895–1981)

American author, poet, and translator. Jeannette Foster also wrote under the pseudonyms Jan Addison, Hilary Farr, and Abigail Sanford. Born Novem-

*Jeannette H. Foster. Photo by Tee A. Corinne.*

ber 3, 1895, in Oak Park, Illinois, she died July 26, 1981, in Pocahantas, Arkansas.

One of the most significant contributions to the study of lesbian literature, Foster's groundbreaking *Sex Variant Women in Literature* was self-published in 1956 by Vantage Press. *Sex Variant Women* critically examines hundreds of occurrences of "variant women" in literature in a number of languages and historical periodxs spanning more than 2,500 years. In her thoroughness, Foster provided all future scholars with the basis for their research.

The germ for *Sex Variant Women*, Foster explains was implanted when she was in college. As a student council member, Foster was called to a secret council meeting to determine the fate of two female students who "locked themselves away together" every chance they got. Foster was perplexed by the need for such a meeting and the need for punishment.

The students in question were placed on probation for the brief remainder of the year. The effect on Foster would last considerably longer; it was then that her search to understand "sex variant" women began. Her research provided her with resources for addressing future conflicts, for managing her own "sexually variant" life, and, ultimately, for an impressive body of work, the crowning jewel of which is *Sex Variant Women*.

A native of Illinois, Foster remained in her home state through 1922, earning a B.S. in chemistry and engineering in 1918 and an M.A. in English and American literature in 1922, both from Rockford College. She then attended Emory University in Atlanta, Georgia, where she earned a B.S. in library science in 1932 before returning to the University of Chicago, where, in 1935, she received her Ph.D. She was a professor of library science, taught writing, literature, and English, and was a librarian at a half-dozen prominent American colleges and universities. Foster was Dr. Alfred Kinsey's first librarian at the Institute for Sex Research, Indiana University at Bloomington, 1948–1952.

Foster called such prominent women as Janet Flanner (1892–1978), May Sarton (1912–1996), and Mary Renault (1905–1983) friends. She had a long-term romantic relationship with Linwood College professor Hazel Tolliver. A number of years later, the two were joined by the head of Linwood's physical education department, Dorothy "Dot" Ross. The three women lived together, moving, upon retirement, to the home they built in Pocohantas, Arkansas.

Foster contributed countless articles, pieces of fiction, and poetry to *The Ladder* in the 1960s. Nearly thirty years of her poetry were published as *Two Women: The Poetry of Valerie Taylor and Jeannette Foster* (1976) and later as *Two Women Revisited: The Poetry of Valerie Taylor and Jeannette Foster* (1991), and her translation of Renée Vivien's *A Woman Appeared to Me* was published in 1976 by Naiad Press.

Barbara Grier (1933–), and Donna McBride (1940–), whose Naiad Press republished *Sex Variant Women* in 1985, donated all of Foster's manuscripts to the main library in San Francisco's Gay and Lesbian Center. Among those manuscripts are unpublished novels and novellas, including *Home Is the Hunter* and *Death Under Duress*, and a considerable number of her poems. Foster also contributed articles to *Library Quarterly* and other professional journals and saw her fiction published in *Harper's*.

Andrea L.T. Peterson

## Bibliography

Foster, Jeannette. Letter to Margaret Anderson, *Forbidden Fires*, Margaret Anderson. Tallahassee, Fla.: Naiad, 1996, p. 154ff.

Kuda, Marie. "Jeannette Howard Foster." In *Gay and Lesbian Literature*. Ed. Sharon Malinowski. Detroit: St. James, 1996, pp. 140–141.

*See also* Flanner, Janet; Grier, Barbara; Kinsey Institute Librarians; Naiad Press; Renault, Mary; Sarton, May; Taylor, Valerie; Vivien, Renée

## France

Large republic in western Europe with a long and rich cultural history, including an expansive history of lesbianism. Information, although fragmentary, is to be found in the fields of politics, religion, literature, philosophy, medicine, and art, among others.

### Early-Modern Era

Aspects of female same-sex love can be found in the history of medieval France, but the recovery of texts from Greek and Roman antiquity in the early-modern period (the Renaissance) gave lesbians a concrete name. They were called "tribades," from the Greek *tribein*, signifying to rub or to rub against each other. In *Lives of Fair and Gallant Ladies*, a fanciful history of the events at the court of France, Pierre de Bourdeilles (ca. 1540–1614), abbot and lord of Brantôme (who also used the word "Lesbian"), identified a tribade as a "counterfeit" who imitates a man, but, because she supposedly does not penetrate her partner, her sexuality is seen as little more than a sham. The printer and essayist Henri Estienne (1531–1598), in his work *Apologia for Herodotus* (1566), distinguishes between tribades and women who use a dildo to penetrate each other.

Although the Renaissance recognized the lesbian as a separate category, it defined her solely in terms of a specific sexual practice. Since their recognition was solely within the context of a devalued sexuality, lesbians were denied social liberties. The occasional transvestite marriages between women that have been uncovered among the French lower classes during the sixteenth century were punished with the same severity as those "crimes against nature" of the sodomite, or male homosexual. In the 1550s, for instance, "a girl from Fontaines, married two years," was discovered and "burned alive" (Estienne 1566). Thirty years later, essayist Michel de Montaigne (1533–1592) mentions a certain Mary, married five months, who was "hung for illicit devices used to compensate for the defect of her sex."

This points to a central contradiction within the culture of early-modern France: Whereas the death penalty awaited those who dared upset social convention as cross-dressers, primarily women of the working and peasant classes, a more tolerant atti-

*Ecole de Fontainebleau, Gabrielle d'Estrées and her sister. Louvre. © Photo R.M.N.*

tude toward upper-class female same-sex couples emerged. At court, and, more particularly, in the Fontainebleau school of painting, lesbian-tinged representations of the classical goddess Diana appeared along with a generally more permissive cultural and sexual environment for women. The famous painting of Gabrielle d'Estrées, the mistress of Henri IV, and her sister naked in the bath is certainly one of the more enigmatic expressions of this period.

These liberal aristocratic attitudes during the early-modern period did not survive the consolidation of power in the hands of the absolute monarchy of Louis XIV (1643–1715), which rested, in part, upon the consolidation of male power and authority. Some women attempted to assert their agency through political action or through literature, contesting the institution of marriage and exalting same-sex love between women. For example, Madeleine de Scudéry (1607–1701) earned the name "Sappho of the Hôtel of Rambouillet." Later, Madame de Murat (1670–1716)—author of fairy tales, including one called *Le Sauvage* (The Savage [1699]), a story of a cross-dressed young girl—was

imprisoned for "debauchery" with women and for denigrating family values that women were supposed to pass on to male children.

## The Eighteenth Century

In the eighteenth century, leaders of the Enlightenment protested against absolutism in its many forms—religion, the monarchy, and masculine hegemony—thus opening the door for some women to live openly homosexual lives. Indeed, lesbian pleasure became a philosophical topic explored most notably by Denis Diderot (1713–1784), not only in the novel *La Religieuse* (The Nun [written in 1760, published in 1796]) but also in the philosophical essay *Le Rêve de d'Alembert* (The Dream of d'Alembert [1769]) and the *Encyclopédie*, in which he redefined the word "tribade."

Society during the Enlightenment, with its openness to new ideas, accepted homosexuals to a certain degree. The actresses Hipployte Clairon (1723–1803) and Françoise Raucourt (1756–1815), the singer Sophie Arnould (1740–1802), and several aristocratic women were regularly written about in underground publications. Far from being shocked, these authors, or "secret observers," recognized lesbians as part of society, going so far as to imagine the existence of a "Secte Anandryne" (Anandryne Sect), presided over by Françoise Raucourt, which supposedly initiated young girls into the joys of Sappho.

As can be seen in Raucourt's life, if one wished to challenge traditional societal values it was better to be an actress on the margins of society. During the French Revolution, Queen Marie Antoinette (1755–1793) learned the cost of transgressing the norm when she shared the "sweet joys of friendship" with the princess of Lamballe (1749–1792) and the duchess of Polignac (1749–1793). Stigmatized for her "sapphic ways" and her foreign origin, she was also accused of being a "bad mother" and a "debauched wife." While the Déclaration des Droits de l'Homme et du Citoyen (Declaration of the Rights of Man and the Citizen [1789]) proclaimed the principle of equality of the sexes, in fact the revolutionaries denied women's civil rights. While the revolutionaries removed sodomy from the category of sexual crimes "against nature," they also committed the first homophobic crime of the new Republic by assassinating the princess of Lamballe in 1792 for her "excessive friendship" with the queen. Although the First Republic (following the revolution) granted sexual liberty to men, the same rights for women were excluded from the new civil code imposed by Napoleon in 1804, a code that resubjugated women to marriage by reinforcing the power of father, brother, and husband.

## The Nineteenth Century

Thus, the early nineteenth century was marked by a triumphant patriarchy. While women still had no civil rights, a general fear of lesbians presisted, which underlined their status as a social danger. Love between women became a disease, as medical and sexological discourses codified and stigmatized "clitorism" or "tribadism" along with other excesses of pleasure. It soon became a moral disease as well: Tribades were considered corrupt and depraved. By the end of the nineteenth century, lesbianism was treated as a mental illness within psychiatric discourse, making this "inverted woman" an example of the dangerous "masculinization" awaiting all women who dared challenge patriarchal beliefs.

Nonetheless, a liberating countercurrent appeared that would exploit the contradictions of the revolution and launch a new theory linking love to social progress. In his *Le Nouveau Monde Amoureux*

(Love in the New World) from around 1816, Charles Fourier argued that Parisian lesbians "defend liberty more than anyone else" and, therefore, deserved a preeminent place in his work. In the 1830s, George Sand (1804–1876), the female followers of the utopian thinker Saint-Simon, and Flora Tristan (1803–1844), pioneer of the Worker's Union, all sought out new models of sexual freedom. Sand was the first novelist to speak of desire and pleasure between women, in *Lélia* (1833), which caused a minor uproar. Tristan was the first to suggest a possible spiritual relationship between women along the lines of Saint John and Jesus.

It was the highly successful painter Rosa Bonheur (1822–1899), though, who braved numerous taboos. The first woman to live openly with another woman, Nathalie Micas (1824–1889), in a quasi-marital relationship that lasted forty years, as well as the first artist decorated by the Legion of Honor, Bonheur showed that lesbianism need not be an obstacle to professional success, provided that the model for success was a masculine one valid for both sexes. In her biography, she confided about Micas: "If I'd been a man, I would have married her, and people wouldn't have invented all these silly stories. I would've started a family, had children and heirs, and no one could have said a thing about it."

Bonheur managed to breach the patriarchal fortress, showing that sexual liberty was inextricably linked to social and cultural liberty, an idea that explains why, from the end of the nineteenth century on, so many lesbians expressed themselves in art and literature. Through art, society began to open up to the reality of lesbian life. For example, in the 1880s, Louise Breslau (1856–1927) painted a number of canvases depicting herself with her lover of forty years, Madeleine Zillhard (1863–1950). Indeed, after the public display of Gustave Courbet's famous painting *Sleep* (*Le Sommeil* [1866]), many artists became fascinated with the sapphic couple. The repetition of this theme served to soften taboos by revealing love between women and forcing society to see those whom it regarded as deviants and sinners.

Literature, as well, responded to the sapphic theme, inspired partly by new fragments of poems by Sappho (ca. 600 B.C.E.) discovered by German archeologists. As the nineteenth century progressed, the word "tribade" fell into disuse as new definitions came to the fore. In 1847, Charles Baudelaire (1821–1867) considered the title *Les Lesbiennes* for his future collection *Les Fleurs du Mal* (The Flowers of Evil [1857]). The feminine form of "homosexual" entered into the illustrated Larousse dictionary (*Nouveau Larousse Illustré*) in 1904, evidence of how medical and scientific language had entered everyday speech.

## The Twentieth Century

Early-twentieth-century France was dominated by a psychiatric theory that pathologized women with "overly masculine" tendencies, a political establishment that labeled sexual emancipation for women as moral, and a feminist movement concerned, above all, with winning civil rights. Hence, culture, by necessity, became the principal medium through which lesbians sought visibility, a trend that would last even through the 1970s.

Natalie Barney (1876–1972), an American writer living in Paris from around 1898, created a salon that was the center of much of this lesbian cultural life. Barney herself became the model for characters in fiction by numerous writers, including her lover Renée Vivien (1877–1909), Liane de Pougy (1869–1953), Lucie Delarue-Mardrus (1874–1945), Colette (1873–1954), Djuna Barnes (1892–1982), and Radclyffe Hall (1880–1943). Romaine Brooks (1874–1970), Barney's lover in later life, painted Barney in her garden on Rue Jacob in Paris.

Not all prominent lesbians worked in the cultural field. Hélène Brion (1882–1962), a teacher who lived for more than thirty years with Marguerite Othon, was a trade unionist and a pacifist. She was accused of "defeatism" during World War I, given a suspended prison sentence of three years, and prohibited from teaching. Editor of the journal *La Lutte féministe* (Feminist Fight [1919–1922]), she transgressed the feminine cultural models of her time by dressing in pants (following the lead of Rosa Bonheur), yet she never dared reveal the strongly ideological underpinnings of her feminism. Another ambivalent figure was the doctor and writer Madeleine Pelletier (1874–1939). Called a "complete feminist," she supported the "masculinization of women" since, "in a social sense, to remain a woman is to remain a slave." But, even though she wore her men's suits like feminist banners, she recommended that women "remain virgins." Perhaps fearing the association of feminism with lesbianism, she wrote to her friend Aria-Ly (1881–1934): "Above all, never fall in love or everyone will sing out 'Lesbos' " (Bonnet 1981, Bard 1992).

Although most available information pertains to lesbianism within middle-class, upper-class, and bohemian circles, some evidence exists of a working-class lesbian culture beginning in the mid-nineteenth century and continuing through World War I (1914–1918). Although there were no laws against lesbianism per se, the negative images, particularly of poor lesbians, created a difficult atmosphere. Homophobia remained unchallenged by leftist organizations representing the working class. For example, when anarchist leader Louise Michel (1830–1905) was accused of lesbianism, her political compatriots vigorously denied it. The French Communist Party, founded in 1920, was indifferent or even hostile to homosexuality.

Nevertheless, authors such as André Gide (1869–1951) and Colette write in their memoirs about lesbianism among domestic servants. Two millinery workers committed suicide in 1898 rather than live apart. Letters of women in jail describe an extensive lesbian culture, and lesbianism among sex workers was well known and documented. Some working-class lesbians even became celebrated, such as Victorine Meurent (1844–1928), a model for painter Edouard Manet (1832–1883), and the dancer Louise Weber (1869–1929), better known as La Goulue, who can be seen in many of Henri Toulouse-Lautrec's (1864–1901) paintings, at times with her lover. A rich vocabulary existed for lesbianism, including *gousse* (garlic clove) for lesbians who took the active role, and *vrille* (tendril) for the passive. Lesbians also referred to one another as *gougnotte* (girlfriend); popular, sometimes derisive, terms for lesbian acts included "to eat garlic" or "to go for the deal."

After World War I (1914–1918), sexual emancipation swept across France, despite the fact that French women were denied the right to vote and saw the imposition, in 1920, of a law curbing abortion and the distribution of birth-control information. The success of Victor Margueritte's *La Garçonne* (The Bachelor Girl [1922]), which sold 300,000 copies within a year, reveals how greatly attitudes had changed in regard to women's sexual freedom. Indeed, this novel portrayed the lesbian as the true liberated woman for the first time, linking economic independence, sexual liberty, and equality with men. Margueritte lost his membership in the Legion of Honor, while feminists, horrified by the "debauchery" and "vice" in his work, refused to support him. Thus, despite the relaxing of moral restrictions after the war, the loss of practically an entire male generation caused the government of the Third Republic, for obvious reasons, to reinforce its control over women and procreation. Women, including feminists, did not protest against the restrictions imposed on them. The accepted social norms allowed married women to engage in limited political activism; single women joined trade unions; and lesbians and liberated heterosexuals enjoyed access to cultural circles. Lesbians continued to have a real visibility within the cultural realm, as international artists inscribed lesbianism within the avant-garde.

The list of outstanding women who lived in lesbian relationships and recreated these in their work is too long to give here. Some of the most celebrated during the period between the world wars include dancer Loïe Fuller (1862–1928), filmmaker Germaine Dulac (1882–1942), photographers Claude Cahun (1894–1954) and Gisèle Freund (1908–), writer Gertrude Stein (1874–1946), painters Marie Laurencin (1883–1956), Mariette Lydis (1894–1970)—creator of the album *Les Lesbiennes* (1926)—and Tamara de Lempicka (1898–1980), and booksellers Adrienne Monnier (1892–1956) and Sylvia Beach (1887–1962). While the economic crisis of 1929 undermined the foundations of their prosperity, World War II would smash this movement. Forced to flee the war, Nazism, and anti-semitism, the majority of them scattered, bringing to an end a golden age to which Natalie Barney had contributed so greatly through her salon.

Women's suffrage, finally won in 1944 with the end of the Nazi occupation, did little to stop a new wave of misogyny, accompanied by a rise in homophobia that forced many homosexuals to live in secret. Despite her many successes and Colette's support, filmmaker Jacqueline Audry (1908–1977) was only barely able to make *Olivia* (1951) and *The Bachelor Girl* (1957). It was only through the help of existentialist philosopher Simone de Beauvoir (1908–1986) that Violette Leduc (1907–1972) could publish her novels. Though prominent gay intellectuals lived openly, lesbians still met with resistance, as Jean-Paul Sartre (1905–1980) showed in his play *Huis Clos* (No Exit [1944]). One of the characters, based on the model of the "damned" lesbian, may have been inspired by the trio he formed with de Beauvoir and Bianca Lamblin, who wrote in her *Mémoires d'une jeune fille dérangée* (Memoirs of a Crazed Young Girl [1993]) how de Beauvoir hid her affairs with women. This may explain why her treatment of both "the lesbian" and "the independent woman" in her masterpiece, *The Second Sex* (1949), strikes many readers as unsatisfactory.

## Lesbians and Feminism

It was not until the wave of demonstrations and general strikes in May 1968 and the emergence of the women's liberation movement that lesbians were able to truly come out. The women's revolt was a key moment in the history of their emancipation. For the first time, society saw a political movement that involved all women, whatever their sexual practice or social class. Also for the first time, a feminist movement held as a fundamental principle that women should define themselves in relation to each other and not solely to men. From that point on, demystifying love between women became a priority in a feminist movement. "Sisterhood is powerful" was a commonplace slogan that recognized the ties of love linking women, reversing oppression, and restoring fragmented identities and lives.

In 1971, the Homosexual Movement for Revolutionary Action (Front Homosexuel d'Action Révolutionnaire) began, inspired by the women's liberation movement. Started by lesbian feminists who wanted an alliance with their "brothers," the Homosexual Movement for Revolutionary Action soon became a men's movement mainly concerned with *plus jouir* (more pleasure). In April of that year, lesbians quit the men's movement and created their own group, called Red Dykes (Gouines Rouges), realizing that their liberation was linked primarily with women rather than with gay men.

The brief time that gay and lesbian militant interests merged was an important moment in the constitution of a new feminist consciousness for lesbians. It not only reinforced the choice to remain separate from men by inserting militant lesbianism in the women's movement, it also underlined the differences between gay men and lesbians, allowing lesbians to link sexuality to the political and the cultural arenas. For the next decade, the women's liberation movement was the location of lesbian struggles for freedom, giving birth to a women's culture that had considerable impact on society.

However, the rise to power of the political Left in 1981, led by socialist President François Mitterand (1916–1996), revealed how fragile the recognition of lesbians was. Some lesbian theorists, such as Monique Wittig (1935–), attempted to create a unique version of "lesbian materialism," influenced by leftist and socialist thought. However, a major conflict over materialist feminism ultimately destroyed the journal *Questions Féministes*, with some materialist feminists attempting to exclude radical lesbianism from the French intellectual scene.

Given this, it is not surprising that the decriminalization of homosexuality in 1982 failed to specifically mention social recognition for lesbians. Christiane Jouve, who founded the monthly magazine *Lesbia* in 1982, noted the "incongruous position of lesbians between marginality and integration," remarking that if those who held to their "right to indifference" wanted to "destroy homosexuality," as for herself, she wanted to "destroy invisibility" (1985). Although this is not a simple task, because of the resistance of social and educational institutions, masculine power structures, and the media, nonetheless, at the end of the twentieth century the French lesbian movement could be said to be particularly dynamic. More than twenty associations in France's largest cities, a monthly publication, *Lesbia*, and a lesbian film festival, Cinéffable, organized and financed by nonprofit sources, existed. At the same time, lesbians were still marginalized by an institutionalized feminism that wished to harvest the fruits of earlier struggles and make peace between the sexes at the expense of lesbians, and by a society that blamed them for attacks on patriarchal authority.

In 1992, the gay and lesbian movement issued a Contract for Social Union (Contrat d'Union Sociale), an attempt to secure the rights afforded heterosexual couples for same-sex couples. Whether this will have any impact on the overall recognition of lesbians seems doubtful, since they have been excluded from the general debate. Women's sexual rights are far from won and will certainly be at issue in the political debates of coming decades. *Marie-Jo Bonnet*

## Bibliography

Bard, Christine. *Madeleine Pelletier (1878–1939): Logique et infortunes d'un combat pour l'égalité* (Madeleine Pelletier [1878–1939]: Logic and Misfortunes in the Combat for Equality). Paris: Côté femmes, 1992.

Benstock, Shari. *Women of the Left Bank: Paris, 1900–1940*. Austin: University of Texas Press, 1986.

Bonnet, Marie-Jo. *Un Choix sans équivoque* (An Unequivocal Choice). Paris: Denoël-Gonthier, 1981. New rev. ed. with additional chapters: *Les Relations amoureuses entre les femmes du seizième au vingtième siècle* (Love Between Women from the Sixteenth to the Twentieth Centuries). Paris: Odile Jacob, 1995.

——. "De l'émanicipation amoureuse des femmes dans la cité, Lesbiennes et féministes au XXè siècle" (On the Sexual Liberation of Women in the City: Lesbians and Feminists in the Twentieth Century). *Les Tempes Moderne* (March–April 1998), 85–112.

Jouve, Christiane. "Détruire l'invisibilité" (Destroy Invisibility). *Lesbia* 30(1985), 3.

Klumpke, Anna. *Rosa Bonheur: The Artist's (Auto)biography*. Tr. Gretchen van Slyke. Ann Arbor: University of Michigan Press, 1997.

Martel, Frédéric. *Le Rose et le noir: Les Homosexuels en France depuis 1968* (The Rose and the Black: Homosexuals in France since 1968). Paris: Seuil, 1996.

Sautman, Francesca Canade. "Invisible Women: Lesbian Working-Class Culture in France, 1880–1930." In *Homosexuality in Modern France.* Ed. Jeffrey Merrick and Bryant T. Ragan, Jr. New York: Oxford, 1996, pp. 177–201.

***See also*** Barnes, Djuna Chappell; Barney, Natalie; Beach, Sylvia; Beauvoir, Simone de; Bonheur, Rosa; Brooks, Romaine; Colette; Delarue-Mardrus, Lucie; Europe, Early Modern; French Literature; Hall, Radclyffe; Leduc, Violette; Marie Antoinette; Michel, Louise; Middle Ages, European; Paris; Raucourt, Françoise; Sand, George; Stein, Gertrude; Tribade; Vivien, Renée; Wittig, Monique

## French Literature

From the Middle Ages through the twentieth century, the figure of the lesbian has appeared in French literature. However, the image and reception of that figure has varied significantly from era to era.

## Middle Ages (A.D. 800–1500)

The medieval period may well be the most problematic, for few relevant texts exist. A number of romances couch attraction between women in terms of a confusion resulting when a cross-dressed woman becomes the love interest of another woman. Typical of this type of tale is *Huon de Bordeaux*, a thirteenth-century romance in which Ide, a cross-dressed woman warrior, marries the daughter of the emperor. When Ide's identity is revealed, both she and her wife are threatened with death by burning, a not uncommon fate for lesbian couples. However, through the intercession of the Virgin Mary, Ide is miraculously transformed into a man, thus restoring the married couple to the "natural" order.

While narratives such as Ide's present a somewhat ambiguous rendering of the couple's consciousness of their trangressive sexuality, a clear portrait of lesbian sexuality appears in the twelfth century. In his *Livre de Manières* (*Book of Manners*), written between 1168–1178, Etienne de Fougères, a clergyman, chastises women who prefer their own sex as partners as rebelling "against the laws of nature" and provides an elaborate metaphoric description of lesbian sexual acts, all characterized by the lack of a penis. Fougères constructs the lesbian couple in terms of the heterosexual model, divided into passive and active partners. His suggestion that lesbians be physically punished and put to death reflects the hostility to lesbians that informed the medieval legal and theological discourses.

Given the prevailing attitudes toward the lesbian in the Middle Ages, it is all the more remarkable that a thirteenth-century poem, addressed to "Lady Maria," the source of "all happiness" for Bieris de Romans (before 1250), exists. The poem is written as a *canso*, the standard form of the Provençal love lyric. When Bieris speaks of her joy, her hope, her desire, she uses the same stylized language and imagery chosen by the male troubadours to express their love and longing for their lady. Were the author male, there would be no controversy over its meaning. The hesitancy to read Bieris's poem as an expression of lesbian love reflects, perhaps, a certain reluctance to recognize the nature of the erotic subject. Still, Bieris de Romans gives a voice to the lesbian writer in France, one that will not be heard as clearly again in French literature for well more than six hundred years.

## Early-Modern Era (1500–1800)

As France recovered from the devastation of the Hundred Year's War, the plague, and ineffectual leadership, the new learning of the Renaissance facilitated a renewed vitality in French literature and an openness to new ideas, at least among the nobility.

Pierre de Bourdeilles (ca. 1540–1614), abbot and lord of Brantôme, composed a "history" of events at the court of France, including a section entitled "Vie des Dames galantes" (*Lives of Fair and Gallant Ladies;* [1666]—written during the 1580s). In his reporting the sexual adventures among the nobles, he includes sexual relations among women at the court and explains that these relations were a "fashion that was brought from Italy by a lady of quality whom I will not name," referring perhaps to the rumored off-duty activities of Catherine de Medici's (1519–1589) ladies-in-waiting. Brantôme

then commences a lengthy discussion of lesbian relations to establish whether they can be considered adulterous; he concludes that lesbian sex is not real sex and, ultimately, cannot be satisfying.

For those of his audience who have not kept up with recent literary history, Brantôme explains: "It has been said how Sappho of Lesbos was a high mistress in this art; indeed, it has been said that she invented it." Brantôme's knowledge of the activities of Sappho (ca. 600 B.C.E.) reflects the rediscovery in the 1550s of a fragment of Sappho's poetry. His use of the term "lesbian" to define women who have sexual relations—this is the first use of the term as such in French—establishes a category distinct from the male homosexual. Although Brantôme's term would be eclipsed for three hundred years by "tribade" (a Greek term for lesbian), his lesbians are women who act as Sappho of Lesbos did.

The apparent tolerance that Brantôme expresses toward lesbian relationships among women at the court is echoed by Pontus de Tyard's (1521–1605) *Elégie pour une dame, enamourée d'une autre dame* (1573, *Elegy for a Lady in Love with Another Lady*). This mid-sixteenth-century text presents the lament of a woman whose female lover has left her. The abandoned lover had hoped their love would counter the abundance of well-known examples of male couples and, in so doing, create a lineage for lesbian couples. While such couples may be tolerated in the court and its literature, a working-class women does not receive the same leeway. Michel de Montaigne (1533–1592), in his *Travel Journal* (1580–1581), recounts the story of the execution of a young woman who had cross-dressed, married, and whose identity was then discovered. Unlike the medieval fictional version of this scenario, no miracle intervened: The "husband" was condemned to death and executed. The anecdote underlines the close connection between cross-dressing and lesbianism both in literature and in life.

The seventeenth century presents few outstanding examples of overt lesbian characters or the theme of lesbianism in French literature. Among many nearly forgotten minor male poets, lesbians or the theme of lesbian love versus heterosexual love appears, with the poets firmly extolling the superiority of the latter. Cross-dressing remains a staple of the baroque theater and novel. A typical example is Honoré d'Urfé's (1567–1625) *Astrée* (1607–1620), in which the hero cross-dresses as a woman to be near his beloved Astrée, who has banished him. Astrée finds herself attracted to this "woman," whose advances she does not reject. The century also sees a substantial increase in the number of women writers, and the cross-dressing motif frequently reappears in fairy tales they write for young girls, although the model of the cross-dresser is that of the warrior-heroine rather than a would-be lover. Henriette-Julie de Castelnau, the countess of Murat (1670–1716), one author of these tales, was herself accused of "monstrous attachments to persons of her own sex," reflecting the divergence between what is acceptable in literature and in life.

As correspondance between nuns dating from the Middle Ages shows, the convent provided a safe haven for relationships between women. This motif as a form of titillation for male readers appears in Jean Barrin's rightly neglected *Venus in the Cloister* (1683). A century later, as the cornerstone of Denis Diderot's (1713–1784) criticism of the institutions of the Catholic Church in *La Religieuse* (*The Nun,* written in 1760, published 1796), a negative image of the lesbian nun—loathsome, unnatural corrupter of innocents—is inscribed into the mainstream of eighteenth-century thought.

Only *Lettres persanes* (*Persian letters* [1721]) by Baron de Montesquieu (1689–1755) offers what might be considered a neutral portrait of female homoeroticism; this work brings to the fore the theme of the exotic lesbian through the author's reference to the relations between women in harems. While this vision of the lesbian appears with regularity in nineteenth-century French painting, feeding a sort of voyeuristic soft-pornographic interest, with the exception of occasional texts, such as *Salammbô* (1863) by Gustave Flaubert (1821–1880), it is less prevalent in literature of that period.

The libertinism that nourished eighteenth-century sexual mores did find its way into a number of texts that are frequently considered pornographic. Works of the Marquis de Sade (1740–1814) mix the heterosexual adventures of heroines Juliette (1798) and Justine (1791) with episodes of lesbian sex, often under the gaze of a male protagonist. Sade's female characters are either the unwilling partners of other women or women who might better be termed bisexuals, who find "true" sexual fulfillment with their male partners.

## Modern Era (After 1800)

A number of nascent (and frequently false) stereotypes relating to lesbians begin to find their way into all genres of French literature in the nineteenth century, although these works often were subjects of public outcry, and, indeed, their publication was censored.

Novels and short stories offer a variety of lesbian themes. In the 1830s and 1840s, Honoré de Balzac (1799–1850) wrote a number of relevant novels, including *Seraphita* (1834), in which the eponymous protagonist is a character who shifts from male to female, creating constant gender confusion throughout the tale. His *Cousine Bette* (1846) offers an example of a relationship between two women that follows the model of the romantic friendship. In *La Fille aux yeux d'or* (*The Girl with the Golden Eyes* [1834–1835]), he tells the tale of Paquita, a young woman sequestered by a lesbian marquise. Paquita betrays the marquise with her own brother, whom she forces to dress as the marquise. When this infidelity is discovered, the marquise murders her captive. Balzac posits the lesbian as a dangerous woman, capable of violence when she does not get her way. Theophile Gautier's (1811–1872) lesbian in *Mademoiselle de Maupin* (1835–1836) is more benign. Although he based his novel on the life of Madeleine d'Aubigny (1670–1707), an actress who dressed as a man so that she might seduce other women, in Gautier's version the male narrator, D'Albret, finds himself attracted to "Theodore," thus adding a second homoerotic complication to the plot.

The bisexual/lesbian prostitute becomes a type in naturalist literature of the late nineteenth century. Sex as a form of power wielded by a bisexual prostitute heroine scandalized the readers of Emile Zola's (1840–1902) *Nana* (1880), yet, perhaps because of the controversial heroine, *Nana* remains Zola's best-known novel. Zola also includes a lesbian couple in his *La Curée* (1871) and, indeed, has many references to lesbians throughout his Rougon-Macquart cycle of novels. Guy de Maupassant (1850–1893) also shows his readers openly lesbian couples in "La Femme de Paul" (*"Paul's Mistress,"* in the collection of short stories *La Maison Tellier* [1881]). In that tale, the discovery that the prostitute he regularly employs can give him up for "Lesbos" drives Paul to drown himself. However, Maupassant does not condemn Madeleine, who finds herself more attracted to Pauline than Paul. Rather, he casts Paul's suicide as overreaction, suggesting a more tolerant view than some earlier writers.

Lesbian themes appear frequently in the poetry of the second half of the nineteenth century. With the publication of *Les Fleurs du Mal* (*The Flowers of Evil* [1857]) and the censored poems of that collection, *Les Epaves* (*The Waifs* [1866]) by Charles Baudelaire (1821–1867), the stereotype of the *femme damnée* enters French poetry. Baudelaire's lesbians are tortured souls, condemned to wander the Earth in joyless sterility. Théodore de Banville (1823–1891) transforms the idea of sterility to a valorization of virginity. In his "Erinna" (published in *Les Exilés* [1867]), Sappho's successor exhorts her charges to chastity. Influenced, perhaps, by his own homosexuality, Paul Verlaine (1844–1896) emphasizes the sensual in his portraits of lesbian couples in *Les Amies* (1867). Unlike Baudelaire's negative portrayal, the "friends" in Verlaine's poems experience sexual pleasure with no regret—except for Sappho, whose death leap for Phaon is interpreted by Verlaine as punishment for her heterosexual affair. At the end of the century, Pierre Louÿs (1870–1925) capitalizes on the taste for both lesbians and the exotic in his *Chansons de Bilitis* (*Songs of Bilitis* [1894]), fake "translations" of ancient Greek poems, purportedly authored by Bilitis, who settles on Lesbos and becomes part of Sappho's circle. Two later volumes published after Louÿs's death, *Chansons inédites* (*Unpublished Songs* [1929]) and *Chansons secrètes* (*Secret Songs* [1931]), contain more sexually explicit passages and clearly pander to male fantasies of lesbian sexuality.

The literature of the nineteenth century was almost entirely dominated by the male writer's voyeuristic gaze. George Sand (1804–1876), who shocked French society by wearing men's clothing and having a liaison with the actress Marie Dorval (1798–1849), figures among the rare exceptions to this rule. Sand depicted an eroticized encounter between two sisters in *Lélia* (1834), and her *Gabriel* (1843), concerning a girl raised as a boy, is often read as her answer to Balzac's *Seraphita*. Rachilde (Marguerite Vallette) (1860–1953), whose career spans the turn of the century, explores gender and sexuality in *Monsieur Venus* (1884) and *Madame Adonis* (1886), which both present transvestite protagonists.

## The Twentieth Century

Twentieth-century literature widens the focus to include texts written by women, many of whom are lesbians themselves. This is not to say that male authors abandon the lesbian or bisexual woman altogether: From Odette and her lovers in Marcel Proust's multivolume *A la recherche du temps perdu* (*Remembrance of Things Past* [1913–1927]), to Romain Rolland's couple *Annette and Sylvie* (1922), to

Victor Margueritte's *La garçonne* (*The Bachelor Girl* [1922]), to the murderous schoolteachers in Boileau-Narcejac's *Celle qui n'était plus* (*The Woman Who Wasn't There* [1952]), the source for the film *Diabolique*, to Inès, the third member of Jean-Paul Sartre's hellish triangle in *Huis Clos* (*No Exit* [1944]), to Mimi, whose one-night stand with another woman leads to her murder by her paraplegic male lover in Pascal Bruckner's *Lune de fiel* (*Bitter Moon* [1981]), male authors frequently include lesbians or bisexual women in their narratives. These characters, portrayed as outcasts or misfits or simply sexually confused, appear as alternative choices to the heterosexual relationships in these texts.

At the turn of the twentieth century, however, Paris become a center for a multinational group of lesbian artists and writers, at the center of which was Natalie Barney (1876–1972), a wealthy American who had moved to Paris. Many of Barney's writings are reminiscences or portraits that give insight to the outstanding gays and lesbians among her acquaintances and to the lesbian literary community in Paris. *Aventures de l'esprit* (*Adventures of the Spirit* [1929]), for example, devoted half to men and half to women, includes sketches of Djuna Barnes (1892–1982), Gertrude Stein (1874–1946), and Barney's lovers, the painter Romaine Brooks (1874–1970) and the poet Renée Vivien (1877–1909). *Traits et portraits* (1963), published when Barney was eighty-six, includes a witty, acerbic defense of lesbianism and male homosexuality as natural and normal lifestyles. Vivien (Pauline Mary Tarn) was English, but, like Barney, settled in Paris and wrote in French. Vivien's poetry consists primarily of finely crafted love poems to other women, such as the collection *Cendres et poussières* (*Ashes and Dust* [1902]). Her novel *Une femme m'apparut* (*A Woman Appeared to Me* [1904]) recounts her meeting with Barney. Vivien also was responsible for the first translation of Sappho's poetry into modern French (1909). Liane de Pougy (1869–1950), another member of the Barney circle, described in her autobiographical *Idylle sapphique* (*Sapphic Idyll* [1901]) the liaison of Annhine (the Pougy character) with an American, Flossie, modeled on Natalie Barney. Sex versus gender informs the adventures of Marion/ Mario, the hermaphrodite who, as the main character in Lucie Delarue-Mardrus's (1874–1945) *L'Ange et les pervers* (*The Angel and the Perverts* [1930]), intrigues both the Paris lesbians and gay men s/he encounters. Mardrus also novelized her affair with Barney in *Nos secrètes amours* (*Our Secret Loves* [1951]).

Colette (1873–1954), too, frequented the Barney enclave and presented her version of the varieties of relationships between and among the women in that group in *Le pur et l'impur* (*The Pure and the Impure* [1932]) and her own liaisons in *Ces plaisirs* (*These Pleasures* [1941]). Many of her novels deal with sexual awakenings, female bisexuality, and the development of a lesbian consciousness in her characters. Colette's earliest success came with the Claudine novels, beginning with *Claudine à l'école* (*Claudine at School* [1900]). Of all of the French writers who came and went in Barney's circle, she remains the most well known.

At least one popular lesbian writer whose career began in the 1920s was not an intimate of the Barney circle. Jeanne Galzy (1885–1980), a member of the jury for the Prix Fémina for some five decades, wrote best-selling semiautobiographical novels. Her *Jeunes filles en serre chaude* (*Young Girls in a Hot House* [1934]) depicted the lives and loves of students and teachers at the prestigious teacher's college the Ecole Normale Supérieure. Toward the end of her life, Galzy published a quartet of novels, *La Surprise de Vivre* (*Life's Surprises* [1969–1976]), taking up themes similar to her early work.

After World War II, Violette Leduc (1907–1972) was among the first lesbian writers to gain recognition for her work, although that recognition came primarily through the intercession of Simone de Beauvoir. Her novels *L'Asphyxie* (*In the Prison of Her Skin* [1946]), *L'Affamée* (*A Woman Starved* [1948]), and *Ravages* (1955) suggest alternate scenarios for her autobiography, *La Bâtarde* (*The Bastard*) (1964), which brought Leduc her first critical success. Françoise Mallet-Joris's (1930–) *Le Rempart des Beguines* (*The Illusionist* [1951]) takes up the theme of sexual awakening and confusion—the young Hélène discovers she is attracted to her father's future wife, whose past hides a lesbian relationship. Eveline Mayhère's (1925–1957) *Je jure de m'éblouir* (*I Will Not Serve* [1958]) treats the tragic tale of Sylvie's love for her convent-school teacher. Sylvie's life, like that of the author, ends in suicide.

While the 1960s produced lesbian writers like Christiane Rochefort (1917–), who wrote *Les Stances à Sophie* (*Poems for Sophie* [1963]), it was only in the 1970s that the work feminist theorists, such as Hélène Cixous (1937–), Luce Irigary (1930–), and Monique Wittig (1935–), began to influence style and themes of literary texts. Of the three, Wittig became most closely associated with the development of a theoretical model for lesbian identity that places her at the forefront of lesbian theory and queer studies. In addition to her theoretical texts, works such as *Le Corps lesbien* (*The Lesbian Body* [1973]) provide a clue to Wittig's project: *le corps*, gendered masculine, becomes lesbian. This "lesbian body" consists of a poem cycle in which *j/e* (I/me) and *tu* (you) share a violent, all-consuming passion. Modeled on the "Song of Songs," it presents a highly charged, disturbing erotic vision, reconciled only at the end when the *j/e* becomes part of society of *amantes* (female lovers).

Wittig's work may be seen as an answer to the strain of French feminist thought developed by Hélène Cixous. Whereas Cixous posits a type of "writing the body" grounded in the feminine and incorporating a bisexuality, Wittig rejects what she considers a type of mistaken essentialism linked to a heterosexist and phallocentric society. Cixous, nonetheless, refused to participate in what she termed the "heterosexist scene" in *Angst* (1977). Texts such as her *Livre de Prométhéa* (*Book of Promethea* [1983]), an experimental fiction that stages female homoeroticism in poetic terms, attempt to break down the binary oppositions of male/female and hetero/homosexual.

The 1970s through the 1990s featured a number of other major figures. Geneviève Pastre, like Wittig and Cixous, is a major figure in scholarly, as well as literary, production. Not only is Pastre an essayist, specializing in classical antiquity, but she also was the founder, in 1985, of the first French lesbian press. Moreover, she is a poet whose collections recall those of Vivien in their treatment of women. Michèle Causse, poet, playwright, and essayist, also translates lesbian-themed literature. She has published Djuna Barnes's *Ladies Almanack* (1928) and edited the memoirs of Berthe Cleyregue, Natalie Barney's houskeeper. Both Pastre and Causse contributed to the now defunct journal *Masques* and are active in lesbian political movements.

In the same period, writers such as Jocylène François returned to the genre of the autobiographical novel. Her trilogy, *Les Bonheurs* (*Times of Happiness* [1970]), *Les Amantes* (*The Lovers* [1978]), and *Joue-nous "España"* (*Play "España" for Us* [1980]), traces the relationship between two women from childhood to adulthood. Autobiographical themes also mark the works of Hélène de Montferrand. She received the prestigious Prix Goncourt for her *Les Amies d'Héloïse* (*Heloise's Girlfriends* [1990]) and soon published its sequel, *Journal de Suzanne* (*Suzanne's Diary* [1991]). Heloise is the central character in both novels, both of which explore themes as wide ranging as the fate of lesbians in World War II, schoolgirl relationships, and political conservatism. Mireille Best was one of the most influential lesbian writers at the end of the twentieth century; among her works are *Camille en octobre* (1988) and *Il n'y a pas d'hommes au paradis* (*There Are No Men in Paradise* [1995]). Moreover, just as the lesbian detective entered American popular fiction, Maud Tabaschnik created Sandra Khan, an American lesbian journalist, who finds herself playing the role of a detective in, among other works, *Le festin de l'araignée* (*The Spider's Banquet* [1996]). Finally, the magazine *Lesbia* provides a space for lesbian writers to come to the fore.

*Edith J. Benkov*

## Bibliography

Benstock, Shari. *Women of the Left Bank, 1900–1940*. Austin: University of Texas Press, 1986.

Bonnet, Marie-Jo. *Un Choix sans équivoque* (An Unequivocal Choice). Paris: Denoël-Gonthier, 1981. New rev. ed. with additional chapters: *Les relations amoureuses entre femmes du seizième au vingtième siècle* (Love Between Women from the Sixteenth to the Twentieth Centuries). Paris: Odile Jacob, 1995.

Dejean, Joan. *Fictions of Sappho*. Chicago: University of Chicago Press, 1989.

Foster, Jeannette H. *Sex Variant Women in Literature*. New York: Vantage, 1956.

Grier, Barbara. *The Lesbian in Literature*. Tallahassee, Fla.: Naiad, 1981.

Mahuizer, Brigitte, Karen McPherson, Charles A. Porter, and Ralph Sarkonak, eds. "Same Sex/Different Text? Gay and Lesbian Writing in French." *Yale French Studies* 90 (1996) (Special Issue).

Stambolian, George, and Elaine Marks, eds. *Homosexualities and French Literature: Cultural Contexts/Critical Texts*. Itahaca, N.Y.: Cornell University Press, 1979.

***See also*** Barnes, Djuna Chappell; Barney, Natalie; Brooks, Romaine; Colette; Beauvoir, Simone de; Europe, Early Modern; France; Leduc, Violette; Mardrus-Delarue, Lucie; Middle Ages, Europe; Paris; Sand, George; Stein, Gertrude; Vivien, Renée; Wittig, Monique

## Friendship

Voluntary relationship, unregulated by the state as family relationships are, characterized by reciprocity (though each friend may give the other something different) and equality (achieved sometimes despite differences of race, class, age, or status around which the larger society constructs inequality). Countless lesbian coming out stories—fictional and nonfictional—make plain that friendship is the frequent vehicle by which lesbians come to recognize their sexual preference in the first place. Nor does friendship's influence cease at coming out. It continues in importance throughout lesbians' lives, sustaining individuals from adolescence through old age. Moreover, friendship is politically, or collectively, significant: It is both the force that binds individuals into lesbian communities and the potent symbol of ideal relations among women that frequently underwrites lesbians' struggles to make those communities sites and agents of cultural transformation.

Since the mid-twentieth century, feminist scholars investigating friendship between and among women have firmly established the fact that friendship is a crucial, although taken-for-granted, dimension of women's lives. Friendship appears to have several major functions. First, it fosters the formation of identity and spurs women's emotional, psychological, and spiritual growth: Friends productively mirror each other, and they provide each other with images of their best selves. No less important, the reciprocal exchange of material gifts that characterizes friendship ensures women's well-being and even, in some cases, survival. If all women need friends, lesbians, who are sometimes outcast by family and marginalized within their communities, sometimes need them even more so.

Yet, despite lesbians' greater need for friendship and the greater value lesbians apparently place on friendship, existing research rarely demonstrates a sustained, critical focus on lesbians' experiences as friends. Lesbians are frequently rendered invisible in discussions of "women's friendship," as though either lesbians don't exist or lesbian practices of friendship are identical to those of heterosexual women. On the other hand, even though the theme of friendship permeates lesbian cultural production, it rarely occupies center stage. What is wanted is a broad synthesis of the voluminous material—now dispersed in lesbian literature, popular culture, and art and in the findings of historians, sociologists, and psychologists—into a coherent account of lesbian friendship.

Such an account would necessarily locate lesbian friendship in the larger context of the intertwined histories of sexuality and "the family," as well as recognize how historical changes in sex-gender systems and divisions of labor influence women's, including lesbians', friendship. The example of "romantic friendship" in Western cultures illustrates the difficulties that must arise upon recognition that current categories distinguishing friendship from sexual relationships, and hetero- from homosexualities, provide an imperfect grid on which to map past practices of friendship and lesbian experience. "Romantic friendships" were first described by Smith-Rosenberg (1975) and more fully analyzed by Lillian Faderman, whose *Surpassing the Love of Men: Romantic Friendship and Love Between Women from the Renaissance to the Present* (1981) surveys their appearance in literature and history from the Renaissance to the present. "Romantic friendships" were intensely emotional, committed, and passionate relationships that were commonplace and apparently respectable in the sex-segregated and supposedly prudish nineteenth century. By twentieth-century standards, romantic friendships seem overtly and unmistakably sexual and, by homophobic standards, clearly deviant. Their significance has been hotly debated, especially the questions of whether they can be described as "lesbian" (did romantic friends "have sex" and does that matter or not?) and whether they supported heterosexuality (by making it bearable for women) or antagonized it (by offering more satisfying alternatives).

In answering such questions, some scholars purposely blur the distinction between friendship and lesbianism, a strategy that has the advantages of normalizing the term "lesbian" and demonstrating the presence of lesbianism throughout history. Rich (1980) assumes such a stance when she advances her notion of the "lesbian continuum" as a tool to analyze women's relationships in the context of compulsory heterosexuality. In a similar fashion, Smith (1977) offers a provocative lesbian interpretation of the relationship between Sula and Nel in Toni Morrison's novel *Sula* (1973). The most important study of women's friendship in this tradition is Janice Raymond's *A Passion for Friends: Toward a Philosophy of Female Affection* (1986). But Rich's paradigm has also been rejected for the way it expands the category of "lesbian" to include virtually every woman, ironically rendering invisible the very women Rich would reclaim, women for whom "lesbianism" is a sexual matter rather than a more diffuse inclination toward other women and homoso-

ciality. Zimmerman (1981) effectively summarizes this debate concerning friendship and argues, against Rich, that definitions of lesbianism ought not to be conflated with female friendship generally, but be historically specific and discriminating.

Zimmerman's argument in favor of historical specificity has implicitly been endorsed by more recent ethnographic and historical studies of lesbian communities. Such studies as Elizabeth Lapovsky Kennedy and Madeline D. Davis's *Boots of Leather, Slippers of Gold: The History of a Lesbian Community* (1993) attend, among other things, to the role of friendship in the creation and sustenance of specific lesbian communities. They not only affirm the validity of feminist research on "women's friendships" for lesbians, but also draw attention to specifically lesbian practices that render the friendships of lesbians unique, different from those of heterosexuals. Lesbians often befriend their ex-lovers, for example, sometimes becoming even "best friends." Also, more lesbians than not reconstitute their friendship networks as "chosen family."

Since the mid-1980s, many lesbians have abandoned a female separatist cultural politics, forming strong personal and political bonds with men that suggest huge territories of lesbian experience, such as AIDS activism and antiracist work, not illuminated by separatist theory and scholarship. New questions arise upon consideration of the fact that lesbian friendships do not involve only other lesbians, or even only other women: Lesbian friendship is also a term appropriate to describe certain relationships with men. Such relationships involve lesbians in different, but not less valuable, struggles for personal growth and fulfillment and social justice.

*Glynis Carr*

### Bibliography

Faderman, Lillian. *Surpassing the Love of Men: Romantic Friendship and Love Between Women from the Renaissance to the Present.* New York: William Morrow, 1981.

Kennedy, Elizabeth Lapovsky, and Madeline D. Davis. *Boots of Leather, Slippers of Gold: The History of a Lesbian Community.* New York: Routledge, 1993.

Raymond, Janice. *A Passion for Friends: Toward a Philosophy of Female Affection.* Boston: Beacon, 1986.

Rich, Adrienne. "Compulsory Heterosexuality and Lesbian Existence." *Signs: Journal of Women in Culture and Society* 5:4 (1980), 631–660.

Shugar, Dana R. *Separatism and Women's Community*. Lincoln: University Nebraska Press, 1995.

Smith, Barbara. "Toward a Black Feminist Criticism." *Conditions: Two* 1:2 (1977), 25–52.

Smith-Rosenberg, Carroll. "The Female World of Love and Ritual: Relations between Women in Nineteenth-Century America." *Signs: Journal of Women in Culture and Society* 1:1 (1975), 1–29.

Zimmerman, Bonnie. "What Has Never Been: An Overview of Lesbian Feminist Literary Criticism." *Feminist Studies* 7:3 (1981), 451–476.

*See also* Coming Out Stories; Community; Family; Lesbian Continuum; Romantic Friendship; Sisterhood

## Fuller, Margaret (1810–1850)

American feminist, writer, and philosopher. Margaret Fuller had a profound impact on American letters and philosophy, as well as on American feminist thought. Her feminist tract *Woman in the Nineteenth Century* (1845) draws on female figures in classical mythology to establish women's right to spiritual, social, and political identity apart from men. Because of her expressions of love for women, her belief that her own identity is both masculine and feminine, and her insistence on crossing gender boundaries in her writing, Fuller has been of interest to current scholars debating definitions of "lesbianism" before the twentieth century.

Scholars have debated the nature of Fuller's relationships with women. Francis B. Dedmond has examined her correspondence with Caroline Sturgis, to whom Fuller wrote: "I build on our friendship now with trust, for I think it is redeemed from 'the search after Eros.'" Fuller described herself at times as an "unnatural" blend of male and female qualities. She identified with French novelist George Sand (1804–1876), whom she described as "a grand, fertile, aspiring, but in some measure distorted and irregular nature."

In the "Conversations" she organized in New England to educate women about philosophical and political issues, Fuller formed powerful relationships that were described by her contemporaries as going beyond traditional friendship. Ralph Waldo Emerson (1803–1882) wrote: "It is certain that Margaret, though unattractive in person, and assuming in manners, so that the girls complained that 'she put upon them,' or, with her burly masculine existence, quite reduced them to satellites, yet inspired an enthusiastic attachment."

Fuller was the editor of the Transcendentalist journal the *Dial* from 1840 to 1842. Transcendentalism maintained that the individual soul could achieve a spiritual connectedness to the higher forces of the universe. In an ongoing dialogue with Emerson, Fuller contributed to Transcendentalist philosophy a recognition of social realities and a belief that "what woman needs is not as a woman to act or rule but as a nature to grow, as an intellect to discern, as a soul to live freely and unimpeded, to unfold such powers as were given her when we left our common home."

Shifting her focus from the state of the soul to direct political action, Fuller moved to Italy in 1847 and joined the cause of the Italian revolution. She became lovers with Giovanni Angelo Ossoli and had a child by him in 1848. In 1850, all three were killed in a shipwreck off Fire Island, New York, as she was returning to America.

*Mary E. Wood*

### Bibliography

Capper, Charles. *Margaret Fuller: An American Romantic Life*, vol. 1: *The Private Years*. New York: Oxford University Press, 1992.

Chevigny, Bell Gale. *The Woman and the Myth: Margaret Fuller's Life and Writings*. Old Westbury, N.Y.: Feminist Press, 1976. Rev. and exp. ed. Boston: Northeastern University Press, 1994.

Wood, Mary E. "'With Ready Eye': Margaret Fuller and Lesbianism in Nineteenth-Century Literature." *American Literature* 65 (March 1993), 1–18.

Zwarg, Christina. *Feminist Conversations: Fuller, Emerson, and the Task of Reading*. Ithaca, N.Y.: Cornell University Press, 1995.

*See also* American Literature, Nineteenth Century; Romantic Friendship; Sand, George

## Furies, The

Lesbian feminist living and working collective formed in Washington, D.C., in 1971. The group's choice of name represented its members' identification with mythological protectors of women and declared anger at injustice as a way to mobilize against women's oppression. By living communally and working collaboratively, group members sought to translate their theory into practice and to produce a publication through which they could record their experiences and disseminate their ideas. Through theoretical writing, the group contributed to the evolution of the lesbian feminist movement in the United States. The collective originally included twelve young white women, all of whom had previously participated in other revolutionary political movements of the time. Their ideology, promulgated through their writing, fused elements of gay liberation's positive affirmation of homosexuality, women's liberation's understanding of the connections between the personal and the political, the New Left's analysis of class, and the hippie counterculture's rejection of mainstream values with their anger at the treatment of gay women by feminists and male gay liberationists.

Their monthly newspaper, *The Furies*, published from January 1972 to June 1973, helped the group gain its notoriety and extend its influence. Here members recorded their theoretical conjectures and their personal struggles to confront homophobia and elitism. The publication also included film reviews, fiction, and photographs. Furies members wrote most of the paper's articles; the publication outlasted the living collective, however. By August 1972, many of the original members had departed, although a smaller group continued to publish the paper.

The Furies committed themselves to ending women's oppression and building lesbian feminist politics and culture. To this end, the group focused on two primary issues that constituted the basis for women's oppression. First, the Furies analyzed the social basis and the political repercussions of heterosexuality and homosexuality. They defined lesbian feminism as a political choice—rather than a matter of sexual orientation—that signified one's commitment to ending male supremacy. By emphasizing that lesbianism represented a political stance, they minimized the importance of sexuality. The Furies argued that heterosexuality constituted a mechanism of social control through which male supremacy kept women economically and emotionally dependent on men, extended social approval to heterosexual women and vilified lesbians, and separated women from one another. Revolutionary change would ensue as gay, feminist women separated from men and straight women in their personal and political lives. They advocated a separatist lesbian feminist movement, bolstered by a national political party, feminist businesses, and new values that replaced misogynist ideas with those that validated women's distinctive characteristics.

Class, the second theme, dominated the group's writing and drove the dynamics within the collective. Articles discussed the evolution of class consciousness, examined the connections between class and heterosexuality, and criticized feminism's exclusion of working-class women. Group members also recorded their own efforts to restructure class by distributing property, salary, and skills within the group.

Former Furies continued to influence lesbian feminism after the collective ended. Photographer Joan E. Biren (JEB), writers Rita Mae Brown and Charlotte Bunch, along with those who established the feminist journal *Quest* and businesses such as Diana Press and Olivia Records, indelibly shaped lesbian feminist politics and culture in the United States.

*Anne M. Valk*

## Bibliography

Berson, Ginny Z. "The Furies: Goddesses of Vengeance." In *Voices from the Underground: Insider Histories of the Vietnam Era Underground Press*. Ed. Ken Wachsberger. Tempe, Ariz.: Mica, 1993, pp. 313–324.

Brown, Rita Mae. *A Plain Brown Rapper*. Oakland, Calif.: Diana, 1976.

Echols, Alice. *Daring To Be Bad: Radical Feminism in America, 1967–1975*. Minneapolis: University of Minnesota Press, 1989.

Fox, Sue. "After the Revolution." *Washington Blade* (June 23, 1995).

———. "The Furies." *Washington Blade* (June 16, 1995).

Myron, Nancy, and Charlotte Bunch. *Lesbianism and the Women's Movement*. Baltimore: Diana, 1975.

Valk, Anne M. "Separatism and Sisterhood: Race, Sex, and Women's Activism in Washington, D.C., 1963–1980." Ph.D. diss., Duke University, 1996.

*See also* Brown, Rita Mae; Class; Lesbian Feminism; Olivia; Publishing, Lesbian; Separatism

# G

## Garbo, Greta (1905–1990)

Swedish actress. Born Greta Lovisa Gustafsson in Stockholm, Garbo made her acting "debut" in advertising films for the department store where she worked in her adolescence. Within a year of this inauspicious start, she was admitted to the Swedish Royal Dramatic Theater Academy, where she came to the attention of Mauritz Stiller (1883–1928), who renamed her and directed her in her first leading role, in the silent film *The Saga of Gösta Berling* (1924). Stiller brought her to Hollywood in 1925, where, under contract to Metro-Goldwyn-Mayer, she soon became one of the most popular and glamorous film stars. Between 1925 and 1941, she starred in twenty-five feature films, in which she typically played an exotic, highly sensual, aloof, and occasionally androgynous femme fatale. The most notable include *The Flesh and the Devil* (1927); her first "talkie," *Anna Christie* (1930); *Mata Hari* (1931); *Grand Hotel* (1932); *As You Desire Me* (1932); *Queen Christina* (1933); *Anna Karenina* (1935); *Camille* (1936); *Conquest* (1937); and *Ninotchka* (1939).

At the age of thirty-six, after the box-office failure of her last film, *Two-Faced Woman* (1941), Garbo retired from acting and lived reclusively in New York City until her death half a century later. The reasons for her withdrawal are the subject of much conjecture. Lesbian film critic Weiss (1993) among others, suggests that scrutiny of her private life by the press and in Hollywood gossip was a likely motivating factor. Garbo was widely known as a participant in the Hollywood gay and lesbian circles that flourished in the late 1920s and early 1930s and exhibited a penchant for cross-dressing and referring to herself, at times, by male pronouns. She was involved, moreover, in a number of unconventional relationships with men and women (although her affectional preference since adolescence was apparently for other women), most notably with the noted photographer Cecil Beaton (1904–1980), who was otherwise gay, and the openly lesbian socialite Mercedes de Acosta (1893–1968). (The latter, Alice B. Toklas [1877–1967] observed, could not be dismissed lightly, as she "has had the two most important women in the United States—Garbo and [Marlene] Dietrich.")

A singular manifestation of Hollywood lesbian subculture may be found in *Queen Christina*. The film's producers attempted to "heterosexualize" the story life of its subject, the seventeenth-century lesbian queen of Sweden who abdicated her throne rather than subject herself to the dynastic marriage that her court and people required. Garbo, with assistance from screenwriter Salka Viertel (1880–1978), with whom she was rumored to be romantically involved during the filming, nevertheless subverts the plot with numerous, if indirect, "lesbian" modes of expression, including a variety of "butch" mannerisms, transvestitism, and a rare filmic example of a shared kiss between two women, and thus creates a sort of cinematic "double discourse."

During Garbo's lifetime, the complexity of her sexuality, while the topic of gossip, was quite purposely obscured. Since her death, several sensitive and well-researched biographies have illuminated this aspect of the life of one of Hollywood's most alluring and mysterious figures.

*Patricia Juliana Smith*

### Bibliography

Acosta, Mercedes de. *Here Lies the Heart*. New York: Reynal, 1960.

Paris, Barry. *Garbo: A Biography*. New York: Knopf, 1995.

Souhami, Diana. *Greta and Cecil*. San Francisco: Harper, 1994.

Vickers, Hugo. *Loving Garbo: The Story of Greta Garbo, Cecil Beaton, and Mercedes de Acosta*. New York: Random House, 1994.

Weiss, Andrea. *Vampires and Violets: Lesbians in Film*. New York: Penguin, 1993.

*See also* Christina of Sweden; Dietrich, Marlene; Film, Mainstream

## Gay Games

Largest and most widely known athletic event for gay, lesbian, bisexual, and transgendered individuals. In fact, as of the 1994 Games, it was the world's largest athletic event of any kind. The Games are an Olympic-style event that is open to all interested participants who are gay, lesbian, bisexual, transgendered, or supportive of these groups. Thomas Waddell (1937–1987), an American Olympic decathlete, founded the Gay Games. His primary goal was to challenge homophobia in traditional sport. Thus, the Gay Games were established on the principles of inclusion, participation, and personal best. They are open to participants of any skill level, age, ethnicity, nationality, physical ability, and sexual orientation. There are no qualifying standards, and winning is not the most salient aspect of the Games. Still, world records have been achieved during the Gay Games.

The Games also are an important cultural event to the gay, lesbian, bisexual, and transgendered community. The organizing body for the Games is the Federation of Gay Games, initially founded in 1980 as San Francisco Arts and Athletics. The fifty-five-member board of directors ensures the continuity of the Games and adherence to the founding principles.

Initially, the Games were called the Gay Olympics. However, shortly before the opening ceremonies of the first Games, in 1982, the organizing committee was served a restraining order from the United States Olympic Committee (USOC), resulting in the removal of the word "Olympics" from anything associated with the renamed Gay Games. After the Gay Games, the organizing committee appealed the order. This legal battle continued until March 24, 1987, when the United States Supreme Court ruled that the USOC had exclusive and proprietary right to use the word "Olympic." However, positive interactions with the USOC occurred during the preparations for Gay Games IV in 1994. With the assistance of the USOC, federation board members met with officials from the United States State Department and Department of Health and Human Services to address the needs of HIV-positive athletes who wanted to participate in the Games. One outcome of this meeting was the enactment of a blanket waiver allowing HIV-positive athletes to enter the United States for the time period of the Games.

The Games offer a rare opportunity for lesbian, gay, bisexual, and transgendered people to participate openly in a friendly and safe sport environment. The Games also provide numerous role models and a socially supportive atmosphere. In many personal accounts of Gay Games participation, athletes have described their experiences as empowering, personally rewarding, and enlightening. The Games serve important social, personal-development, and political purposes for the participants. The athletes in the Gay Games seem to have very positive experiences, which then may generalize to other aspects of their lives beyond sport as they become personally empowered.

Gay Games I was held in San Francisco, California, in August 1982, with 1,350 participants representing twelve countries and competing in fourteen sports. In August 1986, Gay Games II, also in San Francisco, attracted approximately 3,500 athletes from sixteen countries, competing in seventeen different sports. The Games continued to grow, with more than 7,500 athletes participating in twenty-three sports in Gay Games III, in Vancouver, British Columbia, Canada, in August 1990. New York City hosted Gay Games IV, June 18–25, 1994. Still growing, 10,864 athletes, representing thirty-nine countries, participated in thirty-one different sports. Compared to Gay Games I, which had a budget of $125,000, Gay Games IV had a $6.5 million budget. Gay Games IV also benefited from major corporate sponsorship of approximately $1 million in services and cash from twenty-one sponsors. Gay Games V, in Amsterdam, Netherlands, August 1–8, 1998—the first time outside North America—truly marked them as an international event. In Gay Games V, 14,715 athletes, representing eighty-eight countries, participated in thirty official and seven demonstration sports. *Victoria Krane*

### Bibliography
Krane, V., and L. Romont. "Female Athletes' Motives and Experiences During the Gay Games."

*Journal of Gay, Lesbian, and Bisexual Identities* 2: 123–138.

Labrecque, Lisa, ed. *Unity: A Celebration of Gay Games IV and Stonewall.* San Francisco: Labreque, 1994.

Young, P.D. *Lesbians and Gays and Sports.* New York: Chelsea House, 1995.

*See also* Sports, Professional

## Gay Liberation Movement

Post-Stonewall (1969) gay movement shaped by the counterculture of the 1960s, the civil rights movement, radical feminism, and the New Left. Gay liberationists had a revolutionary view of the changes that needed to take place in the lives of lesbians and gay men and in the larger heterosexual society that oppressed them.

One of the most influential organizations was the Gay Liberation Front (GLF). The GLF was constituted out of two divergent groups. One of these groups consisted of former members of homophile organizations such as the Mattachine Society and the Daughters of Bilitis. These organizations had been fighting for equality since the 1950s, and their members emphasized accommodation as a tactic and acceptance by society as their goal. Members of the other group that helped found the GLF were younger, more radical, more idealistic, and more extremist in their approach. Many in this younger core had been active in the antiwar movement and New Left organizations such as SDS (Students for a Democratic Society). This latter group largely ignored the achievements and significance of the homophile movement. Having no patience for lesbian and gay organizations that were more accommodating of mainstream society's oppression of sexual difference, this younger group quickly became the center of the early gay liberation movement.

Gay liberationists argued for fundamental and extensive societal change in the quest for a new order built on egalitarianism, the end of gender bias and discrimination, and a more open, less puritanical attitude toward sex of all kinds. The guiding thread of gay liberation was a rejection of enforced heterosexuality, marriage, traditional gender roles and family arrangements, and sexual privacy—all built upon an understanding of sexual identity as something other than fixed. The Gay Liberation Front of New York City and its namesakes in other urban centers around the country borrowed inspiration from the New Left

analysis that blamed the plight of women and racial and ethnic minorities on deeply ingrained and systemic flaws in society. Similar dynamics and theories also produced gay liberation movements in Canada, the United Kingdom, France, and other European countries, and Australia and New Zealand.

Gay Liberation Front (GLF) members argued that enforced heterosexuality was an evil caused by a sexist culture to protect the power of straight men and that, under this hegemony, homosexuality became prohibited behavior. Carl Whitman's 1969 "Refugees from Amerika: A Gay Manifesto" made the point more stridently clear, arguing that "exclusive heterosexuality is fucked up . . . as it reflects a fear of people of the same sex, it's anti-homosexual, and it is fraught with frustration."

The rejection of heterosexuality was tied to similar disavowals of marriage, family, and sex roles. One member of the New York City feminist collective who produced the newspaper *RAT* argued in 1970 that gay liberationists were "women and men who from the time of our earliest memories have been in revolt against the sex role-structure and the nuclear family structure." Traditional marriage was thought to be an oppressive institution, a contract that smothered both people, denied physical and emotional needs, and placed impossible demands on both members of the contract. Allen Young, one of the central theorists of gay liberation and a Gay Liberation Front member, argued against traditional normative family arrangements:

> The nuclear family, with its man-woman model built in by the presence of parents, is the primary means by which this restricted sexuality is created and enforced. Gays experience rejection by the family in a society where familial love is considered important. The family oppresses women and children as well as gays. The phenomena of runaway teenagers and increasing divorce rates are signs of the erosion of the nuclear family. Gay liberation is another sign. We attack the nuclear family when we refuse to get married and have a family. We are committed to building communal situations where children can grow strong and free (Jay and Young 1992).

For the gay liberationists, the social institutions of marriage and family were suspect, in need of redefinition, if not total elimination, because, like hetero-

G sexuality, they were part and parcel of the very fabric of society that helped oppress lesbians and gays by rendering their lives and loves invisible. The enforced privacy surrounding all discussions of homosexuality made it all but impossible for a teenager in the 1950s and 1960s to learn about other lesbians and gay men. Because of the way it rendered gay existence invisible, GLF members were also critical of the liberal, "straight" notion that sexuality is essentially a private matter. They argued instead that this perpetuated male supremacy and patterns of dominance which are basically sexist and, in the end, antihomosexual.

Although perhaps somewhat utopian in their outlook, the liberationists merged their personal insights and experiences of oppression with a rapidly expanding body of feminist and socialist theory, creating powerful criticisms of the institutions of heterosexuality, marriage, family, and privacy. Many of these criticisms continue to be relevant as young lesbians and gays face oppressive home environments and abusive families when their sexual identity is discovered, although, increasingly, this sad fact is widely acknowledged as a problem. The liberationists' understanding of what it means to be "gay," of what constitutes lesbian or gay *being*, also continued to be radical throughout the late twentieth century. Gay liberationists argued that "heterosexual" and "homosexual" were artificial categories invented by a sexist society, and they made many heterosexuals anxious with their claim that "every straight man is a target for gay liberation." Similarly, the New York City liberationist group Radicalesbians argued that "lesbianism," like male homosexuality, was a category that had meaning only in a sexist society characterized by rigid roles and dominated by male supremacy.

For many liberationists, heterosexuals were the enemy, who could be trusted only if they renounced their heterosexuality and *became* a lesbian or gay person. In the language of the times, one of the central goals of gay liberation was "to reach the homosexuals entombed in heterosexuals," "to liberate our brothers and sisters," "to free the homosexual in everyone." This belief that sexuality was the product of a sexist society, and that heterosexuality and homosexuality were two equally oppressive social roles, was a sophisticated theoretical argument, and many of the liberationist ideas are contained in social-constructionist understanding of sexuality. However, there is an important difference between the gay liberationists of the 1970s and the social constructionists of the 1990s: the issue of choice. While

it is difficult to find a social constructionist who would equate social construction with choice, the liberationists did, indeed, argue that gays and straights alike need only *choose* to be gay to make it so. Far from simplistic, this position seemed carefully developed to help create anxiety and provoke reflection among the heterosexual majority that never had to give a second thought to their sexuality and to the social institutions that support it.

By the mid-1970s many of the most radical ideas of gay liberation were in decline. The GLF faced problems with organizational structure, FBI infiltration, and internal strife. For example, within GLF New York there was a caucus called Gay Liberation Front Women. Many of these women believed that male GLF members were themselves sexist and noted that the word "gay" was coming to be used in the media as a term that referred almost exclusively to men. They broke away and formed their own organizations, often merging with lesbians coming out of the women's liberation movement. With the end of the Vietnam War in 1973 also came the end of more than a decade of political radicalism that had swept the United States, ushering in a more conservative approach to gay activism.

As the 1970s progressed, the notion that sexual identity was a choice or was malleable gave way to a reform model of gay activism that sought integration with the social institutions of society, not their overthrow or replacement. It was easier to argue that gays and lesbians were like everyone else; their sexuality was fixed, immutable, and unchanging. The AIDS epidemic also affected the freer attitude toward sex that gay liberationists had adopted from the counterculture movement of the 1960s. For gay men, a new urban, commercial culture succeeded in creating greater opportunities for men to meet, socialize, and be openly gay. Typified by the Castro in San Francisco and Greenwich Village in New York City, these "gay ghettos" made the liberationist goals of building bridges between all minority groups in an effort to gain freedom and equality seem less immediately necessary and important for many gay men. In lesbian communities, feminist debates about pornography, butch-femme roles, and sadomasochism split the liberationist agenda in unpredictable ways. Still, as the antecedent to the Lesbian Avengers, ACT UP (AIDS Coalition to Unleash Power), and Queer Nation, gay liberation was an important and theoretically sophisticated moment in the history of the gay rights movement in the United States. *Gary Lehring*

## Bibliography

Altman, Dennis. *Homosexual: Oppression and Liberation.* New York: Outerbridge and Dienstfrey, 1971.

Jay, Karla, and Allen Young. *Out of the Closets: Voices of Gay Liberation.* New York: New York University Press, 1992.

Lehring, Gary. "Essentialism and the Political Articulation of Identity." In *Playing with Fire: Queer Politics, Queer Theories.* Ed. Shane Phelan. New York: Routledge, 1997.

Marotta, Toby. *The Politics of Homosexuality.* Boston: Houghton Mifflin, 1981.

*See also* Daughters of Bilitis; New Left; Radicalesbians; Social-Construction Theory

# Gender

Refers variably to socially constructed behavioral and identity distinctions, as in "feminine" and "masculine"; a process, as in "doing gender"; a stratification system or structure, as in "gendered" organizations; or an institution whose main purpose is to create and maintain gender inequality. Should not be confused with "sex," which denotes biological distinctions between females and males.

## Feminist Scholarship

The explosion of scholarship on gender, especially by feminists, followed the emergence of the contemporary women's movement in the 1960s. Early investigations of gender, called "sex-roles" research, focused on individual attributes that are learned via socialization and enforced through social control. "Masculinity" was characterized as encompassing independence, aggression, dominance, emotional detachment, and rationality, while "femininity" was described as entailing dependence, nurturance, passivity, emotion, and irrationality. "Androgyny" referred to a blending of these attributes. Researchers revealed the socially constructed nature of gender by highlighting the changing form and content of gender roles across societies, time, class, ethnicity, age, and sexual orientation.

Later, West and Zimmerman (1987) conceptualized gender not as a property of individuals but as a process of interactional accomplishment enacted continually through various gender displays. For example, men frequently interrupt conversations, while women show interest through eye contact or deferential head tilts. Referred to as "doing gender," the enactment of these interactional processes entails men "doing" dominance and women "doing" submission. According to this perspective, individuals' pursuit of "gender-appropriate" interests and self-presentations reflects a compulsory process of recruitment to gendered identities, where people's perceived competence as members of society is dependent upon their proper enactment of the doing of gender.

Scholars have also conceptualized gender as a structure or stratification system that creates gender differences and then differentially rewards them, with all men ranked above women of the same race and class. Drawing on black feminist thought, recent analysts view gender as part of a matrix of domination containing interlocking systems of oppression based on race, class, gender, and sexual orientation. Hence, researchers refer to the multiplicity of gender, with "hegemonic masculinity" (white, heterosexual, economically successful) being ascendant over both women and "subordinated masculinities," such as gay or working-class men, and "emphasized femininity" being oriented around the accommodation of men's desires.

As a structure, gender legitimates these hierarchies of authority, organizes sexuality and emotion, and divides work in the home and the economy. Relatedly, scholars refer to organizations as "gendered," meaning that advantages and disadvantages are patterned in ways that reflect socially constructed gender distinctions, which typically benefit men. This "gendering" process occurs through the creation of gendered divisions of labor, space, and behavior, as well as symbols, identities, and practices that reinforce those divisions. For instance, job-evaluation systems that employers use to determine pay contain point ratings that systematically ignore or devalue skills found in female-dominated jobs.

Another approach has emerged that conceptualizes gender as an institution in and of itself. This paradigm analyzes gender as simultaneously a process, a stratification system, and a structure. Just as core institutions, such as the family and religion, entail patterns of organization and interaction that serve particular societal purposes, so, too, does gender. According to this perspective, the main purpose of gender as an institution is to construct women as a group to be men's subordinates so that women can be exploited as workers, sexual partners, childbearers, and emotional nurturers.

# G

## Gender, Lesbian Feminism, and Queer Theory

A central theme associated with some tendencies within lesbian feminism—often referred to as "cultural feminism"—is its assumption of fundamental gender differences and its valorization of "female values." In this view, women's traits and values include an ethic of care, cooperation, and pacifism, while men's characteristics encompass an ethic of individual rights, competition, and violence. While some lesbian feminists ascribe to essentialism or biological determinism, others take a social-constructionist approach and attribute these gender differences to socialization.

Lesbian feminism also challenges oppressive standards of gender behavior and appearance. Early lesbian feminists adopted practical, unisex styles of dress and presentations of self that included unshaved legs, no makeup, and short hair. Scholars refer to this as "gender blending." Some recent self-presentation modes incorporate elements of punk culture, while "sex radicals" wear low-cut tops, short skirts, and fishnet stockings. Those who combine these with traditionally masculine items, such as combat boots, adopt a style called "gender fucking." This deliberate "playing" with gender in order to expose it as a social construction also characterizes those identifying as "queer." Queer activists and "queer theorists" aim to explode dominant cultural binaries (man/woman, straight/gay), which are seen as bases of oppression and distortions of human experience.                *Nicole C. Raeburn*

### Bibliography

Acker, Joan. "Hierarchies, Jobs, and Bodies: A Theory of Gendered Organizations." *Gender and Society* 4 (1990), 139–158.

Connell, R.W. *Gender and Power: Society, the Person, and Sexual Politics*. Stanford, Calif.: Stanford University Press, 1987.

Devor, Holly. *Gender Blending: Confronting the Limits of Duality*. Bloomington: Indiana University Press, 1989.

Lorber, Judith. *Paradoxes of Gender*. New Haven, Conn.: Yale University Press, 1994.

West, Candace, and Don Zimmerman. "Doing Gender." *Gender and Society* 1 (1987), 125–151.

*See also* Androgyny; Biological Determinism; Essentialism; Lesbian Feminism; Queer Theory; Social-Construction Theory; Tomboy; Transgender; Women's Liberation Movement

## German Literature

The development of lesbianism, in its broadest definition, as a theme in the literature of Germany is largely linked to the process of women's social and political emancipation in the nineteenth and twentieth centuries. Seen from a historical perspective, the expression of lesbianism in German literature has undergone significant transformations and can be divided chronologically into five major stages, ranging from the aestheticized homoerotic imagery hidden in the correspondence of Romantic women writers to the proud affirmation of radical feminist views in the postmodern novel. In light of the absence of a lesbian aesthetics or a female homoerotic tradition comparable to that of male homoeroticism in Western art and culture, it is important to note that all major works to depict lesbian desire or to include lesbian characters were written by women.

### Romanticism (1780–1880)

The first period that brought about clearly visible traces of female homoeroticism in German literary history is the Romantic period. Though love and relationships between women are not portrayed as explicitly sexual in either correspondence or fiction, many romantic female friendships, such as the ones between Rahel Varnhagen von Ense (1771–1833) and Pauline Wiesel (n.d.) or between Claire von Glümer (1825–1906) and Auguste Scheibe (n.d.), can be labeled lesbian in the sense that both partners were lovingly, and often possessively, devoted to each other in their struggle to be, and remain, together. Bettina von Arnim's (1785–1859) fictional account, in her epistolary novel *Die Günderode* (1840), of her short, but intense, friendship with Karoline von Günderode (1780–1806) demonstrates the amplitude of emotions and the sexual ambiguities women writers of the Romantic period sought to express. Not only does Bettina aspire to the highest form of physical and spiritual closeness with her friend—in one letter, Bettina fantasizes about spending a night together—but she also does it by adopting the language, tone, and imagery of erotic love.

### Sexology and Literature (1880s–1917)

The years of the construction and medicalization of the homosexual by European sexologists ushered in the second stage in the history of German lesbian literature. This period, around the turn of the twentieth century, may be labeled the creation and struggle of what was called the "Uranian" woman, since the literature of this time echoes the medical-scientific debate on homosexuality, on the one hand, and the calls for women's emancipation, on the other. A striking characteristic of male-authored texts depicting female homosexuality is the fact that the lesbian character generally serves to play the role of the deviant and destructive female outsider who is harmful to society and, ultimately, to herself. Such is the case in Alfred Meebold's novella *Dr. Erna Reden's Thorheit und Erkenntnis* (Dr. Erna Reden's Foolishness and Insight [1900]), and in Hermann Sudermann's play *Die Freundin* (The Girlfriend [1913]). Even the legendary Countess Geschwitz, introduced in the final act of Frank Wedekind's drama *Erdgeist* (Ghost [1895]) must realize that there is no place for the lesbian in the world of her times. In *Die Büchse der Pandora* (Pandora's Box), the follow-up play of 1904, Geschwitz, a kind and generous woman, is brutally murdered.

Though not always taking a positive stand on homosexuality, turn-of-the-century women writers clearly join in the feminist movement's call for emotional, spiritual, and political solidarity of women. While some texts, among them Baroness von Puttkamer's lyric cycle *Auf Kypros* (On Cypress [1898]), Mrs. M.F.'s (pseud.) essay *Wie ich es sehe* (As I See It [1901]), and Maria Janitschek's *Die neue Eva* (The New Eve [1906]), seem to endorse common stereotypes, denouncing women's homoerotic desires as sinful and dangerous, others, such as Elisabeth Dauthendey (1854–1918) in her 1906 pamphlet *Die Urnische Frage und die Frauen* (The Uranian Question and Women), argue confidently from a political perspective in an attempt to construct a positive lesbian identity. Unsurpassed in their radicality are the works of the self-proclaimed "women-loving man hater," Helene von Druskowitz (1856–1918), who, due to her subversive and male-threatening views, was imprisoned in a lunatic asylum. Equally outstanding in its realistic insight concerning the social, political, and sexual situation of women at the time is the novel *Sind es Frauen?* (Are These Women [1901]) by Aimée Duc (Minna Adelt, b. 1867). Here women identify as lesbians not because of a congenital drive but, as Faderman and Eriksson (1980) argue, "because they have taken their feminism to its logical conclusion."

### The Weimar Republic and After (1918–1970)

It is hardly surprising, then, to note that an abundance of lesbian literature would result out of the liberal atmosphere that followed Germany's defeat in World War I and that much of it would stand in the light of the social and political activism characteristic of the Weimar Republic (1918–1933). The continuing establishment of women's clubs in the bigger cities and the publication of lesbian magazines, among them *Blätter Idealer Frauenfreundschaften, Frauenliebe, Garçonne,* and *Die Freundin,* further improved communication among women. Through soirees and organized readings, as well as through the publication of articles, book reviews, political essays, and fiction, women's clubs and magazines were instrumental in the creation and distribution of literature concerned with women's and lesbian issues. These were raised particularly by Maria Sauer von Peteani (1888–1960), a Prague-born writer whose many novels were best-sellers in lesbian circles; by Emma Zelenka (n.d.), an activist and writer who, in 1932, appealed to Vienna's lesbians to unite in the fight against mass poverty; and by Edith Cadivec (1879–?), author of the notorious two-volume autobiography, *Unter der Peitsche der Leidenschaft* (Under the Whip of Passion [1931]), who established a club for sadists in Vienna. The best-known works of this period, Anna Elisabet Weirauch's (1887–1970) trilogy *Der Skorpion* (1919, 1921, 1931) and Christa Winsloe's (1888–1944) *Das Mädchen Manuela* (The Girl Manuela [1933]), would find international acclaim.

The advancement in the general emancipation of women, and in the struggle for the rights and recognition of lesbians and gays in particular, came to a sudden halt with Adolf Hitler's rise to power in 1933, forcing many writers and activists into exile. Although the Third Reich failed in its attempts to destroy Germany's lesbian and gay cultures, the severe stigmatization and persecution of homosexuals instigated by the Nazis cast a shadow that would affect the lesbian emancipation movement for no less than four decades. Following World War II, the heightened isolation, the lack of women's presses, and the controlling dominance of men in key positions of cultural production and criticism made it difficult for women writers to reconnect with an earlier tradition and to find a voice of their own. It is, therefore, neither inaccurate nor inappropriate to call the fourth stage in the history of German lesbian literature the Forty Years of Hiding, Reflection, and Renewal.

Indeed, the barricade of speechlessness, the tendency to employ subterfuge, the transposition of heterosexual conventions into homosexual relationships, the adoption of the male gaze to hide lesbian desires, displacement and the search for space, and the escape back into heterosexuality—these themes and techniques have been among the most prominent and enduring in the literature of this stage. They are the keys to understanding not only works in which lesbian desires lurk under the surface, as in Ruth Kempe's *Paria* and Annemarie Schwarzenbach's *Lyrische Novelle* (both 1933), Marie Luise Kaschnitz's *Elissa* (1937), Luise Rinser's *Die gläsernen Ringe* (Rings of Glass [1940]), and Gertrud Isolani's prison-camp documentary *Stadt ohne Männer* (City Without Men [1945]), but also those works in which lesbianism is a more central theme. These include Marlen Haushofer's novels *Eine Handvoll Leben* (A Handful of Life [1955]) and *Tapetentür* (Wallpaper Door [1957]), Ingeborg Bachmann's short story "Ein Schritt nach Gomorrha" (A Step Toward Gomorrah [1961]), Nina Keller's novel *Der Schritt* (The Step [1965]), and the stories "Eine großartige Eroberung" (A Great Conquest [1965]) by Gabriele Wohmann and "Die Klosterschule" (The Convent School [1968]) by Barbara Frischmuth.

**The New Lesbian Movement (1971–)**

The era of a new lesbian movement began to emerge in 1971 with the founding of the political action group Homosexuelle Aktion Westberlin and to take off in 1974 with the creation of the Lesbisches Aktionszentrum (Lesbian Action Center) and the Gruppe L74 (Group L74) (Ewering 1992). Aside from a wave of political and social activism—including the tracing of lesbian history and the establishment of women's presses and lesbian magazines in Germany, Austria, and Switzerland—the following decades would witness a stark increase in the publication of (also French and American) lesbian literature and criticism. In the fiction of the 1970s, lesbians at times still appear hidden in the light of conventional prejudices. However, in groundbreaking works, such as *Häutungen* (Shedding [1975]) by Verena Stefan, *Die Freundinnen* (The Girlfriends [1977]) by Johanna Moosdorf, and *Puppe Else* (Dolly Else [1978]) by Marlene Stenten, the lesbian experience is increasingly becoming a possible and positive alternative to heterosexual relationships.

In the 1980s, the works of Elfriede Jelinek, Waldtraut Lewin, Judith Offenbach, Christa Reinig, Monika Sperr, Marlene Stenten, and Gertrud Wilker, among others, brought about a radical diversification of themes. Lesbians are finally younger than

twenty-five or older than fifty; they die and hide no longer; they are politicians, doctors, mothers, and grandmothers; they appear in wheelchairs and are no longer confined to a marginalized private sphere. Since Germany's reunification in 1990, additional efforts have been made to retrace the history of lesbians in the former German Democratic Republic (East Germany), which have resulted in, among other things, the creation of documentaries (Sillige 1991), biographical sketches (Gutsche 1991), and literary studies (Waberski 1997).     *Christoph Lorey*

*Bibliography*

Ewering, Cäcilia. *Frauenliebe und -literatur.* (*Women's Love and Women's Literature*). Essen: Blaue Eule, 1992.

Faderman, Lillian, and Brigitte Eriksson. *Lesbians in Germany, 1890s–1920s*. Tallahassee, Fla.: Naiad, 1980.

Marti, Madeleine. *Hinterlegte Botschaften: Die Darstellung lesbischer Frauen in der deutschsprachigen Literatur seit 1945* (*Treasured Messages: The Representation of Lesbian Women in German Literature since 1945*). Stuttgart: M und P, Verl. f. Wissenschaft und Forschung, 1991.

Meyer, Adele, ed. *Lila Nächte: Die Damenklubs der Zwanziger Jahre* (*Purple Nights: The Women's Clubs of the 1920s*). Berlin: Frauenbuchverl. Zitronenpresse, 1981.

Schoppmann, Claudia. *"Der Skorpion": Frauenliebe in der Weimarer Republik* (*"The Scorpion": Lesbian Love in the Weimar Republic*). Hamburg: Frühlings Erwachen, 1985.

Tubach, Sally Patterson. "Female Homoeroticism in German Literature and Culture." Ph.D. diss., University of California, Berkeley, 1980.

*See also* Germany; Nazism; Romantic Friendship; Weirauch, Anna Elisabet; Winsloe, Christa

**Germany**

Officially named the Federal Republic of Germany (FRG); the result of the unification between West and East Germany in 1990, a year after the fall of the Berlin Wall. Of its approximately eighty million citizens (including 5.2 million non-German immigrants), sixteen million live in the territory of the former East and sixty-four million in the former West. A large percentage of lesbians and gays live in metropolitan areas, such as Berlin, Cologne, Hamburg, and Munich, rather than in rural or small-town areas, due to their large and visible subcultures, providing a broad variety of community services, meeting places, bars, and bookstores.

## History

One of the earliest records of a German woman who passed as a man and married another woman dates back to a court case in 1721. According to the trial transcript, Catharina Margaretha Linck, disguised as a man, served as a soldier in various German armies. In 1717, after her military service, she worked as a cotton dyer and married a woman. When her wife confessed to her mother that Linck was a woman, the mother brought Linck before the law, and she was imprisoned and tried. The main evidence against Linck was a dildo she had fashioned from leather. Catharina Linck was executed in 1721, based on the verdict that she had committed a "crime against nature."

The death penalty for male and female homosexuality (the term in use at the time was "sodomy") was in effect until its abolishment in 1794. Both male and female homosexuality, however, were treated as criminal offenses until 1851. The legal reform of 1851 excluded women from criminal prosecution by changing the formulation from "men and women" to mention only "men." Female homosexual acts were believed not to occur as frequently as male homosexual acts and, therefore, were ignored by the law. Male homosexual acts between adults ceased to be illegal in East Germany in 1968 and in West Germany in 1969.

The early movement for the liberation of homosexuals was led by Magnus Hirschfeld (1868–1935). In 1897, he and several others founded the Scientific-Humanitarian Committee for the purpose of promoting a scientific discussion of homosexuality and advocating the repeal of all laws persecuting homosexuals. The committee pursued its work until the Nazi rise to power in 1933. Although the committee claimed to be fighting for both male and female homosexuals, it was occupied primarily with the struggle to end the legal persecution of male homosexuals. Thus, the situation of lesbians—who endured more subtle forms of social control and did not have access to the public sphere (women were not allowed to build political organizations until 1908 and only gained the right to vote in 1918)—was not given equal attention.

Despite this ignorance over lesbian concerns, between 1909 and 1911 a broad alliance of both rad-

ical and liberal feminists, individual gay male activists, and the Scientific-Humanitarian Committee successfully fought off government attempts to reincorporate female homosexual acts into the penal code. The attempt to criminalize lesbianism was not directed against female homosexuality per se but was intended to subvert the growing political influence of the women's movement in general. Accordingly, the feminist argument focused almost exclusively on the threat of such a law for all women and argued primarily about women's right to privacy. Except for Johanna Elberskirchen (1864–?) and Anna Rüling (dates unknown), both active in the women's movement and two of the very few female members of the board of the Scientific-Humanitarian Committee, feminists did not take an active and progressive stance on the issue of lesbianism. Most of them shared the sexological view of homosexuality as repulsive and unnatural. Although many of the leaders of the feminist movement lived together in lifetime companionships—for example, Helene Lange (1848–1930) and Gertrud Baeumer (1873–1954), Anita Augspurg (1857–1943) and Lida Gustava Heymann (1868–1943)—none of them ever publicly announced themselves to be lesbian. It was a concept that didn't relate to how they understood their lives, experiences, and relationships.

The history of lesbianism as a medical concept began in 1869 when Carl von Westphal (1833–1890), a German psychiatrist, published a case study of a young woman, Fraulein N., who was attracted to women. Westphal identified the young woman as a "cogenital invert," whose abnormality was not aquired but the result of hereditary degeneration and neurosis. Following Westphal and others, Richard von Krafft-Ebing (1840–1902) developed his theory of female homosexuality as "an inherited diseased condition of the central nervous system," in his book *Psychopathia Sexualis*, first published in 1882. Krafft-Ebing's work would become the most influential theory on homosexuality at the time and was replaced only gradually by the work of Sigmund Freud (1856–1939). Krafft-Ebing's distinction between aquired and inherited homosexuality had an impact on the self-definition of lesbians. In Aimée Duc's 1901 novel *Sind es Frauen?* (Are They Women?), the protagonists proudly identify themselves in the newly available terms, drawing boundaries between "true" members of what was called "the third sex" and those who had never been true inverts. Another example of the proud reclaiming of the sexologist's vocabulary is Anna Rüling's 1904 speech "What Interest Does the

Women's Movement Have in the Homosexual Question?" at the annual conference of the Scientific Humanitarian Committee. Rüling linked female homosexuality to autonomy and independence, thus setting it in a feminist context and also challenging feminism's silence on the "homosexual question."

Although these are early signs of the defiant (and, at times, problematic) reclaiming of the sexologist's ideas on women's part, it took until the Weimar Republic (1918–1933) for a visible lesbian subculture to come into existence. Massive economic, political, cultural, and social transformations in post–World War I German society provided some women with the opportunity to live lesbian lives and build the first lesbian culture in Germany. In the "Roaring Twenties," especially Berlin but other major German cities as well, became the scene of a thriving subculture, consisting of bars, magazines, social gathering places, and associations.

When the Nazis gained power in 1933, they immediately raided and closed all lesbian and gay bars and destroyed the lesbian and gay subculture. Unlike male homosexuals, lesbians were not systematically persecuted. Since it was believed that lesbians were also often heterosexual and, therefore, much less likely than homosexual men to fail to contribute to the birth rate, the Nazi government concentrated on disciplining lesbians through norms of proper femininity, based on racist discourses of the "true" woman—and motherhood. There are relatively few examples of lesbians incarcerated in concentration camps. They would usually be charged with prostitution or "indecent behavior," thus being forced to wear the black triangle for the *Asoziale* (antisocials).

## After World War II

Following World War II, the reconstruction of the economy and the rebuilding of political structures stood on top of the agendas of both West and East Germany. Thus, lesbians and gays did not have a chance to come out of the closet the Nazis had forced them into. During the 1950s and 1960s, however, underground lesbian and gay subcultures developed in both German states. They included friendship circles and bars in major urban centers. During the 1970s and 1980s, these lesbian and gay subcultures in East and West Germany grew stronger, more overtly political, and more visible, creating a historically new sense of pride and assertiveness. In 1972, West Berlin lesbians founded the "women's section" of the gay and lesbian activist group Homosexual Action Westberlin (HAW); in

February 1973, they organized the first lesbian public protest in German history: a leaflet campaign against a series of articles in the newspaper *BILD* on the topic "The Crimes of Lesbian Women." In January 1974, German televion broadcasted the film *And We Take for Ourselves What Is Ours by Right,* which documented personal lives and political activities of lesbians from HAW. Also in 1974, the first autonomous National Lesbian Whitsunday Meeting took place, and Berlin lesbians founded the first autonomous lesbian community center and began publishing the first lesbian journal since the Weimar Republic, *Unsere kleine Zeitung* (Our Little Journal). During the 1970s and 1980s, lesbians adopted feminist ideas and were active primarily in the feminist movement, building a strong, politically active women's community.

The second half of the 1980s witnessed the beginning of two contradictory developments: Lesbians became more visible as lesbians and not just as feminists, demanding more active representation within the feminist movement; at the same time, lesbians of color, disabled lesbians, and Jewish lesbians began to demand recognition within the lesbian community, thus forcing lesbian feminists to take a serious look at the, by then, dominant concept of lesbianism as a feminist or "woman-identified" identity. In the late 1990s, lesbians in Germany became more visible than ever, fighting for cultural and political representation, as well as participating in other political arenas, such as the struggle against racism.

In East Germany, the Homosexuelle Interessengemeinschaft Berlin (HIB; Berlin Association for Homosexual Concerns) was founded in 1974. The semipublic asscociation was established by both women and men and organized mostly private discussion groups and programs. Parallel to these efforts, lesbians and feminists organized separate groups centered on feminist issues. As the Lutheran Church was the only institution strong enough to serve as an umbrella for political work outside the Communist Party, during the 1980s many lesbian and gay activists turned to it to organize publicly and to form discussion groups. Lesbians and gays who were not comfortable with church affiliation continued to fight for recognition by state officials. In 1986, the Sonntags Club (Sundays Club), a group that organized Sunday programs in a regular neighborhood youth club in East Berlin consisting of meetings, discussions, and cultural activities, received official recognition and became the first state-supported lesbian and gay group in the East.

With the collapse of the Communist regime in East Germany and the fall of the Berlin Wall in 1989, history has taken many sharp turns for both (former) East and West Germans. The visibility and critical activity of lesbians in all of Germany, however, remains unabated.

Throughout the 1990s lesbians and gays in both eastern and western Germany became more visible than ever. The annual gay pride parades in Berlin, Cologne, Hamburg, and other major cities grew steadily in numbers, peaking in 1998 with about 350,000 participants in Berlin alone. The growth of gay pride also reflected a renewed interest of both lesbians and gay men to form political, social, and cultural alliances with each other. With the decline of a feminist model of lesbian identity as "woman identification," many lesbians began to associate lesbianism more closely with sexuality than with gender, thus reopening the possibility of forming links with gay men. Feminist politics, however, remained important in lesbian activism, and debates over whether lesbians and gays do indeed share political goals continued.

One of the strongly debated areas between lesbians and gay men in the late 1990s was the struggle for lesbian and gay rights. Whereas many gay men favored gay marriage as the means to legal entry into society, many lesbians adopted a feminist point of view to question if marriage really is the answer to equality for lesbians and gays. These differences notwithstanding, lesbians and gay men agreed that anti-discrimination laws should be one of the primary issues on the political agenda for the next millennium. *Sabine Hark*

## Bibliography

Faderman, Lillian, and Brigitte Eriksson, eds. *Lesbians in Germany, 1890s–1920s*. Tallahassee, Fla.: Naiad, 1980.

Hark, Sabine. *Deviante Subjekte. Die paradoxe Politik der Identitaet* (*Deviant Subjects: The Paradoxes of Identity Politics*). Opladen: Leske and Budrich, 1996.

———, ed. *Grenzen lesbischer Identitaeten* (*Borders of Lesbian Identities*). Berlin: Querverlag, 1996.

Jones, James. *"We of the Third Sex": Literary Representations of Homosexuality in Wilhelmine Germany*. New York: Lang, 1990.

Martin, Biddy. "Extraordinary Homosexuals and the Fear of Being Ordinary." *differences: A Journal of Feminist Cultural Studies* 6:2–3 (Summer/Fall 1994), 100–125.

*See also* Berlin; German Literature; Nazism; Rüling, Anna; sexology

## Gidlow, Elsa (1898–1986)

Poet, freelance journalist, and philosopher. Born in Yorkshire, England, Gidlow's moved with her family to Montreal, Québec, Canada, when she was six. Her childhood was marked by poverty and an often interrupted education. Gidlow wrote poetry from an early age and was a lifelong feminist, having read about suffragists in the United Kingdom as a teenager. In 1920, she moved to New York City, where she became the poetry editor of *Pearson's* magazine, a frequently censored progressive publication.

Her first book of poetry, *On a Gray Thread* (1923), the first openly lesbian poetry collection in the United States, was published by the famous typographer Will Ransom. Gidlow was aware of the social attitudes toward lesbians but believed she had an intrinsic right to publish erotic poetry about women. That she did this without the support of a lesbian community or financial resources to fall back on marks her as a bold and fearless creative spirit.

Her poetry is singularly free of external influences, although she often wrote poetry reminiscent of Japanese haiku, especially in *Wild Song Singing* (1950) and *Makings for Meditation* (1973). *Letters from Limbo* (1956) *and Moods of Eros* (1971) were printed by her own Druid Heights Books. *Sapphic Songs, Seventeen to Seventy* (1976), published by Diana Press, was reissued in a revised and expanded edition, *Sapphic Songs, Eighteen to Eighty* (1982), by Booklegger Press.

In the early 1930s, Gidlow moved to the San Francisco area of California. She was an early supporter of the Daughters of Bilitis and an important member of artistic, philosophical, and bohemian circles, cofounding the Society of Comparative Philosophy in 1962. She counted among her admirers Alan Watts (1915–1973), Kenneth Rexroth (1905–1982), Ansel Adams (1902–1984), Robinson Jeffers (1887–1962), and Del Martin (1921–) and Phyllis Lyon (1924–). She was accused of Communist leanings, and in 1947 the American Civil Liberties Union (ACLU) came to her defense.

In *Ask No Man Pardon: The Philosophical Significance of Being Lesbian* (1975), Gidlow wrote that lesbians are born with different desires and needs but just as nature intended. She appeared in the documentary *Word Is Out* (1978); and in *ELSA: I Come with My Songs* (1986), she chronicles a long

**G**

life of unabashed eroticism, deep spiritual questing, and profound love of women and nature.

*Eloise Klein Healy*

### Bibliography

Rexroth, Kenneth. "Elsa Gidlow's Sapphic Songs." *American Poetry Review* 7:1 (1978), 20.

Wells, Karen. "Part V Sisters All." *Margins* 23 (August 1975), 53–55.

West, Celeste. "Farewell, Elsa Gidlow, Poet-Warrior." *off our backs* (August/September 1986)n n.p.

*See also* Martin, Del, and Lyon, Phyllis; Poetry; Québec

## Girl Scouts

Organization for girls from ages five to seventeen. The Girl Scout organization was founded in Savannah, Georgia, by Juliette Gordon Low (1860–1927) in 1912. Girl Scouts and Girl Guides make up the World Association of Girl Guides and Girl Scouts (WAGGGS), the largest organization of girls and women in the world, with troops on every continent and international centers in England, India, Mexico, and Switzerland. Girl Scouts of the U.S.A. (GSUSA) has had more than sixty million members in the twentieth century. Its national headquarters is in New York City, and there are more than three hundred affiliated but independent councils serving cities and rural areas throughout the United States.

Girl Scouting is devoted to empowering girls to realize their full potential. It encourages self-confidence, independence, and a service ethic through outdoors activities, skill building, character development, and leadership training. Its success is indicated by a 1991 study showing that 64 percent of women in *Who's Who of American Women* were Girl Scouts.

The Girl Scouts has a long-standing commitment to diversity, allowing mixed-race Scout troops and camps during the era of strict segregation, doing outreach in minority communities, publishing information in Spanish, and stressing diversity in its materials. According to a 1994 report by the Nonprofit Academic Centers Council, nearly one-third of GSUSA management positions were filled by people of color, compared to a 14.3 percent national average for nonprofit organizations.

### Lesbians in Girl Scouting

Many lesbians have felt at home in the all-women environments of Girl Scout troops, camps, and council offices, where women do all of the jobs and make all of the decisions. Scouting offers relief from the strain of heterosexual dating and the pressure to be conventionally feminine. In addition, many women who attended Girl Scout camp in their youth found it a refuge from dysfunctional or abusive family situations. While there is no way to determine whether there are more, fewer, or about the same percentage of lesbians in the Girl Scouts as in comparable organizations, estimates from staff members and leadership range from as low as 5 percent of members to as high as 80 percent of administrators.

The official GSUSA position on lesbians was developed in 1980. It states that, while the Girl Scouts does not recruit lesbians, it does not discriminate or intrude into personal matters. It maintains that leaders must provide appropriate role models and that sexual displays or the advocacy of a personal lifestyle or sexual orientation are not allowed. According to GSUSA, appropriate behavior, not orientation, is the issue.

In practice, deep currents of homophobia run through Girl Scouting, reflecting society's stereotypes and fears about homosexuals working with children. Lesbian Girl Scouts, fearful of compromising the organization and of losing their positions, have usually stayed closeted. Despite their caution, many have lost jobs or troops when their sexual orientation became rumored or known. In several camps and councils, executive directors, sometimes themselves lesbians, have conducted periodic "witch-hunts" to rid the organization of lesbians.

In the late twentieth century, with greater social acceptance of gay, lesbian, bisexual, and transgender people, coming out of "the cookie closet" (a reference to the cookie sales that are a primary source of fund-raising for the Girl Scouts) became less fraught with danger. Some Girl Scout councils began adding sexual orientation to their diversity training and to their employment nondiscrimination policies. In several councils, open lesbians began serving on boards of directors, as administrators, and as troop leaders.

Little has been published about lesbians in Girl Scouting. The first article was a 1989 report by Jorjet Harper in New York City's *OutWeek* magazine. The first story, "The Juliette Low Legacy," by Judith McDaniel, appeared in *40 Contemporary Lesbian and Gay Short Stories in 1994*. Also in 1994, *Lesbian Connection*, a bimonthly news and opinion magazine, printed a spirited exchange of letters about the importance of Girl Scouting to many lesbians.

The first book on the subject, *On My Honor: Lesbians Reflect on Their Scouting Experience*, by Nancy Manahan, was published in 1997. It contains essays from thirty-three Girl Scouts, including five women of color and several Scouts who played leadership roles in the organization. This collection encouraged the Girl Scouts to stop compromising its principles of honesty and fairness by acknowledging the contributions lesbians have made to the organization, apologizing for past injustices, adding "sexual orientation" to the GSUSA nondiscrimination policy, incorporating accurate information on sexual orientation into its training materials, and supporting its many dedicated lesbian members.

*Nancy Manahan*

## Bibliography

Manahan, Nancy. *On My Honor: Lesbians Reflect on Their Scouting Experience*. Northboro, Mass.: Madwoman, 1997.

Schultz, Gladys Denny, and Daisy Gordon Lawrence. *Lady from Savannah: The Life of Juliette Low*. New York: Girl Scouts of the U.S.A., 1958, 1988.

*See also* Lesbian Connection

## Gittings, Barbara (1932–)

Homophile and gay rights activist. Founder of the New York City chapter of the Daughters of Bilitis (DOB) in 1958 and editor of the national lesbian magazine *The Ladder: A Lesbian Review* from 1963 to 1966, Barbara Gittings remained active in the struggle for lesbian and gay rights long after the 1969 Stonewall riots and the rise of lesbian feminism in the 1970s.

Born in Vienna, Austria, Gittings moved with her family to Wilmington, Delaware, in the 1940s and decided that she was a homosexual in the early 1950s. In 1951, she moved to Philadelphia, Pennsylvania, and soon began going to gay bars dressed as a butch. (She later rejected what she considered the "role-playing" of butch-femme lesbian culture.) In 1956, Gittings made contact with the homophile movement in California. Two years later, she started the DOB chapter in New York City. In 1961, she met Kay Lahusen [Tobin] (1930–), who became her life partner.

A strong and early proponent of using direct-action tactics in the homophile movement, Gittings marched in lesbian and gay demonstrations beginning in 1965 at Independence Hall in Philadelphia and at the White House and the Pentagon in Washington, D.C. Her support for the controversial strategies of homophile militancy was among the reasons given for her ouster as editor of *The Ladder* in 1966.

In the transformed political climate of the 1970s, Gittings rejected what she considered the extremism of radical gay liberationists, lesbian feminists, and lesbian separatists. Consistently defending lesbian alliances with gay men, Gittings rejected the notion that lesbian activists should work primarily within the context of the women's movement. In the early 1970s, Gittings produced gay exhibits at three annual conventions of the American Psychiatric Association and headed the Task Force on Gay Liberation (renamed the Gay Task Force) of the American Library Association (1971–1986). In 1971, Gittings appeared with six other lesbians on the nationally syndicated television program, *The David Susskind Show*. She also served on the boards of directors of the National Gay Task Force (1973–1982), the Gay Rights National Lobby (1976–1984), and the Delaware Valley Legacy Fund (1994–), which raises and distributes money for lesbian and gay projects.

*Marc Stein*

## Bibliography

Katz, Jonathan. *Gay American History: Lesbians and Gay Men in the U.S.A.* New York: Avon, 1976, pp. 632–651.

Marcus, Eric. *Making History: The Struggle for Gay and Lesbian Equal Rights: An Oral History*. New York: HarperCollins, 1992, pp. 104–126, 213–227.

Perry, Troy, and Thomas L.P. Swicegood. *Profiles in Gay and Lesbian Courage*. New York: St. Martin's, 1991, pp. 153–178.

Tobin, Kay, and Randy Wicker. *The Gay Crusaders*. New York: Paperback Library, 1972, pp. 205–224.

*See also* Daughters of Bilitis; Gay Liberation Movement; *Ladder, The*; Librarians; National Gay and Lesbian Task Force (NGLTF)

## Gluck (Hannah Gluckstein) (1895–1978)

English artist. Born into a wealthy business family, founders of the famed J. Lyons and Company, Gluck chose to attend art school rather than university. At St. John's Wood Art School and during summer visits surrounded by a group of artists in Cornwall, Gluck began to develop her distinctive artistic and

"Gluck" by E.O. Hoppé. The Fine Art Society, London.

sartorial style. Well before it was acceptable, the androgynous Gluck dressed in men's clothing and cut her hair short—never to pass as a man but to violate the rules of fashion as well as of social etiquette. In 1923–1924, the artist Romaine Brooks (1874–1970) captured Gluck's unique persona in a well-known portrait entitled *Peter, a Young English Girl.* E.O. Hoppé (1878–1972) produced a series of photographs of Gluck in 1926 and explained that her "facial contour indicates the qualities expressed in her paintings. . . . To look at her face is to understand both her success as an artist and the fact that she dresses as a man. Originality, determination, strength of character and artistic insight are expressed in every line" (quoted in Souhami [1988]). Gluck's daring tactic to use her own clothing to symbolize the theme of her 1926 "one man" show called *Stage and Country* created a sensation among art critics, who were equally impressed with her work. Throughout her career, Gluck rejected developments in modern art in favor of more traditional subject matter, such as the portrait and the self-portrait, scenes from the theater, still life, and landscape. Biographer Souhami (1988) suggests that the artist's choice of subject was more influenced by the interests of her current partner; Gluck's relationships included journalists Sybil Cookson and Edith Shackleton Heald, flower arranger Constance Spry, and socialite Nesta Obermer. Gluck celebrated her

partnership with Obermer in a 1937 portrait of them both entitled *Medallion,* though the artist referred to it as the "YouWe" picture. After four major exhibitions in the 1920s and 1930s, Gluck disappeared from the art scene, although she continued to paint. In 1973, the gallery with which Gluck had been most closely associated, the Fine Art Society in London's Bond Street, held a major retrospective that revived considerable interest in her work and life.                    *Laura Doan*

### Bibliography

Souhami, Diana. *Gluck: Her Biography*. London: Pandora, 1988.

***See also*** Brooks, Romaine

### Goddess Religion

Contemporary spiritual movement identified as Witchcraft or Wicca, especially the Dianic Tradition, which emphasizes the female principle more than the male. The Goddess is seen as encompassing both the creative life force and the destructive death force and as predecessor of all other gods. She is known by many names and in many aspects, such as the Triple Goddess, Mother/Maiden/Crone, of the Celts; Inanna; Thought Woman; Afrekete; Kali; Diana; Isis; and Ixchel. Some branches of this movement include both men and women as practitioners, but others, such as the Susan B. Anthony Coven of Los Angeles, California, founded by Z. Budapest (1940–), are limited to women. In general, the feminist branches of Wicca seem to have a high percentage of lesbian participants.

Theologian Daly (1973) points to the patriarchal focus of the major religions and how these serve to buttress the power of the fathers in society. For this reason, it is not surprising that the idea of the Goddess and her attendant, the Witch, would become attractive to women, particularly to lesbians. As Adler (1986) notes: "The Witch . . . is an extraordinary symbol—independent, anti-establishment, strong, and proud. She is political, yet spiritual and magical. The Witch is woman as martyr; she is persecuted by the ignorant; she is the woman who lives outside society and outside society's definition of woman."

Philosophically, the roots of the feminist goddess resurgence lie in the ideas of "first wave" feminists, such as Matilda Joslyn Gage (*Woman, Church, and State* [1893]) and Charlotte Perkins Gilman (*His Religion and Hers* [1923]), who sought an alternative culture to the patriarchal society of their time by reviving what they saw as an ancient pre-Christian ideal usually focused on a matriarchy. These ideas resurfaced with the radical feminists in the 1960s and 1970s, who had the same goals of seeking an alternative to what was seen as a death-oriented patriarchal culture.

The Goddess religion is earth-based, celebrating the cycles of the seasons and the moon. The eight festivals, known as Sabbats, and their dates are: Yule/winter solstice, December 20–23; Brigid/Candlemas, February 2; Eostar/spring equinox, March 20–23; Beltane/May Eve (May 1); Litha/summer solstice, June 20–23; Lughnasadh/Lammas, August 1; Mabon/autumn equinox, September 20–23; and Samhain/Halloween, October 31. Visualization or a change of consciousness is the "magic" at the heart of the religion, which seeks to reconcile opposites and, therefore, effect healing for its participants and the earth.

At the end of the twentieth century, Goddess religion had a growing popularity as evidenced by the number of groups identifying themselves with the movement and the intensive workshops held all over the United States by such practitioners as Starhawk (1979), who attempts to restore and acknowledge the spiritual power of women.

*Annette Van Dyke*

### Bibliography

Adler, Margot. *Drawing Down the Moon: Witches, Druids, Goddess-Worshippers, and Other Pagans in America Today*. Boston: Beacon, 1981. Rev. and exp. ed. 1986.

Budapest, Zsuzanna E. *The Holy Book of Women's Mysteries*. 2 vols. Oakland, Calif.: Susan B. Anthony Coven no. 1, 1982.

Daly, Mary. *Beyond God the Father: Toward a Philosophy of Women's Liberation*. Boston: Beacon, 1973.

Starhawk. *The Spiral Dance: A Rebirth of the Ancient Religion of the Great Goddess*. San Francisco: Harper and Row, 1979.

Van Dyke, Annette. *The Search for a Woman-Centered Spirituality*. New York: New York University Press, 1992.

*See also* Spirituality

## Goldman, Emma (1869–1940)

American anarchist and feminist organizer, lecturer, publisher, and writer. As the most influential woman in the international anarchist movement, Goldman included homosexuals among those for whom she demanded justice. Despite criticism from her comrades, who disliked associating anarchism with such "unnatural" topics, she condemned the stigmatization and persecution of homosexuals in lectures on "The Intermediate Sex," drawing primarily on the ideas of Edward Carpenter (1844–1929) but also on those of Havelock Ellis (1859–1939), Richard von Krafft-Ebing (1840–1902), and Sigmund Freud (1856–1939). An early defender of British writer Oscar Wilde (1854–1900) in his 1895 sodomy trial, Goldman attracted to her bohemian Mother Earth circle in New York City a number of gay men and lesbians, including the editor of *The Little Review*, Margaret Anderson (1886–1973), who, according to Goldman, aroused "stirrings" that were "expressive of my previous theoretic interest in sex variation." These "stirrings" may have led Goldman in 1912 to a brief affair with an infatuated admirer, Almeda Sperry, who wrote ecstatically of "the rhythmic spurt of your love juice." But Goldman never acknowledged a relationship with Sperry, and her letters to her great passion, Ben L. Reitman (1879–1942), whose own homosexual attractions she regarded with equanimity, insist that she did "not incline that way."

For all of her outrage at "the social otracism of the invert," Goldman by the 1920s expressed ambivalent feelings toward homosexuality, criticizing the "narrowness" of the lesbians whose "antagonism to the male is almost a disease." In an angry 1923 letter to Magnus Hirschfeld (1868–1935), Goldman denied claims that the great French revolutionist Louise Michel (1830–1905) was a lesbian. Michel's allegedly "masculine" traits were really the attributes of a new type of womanhood. Such women were not only "not homosexual but extremely feminine." In Goldman's view, it was "precisely *because there is no sex element* between them [women] that they can better understand each other (emphasis in original)." While rejecting Victorian definitions of gender, Goldman oscillated between the sexologists' discourse of inversion, which equated homosexuality with cross-gender identification, and a modernist, psychoanalytically influenced discourse of desire, which stressed the independence of sexual orientation and gender identification. Still, Goldman saw sexuality, including homosexuality, as the deepest wellspring of aesthetic expression. Homophobia, not homosexuality, was the problem to be overcome. *Alice R. Wexler*

**G**

*Bibliography*

Chauncey, George. *Gay New York: Gender, Urban Culture, and the Making of the Gay Male World, 1890–1940.* New York: Basic Books, 1994.

Cook, Blanche Wiesen. "Female Support Networks and Political Activism: Lillian Wald, Crystal Eastman, Emma Goldman." In *A Heritage of Her Own: Towards a New Social History of Women.* Ed. Nancy Cott and Elizabeth H. Pleck. New York: Simon and Schuster, 1979.

Falk, Candace, ed. *Emma Goldman: A Guide to Her Life and Documentary Sources.* Alexandria, Va.: Chadwyck-Healy, 1995.

———. *Love, Anarchy, and Emma Goldman.* New Brunswick, N.J.: Rutgers University Press, 1984.

Haalund, Bonnie. *Emma Goldman: Sexuality and the Impurity of the State.* Montreal: Black Rose, 1993.

Wexler, Alice. *Emma Goldman in America.* Boston: Beacon, 1984.

*See also* Anderson, Margaret Carolyn; Michel, Louise

## Gossip

Process of information dispersion and a social interaction, typically dealing with the personal affairs of individuals. Gossip can, thus, refer to news about the affairs of another, to one's experiences, or to any hearsay of a personal nature, whether it is of a positive or a negative nature. Gossip as an activity is a means of passing time, and it helps maintain the fluidity of communication patterns. Gossip is also the repository of folklore and taboo, and, in some cultures, it is a storehouse for social precedents. Gossip is proscribed in principle and generally frowned upon, but, at the same time, it is respected in day-to-day practice because it promotes friendship and group cohesion, helps sustain group norms, and often serves to effectively communicate important information.

### Gossip, Knowledge, and Communication

Lesbian community members frequently rely upon gossip as a source of crucial information inaccessible by other means. It is a very efficient means of acquiring knowledge, in which participants work together to achieve knowledge. Lesbians rely upon gossip as a form of knowledge. Their use challenges the assumption that the informational content of gossip is highly unreliable, although they recognize it is oftentimes unsubstantiated. Gossip serves a variety of needs on the part of the gossipers: It provides information; it reaffirms values and social etiquette; and it serves a tutoring function for new community members. It allows determination of who is lesbian, and it provides for monitoring of members' relationship statuses. Gossip provides a forum for trading news and for providing participants with a cognitive map of the social environment.

As an intrinsically valuable activity, gossip satisfies the basic need to acquire information about the intimate aspects of other people's lives. In lesbian communities, gossip conveys information about personal details of people's lives (love, friendship, sex, violence, money, relationship beginnings and endings) and community politics. Lesbian gossip is not abstract; it is focused on individuals in their concreteness.

This need to acquire knowledge of intimate and personal aspects of other community members' lives occupies a central role in lesbian gossip because there are very few other ways to satisfy this need to acquire accurate information. Often, gossip is more reliable and complete than information released through authorized mechanisms, since candid and open self-description is rare and limited to close friends. Though lesbians must rely on gossip as a source of important community news, it is hard to verify, which is a consequence of the confidential nature of the information conveyed.

Lesbian community members have a need for acquiring knowledge of personal, intimate details of the lives of persons across their social networks and community, and, at times, gossip may well be the only form of inquiry that provides the needed data. Information of such a highly personal nature is not likely to be accessible to the modes of inquiry more standardly perceived as legitimate. Thus, in cases in which the information or knowledge is extremely sensitive (and, frequently, importance is concomitant with sensitivity), acquiring information via the grapevine will be the only form of inquiry available. Such information in likely to be missing from the standard literature or the public storehouse of received knowledge. Gossip allows the indirectness and innuendo that make it safe to talk about certain things.

### Gossip and Community

Another sort of gossip is engaged in strictly for mutual entertainment of the participants. Gossiping for amusement is a reciprocal trade that is derived from the pleasure of talking with other people. This promotes lesbian solidarity through speaking the language of shared experience. Members reveal themselves as they talk of others and construct a joint lesbian culture and social narrative. Like many other kinds of need-satisfying activities, gossip is pleasurable. Really good gossip is usually not just a piece of information but a narrative-style anecdote of interest even to strangers. Gossip is a form of social communication that usually revolves around enjoyable and intriguing information not yet widely known. Gossip functions to construct and maintain lesbian community as speakers and listeners appear to share the same standards of right and wrong behavior. And, although adherence to such standards is often superficial, even the mere appearance of common values establishes intimacy among the participants.

Similarly, giving someone confidential information conveys confidence in that person. Such a use of gossip among friends belies its inherently valuable nature as a friendly activity that strengthens social bonds. It can also solidify a group's sense of itself by heightening consciousness of community boundaries. Trading intimate information satisfies community need and indicates intimate relations among lesbian women. In addition, gossip reaffirms community norms by bringing social pressure to bear on their enforcement. By carefully choosing the audience for gossip, lesbians maintain the boundaries of the very community that the content of gossip potentially exposes. Gossip as an activity is predicated on a trust that the information traded will be confined to those in the community with a legitimate need to know the content of the gossip. This use of gossip functions to demonstrate lesbian unity, and it works to sustain community norms.

Within the lesbian community, as in every community, there is an etiquette for gossiping, and one who doesn't follow the rules is seen and treated as a deviant. In the lesbian community, there is gossip that is considered proper and gossip that is considered improper. Proper gossip is that indulged in by all lesbians; it functions to construct and maintain lesbian community as a unique social world. Improper gossip aims at raising the teller's status at the expense of other lesbians, and, eventually, social constraints will be exerted by community members to rein in this errant member. Because gossip is not merely idle talk, but talk with a social purpose vital to lesbian community functioning, the etiquette of what is proper and improper in gossiping is faithfully controlled by proficient community members.

## The Grapevine

A grapevine is an informal, often secret means of transmitting information, gossip, or rumor from person to person. The term is derived from a popular Civil War–era expression, "a dispatch by grapevine telegraph," which referred to information transmitted by irregular means rather than by regular telegraphic lines. In contemporary practice, a grapevine is an informal communication network involving circles of acquaintances who provide information, often faster than formal communication channels. Participants in a grapevine system work together in a cooperative effort to achieve knowledge, and the grapevine is often an efficient source of crucial information inaccessible by other means.

Since lesbian community members can depend upon few institutional channels to transmit news and information of import to members, it is functional for members to keep an ear to the grapevine, as it were. Members listen carefully to community talk as a means of gleaning information about events that they may be precluded from directly observing. Working the grapevine is an interactive process in which more is going on than speaking and listening. The grapevine participant is constantly sifting through information, evaluating talk, comparing component parts of talk to one another, and judging what is truth, what is falsehood, and what needs further investigation prior to judgment being passed.

Transmitting community information over the grapevine telegraph is an interactive skill that depends on social and storytelling skills. Those engaging in such talk may have no particular focus of interest; in this case, the community member will simply keep an ear to the ground, hoping as much for insight in selecting a particular focus as in acquiring specific information. Users of the grapevine employ community consensus as a primary indication of their proximity to the truth and their own sense of community to discern what bits of information are appropriately accountable as community news.

Success of the grapevine depends upon the quality of the community of relevant correspondents, those qualified to contribute to the investigation, and communication, of a particular concern. Access to accurate information will be limited to those lesbian community members with fairly direct acquaintance with the key individuals affected, nor-

G mally an affinity group small in number. The forum provided by a grapevine network generates its own boundaries or sets of conditions for belonging, and, thus, it creates its own group of insiders and outsiders. The gossipers admitted to the network become insiders, with clearly understood entitlement and privilege within the gossip circle.

## Conclusion

Lesbian gossip serves a crucial function in providing necessary information and in establishing intimacy; thus, it satisfies a lesbian community need. Gossip norms permit or advance social knowledge, as well as serve other social ends. Gossip is an expectation in lesbian community. Not only is engaging in gossip evidence of friendship, but it creates friendship and community. Gossip is a communicative accomplishment that creates, expresses, and sustains lesbian social reality. It is a privilege and even an obligation among lesbians. *Willa Young*

### *Bibliography*

Dunbar, R.I.M. *Grooming, Gossip, and the Evolution of Language*. Cambridge, Mass.: Harvard University Press, 1996.

Goodman, Robert F., and Aaron Ben-Ze'ev, eds. *Good Gossip*. Lawrence: University of Kansas Press, 1994.

Rosnow, Ralph L. *Rumor and Gossip: The Social Psychology of Hearsay*. New York: Elsevier, 1976.

Shibutani, Tamotsu. *Improvised News: A Sociological Study of Rumor*. Indianapolis: Bobbs-Merrill, 1966.

Tebbutt, Melanie. *Women's Talk?: A Social History of "Gossip" in Working-Class Neighborhoods, 1880–1960*. Brookfield, Vt.: Ashgate, 1995.

*See also* Community; Social-Construction Theory

## Gothic

Term used to describe literary and cinematic genres that focus upon and showcase the monstrous, the ghostly, the supernatural, and the perverse. There are many references to nonnormative sexualities and gender expressions within gothic precisely because of the genre's interest in bizarre acts and terrifying embodiments.

There are several different historical periods of intense gothic production. In the 1790s, the gothic novel emerged as an immensely popular literature, generating a huge, mostly female, market. Novels like *The Monk* (1796) by Matthew G. Lewis (1775–1818) and *The Italian* (1797) by Ann Radcliffe (1764–1823) combined eerie windswept settings with elaborate tales of evil (and mostly foreign) monks and aristocrats. Usually, these tales revolved around a gothic heroine. During the nineteenth century, while gothic subplots animated many otherwise conventional novels, the tradition lived on primarily in vampire stories. By the turn of the twentieth century, the gothic novel returned in full force in a series of wildly popular monster stories, including *Dracula* (1897) by Bram Stoker (1847–1912), *Dr. Jekyll and Mr Hyde* (1885) by Robert Louis Stevenson (1850–1894), and *The Picture of Dorian Gray* (1892) by Oscar Wilde (1859–1900). These novels all depend upon the terrifying effects of bodily transformation: Respectable people metamorphose into vampires, blood suckers, cold-blooded murderers, and sexual sinners. The 1890s gothic novel concerns itself far less with gothic buildings and landscapes than in an almost obsessive fascination with bodily abnormality. Finally, in the twentieth century, the advent of cinema brought monstrosity and gothic effect to the silver screen, and the birth of the horror film ushered in a new era of visual horror.

Homosexuality haunts the gothic in all of its manifestations. Many gothic writers of the 1790s and the 1890s were rumored to be "perverse" in some way (William Beckford [1760–1844] and Matthew G. Lewis in the 1790s and Oscar Wilde in the 1890s, most notably), and the gothic itself was always considered to be an abnormal and unhealthy counterpart to bourgeois realism. At the end of the nineteenth century, in particular, gothicism became one of a cluster of discourses dedicated to separating out the normal from the abnormal, the healthy from the perverse, the productive from the unproductive. Medical, psychological, legal, and sexological discourses produced accounts of sexual behavior that resulted in the binary classifications of homo- and heterosexuality.

Many critics have linked lesbianism to gothic texts by describing the "ghosting" of perverse female sexuality. In a classic article on lesbian ghosting, film theorist White (1991) argues that Robert Wise's horror film *The Haunting* (1963) "is one of the screen's most spine-tingling representations of the disruptive force of lesbian desire." In this haunted-house film, as White demonstrates, "we never see the ghost but we do see the lesbian." The identification of lesbian desire with a ghosted effect captures perfectly the ways in which lesbian desire historically has been rendered invisible.

Lesbians are often invisible in the eyes of the law, unremarkable to the psychologist, and inexplicable to the sexologist. Indeed, the lesbian becomes visible only as a specter, on the one hand, or as mannish or aggressive, on the other. Accordingly, within gothic traditions, the lesbian vampire is a counterpart to the lesbian specter. The lesbian vampire is the visible, predatory lesbian who preys upon younger women and seduces them with a phallic bite. The lesbian vampire has been traced by Zimmerman (1981), Auerbach (1995), and others from her first appearance as Carmilla in Joseph Sheridan Le Fanu's (1814–1873) classic text of that name (1872) to contemporary lesbian-made independent films, such as *Because the Dawn* (1988), directed by Amy Goldstein, and novels, including *The Gilda Stories* (1991), by Jewelle Gomez. Presenting an exciting and hypersexualized image of lesbian desire, the lesbian vampire has become a popular cult figure. She represents an alternative to the ghosted and spectral lesbian, and she appropriates stereotypes of predatory lesbian desire. The lesbian vampire is an orally fixated sexual creature who lives among humans, although not one of them, and who lives within an alternative time zone, rising at night and retiring by dawn. Contemporary alternative queer dyke features, such as the Austrian film *Flaming Ears* (1992), directed by Ursula Purrer, Angela-Hans Scheirl, and Dietmar Schipe, tend to feature vampire scenes to emphasize an otherworldly, deliberately perverse, underground dyke scene.

Gothic has long been of particular interest to queer film and literary critics. Queer theorist Eve Kosofsky Sedgwick uses gothic in her seminal work, *Between Men: English Literature and Male Homosocial Desire* (1985), to argue that gothic novels dramatize the "tableau of two men chasing each other across the landscape." This tableau demonstrates both homoerotic longing and paranoia about homoerotic desire. Various gothic conventions, such as doubling and the unspeakable, further code homosexuality into gothic structures. Other critics have examined the various strands that link gothicism to the representation of "perverse" desire.

Contemporary horror film has less obvious links to representations of perverse desire. Low-budget "splatter films," in particular, seem dedicated wholly to the fragmentation of the female body by a murderous heterosexual killer. However, Carol Clover's study *Men, Women, and Chain Saws* (1992) examines what she calls "the final girl" to argue that the horror film provides some of the few representations of tough and androgynous female power in cinema. The "final girl" is the character who survives the carnage and emerges unscathed at the end of the film; she is intentionally gender ambiguous, Clover argues, so that male audiences can identify with both the monster and the victim. What this account leaves out are the powerful potential identifications to be made between queer female viewers and the queer monster killer final girl.

In conclusion, gothicism has essential and important ties to the coded representation of homosexuality within literature and film. Monsters, demons, and vampires represent perverse combinations of pleasure and danger, power and violence, fear and desire. Queers people the gothic as monsters, victims, and survivors, and lesbians, in particular, seem to thrive in its shadow lands.      *Judith Halberstam*

## Bibliography

Auerbach, Nina. *Our Vampires, Ourselves*. Chicago and London: University of Chicago Press, 1995.

Clover, Carol. *Men, Women, and Chain Saws: Gender in the Modern Horror Film*. Princeton, N.J.: Princeton University Press, 1992.

Halberstam, Judith. *Skin Shows: Gothic Horror and the Technology of Monsters*. Durham, N.C.: Duke University Press, 1995.

Sedgwick, Eve Kosofsky. *Between Men: English Literature and Male Homosocial Desire*. New York: Columbia University Press, 1985.

———. *The Coherence of Gothic Conventions*. New York and London: Methuen, 1986.

White, Patricia. "Female Spectator, Lesbian Specter: The Haunting." In *Inside/Out: Lesbian Theories, Gay Theories*. Ed. Diana Fuss. New York: Routledge, 1991, pp. 142–172.

Zimmerman, Bonnie. "Daughters of Darkness: The Lesbian Vampire on Film." *Jump Cut* 24–25 (March 1981), 23–24.

*See also* Film, Mainstream; Vampires

## Grahn, Judy (1940–)

American writer and activist. Born in Chicago, Illinois, to Vera Doris Grahn, a photographer's assistant, and Elmer August Grahn, a cook, Judy Grahn wrote poetry as a child but stopped when she left

# G

*Judy Grahn. © Lynda Koolish.*

home at seventeen. In 1961, she was discharged from the United States Navy for lesbianism. Although she is best known for her poetry, Grahn's contributions to women's publishing and to gay and lesbian and women's cultural history, and her drama, essays, edited collections, and prose fiction have all enriched lesbian culture. Throughout her ouevre, Grahn's writing, in the words of Rich (1978), "over and over . . . calls up the living woman against the manufactured one, the man-made creation of centuries of male art and literature."

In 1963, Grahn picketed the White House with the Mattachine Society, a gay rights group. In 1964, she published an article in *Sexology* magazine under the pseudonym Carol Silver. In 1965, she returned to poetry, including the word "Dyke" in the title of her first long poem to fight the secrecy associated with lesbianism. Although she published a few poems in *The Ladder*, "The Psychoanalysis of Edward the Dyke" was initially unpublishable. In 1969, with her lover, artist Wendy Cadden, Grahn began producing books of poems and graphics. This work formed the basis for the Women's Press Collective, an early hub of the West Coast lesbian feminist movement. In 1971, the Women's Press Collective published Grahn's first poetry collection: *Edward the Dyke and Other Poems*. In 1973, Grahn published seven poems under

the title "The Common Woman." The poems' unsentimental representations of women's lives fed a powerful and growing hunger for authentic, empowering representations of women.

Grahn's definitive political statement on women in Western society occurs in "A Woman Is Talking to Death" (1973), a poem that she told Adrienne Rich "frightened her enough that she'd decided to stop writing poetry for a while." The poem traces the violently tangled historical relations that cause members of disempowered groups, especially women, to abandon each other.

In the 1980s, Grahn's work became more explicitly mythical. In her 1982 American Book Award collection of poetry, *The Queen of Wands*, Grahn explores Helen of Troy from an array of perspectives. *Another Mother Tongue: Gay Words, Gay Worlds* (1984) is based on years of research, interviews, and memories and argues that "gay culture is ancient and has been suppressed into an underground state of being, that everything has meaning, that slang is not necessarily a transitory language form, that old traditions transform, they do not really perish." This theme of persistent, submerged meaning recurs in her play *The Queen of Swords* (1987).

Grahn's novel (1988) *Mundane's World* represents human existence within a web constructed of the experiential and biological lives of "plants, animals, and other natural forms and forces." Her *Blood, Bread, and Roses: How Menstruation Created the World* (1993) was hailed by Alicia Ostriker as a "daring mix of autobiography, anthropology, archaeology and myth." She has also written on butch-femme and the constructed nature of gender identity, in an essay in M.G. Soares's collection *Butch/Femme* (1995).        *Margot Gayle Backus*

## Bibliography

Backus, Margot Gayle. "Judy Grahn and the Lesbian Invocational Elegy: Testimonial and Prophetic Responses to Social Death in 'A Woman Is Talking to Death.'" *Signs: Journal of Women in Culture and Society* 18:4 (1993), 815–837.

Brown, Jayne Relaford. "Judy Grahn." In *The Gay and Lesbian Literary Companion*. Ed. Sharon Malinowski and Christa Brelin. Detroit: Visible Ink, 1995, pp. 213–219.

Carruthers, Mary J. "The Re-Vision of the Muse: Adrienne Rich, Audre Lorde, Judy Grahn, Olga Broumas." *Hudson Review* 36:2 (1983), 293–322.

Case, Sue-Ellen. "Judy Grahn's Gynopoetics: The Queen of Swords." *Studies in the Literary Imagination* 21:2 (1988), 47–67.

Rich, Adrienne. "Power and Danger: The Work of a Common Woman by Judy Grahn." Introduction to *The Work of a Common Woman: The Collected Poetry of Judy Grahn, 1964–1977*. Freedom, Calif.: Crossing, 1978, pp. 7–21.

*See also* Butch-Femme; *Ladder, The;* Poetry

## Greece

Republic located in the southeastern part of Europe. A member of the EEC (European Economic Community), Greece is, at the same time, greatly influenced by the Balkan states that surround it and by Asia Minor. It has a population of almost ten million, and its official religion Christian Orthodox.

For lesbians, Greece is probably best known as the birthplace of Sappho, the famous lyric poet who lived ca. 600 B.C.E. on the island of Lesbos. "Sapphism" and "lesbianism," the two terms that describe female homosexuality, derive, respectively, from the poet and the island upon which she lived. Since late 1970s, Eresos, the town where Sappho was born, has attracted lesbian women from around the world but especially from Europe.

In contrast to the widespread impression of a long male and female homosexual tradition, invisibility seems to be the major characteristic of lesbianism in Greece. As far as is known, there are no written records reporting female homoerotic practices before the late 1970s, when the first gay and feminist groups made their appearance.

AKOE, an acronym for Homosexuals Liberating Movement of Greece, was founded in 1977 in Athens, the capital city. The first organized gay group, it was very active in its time, publishing one of the best gay magazines, *amphi* (Of Both Kinds). One year later, a group of women joined AKOE and, together with women from the feminist group Movement for Women's Liberation, formed the Autonomous Group of Homosexual Women. They left AKOE in 1980 and joined the feminist groups at the House of Women in Romanou Melodou Street in Athens, where they published the lesbian magazine *Lavris* (Labyris; double-axe, a symbol of female power). *Lavris*, which was, until the late 1990s, the only lesbian magazine ever published in Greece, numbered three issues from Spring 1982 to Summer 1983. In the summer of 1983, the lesbian group decided to leave the House of Women in Romanou Melodou because of conflicts with the feminist groups. In 1985, the lesbian group opened another House of Women on Veikou Street, which, for three years, functioned as a meeting point and a group dedicated to self-knowledge.

In 1989, AKOE ceased operations, and the struggle was continued by a new organization, EOK (Greek Homosexual Community), as well as by a lesbian group that met at the Bookstore of Women in Athens. When the bookstore closed in 1990, the Lesbian Group of Athens was formed, sharing lodgings with EOK. In early 1992, AKOE was revived; in 1994, it began to publish *amphi* again.

In Thessaloniki, the second major city of Greece, the lesbian group shared quarters with feminist groups in the House of Women from 1981 to 1987. O.P.O.TH., an acronym for Homosexuals' Initiative of Thessaloniki, was founded in 1988. In 1995, former members of O.P.O.T.H. created a new gay group called Cooperation to Combat Homophobia, which organized public discussions on homosexual issues and publishes a monthly pamphlet, *Vitamin O*.

Small in number and short lived, these lesbian groups seemed to be undecided about whether to cooperate with feminist and/or gay groups. The absence of a tradition of homosexual organizing, the feminist reluctance to embrace lesbians, and the limited effect lesbian groups had on the wider lesbian community prevented the flourishing of an independent lesbian movement and discourse. Moreover, Christian Orthodox tradition and the values of family, kinship, motherhood, and dependent female sexuality, which maintain control in Greek society, condemned lesbianism to invisibility. Even the law ignores female homosexuality. Although homosexual acts in general are not penalized in Greece, since 1933 Code 347 punishes specific homosexual acts (such as for monetary exchange) among men exclusively and differently from heterosexual acts. Same-sex marriage is not allowed, while Paragraph 1578 of the civil code prescribes that courts allow adoption only after examining moral standards along with financial state.

At the end of the 1990s, a group of lesbian women in Athens was publishing a lesbian magazine called *Madame Gou*; another group, the Cyberdykes—was organizing parties and excursions, and women in Crete were publishing Greek lesbian pages on the Internet, the Roz-Mov (Pink and Lavender). Lesbians in Greece, even if they work in small and secluded groups, try to fight against silence and invisibility and struggle to create a discourse to end discrimination and isolation.

*Venetia Kantsa*

## Bibliography

*Amphi. For the Liberation of Homosexual Desire.* Periodical ed. (1978–1988, 1994–). Athens.

*Lavris. Lesbian Discourse and Counter-Discourse.* No. 1 (Spring 1982); No. 2 (Autumn 1982); No. 3 (Summer 1983). Athens.

*Madame Gou.* Lesbian periodical ed. No. 1 (Autumn 1995); No. 2 (March 1996); No. 3 (June 1996); No. 4 (December 1996); No. 5 (November 1997).

Psevdonimou, Xaroula. "Kravges ke psithiri. Gia to lesviako zitima stin Ellada" (Cries and Whispers: About the Lesbian Issue in Greece). In *I Ellada ton ginekon. Diadromes ston horo kai ston topo* (Women's Greece: Stages in Time and Space). Ed. Evtihia Leondithou and Sigrid R. Ammer. Athens: Enallaktikes ekdosis/Gea 1, 1992, pp. 81–95.

*See also* Lesbos, Island of; Sappho

## Greenwich Village

Neighborhood in lower Manhattan in New York City that has maintained a continuous lesbian presence throughout the twentieth century. Bounded by the Hudson River, Broadway, Fourteenth, and Houston streets, it was originally settled in the 1820s and 1830s by New York City's wealthiest families, who moved there to escape a yellow-fever epidemic. At the end of the nineteenth century, it accommodated successive waves of German, Irish, and Italian immigrants.

### 1900–1939

Beginning around 1900, young, single people began moving to the Village. Cultural and political radicals, they were attracted by inexpensive housing they found in converted tenements and stables. Primarily native-born from white, middle-class families, they were determined to repudiate the Victorian values of their parents' generation. They championed artistic, political, and sexual freedom. Most were ardent supporters of feminism who advocated birth control, free love, and other alternatives to the traditional family.

Many lesbian and bisexual women, including arts patron Mabel Dodge Luhan (1879–1962), poet Edna St. Vincent Millay (1892–1950), and writers Margaret Anderson (1886–1973) and Jane Heap (1887–1964), were leaders of this bohemian subculture. They hosted salons, participated in the Heterodoxy and Liberal clubs, and campaigned for the rights of women and workers. They gathered at restaurants such as Polly's and attended frequent costume balls at Webster Hall. Taking advantage of cultural openings that resulted from bohemianism and feminism, they created tolerance for their unconventional lifestyles.

Although lesbians were accepted as individuals before World War I, it wasn't until after the war that they became a collective presence in Greenwich Village. This was due, in large measure, to expansion of the Village's commercial entertainment district. Although rarely enforced after 1923, Prohibition spurred New Yorkers to mock convention, while improved mass transportation made the Village accessible for that purpose. Building on its bohemian reputation, entrepreneurs rushed to open tearooms and speakeasies for white, middle-class tourists. By the mid-1920s, a number of these catered to lesbians and gay men, including the Black Rabbit, the Jungle, and the Bungalow. Some, like the Howdy Club, staged elaborate floor shows for lesbian audiences. In addition, tenement speakeasies and studio parties dotted the neighborhood, attracting lesbians from more varied racial and class backgrounds.

Not all lesbians frequented these establishments, however. In addition to bohemians and tourists, the Village attracted middle- and upper-class women social reformers in long-term relationships with other women, such as Eleanor Roosevelt's associates Esther Lape (1881–1981) and Elizabeth Read (1890–1983), Marion Dickerman (1890–?) and Nancy Cook (1884–1962), Molly Dewson (1874–1962) and her partner, Polly Porter (1884–?); labor activists Pauline Newman (ca. 1890–?) and Frieda Miller (1889–1973); and progressive educator Elizabeth Irwin (1880–1942) and writer Katharine Anthony (1877–1965). Their class privilege fostered interaction with other lesbians in the privacy of their homes, while professional decorum created obstacles to their participation in lesbian nightlife. This nightlife exemplified one of the earliest public lesbian subcultures in the United States, serving as a beacon to women from all over the country who traveled to the Village to vacation or live permanently.

However, by the time Prohibition ended in 1933, Americans had become intolerant of public nightlife and the "excesses" that were associated with it. In addition, psychological theories portraying unmarried women as deviant gained widespread acceptance in the 1930s. New state laws criminalized the presence of those perceived as lesbian or gay in public drinking spaces, paving the way for organized crime to become involved in running these establishments. State laws also censored representations of homosexuality on stage, while many theaters and nightclubs simply folded under economic pressure. These restrictions took their toll on Greenwich Village, making working-class lesbian bars more dangerous and middle-class tourists more discreet, and stigmatizing social reformers who pursued lesbian relationships in private.

Nevertheless, pockets of lesbian resistance appeared in the Village in the late 1930s. In one instance, local lesbians and gay men sought increased tolerance for their lifestyles by collaborating with a group of medical researchers, the Committee for the Study of Sex Variants. Although their hopes were dashed, this effort to educate professionals anticipated a strategy that homophile organizations pursued almost twenty years later.

## World War II and After

World War II drew thousands of lesbians to New York City, where they remained once the war was over. Despite ongoing police harassment, Village bars such as the Welcome Inn, MacDougal's Tavern, Tony Pastor's, and Ernie's Three Ring Circus were important gathering places for working-class lesbians in the 1940s. Middle- and upper-class lesbians continued to socialize in private settings in the Village, which still retained an aura of bohemianism.

Between the 1940s and the 1960s, police harassment of lesbian bars became systematized, and entering the bars became an act of courage. Raids, harassment, and the threat of violence were used to intimidate lesbians. While most bars had short life spans, the bar culture, which was organized on the basis of butch-femme roles, persisted during this period. In the 1950s and early 1960s, bars such as the Pony Stable and the Sea Colony fostered a collective lesbian identity among white, working-class patrons, although they often discriminated against lesbians of color.

In the late 1950s, bars were joined by homophile organizations, which contributed to a collective identity among middle-class lesbians. Founded in 1956, the New York Mattachine Society comprised primarily gay men, although it included a handful of lesbians. Two years later, the New York chapter of the Daughters of Bilitis was formed as a self-help organization for lesbians who sought alternatives to the bars. Both groups maintained a cautious style, which was reflected in their modest membership size over the next decade.

Meanwhile, an oppositional subculture was forming around "beat" artists who congregated in Greenwich Village, representing a rare exception to the cultural and political conformity that characterized American society in the 1950s. By the 1960s, this subculture blossomed, once again turning the neighborhood into an important site of protest activity. Influenced by this, homophile activists helped establish the basis for collective resistance, which erupted on June 27, 1969.

## Stonewall

That night, patrons of a Village bar called the Stonewall Inn fought back against police, igniting a riot that lasted several days and became an international symbol of lesbian and gay liberation. Although few lesbians were present at the bar that night, they have claimed the Stonewall Rebellion as their own.

Soon afterward, a new generation of Village activists organized the Gay Liberation Front and the Gay Activists Alliance. Disillusioned with sexism in the gay liberation movement and heterosexism in the feminist movement, women formed the first lesbian feminist organizations in the Village in the early 1970s. Groups such as Radicalesbians and Lesbian Feminist Liberation absorbed many of those who had been active in the "second wave" of feminism. They rejected both the butch-femme roles of the bars and the cautious style of homophile organizations for more radical forms of activism.

Since the early 1970s, the Village has spawned hundreds of lesbian cultural, political, and social organizations, from Gay Women's Alternative to the Lesbian Avengers. In the 1980s, these began to reflect the sexual, racial, ethnic, and class diversity of New York City's lesbian population. Since 1984, the Village's Lesbian and Gay Community Services Center has housed many of these organizations. In 1990, their political power was reflected in the election of Deborah Glick, the first openly lesbian member of the New York state legislature.

Meanwhile, competition from alternative public spaces, changing attitudes about drinking, and skyrocketing real-estate costs drove many lesbian bars out of business in the late twentieth century. Ironically, high real-estate costs also precluded

G many lesbians from living in the Village during this period, although it remained an important center for lesbian cultural and political activity.

*Christie Balka*

### Bibliography

Chauncey, George. *Gay New York: Gender, Urban Culture, and the Making of the Gay Male World, 1890–1940.* New York: Basic Books, 1994.

Faderman, Lillian. *Odd Girls and Twilight Lovers: A History of Lesbian Life in Twentieth Century America.* New York: Penguin, 1991.

Lorde, Audre. *Zami, A New Spelling of My Name.* Freedom, Calif.: Crossing, 1982.

Schwarz, Judith. *Radical Feminists of Heterodoxy: Greenwich Village, 1912–1940.* Norwich, Vt.: New Victoria, 1986.

Ware, Caroline. *Greenwich Village, 1920–1930: A Comment on American Civilization in the Post-War Years.* New York: Houghton Mifflin, 1935.

***See also*** Anderson, Margaret Carolyn; Daughters of Bilitis; Harlem; Lesbian Avengers; Millay, Edna St. Vincent; Radicalesbians

### Grier, Barbara (1933–)

American publisher, journalist, and editor. Under the pseudonym Gene Damon, Barbara Grier wrote a regular column, "Lesbiana," for *The Ladder* and later became the journal's editor. Grier is cofounder of Naiad Press, the oldest and largest lesbian publishing house in the world.

At age twelve, Grier told her mother that she was a "ho-mo-sex-u-al," and, as Grier tells it, her mother was very supportive, suggesting only that they wait six months before notifying the newspapers. From the start, Grier has been a vocal advocate of coming out. "My one great fear in life," she has said, "is that somebody, somewhere, will, for even a minute, mistake me for a heterosexual."

At eighteen, Grier fell in love with a married librarian in Kansas City, Missouri, and Grier's mother helped the two run away together. They lived together for twenty years and regarded their relationship as a marriage.

During that time, Grier wrote book reviews and letters for *The Ladder*, using fifteen different pseudonyms. "I took one look at *The Ladder*," Grier said, "and fell in love. I remember thinking that this was what I was going to spend the rest of my life doing."

*Barbara Grier. Courtesy of Barbara Grier.*

Under the name Gene Damon, Grier became well known writing the regular column "Lesbiana," serving as poetry and fiction editor from 1966 to 1968 and as the journal's editor from 1968 to 1972. As Gene Damon, Grier also coedited *The Lesbian in Literature* bibliography in 1967, revising it under her own name in 1975 and again in 1981.

Working together on *The Ladder* led Grier to fall in love with Donna J. McBride (1940–) in 1971, and the two have shared their life with lesbian publishing ever since. When *The Ladder* ceased publication in 1972, a newly retired lesbian couple who had supported the journal approached Grier and McBride with the idea of founding a lesbian feminist publishing company, and in 1973 Naiad Press was born in Kansas City, Missouri. In 1974, Naiad published its first novel, Sarah Aldridge's *The Latecomer*, which sold out its initial print run of two thousand copies. Financial success followed popular success, although, for the first nine years of Naiad's existence, Grier and McBride did all of the work of the press without pay, holding down other full-time jobs for income. Naiad's best-known success, Rosemary Curb and Nancy Manahan's *Lesbian Nuns: Breaking Silence* (1985), has sold more than 150,000 copies worldwide.

Grier prides herself on publishing lesbian novels and keeping them in print, along with reprinting classics such as Patricia Highsmith's *The Price of Salt*, Gale Wilhelm's *We Too Are Drifting*, and Ann Bannon's five-novel Beebo Brinker series.

In 1995, Grier and McBride donated their collection of fifteen thousand titles to the new Gay and Lesbian Center in San Francisco's downtown library. The Grier-McBride donation exemplifies Grier's continuing commitment to the preservation of lesbian literature, for it includes books and monographs dating from 1860 to the 1990s, and pulp novels from the 1940s, 1950s, and 1960s.

Maida Tilchen's foreword to the 1981 edition of *The Lesbian in Literature* best describes Grier's contribution to lesbian literature, culture, and survival: "Every time a lesbian finds a reflection of her life in a book, and learns to believe in herself in a world which does all it can to prevent that, the work of Barbara Grier has played a part."     *Greta Gaard*

### Bibliography

Boucher, Sandy. "Clinging Vine (Profile of Barbara Grier)." In *Heartwomen*, by Sandy Boucher. San Francisco: Harper and Row, 1982, pp. 212–230.

Kepner, Jim. "Barbara Grier." In *Gay and Lesbian Literature*. Ed. Sharon Malinowski. Detroit: St. James, 1994, pp. 167–169.

Tilchen, Maida. "The Legendary Lesbian Treasure Map." Foreword to *The Lesbian in Literature*. Comp. Barbara Grier. Tallahassee, Fla.: Naiad, 1981, pp. xi–xvi.

*See also* Bannon, Ann; Bibliographies and Reference Works; *Ladder, The*; Naiad Press; Publishing, Lesbian; Pulp Paperbacks; Wilhelm, Gale

## Grimké, Angelina Weld (1880–1958)

African American poet and playwright. Born in the late nineteenth century to Archibald and Sarah E. Stanley Grimké in Boston, Massachusetts, Angelina Weld Grimké went to some of the best preparatory schools of New England. Her parents separated soon after her birth, and her father reared her. The situation that led to her parents separation is unclear, but Grimké stayed in contact with her mother, sending her letters and her earliest efforts in writing poetry.

Grimké was a small, sad-eyed, introverted woman of mixed heritage. She described herself as having little faith in herself and as being highly critical of friends to the point of insult. At the end of her life, she was reclusive, litigious, and neurotic. Some critics have suggested this turn of personality late in life is connected to paternal expectations, her absentee mother, and failed lesbian relationships.

Grimké's relationship with a woman identified as Mayme is the only close female relationship clearly documented in Grimké's correspondence. From 1898 to 1903, the two women wrote letters, exchanged confidences, and professed undying love and affection in the accepted Victorian fashion of female friendship. This love and affection inspired an unpublished volume of pastoral poetry that extols the beauty of romantic friendship. However, the relationship ended with Grimké washing her hands of love and swearing never to marry or mother children. This event explains the antimarriage theme in her plays.

Grimké wrote two plays, *Rachel*, self-published in 1919, and the unpublished *Mara*. Both plays drew the attention of Harlem Renaissance literati because of the theme of racial injustice. However, *Rachel* also expresses Grimké's negative feelings about marriage and motherhood. This concern for female autonomy was uncommon, and Grimké received criticism for focusing on themes that were so dark in content. The combination of criticism from her father and others led to the self-suppression of Grimké's poetry and her decision to withdraw completely from society. Grimké died in New York City in 1958 after a long illness.

*Stephanie Byrd*

### Bibliography

Abramson, Doris E. "Angelina Weld Grimké, Mary Burrill, Georgia Douglas Johnson, and Marita O. Bonner: An Analysis of Their Plays." *Sage* 2:1 (Spring 1985), 9–12.

Angelina Weld Grimké Papers. Moorland-Spingarn Research Center, Washington, D.C.

Hull, Gloria T. *Color, Sex, and Poetry: Three Women Writers of the Harlem Renaissance*. Bloomington: Indiana University Press, 1987, 107–151.

Young, Patricia Alzatia. "Female Pioneers in Afro-American Drama: Angelina Weld Grimké, Georgia Douglas Johnson, Alice Dunbar-Nelson, and Mary Powell Burrill." Ph.D. diss., Bowling Green University, 1986.

*See also* African American Literature; Harlem Renaissance; Romantic Friendship

# H

## Hall, Radclyffe (1880–1943)

English novelist and poet. Author of *The Well of Loneliness* (1928), acclaimed as the one novel that every literate lesbian in the four decades between 1928 and the late 1960s would certainly have read.

Marguerite Antonia Radclyffe-Hall (known in childhood as Peter and later as John) was born in Bournemouth, Hampshire, on August 12, 1880. Her American mother, Marie Diehl, and her father, Radclyffe Radclyffe-Hall, separated when she was a year old and divorced when she was three. Like her protagonist Stephen Gordon in *The Well*, her relationship with her mother was never close, and her early education came from governesses. Later, she spent a year at King's College London and in Germany. At the age of twenty-one, she inherited her father's and grandfather's estates, enabling her to live as an independent woman, traveling abroad frequently. She began her literary career by writing verses, collected into four volumes of poetry. Many of these, notably "The Blind Ploughman," were set to music by popular Edwardian composers of the day and sung in drawing rooms and concert platforms all over England up to and during World War I. In 1907 Hall met Mabel Batten (1857?–1916), a society hostess, under whose influence she became a Catholic. She lived with her until "Ladye" Batten's death in 1916 and, through her, met Una, Lady Troubridge (1887–1963), who was to become her lifelong lover, companion, and biographer.

Hall's first two novels, *The Forge* and *The Unlit Lamp*, were published in 1924. *Adam's Breed* (1926) was awarded the Prix Femina Vie Heureuse and the James Tait Black Memorial Prize. In 1928, she published *The Well of Loneliness*, a deliberate attempt to confront the subject of lesbianism openly. For her open and polemical stance on this issue, Hall received the Gold Medal of the Eichelbergher Humane Award in 1930. The book's publication brought about the most famous legal trial for obscenity in the history of British law; Brown (1984) argues that the trial was about the protocols of naturalizing the "ugly" facts of medical pathology in a popular novel form that could offer identification and ungoverned discussion about female sexuality. Among those prepared to bear witness in Hall's favor were E.M. Forster (1879–1970), Hugh Walpole (1884–1941), Leonard (1880–1969) and Virginia Woolf (1882–1941), Rose Macaulay (1881–1958), and Vita Sackville-West (1892–1962).

A member of the P.E.N. Club, Hall came to know well such writers as Elinor Wylie (1885–1928), May Sinclair (1863–1946), and Rebecca West (1893–1983). She was also a member of the Society for Psychical Research and a Fellow of the Zoological Society. Her other interests included breeding dogs and riding. A friend of Colette (1873–1954), Romaine Brooks (1874–1970), and Natalie Barney (1876–1972), she and Troubridge moved in the café lesbian society of London and Paris. She spent much of the last nine years of her life in Italy and France in pursuit of another woman, Eugeunia Souline, with whom she was in love. Much of her adult life was lived in Rye, Sussex, where she died of cancer on October 27, 1943.

Although the author apparently did not see her early novel *The Unlit Lamp* as a story of lesbian love, the relationship between Elizabeth and Joan in the novel is passionate, and Joan is represented as something of a sexual misfit, like the central character of *The Well*. This earlier novel is a damning condemnation of the confines of marriage under patriarchy: tyrannical husbands and possessive, demanding mother-love, with relationships and individual freedom and autonomy stifled by possession and dependency. It is one of the strongest descriptions in English fiction of the love—and hate—that can exist between women, mother and daughter, loved and beloved. Some critics argue that this earlier novel is a more skilled literary accomplishment than *The Well*.

Hall decided to write *The Well of Loneliness* to describe and vindicate lesbianism to a hostile public. She publicly associated her novel with the naturist point of view, a theory of homosexual love associated with, among others, the sex reformer Havelock Ellis (1859–1939), who wrote a preface to the first edition. The naturists argued that women do not become lesbians by choice or circumstance but are born with an affliction called "congenital inversion." Troubridge (1961) recounts that Hall had long wanted to write a book on sexual inversion "that would be accessible to the general public who did not have access to technical treatises.... [H]er instinct had told her that in any case she must postpone such a book until her name was made.... [I]t was with this conviction that she came to me (in 1926), telling me that in her view the time was ripe." In fact, a number of novels published in 1928 took the recently developed category of "lesbian" as a theme: Compton Mackenzie's *Extraordinary Women*, Elizabeth Bowen's *The Hotel*, Djuna Barnes's *Ladies' Almanack*, and Virginia Woolf's *Orlando*. Of these, *The Well* alone presents a tragic vision of "inversion," one that does not accord with Hall's own experience directly. It seems that, to achieve her moral purpose, she believed that she had to overstate her case and represent relationships between inverts as doomed to fail. A number of critics have argued that Hall's assertion of inversion as immutable was strategic: The discourse of the sexologists and the image of the mannish lesbian allowed Hall to claim passionate physical desire for lesbians, challenging the asexual model of romantic friendship.

*The Well* has been read as literature, as psychology, as part of the history of censorship, and as autobiography. Recently, debates about the lesbian canon and the cultural history of lesbianism have opened some new perspectives on the novel. In its awareness of the issues of sex and gender, language and literary forms, *The Well* stands as a precursor of later works in the lesbian canon, indicating not only a precedent, but also a part of a tradition that later writers confirm and against which they define themselves. Subsequent lesbian writers have revised Hall's depiction of the "invert," yet the poetics of the novel place it within a contemporary tradition of seeking alternative discourses to represent lesbian desire in fiction.                *Gillian Whitlock*

### Bibliography

Brown, Beverley. " 'A Disgusting Book When Properly Read': The Obscenity Trial." *Hecate* 10:2 (1984), 7–19.

Newton, Esther. "The Mythic Mannish Lesbian: Radclyffe Hall and the New Woman." *Signs: Journal of Women in Culture and Society* 9 (Summer 1984), 559–568.

O'Rourke, Rebecca. *Reflecting on "The Well of Loneliness."* London: Routledge, 1989.

Ruehl, Sonja. "Inverts and Experts: Radclyffe Hall and the Lesbian Identity." In *Feminism, Culture, and Politics*. Ed. Rosalind Brunt and Caroline Rowan. London: Lawrence and Wishart, 1983, pp. 15–36.

Stimpson, Catherine R. "Zero Degree Deviancy: The Lesbian Novel in English." *Critical Inquiry* 8:2 (Winter 1981), 363–397.

Troubridge, Una. *The Life and Death of Radclyffe Hall*. London: Hammond and Hammond, 1961.

Whitlock, Gillian. " 'Everything Is Out of Place': Radclyffe Hall and the Lesbian Literary Tradition." *Feminist Studies* 13:3 (Fall 1987), 555–582.

**See also** Barnes, Djuna Chappell; Barney, Natalie; Bowen, Elizabeth; Brooks, Romaine; Colette; Sackville-West, Vita; Sexology; Woolf, Virginia

### Hamilton, Edith (1867–1963)

American classicist, educator, and writer. Introduced to Latin at age seven by her father, Edith Hamilton was home tutored until enrolled at Miss Porter's School in her late teens. In 1884, she earned an A.B. in Latin and Greek from Bryn Mawr College. After a year as a Bryn Mawr Latin Fellow, a prestigious Bryn Mawr fellowship allowed Hamilton and her sister Alice (1869–1970), the first woman appointed to the Harvard Medical School faculty, to study at the Universities of Leipzig and Munich, where, to the consternation of the chancellor, Edith enrolled as the first woman student. In 1887, faced with the need to support herself, Hamilton became the first headmistress of the Bryn Mawr School in Baltimore, Maryland; over the next twenty-five years, guided by Greek intellectual and moral ideals, her leadership solidified the college preparatory girls' school's high reputation.

Retiring in 1922, Hamilton visited, and then purchased, a house at Sea Wall, Mount Desert, Maine, with Doris Fielding Reid, a 1911 Bryn Mawr School graduate. Her retirement, clouded by her intimacy with Reid, strained family affairs; however, for the next forty years, the two women lived and traveled together, summering at their beloved Sea Wall. From 1923 to 1943, they lived at 23 Gramercy Park in New York City; Hamilton kept house for them, including Reid's nephew Dorian, whom Hamilton adopted, while Reid, from 1929, worked at Loomis, Sayles and Company, an investment firm.

Already well known for poetry and Bible-verse recitation, Hamilton often led extemporaneous discussions on Greek dramatists at afternoon teas. Urged by friends, she reluctantly began writing essays and then published *The Greek Way* (1930) and *The Roman Way* (1932), establishing her second career as a writer. Permeated by her unshakable conviction that the "excellent becomes the permanent," the lively, acclaimed, but undocumented books convey her idealized interpretation of ancient cultures' influences on modern, especially American, civilization. Her popular *Mythology* (1942) retells Greek and Norse myths for the modern reader.

In 1943, Hamilton accompanied Reid to Washington, D.C., and, for the next twenty years, traveled, translated, lectured, and wrote, often about biblical topics. She published *Witness to the Truth: Christ and His Interpreters* (1948) and, when more than ninety, coedited the Bollingen Series *The Collected Dialogues of Plato* (1961).

Although she never professed herself a scholar, Hamilton was awarded four honorary doctorates and numerous awards, including election to the American Academy of Arts and Letters in 1957. Her translated epigrams were often quoted by others, including Robert Kennedy. Enrolled in 1957 as a citizen of Athens at a ceremony in Athens' Theater of Herodes Atticus, she proclaimed: "This is the proudest moment of my life."          *Judith C. Kohl*

### Bibliography

Bacon, Helen. "Edith Hamilton." In *Notable American Women: The Modern Period*. Ed. Barbara Sicherman and Carol Hurd Green. Cambridge, Mass.: Harvard University Press, Belknap Press, 1980.

Hallett, Judith. "Edith Hamilton." In *Biographical Dictionary of North American Classicists*. Ed.

Ward W. Biggs, Jr. Westport, Conn.: Greenwood, 1994, pp. 253–255.

Reid, Doris Fielding. *Edith Hamilton: An Intimate Portrait*. New York: Norton, 1969.

*See also* Mythology, Classical

## Hampton, Mabel (1902–1989)

African American dancer and, later in her life, lesbian activist. Mabel Hampton was born on or about May 2, 1902, in Winston-Salem, North Carolina, where she lived with her grandmother after her mother's death when she was two months old. When Hampton's grandmother died, the seven-year-old girl was taken by an aunt to live in Greenwich Village in New York City.

Hampton began her working life at age eight by singing in the streets of the Village for pennies thrown from windows. That same year, she ran away from her new home to escape her abusive uncle. Taken in by the White family of New Jersey, Hampton worked as a domestic until, at age twenty, she became a member of an all-girl dance troupe performing in Coney Island. She was soon involved in the theatrical life of the Harlem Renaissance, dancing in Harlem cabarets such as the Garden of Joy, appearing in several all-black productions at Manhattan's Lafayette Theater, and attending multisexual parties at the home of A'lelia Walker (1885–1931). During this time, she moved in the circle of "the two Ethels" (Ethel Waters [1896–1977] and her woman lover), Alberta Hunter (1895–1984), and Moms Mabley (1897–1975).

In the early 1920s, after being arrested at a house party, Hampton was incarcerated at the Bedford Hills Reform School for Women on prostitution charges. Upon her release, Hampton continued working to support herself. She was part of a thriving lesbian community, delighting in such events as the 1927 Broadway production of *The Captive*, by Eduoard Bourdet and a proud celebrant of African American culture. She attended the New York concerts of Paul Robeson (1898–1976) and Marian Anderson (1902–1993) and carefully followed the career of Josephine Baker (1906–1975). In these years, she started building her lifelong library of books on black history and culture, gay novels, and metaphysical writings.

In 1932, Hampton met Lillian Foster (1906–1978) while waiting for a trolley car. The two became lifelong partners, remaining together until Foster's

# H

*Mabel Hampton in Eastern Star outfit, in front of poster of Lillian Foster, her lover of forty years, 1984. © Morgan Gwenwald.*

death in 1978. Hampton called Foster her wife, and, to Foster, Hampton was her husband. In 1973, Hampton became an early supporter of the Lesbian Herstory Archives; after Foster's death, she shared the New York apartment in which the archives were housed but always kept close ties to 169th Street in the Bronx, where she and Foster had lived for so many years. In the last ten years of her life, she became an active member of the lesbian and gay community, participating in the Gay Pride demonstrations, appearing in several films about gay history, giving interviews for many publications, and attending as guest of honor many gay and lesbian conferences around the country. In 1984, she addressed the New York City Gay Pride rally: "I have been a lesbian all may life, for eighty-two years, and I am proud of myself and my people. I would like all my people to be free in this country and all over the world, my gay people and my black people."          *Joan Nestle*

## Bibliography

Hampton, Mabel. "I Didn't Go Back There Anymore: Mabel Hampton Talks about the South." *Feminary* 10 (1979), 7–16.

Mabel Hampton Special Collection, including transcripts of oral history. Lesbian Herstory Archives, Brooklyn, New York.

Nestle, Joan. "I Lift My Eyes to the Hill: The Life of Mabel Hampton as Told by a White Woman." In *A Fragile Union* by Joan Nestle. San Francisco: Cleis, 1998.

———. "Surviving and More: An Interview with Mabel Hampton." *Sinister Wisdom* 10 (Summer 1979), 19–24.

*See also* African Americans; Dance; Harlem; Harlem Renaissance

## Hansberry, Lorraine (Vivian) (1930–1965)

American playwright. Born on January 12, 1930, in Chicago, Illinois, Lorraine Hansberry was the daughter of a realtor and banker and the niece of a highly respected scholar of African history at Howard University. Sheltered from some of the "more bestial aspects of white supremacist culture," Hansberry was exposed, at the same time, to many of America's most influential African American thinkers. Her family's move into a restricted white neighborhood in 1937 helped galvanize her resistance to injustice, instilling her with a sense of social activism. She attended the University of Wisconsin and the Art Institute of Chicago and studied in Guadalajara, Mexico, from 1948 to 1950.

Hansberry became interested in theater in high school, pursued this interest in college, then returned to Chicago to study art. She became more politically active after moving to New York City and writing for *Freedom* magazine. She soon met and made friends with Robert Nemiroff, a friendship that survived their marriage and divorce. In 1958, friends encouraged her efforts in writing *Raisin in the Sun*, which became the first play by an African American woman produced on Broadway. She was named "most promising playwright." *Raisin in the Sun* ran for 530 performances from 1959 to 1965; the play closed January 12, 1965, the day Hansberry died from cancer.

Hansberry's work is noted for its cross-gender and cross-cultural views. Her sense of history and the confusing role of women in history are also apparent in her work. Her mindfulness of being an African American woman formed the foundation of a comprehensive worldview that recognized the connectedness of all human suffering. Drafts of her later works suggest the growth of a feminist consciousness, mostly obscured by critical interpretations focusing on race. After her death, Nemiroff completed her works in progress, in some cases changing their theme. Some critics have questioned whether this posthumous publication interfered with the integrity of the artist's feminist voice. Hansberry privately acknowledged her lesbianism and wrote several letters to the lesbian publication *The Ladder* about the economic and psychological stresses that drive lesbians to choose marriage.

*Stephanie Byrd*

### Bibliography

Baldwin, James. "Lorraine Hansberry at the Summit." *Freedomways* 19:49 (1979), 269–272.
Rich, Adrienne. "The Problem with Lorraine Hansberry." *Freedomways* 19:4 (1979), 247–255.
Wilkerson, Margaret B. "The Dark Vision of Lorraine Hansberry: Excerpts from a Literary Biography." *Massachussetts Review* 28 (Winter 1987), 642–650.

*See also* African American Literature; Chicago, Illinois; *Ladder, The*

## Harems

Segregated women's quarters common in upper-class households in the Middle East. The harem, which means a sacred, inviolable place, was a world of its own, separate from the rest of the household, closed to outsiders, and guarded by eunuchs. Concubines in the harem were solely for the sexual pleasure of the patriarch, while wives were expected to produce legitimate heirs.

The harem was institutionalized in a number of societies throughout the Middle East for nearly five thousand years (ca. 3000 B.C.E. to the A.D. 1800s). Although considered to be synonymous with Islam, harems predate the rise of Islam by 3,600 years. Harems were the product of the class-based patriarchal societies of the Middle East. Beginning with the Sumerians in Mesopotamia (now southern Iraq between the Tigris and Euphrates rivers), the state vested in men the control of women both sexually and physically. Women owed complete obedience to their fathers and husbands; adultery by the wife was punishable by death, while men were permitted to have both wives and concubines.

Royalty and upper-class men often maintained large harems to reflect their wealth and power. Over time, the number of women in royal harems increased significantly. An Assyrian king of the twelfth century B.C.E had a harem of forty women. When Alexander conquered Persia in 333 B.C.E., he increased the size of his harem to 365 women to match that of the conquered king. In A.D. 500, another Persian king reputedly had thousands of women in his harem. The rise of the Christian era saw the spread of veiling and women's seclusion throughout the region. It became a prominent feature of upper-class life throughout the Mediterranean Middle East, including Mesopotamia, Persia, Greece, Byzantium (now Turkey), Arabia, Egypt, and Syria, among others. It was also supported by religious thinkers, both Christian and Islamic, who argued that women were primarily sexual and biological creatures who needed to be controlled and veiled, lest they inflame men's lust.

The harem has occupied a large place in the imagination of Europeans. Despite the fact that no European man ever gained admittance to a harem, many opinions were offered as to what took place within them. For many Westerners, it signified a place of heightened sexuality and absolute male dominance over women, as well as the decadence and backwardness of the "Orient." Muslim and European men alike were convinced that the lack of

**H** adequate sexual attention suffered by its inhabitants led these women to look for, in Ibn al-Hajj's words, "satisfaction by perverse and unnatural means" (Ahmed 1992). Religious men frowned on women attending the baths because of the easy, relaxed intimacies of such places. It was feared that such occasions would lead to "numerous corruptions," some unmentionable.

Since women left no written records of their lives in the harem, there is no firsthand accounts of their sexual or erotic relationships. Most stories were based on hearsay or speculation. The most famous lesbian love story comes from Baghdad in the years 785–786. According to Muslim historians, Musa al-Hadi, ruler of the Abbasid Empire, was extremely jealous of the honor and reputation of his royal harem. On hearing that two women in his harem were lovers, he set spies to watch them. When the spies saw the women in amorous embrace, they rushed to tell the king, who immediately had them beheaded. In another account written in 1520, a male writer claimed that women who spend all day at the baths fall in love with each other as a result of their great familiarity in washing and massaging each other. Though based only on hearsay, this account even suggested that, at the baths, one could see a woman in love with another one just like a man and a woman.

A few upper-class European women travelers wrote about their visits to harems but never reported any sexual activity among the women. Lady Mary Wortley Montagu (1689–1762), the wife of the British ambassador to Turkey (1717–1718), visited several royal harems and spoke of the close bonds formed between the women and their female slaves, who served them, danced for them, and groomed them in the baths, yet she makes no mention of erotic attachments. Although much has yet to be learned about the emotional, erotic, and sexual experiences of women in the harem, it is possible that the Western categories of sexuality and lesbianism may be inadequate to express them.

*Evelyn Blackwood*

### Bibliography

Ahmed, Leila. *Women and Gender in Islam*. New Haven, Conn.: Yale University Press, 1992.

Bouhdiba, A. *Sexuality in Islam*. London: Routledge, 1985.

Bullough, Vern L. *Sexual Variance in Society and History*. New York: Wiley, 1976.

*See also* Islam

## Harlem

District of the borough of Manhattan, in northeast New York City. A former village created in 1658 and named New Haarlem, the area was annexed to New York City in 1731. In 1900, a small group of African Americans settled there, and it is now the chief African American quarter of New York, with smaller Italian and Latino sections.

Its growth as an African American enclave coincided with blacks' exodus from the violent racism of the South, which historians have dubbed the "Great Migration" (1915–1940). Often considered the apex of black American culture, its history is rich with its residents' contribution to the popular mainstream culture that defines America today.

### Harlem as Cultural Center

In the 1920s, Harlem developed into a richly vigorous creative center with a thriving underground culture that included black writers, businessmen, artists, and noted blues and jazz singers, such as Gertrude "Ma" Rainey (1886–1939), Bessie Smith (1894–1937), Alberta Hunter (1895–1984), and Gladys Bentley (1907–1960), to name a few, and white society from downtown. Later, Harlem would host some of the most famous and popular big bands that defined the swing era. In 1943, Harlem was the site of a wartime race riot when Harlemites stormed the streets after a white policeman shot a black soldier.

As part of the rebellious, creative culture that has marked Harlem over the years, young gays and lesbians started their own communities, which mingled well within the literary and performance circles.

During its heyday, Harlem was a pulsating cultural center of salons, speakeasies, writer's cliques, and buffet flats (casually decorated apartments rented by several people) that writers and historians still refer to. Located in the northeastern part of Manhattan Island, Harlem came to be known as the "Negro Bohemia," a place that has witnessed the full range of prosperity, from the artistically vibrant days of Prohibition in the 1920s to the economic decline of the Great Depression in the 1930s and continuing into the 1970s and 1980s to the redevelopment of the area in the 1990s.

As early as the 1920s, Harlem was a place where lesbians—and, particularly, bisexual women—intermingled within the musical, literary, and artistic circles and proved itself to be one of the few places where female sexual experimentation, among both whites and blacks, was permitted. Unlike any other locale, Harlem enjoyed a visible black lesbian subculture in the early part of the twentieth century, and, although marriage was still considered the appropriate institution, adherents of the female sexual freedom included some of the most celebrated artists and performers of the day. While many lesbians lived openly together, as a concession to the moral expectations of the mainstream society, apparently heterosexual marriage arrangements were frequent among homosexuals, and even the most unconventional gay artists perfected a bisexual lifestyle.

The area, especially in the 1920s and through the 1940s and 1950s, was a mecca of nightclubs, speakeasies, and salons that were frequented by gays and straights.

Harlem's homosexual subculture was not just for African Americans. Harlem, as well as other enclaves such as Greenwich Village, offered a sort of laissez-faire "morality" that appealed to many whites. Historian Faderman (1991) notes that the interest sometimes suggested a "sexual colonialism" in which many whites used the bustling area as a stimulant to their own sexuality. In Harlem, white women could observe or participate in erotic practices deemed immoral by the mainstream culture. Interracial same-sex affairs were common.

Over the years, dozens of nightclubs catered to a largely homosexual clientele, and huge crowds, mixed in terms of both race and sexuality, gathered to attend frequent and outrageous drag balls in such ballroom haunts as the Rockland Palace and the Savoy Ballroom.

Harlem's lesbian community offered perhaps the era's most visible example of female independence from the masculine social order that dominated the larger society. Freed from economic and emotional dependence upon men, African American lesbians of Harlem controlled their own sexuality, lifestyles, and economic futures.

Women dating women were a common sight during the heady days of Prohibition in Harlem. African American lesbians were particularly visible in the entertainment community. Harlem writers sometimes offered lesbianism as an alternative to a middle-class heterosexual order, as was the case with Nella Larsen (1891–1964), who presented heterosexuality as emotionally empty and sexually stifling in her popular novel *Quicksand* (1928).

Still, several writers have painted a picture of a Harlem where lesbians, although normally unmolested, were not necessarily approved of. Police frequently raided clubs and plays considered interracial and/or homosexual, and, in 1927, officers raided a production of *The Captive* by Edouard Bourdet because of its lesbian themes.

## Decline and Revival

In the 1930s, Adam Clayton Powell, Sr. (1865–1953), influential pastor of Harlem's Abyssinian Baptist Church and an early leader of the Urban League and the NAACP (National Association for the Advancement of Colored People), began a campaign against the homosexual community of Harlem, at one point declaring that sex among women in Harlem "has grown into one of the most horrible, debasing, alarming, and damning vices of present-day civilization, and is . . . prevalent to an unbelievable degree" (Chauncey 1994). Powell suggested that lesbians' refusal to marry posed an insidious threat to the black family.

After nearly a decade of criticism and situations in which moralists publicly named alleged homosexuals (Powell believed that the buffet flats, balls, and gay nightclubs recruited others into "deviancy"), the popularity of the gay institutions began to decline.

By the 1960s, Harlem experienced an economic and social decline that lasted several decades. Crime, drugs, and poverty came to signify the once thriving neighborhood. Once a segregated powerhouse, Harlem came to symbolize black helplessness, racism, and the American underclass. Halls and ballrooms that once teemed with people of all races and sexuality now stood empty and crumbling. Affluent blacks moved away, leaving the neighborhood to the community-destroying activities of drug dealers and pimps.

In the 1990s, Harlem began to rise economically and socially, symbolizing the rebirth of black American self-reliance. Although crime was still high, the crime rate began to fall. Several private- and public-sector developers converged on the area, infusing the community with business deals and development. Investors began to look at numerous opportunities in Harlem, including cable television, restaurants, and performance venues.     *Denise McVea*

### Bibliography

Anderson, Jervis. *This Was Harlem*. New York: Farrar, Straus, and Giroux, 1982.

Chauncey, George. *Gay New York: Gender, Urban Culture, and the Making of the Gay Male World, 1890–1940*. New York: Basic Books, 1994.

Faderman, Lillian. *Odd Girls and Twilight Lovers: A History of Lesbian Life in Twentieth-Century America*. New York: Columbia University Press, 1991.

Johnson, James Weldon. *Black Manhattan*. New York: Arno, 2nd ed. 1968 [1930].

Lewis, David L. *When Harlem Was in Vogue*. New York: Knopf, 1981.

Miller, Neil. *Out of the Past: Gay and Lesbian History from 1869 to the Present*. New York: Vintage, 1995.

*See also* African Americans; Bentley, Gladys; Harlem Renaissance; Rainey, Gertrude "Ma"; Smith, Bessie; Walker, A'Lelia

## Harlem Renaissance

Spanning the time between World War I and World War II (ca. 1917–1935), the Harlem Renaissance, or New Negro movement, was a period of intense flourishing in black arts and letters and the rise of the black middle-class. While not confined to Harlem, the Harlem Renaissance coincided with and was enabled by the Great Urban Migration when many African Americans migrated to Southern and Northern urban centers, in part to flee increased racial violence after the formation of the new Ku Klux Klan in 1915. Many African American writers, artists, jazz and blues singers, actors, and political activists were prolific in their artistic and political endeavors, and philosopher W.E.B. DuBois (1868–1963) dubbed this elite group "the Talented Tenth."

DuBois's insistence that cultural production would lead to racial uplift helped encourage black artists and writers. Organizations like the NAACP (National Association for the Advancement of Colored People) and the Urban League launched magazines—*Crisis* and *Opportunity*, respectively—to publish works by black artists and writers alongside political articles and reports on lynchings. Sociologist Charles S. Johnson, editor of *Opportunity*, instituted annual dinners to award writers in his magazine and to publicize the arrival of black novelists and artists. While these magazines, and others like them across the country, were devoted to racial uplift, it was not uncommon for them to publish writings by and about black lesbians and gay men.

## Lesbian Writers and Artists

For lesbian and bisexual African American women, the Harlem Renaissance was a period in which expressions of erotic desire between women could be both represented in art and literature and publicly displayed. Washington, D.C., was also a place where large networks of black women of varying sexualities gathered and nurtured one another. Georgia Douglas Johnson's (1886–1966) S Street Salon in Washington, D.C., was a regular gathering spot where black women writers and activists met to share work and offer support; Alice Dunbar-Nelson (1875–1935), Angelina Weld Grimké (1880–1958), Gwendolyn Bennett (1902–), Jessie Fauset (1888–1961), and Marita Bonner (1899–1971) were some of the women who took part in Johnson's Saturday evening salon. These evenings established younger writers and offered feedback on writing. Johnson's salon, and others like it, also offered a safe space for women of varying sexualities and a meeting place to discuss politics, race, and sexuality, in addition to writing. Some of these writers chose to write about bisexuality or even lesbianism in their literature; however, most of it is coded by using second-person pronouns, as in the poetry of Dunbar-Nelson, Johnson, and Grimké. Although her writing is also veiled, Nella Larsen's (1891–1964) 1929 novel *Passing* contains a triangulated love relationship between Irene Redfield and Clare Kendry and Irene's husband, Brian. Reading this novel in a contemporary setting allows for readers to decode a largely coded, but highly eroticized, relationship between two "passing" women.

The cultivation of jazz and blues music during this period was due in large part to lesbian or bisexual African American women, such as Gertrude "Ma" Rainey (1886–1939), Bessie Smith (1894–1937), Gladys Bentley (1907–1960), and Ethel Waters (1896–1977). Bentley used her bisexuality for shock value in her performances by hinting at her bisexual desire and also used male drag. Many of these women would sing overtly about their love of women in the lyrics, such as Rainey's rendition of the "lesbian" song "Prove It on Me Blues" (1928). However, Rainey's lesbianism also led to her arrest in 1925 for a "lesbian orgy" at her home with women in her chorus. Not all lesbians or bisexual women in Harlem were as open as Rainey. There were many who married men, either to shield their sexuality, or for economic reasons, or as a safe way to escape rumors about sexuality. Combating racism and lynching were of primary concern to African Americans during the Harlem Renaissance, and, as such, having to endure sexual oppression in addition to racism was secondary.

Harlem, in particular, during the 1920s and 1930s, was a generally accepting community, as evidenced in the number of black lesbians who paired off as butch-femme couples and who even married in large wedding ceremonies. Couples obtained marriage licenses by either having one partner masculinize her name or by having a gay man stand in as the "groom."

The relative acceptance of homosexuality in Harlem was one of the strong attractions that led many white men and women to travel to Harlem, primarily from Greenwich Village, not only to attend jazz shows, parties, and nightclubs, but also to experiment sexually with bisexual men and women in Harlem. This "sexual colonialism" brought a tourist clientele to Harlem businesses and nightclubs, which needed the business of any consumer. Yet the frequency of white men and women in Harlem also created a segregated Harlem. During Jim Crow, when segregation of whites and blacks was legal, having a population of whites in Harlem created an environment in which some nightclubs in Harlem became "white only." Terms designating sexuality also became racialized, with "faggot" and "bulldagger" used in Harlem to describe black gay men and lesbians, whereas whites were termed "gay men" and "lesbians."

The relationship between blacks and whites during the Harlem Renaissance was important and strained in other contexts as well. During this period, white men and women such as Carl Van Vechten (1880–1964), Mabel Dodge Luhan (1879–1962), and Fannie Hurst (1889–1968) served as "patrons," who also held salon gatherings in their homes in Greenwich Village and Brooklyn offering a different kind of support than Johnson's S Street Salon promised. At these gatherings, white publishers and "patrons" would meet with black artists and writers in an attempt to publish and exhibit the work of African Americans. These ties and connections were important, but they also provided novelists with experiences with African Americans that they could use as subjects for their own work, as in Hurst's *Imitation of Life* (1933) and Van Vechten's controversial and problematic *Nigger Heaven* (1926).

While many black artists and writers continued to produce creative work after the decline of the Harlem Renaissance, the onset of the Great Depression and the U.S. involvement in World War II dried up much of the financial resources that had enabled black businesses to flourish, and patronage of black arts and letters declined. Finally, the 1935 Harlem Riot provoked deteriorating urban conditions and the loss of jobs for African Americans in Harlem, which worked to further break down the remnants of the artistic community.      *Marcy Jane Knopf*

## Bibliography

Faderman, Lillian. *Odd Girls and Twilight Lovers: A History of Lesbian Life in Twentieth-Century America*. New York: Penguin, 1991.

Garber, Eric. "A Spectacle in Color: The Lesbian and Gay Subculture of Jazz Age Harlem." In *Hidden from History: Reclaiming the Gay and Lesbian Past*. Ed. Martin Duberman, Martha Vicinus, and George Chauncey, Jr. New York: Meridian, 1989, pp. 318–331.

Huggins, Nathan Irvin. *Harlem Renaissance*. New York: Oxford University Press, 1971.

Hull, Gloria T. *Color, Sex, and Poetry: Three Women Writers of the Harlem Renaissance*. Bloomington: Indiana University Press, 1987.

Knopf, Marcy Jane, ed. *The Sleeper Wakes: Harlem Renaissance Stories by Women*. New Brunswick, N.J.: Rutgers University Press, 1993.

Lewis, David Levering. *When Harlem Was in Vogue*. New York: Oxford University Press, 1979.

**See also** African Americans; Bentley, Gladys; Blues Singers; Bulldagger; Dunbar-Nelson, Alice; Greenwich Village; Grimké, Angelina Weld; Harlem; Rainey, Gertrude "Ma"; Smith, Bessie; Washington, D.C.

## Hawai'i

Archipelago in the Pacific Ocean populated by indigenous people who, for thousands of years, until colonization, lived free of puritanical sexual taboos.

The Hawai'in people call themselves "Kanaka Maoli," the true, original people; or "ka Lahui Hawai'i," the Hawai'in nation. They trace their genealogies back to Papa, the earth mother, and Wakea, the sky father; and then further back to the formation of the earth itself, and further back to the time of the Kumulipo, the source of profound darkness. They originate in *po* (deep darkness).

In modern times, they have been subjected to colonization and missionization. The colonizer teaches that whiteness and light are good, and that blackness and dark are bad; hence, it is no coincidence that the colonizer is white, and the Kanaka Maoli is dark. The missionary teaches that life without sexual taboos is bad, an abomination to their god. The indigenous people's own *kapu* (religious laws) are said to be primitive, savage, something from the long ago, dark, unenlightened past.

Lesbianism as a category did not exist in the indigenous society. Neither did heterosexual monogamous marriage. People formed and ended relationships as they chose. At the same time, they fulfilled the responsibility to produce and care for children. It is well known that male nobles (*ali'i*), such as Kamehameha and others, had *aikane* (homosexual) relationships. Ancient myths contain references to women's romantic desires for each other. It is likely, therefore, that women also engaged in *aikane* relationships.

In 1993, Hawai'i came to U.S. national attention because three same-sex couples sued for the right to marry. The most prominent of the couples is lesbian, Ninia Baehr and Genora Dancel. The same-sex marriage case, *Baehr v. Miike*, and the struggles of the gay communities in Hawai'i to win it, has highlighted tensions and anxieties not only between the conservative/religious political groups and the GLBT (gay, lesbian, bisexual, transgender) communities, but between the GLBT communities themselves. One of those communities is mostly white, with male leaders in prominent roles. Another community is made up of Kanaka Maoli and other people of color, in which women leaders are prominent. Conflicts became apparent when people of color attempted to join in the struggle for same-sex marriage. While Kanaka Maoli activists stressed the need for community coalition building and the linking of the marriage issue to other issues, white activists concentrated on tasks around the marriage issue alone, such as lobbying legislators. It became clear that the goals of the two groups were different. The white activists' goal is to benefit equally with heterosexuals from the current American political-economic arrangement. The Kanaka Maoli activists' goal, on the other hand, is to "decolonize"— that is, be free to engage in political and economic self-determination—and, at the same time, to achieve a decolonization of the mind that allows freedom from the puritanical sexual taboos so foreign to their ancestors.

This is because Kanaka Maoli activists are also active in the indigenous nationalist movement. More than a hundred years have passed since the Hawai'n monarchy was forcibly overthrown by American businessmen. Since then, the Kanaka Maoli have become the poorest, the most unemployed, the most houseless (since Hawai'i remains home), the most imprisoned, and the shortest-lived people in their birth land. Kanaka Maoli cannot help but link the struggle for equality with the struggle for self-determination.                *Noenoe K. Silva*

### Bibliography

Barrett, Paul M. "I Do/No You Don't: How Hawai'i Became Ground Zero in Battle over Gay Marriage." *Wall Street Journal* (June 17, 1996).

Kame'eleihiwa, Lilikala. *Native Land and Foreign Desires Ko Hawai'i 'Aina a me Na Koi Pu'umake a ka Po'e Haole: Pehea La e Pono ai? How Shall We Live in Harmony?* Honolulu: Bishop Museum, 1992.

Ragaza, Angelo. "Aikane Nation: Sovereignty and Sexuality in Hawai'i." *Village Voice* (July 2, 1996).

*See also* Colonialism; Pacific Islands; Pacific Literature

## H.D. (Hilda Doolittle) (1886–1961)

Anglo-American poet. Born Hilda Doolittle in Pennsylvania, H.D. traced her artistic gift through her Moravian mother. She was at Bryn Mawr College with Marianne Moore (1887–1972) and met Ezra Pound (1885–1972) when he was a student at the University of Pennsylvania. Pound idolized her in his "Hilda's Book (1905)"; she recalled their brief engagement in *End to Torment* (1980).

After Pound's departure for Europe, Hilda Doolittle fell in love with Frances Gregg (1884–1941); she would recall their relationship with Pound in *Her* (1981). In 1911, they set sail for Europe, a lesbian idyll traced in *Paint It Today*. In *Asphodel*, another expatriate novel of the 1920s, the Hilda character fails to persuade the Frances character to stay with her in London and continue the artistic tradition of Oscar Wilde (1854–1900). Gregg later resurfaced in H.D.'s life; when she was killed in 1941, "Hilda's Book" was among her possessions.

Hilda Doolittle married fellow poet Richard Aldington (1892–1962) in 1914, acquiring British nationality. They translated ancient Greek poetry and helped Amy Lowell (1874–1925) edit the Imagist anthologies after her split with Ezra Pound. This brought H.D. into contact with D.H. Lawrence (1885–1930), though they were never lovers. The breakup of the Aldington marriage during World War I is presented in *Bid Me to Live* (1960), the only autobiographical novel by H.D. to be published in her lifetime.

In 1918, when H.D. was living with Cecil Gray (1895–1951) and expecting their child, she was discovered by the young writer Bryher (1894–1983). Thus started a vital lifelong relationship. In "I Said" (1920) and "We Two" (1924), H.D. registers their solidarity as lesbians before an uncomprehending world: "We two remain: / yet by what miracle . . . / have we two met within / this maze of daedal paths . . . / where once I stood alone?"

Bryher's wealth allowed H.D. to live for writing rather than by writing. In 1920, they visited Lowell and Ada Russell (1863–1952?) in Boston, Massachusetts, and Marianne Moore in New York City, also traveling to California and Greece. Subsequently, Bryher married H.D.'s lover, Kenneth Macpherson (1902–1971), adopted her daughter, Perdita, and settled in Switzerland. The Macphersons made silent films, including *Borderline* (1930), in which H.D. acted with Paul Robeson (1898–1976). H.D.'s writing at this time occupies psychic, sexual, and racial borderlines: especially her Sapphic lyrics and the experimental fiction of "Kora and Ka" (1934).

In the early 1930s, H.D. was analyzed by Sigmund Freud (1856–1939), recording their sessions in letters to Bryher and prose later published as *Tribute to Freud* (1956). He described her as "the perfect bi-[sexual]," but she continued to be woman identified. While she resisted Freud's theories of femininity and homosexuality, H.D. believed that psychoanalysis powered the "dynamic drive" of her later writings. During World War II, living in London with Bryher, she composed the sustained poetry of *Trilogy* (1944–1946) and her prose memoir, *The Gift* (1983).

H.D. was at the height of her powers, but after the war she suffered a mental and physical breakdown and was sent to a Swiss clinic to recover. There she completed *By Avon River* (1949), celebrating Shakespeare's bisexuality. Later, she wrote *Helen in Egypt* (1961), the revisionary epic that she called "my cantos." After being honored in 1960 by the American Academy of Arts and Letters, she died in Lausanne, Switzerland, the following year. H.D. survives in a body of writing that rivals the achievement of better-known male modernists and extends well beyond her *Collected Poems, 1912–1944* (1983).                    *Diana Collecott*

## Bibliography

Buck, Claire. *H.D. and Freud: Bisexuality and a Feminine Discourse*. New York: St. Martin's, 1991.

Collecott, Diana. *H.D. and Sapphic Modernism, 1910–1950*. Cambridge, England: Cambridge University Press, 1999.

DuPlessis, Rachel. *H.D: The Career of That Struggle*. Brighton: Harvester, 1986.

Friedman, Susan. *Penelope's Web: Gender, Modernity, H.D.'s Fiction*. New York: Cambridge University Press, 1990.

Laity, Cassandra. "Lesbian Romanticism: H.D.'s Fictional Representations of Frances Gregg and Bryher." Introduction to H.D., *Paint It Today*. New York: New York University Press, 1992, pp. xvii–xliii.

***See also*** Bisexuality; Bryher; Lowell, Amy Lawrence; Modernism; Poetry; Psychoanalysis; Sappho

## Health

In health-care research, diagnosis, and treatment, lesbians have often been ignored. The norm for research, diagnosis, and treatment of health and disease in the United States is the white, heterosexual, middle-class male. Doubly distanced from the heterosexual male norm, lesbian health-care and disease issues have failed to receive funding and study. When recognized, lesbians have often been subsumed as a subset of women or homosexuals, so that heterosexual females or homosexual males become the respective norms against which lesbians are measured.

Use of the white, middle-class, heterosexual male as the norm has resulted in the exclusion of women from drug testing, the definition of some diseases that affect both sexes as male diseases, the insufficient study of conditions specific to females, and the ignoring of women's experiences. Ironically, obstetrics/gynecology, the medical specialty centered exclusively on women's health issues, also derives its norms from the heterosexual male. Because of its focus on procreation and heterosexual activity, the centering of women's health in obstetrics/gynecology defines it in terms of their relationships with men. Most women first consult an ob/gyn when they become, or are thinking of becoming, heterosexually active. The possibility of future problems with procreation, difficult periods, the absence of periods, or other problems surrounding menarche bring other women to consult a gynecologist before they become heterosexually active. For many women, the obstetrician/gynecologist becomes the primary-care physician, and reproduction becomes

H a major focus for health care. Defining women's health in terms of men's interests and norms has done more than promote the overmedicalization of normal processes such as pregnancy and childbirth. It has also led to the underfunding of most aspects of women's health not directly related to procreation and heterosexual activity. Thought of as homosexuals and, thus, defined in opposition to their heterosexual counterparts, lesbians become excluded from obstetrics/gynecology, the medical specialty devoted to women's health.

## Research on Lesbians

Although very little health-care research has included separate studies of health-care issues for lesbians, some studies have suggested differences in health and disease processes in lesbians and nonlesbians. For example, it is clear that lesbians have a much lower incidence of certain diseases, such as cervical cancer. Heterosexual intercourse permits the transmission of herpes, trichomoniasis, chlamydia, and the human papilloma virus (HPV), thought to be major causes of cervical cancer. Beginning intercourse at an early age also increases the chances of cervical cancer. Cervical cancer is nonexistent in celibate women and rare in lesbians who have engaged in limited heterosexual intercourse or are not at risk from other factors, such as diethylstilbesterol (DES) exposure and smoking. However, a study by Johnson et al. (1987) demonstrated that lesbians with a history of vaginal intercourse with men have an increased rate of cervical cancer, between 2.7 percent and 2.9 percent, which is in the high-normal range for all women.

Lesbians may be at higher risk for breast, ovarian, and endometrial cancer. As of 1998, however, no prospective population-based study of the comparative incidence of cancers in lesbians had been performed. This lack of research is problematic because general epidemiologic studies of cancer in women have identified specific risk factors that are distributed differently in the lesbian population. Dr. Suzanne Haynes of the National Cancer Institutes estimates that one in three lesbians may develop breast cancer during her lifetime because lesbians are more likely than other women to fall into high-risk categories for the disease. Women who have never had children are at an almost 80 percent greater risk for breast cancer than women who have had children; it may be inferred that lesbians are at increased risk for the disease because lesbians are less likely to have children than are their heterosexual sisters. Never having had children may also con-

stitute a risk for ovarian cancer and may be implicated in endometrial cancer as well.

Failure to identify and fund separate studies of lesbian health issues usually results in lesbians being lumped with heterosexual women in studies of women's health issues. When such lumping occurs in studies of the incidence and/or the causes of sexually transmitted diseases or other gynecological problems from which lesbians are exempt or at low risk because they do not engage in heterosexual intercourse, both lesbians and nonlesbians suffer. Defining such studies generally as research on "women's health issues" rather than "health issues for women engaging in heterosexual sex" leads the general population and some health-care workers to think that lesbians are at risk for diseases that they are unlikely to contract, while obscuring the true risk behavior for heterosexual women.

A related confusion arises when lesbians are not listed as a separate statistical category for frequency of diseases. The Centers for Disease Control in Atlanta, Georgia, does not list lesbians as a separate category in its groups for AIDS infection; homosexual men, bisexual men, and adult men are listed separately. Men are listed not only by sexual orientation but are further subdivided by intravenous drug use and race.

The failure to separate out lesbians as a distinct group for statistics on AIDS leads the public to false understandings of the risk behaviors causing AIDS. It may partly explain the misunderstanding by the public and even by 20 percent of nurse educators that lesbians are at high risk to transmit AIDS (Randall 1989). Lumping lesbians, celibate women, and heterosexually active women together obscures the increased risk of AIDS to women engaged in heterosexual activity, since lesbians and celibate women have very low risk for AIDS from sexual activity. A 1993 survey reported in 1996 by the Council on Scientific Affairs of the American Medical Association of 498 lesbians and bisexual women based upon a random sample of San Francisco and Berkeley, California, residents revealed a 1.2 percent rate of HIV infection. Histories of heterosexual relations or injection-drug use prevented determination of female-to-female transmission. The greatest risk of HIV infection for all women is from injection-drug use and sex with bisexual men. However, female-to-female transmission of HIV can occur through exposure to cervical and vaginal secretions of an HIV-infected woman. The amount of shedding from these secretions likely increases the risk of HIV exposure. Lesbians may also be vulnerable to HIV infection via artificial insemination from an infected donor, as well as from blood transfusions.

Overexamination of, and research centered on, the lesbian population seeking or referred for counseling and therapy have possibly led to misperceptions about the prevalence and severity of problems that sexual orientation causes for lesbians. Since lesbians having fewer problems tend not to seek help, they are underrepresented in the literature or unknowingly lumped with heterosexual women. Presumably, the pattern of overrepresentation of lesbians with problems and underrepresentation of lesbians without problems documented in psychology has been repeated for other aspects of health. This pattern provides health-care practitioners and the general population with a false picture of the prevalence of diseases and difficulties in the lesbian population.

Alcoholism, a problem for lesbians as well as male homosexuals, is thought to be underdiagnosed and undertreated in the lesbian community. A study by McKirnan and Peterson (1989) suggests that the drinking patterns of lesbians are more consistent with national norms for male drinkers than female drinkers. Much of the study of alcoholism in homosexual populations has used the gay bar as a source for estimating and diagnosing the incidence of alcoholism. Limited research suggests that many lesbians, particularly in some geographic areas, such as the South, and from the upper and middle socioeconomic classes, may not frequent lesbian bars. This does not mean that they are not drinking elsewhere and may not be suffering from alcoholism. Similarly, the twelve-step treatment, the model considered to be most successful for treating alcoholics, was developed by two men using themselves (white, middle-to-upper-class heterosexuals) as the norm. Feminists have critiqued the confrontation aspects of the model as less appropriate for many women who seek to avoid conflict. The self-revelation aspects of the model and the involvement of the spouse in Al-Anon or codependency groups are less appropriate for lesbians, who are likely neither to have a spouse nor to reveal much about their personal life in a lesbophobic society. In some cases, Alcoholics Anonymous (AA) is not sensitive to painful prior events such as rape, incest, battering, or other traumas for which alcohol or drug use becomes a symptom.

Ignoring lesbian health issues in research has led to inappropriate diagnoses and treatments for lesbians. For many health-care practitioners, the ab-

sence of lesbians as a group from studies and discussions of lesbian health-care literature has been translated into the assumption that no lesbians seek health-care service or that heterosexual activity should be assumed for all patients. In fact, a significant issue that hinders many lesbians from seeking health care is homophobia and/or insensitivity on the part of health-care practitioners. Stevens's review of nine studies regarding lesbians' experiences with health care between 1970 and 1990 uncovered significant homophobic attitudes on the part of health-care professionals. The Gay and Lesbian Medical Association conducted a study of its membership in 1994 that revealed that 98 percent of respondents felt homosexual patients should disclose their sexual orientation to their physician, but 64 percent believed that, as a result of disclosure, homosexual patients risked receiving substandard care (Schatz and O'Hanlan 1994). Fifty-two percent had observed colleagues denying or providing reduced care to patients because of their sexual orientation.

## Lesbians and Health Care

Because of lesbophobia and the assumption of a heterosexual norm by many health-care practitioners, many lesbians and celibate women refuse routine examinations or delay seeking treatment for serious symptoms because they find questions about contraception and heterosexual activity to be distasteful. Diseases such as endometriosis are unlikely to be diagnosed in lesbians if the practitioner uses pain during intercourse as the major criterion for diagnosis. Some lesbians fear that revealing their sexual orientation to a health-care practitioner may lead to loss of jobs or children if this information is recorded in medical records that may become available to employers or social-service workers.

When a woman does reveal her sexual orientation to a health-care practitioner, she must watch for assumptions on the part of the practitioner that she engages in a particular risk behavior. Risk behaviors, such as anal intercourse, not homosexuality itself, put male homosexuals at risk for HIV. Similarly, not engaging in heterosexual or anal intercourse, not simply current sexual orientation, puts lesbians at less risk for cervical cancer than women who engage in those activities.

Describing specific risk behaviors rather than ascribing them to lesbians because of their sexual orientation will open the way for a better understanding of lesbian health-care issues without reinforcing the status quo of ignorance and oppression

**H** from homophobia. The late-twentieth-century condition of ignoring lesbians and their health-care needs must not continue. It is tragic for lesbians, who remain ignorant about their own health-care issues; health-care practitioners and the nonlesbian population also suffer. When lesbians are ignored in research design, it may lead to their inappropriate inclusion or exclusion from studies of health issues; this obscures the true incidence and cause of some diseases for both lesbian and nonlesbian women. Precious resources may be unnecessarily wasted in overprescribing tests such as Pap smears and tests for STDs when inappropriate inclusion or exclusion from populations sampled becomes translated into inaccurate diagnosis and treatment.    *Sue V. Rosser*

### Bibliography

Council on Scientific Affairs, American Medical Association. "Health Care Needs of Gay Men and Lesbians in the United States." *Journal of the American Medical Association* 275:17 (1996), 1354–1359.

Johnson, S.R., E.M. Smith, and S.M. Guenther. "Comparison of Gynecologic Health Care Problems Between Lesbians and Bisexual Women: A Survey of 2,345 Women." *New England Journal of Medicine* 32 (1987), 805–811.

McKirnan, D.J., and P.L. Peterson. "Alcohol and Drug Use Among Homosexual Men and Women: Epidemiology and Population Characteristics." *Addictive Behaviors* 14 (1989), 545–553.

Randall, Carla E. "Lesbian Phobia Among BSN Educators: A Survey." *Journal of Nursing Education* 28 (1989), 302–306.

Rosser, Sue V. "Ignored, Overloooked, or Subsumed: Research on Lesbian Health and Health Care." *NWSA Journal* 5:2 (1993), 183–203.

Schatz, B., and K. O'Hanlan. *Anti-Gay Discrimination in Medicine: Results of a National Survey of Lesbian, Gay, and Bisexual Physicians.* San Francisco: American Association of Physicians for Human Rights, 1994.

**See also** AIDS (Acquired Immune Deficiency Syndrome); Alcohol and Substance Abuse; Medicine; Nursing; Sexually Transmitted Diseases

### Heroes

Archetypal figures with exceptional qualities who undertake mythic quests and adventures. Heroic figures suffuse lesbian culture, whether public ones appropriated from the mainstream or private ones created out of lesbian thoughts and desires. Heroes are a counterpoint to homophobia, by actualizing lesbian aspirations and fantasies. The heroic epic has survived as the most enduring style of story in many different cultures. The hero-protagonist on a quest for legitimation marks a significant number of lesbian narratives, including Radclyffe Hall's *The Well of Loneliness* (1928), Ann Bannon's Beebo Brinker series (1957–1962), Rita Mae Brown's *Rubyfruit Jungle* (1973), Audre Lorde's *Zami: A New Spelling of My Name* (1982), and Jeanette Winterson's *Oranges Are Not the Only Fruit* (1985). The lesbian hero is a presence everywhere. Consuming her, a metamorphosis takes place through a process of identification and desire: The reader wants the hero, and wants to *be* the hero, whether she be Marlene (Dietrich), Martina (Navratilova), or Madonna.

Zimmerman (1990) suggests that "[t]he lesbian hero, in all her various shapes, journeys through patriarchy to its point of exit, the border of an unknown territory, a 'wild zone' of the imagination." This is a journey of emancipation that assumes that the imagination has a relation to reality and that reading performs a dual function of escape and reconstruction, which introduces the reader back into an imperceptibly changed world on her return. Prevailing categories of the lesbian hero, according to Zimmerman, are outlaws, witches, magicians, androgynes, and artists—all forms adapted to contemporary circumstances and, in the novels Zimmerman describes, to lesbian feminism.

Zimmerman describes how heroic models have modified over the years. In pre-Stonewall (1969) literature, the lesbian longed to return from exile, to be accepted by the dominant culture, and to become normalized and assimilated. On the other hand, in the figure of the lesbian vampire—an erotic spectacle that translated so successfully onto film—she persisted in romantic otherness. The most romantic of these classic forms of the lesbian hero is the butch, her female masculinity offering a potent mixture of agency and idealization for the lesbian reader. The butch is a tragic figure found in novels throughout the twentieth century, from *The Well of Loneliness* (1928) to Leslie Feinberg's *Stone Butch Blues* (1993).

Heroic narratives offer vicarious experiences recognizable as lessons in morality. These quest-stories provide a system of values in the form of a narrative in which the hero must search for and find selfhood. The hero passes from ignorance to knowledge and from passivity to action, guided through the maze by an ethical map. Trials undergone along the way underline the protagonist's role of apprentice and promote understanding of the character and strength of an enemy (such as homophobia). The effect is utopian, offering a vision of how the world *could* be.

Lesbian novels are commonly about becoming, about appropriating power, about finding the heroic in oneself. The positive images of heroes in 1970s fiction evokes the kind of fond embarrassment reserved for naive versions of the self. The lesbian and gay intelligentsia in the 1990s at times adopted a certain distanced snobbery about heroes and positive images in general, which are seen as belonging to a backward and unsophisticated lesbian culture. But these stories are lesbian folktales that have accumulated an elaborate and profound symbolic meaning, adapted and reinterpreted to meet the needs of each new political moment.

For example, *The Gilda Stories* (1991) by Jewelle Gomez offers the black lesbian hero as a vampire. Gomez (1993) described her difficulty in finding black women characters of heroic dimensions, noting: "[W]e have been trapped in the metaphor of slavery . . . [therefore] we are at a loss as to how to extrapolate an independent future." She further identifies two literary archetypes in black fiction, the "bitch," who makes herself the center of her existence, and the "hero," who makes the survival of the community central to her being. In *The Gilda Stories*, Gomez illustrates her own argument by showing her hero figure not as an individualist, but as a woman grounded in her community.

Heroes offer a metaphor of the self in movement, change, and process. Heroism can carry a complex statement of identity and struggle. For example, it does not really matter whether it was a "diesel dyke" who threw the first punch at a police officer outside the Stonewall bar in New York City in 1969. The image is symbolic and has an important function as heroic *legend.*        *Sally R. Munt*

### *Bibliography*

Gomez, Jewelle. "Lye-Throwers and Lovely Renegades: The Road from Bitch to Hero for Black Women in Speculative Fictions." In *Forty-Three Septembers*. Ithaca N.Y.: Firebrand, 1993, pp. 109–128.

Munt, Sally R. *Heroic Desire: Lesbian Identity and Cultural Space*. London: Cassell, 1998.

Zimmerman, Bonnie. *The Safe Sea of Women: Lesbian Fiction, 1969–1989*. Boston: Beacon, 1990.

*See also* Amazons

## Heterosexism

A form of discrimination whereby heterosexuality and heterosexuals are considered superior to lesbians, bisexual men and women, gay men, and queers. Heterosexism prevails in U.S. culture. It not only involves individual acts of mistreatment toward lesbians, but is also built into institutions, such as government and the health-care system. As an institutionalized system of oppression, heterosexism negatively affects lesbians, gay men, bisexuals, and transgender people, as well as some heterosexual individuals who do not subscribe to traditional standards of masculinity and femininity.

### Institutionalized Oppression

The power to create societal definitions of homosexuality has long been the domain of heterosexuals. Throughout history, lesbians and homosexuals have been defined by society in various ways: as sinners, as mentally ill, and as criminals. In the 1990s, heterosexism continued to dictate the illegality of homosexual behavior through the existence of sodomy laws in nearly half of the states. Similarly, most cities with human rights ordinances do not extend legal protection against discrimination to lesbians and gays. Lesbians, gays, bisexuals, and transgenderists are, by and large, not legally protected against discrimination across the United States.

While it varies from city to city and state to state, heterosexism threatens lesbians and other nonstraight individuals in terms of fairness in practices of employment, education, housing, and accommodations. Lesbians, gays, and bisexuals are plagued with concern for safety from physical and emotional harm and the fear of incarceration.

While policy battles were waged across the United States throughout the early 1990s in attempts to gain equal rights and same-sex marriage rights, still only heterosexuals could legally marry. Four nations permitted the registration of same-sex partnerships: Denmark, Sweden, Norway, and Iceland (including Greenland). Despite some differences from heterosexual marriage, partnership registration in these countries is considered to be a legal equivalent. Couples benefit from this status with tax

**H** breaks, the extension of health-care benefits to spouses, and other institutionalized benefits.

## Individual Oppression

On a more personal level, the assumption of individuals' heterosexuality perpetuates heterosexism. For example, a norm exists in U.S. culture that individuals should attend social functions with an other-sex date or partner. Given the fear and intolerance of lesbians, gays, and bisexuals, individuals are faced with the decision of whether or not to attend mainstream events, to go alone, to take a "decoy" date, or to refer to their partner/lover as a "friend." This prescribed pattern serves to keep lesbians in the closet and in fear of the repercussions of being identified as homosexual.

Homophobia and heterosexism remain acceptable in society. It is not uncommon to hear verbal attacks on lesbians, bisexuals, and gay men. Talk about lesbians and gays in negative terms does not receive much, if any, sanction on the street corner, in the home, in the classroom, and or in the popular media.

## Heterosexism and Sexism

Heterosexism and sexism are interwoven systems of oppression. This overlap can be identified at both the institutional and the individual level in society. At an institutional level, for example, women and lesbians particularly are often ignored in medical research. Research on AIDS typically focuses on men. Yet the results of research are assumed to apply to lesbians and other women. While lesbians are considered low risk, the incidence of AIDS among lesbians has risen dramatically from the 1980s to the 1990s. Still, lesbians are ignored in medical research, in general, and often overlooked in AIDS education because of sexism. The invisibility of lesbians in medical research illustrates both heterosexism and sexism because it is discrimination against a particular gender and category of people not involved in heterosexual relationships.

Adherence or the lack thereof to traditional standards of femininity and masculinity can be a "sign" of one's sexual orientation. Beginning at birth, children are socialized to be heterosexual and to fit into traditional gender norms. Boys and girls are sanctioned for transgressive gender behavior with verbal assaults marking them as "other" than heterosexual. Girls who remain tomboys too long may be called "butch" or "dyke," and more effeminate boys may be tagged "sissy" or "fag."

As children grow to adolescents and adults, the connection between heterosexism and sexism remains. Nonconformity in gender is assumed to be equated with nonconformity in sexual orientation. Symbols, such as clothing, jewelry, or hairstyle, can serve to mark nonheterosexuals with the status of "other." Stereotypically, women with short hairstyles, an affinity for flannel and combat boots, and a dislike for makeup may be quickly labeled by straight people as "butch" or "dyke."

Along with the other forms of inequality, heterosexism is a pervasive form of oppression in society. Not only are personal relationships affected by heterosexism, but institutions play a major role in perpetuating this form of inequality.

*Kimberly Dugan*

### Bibliography

D'Emilio, John. *Sexual Politics, Sexual Communities: The Making of a Homosexual Minority in the United States, 1940–1970*. Chicago: University of Chicago Press, 1983.

Harvard Law Review. *Sexual Orientation and the Law*. Cambridge, Mass.: Harvard University Press, 1990.

Pharr, Suzanne. *Homophobia: A Weapon of Sexism*. Inverness, Calif.: Charden, 1988.

***See also*** Discrimination; Heterosexuality; Homophobia; Invisibility; Oppression; Sexism

## Heterosexuality

Term used to refer to sexual behavior limited to male-female interactions, to a sexual preference for, or orientation toward, such interactions, to an identity based on such a preference/orientation, and to the social institutionalization of these. The distinctions are crucial, because, although behavior that could be called heterosexual is a universal, heterosexual institutions and identities are probably not. For, while it is clear that all societies encourage most (though often not all) members to pair heterosexually for the purposes of procreation and lineage, it is not clear that all societies require that members be heterosexual in some essential way. Critical study of heterosexuality is nascent in the late twentieth century and continues to be blocked by the hegemony, or cultural dominance, of heterosexuality. The assumed normality of heterosexuality has impeded the pursuit, even the formulation, of such questions as these: What are the causes of exclusively heterosexual preferences and orientations in individuals? How have heterosexual identities developed historically? How has heterosexuality been institutionalized, and how has this differed for men and women of different societies and social groups?

Historians have found that the term "heterosexuality" did not appear in any European language until 1869, when it—along with its pair, "homosexuality"—was coined in political letters by the German publicist Karoly Maria Kertbeny (1824–1882). It was then used publicly in an anonymous 1880 pamphlet calling for sodomy-law reform, and sexologist Richard Krafft-Ebing (1840–1902) used it in the 1889 edition of his *Psychopathia Sexualis*. Same-gender sexuality, particularly between men, was a primary topic of late-nineteenth-century sexological study, and new terms for it abounded. The invention of a term for its "opposite," heterosexuality, appeared almost as an afterthought. The conceptualization of heterosexuality as an individual sexual preference or orientation seems to have required, and followed, the conceptualization of homosexuality in such terms.

Many scholars have suggested that the hetero/homo distinction was not an important one before that time; Katz (1995) argues that, in Colonial America, for example, the crucial distinction was between procreative and nonprocreative forms of sex and that acts, not desires, were the topic of concern. Social-constructionist and essentialist theorists debate whether there were any heterosexuals, in this sense, before the concept came into being.

Lesbian feminist theorists led the way in the critical analysis of heterosexuality, although most have been less concerned with such questions as the above and more concerned with the place of institutionalized heterosexuality in the subordination of women to men. In her now-classic treatment of this problem, "Compulsory Heterosexuality and Lesbian Existence," Rich (1980) analyzes the forces that have kept women bound to men through heterosexual institutions. Looking at forces ranging from literal enslavement to more subtle ideological pressures, she points out that the denial and distortion of lesbian existence undergirds the portrayal of heterosexual unions as women's only real options. From this point follows the basic lesbian feminist insight that lesbianism is more than an individual sexual preference and is, at least implicitly, a form of resistance to male dominance.

The lesbian feminist analysis, however, is not the only lesbian theoretical approach to heterosexuality. Poststructuralist philosopher Butler (1990) ar-

gues that heterosexuality requires homosexuality, indeed presupposes it. Lesbianism is subversive, then, not in its role as liberatory option, as in lesbian feminism, but through its exposure of heterosexuality as a social construction. This exposure is achieved best by butch-femme "imitation" of heterosexual forms, upon which heterosexuality relies in order to appear to be the "original"; the process parallels the one whereby the social construction of "normal" gender roles is revealed by drag performance.

Perhaps ironically, lesbian analyses of heterosexuality rarely focus on the role of heterosexuality in the lives of lesbians. Research on identity has demonstrated clearly, however, that individuals' sexual behavior does not always "match" their sexual identities, that many women who identify as heterosexual have homosexual experiences, and vice versa. Research on sexual behavior has consistently found higher levels of heterosexual experience among women who identify as lesbians than among men who identify as gay, a gender difference that remains largely unexplained. It is clear, however, that, in light of the actual sexual experiences of lesbians, commonly held beliefs about the immutability of heterosexuality and homosexuality are overstated, particularly for women. The concepts of clearly distinct heterosexuality and homosexuality seem better applicable to men's sexual lives than to women's, which may be more often characterized by flexibility and change.       *Vera Whisman*

### Bibliography

Butler, Judith. *Gender Trouble*. New York: Routledge, 1990.

Katz, Jonathan. *The Invention of Heterosexuality*. New York: Dutton, 1995.

Rich, Adrienne. "Compulsory Heterosexuality and Lesbian Existence," *Signs: Journal of Women in Culture and Society* 5 (1980), 631–660.

Stein, Edward, ed. *Forms of Desire*. New York: Routledge, 1992.

Whisman, Vera. *Queer By Choice*. New York: Routledge, 1996.

**See also** Compulsory Heterosexuality; Heterosexism; Homosexuality; Identity; Lesbian Feminism; Rich, Adrienne; Sexology; Sexual Orientation and Preference

### High Schools, Lesbian and Gay

Educational centers prepared to service students who have, for whatever reason, have dropped out of

H the comprehensive public school system. Created in response to the high numbers of lesbian and gay youth who were not completing their education, lesbian and gay high schools construct an atmosphere of tolerance and acceptance that helps students get back on task to complete a high school diploma or its equivalency.

Students who seek out a lesbian and gay high school have usually experienced some form of violence and gay bashing, verbal and sexual harassment, homelessness, or other kinds of alienating experiences in public school culture. These students, as well as others, may be looking for other lesbian and gay youth for support and community. Often, high school administrators have no policy for dealing with lesbian and gay harassment or refuse to address the issues of bashing and name-calling. The societal oppression and discrimination against the lesbian and gay communities, no access to information and role models, rejection of parental or family love and connection due to their sexual identity, professionals labeling them as pathological and sick, and the extreme homophobia of the high school culture forces some students to leave school and seek out alternatives to finish their education.

In 1998, there were three such programs. In-school support groups, such as Project 10, a program founded in 1985 by Los Angeles Unified School District's Virginia Uribe, also benefit students who are coming out in traditional high schools. Project 10 support groups deal with many of these coming out issues among students and help negotiate a bridge of communication between parents, schools, and students as an afternoon, in-house rap group, usually sponsored by a teacher or an administrator.

The EAGLES Center (Emphasizing Adolescent Gay/Lesbian Educational Services) was started in 1993 by Jerry Battey, an openly gay Los Angeles Unified School District teacher, in response to the publication of the 1991 U.S. Department of Health and Human Services' *Report on Youth Suicide*, which recommended services for homosexual youth because of their much higher than average suicide-completion rates. Although the EAGLES Center emphasizes a lesbian and gay student environment, the school reflects a more inclusive population of youth, including those who identify as bisexual and transgender and other youth who feel solidarity with the "queer" community in Los Angeles. The demographics of the school as of the late 1990s reflected the larger Los Angeles metropolitan area: 70 percent Latino; 10 percent African American; 10 percent white; 6 percent Asian; 2 percent Native American; and 2 percent "other." Boys outnumber girls at the EAGLES Center, constituting at least 70 percent of the student population.

In New York City, the Hetrick-Martin Institute sponsors Harvey Milk High School as part of its overall comprehensive services for lesbian and gay youth. In creating this educational space in its institute, the Hetrick-Martin community has joined social and health services into a comprehensive service environment specifically directed at queer youth. Hetrick-Martin is not only a center where lesbian and gay youth find a tolerant and supportive atmosphere in working toward a high school diploma, but also a space where students can find shelter, health and social services, and a teen drop-in center.

The curriculum for the lesbian and gay high school is queer positive and queer friendly but traditional in approach. Students are required to follow state curriculum guidelines with course work in English, math, science, and social studies. However, because of the high rates of transience of many of the students, much of their course work is based on the Individual Education Plan (IEP), a comprehensive academic plan designed for the student by a team of counselors, teachers, parents (or caregivers), and the student after an assessment of her or his educational needs.

The first priority of the lesbian and gay high school is to allow students access to their cumulative school records. Many students enrolling at these schools are often leaving abusive households and/or schools and are not aware of their status as students. For older students who have been away from school for longer periods of time, the school can also provide classes leading to a General Equivalency Diploma (GED). Students using the IEP pace themselves through their course work and can finish numerous classes in a short span of time.

One criticism of lesbian and gay high schools has been the curriculum, adding lesbian and gay literature and history to an otherwise traditional curriculum. The use of volunteers in designing curriculum for these schools is crucial, and it is through the work donated by people in the lesbian and gay communities that the high schools can provide libraries, guest artists and writers, social and psychological services, internships, and equipment to enrich their curriculum.

Funding is always a problem for the schools. As no-cost items to their local school district budgets, the schools receive no funding beyond teacher salaries, leaving no funds for administrative or instructional staff, facilities, or staff development. Much of the administrative support is provided by volunteers. The EAGLES Center has its particular funding problems. Unlike the Harvey Milk High School, there is no budget for a permanent site, so the EAGLES Center is forced to find community-based organizations that can sponsor sites for the school.

School districts may support these alternative schools for lesbian, gay, bisexual, and transgender youth with teacher salaries but little else. Religious Right organizations have had a tremendous impact in the policymaking of many school districts. With the threat of highly organized blocks of voters, school boards stay politically "neutral" and are hesitant to commit part of school district budgets to support programs for lesbian and gay youth. And, although these educational spaces may keep students from officially dropping out of school, very few of these at-risk lesbian and gay youth are graduating.                    *Cynthia Cruz*

### Bibliography

Remafedi, Gary. *Death By Denial*. Boston: Alyson, 1994.

*See also* Students; Suicide; Teachers

## Hildegard of Bingen, Saint (1098–1179)

German Benedictine abbess, visionary, scientific and theological writer, musical composer, dramatist, and preacher; one of thirty-nine women honored with a place setting in Judy Chicago's art installation *The Dinner Party* (San Francisco, 1979). From childhood, Hildegard experienced religious visions, which she began to record in 1141. These visionary works form a trilogy on Christian doctrine remarkable for its attention to the feminine aspects of theology. Hildegard wrote numerous other works: scientific treatises that combine therapeutic and herbal remedies for diseases with observations on human sexuality and reproduction, astrological lore, and empirical information; the earliest-known allegorical drama in the West; music and lyrics for a cycle of seventy-five poetic songs on liturgical themes; saints' lives; a secret language; and a correspondence of 284 extant items, including letters to popes, cardinals, kings, queens, and emperors. In later life, Hildegard made four tours throughout Germany preaching clerical reform.

Dedicated at the age of eight to the service of God by her aristocratic parents, Hildegard was raised and educated by the anchoress Jutta of Sponheim and spent her life in female religious communities, eventually becoming magistra of a Benedictine convent near Bingen, Germany. She formed social, professional, and emotional friendships with religious and lay women throughout Germany. She corresponded with abbesses, offering them aid and advice, and her work inspired the visionary writing of a protégée, Elisabeth of Schonau, who also wrote to Hildegard and visited her. Hildegard formed a strong emotional attachment to a favorite nun, Richardis von Stade. When Richardis left Hildegard to assume an abbacy, Hildegard protested in writing all the way to the pope, to no avail.

Hildegard's attitude to female homosexuality and homoeroticism varied according to the genre of the discourse in which she wrote. In her visionary moral writing, Hildegard repeated the conventional medieval condemnation of both male and female homosexual acts as "devilish" perversions of so-called natural male (active) and female (passive) roles (*Scivias* 2.6.78). But in her medical writing, Hildegard asserted that woman's sexual pleasure does not depend upon the "touch of a man" (*Causes and Cures* 2.96), and, in both the text and the music of individual poetic songs in her liturgical cycle, the *Symphonia,* Hildegard created female homoerotic tropes that express physical and spiritual desire for the Virgin Mary. In the one extant letter she wrote to Richardis, Hildegard encoded her erotic desire for her favorite nun.                    *Susan Schibanoff*

### Bibliography

Dronke, Peter. *Women Writers of the Middle Ages: A Critical Study of Texts from Perpetua (d. 203) to Marguerite Porete (d. 1310)*. Cambridge: Cambridge University Press, 1984.

Flanagan, Sabina. *Hildegard of Bingen, 1098–1179: A Visionary Life*. London: Routledge, 1989.

Holsinger, Bruce. "The Flesh of the Voice: Embodiment and the Homoerotics of Devotion in the Music of Hildegard of Bingen (1098–1179)." *Signs: Journal of Women in Culture and Society* 19 (1993), 92–125.

Lauter, Werner. *Hildegard-Bibliographie I, II*. Alzey: Rheinhessische Druckwerkstatte, 1970, 1983.

**H**

Newman, Barbara. *Sister of Wisdom: St. Hildegard's Theology of the Feminine.* Berkeley: University of California Press, 1987.

*See also* Religious Communities; Saints and Mystics

## History

The study of same-sex love and sexuality in the past. Until the 1970s, there was no lesbian history. That is, although women in the past had loved and had sexual relations with other women, no body of scholarship documented such lives. With the burgeoning of the women's movement and the gay and lesbian movement throughout the industrialized Western world, academics in the new fields of women's history and women's studies, as well as independent scholars unaffiliated with universities, began to write and publish lesbian history. It was no easy task. But, beginning with attempts to recover the lives of "lost lesbians," scholars have produced a rich and complex history, although one heavily weighted to the experiences of women in the United States, the United Kingdom, and the countries of western Europe.

### Sources for Lesbian History

One big obstacle to the writing of lesbian history is the difficulty of locating sources. Like women's history in general, lesbian history suffers from the fact that societies throughout the world have accorded women less importance than men. Furthermore, gendered illiteracy rates have ensured that women have historically been far less likely than men to be able to write their life stories. In the case of lesbian history, many of the sources have been deliberately destroyed, both by women fearful of leaving a trace and by hostile outsiders determined to wipe out any evidence of the existence of women who loved and had sex with other women.

As a result, historians have had to use ingenuity in writing about lives meant to be invisible. The founding in 1974 of the Lesbian Herstory Archives in New York City represented one response to the problem of sources. The collection of life stories on the local level, beginning with the Buffalo (New York) Women's Oral History Project, was another effort to make sure that scholars of the future would be able to find a history. And the compilation of bibliographies, perhaps most notably J.R. Roberts's *Black Lesbians* (1981), exemplified yet another. Scouring personal papers, literature, newspapers, le-

gal records, and photographs, seeking lesbians willing to share their life stories, researchers have begun to piece together a lesbian history.

Still, a great deal of the literature on gay history ignores women because of the absence of sources. Thus, John Boswell, in his ambitious *Christianity, Social Tolerance, and Homosexuality* (1980), a history of gay people in Europe from the end of the Roman Empire until the fourteenth century, notes the "relative absence of materials relating to women." Taking a different tack, George Chauncey, in his magisterial *Gay New York: Gender, Urban Culture and the Making of the Gay Male World, 1890–1940* (1994), explained that the differences between gay male and lesbian history made it virtually impossible to write a book about both that did justice to each. So, by and large, lesbian history has developed alongside, but apart from, the history of gay men.

### The Meaning of "Lesbian"

It is not only the problem of sources that has plagued the field of lesbian history. Even more troubling has been the question of what is meant by "lesbian." Until the late nineteenth century, the concept and identity of "lesbian" in the modern sense did not exist. Women experienced desires and engaged in behaviors that would now be called "lesbian," and people knew about them. But loving a woman did not place one in a category based on sexual-object choice until Western culture devised a classification scheme that differentiated people known as "heterosexuals" from those considered "homosexuals" around the end of the nineteenth century. So if "lesbian history" means only those who claimed the label and identity, if only to themselves, the field is geographically and chronologically limited.

Early works celebrating lesbianism often called upon history to provide lesbian heroines. Thus, gay liberation activists Sidney Abbott and Barbara Love entitled their 1972 book about lesbianism *Sappho Was a Right-On Woman*, and Dolores Klaich's *Woman + Woman* (1974) named as "historic witnesses" not only Sappho (ca. 600 B.C.E.), but also writers such as Renée Vivien (1877–1909), Natalie Barney (1876–1972), Colette (1873–1954), Radclyffe Hall (1880–1943), Virginia Woolf (1882–1941), and Gertrude Stein (1874–1946). Other famous women, from Queen Christina of Sweden (1626–1689) to U.S. peace activist and social worker Jane Addams (1860–1935) and, later and most notoriously, Eleanor Roosevelt (1884–1962), joined the pantheon of lesbian role models. Were all of these women lesbians? In a classic article, Cook (1977) claimed as lesbians all "women who love women, who choose women to nurture and support and to create a living environment in which to work creatively and independently."

The poet Adrienne Rich, building on developments in the U.S. women's movement, further broadened the definition of "lesbian history" in her influential 1980 article, "Compulsory Heterosexuality and Lesbian Existence." In line with the movement notion of "political lesbianism," Rich offered the concepts of "lesbian existence" and the "lesbian continuum," which included women-identified women who resisted compulsory heterosexuality in a variety of ways. This opened up the possibility of expanding the modern Western confines of "lesbian history" and suggested a way of getting beyond obsessive questions about whether or not one could find "proof of genital contact." Rich placed on her "lesbian continuum" the Beguines of medieval Europe, devout women who lived collectively outside the institutions of both marriage and the convent; African women who formed secret sororities and economic networks; and Chinese marriage resisters.

Not all scholars embraced such a notion, however. The "sex radical" position in the "sex wars" of the 1980s called attention to the denial of sexuality implicit in Rich's definition. And the development of poststructural theory in the emerging area of "queer studies" called for a "problematizing" of identity, an explicit realization that such terms as "lesbian" and even "woman" are profoundly shaped by historical location. Thus, the broad claiming of women across the globe as "lesbians," although responsive to feminist critiques of race and class bias, in fact could perpetuate existing relations of domination by assuming a white, American, middle-class model of "the lesbian."

In response to such theoretical and conceptual discussions, some historians have taken to avoiding "lesbian" as a blanket term. "Female same-sex love and sexuality" describes emotions and behavior that may have occurred at any place at any time without suggesting advance knowledge of the meaning accorded such relationships or acts to the women involved or to the society in which they lived. Rather than assume anything about identity, historians ask what women did, what they felt, and what their actions and feelings meant to them. Even in historical periods and societies in which sexual-object choice did imply that one was a certain type of person, historians take care to specify the terms used, either by women themselves or by the society in which they lived. "Sapphist," "koskalaka," "dyke," "bulldagger," "butch," "femme," "stud," as well as non-gender-specific terms such as "Uranian" or "Third Sex" all emerge from the historical record as externally imposed or proudly claimed descriptions of women who loved and desired women.

The historical evidence tends to point to three quite different phenomena connected to the history of female same-sex love and sexuality: romantic love between women, transgendered behavior, and sexual acts. In almost all cases, uncertainties remain as to what the evidence really means in light of modern conceptions of lesbian life and lesbian identity. In the case of transgendered behavior, it is not even clear that same-sex love and sexuality came into play at all.

## Romantic Friendship

As if echoing Western bourgeois society's association of women with love, evidence of romantic love between women abounds. This is no doubt at least partly a result of the fact that the middle- and upper-class American and European women who engaged in "romantic friendship" had the education and status in society to leave a written trail. Carroll Smith-Rosenberg's pioneering 1975 article, "The Female World of Love and Ritual: Relations Between Women in Nineteenth-Century America," first called attention to what Faderman (1981) would later call "romantic friendships" and "Boston marriages" between eighteenth- and nineteenth-century middle- and upper-class women in the industrialized Western world. Although scholars began in the 1990s to question just how acceptable they were, passionate attachments between women, often lasting through marriage, were, at the very least, relatively common and openly discussed without disapproval. Work by historians such as Everard (1986) and Lützen (1990) has shown how widespread the phenomenon of romantic friendships was in Europe, and others have documented the survival of this form of relationship into the middle of the twentieth century.

Because such relationships required a certain amount of leisure and, in the case of "Boston marriage," economic independence, this was a largely class-bound phenomenon. That romantic attachments crossed the lines of race is clear from the writings of African American poet Angelina Weld Grimké (1880–1958), who formed a romantic friendship with a school friend in the late nineteenth century. In unpublished lyrics and published verses addressed to a gender-unspecified lover, she poured out the pain of an unidentified lost love. We also have evidence of an intense relationship in the mid-nineteenth century between two African American women, Addie Brown (1841–1870), a domestic worker, and Rebecca Primus (1836–1932), a schoolteacher.

Women's expressions of love for one another, during a period in which such declarations did not immediately point to a sexual relationship, leave us uncertain about the actual nature of such ties. Did women, conceptualized by the mainstream society as lacking in sexual desire, love and kiss and caress and sleep with each other but not "have sex"? In the wake of the sex wars, this question came to seem increasingly important. Lillian Faderman has been much criticized for asserting the "asexuality" of such relationships. But, in fact, her *Scotch Verdict* (1983), a re-creation of the case of two Scottish schoolteachers accused of engaging in a sexual relationship in the early nineteenth century, pits opposing interpretations of what happened between the two women and raises the essential question of what exactly we mean by "having sex."

## Passing Women

Another body of historical writing has uncovered stories of women who crossed the gender line by taking on the clothing, work, and social roles of men and marrying women. Faderman, in her monumental work *Surpassing the Love of Men: Romantic Friendship and Love Between Women from the Renaissance to the Present* (1981), collected evidence of such women. Catharina Linck, in eighteenth-century Germany, disguised herself as a man to serve in the army. After her stint in the military, she took on a man's job and married a woman, making a dildo and testicles from leather and pigs' bladders in order, as the court in a similar case put it, to "counterfeit the office of a husband." She was discovered when her wife, after an argument, confessed to her mother that Catharina was a woman. Like other women in early-modern Europe who claimed both the occupational and sexual privileges of men, she was executed for her crimes in 1721.

On the other side of the Atlantic and more than 150 years later, a French-born San Francisco, California, woman by the name of Jeanne Bonnet took to wearing men's clothes. Discovered by the San Francisco Lesbian and Gay History Project, a particularly successful example of community-based historical scholarship, Bonnet's story became part of a nationally touring slide show. Arrested frequently for her penchant for male dress, Bonnet refused to pay a penny of her fines and instead went to jail, proclaiming her intention never to change her ways. In 1875, she organized a gang of former prostitutes who swore off men, arousing the ire of their pimps. Waiting for a gang member who was probably her lover, she was shot to death in 1876.

By the turn of the twentieth century in the United States and Europe, as Bonnet's story begins to suggest, cross-dressing or "passing" women, in the past always isolated from one another, began to come together in urban areas. Within the sexual underworlds of big cities, women who dressed as men but did not try to pass came to be known as "dikes," from the term for a man all dressed up, or "diked out," for a night on the town. Both urban working-class women and wealthy women in bohemian circles affected male dress for a variety of reasons, giving rise to the association made by the early sexologists between same-sex sexuality and gender "inversion." At the height of the Harlem Renaissance, the African American cultural flowering of the 1920s, bisexual and lesbian performers such as Gertrude "Ma" Rainey (1886–1939) and Gladys Bentley (1907–1960) sang of "bulldaggers," connecting a preference for male attire and female company. The butch-femme world of the working-class bars of the 1950s, sketched out by Joan Nestle and painstakingly pieced together for Buffalo by Kennedy and Davis (1993), saw a full elaboration of a gendered lesbian social and sexual system.

If transgressions of the gender line outraged mainstream Euroamerican society and found tolerance in the heady days of the Harlem Renaissance, some Native American cultures, primarily in western North America, included a cross-gender role, at least before the late nineteenth century. Women known as *hwame* (Mohave), *kwiraxame* (Maricopa), *tw!nnaek* (Klamath), *koskalaka* (Lakota), or *warrhameh* (Cocopa) took on the mannerisms, clothing, and work typical of men, and they also married women. Although the cross-gender role had complex spiritual meanings, it is significant that the sex and gender systems of these cultures, prior to the impact of Euroamerican imperialism, made a place for such individuals. Although the cross-gender female became a social male, her sexual behavior with her wife was not considered heterosexual but rather rated its own terminology.

Although many of the cases of women who crossed the gender line give evidence of sexual activity, the historian is left with many puzzling questions. Did the early-modern European and U.S. women who defied their societies and risked death or imprisonment to take on the roles of men do so in order to pursue relationships with women? Or were their motives primarily social and economic, but passing as a man required sexual interaction with women? What about their wives? Should *hwame* and *koskalaka*, who took on the cross-gender role in a spiritual context, be considered lesbians?

## Sexual Activity

Finally, there are examples of sexual acts between women. As already suggested by the case of Catharina Linck, evidence generally comes from court records, notoriously difficult documents to analyze. For one thing, women accused of sexual acts had every reason to deny having committed them, and women caught with other women had cause to portray themselves as innocent victims. In the fascinating case of Benedetta Carlini (1590–1661), discovered almost by accident in the Italian archives by Brown (1986), this Italian abbess was accused of forcing a younger and less powerful sister in the convent to participate in "the most immodest acts." As in the case of Linck, the evidence of a sexual act exists but not its meaning to the women involved.

In Faderman's account of the Scottish schoolteachers, evidence of a sexual act came from an accusing witness, a student born of a liaison between a Scottish officer and an Indian woman. Only the Indian heritage of their chief accuser gave the judges a way out of an impossible choice between believing that respectable romantic friends might lie on top of each other, kiss, and shake the bed, or that decent schoolgirls could make up such tales. Revealing the ethnic and class assumptions of their society, some of the judges concluded that the girl had learned of such behavior in India or at a previous school populated by shopkeepers' daughters and simply used her knowledge to get out of a school she found too strict. That Indian women or lower-class women engaged in such behavior might be entertained, but that respectable Scottish women might do so shook the foundations of the sexual system.

The question for the court was whether the schoolteachers had kissed, caressed, and fondled "more than could have resulted from ordinary female friendship," suggesting a line into sexuality that could be crossed. That such relations did exist

in the guise of romantic friendship is confirmed in the breast-caressing referred to in the correspondence of African American romantic friends Addie Brown and Rebecca Primus and, even more strikingly, in the remarkable nineteenth-century diary of Englishwoman Anne Lister (1791–1840), an upper-class, independent, mannish woman who described her numerous sexual affairs with women, some of them married. Disappointed that the husband of the woman she loved stubbornly refused to die, in 1824 Lister ran off to Paris, where she immediately began to court a widow staying in the same pension. Lister's explicit descriptions of sexuality, recounted in a woman's own words outside the walls of a courtroom, are a historical treasure. Lister was a woman who, before the invention of the term "homosexuality" in 1869 and before the emergence of the first lesbian cultures around the turn of the twentieth century, not only loved and desired women, but also saw this as her defining characteristic.

## Conclusion

Anne Lister's experiences bring together the previously disparate worlds of romantic friends, transgendered women, and same-sex lovers. The standard story of lesbian history in the Western world tells of class-divided experiences, with peasant and working-class women such as Catharina Linck and Jeanne Bonnet serving as forerunners of the butches and femmes of the 1950s, and middle- and upper-class women such as Angelina Weld Grimké, foreshadowing the lesbian feminists of the 1970s. Lister's story makes clear that this is far too simple a depiction. Historians have assumed that, because women did not have access to public space in the same ways that men who cruised the parks and public latrines and taverns of eighteenth-century European cities did, same-sex communities could not form until the turn of the nineteenth century. But perhaps the first "lesbian communities" can be found in the drawing rooms of respectable society, as well as in the ranks of prostitutes and other women within the sexual underworlds of big cities.

By the late nineteenth century, the previously separate strands of female same-sex sexuality became entwined in the category of the "lesbian." Research on the sexologists who defined the lesbian and on the women who provoked, resisted, and embraced the new labeling suggests how complex the process of identity formation could be. As women in the early twentieth century formed communities—

**H** in Berlin and Paris and New York City—and claimed words that described their love for women, modern lesbian history was born.     *Leila J. Rupp*

## Bibliography

Brown, Judith. *Immodest Acts: The Life of a Lesbian Nun in Renaissance Italy*. New York: Oxford University Press, 1986.

Cook, Blanche Wiesen. "Female Support Networks and Political Activism: Lillian Wald, Crystal Eastman and Emma Goldman." *Chrysalis* 3 (1977), 43–61.

Duberman, Martin, Martha Vicinus, and George Chauncey, Jr. eds. *Hidden From History: Reclaiming the Gay and Lesbian Past*. New York: New American Library, 1989.

Everard, Myriam. "Lesbian History: A History of Change and Disparity." In *Historical, Literary, and Erotic Aspects of Lesbianism*. Ed. Monika Kehoe. New York: Harrington Park, 1986, pp. 123–137.

Faderman, Lillian. *Scotch Verdict*. New York: Quill, 1983.

———. *Surpassing the Love of Men: Romantic Friendship and Love Between Women from the Renaissance to the Present*. New York: William Morrow, 1981.

Hansen, Karen V. " 'No *Kisses* Is Like Youres': An Erotic Friendship Between Two African American Women During the Mid-Nineteenth Century." In *Lesbian Subjects: A Feminist Studies Reader*. Ed. Martha Vicinus. Bloomington: Indiana University Press, 1996, pp. 178–208.

Kennedy, Elizabeth Lapovsky, and Madeline D. Davis. *Boots of Leather, Slippers of Gold: The History of a Lesbian Community*. New York: Routledge, 1993.

Lützen, Karin. *Was das Herz begehrt: Liebe und Freundschaft zwischen Frauen* (What the Heart Desires: Love and Friendship Between Women). Hamburg: Ernst Kabel Verlag, 1990.

Rich, Adrienne. "Compulsory Heterosexuality and Lesbian Existence." *Signs: Journal of Women in Culture and Society* 5:4 (1980), 631–660.

Smith-Rosenberg, Carroll. "The Female World of Love and Ritual: Relations Between Women in Nineteenth Century America." *Signs: Journal of Women in Culture and Society* 1 (1975), 1–29.

*See also* Boston Marriage; Buffalo, New York; Bulldagger; Butch-Femme; Harlem Renaissance; Lesbian Herstory Archives; Lister, Anne; Native Americans; Passing Women; Romantic Friendship

## Hoboes

Women who traveled across the United States, hitchhiking or riding freight trains, especially in the 1920s and 1930s, dressed in men's clothes and often passing as men. At the height of transiency caused by the Great Depression in the early 1930s, thousands of women hoboes were on the road in the United States. Much anecdotal and other evidence suggests that many of these women were lesbians.

The majority of women hoboes were young, poor, or working-class women who had been domestic workers, waitresses, or factory workers before becoming unemployed. About one-third had not worked outside the home before they became hoboes. At least 10 percent of women hoboes were African Americans; the majority were native-born women of European descent. Poverty and unemployment forced them into the life and subculture developed by male, migratory, casual workers known as hoboes. They hitchhiked, rode the freight trains, traveled by public transportation, car, and motorcycle, and they walked. They slept in jails, women's shelters, and in the hobo camps called "jungles."

Almost all women hoboes wore men's clothing. Most of them passed as men, at least part of the time. Some of them wore careful disguises and lived as men for years. Many said that they wore men's clothes for convenience and freedom of movement; almost all said that they passed as men to prevent rape or sexual assaults. Passing women are part of a long but hidden American tradition. Some women who passed as men could best be called transgendered; others were butch, or masculine, lesbians. Similarly, many women hoboes undoubtedly were lesbians or transgendered.

After unemployment, the main reason that women gave for being on the road was freedom, especially sexual freedom. Very few women hoboes traveled alone. Almost all of them traveled in couples, some with male companions, most with female companions, although it is not known how many of the women who traveled with female companions were lesbians. Since a large number of women hoboes passed as men, it seems likely that some of the apparently heterosexual couples were also lesbians, with one of the two women carefully disguised as a man.

One hobo term for lesbians was "lady lovers," according to *Sister of the Road* (1937, 1975), Ben L. Reitman's fictionalized account of the life of a woman hobo, "Box-Car" Bertha. Both lesbians and gay men were also called "queers." The male hobo subculture tolerated a high degree of male homosexual activity, with a strong tradition of pairbonding between a male oldtimer and a young newcomer (known as a "gaycat").

In urban centers, the hobo subculture ("hobohemia") overlapped with that of sexual and political radicals in neighborhoods such as New York City's Greenwich Village and Chicago's North Side. In such neighborhoods many women hoboes discovered (or possibly helped transmit) the growing lesbian urban subculture, centered in lesbian bars and cafés, which was thriving by the late 1930s.

*Nan Cinnater*

## Bibliography

Minehan, Thomas. *Boy and Girl Tramps of America*. New York: Farrar and Rinehart, 1934.

Reitman, Ben L. *Sister of the Road: The Autobiography of Box-Car Bertha*. New York: Gold Label, 1937.

Roberts, J.R. "Lesbian Hoboes: Their Lives and Times." *Dyke* 5 (Fall 1977), 39–47.

**See also** Greenwich Village; Passing Women; Transgender

# Hollywood

Area of Los Angeles, California, northwest of the downtown district; from the late 1910s onward, the center of the movie business in the United States.

Lesbians and bisexual women have been involved in almost all facets of the entertainment business in Hollywood. They have made contributions to the motion picture industry as performers, writers, directors, designers, and stuntpeople. Though all have remained "closeted" to the general public, many have been "out" to their colleagues and peers in the entertainment industry. The earliest reliable evidence places lesbians in Hollywood beginning in the late 1910s and early 1920s. Many of these women were quite open about their sexuality within the film community. Toward the end of the 1920s and especially in the 1930s, this atmosphere of relative openness abated somewhat. This change was a result of the increased acceptance of the morbidification of lesbian relationships promoted by some sexologists, the rise of the studio system, and economic hard times. The lesbians and bisexual women in Hollywood during the 1930s and 1940s usually kept their sexual activities a secret from all but other homosexuals. Reflecting the paranoia generated by the Cold War, the late 1940s and the 1950s were fraught with tension for women who loved women in the entertainment industry in Hollywood. It was during this time that many tabloid magazines also began to lift their self-imposed (and studio-imposed) bans on the discussion and identification of homosexuals in Hollywood. These articles could, and did, end the careers of several homosexuals in Hollywood in the 1950s. The 1960s counterculture and the 1970s "second wave" feminism brought about a repeal of reticence within the Hollywood lesbian and bisexual women's community. From this era to the end of the 1990s, lesbians and bisexual women were much more visible on-screen. However, all stars who love other women in Hollywood must still share the beliefs of their foremothers concerning public discussion of their sexuality. With the exception of Amanda Bearse, a television star who came out in the 1990s under threat of a public outing, no female star in the film or television industries in Hollywood had publicly admitted to being lesbian until 1997.

Throughout the history of homosexuals in Hollywood, these men and women have sought to hide or disguise their sexuality. Due to the very public nature of the work and lives of Hollywood stars, this has often not been easy. Many of the lesbians in Hollywood married men, some of whom were gay, to disguise their sexuality from the general public. Though some of these women were actually bisexual, it would be very difficult to separate those who married men for the protection of their reputations and those who married men for pleasure.

## History

Any discussion of lesbians in Hollywood must begin with Alla Nazimova (1879–1945). Nazimova came to the film industry from Broadway, which had a large lesbian and bisexual contingent. In 1918 Nazimova moved to Hollywood, where she bought a large Spanish villa that was to later gain fame as the Garden of Allah, a chic hotel for entertainment industry luminaries. However, when Nazimova lived at this address, the house was well known in Hollywood circles as a meeting place for lesbians in Hollywood, especially those in the entertainment industry. These gatherings were known in the lesbian and gay community as "sewing circles," a phrase Nazimova is credited with coining.

As Metro Pictures highest-paid actress and one of the most popular movie stars in America, Nazimova had enormous power in Hollywood. The actress was also no stranger to scandal. However, due to her fame and her lesbianism, Nazimova's name was rarely seen in print in connection with these scandals. In 1920, Nazimova was alleged to have been the real respondent in Charlie Chaplin's (1889–1977) divorce from his eighteen-year-old wife, Mildred Harris Chaplin (1901–1944). Both of Rudolph Valentino's (1895–1926) wives, Jean Acker (1893–1978) and Natacha Rambova (1897–1966), were "protégées" of Nazimova, and it was she who introduced them to Valentino. After Rambova divorced Valentino in 1926, she alleged that the marriage had never been consummated. Natacha Rambova also played a role in Nazimova's swan song in motion pictures. In 1921, Nazimova left Metro, formed her own motion picture company, and decided to produce a film version of Oscar Wilde's (1854–1900) *Salome*. Nazimova hired Rambova to design the sets and costumes, which were based on the original illustrations by Aubrey Beardsley (1872–1898). As a further "homage" to Wilde, Nazimova employed an all-gay cast and played the lead herself. Unable to find financing for the film, Nazimova used her not inconsiderable personal fortune to pay for the picture. It was a box-office disaster and basically ended Nazimova's reign as a star of the first magnitude in Hollywood.

The atmosphere in the Hollywood lesbian community began to change in the late 1920s and early 1930s. This change was a reflection of three important developments: (1) the increased adoption by the general public of the morbidification of sexual relations between women promoted by some sexologists; (2) the rise of the studio system in Hollywood; and (3) the onset of economic problems connected with the Stock Market Crash of 1929 and the Great Depression. The effect of the heterosexual backlash and the rise of the companionate marriage in the mid- to late 1920s was to push women who loved women further into the closet. The rise of the studio system meant that, were these women ever to venture from that closet and be caught in an embarrassing situation in public, the news media would not print the story. Hard economic times made these women vulnerable to the demands of the studio bosses who protected them—vulnerable enough, for example, to agree to date or even marry a man in order to appear heterosexual when they actually were not. Hollywood had become, in effect, a company town.

Many lesbians and bisexual women in Hollywood in the 1930s and 1940s, especially those from Europe, gathered at the home of Berthold (1885–1953) and Salka Viertel (1889–1978). The Viertels were German émigrés who had come to Hollywood in 1928 to work in the film industry. Like Salka, most of the women who gathered at her home were "Gillette Blades"—that is, their sexuality "cut both ways." Some American-born actresses also fit into this category of actual or apparent bisexuality, while others were lesbians who adhered to the older model of the Boston marriage and lived with their lovers in what was purportedly a platonic relationship.

Following World War II, and with the rise of the Cold War in the late 1940s, the situation of Hollywood lesbians once again underwent a paradigm shift. After Communists, homosexuals were the favorite targets of witch-hunting politicians and bureaucrats, especially those of the House Un-American Activities Committee (HUAC). At this same time, scandal magazines began to print articles that openly identified homosexual stars as such. The tabloid *Confidential* was directly responsible for the end of Lizabeth Scott's (1922–) career in motion pictures when it accused her in print of "unnatural" sexual activity. Many of the lesbians and bisexual women who were married began spending more time with their spouses, and many who were unmarried rushed to the altar. Some of the homosexuals in Hollywood reacted to this climate of fear by becoming reactionary in their politics and cooperating with those carrying out the persecutions. Barbara Stanwyck (1907–1990) and her "beard" husband (a spouse who is taken by a woman who engages in homosexual behavior primarily to help disguise her lesbian activities) Robert Taylor (1911–1969) became archconservatives after World War II. Taylor, who was also gay, was the only actor to "name names" in front of HUAC. Salka Viertel was blacklisted and left the country. This climate of fear and paranoia among Hollywood homosexuals was to last well into the early 1960s.

## The Modern Era

By the mid-1960s, the countercultural revolution and the demise of the studio system helped change the situation of lesbians and bisexual women in Hollywood, at least on-screen. There were many more portrayals of lesbians or women loving women in the films of this era. Most of the lesbian characters were little more than stereotypes whose punishment or death at the end of the film was still a foregone conclusion. Sandy Dennis (1937–1992), an unmarried, lesbian actress, bravely chose to portray a lesbian character in the screen adaptation of D.H. Lawrence's *The Fox* (1968). It is noteworthy that the lesbian character's death was an addition to the screen version. By the early 1970s, "second wave" feminism, with its twin goals of the abolition of sexism and the empowerment of women, was helping improve this situation somewhat. It combated sexism and homophobia on-screen and encouraged women to participate in the creation of their own films and film images, with the result that screen portrayals of lesbians increased in both number and quality throughout the 1970s and 1980s. In the early 1990s, lesbians even enjoyed a brief popularity on-screen as part of the "lesbian chic" fad.

In 1997, television actor Ellen DeGeneres (1958–) broke the code of silence among lesbians in Hollywood. She became the first person in a starring role on television to publicly claim her homosexuality. DeGeneres's "coming out" was accompanied by much media attention. This event was capped off by a highly rated episode of her show in which she also "outed" the character she played on television. During the first season following her coming out, many of the shows addressed Ellen's newly revealed sexual orientation. At the end of the 1997–1998 season, the executives at ABC Television canceled the show. One reason given by the network's president for the cancellation was that the show had become "too gay." *Lisa Rhodes*

### Bibliography

Anger, Kenneth. *Hollywood Babylon*. New York: Bell, 1975, 1981.
———. *Hollywood Babylon II*. New York: Dutton, 1984.
Haleigh, Boze. *Hollywood Lesbians*. New York: Barricade, 1994.
Madsen, Axel. *The Sewing Circle*. New York: Birch Lane, 1995.

*See also* Arzner, Dorothy; Bisexuality; Dietrich, Marlene; Film, Alternative; Film, Mainstream; Garbo, Greta; Television

## Holtby, Winifred (1898–1935)

British novelist and journalist. Winifred Holtby grew up on a farm in Rudston, Yorkshire, a region of England that provides the settings for her first novel, *Anderby Wold* (1923); her third, *The Land of Green Ginger* (1927); and her last and best-known work, *South Riding* (1936). The household was dominated by her mother, Alice Holtby, whose energy and concern for social issues Holtby inherited.

Holtby was educated at Queen Margaret's School in Scarborough and later won a place at Somerville College, Oxford. She went up to Oxford in 1917 but left in the summer of 1918 to serve in the Women's Army Auxiliary Corps in Abbeville, France.

Upon her return to Oxford after the war, Holtby met Vera Brittain (1893–1970), a fellow history student, with whom she formed a lifetime partnership that was only briefly interrupted by Brittain's marriage to political scientist George Catlin (1896–1979). Brittain portrayed Holtby as the tall, golden-haired Daphne Lethbridge in her first novel, *The Dark Tide* (1923).

The bond between Brittain and Holtby was based on their interest in, and support of, each other's writing. Like Brittain, Holtby was a committed feminist, pacifist, and antiimperialist who fought against any form of oppression. In *Women and a Changing Civilization* (1934), Holtby asks for respect for "the richness of variety" in sexual expression. "We do not know how much of what we usually describe as 'feminine characteristics' are really 'masculine,' and how much of 'masculinity' is common to both sexes," she wrote. "We do not even know . . . whether the 'normal' sexual relationship is homo- or bi- or hetero-sexual."

Holtby's relationship with Brittain has been called lesbian by many despite Brittain's consistent denials. In *Testament of Friendship* (1940), Brittain's denial took the form of overemphasizing Holtby's relationship with a lifetime male friend, Harry Pearson (1896–?). Brittain even engineered a marriage proposal from Pearson to Holtby as the latter was dying. It is obvious, though, that Holtby's commitment to Brittain was far greater than her affection for Pearson. Unlike Brittain, Holtby had no fear of the gossip about them, even joking that Brittain's blonde daughter, Shirley, took after her.

In her fiction, Holtby stressed the importance of female friendship, though only once, in *The Crowded Street* (1924), does she portray such a friendship as erotic. Her portrayal of heterosexual marriage is invariably negative. A perceptive literary critic, in 1932 she wrote *Virginia Woolf*, the first book-length study of the author. She died of kidney disease at the age of thirty-six. *Jean E. Kennard*

## Bibliography

Berry, Paul, and Mark Bostridge. *Vera Brittain: A Life*. London: Chatto and Windus, 1995.

Gorham, Deborah. *Vera Brittain: A Feminist Life*. Oxford: Blackwell, 1996.

Kennard, Jean. *Vera Brittain and Winifred Holtby: A Working Partnership*. Hanover: University Press of New England, 1989.

Leonardi, Susan. *Dangerous by Degrees: Women at Oxford and the Somerville College Novelists*. New Brunswick, N.J.: Rutgers University Press, 1989.

*See also* Brittain, Vera Mary; Woolf, Virginia

## Homophobia

Colloquial expression that refers to negative, fearful, or hateful attitudes and behavior toward gays and lesbians. The term is a misnomer in that it implies an irrational fear of homosexuals similar to the panic of claustrophobia. Homophobia is a form of cultural prejudice rather than a manifestation of an individual phobia.

### Containing Sexuality

Like racism, homophobia is a complex social prejudice. Homophobia is an expression of a culture that is confused and inconsistent about sexual behavior. Attitudes and actions reflect both obsession with, and repression of, sexual desire. One basis of tacit agreement is that sexuality is something that must be contained. Homosexuality, along with adultery, prostitution, and pederasty, mark the boundaries by existing outside culturally approved forms of sexuality—what poet Rich (1980) refers to as "compulsory heterosexuality." Heterosexuality is a modern sociopolitical institution that organizes and restricts the expression of sexuality to vaginal-penile intercourse between a monogamous couple who represent gendered difference with the potential for biological reproduction. There are many deviations from this cultural ideal; these also vary in the degree to which they are tolerated. One reason lesbians and gay men are the object of so much cultural fear and loathing may be that homosexual sex is contained neither by gender nor by reproductive expectations of heterosexuality. Social historians note that the emergence of a sexual binary in the nineteenth century posits heterosexuality as natural and socially desirable by contrasting it with homosexuality, which is characterized as unnatural and immoral.

This binary represents the general tendency in modern Western thought to conflate morality and nature. According to this cultural equation, sexual desire is a manifestation of a natural drive to reproduce. The moral, disciplined individual contains this desire within the bounds of heterosexual monogamy. These attitudes are reflected in clinical, social, and religious definitions of the homosexual as cursed, perverted, sexually obsessed, evil, and, until recently, mentally and physically sick. Popular fiction in the 1950s and 1960s depicted lesbians as evil-minded, possessed daughters of the devil, nature's mistakes, and the like.

### Gender

Understanding homophobia is complicated by the strong link between gender and sexuality in U.S. culture. Gender is the basic criterion by which to select sexual partners. The violation of expected gender behavior elicits taunting, prejudice, and physical and social abuse. Frequent targets of this prejudice include the mannish lesbian and the effeminate gay male. Both evoke stereotypes that represent violations of gender expectations and hint of sexual transgressions. Many acts of violence extend to transgendered persons. It is difficult to know if attackers are provoked by what they assume to be a sexual aberration or a gender violation. Given the tight connection between gender and sexuality, it is likely that any deviation is perceived as a threat to heterosexuality. In the 1990s, Lambda Legal Defense documented several cases of murdered transgendered persons in which the murderer was released by the courts. The rationale offered in each case was that to arouse sexual desire in another under "false gender pretense" was to invite violent "self-defense" when the pretense was revealed. This rationale can be interpreted as a manifestation of homophobia; individuals who do not conform to the expected norms of gender and sexuality do not deserve social justice.

### Prejudice, Discrimination, and Violence

Expressions of homophobia include verbal assaults and derisive joking; negative stereotypical media representations; discrimination in employment, education, housing, medical research, and legal defense; physical attack; and tacit approval of gay bashing. Historians D'Emilio and Freedman (1988) report that, during the House Un-American Activities Committee (HUAC) meetings, more people lost their jobs because they were homosexual than because of alleged associations with communism. Their point is that discrimination against homosexuals is driven by homophobia and is persistent and common in the United States. Black Panther leader Huey Newton suggested that homosexuals may be the most feared people in the United States and, therefore, the most oppressed. In 1987, the United States Department of Justice reported that homosexuals are the most frequent victims of hate violence. The extent to which homophobia is an American institution is indicated in the decisions of law-enforcement officials and judges who consider homosexuality sufficient grounds for justifying acts of prejudice, discrimination, and violence. In addition to discrimination in employment, housing, and medical treatment, homophobia affects lesbians through court decisions that use lesbianism as grounds for denying child custody in divorce proceedings.

## Internalized Homophobia

In a culture that marks sex with shame and casts the homosexual as a primary villain, most lesbians and gay men fear negative consequences for revealing their sexuality. The majority experience rejection by their families, friends, and religious and working communities when they reveal their homosexuality. "Coming out" is an ongoing process. A lesbian must decide continually whether or not to voice information indicative of a deviant sexuality in a culture that otherwise assumes she is heterosexual. This process involves wrestling with, and reconciling, family, peer, and religious expectations and personal feelings and experiences. Fear of rejection and a lack of positive role models can lead to confusion and self-hatred. Information compiled by the United States Department of Health and Human Services in 1991 indicates that lesbian youth are two to three times more likely to attempt suicide than their heterosexual peers. Gay and lesbian youth account for 30 percent of all completed youth suicides. In contrast, religious and community organizations that endeavor to understand and support gay and lesbian youth have been successful in reconciling family conflict and keeping these youth off the streets.

## Social Movements

The social protests and political activism associated with lesbian and gay history can be interpreted as a response to widespread, organized manifestations of homophobia. Several observers have suggested that the struggle for gay and lesbian rights is *the*

civil rights issue of the 1990s. This history represents a fight for rights that are constitutionally guaranteed to all Americans but frequently withheld from homosexuals. Many local and national lesbian and gay groups and direct actions have been organized as a direct response to political initiatives designed to legalize discrimination against homosexuals. The federal Defense of Marriage Act (1996), which restricts marriage to a union between a man and a woman, is one such case. Marriage between same-sex couples poses no legal threat or loss of benefits to heterosexual couples. It is difficult to interpret the urgency with which states have pursued legislation to restrict same-sex marriages as anything other than a display of mass homophobia. In the 1990s, there was a focused attempt to enact legislation that would limit the civil rights of gay men and lesbians. These measures included statutory guarantees for such policies as the refusal to hire, the right to fire, the right to refuse housing, the refusal of adoption, and the refusal of marriage rights for lesbians and gays. By the mid-1990s, variations of all or some of these measure had appeared on ballots in forty-two states. This sort of legislation is indicative of the extent to which homophobia is culturally legitimated as an institutionalized form of prejudice. Critics who suggest that antidiscrimination laws are "special rights" fail to comprehend the extensive reach of homophobic actions into the everyday lives of lesbians, gays, bisexuals, and transgendered persons.    *Jodi O'Brien*

### Bibliography

D'Emilio, John, and Estelle Freedman. *Intimate Matters: A History of Sexuality in the United States*. New York: Harper and Row, 1988.

Plummer, Ken. "Speaking Its Name: Inventing a Lesbian and Gay Studies." In *Modern Homosexualities*. Ed. Ken Plummer. London: Routledge, 1992, pp. 3–28.

Rich, Adrienne. "Compulsory Heterosexuality and Lesbian Existence." *Signs: Journal of Women in Culture and Society* 5:4 (1980), 631–660.

Sedgwick, Eve Kosofsky. *Epistemology of the Closet*. Berkeley: University of California Press, 1990.

Singer, Bennett L., and David Deschamps. *Gay and Lesbian Stats*. New York: New Press, 1994.

Tiefer, Lenore. *Sex Is Not a Natural Act*. Boulder, Colo.: Westview, 1995.

***See also*** Coming Out; Discrimination; Gender; Heterosexism; Prejudice; Violence

## Homosexuality

Term originally used to define same-sex attraction. The term itself is a painful philological combination of Greek and Latin elements, the first part, *homo-*, being Greek for "same," and the second part coming from the Latin adjective *sexualis*. Although commonly believed to be an invention of nineteenth-century medical practitioners, the word itself, and the concept it represents, has always been immersed in the politics of state control of individuals and their resistance to that control.

The word first appeared in Germany in 1869 in two political letters anonymously authored by a translator named Karoly Maria Kertbeny (1824–1882). Kertbeny's letters argue against a proposed law that would extend the Prussian antisodomy law to the entire German Confederation. The confusion surrounding the word's invention and its inventor (Kertbeny himself is sometimes identified as a physician) is understandable. Beginning in the second half of the nineteenth century, Europe witnessed an explosion in medical and scientific speculation about the causes of crime and disease. Sodomy, once punished by the church, had been criminalized by many of the central European states. At mid-century, the "cause" of this criminal behavior became the subject of much theoretical investigation, although not exclusively by physicians or scientists. Novelists, criminologists, even tax assessors joined physicians in offering explanations for these criminalized sexual behaviors. With greater frequency as the century progressed, these explanations began to reflect the belief that the preference for same-sex sodomy was inborn, a condition over which the sodomite had little control. By 1869, Kertbeny's belief that same-sex preferences indicated an underlying and unchanging trait was no longer new, but his word for this new identity—*Homosexualitat*—was. By the end of the nineteenth century, it would eclipse the many others terms, such as "inversion" and "contrary sexual instinct," that had been advanced for same-sex attraction.

Many of these early "sexologists," as they called themselves, argued that homosexuals should not be punished as criminals because the homosexual was not someone who chose to break the law or commit a sin. The medicalization of homosexuality—a shift away from notions of sodomy as moral licentiousness and criminal behavior—was extremely important. Magnus Hirschfeld (1868–1935), founder of the Scientific Humanitarian Committee in 1897, claimed that, as a defense witness, his testimony had saved those on trial for sodomy from six thousand years of imprisonment. But not all physicians were interested in defending individuals from state prosecution. For many, homosexuality represented a disease, a physical degeneracy, or a mental illness, the cause for which needed to be diagnosed and the cure for which needed to be discovered. Medical theories about the causes of homosexuality continued to proliferate into the twentieth century, and many who were identified as homosexuals were subjected to physical experimentation, psychiatric examination, and medical institutionalization, often against their will. The search in the late twentieth century for biological and genetic causes of homosexuality indicates how persistent the medical model continues to be.

This understanding of homosexuality as a medical disorder entered official government discourse in the United States early in the twentieth century as a disqualification for military service, and later from all employment with the federal government. It was this repressive history that led many gay liberationists in the second half of the twentieth century to reject the term as one that had been defined and regulated by "experts." They preferred "gay" as a self-ascribed term to indicate same-sex orientation, and, by the 1970s, it had replaced "homosexual" in common usage, even by heterosexuals. During this same period, lesbian feminists argued that both "gay" and "homosexual" were terms that referred primarily to men, and "lesbian" replaced both as the standard for women. Despite the increasingly widespread usage of lesbian and gay during the 1970s, many continued to employ the term "homosexuality." In fact, it was not until July 1987, that the *New York Times* allowed anything but the word "homosexual" to be used in the newspaper's pages to refer to gay men and lesbians.

Homosexuality, both as a concept of same-sex desire and as a term to represent that concept, has undergone many changes in its more than 125-year history. At the center of each of these changes has always been a political struggle between the identification of those individuals society has defined as deviant and the counterassertion of identity by those individuals so defined. Despite the endeavors of science and medicine, homosexuality, as both a concept and a term, was born of resistance and remains firmly entrenched in the territory of politics.

*Gary Lehring*

### Bibliography

Bullough, Vern. *Sexual Variance in Society and History*. New York: Wiley, 1976.

Greenberg, David F. *The Social Construction of Homosexualities*. Chicago: University of Chicago Press, 1989.

Katz, Jonathan. *Gay American History*. New York: Thomas Cromwell, 1976.

Lehring, Gary. "Gay Rights Movement." In *Protest, Power, and Change*. Ed. Roger Powers and William Vogele. New York: Garland, 1997.

Plummer, Kenneth, ed. *The Making of the Modern Homosexual*. London: Hutchinson, 1987.

*See also* Gay Liberation Movement; Sexology

## Human Rights

Right to life, liberty, and security of the person; freedom from torture and from cruel, inhuman, or degrading treatment or punishment; freedom of conscience, expression, and association; inherent dignity of the human person. The concept of human rights refers to both specific rights set forth in international treaties and a system of values premised on the inherent worth and equality of all human beings.

The most important international human rights document, the Universal Declaration of Human Rights (UDHR), was adopted by the United Nations in 1948. It affirms that every human being has, in addition to the rights mentioned above, the right to equal pay for equal work, a standard of living adequate for health and well-being, education, freedom from slavery, and the equal protection of the law, regardless of race, color, sex, language, religion, political or other opinion, national or social origin, property, birth, or other status.

The concept of human rights emerged out of the eighteenth-century European Enlightenment and was referred to then as "natural rights" or the "rights of man." These doctrines held that rights belonged to a person and were not bestowed upon him or her by virtue of citizenship or religion. The United States Declaration of Independence (1776) and the French Declaration of the Rights of Man and of Citizen (1789) are examples of eighteenth-century doctrines of natural rights.

Most early proponents of human rights did not see the concept applying to all humans equally. Despite proclaiming that "all men are created equal," the Declaration of Independence failed to question the institution of slavery, the genocide of American Indians, or the political subjection of women. In *On Liberty* (1859), John Stuart Mill (1806–1873) held

that his doctrine of freedom from government interference should not apply to "barbarians." Although proponents of human rights no longer hold these views, critics of the idea of universal human rights argue that it continues to reflect the interests and perspectives of the West and to ignore cultural differences. Proponents of human rights point out that human rights treaties such as the UDHR are the product of an international consensus that included representatives from a wide range of cultures, political viewpoints, and geographical areas.

Although no international human rights treaties explicitly mention lesbians or sexual orientation, the United Nations and regional intergovernmental bodies, such as the European Court of Human Rights, have begun to interpret these treaties to include and protect lesbian and gay people and those who engage in same-gender sexual practices. Some nongovernmental human rights monitoring agencies have identified the discrimination and mistreatment of sexual minorities as human rights violations. For example, in 1991, Amnesty International changed its policy to consider people arrested for their homosexual identity or for engaging in private, consensual same-gender sex as prisoners of conscience. Other human rights organizations, including the Lawyers' Committee for Human Rights, the International Human Rights Law Group, Human Rights Watch, and the Center for Women's Global Leadership, among others, have followed suit. Locally based human rights groups have also pressed individual governments to end discrimination on the basis of sexual orientation. In 1996, South Africa became the first country in the world to prohibit discrimination on the basis of sexual orientation in its constitution.

Human rights violations against lesbians, bisexual women, women who are single by choice, transsexual, and transgendered women take two forms: persecution carried out by governments ("state-sponsored" persecution) and persecution carried out by families and other private individuals. The most common forms of state-sponsored persecution are violence against sexual minorities carried out by police and paramilitary groups and laws that impose penalties on same-gender sexual practices and lesbian and gay identity. In the United States, some states have laws that punish consensual adult same-gender sex with up to life imprisonment. In the Bahamas, the government's Sexual Offenses and Domestic Violence Act of 1989 punishes same-gender sex with up to twenty years' imprisonment. In

**H** Iran, those who engage in same-gender sexual practices may be executed.

Although lesbians are less likely than gay men to be targeted by these forms of state-sponsored persecution, they are much more likely to suffer from persecution carried out in the private sphere by families and communities enforcing prevailing norms about women's roles. The failure to recognize how profoundly human rights abuses against lesbians are shaped by gender has often obscured important differences between lesbians and gay men and has contributed to the relative invisibility of lesbian-specific issues. Examples of this type of persecution include violence against women suspected to be lesbians or bisexual women by husbands or other male relatives; involuntary psychiatric treatment; rape and forced marriage; and the separation of mothers from their children.

For example, in 1996, the state of Florida denied Mary Ward custody of her daughter, awarding custody instead to her ex-husband, a convicted murderer, on the grounds that, as a lesbian, she was an unfit mother. The story of a twenty-four-year-old lesbian from Zimbabwe is also typical of this type of human rights violation: "My parents decided to look for a husband on my behalf so they brought several boys home to meet me but I was not interested so in the end they forced an old man on me. They locked me in a room and brought him everyday to rape me so I would fall pregnant and be forced to marry him" (quoted in Rosenbloom 1996). Human rights violations against lesbians and women who do not conform to the dominant heterosexual norms of their culture are affected not only by gender, but also by race, nationality, political status, religion, ability, language, class, and age.

Advocates of lesbian human rights urge international organizations and countries to recognize that lesbian human rights include freedom from torture, imprisonment, or execution based on sexual orientation; freedom from forced marriage, rape, physical and psychological violence, and involuntary psychiatric treatment; rights to child custody and visitation, adoption, foster parenting, access to donor insemination, domestic partnership, and same-gender marriage; and equal access to education, employment, and health. Some lesbian rights advocates base these rights claims on established fundamentals of human rights laws, such as rights of freedom of association, conscience, and expression; others base lesbian rights claims on an emerging right of sexual self-determination.

[The author wishes to thank Shannon Minter of the National Center for Lesbian Rights for his help with this article.]     *Paisley Currah*

## Bibliography

Dorf, Julie, and Gloria Careaga Pérez. "Discrimination and the Tolerance of Difference: International Lesbian Human Rights." In *Women's Rights, Human Rights*. Ed. Julie Peters and Andrea Wolper. New York: Routledge, 1995, pp. 324–334.

Heinze, Eric. *Sexual Orientation: A Human Right*. Dordrecht: M. Nijhoff, 1995.

Minter, Shannon. "Lesbians and Asylum: Overcoming Barriers to Access." In *Asylum Based on Sexual Orientation*. Ed. Sydney Levy. San Francisco: International Gay and Lesbian Human Rights Commission and Lambda Legal Defense and Education Fund, 1996, pp. I.B, 3–16.

Rosenbloom, Rachel. "Introduction." In *Unspoken Rules: Sexual Orientation and Women's Human Rights*. Ed. Rachel Rosenbloom. London: Cassell, 1996, pp. ix–xxvii.

*See also* Enlightenment, European; Immigration; Legal Theory, Lesbian; Rights

## Humor

Humor is an engaging social behavior and, therefore, requires that those participating share a common view of the world, with shared values and interpretations. Without a common perspective among members of a group, "humor" falls flat. What one group may find very funny, another will interpret as insulting, degrading, or pointless. Humor is a means of establishing and affirming group membership. Until the second half of the twentieth century, much lesbian humor, humor constructed by lesbians for lesbians, was strictly in-group and occurred only informally, as spontaneous jokes or stories told among lesbians when they gathered in bars or at private parties. Because lesbians did not control any media, jokes were spontaneous and situational and worked only in the contexts in which they occurred. Sigmund Freud (1856–1939) argued that the intent of an in-group joke is to deflect the criticism or hostility directed by the group in power (heterosexuals) against the powerless in-group (lesbians) and convert it into more tolerable forms. More recent work by clinical psychologists not only appears to substantiate Freud's theory regarding this function of in-group humor, but also suggests that such humor provides a means of transcending the pain inflicted by prejudiced people. For example, generations of lesbians have laughed at the unwitting stupidity of the assertion "It's just a phase," because it's been used so often to trivialize their experience. Laughter affirms that shared experience and blunts the hurt.

Informal lesbian humor, the jokes exchanged in social contexts, arises from a shared perspective and serves to deepen the bonds among lesbians. Such humor is highly situational and, often, depending on the context in which it occurs and the women involved, is extended and expanded on as individuals join in with their own contributions. The lesbians who participate in these humorous dialogues become part of the group if they began as strangers; if they were already friends, the humor affirms the bonds within the group. Because the shared joking is part of the bonding process among lesbians, they tend not to use people outside the group as scapegoats but rely instead on experiences familiar to the women within the group. Its subjects, when drawing on lesbian-specific experiences, include the coming out process, lesbian sex and relationships, reactions to the beliefs and behaviors of hostile heterosexuals, and politics.

There were comic moments and humor recorded, both gentle and sharp, in literature produced by lesbians early in the twentieth century, in the writing of Gertrude Stein (1874–1946), for example. Humor grounded in lesbian experience, however, is found only later in the twentieth century, as it sometimes is in the novels of Ann Bannon (1937–). But it was not until the 1970s, as a new group self-consciousness arose, inspired by the women's liberation movement, that lesbian in-group humor drawing on lesbians' experiences emerged. Rita Mae Brown's *Rubyfruit Jungle* (1973) was a huge success, largely because it was a funny lesbian book and there had never been such a thing. In 1974, Meg Christian recorded "Ode to a Gym Teacher," a wry song about a teenage girl's crush on her gym teacher. It was an experience that her audiences could identify with, laughing with her at their own youthful crushes and, thereby, transforming the pain and confusion they felt as adolescent lesbians trying to understand themselves in a hostile society that provided only a very narrow, destructive context in which they could interpret their feelings. Christian offered lesbians a means of laughing together at shared memories, one of the highest func-

tions of humor in U.S. culture. Laughter shared with others is both healing *and* empowering.

By the 1980s, specifically lesbian humor could be found in the full range of genres—as comedy, parody, and satire—and in many formats, ranging from conventional literary forms (the novels of British writer Anna Livia, for example) and newspaper columns and articles (such as those written by Jorjet Harper and Marilyn Murphy in the then-thriving gay and lesbian media, respectively), to cartoons and comic strips (such as those created by Alison Bechdel, Diane Germain, Jennifer Camper, and Diane DiMassa), song lyrics (Sue Fink's "Leaping Lesbians," for example), standup comedy (as performed by Kate Clinton and Karen Williams, for example), skits and monologues (such as Lily Tomlin's), movies (such as *Oranges Are Not the Only Fruit*, based on the prize-winning 1985 novel by British author Jeanette Winterson), and an outpouring of witty slogans found on buttons, bumper stickers, and T-shirts (such as We Are Not Just Friends, Nuke a Gay Whale for Christ, and RU 1 2?).

The topics of contemporary structured lesbian humor, humor designed to be interpreted and repeatable in larger contexts, echo the concerns and experiences of lesbians found in spontaneous in-group humor. In one of her recorded monologues, for example, Kate Clinton reminisces about her Catholic girlhood, gratefully acknowledging the strength and dexterity her tongue developed as she manipulated the communion wafer in her mouth. "Getting the joke" did not require that a lesbian be Catholic or even Christian. In a cartoon, an Alison Bechdel character "cracks" under the strain of trying to decide what to wear to meet another lesbian's parents. Lesbians understood the anxiety such a meeting created, whether they had personally experienced it or not. Lily Tomlin defended her ability to play a heterosexual woman in the film *Moment by Moment* (1978) because she had watched "them" and could imitate how "they" walk and talk, parodying all of the heterosexual actresses who have used a similar explanation for their ability to act lesbian parts.

Debates within lesbian communities have been the most fruitful sources for all kinds of lesbian humor, enabling lesbians to laugh at their most serious preoccupations: vegetarianism, activism, psychotherapy, goddess worship, fashion and style, any behavior that groups of lesbians categorize as PC (politically correct) or PI (politically incorrect). Alix Dobkin once joked that lesbians can all identify

**H** each other because "we all have the same junk on top of our dressers": crystals, shells, labryses, odd feathers, river rocks. The abundance of humor centering on lesbians' lives among their peers drew on the existence of lesbian communities and served to create the sense of a larger lesbian culture to which one might belong. At the same time, lesbian humor is particularly vulnerable to changes in both mainstream (heterosexual) culture and the more visible "gay community."

Humor created to be shared with a larger (listening or reading) audience presupposes that all lesbians have had similar experiences and participate in a more homogeneous lesbian culture. The publishing and recording of lesbian humor on audiocassettes, compact discs, and television, as well as in print media, was primarily a phenomenon of the lesbian feminist movement of the 1970s and 1980s. Although not all lesbian feminists shared *exactly* identical experiences, there were a sufficient number to create laughter across a wide range of media and within a variety of contexts. More recent has been the attempted crossover of lesbian humor into the mainstream media, with, for example, Suzanne Westenhoefer's comedy special on HBO (Home Box Office) and the appearance of lesbian comedians in a gay series hosted by Kate Clinton on PBS (the Public Broadcasting System). The series, however, was short lived, perhaps because there is not sufficient overlap between the lesbian and gay (male) cultures to provide the necessary "shared worldview" that would elicit laughter.

In the 1990s, even as earlier forms of lesbian humor persisted, debates over the meaning of the word "lesbian," the existence of a "lesbian identity," and the diversity of lesbian experience led to a more fragmented, less viable idea of a "lesbian community" and, as a result, new forms of lesbian humor. One might wonder, then, whether lesbians still share the in-group humor of earlier decades. As long as lesbians remain a stigmatized group, denied the rights that heterosexuals take for granted, in-group humor will continue to provide the empowerment and release of laughter. The joyous and raucous reactions at music festivals, concerts, Lesbian and Gay Pride events, and feminist conferences show that a wide range of shared experiences still exists among lesbians that continues to produce a recognizably lesbian humor.

*Susan J. Wolfe*
*Julia Penelope*

## Bibliography

Painter, Dorothy S. "Lesbian Humor as a Normalization Device." In *Communication, Language, and Sex*. Ed. Cynthia L. Berryman and Virginia A. Eman. Rowley, Mass.: Newbury House, 1980, pp. 132–148.

Stanley, Julia [Penelope] and Susan W. Wolfe [Robbins]. "Mother Wit: Tongue in Cheek." In *Lavender Culture*. Ed. Karla Jay and Allen Young. New York: Jove, 1978, pp. 299–307.

Stanley, Julia P., and Susan W. Robbins. "Lesbian Humor." *Women: A Journal of Liberation* 5:1 (1977), 26–29.

Wolfe, Susan J., and Julia Penelope. "Crooked and Straight in Academia." In *Pulling Our Own Strings*. Ed. Gloria Kaufman and Mary Kay Blakely. Bloomington: Indiana University Press, 1980, p. 119.

*See also* Bannon, Ann; Brown, Rita Mae; Camp; Cartoons and Comic Books; Comedy, Standup; Stein, Gertrude

# I

## Identity

An individual's perception or sense of self. Hence, lesbian identity refers to a woman's own perception of herself as a lesbian. The idea of basing personal identity on one's sexuality is found primarily in modern, European-derived cultures, and lesbian identity, in particular, is even more historically and culturally specific. In other cultures and other historical periods, some individuals had sexual contact with members of their own sex, but such individuals were not identified as a different "type" of person from those whose affections ran toward the other sex. Jonathan Katz and other historians have traced the concept of a "homosexual type" of person back to Europe in the 1860s, and Randolph Trumbach argues that its roots can be found in eighteenth-century England. "Gay" identity arose in the United States in the mid-1900s when individuals classified as "homosexual" began to reject beliefs that they were sinful or mentally ill. "Gay" identity originally encompassed gay women as well as gay men. With the advent of the "second wave" of feminism in the late 1960s and early 1970s, however, women who found themselves second-class citizens in both the gay and the feminist movements embraced "lesbian" identity to distinguish themselves, politically and socially, from both gay men and heterosexual women. Since then, lesbians have created additional identities; some women identify themselves as "dykes," "queers," or "lipstick lesbians," and an extensive lesbian subculture has developed.

## Lesbian Political Identity

Because of this history, many women use "lesbian" identity to refer not only to their sexual attractions to and sexual experiences with other women, but also as a reflection of their feminist politics and their participation in lesbian culture. In fact, for some women, politics and culture supersede sexual attractions and behavior as bases for lesbian identity. This "desexualization" of lesbian identity began in the 1970s, as some lesbian feminists—notably the Radicalesbians, the Furies Collective, and Rich (1980)—argued that the heart of lesbianism is "woman-identification" (that is, a political and social commitment to women) and that lesbians were potentially more feminist than heterosexual women because they were independent of men. Redefining woman-identification as the heart of lesbianism made it theoretically possible for any woman to call herself a lesbian. This gave rise to "political lesbians" who identify as lesbian primarily for political reasons and might or might not feel sexually attracted to other women. These women generally see themselves as having "chosen" lesbian identity, whereas other lesbians, dubbed "realesbians" in the 1970s, often believe that their lesbian identities reflect an inherent quality within themselves that they cannot choose to have but can only choose to acknowledge.

The deemphasis of sexuality as a part of lesbian identity facilitated the building of a "lesbian history" that includes women who did not identify as lesbian because they lived in times and cultures without a concept of "lesbianism" and whose sexual lives are unknown to later generations because they were not recorded. For example, women who participated in nineteenth-century "romantic friendships" or "Boston marriages" might or might not have been sexually involved, but many modern lesbians consider them their cultural foremothers because they loved each other psychically and were relatively independent of men. This lesbian history is part of lesbian culture and enhances the belief many lesbians have that lesbianism is a timeless and enduring quality that exists regardless of whether it is recognized by a given individual or in a given culture. Social scientists refer to such a quality as an "essence." When lesbian identity is conceptualized as a reflection of lesbian "essence," as opposed to a chosen political orientation or lifestyle, lesbian identity becomes analogous to racial and ethnic identities. Epstein (1987) and others have described the ways in which modern gay and lesbian identities and politics have been modeled on black/African American and white ethnic identities and political movements.

## Social Construction of Identity

Lesbian, feminist, and "queer theory" scholars generally take a critical view of the concept of lesbian identity as a reflection of lesbian "essence" but do not see it as a matter of choice either. Given the historical and cultural specificity of the concept, many argue that lesbian identity is "socially constructed." In other words, if the concept of a lesbian did not exist, women would not be able to conceptualize or identify themselves as lesbians and would choose another rubric for the description of their feelings, sexual histories, cultural connections, and politics. In a very real sense, then, lesbians would not exist; another type of person would exist instead. Examples include the two-spirit traditions of some Native American groups. A two-spirit person is not considered a man or a woman but, rather, a third gender. A female two-spirit person usually adopts a masculine social role and, in some tribes, marries a woman. Any sexual contact occurring within such a relationship would be between two females, but it is not traditionally conceptualized as homosexual or lesbian. Two-spiritedness involves one's gender, not one's sexuality. In such tribes, lesbians per se do not exist, just as two-spirited people do not exist in traditional Anglo-European cultures.

Carrying social constructionist arguments further, Butler (1990) describes lesbian identity as "performative" (that is, an identity that is created and re-created through symbolic representations of the self). In effect, a woman becomes a lesbian by portraying herself as a lesbian to herself and others. Her identity as a lesbian is her performance of that identity. Alternatively, Fuss (1991) defines identity in terms of "difference," arguing that "homosexuality" (or lesbianism) derives its meaning in distinction from "heterosexuality." Lesbian identity, therefore, provides a woman with a sense of lesbian selfhood and makes her a lesbian by distinguishing her from the alternative—heterosexual women. Another alternative is to understand lesbian identity as a description of a woman's social location. Rust (1996) argues that, by identifying herself as a lesbian, a woman marks herself as living at a certain cultural and historical moment in which that identity is available and describes her social position vis-à-vis other women, social groups, and social institutions. For example, lesbian identity describes a woman as a probable outsider to the institution of legally recognized marriage. Several theorists note that having an identity provides one with a "subject position" (that is, a social position from which to speak). In other words, a woman with a lesbian identity has a different perspective and speaks with a different authority than does a woman with a heterosexual identity, especially on issues involving sexuality and sexual identity.

Because social and political factors enter into a woman's decision to identify as a lesbian, and lesbian identity means different things to different women, women with lesbian identities vary greatly in their actual sexual feelings and behaviors. Several research studies, including studies by Chapman and Brannock (1987) and by Rust (1992), have shown that 80 to 90 percent of women who identify as lesbian have had heterosexual contact, and two-thirds of lesbians say they are sexually attracted to men as well as women. In other words, many lesbian-identified women actually have "bisexual" feelings and sexual histories. But bisexual identity is not as culturally available as lesbian identity, cannot connect one to as extensive a subculture, and is perceived primarily as a sexual, not a political, identity. Both Western mainstream culture and lesbian subculture generally discredit the notion of bisexuality. In lesbian subculture, heterosexual experiences are often explained away as the result of heterosexual socialization, and women who identify as bisexual are encouraged to "finish" coming out as lesbian. As a result, even though adult (age eighteen and older) bisexual experience is ten times more common than exclusively lesbian experience among women, Laumann and his colleagues (1994) found that twice as many women consider themselves "homosexual" (including "lesbian") as "bisexual," with one in a hundred women in the United States identifying herself as "homosexual" or "lesbian."

Identifying as a lesbian involves different issues for women of different racial or ethnic cultural backgrounds. For some Latinas and Asian American women whose cultures of origin emphasize the family rather than personal sexuality as a basis for identity, coming out might be perceived as a rejection of their families and their ethnicity. Latinas, Asian, and African American women, and other women of color, for whom the support of their racial or ethnic communities is important in the face of societal racism, risk losing that support if they come out. Whereas white lesbians find alternative sources of support in lesbian communities, lesbians of color often find that support compromised by the predominantly white character of those communities. Integrating a lesbian identity with a minoritized racial or ethnic identity can be difficult. Some women of color who identify as lesbians are seen by their ethnic peers as succumbing to white influence. The irony is that many non-European cultures were more accepting of same-sex relations prior to contact with white cultures; homophobia, not homosexuality, is the cultural import.                     *Paula C. Rust*

### Bibliography

Butler, Judith. *Gender Trouble: Feminism and the Subversion of Identity*. New York: Routledge, 1990.

Chapman, Beata E., and JoAnn C. Brannock. "Proposed Model of Lesbian Identity Development: An Empirical Examination." *Journal of Homosexuality* 14 (1987), 69–80.

Epstein, Steven. "Gay Politics, Ethnic Identity: The Limits of Social Constructionism." *Socialist Review* 17:2 (1987), 10–54.

Fuss, Diana, ed. *Inside/Out: Lesbian Theories, Gay Theories*. New York: Routledge, 1991.

Laumann, Edward O., John H. Gagnon, Robert T. Michael, and Stuart Michaels. *The Social Organization of Sexuality: Sexual Practices in the United States*. Chicago: University of Chicago Press, 1994.

Rich, Adrienne. "Compulsory Heterosexuality and Lesbian Existence." *Signs: Journal of Women in Culture and Society* 5:4 (1980), 631–660.

Rust, Paula C. "The Politics of Sexual Identity: Sexual Attraction and Behavior among Lesbian and Bisexual Women." *Social Problems* 39:4 (1992), 366–386.

———. "Sexual Identity and Bisexual Identities: The Struggle for Self-Description in a Changing Sexual Landscape." In *Queer Studies: A Lesbian, Gay, Bisexual, and Transgender Anthology*. Ed. Brett Beemyn and Mickey Eliason. New York: New York University Press, 1996, pp. 64–86.

*See also* Bisexuality; Essentialism; Identity Politics; Performativity; Radicalesbians; Sexual Orientation and Preference; Social-Construction Theory; Two-Spirit; Woman-Identified Woman

## Identity Politics

Phrase used to describe those movements, developed largely since the 1960s, that focus on oppressions related to positions of status or identity.

### History and Characteristics

Identity politics began as a concept that distinguished newer social movements, such as civil rights and feminism, from earlier Left, class-centered analyses. These earlier movements often ignored or denied the needs of women, homosexuals, and people of color as they argued that the overthrow of capitalism would end other oppressions. In response, lesbian and feminist groups, such as the Combahee River Collective (Boston, Massachusetts), decided to place their identities and oppressions at the center of their analysis. Rather than try to fit their lives into the framework prescribed by earlier theories, these groups used the particular concerns arising from their daily lives to further understanding of larger social structures.

Early lesbian feminist identity politics linked the oppression of lesbians to the position of women and people of color. The work of lesbians of color has been particularly important to this project. Rather than divert energy from "larger" issues, as opponents sometimes charge, this work inspired many lesbians to make connections between personal life and more traditional "political" issues, such as war, imperialism, and the global economy. An identification as women, or as lesbians, has led many to work across racial and national lines for the common good. At the same time, practitioners of identity politics have called their "home" communities to account for injustice. Lesbians have demanded acceptance and equality within their communities of origin in addition to forming lesbian communities.

### Critiques

Identity politics has come under fire both from conservative critics who disagree with progressive agendas and from other progressives who fear that

I identity politics leads to a splintering and loss of energy. The first group has ridiculed concerns about racism, sexism, and homophobia, suggesting that activists want "special rights" or totalitarian control over public speech and thought. This criticism has largely served as a cover for a reactionary agenda that would roll back the gains made by women, lesbians and gays, and people of color.

The second group of critics is made up of people who often share a political agenda and an identity with those practicing identity politics but who think that the current state of identity politics reduces the possibility of real transformation. Writers such as bell hooks have argued that "identity" becomes too narrow a basis for politics. Rather than ask whether people share a political vision and agenda, practitioners of identity politics may, instead, demand uniformity in the name of a shared identity. For example, lesbian-feminism became embroiled in the 1980s in questions about whether particular practices and, therefore, the people engaged in them were "truly" lesbian. Barry (1982) argued that sadomasochism between lesbians was not "lesbianism," and communities became embroiled in controversies about what "real lesbianism" is. Although the issues raised were important ones, the focus on identity rather than on questions such as Is this a good thing for us to do? and should this be a matter of public concern? often led to polarizations and feelings of rejection. Thus, hooks (1984) argued that, rather than ask whether someone "is a feminist," one should ask whether she or he supports feminism. This allows people to work for change with those who are "different" as well as those with whom they share an identity. Other authors, such as Haraway (1985), have proposed that feminist politics should be based on affinity rather than identity. Because affinity includes both a sense of bondedness and a reflective distance, it is less absolute and inflexible than identity may come to be.

In the 1990s, political theorists began to think in terms of identification rather than identity, to examine the processes whereby groups come to see themselves as "like" some others and to think of themselves as "one of them/us." Such examination allows one to consider the social issues that originally motivated identity politics without excluding as allies those who do not share a full identity.

Along with problems of exclusivity, identity politics faces another challenge. Following the typical pattern of northern European and North American politics, stigmatized groups have increasingly come to focus on mainstream political action. Thus, the National Gay and Lesbian Task Force (NGLTF), the National Center for Lesbian Rights, the Campaign for Military Service (which led the unsuccessful 1993 fight for an end to the ban on queers in the military), and the Human Rights Campaign are all participants in identity politics. With the exception of NGLTF, however, the newer groups do not link the position of lesbians to other major social issues. Instead, they fight in legislatures and the courts for equal rights in employment, marriage, housing, and credit. This sort of activity is not substantially different from mainstream interest-group politics. In such a process, groups jockey to "get theirs" in the system without changing the political, economic, and social structures that continue to generate stigmatized identities.

As long as lesbians are excluded and stigmatized on the basis of their lesbianism, there will be a continuing development of identity politics. For all of its pitfalls, identity politics represents the increasing democratization of politics as people who have been rejected and subordinated challenge their oppressors. The greater danger is that identity politics will disintegrate into interest-group politics. While mainstream tactics are an important part of the battle for groups who are oppressed on the basis of ascriptive characteristics, they run the risk of limiting the more transformative elements of identity politics and reconsolidating privileges along existing lines, as those who are privileged by race or by wealth come to define the issues and agendas of lesbian politics.

*Shane Phelan*

### Bibliography

Barry, Kathleen. "Sadomasochism: The New Backlash to Feminism." *Trivia* 1 (Fall 1982), 77–92.

Haraway, Donna. "A Manifesto for Cyborgs: Science, Technology, and Socialist Feminism in the 1980s." *Socialist Review* 15:2 (1985), 65–108.

hooks, bell. *Feminist Theory: From Margin to Center.* Boston: South End, 1984.

Moraga, Cherríe, and Gloria Anzaldúa. *This Bridge Called My Back: Writings by Radical Women of Color.* New York: Kitchen Table: Women of Color Press, 1981.

Mouffe, Chantal. *The Return of the Political.* London: Verso, 1993.

Phelan, Shane. *Getting Specific: Postmodern Lesbian Politics.* Minneapolis: University of Minnesota Press, 1994.

—————. *Identity Politics: Lesbian Feminism and the Limits of Community.* Philadelphia: Temple University Press, 1989.

***See also*** Combahee River Collective; Identity; National Gay and Lesbian Task Force (NGLTF); Political Theory

## Ideology

The total thought structure of a society, reliance upon which tends to stabilize a social order; distinguished from utopian thought structures, which are used to transform a social order. In particular, ideologies function to explain, rationalize, conceal, or otherwise mystify social relations of dominance and subordination (as, for example, ideologies of racial inferiority have been used justify the subordination of people of color in the United States). Antilesbian ideologies have taken several forms: Medical/scientific, religious, and political ideologies have been particularly powerful in the United States.

Medical/scientific ideologies have been most clearly expressed through theories and research on the etiology of lesbianism. Much of this material is bluntly homophobic, referring to lesbianism as a degeneracy, a failure, or a disorder. But even the literature that takes a more cautious, objective tone, seeking the source of variation rather than pathology, poses the research question so as to explain lesbianism as a departure from heterosexuality and femininity. Such science assumes the normality of heterosexuality and prevailing definitions of femininity, rather than subject these assumptions to analytical scrutiny. As such, it states by implication that lesbianism is abnormal, even as it claims to practice scientific objectivity. Such theories function ideologically by providing justification for antilesbian beliefs and practices.

In recognition of the high status enjoyed in the contemporary United States by medical/scientific knowledge, lesbian and gay rights activists confronted the American Psychiatric Association (APA) in the late 1960s and early 1970s, demanding that homosexuality be deleted from its official diagnostic manual. The APA's subsequent removal of homosexuality from the DSM-III (*Diagnostic and Statistical Manual,* 3rd edition) in 1973 was lauded as a victory not only because many lesbians and gay men would now be spared psychiatric intervention, but also because of the ideological power of psychiatry's official stance in the society at large. Legal reforms, for example, would certainly have proven even more difficult to obtain if the ideology of homosexual psychopathy had remained in the opposition's arsenal.

While in the modern era scientific knowledge holds the most honored claim to a monopoly on truth, that position is generally enjoyed by religion in traditional societies. Yet religion's ideological power is still present—perhaps increasingly so—even in the late twentieth century. Official condemnations of homosexuality from Christianity, Islam, and Judaism are widely influential; U.S. opinion polls consistently find that highly religious respondents display more negative attitudes toward lesbians and gay men than those who are less religious. The correlation is not perfect, however, as there is considerable disagreement among the branches, sects, and churches of the major Western religions on issues of sexuality, homosexuality, and gender. The more liberal bodies frequently take stances against, rather than in support of, the status quo, sponsoring gay and feminist activism. As such, the traditional Marxist view that religion is always ideological, serving as "the opiate of the masses," is too simplistic.

Antilesbian ideologies are found throughout the spectrum of political beliefs, from the revolutionary to the reactionary. Anticolonialist movements have condemned lesbianism and male homosexuality as Western imports, and communist movements have characterized them as examples of capitalist decadence—a point on which fascists have often agreed. These overt condemnations are joined by the much more subtle ideological stance of Western liberalism, with its emphases on tolerance and individual freedom. Lesbian feminists, such as Rich (1980) and Kitzinger (1987), have analyzed the antilesbian ideological implications of portraying lesbianism as an individual issue of sexual preference and lifestyle. In their view, lesbianism is also a form of resistance to compulsory heterosexuality and its role in the subordination of women; to overlook this political significance in favor of a stance that merely advocates the tolerance of individual variations is to contain the valuable threat to the gender order that is implicit in lesbianism.

Strictly speaking, lesbian-positive thought systems are utopian rather than ideological, as they seek to change, rather than uphold, the dominant social order. However, within lesbian communities and cultures, systems of belief do have a certain ideological power. Lesbian feminism, for example, has often been criticized for providing a justification for the stigmatization of butches and femmes within lesbian communities. Lesbian feminists, on the other hand, have pointed out that femmes can be treated as secondary members of butch-femme communities, suggesting that the larger culture's ideology of masculine superiority has its complement there. Such critiques, for all their import, must not overshadow the fact that lesbian-positive thought systems are not the social equals of the various antilesbian ideologies that continue to support the devaluation of all lesbian women. *Vera Whisman*

### Bibliography

Kitzinger, Celia. *The Social Construction of Lesbianism*. London: Sage, 1987.

Mannheim, Karl. *Ideology and Utopia*. New York: Harcourt Brace Jovanovich, 1936.

Rich, Adrienne. "Compulsory Heterosexuality and Lesbian Existence." *Signs: Journal of Women in Culture and Society* 5:4 (1980), 631–660.

*See also* Compulsory Heterosexuality; Etiology; Heterosexism; Homophobia; Lesbian Feminism

## Immigration

The geographical movement of individuals across national borders for the purpose of residing more or less permanently in a country other than the person's country of birth. Historically, the process of immigration is at the core of the United States as a nation. Immigration policy was one of the most important political issues in the United States and the world in the 1980s and 1990s.

### Characteristics

Immigration can be motivated by a desire for better economic conditions or by fear of political or other forms of persecution, including persecution for lesbianism itself. If persecution and danger are the motivating force behind the migration, the person is considered a refugee. The legal distinction between immigrants and refugees is usually colored by the political persuasion of governments.

Many lesbians migrate from their countries seeking to avoid persecution for their sexual orientation or seeking to be able to live a freer, more "out" life in a new country. Other lesbians "come out" years after immigration, as a consequence of the new possibilities for self-expression afforded by the new country. From a psychological perspective,

immigration, even when willingly chosen and eagerly sought, produces a variety of stresses. No matter how glad the immigrant might be to live in a new country, the transitions created by immigration often produce negative experiences and emotional strain. Conversely, the need to adapt to the new environment may open up possibilities hitherto unavailable in the country of birth, including the possibility of living a lesbian life. The immigrant lesbian acculturates to the new society and to the particular lesbian culture in the specific country at the same time. Lesbians who are immigrants or refugees share experiences with heterosexual women in their particular immigrant community, as well as with lesbians in the host culture. They also share experiences with gay men who are immigrants or refugees.

Immigrant communities tend to be intent on preserving cultural traditions in the face of massive cultural transformation. The presence of lesbians in their midst is something not willingly acknowledged by most immigrant communities, which prefer to see lesbianism as one of the "evils" of the host society. The expectations of their communities create emotional pressures on lesbians in immigrant families, particularly for those who "come out" as adolescents. Even as an adult, to be a lesbian in the midst of an immigrant community involves not only a choice about one's own life, but also a choice that affects the community's perception of itself and of the family from which the lesbian comes. "Coming out" may jeopardize not only family ties, but also the possibility of serving the immigrant community itself.

The usual difficulties in obtaining adequate statistics on lesbian populations prevail concerning the numbers of lesbians among immigrants and refugees. Demographic studies have demonstrated that the composition of the gay and lesbian population in North America is very much like the entire population. Thus, it is possible to estimate that large numbers of lesbians and gay men—perhaps as many as two million—exist among the immigrant population in the United States. The numbers are even higher if immigrants and refugees all over the world are considered.

### Legal and Political Institutions

Legislation concerning the immigration of lesbians and gay men to the United States has been mostly restrictive. The Immigration Act of 1917 excluded "persons of constitutional psychopathic inferiority." In the 1952 Immigration and Nationality Act (INA), the prohibition was reworded to exclude "aliens afflicted with psychopathic personality, epilepsy or a mental defect." The legislative history of these acts shows that this language was broad enough to exclude homosexuals and "sex perverts." The 1952 INA was adopted in a climate of national paranoia. Homosexuality was associated with communism not only in the popular mind, but by the government as well, despite the fact that the Communist Party, like mainstream culture, rejected homosexuals.

In 1979, as a consequence of the American Psychiatric Association's 1973 declaration that homosexuality per se does not constitute mental illness, the Surgeon General announced that the Public Health Service, working under the Immigration and Naturalization Service (INS), would no longer exclude aliens because they were suspected of being homosexuals. In 1980, the INS (the federal agency charged with processing immigrants for admission to the country and later for citizenship) adopted new procedures by which arriving aliens would not be asked about sexual orientation. However, a voluntary admission of homosexuality or a disclosure by a third party would still be used to exclude an alien. Finally, the Immigration Act of 1990 rewrote the exclusion section, abandoning the provision excluding homosexuals. As a result, immigrants have the right to enter openly as lesbians. However, those admitted before 1990 can technically be deported because they were admitted at a time when the exclusion was still in effect.

In the mid-1990s, the United States began considering persecution because of sexual orientation a cause for political asylum and, thus, granting refugee status on the basis of sexual orientation. Historically, lesbian and gay aliens were prevented from making an asylum claim for persecution in their countries of birth based on homosexuality. But two cases, following a 1994 directive to the INS from United States Attorney General Janet Reno, held that lesbians and gay men can receive protection under U.S. asylum policy because they can be considered members of a persecuted social group eligible for political asylum, thus eligible for refugee status under the law. Despite Reno's directives, there are still some problems with the laws as written. Interestingly, proving persecution will be harder for closeted lesbians and gays, while open homosexuals will encounter less difficulty demonstrating that they are closely affiliated and share similar interests with other members of the persecuted group, an essential component of the demonstration of the need for asylum.

Despite these positive changes in U.S. immigration policy, the Lesbian and Gay Immigration Rights Task Force, a nonprofit organization advocating the reform of discriminatory immigration laws in the United States that affect lesbians and gay men, was still concerned in the late 1990s with several issues. In particular, although the Immigration and Nationality Act permitted the immigration of a foreign spouse, it discriminated against lesbians and gays because they were still prevented from bringing foreign partners to the United States. Even if same-sex marriage were legalized in the United States, it would take years of legal battles to persuade the INS to recognize these marriages for immigration purposes.                *Oliva M. Espín*

## Bibliography

Cole, Ellen, Oliva M. Espín, and Esther Rothblum, eds. *Shattered Societies, Shattered Lives: Refugee Women and Their Mental Health.* New York: Haworth, 1992.

Espín, Oliva M. "Issues of Identity in the Psychology of Latina Lesbians." In *Lesbian Psychologies: Explorations and Challenges.* Ed. Boston Lesbian Psychologies Collective. Urbana: University of Illinois Press, 1987, pp. 35–55.

Foss, Robert J. "The Demise of Homosexual Exclusion: New Possibilities for Gay and Lesbian Immigration." *Harvard Civil Rights–Civil Liberties Law Review* 29 (1994), 439–475.

Park, Jin S. "Pink Asylum: Political Asylum Eligibility of Gay Men and Lesbians Under U.S. Immigration Policy." *UCLA Law Review* 42 (1995), 1115–1156.

Tremble, Bob, Margaret Schneider, and Carol Appathurai. "Growing up Gay or Lesbian in Multicultural Context." In *Gay and Lesbian Youth.* Ed. Gilbert Herdt. New York: Harrington Park, 1989, pp. 253–267.

United States Committee for Refugees. *World Refugee Survey: 1989 in Review.* Washington, D.C.: American Council for Nationalities, 1990.

*See also* Law and Legal Institutions

## Incest

Sexual abuse of a person by a family member. Estimates of the percentage of the U.S. population that are victims of incest and sexual abuse vary—10–40 percent of women and 5–20 percent of men, depending on the particular study cited. However, many studies do not separate sexual abuse by a non-family member from incest so the incidence of incest is difficult to estimate. Multiple studies have found that lesbians, bisexuals, and gay men are no more likely to be perpetrators than heterosexual individuals. Other studies have found that lesbians are no more likely to be victims of sexual abuse, including incest, than heterosexual women. However, these studies are difficult to conduct, as it is hard to find a normative sample of lesbian women due to fears many have of disclosing their sexuality. Additionally, many lesbians who participate in studies have been in therapy or have other reasons for disclosing this information more readily.

Experts in the field believe that incest has more damaging consequences on a child than sexual abuse by a stranger. This is because sexual abuse by a family member involves a betrayal of trust and an exploitation of the dependency, vulnerability, and love that a child has toward a family member. Not only do victims have to heal from the violation of a traumatic victimization, but they also have to address the profound betrayal of trust and dependency. This betrayal can have a lasting impact on intimate relationships and sense of self. Some aftereffects of incest for adult women are a sense of profound badness or evil, low self-esteem, depression, anxiety, sexual issues, body-image issues, intense rage, sleep disturbances, hyperarousal, posttraumatic stress disorder, and dissociative disorders. Symptoms in child victims are similarly various: depression, anxiety, fearfulness, hypersexuality, intense anger, low self-esteem, changes in normal behaviors, and sleep or eating disorders. Because the aftereffects of incest are so varied and overlap with other disorders, one cannot make a diagnosis of incest or sexual abuse simply from symptoms.

The child victim often takes the blame for the events, thus preserving the relationship to the abusive caretaker. This blame often becomes a sense of personal badness, evil, and a stigmatized identity, which may result in lowered self-esteem, self-destructive behaviors, and other symptoms. Often, as the child matures into adolescence and adulthood, sexuality becomes the focal point for the sense of badness, leading to sexual problems. Other long-term issues are difficulties in basic trust, autonomy, and initiative.

For lesbians, the stigma of incest can increase homophobia and the stigma about being lesbian or bisexual, creating more problems around acceptance of sexual identity. Further, internalized homophobia can lead a woman to blame her lesbian feelings or her lack of feelings for men on the incest. However, no study has shown any relationship between sexual abuse, incest, and lesbian or bisexual feelings. It is important to remember that incest leads a woman to feeling that her sexuality is bad. This is a common issue for all victims of sexual abuse, no matter what their sexual orientation. Lesbian and bisexual women who are survivors of incest have no greater symptoms than heterosexual women.

One of the most striking issues for a survivor can be difficulty protecting herself in intimate relationships. Because an incest survivor did not have safe relationships in childhood, there is no frame of reference for safe relationships as an adult. Cues that relationships or situations are unsafe are not recognized as such. Revictimization or exploitative, depriving, or violent relationships are not uncommon. Victimization is not a goal of victims but is passively accepted. Often, the adult survivor thinks that pain and suffering are the price of love and does not feel entitled to, or does not know what, a loving and safe relationship is.

For lesbians, this difficulty in believing that they are entitled to safety, acceptance, and love can mean the passive tolerance of second-rate status as a lesbian or a woman and may mean taking a more passive role in accepting discriminatory behavior as a lesbian. One of the goals for incest survivors is learning to recognize dangerous situations and feeling entitled to safety and love.

Other goals are establishing safety (physical and interpersonal), reconstructing the trauma story (to lessen self-blame and inappropriate responsibility), and restoring connection between themselves and others (interpersonal relationship and community ties). These issues can take on a moral or spiritual emphasis as they address issues of good, evil, and blameless suffering. In reaching these goals, openness about the trauma, transforming the trauma story into testimony, and a reaffirmation of the personal importance of justice are helpful. Also often helpful are therapy and/or support groups. Survivors need to learn that improvement in symptoms and healing from these traumatic events are possible.

*Judith Glassgold*

## Bibliography

Bass, Ellen, and Laura Davis. *The Courage to Heal.* New York: Harper and Row, 1988.

Finkelhor, David. *Child Sexual Abuse: New Theory and Research.* New York: Free Press, 1984.

Herman, Judith L. *Trauma and Recovery: The Aftermath of Violence—from Domestic Abuse to Political Terror.* New York: Basic Books, 1992.

*See also* Psychotherapy

## India

Situated just above the equator, India, in both its
cultural and geographical diversity, is more a continent than a country. Geographically, it is surrounded
on three sides by water and, on the northern side, by
the Himalayas, the highest range of mountains on
earth. It contains stretches of desert, as well as fertile plains located around an abundance of rivers. Its
historical and cultural realities are equally diverse,
with many different civilizations existing simul-
taneaously. Thus, it is difficult to generalize about
the entire country.

### History

India had a very rich culture of lesbian desire in the
early pre-Vedic cultures prior to 1500 B.C.E. (*Vedas*
are the sacred writings of the Hindu culture that settled in India at that time.) Lesbianism was represented through the concept of *Jami* (the feminine
twins). The notion of twins was not based on a
biological identity but that of a holistic union between women that comprised both erotic and sexual
dimensions.

This notion was later rendered taboo and criminal in the brahmanic (the highest caste in the traditional social structure) texts. The most obvious examples are found in the Laws of Manu (ca. 2
B.C.E.–A.D. 2). According to laws 8.369 and 370:

> A *kanya* [young girl] who does it [*kuryat*]
> to another *kanya* must be fined 200 *panas*,
> pay the double of the bride price and re-
> ceive 10 lashes of the rod. But a *stri* [adult
> woman] who does it [*prakuryat*] to a
> *kanya* shall instantly have her head shaved
> or 2 fingers cut off and be made to ride
> through the town on a donkey.

In spite of these laws, there are many examples of lesbianism in ancient texts, particularly the
texts relating to the independent goddesses (figures
within the religious tradition outside the caste system; these goddesses do not function only as con-
sorts of gods). One such myth tells the story of two
women having sex together and giving birth to a
male child. The child is born without a bone structure because there has been no transmission of
semen.

A series of Islamic invasions, which began in
the twelfth century A.D., was consolidated by different dynasties until the advent of British colonialism
in the eighteenth century. Neither Islamic nor
British rule entirely affected all parts of the country.

Little is known about lesbian sexuality in the
Islamic period or the colonial period. Some literature does demonstrate lesbian desire. For example,
Zeb-un-Nissa (1638–1702) wrote at least one poem
in Persian that suggests desire for another woman.
Bahu Begam (fl. 1855–1865) also wrote about her
fear that a beloved woman might "be crushed by the
burden of my adoring looks."

With the domination of India by the British,
colonial ideologies led to the repression of diverse
lesbian and homosexual traditions. In 1861, the
colonial regime introduced the Indian penal code,
including section 377, which prohibits "carnal intercourse against the order of nature with any man,
woman or animal," punishing it with a fine and imprisonment from ten years to life.

### Contemporary Conditions

Several cases have been reported under this law. One
such was reported in the magazine *India Today*
(April 15, 1990). A woman named Tarulata changed
her sex to marry her girlfriend, Lila Chavda. Muljib-
hai Chavda, Lila's father, went to court, saying that,
since it was a lesbian relationship, the marriage
should be annulled. His petition called for criminal
action to be taken against her under the above law,
contending that "Tarunkumar (Tarulata) possesses
neither the male organ nor any natural mechanism of
cohabitation, sexual intercourse and procreation of
children. Adoption of any unnatural mechanism does
not create malehood and as such Tarunkumar is not a
male." Although the outcome of the case is not
known, activists report that the law is often used as a
coercive weapon to break up lesbian relationships.

The majority of lesbians live silent, private
lives within "the closet," but there have been publicized cases of lesbian marriages and suicides. The
first reported marriage, in 1987, goes back to an
earlier tradition of *gandharva* (noncontractual) marriage. *Gandharvas* were celestial musicians and
linked to divine erotic traditions. The *gandharva*
form of marriage was based on erotic union, the sex
of the partners being unspecified. This is precisely

what two policewomen, Urmilla and Lila, did in a village in Madhya Pradash. They went to a temple and married each other in front of forty witnesses. In retaliation, they were forcibly medically examined and fired from their jobs.

Since 1987, various instances of marriages and friendship contracts between women have been reported. In most cases, these have been broken through coercive tactics, using section 377 of the penal code, although in the minority, when the family has been supportive, the relationship has continued.

The major expression of lesbian oppression is found in numerous examples of lesbian double suicides. One example was reported in a local newspaper in the late 1970s. Malika and Lalitambika, both students at Keralavarma college in Kerala, were very much in love. When they discovered that Lalitambika had passed but Malika had failed her final examinations, they attempted to commit suicide rather than face inevitable separation. The police charged them with attempted suicide and found, among other things, a letter and a greeting card with a silhouette of a kissing couple against a backdrop of a flaming sunset. Inside was a note from Malika: "Lali, after all everybody know about our love, so here's a thousand kisses for you in public." Lalitambika had replied: "Come to me, I shall take you in my arms. I shall cover you with kisses. You shall sleep in my bosom." A letter written before the suicide attempt by Lalitambika to her parents stated: "I cannot part with Malika. Bury us together." It was subsequently reported that their relatives were unable to grasp the implications of their relationship and that Malika's elder brother said that the two had agreed to "forget each other."

The greatest problem in the everyday life of lesbian relationships is the silence over lesbian issues, which leads to terrible isolation. Further, the emotional pressure of compulsory heterosexual marriage in Indian society results in the majority of lesbians marrying, thus allowing only for a closeted and furtive existence. In the large cities, however, some open activity exists, although there are only two formal groups, Stri Sangam (Fusion Between Women) in Bombay and Sakhi (Female Friend, incorporating eroticism) in Delhi. Sakhi, begun in 1990, was the first lesbian group in India. Initially a networking group, it later developed both a political platform and a lesbian archive. Stri Sangam also aims at networking lesbians, as well as making lesbian issues publicly visible. These groups represent a gradual opening up of Indian society around lesbian issues. Human rights groups, too, have challenged the legal code, and, at the close of the 1990s, hope existed that it would be rescinded.

*Giti Thadani*

### Bibliography

Khayal, Utsa, and Susan Heske. "There Are, Always Have Been, Always Will Be Lesbians in India." *Conditions: Thirteen* (1986), 135–146.

Kumar, Mina. "Representations of Indian Lesbianism." In *The Very Inside: An Anthology of Writing by Asian and Pacific Islander Lesbian and Bisexual Women.* Ed. Sharon Lim-Hing. Toronto: Sister Vision, 1994.

Thadani, Giti. *Sakhiyani: Lesbian Desire in Ancient and Modern India.* London: Cassell, 1996.

**See also:** International Organizations; Islam

## Indigenous Cultures

Historical and cultural accounts of female same-sex relationships among native peoples of Asia, Africa, the Americas, and the Pacific.

### Research Problems

The search by Euro-American scholars for lesbians in other cultures has always confronted a number of problems, not the least of which is the difference between Euro-American and native definitions of sexuality. Sexual practices carry different meanings in different cultures. In Euro-American cultures, the term "lesbian," a woman whose primary sexual preference is other women, connotes a permanent sexual identity. Such an identity does not accurately define forms of intimate relations between women or female partners in other cultures.

In many cultures, the only practice that is considered "sex" is sexual intercourse between a woman and a man. Though many other forms of sex practice may be engaged in, including sex between women, in some cultures these physical intimacies fall outside the bounds of sex proper. In a study done in Lesotho, southern Africa, Gay (1986) asked if young women in "mummy-baby" relationships make love like a man and a woman. Most women replied that that was different than the hugging and kissing of the mummy-baby relationship, distinguishing conceptually between what women do together and what women and men do. Kendall (in Blackwood and Wieringa, 1998) was told that women cannot have sex together because there is no sex without a penis. Yet women of Lesotho do have erotic relationships with other women.

Another problem with the anthropological record on lesbian relations is that anthropologists in the past either associated lesbianism with masculinity or assumed that it resulted from heterosexual deprivation. Some identified only masculine women as lesbian, while others confidently asserted that, for instance, among the peoples of Tikopia in Melanesia, women did not engage in lesbianism because so many men were available. Consequently, many sexual or affective relations between women in other cultures have gone unnoticed by naive outside observers, contributing to the small number of such accounts in the ethnohistoric record.

Along with the many problems in the ethnohistorical record, the conquest of indigenous groups contributed to the invisibility of lesbianism. The sixteenth to the nineteenth centuries saw massive incursions by Europeans into native lands. In the process of taking economic and political control, these colonizers imposed their own religious dictates on native peoples. Missionaries controlled native sexualities, in part, by redefining or suppressing native terms for same-sex partners. Words for intimate same-sex friend or sexual partner were translated simply as friend (such as *aikane* in Hawai'in and *takatapui* in Maori), losing their sexual meaning. Anglo officials forbade Native American two-spirit people (formerly *berdache*) to publicly continue in that role and to practice their religious duties. Over time, these words and identities were either forgotten or deeply buried in folk consciousness.

It is only with the globalization of gay liberation that native peoples with alternative sexualities or genders have begun to question colonial histories and to reconstruct their own subjectivities and sexualities. Many are beginning to establish ties between their contemporary gay identities and traditional cultural practices. As Hall and Kauanui (1994) note for the Pacific islands, Western notions about sexuality and homosexuality "are a colonial imposition which only address the realities of a small part of the spectrum of Pacific people who have sexual and love relationships with members of their own sex."

## The Anthropological Record

Despite the limitations of the record, female same-sex sexuality has been noted in a number of indigenous groups. The record suggests that, in indigenous cultures, it is rare to find a segregated community of women involved in affective or erotic relationships (except the sworn sisterhoods of China). Rather, what appears is that women, who are otherwise heterosexually married, engage in a variety of intimate and erotic relationships, including affective or intimate friendships between adult women, adolescent sex play, ritual practices, bond friendships, woman-marriage, and erotic relations between a woman and a transgender female (a female-bodied man). In many cases, the primary relationship for these women may be with men as husbands; in ritual practices, the intent may be to learn and encourage heterosexual relations. In some cultures that allow only two genders or that tie masculinity to erotic attraction to women, some females live as men, taking women as sexual partners or wives. In all cases, these relations are embedded in, and gain their meaning from, wider cultural contexts. For the individuals involved, these relations create social connections and identities, as well as erotic bonds.

The interest in, and availability of, accounts of women's same-sex relationships in indigenous cultures has increased since the 1970s. This entry presents accounts of a variety of relationships that generally fall into five categories: intimate friendships, woman-marriage, ritual practices, adolescent sex play, and transgender practices.

## Intimate Friendships

Although married and raising children, women in many indigenous cultures maintained loving and intimate relationships with other women, often solemnizing these relationships with celebrations and frequent gift exchanges. In some cases, the relationship was between a slightly older and a younger woman, or a married and an unmarried woman, or two young women. This type of relationship is labeled "intimate friendship" because it is often impossible to know whether these relationships are sexual, nor is it necessary to insist on a sexual definition that makes sense only to Western minds.

Azande women of central Africa (now Sudan and the Republic of Zaire) could establish a bond friendship with another woman. Azande society was composed of several kingdoms with noble and commoner classes. Polygamy was the usual form of marriage; each wife had her own dwelling in her husband's compound and her own land to cultivate. Besides the marital relationship, women could establish a formal relationship of exchange and service with another woman, often their cowives. These relationships were formalized by conducting a ritual called *bagburu*, in which the two women exchanged small gifts, then divided a corn cob in half, each one taking a half to plant in her own garden.

Unfortunately, most of what is known about *bagburu* relationships comes from Azande men in the 1930s and reflects their own fears and fantasies about their wives. Men asserted that some women who were bond friends had sexual relations with their partners. The term for lesbian sex was *adandara*. Azande wives had to ask permission from their husbands to begin a *bagburu* relationship. Husbands tried to discourage their wives from developing sexual attachments, however. They believed that, once a woman became her own master and could have sex with another woman when she pleased, not just when a man cared to give it to her, she would want to continue it.

The Nama, an ethnic group of the Khoikhoi of southwest Africa, also maintained the institution of bond friendship, called *sorigus*. The bond was initiated by both partners drinking from the same bowl and signified their willingness to provide mutual assistance. It was considered customary, according to reports from the 1920s, that women in these relationships engaged in sexual practices together.

In southern Africa, other forms of intimate friendship occurred among young women in rural villages and at boarding schools. In the initiation schools of the Lesotho, Venda, and Zulu peoples, an older girl became the mother to a younger girl. The sex education that took place in these schools provided the opportunity for girls to touch and fondle each other physically. Such schools, however, became the target of missionary disapproval and have now all but disappeared.

Bond friendships, or mummy-baby relationships, as they are called, became popular among young girls in southern Africa in the 1950s, particularly at boarding schools. They may have originated in rural women's special affective and gift-exchange partnerships remembered by older women up to the late 1950s. These traditional partnerships, called *motsoalle* in rural Lesotho, were long-term, loving, and erotic relationships that often coexisted with a heterosexual marriage. Such relationships were publicly acknowledged and celebrated by gift giving and feasting that involved the whole community.

In the mummy-baby relationship of Lesotho girls that continues into the present, two young women, the older of whom becomes the mummy and the younger the baby, start a relationship by arranging private encounters and exchanging love letters and gifts. The mummies, being older, provide more substantial goods and may have more than one baby. The girls treat the friendship like an affair or a romance; hugging, kissing, and sexual relations are part of it. These relationships provide emotional, sexual, and material support for the young girls involved. Some relationships continue after the girls leave school and even after marriage.

Whether they were carrying on the traditions of their African foremothers cannot be said, but Afro-Caribbean women on the island of Carriacou near Grenada were known to have intimate relationships with other women. These women were called *madivine* or *zami*. Relationships were usually between an older woman who was married and had children and a younger woman who was more likely unmarried and with little income. The elder partner, who might have several junior partners, particularly if her husband was prosperous, gave her lovers gifts, such as earrings or underwear, while the younger ones gave perfume, as befitted the status of the senior partner. These relationships were noted in the 1950s when little wage labor was available on Carriacou, forcing most men to work overseas for long periods of time and send money home to their wives, who engaged mainly in subsistence farming. This labor pattern led Smith (1962) to claim that it was the long absences of their husbands that led married women to become *madivines*. On the other hand, it was believed that, since women are more sexual than men, only women can satisfy each other. Lorde (1982) referred to the women of Carriacou in her biomythography, asserting poetically that Carriacou women's love for each other is legend in Grenada, as are their strength and beauty.

According to several accounts by anthropologists who worked among different aboriginal Australian groups from the 1930s through the early 1960s, young girls and women engaged in sexual activities with other females. It was said to be quite common among girls, who used an *ininta*, a little stick with string wound around the end, for sexual play. The term *kityili-kityili* referred to a sex practice between adult women that involved tickling the clitoris with the finger, followed by rubbing the genitals together. Sexual intimacy with another woman generally followed the rules of kinship. One's proper sexual partners were one's cross-cousins.

Other sketchy reports of indigenous or diasporic cultures in which women engaged in same-sex practices with other women include the Araucania (Chile) and the Aymara (Bolivia), Haiti and Jamaica in the Caribbean, the Hopi, the Ojibwa, and the

Pawnee of native North America, the Mbundu (Angola) and the Nupe (Nigeria), and the Balinese and the Javanese of Indonesia.

## Woman-Marriage

A common institution throughout sub-Saharan Africa, this practice allows one woman to marry another. Woman-marriage is legally recognized in many African countries and is arranged through the payment of brideprice by the woman for a wife. Whether some of these women have sexual relations with each other has been hotly debated. In some instances, woman-marriage is a nonsexual, economic relationship arranged by a woman to provide offspring for a deceased husband or childless son.

In other cases, a woman who is independently wealthy and powerful takes a wife to establish her own family and compound, of which she is the head. The woman-husband chooses a male consort for her wife, and all resulting children belong to her and inherit her wealth. Although these relationships are not necessarily sexual relationships, some argue that, at least for the Fon of Benin, given the presence of female same-sex practices there, woman-marriages include sexual relations. In discussing woman-marriage in East Africa, Obbo (1976) hinted at the possibility of sexual relations by stating that some women may find woman-marriage more compatible because they cannot lead satisfying lives in a heterosexual marriage. Lacking the voices of the women themselves, however, it remains conjecture whether these women have sexual relations with each other.

## Ritual Practices

Aboriginal Australian customs provide one of the few examples of ritual lesbian practices, which refers to sexual or erotic movements or performances between two women during rituals or ceremonies. Among the aborigines, young girls were initiated into their adult roles at first menstruation through a process of training and ritual that produced a girl's social identity. Initiation ceremonies, which conveyed a number of messages about land, kinship, and social action, included homoerotic and heteroerotic play. This sexual play was determined by the kinship and age of the women and the initiates. Early anthropologists, who seemed reluctant to discuss this aspect of ritual performances, described the movements of the women dancers as sexually suggestive, leading to "simulated intercourse." They insisted that the intent of this action was to ensure heterosexual success (getting or keeping a husband or a male lover). Such ceremonies have rarely been performed since the 1950s in north Australia, but they continue to unnerve Anglo audiences and confuse young aboriginal women, who are now familiar with the Anglo gay identity. Older Belyuen women, however, are not troubled by the homoerotic "digging" (*yedabetj*) of the ritual performances. For them, it is erotic play that initiates young women into the complex social categories within which they will move.

A similar practice was an important part of ceremonies for women in the Solomon Islands in Melanesia. According to Blackwood (1935), women engaged in boisterous sexual play during menstrual and wedding ceremonies, shouting and dancing together suggestively. Observed in the 1920s, this ritual behavior was described in biased terms as an imitation of sexual intercourse, its meaning unclear to the anthropologist, who thought it might be symbolic of marital relations or female sexuality. Similar homoerotic play in ritual dances was noted for women in the nearby Bismarck Archipelago.

## Adolescent Sex Play

Engaging in sex play with members of one's own sex during adolescence may be a common human phenomenon, but for girls it is more typical (or visible) in societies in which virginity is not given heavy weight. Children and adolescents of the egalitarian !Kung San of the Kalahari Desert of southern Africa did engage in homosexual play. Few !Kung now live their nomadic hunter-gatherer lifestyle, having been forced to settle in one place by colonial authorities, but one !Kung woman, Nisa, recounted a life history that shed new light on adolescent sexual practices (Shostak 1981). !Kung adults insisted that they disapproved of childhood sex play, but, when children played in their mock villages or in the bush, they experimented sexually. Nisa watched older girls play sexually with each other and then did the same with her girlfriends as she approached adolescence. The girls would put saliva on their hands, rub it on their genitals, and touch genitals. As the girls got older, they started playing sexually with boys, and all eventually married. But these girls often maintained strong and loyal friendships throughout their lifetimes, even after marriage.

Other indigenous cultures in which anthropologists reported that girls played together sexually included Australian aborigines; some native North American groups; the Fon of West Africa; the Mehinaku, a Brazilian Indian group; the peoples of the

Marquesas Islands and Samoa in Polynesia; and the Alor in Indonesia.

## Transgender Practices

In many indigenous cultures in which the gender system is predicated on two sexes, each with distinct roles, tasks, and behaviors, transgender females live as social men and have sexual relations with women. A wide range of practices fall under this category, from the butch, to the ritual transformer, to the two-spirit, but all derive primarily from the relation between gender, sexuality, and personhood. The sexual division of labor, the importance of kinship and family to the life of the community, and a rigid gender hierarchy act as barriers to individuals who fall outside the norms of appropriate gender. Societies with rigid gender systems force nonconforming individuals to see themselves as belonging to the other gender. In these societies, "masculinity" and erotic attraction to women are constructed as men's behavior. The inability to imagine other models creates the possibility in such cultures of both butch and transgender behavior.

Anthropological accounts of indigenous cultures with female transgenders are less frequent than those with male transgenders, probably owing to the greater constraints on women's sexuality in male-dominant cultures or their greater significance to kin groups and families. According to reports from the 1800s and early 1900s, transgender females were officially acknowledged and respected among some native North American groups and in two northeast Siberian cultures. Among the Chukchi and the Korak of Siberia, the spiritual potency of gender meant that those who ritually transformed themselves into the other gender became the most powerful shamans or healers. Among the Chukchi, female shamans who became men were called *qa cikicheca* (similar to a man). Such a transformed female could marry a woman by going through the customary rites of marriage. If they wanted to have children, they entered into a relationship with a man. Children resulting from that union were considered the transformed shaman's lawful children.

In Southeast Asia, a number of cultures have produced a transgender category in which females who act masculine and are attracted to women appropriate the male gender. In these cultures, sexuality is heavily embedded in rigid gender systems, forcing same-sex couples to rely on, or draw from, dominant cultural images of masculinity and femininity to make sense of their relationship. Called tomboys in Indonesia and toms in Thailand, these butches or transgender females act and dress like men and are sexually involved with women who maintain the customary feminine gender for their cultures. The feminine partners are usually bisexual and may have sexual relationships with men as well. Tomboys are not generally accepted by Indonesians; heavy pressure is brought to bear on females to fulfill family obligations through marriage, forcing many tomboys to migrate to urban areas, where they can live anonymously with their feminine partners. In the Philippines, the tomboy, or *lakin-on,* of the Negros Islands are said to be women with masculine physical characteristics who do tasks primarily regarded as men's work and love only women.

The relation between gender and sexuality is one of the keys to the study of lesbianism in indigenous cultures. Where gender is rigidly hierarchical, some cultures do not construct female same-sex relations as sexual or legitimate, particularly in patriarchal cultures. The great majority of cases of intimate friendships between women occur in indigenous cultures where women have greater control over their sexuality. The data suggest that women engage in a wide range of affective and intimate sexual relations with each other. Through these relationships, they construct meaningful social connections that extend the range of kin and family beyond the heterosexual matrix.

*Evelyn Blackwood*

### Bibliography

Blackwood, Beatrice. *Both Sides of Buka Passage.* Oxford, U.K.: Clarendon, 1935.

Blackwood, Evelyn. "Sexuality and Gender in Certain Native American Tribes: The Case of Cross-Gender Females." *Signs: Journal of Women in Culture and Society* 10:1 (1984), 27–42.

Blackwood, Evelyn, and Saskia E. Wieringa, eds. *Female Desires: Same-Sex Relations and Transgender Practices Across Cultures.* New York: Columbia University Press, 1998.

Evans-Pritchard, E.E. "Sexual Inversion Among the Azande." *American Anthropologist* 72:6 (1970), 1428–1434.

Gay, Judith. "Mummies and Babies and Friends and Lovers in Lesotho." In *The Many Faces of Homosexuality: Anthropological Approaches to Homosexual Behavior.* Ed. Evelyn Blackwood. New York: Harrington Park, 1986, pp. 97–116.

Hall, Lisa Kahaleole Chang, and J. Kehaulani Kauanui. "Same-Sex Sexuality in Pacific Literature." *Amerasia Journal* 20:1 (1994), 75–81.

Hart, Donn V. " The Cebuano Bayot and Lakin-On." In *Oceanic Homosexualities*. Ed. Stephen Murray. New York: Garland, 1992, pp. 193–230.

Lorde, Audre. *Zami, A New Spelling of My Name.* Watertown, Mass.: Persephone, 1982.

Obbo, Christine. "Dominant Male Ideology and Female Options: Three East African Case Studies." *Africa* 46 (1976), 371–389.

Shostak, Marjorie. *Nisa: The Life and Words of a !Kung Woman.* Cambridge, Mass.: Harvard University Press, 1981.

Smith, M.G. *Kinship and Community in Carriacou.* New Haven, Conn.: Yale University Press, 1962.

***See also*** Anthropology; Bisexuality; Butch-Femme; Caribbean; China; Colonialism; Gender; Indonesia; Lesotho; Native Americans; Pacific Islands; Philippines; South Africa; Thailand; Tomboy; Transgender; Two-Spirit

## Indonesia

Sprawling archipelago-nation of great cultural and linguistic diversity. With close to 200 million inhabitants, Indonesia is the fourth most populous nation on Earth and the largest Islamic state. Only in the nineteenth century under Dutch colonial rule did the country become united. This process was accelerated in the early twentieth century by a growing nationalist movement, which propagated the use of a national language, and Islamic revivalism. The national revolution brought Indonesia its hard-won independence in 1949. Nationalist sentiments continued to play a major role, culminating in the invasion of East Timor in 1975. In 1965, a revolt of leftist officers was followed by a wave of propaganda against the strong Communist Party, in which members of the Communist women's movement were accused of having castrated and helped murder the country's top military leaders. In the campaign that followed, probably half a million people were killed, and General Suharto (1921–) rose to power. Suharto's path to development was built on a combination of ruthless capitalist growth, military prowess, and women's subordination.

Ethnographic historical sources reveal a wide variety of same-sex relations among men. Far less mention is made of women's same-sex relations. In Aceh, in northern Sumatra, as well as on the island of Bali, it is reported that women used dildoes made of wax to please each other, while Dayak women in Kalimantan preferred a combination of wood and wax. Male transvestism was, and still, is common in many places in the archipelago, notably on Java. In east Java, cross-dressing women were referred to by the same name as cross-dressing and transgendered men (*wandu* in Javanese or *banci* in Malay). Colonial sources also reveal the existence of women's same-sex relations among the ladies in the royal courts of central Java. The cross-dressing female soldiers at the courts, called "Javanese Amazons" in colonial sources, likewise might have engaged in sexual relations with each other.

There are few historical inscriptions in the temples of Java of women's same-sex activities. On the base of the central Javanese Buddhist temple of Borobudur, some scenes depict women's sexual activities, but the context is not very clear. This "Hidden Foot" was covered again after the renovation of the temple. References to women's same-sex activities in the rich old Javanese literature are likewise scarce and open to various interpretations.

This historical silence on women's erotic friendships and same-sex activities was prepetuated throughout the twentieth century. Indonesian women are supposed to be meek and sexually passive. Women who transgress the boundaries of this moral code of conduct are socially marginalized. Although the term *banci* is still used both for a butch lesbian as for a cross-dressing man, the gendered implications are very different. Male transvestites have found a niche in society in which they can carry out certain occupations (hairdressing, working in beauty salons, or prostitution), and in several cities there are large associations of these men. Masculine lesbian women are ostracized. Occasionally receiving sensationalist press attention, lesbianism is generally regarded as a "deviant" form of sexuality. It is commonly associated with other forms of unacceptable behavior by women, such as prostitution, night life, and drug addiction, and, in general, with a decadent, Westernized lifestyle. There have been cases reported of women who were sent to psychiatric hospitals or who received prison sentences for loving other women. The government actively condemns lesbian women as against the national culture.

Yet women-loving-women in Indonesia carve out their own spaces. Most of them try to avoid the label "lesbian," out of fear of being considered mentally ill or delinquent. There are few public spaces where they can meet, as gay men can. One possibility is the "ladies' night," in which several discotheques offer free access to women. Upper-class women meet in the privacy of their homes, while certain groups of lower-class women meet at eating stalls or shopping malls. The most "visible" lesbians are the butch-femme couples, but there are many other ways in which women express their love for each other. Some internationally oriented women with a command of English have joined meetings of the Asian Lesbian Network. Lesbian women have made several attempts to organize, either within some of the feminist organizations that have emerged or outside. For some time in the early 1990s a small group of lesbian women, Chandra Kirana (Kirana the Shining One), published a bulletin called *Gaya Lestari* (Lesbian Style).    *Saskia E. Wieringa*

## Bibliography

Blackwood, Evelyn, and Saskia E. Wieringa, eds. *Female Desires: Same-Sex Relations and Transgender Practices Across Cultures.* New York: Columbia University Press, 1998.

*See also* Asian Lesbian Network

## International Organizations

Groups of lesbians throughout the world fighting for rights, organizing social activities, doing research, playing sports, sharing artistic contributions, business networking, and many other activities. Such groups are often marginalized within their countries, sometimes practically underground and too often severely underresourced. These groups usually are focused on the women in their local communities; sometimes they are national in scope. Rarely are they international, in the sense of a few or more countries. Some international organizations attempt to be global in scope; others, regional or subregional. Still others call themselves international when they are, in fact, predominantly of one nation but include a handful of members from another country. When determining what international means to an organization, it is important to consider who is representing whom, how decisions are made, and how the group is composed.

## International Networking

Most of the connections that develop among and between lesbian organizations or individuals from different countries are informal in nature—meeting through friends, travel, conferences or, increasingly, on the Internet. This unorganized, organic connecting is important and useful for lesbians interested in international work. Lesbians involved in international nongovernmental organizations (NGOs; the international equivalent of a U.S. nonprofit organization) are often in a privileged position with regard to class and/or race, having either the individual means to travel or having a professional position in an international organization that sends people to attend international conferences or meetings. It is rare that lesbians involved in international work, even from developing countries, would come from a lower- or working-class background or a nonurban area, or would not speak English (the language that dominates most international conferences). On the other hand, lesbian activists working on a local level are more likely to come from a wider range of class and racial backgrounds. This limited representation is a crucial factor in assessing the role and utility of international organizations for lesbian individuals and groups worldwide.

Many lesbian workshops, caucuses, and meetings have been held since the 1970s at international gatherings such as health conferences, U.N. conferences for NGOs, feminist gatherings, the Gay Games, and human rights conferences. Sometimes, attempts have been made to formalize such groups, but few have succeeded in a structured fashion. Nonetheless, such contacts and interactions are extremely useful and important for ongoing work, the sharing of strategies, support, and even advocacy when someone's life has been in danger, not to mention the long-lasting friendships built.

## Lesbian-Only Organizations

As of the late 1990s, there was only one international organization in the world that focused on lesbians exclusively and attempted to include lesbians from the entire world: the International Lesbian Information Service (ILIS). ILIS was formed in the late 1970s by a number of women who reportedly were upset by the sexism and lack of lesbian representation in the International Gay Association (now the International Lesbian and Gay Association or ILGA). ILIS is located in the Netherlands, where a group of dedicated women (all volunteers) have produced a newsletter titled *ILIS* since 1984 in English and Spanish, containing current news and information from lesbians around the world. The group maintains contacts with lesbians from more than sixty countries. In 1986, ILIS held its first and only international conference, in Geneva, Switzerland; approximately two hundred lesbians from about forty countries participated. Although the conference was disrupted by issues of racism and militarism, regional efforts were launched, and many contacts were made among key lesbian activists who have continued organizing in the movement. At least two organizations were formed from the inspiration of this conference—one in Israel and another in the former Yugoslavia. ILIS has maintained its modest goals (with a very modest budget) of increasing communication and information about lesbians worldwide and strategically participating in certain international events, such as the 1995 United Nations World Conference on Women in Beijing, China, and the Gay Games.

The other lesbian-only ongoing international groups are regional in scope and include the Asian Lesbian Network (ALN) and the Encuentros de Lesbianas Feministas, conferences that are organized regularly for lesbians living in Latin America and the Caribbean. The Asian Lesbian Network, formed in 1991 after the first Asian lesbian conference in Thailand, is a loose network of lesbians from more than ten Asian countries, as well as Asian lesbians living outside Asia. The network holds biannual conferences and, in the late 1990s, was the process of formalizing its constitution, membership criteria, and new structure.

The Encuentros de Lesbianas Feministas have been held approximately every three years since 1987 in conjunction with an annual feminist conference for Latin America and the Caribbean. Lesbians have been meeting at the Encuentros Feministas since the early 1980s and continue to meet even if the separate lesbian conference is not on for that year. There is no formal organization or network that hosts this conference, which rotates from year to year.

Other geographic regions have attempted to form such networks, or international organizations, or conferences, but only the Latin American and Asian regions have been able to successfully continue such institutions on a sustainable basis. On the other hand, national lesbian conferences have been plentiful in numerous countries, including Israel, the United States, the Philippines, Brazil, and Chile. Often, women from neighboring countries will attend a national meeting due to a dearth of such opportunities in their own country.

## Lesbians in Mixed Organizations

There are a few other international organizations that, as mixed groups of lesbian, gay, and sometimes bisexual and transgendered people, work on lesbian issues. The oldest such group is the International Lesbian and Gay Association (ILGA), which was formed in 1978 as the International Gay Association. ILGA is a federation composed (as of 1998) of approximately three hundred organizations, which holds a world conference for its members every two years and distributes an English-language bulletin approximately five times per year via its administrative office in Brussels, Belgium. In 1997, ILGA changed its structure from numerous secretariat positions held by member groups to an executive board of individuals from various regions of the world and two secretaries-general that govern the organization between world conferences. The organization maintains a volunteer Women's Secretariat that is charged with keeping lesbian, bisexual, and transgendered women's issues active in the ILGA. With no paid staff, the organization maintains an active presence on the Internet.

The International Gay and Lesbian Human Rights Commission (IGLHRC) is a U.S.-based organization that works on human rights abuses worldwide on the basis of sexual orientation, gender identity, and HIV status. IGLHRC was formed in 1991 to bridge the gap between the mainstream human rights movement and the growing lesbian, gay, bisexual, and transgender movements worldwide. With twelve staff members and offices in New York City and San Francisco, California, IGLHRC monitors, documents, and mobilizes response to human rights violations in partnership with thousands of grass-roots organizations in more than 120 countries. The organization produces regular action alerts in three languages, mobilizing response to urgent situations that need international attention. IGLHRC also provides support to asylum seekers; offers technical assistance to grass-roots lesbian, gay, bisexual, transgender, and other sexual-minority groups in developing countries; and produces human rights reports. IGLHRC was instrumental in ensuring visible, global lesbian participation in the 1995 United Nations World Conference on Women in Beijing and specifically works on lesbian issues within the broader struggle to view sexuality as a human right.

The International Gay and Lesbian Youth Organization (IGLYO), formerly the Union of Gay and Lesbian Youth, has been functioning since 1983 as a loose group of lesbian and gay youth activists. The group, headquartered in Amsterdam, the Netherlands, holds an annual conference and produces a newsletter, *Speak Out*. The Federation of Gay

Games, headquartered in Oakland, California, is another international institution; it has been holding Olympic-style sports and culture events every four years since 1982. The purpose of the federation is to foster and augment the self-respect, dignity, and pride of gay men and lesbians throughout the world and to inspire the respect and understanding of the nongay world.

Numerous religious organizations are becoming more international. The World Congress of Gay and Lesbian Jewish Organizations (London, United Kingdom) had a membership nearing three hundred by the late 1990s; it holds annual conferences, distributes its newsletter among members, and advocates for greater inclusion of lesbian and gay issues in the mainstream Jewish international institutions. The Universal Fellowship of Metropolitan Community Churches, founded in 1968, had more than three hundred churches, primarily in the United States, in the late 1990s, and at least thirty churches in other countries.

Also in the late 1990s, there were about one hundred international lesbian and gay film festivals held around the world on a regular basis. While they feature films and videos from numerous countries, they usually cater to a local or national audience. Film festivals, like Pride marches, are an unsurpassable opportunity to bring together large numbers of people to witness positive images of themselves on the screen and in the streets, particularly given the few opportunities for lesbian visibility.

There are a few organizations that cater to bisexuals and transgendered people that are becoming more international, such as Female-To-Male International (San Francisco, California). There is also an international bisexual conference that is held every three years, although there is no formal international organization. These are primarily European or U.S. dominated but also include a few members from other parts of the world.

Some nonlesbian and nongay international organizations could do constructive work on lesbian issues, such as Amnesty International, the International Women's League for Peace and Freedom, and Planned Parenthood International; however, most of these have historically been reluctant or slow to include lesbian issues in their missions.

Although most lesbian organizations lack sufficient resources to be able to fulfill their missions, there are an increasing number of funding sources for lesbian organizations internationally. These include the Astraea Foundation's International Fund, the Global Fund for Women, the European Human Rights Foundation, and the Dutch government, among others.

*Julie Dorf*

### Bibliography

Dorf, Julie, and Gloria Cariega Pérez. "Discrimination and the Tolerance of Difference: International Lesbian Human Rights." In *Women's Rights, Human Rights: International Feminist Perspectives.* Ed. Julie Peters and Andrea Wolper. New York: Routledge, 1995, pp. 324–334.

ILIS Newsletter, International Lesbian Information Service, Nieuwezijds Voorburgwal 68–70, 1012 Amsterdam, Netherlands.

Reinfelder, Monika, ed. *Amazon to Zami: Towards a Global Lesbian Feminism.* London: Cassell, 1996.

Rosenbloom, Rachel, ed. *Unspoken Rules: Sexual Orientation and Women's Human Rights.* London: Cassell, 1996.

*See also* Asian Lesbian Network; Associations and Organizations; Encuentros de Lesbianas; Gay Games; Human Rights

## Invisibility

As defined by Webster's Third Edition International Dictionary: "intangible, unseen, inaccessible to view; out of sight, of such small size or unobtrusive quality as to be hardly noticeable."

To be visible as a lesbian requires that a woman is known to others as such. This also presupposes being able to participate in an open manner as a lesbian and being included in all areas of life as a lesbian. Throughout history, this has not been the experience of women who define themselves as lesbian. They have lived unseen and largely unnoticed, unacknowledged in their relationships, living secret, stigmatized lives. In public spheres, women in general and lesbians in particular have rarely been clearly and generally acknowledged for their role in society. Lesbians, along with gay men, may be rendered invisible when the media ignores major public events, such as the 1993 march on Washington, D.C., or the Gay Games (athletic competitions held every four years).

Attempts to identify lesbians based on appearance or measurements of physical characteristics have been unsuccessful. Early medical research attempted to prove that lesbians were anatomically more like men than women, but significant differences between heterosexual and lesbian women have not yet been found. More recent research on genetic causes of homosexuality has, as of the late 1990s, included very few women.

Laws against sexual activity by homosexuals usually describe behaviors between men. Often, the laws were not enforced against women, unless they were women who, by cross-dressing, took on more masculine appearance and perogatives. In 1885, when the Criminal Law Amendment was passed in England, Queen Victoria (1819–1901) refused to sign it until all references to women were removed. She did not believe female homosexuality existed and did not wish to blemish women by referring to them in this law about public or private homosexual acts.

Invisibility is a complex issue, compounded by lack of agreement even on how to define lesbians and how to determine who is one. Agreement on lesbianism as biologically determined or chosen does not exist. No one knows how many women have sexual relationships with other women and, of those, how many define themselves as lesbians or how they decide. Women who have sex with women but do not define themselves as lesbian may say, "I am not a lesbian, but my life partner is a woman." Two women who have a close relationship and share living arrangements may seem to others to be lesbians but not see themselves as other than heterosexual.

Invisibility may also be a consequence of the use of the words "gay" or "homosexual," which are generally taken to mean "male homosexual." More specifically, these words are taken to refer to representatives of the dominant culture: white, able-bodied, upper-middle-class men. They exclude lesbian women in general. They also render invisible women of color, the physically challenged, and other groups, all of whom have lesbian members. Similarly, the words "woman" and "feminist" are typically assumed to refer to heterosexual women. Hence, lesbians also remain invisible within the feminist community.

The image of the lesbian is seldom portrayed publicly. When it is, it is usually that of the "butch" or more apparently lower-class, male-identified woman. The more traditionally feminine lesbian is seldom publicly identified. These "femmes" are often derided as "lipstick lesbians" and criticized as not "real lesbians." There is little discussion or representation of butch-butch or femme-femme relationships, again rendering invisible aspects of women's intimate experiences with other women.

This discussion also varies in meaning and in emphasis in different cultures and countries. Lesbians in China and in Turkey, to give two disparate examples, may discuss these issues from very different perspectives than do lesbians in western European or North American countries. Experiences that mark a woman as a lesbian in one culture may not do so in another. Hence, cultural differences may render lesbians invisible to one another.

After decades of neglect, in the late twentieth century, art, music, literature, videos, television, and fiction all began to portray lesbians more frequently. Increasing numbers of lesbian performers—from k.d. lang (1961–) and Melissa Etheridge (1961–) in music to Ellen DeGeneres (1958–) in television—revealed themselves to be lesbians. The analyses of these representations are extensive in both academic and nonacademic works, focusing in part on the language about and images of lesbians. Even within academic circles, there has been a strenuous debate over whether queer theory also renders lesbians invisible.

Social structures, systems, and services are seldom inclusive of lesbians, or, if they are, it is seldom readily apparent. For example, when a counseling center for lesbians and gay men was incorporated into a family-therapy agency, staff were told not to display their lesbian and gay posters where the general public could see them. In this way, invisibility is maintained.

Self-identification as a lesbian varies from instance to instance, with women visible in different ways: less at their children's school, perhaps, and more at home with other lesbians. In most groups of lesbians, there are different comfort levels with visibility and invisibility. Frequently, this is a contentious issue in lesbian families. Visibility requires a knowledge and an acceptance of one's identity and a decision to share that. It also involves truth telling, demanding and occupying a place in the dominant culture, and rejecting homophobia and secrecy.

*Elizabeth L. Massiah*

### Bibliography

Klaich, Dolores. *Woman + Woman: Attitudes Towards Lesbianism.* New York: Simon and Schuster, 1974.

Roof, Judith. *Come As You Are: Sexuality and Narrative.* New York: Columbia University Press, 1996.

Walker, Lisa M. "How to Recognize a Lesbian: The Cultural Politics of Looking Like What You Are." *Signs: Journal of Women in Culture and Society* 18:4 (Summer 1993), 866–890.

**See also** Closet; Heterosexism; Homophobia; Identity; Style

# Ireland

**I** Island located at the northwest extremity of Europe; population, 3.5 million; divided into the Republic of Ireland and Northern Ireland, the latter administratively part of the United Kingdom. Historically, Ireland has struggled against the colonial domination of its more powerful neighbor, England. The Irish Republic won its freedom in 1921. At the end of the twentieth century, Ireland remained a small, divided, postcolonial society whose values are dominated by a misogynist Catholic Church.

Two-thirds of married women in Ireland do not work outside the home. Divorce was unavailable until 1996, and abortion is prohibited by the constitution. Male homosexuality was decriminalized in 1993, establishing an equal age of consent with heterosexuals, yet harassment and constructive dismissal of lesbians and gays in the workplace continued. Numerous incidents of gay bashing have been documented. AIDS claims many lives, and homophobia is an enduring part of the fabric of the culture.

Despite these facts, lesbians have been actively engaged in constructing a "lesbian tradition" in Ireland. One of the places lesbians look to for evidence of a previous lesbian existence is Irish literature. Romantic friendships, androgynous heroines, and women passing as men can all be found in the work of writers such as George Egerton (pseud. of Mary Chavelita Dunne [1859–1945]), Eva Gore-Booth (1870–1926), Martin Ross (pseud. of Edith Somerville [1858–1949] and Violet Martin [1862–1915]), Elizabeth Bowen (1899–1972), and Kate O'Brien (1897–1974). From Egerton's androgynous heroines of the nineteenth century to O'Brien's lesbian realist novel *As Music and Splendour* (1958), there are writers imagining a future for women-loving-women. This tradition is continued in the contemporary work of writers such as Emma Donoghue and Mary Dorcey. Lesbian experiences are validated by this literature and imaginations charged by figures such as Egerton's sketch, in her short story "The Spell of the White Elf" (1893), of "a tall woman with very square shoulders. . . . the flame flickers over the patent-leather of her neat low-heeled boot, and strikes a spark from the pin of her tie."

Other historical figures in an imagined Irish lesbian tradition include the early-eighteenth-century pirate Anne Bonney, whose cross-dressing, daring exploits, and affection for her companion pirate Mary Read make her one of the legendary figures from the Irish past. Equally legendary are the Ladies of Llangollen, two Irish cousins who eloped to Wales in 1778. However, the lives of these women (and, to some extent, the literary women whose privileged backgrounds made it possible for them to lead the lives they did) are, to many contemporary lesbians, only fantasy. In the attempt to fashion what American writer Audre Lorde (1934–1992) calls a "mythography" for Irish lesbians, they are crucial. But in terms of activism or the everyday lives of lesbians in Ireland, it is the work of more recent and collective heroines that has developed the lesbian community.

Work in the gay community in Ireland during the 1970s and 1980s focused on law reform—specifically, the decriminalization of male homosexuality. Paradoxical though it may seem, the very fact that lesbians were not "criminalized" in the first instance points to their invisibility in Irish society. The lack of a political and media focus of attention in the 1980s left lesbians without a public identity. Many lesbians worked with gay activists on law reform, while others joined feminist organizations and the antinuclear movement. Lesbians have been part of every political campaign for women's liberation in Ireland; they have worked for access to contraception and abortion information and in the divorce lobby; they also work in rape crisis centers, trade unions, and environmental groups and have contributed to socialist and nationalist platforms, campaigns against racism, and disability issues. In the 1990s, the focus of social activism narrowed to using European Union—and government-sponsored projects—such as the Lesbian Education and Awareness (LEA) project for training community organizers—to provide facilities for lesbians and target homophobia in the wider community.

At the end of the 1990s, lesbian activism in Ireland was at an all-time high. A cohesive support network of Lesbian (Help)Line groups (a collective organization that operates a countrywide switchboard) around the country—Lesbians Organising Together, the Lesbian Health Network in Cork, and the LEA project—all facilitate the development of the community. The Cork Women's Fun Weekend, which began in 1984, continued to thrive, as did women's weekends in Dublin and Belfast. Talamh na mBan (Women's Land) engaged in fund-raising to buy land for the annual women's summer camps. The study of lesbian experience began to emerge from the excellent work done through women's studies courses around the country, ably supported by the annual Lesbian Lives conference run by the Women's Education Research and Resource Centre at University College, Dublin.

Many questions need to be addressed. Few lesbians in Ireland have successfully gained custody of their children in the courts. In a country in which woman's place in the family is constitutionally enshrined, lesbian parenting is just one of the challenges posed by redefinitions of "the family." Other questions being raised are issues of (un)employment and poverty, problems surrounding alcohol and substance abuse, and differing lesbian "identities" in an Irish social context. In a divided country, cross-border organization of Lesbian (Help)Lines is one way of enabling North-South cooperation. In 1989, the Cork-Belfast Lesbian Line Exchange won a Co-Operation North prize for its efforts. At the end of the 1990s, there was no lesbian-owned venue in Ireland or any lesbian-only space that operated for more than one night a week.

On the other hand, the growing number of non-Irish lesbians who choose to make their homes in Ireland makes a positive statement about the kind of lesbian community that exists. Many women move to rural parts of the west coast, which extends the urban networks. The development of lesbian culture and community through publishing and literature, music and art (Dublin's lesbian and gay choir, Gloria, for example), and education, social work, and therapeutic healing indicates the energetic and constructive work of lesbians in contemporary Ireland.    *Tina O'Toole*

### Bibliography

Bidwell, Emma. "Where Have All the Dungarees Gone?" *Irish Journal of Feminist Studies* 2:1 (1997), 55–62.

Dublin Lesbian and Gay Men's Collectives. *Out for Ourselves: The Lives of Irish Lesbians and Gay Men*. Dublin: Women's Community Press, 1986.

Irish Council for Civil Liberties. *Equality Now for Lesbians and Gay Men*. Dublin: Irish Council for Civil Liberties, 1990.

O'Carroll, Ide, and Eoin Collins. *Lesbian and Gay Visions of Ireland*. London: Cassell, 1995.

O'Leary, Mary. "Lesbianism and Feminism: A Personal Reflection." *Irish Journal of Feminist Studies* 2:1 (1997), 63–66.

Rose, Kieran. *Diverse Communities: The Evolution of Lesbian and Gay Politics in Ireland*. Cork: Cork University Press, 1994.

Walshe, Eibhear. *Sex, Nation and Dissent*. Cork: Cork University Press, 1996.

*See also* Androgyny; Bowen, Elizabeth; Cross-Dressing; Ladies of Llangollen; Lorde, Audre; O'Brien, Kate; Romantic Friendship

# Islam

Youngest of the three Abrahamic religions (also including Judaism and Christianity) professed by Muhammad in A.D. 610. The term "Islam" signifies peace that ensues from complete surrender or submission to God.

## Characteristics

The central tenant of Islam is: "There is no god but God and . . . Muhammad is the Prophet of God." Any one who publicly proclaims this is considered a Muslim. The most authoritative texts for Muslims are the *Quran*, a collection of verses proclaimed by Muhammad (ca. A.D. 570–632) as revelation from God over a period of twenty-two years, and the *Hadith* literature, a record of the practice of the Prophet. In addition, Islam accepts the Bible as revealed scripture and recognizes all of the biblical patriarchs as its own beginning with Adam. Unlike the Shi'i sect, there is no clergy in Sunni Islam, the religion of the majority of Muslims. Scholars' opinions based on the authoritative texts of Islam are of prime importance, and, when scholarly opinion differs, a Muslim is free to accept any one of them. Most of what is called Islamic law (*shariah*) is unenforceable, being rather a manual for personal conduct for one who would practice Islam.

Although Islam originated in Arabia, and the majority of Arabs are Muslims, Arabs form only 20 percent of the Muslim population. Muslims populate vast areas of Africa and Asia. After Christianity, Islam has the largest number of adherents, and it is the fastest-growing religion in the world. A bloc of countries covering North and Central Africa, the Middle East, and Central and South Asia with a Muslim majority are termed "the Muslim world." There are some visible and tangible cultural similarities among these countries. However, local languages, cultures, and customs surviving from before the spread of Islam in these countries define the differences among the various parts of the Muslim world.

## Attitudes Toward Homosexuality

Muslim cultural attitudes toward homosexuality are equivocal. In poetry and literature, it may be celebrated. In biography, it is respected as an intimate and important part of the subject's private life. In Sufi (mystical) lore, it is a common occurrence; in medical lore, a curable disease; and in Islamic authoritative texts, abominable and punishable behavior. From the point of view of orthodox religion, the term "Muslim lesbian" would be an oxymoron, as one cannot identify with both at the same time.

In the Muslim world, which covers a multitude of linguistic and cultural groups, there are several vernacular terms that signify female homoeroticism or homosexuality that are not known outside the particular local cultures. In other indigenous or regional cultures, the emotion and expression of female homoeroticism remains unnamed due to the severity of sexual suppression or reprisals for such behavior. Among the Urdu-speaking Muslims of northern India, references to female homosexuality are found in what is considered erotica or pornographic literature presumably authored by men. Although this poetry is not of literary significance, it nonetheless gives a name for female homosexuality: *chapti khailna* (loosely translated as "playing flat"). In a standard modern Arabic commentary of the *Quran* (Surah IV, verse 15), the term *sihaq* (two surfaces grinding against each other) is used to refer to female homosexuality. There may be several other vernacular Arabic terms for *sihaq*. The fact that Muslim religious (text-based) culture severely condemns homosexuality, and that most Muslims live within oral, nonliteral, gender-segregated, homosocial cultures, makes information regarding female homosexuality quite inaccessible. Among the myriad cultures falling within the Muslim world, there may be long-standing female homoerotic cultures passed down from generation to generation. There also may be individual couples' unnamed, secret, and isolated experience of homoeroticism, and individual feelings that are never understood or recognized by the individual herself due to the absence of cultural representations and models. As of 1998, no systematic field research had been conducted to gather oral histories of Muslim lesbians.

## Literary and Legal Texts

Whereas the religious texts of High Islam have historically condemned homosexuality, the literary and mystical texts have preserved a male homoerotic and homosexual tradition. The relative dearth of references to *sihaq* in classical Arabo-Muslim literary tradition may signify the lack of access to the elite male literary circles with the power to preserve texts for posterity. In the *kitab al-aghani* (The Book of Songs) of the literary historian of the Arabo-Muslim renaissance, Abul Farraj al-Isbahani (ca. A.D. 897–967), there are references to female homoeroticism among the court poets and singers. The *kitab al-aghani* is a yet untapped source for the construc-

tion of a rich chapter in the history of Muslim lesbians. There are references to the Andalusian princess Walladah bint al-Mustakfi (d. 1087), called "the Sappho of Spain," in the works of Al-Maqarri (seventeenth century), prinicipal authority for the literary history of Muslim Spain. About twenty lines of Walladah's amorous poetic exchanges with the great poet Ibn Zaydun (1003–1071) are preserved. There are no known records of her homoerotic poetry, however.

In contemporary literature by Muslim women, an implicit, but undeniable, theme of female homoeroticism can be found in the short stories of the Egyptian Alîfa Rifʿat (n.d.) and the Pakistani Khalida Hussain (1938–). It is not clear whether these authors, who write from within the "protected" and "respectable" environment of a traditional Muslim family, are aware of the undercurrent of female homoerotic engagement in some of their writing. In the provocative fiction of the acclaimed Indian Ismat Chughtai (1915–), one finds a frank exploration of both hetero- and homosexuality. No study of her work focusing specifically on the theme of female homosexuality has been undertaken.

While there is clear textual evidence in the *Quran* that supports the immorality and therefore the illegality of male homosexual behavior, there is no such clear text referring to female homosexual behavior. Surah IV, verses 15–16 of the *Quran,* which is cited by some as prohibiting female homosexual behavior, is, in fact, ambiguous as to the nature of the offense and the gender composition of the couple. Whereas in the earliest extant commentaries of the *Quran* (Ibn Abbas, ca. A.D. 688), this text is understood to refer to heterosexual couples, in more recent times, especially in the twentieth century, the verses have been cited as providing the textual evidence needed to unequivocally condemn female homosexual behavior.

A case cited in Shi'i juristic texts functions similarly to fill in the gap created by the silence of the *Quran* on the issue of female homosexuality. Hasan ibn ʻAli (A.D. 624–669), Muhammad's grandson, and Jafar (A.D. 700–765), Hasan ibn ʻAli's grandson, are said to have ruled on the case. It involves a woman who, subsequent to having sexual intercourse with her husband, engages in sexual activity with a virgin slave, transferring her husband's semen to her female sexual partner, thus causing her partner to become pregnant with the husband's child. Both Hasan ibn ʻAli and Jafar al-Sadiq rule that the married woman is to be stoned to death and the virgin slave's dowry is to be taken away, as she will lose her virginity when she delivers the child. After the child is born, it is to be returned to the father, and the slave woman is to be flogged. The text prescribes the same punishment for female homosexual acts as is prescribed by Islamic law for extramarital heterosexual acts. Regardless of whether the case is a juristic fiction or an actual case, the fact that it is quoted in several Shi'i texts is a recognition of the reality of female homsexuality and a means of condemning and controlling it.

Within Muslim countries at the end of the twentieth century, the public mention of homosexuality is taboo, and, in many places, people perceived as homosexual are ridiculed and/or persecuted. While human rights are a major focus of the political action of the progressive forces, and while women's rights movements are strong in major metropolitan areas, the rights of homosexuals remain, for the most part, publicly unspoken and unspeakable, given that freedom of speech is not guaranteed in most Muslim countries and that most Muslim governments use Islam to legitimize their rule. In the writings on Muslim women by Muslim feminists, there is no mention of female homosexuality; the subject is considered a land mine that could destroy, the progress of women's rights and self-determination. On rare occasions, individual Muslims, such as Ismat Chugtai or the Pakistani poet Josh Malihabadi (1896–1982), have stood for individual freedom and extended it to sexual minorities, protesting their religious and cultural condemnation and political persecution.                    *Ghazala Anwar*

### Bibliography

Duran, Khalid. "Homosexuality and Islam." In *Homosexuality and World Religions*. Ed. Arlene Swidler. New York: Macmillan, 1993.

Ferne, Elizabeth Warnock, and Bassima Qattan Bazirgan. "Walladah bint-al Mustakfi: Andalusian Poet." In *Middle Eastern Muslim Women Speak*. Ed. Fernea and Bazirgan. Austin: University of Texas Press, 1977.

*See also* Arab Literature, Modern; Egypt

## Israel

Country in the Middle East with a population of approximately five million people, of whom four million are Jewish and one million Palestinian Arab. The state of Israel was established in 1948 by the United Nations after years of struggle between the Palestinian Arabs, the Jews, and the British mandate. The Zionist cause gained momentum and achieved considerable international legitimacy in the wake of the Nazi genocide in World War II. After the creation of the state, an influx of immigrants doubled the Jewish population from 600,000 to more than 1.2 million in less than five years. Many of the new immigrants were either Holocaust survivors—mostly Eastern European—or Jews from Arab countries. The rise of the Jewish nation from the ashes of the Nazi genocide and the in-gathering of the Jewish people are two central elements informing Israeli national identity. Israeli identity politics never stray far from the issue of national survival.

### Israeli Gender Construction

Israeli lesbian identity can be understood only in the context of the role gender plays in Israeli society. Gender, in turn, must be evaluated through the lens of social and ethnic background. In spite of the mythology of egalitarianism surrounding the Israeli female soldier and kibbutz life, Israeli society is rigidly gendered. The pervasive militaristic environment constructs and depends upon strict gender roles—men are "just warriors," and women are "beautiful souls." In the same vein, sexual identity is clearly demarcated, wherein masculinity and femininity strictly correlate with male and female heterosexuality and biological sex. The gendered nature of women's role in society is then shaped and exacerbated by the preoccupation with the propagation of the Jewish people, raising the importance of fertility and childbearing to cultish levels. The "cult of fertility," in Hazleton's (1977) coinage, flourishes in Israel's profoundly heterosexist society: Marriage is an assumed and desirable goal, and the family unit is of utmost importance. Lesbianism, historically perceived as a foreclosure on the family unit, generates curiosity, and lesbians are largely pitied or mocked.

### Gay and Lesbian History

Male homosexuality was criminalized until 1988. The criminal code did not mention lesbianism, and, while there was less hostility directed at lesbians than at gay men, the criminal code also contributed to the general antilesbian atmosphere. After the creation of the state, the Israeli Parliament held no specific discussions on the topic of homosexuality. The antisodomy law was carried over from the British mandate. By the 1950s, the general understanding, shared by the legislature, the courts, and the police, was that this law was not to be enforced. In 1970–1971, several Parliament members attempted to overturn the law without success. It would not be until 1988 that the Society for the Protection of Personal Rights (SPPR), Israel's lesbian, gay, and bisexual organization, would successfully spearhead the movement to decriminalize homosexuality.

In the early 1970s, lesbians began organizing themselves and discussing their isolation in Israeli society. These initial attempts at community organizing took place within the fledgling feminist community. Community lore suggests that many of the early feminist activists were either lesbians at the time or came out in future years. However, the feminist community welcomed neither lesbians nor discussions about lesbianism, for fear that the feminist movement and feminism itself would be synonymous with lesbianism. In 1974, at a feminist collective meeting, members, including the lesbian members, voted against starting a lesbian consciousness-raising group. Partly as a result of such attitudes, lesbian feminists organized "underground" activities. In 1976, an informal lesbian network held regular parties and other activities to which only lesbians were invited.

In the spring of the same year, several lesbians participated in a meeting between SPPR and the few publicly supportive parliament members. The previous year, one lesbian and eleven gay men had founded SPPR. Limited participation of lesbians in SPPR has characterized the nature, and determined the direction, of SPPR since its inception. Despite continued involvement in both the lesbian and gay rights movement and the feminist movement, lesbian feminists did not feel represented by, or welcome in, either. For that reason, since 1978 lesbian feminists have established a series of groups to address their invisibility and to fill a social and cultural void. These groups, such as KLaF (Kehila Lesbit feministit; Lesbian Feminist Community), have been increasingly active in the urban centers of Haifa, Tel Aviv, and Jerusalem.

By the late 1980s, lesbians were acknowledged as an integral part of the feminist movement. The feminist movement in Tel Aviv gave a voice to, and a meeting place for, KLaF activities. The feminist center in Haifa, Isha l'Isha (Woman to Woman), recognized lesbians in its mandate. Organizers of the feminist conferences since the early 1990s insist on equal representation for lesbians, Palestinian women, Ashkenazi Jewish women (of European descent), and Mizrahi Jewish women (of Middle East-

ern and North African descent). Nevertheless, homophobia continues to control feminist activity, for, although lesbians stood on the front lines in significant numbers in the women's peace movement of the late 1980s and early 1990s, an unspoken code demanded they remain closeted, lest the general public brand women peace activists as lesbians.

Another aspect of lesbian life is queer bar culture. Until the mid-1990s, there was very little crossover between the feminist lesbian community and lesbian bar culture. This has gradually changed as Israeli lesbians and gay men become more visible in the general public and to one another. Lesbian feminists are exposing themselves to queer culture, and lesbians not affiliated with the feminist community increasingly take part in the political and feminist aspects of gay culture. In the 1990s, Israeli gays and lesbians have made significant strides toward coalition work. Gay Pride celebrations of June 1995 featured a public trial on the issue of lesbian second-parent adoption organized by KLaF and cosponsored by SPPR and other civil rights organizations. In effect this event marked KLaF's, and the lesbian community's, "coming out" event. Two years later, SPPR also came out of the closet when members elected to change the organization's name and to represent its constituency: the Association for Lesbians, Bisexuals, and Gay Men. These public events came in the wake of several important legislative gains. In 1992, sexual orientation was added to the Equal Rights in the Work Place law. In 1993, the military amended its regulations to prohibit discrimination on the basis of sexual orientation. In 1995, the Israeli Supreme Court recognized lesbian and gay domestic partnership when it ruled in favor of a gay flight attendant who sued for spousal benefits for his lover.

On an individual basis, Israeli lesbians (and gay men) are slow to take advantage of these political and legislative gains. The personal coming out process is made more complicated and frightening by Israel's small size and familial feeling: Coming out publicly is tantamount to coming out to the entire nation. Subsequently, some would argue that the vast majority of Israeli lesbians do not participate in public lesbian life.

Nevertheless, 1998 saw an outpour of lesbian and gay pride. In May of that year, Dana International, an Israeli male-to-female transgendered vocal artist, represented Israel in The Eurovision, an annual European song contest, which she won. Her selection as the Israeli representative and her participation generated considerable media attention and public debate.

Within the lesbian community, the issue of hostility to transgendered persons came to the fore. Dana International's victory largely silenced the disagreements among lesbians, and she was fully embraced as a hero by the queer community as well as by many heterosexual secular allies. In June 1998, for the first time in Israel and the entire Middle East, the Israeli queer community took to the streets of Tel Aviv for a Gay Pride march, sponsored by multiple organizations working in concert.

*Ruti Kadish*

## Bibliography

Freedman, Marcia. *Exile in the Promised Land: A Memoir*. Ithaca, N.Y.: Firebrand, 1990.

Hazelton, Lesley. *Israeli Women: The Reality Behind the Myths*. New York: Touchstone, 1977.

Moore, Tracy. *Lesbiot: Israeli Lesbians Talk About Sexuality, Feminism, Judaism, and Their Lives*. New York and London: Cassell, 1995.

Safir, Marilyn P., and Barbara Swirski, eds. *Calling the Equality Bluff: Women in Israel*. New York: Pergamon, 1991.

*See also* Antisemitism; Judaism; Nazism

## Italy

Republic located in southern Europe, with a population of about 56 million. First unified as a kingdom in 1861, the written history of the Italian peninsula goes back more than two millennia. A hypothetical lesbian history of Italy might begin with the presence of the Greek poet Sappho (ca. 600 B.C.E.) on the island of Sicily in 596 B.C.E. and continue with references to the sexual behavior of Roman courtesans mentioned in classical Latin texts.

After the decline of the Roman Empire (ca. A.D. 476), the Italian peninsula was conquered by different populations (Arabic and Turkish from the south, "barbarians" from northern Europe) and split into a number of independent regions, city-states, and kingdoms, many of which were dominated by the papacy and by foreign powers. Information about lesbianism is scattered throughout different types of documents.

## History

In the fourteenth century, the statutes of the cities of Ferrara and Florence condemned women for sodomy. However, given the lack of clarity in the definition of this crime, it is not obvious whether these statutes referred to heterosexual or homosexual acts. On the other hand, at the beginning of the fifteenth century, Saint Antoninus (1363–1451) made explicit mention of sexuality between women as the eighth of nine kinds of lust, and, at the end of the century, the Florentine political and religious leader Fra Girolamo Savonarola (1452–1498) was equally explicit in his condemnation. In 1539, Annibal Caro (1507–1566), perhaps for the first time in the Italian language, used the word "tribades" of Lesbos; "lesbian" as a noun appeared only at the beginning of the twentieth century, first in literary texts. In 1574 in Treviso, women guilty of this crime were condemned to be burned at the stake outside the city gate.

In the seventeenth century, the French libertine writer Pierre de Bourdeilles (ca. 1540–1614), abbot and lord of Brantôme, describing the customs of French courtly women, asserted that these are "manners brought from Italy by a highly placed woman whom I will not mention." But, at the same time, his contemporary Italian jurists strongly condemned this crime.

The women identified as lesbians during this period included noblewomen, courtesans, and nuns. In 1626, Benedetta Carlini (1590–1661), the abbess of a convent, was sent to prison, where she spent thirty-five years, for, among other reasons, having seduced a novice, Bartolomea Crivelli, assuming for this purpose the masculine identity of an angel she called Splenditello. Others were intellectuals, influenced by the recovery of ancient texts such as those of the philosopher Plato (427?–347? B.C.E.).

In the eighteenth century, lesbianism was common among aristocratic women. Turin saw the birth of Maria Teresa of Savoia Carignano (1749–1792), who later became princess of Lamballe and Marie Antoinette's (1755–1793) reputed lover. Even Maria Carolina, queen of Naples (1752–1814), sister of the beheaded queen of France, had at least one woman lover, Emma Hamilton (1730–1803), who had been the lover of the British naval hero Lord Nelson (1758–1805). On the other hand, in 1739, a woman accused of witchcraft who had experienced carnal pleasures with another woman was brought to trial in Reggio Emilia. And in Rome, a woman who had lived for eight years dressed as a man was convicted in 1743.

In the nineteenth century, a vulgar satire accused some Venetian women, several of whom were Jewish,

I of the crime of tribadism. During the same period, in the isolated mountains of Pollino on the border between the southern regions of Basilicata and Calabria lived a number of masculine lesbians called *sbraie* who, reputedly, were endowed with magic powers.

In 1861, Italy was unified into a single state, and, in 1889, the articles in the penal code that condemned homosexuality (between men) were abolished. As Italy moved into the modern era, it is known that a number of famous artists and feminists engaged in same-sex relationships, such as the actress Eleonora Duse (1858–1924), who had numerous women lovers, including Isadora Duncan (1878–1927). There were strong attachments between numerous feminist leaders, including Armida Barelli and Teresa Pallavicino (both active in the early twentieth century) and Giacinta Pezzana (1841–1919) and Alessandra Ravizza (1846–1915), among others.

Italy was a popular destination for foreign women, including many who had same-sex lovers, beginning with Queen Christina of Sweden (1626–1689), who, after abdicating in 1654, came to live in Rome (and is buried in Saint Peter's Cathedral). In the nineteenth century, American actress Charlotte Cushman (1816–1876) and her partner, Emma Stebbins (1815–1882), along with artists Harriet Hosmer (1830–1908) and Edmonia Lewis (ca. 1843–after 1911), also settled in Rome. Evangeline Marss Simpson (Whipple) (d. 1930) and Rose Elizabeth Cleveland ([d. 1918]; sister of the American president) left the United States in 1910 for a small Tuscan town, Bagni di Lucca, where they are buried in twin tombs. Vernon Lee, pseudonym of Violet Page (1856–1935), an eminent Victorian writer, lived in Florence from 1873 to 1935. British composer Ethel Smyth (1858–1944) spent more than a year there as well. Gertrude Stein (1874–1946) and Alice B. Toklas (1877–1967) were guests of American hostess Mabel Dodge Luhan (1879–1962) in Fiesole in 1910. British novelist Radclyffe Hall (1880–1943) lived there on several occasions in the 1920s and 1930s with her partner, Una Troubridge (1887–1963), and with Souline, the last woman with whom she fell in love. Natalie Barney (1876–1972) and Romaine Brooks (1874–1970), who was Italian by birth, left France for Italy during World War II. A colony of famous homosexual women and men flourished on the island of Capri in the 1920s. From 1955 until her death, Violet Trefusis (1894–1972), Vita Sackville-West's (1892–1962) lover (who was portrayed as Sasha in Virginia Woolf's [1882–1941] novel *Orlando,* 1928), spent part of each year in Flo-

rence. A network of relations existed between foreign and Italian women, as can be seen from the letters and visits that they exchanged and the common circles that the expatriates frequented.

The work of German sexologists began to influence Italian intellectuals at the end of the nineteenth century. In 1883, the first Italian case of "sexual inversion" was described, and it concerned a woman. At the turn of the twentieth century, scientists, criminologists, and anthropologists circulated information about "abnormal" women through meticulous descriptions of prostitutes, schoolgirls, incarcerated women, and madwomen and published love letters from nurses and students and transcripts of legal cases involving separations due to the lesbianism of the wife.

Under the Fascist government of Benito Mussolini (1922–1945), it is known that lesbianism survided in the boarding schools and sports academies (in Orvieto, for example) and that some women were accused of tribadism and condemned to internal political exile. Surprisingly, in 1930, at the height of Fascism, Radclyffe Hall's *The Well of Loneliness* (1928)—a book that had been censured in England, a much more liberal country—was translated and published in Italy.

## Lesbians in Modern Italy

Women in Italy voted for the first time in 1946, and the period after the war was dedicated to the economic rebuilding of the newborn republic. Therefore, in the 1950s and 1960s, the only spaces for women were home and church. The homosexual movement that emerged in the early 1970s did not have a large following among lesbians, who preferred to ally themselves instead with feminists in the struggle for abortion and, thus, defined themselves as "separatists" (working apart from gay men). In the 1980s, the movement in Rome coined the name "lesbofeminist" and gave birth to the CLI (Connection of Italian Lesbians), which, as late as 1998, still published its *Bulletin.* In the same period, an influential group from Milan had developed a feminist theory that rejected "lesbianism" as a politically useful category; in spite of this, lesbians from various groups, both separatist and nonseparatist, organized several conventions (the last in 1997) and lesbian weeks (in 1990, 1996, and 1998). In the 1990s, new alliances between lesbians and gay men began to develop.

The Italian situation, while apparently favorable to lesbians, has not been sufficient to promote visibility: No "famous" women writers, actors, directors, or singers have publicly declared themselves to love or to have loved other women. And those who, in the wake of the first feminist wave (ca. the late 1970s), had done so—for example, writer Dacia Maraini (n.d.)—later denied it. In practice, then, one cannot mention the name of a living Italian lesbian without the threat of legal action. This reticence also concerns "lesbian studies," which, with rare and notable exceptions, is still absent from the universities and from research in general. A Web site, Pagine Lesbiche (Lesbian Pages) at http://www.women.it/les, was added in the late 1990s to the meager sources of information at the disposal of Italian lesbians.          *Nerina Milletti*

**Bibliography**

Danna, Daniela. *Amiche, compagne, amanti: storia dell'amore tra donne* (Friends, Companions, Lovers: A History of Love Among Women). Milan: Mondadori, 1992.

Macrelli, Rina. "Vacca d'Israele" (Cow of Israel). *Squaderno* 1 (1989), 45–72.

Milletti, Nerina. "Analoghe sconcezze. Tribadi, saffiste, invertite ed omosessuali: categorie e sistemi sess/genere nella rivista di antropologia criminale fondata da Cesare Lombroso (1880–1949)" (Analogous Indecencies: Tribades, Sapphists, Inverts, and Homosexuals: Sex/Gender Categories and Systems in the Journal of Criminal Anthropology Founded by Cesare Lombroso [1880–1949]). *DWF donnawomanfemme* 4:24 (1994), 50–122.

———. "Bagni di Lucca: A Place To See. Il ricordo di una storia durata 18 anni" (Bagni di Lucca: A Place To See: Remembrance of an 18-Year-Long Story). *Quir* 6 (1993), 26–29.

———. "Calavrisella mia, facimmu 'amuri? La storia delle lesbiche contadine italiane attraverso le tradizioni orali" (Little Calabrese Woman of Mine, Shall We Make Love? The History of Italian Lesbian Peasant Women Through Oral Tradition). *Quir* 11 (1994), 23–26.

———. "Due Violette a Firenze. Violet Paget (1856–1935) e Violet Keppel (1894–1972)" ("Two Violets in Florence: Violet Paget [1856–1935] and Violet Keppel [1894–1972]). *Quir* 13 (1994), 25–28; *Quir* 14 (1994), 29–30.

———. "Pas d'oubli: Eleonora Duse (1858–1924) a Firenze" (No Forgetting: Eleonora Duse [1858–1924] in Florence). *Quir* 17 (1995), 20–24.

***See also*** Europe, Early Modern; Libertinism; Religious Communities; Sappho

# J

## James, Alice (1848–1892)

American diarist. Known in her day chiefly as the daughter and sister of famous men (Henry James [1811–1882], father; William James [1842–1910] and Henry James [1843–1916], brothers), Alice James now stands on her own merit as a writer and personality. The publication of an edition of her diary, edited by Leon Edel, in 1964; an excellent biography by Jean Strouse in 1980; a selection of her letters, edited by Ruth Yeazell, the following year; a chapter in R.W.B. Lewis's *The Jameses: A Family Narrative* (1991); and the rise of feminist literary studies have all contributed to the reassessment of Alice James.

Denied a public sphere by her gender and suffocated by her family, James became an invalid, eventually dying of breast cancer. She was too high spirited to let illness define her, however, and, near the end of her life, she pleaded with her brother William: "Pray don't think of me simply as a creature who might have been something else."

Both her diary and her letters reveal her trenchant, sarcastic wit, her unsparing and mordant view of herself, and her irreverent, iconoclastic view of the world. More egalitarian than her brothers and more compassionate toward the poor, she ardently supported Home Rule for Ireland.

In the 1870s in Boston, Massachusetts, James joined the Society to Encourage Studies at Home, which linked educated women to women correspondents around the country. A history teacher at the society, Katharine Loring (1849–1943), became her life partner. Often kept from James's side by family duties, Loring took a few holiday trips with James and nursed her in London during the last months of her life. The other Jameses acknowledged that their relationship was equivalent to a marriage. Strouse, Yeazell, and Lewis have not been as forthright, however. Inability to deal candidly with lesbianism also characterizes Susan Sontag's 1993 play *Alice in Bed*. On the contrary, James exclaimed in a letter: "Oh Lord, how thankful I am I didn't take to refined spinsterhood." Portraying James as an inactive or failed heterosexual not only falsifies history, but also foists upon her the very role she emphatically rejected.

James described Loring to her Cambridge friends in 1879 as "a most wonderful being. She has all the mere brute superiority which distinguishes man from woman combined with all the distinctively feminine virtues. There is nothing she cannot do from hewing wood & drawing water to driving run-away horses & educating all the women in North America" (Strouse 1980). The love relationship between Alice James and Katharine Loring deserves a lesbian feminist interpretation.

*Margaret Cruikshank*

### Bibliography

Edel, Leon, ed. *The Diary of Alice James*. New York: Dodd, Mead, 1964.

Lewis, R.W.B. *The Jameses: A Family Narrative*. New York: Farrar, Straus, and Giroux, 1991.

Sontag, Susan. *Alice in Bed: A Play*. New York: Farrar, Straus, Giroux, 1993.

Strouse, Jean. *Alice James: A Biography*. Boston: Houghton Mifflin, 1980.

Yeazell, Ruth, ed. *The Death and Letters of Alice James*. Berkeley: University of California Press, 1981.

***See also*** Diaries and Letters

# J

## Japan

Archipelago in the Pacific Ocean off the Asian mainland, consisting of four main islands—Honshu, Hokkaido, Kyushu, and Shikoku–and 3,900 smaller ones. The majority of the population of 123 million is concentrated in Honshu between the capital city of Tokyo and Osaka. Japanese is the official language, although there are numerous (sometimes mutually incomprehensible) regional dialects in addition to the languages spoken by historical minority groups, including Ainu, Chinese, Korean, and Okinawan. Buddhism and Shinto represent the major religious traditions, although there is a significant population of Christians and also hundreds of alternative religious organizations.

In the nineteenth century, Japan merged as an imperial power after 250 years of virtual seclusion under the xenophobic Tokugawa Shogunate. The first half of the twentieth century saw the dramatic rise and collapse of the Japanese Empire, which stretched over much of the Pacific Rim. Centuries of military rule ended with Japan's unconditional surrender in World War II following the U.S. atomic bombings of Hiroshima and Nagasaki in August 1945. The postwar constitution, drafted in part by the Americans, who occupied Japan from 1945 to 1952, is distinguished by Article 9, which renounces war and the right to possess an offensive military force, and by an Equal Rights Amendment, largely ignored until reactivated in 1986 by Japanese feminists and women's groups.

The stereotype of the Japanese people as constituting a homogeneous group has effectively whitewashed a colorful variety of gender identities and sexual practices. More often than not, the differing experiences of female and male members of Japanese society continue to be underacknowledged and/or collapsed with dominant, naturalized gender ideals (for example, "*the* Japanese" housewife and "*the* Japanese" businessman). A brief review of the discourses about gender and sexuality that emerged at different historical junctures in Japanese cultural history provides an opportunity to dismantle some of the more tenacious stereotypes of Japanese women and men of domestic and foreign creation alike, although here the focus will be primarily on girls and women.

### Cross-Dressing Practices

For centuries, cross-dressed performances have characterized shrine festivals and theatrical performances; they have lent spice to many novels and even figured in the eighth-century mytho-histories. However, it was during the Edo period (1603–1867), in particular, that sexual and gender transformations became a subject of popular and legal fascination. There has long been a close connection made in Japan between androgyny—a body that is read as both masculine and feminine (in a conventional sense) or neither masculine nor feminine—and same-sex sexuality and "homosexual" practices.

The Kabuki theater, which dates to ca. 1600, originally included females who performed men's roles, while male actors often took women's roles. However, female actors were banished from the stage in 1629. Apparently, the Confucian Shogunate was disturbed by the general disorder, including unlicensed prostitution, associated with women's Kabuki. Eventually, the prohibition of females and, later, of boys, whose nubile, androgynous eroticism also upset convention, prompted the sanctioned emergence of the *onnagata*, adult males who specialized in femininity and who often lived as women offstage and often engaged in same-sex sexual practices. Contrarily, females who appropriated masculinity as a social guise were criminalized. This double standard was illustrated poignantly by the case of a woman named Take, who, in the 1830s, openly defied the sex-gender hierarchy by passing as a man—and as a magistrate. When apprehended, she was charged with the newly coined crime of "corrupting public morals," fined, imprisoned, and subsequently exiled.

By the turn of the twentieth century, some intrepid females passed as men to secure employment as rickshaw drivers, construction supervisors and laborers, fishers, department-store managers, grocers, and so on. Unlike the Edo-period Shogunate, social critics writing in the early twentieth century associated male impersonation with sexual deviancy only when practiced by urban middle- and upper-class girls and women who, they argued, wore masculine attire not to secure a livelihood, but as an outward expression of their "moral depravity." As privileged and educated—in short, bourgeois—girls and women, they were supposed to fulfill the normative gender role of "Good Wife, Wise Mother" sanctioned by the Meiji (1867–1911) state. This role was strictly enforced in the pro-natalist climate that characterized modern Japanese society, especially in the context of military mobilization in the 1930s and 1940s. The Good Wife, Wise Mother persisted through the 1990s as the dominant model of adult female gender.

## Twentieth-Century Sexologists

In the early twentieth century, critics were joined by sexologists in singling out girls' schools and their (unmarried) female instructors and students as the primary sites and agents of homosexuality among females. Distinctions were drawn between two types of passionate relationships between females: *dôseiai* (same-sex love) and *ome no kankei* (male-female relations). *Dôseiai* is now used as a generic term for "same-sex love" or homosexual relationships. However, when it was coined in the early twentieth century to distinguish intimate relations between girls and women from those between boys and men (upon which the existing terminology was based), *dôseiai* had the specific meaning of an essentially platonic, if passionate, relationship between two females. Such friendships were also referred to as "S" or "Class S" (*kurasu esu*), with the "S" standing for *shisutâ* (sister), *shôjo* (girl), *sekusu* (sex), and/or *shon* (the Japanese pronunciation of the German word *schön,* or beautiful). Class S continues to conjure up the image of two schoolgirls, often a junior-senior pair, with a crush on each other. *Ome*, on the other hand, is an abbreviation of *osu* (male) and *mesu* (female), terms reserved for plants and animals and applied pejoratively to humans, including lesbians. Many Japanese pundits blamed the popular all-female-revue theater and its hallmark man's-role players with stimulating the emergence of a "butch-femme"-like lesbian subculture in the early twentieth century.

Since the turn of the twentieth century and even earlier, Japanese scholars have been adept at selectively adapting for domestic (and often dominant) purposes, institutions and terminologies that were coined and first popularized outside Japan. With respect to sexological terms, Euro-American loanwords and Japanese neologisms rapidly made their way into professional and lay parlance alike, evidenced not only in a wide range of printed media, including translations of foreign texts, but also by the many dictionaries devoted to introducing and defining such words. Loanwords and Japanese social-scientific neologisms that became household words in the early twentieth century included *rabu retâ* (love letter); *rezubian* (lesbian); *dôseiai* for homosexuality (also referred to as *homosekushuaru*); and *iseiai* for heterosexuality (also *heterosekushuaru*). Other loanwords referring to sexual practices that were introduced at this time included *saffuo* (sapphism), *tsuribadeizumu* (tribadism), and *uranizumu* (uranism). Obviously, social and sexual practices labeled and categorized in the "feudal" Edo period were undertaken and perceived differently in the early twentieth century, when the country was embarked on a course of massive modernization, industrialization, selective Westernization, and imperialism. In fact, a new interpretation of sexual relations between females prompted the introduction of the term *dôseiai*, noted above.

Among the indigenous terms for lesbians are *tachi* (an abbreviation of *tachiyaku*, or "leading man," similar in meaning to "butch"), *neko* (cat, similar in meaning to "femme"), *onêsama* (older sister), *imoto* (younger sister), *join* (female licentiousness), *joshoku* (female eroticism), *gôin* (joint licentiousness), *tomogui* ("eat each other"), *shirojiro* (pure white, with etymological implications of falseness and feigned ignorance), and *kaiawase* (matching shells). Japanese lesbian feminists translate butch and femme as *tachi* and *neko*, respectively, and often use the loanwords *butchi* and *fuemu*. Another Japanese term for "butch" often encountered today is *onabe* (shallow pot), a play on *okama* (deep pot), a slang word for a feminine (passive) homosexual male.

## Sexuality and Everyday Life

Contrary to normative ("commonsense") assumptions, marriage is not an indisputable marker of exclusive heterosexuality. But, precisely because it is commonly thought to be, marriage has served—at least in the twentieth century in industrialized countries, including Japan—as a convenient cover for various unconventional sexual practices, including homosexual practices. Although historically in Japan the broad spectrum of sexual practices available to males has been openly acknowledged—and, in some cases, has been the rule—the sexuality of Japanese females invariably has been equated with procreation and/or male recreation. Homophobia in Japan is, thus, rationalized less on religious premises than on the idea that a female sexuality not directed toward either childbirth and, by extension, household posterity, or pleasuring males is unacceptable and represents the disruption of the gendered social hierarchy. Accordingly, the vast majority of Japanese women marry, and the lesbians among them are actually freer to initiate or continue same-sex relationships under the protective umbrella of wife- and motherhood. Japanese females who identify as lesbians, whether in terms of sexual practices, or politics (feminism), or both, continue to assume a very low, mostly closeted, public profile. With the exception of a few "out" critics and groups, such as the Re-gumi (Re-association, from *rezubian,* or lesbian) in Tokyo, most feel obliged to conduct their relationships in a

**J**

clandestine fashion, including passing as a male-female couple.                    *Jennifer E. Robertson*

**Bibliography**

Robertson, Jennifer. *Takarazuka: Sexual Politics and Popular Culture in Modern Japan*. Berkeley: University of California Press, 1998.

*See also* All-Female Reviews (Japan); Miyamoto Yuriko; Yosano Akiko; Yoshiya Nobuko

### Jay, Karla (1947–)

American scholar, educator, and activist. Karla Jay's best-known contributions to the post-Stonewall (1969) gay liberation movement are three anthologies (coedited with Allen Young): *Out of the Closets: Voices of Gay Liberation* (1972; reprinted in 1992), *After You're Out: Personal Experiences of Gay Men and Lesbian Women* (1975), and *Lavender Culture* (1978; reprinted in 1994).

Written in the context of the 1960s counterculture, the black civil rights movement, the New Left, and radical feminism, the essays in *Out of the Closets* envisioned gay liberation as part of a larger, revolutionary social transformation. With essay after essay emphasizing gay pride, self-affirmation, and

*Karla Jay, 1995. Photo by Jill Posener.*

self-assertion, *Out of the Closets* was welcomed as the first positive collection of writing by, about, and for gay people. It achieved the goal set for it by Jay and Young: "No one need grow up again thinking that he or she is the only gay person in the world."

*After You're Out* continued the project of the first anthology, addressing the variety of gay and lesbian identities and offering strategies for surviving in a heterosexual world and for building gay communities of support. Essays on love relationships, gay parenting, legal issues, gay history, and racism in the gay community all began discussions still relevant today. *Lavender Culture* used the standard features of culture—art, dance, theater, literature, and music—to suggest that gay communities form a unique culture, distinct from heterosexual culture. Essays on sexual practices, the bars, growing up gay, aging, race, economics, lesbian separatism, and sports augmented the message.

Although Jay's reputation could rest on these three books alone, her work continues to contribute to the development of gay and lesbian literature and culture. Jay's *The Amazon and the Page: Natalie Clifford Barney and Renée Vivien* (1988), her coedited (with Joanne Glasgow) *Lesbian Texts and Contexts: Radical Revisions* (1990), her anthologies *Lesbian Erotics* (1995) and *Dyke Life* (1995), and her editorship of the New York University Press series The Cutting Edge: Lesbian Life and Literature all prove Jay's unswerving commitment to the creation, recovery, and preservation of lesbian literature and culture.        *Greta Gaard*

**Bibliography**

Duberman, Martin. "Karla." In Martin Duberman, *Stonewall*. New York: Dutton, 1993, pp. 14–20.

Jay, Karla. *Tales of the Lavender Menace: A Memoir of Liberation*. New York: Basic Books, 1999.

Jay, Karla. "A Journey to the End of Meetings." In *Lavender Culture*. Ed. Karla Jay and Allen Young. New York: Jove/Harcourt, Brace, Jovanovich, 1978. Reprint. New York: New York University Press, 1994, pp. 452–57.

———. "Portrait of the Lesbian as a Young Dyke." In *Out of the Closets: Voices of Gay Liberation*. Ed. Karla Jay and Allen Young. New York: Jove/Harcourt Brace Jovanovich, 1972. Reprint. New York: New York University Press, 1992, pp. 275–277.

Kuda, Marie J. "Karla Jay." In *Gay and Lesbian Literature*. Ed. Sharon Malinowski. Detroit: St. James, 1994, pp. 198–200.

*See also* Gay Liberation Movement; Radicalesbians

## Jewett, Sarah Orne (1849–1909)

American writer. Born in South Berwick, Maine, Sarah Orne Jewett often left school and joined her doctor father, Theodore, on his rounds. Country life and visiting friends, healing the spirit, and connection to Maine as a place characterize Jewett's interests throughout her life and her life's work as a writer. Jewett published eighteen books, most of which were collections of sketches and short stories, and worked closely with editors William Dean Howells (1837–1920) and Horace Scudder (1838–1902).

From her earliest diary entries as a young woman to the series of sketches that became the basis for her first published book, *Deephaven* (1877), Jewett discovered that writing and friendship, especially her friendships with women, mutually reinforced each other. Jewett portrayed empathic connection as the center of these friendships, as well as the source of the listening that produced the stories, as in her best work, a novelistic collection of sketches, *The Country of the Pointed Firs* (1896).

After the death of her beloved father in 1878, Jewett became friends with Annie Adams Fields (1834–1915), the wife of publisher and editor James T. Fields (1817–1881). Following James Fields's death, Jewett and Annie Fields became intimate, traveling to Europe together in the spring and summer of 1882 and establishing their primary residence at the Fieldses' 148 Charles Street home, which had been, and would continue to be, Boston's literary center. Jewett began the pattern she would continue throughout her "Boston marriage" with Annie Fields and, indeed, for the rest of her life, alternating seasons with Fields in Boston or at Manchester-by-the-Sea, where the Fieldses had built a summer house, with seasons at home in South Berwick with her invalid mother and sister Mary, where she focused on her writing.

While her biographers have agreed that Jewett's Boston marriage more closely resembled the nineteenth-century "romantic friendship" than the twentieth-century lesbian relationship, Willa Cather (1873–1947) recognized in Jewett a personal, as well as a literary, mentor during the year they knew each other before Jewett's death. Furthermore, Jewett's letters to Fields, her fictional character Nan Prince in *A Country Doctor* (1884), and her advice to Cather that she could have written a male lover as female ("[A] woman could love her in that same protecting way—a woman could even care enough to wish to take her away from such a life, by some means or other") all suggest that Jewett recognized herself and her relationship with Fields as lesbian, whether or not anyone else would have done so.

The sketches and stories (in addition to the three books already mentioned) that scholars and biographers have most frequently identified as revealing Jewett's interest in sexuality include "An Autumn Holiday" (1880), "Tom's Husband" (1882), "A White Heron" (1886), and "Martha's Lady" (1899). "Martha's Lady" also brings into focus class differences that separated women and Jewett's perception that women who occupied different class positions might also be gendered and sexualized differently.

*Marjorie Pryse*

### Bibliography

Blanchard, Paula. *Sarah Orne Jewett: Her World and Her Work*. Reading, Mass.: Addison-Wesley, 1994.

Donovan, Josephine. "Nan Prince and the Golden Apples." *Colby Library Quarterly* 22 (1986), 17–27.

Fetterley, Judith. "Reading *Deephaven* as a Lesbian Text." In *Sexual Practice/Textual Theory: Lesbian Cultural Criticism*. Ed. Susan J. Wolfe and Julia Penelope. Cambridge, Mass., and Oxford, England: Blackwell, 1993, pp. 164–183.

Pryse, Marjorie. "Archives of Female Friendship and the 'Way' Jewett Wrote." *New England Quarterly* 66 (March 1993), 47–66.

*See also* American Literature, Nineteenth Century; Boston Marriage; Cather, Willa; Romantic Friendship

## Jewsbury, Geraldine (1812–1880)

English novelist. Geraldine Jewsbury wrote six novels, one of which, *Zoe* (1845), was regarded as daring and improper for its hints of adultery and sexual passion in women. She also wrote children's stories and contributed articles to Charles Dickens's *Household Words*. For thirty years, Jewsbury reviewed fiction for the *Athenaeum*.

In 1854, Jewsbury moved from Manchester to London to be near her intimate friend, Jane Carlyle (1801–1866). Their intense friendship lasted twenty-five years until Carlyle's death. In October 1841, Jewsbury wrote: "[Y]ou will laugh but I feel towards you much more like a lover than a female friend!" In another letter, she playfully proposed that the two women run off together and "take a cottage . . . on a moor or on a mountain." Because Jewsbury destroyed all correspondence from Carlyle (at the latter's request), only a partial record of their shared lives exists.

Literature was an important element of their friendship. Jewsbury urged Carlyle to step out from the shadow of her famous husband, Thomas (1795–1881), by becoming a writer herself, and Carlyle found a publisher for Jewsbury. They were keenly aware of the limitations of their lives. "We are indications of a development of womanhood which as yet is not recognized," Jewsbury wrote to Carlyle, describing them both as hints of "higher qualities and possibilities that lie in women."

In her essay "Geraldine and Jane" (1929), Virginia Woolf (1882–1941) brings to life the great friendship of the two women. She contrasts the poetic and imaginative Jewsbury to the direct and practical Carlyle, whose mind had "a hawk-like swoop and descent" on facts. *Margaret Cruikshank*

### Bibliography

Ireland, Mrs. Alexander, ed. *Selections from the Letters of Geraldine Ensor Jewsbury to Jane Welsh Carlyle.* London: Longmans, Green, 1892.

Cruikshank, Margaret. "Geraldine Jewsbury and Jane Carlyle." *Frontiers: A Journal of Women Studies* 4:3 (Fall 1979), 60–64.

Langstaff, Eleanor. "Geraldine Ensor Jewsbury." In *An Encyclopedia of British Women Writers*. Ed. Paul Schlueter and June Schlueter. New York: Garland, 1988.

Woolf, Virginia. "Geraldine and Jane." *Times Literary Supplement* (February 22, 1929), p. 150.

*See also* Woolf, Virginia

### Joan of Arc (Jeanne d'Arc) (1412–1431)

Cross-dressing warrior and French national heroine. Jeanne led a troop of French soldiers and served as a temporary focus of French resistance to English occupation in a late phase of the Hundred Years' War (conventionally dated 1337–1453). Tried and convicted by the Inquisition, she was canonized in 1920 by the same church that martyred her.

Born the fourth child of French peasants, Jeanne began to hear the voices of Saint Michael, Saint Catherine, and Saint Margaret when she was thirteen. Her voices told her to go to the aid of the French dauphin (the future Charles VII) in his fight against the English.

*Carolyn Gage in* The Second Coming of Joan of Arc. *Photo by Linda C. Russell.*

After the rejection of her first appeal for a military escort, Jeanne adopted male clothing, and her second appeal met with success. The dauphin was duly impressed and granted her a suit of armor and permission to ride with the army. Under her charismatic leadership, the French lifted the siege at Orleans, and, on July 16, 1429, Jeanne accompanied Charles to his coronation at Rheims, the high point of her career.

Hampered by Charles's indecisiveness, Jeanne's attack on Paris failed. Finally, in May 1430, she went to the defense of Compiègne, where she was captured. In a shocking betrayal, the king refused to ransom her, and Jeanne was turned over to the English to be tried for heresy.

She was accused of witchcraft and charged with "leaving off the dress and clothing of the feminine sex, a thing contrary to divine law and abominable before God, and forbidden by all laws" to wear "clothing and armor such as is worn by man." Jeanne, in her spirited defense at the trial, insisted that "she did not take this dress nor do anything at all save by the command of Our Lord and the angels" (Scott 1956).

Forced to recant and wear a dress, Jeanne was raped in her cell, after which she defiantly resumed her male attire. Jeanne, nineteen, was burned at the stake on May 30, 1431. Her naked body was displayed publicly to dispel any doubts about her sex.

*Carolyn Gage*

## Bibliography

Feinberg, Leslie. *Transgender Warriors: Making History from Joan of Arc to RuPaul*. Boston: Beacon, 1996.

Sackville-West, Vita. *Saint Joan of Arc*. Boston: G.K. Hall, 1984.

Scott, W.S., trans. *The Trial of Joan of Arc, Being the Verbatim Report of the Proceedings from the Orleans Manuscript*. Westport, Conn.: Associated Booksellers, 1956.

Warner, Marina. *Joan of Arc: The Image of Female Heroism*. New York: Knopf, 1981.

*See also* France; Passing Women; Transgender

## Johnston, Jill (1929–)

American critic and writer. Jill Johnston, best known as the author of *Lesbian Nation: The Feminist Solution* (1973), began her writing career as an arts critic in the mid-1950s, writing for the *Village Voice* beginning in 1960. Johnston's major project has been connecting the personal to the political and the artistic through biographical criticism and the autobiographical form. In her *Voice* column, she came to focus on her own life as a central topic, coming out in print in "Lois Lane Is a Lesbian" in 1970. Johnston also became known as an iconoclastic participant in art-world and cultural events. She wrote of that period in *Lesbian Nation*: "I had the correct instinct to fuck things up, but no political philosophy to clarify a course of action." Without a political philosophy and before the 1970s "lesbian/feminist revolution" when "[t]here was no lesbian identity. There was lesbian activity," Johnston also broke and remade herself, undergoing hospitalization twice for schizophrenia and writing herself out of a third episode.

*Lesbian Nation* narrates the constitution of a political consciousness and an identity termed "lesbian" that could be the intersection of the personal and the political. Johnston places this possibility at the intersection of the "gay/feminist" movement; yet this alliance was difficult to materialize. Some of the actions for which Johnston was most (in)famous—swimming topless at a feminist fund-raiser and participating in a lesbian demonstration at a panel discussion focused on Norman Mailer (1923–) and Germaine Greer (1939–)—were precisely challenges to a consolidation of the women's movement that excluded the (politicized) lesbian. The continuing failure of alliance shifted the social possibilities for lesbian-feminism. The conjunction of lesbian and feminism came to name not alliances, but separation—separation from various forms of feminist politics, as well as from men, including gay men. Thus, although Johnston refers to "gay/feminist" much more frequently than to "lesbian nation" as the title of her politics, it is the title of the book, and Johnston herself, that become the founding icons of a particular form of lesbian feminism.

In the end, Johnston expressed ambivalence about her place as both movement icon and iconoclast. She never repudiated lesbian politics, but she did quell the distribution of the 1976 lesbian feminist Canadian film *Jill Johnston: October 1975*. Over time, changes in both lesbian and feminist politics led to a similar ambivalence over the iconographic legacy of *Lesbian Nation*, which came under attack as the marker of a monolithic community with overly rigid boundaries that ultimately separated itself from engagement with politics. Yet Johnston was never comfortable with a monolithic movement, and her style in *Lesbian Nation*, frequently described as irreverent, produces a text that is suffused with irony and complexity. Johnston continued writing, mostly autobiography, and she later returned to arts criticism, once again connecting life and art, the personal and the political, as she wrote in *Secret Lives in Art* (1994): "As we write ourselves into existence, the class, race, and sexual political structures of society inevitably change. . . . And as this happens, the culture will expand."

*Janet R. Jakobsen*

## Bibliography

Banes, Sally. *Writing Dancing in the Age of Postmodernism*. Middletown, Conn.: Wesleyan University Press, 1994, pp. 3–10.

Ross, Becki L. *The House That Jill Built: A Lesbian Nation in Formation*. Toronto: University of Toronto Press, 1995.

*See also* Lesbian Feminism; Lesbian Nation

## Journalism

Coverage of lesbians in the news media, including lesbians as journalists. Although groups devoted to lesbian and gay concerns have existed in the United States since the turn of the twentieth century, both lesbians and gay men have historically been invisible in the mainstream media. Until the 1980s, the little coverage these communities received was dominated by reports of vice and crime, almost always involving gay men. In the 1950s and 1960s, local newspapers covered gay-bar raids and arrests as crime stories and only from the perspective of the police.

## Media Coverage After Stonewall

When hundreds of lesbians and gay men rioted in 1969 to protest a raid by vice officers at the Stonewall Inn in New York City's Greenwich Village, the event received little attention outside the gay community. The *New York Times* ran an inconspicuous five-inch story on page thirty-three under the headline "Four Policemen Hurt in Village Raid." No mention was made of the political nature of the event—of the condemnations of police read to the crowd or of the "support gay power" and "legalize gay bars" graffiti that appeared on the boarded-up windows of the Stonewall Inn. Neither was any mention made of the lesbians involved. Rioters were uniformly described as "young men."

The Stonewall Rebellion marked the beginning of a radically changed lesbian and gay movement in the United States and of a new relationship with the media. Prior to the 1960s, a number of lesbian and gay groups existed. Their function was primarily social, although some efforts were made to reach out to and educate the heterosexual public. After Stonewall, lesbians and gays began to organize in greater numbers. They soon learned from the tactics of antiwar and civil rights protesters that the mainstream media would pay attention to colorful and dramatic events, such as parades, marches, and demonstrations.

While the beginning of the 1970s witnessed a significant increase in media attention to the gay and lesbian movement, the coverage paid scant attention to the substance of movement issues and was generally characterized by a simplistic reliance on stereotypes. Flamboyant drag queens provided the photo or video shot of choice, and, when lesbians were noticed at all, it was the stereotypical image of "dykes on bikes" (motorcycles) that was presented. Ignored by the mainstream media were the hundreds of others who made up the diversity of the community.

Counterprotesters were another favorite focus of the media at Gay Pride events. In the guise of presenting "balanced" coverage, reports of lesbian and gay events almost always included quotes from antigay hecklers and often a visual image of a religious fundamentalist holding a sign declaring "Gays Repent" or a similar sentiment.

Such a focus on conflict and controversy fueled much of the news coverage of lesbians and gays in the 1970s and early 1980s. The new visibility of the movement inspired a backlash from conservatives such as singer Anita Bryant and California State Senator John Briggs, who spearheaded antigay campaigns in the 1970s. Media scrutiny of such legal challenges to the rights of lesbians and gays made the movement visible for the first time to many Americans. But the tone of the coverage, the way in which the conflict was framed as America's response to the lesbian and gay "threat," did little to draw attention to the overall goals and aims of the movement.

Lesbians and lesbian concerns were rarely the focus of the mainstream news media. When they were singled out for attention, it was generally in reference to the lesbian "problem" in the feminist movement. When Kate Millet (1934–) came out as a bisexual in the early 1970s, for example, *Time* magazine featured her on its cover and ran a divisive story about the rift between heterosexuals and lesbians within the feminist movement.

## The AIDS Crisis

By the mid-1980s, media attention to gay men (rarely lesbians) was dominated by coverage of the AIDS crisis. The mainstream media were slow to pick up what they eventually came to call the "gay plague" story. As the numbers of deaths increased, however, and began to include prominent personalities such as Rock Hudson, the media finally responded with coverage of the community that focused almost exclusively on AIDS.

The disease played a major role in mobilizing the gay movement of the 1980s, as the specter of sick and dying friends motivated large numbers of lesbians and gays to come out and to engage in political action for the first time. This surge in lesbian and gay visibility, particularly the dramatic actions of new activist groups such as ACT UP (AIDS Coalition To Unleash Power) and Queer Nation, succeeded in capturing greater mainstream media attention than ever before.

But the blessings of mass-media recognition of the AIDS crisis were mixed. While the media focused much-needed attention on a major concern of the gay community, they did so to the near exclusion of all other community concerns. News coverage of the community became synonymous with AIDS coverage in the 1980s. Press reports of the 1987 National March on Washington for Lesbian and Gay Rights, for example, were dominated by the AIDS issue. At least one major metropolitan newspaper— the *Chicago Tribune*—devoted its march coverage exclusively to AIDS, making no mention of the civil rights demands that were also being stressed by the movement.

The most obvious omission in media coverage of the movement in the 1980s was the role of lesbians. Lesbians experience a rate of AIDS infection lower than that of all adult segments of the population, but mainstream news-media coverage of AIDS in the gay community rarely made note of this fact. Subsequently, lesbians were virtually ignored in media coverage of gays that was dominated by AIDS.

By the 1990s, mainstream-media interest in AIDS began to wane as hopes for a cure remained distant, and reporters failed to come up with new angles on the story. In the course of covering the AIDS crisis, however, reporters had developed a variety of lesbian and gay sources who had begun to familiarize them with other issues affecting the community. When Democratic Party candidate Bill Clinton openly courted the lesbian and gay vote during his 1992 presidential campaign, assignment editors developed a sudden interest in the community, and, at many news outlets, what had been the AIDS "beat" gradually became, either officially or unofficially, the lesbian and gay beat.

## Media Coverage of Lesbians

President Clinton's outreach to lesbians and gays helped make them a "safe" topic for mainstream news media to cover. By acknowledging issues of concern to the community, Clinton gave it a new legitimacy in the eyes of the news media. Subsequently, lesbian and gay issues became rather commonplace in the mainstream news media during the early 1990s. The issue that received the most coverage during this time was the debate over gays in the military. After Clinton announced his intent to eliminate the ban on gays, the media were saturated with stories—many of which were uncharacteristically sympathetic to the plight of the gay soldier. Few of these stories, however, focused on lesbians in the military. Although women were, at the time, much more likely than men to be the targets of "witch-hunts" designed to ferret out homosexuals in the

military ranks, the vast majority of news coverage focused on gay men in the military.

Indeed, up to this point, lesbians had generally been treated by the mainstream media as an afterthought. In spite of the presence of women in leadership positions at national lesbian and gay organizations, the bulk of the focus remained on gay men. Lesbians have never received the amount of coverage that gay men have. Lesbian marches held as adjunct events to gay pride marches, for example, are treated in the mainstream media as footnotes, if they are mentioned at all. And female groups such as the Lesbian Avengers have never received the kind of press that primarily male groups such as ACT UP have.

However, the mainstream media suddenly discovered lesbians in the 1990s. A *Newsweek* magazine cover featured two all-American, wholesome-looking women posing together with the headline "Lesbians" above them. "Lesbian chic" was born, and news-media outlets rushed to feature their own lesbian story. In August 1993, *Vanity Fair* magazine ran a suggestive cover photo of lesbian singer k.d. lang with model Cindy Crawford. Newspapers and television news magazines featured stories on lesbian communities, such as Northampton, Massachusetts. While such mainstream-media acknowledgment was to some a welcome change, its overwhelming focus on white, middle-class, often "straight-looking" women failed to capture the vast diversity of the lesbian community.

Media fascination with the newly "discovered" lesbians, however, faded quickly, and the media moved on to other new trends. In 1996, however, lesbians were back in the limelight when *Newsweek* again featured lesbians on the cover when it ran a photo of lesbian rock star Melissa Etheridge and her partner, Julie Cypher, under the headline "They're Having a Baby." Inside was an in-depth (if belated) look at the lesbian and gay "baby boom." The article was thorough and generally supportive—a great improvement over the "gay threat" approach taken by the mainstream news media in the preceding decades.

The *Newsweek* "baby boom" cover story is indicative of much of the coverage of lesbians and gays found in the mainstream news media by the middle of the 1990s. Television news, news magazines, news wire services, and big-city newspapers have increasingly devoted time and resources to cover in-depth issues such as marriage laws, military policy, AIDS policy, antidiscrimination statutes, and others that affect the community.

**J** Nevertheless, coverage in the mainstream media is far from perfect. Content varies geographically, with news outlets in more politically conservative regions of the country less likely to use stories about lesbians and gays out of fear of "offending" their readers, viewers, or listeners. Mainstream news media in all areas of the country also have a tendency to "balance" stories about lesbians and gays with commentary from questionable "experts" representing the "other side." For example, representatives of the Christian Coalition are often called upon by the media to comment on policy issues such as gay marriages and antidiscrimination legislation—a practice described by lesbian and gay leaders as akin to asking leaders of the Ku Klux Klan to provide commentary on affirmative action. Lesbians and gays, however, continue in their attempts to educate the mainstream news media, often from within the newsroom itself. In addition, the Gay and Lesbian Alliance Against Defamation (GLAAD) issued in 1994 a *Media Guide to the Lesbian and Gay Community* to provide professionals with story ideas, background information, and a glossary of terms and usages.

## Lesbians in the Newsroom

Lesbians and gay men have always worked in the mainstream media, although, until the mid-1980s, few had been out on the job. Esteemed journalists from the past who were lesbian or bisexual include Margaret Fuller (1810–1850), a journalist for the *New York Tribune*; Janet Flanner (1892–1978), a foreign correspondent and *New Yorker* columnist who wrote under the pen name Genêt; Dorothy Thompson (1893–1961), one of the first female foreign correspondents; and Lorena Hickok (1892–1968), an accomplished Associated Press White House correspondent who is best known for her relationship with Eleanor Roosevelt (1884–1962).

Like members of most other professions, journalists have considered the possibility of coming out on the job a risky proposition. Mainstream newsrooms, historically populated by white males, have traditionally been hostile workplaces for lesbians and gays. *New York Times* publisher Arthur Ochs banned use of the word "gay" in 1975, insisting instead on the more clinical "homosexual." Ochs's ban was not overturned until 1987. The *Wall Street Journal* banned use of the word from 1978 to 1984. The few lesbians and gays who came out in such an antagonistic environment in the 1970s and 1980s often found their ability to be objective journalists and report the news without bias called into question. Others have suffered from more direct discrimination. In 1987, Christine Madsen, a seven-year veteran reporter at the *Christian Science Monitor*, was fired when she refused to seek "healing" for her lesbianism.

Gays and lesbians were increasingly likely to come out in the 1990s. The National Gay and Lesbian Journalists Association was established in 1990 to increase the visibility and defend the rights of lesbian and gay journalists. The association has been instrumental in improving the work environment for lesbians and gays in the newsroom. Nevertheless, revealing one's sexuality can still have negative consequences in the news business. Sandy Nelson, a reporter at the Tacoma, Washington, *Morning News Tribune*, was demoted in 1990 when she spoke out publicly in support of antidiscrimination legislation. She subsequently lost a lawsuit she filed against the newspaper. Also in 1990, United Press International reporter Julie Brienza was fired after an evangelical broadcaster attacked her on the airwaves for her freelance work for a gay newspaper. Brienza eventually collected $255,000 in damages from the evangelist in an out-of-court settlement of a $10 million libel suit she had filed against him.

In spite of the continuing danger of coming out in the newsroom, there have been major strides made within mainstream media. In 1991, Linda Villarosa, then a senior editor at *Essence* magazine, came out in the magazine in an article she cowrote with her mother. Villarosa suffered no repercussions on the job; indeed, in 1994 she was promoted to the magazine's top position of executive editor, the highest-ranking post for an out lesbian in mainstream media at the time.

In 1992, the *Detroit News* began publishing the first regular column by an openly lesbian commentator, Deb Price, an editor at the paper. Price's syndicated column has since been picked up by other newspapers throughout the country. The success of Price's groundbreaking column led to the launching of columns by other lesbians and gay men, including Victoria Brownworth at the *Philadelphia Daily News* and Amy Adams Squire Strongheart at the *St. Louis Post-Dispatch*.

Since the late 1940s, lesbians have produced their own alternative media to report news of interest to the community. The first lesbian publication was *Vice Versa*, a newsletter that circulated from 1947 to 1948. *The Ladder*, a monthly publication of the Daughters of Bilitis, was produced from 1956 to 1972. In the 1970s, a number of lesbian feminist publications, such as *the Lesbian Tide* (Los Angeles, California), *The Furies* (Washington, D.C.), and *Lavender Woman* (Chicago, Illinois), were launched to meet the information needs that were not being met by male-centered gay publications such as the *Advocate*. By the 1990s, a variety of specifically lesbian publications existed, and lesbians were prominently featured on the staffs of the *Advocate* and *Out*, the two most popular national gay and lesbian magazines.                     *Jane R. Ballinger*

## Bibliography

Alwood, Edward. *Straight News*. New York: Columbia University Press, 1996.

Cruikshank, Margaret. *The Gay and Lesbian Liberation Movement*. New York: Routledge, 1992.

Faderman, Lillian. *Odd Girls and Twilight Lovers: A History of Lesbian Life in Twentieth-Century America*. New York: Columbia University Press, 1991.

Gross, Larry. "Out of the Mainstream: Sexual Minorities and the Mass Media." *Journal of Homosexuality* 21:1–2 (1991), 19–46.

Price, Deb, and Joyce Murdoch. *And Say Hi to Joyce: The Life and Chronicles of a Lesbian Couple*. New York: Doubleday, 1995.

Signorile, Michelangelo. *Queer in America: Sex, the Media, and the Closets of Power*. New York: Random House, 1993.

**See also** Flanner, Janet; Fuller, Margaret; *Furies, The; Ladder, The;* Periodicals

## Juana Inés de la Cruz, Sor (1648–1695)

Seventeenth-century Mexican nun, scholar, poet, and playwright, known as "the first feminist of the Americas." Born in the small town of San Miguel de Nepantla on the outskirts of Mexico City, Juana Inés was, according to her baptismal records, the third "natural" daughter of Doña Isabel Ramírez. Self-educated since the age of three—at six, she requested that her mother dress her as a boy so she could attend the University of Mexico—Juana Inés entered the Order of Saint Jerome at the age of twenty. Her reputation as a girl-scholar won her the admiration of nobles, scholars, and clergy across the realm; yet it would prove to be a double-edged sword that both empowered and injured her throughout her life.

In an age when learning was the exclusive domain of men, she was viewed simultaneously as a prodigy and an aberration to her sex, a distinction that compromised her "salvation" when she donned the habit. She writes in her autobiographical *Respuesta a Sor Filotea* (1691; Reply to Sor Filotea) that she joined the convent because of her "total antipathy toward marriage" and because it was possible there to pursue a life of learning. In her two-story cell, she amassed a library of nearly four thousand books and collected many musical and scientific instruments, and her prolific pen produced a body of work now anthologized in four separate volumes. Of these, her more famous pieces are *Respuesta*—her defense of a woman's right to learn and discourse—and her philosophical satire on "stubborn men who malign / women without reason / dismissing yourselves as the occasion / for the very wrongs you design." In her love poetry to two Vicereines—the one whom she attended at court before entering the convent, Leonor Carreto, Marquesa de Mancera, and the one with whom she shared a "platonic love-friendship" for eight years, María Luisa Manrique de Lara, Condesa de Paredes—one finds the true nature of what she calls her "inclination." It was la Condesa, editor of the first two volumes of Sor Juana's work, who gave her the epithet "tenth muse"—what Plato had called Sappho two millennia earlier. Though some scholars explain her "Sapphic tendencies" as excessive libido that had no outlet in the opposite sex, a consequence of what Paz (1988) calls her "illegitimacy," or a combination of other psychic traumas such as manic-depression, subjection to the Catholic Church, or penis envy, it is evident from her own primary documents that Sor Juana not only refused to submit to the male construction of her gender, but also rejected compulsory heterosexuality by joining a separatist community and cross-dressing as a nun.

Two years after scandalizing her superiors in religion with her *Respuesta*, she was issued an ultimatum: either renounce her scholarly life and prostrate herself to the Catholic Church or suffer the Inquisition. In 1694, she renewed her vows, using her own blood for ink, and submitted to all of the Church's demands, selling her library and instruments and forfeiting all that had constituted her passion, her devotion, and her enlightened subjectivity. In 1695, at the age of forty-six, attending to her sick sisters, she died of the epidemic infesting the convent, leaving behind a legacy of colonial feminism and a cloistered identity that would not find expression for three hundred years: "And if my intention is guilty / my affection is also damned, / for loving you is a transgression / of which I will

**J**

never repent." [Translations of Sor Juana's verses are by the author.]    *Alicia Gaspar de Alba*

### Bibliography

Arenal, Electa, and Amanda Powell, trans. *The Answer/La Respuesta* (Translation of Sor Juana's *Respuesta a Sor Filotea*). New York: Feminist Press, 1994.

Gaspar de Alba, Alicia. "Excerpts from the Sapphic Diary of Sor Juana Inés de la Cruz." In *Tasting Life Twice: Literary Lesbian Fiction by New American Writers*. Ed. E.J. Levy. New York: Avon, 1995, 182–190.

Merrim, Stephanie, ed. *Feminist Perspectives on Sor Juana Inés de la Cruz*. Detroit: Wayne State University Press, 1991.

Paz, Octavio. *Sor Juana; or, the Traps of Faith*. Trans. Margaret Sayers Peden. Cambridge, Mass.: Harvard University Press, 1988.

*See also* Mexico; Religious Communities

## Judaism

For most of its three-thousand-year history, lesbianism has been a subject of little interest in Jewish texts and societies. Only in the late twentieth century have Jewish scholars and communities faced the issue of erotic love between women.

### Biblical Times (1000–165 B.C.E.)

Lesbianism is not mentioned in the Hebrew Bible (Old Testament), in contrast to male homosexual behavior, which is expressly forbidden as a capital crime. The absence of discussion of lesbianism in this context has raised scholarly interest. Biblical criticism suggests that this difference exists because female homoerotic behavior would not have been considered sexual behavior, which, in ancient times, was understood to require the emission of semen. A related theory suggests that nothing women did without men would matter because women were not full persons by biblical standards. More traditional Jewish scholarship suggests that the writers of the Bible knew nothing of erotic attraction between women and could not prohibit something about which there was no knowledge or awareness. Another traditional interpretation is that the behavior was obviously prohibited because what applied to men applied to women. Feminist interpreters posit that biblical society accepted erotic love between women as a matter of course. Without further evi-

dence, all arguments are inconclusive. There is extant no information about erotic love between women in this time period in Jewish history.

### Rabbinic Times (165 B.C.E.–A.D. 900)

The first discussion of female homoeroticism in Jewish texts is found in *Sifra*, a postbiblical commentary on the Book of Leviticus, edited in the second century of the common era. The reference is to a passage in Chapter 18 of the Book of Leviticus that prohibits Israelite participation in acts deemed "the doings of Egypt." The commentator in *Sifra* suggests that lesbian marriage was one of the acts that would be included in this category. What one can infer from this text is that, at the time of the writing of *Sifra,* Jewish communities were cognizant of the Roman practice of women marrying other women.

The Talmud, a compendium of Jewish law and practice compiled in the fifth century of the common era, includes passages about female homoerotic behavior (*mesolelot*), not lesbian marriage. The word *mesolelot* is understood by later commentators to refer to the practice of tribadism (women rubbing genitals against each other). A passage in the Talmud (*Yevamot* 76a) questions whether women who practice *mesolelot* are eligible to marry priests. Virginity is the criterion upon which eligibility for priestly marriage is based, so, for example, a divorced woman or a widow is not allowed to marry a priest. The *Mishnah* (a compilation of Jewish law dating from c. A.D. 200) gives two opinions about the eligibility for priestly marriage of one who practices *mesolelot*. The accepted opinion is that such a woman is eligible, although the minority opinion is that she is not. In the majority opinion, lesbian behavior is considered a minor infraction. This passage establishes the existence of female homoeroticism in Jewish communities in ancient times. It also suggests that this behavior was understood by rabbinic authorities as a specific practice, not as a person's sexual orientation, as the question is raised in the context of marriage to a man. Some authorities place it in the category of sexual practice, and, as such, it disqualifies the practitioner from the category of virgin.

There is one other discussion in the Talmud about lesbianism. In *Shabbat* 65a, Rabbi Samuel is quoted as saying that he does not permit his daughters to sleep under the same blanket. Elsewhere, the Talmud prohibits men from this behavior because of fear of homosexual contact. One of the Talmudic commentators suggests that Rabbi Samuel is following the minority opinion and making sure that his daughters will be eligible for priestly marriage. But the text also gives several reasons, unrelated to lesbianism, for prohibiting the young women from sleeping together.

## Middle Ages (A.D. 900–1700)

There is one significant discussion of female homoerotic behavior in the medieval era. This is found in a compilation of laws known as the Mishneh Torah, written by legal scholar and philosopher Moses Maimonides (1135–1204) in the twelfth century. Maimonides reiterates the connection to the Levitical prohibition against the "doings of Egypt" but also suggests that this behavior should not disqualify a woman from marrying a priest because it is still only a minor infraction. Maimonides goes on to suggest that the courts administer a flogging to a woman who is caught engaging in homoerotic behavior. Finally, Maimonides warns men to keep their wives from visiting with women who are known to practice *mesolelot* with other women. This text views lesbian behavior as threatening to the institution of marriage and worthy of punishment.

## Modern Era (A.D. 1700–1945)

During the modern period, female homoeroticism is mentioned infrequently in Jewish sources. Most references are from fictional writings. An early example is found in a Yiddish play produced by Sholem Asch (1880–1957) for the American theater, entitled *The God of Vengeance*. Written in 1907, it was performed in many European countries as well. The plot focused on a lesbian relationship between a prostitute and the daughter of a brothel owner and included several explicit homoerotic scenes. Noted Yiddish author Isaac Bashevis Singer (1904–1991) also wrote several short stories about lesbian love.

During the modern period, Jewish sources also document the existence of women whose behavior does not conform to stereotypic notions of gender. One such historical character is the Maid of Ludmir, a nineteenth-century Hasidic teacher. Rachel Webermacher lived, dressed, and taught as a man for many years. She had a large following who listened to her preach from the other side of a curtain, since women were not allowed to speak publicly. Hasidic leaders forced her to marry so that she would stop teaching, but their efforts ended in failure. Webermacher was the model for the "Yentl" character created by Singer.

The first Jewish novel by a woman that explored lesbian themes was *The Wasteland* (1948),

written by Ruth Seid (1913–) under the pseudonym of Jo Sinclair. The heroine was open about her sexuality to her family. The novel is about her brother's effort to come to terms with her lesbianism. This frank discussion of lesbian themes, and the portrayal of lesbianism as a psychologically healthy alternative, was unusual for its time.

During the early part of the twentieth century, women began to live openly as lesbians, including Jewish women. Gertrude Stein (1874–1946) and Alice B. Toklas (1877–1967) are perhaps the best-known examples. Pauline Newman (ca. 1890–?), an organizer of the Jewish labor movement, lived openly with her partner in New York City's Greenwich Village, where they raised a child together. But, for the most part, women who loved women prior to the 1960s neither identified publicly as lesbian nor had the opportunity to live openly in partnerships.

## Lesbians and Contemporary Judaism

One result of the feminist and gay liberation movements in the 1960s and 1970s was that large numbers of women began to claim lesbian identity. It was in the context of these movements that lesbians began to explore Jewish identity as well. The early 1980s witnessed an explosion of small groups of lesbians who were beginning to make connections to their Jewish identities. The members of these groups identified their simultaneous rejection as Jews in the lesbian community and as lesbians in the Jewish community. Evelyn Torton Beck made these issues visible in her groundbreaking anthology of writings by Jewish lesbians, *Nice Jewish Girls: A Lesbian Anthology* (1982, 1989). Many lesbian novels with Jewish themes were published by women's presses. Progressive Jewish organizations, such as New Jewish Agenda, began discussions of how to incorporate the needs of gay men and lesbians in Jewish life.

Jewish lesbians also made inroads in religious movements. The gay and lesbian synagogue movement, which began in the early 1970s, provided a locus for lesbians to explore religious identity. In the 1980s, women rabbis like Stacy Offner and Linda Holtzman began to disclose their lesbian identities, and many lost their jobs. The Reform and Reconstructionist movements developed policies that sanctioned the ordination of lesbian and gay rabbis and raised the issue of performing commitment ceremonies for lesbian and gay couples. The Conservative and Orthodox movements remained intransigent. The Conservative movement struggled over permitting lesbians and gay

**J** men to teach in religious schools. Orthodox leaders publicly denounced lesbianism as a sin.

The 1990s bore witness to a growing interest in lesbian issues in the Jewish community. Articles were published in the Jewish press. Symposia and conferences were held by mainstream Jewish organizations. Some synagogues incorporated discussions of lesbian issues into their agenda and actively welcomed lesbian and gay members. These activities made it possible for lesbian Jews to feel welcome in the Jewish community. Yet lesbian Jews continued to voice concerns that go beyond acceptance and toleration. They sought a reinterpretation of Jewish values, including the assumption that heterosexuality is normative. They desired an inclusion of their visions and stories as part of a reconstructed Jewish textual tradition. And they aimed to create an environment of complete comfort in which to claim their identity and celebrate the occasions of their lives.          *Rebecca T. Alpert*

### Bibliography

Alpert, Rebecca. *Like Bread on the Seder Plate: Jewish Lesbians and the Transformation of Tradition*. New York: Columbia University Press, 1997.

Balka, Christie, and Andy Rose, eds. *Twice Blessed: On Being Lesbian or Gay and Jewish*. Boston: Beacon, 1989.

Beck, Evelyn Torton, ed. *Nice Jewish Girls: A Lesbian Anthology*. Rev. and updated. Boston: Beacon, 1989.

Biale, Rachel. *Women and Jewish Law: An Exploration of Women's Issues in Halakhic Sources*. New York: Schocken, 1984.

Kaye/Kantrowitz, Melanie, and Irena Klepfisz, eds. *Tribe of Dina: A Jewish Women's Anthology*. Montpelier, Vt.: Sinister Wisdom, 1986.

Moore, Tracy, ed. *Lesbiot: Israeli Lesbians Talk About Sexuality, Feminism, Judaism, and Their Lives*. London: Cassell, 1995.

Rogow, Faith. "Why Is This Decade Different from All Other Decades? A Look at the Rise of Jewish Lesbian Feminism." *Bridges* 1 (Spring, 1990), 67–79.

***See also*** Antisemitism; Israel; Synagogues

# K

## Kahlo, Frida (1907–1954)

Mexican painter. One of Mexico's most original artists, whose work combines realism with the fantastic, Frida Kahlo is often associated with Surrealism in spite of her protestations that "I never painted dreams. I painted my own reality." Her reality included a great deal of physical and psychic pain, which informed her paintings. In more than fifty-five striking self-portraits (almost a third of her oeuvre), Kahlo constructed and revealed herself even as she masked her deepest feelings (*The Mask* [1945]).

Born to a Hungarian-German-Jewish father and a Spanish-Indian-Catholic mother, Kahlo made her multiple heritage a central theme in her work by combining European influences with indigenous Mexican iconography (*The Two Fridas* [1939]; *Tree of Hope* [1946]). A bout with polio when she was six and a near fatal bus accident at eighteen made her keenly aware of the body's vulnerability. Further degeneration led to a series of painful pelvic and spinal operations that left her unable to bear a child. Kahlo mourned this fate and made the experiences of her miscarriages and operations public in graphic paintings that are singular in Western art (*My Birth* [1932]; *Henry Ford Hospital* [1932]; *Remembrance of an Open Wound* [1938]). Her obsessive love-hate relationship with her husband, the well-known Mexican muralist Diego Rivera (1886–1957), whom she had married in 1929 (when she was twenty-two and he forty-three), also made its way into her work.

Much has been made of Rivera's well-documented womanizing (including an affair with Kahlo's sister) and Kahlo's numerous affairs with both men and women. What is often minimized in the narrative of Kahlo's life is her abiding passion for women, which began in early adolescence and not, as some suggest, in response to Rivera's chronic unfaithfulness. Kahlo biographers agree that her first sexual encounter at thirteen was with a woman teacher, an affair that ended abruptly when her mother discovered the liaison and moved Kahlo to a different school. A family photograph taken by her father in 1926, which shows Kahlo in male clothing, is often dismissed as a sign of the young Frida's high spirits or is taken as a symbol of rebellion against her bourgeois family.

Kahlo *was* rebellious—by taking herself seriously as an artist, by allowing herself sexual pleasure with men and women, by joining the Communist Party and taking a public stand against political oppression and imperialism, and, not least, by refusing conventional role expectations for women of her social class—but it was not rebellion that drew Kahlo to the many women with whom she was lovingly and sometimes amorously intimate throughout her life (*Two Nudes in the Jungle* [1939]). Yet, in spite of these many same-sex relationships that clearly nourished her, Kahlo's paintings exude a deep sense of loneliness and isolation, as well as vitality and hope. Her innermost longings are recorded in her *Diary* (published in 1995) in powerful, freely flowing language and in paintings wrought in a style far less controlled than the work she allowed the public to see.

Although Kahlo's paintings were exhibited and given critical attention in her lifetime, after her death in 1954 her name passed into near oblivion. In the 1970s, her work was reclaimed by feminist scholars as a prime example of an artist who had been "lost to history" because she was a woman whose work reflected a woman's life experiences. In the late 1990s, her popularity continued to grow

**K** (and her market value gained) as her work also converged with growing public interest in non-European indigenous cultural expression.

*Evelyn Torton Beck*

### Bibliography

Collins, Amy Fine. "Diary of a Mad Artist." *Vanity Fair* (September 1995), 176, 229.

Herrera, Hayden. *Frida: A Biography of Frida Kahlo*. New York: Harper and Row, 1983.

———. *Frida: The Paintings*. New York: Harper-Collins, 1991.

Lowe, Sarah M. *Frida Kahlo*. New York: Universe Books, 1991.

*See also* Art, Mainstream; Mexico

### King, Billie Jean Moffitt (1943–)

Tennis champion; born into a white, working-class family in Long Beach, California, on November 22, 1943. The Moffitt family, including younger brother, Randy, was active in sports and encouraged Billie Jean at a young age; she enjoyed baseball and football with neighborhood boys and played championship girls softball at age ten. At eleven, her parents encouraged her to pick a "girl's" sport. King recalled that the first time she hit a tennis ball she knew it was her game; she told her mother she was going to be the number one tennis player in the world.

King states in her 1974 autobiography, *Billie Jean King*, that she knew she was different because her interest in sports and wanting to excel were considered unusual for a girl. Growing up in the 1940s and 1950s, she was labeled "tomboy" though she was uncomfortable with the definition. The media often deemed her skills "masculine." By the 1960s, the term "tomboy" intimated "innate and immutable traits that were allegedly incompatible with femininity and hetereosexuality," according to one sports historian. Thus, King shunned the tag.

King won her first Wimbledon singles match in 1966. She was then married to Larry King, a college boyfriend. Their marriage endured from 1965 to 1985. However, on May 8, 1981, King was forced to call a press conference, at which she admitted to a lesbian affair with her former hairdresser and secretary, Marilyn Barnett. Barnett filed a now famous palimony lawsuit seeking financial support from the Kings. Though King admitted to the affair, which began in 1972, she also deemed it a mistake. This angered gay activists and feminists alike. One

*Newsweek* (1981) columnist wrote: "[T]he women's rights movement, of which Billie Jean King has been a champion for years, taught many of us that there is more than one way for women to live. . . . We got to know women for whom homosexuality was a workable alternative to the traditional way of life." For many years after the exposé, King refused to embrace a lesbian identity, although, during a fund-raising event for the 1994 Gay Games, she thanked Martina Navratilova (1956–) for helping her understand her own sexuality. Finally, at the age of 55, King came out, stating that she had "settled into an enduring relationship with another woman," and that dealing with her sexuality had been the hardest battle of her life.

Throughout her tennis career, King was ranked number one in the world five times and number one in the United States seven times. She retired in 1984. Her many honors include induction into the National Women's Hall of Fame (August 1990) and the International Tennis Hall of Fame (July 1987). She continues to promote women's tennis globally.

*Mary Johnson*

### Bibliography

Bianco, David. "How did Billie Jean King Come Out?" *Impact* (September 1996). Available: http://www.impactnews.com/pastout.htm

King, Billie Jean, and Frank Deford. *Billie Jean King*. New York: Viking, 1982.

King, Billie Jean, and Kim Chapin. *Billie Jean King*. New York: Harper, 1974.

Roberts, Shelly. "Bad Form Billie Jean King." *Newsweek* (May 25, 1981).

Taylor, Anne. "The Battles of Billie Jean King." *Women's Sports and Fitness* (September/October 1998), 131–134, 168–171.

*See also* Navratilova, Martina; Sports, Professional; Tomboy

### Kinsey Institute

Founded by Alfred Kinsey (1894–1956) and incorporated in 1947 as the Institute for Sex Research, it is now named the Kinsey Institute for Research in Sex, Gender, and Reproduction. Housed at Indiana University, the Kinsey Institute is one of the largest collections of materials on sexuality in the world. In addition to extensive textual and archival holdings, its collection of erotica contains drawings, paintings, etchings, photographs, and old "stag" films.

Also the home of a network of sex researchers, the Kinsey Institute is probably best known for its studies on male and female sexual behavior, as released in *Sexual Behavior in the Human Male* (SBHM) (1948) and *Sexual Behavior in the Human Female* (SBHF) (1953). Based on sex histories from almost twelve thousand men and women, the Kinsey reports were an unprecedented glimpse at the sexual lives of white Americans (although Kinsey and his associates studied African American women and men, they did not include that data in SBHM or SBHF because they believed their sample was not large enough). The Kinsey reports had a huge impact on postwar culture in the United States and, in particular, shaped the emerging lesbian and gay communities in the 1950s.

The well-known Kinsey Scale challenged the notion of fixed sexual identities and instead suggested that individuals might be located on a 0–6 continuum from exclusively heterosexual to exclusively homosexual in sexual involvement and interest. The popular slogan that one in ten adults is homosexual is widely attributed to the Kinsey research. The statistic derives from Kinsey's finding that 10 percent of males were "more or less exclusively homosexual" (that is, they would rate a 5 or 6 on the Kinsey scale) for at least three years between the ages of sixteen and fifty-five. The figure was lower for women: 3 to 8 percent of unmarried women rated between 4 and 6 on the Kinsey Scale in each of the years between twenty-five and thirty-five. Kinsey found, however, that much larger numbers of men and women reported some level of same-gender sexual involvement. In the 1950s, a writer in the lesbian publication *The Ladder* said: "Probably the reams of material written in passionate defense of the homophile have done less to further the cause of tolerance than Kinsey's single, detached statement that 37 percent of the men and 19 percent of the women whom he interviewed admitted having had overt homosexual relationships." Kinsey was widely perceived as an ally of lesbian and gay communities.

Throughout the 1970s and early 1980s, the Kinsey Institute conducted major studies on homosexuality. The findings from ethnographic research on gay male communities in San Francisco, California; Amsterdam, Netherlands; and Copenhagen, Denmark; were published in *Male Homosexuals: Their Problems and Adaptations* (1974) by researchers Martin Weinberg and Colin Williams. Data from studies on both lesbians and gay men were released in Alan Bell and Martin Weinberg's *Homosexualities: A Study of Diversity Among Men and Women* (1978) and Alan Bell, Martin Weinberg, and Sue Hammersmith's *Sexual Preference: Its Development in Men and Women* (1981). Researchers at the Kinsey Institute have also studied topics such as sex offenders, nudists, adolescent sexuality, and puberty.         *Janice M. Irvine*

## Bibliography

D'Emilio, John. *Sexual Politics, Sexual Communities: The Making of a Homosexual Minority in the United States, 1940–1970*. Chicago: University of Chicago Press, 1983.

Irvine, Janice. *Disorders of Desire: Sex and Gender in Modern American Sexology*. Philadelphia: Temple University Press, 1990.

Pomeroy, Wardell. *Dr. Kinsey and the Institute for Sex Research*. New York: Harper and Row, 1972.

*See also* Sexology

## Korea, South

Peninsula located in eastern Asia, between China and Japan. Choson Dynasty, known as Korea in the twentieth century, was partitioned into North Korea (Democratic People's Republic of Korea) and South Korea (Republic of Korea) when the Korean War ended in 1953. This entry addresses only South Korea.

Accounts of homosexual behavior among women in South Korea are scarcely recorded in official history. One of the rare exceptions is a royal record from the fifteenth-century Choson Dynasty (1392–1910), during the reign of King Sejong, which reports that the king's daughter-in-law, Bongsi, caused a scandal for "mimicking" heterosexual relations with another woman. It is said that she preferred the company of other women to her husband and frequently slept with her maidservants. The royal cabinet stripped her of nobility and expelled her from the palace with accusations of lying, shaming the king, and harboring improper jealousy. There are very few other historical sources that document the lives of peasants and other commoners.

Fortunately, oral histories help provide contemporary information about the more informal social networks of women. By several accounts, a women's café, Chanel, thrived in the late 1960s in Myong-dong district of downtown Seoul, the capital. A brainchild of a well-traveled Korean man who admired the free-spiritedness of the European countries he had visited, the women-only café attracted lesbians from all across the country. Because there

**K** is a strong social taboo against women smoking cigarettes in public, Chanel also became known as a place where women went to freely smoke cigarettes. Men were asked to leave or were forcibly removed if they refused to cooperate. Some discontented men eventually started a rumor that Chanel fostered marijuana smoking, and, at the height of the military dictatorship and drug enforcement, Chanel was raided by the police in 1968. Because many women feared the increase in public attention and potential humiliation, they stopped coming to the café. Chanel closed its doors soon after the raid.

A more organized instance of networking was the Women Taxi Drivers Association in the city of Taejon, which formed around 1965. About 90 percent of its members were taxi drivers, but women entrepreneurs and artists also joined the group. On the surface, the association appeared to be an advocacy group for women in a profession that is overwhelmingly occupied by men. Members of the association did not identify as homosexual or lesbian, but as "single"—a term commonly used in Korea to denote a person who chooses not to marry.

The women in the association followed a rigid hierarchy based on age and butch-femme roles. The butch women, who took on the characteristically masculine roles, were called *baji* (pants), and the femmes were called *chima* (skirts). Younger pants had to defer to the older pants as *hyong*, a term usually reserved for men to call older men. The membership grew steadily over the years, and it is said that at least 1,200 to 1,300 women would gather for events. The members took care of one another by planning funerals, celebrating birthdays, and organizing other activities that are traditionally associated with the family. There were also occasional marriages, which were held at Buddhist temples or wedding halls and attended by hundreds. Some women even adopted and raised children. Even though the individual members were not willing to seek visibility in the public eye, they sought institutional visibility. The Women Taxi Drivers Association filed legal papers to become a public organization in the early 1980s but disbanded in 1984 after a divisive election.

In November 1991, a group called SAPPHO formed in Seoul, consisting mostly of American women who were teaching English or stationed on military bases. The group also included women from Belgium, Canada, Sweden, and Australia, as well as women from all over the Korean diaspora. In December 1993, two Korean Americans and several Korean gay men and lesbians formed an organization called Chodonghwe. Students at major universities, such as Seoul National University, Yonsei University, and Koryo University, have also organized campus groups for gays and lesbians. A Korean lesbian organization called Kirikiri (Among the Likes) was officially launched in 1994, and a café/bar called Lesbos in Mapodong in Seoul opened in 1995. Both were covered by a popular news program in 1996, after which Kirikiri's membership grew and Lesbos received more than sixty phone inquiries a day. The 1990s also saw further visibility in the media, including a 1995 made-for-television movie, called *Two Women's Love*, a story about a woman who commits suicide when the woman with whom she is in love marries a man. In June 1997, the first public gay and lesbian rights rally took place in Chongno in Seoul.

*Ju Hui Judy Han*

### Bibliography

Bruining, Miok. "A Few Thoughts from a Korean, Adopted, Lesbian, Writer/Poet, and Social Worker." In *Lesbians of Color: Social and Human Services*. Ed. Hilda Hidalgo. New York: Harrington Park, 1995, pp. 43–60.

Eng, David L., and Alice Y. Hom. *Q & A: Queer in Asian America*. Philadelphia: Temple University Press, 1998.

***See also*** Asian Americans; International Organizations

# L

## Labeling

Sociological term refering both to the process by which something comes to be defined as "deviant" and to a theoretical perspective about the significance of that process. The latter is an approach to deviance that emerged in the 1960s; prior to this, sociology's approach to deviance, like criminology's to crime or psychology's to individual pathology, had been to treat it as a departure from some standard of normality and to explain the cause of the departure. Labeling theorists turned such questions on their heads, noting that nothing is inherently or universally deviant and opening the door for examining both the causes and the effects of the social reaction that places something or someone into the deviant category. The relativism of the labeling approach provided a useful opening for a new academic approach to lesbian and gay lives, cultures, and communities. Most of the sociologists who pioneered these studies were grounded in labeling theory. (Significant members of this first generation include Barry Adam, Philip Blumstein, Barry Dank, John Gagnon, Martin Levine, Barbara Ponse, Pepper Schwartz, Richard Troiden, and Carol Warren.)

Labeling processes impact lesbians at every level, from the societal to the inter- and the intrapersonal. Historical studies demonstrate that, in the European and U.S. middle and upper classes, intense, loving, exclusive relationships between women, termed "romantic friendships," were not only acceptable but honorable prior to the late nineteenth and early twentieth centuries. At that time, such relationships came to be seen as both lesbian and deviant, and, eventually, the once widespread practice of romantic friendship became virtually extinct. The history of romantic friendship demonstrates two central points about the labeling process. First, a behavior viewed as "normal" can come to be labeled deviant over time; relationships between women are not intrinsically deviant. Second, once the deviant label adheres to a behavior, it changes the experience of that behavior; it became nearly impossible for a woman to feel a sensuous, loving attachment to another woman without considering the possibility that she might be a lesbian. What had been a widespread behavior in which any woman might participate had become an indicator that the participant was a particular type of woman.

The effects of this modern lesbian label have been contradictory. On the one hand, a new form of stigma was created, removing the aura of innocence that had surrounded romantic friendships, driving much expression of affection between women into hiding. On the other hand, the lesbian label made it possible to define a relationship between women as explicitly sexual, and, as such, the label was welcomed by some women in spite of the stigma attached to it. The lesbian communities, cultures, and, eventually, social movements that have grown over the course of the twentieth century have been built upon the very lesbian label that originated as a stigma.

As a result of these changes on the societal level, a modern individual may self-label, or identify, as a lesbian in a manner not found in the historical past. This process of identification, often listed as the first stage of coming out, must be understood as an achivement, as a lesbian identity does not automatically follow from any particular behaviors or desires. As a number of studies from the 1970s, 1980s, and 1990s have demonstrated, a woman who has never had a sexual experience with another woman might identify as a lesbian, while a woman who is involved in a serious relationship with another woman might not identify as a lesbian. While many within and outside lesbian communities would be inclined to see women such as these as mistaken about their own identities, such judgments would miss the point that one's self-label, or identity, is significant regardless of its "accuracy" of self-description. A woman who does not identify as a lesbian, who perhaps sees herself as attracted only to a particular woman, rather than to women per se, will make life decisions (such as whether or not to become involved in political activism on lesbian issues) based on that identity.

The lesbian label is not always chosen by the individual, however, but is also a label applied by others, usually to stigmatize. As such, the use of the lesbian label to refer to women who are strong and independent, such as athletes, feminists, and women in positions of authority, is intended to discourage these women and others who might admire them, regardless of the actual "accuracy" of the label. As such, many feminists consider the destigmatization of the lesbian label a crucial goal of the women's movement.                                    *Vera Whisman*

### Bibliography

Faderman, Lillian. *Surpassing the Love of Men: Romantic Friendship and Love Between Women from the Renaissance to the Present*. New York: William Morrow, 1981.

Ponse, Barbara. *Identities in the Lesbian World*. Westport, Conn.: Greenwood, 1978.

Schur, Edwin. *Labeling Women Deviant*. New York: Random House, 1984.

*See also* Coming Out; Feminism; Identity; Romantic Friendship; Stigma

## Labor Movement

The wide range of organizations dedicated to maintaining workers' rights to organize unions, to negotiating employment contracts as members of collective bargaining units, and to advocating all workers' rights in society. In the United States in 1995, 15 percent of the employed workforce consisted of union members; how many of those organized workers were lesbian, gay, bisexual, or transgendered was unknown. Still, since the mid-1980s, many unions have provided an opportunity for lesbian members to develop their strengths as organizers for workplace democracy.

Visible lesbian contributions to union activism come on the heels of two decades of feminist union work. Labor feminists who have been successful in enforcing principles of wage equity in union contracts and who have achieved respect in leadership positions have come out to organize lesbian and gay committees. Other, heterosexual supporters have encouraged the efforts of gay and lesbian coworkers to organize caucuses.

Lesbian and gay activists of Service Employees International Union (SEIU) Local 503, the state employees of Oregon, were critical coalition builders in the "No on 9" and "No on 13" battles of the early 1990s. These electoral campaigns twice successfully defeated statewide referendum proposals that would have mandated discrimination against lesbian and gay citizens. Feminists from that local had led pay-equity-contract campaigns in the 1980s; defending gay rights was an important advance in Local 503's progressive program. The organizers' public speeches at union halls throughout Oregon helped defeat the statewide antigay referendum proposals.

In the highly organized public and service work sectors, where women's union participation is especially forceful, unions such as the SEIU and the American Federation of State, County, and Municipal Employees (AFSCME) have chartered lesbian and gay committees. Along with other public employee unions, such as the American Federation of Teachers (AFT) and the American Postal Workers Union (APWU), they have articulated in their constitutions clear principles of nondiscrimination for sexual orientation.

Lesbian union work takes many forms, depending on the needs of workers and the strength of support available from communities and local and national unions. Domestic-partner benefits have been a popular issue since the mid-1980s. AFSCME and SEIU members have bargained benefit equity into contracts with the cities of Seattle, Washington; San Francisco and Berkeley, California; and New York City. In private-sector contracts, Hotel and Restaurant Employees (HERE) Local 26 in Boston and Local 6 in New York City have achieved similar gains.

Lesbians experience homophobia as a constant workplace hazard in the unionized but male-dominated occupations in which feminism has been less influential, such as the building trades. Women construction workers, both gay and straight, often endure grueling harassment from male coworkers, and rarely are their local unions responsive to complaints. Yet unionized nontraditional jobs attract lesbians because the complex skills needed for construction work are matched by high wages.

Since the mid-1980s, regionally based lesbian and gay labor coalitions have been successful in campaigns against homophobic employers (for example, the Coors beer boycott, which began in 1973 and continued until 1987); they have supported individual workers isolated by harassment; they have encouraged union locals to bargain for domestic-partner benefits; they have contributed to AIDS fund-raising; and they have supported the unionization of employees of gay-owned businesses. In 1994 these regional groups formed Pride at Work (PAW), a national organization, and in 1997 PAW became an official constituency group of the AFL-CIO. Pride at Work has established international links with lesbian and gay committees active in labor unions in New Zealand and in Canada, as well as in several countries of the European Economic Community, including Germany, the Netherlands, and the United Kingdom.               *Miriam Frank*

### Bibliography

Frank, Miriam. "We Are Everywhere: How (and Why) To Organize Lesbian/Gay Union Committees." In *America's Working Women: A Documentary History*. Ed. Rosalyn Baxandall and Linda Gordon. Rev. and updated. New York: Norton, 1995, pp. 324–327.

Frank, Miriam, and Desma Holcomb. *Pride at Work: Organizing for Lesbian and Gay Rights in Unions*. New York: Lesbian and Gay Labor Network, 1990.

Hunt, Gerald, ed. *Laboring for Rights: An International Assessment of Organized Labor's Response to Sexual Orientation*. Philadelphia: Temple University Press, 1998.

Montague, Ann. "We Are Union Builders Too." *Labor Research Review* 20 (Spring/Summer 1993), 79–83.

**See also** Class; Coalition Politics; Community Organizing; Domestic Partnership; Economics; Work

### Ladder, The

Lesbian periodical (1956–1972) published by the Daughters of Bilitis (DOB), a women's homophile organization established in San Francisco, California, in 1955. Although not the first lesbian publication in the United States, *The Ladder* was the first that was printed, widely circulated, and long running. Begun as a small, mimeographed monthly newsletter with a readership of less than two hundred, *The Ladder* advertised DOB events and published short fiction, poetry, book reviews, essays, news clippings, and letters to readers. By its last issue in 1972, *The Ladder* was a polished forty-four page publication sent to approximately 3,800 people, including DOB members in seven countries.

The mission of the Daughters of Bilitis was printed in each issue. This mission included education of the female homophile to enable her to "make her adjustment to society"; public education, which DOB hoped would lead eventually to a breakdown of taboos and prejudices; participation in research projects by psychologists and other recognized experts; and investigation of the penal code. In *The Ladder*'s early years, under the editorships of Phyllis Lyon (1924–) and Del Martin (1921–) (who continued their work and became important lesbian activists), the publication promoted a firmly integrationist stance, working to promote personal and social acceptance of the female "variant" and promoting a "feminine viewpoint" within the homophile movement. In keeping with the goal of gaining increased acceptance of individual lesbians, early issues of *The Ladder* counseled readers on issues of dress and appearance and emphasized accommodation to the mores of middle-class heterosexual society. To help counter the extreme stigma attached to lesbianism in the 1950s, it emphasized that both heterosexuals and homosexuals read *The Ladder,* and it published the views of those few professionals who were sympathetic to lesbians.

During the early and mid-1960s, with Barbara Gittings (1932–) as editor, the publication became more firmly allied with the militant and male-dominated segment of the homophile movement, which rejected accommodationist politics and embraced tactics then considered radical, such as picketing. The magazine published controversial arguments (for example, that homosexuality was not an illness but an orientation or preference akin to heterosexuality) and news about militant homophile organizations and actions. In 1966, under the editorship of Helen Saunders, *The Ladder* shifted emphasis again. This time, *The Ladder* moved away from the male-dominated homophile movement and focused on women's issues and the emerging feminist movement. Articles critical of the male homophile movement and its tactics and issues appeared, along with news and viewpoints positive of the women's movement. In 1970, *The Ladder* became an independent women's liberation movement publication, unaffiliated with the Daughters of Bilitis and edited by Gene Damon (pseud. of Barbara Grier [1933–]). Throughout the magazine's history, short stories and poems showing positive images of lesbians were an important feature, as were reviews of books published by and/or about lesbians. Many of the reviews were reprinted in Barbara Grier's *Lesbiana: Book Reviews from the Ladder, 1966–1972* (1976).

Kristin G. Esterberg

### Bibliography

Esterberg, Kristin. "From Accommodation to Liberation: A Social Movement Analysis of Lesbians in the Homophile Movement." *Gender and Society* 8 (1994), 424–443.

———. "From Illness to Action: Conceptions of Homosexuality in *The Ladder*, 1956–1965." *Journal of Sex Research* 27 (1990), 65–80.

Martin, Del, and Phyllis Lyon. *Lesbian/Woman*. Twentieth Anniversary Edition. Volcano, Calif.: Volcano, 1991.

Grier, Barbara. *Lesbiana: Book Reviews from the Ladder, 1966–1972*. Reno, Nev.: Naiad, 1976.

**See also** Daughters of Bilitis; Gittings, Barbara; Grier, Barbara; Martin, Del, and Lyon, Phyllis

## Ladies of Llangollen

Lady Eleanor Butler (1739–1829), and the Honorable Sarah Ponsonby (1755–1831), Irish diarists. Known as the Ladies of Llangollen after the Welsh valley where they lived for half a century, Sarah Ponsonby and Eleanor Butler are probably the most famous pretwentieth-century example of a female couple.

Both grew up as members of the gentry in Kilkenny, Ireland. In 1778, Butler was under pressure to save her family trouble and money by becoming a nun, and Ponsonby, her friend of ten years, was fighting off the advances of her guardian, who expected his wife to die soon. The two women ran away together in men's clothes (for safer travel) but were brought back by their families, locked up, and starved. On the second attempt, they and their devoted maid, Mary Carryll, managed to cross the Irish Sea. One of Ponsonby's relatives commented that at least "there were no gentlemen concerned, nor does it appear to be anything more than a scheme of Romantic Friendship."

*The Ladies of Llangollen, pirated version of engraving by Lady Leighton. Courtesy of Emma Donoghue.*

After two years of travel, they settled in north Wales, because it was cheaper than England. There they shared a rural, studious, devoted life in a cottage they named, significantly, Plas Newydd (New Place). Over the years, they redecorated it in Gothic style with stained glass and carved oak and planted a famous garden. Money was always short—Mary Carryll got no wages—but, eventually, their families became resigned to the situation and gave them small stipends to live on, and in 1787 Ponsonby got an annual pension of £100 from the king.

The Ladies' story of noble birth, resistance, and escape appealed to the late-eighteenth-century imagination, and their lifestyle seemed to combine all of the best aspects of romantic friendship between women: unworldly motives, rural seclusion, Anglican piety, scholarliness, lifelong virginity, and faithful love. Well aware of being legends in their own lifetime, the Ladies wrote up what they called their "heavenly" days as they went along, in letters (signed jointly), diaries recording how they spent every hour, and books of recipes, medicines, notes on tradesmen, weather, health, extracts from their reading, and future plans. Despite their scandalous "elopement," they were in no sense radicals; they prayed for the king and dismissed servants for pregnancy and venereal disease.

Their journals, though marked by a certain smugness, offer an unparalleled, vivid picture of a shared life that so many other "romantic friends" could only dream of. The Ladies referred to each other as "my sweet love," "my Beloved," "my Heart's darling," and "my better half." One poem of Ponsonby's celebrated serene "Love" over "Vulgar Eros," and, in her day book, she commented: "Those that have loved longest love best." The Ladies became an object of pilgrimage for visitors from all over Europe. William Wordsworth (1770–1850) celebrated them in a sonnet as "Sisters in love"; Anna Seward (1747–1809) wrote many poems about their "Davidean friendship" (recalling that between David and Jonathan), including one that prayed that when they had to die it would be under a single bolt of lightning.

In the early nineteenth century, some visitors saw them, with their old-fashioned cropped hair and mannish riding-habits, as androgynous figures of fun. After a visit in 1822, Anne Lister (1791–1840) speculated with her lover about whether the Ladies' bond had always been "platonic" or was "cemented by something more tender still than friendship." Such suspicions were not new; in 1790, the Ladies had been so incensed by a hinting article entitled "Extraordinary Female Affection" in a local paper that they asked their friend Edmund Burke (1729–1797), who had fought innuendo about his own sexuality in court, whether they should sue. One friend who had highly ambivalent attitudes to the Ladies was the writer Hester Thrale Piozzi (1740–1821); in most of her diaries, she referred to them as "fair and noble recluses," but, in an unpublished diary (unearthed by Liz Stanley), she called them "damned Sapphists," claiming that women were scared to spend a night at Plas Newydd unless accompanied by men.

After their deaths, the Ladies lived on in poetry, plays, and a semifictional biography, *The Chase of the Wild Goose* (1936) by Mary Gordon, who was convinced that she had talked to their ghosts. They still have a central place in the controversy over the extent to which the female couples of the eighteenth, nineteenth, and twentieth centuries can be considered "lesbians." In her study of the Ladies, Mavor (1971) resurrected what she called the "more liberal and inclusive" eighteenth-century term "romantic friendship" to describe their "homoerotic" rather than "homo-sexual" relationship. But, as she points out, it is arguable that the frequent references to headaches and mutual nursing in Butler's diary may stand (consciously or not) for a sexual connection.          *Emma Donoghue*

## Bibliography

Colette. *The Pure and the Impure*. Reprint. New York: Farrar, Straus, and Giroux, 1967.

Faderman, Lillian. *Surpassing the Love of Men: Romantic Friendship and Love Between Women from the Renaissance to the Present*. New York: William Morrow, 1981.

Mavor, Elizabeth. *The Ladies of Llangollen: A Study in Romantic Friendship*. London: Michael Joseph, 1971.

Stanley, Liz. "Epistemological Issues in Researching Lesbian History: The Case of Romantic Friendship." *Women's History Review* 1:2 (1992), 193–216.

*See also* Couples; Diaries and Letters; English Literature, Eighteenth Century; Ireland; Lister, Anne; Romantic Friendship; United Kingdom

## Lagerlöf, Selma (1858–1940)

Swedish author. In 1909, Selma Lagerlöf became the first woman to win the Nobel Prize in literature. She grew up at Mårbacka, a small manor in Värmland, and attended the Royal Teacher's College for Women in Stockholm, where she encountered new ideas and met women who became her lifelong friends. Before Lagerlöf could make a living from her pen, she worked as a teacher for ten years.

Lagerlöf's first novel, *The Story of Gösta Berling* (1891), was a bold breakthrough with a new type of prose poetry in a symbolistic, romantic vein. Her subsequent work was more traditional in form but did contain deep psychological insights that were often symbolically framed. Conflicts concerning female creativity and desire could be written into male characters. She won her greatest acclaim with two books characterized by their nationalist symbolism: *Jerusalem* (1901–1902) and *The Wonderful Adventures of Nils Holgersson* (1906–1907). Before entering the literary field, Lagerlöf voiced a high confidence in her own genius as a writer. Later, she resigned herself to the position of moralist spinster, telling fairy tales from Värmland, a role she was assigned by sexist critics.

All of her life, Lagerlöf had close emotional ties to other women and was in tune with bourgeois feminist ideas. The more than 2,500 letters Lagerlöf wrote to her most intimate friends were sealed until fifty years after her death. These letters reveal a woman full of passion. In 1894, she fell in love with the widowed author Sophie Elkan (1853–1921). Her first letters to Elkan give self-disclosing evidence of her negotiations over her sexual identity. Lagerlöf's feelings were evidently sexual, but Elkan seemed reluctant to live out the physical side of the relationship, which lasted as a friendship until the death of Elkan in 1921. The more sophisticated Elkan introduced Lagerlöf to new circles, and together they traveled extensively throughout Europe. In 1902, Lagerlöf met Valborg Olander (1861–1943), a teacher, who became her lover and close companion. Although they never lived together, Olander supported Lagerlöf and her work in different ways throughout her life. At her death, Lagerlöf's family home, Mårbacka, became a museum, which is open to the public as a living memory of her life and work.

Lisbeth Stenberg

### Bibliography

Berendsohn, Walter A. *Selma Lagerlöf: Her Life and Work.* Preface by V. Sackville-West. London: Nicholson and Watson, 1931.

Larsen, Hanna Astrup. *Selma Lagerlöf: A Short Biography of the First Woman Winner of the Nobel Prize for Literature.* New York: Doubleday 1935.

Stenberg, Lisbeth. "Och forkladnad. En lasning av Selma Lagerlöf's novell *En fallen kung*" (Text in Disguise: An Analysis of Selma Lagerlöfs Short Story "A Fallen King"). *Lambda Nordica* 2:2 (1996), 34–47.

*See also* Sweden

## Land

Movement of self-consciously lesbian women to rural settings with the intent to create autonomous lesbian culture. Although lesbians have always lived on land, as a definable movement it can be said to have begun in the late 1960s and early 1970s, in North America, western Europe, Australia, and New Zealand, as part of a countercultural back-to-the-land movement, following which many of the women came out as lesbians. The other primary genesis was lesbian separatism.

The movement of lesbians to land creates two opportunities: to live secluded from the continual presence of patriarchal "culture" and, in the absence of that pressure, to develop an authentic definition of lesbian culture and identity. Land experiences are of varied durations. Festivals and encampments bring lesbians together in a lesbian-centered society for a weekend or a week. Wandering bands may squat or be received by rural lesbian homesteaders for a summer. Lesbian individuals, partners, or intentional communities may create both a home for themselves and a refuge for others. And community land trusts create and preserve lesbian space on land "in perpetuity."

Anthropologically, "landyke culture" exists as a definable culture distinct from both rural society of the general population and urban lesbian culture. Some of the features of this culture include gynecentricity; having no or limited male presence; decision making by resident consensus; attending to rhythms of menstruation, birth, and menopause in the planning of activity; organic-ecological methods: growing all or part of their food supply by organic, veganic, or bioenergetic methods in cooperation with the natural forces; hospitality: accommodating multiethnic, multigenerational friends and strangers in need for economic, health, and mental-health reasons; appropriate technology: using low-impact methods and machinery that can be made or repaired by the community favoring sun, wind, and water power; teacher-mentor ethic: developing skills and empowering new residents, visitors, and neighbors with information and opportunity to practice; diversity: superseding constrictions of age, race, ethnicity, ability, education, and class to bring in varied traditions of how to accomplish self-sufficient living; and natural healing: replacing paid health care, either allopathic or alternative, with the use of plants and techniques at hand. In addition, a higher percentage of rural lesbians than urban are visibly "out" in all kinds of local encounters, whether by choice, difference from neighbors, or the efficiency of rural gossip. Given the demands of self-sufficient living, few participate in the cash economy on more than a casual basis, but many support a barter economy by crafts production done on the land using materials readily available. A large proportion of lesbian cultural producers live on land and create art, music, books and periodicals, and gatherings and conferences for the larger lesbian community.

Lesbians who live on land have learned most of their land skills since moving to a lesbian land community, whether they grew up rural with land skills or urban. Often, new land communities locate near existing ones, providing companionship, exchanges, and safety. There are pockets of lesbian land communities with members in the hundreds, many of whom know one another. More commonly, lesbians settle on land within driving distance of an established urban lesbian community for resources such as visitors, bookstores, and concerts, as well as outlets for market gardens and crafts.

While some communities endure for decades, others dissolve in conflict. Close living and interdependence raise issues of race, class, and able-bodied assumptions. Communities are often overrun with visitors in extreme situations who lack resources and deplete resident energy. Some women find the demands of self-sufficiency and isolation overwhelming, and others simply move on to new communities, new lovers, new jobs.

It is commonly understood that land cannot be owned or be an investment. Although more land is purchased and developed by private ownership than by nonprofit-corporation land trusts, many private owners convert or bequeath their homesteads to community ownership, creating lesbian legacies. Because land is a resource that generates other resources, such as food, fuel, shelter, water supply, and fiber, the lesbian land movement is a core element of lesbian autonomy and social freedom. A goal of the lesbian land movement is to keep lesbian land in lesbian hands and to create spaces in which lesbians may live out their whole lives.    *Nett Hart*

## Bibliography

Cheney, Joyce, ed. *Lesbian Land*. Minneapolis: Word Weavers, 1985.

Sue, Nelly, Dian, Carol, and Billie. *Country Lesbians: The Story of the WomanShare Collective*. Grants Pass: WomanShare, 1976

Tetrault, Jeanne, and Sherry Thomas. *Country Women*. New York: Doubleday, 1976.

*See also* Ecology and Ecofeminism; Economics; Lesbian Nation; Music Festivals; Separatism; Small Towns and Rural Areas

## Landowska, Wanda (1879–1959)

Polish-born French harpsichordist, pianist, and pedagogue. Wanda Landowska was one of the most celebrated performers of seventeenth- and eighteenth-century keyboard music and a pioneering figure in the revival of the harpsichord. She toured Europe extensively as a harpsichordist, performing early music and educating the public about long-neglected musical repertoires of the past. In 1925, Landowska founded her own school of early music, the École de Musique Ancienne, in St.-Leu-la-Forêt, north of Paris, which included a vast library

and collection of harpsichords and attracted an international student body.

Landowska's highly respected work is well documented on numerous recordings and in her own published writings on harpsichord technique, music interpretation, style, and history. She revitalized works by Domenico Scarlatti (1685–1757) and George Frideric Handel (1685–1759) and is best known for her authoritative performances of Johann Sebastian Bach (1685–1750), drawing out the poetic and sensuous qualities she believed were overlooked in his music. In addition, she commissioned both Manuel de Falla (1876–1946) and Francis Poulenc (1899–1763) to compose modern harpsichord concertos for her in 1925 and 1929, respectively.

Landowska was apparently quite open about her lesbianism with her students and colleagues. She participated in the Parisian lesbian scene by attending, and occasionally performing at, the famous salons of Natalie Barney (1876–1972) and Gertrude Stein (1874–1946). Her performances of keyboard music were marked by a vigorous passion that is often considered excessive but can be heard as the work of a lesbian musician clearly devoted to promoting the beauty, subtlety, and status of the harpsichord in the classical-music world.    *Martha Mockus*

## Bibliography

Landowska, Wanda. *Music of the Past*. Trans. William A. Bradley. New York: Knopf, 1924.

Restout, Denise, ed. *Landowska on Music*. New York: Stein and Day, 1964.

Rogers, W.G. *Ladies Bountiful*. London: Victor Gollancz, 1968.

Salter, Lionel. "Wanda Landowska." In *The New Grove Dictionary of American Music*, vol. 3. Ed. H. Wiley Hitchcock and Stanley Sadie. London and New York: Macmillan, 1986, pp. 8–9.

*See also* Barney, Natalie Clifford; Music, Classical; Stein, Gertrude

## lang, k.d. (Kathryn Dawn) (1961–)

Canadian singer and songwriter. In the early 1980s, k.d. lang studied voice at Red Deer College, Alberta, and worked as a performance artist. She recorded *A Truly Western Experience* in 1984 with Bumstead, a Canadian independent label. In 1987, she signed on with Sire Records and recorded *Angel with a Lariat* (1987), *Shadowland* (1988), *Absolute Torch and Twang* (1989), *Ingénue* (1992), *All You Can Eat*

(1995), and *Drag* (1997). In 1993, she co-composed (with Ben Mink) and performed the sound track for Gus Van Sant's film *Even Cowgirls Get the Blues*.

lang's early musical style is a mischievous blend of honky tonk and rockabilly, and her extraordinary mezzo voice often recalls the late Patsy Cline (1932–1963). lang's powerful vocal style includes bluesy melancholy, rambunctious yodels and hiccups, and langorous phrasing. While some critics find her music overwrought, others admire its exquisite passion, humor, and camp. The Nashville establishment held k.d. lang and the reclines (her band) in suspicion, even though lang befriended Minnie Pearl (1912–1996) and recorded with Brenda Lee (1944–), Loretta Lynn (1935–), Kitty Wells (1919–), and Roy Orbison (1936–1988). She presented an unabashedly butch image to the world: short spiky hair, men's clothing, no makeup, and no mention of boyfriends in her song lyrics and interviews. Furthermore, she identified as a feminist, and her music was banned from many midwestern country music radio stations in 1990 when she publicly promoted vegetarianism on television.

Although lang was consistently referred to as "androgynous" in the music press, her lesbianism was only a semisecret to her lesbian and gay fans. Such songs as "Big Boned Gal," "It's Me," and "Big Big Love" are easily heard as raucous lesbian anthems. lang often adopts the stage antics of Elvis Presley (1935–1977), Buddy Holly (1936–1959), and Wayne Newton (1942–). And, in her mid-1980s' performances of "Bopalena" and "Polly Ann," which are included on her 1992 video *Harvest of Seven Years (Cropped & Chronicled)*, she enacts outrageous girl drag. In 1992, lang moved away from country music (on *Ingénue*) and came out publicly as a lesbian in the *Advocate*, one of the first visible women in popular music to do so. She also made her film debut, portraying a butch lesbian in northern Alaska, in Percy Adlon's *Salmonberries* (1991).

After coming out, a queer strain continued to shape lang's work. In her 1992 video of "Miss Chatelaine," she donned prom-dress drag, and her musically pared down, funk-inspired *All You Can Eat* made explicit reference to a female lover.

*Martha Mockus*

### Bibliography

Bennets, Leslie. "k.d. lang Cuts It Close." *Vanity Fair* 56:8 (August 1993), 94–99, 142–146.

Lemon, Brendan. "Virgin Territory: k.d. lang." *Advocate* 605 (June 12, 1992), 34–46.

Mockus, Martha. "Queer Thoughts on Country Music and k.d. lang." In *Queering the Pitch: The New Gay and Lesbian Musicology*. Ed. Philip Brett, Elizabeth Wood, and Gary C. Thomas. New York: Routledge, 1994, pp. 257–271.

Rich, B. Ruby. "On Standing by Your Girl." *Artforum* 30 (Summer 1992), 17–19.

*See also* Camp; Music, Popular

## Language

The study of lesbian language did not begin until the last two decades of the twentieth century. It has its origins in two rather different fields of inquiry. The first concentrated on language and sexuality, while the second looked at language and gender. Early studies of language and sexuality mostly took the form of investigations into gay slang. The creation of a specialized gay vocabulary was seen as an integral part of establishing group cohesion and identity. Glossaries of gay slang, including the words used, their meanings, and origins, began appearing as early as 1941 with Gershon Legman's "The Language of Sexuality: An American Glossary." A tacit assumption of many researchers was that lesbian slang could be subsumed under a general "homosexual" heading. Two methods were used to gather the data. Researchers would circulate questionnaires to places where gay people gathered, such as bars, asking respondents to list the gay words they knew for various activities and people, such as "having sex" or "lesbian." Alternatively, as participant observers who were themselves gay or lesbian, they would provide information about their own and their friends' use of gay slang.

These early studies proved of limited value to the investigation of lesbian language for several reasons. Participant observation necessarily limits its findings to the insights of the informant/researcher and his or her acquaintances, while questionnaires that ask only for a series of discrete lexical items lose vital information, such as the context of use and the role the words play in creating community. Although it is interesting to note that the majority of San Francisco Bay Area lesbians are familiar with the expressions "butch bottom" (a lesbian of masculine appearance who takes a relatively passive role in bed), "rug munching" (performing oral sex), and "packing" (wearing a dildo), this does not tell when and how these terms are used, by whom, nor what their connotations are. Nevertheless, the early glossaries and slang dictionaries did help show that the language of lesbians was a valid area of study.

The gay slang glossaries listed relatively few terms for lesbian activities, a fact that Penelope and Wolfe (1979) investigated. They observed that "lesbians know few of the terms usually regarded as gay slang and use even fewer" because, according to them, slang itself mostly consists of derogatory terms for women. Since, as they concluded, "lesbians do not possess a unique vocabulary," Penelope and Wolfe turned their investigations in another direction, asking not what lesbian slang consists of, but what other social mechanism is used by lesbians to create cohesion among themselves. Penelope and Wolfe began to analyze lesbian verbal humor instead of concentrating on single words.

This development in lesbian linguistics proved both useful and detrimental. It temporarily shelved the investigation into lesbian slang by stating that slang was not a fruitful area of research, implying even that such research was antifeminist. On the positive side, it moved the emphasis away from individual words and looked at the discourse context and the cooperative creation of verbal texts.

The second field of inquiry that has contributed important concepts and analytical tools to the study of lesbian language is conversational analysis, especially the analysis of language and gender. Specialists in the study of language and gender, such as Robin Lakoff, Jennifer Coates, Deborah Cameron, and Deborah Tannen, examined three principle areas: (1) the differing connotations of words applied to members of each sex; (2) the differing speech patterns of men and women; and (3) the cultural effects of linguistic gender in languages such as Spanish or Hindi, which classify nouns as masculine or feminine.

This approach provided a robust and complex framework for the analysis of lesbian language. It showed, for example, that conversational concepts such as "no gap, no overlap," which assumed that silences, interruptions, or overlaps in conversation were signs that something was amiss, were not only culturally limited (not applicable in cultures where several people speaking at once might be encouraged as a valued skill), but also of limited application in all-female groups. An overlap might well be a sign of agreement or cooperation, since cooperative speech is more characteristic of women, while competitive speech is more characteristic of men. Since the study of lesbian language is, to a large extent, the study of all-female discourse groups, these

findings have been useful to researchers looking at lesbian language. Kathleen Wood and Ruth Morgan, in a study of lesbians' informal conversation, demonstrate that such talk tends to be highly collaborative, employing not only cooperation, but also co-construction of narratives. One lesbian will begin a description with a word or phrase, and others will build on that description by offering new elements. These new elements are not considered interruptions of the first speaker's turn, but embellishments; not a takeover bid, but a group effort.

A great disadvantage of the "language and gender" approach, on the other hand, is that it assumes that the concepts "masculinity" and "femininity" are directly related to anatomical men and women. In other words, it accepts as unproblematic that men use masculine modes of speech while women use feminine modes of speech. It leaves no space for linguistic gender transgression or performativity. It cannot account for the speech characteristics of butch women or effeminate men, for example.

Both approaches, the "language and sexuality" approach and the "language and gender" approach, have been criticized by modern theorists as reductive. The former assumes that shared homosexuality can cancel out gender differences. It also views language as a collection of words, a lexicon, rather than as a system that works on many levels, principally those of sound (phonology), vocabulary (lexicon), grammar, meaning, and discourse (or language in context). Any of these levels may be used by lesbians to distinguish their speech from that of heterosexual women. For example, Birch Moonwomon (Livia and Hall, 1997), in a pioneering study of lesbian phonology, showed that lesbians tended to stick to the lower vocal range and did not employ the full range of pitch modulation with the steep ascents and descents observed in heterosexual women's speech. William Leap, a gay anthropologist working in the field of language and homosexuality, titled his lesbian and gay linguistics anthology *Beyond the Lavender Lexicon: Authenticity, Imagination, and Appropriation in Lesbian and Gay Languages* (1995), in humorous recognition of the earlier single-minded focus on individual words.

In the 1990s, a more rounded picture of lesbian language began to emerge. Language was considered in all of its aspects (not just lexicon). Lesbians themselves were seen not only as distinct from heterosexual women on the one hand and gay men on the other, but also as belonging to different "communities of practice," or different groups that come together for different purposes, bound by different identities. Early studies tended to look only at the language of white American lesbians, whereas in the 1990s greater emphasis was placed on lesbian communities in other parts of the world and in a variety of different ethnic and social groups.

It is impossible to state exactly what lesbian language consists of; any generalization would risk being reductive. Moonwomon demonstrated that, in Northern California, lesbians are believed by straight outsiders to have an assertive, emotional, talkative manner and a direct, "engaged" style with little use of hedges and qualifiers. Research on fictional representations of butch-femme speech, on the other hand, shows that the fictional butch (usually taken as the archetypal lesbian) speaks little, betrays few emotions, and often allows the words of popular songs to speak for her (Livia, 1995). The popular perception of the way real lesbians speak and the fictional portrayal of butch lesbian speech would appear to be completely at odds. The real lesbian is seen as talkative and expressive; the fictional butch is seen as taciturn and unemotional.

To add a further complication to an already complex picture, these portrayals, although valid for what they show of the perceptions of lesbian language, do not take account of the actual speech of lesbians in specific contexts. A study by Barbara Joans (Leap, 1995) comparing the speech of the lesbian motorbike group Dykes on Bikes with that of the predominantly heterosexual group Ladies of Harley shows that, although members of the first group engage in identifiably lesbian language and topics when talking about their lives outside the bike group, when they go on rides their "bike talk" is indistinguishable from that of the heterosexual group. Another problem one needs to be aware of is the fact that linguistic scrutiny itself may change the nature of the discourse. As Mary Porter (Leap, 1995), reporting on Swahili terms for lesbians in Kenya, observes: "[T]he scrutiny of female friendship is itself disturbing. . . . It is troublesome to think that increased self-consciousness may inhibit the very friendships on which women most depend."

Lesbian language is a complex, multifaceted, and essential part of group identity, cohesion, and expression. It cannot be reduced to one uniform set of practices. *Anna Livia*

## Bibliography

Hayes, Joseph. "Language and Language Behavior of Lesbian Women and Gay Men: A Selected Bibliography [Parts One and Two]." *Journal of Homosexuality* 4:2 (Winter 1978), 201–212; 4:3 (Spring 1979), 299–309.

Leap, William, ed. *Beyond the Lavender Lexicon: Authenticity, Imagination, and Appropriation in Lesbian and Gay Languages*. Buffalo, N.Y.: Gordon and Breach, 1995.

Livia, Anna. "I Ought To Throw a Buick at You: Fictional Representations of Butch/Femme Speech." In *Gender Articulated: Language and the Socially Constructed Self.* Ed. Kira Hall and Mary Bucholtz. New York: Routledge, 1995, pp. 245–278.

Livia, Anna, and Kira Hall, eds. *Queerly Phrased: Language, Gender and Sexuality*. New York: Oxford University Press, 1997.

Penelope, Julia, and Susan Wolfe. *Sexist Slang and the Gay Community: Are You One, Too?* Ann Arbor: Michigan Occasional Paper No. 14 (Summer 1979).

*See also* Gossip; Penelope, Julia; Slang

## Latin American Literature

A body of literature produced by Latin American writers that goes beyond simple representations of lesbian themes and motifs to privilege a lesbian perspective. This literature concerns itself mainly with erotic, autobiographical, and sociopolitical themes. However, in many texts, these are so intertwined that their classification is difficult to discern.

As a consequence of women's and feminist movements, the decades of the 1970s, 1980s, and 1990s favored the emergence and development of this type of literature. Still, the limited critical attention that lesbian literature has received speaks to the denial that exists when it comes to lesbianism. Traditionally, writers interested in lesbian issues and themes have resorted to the strategy of hiding meanings or transforming them into socially acceptable forms. Hence, the history of lesbian literature has to be liberated from the silence that society has imposed on it.

### Key Literary Figures

While the omission of lesbian issues is the norm in Latin American literary critical discourse, some critics have begun to rescue from heterosexist views two key literary figures: Sor Juana Inés de la Cruz (Juana de Asbaje, Mexico [1648–1695]) and Nobel Prize winner Gabriela Mistral (pseud. of Lucila Godoy, Chile (1889–1957]).

Sor Juana Inés de la Cruz, a Carmelite nun, is well known for her lyric and philosophical poetry, essays, and drama in which she rebels against patriarchal structures. Her love poetry, dedicated to noblewomen, the Countess of Paredes and the Marquise de Laguna, among others, has provided the basis for lesbian interpretations of her works and, thus, of her life. Poems such as "En que describe racionalmente los efectos irracionales del amor" (In which she describes rationally the irrational effects of love), "Filis," and "Divina Lysi mía" (My Divine Lysi) suggest a lesbian love discourse.

Central to Gabriela Mistral's poetry are the themes of loneliness, love, and frustration, reflecting the consciousness of a woman identified at different emotional levels with other women. Her female friendships and the existence of a female partner have been overlooked in Mistral's life, as critics have focused on her desolation because of a male lover's death.

As with Sor Juana Inés's and Gabriela Mistral's lives, literary critics have dismissed female bonding in the life of prose writer Teresa de la Parra (pseud. of Ana Teresa Parra Sanojo, Venezuela [1889/1890–1936]). Moreover, de la Parra's close friendship with anthropologist and writer Lydia Cabrera (Cuba [1900–1991]) provides a basis for a lesbian reading.

## Late Twentieth Century

In the second half of the twentieth century, the works of Alejandra Pizarnik (Argentina [1936–1972]) and Cristina Peri Rossi (Uruguay [1941–]) intertwine eroticism with the investigation of the process of writing and sociopolitical concerns. Considered mainly a poet, Pizarnik, in *La condesa sangrienta* (The Bloody Countess [1971]), a work based on Valentine Penrose's *Erzébet Bathóry: La Comtesse Sanglante* (1963), mixes lesbian eroticism with death, power, and torture. This mosaic of eleven prose vignettes is a metaphor for her country's political situation.

Short-story writer, journalist, poet, and novelist Peri Rossi is the author of two books, among many novels and poetry collections, that contain lesbian themes: *Evohé* (1971) and *Lingüística general* (General linguistics [1979]). The epigraph of the former, a poem by Sappho (ca. 600 B.C.E.), is an obvious reference to the theme of lesbianism. In *Evohé,* Peri Rossi assumes a male voice to speak of desire for the female body. Through the use of male and female pronouns, the author encodes her meanings and, thus, avoids political censorship.

While Peri Rossi encodes eroticism and love in *Evohé, Lingüística general* addresses lesbianism openly. Here, the poet continues to explore the relationship of language, meanings, grammar, gender categories, and, in several poems, lesbian love. In "3ra. Estación: Campo de San Barnaba," for example, lesbian meanings are clearly expressed and the female voice proclaims her love for another woman. In "4ta. Estación: Ca Foscari," one of her most beautiful lesbian love poems, the exchange of the women's identities is prominent: "I love you tonight and some others / our identifying marks exchanged / the way we joyfully exchange our clothes / and your dress is mine / my sandals yours / my breast / your breast."

The decade of the 1980s witnessed the emergence of other lesbian poets, such as Magaly Alabau, Nancy Cárdenas, Diana Bellessi, Mercedes Roffé, Nemir Matos, and Sabina Berman. With the exception of Roffé, this poetry is characterized by an openly lesbian erotic discourse. However, eroticism has acquired diversified manifestations in these women's works. In some of them, for example, eroticism is intertwined with rivalry and violence, while in others it is connected with the act of writing.

Among the numerous poetry collections published by Magaly Alabau (Cuba [1945–]), *Electra/Clitemnestra* (1986) and *Hermana* (Sister [1989]) focus on lesbian love, eroticism, and intimacy. In her first book, the author adapts and elaborates on the Greek myths of Electra and Clytemnestra. Through the process of reinterpreting these classical myths, Alabau transforms their heterosexual context into lesbian meanings. While, in her first collection, violence and rivalry are features of the female protagonists' relationships, in *Hermana* she presents the possibility of emotional bonding between women.

Sabina Berman, Nancy Cárdenas, and Rosamaría Roffiel, all Mexican, have produced erotic, sociopolitical lesbian literature. In the erotic vein is the poetry collection *Lunas* (Moons, 1988) by playwright, novelist, and actress Berman (1955–). Cárdenas (1934–1994), poet, playwright, and theater director, was, until her death in April 1994, an activist for lesbians' rights in Mexico City. Her book *Cuaderno de amor y desamor* (Book of Love and Absence of Love, [1994]) articulates an openly lesbian erotic discourse that, as the title indicates, centers on either celebratory or unrequited love. The grammatical markers (the use of an "I" identified as female and a "she") make clear that the female speaker is invoking a woman lover and specifies its

**L** lesbian nature. Moreover, the first pages of the book allude to a new genesis, a reinterpretation of the foundational myth of the Western world. Here, Adam and Eve have been replaced by two women, who, alone and naked, will write their own history.

Rosamaría Roffiel (Mexico [1945–]) is the author of a collection of poetry, *Corramos libres ahora* (Let's Run Freely Now [1986]); a documentary narrative, ¡*Ay Nicaragua, Nicaraguita!* (Oh, My Dear Nicaragua [1987]); and a lesbian novel, *Amora* (Love in the Feminine [1989]). Most of the poems of *Corramos libres ahora* deal with the theme of love and intimacy among women. In *Eroica*, Diana Bellessi (Argentina [1946–]) presents a passionate lesbian erotic discourse characterized by a celebratory tone. In *Eroica*'s section "Dual," as in Peri Rossi's "4ta. Estación: Ca Foscari," the speaker emphasizes the reciprocity of the lovers' desire. Nemir Matos (Puerto Rico [1949–]), the first writer on the island to deal openly with lesbian issues, also deals with the mutuality of desire in her two collections of poetry, *Las mujeres no hablan así* (Women Should Not Speak That Way [1981]) and *A través del aire y del fuego pero no del cristal* (Through Air and Fire but not Glass [1981]). Unlike the previously mentioned poets, Mercedes Roffé (Argentina [1954–]), author of three poetry collections, *Poemas 1973–1975* (1978), *Cámara Baja* (Lower Bedroom [1987]), and *La noche y las palabras* (Nights and Words [1996]), deals with the experience of the lover's absence.

Lesbian prose writers in Latin America have been less prolific than poets. Most lesbian narrative concerns itself with the autobiographical and the erotic. In the biographical mode is the novel *Monte de Venus* (1976) by Reina Roffé (Argentina [1951–]). Censored in Argentina because of its portrayal of political problems and lesbianism, the novel revolves around a lesbian whose life experiences reflect the marginality she suffers in a homophobic society.

During the 1980s and the 1990s, three significant novels dealing with lesbian issues were published. *En breve cárcel* ([1981]; translated as *Certificate of Absence*, [1989]) by literary critic Sylvia Molloy (Argentina [1938–]) explores the link between eroticism and the act of writing. Rosamaría Roffiel's novel *Amora* intertwines a love story, an autobiography, and a social and political commitment to women's causes with a reflection upon women's position of inequality in Mexican society. The novel's epigraph alerts the reader to the fact that it is an autobiographical account based upon real characters and plot. Furthermore, the book's dedication clearly states its lesbian character: "Para todas las mujeres que se atreven a amar a las mujeres" (To All Women Who Dare to Love Women). The controversy caused by the publication of the autobiographical novel *Dos Mujeres* ([1990]; translated as *The Two Mujeres* [1991]) by Sara Levi Calderón (Mexico [1942–]) speaks to the denial and silence that still prevails regarding lesbianism in Latin America.        *Elena M. Martínez*

### Bibliography

Foster, David William. *Gay and Lesbian Themes in Latin American Writing*. Austin: University of Texas Press, 1991.

Martínez, Elena M. *Lesbian Voices from Latin America: Breaking Ground*. New York: Garland, 1996, pp. 12–33.

Rodriguez Matos, Carlos. "Nemir Matos." In *Latin American Writers on Gay and Lesbian Themes. A Bio-Critical Sourcebook*. Ed. David William Foster. Westport, Conn.: Greenwood, 1994, pp. 216–217.

**See also** Juana Inés de la Cruz, Sor; Mistral, Gabriela; Parra, Teresa de la; Sappho

## Latina Literature

Literature written by U.S. women writers whose ethnic identity originates from Mexico, Central America, South America, and Spanish-speaking countries of the Caribbean.

U.S. Latina lesbian literature became widely available and visible only with the publication of *This Bridge Called My Back: Writings by Radical Women of Color* (1981). Prior to its publication, the very concept of a Latina lesbian was met with cultural and social resistance. The editors of *This Bridge*, Cherríe Moraga (1952–) and Gloria Anzaldúa (1942–), introduced into American literature for the first time the voices of openly lesbian Latinas, as well as those of other women of color. As Latina literature proliferated after 1981, so, too, did lesbian literature. By 1998, two anthologies were specifically devoted to Latina lesbian literature. Additional work in this field is increasing as Latina lesbians continue to write and publish literary texts.

### Terms and Origins

One needs to clarify the use of the terms "Latina," "Chicana," and "Hispanic" to recognize the specific differences within the community. "Latina" is an umbrella term that includes women whose ethnic heritage and culture include most of the Spanish diaspora (the originally homogeneous population now dispersed around the world) from Central and South America. "Chicana" refers specifically to women of Mexican American descent who are politicized; the term also attempts to include a recognition of the indigenous heritage. These terms are often used interchangeably, but the distinctions should be acknowledged. "Hispanic" is an umbrella term primarily used by mainstream acculturated communities to describe Latinos in the United States. Latina lesbians rarely use "Hispanic" because it is not considered to be a radically politicized term.

Latina/o literature can trace its beginnings to the protest literature of the civil rights movements in the 1960s. The early published writings of Latinas/os were specifically preoccupied with attempts to identify the community in relation to mainstream American society. Many of the poets and prose writers were male nationalists interested in defining the Latino community in opposition to mainstream society; this included an affirmation of the traditional place of the woman in the Latino community, a rigidly defined domestic space. In response to this narrow definition of women, Latinas began telling their own stories in opposition to both Latino writers and the mainstream society. Many Latinas found themselves active in mainstream feminist organizations in the 1970s, as well as in politicized Latino organizations. Within both movements, however, Latinas found themselves invisible.

In 1980, two works of major significance to the development of Latina writing were published: Margarita Melville's *Twice a Minority: Mexican American Women* and Dexter Fisher's *The Third Woman: Minority Women Writers of the United States*. These two works introduced the concept of Latina—specifically, Chicana—women as writers in contrast to more traditional female role models. However, it was the challenge made by Moraga and Anzaldúa in 1981 that, in many ways, marks the beginning of the contemporary Latina feminist literary period.

## Major Figures

An essayist and editor, as well as one of the founders of Kitchen Table: Women of Color Press, Cherríe Moraga invests her poetry and drama with both personal and political dimensions. Her first collection of work, *Loving in the War Years/Lo que nunca paso por sus labios* (1983), is one of the first articulations of Latina lesbian existence and the cultural politics involved in such an existence. Moraga acknowledges the influence and importance of the African American feminist movement—specifically, the radical manifesto of the Combahee River Collective of 1977—and its role in developing a framework that includes the intersections of race, class, and sexual orientation. Her mixed format of memoir, essay, and historical retelling represents a significant literary development for Chicana writers, as it introduced the literary form that would be followed by later Latina lesbian intellectuals.

In 1983, Kitchen Table: Women of Color Press published *Cuentos: Stories by Latinas*. This collection of stories, edited by Alma Gomez, Cherríe Moraga, and Mariana Romo-Carmona, is one of the earliest collection of stories by not only Latina lesbians, but also heterosexual Latinas. It introduced authors who would later go on to be recognized as the premier Latina lesbian writers.

Gloria Anzaldúa is a poet and an essayist who also questions and revises traditional conceptions of literature. Her highly influential theoretical/poetic, *Borderlands/La Frontera: The New Mestiza* (1987), breaks completely with traditional forms of narrative or essay. Through metaphor, poetry, the retelling of cultural myths, and her own personal narrative, Anzaldúa defines a space that underscores the ambiguity and multiplicity of sexuality in both U.S. mainstream society and the Chicana/o community. In this way, Anzaldúa can be credited with introducing a unique blend of Chicana feminism and queer theory. Anzaldúa, like Moraga, began the articulation of lesbian Latina literature, and both continued through the 1990s to be tireless cultural workers who challenged the stereotyping of Latina sexuality and gender roles.

## Expansion and Continuations

In 1987, a second important anthology was published, *Compañeras: Latina Lesbians: An Anthology*, compiled and edited by Juanita Ramos. This text was the first collection devoted completely to Latina lesbian writings. Published initially by the Latina Lesbian History Project and republished in 1994 by Routledge, a mainstream press, *Compañeras* continued the work of *This Bridge*. One way it did so was by including writers from a variety of specific Latina identities. Like the later works of Anzaldúa and Moraga that use essay, fiction, poetry, and drama, *Compañeras* attempts to break down the traditional lines between genres and explore other means of communicating the complexity of sexuality and its constructions. This anthology introduced the work of Mariana Romo-Carmona, as well as the first writings of previously unpublished lesbian Latinas.

In 1991, an anthology featuring only Chicana lesbians and edited by Carla Trujillo was made available by one of the important small presses that publishes the work of Latina lesbians, Third Woman Press. *Chicana Lesbians: The Girls Our Mothers Warned Us About* can be read as a "coming of age" work by Chicana lesbians, who were ready to assert an identity separate from that of other Latinas. Like its predecessors, *Chicana Lesbians* compiles fiction, poetry, and essays into a text that continues to deconstruct traditional literary genres and also represents the diversity and complexity of the identity "Chicana lesbian." *Chicana Lesbians* also continued the work of *This Bridge* by introducing Chicanas into the previously Anglo-dominated discussions of lesbianism and by interjecting such theorists as Ana Castillo, Emma Perez, and Yvonne Yarbro-Bejarano into the debates over what was coming to be known as queer theory.

The work of writers such as Castillo and Perez points to the continued health of the field. An essayist and a novelist, Castillo has always presented work that is groundbreaking, prolific, and experimental. Among her more recent writing is a collection of essays, *Massacre of the Dreamers: Essays on Xichanisma* (1994), that explores the realm of a feminism indigenous to the cultures to which Castillo belongs. Using both personal and scholarly essay forms, Castillo takes up many of the same issues Moraga and Anzaldúa articulated in their own essays. Castillo's prose, fiction, and poetry represent one of the more complex voices among Latina lesbians.

Latina lesbian writers also have worked with the short story and poetic forms. Achy Obejas's collection of humorous and entertaining short stories, *We Came All the Way from Cuba So You Could Dress Like This?* (1994) incorporates some of the major themes Latina lesbians address in their creative works, such as resistance and rejection by family and community, interracial and interethnic relationships among women, and the complexities of coming out. Prominent Latina lesbian poets of the 1980s and 1990s, in addition to Anzaldúa and Moraga, include Mariana Romo-Carmona, Julia Perez, and Luz Maria Umpierre.

One of the unique aspects of Latina lesbian literature is the use of bilingualism, usually Spanish and English, but also the informal oral languages of "Tex-Mex," "Spanglish," and specific regional dialects. The poetry in *Chicana Lesbians* and other collections, for example, includes bilingualism as a fundamental characteristic. Terri de la Peña's novel *Margins* (1992) includes an explicit statement of purpose about her use of bilingualism within the dialogue, which attempts to reflect accurately the aural experience of Latina lesbians, as well as the emotional and physical experiences as she understands them. In *Margins*, de la Peña explores a unique and particular Chicana lesbian community defined primarily by relationships and not necessarily by a one-dimensional, or "essential," identity.

In 1996, historian Emma Perez published *Gulf Dreams*, a short novel that produced yet another new space for the articulation of desire and intellect. Influenced by postmodern scholarship, Perez recognized how late-twentieth-century theorists have erased the traditional boundaries between sexual desire and intellectual concepts. Hence, *Gulf Dreams* pushes Latina lesbian sexuality and theory further into the postmodern space known as queer theory.

At the end of the twentieth century, Latina lesbian literature was still in its nascent stages. However, language is now available for the articulation of sexuality and desire within the framework of cultural diversity, which leaves ample space for new and invigorating creative work. *María C. González*

### Bibliography

Anzaldúa, Gloria. *Borderlands/La Frontera: The New Mestiza*. San Francisco: Spinsters/Aunt Lute, 1987.

Castillo, Ana. *Massacre of the Dreamers: Essays on Xicanisma*. New York: Plum, 1994.

Gomez, Alma, Cherríe Moraga, and Mariana Romo-Carmona, eds. *Cuentos: Stories by Latinas*. New York: Kitchen Table: Women of Color Press, 1983.

Morag, Cherríe. *Loving in the War Years/Lo que nunca paso por sus labios*. Boston: South End, 1983.

Moraga, Cherríe, and Gloria Anzaldúa, eds. *This Bridge Called My Back: Writings by Radical Women of Color*. Watertown, Mass.: Persephone, 1981.

Ramos, Juanita, ed. *Compañeras: Latina Lesbians: An Anthology*. New York: Latina Lesbian History Project, 1987. Republished New York: Routledge, 1994.

Trujillo, Carla, ed. *Chicana Lesbians: The Girls Our Mothers Warned Us About*. Berkeley: Third Woman, 1991.

*See also* Anzaldúa, Gloria E.; Combahee River Collective; Latinas; Moraga, Cherríe

## Latinas

Diverse community of women living in the United States, as well as a movement for social change that emerged in the 1970s. Latina lesbian identity involves a complex blend of ethnic, gendered, and sexual characteristics and experiences. As people of color, as women, and as lesbians, Latinas have been marginalized in U.S. society yet also have successfully created a distinct culture. Often underlying the identity of Latina lesbians is the refusal to give up or to prioritize one part of their identity over another.

### Diversity

While they share an identity based on cultural, ethnic, and linguistic factors, like the Latino population as a whole, the Latina lesbian community is quite heterogeneous. Latino cultures in the United States represent a fusion, to varying degrees, of specific Latin American cultures with national and regional U.S. cultures. Latin America itself represents a fusion, again to varying degrees, of indigenous, African, and European cultures emanating from more than three hundred years of Spanish colonial rule and racial intermixture.

The designation "Latina" is an umbrella term referring to women of Spanish-speaking heritage in the United States and includes both Latin American and U.S.-born women. The term is often chosen in conscious opposition to the term "Hispanic," which is perceived by many women to be an artificial label imposed by the media and the government. As members of particular communities, Latina lesbians may refer to themselves by more specific labels, such as Puertoriqueña, Chicana, Mexican American, or Cuban. Some Latina lesbians refer to themselves simply as American. Regional identities are also important. For some Chicana lesbians, for example, identities such as Tejana (Mexican Texan) and Hispana (New Mexican) are primary.

Adding to the diversity among Latina lesbians is the presence of both U.S.-born and immigrant women. While a significant part of Latino history in the United States is rooted in the immigration experience, some communities, particularly in the Southwest, trace their beginnings to Spanish-Mexican settlements in the seventeenth and eighteenth centuries. As a consequence, the Latina lesbian community includes a wide spectrum of women, from recent immigrants to women whose families may trace their presence in what is now the United States back many generations.

Immigrant women bring distinct experiences and viewpoints to the Latina lesbian community. They often carry with them specific ways of "being" lesbian, learned in their country of origin, and may not even use the word "lesbian" to describe themselves. In addition to mastering survival in a new culture and country, they must also negotiate what may be a very different lesbian identity once in the United States. Moreover, immigrant women, like Latinas in general, may feel great pressure to represent their communities to the larger society and may, therefore, feel conflicted about living openly lesbian lives.

While the Spanish language is one unifying factor, it also reflects the diversity of the population. The Latina lesbian community includes bilingual women, as well as monolingual English- or Spanish-speaking women. Differences in language among the distinct Latina lesbian communities are illustrated by the spectrum of terms of self-designation used by Latina lesbians. For example, while a Chicana or Mexican lesbian might refer to herself as a *tortillera* (slang for lesbian, literally a woman who makes *tortillas*), another Latina might call herself a *cachapera* (slang for dyke, probably from the word *cachapa*, a pancake).

Economic class is yet another factor that adds to the diversity within the Latina lesbian community. While many women come from working-class backgrounds, others derive from middle- or upper-middle-class backgrounds. Economic class is often associated with particular groups within the Latino population. Historically, many population movements are representative of particular socioeconomic classes. For example, Mexican immigration to the United States in the early part of the twentieth century was predominantly working class, while the Cuban migration of the 1950s and 1960s was chiefly middle class.

Thus, there is no one Latina lesbian identity or experience. Rather, there are a range of experiences defined by individual, regional, and group backgrounds and histories. Despite the many sources of diversity, however, Latina lesbians often share a sense of collective identity based on the common experiences of women who identify both as Latinas and as lesbians. These shared experiences frequently include both the embrace and the critique of traditional cultural values.

## Commonalities

One deeply held value, in both Latin America and among Latinas and Latinos in the United States, is a strong orientation toward family. For Latinos in the United States, identification with the family has served as a survival strategy. Since Latinos have faced deep-seated discrimination and prejudice in the United States, family has often provided a refuge and a place to maintain traditional ethnic culture. An already-strong family orientation, therefore, has been reinforced by the experience of exclusion and segregation. This has had contradictory consequences for Latina lesbians. On the one hand, strong family ties and the fear of being ostracized from the family have made it more difficult for some Latinas to come out as lesbians. Yet, for other women, strong family loyalty has meant a certain level of family acceptance of their lesbianism despite an underlying disapproval.

Another powerful cultural value within Latino societies revolves around the protection of women from outsiders, especially men. The resulting sex segregation has limited women's abilities to move about in society, but also has provided women with opportunities to form intimate and intense relationships with other women. Although the individuals in these woman-centered relationships may not refer to themselves as lesbians, the relationships involve important components of lesbian relationships, including devotion, affection, intimacy, and love.

While religion is by no means a monolithic institution within the Latino community, it has supplied Latinas with another common link. Although Protestant denominations have made important inroads into Latino communities in the twentieth century, Latinos have traditionally identified with the Roman Catholic Church. The Catholic Church maintained religious dominance in Latin America through three hundred years of colonial rule. It influenced every aspect of life. Yet it, too, was modified by its contact with indigenous and African spiritual systems. Latin American spiritualities, therefore, reflect a fusion of Catholic beliefs and practice with indigenous, African, and folk beliefs and practice. In Mexico, for example, Catholicism has been infused with a variety of indigenous worldviews. The patron of Mexico, and of the Americas, Our Lady of Guadalupe, is a dark-skinned virgin who is said to have appeared to an Indian man in 1531. She asked that a temple be built to her on the site of a previous temple to the goddess Tonantzin. The Catholic Church, with its stance against homosexuality, has

made it difficult for Latina lesbians to be open, particularly within strictly Catholic households. Yet many Latina lesbians have maintained ties with the Catholic Church and have continued to practice their specific forms of spirituality.

These connected, yet distinct, religious backgrounds have had differing consequences for Latina lesbians. Spirituality may open up spaces for lesbians. In the Caribbean, Catholicism has been imbued with African spiritual beliefs. Santeria, a spiritual system derived from the Yoruba people of western Africa, often disguised itself as Catholicism in the Caribbean, where it has flourished, although often underground, since colonial times. There is evidence of a strong lesbian presence within Santeria in the nineteenth century. That presence was powerful enough to merit a divinity, a protector of lesbians, the hermaphroditic Inle. Like other culturally held values and beliefs, religion has served to both limit Latina lesbians and allow them places to exercise some control over their own lives.

Along with shared cultural values, an experience of exclusion from predominantly heterosexual Latino communities and predominantly white lesbian communities has also reinforced the creation of a Latina lesbian identity. Heterosexual Latinos and Latinas sometimes label lesbianism as "acting white" in an effort to control the sexuality of Latina lesbians. Out lesbians have been labeled "sellouts" (*vendidas*) by straight Latinos and Latinas who see lesbianism as an intrusion of American culture. Latina lesbians have also been accused of being *antifamilia* by others who believe that maintaining traditional culture is paramount to the survival of peoples of color. These debates have been most visible within the political arena, particularly during times of intense cultural nationalism.

## Latina Politics

As a consequence of the conflicts and debates between Latina lesbians and cultural nationalists, who believe that "culture" should remain unchanged, Latinas have responded politically in several different ways. Some have continued to work within broad ethnic groups, others left to work with lesbian-only organizations, while others formed separate Latina lesbian groups.

The move to lesbian-only groups presented difficulties. Within predominantly white lesbian organizations, Latina lesbians frequently experienced racism and exclusion. In the 1970s, many Latina lesbians believed that what was then termed "women's culture" was actually "white women's culture." Within such settings, Latina lesbians often felt pressured to speak only English, to set aside cultural practices and values, and to disregard concerns over racism in favor of a focus on sexism. Despite the feelings of exclusion arising from their interactions with both heterosexual Latinos and white lesbians, Latina lesbians have continued to work within both communities.

While there have been Latinas who fit the definition of "lesbian" throughout the twentieth century, the term "Latina lesbian" emerged from the particular historical circumstances of the late twentieth century. The movement of Latina lesbians working for social change derives from a particular political orientation that deems ethnicity, gender, and sexuality equally worthy of consideration.

As a political movement, Latina lesbians draw inspiration and experience from several other movements, including the civil rights movement, the Chicano movement, the gay and lesbian liberation movements, and the feminist movement. Since the 1970s, Latina lesbians have organized politically in a number of ways around a number of issues. Although Latina lesbians have always been present within their communities, their visibility as a distinct politicized group dates from the 1970s.

Shortly after the Stonewall Rebellion (1969) in New York City's Greenwich Village, Latina lesbians and Latino gay men created organizations that fought racism and homophobia in a variety of ways. In the 1970s, organizations included El Comite de Orgullo Homosexual Latinoamericanos (New York City), Comunidad de Orgullo Gay (Puerto Rico), Greater Liberated Chicanos (Los Angeles, California), and the Gay Latino Alliance (San Francisco, California). By the 1980s, Latina lesbians were creating separate organizations, including Latinas Lesbianas Unidas (Los Angeles), Ellas (Texas), Las Buenas Amigas (New York City), and Lesbianas Latinas de Tucson (Arizona). The 1980s also saw the formation of the first national organization of Latina lesbians and Latino gay men, Latina/o Lesbian and Gay Organization (LLEGO). By the early 1990s, Latina lesbians were also working within organizations focused on creating linkages between Latina lesbians in the United States and lesbians in Latin America. In 1994 Adelante con nuestra vision: First National Latina Lesbian Leadership and Self-Empowerment Conference, Latina lesbians from throughout the United States attended in Tucson, Arizona.

Simultaneously, Latina lesbians have continued creating and re-creating a Latina lesbian culture that reflects the diverse Latina lesbian visions through literature and art. Beginning in the 1980s, Latina lesbian newsletters and journals undertook the task of diffusing these visions regionally and nationally. One important avenue for this process was the journal *esto no tiene nombre* (this does not have a name) from Miami, Florida, which published work by Latina lesbians from 1991 through 1994.

Latina lesbians, like other lesbians of color, represent a diverse, and still evolving, community of women who identify as Latinas and as lesbians.

*Yolanda Chavez Leyva*

## Bibliography

Alarcón, Norma, Ana Castillo, and Cherríe Moraga. *The Sexuality of Latinas*. Berkeley: Third Woman, 1989.

Espín, Oliva. "Cultural and Historical Influences on Sexuality in Hispanic/Latin Women: Implications for Psychotherapy." In *Pleasure and Danger: Exploring Female Sexuality*. Ed. Carole S. Vance. Boston: Routledge, 1984, pp. 149–164.

Garcia, Alma. "The Development of Chicana Feminist Discourse." In *Unequal Sisters: A Multi-Cultural Reader in U.S. Women's History*. Ed. Vicki L. Ruiz and Ellen Carol DuBois. New York: Routledge, 1994, pp. 531–544.

Leyva, Yolanda Chavez. "Breaking the Silence: Putting Latina Lesbian History at the Center." In *The New Lesbian Studies: Into the Twenty-First Century*. Ed. Bonnie Zimmerman and Toni A.H. McNaron. New York: Feminist Press, 1996, pp. 145–152.

Moraga, Cherríe, and Gloria Anzaldúa, eds. *This Bridge Called My Back: Writings by Radical Women of Color*. Watertown, Mass.: Persephone, 1981.

Ramos, Juanita, ed. *Compañeras: Latina Lesbians*. New York: Latina Lesbian History Project, 1987.

Trujillo, Carla, ed. *Chicana Lesbians: The Girls Our Mothers Warned Us About*. Berkeley: Third Woman Press, 1991.

*See also* Caribbean; Immigration; Latina Literature

## Law and Legal Institutions

Lesbian lives are affected on a daily basis by the law and legal institutions. The law often determines whether lesbian sexual practices will be punished or tolerated, whether children will be removed from lesbian households, whether or not lesbian relationships will be valued, whether or not lesbians will be able to immigrate, and whether or not lesbians will be discriminated against in employment, housing, and other necessities. While the law and legal institutions do not necessarily determine social realities, the law does have an important practical and symbolic role. In advocating for the betterment of lesbian lives, there is controversy about how much the law and legal institutions should be utilized to effect change for lesbians.

In a little less than half of the states in the United States and in many nations, lesbian sexual practices are illegal. The criminalization of lesbian sexual practices is often the linchpin that supports other forms of discrimination. For example, in child-custody disputes, courts have often used the "criminal" status of the mother's sexual practices to deprive a lesbian mother of custody. While there has been some liberalization in lesbian child-custody cases since the 1960s, lesbian mothers continue to be deprived of custody of their children—even in cases in which such a deprivation requires the court to award custody of the child to a person convicted of murder or a person, such as a grandparent, who is in the ordinarily much less favored legal position of a nonparent. For lesbian nonbiological parents, the law has not recognized their status as parents. This means that, if there is a separation or if the legal parent dies, the nonlegal parent has little claim for custody or even visitation of the child. However, several states have begun to recognize second-parent adoptions, which allow the nonbiological parent who is a partner of the biological or adoptive parent to adopt the child—thus, becoming a legal parent.

## Relationships

Regarding lesbian relationships, the traditional stance has been a denial of legal status. This can cause problems because the law routinely accords other relationships legal status. For example, a lesbian's "next of kin" for medical determinations and inheritance purposes could be a biological relative she has not seen for twenty years rather than the lover with whom she has been living for those twenty years. With the advent of statutes allowing health-care proxies in almost every state and many nations, a lesbian can select the person(s) she wishes to make her decisions should she become incapacitated. In terms of inheritances, the will of a lesbian devising her property to her lover(s) was once easily contested by biological relatives under the legal

doctrine of "undue influence," and such wills were set aside by judges who believed that biological relatives, not lesbian lovers, were the "natural objects of a person's bounty." In the 1990s, however, such will contestations ceased to be generally successful. Nevertheless, unless there is a legal document, such as a health-care proxy or a valid "last will and testament," the law continues to operate to privilege biological relations and obliterate lesbian relations.

The legal nonrecognition of lesbian relations can also cause a lesbian partner to be denied private insurance benefits, Social Security benefits, and a host of other benefits available to "spouses." In a growing number of cases, municipalities, universities, and corporations have adopted domestic-partnership policies that attempt to recognize certain long-term lesbian relationships for benefit purposes. However, such policies remain the exception rather than the norm.

Thus, many advocate for the extension of legal marriage to same-sex couples. The traditional legal view has been that legal marriage can be extended only to couples who are composed of one man and one woman, although there were certainly factual exceptions in the cases of passing women and of transsexuals who changed gender identity after the marriage occurred. In the 1990s, however, there have been glimmers of change. Several Scandinavian nations, as well as the Netherlands, allow some form of same-sex marriage, although not on the same terms as traditional male-female marriages. In the United States, although during the 1970s many state courts had rejected legal challenges to the limiting of marriage licenses to couples consisting of a male and a female, in 1993 the Hawai'i Supreme Court ruled that such treatment might constitute sex discrimination (*Baehr v. Lewin*). The court relied upon its state constitutional provision prohibiting sex discrimination and held that, unless the state could demonstrate a compelling interest for the limitation of marriage to male-female couples, the practice must be discontinued, and same-sex couples must be allowed to avail themselves of legal marriage. When the case was remanded for trial, the trial court found that the state did not satisfy its burden of demonstrating a compelling reason. A 1999 referendum empowered the legislature to ban same-sex marriages, though no such law has been passed, nor has the Hawai'i Supreme Court ruled on the court decision. Although the validity of Hawai'in same-sex marriages in other states is unclear, in response to the Hawai'i litigation, in 1996 Congress passed the Defense of Marriage Act (DOMA), which attempts to make it clear that states need not recognize Hawai'in same-sex marriages. Many states have passed similar statutes providing that the state will not recognize same-sex marriages even if such marriages are legally valid in other states. These state laws, as well as DOMA, contradict the general practice of states recognizing as valid marriages that are valid in other states, a practice that is possibly mandated by the "full faith and credit" clause of the United States Constitution.

Yet lesbians do not universally advocate same-sex marriage. For some lesbians, legalizing same-sex marriage is overwhelmingly positive: It will afford some individual lesbians concrete benefits, and it has the potential to erode the gendered configuration of marriage and to liberalize, and perhaps even liberate, the institution of marriage from its patriarchal roots. For other lesbians, the availability of marriage will have negative effects: It will cause a rift between "good" lesbians, who inhabit monogamous long-term relationships, and "bad" lesbians, who do not, and will mean that lesbian couples will be assimilated into the institution of marriage with all of its defects, including its patriarchal history devaluing women.

The availability of lesbian marriage would also affect the immigration laws of the United States and many other nations that give preference to noncitizens related by blood or marriage to citizens. This privileging can result in the denial of a preferential immigration status to the noncitizen partner of a lesbian citizen. Further, the immigration laws of many nations provide for the exclusion of persons who have committed crimes or are morally unfit, both of which can be applied to lesbians, although in recent years this application has become increasingly rare. Increasingly, legal advocates have argued that the laws allowing political asylum for persons who have a justified fear of persecution in their countries should be applied to lesbians and gay men who have a fear of persecution because of their sexuality.

## Legalized Discrimination

"Persecution," in the immigration/asylum context, usually means fear of death in the home nation, but every nation seems to have an unacceptable level of violence against lesbians. A less dramatic form of persecution and violence occurs against lesbians in the form of legalized discrimination. In the United States, it is unlawful for any government and most private entities to discriminate against a person on the basis of race, national origin, sex, or religion. Although such discrimination undoubtedly occurs, it is, nevertheless, illegal, and a person who could prove, for example, that a landlord would not rent to her because she is Asian, or from Japan, or a woman, or a Buddhist, could bring a lawsuit and be awarded money damages. However, if the landlord told her he would not rent to her because she is a lesbian, in all but a handful of states or cities she would have no legal remedy. In the places that do prohibit discrimination on the basis of sexual orientation, however, it would also be illegal for a lesbian landlord to refuse to rent to a heterosexual man on the basis of his heterosexuality. Since 1995, the United States Congress repeatedly considered, but refused to pass, a federal law that would prohibit discrimination on the basis of sexual orientation.

In the United States, perhaps the most visible legal discrimination has occurred in the military, which discharges women on the basis of lesbianism in numbers disproportionate to the number of women serving in the military. According to anecdotal evidence, many women discharged or forced to resign may not be actual lesbians, but may have merely resisted the sexual advances of male service members and have then been subjected to lesbian baiting. In other cases, lesbians who have simply stated that they are lesbians have been discharged. The courts have generally upheld these discharges, giving great deference to the military and rejecting various arguments, including that the discrimination is unconstitutional under the "equal protection" clause or that the discharge violated the lesbian's constitutional right to free speech.

For many years, the United States Supreme Court has not been receptive to lesbian arguments for equality, most often refusing to even hear cases in which lower courts had allowed discrimination or other forms of inequality. In 1986, the Court rendered its notorious decision in *Bowers v. Hardwick,* which held that states could constitutionally criminalize minority sexual practices. Perhaps less well known, but equally offensive, was the Court's decision (1987) in *San Francisco Arts and Athletics v. United States Olympic Committee,* in which the Court held that the United States Olympic Committee "owned" the word "Olympics" and could seek an injunction against the Gay Olympics for infringement, despite granting the use of the term "Olympic" to other groups (such as the Explorer Olympics) and its failure to enforce its right against

**L** other groups (such as the Crab-Racing Olympics). Similarly, in *Hurley v. Irish American Gay, Lesbian, and Bisexual Group of Boston* (1995), the Court overruled the Massachusetts Supreme Court—which had held that the group organizing Boston's St. Patrick's Day Parade violated state laws by excluding gay, lesbian, and bisexual Irish Americans from the parade—arguing that the parade organizers had a First Amendment right to determine the content of the parade.

In 1996, however, the United States Supreme Court, for the first time, ruled in favor of lesbians, gay men, and bisexuals. In *Romer v. Evans,* the Court ruled that Amendment 2 to the Colorado State Constitution, passed in a referendum by Colorado voters, was unconstitutional. The amendment itself was a backlash to some policies and ordinances in Colorado that had made discrimination on the basis of sexual orientation unlawful. Amendment 2 provided that the state or any of its subdivisions could not enact or adopt any policy "whereby homosexual, lesbian or bisexual orientation, conduct, practices or relationships shall constitute or otherwise be the basis of or entitle any person or class of persons to have or claim any minority status, quota preferences, protected status or claim of discrimination." In declaring Amendment 2 unconstitutional, the Court held that Amendment 2 "classifies homosexuals not to further a proper legislative end but to make them unequal to everyone else. This Colorado cannot do. A State cannot so deem a class of persons a stranger to its laws."

Many advocates on behalf of lesbian legal rights believe that *Romer v. Evans* marked a new beginning in the law's treatment of lesbians and other sexual minorities. Although most agree that this case does not guarantee that lesbian sexual practices will no longer be punished, or that children will not be removed from lesbian mothers, or that lesbian relationships will not continue to be devalued, or that lesbians will not continue to be lawfully discriminated against, most also agree that perhaps the law's hostility toward lesbian may be waning.

*Ruthann Robson*

### Bibliography

Herman, Didi, and Carl Stychin, eds. *Legal Inversions: Lesbians, Gay Men, and the Politics of Law.* Philadelphia: Temple University Press, 1995.

Leonard, Arthur. *Sexuality and the Law: An Encylopedia of the Major Legal Cases.* New York and London: Garland, 1993.

Robson, Ruthann. *Lesbian (Out)Law: Survival Under the Rule of Law.* Ithaca, N.Y.: Firebrand, 1992.

———. *Sappho Goes to Law School: Fragments in Lesbian Legal Theory.* New York: Columbia University Press, 1998.

Rubenstein, William, ed. *Lesbians, Gay Men, and the Law: Cases and Materials.* New York: Free Press, 1993.

Wilson, Angela, ed. *A Simple Matter of Justice?* London and New York: Cassell, 1995.

*See also* Adoption; Custody Litigation; Discrimination; Domestic Partnership; Legal Theory, Lesbian; Privacy; Rights

## Leather

Term that can refer to clothing, a fetish, sexuality, a lifestyle, or a subculture with its own vocabulary and codes. There is no universal profile of a lesbian who has interests in leather or in the leather community. Many lesbians involved within the leather scene explain that their interests, fetishes, or practices are merely matters of personal choice and expression of sexual autonomy and radical sexuality.

In the 1990s, the community represented itself as pansexual and inclusive of different sexualities, persuasions, and varying degrees of interest in leather. The importance of a subculture and a vocabulary for leather lesbians is an affirmation of their self-knowledge, sexual taste, and lifestyle. Attraction to leather can extend into personal dress, sexuality, or leather fetish. Despite popular stereotypes, not everyone interested in leather has an interest in sadomasochism.

During the late 1960s and early 1970s, the lesbian leather community was small, but it flourished even though there were no lesbian leather bars or organizations. Instead, many leather women met within the men's leather bars, which had existed since the late 1950s. Several sources corroborate that there was an increased curiosity in leather within the lesbian community in the late 1970s. In 1978, a group of leather women in San Francisco, California, founded a group, Samois, which was one of the first organized support groups that catered to lesbians interested in leather or sadomasochism. The name "Samois" comes from the estate of the lesbian dominatrix Anne-Marie in the *Story of O* (1965) by Pauline Réage (pseud. of Dominique Aury). Samois' membership grew large enough to rent space at the Catacombs, a privately owned leather/sadomasochism men's space, the Hothouse, and other places that welcomed their activities.

The effort to publish their booklet *What Color Is Your Handkerchief?* (1980; out of print) and their book *Coming to Power: Writings and Graphics on Lesbian S/M* put a strain on the members, and, by 1983, the group disbanded. Initially, Samois' publications were banned from the shelves of most feminist bookstores. They and other leather women were attacked for what was perceived as male-identified sexuality and the violence attributed to leathersex. Acceptance from the feminist community was nonexistent at the time and is still controversial. After Samois' demise, other leather woman founded the Outcasts in San Francisco in 1984. They published groundbreaking works that dealt with leather lesbian sexuality and sadomasochism, published by Alyson Publications. Attention to "leather dykes" has surrounded lesbian scholarship during the decades of the 1980s and 1990s.

The 1980s saw a proliferation of lesbian or woman-friendly leather clubs in most major cities in the United States, such as the Lesbian Sex Mafia in New York City (1981); the Outer Limits in Seattle, Washington (1988); and Female Trouble in Philadelphia, Pennsylvania (1989). Most organizations are affiliated with the National Leather Association. These organizations and countless others, cater to women interested in the leather or sadomasochist (S/M) culture. At the end of the 1990s, most major cities had leather-related groups, and many Internet sites that cater to lesbians existed, offering workshops, conferences, and contests to members and others.                          *Janni Aragon*

## Bibliography

Califia, Pat. "A Personal View of the History of the Lesbian S/M Community and Movement in San Francisco." In *Coming To Power: Writings and Graphics on Lesbian S/M*. Ed. Samois. San Francisco: Samois, 1981. 3rd ed. Boston: Alyson, 1987, pp. 245–284.

Califia, Pat, and Robin Sweeney, eds. *The Second Coming: A Leatherdyke Reader*. Los Angeles: Alyson, 1996.

Rubin, Gayle. "The Catacombs: A Temple of the Butthole." In *Leatherfolk: Radical Sex, People, Politics, and Practice*. Ed. Mark Thompson. Boston: Alyson, 1991, pp. 119–141.

*See also* Sadomasochism

## Leduc, Violette (1907–1972)

French writer whose works reflect the complex interplay of autobiography and fiction. Violette Leduc's fictional works stand as counterpoints to the autobiography she would later write. Indeed, it was only through the publication in 1964 of *La Bâtarde* (The Bastard), the first volume of her autobiography, that Leduc began to receive any recognition as a writer.

The stigma of illegitimacy marked Leduc's childhood, as her mother shifted the burden of her own disgrace onto the child. She taught her to distrust men and fear pregnancy and, at the same time, criticized her unattractiveness and unfeminine behavior. Although her grandmother's love counterbalanced her mother's lack of affection, her grandmother's death when Leduc was nine brought an abrupt end to any happiness she might have known in the context of her family. With her mother's marriage and the birth of a legitimate child, a son, Leduc's alienation was complete. The rest of her youth would probably have been spent at boarding school had she not been expelled for a lesbian relationship with one of the teachers.

Leduc quit high school and went to work for a while as a secretary and publicity writer for the publishing house Plon. She also began another liaison with a woman. Illness forced her to give up her job, and, soon afterward, the breakup of her relationship left Leduc with few resources. She worked at odd jobs, was married, albeit briefly, and maintained contact with some of the writers she knew from Plon. After the onset of World War II, she fled to the Normandy countryside with the flamboyant writer Maurice Sachs (1906–1945). Under Sach's aegis, Leduc not only became a successful trader on the black market, but also completed the draft of her first novel, *L'Asphyxie* (In the Prison of Her Skin). The return to Paris at the end of the war introduced Leduc to the circle of Simone de Beauvoir (1908–1986) and Jean-Paul Sartre (1905–1980). Beauvoir shepherded the publication of *L'Asphyxie* (1946) and became one of Leduc's strongest supporters. She helped Leduc during her nervous breakdown and assured her financial stability through a monthly stipend from the publishing house Gallimard. For her part, Leduc had long idolized Beauvoir. In a sense, all of her works, be they fiction or autobiography, were written with Beauvoir as their intended reader. Her ambiguous, very much one-sided, relationship with Beauvoir became, as all of Leduc's life, matter for both her novels and her autobiography.

With Beauvoir's encouragement and despite the lack of immediate critical success, Leduc continued living in Paris and writing. Then, in 1964, *La Bâtarde*, the autobiography behind the fiction of *L'Asphyxie,* appeared and instantly became a *succès de scandale* of the year. After experiencing the recognition of her talent and the fame she had long hoped for, Leduc spent increasing amounts of time, devoted to writing, in the southeast of France, where she died of cancer in 1972.          *Edith J. Benkov*

### Bibliography

Courtivon, Isabelle. *Violette Leduc*. Boston: Twayne, 1985.

Evans, Martha Noel. "Violette Leduc: The Bastard." In *Masks of Tradition: Women and the Politics of Writing in Twentieth-Century France*. Ed. Martha Evans Noel. Ithaca, N.Y.: Cornell University Press, 1987, pp. 102–122.

***See also*** Beauvoir, Simone de; French Literature

## Lee, Vernon (1856–1935)

British woman of letters. Born Violet Paget to an English mother of West Indian origins and a Polish father in Boulogne, France, on October 14, 1856, she was multilingual with an internationalist perspective, having spent most of her life on the Continent with annual visits to England. At age fourteen, on the publication of her first short story, she adopted a pseudonym to protect her identity from the all-male literary establishment. "Lee" was a tribute to her half-brother, the poet Eugene Lee-Hamilton (1845–1907), but the other major influences in her life were women, including her mother, Matilda, and the novelists Cornelia Turner (d. 1874) and Henrietta Camilla Jenkin (1807?–1885).

In 1880, she published her most widely acclaimed work, *Studies of the Eighteenth-Century in Italy*, which revived scholarly and popular interest in the art and music of the Italian eighteenth century. She would write more than forty other books, including supernatural and historical fiction, fairy tales, a play and a biography, and collections of essays on traveling, literary and aesthetic criticism, and philosophical, political, and social issues. She also published well over two hundred articles throughout her lifetime, many in major journals and newspapers. Brilliantly outspoken in her spectacles and tailored dress, Lee was oftentimes both deeply admired and harshly attacked, most especially for her antiwar activism and writing during the Great War.

Her most intensely personal writing appears in her correspondence with Kit Anstruther-Thomson (1857–1921), a painter, who was her lover and collaborator from 1887 until 1898 and thereafter her special friend until Anstruther-Thomson's death in

*Vernon Lee [Violet Paget]. Special Collections, Miller Library, Colby College, Waterville, Maine.*

1921. Although she never identified herself as lesbian, Lee's romantic attachments were exclusively with women. She also had an extensive network of literary and artistic friends with whom she corresponded and exchanged visits, including Henry James (1843–1916), Edith Wharton (1862–1937), John Singer Sargent (1856–1925), Mary Cassatt (1845–1926), Ethel Smyth (1858–1944), Sarah Orne Jewett (1849–1909), and Bernard Berenson (1865–1959). By the early 1930s, Lee suffered increasing isolation resulting from her loss of hearing and the almost total neglect into which her work had fallen. She died at her home outside Florence on February 13, 1935.          *Phyllis F. Mannocchi*

## Bibliography

Gunn, Peter. *Vernon Lee: Violet Paget, 1856–1935.* Oxford: Oxford University Press, 1964. Reprint. New York: Arno Press, 1975.

Mannocchi, Phyllis. " 'Vernon Lee': A Commentary and Primary Bibliography." *English Literature in Transition, 1880–1920* 26 (1983), 231–267.

———. " 'Vernon Lee and Kit Anstruther-Thomson: A Study of Love and Collaboration Between Romantic Friends." *Women's Studies* 12 (1986), 129–148.

Markgraf, Carl. " 'Vernon Lee': A Commentary and Annotated Bibliography of Writings About Her." *English Literature in Transition, 1880–1920* 26 (1983), 268–312.

*See also* Jewett, Sarah Orne; Smyth, Dame Ethel Mary

## Legal Theory, Lesbian

Ideas about lesbians and law. Since surfacing as a self-conscious enterprise in the late 1980s, lesbian legal theory has become a robust, yet controversial, field for law professors, lawyers, and others. Lesbian legal theory offers a critique of, and a theoretical framework for, ongoing efforts to obtain enhanced legal protections for lesbians through litigation, legislation, and other political strategies.

One root of lesbian legal theory was Patricia Cain's challenge to the invisibility of lesbian experience in feminist legal theory. Cain (1989) pointed out that inclusion of lesbian experience in feminist legal scholarship lagged far behind scholarship in other disciplines. This omission was especially wrong given that a basic project of feminist legal theory is to use women's experience to reveal the entrenched male bias permeating avowedly neutral legal theory and doctrine.

At approximately the same time, Ruthann Robson unleashed her groundbreaking work developing lesbian legal theory. Robson's landmark book, *Lesbian (Out)law: Survival Under the Rule of Law* (1992), included a critique of feminist legal theory similar to that made by Cain. But Robson, in *Lesbian (Out)law* and numerous articles, ambitiously declared the need to develop a lesbian legal theory distinct from feminist jurisprudence and undertook that task.

As developed by Robson, lesbian legal theory is a theory of law that has as its purpose lesbian survival. It constitutes a way to examine the law from both individual and community lesbian perspectives and is committed to being "relentlessly lesbian," putting lesbians, rather than law, at the center. For example, in *Lesbian (Out)law*, Robson argues that the law's traditional categories and themes sacrifice and damage lesbians. She reveals the centuries of legal punishment of lesbians, hidden behind the myth of lesbian impunity.

According to Robson's vision, lesbian legal theory respects a variety of lesbian traditions and does not emphasize some elements of lesbian identity over others. It understands the inevitability of the law's influence but is not knowingly complicit in the creation of the law's dominance. It makes lesbians visible in the law and challenges what Robson calls the domestication of lesbians by the law, or the diminishment of lesbians through interaction with laws. For example, Robson argues that reform of marriage laws to include lesbian relationships would further domesticate lesbians, reforming lesbians as much as the law. Robson has examined legal history, lesbians as criminal defendants, the use of contract law by lesbian couples, intralesbian intimate violence, and family law, among other areas.

Although Robson began as an almost solitary pioneer in the field of lesbian legal theory, she has been joined by a number of lawyers and legal academics developing and applying lesbian legal theory to immigration law, family law, contract law, lesbian marriage, criminal law, nondiscrimination law, legal history, and other subjects.

Those working to develop lesbian legal theory assert that elimination of sexism will not necessarily eliminate heterosexism and, thus, that feminist jurisprudence does not adequately address the situations of lesbians. Lesbian legal theory is needed, for example, because feminist jurisprudence's preoccu-

L pation with women compared to men suggests a heterosexual bias and because lesbian lives are not explained solely by either sex or gender.

Lesbian legal theory also implicitly critiques legal theories, sometimes called "queer law," that combine claims or rights related to lesbians with those related to gay men. In putting lesbian experience first, lesbian legal theory suggests that sex and gender differences distinguish the lives and experiences of lesbians from those of gay men in meaningful ways. Lesbian legal theory, thus, differs from the dominant theory of lesbian law reform, which focuses on sexual-orientation discrimination, combining the interests of lesbian and gay men in human rights law, constitutional litigation, contract law, employment discrimination, housing, domestic-partnership litigation, and other legal controversies.

However, the very notion of lesbian legal theory has brought criticism from both opponents and proponents of legal advances for lesbians and gay men. Traditionalists within the legal academy scorn the idea of lesbian legal theory as simultaneously trivial and grandiose. The more serious criticism, however, comes from progressive legal theorists, including feminists and lesbians, who identify serious dangers in the development of explicitly lesbian legal theory. Lesbian legal theory has evolved in the context of other legal theories based on identities or standpoints, including critical race studies, and provokes the same criticisms as these other identity- or standpoint-based theories.

Many academics understand lesbian identity, like other identities, to be socially constructed, diverse, contingent, and mutable. Eaton (1994) and others warn that developing a lesbian legal theory risks universalizing one version of lesbian identity through submersion of racial, class, and other aspects of identity. Arriola (1994) has charged that the attempt to develop lesbian legal theory necessarily and wrongfully privileges lesbian identity, suggests that identity is constituted by a singular trait, and dichotomizes "lesbian" and "woman." Herman (1994) questions why any one identity should be chosen as the basis of unity (lesbian identity rather than, for example, Jewish identity), given that each person holds multiple and often contradictory identities.

Considering these dangers, Cain (1994) concludes that, although lesbian-centered theorists must be careful not to universalize lesbian experience or valorize lesbian over any other experience, the experience of becoming and/or discovering oneself a lesbian is transforming in a way that suggests that "lesbian" is a meaningful identity to place at the center of a legal theory.

In related critique of lesbian legal theory, Herman (1994) and other critical theorists question the goal of developing any all-encompassing theory of law. Although, by its own terms, Robson's lesbian legal theory does not aspire to become a paradigmatic, objective, or authoritative account of law, critics argue that the very enterprise of lesbian legal theory implies the goal of overarching principles. Eaton addresses this concern—and perhaps qualifies Robson's project—by suggesting that lesbian legal theory be contextualized, find different shapes in different controversies, and even disappear when lesbian identity is not distinctive within a particular legal arena, such as stranger violence against women or some economic issues.

Lesbian legal theory in English-speaking countries followed the growth of lesbian movements for legal rights and the inclusion of lesbian activists in the legal academy. The important advances in lesbian rights around the globe, including the explicit protection for lesbians and gay men in the South African constitution and the greater advocacy of lesbian rights through international human rights provisions, suggest the possibility of ever-expanding, global lesbian legal theories.     *Joan W. Howarth*

## Bibliography

Arriola, Elvia. "Gendered Inequality: Lesbians, Gays, and Feminist Legal Theory." *Berkeley Women's Law Journal* 9 (1994), 103–143.

Cain, Patricia A. "Feminist Jurisprudence: Grounding the Theories." *Berkeley Women's Law Journal* 4 (1989–1990), 191–214.

———. "Lesbian Perspective, Lesbian Experience, and the Risk of Essentialism." *Virginia Journal of Social Policy and Law* 2 (1994), 43–73.

Eaton, Mary. "At the Intersection of Gender and Sexual Orientation: Toward Lesbian Jurisprudence." *Southern California Review of Law and Women's Studies* 3 (1994), 183–218.

Herman, Didi. "A Jurisprudence of One's Own? Ruthann Robson's Lesbian Legal Theory." *Canadian Journal of Women and Law* 7 (1994), 509–522.

Herman, Didi, and Carl Stychin, eds. *Legal Inversions: Lesbians, Gay Men, and the Politics of Law.* Philadelphia: Temple University Press, 1995.

Robson, Ruthann. *Lesbian (Out)law: Survival Under the Rule of Law.* Ithaca, N.Y.: Firebrand, 1992.

———. *Sappho Goes to Law School: Fragments in Lesbian Legal Theory*. New York: Columbia University Press, 1998.

***See also*** Law and Legal Institutions

## Lesbian

Term derived from the Greek island of Lesbos, home of the seventh-century B.C.E. poet Sappho. In the twentieth century, "lesbian" has come to refer almost exclusively to female same-sex practices in which Sappho reputedly engaged and which she celebrated in her lyric poetry.

The equivocal grammatical status of "lesbian," as both noun and adjective, captures the historical difficulty and the controversy over its definition. Whereas the former names a substantive category of persons—female homosexuals—the latter refers to a contingent attribute.

The use of the term to denominate a particular kind of woman, one whose sexual desire is directed toward other women, originated in the late nineteenth century with the formulation of types of sexual deviance, especially homosexuality. European sexologists at the time invented the lesbian as a personage with a pathological medical and mental profile. The term typically designates a woman whose sexual orientation is believed to be caused by a biological (genetic or hormonal) anomaly or by an abnormal psychological development. The lesbian's defining trait was her alleged manliness, manifested in her dress and behavior and in her envy of the penis. According to popular opinion, buttressed by Freudian theory, her desire for other women issued from her wish to be a man—her sexual inversion. Although this belief was largely abandoned in the 1970s, the assumption that the lesbian is a unique and specific type of person, different from heterosexual women, remains prevalent.

Taking "lesbian" as an adjective, however, implies that female same-sex desire is a detachable modifier, a relative characteristic rather than an essential, or core, substance. Describing an object or activity as lesbian may simply reflect its contingent affiliation or association with female homoeroticism. Such an understanding of the term was common in Western societies before the twentieth century and remains so in non-Western cultures that do not sharply distinguish female homosexuality from heterosexuality.

The best-known use of "lesbian" as an adjective is in the phrase "lesbian feminism," which became widespread in the 1970s to refer to a political movement that joined feminist ideology to lesbian sexual practices. In its earlier form, this movement criticized the heterosexist categorization of lesbians and advocated the concept of a "lesbian continuum," Adrienne Rich's (1929–) phrase for the broad range of affective and erotic bonds among women. Championed as a "woman-identified woman," the lesbian was a figure for the defiant rage of all women, whether or not they fit the sexological profile of the lesbian deviate. With the waning of feminism as a political force in the 1980s, lesbianism became increasingly defined in cultural and psychological terms.

To be a lesbian, at end of the twentieth century in the United States, typically means to embrace an identity and to participate in a lesbian subculture. The clothing styles and sexual practices that signify the lesbian have diversified in the aftermath of disputes over pornography, S/M (sadomasochistic) sex, and the vogue of 1990s "lipstick" (conventionally feminine) lesbians. The mainstreaming of lesbian subculture and its growing commodification, especially in the entertainment industry, suggest that "lesbian chic" will come to serve as an advertising ploy and that lesbians will gain a commercial niche. While some critics deplore this trend, others see it as a means of infiltrating the dominant culture and subverting the homophobic notion of the lesbian as a freak of nature. In this view, she is a consumer whose desires are constituted and manipulated by social and market forces.

Academic debates concerning the meaning of lesbianism in the last quarter of the twentieth century frequently have turned upon the interpretation of same-sex desire and identification within psychoanalytic theory. Influenced by the writings of Julia Kristeva (1941–), Luce Irigaray (1930–), Hélène Cixous (1937–), and Melanie Klein (1882–1960), many theorists argue that the crux of lesbian desire lies in the preoedipal relation between mother and daughter, which they privilege as a primordial intimacy. In keeping with the lesbian feminist precept of female identification, this line of thought has led to a preoccupation with identity politics. However, theorists indebted to the poststructuralist thought of Jacques Derrida (1930–) and Jacques Lacan (1901–1981) criticize gender and sexual categories, claiming that "woman" and "lesbian" are social inscriptions. Rather than springing from a natural origin, the lesbian is produced through coerced and regulated enactments of that role, a process Butler (1991) calls "performative repetition."

The controversy between these essentialist and constructionist views, corresponding to the difference between "lesbian" as a noun and as an adjective, has resulted in a disciplinary rift in the late twentieth century. On the one hand, some scholars seek to establish lesbian history and literature as academic fields, while, on the other hand, queer theorists question the fundamental distinction between homosexuality and heterosexuality and, like Sedgwick (1990), replace "lesbian and gay" with the multivalent and contested term "queer."

A persistent problem with the use of "lesbian" is its historical and cultural relativity. Most non-Western cultures lack a corresponding category and term, while most Western cultures possess a similar linguistic expression but attach different significations to it. These barriers to a universal or unified definition of "lesbian" are exacerbated by heightened attention, at the end of the twentieth century, to bisexuality and transgendering. Both phenomena elude the conceptual boundaries of lesbianism and threaten its coherence.

If to describe is also to prescribe, any definition of the term "lesbian" is also an implicit validation of a particular meaning as normal and, hence, normative. Such a tacit endorsement, under the guise of an accurate representation, is especially the case with encyclopedias, which aim to instruct on the basis of their claim to objective authority. Admittedly, the foregoing account of "lesbian" encourages consideration of the contingent, or adjectival, understanding of the term. Instead of searching for a nominative essence, one might recall the archaic sense of the word "lesbian" as (according to the *Oxford English Dictionary*) a pliant and accommodating principle of judgment that, like a mason's rule, rather than going in a straight line, bends to fit its object. *Colleen Lamos*

### Bibliography

Butler, Judith. "Imitation and Gender Insubordination." In *Inside/Out: Lesbian Theories, Gay Theories*. Ed. Diana Fuss. New York: Routledge, 1991, pp. 13–31.

Doan, Laura, ed. *The Lesbian Postmodern*. New York: Columbia University Press, 1994.

Faderman, Lillian. *Surpassing the Love of Men: Romantic Friendship and Love Between Women from the Renaissance to the Present*. New York: William Morrow, 1981.

Rich, Adrienne. "Compulsory Heterosexuality and Lesbian Existence." In *The Lesbian and Gay Studies Reader*. Ed. Henry Abelove, Michèle Aina Barale, and David M. Halperin. New York: Routledge, 1993, pp. 227–254.

Sedgwick, Eve Kosofsky. *Epistemology of the Closet*. Berkeley: University of California Press, 1990.

*See also* Bisexuality; Essentialism; Lesbian Continuum; Lesbian Feminism; Performativity; Postmodernism; Psychoanalysis; Queer Theory; Sappho; Sexology; Woman-Identified Woman

## Lesbian Avengers

In 1992, writer and activist Sarah Schulman and five friends, Ana Maria Simon, Anne-Christine D'Adesky, Maxine Wolfe, Marie Hoban, and Ann MaGuire, responded to a lack of attention given to lesbian issues by founding a direct-action group, the Lesbian Avengers, dedicated solely to lesbian visibility. In *My American History: Lesbian and Gay Life During the Reagan/Bush Years* (1994), Schulman provides a detailed account of the group's history up to 1994. Highlights of their first year included the *New York Times'* appellation of the group as the Lesbian Agenda and "zaps" (quick, small-scale political actions) against Denver Mayor Wellington Webb. The group's organization of the "first ever Dyke March on the White House" during the 1993 March on Washington provided the Avengers with the opportunity to contact lesbians from around the country.

The "Lesbian Avenger's Handbook" (included in *My American History*) is the best guide to the group's philosophy and tactics. Organizing an action includes answering questions concerning tactics and logistics, as well as more conceptual concerns—all summarized in the Avenger Action checklist and a task roster. Their tactics are inherently theatrical, many borrowed from the guerrilla-theater troupes of the 1960s and 1970s. The handbook's authors emphasize that meetings must be focused: A trained facilitator ensures that members make concrete suggestions, propose alternatives, and take responsibility for their ideas.

Two important actions undertaken by the Lesbian Avengers demonstrate their verve. First, their 1993 "Freedom Ride" through New England to help members of the gay, lesbian, and bisexual community of Lewiston, Maine, resist the repeal of their city's antidiscrimination measure, Equal Rights Protection, succeeded in opening many closet doors. Second, the Lesbian Avengers' 1994 grass-roots, pro-gay and lesbian organization in Idaho, the Lesbian Avengers Civil Rights Organizing Project (LACROP), which clashed with the more conservative local group, NO on One, influenced the defeat of a measure aimed at prohibiting antidiscrimination legislation. LACROP also produced and reproduced gay-positive literature, directly delivering it to rural gays lesbians, and straight people, and inspired two Lesbian Avenger chapters, in addition to several local gay and lesbian support groups and an "Out Against the Right" handbook. The Lesbian Avengers remain as impetuous as their name implies.

*Amy Gilley*

## Bibliography

Metz, Holly. "Sarah Schulman." *Progressive* 58 (October 1994), 37–41.

Pursley, Sara. "With the Lesbian Avengers in Idaho." *Nation* 260 (January 23, 1995), 90ff.

Schulman, Sarah. *My American History: Lesbian and Gay Life During the Reagan/Bush Years.* New York: Routledge, 1994.

*See also* Associations and Organizations

*Lesbian Connection: Twentieth Anniversary Issue.*

## Lesbian Connection

Longest-running publication for lesbians in the United States. Continuously published since 1974, the *Lesbian Connection* (*LC* or Elsie) is a twenty-eight page forum for information exchange and dialogue among lesbians. *LC* is the premier example of a publication creating a national and international network for lesbians, with a worldwide circulation of more than twenty thousand subscribers. *LC* is free to lesbians and is published six times annually in East Lansing, Michigan, by the Elsie Publishing Institute, a not-for-profit corporation.

*LC* was founded on lesbian feminist principles by a collective called the Ambitious Amazons to address the lack of safe, reliable, and targeted information channels for lesbian groups and individuals. Margy, one of the original Ambitious Amazons, described its genesis (quoted in Baker, 1996): "We figured if LC was to be for every lesbian it should be written by its readers, not by us, thereby becoming the space for a wide-ranging lesbian dialogue. We thought of ourselves as the caretakers of this forum."

The content and the structure of *LC* adhere to the characteristics of a feminist publication detailed by Steiner (1992), including the use of egalitarian management practices and consensus-based, horizontal decision making. The newsletter is funded by advertising, donations, and fund-raising. It provides generous space for reader submissions, and the discussion topics are all encompassing.

Begun on a donated budget of $33, the first issue of *LC* was a four-hundred-piece mimeographed mailing with hand-addressed labels. In 1997, the subscriber mailing was more than twenty thousand, costing about $55,000 per issue. Its "look" has since evolved to a "desktop published" design. *LC* is distributed primarily through subscriptions, alternative bookstores, and music festivals. Its content includes Letters and Responses (discussions of wide-ranging issues); Articles and News; Festival Forum (information about upcoming music festivals and letters discussing recent festivals); To Our Health; Reviews (reader reviews of books, films, art, and music); classified and display advertisements; and the Contact Dyke Directory (listing by state and country of women who are willing to act as contacts for travelers, visitors, or women relocating to their area). Joan Nestle (in Streitmatter, 1995) credits the Contact Dyke section of *LC* with liberating American lesbians by connecting them.

*Laurie J. Baker*

# L

*Bibliography*

Baker, Laurie J. "Ritual Argument: Creating and Maintaining Identity Through Dialogue in the *Lesbian Connection*." Master's thesis, North Dakota State University, 1996.

Steiner, Linda. "The History and Structure of Women's Alternative Media." In *Women Making Meaning: New Feminist Directions in Communication*. Ed. Lana Rakow. New York: Routledge, 1992, pp. 121–143.

Streitmatter, Roger. *Unspeakable: The Rise of the Gay and Lesbian Press in America*. Boston: Faber and Faber, 1995.

*See also* Lesbian Feminism; Periodicals

## Lesbian Continuum

A spectrum of female relationships that can, to varying degrees, be termed "lesbian." First coined by Adrienne Rich in "Compulsory Heterosexuality and Lesbian Existence" (1980), the term "lesbian continuum" suggests that there is a lesbian presence that has existed across cultures and historical periods. Rather than restrict her definition to women who self-identify as "lesbian" and engage in same-sex sexual relationships, Rich expands the term to include many kinds of practices and beliefs that express both resistance to male domination and political and emotional commitment to women. The term, therefore, incorporates feminism into a definition of lesbianism and reclaims many forms of behavior that had not previously been recognized as lesbian, such as marriage resistance and women's intense personal friendships.

In the early stages of "second wave" U.S. feminism, which emerged in the late 1960s, lesbianism, when not demonized as a deviant sexuality, was often considered irrelevant to the cause of feminism. Rich's analysis was important as an assertion that lesbianism is not antifeminist and that lesbian relationships are not merely sexual. By arguing that there is a long line of resistance to male domination and compulsory heterosexuality that can be traced throughout history, and by naming this line "lesbian," Rich proposes that the impulse toward woman-identification (feminism) and lesbianism strongly overlap. She sees the erasure of lesbians from history as a great loss for feminism, because it leaves the impression that women have never resisted patriarchy and that the hatred and violence lesbians face is particular to them as a minority, rather than an extension of the coercion all women face to remain subservient to men.

Some critics argue that the term "lesbian continuum" deemphasizes, or even erases, the sexuality of lesbian relationships by defining feminism rather than attraction to women as the primary element of lesbianism. The concept has also been criticized as being inattentive to historical and cultural differences, especially by feminist historians and other critics who think that it erases the specificity of lesbian experience by naming any feminist or close female relationship "lesbian." In her 1986 afterword to "Compulsory Heterosexuality," Rich herself admits that the term could easily be misused in this way. She argues, however, that her intention was not to erase differences between heterosexual and lesbian women, but to define lesbianism broadly in her search across cultures and times for a continuity of lesbian and feminist resistance to patriarchy.

While the idea of a lesbian continuum has caused much controversy, it has also been widely used in women's studies and lesbian and gay studies, often in discussions of the difficulty of defining and applying the term "lesbian" in scholarship on women's history, literature, and media representation.     *'Becca Cragin*

*Bibliography*

Keohane, Nannerl, Michelle Rosaldo, and Barbara Gelpi, eds. *Feminist Theory: A Critique of Ideology*. Chicago: University of Chicago Press, 1982.

King, Katie. "The Situation of Lesbianism as Feminism's Magical Sign: Contests for Meaning and the U.S. Women's Movement, 1968–1972." *Communication* 9 (1986), 65–91.

Rich, Adrienne. "Compulsory Heterosexuality and Lesbian Existence." *Signs: Journal of Women in Culture and Society* 5:4 (1980), 631–660. Reprinted in Rich, *Blood, Bread, and Poetry, Selected Prose, 1978–1985*. New York: Norton, 1986.

Thompson, Martha. "Comments on Rich's 'Compulsory Heterosexuality and Lesbian Existence.'" *Signs: Journal of Women in Culture and Society* 6:4 (1981), 790–794.

*See also* Lesbian; Rich, Adrienne

## Lesbian Feminism

A political movement and philosophy that began in the early 1970s, the basic tenet of which is that lesbianism is a political choice that any woman can make, not an essential identity. The early movement slogan "Feminism is the theory; lesbianism is the practice" indicates the belief that lesbianism is a self-conscious enactment of an antipatriarchal politics, a profoundly political act of rejecting heterosexist norms that oppress women. Beyond the basic commitment to lesbianism as a political choice, lesbian feminists differ widely in terms of political beliefs and activism. The growth of lesbian feminism out of radical feminism in the early 1970s would seem to indicate a sole focus on gender politics, but many lesbian feminists were and are multi-issue activists.

## Origins

The earliest articulation of lesbian feminist theory is in "The Woman Identified Woman," a political manifesto written in 1970 by the New York group Radicalesbians in response to radical and reformist feminists' dismissal of lesbianism as a serious issue for the movement. The manifesto was first distributed in 1970 at the Second Congress to Unite Women, after a protest led by Rita Mae Brown (1944–) designed to heighten lesbian visibility in the women's movement. Brown had left a leadership post in the National Organization for Women (NOW) in 1969 after NOW's cofounder Betty Friedan (1921–) dubbed lesbian issues a "lavender menace" for feminism. "The Woman-Identified Woman" was the first important document to propose lesbianism as a political strategy, critiquing the institution of heterosexuality and arguing that all women are potential lesbians. Its famous opening reads: "What is a lesbian? A lesbian is the rage of all women condensed to the point of explosion."

Brown was also a member of the influential lesbian feminist Furies collective, a Washington, D.C.–based group that included writer and activist Charlotte Bunch (1944–), photographer Joan E. Biren (JEB, 1944–), and Ginny Berson, cofounder of Olivia Records, among others. The Furies lasted only one year (1971–1972), but it influenced the lesbian feminist movement profoundly, largely through its newspaper, *The Furies*, which was published until the summer of 1973. The group's radical politics shaped the terms of the "gay-straight split" that developed among radical feminists in the early 1970s. The Furies advocated a brand of lesbian separatism, arguing that lesbianism was the only choice for feminists committed to fighting male supremacy. The group's materialist, anticlassist politics mark its

work as an important early attempt to grapple with classism within the women's movement.

Despite the oppositional status of these early lesbian feminists in the women's movement, the emergence of the "second wave" of U.S. feminism in the late 1960s was crucial to many women's coming out and politicization as lesbians. At conferences, marches, and in consciousness-raising groups, a mass movement of feminists protested traditional female roles, including roles within the heterosexual nuclear family. Many members of the previously underground, despised lesbian community came out of the closet into a political movement whose slogans called for women's liberation, and they decided that meant their liberation as lesbians as well. Other lesbians who came out in the late 1960s and the 1970s discovered their love for women through their feminist activism.

Among the most extreme statements of lesbianism as a political stance was Jill Johnston's book *Lesbian Nation: The Feminist Solution*, which was published by a large mainstream press in 1973. Johnston (1929–) argued that lesbianism is the political vanguard of feminism: "Feminism at its heart is a massive complaint. Lesbianism is the solution. . . . Until all women are lesbians there will be no revolution. No feminist per se has advanced a solution outside of accommodation to the man." Johnston repudiated the butch-femme identities so common before the women's movement as antifeminist and considered bisexuality "a fearful compromise . . . a continued service to the oppressor." Unlike the work of most early lesbian feminists, Johnston's theory included a large dose of biological essentialism, with a twist, in which "the lesbian is woman prime."

In contrast, the French-born lesbian feminist writer Monique Wittig (1935–) argued in 1981 that lesbians are not women at all because they do not conform to female social roles. In "One Is Not Born a Woman," Wittig argued for a strong social-constructionist lesbian feminism: "The refusal to become (or to remain) heterosexual always means to refuse to become a man or a women, consciously or not."

## Development

Many lesbian feminists have disagreed with Johnston's biological determinism and separatism. But, for many white lesbians in the 1970s, the burgeoning feminist and lesbian feminist movements led to a belief that the shared bond of woman-identification transcended differences among women, rendering

**L** those differences less important. The desire to express this perceived bond, and to be able to spot other lesbians, led to a conformity of style among many white lesbians. The "clone look"—featuring flannel shirts, jeans, boots or Birkenstock sandals, short hair, and no makeup—expressed an androgynous, feminist refusal of the trappings of traditional femininity.

The emphasis on sameness and the erasure of difference was criticized by some lesbian feminists, especially working-class lesbians and lesbians of color, who were often involved in more than one liberation movement simultaneously. Members of the Combahee River Collective explained, in their "Black Feminist Statement" (1977), that separatism amounts to "fractionalization," that they "feel solidarity with progressive Black men," and that "as Black women [they] find any type of biological determinism a particularly dangerous and reactionary basis upon which to build a politic."

Ample evidence shows that working-class lesbians and lesbians of color were active in both lesbian feminism and the women's liberation movement in the 1970s; however, attempts to describe the racism of many white feminists and lesbian feminists have often led historians and other commentators to misrepresent lesbian feminism as a white, middle-class women's movement. Sandoval (1991) explains that women of color were both active within and "at odds with" white feminism "from the beginning of what has been known as the second wave of the women's movement." Their participation has been overlooked by historians describing lesbians who were politically active only "as lesbians"—that is, white, middle-class women who were not identified also by race and class.

Prominent lesbian feminists as early as the 1970s (and beyond) included such writers and activists as working-class-identified African Americans Pat Parker (1944–1989) and Audre Lorde (1934–1992); Asian American Willyce Kim (1946–); and white, working-class-identified Judy Grahn (1940–). Grahn (1985) described the diversity of women involved in early feminism and lesbian feminism, including black lesbians, Asian American lesbians, Jewish lesbians, and white, working-class lesbians. The diversity of the lesbian feminist community became much more obvious in the 1980s, when both multiculturalism and racism were highlighted by lesbian writers and activists of color.

Many lesbian feminist theorists and activists are best known for their work within literary or academic contexts. Among the most prominent are the poet and essayist Adrienne Rich (1929–), the historian and literary scholar Lillian Faderman (1940–), and the philosopher Mary Daly (1928–). Rich, in her essay "Compulsory Heterosexuality and Lesbian Existence" (1980), and Faderman, in her book *Surpassing the Love of Men: Romantic Friendship and Love Between Women from the Renaissance to the Present* (1991), made the important contribution of broadly defining lesbian identity as intimacy between women, claiming a wide range of behavior, not necessarily sexual, as evidence of historical lesbian existence.

Beginning in the 1970s, lesbian feminists founded many institutions that constituted "women's culture" and lesbian communities in the United States. Bookstores, coffeehouses, publishing houses, health centers, credit unions, newspapers, magazines, music festivals, and record labels created a nationwide network of feminist and lesbian feminist communities. They attempted to set up an alternative to the exploitative, patriarchal institutions that dominate U.S. society. This movement was dubbed "cultural feminism" by radical feminist detractors, who decried the cultural feminists' celebration of essential femaleness and their perceived withdrawal from engagement in direct struggle against the patriarchal system. "Cultural feminism" largely supplanted radical feminism among lesbian feminists by the late 1970s.

For some lesbian feminists, separatism was the logical next step. Separatists dissociate themselves from men in every way possible, sometimes forming rural land collectives; some lesbian separatists dissociate from heterosexual women and from lesbians who are not separatists. Generally, lesbian feminists have lived in separate subcultures from gay men, who have been seen as sharing with heterosexual men both male privilege and a tendency toward sexism. This has changed, to a large degree, since the onset of the AIDS crisis in the early 1980s, which brought together lesbian and gay activists in many communities. While lesbian separatism has provided much of the energy for the creation of lesbian feminist culture, it is not synonymous with lesbian feminism. Women who consider themselves lesbian feminists may be separatists, cultural feminists, radical feminists, liberal feminists, or some combination of these categories.

Confusion about the definition of lesbian feminism stems both from the various ways of expressing lesbian feminism and from the hostility of other lesbians toward the movement's basic principles. Lesbians who believe that they are born homosexual ("essentialist" lesbians) criticize lesbian feminism's emphasis on lesbianism as a conscious, if socially constructed, choice. Postmodern "queer" lesbians reject the implicit separatism of lesbian feminism and consider lesbian feminism to be essentialist.

## Lesbian Feminism and Queer Theory

The excoriation of lesbian feminism by some female academic "queer theorists" has led to splits between activist theorists who often share many goals but whose critical tools and academic reference points differ. This is sometimes expressed as a divide between older "1970s feminists" and younger "queer" lesbians, but, in fact, the generational divide is not absolute.

Some "queer theorists" in the 1990s who opposed lesbian feminism wrote about the movement as if it were over, but many lesbian feminists continued to organize politically and to publish their work throughout the decade. The discord between postmodern queer theorists and activist lesbian feminists was exacerbated by some British and Australian lesbian feminist publications such as Sheila Jeffries' (1993) in the mid- to late-1990s that accused postmodernists of academic elitism and of lacking a radical political agenda. The existence of the British and Australian publications, in addition to continued lesbian feminist activism and writing in the United States, makes clear that the lesbian feminist movement and community continue.

*Linda Garber*

## Bibliography

Cruikshank, Margaret. *The Gay and Lesbian Liberation Movement.* New York and London: Routledge, 1992.

Echols, Alice. *Daring To Be Bad: Radical Feminism in America 1967–1975.* Minneapolis: University of Minnesota Press, 1989.

Faderman, Lillian. *Odd Girls and Twilight Lovers: A History of Lesbian Life in Twentieth-Century America.* New York: Columbia University Press, 1991.

Garber, Linda. "Lesbian Identity Poetics: Judy Grahn, Pat Parker, and the Rise of Queer Theory." Ph.D. diss., Stanford University, 1995.

Grahn, Judy. *The Highest Apple: Sappho and the Lesbian Poetic Tradition.* San Francisco: Spinsters Ink, 1985.

Jeffries, Sheila. *The Lesbian Heresy: A Feminist Perspective on the Lesbian Sexual Revolution.* North Melbourne, Australia: Spinifex, 1993.

Sandoval, Chela. "U.S. Third World Feminism: The Theory and Method of Oppositional Consciousness in the Postmodern World." *Genders* 10 (Spring 1991), 1–24.

***See also*** Biological Determinism; Bisexuality; Brown, Rita Mae; Butch-Femme; Combahee River Collective; Essentialism; Faderman, Lillian; Furies, The; Grahn, Judy; Johnston, Jill; Lorde, Audre; National Organization for Women (NOW); Parker, Pat; Postmodernism; Queer Theory; Radicalesbians; Rich, Adrienne; Separatism; Social-Construction Theory; Wittig, Monique; Woman-Identified Woman

## Lesbian Herstory Archives

The Lesbian Herstory Archives (LHA) of the Lesbian Herstory Educational Foundation is a popular and perhaps the best-known collection of lesbian archival material. LHA began in 1974, when lesbians who had met the year before in New York City's chapter of the Gay Academic Union began to formulate and publicize the project. Cofounders Joan Nestle (1940–) and Deborah Edel (1944–) are two central figures of the original group who have

*Lesbian Herstory Archives building in New York City. Photo by Saskia Scheffer.*

**L** remained active with the archives. Following publication of the first LHA newsletter in 1975, the archives opened for community use in 1976. It was located in Nestle's Upper West Side Manhattan apartment, which she shared with Edel and, subsequently, others involved in the project. The opening and growth of the collection shaped and reflected efforts to involve a broad-based lesbian constituency in the construction and ownership of the archives, including lesbian sexualities marginalized or ostracized by dominant lesbian feminist politics in the 1970s. Archives organizers welcomed any lesbian to help with the project's work and invited, in Nestle's (1990) words, "any woman who has had the courage to touch another woman," to have her life reflected and remembered by becoming part of the collection.

Founders positioned LHA as a community-based institution designed to rectify the deprivation and invisibility of lesbian lives and history. Nestle wrote in the Spring 1979 *Lesbian Herstory Archives Newsletter*: "The roots of the Archives lie in the silenced voices, the love letters destroyed, the pronouns changed, the diaries carefully edited, the pictures never taken, the euphemized distortions that patriarchy would let pass."

From the inception of the organization, the LHA newsletter and slide shows were educational and organizing tools designed to reflect a broad range of lesbian life, identity, and experience. LHA founding principles reflect lesbian-centered, feminist, class-conscious, antiracist, pro-sexual diversity politics situating the archives within a "lesbian community," distinct from mainstream libraries and archives. In 1979, the LHA became one of the early lesbian and gay groups to obtain nonprofit status in New York state, incorporating as the Lesbian Herstory Educational Foundation Inc. The Lesbian Herstory Archives of the Lesbian Herstory Educational Foundation has resisted reliance on state or corporate funding, soliciting financial donations exclusively from individual lesbians and radical funding sources supporting lesbian-focused projects.

LHA continues to be an all-volunteer effort governed by a committee of volunteer lesbian coordinators. In 1993, after several years of fund-raising, LHA reopened in a three-story brownstone in Brooklyn's Park Slope—the first building owned by a lesbian organization in New York City. The collection contains extensive archival holdings donated by lesbians and organizations with exclusive or significant lesbian participation. Collections include writings, art, photographs, clothing, personal records, memorabilia, and other assorted objects. LHA houses books, periodicals, and electronic recordings (spoken word, music, and visual), and volunteers maintain clipping files arranged by subject, organization titles, and individual names. LHA sponsors traveling exhibits (the largest is the 1991 "Keepin' On" exhibit about African American lesbians), slide shows, social events, and presentations featuring lesbian activists, artists, and other public figures. The building and collections are open to visitors and researchers by appointment.     *Polly Thistlethwaite*

### Bibliography

Edel, Deborah. "The Lesbian Herstory Archives." *Woman of Power* 16 (Spring 1990), 21–22.

Lesbian Herstory Educational Foundation/Lesbian Herstory Archives. P.O. Box 1258, New York, N.Y. 10116.

Nestle, Joan. "The Will To Remember: The Lesbian Herstory Archives of New York." *Feminist Review* 34 (Spring 1990), 86–94.

*Not Just Passing Through*. Videocassette. Jean Carlomusto, Dolores Perez, Catherine Saalfield, and Polly Thistlethwaite Producers/Directors. 52 mins. New York: Women Make Movies, 1994.

*See also* Archives and Libraries; Nestle, Joan

### Lesbian Impunity, Myth of

The term "myth of lesbian impunity" was brought to scholarly attention by Louis Crompton in a 1980 essay. It designates the frequently held belief that lesbians are, and have historically been, more "acceptable" to heterosexuals and straight society than homosexual men. It is assumed that they encounter less violence on the street, that state laws and local ordinances have been less often aimed at them, and, thus, that their lives are much easier. This view is contested by lesbians, who, overtly and covertly, struggle with complex issues of survival and (in)visibility in daily life.

An overview of European laws and legal cases before 1791 shows that lesbians, indeed, have faced capital punishment over the centuries in several countries, including France, England, and Germany, as well as other forms of punishment.

The nineteenth-century medical profession did not treat lesbians kindly; in France, doctors were likely to recommend the psychiatric incarceration of lesbians, and, in the 1820s, they performed clitoridectomies (removal of the clitoris) on lesbians to cure them of their "affliction," assumed to be caused by an enlarged, penislike clitoris.

In the United States, there is ample documentation of harsh police brutality in the 1940s through the early 1960s, as laws banning the wearing of male clothing resulted in arrests, beatings, rapes, and incarceration. Laws banning same-sex contact (dancing, touching, kissing) in social spaces such as bars applied to lesbians just as much as to gay men. In France, the Napoleonic Code forbade women to wear men's clothing (a situation that changed only in the 1960s), and, in the 1950s, lesbians were still routinely harassed outside bars by the police.

Lesbians in the United States Armed Forces did not fare well after World War II. A wave of repression, in many cases enforced by closeted lesbian officers themselves, aimed at destroying the intense lesbian networks and subculture within the Women's Army Corps. Lesbian personal histories are filled with detail about the immediate dangers of public identification on the job, particularly in nontraditional professions for women, such as the construction trades.

The enormous amount of implied or direct violence aimed at women who transgress the order of male/heterosexual prerogatives is the other side of legal repression against lesbians. The street and many workplaces are hazardous spaces for all women. The violence meted out at lesbians (taunts such as "Can you fight like a man?" and punitive rapes) makes visibility particularly dangerous for lesbians, especially butch-identified ones. For instance, near Falls City, Nebraska, twenty-one-year-old Teena Brandon, who dressed and passed as a man, was kidnapped, sexually assaulted, and murdered by two men on December 25, 1993, along with the woman she lived with and a friend.

Thus, if lesbians appear less visible and, therefore, more "acceptable" and less vulnerable to punishment, it is because of the subsumed status of women and the brutal enforcement of gender normativity against them. A full discussion of dissident sexualities among women requires that serious scholars devote further attention to the history of lesbian resistance before concluding that lesbianism is a low-risk path in life.    *Francesca Canadé Sautman*

## Bibliography

Bond, Pat. "Tapioca Tapestry." In *Long Time Passing: Lives of Older Lesbians*. Ed. Marcy Adelman. Boston: Alyson, 1986, pp. 164–176.

Bonnet, Marie-Jo. *Les Amours entre Femmes* (Love Between Women). Paris: Editions Odile Jacob, 1995.

Crompton, Louis. "The Myth of Lesbian Impunity: Capital Laws from 1270–1791." *Journal of Homosexuality* 6 (1980–1981), 11–25.

Nestle, Joan. *A Restricted Country*. Ithaca, N.Y.: Firebrand, 1987.

Sautman, Francesca Canadé. "Invisible Women: Lesbian Working Class Culture in France, 1880–1930." In *Homosexuality in Modern France*. Ed. Jeffrey Merrick and Bryan T. Ragan, Jr. New York and Oxford: Oxford University Press, 1996, pp. 177–201.

***See also*** Law and Legal Institutions

## Lesbian Nation

Lesbian nation was conceived by Jill Johnston (1929–) in 1973 in the form of the book *Lesbian Nation: The Feminist Solution,* which consists of a collection of essays written by her for a regular column in the the *Village Voice* newspaper. The essays are focused on the political and cultural events of the late 1960s and early 1970s in the United States from her point of view as a social critic, political activist, anarchist, and lesbian. Her conflict with the antilesbian membership of the women's liberation movement led Johnston to argue that the best thing to do was retreat and "build lesbian nation from the grass roots out of your own community of women." The constituents of the gay and lesbian liberation movements also had links with wider civil rights movements that encompassed the politics of the Left. The political arena included the appeal to black nationalism and to indigenous American Indian claims to sovereign nationhood. Lesbian nation was also a response to what Johnston refers to as the cultural desert of lesbian life in the period before the 1960s. She wrote: "Most of us didn't know yet that it was wrong to be a woman but we did know it was wrong to be lesbian [though we] were acquiring the rudimentary emotions of gay consciousness." Johnston and other radical lesbians operated from the perspective that the heterosexual institution was the prototype for all other dyadic structures of oppression. Lesbian nation is, therefore, a metaphor constituted in opposition to widespread women's suffering in what Johnston referred to as "stag nation."

Zimmerman (1990) suggests that, while the purpose of lesbian fiction is to map out the boundaries of lesbian nation, " 'lesbian' is not an ethnic or national designation, nor is it a stylistic or historical one, although it combines elements of each." Zimmerman (1990) refers to the lesbian myth of origins as "articulating a vision of the world before patriarchy and offering this vision as a model for lesbian nation." She (1995) suggests that "space is a profound metaphor for lesbian writers which has a lot to do with the fact that we were scattered in such a way that we must create a concept of space because that space is not given to us."

In *Sisters, Sexperts, Queers: Beyond the Lesbian Nation* (1993) Arlene Stein regards lesbian nation as "a lesbian refuge from society's ills somewhere between metaphor and reality." However, in the early 1980s, she says, there was "an explosion of discussion about sex and race [which] echoed across the country. The geography of the lesbian nation would never be the same." For Stein, this means that "once there was a dream of a Lesbian Nation—a sisterhood with a shared identity, a common agenda. Today that first wave of pride has given way to a far more complex sense of community. From lesbian marriage to the seductive pleasures of butch-femme to the untidy class difference that divide the lesbian community . . . a lesbian culture of tremendous diversity . . . is reinventing itself for the nineties."

In the 1990s, Parker and colleagues (1992) argue, nationalism and sexuality are "two of the most powerful global discourses shaping contemporary notions of identity." This is evidenced in the emergence of queer nation as a discourse of resistance whose origins can be found in the idea of a lesbian nation that much earlier disrupted the narrative of a homogeneous heterosexual nation.　　*Susan Sayer*

### Bibliography

Johnston, Jill. *Lesbian Nation: The Feminist Solution*. New York: Simon and Schuster, 1973.

Parker, Andrew, Mary Russo, Doris Sommer, and Patricia Yaeger, eds. *Nationalisms and Sexualities*. New York and London: Routledge, 1992.

Stein, Arlene, ed. *Sister, Sexperts, Queers: Beyond the Lesbian Nation*. New York: Plume, 1993.

Zimmerman, Bonnie. *The Safe Sea of Women: Lesbian Fiction, 1969–1989*. Boston: Beacon, 1990.

———. "From Lesbian Nation to Queer Nation." Interview with Susan Sayer. *Hecate* 21:2 (1995), 29–43.

*See also* Community; Johnston, Jill; Queer Nation; Separatism

## Lesbian Studies

The production of knowledge about lesbians (and other matters) from various lesbian perspectives.

### Origins

Lesbian studies in the United States began outside academia as a product of social movements of the 1960s and 1970s, most notably the women's liberation and the gay liberation movements. As homophobia and hostility toward lesbians were problematic in the feminist movement, so also sexism and misogyny worked against full lesbian involvement in gay liberation struggles. Lesbians frustrated with these movements, as well as those coming from lesbian organizations such as Daughters of Bilitis or as individuals looking for community, convened locally in many areas or connected by circulating mimeographed writings and newsletters to form various autonomously identified lesbian groups. These groups ignited a new collective process of thinking together, researching, and interpreting lesbian worlds and ideas from lesbian perspectives— the beginning of lesbian studies. Emerging outside universities and colleges, this early work gave voice and print to ideas that threatened the closet of many lesbian academics as it challenged the assumptions of mainstream feminism.

First-generation (ca. 1970s) community-based lesbian scholars published lesbian journals such as *Conditions*, *Trivia*, and *Sinister Wisdom*, started small lesbian presses such as Naiad Press, Frog in the Well, Spinsters Ink, Cleis Press, and the Institute for Lesbian Studies, and circulated newsletters and newspapers such as *Matrices*, *Lesbian Insider/Inciter*, *Lesbian Tide*, *C.L.I.T.*, and *Lesbian Connection*. This grass-roots intellectual movement included J.R. Roberts, a librarian and community activist, who compiled *Black Lesbians: A Bibliography*, finally published by Naiad Press in 1981, along with *Sinister Wisdom* which created a special 1976 issue on lesbian literature. *Sinister Wisdom* also published the proceedings of lesbian panels at the meetings of Modern Language Association and some of the early work of lesbian philosophers, such as Marilyn Frye and Sarah Lucia Hoagland, as well as Audre Lorde, Adrienne Rich, and Mary Daly.

In several cities, lesbian archives, libraries, and resource centers, along with feminist bookstores, were established; among the oldest of these are the Lesbian Herstory Archives in Brooklyn, New York, and the Amazon Bookstore in Minneapolis, Minnesota. During the 1970s, influential texts—such as

*Sappho Was a Right-On Woman* (1972) by Sidney Abbott and Barbara Love, *Woman Plus Woman* (1974) by Dolores Klaich, *The Wanderground* (1978) by Sally Gearhart, *Gyn/Ecology* (1978) by Mary Daly, *Amazon Odyssey* (1974) by Ti-Grace Atkinson, and *Lesbian/Woman* (1972) by Del Martin and Phyllis Lyon—began circulating among lesbian readers, who also found community in new lesbian music, theater, film, and a coffeehouse social life that overlapped, although somewhat contentiously, with lesbian bar cultures and a long history of closeted gay suffering and heroic survival.

## Lesbian Studies and Women's Studies

Lesbian studies in universities and colleges found an emergency home in a few women's studies classes that began to include lesbian readings and discussions on homophobia and lesbian oppression. In the 1970s, titles of the early lesbian-friendly women's studies courses were vague but suggestive, such as Women Bonding with Women, Woman-Identified Woman, and Woman Plus Woman, but, by the mid-1980s, course titles had become more explicit, as in Lesbian Cultures, Lesbian Lives, Lesbian Ethics, and Lesbians in Film, Literature, and Theory. These courses were offered during a time when homophobia and misogyny continued to wage unchecked violence against the lives and careers of lesbian professors and students, making the shelter of women's studies and a few small spaces in other disciplines the only venue for these courageous moments in lesbian studies.

Women's studies, however, was at times a reluctant home, often bristling with its own homophobia and fear of lesbian visibility, rendering lesbian academic presence in women's studies difficult for lesbian-identified scholars and threatening for women's studies departments overly burdened with antilesbian and antifeminist bashing from those hostile to women's studies. While women's studies was a venue where inclusive and radical scholarship on women was supported, the tension between heterosexual feminists and lesbians in women's studies has been a theme of historical struggle on campuses and in the National Women's Studies Association.

In the 1980s, lesbian studies maintained a small but viable presence in academia. Lesbian scholarship began to appear in special issues of academic journals, such as *Frontiers* (one of the first women's studies journals), *JumpCut*, *Radical Teacher*, *Signs*, and *Feminist Studies*. Caucuses and divisions flourished in many professional organizations, and lesbian students and professors continued to create classrooms for open lesbian inquiry, despite tenure and promotion decisions and admissions and evaluation procedures still driven by homophobia and antilesbian hatred. During this decade, the writings of Jeffner Allen, Nichole Brossard, Claudia Card, Mary Daly, Lillian Faderman, Marilyn Frye, Sarah Hoagland, Karla Jay, Toni McNaron, Julia Penelope, Joyce Trebilcot, Monique Wittig, and Bonnie Zimmerman configured an approach to academic lesbian feminism that problematized lesbians as objects of sexist and antilesbian oppressions and as subjects of heightened epistemic and revolutionary (often coded as separatist) potential.

Supported on the margins of academic feminism, lesbian feminism generated a more inclusive dialogue on lesbians and lesbian existence, as can be seen in the rich cross-currency of writings emerging from U.S. lesbians of color, lesbians living with disabilities, working-class lesbians, and lesbians with various "other" identities. In the United States during the 1980s, these included the work of Gloria Anzaldúa, Beth Brandt, Chrystos, Jewelle Gomez, Audre Lorde, Joan Nestle, Cherríe Moraga, Sarah Schulman, and Barbara Smith, all of whom challenged what many perceived as socially privileged representations of lesbians in academic lesbian feminist work. As Bernice Reagon (in Smith, 1983) described this period, feminist community in academia and outside was no longer coded as a home, a "safe place" built upon the parochial complacency of sameness. By the mid-1980s, Margaret Cruikshank's collective naming of "lesbian studies," Lillian Faderman's "romantic friendship," Barbara Smith's "home girls," Adrienne Rich's "lesbian continuum," and radical women of color's evocation of "this bridge called my back" were notions widely circulating in feminist academic readings as identity politics developed new models of coalition struggle and multiple-identity theory.

## Queer Theory

The attention to difference in lesbian studies did not end with questions of how race, class, ethnicity, disability, generation, and other multiple social differences influence, and are influenced by, lesbian sexual politics and identity. Sex itself was to be questioned and reshaped by the sex wars of feminism in the 1980s, by the male-driven gay insurgency emerging in the AIDS crisis, and by the popularity of queer theory in academic circles. Signaled significantly in 1984 by Gayle Rubin's essay "Thinking Sex" (in Abelove, 1993), a new space for sexuality studies was positioned separately from lesbian feminism and oppositionally to heterosexual normativity. Queer theory represented lesbian feminism as a gender-separatist framework that was too soft on sex, too inhibited by sexual politics, and too much inclined to understand female sexuality as a function of women's oppression rather than as a function of women's erotic and pornographic agency in pleasure, danger, and power.

The space opened up by the feminist sex wars intersected with queer theory and the emerging queer studies movement. Lesbian studies was endangered by this move not only because of its past commitment to feminism and feminist method, often represented as a separate and gender-specific endeavor, but also because the category "lesbian" itself was dissolving. The idea of "queerness" relies heavily on the social-constructionist thesis that categories of sexual identity are cultural fictions that are less stable, unified, and coherent than they are assumed to be and more fragile and fluid than the categories of masculine/feminine, male/female, hetero/homo, lesbian/gay presume. "Lesbian" is a category that dissolves into a multiple-gendered and sexually pluralistic space of queerness, in which any attempt to name a difference that is lesbian is immediately rejected as a historical, ethnocentric, essentialist, or sexually repressive and dishonest.

On the other hand, critics argue, queer studies allies itself with a radical politics of sexual transgression, while too easily ignoring the questions of mutiple social differences, such as race, class, generation, disability, and political ideology, raised by lesbian feminists in the 1980s. Likewise, the significance of social relations of power in maintaining white male dominance is often reduced to contextualized "performative" acts only distantly related to the real effects of the sex/gender economy on the lives of women. This is a subject matter of urgent and vital interest to feminists.

Although lesbian sexual identity may be a cultural fiction, it is necessary fiction with real effects on women (and men). The question of lesbian difference in the 1990s continued to establish the need for lesbian studies wherever it could find a margin or corner to claim as its own inside the academy. Lesbian studies continued as a viable academic project, often sheltered by women's studies, gender studies, cultural and literary studies, or queer studies, but also on its own turf. The results have led to scholarship and research in the areas of lesbian his-

toriography and social movement theory; lesbian literary, film, and cultural studies; lesbian ethnography and anthropology; lesbian sociology, psychology, and psychotherapy; lesbian policy studies and international studies; lesbian theory and philosophy; and various explorations of lesbian identities and identification strategies. In academia, lesbians are everywhere and going somewhere, often situated on the cutting (although also marginalized) edge of disciplines, interdisciplines, and academic trends.

## Lesbian Studies at the End of the Twentieth Century

Lesbian studies at the end of the twentieth century is located in an academic space opened up historically by the theoretical and practical inadequacies of women's studies, feminist theory, gender studies, queer theory, ethnic, race, and global studies, postmodernism, poststructuralism, cultural studies, social movement theory, and a variety of movement politics emerging from, or since, the 1970s. In addition, lesbian studies is a positive space in which knowledge is produced from lesbian perspectives, leaving open to intellectual and political debate what determines such perspectives and criteria for knowing.

Although not limited to to the study of lesbians, lesbian studies is a primary means of producing new knowledge about lesbians, often in opposition to more traditional and heterosexually biased misrepresentations of lesbian existence, leaving open to intellectual and political debate what counts as a more accurate or more reliable representation. In addition, an important component of lesbian studies and life as a lesbian scholar is the creation of a space in which "lesbian" is more than an object of study but also a place where agency——possessing the knowing authority to speak, look, listen, read, think, and create—is signified as lesbian. In other words, "lesbian" is recognized as a legitimate position from which to begin inquiry and creative work.

While lesbian studies also emerges within the disciplines, it may best be conceived as an interdisciplinary and multidisciplinary intellectual project that transforms how disciplines produce knowledge, including knowledge about lesbians or sexuality more generally. Lesbian studies also refuses the confines of any one discipline, without vanishing into one of several interdisciplinary foster homes such as women's studies, gender studies, cultural and literary studies, and/or queer studies. Although it seldom has its own institutional infrastructure—as a program or a department of lesbian studies—the dispersed and disruptive project of lesbian studies can create instability in more established locations. Others may argue, however, that having an identifiable institutionalized base, such as a department, program, or area studies, creates a more effective intervention in the academy and better assistance in the disciplines to scholars advancing the work of lesbian studies who are still isolated, ignored, and harrassed. The emergence of LGBT (lesbian, gay, bisexual, and transgender) studies and queer studies, however, seems to override the institutional formation of a more autonomous lesbian studies.

In spite of this, lesbian feminist inquiry persists in raising the question of lesbian difference as it continues to investigate the mechanisms of white male power and lesbian-specific oppressions, the meaning and centrality of sex and gender in lesbian identity, the differences among and between lesbians from different cultures and stations in life, the differences between women and men, and the material effects of gendered life on the lesbian subject. Its strength and endurance is evidenced by the numbers of active scholars and students not only in the United States, but also in Canada, Australia, New Zealand, the United Kingdom, the Netherlands, and other European countries, as well as the promise of its emergence throughout the world.          *Jacqueline N. Zita*

### Bibliography

Abelove, Henry, Michèle Aina Barale, and David M. Halperin. *The Lesbian and Gay Studies Reader.* New York and London: Routledge, 1993.

Garber, Linda. *Tilting the Tower: Lesbians Teaching Queer Subjects.* New York: Routledge, 1994.

Griffin, Gabriele, and Sonya Andermahr. *Straight Studies Modified.* London: Cassell, 1997.

Medhurst, Andy, and Sally R. Munt. *Lesbian and Gay Studies: A Critical Introduction.* London: Cassell, 1997.

Moraga, Cherríe, and Gloria Anzaldúa, eds. *This Bridge Called My Back: Writings by Radical Women of Color.* Latham, N.Y.: Kitchen Table: Women of Color Press, 1981.

Smith, Barbara, ed. *Home Girls: A Black Feminist Anthology.* New York: Kitchen Table: Women of Color Press, 1983.

Wilton, Tamsin. *Lesbian Studies: Setting an Agenda.* New York: Routledge, 1995.

Zimmerman, Bonnie, and Toni A.H. McNaron, eds. *The New Lesbian Studies: Into the Twenty-first Century.* New York: Feminist Press, 1996.

*See also* Cruikshank, Margaret; Cultural Studies; Lesbian Feminism; Performativity; Queer Theory; Social-Construction Theory; Women's Studies

## Lesbos, Island of

Birthplace of the famous Greek poet of the seventh century B.C.E., Sappho, many of whose lyrics focused on homoerotic desire; thus, the name of her island furnished the nineteenth-century term "lesbian" to refer to erotic love between women.

Lesbos is the third-largest island in the Aegean Sea (665 square miles) and lies a few miles off the coast of modern-day Turkey. The historical evidence suggests a long tradition of cultural development that produced not only Sappho but several other poets as well, including Sappho's contemporary, Alkaios, who refers to her by name in a short fragment.

According to ancient legend, Sappho was born on the southwest coast, at the town of Eresos (modern Skala Eressou). On the acropolis overlooking the modern village, there survive a few scattered ruins, including traces of polygonal stone walls that may date to Sappho's time. Little is known of life on the island in that early period, but it would appear that upper-class women, at least, enjoyed more freedom than they did elsewhere in Greece.

In the twentieth century, Lesbos became a place of interest for many lesbians seeking to make a pilgrimage to the island of Sappho's birth. The poet Renée Vivien (1877–1909) and her lover, Natalie Barney (1876–1972), for example, fancied themselves latter-day followers of Sappho and traveled to Lesbos in 1904 in pursuit of their spiritual past.

The chief city of the island, Mytilene, features a large modern statue of Sappho playing the lyre.
          *Jane McIntosh Snyder*

### Bibliography

Paraskevaïdis, M. "Lesbos." In *Princeton Encyclopedia of Classical Sites.* Ed. Richard Stillwell. Princeton, N.J.: Princeton University Press, 1976, pp. 502–503.

Schaus, Gerald P., and Nigel Spencer. "Notes on the Topography of Eresos." *American Journal of Archaeology* 98 (1994), 411–430.

Snyder, Jane McIntosh. *Sappho.* New York: Chelsea House, 1995.

*See also* Barney, Natalie Clifford; Lesbian; Sappho; Vivien, Renée

## Lesotho

Small and impoverished African country with a homosocial society in which romantic, and sometimes erotic, personal relationships between women appear to be normative. As more Basotho (term referring to people from Lesotho) women are exposed to Western ways and customs, homophobia is entering the country, but, as recently as the 1950s, women in rural areas were celebrating their love relationships with other women by means of public and socially approved feasts. Although there is no written documentation of women's social history prior to colonization by the British in 1868 following the Boer War, there is evidence in rituals that survived the missionary period (beginning in 1833 and continuing through the early twentieth century) that love between women—though not conceptualized as "sexual," not constructed as an "identity," and not considered to conflict with (compulsory) heterosexuality—was a feature of precolonial life in Lesotho.

Basotho women are brought up separately from Basotho men, work hard all their lives, and many endure physical abuse from men. Except in the wealthiest families, girls and women are responsible for hauling water, gathering firewood, washing and mending clothing, rearing and educating children, gathering wild vegetables, cultivating and harvesting small gardens and large fields, cooking, cleaning, earning whatever cash income they can, and decorating their homes. Women's legal status is nil. All women are legally minors in Lesotho under customary law; under common law women are minors until age twenty-one, but they revert to minor status if they marry, attaining majority status only if single or widowed. Women cannot hold property; they have no custody rights in the case of divorce; they cannot inherit property if they have sons; they cannot borrow money, own or run property or businesses, sign contracts, or buy and sell livestock, land, or "unnecessary" goods. Nor can they obtain a passport without a husband's or father's consent. A woman whose husband and father are dead must obtain permission from her local chief (97 percent of whom are male) to conduct "adult" business.

Marriage is socially compulsory, and wife beating is expected. Divorce is very expensive; the divorce rate is only 1 percent for this reason. Yet women manage up to 60 percent of the households on their own, owing to the fact that men often work away from their homes, may abandon their families, or may be abandoned by women who tire of physical abuse. Date rape and marital rape are norms; in fact, according to precolonial tradition, a man claimed a woman as a wife by raping her, and this custom is still common in rural areas. In this context, it is not surprising that women find emotional nourishment, understanding, and love in the arms of other women. A fairly modern phenomenon is the practice of boarding-school girls choosing female partners; this is strikingly similar to the custom of their grandmothers choosing female "wives" (batsoalle).

*Kendall*

### Bibliography

Blacking, John. "Uses of Kinship Idiom in Friendships at Some Venda and Zulu Schools." In *Social System and Tradition in Southern Africa*. Ed. John Argyle and Elinor Preston-Whyte. Cape Town: Oxford University Press, 1978, pp. 101–117.

Gay, Judith. "Mummies and Babies and Friends and Lovers in Lesotho." *Journal of Homosexuality* 2:3–4 (Summer 1985), 97–116.

Gill, Debby. *Lesotho: A Gender Analysis*. Lesotho: SIDA, 1992.

Kendall. "Women in Lesotho and the (Western) Construction of Homophobia." In *Female Desires: Same-Sex Relations and Transgender Practices Across Cultures*. Ed. Evelyn Blackwood and Saskia Wieringa. New York: Columbia University Press, 1998.

Nthunya, Mpho. "When a Woman Loves a Woman." In *Singing Away the Hunger: The Autobiography of an African Woman*. Bloomington: Indiana University Press, 1997.

*See also* Indigenous Cultures

### Lewis, Mary Edmonia (ca. 1843–after 1911)

American sculptor. Born to an Ojibwa (Chippewa) mother and an Afro-Haitian father, Edmonia Lewis was a woman whose ancestry was both a source of fascination for critics and cultural observers and a site for her own self-invention. An expatriate who lived in Rome in the late 1860s and the 1870s, Lewis associated with the "White Marmorean flock," the name Henry James (1843–1916) gave to a circle of Euro-American women artists and poets who worked in Italy and formed same-sex relationships with each other. Lewis's marble statuary, accomplished in the neoclassical style favored by late-nineteenth-century American artists, is a complex matrix of American romanticism, European conven-

*Edmonia Lewis by Henry Rocher. Collection of the Boston Athenaeum.*

tion, and a related veneration of ancient Greco-Roman ideals.

Lewis attended Oberlin College (1859–1864), then, in 1865, moved to Boston, where she studied sculpture with the artist Edward Brackett (1818–1908). She made her living sculpting portrait busts and medallions that were replicated and sold. Her work depicted Euro-American figures well known to the New England community of abolitionists and Transcendentalists, among them the poets Henry Wadsworth Longfellow (1807–1882) and Anna Quincy Waterston (1812–1899), and Robert Gould Shaw (1837–1863), the fallen commander of a Union Army regiment of black soldiers. Lewis took up allegorical and literary subjects as well. *Hagar in the Wilderness* (1875) was inspired by the eponymous biblical heroine who was impregnated by her master, Abraham, and subsequently banished to the wilderness. *Old Arrow Maker and His Daughter* (1872) is one of several sculptures based upon Longfellow's popular epic poem *The Song of Hiawatha* (1855). Interestingly, Lewis's portrayal of fe-

male Native Americans, like that of the Egyptian Hagar and the emancipated black American woman of Lewis's 1867 sculpture, *Forever Free*, adheres to a Greco-Roman paradigm of beauty. Buick (1996) has argued that Lewis's female portraiture consistently indicates an aderence to "the Cult of True Womanhood," in contrast to her ethnically marked male figures, such as the hook-nosed Native arrowmaker and the curly-haired black male in *Forever Free*.

Lewis's own identity was far more complex than her contemporaries reckoned. In response to the public's expectations of her primitivism and exoticism, Lewis seemingly embellished the circumstances of her upbringing, downplaying her boarding-school education in favor of anecdotes of hunting, fishing, and wigwams. Furthermore, her association with the circle of female couples in Rome (centered on actress Charlotte Cushman [1816–1876]) and her own androgynous dress and appearance have fueled speculation about her sexual identity. As Holland (1995) has hypothesized, Lewis's shaping of her own story may be a measure of her agency and resistance. *Jacqueline Francis*

## Bibliography

Buick, Kirsten P. *Edmonia Lewis in Art History: The Paradox of the Exotic Subject, in Three Generations of African-American Women Sculptors*. Philadelphia: Afro-American Historical and Cultural Museum, 1996, 12–15.

Hartigan, Lynda R. *Sharing Traditions: Five Black Artists in Nineteenth-Century America*. Washington, D.C.: Smithsonian Institution Press, 1985.

Holland, Juanita M. "Mary Edmonia Lewis's *Minnehaha*: Gender, Race, and the 'Indian Maid.' " *Bulletin of the Detroit Institute of Arts* 69 (1995), 26–35.

Richardson, Marilyn. "Edmonia Lewis's *The Death of Cleopatra*: Myth and Identity." *International Review of African-American Art* 12 (1995), 38–52.

*See also* Cushman, Charlotte

## Liberalism

Philosophy founded on the belief that each individual has an inalienable right to realize full selfhood. This sovereign individual, through the use of free will, steps out from the private realm to make a contract with society and become a member of a public world. In the modern era, two discourses—liberalism and humanism—have consolidated the making of Western societies and, through the colonial expansion that followed, shaped the rest of the world. Humanism is based on the idea that people everywhere have in common an essential human nature, a universal truth, which, with the power of reason and the benefit of culture, fuels human progress to a better world. Democracy is founded on the principle of making a choice for the greater good. Liberal humanists maintain that culture brings moral enlightenment, through setting up as an ideal the best, most beautiful, virtuous, or intellectual aspirations of society for the multitude to follow.

Liberal humanists believe that all individuals, because of their intrinsic humanity, deserve respect and an opportunity to explore their full potential through the pursuit of liberty and happiness. The freedom to express oneself, so long as one does not cause harm to others, is more important than any interference by the state to control liberty.

Liberalism has been a useful ally for lesbians. First, as an ideology based on the rights of the individual, it has been used to justify a number of modern civil rights movements. Martin Luther King, Jr. (1929–1968) realized this in his 1963 March on Washington speech ("I have a dream") when he envisioned "that one day this nation will rise up and live out the true meaning of its creed: We hold these truths to be self-evident, that all men are created equal." The progressive, liberating side of liberal humanism has been used as a rhetoric to end slavery, to argue for women's right to vote, and to inaugurate affirmative-action programs, including partnership rights for lesbian couples.

In the liberalization of homosexuality in the West, the most prevailing argument has been the forceful defense of privacy for sexual behavior. Liberal feminism, introduced by Mary Wollstonecraft (1759–1797) in her *Vindication of the Rights of Woman* (1792), argued for equal rights for women in economic and social spheres. In the 1960s, liberal feminism became the dominant feminist ideology, centering on the right to control one's own body principally through reproductive choice (the idea that people "own" their bodies is a liberal one). Liberal feminists were wary of lesbians, however— Betty Friedan (1921–) coining the term "lavender menace," for example—which may have been a logical move for a political movement committed to improving the status quo. Lesbian feminism adopted the liberal respect for privacy, turning it into a fierce defense of "personal space"—a concept not too distant from the liberal notions of private property and separate spheres. Perhaps the most intense inheritors of liberalism are lesbian sadomasochists, whose activist libertarianism defends the right to free sexual conduct. They offer the concomitant justification that S/M in the bedroom is separate from the eroticism of public (state) power, that sex is only sex, and that consent is given as an autonomous act of will.

In 1995, philosopher Ernest Gellner wrote in the British newspaper, the *Guardian:* "Liberalism has become the world's dominant political theory, but its political foundations remain uncertain and its capacity to deal with brutal realities unsatisfactory." Certainly for lesbians, the use of liberal concepts to argue for lesbian and gay rights has been problematic. First, the growth of liberal humanism reflected the concerns of white heterosexual propertied males' needs and desires. Their "human nature" depended on defining itself against "the Other"—be that female, black, lesbian or any marginal, disenfranchised classification. In the latter part of the twentieth century, a new pluralistic vision based on categories of difference and diversity raised questions about these assumptions of liberal humanism. This new vision, in turn, became subject to accusations of moral relativism, resulting in paralysis in response to injustice. Second, the argument for rights is said to be a reformist one, therefore perpetuating an intrinsically discriminatory system, perpetuating dependency on the "nanny" (welfare) state, and keeping petitioners in a permanent position of victimhood. Third, liberal humanism romanticizes individualism, thus failing to recognize the social and communitarian needs of subcultural groups, such as lesbians, who need to facilitate a sense of belonging, create affectional bonds in an imagined community, and who, for political reasons, wish to create an ethics of social responsibility.  *Sally R. Munt*

## Bibliography

Phelan, Shane. *Getting Specific: Postmodern Lesbian Politics*. Minneapolis: University of Minnesota Press, 1995.

Sullivan, Andrew. *Virtually Normal: An Argument About Homosexuality*. New York: Knopf, 1995.

Weeks, Jeffrey. *Invented Moralities: Sexual Values in an Age of Uncertainty*. Cambridge: Polity, 1995.

*See also* Enlightenment, European; Essentialism; Privacy

## Libertinism

Style of aristocratic masculinity that developed in France in the sixteenth century, traveled to England with the Restoration court of Charles II (1630–1685) in the seventeenth century, and underwent sea changes in the eighteenth century; it became socially unacceptable only in the nineteenth century after the revolution in France and the rise of the ideals of companionate family life and sentimental masculinity in England. Libertinism originally meant a desire for religious freedom but soon grew into a religion of sexuality. In the words of historian Trumbach (1993): "This religion can be defined as believing, in contradistinction to orthodox Christianity, that sexual experience was central to human life and that sexual desire and pleasure were good and natural things. The sexual organs and acts of sexual intercourse were, therefore, symbols of a great life-giving force and were as worthy of human worship as the symbols of the Christian sacraments and the grace that was the life of the soul." Libertines were materialist, pleasure seeking, and anti-Christian; they were also, at least in the seventeenth century, attracted to both boys and women.

Many explicit early-modern representations of female-female sexuality occur in the works of libertine writers, from Pierre de Bourdeille de Brantôme (1527–1614) to the Marquis de Sade (1740–1814). Representations of female-female sexuality were as titillating to early-modern audiences as they are to consumers of pornography today. Libertinism supported many theories of gender, the best known being, in the words of the poet Alexander Pope (1688–1744) that "every woman is at heart a rake." Identification—the notion that women are just as sexually predatory and excitable as men—underlay libertine representations of female sexuality. Libertines such as John Wilmot, Earl of Rochester (1647–1680), and the fictional Robert Lovelace in Samuel Richardson's *Clarissa* (1747) were both passionately enamored of women and terrified of their hidden sexual power. Proof of women's innate sexual appetitiveness was the lesbian phase they went through on the way to finding mature sexual fulfillment with men. Here is Brantôme in the erotic *Lives of the Fair and Gallant Ladies* (1901): "How many of these Lesbian dames have I seen who, for all their friggings and mutual frictions, yet fail not at the last to go after men! Even Sappho herself, the mistress of them all, did she not end by loving her fond, favorite Phaon, for whose sake she died?"

A stock character in libertine writings is the older masculine woman who initiates girls into the mysteries of sexual pleasure. In John Cleland's pornographic novel *Fanny Hill: or, Memoirs of a Woman of Pleasure* (1748), "the hackneyed, thoroughbred Phoebe," procuress of the brothel in which the heroine Fanny finds herself, makes Fanny aware of genital pleasure. Yet, despite Phobe's "lascivious touches" and probing fingers, Fanny retains her virginity, bestowing it on her first male lover.

In their pansexual love of pleasure and their pursuit of aggressively phallic relations with other women, some lesbians achieved their own libertine notoriety. London actress Charlotte Charke (1713–1760) wrote a 1755 autobiography describing her cross-dressed seductions of women; the novelist and satirist Henry Fielding (1707–1754) based his pamphlet *The Female Husband* (1746) on Charke's adventures, describing a dildo-sporting cross-dresser who marries an unsuspecting woman.

*Blakey Vermeule*

### Bibliography

Barker-Benfield, G.J. "The Reformation of Male Manners." In *The Culture of Sensibility: Sex and Society in Eighteenth-Century Britain*. Chicago: University of Chicago Press, 1992.

Brantôme, Pierre de Bourdeille de. *Lives of the Fair and Gallant Ladies*. Trans. A.R. Allison. 2 vols. Paris: Charles Carrington, 1901.

Trumbach, Randolph. "Erotic Fantasy and Male Libertinism in Enlightenment England." In *The Invention of Pornography: Obscenity and the Oriins of Modernity, 1500–1800*. Ed. Lynn Hunt. New York: Zone, 1993, pp. 69–85.

*See also* Charke, Charlotte; Erotica and Pornography; Europe, Early Modern

## Librarians

From its earliest days of academic training, librarianship has been a predominantly female profession. When Melvil Dewey (1851–1931) created the first professional library school in 1887 at Columbia College in New York City, women were in the majority. Although Dewey lost his job for allowing women to enroll in the heretofore all-male Columbia College, he did open the doors to a new and different opportunity for women. Historians of the development of U.S. librarianship hotly debate Dewey's reasons for championing women as librarians. Their arguments range from the benevolent, a desire on his part to encourage women, particularly middle-class women, in their pursuit of a profession, to the far more negative assessment that Dewey engaged both in a form of social control (libraries and librarians as civilizing forces) and, at the same time, ensured that libraries would be staffed by well-educated but low-paid female workers. Whatever the real motives were, at the end of the nineteenth and the beginning of the twentieth century, librarianship offered one of the few opportunities for women to earn a living, albeit a frugal one, as a professional.

In any female-intensive occupational category, one will find lesbians. Librarianship is no exception. Drawn to it for a number of reasons, not the least of which was a kind of genteel respectability the profession bestowed upon its practitioners, lesbian librarians were no more visible than lesbians in teaching, nursing, or social work until the rise of the "second wave" of feminism in the 1960s. Feminism did not, however, automatically translate into a specifically lesbian form of activism, even among progressive librarians. While many lesbian librarians were involved in the growing number of women's groups and caucuses in professional organizations on the national, regional, and state levels, a chasm existed between these women and the smaller number who allied themselves with the American Library Association's Social Responsibilities Gay Task Force. The Gay Task Force was the creation of a small group, some of whom were librarians by vocation, others by avocation. Led for many years by Barbara Gittings (1932–), an important voice in the early homophile movement, the Gay Task Force had the odd distinction of being perceived, in spite of Gittings's leadership position, as a space for men. Lesbians were apt to find a more conducive home in the Feminist Task Force, the Committee on the Status of Women in Librarianship, and groups such as Wisconsin Women Library Workers. The structure of the American Library Association (ALA), with its dues schedule and heavy fees for conference attendance, tended to limit participation in organized groups to degreed librarians (people with advanced degrees in library and information science), effectively eliminating all but the most dedicated and tenacious "nonprofessionals."

In spite of the tensions between the Gay Task Force and women's groups in the ALA, there was a sufficient degree of cross-fertilization to permit the groups to benefit from each other's existence. Through co-sponsorship of programs, development of bibliographies, and discussion of outreach efforts, lesbian librarians became more involved in professional and association activities that marked them as lesbian. After some years of struggle and debate, the Gay Task Force changed its name to the Gay and Lesbian Task Force, and the Gay Book Award, one of the first of its kind anywhere, added Lesbian to its title and made a concerted effort to ensure gender equity in the nominations and selections process. While still predominately male, the Gay and Lesbian Task Force has made great strides in incorporating lesbian librarian voices and perspectives.

While the lesbian librarian presence in professional organizations continues to grow, the most obvious manifestation of lesbian librarians continues to be in less traditional arenas. The creation of specialized libraries such as the Lesbian Herstory Archives in Brooklyn, New York, and the June Mazer Collection in West Hollywood, California, started by women who did not identify as librarians, has been helped along by lesbian librarians who have found in them an outlet that combines political activism with professional expertise. As these community-based libraries expand, adding different sorts of materials to their collections, lesbian librarians trained to catalog music or organize manuscript collections have provided invaluable service to the individual libraries and to the preservation of the lesbian past. Some of the most exciting sites on the World Wide Web and some of the liveliest discussion groups in cyberspace have been developed and nurtured by lesbian librarians.

Lesbians have always been a presence in librarianship. While a number of variables, including the type of library in which one works and where it is located, impact the degree of openness, an increasing number of lesbian librarians are coming out and taking leadership roles in issues as wide-ranging as domestic-partnership legislation and the provision of library services to lesbian and gay teenagers. While some members of the American Library Association have expressed outrage at this openness, demanding that lesbian librarians return to the closet, that is highly unlikely. Whether in organized groups or as individuals, lesbian librarians have found their voice in the information age and, in so doing, have given rise to new and significant considerations of the role of all women in librarianship.

*Ellen Broidy*

## Bibliography

Gough, Cal, and Ellen Greenblatt, eds. *Gay and Lesbian Library Service.* Jefferson, N.C.: Mc-Farland, 1990.

Kester, Norman, ed. *Liberating Minds: The Stories and Professional Lives of Gay, Lesbian, and Bisexual Librarians and Their Advocates.* Jefferson, N.C.: McFarland, 1997.

*See also* Archives and Libraries; Gittings, Barbara; Lesbian Herstory Archives

## Lister, Anne (1791–1840)

English diarist. The Lister journals in Calderdale Archives, Yorkshire, England, comprise more than four million words (three times as many as those of Samuel Pepys [1633–1703]), a sixth of them in code. They represent an extraordinary document of an early-modern lesbian life.

Anne Lister grew up in rural Yorkshire and attended a boarding school where she met her first lover, Eliza Raine (n.d.), a "girl of colour." From 1806, Lister spent most of her time at Shibden Hall, Halifax, choosing to live with her unmarried uncle and aunts rather than her less genteel family; she inherited Shibden in 1826.

From 1817 until her death, Lister kept a daily diary. She devised a secret code to veil her references to money, clothes, menstruation, and, above all, her overlapping love affairs with women. Lister's money and position as a landowner allowed her to refuse all pressure to marry a man. She pursued a rigorous course of self-education, learning French, German, Latin, Greek, mathematics, history, the flute, and the harpsichord. She enjoyed walking, riding, and hunting; she managed her estates herself, developed coal mines, and used her influence to win Tory votes. Although she never wore trousers in public, her severe black dresses, cloaks, and partly cropped hair won her the nickname of "Gentleman Jack" and regular harassment from men, one of whom she beat off with her umbrella.

None of this seems to have troubled her very much; her diaries reflect her remarkable confidence. Lister does not seem to have thought of herself as transgendered, but rather, as an androgynous "oddity" created by nature, a woman to whom "gentleman-like" manners and the love of women came naturally. "I love, & only love, the fairer sex," she declared in 1821; "my heart revolts from any other love than theirs." Ever frank, she recorded her fantasies (including one of seducing a servant, another of "having a penis"), her busy sex life of "grubbling" (groping) under petticoats and long "kisses" (tribadism, most likely), her fear of passing on her venereal disease, and her longing for a "wife" to run her household.

Lister's many lovers in England and France—several married to men—did not share her sense of a distinct sexual identity, but the diaries reveal a female continuum of romantic friendship, flirtation, and discreet sex. Lister pursued a nonmonogamous lifestyle with varying degrees of honesty until she settled down with a local heiress, Ann Walker, in 1832. They took the Eucharist together as a sort of wedding, and Lister rewrote her will to leave a lifetime interest in Shibden to her "friend and companion." On their travels, Lister succumbed to plague in Georgia at the age of forty-nine.

Uncontroversial, censored excerpts from the diaries were published on and off from the 1880s until, in 1988, Helena Whitbread brought out a frank selection from the years 1817–1824. These were published in the United States under the titles *No Priest But Love* and *I Know My Own Heart* (both 1992). Points of controversy since have included the authenticity of the papers, Lister's gender identity, and the extent to which she should be seen as unique, or representative of other secret lives. Work on the Lister papers, which include more than a thousand letters, has barely scratched the surface of this treasure trove.

*Emma Donoghue*

## Bibliography

Castle, Terry. "The Diaries of Anne Lister." In *The Apparitional Lesbian: Female Homosexuality and Modern Culture.* New York: Columbia University Press, 1993, pp. 92–106.

Donoghue, Emma. "Liberty in Chains: The Diaries of Anne Lister (1817–1824)." In *Breaking the Barriers to Desire.* Ed. Kevin Lano and Claire Parry. Nottingham: Five Leaves, 1995, pp. 79–86.

Liddington, Jill. "Anne Lister of Shibden Hall, Halifax (1791–1840): Her Diaries and the Historians." *History Workshop* 35 (1993), 45–77.

Moore, Lisa. " 'Something More Tender Still Than Friendship': Romantic Friendship in Early-Nineteenth-Century England." *Feminist Studies* 18:3 (1992), 499–520.

*See also* Androgyny; Diaries and Letters; Romantic Friendship

# Literary Criticism

An approach to literature that analyzes and evaluates the lesbian elements in a literary work or that interprets it from a lesbian perspective. Lesbian literary criticism is an evaluative and descriptive response, usually written, to literatures the critic or others identify as lesbian. To a lesser extent, lesbian literary criticism refers to reading any literature from a lesbian perspective. It has existed since readers' first comments on Sappho (ca. 600 B.C.E.), but it has flourished primarily in the twentieth century. It is not a single approach to literature; it does not concentrate on one type of literature; nor does it appear in one type of publication. Because different critics or schools of criticism make different assumptions about what makes literature lesbian and what constitutes good or effective lesbian literature, no one way of analyzing or evaluating literature constitutes lesbian literary criticism. This type of criticism addresses traditional literary forms, such as the novel, short story, poetry, and drama, as well as less traditional but now accepted genres, such as autobiography, essay, and film; it encompasses what is generally considered "popular" literature, as well as what in some circles is called "high" literature. It also exists wherever lesbian literature is discussed, from the dyke on the street who reviews a lesbian book for the local women's press to the academic who offers a book on postmodern lesbian literary theory for her tenure review. Variety is its key.

## History

Although lesbian literary criticism exists primarily as a twentieth-century phenomenon because of the relative obscurity of lesbians and lesbian literature prior to the late nineteenth century, it also has an earlier history. However, most of the early literary comments about what might be identified as lesbian literature today were written by men who often condemned or ignored the lesbian elements in a work of art. Commentary on Sappho is a case in point. Some of Sappho's early commentators denied or ignored her obvious lesbianism and instead identified her lyrical style as the essence of "Sapphic" and as a model for their own poetry. Early women writers who were accorded the name of Sappho—for instance, the English poet Katherine Philips (1632–1664) was called the "English Sappho"—gained that title as much by virtue of their poetic lyricism as by their attachment to women.

But it is the twentieth century, especially since the 1970s, that has been central to the activity that would be called lesbian literary criticism, a criticism written primarily by lesbians explaining, appreciating, and analyzing literature that is identified as lesbian. Some of this criticism is designed for a specific lesbian reading community, which, in the early part of the twentieth century, was a small, educated, and wealthy elite; at mid-century, an underground, but more diverse, group of readers; and at the end of the century, the lesbian community at large. Some of the criticism of the 1970s and later has been directed specifically to the academic community. Lesbian literary criticism can be found in underground journals like *The Ladder* (1956–1972); in community-based magazines such as *Sinister Wisdom* and *Conditions*, both begun in the 1970s; and, since 1994, in the *Lesbian Review of Books*, which reviews general texts on lesbian life and work, lesbian literature, and academic books on lesbian topics. Lesbian literary criticism also appears in books addressed to a general reading public, such as Jane Rule's (1931–) *Lesbian Images* (1976), and in anthologies of essays addressed primarily to the academic world. The latter can appear as highly theoretical writing, as with the queer theorists or postmodern critics of the 1990s. Creative writers—to mention only a few, Adrienne Rich (1929–), Judy Grahn (1940–), Monique Wittig (1935–), Bertha Harris (1937–), and Audre Lorde (1934–1992)—have written a unique form of lesbian literary criticism in which they respond to other lesbian writers or, more important, explain their own literary impulses. Lesbian literary criticism also appears in introductions to anthologies of lesbian writing. Lastly, lesbian criticism can be found in coded form in works such as Virginia Woolf's (1882–1941) *A Room of One's Own* (1929).

Once lesbianism became more visible in the early twentieth century, lesbian writing and criticism as we know it surfaced. But while the lesbian writers of the early part of the twentieth century at times wrote self-consciously about lesbianism, they often coded not only their fictional characters, but also their comments on lesbian literature. Given the relative difficulty early writers experienced when coming out—Radclyffe Hall's (1880–1943) trial for writing *The Well of Loneliness* (1928) is a case in point—a literature that depends on codes may be seen as one option these writers had. Lesbian literary-critical works like *A Room of One's Own* may also participate in this method of writing. Although not universally acknowledged as lesbian, *A Room* is surrounded by lesbianism: Woolf wrote this critical text at the same time as her lesbian fantasy story of her lover, Vita Sackville-West (1892–1962), *Orlando* (1928); Woolf herself imagines in her diary that the critics of *A Room* will call her a "Sapphist"; and she refers in the book to the fantasy female friends Chloe and Olivia. The central topic that defines its lesbian concern may be the notion of androgyny, which some have seen as a flight from feminism and lesbianism, but which may be read as a code word for homosexual. For while the notion of androgyny was used negatively by the sexologists at the turn of the twentieth century, it was used positively by some homosexuals and bisexuals of Woolf's era. Woolf incorporates that sense of androgyny when she describes the ideal position from which a woman should write literature. The difficulty of recognizing the lesbian elements in *A Room* is indicative of the problem of identifying writings that may have been intended, in part or wholly, as works of lesbian literary criticism. Much of this literary criticism may remain unknown.

## Lesbian Criticism from 1970

The work of lesbian literary criticism, however, has flourished openly since the 1970s. When this criticism did stand in the open, it naturally developed arguments about what constituted lesbian literature. Although the term "lesbian literary criticism" implies an agreed upon definition of lesbian literature—literature by and about women who are sexually attracted to other women—it does, in fact, involve a variety of approaches to, and definitions of, this literature. Each approach is determined both by the critic's definition of "lesbian" and by the critic's assumption about what constitutes effective or good literature. What could be a simple issue, then, has become a complex problem of definition. In other words, the basis on which a literary work is descibed, analyzed, and evaluated can be radically different, depending the the leaning of the critic.

The most common critical approach assumes that lesbian literature must be written by a lesbian, display lesbian characters, and contain overt lesbian themes. This form of lesbian literary criticism attempts to identify literatures that have been previously ignored, to judge the accuracy of the portrayal of lesbians, and to identify imagistic similarities among a diverse group of books. It is a criticism that often advocates for literature that takes a strong political stance and literature that represents lesbians in an unbiased, if not powerful, way. This form of criticism can be identified with American lesbian feminism since the 1970s, with some ethnic criticism, and with the popular critical forums like *The Ladder*, especially the reviews written by Gene Damon (pseud. of Barbara Grier, 1933–). Often addressed both to the academic community and the larger lesbian community, like Bonnie Zimmerman's (1947–) work, its strong points are its ability to bring to light previously ignored lesbian literature, its refusal to speak obliquely about obvious or even subtle lesbian texts, and its insistence that lesbian literature reflect lesbian experience. Organizing and evaluating the literary themes and images becomes the primary way the critic approaches literature.

The American lesbian feminists of the 1970s also proposed a larger definition of "lesbian," which, in turn, expanded the literary works that could be considered lesbian. Lesbian was defined by a woman's political stance, not necessarily her sexual activity; thus, lesbian could mean the rage of all women, the creative energy in each woman, or the primary intensity of women with one another, what Adrienne Rich (1929–) termed the "lesbian continuum." This wider definition also includes Lillian Faderman's (1940–) phrase "romantic friendship," as a passionate attachment of women for one another especially in pre-twentieth-century eras. These larger, metaphoric definitions allow as lesbian literary works by Emily Dickinson (1830–1886), who wrote passionate letters to her sister-in-law; a story by Isak Dinesen (1885–1962), "The Blank Page" (1957), which contains no lesbian character or direct lesbian reference but may imply a lesbian topic; and Toni Morrison's (1931–) *Sula* (1973), whose primary characters critic Barbara Smith (1946–) has called lesbian. This wider critical approach allows more literature to be named lesbian, including literature by women who are not necessarily lesbian. It may also allow for a deeper understanding of these texts.

Ethnic, racial, and class perspectives on lesbian literary criticism also complicate what, in the early stages of lesbian feminism, was represented as an unproblematic, generic definition of lesbian. Especially an American phenomenon since the late 1970s, this insistence on difference once again expands and complicates what can be called lesbian literature and how it can be talked about. African American Audre Lorde (1934–1992) insists on the complicated issues of divided loyalty when someone is lesbian and black in America; Dorothy Allison (1949–) considers class more important than sexual identity; and Gloria Anzaldúa (1942–) recounts the magical place gay people held in her native culture. These critical perspectives emphasize the way in which lesbian experience functions differently in different cultural contexts and in different literary traditions (for example, Native American myths). It forces the literary critic to see lesbianism as part of a cross-current of identities, rather than the only one, and to analyze literature as part of different literary traditions.

### Theory and Criticism

In the 1970s in France and in the 1980s and 1990s in the United States, academically oriented literary critics developed a highly theoretical form of lesbian literary criticism. Based primarily on the European philosophical tradition from Friedrich Nietzsche (1844–1900) through Michel Foucault (1926–1984), this lesbian criticism disagrees with U.S. lesbian feminist criticism by questioning realism as an effective type of lesbian literature, by refusing the meaning of "lesbian" as either a stable term or a metaphor for all women, and by centering work on disruptive postmodern fiction, film, and drama. Monique Wittig (1935–), a French lesbian writer of fiction and theory, and queer or postmodern critics such as Elizabeth Meese (1943–) and Judith Roof (1951–) assume that, because Western literature is a male and heterosexual system of meaning, lesbian literature will fail if it uses the same forms. These critics favor writings that are nonlinear and disruptive, such as literature by Gertrude Stein (1874–1946) and Jeanette Winterson (1959–). The strengths of this form of literary criticism are its attention to literary structure rather than content, its interdisciplinary emphasis, and its recognition of differences; its weaknesses are its dismissal of more popular lesbian literature and, for some, its alliance with gay men instead of straight women. Many of the essays from this perspective appear in anthologies devoted to interdisciplinary topics from both gay and lesbian critics.

Finally, and most broadly, lesbian literary criticism can be considered a way of reading any literature, whether the literature is written by a lesbian, a straight woman, a gay man, or a straight man. This reader may be the lesbian who, while reading works highlighting straight culture, must reinterpret the literary work for herself, or the reader may be someone who is straight or gay and desires to approach a text from a lesbian perspective. For instance, a critic reading from a lesbian perspective could read John Milton's (1608–1674) *Paradise Lost* not as a lesbian text but as a work of literature that incorporates lesbian anxiety and lesbian potential in a crucial scene in which Eve falls in love with her own image. Although this approach is not the usual way to define lesbian literary criticism, it is an interesting addition to an expanding way of talking about literature. In this fashion, all of literature would be open to lesbian readings.

Lesbian literary criticism, then, encompasses a wide variety of approaches to literature, but these perspectives do have one thing in common: They end the silence that has surrounded lesbian writing and lesbian issues in literature.

*Marilyn R. Farwell*

### Bibliography

Anzaldúa, Gloria. *Borderlands/La Frontera: The New Mestiza*. San Francisco: Aunt Lute, 1987.

Faderman, Lillian. *Surpassing the Love of Men: Romantic Friendship and Love Between Women from the Renaissance to the Present*. New York: William Morrow, 1981.

Grier, Barbara (pseud. Damon, Gene). *Lesbiana: Book Reviews from The Ladder, 1966–1972*. Reno, Nev.: Naiad, 1976.

Jay, Karla, and Joanne Glasgow, eds. *Lesbian Texts and Contexts: Radical Revisions*. New York: New York University Press, 1990.

Munt, Sally, ed. *New Lesbian Criticsm: Literary and Cultural Readings*. New York: Columbia University Press, 1992.

Roof, Judith. *A Lure of Knowledge: Lesbian Sexuality and Theory*. New York: Columbia Universty Press, 1991.

Rule, Jane. *Lesbian Images*. New York: Pocket Books, 1976.

Smith, Barbara. "Toward a Black Feminist Criticism." Conditions: II, 1, 2 (1977), 25–43.

Zimmerman, Bonnie. *The Safe Sea of Women: Lesbian Fiction, 1969–1989*. Boston: Beacon, 1990.

***See also*** Anzaldúa, Gloria E.; Cultural Studies; Faderman, Lillian; Grier, Barbara; *Ladder, The;* Lesbian Feminism; Lesbian Studies; Lorde, Audre; Philips, Katherine; Postmodernism; Queer Theory; Rich, Adrienne; Sappho; Smith, Barbara; Wittig, Monique; Woolf, Virginia

## Literary Images

Images of lesbians in Western literary traditions have been in circulation only since the late nineteenth century. However, expanding definitions to include images of any female same-sex erotic attachments or women who violate demands for female/feminine behavior, reveals a much larger and longer tradition of images that were deployed by both these women and others who wrote about them.

The image of amazons has long been considered one of female strength and resistance, an image found attractive by many lesbian writers. Persistent legends of amazons can be found in Western classical and in non-Western mythologies. Roman colonial rule of Celtic tribes was almost overthrown by the first century A.D. Queen Boudica (from whom Judy Grahn suggests the word "dyke" derives). Other stories originate in northwest Africa, where amazons were known as warriors and founders of cities throughout North Africa, Egypt, and the islands of Greece. One of the cities said to be founded by these amazons, Mytilene, later became the home of Sappho (ca. 600 B.C.E.).

Many lesbian writers in the twentieth century came to utilize the images of amazons found in earlier eras. While writers such as Natalie Barney (1876–1972) and Renée Vivien (1877–1909) harkened back to the ancient Greek mythology and the poetry of Sappho as sources of a liberatory personal and literary aesthetic, it wasn't until the late twentieth century that feminist and lesbian feminist writers reinvoked the images of amazons in more complete and political (and perhaps idealized) terms. Thus, the amazon figure not only was a strong woman, but also became a woman who waged war against patriarchy and violence against other women. Poets frequently utilized the image. Audre Lorde (1934–1992), in her poem "125th Street and Abomey," (1978) writes: "I surrender to you as libation / . . . take my fear of being alone / like my warrior sisters / who rode in defense of your queendom / disguised and apart / give me the woman strength / of tongue in this cold season." Fiction writers, too, found the image of strong women and all-female societies alluring. Elana Nachman, in her novel *Riverfinger Women* (1974), writes that "some of us began our resistance, learned to change (acid on stone) who we thought we were doomed to be into who we are. Tough, strong, proud: free women."

It is, perhaps, these images of amazons that also gave birth to one of the more ubiquitous images of lesbians: that of the "mannish" woman. While most nineteenth-century feminists wore traditional women's clothing, a number of primarily upper-class women cross-dressed as a symbol of their feminism. This cross-dressing came to be increasingly associated with sexual inverts, women who were by temperament and dress "mannish." In this way, the popular imagination converted the strong amazon figure into a woman who was mannish in some fashion.

This conflation of gendered dress and behavior with sexuality produced one of the best-known figures in lesbian literature: Stephen Gordon, the hero of Radclyffe Hall's (1880–1943) *The Well of Loneliness* (1928). In the 1950s and early 1960s, the butch character in pulp novels, such as Ann Bannon's (1937–) *Beebo Brinker* (1962), took the place of the invert of Hall's famous novel. Cheryl Clarke's (1947–) poem "Of Althea and Flaxie" (1982) celebrates the mannish woman or butch: "In 1943 Althea was a welder / very dark / very butch / and very proud / loved to cook, sew, and drive a car / and did not care who knew she kept company with a woman." While some lesbian feminists in the 1970s and 1980s critiqued this particular image as belonging to a patriarchal pornographic imagination (and, indeed, the image of the mannish woman is found in many works by male writers as well), others saw the mannish woman, or butch, as a proud carrier of a working-class lesbian literary tradition. This may be best exemplified in Leslie Feinberg's *Stone Butch Blues* (1993), a novel that chronicles a young butch lesbian's decision to pass as a man when she needs to work.

While women who took "male" prerogatives were considered "mannish," it is in the figure of the unnatural woman, the evil monster, that patriarchy's worst fears of female autonomy can be found. This "otherness" of the lesbian can be found in nineteenth-century literature, especially French decadent literature. Emile Zola (1840–1902), Guy de Maupassant (1850–1893), and Alphonse Daudet (1840–1897) all contributed works that emphasized lesbian evil. Honoré de Balzac's (1799–1850) *The Girl with the Golden Eyes* (1835) illustrates this theme. Balzac's androgynous Marquise de St. Réal purchases pretty young Paquita from her mother and holds her in sexual slavery; when she telepathically discovers that Paquita has been sexual with a man (her half-brother, no less), she barbarously murders her. Writers such as Charles Baudelaire (1821–1867), Algernon Swinburne (1837–1909), Pierre Louÿs (1870–1925), and Paul Verlaine (1844–1896) all utilized images of monstrous (and often exotic) lesbian evil, which proved a popular theme well into the twentieth century. Even the American Mary Wilkins Freeman (1952–1930) (who had close friendships with women) wrote "The Long Arm" (1895), which depicts a romantic friendship in which the more masculine, unnatural woman murders her partner's male suitor, continuing this particular image of lesbian monstrosity.

Lesbians themselves have often utilized the image of lesbian evil or monstrosity in their works. Djuna Barnes' (1892–1982) Robin Vote in *Nightwood* (1936) invokes this succubus-like character. It was not until the lesbian feminist writers of the 1970s that the image of the monster was reappropriated as an outlaw figure, a source of female-centered power outside patriarchal reach. Adrienne Rich's (1929–) poem "Planetarium" (1971) begins: "A woman in the shape of a monster / a monster in the shape of a woman / the skies are full of them."

Judith Katz's novel *Running Fiercely Toward a High Thin Sound* (1992) follows the adventures of Nadine Pagan, who is mythologized by her sisters as half-girl, half-wolf. (In early published exerpts, the novel was titled *The Monster in My Mother's House.*) Nadine's mother believes "[t]here's a *dybbuk* inside her!" Nadine is perceived as tainting the family and its place in the larger Jewish community, especially after hiding in, and falling out of, the Ark at her sister's wedding. A similarly devilish figure employed by Chicana lesbian writers is that of the Aztec princess Malinche, who, as translator and courtesan to Hernando Cortez, betrayed her Indio people and symbolically gave birth to mestizo/Mexicano people. For a writer like Cherríe Moraga (1952–), Malinche symbolizes the way Moraga, in her *Loving in the War Years* (1983), "further betrays my race by choosing my sexuality which excludes all men, and therefore most dangerously, Chicano men."

The crossing of same-sex eroticism, sexuality, and danger led to literary works that are notable for their use of vampire characters and vampiric imagery. The English romantic Samuel Taylor Coleridge's poem "Christabel" (1817) and Irish writer Joseph Sheridan LaFanu's short story "Carmilla" (1872) feature two well-known examples of vampire-like women who erotically drain the life force out of other women. Raymond McNally, a noted vampire scholar, suggests that the birth of the myth of the vampire is actually traceable to a Hungarian countess, Elizabeth Bathory (1560–1614), who sexually preferred young women and liked to dress in men's clothing (cited in Keesey, 1993). These origins are overlooked in most vampire fiction.

Vampires became popular images used by lesbian writers in the 1980s and 1990s, although the lesbian-as-vampire character clearly existed well before that time. Lesbian writers both rewrite old stories and remythologize new ones. Perhaps the best-known writer of lesbian vampire stories is Jewelle Gomez (1948–). Her collection *The Gilda Stories* (1991) tells of a black lesbian feminist vampire who escapes from slavery and searches for her place in the world. Commenting on the writing of vampire fiction, Gomez has said: "I feel I can remake mythology as well as anyone. . . . I was certain I could create a mythology to express who I am as a black lesbian feminist" (Keesey, 1993). Other lesbian writers of the 1980s and 1990s who have explored the image of the vampire include Judith Katz, Katherine Forrest, and Pat Califia.

Lesbians have been represented in many modes and manners in both mainstream and alternative literature. In addition to the amazon, the mannish lesbian, the monster, and the vampire, lesbian writers (and others writing about lesbians) have drawn upon the images of the schoolgirl, the athlete, the alcoholic, and the aristocrat, among others. While mainstream literature has not always been complimentary to lesbian images, lesbians often reclaim and revise some of these images, making them over in ways that better reflect how lesbians perceive themselves within their own social and cultural paradigms.

*Linnea A. Stenson*

### Bibliography

Faderman, Lillian. *Surpassing the Love of Men: Romantic Friendship and Love Between Women from the Renaissance to the Present*. New York: William Morrow, 1981.

Foster, Jeannette H. *Sex Variant Women in Literature*. Tallahassee, Fla.: Naiad, 1956, 1985.

Keesey, Pam. "Introduction." In *Daughter of Darkness: Lesbian Vampire Stories*. Ed. Pam Keesey. Pittsburgh, Penn.: Cleis, 1993.

Newton, Esther. "The Mythic Mannish Lesbian: Radclyffe Hall and the New Woman." *Signs: Journal of Women in Culture and Society* 9:4 (Summer 1984), 557–575.

Zimmerman, Bonnie. *The Safe Sea of Women: Lesbian Fiction 1969–1989*. Boston: Beacon, 1990.

*See also* Amazons; Bannon, Ann; Barnes, Djuna Chappell; Barney, Natalie Clifford; Butch-Femme; Hall, Radclyffe; Lorde, Audre; Moraga, Cherríe; Pulp Fiction; Rich, Adrienne; Romantic Friendship; Sappho; Stereotypes; Vampires; Vivien, Renée

## London

Capital of the United Kingdom, as well as its lesbian capital. Many famous lesbians have lived in London over the years: The *Pink Plaque Guide* lists the addresses of, among others, writers Bryher (1894–1983), Charlotte Charke (1713–1760), Mary Renault (1905–1983), and Sylvia Townsend Warner (1893–1978), the artist Gluck (1895–1978), and the composer Ethel Smyth (1858–1944). Radclyffe Hall (1880–1943) lived at several London addresses and died there. Her novel *The Well of Loneliness* (1928) was successfully prosecuted for obscenity at Bow Street Magistrates Court (opposite Covent Garden Opera House) in 1928, and she worshiped at the Roman Catholic Church in Maiden Lane nearby (her name, and that of Lady Una Troubridge [1887–1963], her lover, are still attached to the pew they occupied).

In the late nineteenth and early twentieth centuries, there were lesbian groupings around the theater, the art world, and women's colleges, as well as feminist activism. Less is known of working-class lesbian culture at that time, but after World War II, the Gateways Club, immortalized in the film *The Killing of Sister George* (1969), flourished in Bramerton Street, SW3. It closed in 1985.

Modern lesbian organizing began in London. In the 1960s, women associated with the pioneering lesbian magazine *Arena 3* organized monthly meetings at the Shakespeare's Head pub in Carnaby Street. Kenric, a social group for lesbians that still flourishes nationwide, was set up by two *Arena 3* members from the London boroughs of Kensington and Richmond; hence, its name. When *Arena 3* ceased publication in 1971, women continued to meet at the Museum Tavern in Museum Street—opposite the British Museum—which led to the founding of *Sappho* in 1972. This was both a magazine (which ran until 1981) and a social group, whose collective organized discos (until 1982) and weekly meetings in a West End pub, usually with speakers and discussion. These meetings still take place. London Friend, which began as the counseling arm of the Campaign for Homosexual Equality in 1971, still reaches out to newly arrived lesbians and gays from its Caledonian Road premises.

Radical activism in the 1970s gave London lesbians a higher public profile. They were involved in the Gay Liberation Front and, especially, the women's liberation movement. A successful Lesbian Sex and Sexual Practice Conference was held in London in 1983, followed by a Lesbian Studies Conference in 1984. These inspired the setting up of lesbian studies classes, the Lesbian Archive, and the Lesbian History Group. In 1985, the Greater London Council (GLC), London's municipal authority, opened a Lesbian and Gay Centre in London and published *Changing the World: A London Charter for Lesbian and Gay Rights*. Their lead was followed by several left-wing local authorities in London but soon gave way to an antigay reaction that not only prompted the passing of Section 28 of the Local Government Act 1988 (known as Clause 28 before the act was passed)—which prohibits the "promotion" of homosexuality in some state-funded venues—but was also partly responsible for the abolition by the Conservative Party government of the gay-friendly GLC itself.

By the end of the 1990s, the feminist focus of London lesbianism had largely been replaced by an emphasis on lesbian style. The London Lesbian and Gay Centre was destroyed by internal wrangling and the withdrawal of funding. Funding cuts also forced the Lesbian Archive to move to Glasgow, Scotland. Nonetheless, a lively bar and club scene remained. At the former London Women's Centre, renamed the Wheel (in Wild Court, off Kingsway WC1), many lesbian groups continued to meet or maintain a mailbox. For example, although the Lesbian History Group folded in 1994, it was replaced by two radical lesbian feminist discussion groups, Lesbian Viewpoints and RADS. Also at the Wheel were groups such as the Lesbian Avengers and the Older Lesbian Network, and groups for black and ethnic-minority lesbians. Silver Moon Bookshop in Charing Cross Road, Europe's biggest women's bookshop, continued to offer a large selection of lesbian books and magazines.

Among the lesbian institutions in London, three deserve highlighting: the annual Gay Pride march through central London to Hyde Park, which has taken place every June since 1972; the lesbian pantomime at Christmas at the Drill Hall in Chenies Street, another popular venue for classes, shows, and meetings; and the Ladies' Pond on Hampstead Heath, free to all women and a delightful place to spend a summer Sunday afternoon.

Information on London events can be found in *Time Out*, a weekly informational magazine for London, and the *Pink Paper,* a free gay weekly paper, or through the Lesbian and Gay Switchboard or Lesbian Line, which also provide counseling and information about accommodation.

*Rosemary Auchmuty*

### Bibliography

Duffy, Maureen. *The Microcosm*. New York: Simon and Schuster, 1966.

Elliman, Michael, and Frederick Roll. *The Pink Plaque Guide to London*. London: GMP, 1986.

Neild, Suzanne, and Rosalind Pearson. *Women Like Us*. London: Women's Press, 1992.

*See also* United Kingdom

## Lorde, Audre (1934–1992)

African American lesbian, feminist, poet, warrior, and mother. Audre Lorde was one of the foremost lesbian thinkers of the twentieth century, who inspired many other women, regardless of their sexuality, to think deeply about the interconnections between racism, sexism, and homophobia. She kept a wide circle of women poets and scholars as close friends, including Cherríe Moraga (1952–), Gloria Hull, Adrienne Rich (1929–), Judy Grahn (1940–), and Barbara Smith (1946–).

Raised by Grenadian parents who came to the United States in 1924, Lorde recalled her early life in Harlem in her biomythography, *Zami: A New Spelling of My Name*, remembering that, "underneath it all as I was growing up, *home* was still a sweet place somewhere else which they had not managed to capture yet on paper, nor to throttle and bind up between the pages of a schoolbook." Using the sights, sounds, and material memory of her

*Audre Lorde. Photo by Tee A. Corinne.*

childhood as fodder for her vision as a poet, Lorde wove an incredible life from an early childhood of silence and near blindness. Lorde's description of her early life in *Zami,* paints a portrait of a young woman constantly trying to negotiate the racism and sexism of America in the 1950s. She said about becoming a poet: "[W]hen the strongest words for what I have to offer come out of me sounding like words I remember from my mother's mouth, then I either have to reassess the meaning of everything I have to say now, or reexamine the worth of her words." Her memories of childhood are enmeshed with memories of her mother's simultaneous softness and harshness; this relationship is always bittersweet, and, throughout much of Lorde's work, the mother comes forward as a figure of both construction and destruction. The bittersweet nature of the mother-daughter bond is closely linked to the erotic connection to women that Lorde finds early in her life. Speaking of the sacred and the profane in one breath, Lorde reminds her readers at the end of *Zami* that "the desire to lie with other women is a drive from the mother's blood."

What appears to be one of Lorde's first poems was written in May 1949, after the suicide death of a close high school friend. The piece is illustrative of an early poetry wrought with visceral images of birth and death. Creating poetry at a time of intense production by women artists, poets, and educators, Lorde had her first volume of poetry, *The First Cities*, published in 1968. Always hurt and dismayed by the response of other African Americans to her work, Lorde once remarked in an interview: "[I]n the forties and fifties my life-style and the rumors about my lesbianism made me persona non grata in Black literary circles.... [W]hy do you think my last book, *The Black Unicorn*, has not been reviewed, nor even mentioned, in any Black newspaper or Black magazine within the thirteen months since it appeared?" (in Evans, 1984).

Her refusal to forget the fact of her lesbianism posed a challenge for Lorde throughout her career. Consistently, she took the feminist maxim "the personal is political" and made it a reality in her work and life. Recording her own personal tragedy and triumphs so that others might gain strength from her insight, Lorde spoke openly of her own struggles with racism, sexism, and homophobia. But perhaps her most profound impact on the feminist and lesbian communities was the chronicling of her own fight with cancer in *The Cancer Journals* (1980). In the introduction to the work, Lorde writes: "[F]or other women of all ages, colors, and sexual identities who recognize that imposed silence about any area of our lives is a tool for separation and powerlessness, and for myself, I have tried to voice some of my thoughts about the travesty of prosthesis, the pain of amputation, the function of cancer in a profit economy, my confrontation with mortality, the strength of women loving, and the power and rewards of self-conscious living."

Author of more than nine volumes of poetry, two collections of essays, and two autobiographical works, Lorde will be remembered for the intensity of her words, the beauty of her presence, and the insight of her work. Of her essays, "Uses of the Erotic: The Erotic as Power" and "The Masters Tools Will Never Dismantle the Master's House," both in *Sister Outsider* (1984), will be long remembered because of Lorde's attention to the way in which the patriarchy robs women of their own power and, therefore, their ability to speak clearly and lovingly to one another. Some of her best-known poems are "Coal" (1970), "A Litany for Survival" (1978), and "Power" (1978), all of which utilize contemporary politics as the backdrop for creative production. Lorde was a prolific poet; her work spanned three decades—from the poetic style of the Black Arts Movement to the postmodern aesthetic evidenced in her last book of poetry, *Undersong*, published posthumously in 1992.

Lorde died from breast cancer that had metastasized to the liver in November 1992. Her passing was deeply felt by all of those whom she touched with her words and her vision of a place of understanding for humanity.          *Sharon P. Holland*

## Bibliography

Evans, Mari, ed. *Black Women Writers (1950–1980): A Critical Evaluation.* New York: Anchor, 1984.

Perreault, Jeanne. *Writing Selves: Contemporary Feminist Autography.* Minneapolis: University of Minnesota Press, 1995.

Tate, Claudia, ed. *Black Women Writers at Work.* New York: Continuum, 1989.

*See also* African American Literature

## Los Angeles, California

Largest city in California; noted in particular for its ethnically diverse population and its central role in the entertainment industry. Prior to the Stonewall Rebellion (1969) in New York City, lesbians in Los Angeles gathered in private homes and bars, at softball games and beauty contests on the Venice Beach boardwalk, and on discrete strips of local beaches. Some were active in homophile groups, and many in social movements not their own. Recorded lesbian activism in Los Angeles began with resistant gestures like that of Lisa Ben (a pseudonym constructed from "lesbian"), who clandestinely published and circulated the first lesbian newsletter (*Vice Versa*) in 1947–1948. In the 1950s, when homophile groups formed, lesbians were notably active in *ONE* and the local chapter of Daughters of Bilitis (DOB). Shortly after Stonewall, a handful of lesbians joined the Los Angeles Gay Liberation Front (GLF) but were soon alienated by the sexism of GLF males. A developing feminist consciousness and memories of sexist experiences in other movements led some to form a GLF women's caucus and then an entirely separate group, Lesbian Feminists (LF). Housed at the Crenshaw Women's Center, LF was an energetic group that helped organize gatherings such as the Gay Women's West Coast Conference (1971), ran a coffeehouse and a speakers bureau, participated in the movement against the Vietnam War, sponsored "gay-straight dialogues," and worked with National Organization for Women (NOW) members to help pass NOW's historic pro-lesbian resolution in 1971.

In 1971, the *Lesbian Tide* became the first lesbian publication to use the "L" word on its masthead. Its publisher, Jeanne Cordova, was an activist whose local credits included coorganizing the 1973 West Coast Lesbian Conference. This second national lesbian conference (DOB held the first one in 1960) was held at the University of California, Los Angeles, with more than 1,500 women attending.

In the 1970s and 1980s, Los Angeles lesbians working alone and with allies created an institutional and cultural base that included centers like the Gay Women's Service Center (possibly the first in the United States), the Westside Women's Center, the Alcoholism Center for Women, and Connexxus Women's Center/Centro de Mujeres; bookstores, including Sisterhood Books and Page One; support and advocacy groups, such as Fat Underground, Z Budapest's Wicca, Radical Therapy Collective, and rape hotlines; actions like the First National Lesbian Kiss-In (1973); gatherings such as the Lesbian History Exploration (1975), the National Lesbian Feminist Organization Founding Conference (1978), and the West Coast Old Lesbian Conference (1987); cultural events and groups, including the Great American Lesbian Art Show at The Woman's Building, L.A. Women's Community Chorus, and the West Coast Music Festival; the first lesbian sorority in the United States (Lambda Delta Lambda) founded at UCLA in 1988. Important publications that continued to publish through the 1990s include the *Lesbian News*, cofounded by Jinx Beers in 1975; *Lesbian Ethics*; and the *L.A. Women's Yellow Pages*.

The diverse lesbian community of Los Angeles also had its share of painful internal struggles over issues of class, race, roles, separatism, sadomaschism, AIDS, sexism, and generational differences in perspective and style. Lesbians of color who were unhappy with the racism in lesbian organizations and the sexism in gay people of color organizations formed groups such as Lesbianas Latinamericanas (formed in 1974), Debreta's (1977), Lesbianas Unidas (1984), Asian Pacific Lesbians and Friends (1985), and United Lesbians of African Heritage (1990). Lesbians of Color (LOC), founded in 1978, organized the first National LOC Conference in 1983. Working with allies from White Women Against Racism, Connexxus, and Califia (an organization known for its week-long camps and workshops on racism and classism), LOC also conducted numerous racism workshops.

In the late 1970s and the 1980s, amidst a homophobic backlash, the AIDS epidemic, and the inevitable life-cycle changes that individuals and social movements are heir to, the momentum of lesbian-focused activism shifted. Beginning in 1977, lesbians from many segments of the community worked in co-gender coalitions to stop various homophobic propositions, including the infamous Briggs Initiative, which was an attempt to prohibit any discussion of homosexuality in public schools; it was defeated by California voters in 1978. These efforts required new strategies and styles. Activist lesbians increasingly worked with co-gender projects (the Municipal Elections Committee of Los Angeles and the multimillion-dollar Gay and Lesbian Community Services Center, which hired its first lesbian director, Torie Osborne, in 1988) and in mainstream venues (Jackie Goldberg was elected to the Los Angeles City Council in 1993, and Sheila Kuehl to the California State Assembly in 1994; Jean O'Leary was appointed to the Democratic National Committee in 1994). By the mid-1990s, lesbian-focused projects and groups, such as Southern California Women for Understanding, the June Mazer Lesbian Collection, lesbians-of-color groups, and the (Internet) Lesbian History Project, were

small in number, a sign that the "golden days" of lesbian activism were gone or in abeyance mode.

*Yolanda Retter*

### Bibliography

Kepner, Jim. "The Women of ONE." URL: http://www.lib.usc.edu/~retter/onewomen.html

Retter, Yolanda. "Lesbian Spaces in Los Angeles, 1970–1990." In *Queers in Space: Communities, Public Spaces, Sites of Resistance*. Ed. Gorden Brent Ingram, Anne-Marie Bouthillette, and Yolanda Retter. Seattle: Bay Press, 1997, pp. 325–337.

*See also* Daughters of Bilitis; Gay Liberation Movement; Hollywood; Music Festivals; National Organization for Women (NOW); Sororities

# Love

Intense affection, sexual passion, or deep devotion. Love poetry and letters constitute the earliest written evidence of love between women. Poetry has been used to express the passion, turmoil, and tenderness of lesbian love throughout the ages, beginning with Sappho (ca. 600 B.C.E.). Love letters were a second major means of communicating a transgressive love and have provided the basis for understanding the rise of romantic friendships in the United States from the eighteenth century to the early twentieth century. Women in romantic friendships, also known as Boston marriages, avowed a deep, abiding love for each other, although the extent to which the relationships included a sexual dimension is uncertain. Multiple positive images of lesbian love evolved in the late twentieth century, paralleling the development of a modern lesbian community. These images celebrated the sensuality, intensity, danger, and comfort of love between women. Concurrent with women's own accounts of love, lesbian love also has been stereotyped as depraved, sick, or titillating in religious, medical, and pornographic representations.

## Characterizations of Lesbian Love

Research on lesbian love in Western societies has found that choice, equality, intimacy, sensuality, and independence are highly characteristic of and valued in lesbian relationships, although individual variations exist (Peplau, 1993). Lesbians generally make a free, affectionally based choice of partners. Equality is enhanced by the equal gender status of partners and feminist values that emphasize the importance of equity in relationships. Female gender socialization contributes to high levels of intimacy, including the desire to have an emotionally close and relatively secure love relationship. Sensuality encompasses physical affection, as well as explicit erotic acts. Independence refers to the high level of personal autonomy preferred by many lesbians, including having separate interests, friendships, and earnings.

Variation in the strength of particular elements may be associated with specific outcomes in lesbian love relationships. Couples who emphasize choice, equality, and intimacy may seek stable, close monogamous relationships. A pattern of high intimacy and low independence in couples has been associated with "fusion" or "merger," or the problem some lesbians have with maintaining a separate identity when they are in a couple. High levels of intimacy may contribute to a low rate of sexual desire or activity, also known as "lesbian bed death." If both intimacy and independence are highly valued, a pattern of serial monogamy or nonmonogamy may result, with high independence making it possible for lesbians to seek a more satisfying relationship if expectations for intimacy are not met.

## Lesbian Love Scripts

Three primary lesbian love scripts have emerged in the United States since the 1960s: friendship/companionate, romantic, and erotic. A script represents a cognitive schema concerning why, when, where, how, and with whom one should love, as prescribed by the individual's culture. Lesbian love scripts have been derived partly from heterosexual love scripts and partly from social norms as represented in lesbian popular culture, such as fiction and comedy. The three scripts are distinguished by the different emphasis each places on intimacy, sexuality, and commitment.

The friendship, or companionate, love script among lesbians combines feelings of deep attachment, intimacy, and commitment, with little or no emphasis placed on sexuality. It is highly valued by some lesbians because it promotes equality and is a preferred courtship script, particularly in first relationships. If friendship is not present prior to sexual involvement, lesbians generally act quickly to establish one. The priority given friendship love also is shown by a frequently expressed fear that becoming sexual with a friend might jeopardize the friendship.

The romantic love script combines emotional intimacy and sexual attraction. An emotional or sexual awakening aroused by the beloved is a key component of the lesbian romantic love script. An intense longing for union with the loved one, if reciprocated, is associated with ecstasy and fulfillment. Separation or unrequited romantic love elicits feelings of anxiety and despair. During courtship, the intensity of romantic love can be increased by cultural barriers to lesbian love and the uncertainty of a new relationship.

The erotic love, or sexually explicit, script celebrates the active pursuit of sexual pleasure and variety. Sensuality and lust motivate the connection, rather than feelings associated with romantic or friendship love, such as duty, anxiety, or jealousy. Initiation of the relationship is direct and goal oriented. Erotic love scripts sometimes explicitly include role playing to stimulate desire, including butch-femme or sadomasochistic roles. In long-term erotic relationships, a friendship may be established but is not intertwined with the sexual component as it is in the case of romantic love.

Love scripts may be fluid, with changes in preferred script occurring over the course of a relationship or the life span. Friendship or erotic love may develop into romantic love or vice versa. The sexual component of romantic and erotic love declines substantially for most couples after two years; even so, most lesbians report high levels of sexual satisfaction and orgasm in relationships. Friendship love appears to remain strong even when a romantic or an erotic relationship has ended, accounting for the phenomenon among many lesbians of having ex-lovers as friends and extended family. Scripts also may overlap. In romantic friendships or Boston marriages, lesbians are highly committed to each other and view themselves as a couple but are asexual. Finally, love scripts are not mutually exclusive. For example, a lesbian might have an erotic and a romantic relationship with different partners simultaneously.

Little research has been conducted about the effect age, race, class, or disability have on lesbian love in Western, industrial societies. A majority of white lesbians fall in love with partners who are similar on these dimensions. Most also tend to choose partners based on companionate traits rather than physical beauty and to emphasize the importance of emotional connection over sexual intimacy. Lesbians of color appear to follow a similar pattern in terms of partner choice but often describe having to subordinate their lesbian desires to maintain the support of their own ethnic community. Barriers to love reported by interracial couples include societal and internalized racism and negative reactions from family and community.

# L

Although heterosexist cultural scripts had a strong influence on lesbian love scripts in the past, new themes introduced in the late twentieth century are having an impact, including increased gender blending of individual identity and roles, debates about same-sex parenting and marriage, the salience of race and culture in defining relationships, and the importance of extended friendship networks as a chosen family for lesbians. These themes are likely to result in the evolution of future love scripts that are more clearly lesbian defined.      *Suzanna Rose*

## Bibliography

Mays, Vicki M., Susan Cochran, and Sylvia Rhue. "The Impact of Perceived Discrimination on the Intimate Relationships of Black Lesbians." *Journal of Homosexuality* 25:4 (1993), 1–14.

Pearlman, S. "Loving Across Race and Class Divides: Relational Challenges and the Interracial Lesbian Couple." *Women and Therapy* 19:3 (1996), 25–35.

Peplau, L. Anne. "Lesbian and Gay Relationships." In *Psychological Perspectives on Lesbian and Gay Male Experience*. Ed. Linda D. Garnets and C. Kimmel Douglas. New York: Columbia University Press, 1993, pp. 395–419.

Rose, Suzanna. "Lesbian and Gay Love Scripts." In *Preventing Heterosexism and Homophobia*. Ed. Esther D. Rothblum and Lynne A. Bond. Thousand Oaks, Calif.: Sage, 1996, pp. 151–173.

Rose, Suzanna, Deborah Zand, and Marie Cini. "Lesbian Courtship Scripts." In *Boston Marriages: Romantic but Asexual Relationships Among Contemporary Lesbians*. Ed. Esther D. Rothblum and Kathleen A. Brehony. Amherst: University of Massachusetts Press, 1993, pp. 70–85.

*See also* Boston Marriage; Butch-Femme; Couples; Friendship; Monogamy and Nonmonogamy; Romantic Friendship; Sadomasochism; Sexuality

## Lowell, Amy Lawrence (1874–1925)

American poet. Born into a distinguished and wealthy family in Brookline, Massachusetts, Amy Lowell was educated privately. For a brief period, she was associated with Ezra Pound (1885–1972), but she broke with him to go her own way. In fact, her imagist poetry is quite different from that of Pound's circle.

Lowell described herself in her adolescent diary as "a great, rough, masculine, strong thing." Although she had very strong crushes on young males during that adolescent period, it was her crushes on her female friends that appear to have first led to her writing poetry; one of her earliest extant poems came out of her adolescent crush on her girlfriend, "Louly W."

Lowell's first published volume of poems, *A Dome of Many Coloured Glass* (1912), contains a number of seemingly homoerotic poems, addressed to two women. But the most significant body of her experiential love poems was written to, and for, the actress Ada Russell (1863–1952?).

Lowell first encountered Russell in 1909. They spent part of the summer of 1912 together, and, for the next two years, the poet tried to persuade the actress to live with her. This courtship is reflected in approximately twenty poems of *Sword Blades and Poppy Seed* (1914). Russell finally yielded to Lowell's pursuit in the spring of 1914. She quit the stage and went to live with Lowell in her Brookline mansion, Sevenels, ostensibly as her paid companion but, in fact, as her mate. The two lived together until Lowell's death in 1925.

Several of Lowell's later volumes contain love poems about the relationship between the two women, including *Pictures of the Floating World* (1919)—especially the forty-three poems in the "Two Speak Together" section—and two posthumous volumes, *What's O'Clock* (1925) and *Ballads for Sale* (1927).

The usual critical observation that Lowell was an overweight, pathetic, and lonely unmarried woman is not borne out by the body of Lowell's poetry. The preponderance of her experiential poems suggest a life and a relationship that were extremely happy and productive. Lowell admitted to her acquaintances that such love poems were about Russell.

In a scurrilous study published one year after Amy Lowell's death, Clement Wood argued that Lowell was not a good poet because many of her poems were homosexual; therefore, they did not "word a common cry of many hearts." Lowell, he concluded, may qualify "as an impassioned singer of her own desires; and she may well be laureate also of as many as stand beside her," but nonlesbian readers will find nothing in her verse.

*Lillian Faderman*

## Bibliography

Gould, Amy Jean. *The World of Amy Lowell and the Imagist Movement*. New York: Dodd, Mead, 1975.

*See also* Poetry

# M

## Mâhû

Indigenous to the Hawai'in Islands and Society Islands (French Polynesia), the term *mâhû* is translated as "half-man, half-woman" by Polynesians of the Society Islands. References to *mâhû* date back to eighteenth-century European narratives identifying *mâhû* in the entourages of Polynesian queens and kings and in everyday life. While most historical and ethnographic accounts suggest *mâhû* is a gender category available only to males, recent ethnographic and historical work demonstrates that females have also been, and are, *mâhû*.

In the Hawai'in and Society Islands, *mâhû* refers to females or males who adopt complex combinations of masculine and feminine gender signs: There are crucial distinctions here between sex differences (female, male), gender categories and behaviors (woman/feminine, man/masculine, *mâhû*), and sexual practices. *Mâhû* adopt styles of dress, work, and embodied expressions (gestures, stances, speaking styles, voice pitch) that, while incorporating both, privilege one over the other. Female *mâhû*, for example, often dress and behave more like men than women. Analogous categories with similarly long histories are found elsewhere in Polynesia: *fa'atama* (for females) and *fa'afâfine* (for males) in Samoa; and *fâfine tangata* or *fakatangata* (for females) and *fakafâfine* or, more recently, *fakaleitî* (for males) in Tonga.

In Hawai'i, *mâhû* means "a homosexual of either sex who adopts the opposite gender role." This gendering of *mâhû* in ways lying beyond the binary man/woman is its most significant aspect, but homosexuality is also involved. In French Polynesia, however, *mâhû* is primarily a gender, not a sexual, category. While the category *mâhû* often connotes homosexual practices, these are culturally understood in terms of the *mâhû*'s complex gender status as "half-man, half-woman": It is, for example, because a female *mâhû* is "half-man" that s/he is attracted to women (Tahitian, *vahine*) as lovers. However, homosexual practices are not necessarily part of *mâhû* behavior since many, but not all, *mâhû* take same-sex lovers. An important corollary of the complex relationship between gender and sexual practice throughout Polynesia, however, is that the lovers of *mâhû* are either men (*tane*) or women (*vahine*) and never other *mâhû*.

In urban Papeete (French Polynesia), for example, where a butch-femme model structures sexual relationships among many females, *mâhû* are butches who, in local terms, behave "in the manner of men." In the context of their butch-femme relationships, this means female *mâhû* are sexually attracted, like heterosexual men, to women. Femmes, on the other hand, behave (in style, dress, and gender-coded work), and are culturally treated, as women. Femmes, then, unlike their female *mâhû* lovers, are not linguistically or socially marked as anything other than women, even though they have sexual relationships with females.

This is a telling aspect of the ways in which gender and sexuality are both separate and interrelated in these Polynesian societies: *Mâhû* is primarily meaningful as a complex gender category, and with its set of masculine and feminine gender significations comes the possibility of taking same-sex lovers; yet, in these societies, women (and men) may also take same-sex lovers without these homosexual practices rendering them *mâhû*.

[The author wishes to thank J. Kehaulani Kauanui, Lanuola Asiasiga, and her *mâhû* and non-

# M

*mâhû* teachers in French Polynesia for their guidance and insights.] *Deborah A. Elliston*

**Bibliography**

Besnier, Niko. "Polynesian Gender Liminality Through Time and Space." In *Third Sex, Third Gender: Beyond Sexual Dimorphism in Culture and History*. Ed. Gilbert Herdt. New York: Zone, 1993, pp. 285–328.

Hall, Lisa Kahaleole Chang, and J. Kehaulani Kauanui. "Same-Sex Sexuality in Pacific Literature." *Amerasia Journal* 20:1 (1994), 75–81.

James, Kerry E. "Effeminate Males and Changes in the Construction of Gender in Tonga." *Pacific Studies* 17:2 (1994), 39–69.

Oliver, Douglas L. *Ancient Tahitian Society*. 3 vols. Honolulu: University Press of Hawai'i, 1974.

**See also** Anthropology; Butch-Femme; Hawai'i; Pacific Islands; Transgender

## Mansfield, Katherine (1888–1923)

New Zealand short-story writer. Born Kathleen Mansfield Beauchamp in Wellington, she was sent to England at fourteen to complete her education at Queen's College, London. Returning home at seventeen, she started to publish short fictions, which she had begun writing at school, but soon grew bored and dissatisfied with the provinciality of her homeland and returned to England with an allowance from her family. While still in New Zealand she also began her ongoing exploration of what she called "the complete octave of sex," although her adolescent affairs were primarily with other young women. In London, she was reunited with Ida Baker (b. 1888; also androgynously known as Leslie Moore or L.M.), whom she had met at Queen's College. L.M. became her lifelong devotee, even during Mansfield's relationships with men.

Within a year of her return to England, Mansfield became pregnant by one man and quickly married another, whom she left the evening of the wedding. Soon after, her mother arrived in London and swiftly removed her to Bavaria (where she miscarried) and disinherited her. Late-twentieth-century biographers have suggested that this was not so much a response to Mansfield's pregnancy (of which her mother may not have been aware) as it was to speculation about lesbianism between Mansfield and L.M., who was also dispatched abroad by her own family.

In the wake of this episode, Mansfield embarked upon a serious writing career and became acquainted with such literary figures as Virginia Woolf (1882–1941), D.H. Lawrence (1885–1930), and John Middleton Murry (1889–1957), with whom she lived for many years and eventually married. While her working relationship with Woolf was intense, it was not without hostility ("I thought her cheap, and she thought me priggish," Woolf wrote to Vita Sackville-West [1892–1962]), and each sharply criticized the other's work.

With the exception of "Bliss" (1920), which Woolf found indicative of Mansfield's "callousness and hardness," her stories, while often detailing women's dissatisfaction with traditional gender roles, rarely examine desire between women. Because of Mansfield's chronic ill health and early death from tuberculosis, her literary output is small, although often exquisite in its execution. Her diaries, however, provide much insight into her complex bisexuality. *Patricia Juliana Smith*

**Bibliography**

Alpers, Antony. *The Life of Katherine Mansfield*. New York: Viking, 1980.

Boddy, Gillian. *Katherine Mansfield: The Woman and the Writer*. Ringwood: Penguin Australia, 1988.

Moore, Leslie. *Memories of L.M.* London: Virago, 1985.

Tomalin, Claire. *Katherine Mansfield: A Secret Life*. New York: Knopf, 1988.

**See also** New Zealand; Sackville-West, Vita; Woolf, Virginia

## Marches and Parades

Organized public displays and celebrations, sometimes expressing a political agenda.

### History and Characteristics

Although Chicago, Illinois, had had a small gay and lesbian celebration in 1967, it was the 1969 Stonewall Rebellion in New York City that initiated the era of gay pride parades. The first of these came the year after Stonewall, as a demonstration for gay civil rights and liberties. Originally small and limited mainly to gays and lesbians who were publicly "out," parades and marches mushroomed in numbers of locations and participants, varying in size from thirty to more than 500,000. In West Hollywood, California, for example, the gay and lesbian parade is the third largest of any parades held in the Los Angeles region; with an estimated 400,000 participants, it is smaller only than the Tournament of Roses and Christmas parades.

In 1996, there were more than 127 separate international gay pride celebrations held as annual events. In addition to those in the United States, in both large and small cities, there were parades in Mexico, Canada, Australia, New Zealand, South America, and Europe. Tokyo, Japan, had its first parade in 1994, with one thousand participants marching three miles between two commercial areas. Sydney, Australia, boasts the world's largest annual parade, which began in 1978 as a protest against lesbian and gay oppression.

By the late 1990s, Pride marches and festivals had become a major enterprise in large U.S. urban centers, with individuals and organizations spending most of the year planning for the annual event. Pride parades begin in the spring and last throughout the summer and into the fall, although the largest number are clustered during the last weekend in June, in commemoration of the Stonewall Rebellion. Many marches and parades include the bisexual and trangendered communities, as well as allies, friends, and family members, some of whom are members of the organization PFLAG (Parents and Friends of Lesbians and Gays). In many communities, the march or parade is the culmination of a week, or several-day-long series, of events, including dances and other social events; film series and cultural performances; political rallies that highlight civil rights issues and protests against discrimination; and festivals that include music and dancing, arts and crafts fairs, and booths purveying information about community-based organizations and social services. The highlight is the parade itself, complete with floats, marching bands, and politicians and celebrities. What is primarily notable is the fun, festiveness, and pageantry of it all: from drag queens to "dykes on bikes"; people attired in leather or little at all to mainstream lesbian moms and gay dads. Members of organizations and businesses march together, as do people who live in the same neighborhood or who share professions, such as gay and lesbian dentists, lawyers, teachers, or electricians. In all, Pride parades create the largest gathering of lesbian and gay people together in a protected space.

Gay and lesbian parades are often heralded as a commemoration of the gay rights movement.

Themes often pay homage to Stonewall—for example, "Stonewall XX: A Generation of Pride" or "San Francisco to Stonewall: Pride and Protest." Most participants in the parades see them as sources of pride; for some, it is the only time of the year that they are "out." Despite their size and community appeal, media coverage of the parades may be spotty and participant counts inaccurate. Although counterprotests may occur, by the end of th 1990s these had become quite small and inconsequential.

In some cities, exclusively lesbian events, or "Dyke Marches," precede the larger lesbian, gay, bisexual, and trangender marches by a day. In the 1970s and early 1980s, these were often protests against the growing commercialism and pageantry of the larger, inclusive parades and carried a more explicitly political and confrontational message. In the 1990s, Dyke Marches were organized by groups like the Lesbian Avengers as a way of demonstrating lesbian visibility.

## Slogans and Symbols

Slogans—chanted during marches, printed on T-shirts, written on placards and posters held up during demonstrations, and reproduced on buttons and stickers—are a political mainstay, sources of gay and lesbian pride. Slogans are designed to raise consciousness, to provoke reaction, to educate, to assert and build communities, to fight heterosexism and sexism, and sometimes just to have fun. Many slogans reclaim the formerly negative word "dyke," turning it into a self-affirming positive word. Others challenge lesbian invisibility, both within society at large and the gay movement specifically, and heterosexist assumptions. There are also numerous examples of familiar symbols, such as the rainbow, adopted as the symbol of the lesbian, gay, bisexual, transgender, and queer movement; the pink triangle, taken from the Nazi persecution of homosexuals; the red ribbon, in memory of those who have died from AIDS; and the entwined double-women's symbol and the labyris (a double-headed axe) that specifically represent lesbians. Like the marches and parades that they adorn, slogans and symbols respond to contemporary social and political events and debates.

*Akilah Monifa*

### Bibliography

Blasius, Mark, and Shane Phelan, eds. *We Are Everywhere: A Historical Sourcebook of Gay*

# M

*and Lesbian Politics.* New York: Routledge, 1997.

International Association of Lesbian/Gay Pride Co-ordinators, Inc. Web site through Queer Resources Directory: http://www.qrd.com

*See also* Demonstrations and Actions; Lesbian Avengers; Symbols

## Marie Antoinette (1755–1793)

Queen of France (1774–1792). Born an Austrian princess and married in 1770 to the French dauphin, Marie Antoinette was executed for treason during the French Revolution. She died a singularly unpopular queen, a symbol of the threat posed by women who transgressed upon men's sphere and entered public life. Nicknamed "Madame Deficit" and "Austrian wolf" in the popular press and reviled as "perverse" and "immoral" in the bill of indictment against her, she was denounced by the official newspaper, the *Moniteur universel,* as "a bad mother, a debauched spouse." The printed campaign against the queen, disseminated in newspapers and in pornographic political pamphlets, typically interwove political with sexual themes, from corruption to conspiracy, and adultery to incest. The allegation that Marie Antoinette was a tribade—a term commonly used in the eighteenth century to describe women who had sex with other women—proved to be one of the most persistent, and politically damaging, charges.

Rumors of Marie Antoinette's illicit liaisons began shortly after her marriage, fueled by rivalries at court. The queen's disregard for royal etiquette and her taste for private audiences with her "female favorites" at the Petit Trianon, a private retreat on the grounds of Versailles that she had constructed on the model of an Austrian hamlet, did nothing to allay public suspicions. Over the next two decades, rumor convicted Marie Antoinette of betraying both her husband, Louis XVI (1754–1793), and the French people as a whole. Pamphleteers of different political leanings soon took up the charges of adultery that had originated at court. Pamphlets and engravings that represented Marie Antoinette in graphic sexual poses eluded royal censors and played an important role in eroding support for a regime already wracked by political schism and financial woes. Pornography that targeted the queen proliferated during the revolution. In this pornographic literature, Marie Antoinette appeared in the embrace of partners as diverse as the king's brother and his manservant, the queen's ladies in waiting, and the royal dog. In one pamphlet, she managed to copulate with her father while still in her mother's womb. Images such as these cast doubt upon the royal succession, Louis XVI's virility, and the very nature of royalty and served as a staple of revolutionary culture.

The allegation that the queen was a tribade also expressed the considerable anxiety of Enlightenment Europe in general and French revolutionaries in particular over shifting sexual identities and models of sexual difference in the late eighteenth century. At a time when dominant legal and medical opinion defined each sex as attracted exclusively to its opposite, Marie Antoinette's alleged transgression was her insatiable desire for both men and women. Her ability to satisfy her own lust by assuming the "male" prerogative in sex further violated the sexual taboos of the period. The significance of representations of Marie Antoinette as a tribade, then, lie less in their historical plausibility than in their implications for the political and sexual order of late-eighteenth-century France.                    *Elizabeth Colwill*

### Bibliography

Colwill, Elizabeth. "Pass as a Woman, Act Like a Man: Marie Antoinette as Tribade in the French Revolution." In *Homosexuality in Modern France.* Ed. Bryant T. Ragan and Jeffrey Merrick. New York: Oxford University Press, 1996, pp. 54–79.

Hunt, Lynn. *The Family Romance of the French Revolution.* Berkeley: University of California Press, 1992.

———. "Pornography and the French Revolution. In *The Invention of Pornography.* Ed. Lynn Hunt. New York: Zone, 1995, pp. 301–339.

*See also* Erotica and Pornography; France; Tribade

## Marriage Ceremonies

Rituals that solemnize same-sex relationships have been documented in many different historical contexts and cultural settings throughout the world, offering evidence that marriage is a concept as variable as any other associated with sex and gender. Boswell's (1994) research on early Christianity indicates that such rituals may have been common in Greco-Roman and Byzantine cultures. And descriptions of the Harlem Renaissance contain numerous references to lesbian unions, including some cases in which marriage licenses were obtained when one partner posed as a man or had a man apply for the license in her place. But the performance of rituals symbolizing lesbian and gay partnerships—whether they be called "weddings," "commitment ceremonies," "holy unions," "handfastings," or "celebrations"—has become increasingly visible in the United States and other Western countries in recent years, along with a growing demand by lesbians and gay men that they be legally allowed to marry.

At the same time, opinions in the lesbian and gay communities are sharply divided over the importance of marriage ceremonies or legal marriage as civil rights issues. Some argue that marriage as an institution is at the heart of patriarchy and cannot contribute to the liberation of women from constricting gender roles; others claim either that same-sex marriage has revolutionary implications for mainstream culture or that lesbians and gay men have similar aspirations to other citizens and want only the right to have their relationships recognized and supported.

Same-sex wedding ceremonies in America take a variety of forms, depending upon the political and religious inclinations of the couple and their families. Although the Catholic Church and most mainline Protestant denominations refuse to recognize such unions as equivalent to heterosexual marriage and enjoin their clergy from officiating, ceremonies drawing on virtually all religious traditions occur. The pioneer in this area was the predominantly gay Metropolitan Community Church, founded by the Reverend Troy Perry in 1968, which, since the early 1970s, has performed rituals it calls "holy unions" for both female and male couples. Some of the more liberal Protestant churches, such as the Unitarian-Universalist and the United Church of Christ, also perform same-sex weddings or commitment ceremonies, as do the Reform and Reconstructionist movements in Judaism. Individual clergy and congregations in other denominations have also shown support for same-sex marriage, though these activities have sparked sharp debate among these groups and, in some cases, have led to the expulsion of particular clergy or churches from national or regional denominational organizations; conflict over this issue has been particularly intense in recent years among Presbyterians, Lutherans, Episcopalians, and Baptists. Same-sex ceremonies, particularly among lesbians, sometimes draw on alternative religious or spiritual movements, such as Wicca, goddess worship, Buddhist or other Eastern traditions, or Native American rituals, and many ceremonies are eclectic in their choice of spiritual elements or in the balance they establish between religious and secular dimensions.

At the same time that lesbian and gay couples are choosing to solemnize their relationships without benefit of legal recognition, the issue of legal marriage for same-sex couples has become a prominent element of the civil rights agenda of the 1990s. At national gay and lesbian rights marches in Washington, D.C., in both 1987 and 1993, a massive wedding was held outside the headquarters of the Internal Revenue Service, symbolizing the exclusion of gay people from the many layers of financial and legal benefits accorded to married heterosexuals. A number of legal challenges to the prohibition of same-sex marriage have been lodged over the years, with the most significant one to date resulting in a 1993 ruling by the Hawai'i State Supreme Court that limiting marriage to opposite-sex couples appeared to constitute gender discrimination. The Supreme Court returned the case, *Baehr v. Lewin,* brought by one lesbian and two gay male couples, to a lower court, saying that only if the court could demonstrate a compelling state interest against same-sex marriage would it prohibit it in the future. While no final determination in this case had been reached by mid-1999, and progress had stalled in the wake of a determined campaign against same-sex marriage, in anticipation of an outcome favorable to same-sex couples, many states have drafted legislation denying recognition of same-sex marriages performed in other states. It was expected that legalization of same-sex marriage in any state would lead to protracted legal action around the country, as couples married there sought to have their unions recognized by other states and by the federal government.

*Ellen Lewin*

### Bibliography

Ayers, Tess, and Paul Brown. *The Essential Guide to Lesbian and Gay Weddings*. San Francisco: HarperCollins, 1994.

Boswell, John. *Same-Sex Unions in Premodern Europe*. New York: Villard, 1994.

Butler, Becky, ed. *Ceremonies of the Heart*. Seattle: Seal, 1990.

Lewin, Ellen. *Recognizing Ourselves: Ceremonies of Lesbian and Gay Commitment*. New York: Columbia University Press, 1998.

Sherman, Suzanne, ed. *Lesbian and Gay Marriage*. Philadelphia: Temple University Press, 1992.

***See also*** Domestic Partnership; Hawai'i

## Martin, Del (1921–) and
## Lyon, Phyllis (1924–)

American activists and writers. Del Martin was born in San Francisco; Phyllis Lyon, in Tulsa, Oklahoma. Both women studied journalism, Lyon at the University of California, Berkeley, and Martin at San Francisco State College. Each faced heavy gender discrimination trying to pursue a journalism career in the 1950s. Meeting on their jobs at a Seattle trade-journal publishing company in 1949, Martin and Lyon fell in love. In 1953, they moved to San Francisco, California, and began living together, dating their commitment from Valentine's Day. The couple "knew practically nothing about homosexuality," and what little they found in the library branded lesbians as sick. Martin had even considered suicide when she discovered, during her brief prior marriage, that she was attracted to women. Their first year was stormy. Lyon was still dating an old boyfriend; Martin's young daughter spent their honeymoon with them; and they knew no other lesbians. However, their love endured and provided the foundation for decades of visible lesbian activist leadership.

After setting up house together, they found it extremely difficult to connect with other lesbians. When they went to lesbian bars, the only social outlet at the time, they were too shy to speak to the women there. When one of their few lesbian acquaintances invited them to help start a lesbian social club, Martin and Lyon jumped at the chance, founding Daughters of Bilitis (DOB) in 1955 with eight members.

"The fifteen years that followed were to be rich ones," they wrote in *Lesbian/Woman* (1972). Martin and Lyon devoted long hours to the organization, which "put us in touch with countless lesbians around the world." In the process, the couple strengthened their own self-definition and pride. They met individually at the DOB office with hundreds of lesbians, many of whose stories found their way into Martin and Lyon's first book, *Lesbian/Woman*.

The couple became pioneering "out" lesbians in the American media and on the college and religious lecture circuit. DOB grew to become a national organization with chapters in other large cities. Its magazine, *The Ladder*, was virtually the only resource for lesbians through the 1960s. Lyon edited *The Ladder* from 1956 to 1960; Martin, from 1960 to 1962.

Martin and Lyon wrote in *The Lesbian Path* (1980) that they believed that "the church was at the core of all our problems" gaining acceptance in mainstream society. Consequently, they pushed for dialogue with religious leaders, even if it meant a reverend coming to DOB's national convention and declaring homosexuality a sin. Their work led the couple to join with other activists and clergy to found the Council on Religion and the Homosexual in 1964. The organization became a vehicle for attempts to increase acceptance for gay people within organized religion.

Martin and Lyon published *Lesbian/Woman* in 1972. It was one of the earliest affirming nonfiction books on lesbians, passed around eagerly from coast to coast, and served as a primer for women coming out in the ensuing years. Their second collaboration, *Lesbian Love and Liberation*, was published in 1973.

In 1972, Martin and Lyon were among the founders of the Alice B. Toklas Memorial Democratic Club, a pioneering organization set up to endorse, campaign for, and elect pro-gay Democrats to office.

Lyon went on to earn a Ph.D. in human sexuality in 1976, helping found, and later serving as professor and registrar at, the Institute for Advanced Study of Sexuality in San Francisco (1976–1987). Martin wrote *Battered Wives* (1976), the first nonacademic book on the subject.

Indefatigable activists, they founded and served as leaders of dozens of organizations and have been members of many more. They also took posts on government commissions and task forces. Among them, Martin cofounded the Lesbian Mothers' Union (1971) and the San Francisco battered women's shelter La Casa de Las Madres (1976). She chaired the San Francisco Commission on the Status of Women (1976–1977) and served on the national board of the National Organization for Women (NOW). Lyon cofounded and served on the board of Citizens Alert, a coalition of ethnic minorities and gays dealing with police harassment and brutality (1965–1972), cofounded the National Sex Forum (1968), and served on the San Francisco Human Rights Commission (1976–1987), chairing it in 1982–1983.

A lesbian health clinic in San Francisco was named in their honor. Both women received numerous awards for their writing and activism. In 1978, the San Francisco Board of Supervisors issued a Certificate of Appreciation commemorating their twenty-fifth anniversary. About that occasion, they wrote: " 'The integration of the homosexual into so-

*Del Martin, left, and Phyllis Lyon. Photo by Ruth Mountaingrove.*

ciety' had been an early—and seemingly impossible—goal of the Daughters of Bilitis. We are proud to have played a role in making the impossible possible" (Martin and Lyon, 1980).     *Judy MacLean*

### Bibliography

Jurgens, Jane. "Del Martin." In *Gay and Lesbian Literature*. Ed. Sharon Malinowski. Detroit: St. James, 1994, p. 249.

Martin, Del, and Phyllis Lyon. "Anniversary." In *The Lesbian Path*. Ed. Margaret Cruikshank. Monterey, Calif.: Angel, 1980.

———. "Reminiscences of Two Female Homophiles." In *Our Right to Love*. Ed. Ginny Vida. Englewood Cliffs, N.J.: Prentice-Hall, 1978. Rev. ed. New York: Simon and Schuster, 1996.

**See also** Daughters of Bilitis; *Ladder, The;* National Organization for Women (NOW); San Francisco, California

## Masturbation

The production of sexual excitement through self-stimulation. In the Euro-American context, masturbation has traditionally been viewed as a narcissistic and socially useless erotic indulgence. During the eighteenth-century Enlightenment, polemics against the practice took on a focused sense of alarm, casting it as a pernicious danger of near-epidemic proportions. The anonymously published compendium *Onania or the Heinous Sin of Self-Pollution* (1723), which appeared in England in the early part of the eighteenth century, detailed dozens of stories of addictive masturbation and the woes it was said to bring. Later in the century, the Swiss physician Samuel Tissot's *L'Onanisme* (1760) became the first medical tract to deal extensively with the ailments caused by masturbation.

By the nineteenth century, the campaign against masturbation in both Europe and the United States had intensified. Writings against masturbation in this period straddled the line between public health and pornography, identifying and even inciting sexual desire in order to manage and control it. Accounts linked masturbation to a long list of physical and psychological problems, including consumption, insanity, sterility, and death. It was also held to erode the moral faculties and undermine the will, resulting in addiction to sexual vice. Antimasturbation tracts proclaimed that indulgence in "the solitary vice" made one averse to matrimony. The

**M** dominant conception of heredity resulted in a belief that chronic onanists could transmit these weaknesses to their offspring.

Masturbation was directly associated with homosexuality, as the idea that masturbation created aversion to marriage evolved into the popular belief that masturbation caused homosexuality. Homosexual exchange was viewed not only as an effect of masturbation, but also as its cause. In nineteenth-century polemics, the habit of masturbation was often seen to originate in homosocial contexts, especially the single-sex boarding school or college. The line between self-titillation and homosexuality in these accounts was blurry. The medical model of the homosexual, which became visible at the end of the nineteenth century, incorporated many of the characteristics of the addictive onanist.

The question of women's masturbatory practices fascinated late-nineteenth-century sexologists. Particularly intriguing were the use of dildoes and other insertive objects and the belief that many women had perfected the art of masturbation to the point that they did not need to touch themselves in any way. These fixations reflect an anxiety that female masturbation was taking place outside masculine knowledge and control.

In the twentieth century, medical prohibitions against masturbation eroded, and the practice was increasingly seen by medical and psychological professionals as normal and healthy. During the sexual and women's liberation movements of the 1960s and 1970s, masturbation was endorsed as a vehicle for women's erotic self-exploration. Women were encouraged to take charge of their own sexual pleasure and to become familiar with their bodies through masturbation. However, the stigma against the practice never fully disappeared; in 1994, the surgeon general of the United States, Dr. Jocelyn Elders (1933–), was forced to resign after a scandal erupted over her statement that children should be taught that masturbation is not unhealthy.    *Dana Luciano*

### Bibliography

Anonymous. *Onania, or; The Heinous Sin of Self-Pollution*. London: 1723. New York: Garland, 1986.

Bennett, Paula, and Vernon Rosario. *Solitary Pleasures: The Historical, Literary, and Artistic Discourses of Autoeroticism*. New York: Routledge, 1995.

Bullough, Vern L., and Bonnie Bullough. "The Secret Sin." In *Sin, Sickness, and Sanity: A History of Sexual Attitudes*. New York: Garland, 1977, pp. 55–73.

Dodson, Betty. *Liberating Masturbation: A Meditation on Self-Love*. New York: Dodson, 1974.

Ellis, Havelock. *Studies in the Psychology of Sex*. Philadelphia: F.A. Davis, 1900–1928.

*See also* Sex Toys; Sexology

### McCullers, Carson (1917–1967)

American novelist and playwright. McCullers was born Lula Carson Smith in Columbus, Georgia. After attending Columbia University and New York University, both in New York City, between 1935 and 1937, she married Reeves McCullers in 1937. They divorced in 1940 but remarried in 1945; their marriage ended when Reeves committed suicide in 1953. The relationship proved to be an unusual one, as both Reeves and Carson were attracted to members of their own sex. Carson was rumored to have been involved with Greta Garbo (1905–1990), Katherine Ann Porter (1890–1980), and Gypsy Rose Lee (1914–1970).

Carson McCullers burst on the American literary scene with her first novel, *The Heart Is a Lonely Hunter* (1940). In this work, along with the theme of racial prejudice, McCullers explores the love Singer feels for his hospitalized friend, Antonapoulos. When Singer kills himself after his friend's death, his action is incomprehensible to the other characters, who are unable to understand the life these two have shared together. *Reflections in a Golden Eye* (1941) is a less subtle treatment of homosexuality, focusing on the sexual obsession an Army captain feels for an enlisted man. *The Ballad of the Sad Cafe* (a novella serialized in 1943) recounts androgynous Amelia's love for her cousin Lymon, a dwarf, and the cafe she opens to provide their town with a healing center. In *The Member of the Wedding* (1946), McCullers creates one of her more memorable characters in Frankie Addams, an adolescent whose fluid gender and sexual identity is finally vanquished by the culture's demands that she mature into a proper young white woman. Finally, in *Clock Without Hands* (1961), the grandson of a bigoted, homophobic Southern congressman falls in love with his grandfather's secretary, a mixed-race man. In all of McCullers's works, the themes focus on how issues of race, gender, and sexuality are utilized by society to isolate and alienate individuals from one another.

McCullers received some criticism for the grotesqueness or freakishness of many of her characters. While some of these characteristics are due to her writing in Southern Gothic traditions, some seem due to her ambiguous sexuality and her own physical ailments. She was stricken early in her life with rheumatic fever anemia, pleurisy, and other respiratory illnesses. Following three strokes, McCullers was partly paralyzed before she was thirty. Nonetheless, those who inhabit her literary worlds are not abnormal. She once wrote: "Nature is not abnormal, only lifelessness is abnormal. Anything that pulses and moves and walks around the room, no matter what thing it is doing, is natural and human to the writer." McCullers, in both life and art, strove to invert the normalized categories that govern social ideals of gender, sexuality, and love.

Linnea A. Stenson

## Bibliography

Carr, Virginia Spencer. *The Lonely Hunter: A Biography of Carson McCullers*. Garden City, N.Y.: Doubleday, 1975.

———. *Understanding Carson McCullers*. Columbia: University of South Carolina Press, 1990.

*See also* American Literature, Twentieth Century; Garbo, Greta

## Medicine

Research on the experiences of lesbians in medical school began to emerge in the 1990s. One scholar in this area, Cathy Risdon, has argued that "there needs to be some institutional [acknowledgment] that there are gay and lesbian medical students" (Robb, October 1996). While improving the social climate for lesbian and gay medical students is the focus for some, others, such as Dr. Gary Gibson, a professor of family medicine at the University of Western Ontario, have proposed curriculum changes that would ensure more thorough coverage of lesbian health issues during medical training.

Many medical schools have begun gay and lesbian students' associations. These organizations may account for the tolerance, acceptance, and understanding that, according to a 1994 survey by the Gay and Lesbian Medical Association (GLMA), many say existed during their medical training. In their 1996 study of lesbian and gay medical students and residents, the *Canadian Medical Association*

*Journal* found that a small but outspoken cluster of homophobic voices was present at their schools. Reported were gay-bashing jokes and nonverbal homophobic gestures, such as the limp-wrist portrayal suggesting a gay man (Robb, October 1996).

A particularly difficult area for lesbian medical students is the mentoring system, which is important in medical training. Mentoring thrives on the development of close relationships between residents and staff physicians. It is through this relationship that the latter socialize a doctor-in-training into the larger profession. Yet lesbians can be at a distinct disadvantage in such a system. If she perceives that the atmosphere is homophobic, a lesbian resident is unlikely to reveal personal information about herself. This weakens the relationship and, therefore, the training and networking.

In particular, heterosexist assumptions have created difficulties for lesbian residents with their mentors. For example, one woman noted that her mentors had advised her to develop stronger relationships outside work (Robb, October 1996). They gave this advice based on the observations that she did not have male escorts at social functions and that they knew little of her outside life. When she explained that her social network was wonderful, one male mentor urged her to be honest with herself. Ultimately, this resident had a male friend posture as her boyfriend for professional functions. She received greater acceptance after that.

Finding adequate mentors for lesbian medical students can be problematic because of structural homophobia and heterosexism. Finding lesbian, or even lesbian-friendly, mentors, is often difficult because many remain closeted. This closeted stance is understandable. Results of the 1994 GLMA study revealed that 59 percent of its U.S. members reported that they, personally, had experienced job-related discrimination because of their sexuality. Despite this reporting of discrimination, Dr. Jill Tinmouth of Toronto, Ontario, and a member-at-large of GLMA, has urged lesbian and gay physicians to come out to serve as resources for colleagues and students (Robb, October 1996). She also argues that being "out" is generally healthier for lesbian physicians, since the price paid in terms of active discrimination may be outweighed by the price paid by remaining in the closet.

Besides the changing social climate at medical schools, some schools are addressing curriculum issues. For example, in 1996 the Canadian Medical Association endorsed a gay and lesbian curriculum

**M** for postgraduate family medicine created by Gibson, who has noted that most family medicine departments do not have any structured segment on lesbian and gay health, except during discussions of HIV (Robinson and Cohen, 1996). Moreover, most information addresses gay men's issues, with far less coverage of lesbian health issues. Addressing sexuality only in relation to illness and disease is likely to stigmatize and ostracize lesbian and gay doctors in training and patients. Studies have shown that physicians have witnessed colleagues cut back on treatment, give inappropriate care, and, occasionally, refuse treatment all together upon discovery of a client's lesbian or gay identification.

Overall, homosexuality is discussed very little during medical training. Results of a 1991 survey of all U.S. medical schools showed that the mean amount of time during which homosexuality was discussed was three hours and twenty-six minutes (Wallick et al., 1992). Differences existed across geographic regions, with the western region mean at five hours and fifty-six minutes. Of those that did cover homosexuality, the most frequent style of education involved lectures during a human sexuality sequence. Panel presentations and meetings with gay and lesbian health professionals and potential patients followed this strategy distantly. Of the eighty-two responding schools, eight reported that the topic of homosexuality was wholly absent; one reported that it covered the topic only during discussions of HIV; twelve others said they taught or mentioned it during discussions of AIDS. Largely, many agree that much anxiety surrounds sex and sexuality discussions during medical school training.

Organizations have arisen to help address these issues. The GLMA, founded in 1981, is one of several professional associations that dedicates itself to combating homophobia in the medical profession and in society. It also promotes the best possible health care for lesbian and gay patients. Nearly half of the member are women and physicians of color, and the group offers an annual conference on "Women in Medicine." It also sponsors the Lesbian Health Fund, which provides grants for medical research on lesbian health issues and education of health workers about health needs of lesbians. It also educates lesbians regarding early diagnosis procedures for health problems and addresses the manner in which lesbian and gay health is taught in medical school. Four other professional associations are the Southern Ontario Gay and Lesbian Association of Doctors (SOGLAD); the Gay and Lesbian Association of Doctors and Dentists (GLADD); Lesbian, Gay, Bisexual People in Medicine (LGBPM); and the National Lesbian and Gay Health Association (NLGHA)—all based in the United States.                              *Christy M. Ponticelli*

### Bibliography

O'Hanlan, Katherine A. "Lesbian Health and Homophobia: Perspectives for the Treating Obstetrician/Gynecologist." *Current Problems in Obstetrics, Gynecology, and Fertility* 18:4 (1995), 97–127.

Robb, Nancy. "Fear of Ostracism Still Silences Some Gay MDs, Students." *Canadian Medical Association Journal* 155:7 (October 1, 1996), 972–977.

———. "Medical Schools Seek to Overcome 'Invisibility' of Gay Patients, Gay Issues in Curriculum." *Canadian Medical Association Journal* 155:6 (September 15, 1996), 765–770.

Robinson, Gregory, and Mary Cohen. "Gay, Lesbian, and Bisexual Health Care Issues and Medical Curriculum." *Canadian Medical Association Journal* 155:6 (September 15, 1996), 709–711.

Wallick, Mollie M., Karl M. Cambre, and Mark H. Townsend. "How the Topic of Homosexuality Is Taught at U.S. Medical Schools." *Academic Medicine* 67:9 (September 1992), 601–603.

*See also* Health; Nursing; Psychiatry

### *Mestizaje*

A Spanish word meaning racial/cultural hybridity. The cultural construction of *mestizaje* was critical to the formation of collective identities in Latin America. Unlike the ideologies of racial purity embodied in the English word "miscegenation," the discourse of *mestizaje* celebrates the mixture of races and the birth of a new, racially mixed body— "*la mestiza/el mestizo.*" *Mestizaje* refers to the cultural and racial fusion of native, European, Asian, and African peoples that began with the Spanish conquest of the Americas in 1521. This cultural and racial mixture began in the context of conquest, and, as such, it was forced upon the native inhabitants of the Americas against their will. The original "mixing" is the direct outcome of a violent and sexual confrontation between colonizer and colonized, in particular between the Spanish men who came to conquer and the native women who bore their children.

In Latin America, both elites and popular movements have at various times embraced ideologies that regard *mestizaje* as a positive outcome of conquest. The central philosophical text that developed and popularized the celebratory discourse of *mestizaje* is José Vasconcelos's *La raza cósmica* (The Cosmic Race [1925]). Vasconcelos posited the emergence of a fifth race in Latin America, "the cosmic race," envisaged as a synthesis of the best aspects of all of the world's races. Although fraught with Social Darwinism and psuedoscientific ideologies of race, *La raza cósmica's* challenge to notions of racial purity and its importance to the formation of collective ethnoracial identities make Vasconcelos's text a critical starting point for discussions of Latino/a racialization.

In *Borderlands/La Frontera: The New Mestiza* (1987), Chicana queer theorist Gloria Anzaldúa (1942–) reworks Vasconcelos's concept of genetic *mestizaje,* positing a "new *mestiza*" defined not by genes but by positionality, by the psychic and cultural spaces she occupies. Anzaldúa sets up the conflict: "The coming together of two self-consistent but habitually incompatible frames of reference causes *un choque,* a cultural collision." Anzaldúa describes the collision as a space that creates "ambivalence," "internal strife," and "psychic restlessness," yet the ambiguity of the space opens up the possibility of a "*mestiza* consciousness," a consciousness that challenges binaries. Anzaldúa writes: "The new *mestiza* copes by developing a tolerance for contradictions, a tolerance for ambiguity. She learns to be an Indian in Mexican culture, to be a Mexican from an Anglo point of view. She learns to juggle cultures." This juggling act becomes part of the repertoire of an increasing number of queer and diasporic peoples in late capitalist social formations.

Identification with *mestizaje* informs much Latina/Chicana lesbian writing, both literary and theoretical. Because the site of *mestizaje* embodies ambiguity, it becomes an important theoretical framework for the multiple and contradictory subject positions of the Latina/Chicana lesbian, who is often forced to reconcile her ethnoracial identity with her lesbianism. In a society in which Latina identity is often coded as heterosexual, and lesbian identity is often coded as white, the Latina lesbian can utilize "*mestiza* consciousness" to navigate the spaces between these codings and to challenge her exclusion.                              *Luz Calvo*

## Bibliography

Anzaldúa, Gloria. *Borderlands/La Frontera: The New Mestiza.* San Francisco: Aunt Lute, 1987.

Perez, Emma. "Sexuality and Discourse: Notes from a Chicana Survivor." In *Chicana Lesbians: The Girls Our Mothers Warned Us About.* Ed. Carla Trujillo. Berkeley: Third Woman, 1991, pp. 159–184.

Raiskin, Judith. "Inverts and Hybrids: Lesbian Rewritings of Sexual and Racial Identities." In *The Lesbian Postmodern.* Ed. Laura Doan. New York: Columbia University Press, 1994, pp. 156–172.

Vasconcelos, José. *La raza cósmica: misíon de la raza iberoamericano.* Mexico City: Espasa-Calpe, S.A., 1982.

**See also** Anzaldúa, Gloria, E.; Latina Literature; Latinas

## Mew, Charlotte (1869–1928)

English author of poetry, short stories, essays, and plays. In 1924, Virginia Woolf (1882–1941) told Vita Sackville-West (1892–1962) that Charlotte Mew was "the greatest living poetess." Thomas Hardy (1840–1928) agreed, predicting she would still be read "when others are forgotten." Mew's work appeared between 1894 and 1914 in major periodicals, including the *Nation, Athenaeum, Academy, Englishwoman, New Statesman,* and the infamous *Yellow Book,* a provocative 1890s periodical associated with Oscar Wilde (1854–1900). Harold and Alida Monro's Poetry Bookshop published *The Farmer's Bride* (1916, 1921) and *The Rambling Sailor* (1929). Yet, despite her literary success, Mew was isolated and unhappy. She killed herself at age fifty-nine.

Mew's life was full of intense attachments to other women, including her sister Anne, whose death from cancer in 1927 precipitated Mew's decline and suicide. As a schoolgirl, Mew had a crush on her headmistress, the suffragist Lucy Harrison (1844–1915), who fell in love with another teacher and moved with her to Yorkshire. Mew evidently fell in love with Ella D'Arcy (1856/1857?–1937?), another *Yellow Book* contributor, whom she visited in France in 1902, but that love, too, was unrequited. In 1914, she apparently made a sexual overture to a friend, novelist May Sinclair (1863–1946), who rebuffed and subsequently lampooned her. In her final years, Mew grew close to Kate Cockerell (1872–1949), who received her last letter.

*Charlotte Mew. Photograph from* The Bookman. *By courtesy of the National Portrait Gallery, London.*

Mew's friends described her as masculine in her clothing, voice, and demeanor and defiant in her self-presentation. They remarked upon her "double personality" and her obsessive concern for appearances. She was rumored to have several trunks full of unpublished poems, which she used for lighting cigarettes. Mew was probably struggling with prohibited lesbian feelings. Her work shows strong evidence of love for women, sexual frustration, and a sense of being an outcast. Persistent images include closets, keys, "fallen women," intimate bed scenes, and being buried alive. The natural landscape is characteristically rendered in sensual female imagery. Dramatic monologues with male speakers ("The Farmer's Bride" 1912) and Fête love poetry with "I/thou" constructions ("Fin de Fete" 1923) or ambiguous gender references ("The Forest Road" 1916) are prevalent. In its appreciation of erotic female beauty and its renunciatory aesthetic, Mew's work has been said to resemble that of Christina Rossetti (1830–1894). *Kathleen Hickok*

### Bibliography

Fitzgerald, Penelope. *Charlotte Mew and Her Friends*. London: Collins, 1984. New York: Addison-Wesley, 1988.

Leighton, Angela. *Victorian Women Poets: Writing Against the Heart*. Hemel Hempstead, England: Harvester Wheatsheaf, 1992. Charlottesville, Va.: University Press of Virginia, 1992, pp. 266–298.

*See also* English Literature, Twentieth Century; Poetry; Sackville-West, Vita; Woolf, Virginia

## Mexico

Country in North America situated between the United States to the north and Central America to the south. Lesbian life in Mexico is constrained by a culture that rigidly controls sexuality through silence. Homosexuality can be tolerated as an unavoidable individual sin, as long as it is discreet and does not confront dominant norms and beliefs. In this context, lesbians have lived, for the most part of their concealed history, married to men or "keeping company" with each other, without social spaces or economic options to live their emotional and sexual lives openly.

### History

Little research has been done into the varieties of same-sex affection among women or behaviors that transgressed gender norms. The life and writing of the seventeenth-century nun Sor Juana Inés de la Cruz (1648–1695) have been a rich source of speculation about homoeroticism among women in colonial Mexico. Other possibilities may lie in the cross-dressing *soldaderas* (female soldiers) who fought during Mexico's wars of independence. Although ostensibly heterosexual, their similarity to passing women in other countries does at least raise interesting questions.

In more recent times, bohemian and artistic circles provide some evidence of lesbianism and female bisexuality. The famous artist Frida Kahlo (1907–1954), for example, exhibited both gender transgression and love for other women in her life and her paintings. The late 1940s and 1950s were years of splendor for Mexican popular culture, which was exported to all of Latin America. The most famous women singers, such as Chavela Vargas (1919–), interpreted passionate love songs (written by male lyricists) that were dedicated to other women. This practice did not necessarily elicit suspicion of "irregularity," although it is not known for sure to what extent closeted lesbians may have found personal validation in listening to these performances. By the late 1960s, however, these songs began to be heard in the context of a counterculture that began to challenge the rigid gender system that had rendered lesbians unimaginable, and, accordingly, the lyrics began to be modified.

## The Emerging Lesbian Movement

Lesbianism was publicly acknowledged for the first time by the Mexican press in regard to the United Nations' first International Women's Year Conference, held in Mexico City in 1975. The press portrayed it as an imported extravagance, completely alien to Mexican women and to the legitimate interests of Third World women. As a leading editorialist in *Excelsior*, the newspaper with the largest circulation in Mexico and a reputation for progressive social politics, wrote: "What are the lesbians doing here? What can they ask for? Do they want to inscribe their pathological irregularity in the Charter of Human Rights? Are they claiming the pathetic 'right' to boast about their sexual aberration? This unawareness of their illness just proves how severe these clinical cases are. . . . They have discredited this Conference and distorted the true purposes of woman's emancipation."

Although in 1971 an underground lesbian community had started to read and write about Mexican law and sexual liberation, its members did not feel prepared to challenge the media. The groups primarily engaged in informing journalists, intellectuals, and psychologists and psychiatrists in private sessions about the seriousness of social discrimination against lesbians and gay men.

The late 1970s in Mexico was a period of rising social expectations, caused by a brief period of apparent economic affluence, fueled by the oil boom, and state-led political reform. During this time, a lesbian and gay movement emerged, preceded by the feminist movement, which had begun to organize earlier in the decade. One of the particular characteristics of social movements in Latin America is that they tend to look to the political Left and socialism for their ideas, language, and goals. Accordingly, the emerging lesbian and gay movement endorsed the general demands of the Left, while also raising the cry for sexual freedom. In 1978, a small contingent of lesbians and gay men joined a major demonstration against political repression. They were viewed uneasily by some left-wing groups who represented themselves through the attributes of "virility" (manliness) and uncritically endorsed procreation and domesticity for women.

In the early years of the movement, lesbians rarely claimed specific rights, but instead stated their goal as the end of exploitation and "sexual misery" of the whole population. Concepts familiar to other lesbian movements, such as "identity politics" or "alternative lifestyles," were rarely advanced. At best, sexual liberation in the late 1970s in Mexico was mistaken as a sexological enterprise, which would provide assistance to those who wished to engage in "peculiar" sexual activities. Although some groups strongly opposed sexology, sexological language did open up spaces for a new understanding of sexuality. The First World Sexology Congress was held in Mexico City in 1979 at the National Medical Center. A group of lesbians brought a statement to the forum that criticized sexology because it tried "to obscure the subversive potential of sexual dissidence." Instead, they argued, "[c]oming out as lesbians means shedding prescribed guilt and assigned shame; it means renouncing an imposed clandestinity and a silent complicity with institutionalized repression."

This statement reflects the influence of feminism, with its radical critique of sexual oppression, upon lesbians. It was through the feminist challenge of the arbitrary gender-role system that lesbian feminists also questioned heterosexual feminists' fear of discussing lesbianism. A main focus of the feminist movement was the development of what was termed a "voluntary motherhood" campaign for reproductive freedom. Lesbian feminists argued that reproductive freedom could not exist without a full range of sexual options. As a result, some feminist groups attempted to create distance from the lesbian organization to avoid being stigmatized. Unwelcome in feminist groups, many lesbians tried, instead, to work within gay male organizations.

In the early 1980s, a number of factors, including economic crisis, defeat of abortion rights, and the rise of a political right wing, led to a temporary demobilization of the feminist movement, including lesbian feminist groups. In particular, the worsening of economic conditions made it increasingly difficult for lesbians to gain the economic independence needed to live openly as lesbians. Many had to return to their families for survival, while others had to work longer hours, thus making it more difficult to maintain political activism. Some of the most visible lesbian groups in Mexico City dispersed or merged with others. These new organizations carried on some of the projects of the lesbian feminist movement, such as the annual celebration of Lesbian and Gay Cultural Week. By the mid-1980s, the continuing economic crisis propelled many women into street demonstrations, union organizing, and electoral politics. This new grass-roots constituency, as well as the emergence of feminism in other Latin American countries, revitalized the feminist movement.

In 1987, the First Regional Lesbian Encuentro (conference) was held in Mexico. By the end of the same year, the National Coalition of Lesbian Feminists was organized. In 1990, the right to a "free sexual option" became one of the three central issues of the Mexico City Feminist Coalition agenda (Coordinadora Feminista del Distrito Federal), along with opposition to domestic violence and voluntary motherhood.

## Contemporary Mexico

In the 1990s, lesbians gained some greater visibility in Mexico even as they continued to face many of the same problems and dilemmas. A number of prominent literary figures published explicit lesbian texts, including playwright, novelist, and actress Sabina Berman (1955–) and poet, playwright, and theater director Nancy Cárdenas (1934–1994). In 1989, Rosamaría Roffiel (1945–) had published *Amora* (Love in feminine), an autobiographical novel dedicated to all women who love women, while Sara Levi Calderon's (1942–) *Dos Mujeres* (Two Women), a love story between two upper-class Jewish women, caused controversy when published in Mexico in 1990; it was translated and published in the United States a year later.

In 1991, the Thirteenth Annual Conference of the International Lesbian and Gay Association (ILGA) was scheduled to be held in Guadalajara, the first time in a developing nation. However, due to the joint effort of the local authorities and the Catholic Church, a campaign of harassment and intimidation forced the organizers to move the conference to the city of Acapulco, where a "tourist" culture was seen as the appropriate "space" for that kind of meeting.

Lesbian activists in the 1990s kept close connections with different U.N. conferences. On the one hand, these events permitted lesbians to network and advance their platform on sexual rights. On the other hand, they were sober reminders of the different kinds of violence and discrimination that lesbians face around the world. Moreover, these international events focused the tensions that still exist between mainstream feminism and lesbian feminist groups. The former continued to marginalize lesbians in order to advance what was considered a "negotiable" feminist agenda. Hence, two major challenges for lesbians in Mexico are to explore the meaning of compromising lesbian visibility for the future of the women's movement, and to link the lesbian movement's agenda to the debates on the construction of democracy in the country. Ultimately, lesbian visibility in Mexico can only be understood as an integral part of a broader struggle toward the creation of a new political culture that includes all people and of the conditions that enable all women's economic empowerment and self-determination.

*Claudia Hinojosa*

## Bibliography

Schaefer, Claudia. *Danger Zones: Homosexuality, National Identity, and Mexican Culutre.* Tucson: University of Arizona Press, 1996.

*See also* Encuentros de Lesbianas; International Organizations; Juana Inés de la Cruz, Sor; Kahlo, Frida; Latin American Literature; Passing Women; Vargas, Chavela

## Michel, Louise (1830–1905)

French revolutionary anarchist associated with the Paris Commune of 1870–1871. Questions concerning Louise Michel's sexual identity were first posed by the military tribunal investigating the uprising, which concluded that her revolutionary ardor stemmed from her passion for fellow Communard Théophile Ferré.

Michel's public denials of such feelings spawned new rumors. Charges of lesbianism arose during her New Caledonian exile and focused on her relationship with fellow anarchist and communard Natalie Lemel (1827–1921). From this time, Michel's dossier at police archives alleged that she had "tastes against nature." Later police reports seized on her relationship with socialist activist Paule Minck (1839–1901).

Although the inquiry into Michel's private life was originally begun by her detractors, her life also became the focus of researchers in the emerging sexology movement of the late nineteenth century. One of the first biographies of Michel appeared in the 1905 *Jahrbuch für sexuelle Zwischenstufen* (Yearbook for Intermediate Sexual Types), the official journal of Magnus Hirschfeld's (1859–1939) Scientific Humanitarian Committee, usually credited with being one of the earliest gay liberation organizations. The entry, by German doctor Karl von

Levetzow, is instructive for what it reveals about the biases of early sex researchers, all of whom linked masculine traits and homosexuality in women. Thus, von Levetzow highlighted Michel's virile appearance, her lack of interest in clothes, her youthful preference for tomboyish pastimes, her militaristic revolutionary activities, her failure to marry, and her apparent dislike for men. Von Levetzow's findings about Michel were later repeated by Havelock Ellis (1859–1939), whose *Sexual Inversion* (1936) long remained one of the most influential treatises on the subject to appear in English.

The debate over Michel's sexuality was continued by her friends, notably anarchist Emma Goldman (1869–1940), who penned an impassioned rebuttal to Hirschfeld. Most subsequent biographers have carefully skirted the controversy, choosing either to emphasize her passion for Ferre or, more commonly, to highlight the asexual, saintly, and ascetic nature of the legendary "Red Virgin." Michel's historiographical treatment is most instructive for what it reveals about historical social attitudes toward women as private and public beings and about the way biographers have dealt with those attitudes.

*Marie Marmo Mullaney*

### Bibliography

Ellis, Havelock. *Sexual Inversion*. New York: Random House, 1936.

Hirschfeld, Magnus. *Sexual Anomalies*. New York: Emerson, 1948.

Mullaney, Marie Marmo. "Sexual Politics in the Career and Legend of Louise Michel." *Signs: Journal of Women in Culture and Society* 15:2 (1990), 300–322.

Thomas, Edith. *Louise Michel*. Trans. Penelope Williams. Montreal: Black Rose, 1980.

*See also* France; Goldman, Emma

## Middle Ages, European

Period of European history conventionally dated from the fall of the Roman Empire in A.D. 476 to the emergence of the early-modern period. The end of the Middle Ages varies greatly from country to country (the late fourteenth century in Italy to the early sixteenth century in France, England, and Spain, for example). The greatest challenges posed by any discussion of lesbians in the medieval period are that the discourses of that era—be they legal, theological, medical, or literary—had not themselves come to terms with how a "lesbian" might be defined and that few personal records attesting to affective and/or sexual relationships between women exist. Indeed, the noun "lesbian" with its modern meaning had not yet entered the vernacular. However, if no familiar term existed for a woman who had a sexual and emotional relationship with another woman, medieval society was well aware of the "lesbian," and it was not entirely devoid of women who might be considered "lesbians."

### Theological Writings

Most medieval ecclesiastic writers took their lead from Saint Paul's (d. ca. A.D. 67) condemnation of the vices of Roman women, who "did change the natural use into that which is against nature" (Romans 1:26). This epithet "against nature" becomes typically associated with the sin of sodomy (a sin broadly construed to include any type of "unnatural" form of sexual intercourse, be it hetero- or homosexual). Although Saint Paul's words are repeated and glossed throughout the Middle Ages, not all of the early-medieval theologians explicitly included women in their interpretations. Nonetheless, a number of medieval theological tracts do make mention of sexual relations between women. Indeed, in his *Commentary on St. Paul*, the twelfth-century French theologian Peter Abelard (1079–1142) underscores the importance of relations between women through his gloss: "against nature, that is, against the order of nature, which created women's genitals for the use of men and not so women could co-habit with women." In the thirteenth century, both Albertus Magnus (ca. 1200–1280) and Thomas Aquinas (1225–1274) in his *Summa Theologica* (1267–1273) clearly state that the sin of sodomy includes men with men and women with women. Notions such as these are typical of the formulations found in the writings of medieval theologians and inform the discourse of the vast majority of male medieval writers.

Medieval handbooks of penance classified sodomy between women under the rubric of the sin of fornication. The seventh-century *Penitential* of Theodore, which imposes a penance of three years upon "a woman who practices vice with a woman," indicates that relations between women were, in general, judged less harshly than those between men. However, while sodomy or fornication encompasses sexual relations between women, the medieval definition of those relations remains ambiguous: What acts between women can be considered sodomy? These same penitentials provide a bountiful source of what constituted irregular sexual acts. They include examples of sinful behavior to guide the priest through his interrogation of the penitent and to help him elicit confessions of all the parishioners' sins. "Unnatural" frequently came to be interpreted in penitentials as nonprocreative intercourse and, by extension, the use of any member not intended for procreation. The ninth-century theologian Hincmar of Rheims elaborated on this formulation in relation to female sodomy, citing women who use "diabolical instruments to excite desire." Thus, in broad terms, medieval theological discourse constructs the lesbian as a sinful, unnatural woman and associates her with the devil. The link between lesbian sexuality and satanic forces appears repeatedly, relating "unnatural" sexual relations with heretical beliefs or with sorcery.

## Religious Communities

It may, then, be considered ironic that the convent appears to have been an environment in which affective relationships between women developed. Circumstances that led women to the convent varied and did not necessarily indicate a vocation. Medieval comic literature often pokes fun at the loose ways of nuns, yet it sidesteps any overt reference to too affectionate sisters. Although the walls of the cloister seem to have kept relationships between nuns from becoming common knowledge, relationships between members of these communities were not unknown. As early as the sixth century, Saint Augustine (354–430) warned his sister against them: "[T]he love you bear for one another ought not to be carnal, but spiritual." Ecclesiastic leaders, then, were clearly aware of the possibility of lesbian relationships in the convent. Moreover, it is likely that their uneasiness concerning relationships between nuns inspired a number of the more common regulations of convent life: Nuns were prohibited from sleeping together; they were to sleep clothed; they were required to have lamps burning all night in their dormitories; they were to stay out of each other's cells at night; they were to leave their doors unlocked at night; and finally, they were exhorted *not* to form special ties of friendship within the convent.

It is, then, all the more remarkable that any positive record of a relationship between nuns has survived. Yet, from the evidence found in twelfth-century anonymous Latin verse letters composed in a Bavarian convent by one nun for another, it seems likely that the women in question had a relationship

that was both spiritual and physical. A parallel exists between this epistolary poem and a letter of Hadewijch, a thirteenth-century Beguine, to one of her fellow Beguines, Sara. Similarly, Hildegard of Bingen (1098–1179), who, in her official writings, echoed the opinions of her male counterparts, voiced her feelings for another woman, Richardis von Stade, in terms that hint at a more than sisterly love. Although there is no way to determine whether there existed a physical, erotic component to these relationships, the women involved might well be deemed "particular friends." The complex relations of medieval nuns, in which the spiritual and the physical might often overlap, nonetheless serve to delineate at least one facet of medieval lesbian identity.

## Legal and Medical Discourses

Secular legal discourse presents another side to this configuration. The elision of the lesbian into the sodomite often makes it difficult to distinguish the male from the female transgressor in multitudes of customaries (written collections of laws used in different regions of France) and codes in vigor at different moments of the medieval era. The earliest legal text to mark out a space for lesbian relations distinct from male homosexual relations appears to be the *Livre de Jostice et de Plet* (Book of Justice and Suits), a customary from the Orleanais district in France, compiled ca. 1270. Following the paragraph treating male sodomites, paragraph 23 lists the penalties for females: dismemberment for the first two convictions and burning for the third. Italian legists, influenced by Roman law, follow a similar path. Cino da Pistoia (ca. 1270–1336/1337), for example, in a gloss on the *lex foedissimam* (Roman law treating rape and later interpreted to cover other sexual crimes), interprets it as including "women who exercise their lust on other women and pursue them like men." By 1400, Bartolomeus of Saliceto, in another gloss on the *lex foedissimam* prescribes the death penalty for the defilement of a woman by another woman. Although Bartolomeus's gloss was not official, such pronouncements by noted legal scholars often carried the weight of law. Judicial discourse, then, constructs lesbian sexual relations not merely as illegal, but as a capital offense. Indeed, by the end of the Middle Ages, the death penalty for lesbian relations does appear to be the norm in continental Europe. The 1507 *Constitutio criminalis* of Bamberg, for example, decrees that women "who have lain with other women" be burned at the stake. Significantly, this same condemnation becomes, through its inclusion in the *Constitutio criminalis carolina* (1532, the criminal code of the Emperor Charles V), the penalty for lesbians throughout the Holy Roman Empire during the sixteenth century. While secular justice was involved with punishing criminals, it must be noted that those crimes punished were often the result of condemnations by clerical authorities. Thus, the punishment for heresy or sorcery, like that for convicted lesbians, was death. Since these three crimes were repeatedly linked in the theological discourse of the late middle ages, the death penalty for lesbianism is, perhaps, not unexpected.

Medieval medical discourse parallels the legal and theological discourses in its negative construction of the lesbian. Supposedly following Galen (A.D. 129–ca. 216), an early Arabic text recommended drugs to rid women of the desire for other women. By the thirteenth century, a woman's desire to engage in sexual relations with another woman had a particular pathology. As explained in William of Saliceto's *Summa conservationis* (1285), the disease of ragadia, fleshy growths similar to an elongated clitoris, supplies a physical cause for lesbian desire. Thus, William remedies woman's lack of a phallus and offers a naturalizing explanation for what, in legal and theological terms, remains "unnatural" behavior. To eliminate the cause of the aberrant behavior and, thus, cure the disease, William recommends cauterization or clitoridectomy. This medical treatment, inspired perhaps by African customs, comes in and out of vogue in Europe for the next six centuries.

Given the antagonistic climate of the Middle Ages, it is not hard see why so few traces of lesbians can be found. We have no count of how many women might have been diagnosed with "ragadia." It is equally difficult to estimate how many woman may have run afoul of the law. Two women were put to death for their relationship in the town of Speyer in 1474, and scattered references to others who met other forms of punishment document a lesbian presence in legal records of medieval Europe. While the Catholic Church clearly acknowledged that "unnatural" women existed, the privilege of the confessional cloaks whatever secrets the priests may have heard in silence. Thus, the historical lesbian remains an elusive figure in the Middle Ages.

## Literary Texts

Literary texts complete the portrait of the lesbian in the Middle Ages. Etienne de Fougères, a high-ranking member of the clergy, describes lesbian sexual relations in his *Livre de Manières* (Book of Manners, composed between 1168 and 1178), a didactic treatise. In his discussion of women, he describes the proper role for women in society: motherhood followed by a life of devotion to the church. The originality of de Fougères' text lies in his inclusion, in an otherwise conventional presentation, of women who choose female partners. His condemnation of such women as "against the laws of nature" echoes theological and legal discourses, but his lengthy description of women's sexual activities slips into a metaphor-laden style that recalls the Old French *fabliaux* (comic verse tales popular in thirteenth- and fourteenth-century France). He defines lesbian by the lack a penis and, following a heterosexual model, notes that there is a passive and an active partner. Fougères' conclusion that the lesbian should be stoned, beaten, or killed aligns him with the norms of the period.

A number of medieval romances include cross-dressed women who develop romantic attachments with other women. These relationships end, almost without exception, when the true identity of the cross-dresser is revealed. The odd variant comes in an episode of *Huon de Bordeaux* (a thirteenth-century French romance), in which the couple is threatened with death. However, the Virgin Mary intercedes and transforms the cross-dresser into a man, thus eliminating the lesbian nature of the affection. The ambiguity of these texts—lesbians who are not lesbians—offers a glimpse into the possibility of a transgressive sexuality without ever defining it as such.

Perhaps, then, the most unexpected text of all is a thirteenth-century poem by Bieris de Romans, a Provençal writer, who appropriates the male-voiced courtly lyric and addresses her poem to another woman, Maria. The reading of this work as an example of a lesbian love poem has met with some resistance. Nothing is known of Bieris or Maria, and there is no precedent in medieval vernacular literature for such a poem. The scarcity of women-authored texts from the period might explain the lack of like-themed works. Moreover, given the complexity of relationships between women, as evidenced by the letters of nuns and beguines, the homoerotic elements of Bieris's poem to Maria cannot be dismissed out of hand. On a textual level, the relationship between the "I" of the poem and Maria could be considered lesbian.

Thus, while the overwhelming majority of medieval sources present lesbian relations in a negative

**M** or even criminal light, documents authored by women, be they poems or letters, provide a more positive vision of their relationships.

The history of women who had homoaffective or homoerotic relationships in the Middle Ages is just now being written. As research continues in the area of medieval conceptions of sexuality and in women's history, the gaps in our understanding of the period will begin to be filled in.        *Edith J. Benkov*

### Bibliography

Brown, Judith C. "Lesbian Sexuality in Medieval and Early Modern Europe." In *Hidden from History: Reclaiming the Gay and Lesbian Past.* Ed. Martin Duberman, Martha Vicinus, and George Chauncy Jr. New York: Meridian, 1989, pp. 67–75.

Bullogh, Vern L. "The Sin Against Nature and Homosexuality." In *Sexual Practices and the Medieval Church.* Ed. Vern L. Bullogh and James A. Brundage. Buffalo, N.Y.: Prometheus, 1982, pp. 55–71.

Crompton, Louis. "The Myth of Lesbian Impunity: Capital Laws from 1270–1791." *Journal of Homosexuality* 6 (Fall/Winter 1980–1981), 11–25.

Matter, E. Ann. "My Sister, My Spouse: Woman-Identified Women in Medieval Christianity." *Journal of Feminist Studies in Religion* 2 (1986), 81–93.

Murray, Jacqueline. "Twice Marginal and Twice Invisible: Lesbians in the Middle Ages." In *Handbook of Medieval Sexuality.* Ed. Vern L. Bullogh and James A. Brundage. New York and London: Garland, 1996, pp. 191–222.

Rieger, Angelica. "Was Bieris de Romans Lesbian? Women's Relations with Each Other in the World of the Troubadours." In *The Voice of the Trobaritz.* Ed. W. Paden. Philadelphia: University of Pennsylvania Press, 1989, pp. 73–94.

***See also*** Christianity, Early; Clitoris; Crime and Criminology; Law and Legal Institutions; Religious Communities; Witches, Persecution of

### Military

The ground, air, and naval forces of a government whose mission, historically, is to prepare for and, if necessary, engage in warfare. The lengthy history of women's participation in the armed forces would be incomplete without first mentioning the women who passed as men so that they might serve their countries. For some, this decision was based on the desire to join their male partners as they traveled with the military; for others, it was simply the fact that they wanted to participate in an occupation, whether for livelihood or patriotism, in which women were prohibited. The sexuality of these women has often been the focus of inquiry into their lives. Some would readily have identified as lesbians; others were so male identified that they would not have perceived themselves as women-loving women. Thus, lesbians have served in the military as long as women have served in the military, and even before women, recognized as such, were permitted to do so.

But women have always served *with*, if not *in*, the military. Before holding any official status as members of the U.S. military, women served as cooks, laundresses, seamstresses, and nurses. In World War I, 34,000 women served as telephone operators, clerks, and nurses, yet the nurses were not granted "official status" until World War II. In World War II, the military found that it needed far more personnel than could be obtained if it recruited only men. Women would now be recruited for such positions as teletype operators, aircraft electricians, aircraft mechanics, machinists, metal workers, radio mechanics, and glider instructors, to name a few. All told, approximately 271,600 women served in the military during World War II.

### Sexuality and the Military

Although it is clear that lesbians have served as long as have women, discussions about sexuality and the military have generally focused on gay men. Indeed, during World War II, much of the psychiatric screening was aimed at male recruits. In general, criminal law ignored sexual acts between women, and the military followed suit. This is not, to say, however, that the issue of women's sexuality was ignored. Quite the contrary, it was a central issue in the debate over the entrance of women into the military.

One of the initial concerns was that women would be either too frail to do the work or too masculine to foster a "good public image." Oveta Culp Hobby, the chief of the women's interests section of the War Department's Bureau of Public Relations, is reported in a 1942 *New York Times* article to have said that members of the Women's Army Auxiliary Corps would be neither "Amazons rushing into battle" nor "butterflies fluttering free." There were fears that women who would seek to join the military could be compared to "naked Amazons . . . and the queer damozels of the Isle of Lesbos" (Treadwell, 1953). There was a considerable amount of panic that military women would all end up as lesbians or, at the very least, divested of any sense of moral decency.

Yet not all of the concern was focused on the notion of lesbianism. The military was also concerned with how to simultaneously downplay and highlight women's femininity and heterosexuality. For example, there was considerable debate over whether women's jackets should have breast pockets, as the men's did. On the one hand, the military wanted uniformity; on the other hand, it was believed that the pockets might place undue emphasis on the fact that women had breasts.

The image of the servicewoman that was marketed was one of femininity and (hetero)sexual attractiveness. Ultimately, the military managed; women were recruited and served honorably. At the close of the war, a great deal was made of the fact that the military had not tarnished women's femininity or their ability to be good wives and mothers. Thus, the military might be described as being concerned that women in general, and lesbians in particular, would ruin the military and that the military would ruin women, heterosexual women in particular. Lesbians, after all, were already "ruined." Heterosexual women, the military worried, would distract the men, get pregnant, and/or transmit venereal disease. But, despite the frequent discussion about women's sexuality, there was a war to be fought. And it is common knowledge that, during war, things that might engage one's energies during peacetime are often ignored.

In fact, one of the most frequently told tales of World War II concerns Johnnie Phelps and General Dwight D. Eisenhower (1890–1969). The general gave Sergeant Phelps an order to "find the lesbians" in the WAC (Women's Army Corps) battalion and get rid of them. Reportedly, Phelps replied: "Sir, if the General pleases, I'll be happy to check into this and make you a list. But you've got to know, when you get the list back, my name's going to be first." Eisenhower's secretary then indicated that, no, her name would be first. Apparently, Eisenhower was then reminded about the outstanding performance of the battalion since its assignment and the fact that he would lose many of his most valuable personnel. His response was: "Forget that order. Forget about it" (Humphrey, 1990). While much of the emphasis

on expulsion was directed at gay men, and stories such as the above are not unusual, lesbians were the victims of investigations and purges—and continue to lose their careers because of the prohibition on lesbians and gay men in the military.

## Prohibition and Persecution

From the World War II era through much of the 1970s, the military retained a degree of flexibility regarding lesbian and gay service members. In those instances in which it was clearly in the military's best interest to retain the individual, it did so. In the late 1970s, the policy was revised to state that "homosexuality is incompatible with military service." Because the previous policy had allowed for some lesbians and gay men to remain in the service, some thought that the loopholes that allowed for those cases must be closed. The solution was to make the policy more rigid. President Jimmy Carter would be seeking reelection in 1980, and drafting a new and less vulnerable policy was seen as a good way to court the conservative electorate. The process took longer than anticipated and in January, 1981, days before Ronald Reagan took office, a new Department of Defense directive was announced. The new policy stated flatly that "homosexuality is incompatible with military service." Because the previous policy had allowed some lesbians and gay men to remain in service, some felt the loopholes that allowed for those cases needed to be closed. The solution was to make the policy more rigid. The new policy would also allow for the discharge of personnel believed to "demonstrate a propensity to engage in homosexual conduct." Prior to this, the military had to "prove," so to speak, that an individual was "actually" a homosexual. The political climate was changing, as was the military, and it became increasingly more difficult for lesbians who wished to serve to do so.

During the 1980s, there were a number of high-profile cases involving the discharge of lesbian service members, including Miriam Ben-Shalom, Barbara Baum, and Dusty Pruitt. And the numbers of women whose cases did not make the papers are vast according to the United States General Accounting Office (1992). While there were cases of women who survived administrative hearings and were retained in the military, many were not so fortunate. In September 1990, shortly after the United States sent troops to the Persian Gulf, one Navy admiral issued a memo to his subordinates indicating that, although lesbians were often the top perform-

**M** ers, they were to be discharged nonetheless. Then, when it became apparent that this might be a deployment of some duration, *claiming* to be a lesbian did not guarantee expulsion, at least not until the war was over. Discharges and inquiries were, for the most part, halted.

One of the most prominent cases is that of Margarethe Cammermeyer, chief nurse of the Washington Army National Guard. In 1989, Cammermeyer was preparing to attend the Army War College, a move necessary before she could be considered for promotion to brigadier general. This required that she undergo an extensive security investigation. In the course of the investigation, Cammermeyer chose not to lie and revealed that she was a lesbian. Thus began a legal battle that ultimately resulted in her reinstatement, in 1994, as a member of military. In 1997, Colonel Cammermeyer retired from military service. While hers is not the only "success" story, it is certainly one of the most well known.

One of the most interesting aspects of the military's treatment of lesbians is the fact that lesbians are discharged in numbers quite disproportionate to their representation. It is not known how many lesbians there are in the military, but, given the percentages of women compared to men in the military, lesbians are discharged at a much higher rate than are gay men. Some believe that this is part of a larger backlash against women serving in the military. This is not a radical argument, considering that any women, regardless of sexual orientation, may be subject to "dyke baiting" and many have lost careers because of accusations of lesbianism. The threat of being labeled a lesbian may serve to keep women from forming close bonds with their female peers and from performing to their utmost ability and also may function as a weapon by which women are encouraged, or even forced, to engage in sexual relations with men when they might not otherwise do so. Thus, while "banning" gay men may serve, falsely, to ensure the military's image as a bastion of masculinity, "banning" lesbians may help, quite literally, to keep the military more male dominated.

**Lifting the Ban**

In late 1992, Democratic presidential candidate Bill Clinton made an election-year promise to eliminate the ban on lesbians and gay men in the military. It is likely that no one expected that, shortly after his inauguration, Clinton would announce his intention to "lift the ban." Thus ensued what might be considered one of the most intense debates in congressional history. Senate hearings were held on the subject, with testimony both for and against lifting the ban. Again, debate focused on male sexuality, but it was clear that the careers of women were also at stake. The debate resulted in Congress codifying "the ban" into federal law, whereas it had been a military regulation. As a regulation, it could have been changed by the Department of Defense. Changes would now have to come via congressional vote.

During the debate on lifting the ban, there was a great deal of attention to what other countries, specifically NATO (North Atlantic Treaty Organization) countries, do about lesbian and gay service members. Although their policies also experience periodic revision, most, either officially or informally, are more lenient than the policy of the United States. As of June 1992—as reported by the United States General Accounting Office—only four of seventeen countries, not including the United States, specifically excluded lesbians and gays. Since that time, Canada eliminated its restriction. Some of the countries that have no overall exclusion policy do have restrictions on the types of positions that can be held.

In the late 1990s, the fight continued. Lesbians continue to serve in the U.S. military. Cases continue to make their way through the courts. There have been various decisions at different levels in the judicial system: some wins, some losses. Most agree that it will take having a case heard by the United States Supreme Court to make the final determination as to whether those who wishes to serve their country may do so, regardless of sexual orientation.

*Melissa S. Herbert*

### Bibliography

Berubé, Allan. *Coming Out Under Fire: The History of Gay Men and Women in World War II*. New York: Free Press, 1990.

Herbert, Melissa S. *Camouflage Isn't Only for Combat: Gender, Sexuality, and Women in the Military*. New York: New York University Press, 1998.

Humphrey, Mary Ann. *My Country, My Right To Serve*. New York: HarperCollins, 1990.

Treadwell, Mattie E. *The Women's Army Corps*. United States Army in World War II, Special Studies. Washington, D.C.: Office of the Chief of Military History, Department of the Army, 1953.

United States General Accounting Office. DOD's *Policy on Homosexuality*. GAO/NSIAD–92–98. Washington, D.C.: GAO, June 1992.

Wheelwright, Julie. *Amazons and Military Maids: Women Who Dressed as Men in Pursuit of Life, Liberty, and Happiness*. London: Pandora, 1989.

*See also* Norton Sound Incident; Passing Women

## Millay, Edna St. Vincent (1892–1950)

American poet, playwright, and essayist. Raised in Camden, Maine, in a close-knit, creative household by her divorced mother, Cora, Edna St. Vincent Millay published her first poem, "Forest Trees," in 1906; six years later, her celebrated poem, "Renascence," was included in *The Lyric Year* (1912), bringing the young poet to national attention and enabling her enrollment in Vassar College (1913–1917), where the rebellious Millay excelled in languages and literature, especially drama. In several works, Millay invokes her powerful loves formed within a clique of Vassar women, especially Charlotte Babcock, the model for one of the devoted stepsisters in *The Lamp and the Bell* (1921), and Dorothy Coleman, whose premature death prompted "Memorial to D.C." (1920), an elegy sequence commemorating friendship and Sapphic love. Years later, to a personal question, Millay retorted: "Oh, you mean I'm homosexual! Of course, I am, and heterosexual too."

Following graduation, the vivacious, independent Millay acted with the Provincetown Players (New York City) and directed her antiwar verse play, *Aria da Capo* (1919). Vincent supported the animated Greenwich Village household formed with her mother and younger sisters by publishing short fiction and popular essays under the pseudonym Nancy Boyd in *Ainslee's*, the *Dial,* and *Vanity Fair*. The first woman to win the Pulitzer Prize for poetry (1922), Millay, in *A Few Figs from Thistles* (1920), champions the liberation of women and captures her intoxicating Village life in the famous lines "My candle burns at both ends; it shall not last the night."

Several Village acquaintances intricately influenced Millay's life: Edmund Wilson (1895–1972); playwright and *Masses* editor Floyd Dell (1887–1969); poet Arthur Ficke (1883–1945), and Eugen Boissevain (d. 1949), whom she married in 1923. Millay dedicated her poem "The Pioneer" (1923) to Boissevain's first wife, the feminist Inez Milholland (1886–1916). In 1925, Millay, henceforth in deteri-orating health but now protected by Boissevain, withdrew to Steepletop, their country retreat in Austerlitz, New York. Meanwhile, she completed the libretto for Deems Taylor's *The King's Henchman* (1927); *Fatal Interview* (1931), the passionate sonnet collection dedicated to the cherished memory of poet Elinor Wylie (1885–1928); and, notably, two additional elegiac sequences for women, one lamenting her mother published in *Wine from These Grapes* (1934) and the other mourning Wylie in *Huntsman, What Quarry?* (1939). After protesting the Sacco and Vanzetti case (1927) and fascism, Millay supported British War Relief; although increasingly reclusive, she continued giving public readings, dressed in her trademark flowing chiffon gowns. Shattered by Boissevain's death in 1949, Millay remained alone at Steepletop until her death on October 18, 1950. The Millay papers are held in the Vassar College Library, Poughkeepsie, New York.                *Judith C. Kohl*

### Bibliography

Cheney, Anne. *Millay in Greenwich Village*. University: University of Alabama Press, 1975.

Gould, Jean. *The Poet and Her Book*. New York: Dodd, Mead, 1969.

Gurko, Miriam. *Restless Spirit: The Life of Edna St. Vincent Millay*. New York: Crowell, 1962.

*See also* Colleges, Women's; Greenwich Village; Poetry

## Millett, Kate (1934–)

American feminist. Born into an Irish American family in St. Paul, Minnesota, Kate Millett was first introduced to politics listening to her family talk about the Irish political situation.

Her family found out she was in love with another woman while she was in college. This forced Millett to accept, as she wrote in *A.D.: A Memoir* (1995), the "renegade life I have sold myself into, like some secret society banned by the police . . . a secret leper, a secret everywhere except with two or three other souls in history."

After her family's discovery, Millett went abroad and studied at Oxford University in England. In 1959, she moved to New York City to become an artist. New York proved inhospitable, and she went to Japan, where she had her first sculpture show, in 1963. That same year she returned to New York City, where her work became increasingly political. In the

**M** mid-1960s, Millett became involved in the women's movement and began work on a Ph.D. at Columbia that culminated in *Sexual Politics* (1970), a critique of cultural assumptions in the portrayal of women in fiction.

*Sexual Politics* became a best-seller in 1970. However, the publicity surrounding the book created problems for Millett. She spoke publicly about gay liberation alarming moderate feminists, while lesbians were confused because she did not publicly come out about her lesbianism. When she did publicly acknowledge her lesbianism in 1970, *Time* magazine claimed this disclosure would discredit both her and the movement. The publicity surrounding this event became an early turning point in the feminist movement by making lesbianism a high-profile and controversial issue.

Afterward, Millett found herself on the margins of the women's movement. She continued to write and speak publicly on feminist and lesbian issues. In *Flying* (1974), she wrote about her life, and the book became an underground lesbian classic. Continuing to write about her life and the evolving lesbian culture, Millett wrote *Sita* (1977), *Elegy for Sita* (1979), and *A.D.* (1995). Millett's work also includes *The Loony-Bin Trip* (1990), an autobiographical expose of the mental health system, and *The Politics of Cruelty* (1994), an examination of the use of torture in the twentieth century. She founded an art colony outside Poughkeepsie, New York, for women artists in 1978 and continues to work as a sculptor. *Anne B. Keating*

### Bibliography

Keating, Anne B. "Kate Millett." In *Contemporary Lesbian Writers of the United States: a BioBibliographical Critical Sourcebook*. Ed. Sandra Pollack and Denise Knight. Westport, Conn.: Greenwood, 1993, pp. 361–369.

———. " 'A World We Have Invented Here': Exploring Community, Identity, and Art in the Construction of 'The Farm,' Kate Millett's Feminist Art Colony, 1978–1994." Ph.D. diss., University of Maryland, College Park, 1995.

Juhasz, Suzanne. "Towards a Theory of Feminist Autobiography: Kate Millett's *Flying* and *Sita*; Maxine Hong Kingston's *The Woman Warrior*." In *Women's Autobiography: Essays in Criticism*. Ed. Estelle Jelinek. Bloomington: Indiana University Press, 1980, pp. 221–237.

Kolodny, Annette. "The Lady's Not for Spurning: Kate Millett and the Critics." In *Women's Autobiography: Essays in Criticism*. Ed. Estelle Jelinek. Bloomington: Indiana University Press, 1980, pp. 238–259.

*See also* Autobiography; Feminism; Gay Liberation Movement; Women's Liberation Movement

## Misogyny

Woman hating; includes antifeminist, along with antifemale, beliefs and behaviors and hostility for women as a sex, as well as for that which is culturally understood as feminine. Misogyny, although characteristic of men's sexism, also infects women's attitudes toward themselves and other women.

Hostility toward woman as the "other" is a recurrent theme in all manner of patriarchal ideology, social organization, and practice. The male is the norm, and the female an imperfection, a deviation, a monstrosity. Judeo-Christian religious belief decrees divinity to be all-male and associates sin, evil, and apocalypse with the female. Women's sexual functions, in science as well as religion, are viewed as redolent of impurity and/or disease.

Realms of all-male fraternal bonding—sport, politics, the military, religion, and social clubs—provide potent sites for the promulgation of misogyny. Misogyny is institutionalized in many forms of violence, including sexual slavery, war crimes, battery, rape, and femicide (male killing of women for reasons of hatred, pleasure, or sense of ownership). The latter is epitomized in practices from witch burnings through spousal and sex murder. Narratives and images of such violence then are channeled into art, both elite and popular, in museums and mainstream media, in pornography, children's stories, jokes, and songs.

Misogyny declares women to be either evil or impossibly good, domineering or completely submissive (whorish or asexual, disgustingly ugly or fatally beautiful), as well as petty, treacherous, manipulative, stupid, illogical, gossipy, castrating, hyperemotional, or childlike. Such beliefs are enshrined in stereotypes, including the welfare queen, the dumb blonde, the femme fatale, the Jewish mother, the hot tamale, the shrewish mother-in-law, the nymphet, and the man-hating dyke.

Stereotypically, patriarchal heroes are men who bond with other men, shun, and even violate women. Men who aggress against women are celebrated, often covertly, as heroes in both the real and the fictional world, as evidenced by the cult of celebrity that has grown around the serial killer. Such extremely misogynist men are heroes because they represent the core values of male supremacy and serve as enforcers of that order. Ironically, with the exception of feminist thinking, the phenomenon of sex killers is rarely understood as based in culturally endorsed misogyny, but is instead attributed to individual, and usually inexplicable, deviance. However, Aileen Wuornos, a woman who was convicted of murdering seven men in Florida between 1989 and 1991 (despite her claim of self-defense), has been branded a man-hating lesbian.

Psychoanalysis enshrines the misogynist notion that, in order for boys to become men, they must separate from the mother and root out any lingering trace of femininity. The worst thing a male can be is a "pussy." Racism and colonialism fundamentally rest upon misogynist principles in that the "lower orders" are invariably deemed inferior because they have not been able to shuck off what the oppressor cultures perceive as the dominance of the feminine. Similarly, misogyny informs the violence that male supremacist cultures characteristically direct against the land, the Earth, nature—all entities that traditionally have been associated with women.

Misogyny ordains that all traits valued in a culture—bravery, independence, tough-mindedness, logic, strength—are deemed masculine, the property of males. Female masculinity, then, especially that associated with lesbianism, is most hated. Ironically, lesbians are deemed "unnatural" women. Yet, by virtue of that perceived monstrosity, lesbians are concomitantly understood to be the most "other" and, therefore, the most "woman" and the most despised. Any woman who sparks the ire of a misogynist is likely to find herself anathematized as "dyke." *Jane Caputi*

## Bibliography

Caputi, Jane. *The Age of Sex Crime*. Bowling Green, Ohio: Bowling Green State University Popular Press, 1987.

Daly, Mary. *Gyn/Ecology: The Metaethics of Radical Feminism*. Boston: Beacon, 1978, 1990.

Hart, Lynda. *Fatal Women: Lesbian Sexuality and the Mark of Aggression*. Princeton, N.J.: Princeton University Press, 1994.

Radford, Jill, and Diana E.H. Russell, eds. *Femicide: The Politics of Woman Killing*. New York: Twayne, 1992.

*See also* Heterosexism; Sexism

## Mistral, Gabriela (1889–1957)

Poet, first Latin American Nobel laureate (1945). Born Lucila Godoy Alcayaga in Vicuña, Chile, she published under her pseudonym *Desolacion* (1922), *Lecturas para mujeres* (Readings for Women [1924]), *Ternura* (Tenderness [1926]), *Tala* (Felling Trees [1938]), *Lagar* (Wine Press [1954]), and the posthumous *Poema de Chile* (1972) and *Lagar II* (1992). Her collected prose, some five hundred essays, is also widely read.

The canonized figure of Gabriela Mistral appears on postage stamps, banknotes, public schools, and parks throughout Latin America, reflecting the erasure of sexuality attending women's access to the public sphere. Contradicting this erasure are her earliest publications, stressing introspection, the alternative spirituality of theosophy, educational reform, and the redemptive power of art. Critics seized on a handful of earlier poems, however, which they built into a soap-operatic story of a (male) lover's suicide and the poet's subsequent renunciation and transformation into a symbolic mother. This narrative overlooks the all-female worlds in which the poet lived, especially Chile's Liceo de Niñas (girls' high schools), where women teachers lived together on the premises. It also overlooks the extensive network of women's clubs and professional associations that constituted an important audience for Mistral.

As Mistral became a celebrity, she chose the relative anonymity of exile, often outside Latin America. She changed residences frequently, preferring women-centered households on the outskirts of cities. Her itinerary resembles that of many other similarly rootless Latin American intellectuals: Paris in the 1920s, Madrid in the early 1930s, variously Brazil, Italy, return to Mexico, California, New York.

Mistral's poetry encodes a lesbian sensibility "through the treatment of certain themes as well as in the tendency to avoid grammatical pronouns that mark gender. The themes of frustration, prohibition, absence, and exile may be identified with the marginal position of lesbians in society" (Martínez, 1996). Writing of motherhood allows Mistral to dwell on the female body, an area of discourse prohibited to men. Matricide emerges in her later work: A number of critics call for a lesbian interpretation to revise the ideal of Mistral's relation to motherhood. The case of Gabriela Mistral, both as a text and a producer of texts, reveals the emergence of a specifically female-centered identity, expressed as

# M

prohibited longing and disguised as fascination with the female body, above and beyond male desire.

*Elizabeth Rosa Horan*

## Bibliography

Fiol-Matta, Licia. "Gabriela Mistral: Maestra de América." In *Entiendes: Queer Readings, Hispanic Writings.* Ed. Emilie L. Bergmann and Paul Julian Smith. Durham, N.C.: Duke University Press, 1995, pp. 201–227.

Horan, Elizabeth Rosa. "Gabriela Mistral." In *Latin American Writers on Gay and Lesbian Themes: A Bio-Critical Sourcebook.* Ed. David William Foster. Westport, Conn.: Greenwood, 1994, pp. 221–235.

———. *Gabriela Mistral: A Poet and Her People.* Washington, D.C.: Organization of American States, 1994.

Martínez, Elena M. *Lesbian Voices From Latin America: Breaking Ground.* New York: Garland, 1996.

Rubio, Patricia. *Gabriela Mistral Ante La Critica: Bibliografia Anotada* (Gabriela Mistral Regarding Criticism: An Annotated Bibliography*).* Santiago, Chile: Direccion de Bibliotecas, 1995.

*See also* Chile; Latin American Literature; Poetry

## Mitchell, Alice (1873?–1898)

American murderer. With four slashes of a razor, Alice Mitchell became one of the most notorious women in 1890s America. A woman killing her lover, although shocking enough, would not normally have grabbed headlines throughout the country. But the nineteen-year-old Mitchell's sweetheart was no dashing young man, but her seventeen-year-old lesbian lover.

The death of Freda Ward stunned Victorians for a number of reasons. Apart from the sheer brutality of Ward's killing, Mitchell's act challenged popular ideas about female sexuality. In an era in which homosexuality went unrecognized and women were not thought to have much of a sexual appetite, the American public struggled to explain the attraction between Ward and Mitchell. The sensational trial of Mitchell forced the public at large to question what it meant for a woman to love another woman.

By 1892, Mitchell and Ward had been friends for several years. Both Tennessee schoolgirls, their relationship was classed as romantic friendship, an intimate relationship that prepared women for marriage. Kissing, embracing, and writing love letters to each other, the two girls behaved much like the other young women of the era and caused no concern to their families. Planning to elope together, however, marked them as somewhat different from other romantic friends. Mitchell gave Ward a ring in 1891, and both considered themselves engaged. Mitchell planned to assume the male persona of Alvin J. Ward, find a job, and support Ward as would a husband. When Ward's sister caught her waiting, fully dressed and packed, for Mitchell to arrive in the middle of night, the Ward family stopped all contact between the girls. Angered by this rejection and rumors that Freda had subsequently become romantically involved with a man, a jealous Mitchell accosted her one afternoon on a ferryboat dock. In a brief skirmish, Mitchell cut Ward's throat. Arrested at home that same night, on January 25, 1892, Mitchell pled insanity.

Mitchell's trial began on July 18, 1892, in a packed courthouse. Enormous amounts of newspaper coverage had made the murder case into a national sensation. Blaring headlines announced that this was "A Very Unnatural Crime" in which the murderess claimed to have loved her victim so much that she killed her rather than live estranged from her. After a ten-day trial, which included the testimony of several medical experts, the jury declared Mitchell insane, and the judge remanded her to the Tennessee State Insane Asylum at Bolivar, Tennessee, until she was fit to stand trial. Mitchell was reported to have died from tuberculosis at the asylum in 1898, but one of her lawyers later stated that she had committed suicide by jumping into a water tower.

Nineteenth-century America could understand the motivations behind the murders of spouses and sweethearts, as long as a man was somehow involved. But the lack of a male presence in this killing baffled the public and turned the story of Mitchell and Ward into a topic of newspaper coverage and sexological debate well into the twentieth century. The case played a critical role in the definition of lesbianism by drawing a line between the acceptable model of romantic friendship and the emerging figure of the deviant, mannish lesbian.

*Caryn E. Neumann*

## Bibliography

Duggan, Lisa. "The Trials of Alice Mitchell: Sensationalism, Sexology, and the Lesbian Subject in Turn-of-the-Century America." In *Gender and*

Scientific Authority. Ed. Barbara Laslett, Sally Gregory Kohlstedt, Helen Longino, and Evelynn Hammonds. Chicago: University of Chicago Press, 1996, pp. 217–240.

Lindquist, Lisa J. "Images of Alice: Gender, Deviancy, and a Love Murder in Memphis." *Journal of the History of Sexuality* 6:1 (July 1995), 30–61.

*See also* Crime and Criminology; Romantic Friendship; Sexology

## Miyamoto Yuriko (1899–1951)

Japanese novelist. One of the most talented proletarian writers, Miyamoto Yuriko started writing as an idealistic humanist who was disturbed by the alienation of elite intellectuals from the masses. Her awareness of women's condition and her own experience of marriage and divorce led her to become a feminist and a Communist.

Born in Tokyo as the first child of a prosperous architect, in 1918 she accompanied her father to New York City. While studying at Columbia University there, she married a scholar of Oriental linguistics fifteen years her senior. Their marriage brought five years of psychological struggle and creative stagnation that continued until the couple divorced in 1924. Miyamoto's traumatic experiences during what she called her "swamp period" were soon to become the basis of her first masterpiece, *Nobuko* (1923), which, like all of her subsequent novels, is highly autobiographical. Nobuko, Miyamoto's alter ego, comes to recognize the traps created by women's vulnerability to the idealization of romantic love and marriage, a realization that leads her to explore love relations that are not based on either. *Nobuko* was followed by two sequels: *Futatsu no niwa* (Two Gardens [1947]) and *Dôhyô* (Road Sign [1950]).

After the divorce, Miyamoto lived with Yuasa Yoshiko (1896–?), a woman translator of Russian literature who appears in Miyamoto's fiction under the name of Motoko. In Miyamoto's fiction, her alter ego Nobuko comes to realize the prejudices to which single women are subject in a male-oriented society: They force themselves unnaturally to behave like men, yet they are more vulnerable than married women and more conscious of themselves as sexual objects. Thus, she comes to reject the androgynous existence she once thought necessary.

Miyamoto returned to Japan in 1930 and joined the Japan Communist Party in 1931. The following year, she married Miyamoto Kenji (1908–1988), a young Communist and literary critic. From 1932 on, her works became subject to strict government control. Between 1932 and 1943, she was arrested six times because of her affiliation with the Communist Party, spending approximately two years in prison.

Despite these hardships and the torture she experienced in prison, Miyamoto refused to give up her ideological beliefs. The years between 1945 and her sudden death in 1951 were the most active and productive period of her life. Her major achievement is clearly in her autobiographical novels, throughout which the protagonist tries to liberate herself from her own feudal-bourgeois class background and to contribute to human welfare by fighting against sexism, war, and exploitation of the working class.                    *Richmod Bollinger*

### Bibliography

Lippit, Noriko Mizuta. "Literature, Ideology, and Women's Happiness: The Autobiographical Novels of Miyamoto Yuriko." *Bulletin of Concerned Asian Scholars* 10:2 (1978), 2–9.

*See also* Japan

## Modernism

Literary and artistic movement. Though there is no exact formula for the time frame or definition of modernism, critics generally date the movement as occurring between 1890 and 1940, though modernist works and artists both precede and follow this time.

### History and Characteristics

Viewing this era as a period of cultural crisis, many painters, musicians, and writers responded by expressing a sense of chaos and disruption through artistic experiment, specifically, according to Bradbury and McFarlane (1976), "anti-representationalism in painting, atonalism in music, *vers libre* [free verse] in poetry, stream of consciousness narrative in the novel." Modernist art forms included architecture, dance, and film as well. Many modernists, at some point in their careers at least, sought to depict through experimental means the degradation, disharmony, isolation, and confusion of the modern condition. Form was designed to be inseparable from content.

In literature, T.S. Eliot (1888–1965) wrote criticism focusing on the idea that the work of art should

**M** be considered by itself, independent of its historical or biographical context. In the middle of the twentieth century, this exclusive focus on the formal qualities of the art work became the basic practice of New Criticism, a critical school influencing literary studies in British and U.S. colleges and universities for several decades. In conventional accounts, the 1920s came to be seen as the decade during which "high modernism" flourished because of the preponderance of stylistically experimental works that appeared during that period. In addition, several New Critics and others advanced the year 1922 as a high point of literary modernism inasmuch as it featured the publication of modernist classics like Eliot's poem "The Waste Land" and James Joyce's (1882–1941) epic novel *Ulysses*. Besides artistic experimentalism, another key feature of the movement was cultural iconoclasm. Despite this subversive component, early conventional studies of modernism centered on the work of white, male, often Christian, artists, such as Joyce, Eliot, Ezra Pound (1885–1972), and William Butler Yeats (1865–1939) in literature; Pablo Picasso (1881–1973) and Henri Matisse (1869–1954) in art; Igor Stravinsky (1882–1971) and George Antheil (1900–1959) in music; Sergei Diaghilev (1872–1929) in dance; and Sergei Eisenstein (1898–1948) in film.

By the 1970s, however, the cultural and scholarly influence of feminism and other emergent movements in the United States and Europe had begun to make inroads into the largely academic construction of modernism as a movement practiced and analyzed primarily by white men. In opposition to the New Criticism, many feminists and other scholars began to insist on the significance of biography and cultural context as constituents of critical evaluation. Feminists were also discovering a range of overlooked or undervalued female modernists to consider. Women dancers, such as Isadora Duncan (1878–1927); painters, including Marie Laurencin (1883–1956); and writers, such as Dorothy Richardson (1873–1957) and Katherine Mansfield (1888–1923), became subjects of study; female modernists such as Gertrude Stein (1874–1946) and Virginia Woolf (1882–1941), sometimes mentioned in earlier accounts of the literary canon, became the objects of serious, respectful inquiry.

## Feminist and Lesbian Perspectives

The 1980s witnessed several important thematic and recuperative studies expressing a feminist perspective on the modernist period. Shari Benstock's *Women of the Left Bank* (1986), for example, combined biography and literary criticism in its examination of the intersection of female artists and writers, many of them lesbian, in a single section of Paris during the modernist years. Sandra Gilbert and Susan Gubar, in a three-volume thematic study, *No Man's Land: The Place of the Woman Writer in the Twentieth Century* (1988–1994), traced the movement as an arena of struggle for women modernists, whom Gilbert and Gubar present as engaged in a professional and personal battle of the sexes. Feminist book-length biographies, as of U.S. novelist Willa Cather (1873–1947), and critical treatments, as of U.S. expatriate writer H.D. (Hilda Doolittle) (1886–1961), also began to appear in the 1980s. And in *Writing for Their Lives* (1987), Gillian Hanscombe and Virginia Smyers, besides considering writers, turned biographical and historical attention to women publishers, editors, and patrons during the modernist period, further expanding the designation of "modernist" beyond the exclusively artistic. Much of the feminist work on modernist women revealed the lesbianism, bisexuality, and otherwise strong personal and professional affiliations among female modernists in Paris, London, New York City, and Berlin, the urban capitals of this international movement.

Within the artistic domain, critics began to question the notion of stylistic "experimentalism" as a key indicator of literary modernism, proposing as a modernist feature subversive content expressed in conventional literary style. Similarly, writing in the 1990s, critics Elliott and Wallace (1994) examined the artistically subversive strategies in the apparently conventional portraits by neglected lesbian painter Romaine Brooks (1874–1970), juxtaposed to the nonexperimental, yet oppositional, writings of her longtime lover, Natalie Barney (1876–1972). This line of argument, that conventional style expressing anticonventional subject matter is a characteristic of modernism, led lesbian publisher and critic Jay (1995) to advance Radclyffe Hall's (1880–1943) lesbian classic *The Well of Loneliness* (1928) as an example of what Jay called "lesbian modernism." Because this novel is written in a representational style, follows a chronological plot, and includes conventional characterization, Jay suggested that Hall's unswerving treatment of the culturally insurgent subject of lesbianism disrupts reader expectation particularly effectively.

Besides *The Well of Loneliness*, critic Benstock (1990) included French writer Colette's (1873–

1954) *The Pure and the Impure* as an example of what Benstock called "sapphic modernism." While Colette and Hall drew on traditional forms in their works centering on lesbianism, Benstock also identified as examples of sapphic modernism some experimental works that presented lesbianism in codes, as in the work of Stein, or disguised lesbian content behind an ostensibly heterosexual narrative, as in some writing of Woolf and H.D. Benstock and others also point to certain stylistic characteristics as sometimes representing lesbianism—such as ellipses and dashes, markers that disrupt the flow of language and suggest the rupture of the cultural narrative of heterosexuality.

Jay (1995) observed that, unlike many male modernists, lesbian modernists in general distrusted the ideas of Sigmund Freud (1856–1939) (except H.D., who underwent psychoanalysis with him). Rather, lesbian modernists, according to Jay, favored the theories of sexologist Havelock Ellis (1859–1939), which considered lesbianism as genetic, biological, and, therefore, not subject to the "cure" ostensibly offered by Freud and his followers. Like Benstock, Jay also advanced coding and experimentalism as strategies employed by lesbian modernists to present their revolutionary subject matter. Among these tactics, Jay includes private printing and distribution as well. The 1928 obscenity charges in England against *The Well of Loneliness* alarmed lesbian modernists considerably, according to Jay, yet the year itself may be described as the high point of lesbian modernism. Besides Radclyffe Hall's novel, 1928 saw the private publication of U.S. expatriate writer Djuna Barnes's (1892–1982) *Ladies Almanack*, a spoof on Natalie Barney's Paris lesbian circle. Virginia Woolf's *Orlando*, a comic depiction of gender switching, dedicated to Woolf's female lover, writer Vita Sackville-West (1892–1962), was brought out the same year, as was African American novelist Nella Larsen's (1891–1964) *Passing*, a novel containing perceptible lesbian undertones. All of these novels present clear illustrations of the ways lesbianism was treated by female modernists.

Besides Colette, Djuna Barnes, Katherine Mansfield, Gertrude Stein, Natalie Barney, and Virginia Woolf, the list of prominent female modernists who are lesbian or bisexual is long and wide ranging. U.S. expatriate editors Margaret Anderson (1886–1973) and Jane Heap (1887–1964), who printed Joyce's *Ulysses* in their periodical, the *Little Review,* and were brought up on consequent obscenity charges, were lovers for many years. In the *Little Review*, Anderson and Heap provided engaging cultural commentary and an important place for male and female literary modernists to circulate their work. Similarly, bookseller Sylvia Beach (1887–1962), who published Joyce's controversial volume and operated a store in Paris called Shakespeare and Company, was a longtime intimate with French bookseller Adrienne Monnier (1892–1956), who owned a store across the street. Both establishments became important cultural meeting places for the U.S. expatriates and French literati during several modernist decades. In the United States, poet Amy Lowell (1874–1925) and novelist Willa Cather presented lesbian modernism in traditional forms. In the United Kingdom, H.D.'s partner of more than forty years (though both women were married for some of that time), heiress Winifred Ellerman, who called herself Bryher (1894–1983), wrote novels and memoirs and provided lifelong emotional support for H.D. and critical financial backing for several female modernists. Other lesbian modernists include British writer Charlotte Mew (1869–1928), Anglo American poet and novelist Renée Vivien (originally Pauline Tarn [1877–1909]), Australian fiction writer Henry Handel Richardson (1870–1946), and Harlem Renaissance writer Angelina Weld Grimké (1880–1958).

## Conclusion

Despite ongoing elaborations of the description of the movement of modernism, the late twentieth century witnessed modernist studies brought to a pivotal point. The inclusion of the work of lesbians and other marginalized groups, like artists of the Harlem Renaissance, into the modernist framework has raised questions about the value of assimilating divergent artistic productions into an overarching critical construct. Several scholars have suggested that, in the late twentieth century, instead of trying to incorporate different styles and artists into a somewhat vaguely defined artistic and literary movement, it may be more accurate to speak of modernisms and consider clusters of writers and works separately. Some critics have suggested abandoning the term "modernism" altogether in favor of a broader designation like "early-twentieth-century studies." Whatever the outcome of the critical debate, it is clear that the artistic impulse in Europe, the United States, and elsewhere (the geographical scope of modernism is expanding) during the time period in question was critically influenced by lesbians.

*Anne Charles*

# M

## Bibliography

Benstock, Shari. "Expatriate Sapphic Modernism: Entering Literary History." In *Lesbian Texts and Contexts: Radical Revisions*. Ed. Karla Jay and Joanne Glasgow. New York: New York University Press, 1990, pp. 183–203.

Bradbury, Malcolm, and James McFarlane, eds. *Modernism: 1890–1930*. New York: Penguin, 1976.

Elliott, Bridget, and Jo-Ann Wallace, eds. *Women Artists and Writers: Modernist (Im)positionings*. New York: Routledge, 1994.

Felski, Rita. *The Gender of Modernity*. Cambridge, Mass.: Harvard University Press, 1995.

Jay, Karla. "Lesbian Modernism: (Trans)Forming the (C)Anon." In *Professions of Desire: Lesbian and Gay Studies in Literature*. Ed. George E. Haggerty and Bonnie Zimmerman. New York: Modern Language Association, 1995, pp. 72–83.

Kershner, R.B. *The Twentieth-Century Novel: An Introduction*. Boston: Bedford, 1997.

Perloff, Marjorie. "Modernist Studies." In *Redrawing the Boundaries: The Transformation of English and American Literary Studies*. Ed. Stephen Greenblatt and Giles Gunn. New York: Modern Language Association, 1992, pp. 154–178.

*See also* American Literature, Twentieth Century; Anderson, Margaret Carolyn; Barnes, Djuna Chappell; Barney, Natalie; Beach, Sylvia; Brooks, Romaine; Bryher; Cather, Willa; Colette; English Literature, Twentieth Century; Grimké, Angelina Weld; H.D. (Hilda Doolittle); Hall, Radclyffe; Harlem Renaissance; Lowell, Amy Lawrence; Mansfield, Katherine; Mew, Charlotte; Sackville-West, Vita; Stein, Gertrude; Vivien, Renée; Woolf, Virginia

## Monogamy and Nonmonogamy

Terms societies employ to differentiate between people who have sexual and/or emotional relationships with just one person and those who have relationships with more than one person simultaneously. Generally, the designations refer to sexual relations confined to one person or sexual relations outside of marriage. These distinctions and restrictions grew out of the formalizing of the institution of marriage. Marriage can be interpreted as the joining together of two people (generally male and female) in a special kind of social and legal dependence for the purpose of founding and maintaining a family. Monogamous is defined as "mono-" "gamos," one marriage only during a life or marriage with one person at a time.

Feminist scholars state that the origins of monogamy can be traced back five thousand years to the establishment of patriarchal rule. In the hierarchical, social construction of patriarchy, women were regarded as inferior to men. Viewed as the possessions of the male, women were used for barter and/or procreation. This concept of women as personal property gave rise to the precept of patrimonial inheritance, and male heirs inherited only if they were the legitimate sons of the father. Legitimacy of a child relates to the acknowledgment of the child's father, not to the child's mother. This definition of legitimacy is still a legal reality in many cultures, and children born to unmarried females are classified as illegitimate. To maintain a line of inheritance and to assure a father of the legitimacy of the male heir, the female must be confined in her sexual activities. Monogamy is, therefore, a necessity in marriage and patriarchy in terms of the bequeathing of familial inheritances of material goods and properties to heirs. In a patriarchal society, marriage and female fidelity are requirements for heterosexual relationships.

In the nineteenth century, Marxist philosophers considered both marriage and monogamy restrictive states reflective of the theories of capitalism, ownership of goods and of people. By the twentieth century, the institution of marriage and the belief in the natural state of monogamy have been so integrated into present-day thinking that they are both sanctioned as the normal mode of behavior in human relations. In present psychological texts, practicing monogamy has been viewed as a sign of stability and maturity, while nonmonogamy, especially for females, has been labeled as immature or, worse, transgressive behavior, punishable in some cultures by death.

For many centuries, scientists attempted to reinforce the supposition that humans were naturally monogamous by citing examples of monogamous coupling in other animal species. This has since been disproved by social scientists who attribute linking of human behavior to behavior of other animals as anthropomorphic (human-centered) thinking. In terms of sexuality, human beings cannot be compared to other animal species since they mate whenever they desire, not only when the female comes into heat.

There are a small number of societies in the world that do not proscribe multiple partners; however, in those cultures in which monogamous relationships have been endorsed as the ideal, clandestine nonmonogamy is widely practiced. Serial monogamy has also been a product of the concept of monogamy, facilitating the rejection of one person for the next.

The socialized patterns of monogamy and its historical derivations go largely unquestioned by lesbians. The implications of the historical prerogative of male inheritance has little relevance for the lesbian community, but the social values and behavioral modes of the larger heterosexual community have been firmly implanted within the larger lesbian population.

In the late 1960s through the 1970s, the "second wave" of feminism in the United States questioned all forms of heterosexual sexual practices, and monogamy was considered, by some, a restrictive tool used by the patriarchy to thwart women's sexual energies. Soon though, in the 1980s, the general backlash against women's equality began. The Barnard Women's Conference on Sexuality (New York City) in 1982 created a major furor between feminists when the conference organizers attempted to include representative speakers expressing the diversity of women's sexual experiences. Nonmonogamy was viewed by some as promiscuous, imitative of masculine behavior, and not politically correct.

There is still no positive word that has been generally adopted to express involvement with more than one person simultaneously, although "polyfidelity" or "polyamory" have both been used. Nonmonogamy is practiced, openly, by only a minority of the lesbian population, and lesbian nonmonogamy (polyamory) can be differentiated from heterosexual nonmonogamy as its purposes are intrinsically related to the structures that characterize the wide variety of lesbian lives. Lesbian nonmonogamy can be a political statement that rejects the confining heterosexual models of monogamy as not applicable to the diverse nature of lesbians. Nonmonogamy may also be a response to personal situations in which individual lesbians do not feel the needs for constraint in a relationship that has not been legally sanctioned, or it can be a way for two women to define autonomy within a coupled situation and avoid the intense bonding typical of some lesbian partners. Nonmonogamy can also be a method of extending friendship or a manifestation of friendship. Often, as in the heterosexual model, it is a way to make a transition from one monogamous relationship into another monogamous relationship.

The forms of nonmonogamy for lesbians vary. Within a partnered situation, one or both women might agree to having connections outside the primary one. Within the couple scenario, there can be additional people added to the couple to produce a triad, a quartet, or a shared lover. Although the forms and requirements of these setups vary from person to person, the general rules and guidelines for nonmonogamy are agreed to by both partners. Unpartnered nonmonogamous lesbians, whether by preference or chance, can choose to be open to various levels of involvement with other women, ranging from casual sex to intense personal commitments in friendships and loyalties.

Lesbian nonmonogamy can be an active force reflecting the openness and willingness of the participants to view nonmonogamy as a positive, and not a negative, aspect to their lives. The boundaries of lesbian nonmonogamy are continually being reset and invented, depending on personal arrangements and agreements.

*Judith P. Stelboum*

## Bibliography

Anapol, Deborah. *Love Without Limits: Responsible Nonmonogamy*. San Raphael, Calif.: Intinet Resource Center, 1992.

Eisler, Riane. *The Chalice and the Blade*. San Francisco: Harper, 1988.

Hall, Marny. *A U Haul Named Desire*. New York: HarperCollins, 1997.

Johnson, Sonia. *The Ship That Sailed into the Living Room*. Estancia, N.M.: Wildfire, 1991.

Kassof, Elizabeth. "Nonmonogamy in the Lesbian Community." Ph.D. diss., California School of Professional Psychology, 1985.

Stelboum, Judith, and Marcia Munson. *Lesbian Polyamory*. New York: Harrington, 1998.

West, Celeste. *Lesbian Polyfidelity*. San Francisco: Booklegger, 1996.

**See also** Couples

## Moraga, Cherríe (1952–)

Chicana lesbian playwright, poet, essayist, and teacher. Raised in the San Gabriel Valley by an Anglo father and a Chicana mother, Cherríe Moraga confronted the subtle effects of Southern California–style racism from the onset. With fair skin and a

M

*Cherríe Moraga. Photo © Patrick "Pato" Hebert. Courtesy of Cherríe Moraga.*

European surname, she was pushed to assimilate into Anglo society in order to excel. Moraga discovered the impact of this assimilation on her life during her years at a small private college in Los Angeles. As she began to acknowledge her sexual desire for women and confront the absolute silence imposed upon her, the depth of race and class oppression began to emerge in her consciousness. This awakening led her back into her mother's experience of oppression, "due to being poor, uneducated, and Chicana." Since this revelation, she has continued to argue the connections between oppressions, exploring the specificity of each condition and searching for the respective paths for empowerment and the creation of coalitions.

During the late 1970s and early 1980s, she co-founded Kitchen Table: Women of Color Press and began working on an anthology of writings by radical women of color. What began as a thesis project for her master's degree in feminist literature at San Francisco State University became a groundbreaking collection of voices testifying to the multiple oppressions levied against women of color. In addition to the women-of-color communities who immediately benefited from the broken silence, *This Bridge Called My Back: Writings by Radical Women of Color* (1981), coedited with Gloria Anzaldúa, was adopted by women's and ethnic studies courses throughout the nation and was awarded the Before Columbus Foundation Book Award in 1986. It became an important resource for the women's movement and feminism by critically exploring the deep-rooted racism within these groups. In the early 1980s, Moraga moved to New York City and became involved with a community of writers active at that time, including Audre Lorde, Barbara Smith, Gloria Anzaldúa, Myrtha Chabran, Amber Hollibaugh, Jewelle Gomez, and Dorothy Allison, among others.

In 1983, she published *Loving in the War Years/lo que nunca paso por sus labios*, a collection of essays, short stories, and poetry. In this work, she describes the painful consequences of her early separation from Mexican culture and history and the difficult process of reclamation. The text is noted for its revolutionary mixed-genre style and the essay "A Long Line of Vendidas," which explores the origins and implications of betrayal between Chicanas. Moraga utilizes her physical body as a site that informs her theory, examining the damages incurred, as well as the possibilities for healing. In 1993, *The Last Generation* appeared, incorporating both queer and bicultural theory. She has been anthologized in dozens of literary collections published by such notable presses as Norton, Routledge, Harper, and St. Martin's.

Eager to expand the autobiographical voice, Moraga began to focus her attention on playwrighting, allowing multiple expressions from families and communities to enter into her work through fictional characters. Since 1985 when Moraga turned to theater, she has written eight plays, including *Giving up the Ghost* (1987), *Shadow of a Man* (1990), *Heroes and Saints* (1992), and *Watsonville* (1995), which have been produced across the country. They address issues related to Mexican womanhood, Chicano/a and Mexicano/a cultural values, environmental racism, illegal immigration, the conditions of migrant farmworkers, indigenous and Mexican Catholic spirituality, contradictory strategies for female survival, the necessity of exposing secrets, and the impact of sensual, desperate desires.

Moraga makes her home in San Francisco with her son, Rafael Angel Moraga (b. 1992), where, in the late 1990s, she continued to write and teach chicana/o studies, women's studies, writing, and theater as an artist-in-residence at Brava Theater Center and Stanford University. As theorized in her literary works, she practices in her classrooms her conviction of creating radical change through the embrace of the stories and experiences of the silenced.

*Karleen Pendleton Jiménez*

## Bibliography

Yarbro-Bejarano, Yvonne. "Deconstructing the Lesbian Body: Cherríe Moraga's Loving in the War Years." In *Chicana Lesbians: The Girls Our Mother Warned Us About.* Ed. Carla Trujillo. Berkeley, Calif: Third Woman, 1991, pp. 143–155.

*See also* Anzaldúa, Gloria E.; Latina Literature; Lorde, Audre; Smith, Barbara; Theater and Drama, Contemporary

## Mothers, Lesbian

Lesbian mothers have probably always existed, but, for the same reasons that accurate demographic data on lesbians are rarely available, their absolute numbers or the proportion of all mothers who can be defined as lesbian cannot be established. Beyond this, because of the popular tendency to assume that women with children must be heterosexual, lesbian mothers have sometimes tended to be even more invisible than other lesbians.

The visibility of lesbian mothers increased, however, in the 1970s, when a number of highly publicized custody disputes, such as the Mary Jo Risher case in Texas and the case of Sandy Schuster and Madeleine Isaacson in Washington state, brought their existence to the attention of both the lesbian community and the wider society. The lesbian mothers involved in cases such as these had nearly all had their children during heterosexual marriages; disputes with former husbands either at the time of their divorces or later brought them into the legal system.

In virtually all of the publicized contested custody cases from this period involving lesbian mothers, judges removed children from their mothers' homes. The justifications used for these decisions rested on many of the same assumptions about gender and sexuality that also have prevailed in nonlesbian custody determinations. Judges have tended, for example, to assume that lesbian sexuality (or, indeed, any sexuality) implies promiscuity, self-indulgence, and an absence of the level of altruism and nurturance assumed to be necessary for adequate mothering. Even when evidence indicates that mothers offer their children excellent homes, judges have still accepted claims that children's psychological, social, or sexual development will be harmed by life in a lesbian household or that the stigma they may suffer because of their mother's sexual orientation will be a serious burden to them. The fear that any encounter with the legal system may lead to loss of custody has led lesbian mothers either to conceal their lesbianism from ex-husbands, children, and others or to forgo claims to property and child-support payments in exchange for usually informal agreements not to challenge custody. Their best defense against a threat that is all too real has required them to avoid the surveillance of the legal system, and this means that only a small proportion ever expose themselves to judicial scrutiny. Not surprisingly, these maneuvers have tended to compromise the economic status of lesbian mothers and their families, much as similar pressures have affected nonlesbian, formerly married mothers who had had to cope with custody challenges.

In response to the concerns about children's welfare raised in these cases, a number of psychologists have undertaken carefully controlled studies comparing the children of lesbian and heterosexual mothers; virtually all of this research has shown conclusively that no emotional or cognitive differences between children can be traced to their mother's (or father's) sexual orientation. In fact, studies that examine the later development of children of lesbian, gay, or transsexual parents in comparison with those from other families that have experienced divorce or separation reveal virtually no systematic differences. Despite the solidity of this body of research, however, and the appearance of some of the experts as witnesses in lesbian-mother custody cases, courts continue to discriminate against lesbian mothers, awarding children to their fathers and, occasionally, to other relatives when the mother's sexual orientation is made public. The 1993 case of Sharon Bottoms in Virginia, in which a lesbian mother's mother was awarded custody despite evidence that the grandmother's husband was prone to be sexually abusive, illustrates the depth of prejudice lesbian mothers experience in court.

Although there have probably always been some lesbians who have chosen motherhood outside of heterosexual marriages, these families became a more prominent part of the community in the 1980s, as the women's health movement and feminist clinics made donor insemination more readily available to unmarried women. Because many more lesbians began to choose motherhood during this period,

**M** through either donor insemination (sometimes jokingly called the "turkey baster" method), or a deliberate sexual encounter, or adoption, many observers began to refer to the existence of a "lesbian baby boom." But the appearance that a baby boom was under way very likely had as much to do with increasingly open lesbian community life as with actual increases in the numbers of lesbians choosing to become mothers.

In some cases, single lesbians or lesbians and their partners are raising children together, and, in a few states, the nonbiological mother has been able to adopt the children as a "second parent." In other instances, probably less frequently, lesbians and their children's fathers or donors have created alternative family arrangements, sometimes with the involvement of additional adults, such as mothers' or donors' lovers. All of these family forms have been, at times, strengthened by input from other adult caretakers, including friends and ex-lovers of mothers. The emergence of these seemingly new family constellations has stimulated discussion of lesbian and gay kinship and popularized the imagery of "families we choose" as a feature of lesbian community life. Still, research by Lewin (1993) indicates that lesbian mothers are likely also to maintain ongoing relationships with their biological families and to place particular emphasis on the symbolic importance of traditional kin ties. Lewin also found that lesbian mothers interact with other women who are mothers, regardless of their sexual orientation, and may perceive their identity as "mothers" to supersede or overwhelm that as "lesbians." Being mothers, in short, brings lesbians' lives closer to those of other women; while lesbian motherhood undermines the notion that only heterosexual women may be mothers, it also can enable lesbians to view themselves as women very much like others.

While earlier legal discussions of lesbian mothers tended to be preoccupied with custody problems and strategies for overcoming them, more recent legal concerns have surrounded relations with anonymous and known donors and problems that may arise between women when lesbian parents end their relationships. Because known donors may be legally regarded as fathers, lesbian mothers must often create elaborate contractual arrangements that restrict donors' rights; even when such documents exist, however, known donors may intrude more on lesbian mothers and their families than was originally planned. To avoid these hazards, which may even lead to custody and visitation rights going to a donor, many lesbians who wish to become mothers choose anonymous donors, using commercial sperm banks or go-betweens to locate suitable donors. But such arrangements do not resolve the issues of custody and visitation that may arise when lesbian coparents break up, which may leave the nonbiological mother without legally enforceable rights to see the children and may also allow the biological mother no way to claim support from her former partner.                              *Ellen Lewin*

### Bibliography

Burke, Phyllis. *Family Values.* New York: Random House, 1993.

Lewin, Ellen. *Lesbian Mothers: Accounts of Gender in American Culture.* Ithaca, N.Y.: Cornell University Press, 1993.

Maggiore, Dolores J., ed. *Lesbians and Child Custody: A Casebook.* New York: Garland, 1992.

Martin, April. *The Lesbian and Gay Parenting Handbook.* New York: HarperCollins, 1993.

Weston, Kath. *Families We Choose.* New York: Columbia University Press, 1991.

**See also** Adoption; Children; Custody Litigation; Donor Insemination; Family

## Music, Classical

Although classical music—music written in the Western art tradition—has been an extremely male-dominated arena and its history relies almost entirely on written documents, the diverse sounds of all-female musical communities throughout various periods of classical-music history can be heard. The presence of lesbians in classical music emerges primarily through highly suggestive contextual clues rather than documented "evidence." "Lesbian" and its related terms rarely, if ever, appear in musical discourse before the nineteenth century, but female homosocial musical traditions and representations of lesbian eroticism in musical texts invite one to challenge, reinterpret, and revise "official" histories of classical music.

### Medieval and Early-Modern Europe

Convents in Europe during the medieval period offered women an alternative to marriage and created all-women communities for making music. Medieval nuns composed, arranged, and sang liturgical music—plainsong and polyphony—as a central form of Christian worship and communal activity.

Twelfth-century nuns, such as Herrad of Hohenburg, Mechtilde of Magdeburg, Adelheid of Landau, Héloise, Marie of Oignies, Constance of Le Ronçeray, and Hildegard of Bingen (1098–1179), are known to have composed sacred music. Hildegard's numerous compositions survive, and many of her chants address female saints, as well as the Virgin Mary, in highly sensuous and erotic language and music.

In the medieval secular domain, the single remaining musical example of lesbian love is the song "Na Maria, pretz e fina valors" (Lady Maria, in you merit and distinction) by the thirteenth-century *trobairitz* (woman composer-poet) Bieiris de Romans.

Convents in fifteenth- and sixteenth-century Ferrara, Milan, Modena, and Bologna fostered all-female music making. The nuns at the San Vito Convent in Ferrara were led by organist and composer Sister Raffaella Aleotti and were admired for their high degree of musicianship as both vocalists and instrumentalists. In addition to their own liturgical music, these nuns performed public concerts and played instruments, such as cornetti and trombones, that were considered inappropriate for women. However, the Council of Trent (1545–1563) eventually restricted the musical educations of nuns and prohibited them from performing concerts.

The lives and careers of three women composers from the sixteenth and seventeenth centuries invite lesbian interpretations of their music. Madalena Casulana (ca. 1540–ca. 1590) was a well-respected singer and madrigal composer and the first woman to publish her music. Thomasin LaMay persuasively suggests that Casulana may have written the vast majority of the poems herself in her *Primo Libro dei madrigali à quattro voci* (First Book of Madrigals for Four Voices, published in 1568 and dedicated to Isabella de' Medici), and most of these poems address passion for a woman, sometimes with erotic imagery of the female body. Francesca Caccini (1587–1641?) was also a highly successful professional singer and composer of both sacred and secular music. She is recognized as the first woman opera composer, and in 1625 she wrote the Florentine court opera *La liberazione di Ruggiero dall' Isola d'Alcina* (The Liberation of Ruggiero from the Island of Alcina), based on Ariosto's *Orlando Furioso* (1516) and commissioned by Archduchess Maria Maddalena of Austria. Cusick (1993) argues that Caccini's gynocentric opera revolves around the struggle for power between two sorceresses, Melissa

and Alcina, over the young knight Ruggiero and is unusual in its absence of god figures to whom the women might appeal. Rather, this opera can be understood as a model of how its woman patron, Maria Maddalena, might rule sucessfully within the systems of patriarchy and monarchy. The later years of Caccini's career often centered on other women: Cusick believes she probably taught music to princesses Anna de' Medici and Vittoria della Rovere and taught, coached, and composed music for women in Florentine convents. Isabella Leonarda (1620–1704) entered the convent at age sixteen and published her first composition at age twenty. She composed both vocal and instrumental music for the church, and her passionate devotion to the Virgin Mary is borne out in her double dedications of her compositions—to the Virgin and to a human patron. It is likely that she wrote her own texts, and some of the most beautiful are addressed to the Virgin.

Next to convents, the Venetian *ospedali* (conservatories) of the seventeenth and eighteenth centuries stand as one of the most important musical institutions for the study of female-centered networks and musical practices. There were four *ospedali* in Venice, each with its own choir and orchestra of girls: the Ospedale della Pietà (where Antonio Vivaldi [1678–1741] taught), i Mendicanti, gli Incurabili, and i Derelitti, or l'Ospedaletto. The *ospedali* housed and educated orphaned and abandoned girls, and those with musical talent were given excellent musical training that required ten years of rigorous study. Each *ospedale* gave public concerts and attracted audiences from all over Europe. The best musicians could remain in the *ospedale* as *maestrae* and teach alongside the male masters. Such a career in music offered the *maestrae* an alternative to both marriage and the convent. The predominant genres of music cultivated and performed at the *ospedali* were concertos, choral music for treble voices, and oratorios (more than two hundred libretti for *ospedali* oratorios survive). Two of the most celebrated women violinists from the *ospedali* are Maestra Anna Maria della Pietà (for whom Vivaldi composed many violin concertos) and Maestra Maddalena Lombardini, who toured Europe with her violinist husband, Ludovico Sirmen, and composed her own concertos—the only woman trained in the *ospedali* known to have done so.

## Modern Era

In the late nineteenth century, all-women symphony orchestras and brass bands in Europe and North

**M** America offered women performers meager professional opportunities in music. These ensembles, particularly the orchestras, were modeled on the Vienna Ladies Orchestra, which toured America in 1871. They performed "light" classical music and were often led by male conductors; the musical public regarded them as a curious novelty. However, some of these orchestras were founded by women: the Philadelphia Women's Symphony by Mabel Swint Ewer in 1921, the British Women's Symphony Orchestra by Gwynne Kimpton in 1922, the Orchestrette Classique by Frédérique Petrides in 1932, and the New York Women's Symphony Orchestra by Antonia Brico in 1934. Most of the all-women's orchestras lasted between five and twenty years, and nearly all of them were forced to disband after the economic and social constraints that followed World War II.

The rise of feminist activism, particularly the suffrage movement, in the early decades of the twentieth century functions as an especially rich context for lesbian music making. Although lesbianism among the suffragists in Britain is still a story in waiting, Wood (1995) argues that several compositions by Ethel Smyth (1858–1944), such as her *Songs of Sunrise*, are inextricably linked both to her passion for Emmeline Pankhurst (1858–1928) and to her devotion to the suffragists, with whom Smyth engaged in militant feminist action in the years 1910–1912.

The Parisian salons of such notable lesbians as Natalie Barney (1876–1972), Gertrude Stein (1874–1946), and the Princess de Polignac (née Winaretta Singer [1865–1943]) were extremely important international gathering places for lesbian artists, including musicians. Among musical circles in Paris, Nadia Boulanger's work is of towering importance. Boulanger (1887–1979) helped found the American School at Fontainebleau and is regarded as the greatest composition teacher of the twentieth century. Some of her women students were Ruth Anderson (1928–), Cécile Armagnac (n.d.), Marion Bauer (1882–1955), Suzanne Bloch (1907–), Peggy Glanville-Hicks (1912–1990), Helen Hosmer (n.d.), Thea Musgrave (1928–), Priaulx Rainier (1903–1986), and Louise Talma (1906–1996). Boulanger formed lifelong friendships with Armagnac, Hosmer, and Talma. Many of her male students, such as Aaron Copland (1900–1990), Gian Carlo Menotti (1911–), Ned Rorem (1923–), and Virgil Thomson (1896–1989), were openly gay and accepted by her. Boulanger never married and lived most of her life with her mother, Raïssa, and personal assistant, An-

nette Dieudonné; at the time of her death, Dieudonné and Armagnac were her principal heirs. She was also tirelessly devoted to promoting the music of her younger sister, Lili Boulanger (1893–1918), who, in 1913, was the first woman composer to win the prestigious Grand Prix de Rome. As a Catholic, Boulanger held conflicting views about politics and sexuality. She rejected overtly feminist ideology, but, in practice, she was supremely critical of marriage for her women students and was keenly aware of the sexism those women would face in the music world. Her biographer, Rosenstiel (1982), writes that the salon of Princess de Polignac (whose lesbianism was well known) was extremely important to her career, but she avoided Stein's salon because the "flagrant homosexuality of many of its members [was] antithetical to [Boulanger's] belief in discretion and elitism." Rosenstiel further speculates that Boulanger was quite possibly a lesbian, but she was not allowed access to Boulanger's private diary.

## Opera

Sprinkled throughout the opera repertory are male characters sung by female singers ("breeches" or "trouser" roles), usually mezzo-sopranos or contraltos. These roles, and the women who sang them, support lesbian interpretations of these operas: Orfeo in Christoph Gluck's *Orfeo ed Euridice* (1762), Cherubino in Mozart's *The Marriage of Figaro* (1786), Arsace in Gioacchino Rossini's *Semiramide* (1823) and the title role in his *Tancredi* (1813), Romeo in Vincenzo Bellini's *I Capuleti ed i Montecchi* (1830), the title role in Jules Massenet's *Le Jongleur de Notre Dame* (1902), and Octavian in Richard Strauss's *Der Rosenkavalier* (1911). Explicitly lesbian characters can be found in Camille Erlanger's *Aphrodite* (1906), Alban Berg's *Lulu* (1929–1935), and Peggy Glanville-Hicks's *Sappho* (1960), opera's most illustrious lesbian composer, Ethel Smyth, wrote six operas. While none of them feature lesbian roles, *Fantasio* (1894), *The Boatswain's Mate* (1914), and *Fête Galante* (1923) resonate clearly with Smyth's notions of lesbian desire and her political work with the British suffragists. Groundbreaking scholarly work by Castle (1993) and Wood (1994) on opera divas and lesbian audition has prompted a reexamination of the opera repertory and its connections to lesbian cultural life, past and present.

## "Second Wave" Feminism

The "second wave" of the feminist movement in the 1960s encouraged women in classical music to revisit the institution of professional female orchestras. In 1978, lesbian composer-conductor Kay Gardner cofounded, with Nancy Barrett Thomas and Leslie Judd, the New England Women's Symphony; in 1981, flutist Nan Washburn helped found the Bay Area Women's Philharmonic in San Francisco, California. Both groups have women conductors and were formed with the feminist aim of seeking out and performing music written specifically by women composers, both historical and contemporary. Similarly, the European Women's Orchestra, based in Britain and conducted by Odaline de la Martinez, features repertoire by women composers. The Minnesota Philharmonia is nonprofessional and the first lesbian and gay community orchestra of its kind; ironically, this group does not perform music by lesbian or gay composers, and its conductor, James Touchi-Peters, is heterosexual (though queer supportive).

Although her work does not involve the women's symphony orchestra circuit, guitarist Sharon Isbin came out in 1995. One of the only "out" lesbians in professional classical music, Isbin teaches guitar at the Julliard School of Music in New York City and has commissioned many new works for guitar, including the *Troubadour Concerto* (1993) by John Corigliano, a composer who addressed the tragedy of AIDS in his *Symphony No. 1* (1991).

The most overtly lesbian context for making classical music is the tradition of grass-roots feminist community choruses that began in earnest in 1975. While influenced, in part, by the popularity of "women's music," women's choruses in Europe, North America, and Australia do not limit themselves to singing the more folk-inspired "women's music"; rather, they recover historical music by women composers and perform new music by women as well. Choral music by male composers that feature texts by women and/or lesbian poets are also sought. Groups such as the Calliope Women's Chorus (Minneapolis), the Anna Crusis Women's Choir (Philadelphia), Muse: Cincinnati Women's Choir, the Bread and Roses Feminist Singers (Maryland), and the Portland (Oregon) Lesbian Choir, to name only a few, include both lesbians and straight women and often program music with texts that address lesbian eroticism. Most of these choirs belong to the Sister Singers Network and the Gay and Lesbian Association of Choruses; many have produced compact discs and are well known in the lesbian community. In addition to classical music of all periods, many women's choruses turn to non-Western repertoires (especially traditional African and Latin American music) and actively commit themselves to abolishing racism and ethnocentrism in musical performance.

[The author thanks Sophie Fuller, Chip Whitesell, and Elizabeth Wood for their assistance in preparing this entry.]                    *Martha Mockus*

## Bibliography

Blackmer, Corrine E., and Patricia Juliana Smith, eds. *En Travesti: Women, Gender Subversion, Opera*. New York: Columbia University Press, 1995.

Castle, Terry. *The Apparitional Lesbian: Female Homosexuality and Modern Culture*. New York: Columbia University Press, 1993.

Cusick, Suzanne G. "Of Women, Music, and Power: A Model from Seicento Florence." In *Musicology and Difference: Gender and Sexuality in Music Scholarship*. Ed. Ruth A. Solie. Berkeley: University of California Press, 1993, pp. 281–304.

Holsinger, Bruce Wood. "The Flesh of the Voice: Embodiment and the Homoerotics of Devotion in the Music of Hildegard of Bingen (1098–1179)." *Signs: Journal of Women in Culture and Society* 19:1 (1993), 92–125.

Jackson, Barbara Garvey. "Musical Women of the 17th and 18th Centuries." In *Women and Music: A History*. Ed. Karin Pendle. Bloomington: Indiana University Press, 1991, pp. 54–94.

Rosenstiel, Léonie. *Nadia Boulanger: A Life in Music*. New York: Norton, 1982.

Wood, Elizabeth. "Performing Rights: A Sonography of Women's Suffrage." *Musical Quarterly* 79:4 (Winter 1995), 606–643.

———. "Sapphonics." In *Queering the Pitch: The New Gay and Lesbian Musicology*. Ed. Philip Brett, Elizabeth Wood, and Gary C. Thomas. New York: Routledge, 1994, pp. 26–66.

Yardley, Anne Bagnall. "'Ful weel she soong the service dyvyne': The Cloistered Musician in the Middle Ages." In *Women Making Music: The Western Art Tradition, 1150–1950*. Ed. Jane Bowers and Judith Tick. Urbana: University of Illinois Press, 1986, pp. 15–38.

*See also* Choruses, Women's; Composers; Hildegard of Bingen, Saint; Landowska, Wanda; Music, Women's; Opera; Religious Communities; Smyth, Dame Ethel Mary

# M

## Music Festivals

Primary public venue for the live presentation of music by women and "women's music"; coffeehouses also function as the smaller, local counterpart to festivals. There are about twenty women's music festivals in North America that occur annually in rural settings during the summer months, between May and September, and draw between five hundred and ten thousand women each. These festivals expose lesbian audiences to new music that is otherwise difficult to obtain and allow women's record labels to investigate the potential popularity of a given artist. The Michigan Womyn's Music Festival, founded in 1975, is the largest ongoing festival. A veritable lesbian cultural institution, this six-day event is held in the woods of Oceana County and features three stages and an increasingly diverse program, ranging from established artists, such as Margie Adam, Alix Dobkin, and Sweet Honey and the Rock, to brand-new women musicians. It is probably the most international festival of its kind, having booked artists from Japan and South Africa and drawing crowds of women from all fifty states, every Canadian province, and more than twenty other countries. In addition to the music, there are open mikes and workshops addressing issues of race, class, health, and sexuality. This festival has set a precedent for other lesbian and feminist events (musical or otherwise) by including sign-language interpreters, wheelchair accessibility, and child-care facilities.

While women's music festivals are open to all women, the vast majority of organizers, producers, artists, and audiences are lesbians. The National Women's Music Festival, begun in 1974 in Champaign-Urbana, Illinois, is held in Bloomington, Indiana. Smaller venues include the West Coast Women's Music and Comedy Festival (California) (begun in 1979) and the Women's Jazz Festival in Kansas City, Missouri (begun in 1978), as well as the Gulf Coast Women's Festival (Mississippi), the Southern Women's Music and Comedy Festival (Georgia), the East Coast Lesbians' Festival (Massachusetts), the Northampton Lesbian Festival (Massachusetts), and Sisterfire (Maryland), all of which started in the 1980s. In 1987 the Sisterfire Festival was notable for including a Deaf Stage and for placing the child-care area, called the Hearth, at the center of the festival rather than at the periphery. Sisterfire is also considered a leader in programming multicultural music (Asian, Latina, and Native American artists) and challenging the stereotype of women's music as acoustic white folk music.

Newer festivals are Rhythmfest (North Carolina), which began in 1990, and the Lone Star Women's Music Festival (Texas), started in 1994.

Several festivals are held in Canada, although not all are annual events. Among these are the Vancouver Women's Music Festival (1988), the Canadian Women's Music and Cultural Festival (Winnipeg, 1984), Women in View: A Festival of Performing Arts (Vancouver, 1989), the Western Canadian Women's Music Festival (once only in 1976), the Kingston Womyn's Music Festival (Ontario, 1984), and the Festival International de Musiciennes Innovatrices (Québec, 1988), which featured avant-garde and experimental music.

Each festival has its own character, and, in addition to musicians, many festivals feature dancers, performance artists, and stand-up comics, such as Robin Tyler, Kate Clinton, Pat Harrison, and Lynn Lavner. The Women's Jazz Festival, organized by Carol Comer and Dianne Gregg, showcases jazz by women musicians but includes male performers as well.

Most of these festivals are for women and girls only, although preadolescent boys are usually allowed. A storm of controversy has surrounded the Michigan festival, in particular, for its exclusion of transsexual and transgender women. Several festivals are run cooperatively and require women to share certain work duties so that the admission price remains affordable to everyone.　*Martha Mockus*

### Bibliography

McBride, Renee, and Yolanda Retter. "Festivals: Born from Womyn's Music." *Lesbian News* 21:1 (August 1995), 31–32, 36.

Petersen, Karen E. "An Investigation into Women-Identified Music in the United States." In *Women and Music in Cross-Cultural Perspective*. Ed. Ellen Koskoff. Urbana: University of Illinois Press, 1987, pp. 203–212.

*See also* Land; Music, Popular; Music, Women's

## Music, Popular

Music that has wide public appeal. Central to this appeal is the ability of music to evoke our deepest desires and identifications. At the same time, popularity is typically synonymous with commercial success, particularly in the United States. Hence, popular music typically positions women as objects of male desire. To achieve commercial success, female performers have been required to project a sense of (hetero)sexual availability.

While images of heterosexuality dominate popular music, they have not gone unchallenged. Lesbians, for example, have always found ways to listen to popular music against the grain—changing the pronouns of songs in their heads and projecting their fantasies upon their favorite performers. The fantasies lesbians construct about particular performers' identities, and about themselves in relation to these identities, are a collectively shaped and shared part of lesbian experience.

Lesbian-identified artists have also struggled for greater representation in musical production, both by explicitly encoding lesbian references into their music and by using more implicit, ambiguous coding.

## Pioneers

Lesbian performers have long participated in the creation of popular music in the United States, although relatively few have openly identified themselves as such. Generally, overt homosexuality has been seen as a threat to the popularity of commercially successful artists. Large record companies, organized to minimize risk, seek out the "lowest common denominator" and hold back potentially discreditable information about a performer from the public.

The presence of lesbians in the entertainment field has been a guarded secret. But at certain times and places, such as Paris and Harlem in the 1920s and 1930s, female homosexuality became a source of musical inspiration and a subject of fascination and intrigue.

References to gender and sexual nonconformity made their way into the art of a number of female blues singers in the United States during the Jazz Age. Bessie Smith (1894–1937) puzzled over "mannish-acting women" in her "Foolish Man Blues" (1927), and Gertrude "Ma" Rainey (1886–1939) confessed that she liked to "wear a collar and a tie" in her "Prove It on Me Blues" (1928). "They say I do it, ain't nobody caught me, they sure got to prove it on me," sang Rainey, about the friends who "must've been women, cause I don't like no men." Blues singers Ethel Waters (1896–1977) and Alberta Hunter (1895–1984) were also said to have had romantic relationships with women.

Gladys Bentley (1907–1960), a 250-pound tough-talking cross-dressing singer, enjoyed a successful twenty-year career in Harlem's jazz scene, until the repressive climate of the 1950s forced her to sanitize her act, begin wearing dresses, and bury her lesbian image.

In the 1960s, the "girl group" sound spawned singers such as Leslie Gore (1946–) and Dusty Springfield (1939–1999), who achieved mass popularity and a loyal lesbian and gay following. In 1970, Fanny became the first all-woman rock and roll band to be signed and promoted extensively by a major label.

## Women's Music

In the 1970s, the feminist movement provided the impetus for many women to create their own fiction, visual art, and music and to openly incorporate their sexual identities into their creative work. Though not always explicitly lesbian, women's music was created and performed primarily by lesbian feminists. It was imbued with a belief in a universal female sensibility, expressed in the idea of "woman identification," and defined, in large part, by its opposition to masculinist forms of culture, such as mainstream rock and roll.

In addition to encouraging innovation in terms of musical content, women's music politicized the process of music production. Its producers sought to redress the fact that women in general, and lesbians in particular, had been shut out of positions of power in the music industry. They believed that it was important to erase the distinctions between the industry, the performers, and the audience—distinctions that were central to commercially produced music.

The vision of women's music was an ambitious one. In positively valuing lesbian lives and accomplishments and serving as an organizing tool, it played an important role in the development of lesbian feminist culture. However, the narrow way in which women's music was defined—as music produced by, of, and for feminists—may have inadvertently limited its appeal.

By the 1980s, the most loyal sectors of the women's music audience had aged, shedding some of their political commitments to alternative women's culture. Some suggested that women's music had been firmly entrenched in what was, for the most part, a European tradition. Others criticized women's music for its stylistic conservatism. The feminist movement had helped create an audience that was beginning to outgrow the counterculture.

## Crossover Stars

While lesbian musicians of the 1970s were forced out of the mainstream in order to achieve some creative autonomy, fifteen years later there were signs of new openings. In the late 1980s, a new wave of "androgynous" women began to find their way onto major record labels and into mainstream tastes.

Tracy Chapman's carefully crafted folk albums garnered her millions of fans. The Indigo Girls, an Atlanta-based duo, performed soul-searching folk-rock ballads, drawing upon folk and country influences. k.d. lang, a cross-dressing crossover artist, flaunted a butch image, blending pop and country music. Melissa Etheridge, clad in jeans and vest, prowled and kicked at her guitars and produced hard-driving rock and roll. Michelle Shocked blended feminist and anarchist sympathies with traditional folk and blues influences.

Even if they tended to skirt clear identifications, these artists weren't particularly heterosexually identified either, studiously avoiding male pronouns in romantic ballads and carefully constructing their personas to assert a strong, if sexually ambiguous, presence. This ambiguity appealed to a lesbian and gay audience and garnered mass appeal.

On the heels of the feminist movement, female performers and fans became commercially important "properties" and "markets," giving both musicians and fans new power. The trail was blazed by women's music and by a number of commercially popular performers who broke with conventions of femininity in popular music. Beginning in the late 1970s, Joan Armatrading attracted a large feminist and gay following for her finely crafted and sexually ambiguous rock and folk ballads. Madonna, one of if not the most successful female stars of the 1980s and 1990s, exuded sexual power and invincibility, at times making allusions to lesbianism, as on her "Justify My Love" video, which was banned by MTV (Music Television) at the end of 1990. Queen Latifah challenged the sexism of rap music in such albums as *Nature of a Sista'*. Even country music, which had never been known for its gender and sexual nonconformity, produced such artists as Nanci Griffith and Mary-Chapin Carpenter, who departed from Nashville's "stand by your man" approach.

At the same time, a few artists recording on major independent labels made lesbianism an integral part of their art. Phranc, calling herself a "Jewish lesbian folksinger," made several records, including the 1989 album *I Enjoy Being a Girl*, which pictured her in a flat-top haircut, alongside a blurb that sang her praises as a "little daughter of bilitis." The Austin, Texas, trio Two Nice Girls made no bones about identifying as lesbians and, indeed,

flaunted it. Their tongue-in-cheek "I Spent My Last $10 (On Birth Control and Beer)," was a country-and-western "tale of woe" about a lesbian who breaks up with her girlfriend and unexpectedly finds love in the arms of a "strong hairy man."

By the early 1990s, these and other developments made it possible for a few mainstream artists to "cross over" and achieve commercial success as "out" lesbian performers. Lang and Etheridge came out as lesbians to great fanfare within lesbian and gay circles and even greater commercial success. They were able to openly integrate their sexual identities into their art. Singer-songwriter Janis Ian, who had a series of hits in the 1960s and 1970s, including "Society's Child," one of the first songs to tackle the theme of interracial romance, followed suit.

But there were limits to the crossover artists' newfound power. Lesbian performers were still generally seen as marketable only when their sexuality was muted. A woman singing a love song to another woman was, for the most part, still taboo, as Phranc sang: "Androgyny is the ticket or at least it seems to be. Just don't wear a flat-top and mention sexuality, and girl you'll go far, you'll get a record contract and be a star." Few, if any, major record labels specifically targeted a lesbian audience. In the mainstream, the classic dilemma persisted: A performer either became known as a "lesbian artist" and was, thus, doomed to marginality, or she watered down her lesbianism to appeal to a mass audience.

## Alternative Rock

Even as lesbians enjoyed greater visibility than ever in popular music in the 1990s, many artists and fans had little interest in crossing over to the mainstream. They shared with their lesbian feminist predecessors a disdain for commercialism, a belief in the capacity of anyone to create music, and a desire to create cultural space for women. But they rejected the feminist belief that brashness is inherently male, and they created a music that was loud and, often, rude. Rather than abandon rock and roll as inherently misogynistic, as women's music did, they reclaimed it.

This tradition of performers could trace its roots to artists such as Patti Smith, Pat Benatar, Janis Joplin, and others who had defied conventions of gender since the 1960s. Proto-punk singer-songwriter Patti Smith proclaimed, "As far as I'm concerned, any gender is a drag," and wore men's shirts and ties, affecting a street-tough, androgynous style. Grace Jones struck a gender-bending Amazonian pose.

In England, Annie Lennox, lead singer of the Eurythmics, accepted a 1984 Grammy Award decked out in full Elvis Presley–style drag. The Au Pairs poked fun at heterosexual antagonisms, and Siouxsee Sioux sang love songs to women. Bands such as the Slits and the Raincoats provided alternative images of women and sometimes made allusions to lesbianism.

Inspired by these and other performers, throughout the 1980s, in San Francisco, Boston, New York City, and other cities, local bands with names such as Mermaid Tatoo, Lesbian Snake Charmers, Gutter Sluts, and Mudwimmin created a new kind of musical presence within the lesbian community. They embraced punk and other "bad girl" styles, unabashedly flaunted their sexuality, and mocked the image of the sexy girl group. A few, such as 4 Non Blondes and Tribe 8, achieved some commercial success.

A cosexual "queer" youth subculture emerged alongside this music scene, partly through the medium of fanzines, photocopied homemade magazines with names like Homocore and JD's (Juvenile Delinquents) that featured long, rambling subscriber mail from alienated youth in far-flung places, short stories and graphics, and interviews with musicians. Queer punks shared a feminist and anarchist politic and a disdain for professionalism, commercialism, and anything that reeked of "mainstream" values.

In the 1990s, a subculture that first emerged in the Pacific Northwest and the Northeast, made up of young, angry women engaged in cultural production—fanzines, music, performance events—came to be known as "riot girls." Bands such as Bikini Kill, Hole, Babes in Toyland, and Team Dresch, some of whom included out lesbians, blended anarchism and punk and were clearly influenced by feminist/lesbian sensibilities.

Singer-songwriter Ani diFranco won a huge cult following for her live performances of hard-edged folk music that spoke unabashedly of bisexuality. Shunning the commercial record industry, she formed her own company to distribute her music to her young, largely female fans. DiFranco's songs, which blended the soul-searching quality of women's music and the raunchy abandon of riot-girl punk, embodied the gender/sexual sensibilities of a new generation of women.          *Arlene Stein*

### Bibliography

Gaar, Gillian. *She's a Rebel: The History of Women in Rock and Roll*. Seattle: Seal, 1992.

Griffin, Gabriele, ed. *Outwrite: Lesbianism and Popular Culture*. London: Pluto, 1993.

Hamer, Diane, and Belinda Budge, eds. *The Good, the Bad, and the Gorgeous: Popular Culture's Romance with Lesbianism*. London: Pandora, 1994.

Lewis, Lisa. *Gender Politics and MTV: Voicing the Difference*. Philadelphia: Temple University Press, 1990.

McDonnell, Evelyn, and Ann Powers, eds. *Rock She Wrote*. New York: Delta, 1995.

Stein, Arlene, ed. *Sisters, Sexperts, Queers: Beyond the Lesbian Nation*. New York: Plume, 1993.

***See also*** Bentley, Gladys; Blues Singers; lang, k.d. (Kathryn Dawn); Music, Women's; Rainey, Gertrude "Ma"; Smith, Bessie; 'zines

## Music, Women's

Genre of popular music that emerged in the early 1970s as music by, for, and about women. Women's music is defined in *The Ladyslipper Catalog and Resource Guide and Catalog of Records and Tapes by Women* as "music springing from a feminist consciousness, utilizing women's talent . . . with production, presentation and finances controlled by women." It is the music most closely connected to the "second wave" of feminism, and communities of lesbians were (and still are) its main audience. Its primary precursors were the women's suffrage music of the early twentieth century, the blues queens of the 1920s, and Malvina Reynolds's (1900–1978) political songs.

### Characteristics

Also referred to as "woman-identified music," "women's music" is something of a euphemism for "lesbian music" since the vast majority of the artists, production companies, and audiences were lesbians. Founding artist Alix Dobkin asserted in a 1992 article in the *Lesbian News* (Los Angeles, California) that "women's music is second only to softball in creating and sustaining a culture and having a profound effect on lesbians." This was the first musical context in which lesbian life, desire, and sexuality were sung about openly. Lesbian relationships and the feminist critique of patriarchy, misogyny, and homophobia, as well as the desire for independence from men, were concerns that were not sufficiently expressed in mainstream, male-dominated popular music of the late 1960s and early 1970s. In this respect, women's music was an extremely important stimulus in the formation of the lesbian feminist community.

Stylistically, women's music draws most heavily from the folk tradition, although the traces of rock, pop, jazz, reggae, and classical music are often heard. Women's music usually features autobiographical lyrics and an emphasis on acoustic instruments: guitar and/or piano as primary accompaniment, and light percussion, strings, or winds as secondary timbres.

Women's music was not broadcast over radio or television, but promoted through women-owned and -operated record labels and production companies, which had no precedent in twentieth-century Western music. The grass-roots, low-budget effort provided women with the opportunity to record, engineer, produce, and distribute recordings in a feminist environment and to be trained in the various aspects of the music business. Olivia Records was founded in 1973 in the Washington, D.C., area and soon moved to Los Angeles, California; in late 1977, Olivia settled in Oakland, California. Other women's music labels include Women's Wax Works, Redwood Records (established by Holly Near in 1973), Kay Gardner's Urana Records (New York City), and Margie Adam's and Barbara Price's Pleiades Records (Berkeley, California). Ladyslipper (based in Durham, North Carolina) began in 1977 and is the largest distributor of women's music. While many of these labels and distribution companies were short-lived, Olivia Records has remained the most successful, despite the economic decline of the late 1980s. The Reagan-Bush era (1980–1992) was particularly difficult for the women's music business, forcing Olivia to sponsor all-lesbian vacation cruises, and in 1989 Redwood became a nonprofit organization.

## Performers

The New Haven Women's Liberation Rock Band, the Chicago Women's Liberation Rock Band, Family of Women, and New Harmony Sisterhood Band were all-women's acoustic folk bands that started up ca. 1972–1973. However, solo singer-songwriters were far more well known than bands.

Maxine Feldman is usually credited with performing the first lesbian song, "Angry At This," in 1969 in Los Angeles; this was later recorded on her album *Closet Sale* (1979) with Galaxia Records. However, the first album of women's music was *Lavender Jane Loves Women* (1973), recorded by

Alix Dobkin with Kay Gardner on the Women's Wax Works label. Dobkin performed folk music in New York City coffeehouses in the late 1960s, and, in 1971, she decided to focus on writing songs about women's experiences. She also recorded *Living with Lesbians* (1976), *XXAlix* (1980), *Never Been Better/These Women* (1986), and a compilation CD *Love and Politics: A 30-Year Saga* (1992), all on the Women's Wax Works label. Dobkin continues to perform at women's music festivals throughout North America. Her musical style falls in the folk tradition, and her songs often address the issues of women's relationships with women—as mothers, daughters, lovers, and friends. As an openly lesbian feminist, Dobkin is an iconoclastic figure for the women's music community; she has also performed in conjunction with Jewish political groups and remains active in the struggle against antisemitism.

Cris Williamson produced her first album, *The Changer and the Changed* (Olivia), in 1975. It was the widest-selling album in women's music (more than 250,000 copies) and is regarded as a classic in the genre. Williamson is one of the pioneers in women's music, along with Dobkin, Margie Adam, Meg Christian, and Holly Near. Her music combines folk, country, and pop sounds with soulful lyrics of lesbian passion. She has performed regularly at women's music festivals, remains active in the lesbian feminist community, and has produced nearly a dozen albums since *The Changer*, including *Blue Rider* (1982), *Prairie Fire* (1985), and *Wolf Moon* (1985), all on the Olivia label. She collaborated with Tret Fure on *Postcards from Paradise* (1993), also on Olivia, and Teresa Trull on *Country Blessed* (1989) on Second Wave. When she is not touring, she teaches music at small universities and colleges. In 1990, Olivia released a documentary videotape, *The Changer: A Record of the Times*, which chronicles the early history of women's music and includes interviews with Williamson, Christian, Bonnie Raitt, Near, and Adam, as well as rare concert footage from the mid-1970s.

Meg Christian grew up in Lynchburg, Virginia, and completed a degree in music from the University of North Carolina. She studied classical guitar, folk, and Appalachian music. In the early 1970s, she involved herself in radical feminism and performed extensively at women's music festivals. In 1974, she recorded her first album, *I Know You Know* (Olivia), which included both original material and songs by other artists. Christian's own tunes deal openly with various aspects of lesbian life, and her "Ode to a

Gym Teacher" remains one of her best-known songs. In 1977, she recorded *Face the Music* (Olivia), on which she sings "Leaping Lesbians" (by Sue Fink and Joelyn Grippo), and collaborates with Sweet Honey in the Rock, Near, Linda Tillery, and Trull. For Olivia, she recorded *Turning It Over* in 1981, the double album *Meg/Cris at Carnegie Hall* (Second Wave Records) in 1983, and *From the Heart* in 1984; soon after, she left the women's music scene to study Syda Yoga with Guruyami Chidvilasananda in India. She recorded a tape in 1986, *The Fire of My Love: Songs for Guruyami Chidvilasananda* (Ladyslipper).

Many leading figures in women's music are African American and African Canadian. Mary Watkins trained as a classical pianist, studied music at Howard University, and later moved into jazz. Her own compositions draw from jazz, rhythm and blues, gospel, and soul traditions. She has recorded three albums: *Something Moving* (1978) (Olivia), on which four pieces are purely instrumental compositions; *Winds of Change* (1982) (Palo Alto Records); and *Spiritsong* (1985) (Redwood). She often collaborates with Linda Tillery, both of whom are extremely dedicated to the women's music scene, have produced records for other musicians, and have played on the albums of other women's music artists. Tillery is a singer, songwriter, and percussionist whose style is most inspired by rhythm and blues. She recorded *Linda Tillery* (Olivia) in 1977, *Secrets* (411 Records) in 1986, and *Good Time, A Good Time* (Tuizer Music), a collection of blues and sprituals with the Cultural Heritage Choir, in 1995. Many of her songs address political oppression, liberation, and religious hypocrisy. Déidre McCalla earned a degree in theater from Vassar College and established her career as an out lesbian in women's music as a guitarist and songwriter who works mainly in the folk music tradition. She has recorded *Fur Coats and Blue Jeans* (1973) on the Roulette label and *Don't Doubt It* (1985), *With a Little Luck* (1987), and *Everyday Heroes and Heroines* (1992) for Olivia. Faith Nolan of Toronto is also a folk-blues guitarist and songwriter, who often sings about the lives of blacks in Canada. Her recordings include *Africville* (1986) and *Sistership* (1987), both on the Multi Cultural Women in Concert (MCWIC) label, and *Freedom to Love* (1989) (Redwood), a collection of protest songs.

Holly Near is a groundbreaking figure in women's music and maintains a prolific career as a songwriter, performer, actress, and recording artist.

In 1973, she recorded *Hang in There* (Redwood). She has recorded more than ten albums and continues to be one of the most visible figures in women's music, performing at festivals, benefit concerts, and at larger venues, where her music has attracted mainstream folk audiences.

Many of these artists can be heard on Olivia's *Lesbian Concentrate: A Lesbianthology of Songs and Poems* (1977), a collective project designed to counteract Anita Bryant's homophobic campaign of the mid-1970s.

## Conclusion

The heydey of women's music subsided ca. 1985 when both socioeconomic pressures and changes in mainstream popular music shifted the focus away from a "woman-identified" musical culture. Successful women musicians of the late 1980s and the 1990s—several of whom are out lesbians—such as k.d. lang, Tracy Chapman, Shawn Colvin, Melissa Etheridge, Michelle Shocked, Suzanne Vega, The Indigo Girls, and Sinead O'Connor—offered strong alternative sounds and messages to lesbian listeners while recording on mainstream labels, making the Top Forty, producing videos, winning Grammy Awards, and performing for general audiences. While critics of women's music argue that its overall musical style lacked interest and innovation, supporters claim that the success of contemporary mainstream women artists has a great deal to do with the political passion and commitment of women's music. Newer artists, such as Phranc (née Susie Gottlieb), Girls in the Nose, and Two Nice Girls, are out lesbians whose music crosses over between lesbian and general audiences.

*Martha Mockus*

### Bibliography

Dlugacz, Judy. "If It Weren't for the Music: 15 Years of Olivia Records." *Hot Wire: The Journal of Women's Music and Culture* 4:3 (July 1988), 28–31, 52.

Near, Holly with Derk Richardson. *Fire in the Rain, Singer in the Storm*. New York: Morrow, 1990.

Pipik, Jane E. "Woman-Identified Music: Moving On." *Heresies* 10 (1980), 88–90.

Pollock, Mary S. "The Politics of Women's Music: A Conversation with Linda Tillery and Mary Watkins." *Frontiers: A Journal of Woman Studies* 10:1 (1988), 14–19.

———. "Recovery and Integrity: The Music of Meg Christian." *Frontiers* 9:2 (1987), 29–34.

Post, Laura. *Backstage Pass: Interviews with Women in Music.* Norwich, Vt.: New Victoria, 1997.

*See also* Community; lang, k.d. (Kathryn Dawn); Lesbian Feminism; Music Festivals; Music, Popular; Olivia

## Mystery and Detective Fiction

The lesbian mystery novel has its origins in lesbian pulp fiction works of the 1950s and early 1960s. Their glimpse into an underworld of intrigue and suspense is redelivered in the lesbian crime novels that proliferated in British and North American feminist publishing houses during the 1980s. They allow the reader to step into, relish, and then render safe a quagmire of sex, violence, and death. Lesbian crime novels are also about discovering, and exploring, lesbian identities.

The first lesbian feminist crime novel was M.F. Beal's *Angel Dance* (1977). Its angry, complex, visionary indictment of hetero/patriarchal capitalism is replete with the peculiar energy of 1970s protest culture. The Chicana detective and first-person narrator, Kat Guerrera, is a subversive whose character embodies the way class, race, gender, and sexuality interface to uphold the dominant order of law. The corrupt power of the state is represented as being so extensive that the concept of justice can no longer be invoked.

This figure of the lesbian guerrilla—an icon of 1970s resistance culture—was distilled by French materialist philosopher Monique Wittig in her 1971 novel *Les Guérillères*. This invention of a new, militant category of lesbian, inspired by the myth of the Amazon, invigorated a whole community of women to wage "war" on the political institution of heterosexuality. The early lesbian detectives reproduced this figure.

The traditional crime novel is a site for the expression of anxieties about society in which the enemy is named and destroyed. In the lesbian and feminist crime novel, the terms often become inverted, so that the state is identified as the corrupt enemy, and the lesbian sleuth, normally the feared and hated Other, is the victor. The narrative resolution of the mystery is resolved in two stages: First, by using the process of individuation intrinsic to the thriller mode, the lesbian hero achieves self-determination; and, second, she becomes integrated into a community. The first phase is often represented by coming out; the second, by finding love, in the form of the romance, and/or discovering the lesbian community, in a movement toward politicized self-integration.

Lesbian mystery fiction has consistently problematized the use of the heroic. A type of novel predominant in the mid-1980s self-consciously appropriated the image of the avenging knight, offering a sexy superdyke striding the city streets in her steel-capped boots, swinging her double-headed axe, leaving slain patriarchs in her wake. This was one form of transgressing the boundaries of the genre. Later manifestations tended to produce antiheroes, such as the unnamed protagonist in Sarah Schulman's novel *After Delores* (1988).

Lesbian mystery fiction often makes more explicit the representation of butch culture. As a subcultural stereotype, the butch detective works at two levels of identification for the reader. Not only does the reader desire the butch, who is a figure of eroticized power, she also wants to be the butch or, at least, procure her sense of agency. Femme lesbian detectives are rare, since the conflation of the masterful detective hero with femininity can be jarring. Paradoxically, the most convincing super-femme sleuths are heterosexual: novelists Sara Paretsky, Sue Grafton, and Patricia Cornwell have all produced fantasy femme protagonists in the 1980s and 1990s.

In genre theory, detective fiction has been most likened to satire. Classic Greek satire, in its simplest form, consists of a dialogue between stylized characters who merely mouth ideas. The two speakers are an *eiron*, the hero, and an *alazon*, someone usually revealed to be a deluded and pompous fool. The lesbian crime-fiction detective's dramatic function is to expose alazons using her powers of reasoning, thus leading the reader into a changed and enlightened consciousness. The feminist ideological project presents patriarchy and heterosexism as synonymous with foolishness. Thus, "false consciousness" is exposed by an investigation into gender relations. It is a persuasive structure artfully seducing the proto-feminist reader. The protagonist, or *eiron,* is able to scrutinize the hysterical excesses of masculinity with a deflationary gaze. Masculinity, in these narratives, usually ends up shooting itself in the foot.

The most effective lesbian crime novels have been those that have most enthusiastically embraced the need to entertain the reader, to interweave suspense with pleasure. Those, such as *She Came Too Late* (1986) and *She Came in a Flash* (1988) by

Mary Wings, that arguably reproduce most faithfully the classic element of satire, succeed most—if readership is anything to go by—as popular novels. Lesbians as a group tend to be highly self-conscious and ironically self-referential; along with other minority cultures, they have recognized the destabilizing potential of parody. Having a sense of humor is an essential survival tool for lesbians, necessary to deflect some of the damage that dominant homophobic and misogynistic discourses inflict upon them. Thus, lesbian crime novels, by their double deflationary gaze—at the sex/gender system and at lesbians themselves—swing the two-headed axe liberally not just to destroy, but also to carve out and recombine new kinds of identities for lesbians to inhabit.

The crime novel, with its legacy of socialist critique (Dashiell Hammett [1894–1961], creator of the famous detective Sam Spade, for example, was a Communist), its formal relationship to parody, and its tendency to produce antiheroic narratives, contains elements favorable to countercultural appropriation. But the lesbian crime novel had its heyday under the individualistic era of Reaganism/Thatcherism during the 1980s, often posing a response to crime and social problems in the form of personal, rather than structural, acts of justice. This did not gel with the more communitarian impulses of 1970s lesbian feminism, nor with the coalition activisms of the late 1980s and the 1990s. The limits of its political vision, although palliative, meant that few of these fictions endured into the 1990s.          *Sally R. Munt*

## Bibliography

Munt, Sally R. *Murder by the Book: Feminism and the Crime Novel*. London and New York: Routledge, 1994.

Palmer, Paulina. "The Lesbian Feminist Thriller and Detective Novel." In *What Lesbians Do in Books*. Ed. Hobby Elaine and Chris White. London: Women's Press, 1991, pp. 9–27.

*See also* Pulp Paperbacks; Wittig, Monique

## Mythology, Classical

References in Greek and Roman mythology and ritual to same-sex love among women. There is little historical evidence available about erotic relationships among women in classical Greece and, aside from the poetry of Sappho (ca. 600 B.C.E.), no written accounts by women of their own experience of such love or of its mythical representation. (In the ancient world, "lesbian" referred to fellatio, not to female homosexuality.) Same-sex love (at least among men) was not only accepted, but also given religious validation and important educational and social functions. The socially validated expression of male homosexuality involved the love of an older man for a youth and was seen as part of the youth's initiation into full manhood. Its purpose was the transfer of phallic potency from the older to the younger. What little evidence there is suggests that, in female-female relationships, the dominance/submission pattern so central to male-male love was absent. Although the written accounts of classical mythology reflect male perspectives, study of non-literary sources and imaginative reconstruction have enabled contemporary feminist scholars to discover something of what the tales and rituals may have meant to the women of the ancient world.

Aside from Sappho's poetry, the only explicit literary reference to love between women appears in the myth in Plato's (427?–347? B.C.E.) *Symposium* about the primordial "round people" (some of whom were hermaphrodite, some male, some female), who were cut in two as punishment for daring to challenge the gods. The same desire for reunion with their lost other half is said to animate the yearning of heterosexuals, of homosexual men, and of lesbians.

Both Amazons and Maenads are mythical groups of women sexually involved with each other. The Amazons were a society composed entirely of women whose sexuality was mostly lived out among themselves, although once a year they would seek out the men of neighboring tribes for intercourse, solely for the sake of reproduction. Girl children were kept and raised; boys were either exposed to the elements and left to die or sent away. Because to master the Amazons sexually was seen as an essential part of challenging their monstrous claim to live as self-sufficient women, many myths show the most celebrated Greek heroes testing their manhood against the fearsome Amazon warriors.

Myths picture the Maenads as women who temporarily left their conjugal lives to be with one another for a ritual period, during which they were free to release energies ordinarily suppressed. Maenadic enthusiasm was a communal, not an individual, experience. Participation in the ecstatic rites represented an initiation of women by women into women's own sexuality, into arousal for its own sake. The excesses sometimes associated with maenadic frenzy were understood to express what happens when women are cut off from access to their own desire and power and from one another.

Several of the Greek goddeses are involved with women in ways that illuminate some aspect of same sex love. None are shown as fitting easily into the normative pattern of heterosexual relationship. Myths describe Demeter as a determinedly woman-identified goddess who allows Zeus to father her child but refuses him any participation in the child's rearing. Her daughter, Persephone, is to be hers alone and to be the object of all her love. Demeter hopes to maintain their closeness forever and to protect their bond from any male intruder. Almost inevitably, her daughter ends up being abducted by the male god of the underworld, Hades, and Demeter ends up devastated. Nonetheless, what is most important about Demeter is her association with the love that flows between mothers and daughters and, more generally, between one woman and another. The major all-women's ritual associated with Demeter encouraged abandonment. It gave participants an opportunity to vent their anger against men and to indulge in "obscenity"—that is, in a taboo-free sexuality. In the temple of the mother, all was permitted. Demeter reconnected her worshipers to a time when there were no boundaries, when lover and beloved were one.

There is no agreed-upon evidence of rituals in ancient Greece in which pubertal girls were initiated into female sexuality and identity by older women parallel to the male pattern. Many scholars believe that an initiation into female sexuality that would help prepare a young girl for marriage may have played an important role in Sappho's circle. Plutarch attests that, in archaic Sparta, education for womanhood involved sexual relationships between aristocratic women and young girls. In the classical period, Athenian maidens were sent to Artemis's temple at Brauron for an extended initiation just before they reached marriageable age, and there are hints that the priestesses there may have presided over sexual initiations.

A virgin goddess, Artemis claims her sexuality is her own, not possessable by any man. Refusing all association with men, she spends her time alone or in the company of her nymphs, maidens dedicated to remain virgins, to stay true to the virginal goddess. One day, Zeus came upon Callisto, Artemis's favorite nymph, alone in the forest and desired her. Knowing she would not accept advances from a man, he disguised himself as Artemis and was warmly wel-

comed. Callisto responded to his first kisses but drew back in horror when she felt his erection. She fought him off with all her strength, but Zeus had his way with her and left her ashamed and pregnant. When Artemis discovered what had happened, she banished the nymph. Callisto's unsurprised responsiveness to what she takes to be Artemis's embrace suggests that the nymph considered physical contact with the goddess comfortable and familiar. Given Artemis's identification with the female body and with the instinctual, the relationship between her and the nymphs was clearly not viewed simply as a spiritual bond. But to understand this bond in primarily erotic terms would be to misunderstand Artemis, who is essentially chaste, virginal, and solitary, who does not give herself to any other, male or female, and who, as the myth suggests, can be unforgiving toward those who do, even unwillingly.

Though Artemis was the goddess of the Amazons, Aphrodite was the goddess of Sappho. Goddess of all erotic love, all sensual pleasure, all delight in beauty, Aphrodite, rather than Artemis, is the goddess most associated with the explicitly erotic, physical, orgasmic dimension of love among women. She blesses all lovemaking that is dedicated to mutual enjoyment (rather than to domination of another or to procreation), whether marital or adulterous, heterosexual or homosexual, between men or between women. Though not specifically a goddess of women, she models women's affirmation of their own sexuality as powerful, beautiful, and sacred. Sappho and Plato valued her association with a love that is not just physical but truly directed toward the other's being, the other's soul. They saw her as perhaps more truly present in same-sex love than in heterosexual love because the latter was, in ancient Greece, viewed primarily in relation to physical reproduction, not to emotional intimacy or intellectual stimulation.

The Latin poet Ovid (43 B.C.E.–A.D. 17/18) relates an otherwise unknown myth of a woman's love for a woman. The story begins with a poor peasant telling his pregnant wife that he hopes their child will be a son, for if they have a girl they will be forced to expose her. The wife is in despair until the goddess Isis comes to her and, telling her not to worry, advises her that, if she has a daughter, she should simply deceive her husband and raise her as a boy. The woman gives birth to a girl, Iphis, whom she rears as the goddess had advised. All goes well until Iphis turns thirteen and the father arranges a marriage with Ianthe, the most beautiful girl on the island. The two had gone to school together and already love each other. Ianthe is happy and looks forward to marrying the boy she already loved, but Iphis, of course, knows that she is really a girl in love with another like herself. She believes her love to be a strange and unnatural love that none has known before and that cannot happily be consummated. Her mother, too, is in despair; she cannot postpone the wedding forever. Finally, the two go to the temple, and the mother asks Isis to come to her aid again. As they walk home together, Iphis begins to take longer strides, her features sharpen, she becomes a man. The myth recognizes the love the two girls feel for each other and shows the confusion this engenders in Iphis, who does not know that women have ever before been drawn to women. Like the male authors of the classical world who cannot imagine sexuality without a phallus, Iphis cannot imagine how such a love might be lived out except by her becoming a man. In Ovid's myth, lesbian desire is acknowledged but not the possibility of its fulfillment. *Christine Downing*

## Bibliography

Cantarella, Eva. *Bisexuality in the Ancient World.* New Haven, Conn.: Yale University Press, 1992.

Dover, K.J. *Greek Homosexuality.* Cambridge, Mass.: Harvard University Press, 1978.

Downing, Christine. *Myths and Mysteries of Same-Sex Love.* New York: Continuum, 1989.

*See also* Amazons; Antiquity; Classical Literature

## Mythology, Nonclassical

Mythology—the prehistorical origin accounts of superhuman, often divine, beings and events—has its source in each culture's oral traditions and exists in numerous literary and nonliterary forms. Although English-speaking peoples in Western cultures generally associate mythology with the Greco-Roman tradition, nonclassical mythology, which encompasses the origin stories derived from preclassical Indo-European and non-European cultures, can be found throughout the world and provides a rich source of alternative imagery and worldviews.

## Characteristics

Generally, mythologies are associated with a culture's foundational accounts; they explain the beginnings of everything, from the universe, divine beings, and humankind to the existence of a specific river or mountain range. As such, mythic narratives serve a number of ideological purposes: They provide concrete explanations of philosophical and metaphysical issues, such as the cause of good and evil or the meaning of "truth"; they establish and reinforce a variety of social institutions and mores, including gender roles, sexual norms, and kinship systems; and they influence a community's religious institutions and experiences. Myths function on several levels: For some people—especially those within the specific culture in which the myths originate—they are believed to be literally true; for others, they represent unsophisticated, inaccurate, naive beliefs and a nostalgic worldview; and for others, myths reveal archetypal and psychological truths about human nature.

Nonclassical mythology's prehistorical status creates a number of problems for twentieth-century people, especially those trained in Western educational systems. To begin with, because these stories were transmitted orally from generation to generation and subtly reshaped to meet each generation's changing needs, as well as each culture's interactions with other cultures, they have undergone many undocumented alterations. These changes make it impossible to attain absolute knowledge about the original myths. And, because these revisions reflect the perspectives of increasingly male-dominated, hierarchical power structures and social systems, the commonly accepted twentieth-century versions contain a deeply embedded masculine, Eurocentric bias. In such accounts, complex female images with multiple forms and functions have been altered both by the successive generations of patriarchal cultures who inherited and revised the various mythic systems and by nineteenth- and twentieth-century Western scholars who recorded and interpreted nonclassical myth.

Whereas prepatriarchal goddess figures represented highly sophisticated female beings with the power to create, destroy, and regenerate, their patriarchal versions have been heterosexualized and transformed into benign mother goddesses and omnipotent male gods, redefined to indicate the dangers of female sexuality and control, or in other ways simplified and disempowered. Thus, for example, when the Aztecs conquered the Toltecs, they divided Coatlicue, a Mesoamerican creatrix figure with all-inclusive, cosmic powers, into two parts: As Tlazolteotl/Coatlicue, she was restricted to the underworld and reduced to the embodiment of darkness, materiality, and female evil; as Tontantsi/ Guadalupe, she was purified and transformed into the "good mother" and heterosexual consort of more powerful male gods. After the Spanish conquest, this latter mythic figure underwent further changes; she was Christianized and identified with Mary, the holy virgin mother. Similarly, Kali Ma—the Hindu Triple Goddess who, in her earliest forms held unlimited power to create, protect, and destroy—is now known to Western readers primarily as an entirely destructive, terrifying female figure and the wife of Shiva. Her all-encompassing powers have been redistributed to three male gods: Brahma the creator, Vishnu the preserver, and Shiva the destroyer. In other instances, such as the Mayan mates and partners Xmucane and Xpiyacoc, female divinities who together created the world are changed into heterosexual couples. Western-trained scholars have further diminished prepatriarchal female figures' power by attributing it to non-Western cultures' superstitious, inaccurate worldviews. Parthenogenic goddess figures such as the Laguna Keres Thought Woman, the Old European Bird Goddess, and the Navajo Hard Beings Woman—whose creative powers had their source in their own bodies or minds, with no need for male insemination—were redefined as fertility goddesses created by simpleminded tribal peoples incapable of recognizing men's role in reproduction.

## Feminist Critiques

Not surprisingly, then, Gloria Anzaldúa (1942–), Mary Daly (1928–), Adrienne Rich (1929–), and many other feminists have argued that, in its patriarchal Western versions, mythology is inhospitable to women. Whereas men find a wide range of male gods and heroes engaged in an equally wide variety of actions with which to identify, women do not. Instead, they find a series of passive female mythic figures who function primarily as brides, wives, mothers, and daughters of the male gods and heroes, often as the reward at the end of the quest or the helpless victim in need of salvation. When women are portrayed as powerful agents, their power is often undermined and viewed as negative. In Judeo-Christian tradition, for example, Eve, the woman created to fulfill Adam's need for companionship, is associated with temptation, the fall from Paradise, and the introduction of evil into the world. Lilith, the woman who, in Jewish creation accounts, was created to be Adam's mate yet rejected his sexual advances, has been entirely erased from Christian

origin stories and demonized in Jewish myth. This masculine bias has had a negative impact on women. Because mythology embodies deep-seated, often unacknowledged, and, therefore, unquestioned cultural assumptions about human nature, value systems, and social structures, patriarchally shaped mythic stories play a powerful—though rarely recognized—role in naturalizing women's insubordinate status. And, by focusing on women's relationships to men, such myths normalize and reinforce heterosexual systems of gender.

Twentieth-century women have reacted to these misogynist depictions of women in a number of interrelated ways: They critique how the existing (masculine) mythic stories silence women; they appropriate and transform patriarchal myths by permitting the women silenced in these accounts to tell their side of the story; they recover previously erased stories and perspectives; and they invent new myths valorizing female power. Despite the many differences among them, these various forms of revisionist mythmaking are motivated by the belief that myth, when reshaped to provide positive representations of women, can bring about concrete material change. Nonclassical mythology plays a vital role in this revisionary process, for it offers a wide variety of non-Western perspectives on gender roles, sexual norms, and female identities. By reclaiming and rewriting the stories of Lilith, Kali, and other mythic figures, twentieth-century women scholars and creative writers challenge patriarchal constructions of womanhood and invent new descriptions of reality that affirm women's experiences. Their revisionist myths offer new models for female subject formation: Women see themselves differently; they identify with these mythic female images of the divine and recognize the sacredness of their own being. No longer silenced by feelings of inferiority, they reject masculinist definitions and begin affirming their own power.

## Lesbian Mythmaking

For self-identified lesbians, revisionist mythmaking takes on an additional purpose as well, for it allows them to move beyond the existing heterosexual system of gendered relations and invent alternative definitions of female identity and power that celebrate women's same-sex relationships. Nonclassical mythology offers an especially wide range of strong, nonheterosexual female images for twentieth-century lesbian writers. In *Another Mother Tongue: Gay Words, Gay Worlds* (1984), for instance, Judy

Grahn (1940–) uses a variety of non-Western mythic figures, including the South Asian Indian goddess Kamar, the Brazilian-West African Oya, and the Hebrew goddess Daath, to validate lesbian women's spiritual and historical roots. Similarly, by reclaiming and rewriting West African mythology, Audre Lorde (1934–1992) simultaneously critiques existing conceptions of womanhood modeled on European beauty standards and social roles and invents new definitions that more accurately reflect her own experiences as a lesbian woman of African descent. Like Lorde and Grahn, Paula Gunn Allen (1939–) uses revisionist mythmaking to subvert the dominant ideology's male, heterosexist, Western bias. Throughout *The Sacred Hoop: Recovering the Feminine in American Indian Traditions* (1986), her collection of academic essays, she exposes the sexism and ethnocentrism in English-speaking scholars' interpretations of indigenous mythologies and maintains that their references to fertility goddesses and heterosexually paired mythic figures represent later patriarchal interjections into earlier gynecentric texts. Drawing on a wide variety of indigenous North American mythologies, she describes her mythic figures in distinctly nonheterosexual terms. When she retells the Laguna Pueblo creation story of Tse che nako, or Thought Woman, for example, she emphasizes that creation did not occur through heterosexual biological reproduction, but, rather, through Thought Woman's intellectual and linguistic powers. And when she retells the Navajo creation story of Hard Beings Woman, she points out that creation did not result from male/female sexual intercourse, but from the merger of two "feminine" elements—woman and water. Although Allen does not explicitly lesbianize these female creatrix figures, her repeated emphasis on their nonbiological creative powers undermines readers' heterosexist assumptions.

This retrieval of Native American, West African, and other nonclassical mythic figures enables Allen, Lorde, Grahn, and other twentieth-century women writers to intervene in existing systems of heterosexually gendered meaning. Their mythic women represent an innovative departure from those reclaimed from classical mythology. By replacing European-based, masculine images of benign Mother Goddesses and other male-identified mythic women, they challenge Western culture's ethnocentric bias and provide all women with new models of subject formation.                    *AnaLouise Keating*

### Bibliography

Alarcón, Norma. "Chicana's Feminist Literature: A Re-Vision Through Malintzin/or Malintzin: Putting Flesh Back on the Object." In *This Bridge Called My Back: Writings By Radical Women of Color*. Ed. Cherríe Moraga and Gloria Anzaldúa. Watertown, Mass.: Persephone, 1981. New York: Kitchen Table: Women of Color Press, 1983, pp. 182–190.

Anzaldúa, Gloria. *Borderlands/La Frontera: The New Mestiza*. San Francisco: Spinsters/Aunt Lute, 1987.

Keating, AnaLouise. *Women Reading Women Writing: Self-Invention in Paula Gunn Allen, Gloria Anzaldúa, and Audre Lorde*. Philadelphia: Temple University Press, 1996.

Walker, Barbara G. *The Woman's Encyclopedia of Myths and Secrets*. San Francisco: Harper and Row, 1983.

***See also*** Allen, Paula Gunn; Anzaldúa, Gloria E.; Grahn, Judy; Lorde, Audre; Rich, Adrienne

# N

## Naiad Press

Lesbian publishing house. Cofounded by Barbara Grier (1933–) and Donna J. McBride (1940–) in January 1973, Naiad Press is the largest and most enduring lesbian publishing company in the world. In its first twenty-three years of operation, Naiad published 350 titles. Its mailing list comprises more than 26,400 people, and its books are carried by more than 2,800 booksellers worldwide. Since its creation, Naiad has been committed to providing readers with affirmative lesbian materials, to reissuing lesbian classics, and to keeping its titles from going out of print.

In October 1972, following the dissolution of *The Ladder* (1956–1972), Grier and McBride borrowed $2,000 in seed money from Anyda Marchant (1911–) and Muriel Crawford (1914–) to start a lesbian publishing house. Marchant, who had contributed to the final two issues of *The Ladder* under the pen name Sarah Aldridge, provided the press with its first three titles. *The Ladder* mailing list furnished Naiad with its initial market for its publications. Grier and McBride, both working at day jobs, ran the press from their home in Kansas City, Missouri, before moving it to Tallahassee, Florida, in 1980. It was not until 1982 that the cofounders began to run the enterprise full-time and to draw salaries from the business.

The success of Naiad Press is largely due to its concentration on genre fiction with positive lesbian content. Mysteries and romances, plot-driven narrative forms that are both popular and profitable, account for much of Naiad's list. Although Naiad is best known for its fiction, particularly novels by Katherine V. Forrest, Lee Lynch, Jane Rule, Dianne Salvatore, Ann Allen Shockley, and Sheila Ortiz Taylor (all of whom published with Naiad in the 1980s), it has also published numerous nonfiction works and reference volumes. Such publications as Anita Cornwell's *Black Lesbian in White America* (1983), Jeannette Foster's *Sex Variant Women in Literature* (1985), Rosemary Curb's and Nancy Manahan's *Lesbian Nuns: Breaking Silence* (1985), and Clare Potter's *The Lesbian Periodicals Index* (1986) attest to the range of lesbian expression that Naiad fosters.

Even as Naiad Press has expanded, branching out into video sales, it continues to prove that publishing lesbian books is good business.

*Alisa Klinger*

### Bibliography

Brandt, Kate. "Barbara Grier: Climbing *The Ladder* to Success: Naiad Press." In *Happy Endings: Lesbian Writers Talk About Their Lives and Work*. Tallahassee, Fla.: Naiad, 1993, pp. 99–108.

Gambill, Sue. "The World's Oldest and Largest Lesbian–Feminist Publishing House Naiad Press." *Hot Wire* 3:2 (March 1987), 18–19, 59.

Klinger, Alisa Margaret. "Paper Uprisings: Print Activism in the Multicultural Lesbian Movement." Ph.D. diss., University of California at Berkeley, 1995.

*See also* Businesses, Lesbian; Cornwell, Anita; Foster, Jeannette Howard; Grier, Barbara; *Ladder, The*; Mystery and Detective Fiction; Publishing, Lesbian; Rule, Jane Vance; Shockley, Ann Allen

## Namibia

An arid country situated on the west coast of southern Africa. Namibia was sparsely inhabited by a number of different African peoples when it was colonized by Germany in 1884. After World War I, Namibia was placed under British mandate but was administered and economically exploited by white-ruled South Africa until 1989.

Even before colonization, Christian missionaries from Europe were active in Namibia, combating traditional beliefs and practices such as polygyny with nineteenth-century European morality and Christian beliefs. South Africa subsequently imposed its rule of apartheid onto Namibians.

The traditional powers and rights of women vary among the different African peoples in Namibia, with several having a history of women rulers. However, under the Roman-Dutch law introduced by South Africa, married women became legal minors, dependent on their husband's permission to engage in any kind of legal transactions.

During the long struggle for liberation, women experienced empowerment, in particular, through their political and military involvement. Women's equality became part of the liberation agenda. But until 1990, political independence remained the paramount goal.

Since independence, the Namibian government has been active in abolishing legal discrimination against women and has shown concern over the rising tide of violence against women and children. However, contrary to the new ethos of equality and human rights enshrined in Namibia's constitution, the state president and a number of senior ministers have lashed out repeatedly against any public manifestations of homosexuality, claiming it to be an immoral and un-African import from the West.

Research published in 1926 by the German Kurt Falk shows that homosexuality existed not only among men working as migrant laborers in the diamond fields or other mines, but also among women and men in all Namibian communities he visited. As of the late 1990s, no other research had been conducted, but a growing number of Namibian lesbians and gays were coming out to the nation as proud African homosexuals in response to the attacks of the politicians.

Support for lesbian and gay rights has been slow to develop in the newly independent country, which is still divided racially, ethnically, culturally, and economically by the legacies of apartheid and colonial rule. Most women's and other groups are engaged in single-issue struggles to overcome poverty, violence, or AIDS.

The Sister Namibia Collective, founded in 1989, is the first organization to speak out for lesbian rights as part of its feminist multiissue politics. From 1993, articles, short stories, poems, and letters dealing with lesbian life and lesbian issues have been published in the bimonthly *Sister Namibia* magazine, as well as in an anthology of women's writings produced by the collective in 1994.

In 1997, the Sister Namibia Collective received one of the three Felipa de Souza Awards of the International Gay and Lesbian Human Rights Commission. The same year saw the birth of the Rainbow Project, in which lesbians and gays in Namibia began to join together to fight for their rights.

*Liz Frank*

### Bibliography

Falk, Kurt. "Homosexualitat bei den Eingeborenen in Sudwest-Afrika" (Homosexuality Among the Indigenous Peoples of South West Africa). In *Geschlecht und Gesellschaft* (Sex and Society) 13 (1926), 203–214.

Frank, Liz, and Elizabeth Khaxas. "Black Sisters: Lesben (Lesbians)." In *Namibia: Frauen mischen sich ein* (Namibia: The involvement of Women). Ed. Florence Herve. Berlin: Orlanda Frauenverlag, 1993, pp. 107–111.

———. "Lesbians in Namibia." In *Amazon to Zami: Towards a Global Lesbian Feminism*. Ed. Monika Reinfelder. London and New York: Cassell, 1996, pp. 109–117.

*See also* South Africa

## National Gay and Lesbian Task Force (NGLTF)

A national organization, based in Washington, D.C., whose goal is the creation of a society in which lesbians and gay men can live openly, free from violence, bigotry, and discrimination. Since its founding in 1973, NGLTF's main activities have focused on lobbying, research, and education.

An early victory for the Task Force came in 1973–1974 when its efforts helped persuade the American Psychiatric Association to declassify homosexuality as a mental illness. In 1975, NGLTF lobbying led to the United States Civil Service Commission's ruling that officially allowed lesbians and gay men to serve as federal employees. The group's successes in the congressional arena include lobbying efforts to defeat the 1981 Family Protection Act, increase AIDS funding and programming, remove restrictions against the immigration of lesbians and gay men in the 1990 Immigration Reform Act, include people with AIDS and HIV infection in the 1990 Americans with Disabilities Act, and include crimes against lesbians and gay men in the 1990 Hate Crimes Statistics Act. Items remaining on NGLTF's congressional agenda include the extension of civil rights protections to gay men and lesbians, recognition and protection of lesbian and gay family relationships, and elimination of discrimination in the military.

NGLTF also provides support for organizations throughout the country in their attempts to enact state and local laws decriminalizing lesbian and gay sex, recognizing and protecting domestic partnerships and lesbian and gay parenting, and banning discrimination on the basis of sexual orientation. Since 1988, NGLTF has held annual "Creating Change" conferences, which bring together lesbian and gay activists from around the country for skill building and strategy sessions.

In the area of research and education, NGLTF and the NGLTF Policy Institute collect, analyze, and distribute information on a variety of issues, including employment and violence. In 1984, the organization released the first national survey of violence directed against lesbians and gay men. NGLTF updated that report in 1986 and has produced and distributed annual reports about violence against gays and lesbians since then. In the area of employment, the organization has conducted surveys to identify employment discrimination, produced informational brochures for employers about lesbian and gay employees, and coauthored a 1995 book on the best and worst companies in the United States for gays and lesbians to work.

While it was founded under the name the National Gay Task Force (NGTF), adding the word "lesbian" to its title only in 1985, both lesbians and gay men have played key leadership roles on the board and staff of the organization since its inception. Founders and early board members reflected the variety of gay and lesbian politics during the 1970s. Among them were activists from the Daughters of Bilitis and the Mattachine Society (homophile organizations founded in the 1950s), lesbian feminists, and activists from gay liberation organizations founded after the Stonewall Rebellion of 1969. Among the lesbians who have served as executive director or codirector are Jean O'Leary, Virginia Apuzzo, Urvashi Vaid, Torie Osborne, Peri Jude Radecic, and Melinda Paras.          *Davida J. Alperin*

## Bibliography

Adam, Barry D. *The Rise of a Gay and Lesbian Movement*. Boston: G.K. Hall, 1987.

Blumenfeld, Warren J., and Diane Raymond. *Looking at Gay and Lesbian Life*. Boston: Beacon, 1988. 2nd ed. New York: Farrar, Straus, and Giroux, 1993.

Marcus, Eric. *Making History: The Struggle for Gay and Lesbian Civil Rights, 1945–1990: An Oral History*. New York: HarperCollins, 1992.

Moratta, Toby. *The Politics of Homosexuality*. Boston: Houghton Mifflin, 1981.

Vaid, Urvashi. *Virtual Equality: The Mainstreaming of Gay and Lesbian Liberation*. New York: Anchor, 1995.

*See also* Associations and Organizations; Daughters of Bilitis; Gay Liberation Movement

## National Organization for Women (NOW)

The National Organization for Women (NOW) is the largest women's rights group in the United States and focuses on promoting equality for all women.

### History

NOW was formed on October 29, 1966, during a luncheon of women at the National Conference of State Commissions in Washington, D.C. NOW was created when conference participants were blocked from passing a resolution pressing the Equal Employment Opportunities Commission (EEOC) to use greater force in investigating sex-discrimination cases. Founding members include Betty Friedan (1921–), author of the *Feminist Mystique* (1963); lawyer and civil rights activist Pauli Murray (1910–1985); and Kay Clarenbach (1921–1994), head of the Wisconsin Commission on the Status of Women.

Modeled after the National Association for the Advancement of Colored People (NAACP), NOW had as its original goal the expansion of women's economic rights and responsibilities by fighting sex discrimination in the workforce. In one of its first actions, NOW pressured the EEOC to end the practice of sex-segregated help-wanted advertisements in newspapers. Along with employment and economic issues, NOW eventually formed task forces to deal with areas of discrimination in education and religion, family rights, women's image in the mass media, political rights and responsibilities, and problems facing poor women.

Starting with twenty-seven members, the founding mothers originally intended to create a small group of activists who could work quickly to effect change through the legal system. However, the organization began to grow: NOW had three hundred members by the end of 1967, three thousand by 1970, and 46,500 by 1974. A combination of events in the 1980s and 1990s increased the membership to 250,000. Those events included the 1987 nomination of Robert Bork to the United States Supreme Court, the erosion of abortion rights in the late 1980s, and the 1991 Anita Hill–Clarence Thomas sexual harassment hearings.

The "second wave" of the women's movement in the 1970s developed in two different "branches," of which NOW is characterized as belonging to the older, more mainstream branch. The younger, more radical branch of the movement developed, to a large degree, from the New Left and focused on women's "liberation" from the system. The older, more mainstream branch emphasized women's "rights" within the system. However, with the demise of many radical groups and an influx of younger women into the organization in the late 1970s, NOW came to be seen as the main organization of the women's movement.

The first members of NOW were primarily white, middle-class women who were mostly middle-aged, married, and had working experience. In the 1990s, NOW continued working to become a more racially diverse organization.

## Characteristics

NOW continues to work on issues of employment discrimination, in particular gaining recognition for the value of women's work both inside and outside the home. Related to these concerns is NOW's continuing goal of passing the Equal Rights Amendment (ERA). In the 1970s, NOW joined other organizations in working to pass the amendment. Despite the ERA's failure, the national and state-level efforts encouraged thousands of women and men to join the organization and brought about the formation of a feminist activist network. The process of working for the ERA convinced NOW leaders that more women needed to become part of the political process. NOW began to press for women, especially feminists, to run for political office at a variety of levels. In 1992, NOW encouraged voters angry at the chipping away of abortion rights and the United States Senate's treatment of law professor Anita Hill to "Elect Women for a Change."

In the 1980s, the organization put much of its efforts into maintaining abortion rights for all women. NOW organized efforts to stop antichoice activists from blocking access to women's health clinics by training members as clinic defenders. In 1994, the organization won a Supreme Court victory in *NOW v. Schiedler*. The ruling found that antiracketeering laws could be applied against antichoice activists restricting patients and staff from entering clinics. NOW continues to work on other issues—opposing racism, ending sexual harassment, and stopping violence against women, to name a few.

NOW embraces both traditional and nontraditional forms of activism. Activists on all levels do electoral, judicial, and legislative work, such as bringing lawsuits, lobbying officials, supporting feminist candidates, and running for office themselves. NOW has also organized rallies, mass marches, pickets, and civil-disobedience actions. In 1978, an estimated 100,000 people marched for the ERA in Washington, D.C. The March for Women's Lives, in 1992, drew an estimated 750,000 participants. On both the local and the national level, NOW encouraged activists to participate in "zap actions" (demonstrations responding quickly to women's rights issues).

NOW's structure is hierarchical with a small national level, intermediate state and regional levels, and a large and loosely structured grass-roots level. NOW's expansion from the national to the grass roots was not without problems. The first chapters were formed in the late 1960s and the early 1970s, and, in the following years, tension between the national and the local levels rose because of such issues as the division of members' dues. In 1998, NOW had 550 chapters, fifty state groups, nine regional groups, and thirty staff members.

At yearly national conferences, the membership decides NOW's policies and goals. This style of leadership has sometimes resulted in dissension and controversy. When the issues of the ERA and abortion came up at the second annual conference, in 1968, the membership splintered. Arguing that the issues were too controversial and diverted NOW from its original intent, some members formed the more conservative Women's Equity Action League.

## Lesbians in NOW

Since NOW's inception in 1966, lesbians have been members of the organization. Yet many felt pressured to keep their sexuality hidden from the public and other NOW members. From 1968 to 1971, the issue threatened to divide the group. Several prominent lesbian leaders resigned from the organization because of NOW's unwillingness to address lesbian rights. In 1968, Ti-Grace Atkinson, president of New York City NOW, left to form The Feminists, a more militant group. In 1969, Rita Mae Brown forced NOW to confront lesbian issues at a panel discussion on women discriminating against other women. Afterward, Brown was told not to talk about the issue and consequently resigned from NOW.

Responding to rumors that lesbians wanted to take over the organization and change its focus to lesbian rights, then-president Betty Friedan called lesbianism a "lavender menace" threatening the credibility of the women's movement and detracting from the purpose of NOW. Friedan later recalled, "I didn't want to be a 'straight woman' fronting for a lesbian cabal. I didn't want the issue to surface and divide the organization" (1976).

In a defining action at the 1970 Second Congress to Unite Women, a number of lesbians took over the stage wearing lavender T-shirts identifying them as the "Lesbian Menace." They were joined by other women from the audience. They later formed the group Radicalesbians. After much infighting, debate, and conflict, the organization passed a resolution in the 1970s stating that "a woman's right to her own person includes the right to define and express her own sexuality and to choose her own lifestyle; therefore[,] we acknowledge the oppression of lesbians as a legitimate concern of feminism."

Since then lesbian rights have been one of NOW's priority issues and was the theme of national conferences in 1984 and 1988. In addition, lesbians are a visible presence in the leadership of NOW. For instance, lesbian Rosemary Dempsey came to NOW for assistance with her 1979 custody case and later became a national officer.

Despite NOW's attention to lesbian rights and lesbian leadership, the connection drawn between feminism and lesbianism continues to plague the organization. When President Patricia Ireland admitted to having a female companion in 1991, antifeminist groups used her admission as evidence that all feminists are lesbians. Ireland, by not identifying as a lesbian or bisexual, also stirred debate among the NOW membership with lesbian and progay members feeling betrayed by her lack of identification, and others seeing her admission as weakening the organization's assertion that it represents women of all sexual orientations. *Jo Reger*

## Bibliography

Carden, Maren Lockwood. *The New Feminist Movement*. New York: Russell Sage Foundation, 1974.

Davis, Flora. *Moving the Mountain: The Women's Movement in America*. New York: Simon and Schuster, 1991.

Deckard, Barbara. *The Women's Movement*. New York: Harper and Row, 1979.

Friedan, Betty. *It Changed My Life: Writings on the Women's Movement*. New York: Random House, 1976.

*See also* Associations and Organizations; Brown, Rita Mae; Radicalesbians; Women's Liberation Movement

## Native Americans

Intimate relationships between females have been (and are) a feature of many Native nations of North America. Because traditional Native American understandings of gender and sexuality do not necessarily correspond with Western conceptions, it is difficult to label such females as "women" or such relationships as "lesbian" in the Euro-American sense of these terms. Each American Indian society has its own words for female (and male) "two-spirited people," along with culturally specific understandings of them. The Mojave, for instance, have four different gender roles: female, male, *hwame* (female two-spirit), and *alyha* (male two-spirit). While the *hwame* is physiologically female, she does not generally engage in gender-role activities appropriate to women. Nor is the *hwame*'s partner considered a lesbian in the Western sense. She is a woman, and her partners are as likely to be male as they are to be female. The case of the Mojave should not be taken as illustrative of all Native American traditional understandings of gender and sexuality, however. It does demonstrate, though, the limitations of Euro-American concepts for discussing lesbianism, homosexuality, bisexuality, and transgenderism in American Indian communities.

While each First Nation has its own words for women-loving females and men-loving males, many Native people have begun to use the term "two-spirited" or "two spirit" in the English language. Scholars do not know much about two-spirits in general, and even less is known about female two-spirits and community regard for them. In part, information is not available because, for Native Americans generally, sex is often considered a private matter. Where there is information, much of it is based on accounts by male explorers, missionaries, and anthropologists, most of whom spoke with, and observed, men. As outsiders to American Indian communities, they generally did not consider women's activities important, and they did not have the opportunity to interact with females regularly due to the sex segregation that is common in Native American societies. It is also difficult to determine indigenous understandings of two-spirited life prior to contact with Europeans. The Christianization of American Indians has often resulted in communities that, to a greater or lesser degree, reflect Euro-American conceptions of sexuality and gender, as well as their generally negative attitudes toward homosexuality. Loss or change of indigenous religious traditions through acculturation and urbanization has also led to a loss of traditional roles and ways of life, including those of the two-spirited. Nonetheless, an impression of this way of life can be gleaned from the small but growing literature on the subject.

The Gay American Indian (GAI) History Project began in 1984 to review and index sources reporting the existence of female and male two-spirits in various North American tribes. By 1988, they had found evidence of many First Nations with two-spirits, along with terms indicative of them in indigenous languages. Organized below by region, those nations with a known tradition of female two-spirits and the native words for them are:

Alaska: Bering Strait Eskimo and Chugach;

Northwest: Haida, Haisla, Nootka, Quileute, Quinault (*tawkxwa'nsixw*—"man acting"), and Tlingit;

Columbia Plateau: Flathead (*ntalha*), Kalispel, Klamath (*tw!inna'ek*), Kutenai (*titqattek*—"pretending to be a man"; *kocomenepeca*—"manlike woman"), Lillooet, Okanagon, Sanpoil (*sinta'xlau'wam*—"female homosexuality"), and Thompson;

California: Achumawi, Atsugewi (*brumaiwi*), Nisenan, Shasta, Tipai, Wappo, Wintu, Wiyot, Yuki (*musp-iwap naip*—"woman mangirl"), and Yurok;

Great Basin: Northern Paiute (*moroni noho*), Shoshoni (*nuwuduka, waippu sungwe*—"woman half"), Ute, and Washo;

Southwest: Apache, Cocopa (*warhameh*), Hopi, Isleta, Maricopa (*kwiraxame'*), Mojave (*hwame*), Navajo (*nádleeh*—"that which

changes," "hermaphrodite"), Papago, Pima, Santo Domingo, Yavapai, Yuma (*kwe'rhame*), and Zuni (*katsotse*—"girl-boy");

Subarctic: Carrier, Chipewyan, Cree, Ingalik (*chelxo-delean*[e]), Kaska, and Ojibwa (*okitcitakwe*—"woman warrior");

Plains: Assiniboin, Blackfeet (*sakwo'mapi akikwan*—"boy-girl"), Cheyenne, Crow, Dakota (*koskalaka*—"woman who doesn't marry," although an alternative interpretation is "male youth or postpubescent male"), and Pawnee;

Northeast: Illinois (*ickoue ne koussa*—"hunting women"), Ottawa, Potawatomi, and Winnebago; and

Southeast: Timucua.

To this GAI list could be added the Bella Coola (Northwest), Yokuts (California), Southern Ute (Great Basin), and Southern Paiute (Great Basin) (Blackwood [1984]).

While there is variation among American Indian cultures as to the lifeways of two-spirited females, some commonalities have been noted. Historically, they often demonstrated an inclination early in childhood toward activities appropriate to the male gender role, such as hunting and war. Upon observation of these tendencies, the child's relatives may have tried to discourage her from this path. Such attempts at influencing her may have been limited, however, because of the latitude given for individual differences and because of the perceived involvement of supernatural powers in her preferences and talents. For instance, visions and dreams may have played a role in her becoming a two-spirit, especially if she were from one of the Southwestern nations.

In fact, it is the involvement of such powers that particularly differentiates two-spirits from Euro-American lesbians, gay men, bisexuals, and transgendered people. For two-spirits, one's identity is often based on spiritual and communal orientations, not sexual or affectional ones. Some two-spirits have been known for their spiritual acumen, although "two-spirit" is by no means synonymous with "medicine woman" or "medicine man." Two-spirits are not necessarily spiritual leaders of any kind. However, a female two-spirit's spiritual strength may have been looked upon favorably by potential partners; historical accounts report that, because of her relationship with spirits, she is often "lucky" as a hunter and, hence, a good provider.

While two-spirits have often worn traditionally male clothing, this practice has not been true for all nations. Some two-spirits engaged exclusively in men's work, but there is evidence that, in some cultures, they performed both women's and men's work. It should be pointed out, however, that some women, particularly among Plains peoples, participated in hunting or warfare, traditionally male pursuits, although these "warrior women" were not two-spirited. Such activities were allowable within their roles as women. Regarding the partners of two-spirits, scholars disagree as to whether, historically, they were usually women who followed traditional gender roles, including wife and mother, or whether they were two-spirited themselves. Blackwood (1984), in her study of what she calls "cross-gender females" in western North America and the Plains, argues that "two cross-gender females did not marry." Williams (1986), though, states that "relationships between two women-identified women were probably more common." Marriage has been permitted in many nations, although more informal relationships between females have existed as well.

A brief look at particular Native American cultures and two-spirits known historically sheds light on some of the specifics of being two-spirited. Among the Kaska of the Subarctic, a daughter might be selected to "be like a man" if a family or community needed a son to hunt. In this case, a female is transformed through a ceremony designed to prevent menstruation and pregnancy. Thereafter, she dressed like a man, was taught to do male tasks, and had sexual relationships with women only.

The Mojave *hwame*, mentioned earlier, is said to have dreamed about her role in the womb. She refused to play with girls' toys or do traditionally feminine tasks. Through an initiation ritual, she was authorized to dress, work, and engage in sexuality appropriate to her gender. The Mojave believe that she does not menstruate. This may have been the case, although they may have chosen to ignore it or she may have hidden it from then. In addition to marrying a woman, a *hwame* could become the father of her partner's child. If the "wife" had been impregnated by a man but later marries a female two-spirit, the *hwame* is considered to be the child's father.

One particular *hwame* was named Sahaykwisa. As a masculine name, it suggests that she had already been initiated. Though she was a prostitute for white men, she had several wives during her life. Through prostitution and her abilities as a hunter and a farmer, she was prosperous. It was also known that she could heal, curing people from venereal diseases.

Among the Kutenai in the nineteenth century was another well-known two-spirit. After leaving her homeland and marrying a white man, she returned home, stating that her husband had transformed her into a man. She changed her name to "Gone-to-the-spirits" and began to wear men's clothes, court women, and fight as a warrior. In the stories passed down about her, she is remembered for marrying several women and for her supernatural powers. She had the ability to see into the future and to cure illnesses.

One final example is of the nineteenth-century Crow leader Woman Chief. Though the female two-spirit tradition is relatively rare among Plains nations, she was an exception. In actuality, she was of the Gros Ventre people but had been captured by the Crows and had lived with them since she was ten years old. Very skilled on horseback, in hunting, and in war, she was known in her adult years for her acts of bravery, which contributed to her earning the third-highest rank in the nation. She is said to have at first married one woman and later three others.

These accounts may lead one to believe that the two-spirit tradition is a relic of the past. On the contrary, two-spirits exist today in many Native nations. Some have established organizations, including American Indian Gays and Lesbians (Minneapolis, Minnesota), Gay American Indians (San Francisco, California), WeWah and BarCheeAmpe (New York City), Gays and Lesbians of the First Nations (Toronto, Canada), 2-Spirited People of the First Nations (Toronto, Canada), and Nichiwakan N.G.S. (Winnipeg, Canada). Others have been involved in producing the newsletter *Two Eagles: An International Native American Gay and Lesbian Quarterly* (Minneapolis, Minnesota). Two-spirited people have also been meeting for the past several years in international gatherings. One result of this organizing has been the concerted effort to educate scholars, especially in anthropology, about indigenous perspectives on two-spirit ways of life (Jacobs et al. 1997).

Probably the most important and accessible source for understanding the perspectives of female two-spirits is the body of literature that they have produced. In "Giveaway: Native Lesbian Writers" (1993), Beth Brant (Mohawk) describes some of this poetry and prose and its importance to her as a two-spirit writer: "Being a Native lesbian is like living in the eye of the hurricane—terrible, beautiful,

# N

filled with sounds and silences, the music of life-affirmation and the disharmony or life-despising. To balance, to create in this midst is a gift of honor and respect." Several two-spirit writers are giving such a gift, voicing the complexities that often characterize life on the borders between Native and non-Native, traditional spirituality and Christianity, two-spirited ways and lesbianism. In addition to Brant, other well-known two-spirited writers of the late twentieth century are Paula Gunn Allen (Laguna and Lakota), Chrystos (Menominee), Janice Gould (Maidu), and Vickie Sears (Cherokee). The works of many others are beginning to make their way into print as well. It is the works of both established and new writers, along with those of their brother two-spirits, that will revolutionize understandings of two-spirited life, both historically and through the twenty-first century.                                        *Mary C. Churchill*

## Bibliography

Allen, Paula Gunn. *The Sacred Hoop: Recovering the Feminine in American Indian Traditions.* Boston: Beacon, 1986.

Blackwood, Evelyn. "Sexuality and Gender in Certain Native American Tribes: The Case of Cross-Gender Females." *Signs: Journal of Women in Culture and Society* 10:1 (Autumn 1984), 27–42.

Brant, Beth. "Giveaway: Native Lesbian Writers." *Signs: Journal of Women in Culture and Society* 18:4 (Summer 1993), 944–947.

Brown, Lester B., ed. *Two Spirit People: American Indian Lesbian Women and Gay Men.* New York: Haworth, 1997.

Jacobs, Sue-Ellen, Wesley Thomas, and Sabine Lang, eds. *Two-Spirit People: Native American Gender Identity, Sexuality, and Spirituality.* Urbana: University of Illinois Press, 1997.

Medicine, Beatrice. " 'Warrior Women'—Sex Roles Alternatives for Plains Indian Women." In *The Hidden Half: Studies of Plains Indian Women.* Ed. Patricia Labers and Beatrice Medicine. Lanham, MD: University Press of America, 1983, pp. 267–279.

Roscoe, Will. *Changing Ones: Third and Fourth Genders in Native North America.* New York: St. Martin's, 1998.

———, ed. *Living the Spirit: A Gay American Indian Anthology.* New York: St. Martin's, 1988.

Williams, Walter L. *The Spirit and the Flesh: Sexual Diversity in American Indian Culture.* Boston: Beacon, 1986.

*See also* Allen, Paula Gunn; Indigenous Cultures; Two-Spirit

## Navratilova, Martina (1956–)

American tennis player. Born in Prague in the former Czechoslovakia, Martina Navratilova began playing tennis as a young child. When she defected to the United States in 1975, Navratilova aspired to be the top women tennis player in the world. By the time she retired in 1994, she had won more overall titles than any other woman or man in tennis history. She was the first professional athlete to proclaim her lesbianism and the only twentieth-century sports legend to become an outspoken advocate of lesbian and gay rights.

Navratilova is an accomplished athlete who changed the look and style of women's tennis. She introduced the concepts of healthy eating and physical conditioning to the women's tour. In her twenty-two-year professional career, Navratilova earned eighteen Grand Slam singles titles, 167 career singles titles (including a record nine Wimbledon titles), and 166 doubles titles (including thirty-one Grand Slam titles). She held the record for 109 consecutive doubles wins (with Pam Shriver [1962–]), and the longest continuous winning streak (seventy-four matches). By the end of 1994, when she retired, she had won a total of 1,438 matches, and her career earnings exceeded $20 million. She has been named Athlete of the Year numerous times, as well as Athlete of the Decade for the 1980s.

After her retirement, Navratilova served as president of the Women's Tennis Association Tour Players Association, played in the Virginia Slims "Legends" Tour, and represented the United States in the Federation Cup. She became a television commentator for Grand Slam tournaments, impressing viewers with her insight, candor, and humor. Navratilova reached a wider audience with her editorials on sexism and homophobia in sports. She also published two tennis-themed mysteries, *The Total Zone* (1995) and *Breaking Point* (1996), and became a leading speaker on the international lecture circuit.

Martina Navratilova has been an influential advocate of lesbian and gay civil rights. In 1992, she took an active role in working to overturn Colorado's Amendment 2, a law that would have severely curtailed the civil rights of lesbians and gays. At the 1993 National Lesbian, Gay, Bisexual, and

*Martina Navratilova. Photo by Greg Gorman. Courtesy Linda Dozoretz Communications.*

Transgendered March on Washington, D.C., Navratilova was a keynote speaker. She spoke passionately about the importance of coming out and being visible as lesbian and gay people: "I believe the biggest, strongest weapon of our movement for equality is visibility, and the best way to get it is to come out. . . . [B]eing a lesbian . . . is what I am. Nothing more and nothing less."

In 1995, Navratilova became the spokesperson for the Rainbow Foundation, founded that year. This American-based nonprofit organization donated more than $100,000 in its first year to lesbian and gay health, cultural, and civil rights organizations, such as the Astraea National Lesbian Action Foundation, the National Breast Cancer Coalition, the National Center for Lesbian Rights, and the National Lesbian and Gay Health Association.

In 1996, Navratilova was awarded an honorary doctorate in public service from George Washington University.                    *Nanette K. Gartrell*

### Bibliography

Navratilova, Martina, with George Vecsey. *Martina.* New York: Knopf, 1985.

*See also* King, Billie Jean Moffitt; Sports, Professional

## Nazism

Acronym for National Socialism, the political philosophy and movement that dominated Germany in the years 1933–1945 and influenced many other countries throughout Europe and the rest of the world. Homosexuality was fundamentally condemned by National Socialism, because it called into question Nazi norms of sexual behavior, which were oriented toward the production of healthy "Aryans" (Nordic, non-Gypsy gentiles). However, after the takeover of power in 1933, Nazi policy toward homosexuals was differentiated. Its aim was not the physical destruction of all homosexuals, but, rather, "deterrence through punishment." Furthermore, homosexual men and women were treated differently. This distinction between the sexes made the Nazi persecution of homosexuals fundamentally different in kind from the racial war of destruction that the regime waged against the Jewish population and against Sinti and Roma (Gypsies).

After January 1933, one of the most urgent tasks for Nazi policy on sexual matters was to destroy the organized public homosexual movement. Informal communications networks were smashed, and pubs and bars were closed or placed under surveillance. Raids and denunciations contributed to a climate of fear and led many lesbians to withdraw into the private sphere or to break off all of their contacts.

Some lesbians in Nazi Germany were at risk on the grounds of their ethnic identity, their political affiliation, or for other reasons. However, for those who were not at risk on these grounds, the crucial factor defining the circumstances under which they lived was their status as women. The Nazi state saw motherhood and marriage as the fundamental destiny of a woman who was "Aryan" and "hereditarily fit." A population policy aimed at increasing the number of "desirable" births was the essential precondition for the National Socialist goal of conquest through war. After 1933, many of the estimated one million lesbians in Germany got married to escape social pressure and, in some cases, to avoid losing their jobs.

The criminalization of male homosexuality was never questioned, and the criminal law (paragraph 175 of the criminal code, which since 1851 had criminalized only sexual acts between men) on male homosexuality was severely tightened up; fifty thousand men were convicted on the basis of paragraph 175, and about fifteen thousand were sent to concentration camps. Yet the Ministry of Justice decided in 1935 to reject proposals to extend paragraph 175 to women. (Only in Austria, after the annexation in 1938, did the Nazi regime prosecute lesbians in the courts: In Austria, lesbianism had long been a criminal offense.) The ministry's decision of 1935 was justified with reference to socially defined gender roles. Government officials pointed out that male homosexuality posed a greater menace than female homosexuality to public life and political institutions, largely because of women's generally subordinate status and their exclusion from positions of power. Another argument against the criminalization of female homosexuality was derived, on the one hand, from assumptions about marital relationships and, on the other, from the stereotype of the lesbian who was only "pseudo-homosexual" and, thus, "curable." Most lawyers and population experts took the view that the danger of women being "seduced" into homosexuality was less of a danger for the state, since "a woman seduced in this way is not permanently withdrawn from normal sexual intercourse, but retains her utility for population policy purposes" (in Schoppmann, 1996).

There are only a few known cases in which women were persecuted because of their lesbianism; officially, they were usually accused of other "offenses," such as "political unreliability" or "subversion of national defense." As they were not—unlike homosexual men—marked with a pink triangle in concentration camps, their lesbianism was kept invisible. Lesbians were probably threatened to a greater degree by the persecution of the so-called asocials, which was based on Heinrich Himmler's decree of December 1937 on "preventive measures to combat crime." As a result, persons who had committed no criminal offense but who were in some way socially deviant were labeled "asocial" and taken by the police into concentration camps. The major targets of this drive against the "asocial," who were marked in the camps with a black triangle, were homeless people, the unemployed, and prostitutes, but also lesbians and Sinti and Roma.

How many women endured the horrors of the concentration camps because of their lesbianism? All that can be said is that there was no systematic persecution of lesbians comparable to the persecution of gay men in the Third Reich. Most lesbians were spared the fate of the camps as long as they were not endangered for other reasons and were prepared to conform to the regime's norms. The majority tried not to attract attention. Some were forced to leave their homeland—either because of their involvement in antifascist activities or because of their Jewish origins.                    *Claudia Schoppmann*

### Bibliography

Grau, Günter, ed. *Hidden Holocaust? Gay and Lesbian Persecution in Germany, 1933–45.* London: Cassell, 1995.

Schoppmann, Claudia. *Days of Masquerade: Life Stories of Lesbians During the Third Reich.* New York: Columbia University Press, 1996.

———. *Nationalsozialistische Sexualpolitik und weibliche Homosexualität* (National Socialist Sexual Politics and Female Homosexuality). Pfaffenweiler: Centaurus, 1991. Rev. ed. 1997.

*See also* Austria; Germany

## Nestle, Joan (1940–)

Essayist, editor, poet, historian, archivist, educator, and cofounder of the Lesbian Herstory Archives in 1973. The Lesbian Herstory Archives resided in Nestle's Upper West Side Manhattan apartment from 1974 to 1992, with Nestle opening her home and the archives to visitors, researchers, and public events. Born in the Bronx, Joan Nestle graduated from Queens College of the City University of New York in 1963 and earned an M.A. in English from New York University in 1965. She taught literature and composition in the SEEK program at Queens College from 1966 until her retirement in 1995.

Nestle's political vision and grass-roots scholarship has been central to constructing the nature and content of lesbian history. As she wrote in *A Restricted Country* (1987): "To live without history is to live like an infant, constantly amazed and challenged by a strange and unnamed world. There is a deep wonder in this kind of existence. . . . But a people who are struggling against a world that has decreed them obscene need a stronger bedrock beneath their feet."

Citing her own experience as a working-class femme who frequented lesbian bars beginning in the late 1950s, Nestle, in her historical work, honors the "sexual courage" and erotic complexity of femme and butch lives and relationships. Her embrace of marginalized sexualities—butch-femme, sadomasochism (S/M), prostitution—challenged lesbian feminists, who protested, during the early 1980s "sex wars," that Nestle represented "heterosexual, exploitative, dominant/submission butch-femme

*Joan Nestle. © Morgan Gwenwald.*

sexuality." Nestle wrote in 1983: "It is tempting to some Lesbians to see themselves as the clean sex deviant, to disassociate themselves from public sexual activity, multiple partners, and intergenerational sex. While this may be the choice for some of us, it is not the reality of many others, not now and not in the past" (in *A Restricted Country*). With the wide readership of *A Restricted Country* and *The Persistent Desire* (1992), however, Nestle has become well known and revered for her sexual politics and historical vision.

Nestle's writing incorporates a constellation of themes and influences, including the political oppression of the McCarthy era of the early 1950s; her civil rights activism; growing up Jewish, the daughter of a single mother; and coming of age in a lesbian world rich in erotic power and cultural resistance. Nestle characterizes "lesbian" as an array of erotic identities, desires, and sensibilities. She wrote in *A Restricted Country*:

But my body made my history—all my histories. Strong and tough, it allowed me to start working at thirteen; wanting, it pushed me to find the lovers I needed; vigorous and resilient, it carried me the fifty-four Alabama miles. Once desire had

a fifties face: now it is more lined. But still when I walk the streets to protest our military bullying of Central America, or the Meese Commission on pornography, or apartheid in South Africa and here, my breasts and hips shout their own slogans. As a woman, as a lesbian, as a Jew, I know that much of what I call history others will not. But answering the challenge of exclusion is the work of a lifetime.

*Polly Thistlethwaite*

## Bibliography

Metz, Holly. "Interview with Joan Nestle." *American Voice* (Winter 1990), 72–84.

***See also*** Butch-Femme; Lesbian Herstory Archives

## Netherlands

Constitutional monarchy since 1815, located in northwest Europe; capital, Amsterdam. With a population of 15.5 million, mainly in urban centers, the Netherlands has a history of social tolerance since the seventeenth century.

### History

The history of lesbianism in the Netherlands might be said to start either in 1730, when the dictionary of Van Hoogstraten en Schuer mentioned Sappho's love for "her own sex," or in 1892, when the expression "homosexual" was first used in an article by a psychiatrist. Between these two dates there is a shadowy period in which different elements of same-sex relationships or prelesbian configurations can be recognized. If transgressive behavior and societal condemnation of cross-dressing and nonconformist sexual behavior can be considered prelesbian configurations, then lesbianism starts with seventeenth- and eighteenth-century female soldiers and sailors, sexual relationships among women of the lower classes, and love poems written by educated seventeenth- and eighteenth-century women, such as writers Betje Wolff and Aagje Deken (both fl. ca. 1780). However, the dichotomy between homosexual and heterosexual had not yet been established, and in none of these cases does same-sex preference seem to have been exclusive.

At the end of the nineteenth century, under the influence of scientific studies from Germany and France, male and female homosexuality began to be

**N** seen as a personality trait caused by biological inversion (the "wrong" sex trapped in the opposite body). The word *homosexualiteit* was used for a time in competition with other words, such as *Uranier/Urninde* (which refers back to the classical period) and *tegennatuurlijke geslachtsdrift* (contrary sexual drive). The discussion informed the general public about a phenomenon that had hitherto been unknown and was thought to derive from France. Colloquially, these women were called *lollepot*, which had previously meant "immodest woman." *Lollepot* has since been abbreviated to *pot* ("dyke") and, in the late twentieth century, was a common expression. The term "lesbian" became common only after World War II.

The increasing visibility of homosexuality at the turn of the twentieth century led to a backlash, put into effect by the conservative majority, who won the 1906 elections. As a result, in 1911 section 248bis, which prohibited same-sex sexuality between adults and minors (under twenty-one), was put into the penal code. Contrary to the situation in most surrounding countries, where laws also were being tightened, this section applied to women as well as men. The impending introduction of this article led to the formation, by J.A. Schorer, of the first emancipation organization in the Netherlands, het Nederlandsch Wetenschappelijk Humanitair Komitee (NWHK; Dutch Scientific Humanitarian Committee). It distributed scientific information on homosexuality in the belief that the public would be more positively inclined toward homosexuality if they knew its biological origins. In reality, the NWHK was very much a one-man show, although it attracted the attention of a number of early feminists who were opposed, in principle, to state intervention in private lives. In the course of its sixty-year existence, nearly five thousand men and fifty women were convicted under section 248bis. More significant, it was used as an instrument to render homosexuality and lesbianism virtually invisible in Dutch society. Whenever homosexuals and lesbians began to organize, it was used by the police to quell their activities. Cross-dressing was forbidden by local police bylaws, which were used to pick up women in masculine trousers. Personal advertisements were also closely monitored by the police. It is, therefore, not surprising that there was very little subcultural activity before World War II.

There were some signs before the war of an emerging subculture in the lower-class honky-tonk bars and cafés in the "red light" districts of Amster-

dam and The Hague, where sex workers could be wooed by ladies with money, such as sculptor Saar de Swart (1861–1951), one of the first more or less open lesbians in the country. Sometimes men and women joined one another at sedate parties in private homes. Women with financial means also traveled to foreign countries.

During the 1930s, the first novels with lesbian themes began to appear, such as *Twee meisjes en ik* (Two Girls and Me [1930]) by A.H. Nijhoff and *Terug naar het eiland* (Back to the Island [1937]) by Josine Reuling. These novels are always set in foreign places, such as Paris, Berlin, the Alps, or Italy, reflecting the apparent reality of lesbian life at that time. A book of autobiographies, *De Homo-sexueelen*, published in 1939, reflected another piece of lesbian reality: butch-femme relationships closely adhering to the third-sex image propagated by the NWHK, which commissioned the book.

During World War II, the Netherlands was occupied by Nazi Germany, which had a paradoxical effect on homosexuals. Although the German occupation prohibited all male homosexuality, in practice, persecution was limited to those who had contacts with Germans. Lesbians appear not to have been persecuted at all. Nevertheless, many lesbians and gays went into the Resistance. Being illegal was, for the first time, an asset rather than a liability. Because "red light" districts were out of bounds to the German soldiers, bars such as Bet van Beeren's famous Het Mandje on the Zeedijk in Amsterdam, were used as arms depots for the Resistance.

## Postwar Organizing

After the war, there was a general feeling among the population that it should be possible to break through the old conservative prewar structures. At the same time, moral panic arose over the general looseness of behavior of the American and Canadian soldiers who liberated the country. In this climate, the COC (Cultuur-en Ontspannings Centrum; Center for Culture and Relaxation), a homosexual group, was founded on December 7, 1946. At the first meeting, three women were present. It was tolerated by the authorities, in part because their impeccable behavior during the war had given homosexuals some credit.

The COC's objective was twofold. Publicly, it aimed at abolishing section 248bis, which had been reinstated after the war and rigorously enforced during the 1950s. Privately, it wanted to provide a safe haven for its members. For the COC, the morality of its members was the ultimate proof that homosexuals had the right to be treated like other upstanding citizens. Therefore, it condemned sexual license and cross-dressing, which, until the late 1950s, included the wearing of pants by its "lady-members." Although, in principle, the COC was a mixed organization, in fact it was male-dominated in its early years. Throughout the 1950s and 1960s, the percentage of women members never rose above 20 percent. Very few women visited the COC because they thought they had little chance of meeting other women there, or they were afraid they might lose their girlfriends if they did meet other women. The organizational structure of the COC was tightly regulated, with a strong board and endless meetings, which also was unappealing to most women. The human rights perspective of the COC left no space to discuss male-female differences or any possibility for organizing separately. After 1961, a one-day women's convention was held infrequently, and the COC magazine began to include lesbian pages.

Outside the COC, a lesbian subculture was slow to develop. Many lesbians lived in the cities of Amsterdam and The Hague, attracted by the job opportunities in a sex-segregated employment market. Housing was difficult to find, as one-third of the country's infrastructure had been demolished during the war and single people had no individual right to housing. Lesbian lifestyles included a butch-femme culture, as well as "bar-dancers"—women with lower-to-middle-class jobs who went out in large circles to lead a life of fun and drink. Other women met privately, with a couple of friends in their own rooms. Overall, there was very little visible lesbian life, although the lesbianism of women such as novelist Anna Blaman (1905–1960) and pianist Pia Beck (1925/1926–) was well known. Books written during this period with lesbian themes include Dola de Jong's *De Thuiswacht* (The Tree and the Vine [1954]) and A.H. Nijhoff's *De Vier doden* (The Four Dead [1950]).

## Lesbian Feminism

During the 1960s, the social position of homosexuals slowly began to change, thanks to the strategy of the COC, whose members worked for full integration into society. The advent of feminism in the early 1970s touched a sore spot, however: The integration strategy did not permit women to organize separately. In 1971, a breach occurred, and groups like Lavender September and Group 7152 split off from the COC. Women's houses and cafés began to attract many women, some of whom left their husbands. New divisions occurred—between "old" lesbians (who had been "out" before the feminist movement) and "new" lesbians, between lesbians in Amsterdam, who saw themselves as the vanguard of the lesbian feminist movement, and those in the rest of the country. Using the feminist motto "the personal is political" and under the influence of U.S. poet and theorist Adrienne Rich (1929–), Lavender September stated that being lesbian was a political position. The country needed a "cultural guerrilla" movement against patriarchy with its strategy of enforced heterosexuality. In the *Lesbisch prachtboek* (The Lesbian Deluxe-Book [1979]), this strategy was fully developed. Although Lavender September was a very small group in reality, its public-relations campaign was excellent, and, within weeks, its demands had become well known. The first structure that had to be changed was language itself; therefore, the members communicated in a self-fabricated odd archaic style, which also served as a kind of code to distinguish them from others. Lavender September influenced mainstream feminism by insisting that a "real" feminist should be a lesbian. For a period of time in the early 1970s, many heterosexual feminists experimented with lesbianism, although few continued, which led to frustration on both sides. For example, it was known within the movement that lesbians had been leaders in the defense of the first abortion clinic, Bloemenhove, but lesbians increasingly complained that heterosexual feminists could not be convinced to support lesbian demands.

During this period, some women chose to remain within the COC, where a split occurred between those women who still wanted to work together with the men—later known as "mixed" women—and those who wanted an autonomous position within the COC. In 1981, this led to the establishment of a federated structure, in which most chapters had a gender-mixed committee alongside a women-only committee. One of the women's demands was for an exclusive women's night, since gay male culture had grown extensively during this period but there was still hardly any women's space.

At the end of the 1960s, author Andreas Burnier wrote novels such as *Een Tevreden Lach* (Satisfied Laughter) and *Het jongensuur* (The Boys Hour) that gained wide acclaim among lesbians and the public at large. Much foreign acclaim was given to Anja Meulenbelt's *The Shame Is Over*, a story of personal growth that contained lesbian elements.

The 1980s saw a tremendous rise of the organized lesbian movement. Special lesbian magazines such as *Diva* and the literary *Lust and Gratie* (Lust and Grace), began publication. Lesbian and gay studies programs were established at several universities. A riot at the Pink Pride Demonstration in 1982 initiated a new dialogue with the government, which led to the formulation of political demands on both national and local levels. The government increasingly provided money for organization and research. It even funded projects for lesbians in Latin America and Asia. It also put lesbian demands on the agenda of the United Nations Women's Conference in Nairobi in 1985.

## Contemporary Perspectives

By the end of the 1980s, feminism had lost its sway over lesbian activists. Younger lesbians were likely to be involved in mixed political movements and adopted a new lifestyle, including small-scale forms of enterprise, such as restaurants and bookshops. Other women chose motherhood, aided by changes in technology and public attitude. Since few clinics would inseminate single women, they turned to gay male friends as donors. This led not only to new coalitions with gay men, but also to intricate forms of parenthood by both lesbians and gay men.

The advent of AIDS in the 1980s focused the movement on providing social services, as a result of the influx of government money into AIDS prevention. In a changing modern society, separatism no longer seemed an effective strategy. New government policies made people more responsible for themselves; less money from state subsidies had to be spent more economically. All of these trends led to a smaller, more professionalized movement.

After fifteen years of political struggle, the Equal Rights Act became law in 1994. With this, the formal equality of homo- and heterosexuality became a fact in Dutch society. Progress toward absolute equality within all laws and regulations—such as domestic partnerships and gay marriages and, especially, the position of children within such units—will take a longer time.    *Judith Schuyf*

## Bibliography

Everard, Myriam. *Ziel en Zinnen. Over liefde en lust tussen vrouwen in de tweede helft van de achttiende eeuw* (Soul and Senses: About Love and Lust Between Women in the Second Half of the Eighteenth Century). Groningen: Historische Uitgeverij, 1994.

Meijer, Irene Costera. *Het persoonlijke wordt politiek. Feministische bewustwording in Nederland, 1965–1980* (The Personal Becomes Political: Feminist Consciousness in the Netherlands, 1965–1980). Amsterdam: Het Spinhuis, 1996.

Schuyf, Judith. *Een stilzwijgende samenzwering. Lesbische vrouwen in Nederland, 1920–1970.* (A Conspiracy of Silence: Lesbians in the Netherlands, 1920–1970). Amsterdam: IISG, 1994.

Tielman, Rob. *Homoseksualiteit in Nederland. Studie van een emancipatiebeweging* (Homosexuality in the Netherlands: Study of an Emancipation Movement). Meppel: Boom, 1982.

*See also* Blaman, Anna; Butch-Femme; Cross-Dressing; Rich, Adrienne

## New Left

Umbrella term used to describe the loosely linked groups of men and women who challenged the basic values and institutions of American society in the 1960s. Among their targets were racism and the American political process. The New Left emphasized personal freedom and direct democracy and raised individual freedom as its highest goal. Both the lesbian and gay movement and the women's movement were shaped by the New Left, and lesbians during the 1960s held multiple memberships in a range of New Left movements from civil rights groups to antiwar groups.

It is possible to trace the origins of a New Left political sensibility in the earliest modern lesbian political organizations. While the Daughters of Bilitis (DOB) adopted the conservative policy of helping lesbians adjust to society, not all lesbians within DOB were comfortable with this policy. In 1965, DOB member Ernestine Eckstein (pseud.), who had been active in the National Association for the Advancement of Colored People (NAACP), attempted to make DOB New York more militant. Eckstein argued that DOB should change its policies in favor of a program of direct action to secure full equality for homosexual citizens.

By the late 1960s, new organizations formed whose political agendas were more directly in line with New Left political agendas. In 1967, Rita Mae Brown helped found the Student Homophile League, the first New Left gay student group at Columbia University. In 1969, the Stonewall Rebellion in New York City became the critical turning point for lesbian and gay New Left activism. Although Stonewall was not an organized political action, it served as a catalyst for lesbians and gays in the New Left to examine their status in American society.

The Gay Liberation Front (GLF), a powerful new homosexual rights organization, emerged in the wake of Stonewall. Though Marxist in nature, GLF was a catalyst for the lesbian and gay movement, but, early on, GLF women felt that GLF men did not value their concerns as lesbians. In this, they echoed the sentiments of many lesbians who, tired of the sexism they encountered, left New Left organizations to join the women's movement.

Thus, in early 1970, Martha Shelley and Lois Hart of GLF formed the women's caucus of GLF, which eventually became the Radicalesbians. The Radicalesbians produced the critical theoretical treatise "Women-Identified Woman" (Koedt et al., 1973) and, in May 1970, took over the Second Congress to Unite Women, demanding better treatment for lesbians within the women's movement. This action became a watershed event in contemporary lesbian history.

In August 1970, Huey Newton, a leader of the Black Panthers, a Black Power organization, wrote a letter arguing that, despite personal opinion, the Panthers should unite with homosexuals politically. Shortly after the letter was published, the Panthers held their Black Panther Constitutional Convention. Hart, Brown, Shelley, and Charlotte Bunch were among the lesbians who went to the convention, which drew six thousand participants, to discuss gay liberation, among other topics. Twenty lesbians attended the women's workshop.

In this time of increased Left militancy, lesbian groups began to identify with more militant leftist groups. In Washington, D.C., Bunch went on to help found the leftist group the Furies, the members of which identified themselves as true revolutionaries, most like the Weathermen, a militant faction of the Students for a Democratic Society. As radical "outlaws," leftist lesbians had a special place in the women's liberation movement. It was believed that if the revolution was to be led by the most marginalized outcast groups, then lesbians were the vanguard of the revolution. This outlaw status was further heightened by the fact that the Federal Bureau of Investigation (FBI) infiltrated lesbian and women's groups in this period.

As heroic as this outlaw status was in this period, the early 1970s were also mercurial years for radical activist lesbians, and Robin Morgan's 1970 essay in the counterculture newspaper *Rat*, "Goodbye to All That," reflected a growing sense that women's liberation was turning away from the New Left. Morgan wrote: "Goodbye, goodbye forever, counterfeit Left . . . male-dominated cracked-glass-mirror reflection of the Amerikan Nightmare. Women are the real left." The militancy and violence of the Left came under fire both in the mainstream and critically in the women's movement. This turning away from leftist radical politics became clear when Susan Saxe, a Weatherman and a lesbian, was arrested in March 1975. Many in the lesbian feminist community blamed her for the presence of the FBI in their community. This reaction to Saxe's capture signaled a critical shift in lesbian political thought away from a radical leftist brand of politics and toward the inward-focused community-building efforts of cultural feminism of the late 1970s.

*Anne B. Keating*

### Bibliography

Echols, Alice. *Daring To Be Bad: Radical Feminism in America, 1967–1975*. Minneapolis: University of Minnesota Press, 1989.

Faderman, Lillian. *Odd Girls and Twilight Lovers: A History of Lesbian Life in Twentieth-Century America* New York: Columbia University Press, 1991.

Jay, Karla, and Allen Young, eds. *Out of the Closets: Voices of Gay Liberation*. New York: Douglas, 1972.

Marotta, Toby. *The Politics of Homosexuality*. New York: Houghton Mifflin, 1981.

Radicalesbians. "The Woman Identified Woman." In *Radical Feminism*. Ed. Anne Koedt, Ellen Levine, and Anita Rapone. New York: Quadrangle/New York Times Book Co., 1973, pp. 240–245.

Teal, Donn. *The Gay Militants*. New York: Stein and Day, 1971.

***See also*** Brown, Rita Mae; Daughters of Bilitis; Furies, The; Gay Liberation Movement; Radicalesbians; Socialism

## New Right

A conservative segment of political life that shifted right-wing politics away from a strictly economic stance to one that emphasizes values and morality. The political spectrum in the United States is typi-

**N** cally characterized along a continuum, with conservatism on the right end or "wing" and liberalism on the left. The right wing comprises a range of conservative political ideals and motivations. For some, organized religion provides the moral basis for their conservative political activism. Others are motivated by capitalist principles that challenge the government's role in the marketplace. Since in the early 1970s, this dominant political force in the Republican Party has been referred to as the "New Right."

## Characteristics

The "New" label distinguishes this constituency from its conservative predecessors, the "Old" Right. Characterized largely by its focus on economic and militaristic goals, the older division led the nation in the struggle against a perceived Communist threat to capitalism. Since the 1970s, there has been a change in the Right's ideological focus. Its political agenda now includes social and moral issues. The New Right agenda involves challenges to such diverse personal-life concerns as a woman's right to choose abortion; the rights of lesbians, bisexuals, and gay men; the humanity and rights of so-called illegal immigrants; and intense campaigns to remove gun-control legislation and to limit government financial and other assistance to poor, single parents for themselves and for their children.

While the concept New Right implies one unified group of conservatives, those who constitute this group are not monolithic in their views. The New Right can be divided into various organizations representing distinct interests. One identifiable segment is composed of those typically referred to as the Christian, or Religious, Right. The Christian Right's fundamentalist views on sexuality, family, and society in general drive its adherents' political agenda to restore "traditional family values." Its "family values" campaign promotes traditional gender relations and procreative and marital sexual relations. Often referred to as the "pro-family" movement, this segment of the New Right has gained considerable recognition and legitimacy from the Republican Party and some factions of the Democratic Party, as well as the mass media and the public.

Another faction consists of those whose stance on specific social issues drew them into coalition with the larger New Right. Many of the views of these "single-issue" conservatives are shared with the Christian Right. Historically, many single-issue conservatives became politically active with the New Right as they mobilized to oppose such progressive issues as the Equal Rights Amendment, abortion rights, and lesbian and gay rights, as well as issues involving gun control, euthanasia, and capital punishment.

Like their conservative predecessors, the third segment of the New Right campaigns around capitalist interests. Emergent from business, elite, and political segments of society, these individuals and organizations strive for a marketplace free from government intervention and regulation. Some scholars have noted that professional organizers often come from this segment of the New Right. While pushing for their economic and social agenda, these organizers facilitate coalition and organization among the different constituencies of the New Right.

## Goals

The New Right economic campaign of the 1990s centered on the reduction and elimination of the federal budget deficit. The means proposed to abolish the deficit involve spending cuts on programs such as public assistance and other lower- and middle-income social welfare programs. New Right proponents also advocate an income-tax reduction.

In support of its social agenda, the New Right channels considerable resources into campaigning for legislative and cultural change. After the United States Supreme Court's *Roe v. Wade* decision (1973) legalizing abortion, the New Right launched numerous attacks on adult and minor women's right to obtain safe and legal abortion upon demand. They were successful in their legislative attempts in many states to limit the power of *Roe v. Wade*. Likewise, New Right forces have blocked abortion clinics, set up their own pro-life clinics, and held marches to gain support and prevent abortion.

In the late 1980s and the 1990s, a shift occurred in the New Right's social priorities, with the battle against lesbian, gay, and bisexual rights becoming primary agenda item. The Right created a well-funded, well-organized challenge to the lesbian, gay, and bisexual movement. In the early 1990s, for example, it was successful in legislating antigay laws in a number of localities across the United States. Colorado was the first state to have voters pass a law that allowed for discrimination against lesbians, gay men, and bisexuals in employment, housing, and accommodations. The constitutionality of this and other similar initiatives have been challenged in the courts, with Colorado's law declared unconstitutional by the United States Supreme Court in 1996.

Along with such legislative campaigns, the New Right has attacked lesbians, gays, and bisexuals in other critical areas. Campaigns have been launched in the schools against multicultural and sex-education curricula supportive of lesbians, gay, and bisexual rights. New Right proponents oppose any positive portrayal of what they term a "homosexual lifestyle" in the schools and in the media. Private organizations have also been affected by the New Right antigay campaign. For example, as late as 1998, the Boy Scouts of America discriminated on the basis of sexual orientation in their national policy despite court challenges in different locations and at least one state supreme court decision against the organization's policy. These are just a few of the targets of the New Right. A major component of the Right is determined to create a society based solely on the notion of "traditional family." In the 1990s, the New Right stood as a major opponent with which lesbians, gay men, and bisexuals had to contend in the struggle for equality.    *Kimberly Dugan*

## Bibliography

Adam, Barry D. *The Rise of a Gay and Lesbian Movement.* Boston: Twayne, 1987.

Diamond, Sara. *Spiritual Warfare: The Politics of the Christian Right.* Boston: South End, 1989.

Himmelstein, Jerome L. "The New Right." In *The New Christian Right: Mobilization and Legitimation.* Ed. Robert C. Liebman and Robert Wuthnow. New York: Aldine, 1983, pp. 13–30.

Klatch, Rebecca E. *Women of the New Right.* Philadelphia: Temple University Press, 1987.

Mueller, Carol. "In Search of a Constituency for the 'New Religious Right.' " *Public Opinion Quarterly* 47 (1983), 213–229.

*See also* Electoral Politics; Law and Legal Institutions

## New Woman

A term developed by social commentators in the late-nineteenth- and early-twentieth-century industrial cities of Europe and North America, indicating a new independence and including, in some usages, the choice of emotional or sexual partnerships with women over dutiful daughterhood or marriage to men.

The New Woman offered a challenge to Victorian womanhood that stemmed from wage earning or extended education that removed a daughter from the domestic sphere of her parental home and took her into public space. New Women included factory and clerical workers and early college students alike, and they were often active in labor unions, social reform and radical movements, or the women's suffrage movement. They thereby claimed more space in traditionally male arenas than previous generations. The "New Negro Woman" of the 1920s in the United States, for example, was portrayed as an intelligent and aggressive partner with the black man in political activity to liberate their race. New Women also resisted older, more demure forms of womanhood and claimed male privileges through physical activity, dress, and manners—walking the streets, riding bicycles or driving cars, wearing shorter, lighter clothing, smoking cigarettes, or cutting long hair.

Historians have developed both a heterosexual and a lesbian story about sexual independence as a component of New Womanhood. The first story marks late-nineteenth-century working-class "tough girls" or "charity girls" as originators of a more assertive heterosexual style. These women pioneered dating as a form of courtship at commercial amusements like dance halls, away from family scrutiny. Class difference made them targets for attributions of "immorality" from middle-class exemplars of Victorian sexual restraint, but low wages did underlie the dating exchange of sexual favors for male treating at entertainments. Feminist bohemians of the 1910s and flappers of the 1920s adapted these styles and dating patterns for middle-class women, but their relative freedom remained in tension with heterosexual relationships and usually ended with marriage.

A second historical account of New Womanhood traces the shifting of same-sex relations among middle-class women from the model of romantic friendship in the nineteenth century to one of lesbian relations, with acknowledged sexuality, in the twentieth. Smith-Rosenberg (1985) and Newton (1984) argue that the first generation of New Women asserted their autonomy primarily by denying the family claim of motherhood and choosing lives of public service. Many declined marriage in favor of long-term partnerships, or "Boston marriages," with other women, not usually considered sexual (whatever their daily reality). Public discussion of sex in the early twentieth century both encouraged sexual consciousness in second-generation New Women and stigmatized them for rejecting not just motherhood but men. If not actively heterosexual, a New Woman might be labeled either a "mannish lesbian" or a repressed "lady in lavender." Twentieth-century lesbian New Women sometimes created an androgynous sexuality, sometimes embraced butch styles, and sometimes continued to understand themselves as Victorian romantic friends.

*Christina Simmons*

### Bibliography

Freedman, Estelle. "The New Woman: Changing Views of Women in the 1920s." *Journal of American History* 61 (1974), 372–393.

Newton, Esther. "The Mythic Mannish Lesbian: Radclyffe Hall and the New Woman." *Signs: Journal of Women in Culture and Society* 9 (1984), 557–575.

Peiss, Kathy. *Cheap Amusements: Working Women and Leisure in Turn-of-the-Century New York*. Philadelphia: Temple University Press, 1986.

Smith-Rosenberg, Carroll. "The New Woman as Androgyne: Social Disorder and Gender Crisis, 1870–1936." In Smith-Rosenberg, *Disorderly Conduct: Visions of Gender in Victorian America*. New York: Knopf, 1985, pp. 245–296.

*See also* Androgyny; Boston Marriage; Butch-Femme; Romantic Friendship

## New Zealand

Also called by its Maori name Aotearoa. Group of islands located in the South Pacific, about 1,200 miles southeast from Australia and bordered by the Tasman Sea to the west and the Pacific Ocean to the east. There are two major islands: the North Island and the South Island. The population is four million, the capital is Wellington, and the largest city is Auckland, both in the north. Other large cities are Christchurch and Dunedin, both in the south. The country is bicultural: Maori, the indigenous people, arrived before A.D. 1000, and Pakeha, descended from mainly British settlers, arrived in the nineteenth century. The founding document is the Treaty of Waitangi, signed between Maori tribes and the British Crown in 1840. There are, in addition, many ethnic groups from the South Pacific, Asia, and Europe. Aotearoa/New Zealand is a self-governing member of the British Commonwealth with a parliament, elected every three years, that selects a prime minister and cabinet.

## History

There have always been women who loved other women in Aotearoa/New Zealand. The Royal Commission on Social Policy said in 1988 that "homosexuality—female and male—was not uncommon in pre-European times and . . . it was in fact more readily accepted than today." During the nineteenth and early twentieth centuries, numbers of settler women arrived. There are documented cases of women passing as men to marry other women or to gain access to male employment opportunities. Romantic friendships were common among women of the upper and middle classes, married or unmarried. However, not all such friendships were as publicly acknowledged as that of poet Ursula Bethell and her companion, Effie Pollen, who lived together from 1904 until Pollen's death in 1934. Some upper-class women who loved women moved overseas. Katherine Mansfield (1888–1923), for example, following intense relationships with Wellington artist Edith Kathleen Bendall (later Robison [1877–1983]) and with Maata Mahupuku (1890–1952) in Wellington, moved to London and continued her relationship with Ida Baker (1888–1978) until her death in 1923.

Little research has been done on the occupational networks of lesbian women (hospitals, post office and telephone exchange, nursing, teaching, and the military) that existed prior to the 1950s. By the early 1960s, the rapid urbanization of Maori during the post–World War II period meant that numbers of Maori "kamps" (a word meaning homosexual introduced by "ship-queens" on British boats) met in hotel bars in the port cities of Auckland and Wellington, together with Pakeha working-class kamp girls. The first lesbian club was the KG Club—the Karangahape Road Girls' Club, also known as the Kamp Girls Club, started in Auckland by Maori lesbians in 1970. In addition to this and other visible groups, networks of middle-class Pakeha women (many also calling themselves kamps) met in private homes.

## Lesbian Organizing

The late 1960s brought new ideas to Aotearoa/New Zealand from the United States—black, women's, and gay liberation. In the late 1960s, the first women's liberation groups began; the first gay liberation group was started in 1972 at the University of Auckland. The words "gay" and later "lesbian" and "dyke" replaced "kamp" in common usage. From the 1980s, the Maori word *takatapui* or *takatapuhi* ("beloved and intimate friend of the same gender") was used by Maori lesbians and gays.

In 1973, the first national lesbian political organization, Sisters for Homophile Equality (SHE), was formed. The Wellington branch produced the *Circle*, a national lesbian magazine, from December 1973 until 1986. Wellington SHE began Club 41, the first lesbian club there, and held the first National Lesbian Conference in 1974. Christchurch SHE started the first Women's Refuge in 1975 and operated regular lesbian summer camps. The group also was active in the women's art and literature movements, including the production of *SPIRAL*, the women's art magazine, in 1976.

After conflicts between lesbians and heterosexual feminists at the United Women's Conventions (1977 and 1979) and the Radical Feminist Caucus (1978), more lesbians organized separately. The first Lesbian Center was started in Wellington in 1978. In 1979, Breathing Space, a discussion and social group for women who were "coming out" as lesbians, was formed; continued into the late 1990s. All of these groups had a lesbian agenda, and this tradition of lesbian-only groups and events continued through the 1990s. In smaller centers, lesbians often worked, and continue to work, in organizations with feminists or with gay men—for example, MALGRA (Manawatu Lesbian and Gay Rights Association), established in Palmerston North in 1977.

During the 1980s and 1990s, lesbian groups and organizations grew in numbers and scope. Lesbian phone lines were started in various parts of the country, including Christchurch (1981), Wellington (1983), and Dunedin (1984). By the early 1990s, services operated in smaller towns, such as Nelson, Palmerston North, Timaru, Wanganui, and Hamilton.

Many lesbian newsletters and magazines came and went in the last three decades of the twentieth century, including the Wellington *Lesbian Network Newsletter*, the *Grapevine, Behind Enemy Lines*, *Lesbian LIP, Dykenews*, and *Glad Rag*; the Auckland *Juno, LIP* (Lesbians in Print), and *Bitches, Witches, and Dykes*; the *Hamilton lesbian News*; and, in Dunedin, *Against All Odds*. The 1990s produced the *Wellington Lesbians Newsletter*, the *Otautahu Lesbians Newsletter* (Christchurch), and the *Tamaki-Makarau Lesbians Newsletter* (Auckland), among others. There are also some important national lesbian and gay publications, such as the *Express* newspaper, published in Auckland.

Lesbians worked for homosexual law reform and human rights in the 1970s and 1980s. In 1985 and 1986, the participated in the Homosexual Law Reform Bill campaign. The bill was introduced by Labor Member of Parliament (MP) Fran Wilde in two parts: to decriminalize male homosexuality and to amend the Human Rights Act by adding sexual orientation to the grounds for prohibiting discrimination. Some lesbians worked in lesbian and gay organizations (Gay Task Force, Campaign for Homosexual Equality), others in lesbian, gay, straight coalitions (Coalition for the Bill), and others in lesbian organizations (Lesbian Coalition), especially opposing the nationwide door-to-door petition against the bill organized by fundamentalist Christians using American advisers. The first part of the bill was passed in 1986 and male homosexuality was decriminalized, but part two, the human rights section, was lost. It reintroduced by national MP Katherine O'Regan in 1991 as the Human Rights Amendment Bill and was approved, adding sexual orientation (defined as lesbian, homosexual, bisexual, or heterosexual) to the Human Rights Act. Christchurch-based LAVA (Lesbian Action for Visibility in Aotearoa) was a prominent lesbian group active on this campaign.

Lesbian involvement in women's organizations is also considerable. Lesbians started women's centers, rape crisis and sexual abuse help centers, women's refuges, and antiracism groups and have initiated many feminist actions.

In Wellington, DOODS (Dykes out of Debt) held monthly dances as fund-raisers for local lesbian services, and there were regular Over-35's lesbian dances. LILAC (Lesbian Information, Library, and Archives Collective) in Wellington runs a lending library and is developing archives. The Lesbian Overland and Cafe Club organizes outdoor activities in Wellington, and, in Auckland, POLLY (Proud Older Lesbians Like You) arranges events for older lesbians. Lesbian Balls, which are formal-dress and ballroom-dancing events, are held annually in the main centers, attracting hundreds of partipants: The Wellington Ball is held in the Town Hall; the Dunedin Ball, at Larnach's Castle. There are many lesbian sports clubs: the Wellington Amazon Softball Club was the first (1977), followed by Auckland's Circe Softball Club (1979) and Soccer Club (1980), to name just three.

Lesbian radio broadcasting started on Wellington Access Radio in 1984 with a weekly show that continued to broadcast through the 1990s. Lesbian programs have been broadcast in Auckland, Christchurch, Dunedin, and Nelson. There is a national lesbian and gay weekly television program called *Out*

# N

*There* with a lesbian copresenter. Lesbian playwright Lorae Parry, actor Madeline Macnamara, and musicians Sue Dunlop and the Topp Twins made significant contributions to lesbian visibility in the 1980s and 1990s, as did fiction writers Frances Cherry, Ngahuia Te Awekotuku, and Cathie Dunsford and nonfiction writers Miriam Saphira and Julie Glamuzina.

National Lesbian Studies Conferences were held in Wellington, in 1993 and 1995, attracting more than three hundred lesbians. Lesbian studies are included at some universities, especially women's studies at Victoria University in Wellington. Lesbians are also active members of GLEE (Gays and Lesbians in Education Everywhere) (primary, secondary, and tertiary), which holds regular national conferences. There are also lesbian and gay student and youth groups at the universities. In Wellington, the Alexander Turnbull Library, situated in the National Library, houses LAGANZ (Lesbian and Gay Archives of New Zealand).

Some lesbian and gay events are particularly significant, especially the HERO festival in Auckland and DEVOTION in Wellington. These are weeklong festivals that include major street parades, dance parties attracting thousands of partipants (open to anyone), theater performances, and historical walks. In Christchurch, a lesbian and gay Futures Forum discusses current directions. International lesbian influences remain significant, especially through books and magazines from the United States and electronic connections through the Internet. *Alison J. Laurie*

## Bibliography

Coney, Sandra, ed. *Standing in the Sunshine: A History of New Zealand Women Since They Won the Vote.* Auckland: Viking, 1993.

Du Plessis, Rosemary, Phillida Bunkle, Kathie Irwin, Alison J. Laurie, and Sue Middleton, eds. *Feminist Voices: A Women's Studies Text for Aotearoa/New Zealand.* Auckland: OUP, 1991.

Else, Anne, ed. *Women Together: A History of Women's Organisations in Aotearoa/New Zealand.* Wellington: Internal Affairs/Brigid Williams Books, 1993.

Glamuzina, Julie. *Outfront: Lesbian Political Activity in Aotearoa, 1962–1985.* Hamilton: Lesbian Press, 1993.

Laurie Alison J. "From Kamp Girls to Political Dykes." In *Finding the Lesbians.* Ed. Julie Penelope and Sarah Valentine. Freedom: Crossing, 1990.

———. "Katherine Mansfield: A Lesbian Writer?" *New Zealand Women's Studies Journal* (December 1988), 48–70.

*See also* Mansfield, Katherine; Pacific Literature; Romantic Friendship

## Nin, Anais (1903–1977)

French-American writer. Born outside Paris to a French-Danish singer and a sexually abusive father who was a Spanish composer, Anais Nin is most frequently associated with the Parisian literary and artistic scene of the 1930s and with her sexually volatile relationships with Henry (1891–1980) and June Miller (1902–after 1977?). As a writer, she is best known for her voluminous diaries, which began publication in 1966. A prolific writer, Nin published thirteen volumes of diaries, twelve novels, and several volumes of criticism and pornography. She lectured widely after her diaries were published and attained an almost iconic status with many feminists in the United States, where she settled at the outbreak of World War II.

Nin's diaries have received considerable attention, in part, for their record of her compulsively voracious sexuality, including her experiences with women. Although ambiguity surrounds Nin's actual engagements with women—biographers describe Nin as a rapacious liar who fabricated much in both her diaries and her life—she wrote frequently of feeling tremendous passion for women. Nin has been celebrated for depicting female sexuality in a groundbreaking manner; however, her emphasis on female masochism and the psychic scars left on her as a result of paternal incest mitigate the ability of her work to speak to a broad spectrum of female sexual experiences. Nevertheless, in her writings, lectures, and interviews, she was a consistent, if problematic, voice for free sexual expression, especially for the expression of intense emotional and sexual feelings between women.

Nin's views of women and sexuality were profoundly affected by years of psychoanalysis, including analysis with Otto Rank (1884–1939), with whom she also had a sexual relationship. Nin trained as a psychoanalyst herself, although she infrequently worked with patients. While she has stated that she experienced homosexual relations as immature and narcissistic, she viewed lesbianism as a positive force in women's lives. She believed that feminist and lesbian anger toward men created an additional layer of problems in regard to male/female estrangement that would eventually require psychological energy and attention. Hence, unlike many other feminists, she eschewed the inevitability of such anger. Ultimately, for Nin, it was the internal world of dreams, passion, and feeling that held the greatest reality. The quest for self-realization was her life's work. Her novels and diaries serve as the complex record of that quest.          *JoAnn Pavletich*

### Bibliography

Bair, Deirdre. *Anais Nin: A Biography*. New York: Putnam, 1995.

Fitch, Noel Riley. *Anais: The Erotic Life of Anais Nin*. Boston: Little, Brown, 1993.

*See also* Diaries and Letters; Psychoanalysis

### Noble, Elaine (1944–)

U.S. political figure, and the first open lesbian elected to a state assembly. Born in 1944 near Pittsburgh, Pennsylvania, she graduated from Boston University and later earned a master's degree in speech from Emerson College (Boston) and a master's degree in education at Harvard University. After she came out in the late 1960s, she helped found the Boston chapter of the Daughters of Bilitis and produced one of the first lesbian and gay radio programs (Gay Way). Later, she served as director of the Massachusetts Womens Political Caucus and gained valuable skills lobbying the state legislature on behalf of women's issues. During this time she also taught speech at Emerson College.

Noble ran for the Massachusetts State Assembly on a multi-issue platform in 1974 and won the first of two terms. Members of the "old boys' network" in the legislature grew to like and respect their personable colleague. In 1977, Noble was part of a delegation of lesbians and gays who met with representatives of President Jimmy Carter's administration. In 1978, her district was redrawn and she decided not to run for a third term. Barney Frank, who came out himself in 1987, won the seat Noble had held.

After Noble left the Assembly, she worked for Boston Mayor Kevin White's office of intergovernmental affairs. There she became involved in an FBI investigation aimed at White's administration but was exonerated of any wrongdoing. After leaving her position with the city, she cofounded in the early 1980s the Pride Institute, a gay and lesbian alcohol and drug treatment center in Minneapolis, Minnesota. She later ran unsuccessfully in Massachusetts for the U.S.

Senate (1980), and twice for the Cambridge City Council (1991 and 1993). In 1998, she continued to live in Boston, and also managed the Pride Value Fund (a lesbian and gay investment fund).

As the first high-profile, out lesbian political official (Kathy Kozachenko had served as a member of the Ann Arbor, Michigan, City Council in 1973), Noble was the target of unrealistic expectations from the gay and lesbian community. In one interview she recalled that "I had not only more work, but got more flack, more criticism, more heartache from the gay community than from the people who elected me" (quoted in Thompson, 1994). Yet she was an inspiration to the many openly lesbian and gay elected official who followed her in the United States.          *Yolanda Retter*

### Bibliography

Retter, Yolanda. "Herstory: Elaine Noble." *The Lesbian News* (September 1998), 52.

Thompson, Mark, ed. *Long Road to Freedom: The Advocate History of the Gay and Lesbian Movement*. Foreword by Randy Shilts. New York: St. Martin's, 1994.

*See also* Electoral Politics

### Norton Sound Incident

Investigation into alleged lesbianism aboard a United States naval ship. In May 1980, at the request of a member of the United States Congress, the Naval Investigative Service (NIS) began an investigation into life aboard the ship USS *Norton Sound*. Allegations of stabbings, drug dealing, and loansharking had been made, yet initial investigation into these crimes revealed nothing. But, when an agent asked one woman about lesbians aboard the ship, she provided a four-page statement claiming that twenty-three of the sixty-one women serving on the *Norton Sound* were lesbians. Significant in this statement, eight of the nine African American women aboard the ship were identified as lesbians. This was all the NIS needed to undertake a full-scale investigation focusing solely on homosexuality. Investigations of homosexuality were viewed as an easy means of demonstrating that the much maligned NIS was doing its job and provided an opportunity for investigators to "improve" their image.

The NIS called in the thirty-eight women who had not been identified as lesbian, assumed they were heterosexual, gave them a list of female crew members, and asked them to identify who they thought might be lesbian. The NIS engaged in questioning that was lewd and embarrassing ("Did you lick her juices?") and used lies and coercion to obtain information. Although no one indicated having observed sexual behavior between any women, these tactics resulted in nineteen women being threatened with discharge.

Unlike other "witch-hunts," some of the accused decided to seek outside help. They turned to the American Civil Liberties Union and other organizations with experience in dealing with the issue of lesbians and gays in the military. The case also gained the attention of the increasingly politicized lesbian and gay community. It is the degree to which this witch-hunt was made public that may have saved some women's careers. Before administrative hearings were begun, charges against eleven of the women were dropped, and those against the other eight were reduced from unsuitability to misconduct.

The first two women on whom hearings were conducted were able to provide testimony from men with whom they had had sexual relations. They were recommended for retention. The next two women were unable to provide such testimony. Their hearings resulted in discharge. The Navy then decided to drop the charges against the remaining four women due to "insufficient evidence." It appeared to many that the Navy, having started the investigation, had to convict someone. Now that it had, it could drop the charges against the others.

Although the *Norton Sound* incident is only one of many witch-hunts that have occurred throughout the military, it is viewed by some as one of the most egregious examples of intimidation and harassment. It is also recognized by many as a turning point for military personnel in that they learned that using the press to their advantage was possible, and, perhaps most important, many learned that they were not alone. In the end, the investigation of the *Norton Sound* ruined more careers than those of the two women who were discharged, but it was one of the first cases to bring to the public the issue of lesbians and gays in the military and the McCarthy era tactics often employed by military investigative units. *Melissa S. Herbert*

### Bibliography

Shilts, Randy. *Conduct Unbecoming: Lesbians and Gays in the U.S. Military*. New York: St. Martin's, 1993.

*See also* Military

## Nursing

Women's profession and scientific discipline. Nursing is the care and nurturance of the health of both healthy and sick people in any setting. Nursing is performed by nurses, and there are many types of nurses.

### Characteristics

Registered nurses (RN) may have two, three, four, or more years of basic nursing education. Licensed practical (or vocational) nurses (LPN, LVN) typically have twelve to eighteen months of basic education. Advanced practice nurses (APN) have graduate degrees and specialize as nurse practitioners, nurse anesthetists, nurse midwives, and clinical nurse specialists. Each level of nurse has different skills. Multiple types and levels of nurses create a problem for nursing because people who are not aware of differences among nurses tend to think that "a nurse is a nurse."

Nurses are the largest number of workers in the health field. Most nurses engage in nursing practice, and the largest number of nurses practice in hospitals. Other nurses work as educators, researchers, and administrators. Nursing offers a wide variety of career options.

More than 90 percent of nurses are women. Historically, nursing was one of the few professions that women were allowed to enter. Florence Nightingale (1820–1910) is considered the founder of modern nursing. The image of Nightingale as the "lady with the lamp" is a stereotype that nurses continue to endure (coincidentally, many of Nightingale's own relationships with women were intense, "romantic" friendships). Nurses, as women, are viewed as nurturant, self-giving, and altruistic. Nurses are often thought less important than physicians, and they make less money and have less social recognition than physicians. There are at least two reasons for this: Society does not view nursing as a profession, and people are socialized to value cure (what physicians are educated to do) more than care (what nurses are educated to do).

### Lesbians in Nursing

Most nurses, both women and men, are heterosexual; however, the representation of lesbians in nursing should be similar to that of lesbians in society. Lesbian nurses often recognize one another, even if they are not recognized by their heterosexual colleagues, and they believe that their is a substantial number within the field. A majority of lesbian nurses, however, do not reveal to their colleagues that they are lesbian because internalized homophobia causes them to fear what might happen if they do "come out of the closet." Indeed, there are real risks. Deevey (1993) writes that nurses risk physical violence; loss of job, income, nursing license, and professional reputation; and shunning by colleagues and family.

Nursing has a reputation for caring—about all kinds of people. Nursing education emphasizes being nonjudgmental, but research shows that nurses, nursing students, and nursing educators (as well as other health-care professionals) have homophobic attitudes, which affect lesbian colleagues, as well as gay and lesbian clients. Although multiculturalism is spreading, many people do not consider valuing lesbians as part of being multicultural. When nurses report that they do not know any lesbians, they are probably wrong.

Still, being closeted results in feelings of isolation, loneliness, powerlessness, and anger. Revealing one's true self to colleagues is freeing and empowering, if difficult for some nurses. Deevey's suggestions for approaches to coming out on the job came from her experience as a nurse, but they are relevant to any job situation.

An Australian study (Jackson 1995) suggests that one explanation for homophobic attitudes among nurses is that nursing textbooks have little or no information about lesbians (and gay men) and that, when information is present, it is negative. For example, pediatric nurse practitioners are taught that children of lesbians are socially isolated. Stevens and Hall (1991) attribute homophobic reactions of nurses and other health professionals to the larger, historical construction of lesbians as pathological.

The Acquired Immune Deficiency Syndrome (AIDS) epidemic has played a role in helping lesbian nurses come out professionally. Lesbian nurses became unwilling to ignore homophobic attitudes directed toward the large numbers of gay men who were among the first diagnosed with AIDS in the United States. Research shows that homophobia among many health-care professionals, including nurses, has decreased since AIDS appeared.

Lesbians are increasingly a visible presence in nursing. Since the late 1980s, several nurses have disclosed their lesbianism in nursing publications, and more have published on lesbian topics without specifically disclosing their sexuality. Many of these nurses reported at least as many positive responses from colleagues as negative ones.

These nurses are making a difference in nursing curricula; they are conducting research on issues of importance to the life and health of lesbians; and they serve as role models for lesbian students. Lesbian nurses such as Christine Tanner at Oregon Health Sciences University in Portland are working for the legal right to domestic-partner benefits in places of employment. Young lesbians in the 1990s are more likely than lesbians in the past to be out, and they seek support from older colleagues in their chosen fields.

## Organizing Efforts

In the United States, there have been several attempts to organize lesbian and gay nurses. Carolyn Innes and David Waldron founded the Gay Nurses Alliance (GNA) in Pennsylvania in August 1973. GNA emerged nationally after Innes and Waldron presented the organization at the American Nurses Association (ANA) convention in June 1974, which by chance, was held in San Francisco, California.

The purposes of GNA were to raise awareness within nursing about the numbers of gay nurses, provide a forum for gay nurses, work for the civil rights of gay nurses, and sensitize health professionals to the needs of gay patients. Several local chapters developed, but most action was national and focused on ANA. The organization lasted for about ten years before disappearing, and a newer generation of lesbian nurses did not know that GNA existed.

But lesbian nurses, like other lesbians, often find ways to network with one another, both socially and professionally. Lesbian nurses in California began organizing in the San Francisco Bay Area in 1989 and only later discovered that a group of lesbian nurses had been meeting in Los Angeles since 1985. The mid-1990s brought another organization, Lavender Lamps, the National Lesbian and Gay Nurses Association, which is trying to become known in nursing. The need for a national presence of lesbian nurses remains. *Linda A. Bernhard*

### Bibliography

Deevey, Sharon. "Lesbian Self-Disclosure: Strategies for Success." *Journal of Psychosocial Nursing* 31 (1993), 21–26.

Jackson, Debra. "Nursing Texts and Lesbian Contexts: Lesbian Imagery in the Nursing Literature." *Australian Journal of Advanced Nursing* 13 (1995), 25–31.

**N** Oakley, Ann. "On the Importance of Being a Nurse." In *Telling the Truth About Jerusalem: A Collection of Essays and Poems*. Ed. Ann Oakley. New York: Blackwell, 1986, pp. 180–195.

Stephany, Theresa M. "Nursing as a Lesbian." *Sexuality and Disability* 10 (1992), 119–124.

Stevens, Patricia E., and Joanne M. Hall. "A Critical Historical Analysis of the Medical Construction of Lesbianism." *International Journal of Health Services* 21 (1991), 291–307.

***See also*** Health; Medicine; Romantic Friendship

# O

## O'Brien, Kate (1897–1974)

Irish novelist, playwright, travel writer, and journalist. Romantic friendships between women, lesbian heroines, the dilemma of women's identity in a rigidly sex-stereotyped society, are all grist to the mill of Irish writer Kate O'Brien.

Born in Limerick in 1897, O'Brien went to the French convent school Laurel Hill. *The Land of Spices* (1941) is a fictionalized account of her time there. Graduating in 1919 from University College Dublin, she worked for two years as a journalist and a teacher in England, where the painter Mary O'Neill became her lifelong friend and, later, literary executor.

Considering marriage to Dutch journalist Gustaaf Reiner in 1922, O'Brien spent a year in Bilbao. Spain became her most enduring love, and her novel *Mary Lavelle* (1936) was based on her experiences there. Subsequently, she set the novel *That Lady* (1946) in Spain, and, because of her criticism of the regime of Francisco Franco (1892–1975) in *Farewell Spain* (1937), she was barred from the country. Following her year in Bilbao, O'Brien returned to London and married. The union lasted only eleven months, and she later referred to her ex-husband as "poor Gustaaf, now in the grave" despite the fact that he outlived her.

O'Brien began her literary career in 1926 with the play *Distinguished Villa*, which she wrote for a bet. On the strength of its success, O'Brien wrote her first novel, *Without My Cloak* (1932). The sequel, *The Ante Room* (1934), and *Mary Lavelle*, her first novel to be banned by the Irish censor, followed.

During World War II, O'Brien lived in Oxford, publishing *Pray for the Wanderer* in 1938. She wrote the novel *The Last of Summer* (1942) while staying at the home of novelist E.M. Delafield (1890–1943). *That Lady*, her only historical novel, was filmed in 1955.

The lesbian "fairytale" *The Flower of May* (1953) and a study, *Teresa of Avila* (1951), were written in Ireland. In her last novel, the lesbian realist text *As Music and Splendour* (1958), O'Brien forges a link between women's autonomy and the rejection of the heterosexual contract.

Critically neglected, she spent her last fourteen years in England. She died in 1974 in Canterbury, where her grave bears the inscription "pray for the wanderer."                                   *Tina O'Toole*

### Bibliography

Dalsimer, Adele. *Kate O'Brien: A Critical Study*. Dublin: Gill and Macmillan, 1990.

Reynolds, Lorna. *Kate O'Brien: A Literary Portrait*. New Jersey: Barnes and Noble, 1987.

Walshe, Eibhear, ed. *Ordinary People Dancing*. Cork: Cork University Press, 1993.

***See also*** Ireland; Romantic Friendship

## Olivia

Founded in 1973 as a record company to support the creativity of women singers, songwriters, musicians, engineers, and producers, Olivia Records grew to become one of the largest independent record labels in the 1970s and 1980s. In the 1990s, Olivia became the premier travel company for lesbians.

Olivia recorded more than forty albums, with sales of more than a million records, and produced hundreds of concerts, including three sold-out events at Carnegie Hall. Olivia Records was the forerunner for the late-twentieth-century boom of lesbian performers, having recorded and promoted "out" lesbians since its inception.

Olivia's most successful artist, Cris Williamson (1947–), recorded her best-selling classic *The Changer and the Changed* in 1975. Over the course of twenty-one years, Cris recorded fourteen albums and the documentary video (aired on the Public Broadcasting System) *The Changer: A Record of the Times*, for Olivia. The roster of artists who recorded on Olivia during the 1970s and 1980s includes Meg Christian, Teresa Trull, Lucie Blue Tremblay, Tret Fure, Linda Tillery, Dianne Davidson, Deidre Mc-Calla, Mary Watkins, June Millington, Nancy Vogl, BeBe K'Roche, Pat Parker, and Judy Grahn, among others. All are featured on a compilation called *Lesbian Concentrate: A Lesbianthology of Songs and Poems*, released in 1977 as a response to Anita Bryant's antigay campaign. *Lesbian Concentrate* was one of the first recordings ever made with the word "lesbian" in the title.

In 1990, Olivia Records expanded into Olivia Cruises and Resorts, the leading travel company chartering entire cruise ships and resorts exclusively for women. Between 1990 and 1996 alone, Olivia chartered more than thirty cruises and resort vacations for more than fifteen thousand women, with destinations including Alaska, Hawai'i, Greece, the Caribbean, Mexico, the Mediterranean, Canada, Costa Rica, and Tahiti. As with the record label, Olivia Travel created a path for lesbians, where none had existed before, and became the largest "out" lesbian business in the United States.

Since 1973, Olivia's founder, Judy Dlugacz, has dedicated herself to building visibility for the lesbian community. She was instrumental in the creation of the cultural phenomenon called "women's music" and later developed exclusive vacations for women. She also manages actor-comedian Suzanne Westenhoefer and coproduced Westenhoefer's 1994 out lesbian Home Box Office (HBO) comedy special, a first ever on television, which received a CableACE nomination.          *Judy Dlugacz*

### Bibliography

Berman, Leslie. "Olivia Turns Fifteen." *High Fidelity* 39:3 (March 1989), 51.

Davis, Riccardo A. "Sky's the Limit for Tour Operators." *Advertising Age* 64:3 (January 18, 1993), 36–37.

*See also* Businesses, Lesbian; Music, Women's; Tourism and Guidebooks

## Opera

Art form characterized by extended dramatic compositions in which all parts are sung to instrumental accompaniment.

### Historical Roots

The medieval mystic Hildegard of Bingen (1098–1179) and her nuns created the first musical drama, *Ordo Virtutum* (1158), which concerns the efforts of a female soul to resist worldly (that is, heterosexual) temptation and rejoin her female religious community. The art form recognized today as opera, however, originated in seventeenth-century Venice, where an enthusiastic public audience and aristocratic patronage encouraged its development. While it cannot be known whether members of the so-called Academy of the Anonymous, who worked to promote this new genre, were homosexual, their secular outlook made opera a friendly forum for homoerotic representations. Baroque opera, denounced by its enemies as "decadent," presented Greco-Roman narratives of male and female homosexual desire and gender-role subversion through the means of cross-dressed performers.

Claudio Monteverdi (1567–1643) was responsible for operatic constructions of madness and desire. Accordingly, both male and female characters could be portrayed as losing control of reason through anger, passion, or grief. For example, *L'incoronazione di Poppea* (1643) portrays Poppea, a Roman courtesan, employing her vocal prowess to scheme her way into power as empress. The characters of Ottone, her former lover, and Nero are soprano roles for male castrato or female soprano. The early depiction of female homoeroticism and protolesbianism reaches its pinnacle, however, in George Frideric Handel's (1685–1759) *Serse* (1738). Serse dramatizes, through an elaborate series of starcrossed and cross-dressed loves, the complicated plottings of the rivalries of King Serse and his "brother" Arsemenes (sung by a female mezzo-soprano) for the love of Romilda, whose sister Atalanta is secretly in love with Arsemenes.

The gradual suppression of the practice of castrating young male singers to retain their high *tessatura* (vocal ranges) caused a shift in the casting of male roles to female mezzo-sopranos, resulting in the *travesti*, or trouser, role. For example, Christoph Willibald Gluck (1714–1787) wrote the male lead of *Orfeo ed Euridice* (1762) for a castrato; when the opera was revived in 1859, however, Orfeo was sung by the famous mezzo-soprano Pauline Viardot (1821–

Der Rosenkavalier: *Gwyneth Jones (left) as the Marschellin and Tatiana Troyanos as Oktavian. Winnie Klotz/Metropolitan Opera.*

1910). Subsequent opera composers made further developments in the *travesti* role. Wolfgang Amadeus Mozart's (1756–1791) *Le Nozze di Figaro* (1786) takes the occasion of the waning of male aristocratic privilege to explore the subversive meanings of female-female love. Cherubino, played by a mezzo-soprano, is the womanizing page of Countess Almaviva; while in love with the countess, "he" seduces Barbarina, the gardener's daughter. Cherubino sings an aria in which "he" proclaims: "Every woman makes me change color, every woman makes me tremble." This character type later reappears as Oktavian in Richard Strauss's (1864–1949) *Der Rosenkavalier* (1911), which makes the female homoeroticism in *Nozze* quite apparent. Subsequent trouser roles of note include Siebel in Charles Gounod's (1818–1893) *Faust* (1859), Count Orlovsky in Johann Strauss's (1825–1899) *Die Fledermaus* (1874), and Nicklausse in Jacques Offenbach's (1819–1880) *Les Contes d'Hoffmann* (1881).

In contrast to Mozartian opera, in which *travesti* roles are comic, Gioacchino Antonio Rossini's (1792–1868) female "armor" roles are typically heroic figures who perform such actions as fighting duels, leading armies to victory, and romancing the soprano heroines. In *Semiramide* (1823), for example, Queen Semiramide falls in love with the mezzo-soprano Arsace, commander of her army and, unknown to her, her long-lost son. Arsace is in love with Princess Azema and seeks vengeance for the murder of "his" father, who was killed, not coincidentally, by Semiramide. Vincenzo Bellini (1801–1835), however, deployed his more psychologically convincing *travesti* roles to romantic ends. His *I Capuleti e I Montecchi* (1830) features a mezzo in the role of Romeo in this homoerotic adaptation of the story of Shakespeare's star-crossed lovers. Moreover, in *Norma* (1831), romantic friendship between women is given eloquent, impassioned expression. In their duet, Adalgisa and Norma, who had once been rivals for the love of the same man, swear their eternal love to each other, concluding: "With you I shall set my face firmly against the shame which fate may bring, as long as I feel your heart beating next to mine."

## The Twentieth Century

The early twentieth century witnessed the creation of new modes of gay and lesbian representation, beginning with the antibourgeois aesthetics of Richard Strauss's *Elektra* (1909) and Alban Berg's (1885–1935) *Lulu* (1937). Since the 1980s, productions have increasingly portrayed the title character of Elektra as a lesbian gripped by the Freudian "Elektra complex," identifying with her father against her mother and engaging in an incestuous relationship with her sister Chrysothemis. Lulu, based on Frank Wedekind's (1864–1918) plays, features opera's first openly lesbian character, the heroic Countess Geschwitz, who dies as the result of her unrequited love for the amoral protagonist, Lulu, and emerges as the only sympathetic, humane character in the opera.

The American gay composer Virgil Thomson (1896–1989) collaborated with his librettist Gertrude Stein (1874–1946) to produce two original operas that not only eschew conventional heterosexual plotting but also illuminate the social and spiritual parameters of homosocial community. *Four Saints in Three Acts* (1934) takes place in Spain and explores the lives of a group of male and female Carmelites who work together harmoniously to achieve collective sainthood. *The Mother of Us All* (1946) is a homage to the nineteenth-century American suffragist Susan B. Anthony (1820–1906), which focuses on the romantic friendship between Anthony and her lifelong companion, Anne.

## Lesbian Subculture

In the twentieth century, opera also became a significant force in lesbian subculture. Leading singers such as Mary Garden (1874–1967), Emma Calvé (1858–1942), Geraldine Ferrar (1882–1967), and Kathleen Ferrier (1912–1953) became cultural icons to lesbian opera fans. The American lesbian novelist Willa Cather (1873–1947), a devotee of opera, wrote *The Song of the Lark* (1915), a fictionalized biography of the Wagnerian soprano Olive Fremstad (1871–1951). Opera has thus served lesbians as a vehicle for camp masquerade and diva identification. More recent works by gay composers, however, deal more seriously with homosexual-related themes, such as social exclusion, persecution, and the price of being different, all of which gained urgency in the wake of the Holocaust and the subsequent emergence of gay and lesbian politics. Francis Poulenc's (1899–1963) woman-centered tragic opera *Dialogues des Carmélites* (1957) returns to the scene of the French Revolution to explore how a homosocial community of women, the Carmelite nuns of Compiègne, respond to their scapegoating and martyrdom at the hands of the all-male revolutionary authorities. The increasing visibility of gay and lesbian artists and audiences has contributed not only to the revival of queer Baroque operas, but also to production of mainstream operas that explore the homoerotic possibilities of ostensibly heterosexual plots.      *Corinne E. Blackmer*

### Bibliography

Blackmer, Corinne E., and Patricia Juliana Smith, eds. *En Travesti: Women, Gender Subversion, Opera*. New York: Columbia University Press, 1995.

Brett, Philip, Elizabeth Wood, and Gary C. Thomas, eds. *Queering the Pitch: The New Gay and Lesbian Musicology*. New York: Routledge, 1994.

Clément, Catherine. *Opera: or, the Undoing of Women*. Minneapolis: University of Minnesota Press, 1988.

Koestenbaum, Wayne. *The Queen's Throat: Opera, Homosexuality, and the Mystery of Desire*. New York: Poseidon, 1993.

Leonardi, Susan J., and Rebecca A. Pope. *The Diva's Mouth: Body, Voice, Prima Donna Politics*. New Brunswick, N.J.: Rutgers University Press, 1996.

McClary, Susan. *Feminine Endings: Music, Gender, and Sexuality*. Minneapolis: University of Minnesota Press, 1991.

*See also* Anthony, Susan B.; Cather, Willa; Hildegard of Bingen, Saint; Music, Classical; Stein, Gertrude

## Oppression

According to Webster's (1997) dictionary, oppression is the "unjust exercise of power." The oppression of lesbians occurs through two wedded systems of domination: sexism, beliefs and practices that enforce male dominance and female subordination; and heterosexism, beliefs and practices that enforce heterosexuality as the only normal and natural form of sexual expression. The oppression of lesbians occurs at the interpersonal, organizational, and institutional (cultural) levels of social life.

Because lesbians vary according to nationality, race, ethnicity, gender identity, class, ability, age, and religion, they experience oppression as lesbians in multiple and varied ways. However, as women and homosexuals, lesbians commonly share being perceived, and treated, as inferior to men and as sexually deviant. Regardless of the many axes along which lesbians may experience oppression and privilege (for example, race and class), both sexism and heterosexism, as systems of oppression, shape lesbian experience.

At the interpersonal level, lesbians face prejudice, harassment, and violence in everyday life. Although public attitudes toward lesbians and lesbianism have become more tolerant, in the 1990s hate crimes against lesbians in the United States reached an all-time high (National Gay and Lesbian Task Force Anti-Violence Project 1997).

At the organizational level, lesbians face legal oppression, typically in the form of discrimination. Because U.S. federal legislation does not forbid discrimination on the basis of sexual orientation, lesbians face legal discrimination in employment, housing, and public accommodations. Further, sexual relations between adult, consenting women are criminalized in twenty of the United States; these so-called "sodomy" laws are invoked to take children away from their lesbian mothers and to justify other forms of organizational discrimination. The lack of legal protection of lesbians and legal acknowledgment of their relationships denies lesbian families many social and economic privileges granted to married couples, including the right to visit one another in the hospital in an emergency and to take a leave of absence to care for a sick partner under the Family Medical Leave Act of 1993.

Institutional, or cultural, oppression of lesbians includes the annihilation, exclusion, and marginalization of lesbian experience and representations in social consciousness and in social institutions, such as family, education, art, religion, literature, media, and language.

Lesbians are not merely victims of oppression; they also resist sexist and heterosexist systems of domination. Lesbian resistance in the United States is evident in lesbians' existence as a political force as individuals, in lesbian communities, and in larger social movements. At the individual level, lesbians are working toward social change by coming out as lesbians and forming lesbian relationships and families. Lesbians also form communities to affirm their identities as lesbians and to provide social and material support for themselves. These communities often provide a social context for political mobilization against oppressive beliefs and practices. Lesbians have also been instrumental in larger social movements, such as women's and gay liberation movements. Lesbian resistance and activism has contributed to the repeal of sodomy laws in more than half of the states, the declassification of homosexuality as a mental disorder, the institution of sexual-harassment legislation, and the establishment of domestic-partner policies and legislation. Lesbian resistance has often targeted both male and heterosexual privilege.

*Christine Robinson*

### Bibliography

Esterberg, Kristin G. *Lesbian and Bisexual Identities: Constructing Communities, Constructing*

*Selves*. Philadelphia: Temple University Press, 1997.

National Gay and Lesbian Task Force Anti-Violence Project. *Annual Report*. Washington, D.C.: NGLTF, 1997.

*See also* Heterosexism; Law and Legal Institutions; Sexism

## Oral History

Using memory as a source for history. Because of the paucity of written records on lesbians before 1970, oral history has become central in creating knowledge about twentieth-century lesbians. It expands the factual base of lesbian history and provides insight into lesbian consciousness and subjectivity.

The triumvirate of lesbian oppression—that it was sinful, sick, and criminal—made it extremely unlikely that, before the feminist and lesbian liberation movements, women would leave written records of their erotic attachments to other women. The primary public records available for the historical study of lesbianism were those of the criminal justice system, which recorded prosecution for transgressing sexual norms, or of the medical profession, which treated lesbians as cases of perversion. Although necessary for writing a history of lesbianism, these documents are not sufficient, because of their bias and because they cannot adequately convey the breadth of women's experience or their consciousness of it.

Without oral histories, the only insights into women's consciousness about their erotic attachments with women were provided by a few far-sighted women who donated their letters and diaries to archives, usually with the stipulation that they not be open to the public until after their death. No matter how valuable these few records, they also do not serve as a sufficient basis for constructing lesbian history. They represent a very elite group of women, those with the leisure and training to write.

In the mid-1970s, the lesbian and gay liberation movements were motivated to understand their histories in order to gain insight into the present and the future. Grass-roots gay and lesbian history projects sprang up throughout the United States and, subsequently, around the world; among them were the San Francisco Gay and Lesbian History Project and the Lesbian Herstory Archives. Armed with tape recorders, questions about the past, and the de-

sire to listen, project members went out to record memories before they were lost. Oral history provided the opportunity to include all voices and visions of the lesbian past: those bourgeois women who were not women of letters and did not leave diaries and letters and, most important the many working-class women of all racial and ethnic groups, whose lives would be completely invisible if they were not recorded through oral history.

Oral histories have played a crucial role in all of the major publications on lesbian and gay history of the 1970s, 1980s, and 1990s. In 1976, in the first collection of documents on gay and lesbian history, Katz (1976) included his oral history interviews with the founders of the Mattachine Society and Daughters of Bilitis. D'Emilio (1983) and Duberman (1993) both use extensive oral histories, along with archival sources, to write a complex history of the development of the homophile movement and the gay and lesbian liberation movements, respectively. Oral histories have not only documented political activism, but also illuminated daily life. Numerous collections of individual life stories, such as the one edited by the Hall Carpenter Archives Lesbian Oral History Group (1989), demonstrate the various ways of being lesbians. In addition, scholars such as Newton (1993) and Kennedy (1995) and Davis (Kennedy and Davis 1996) have constructed histories of wealthy and working-class communities based on oral histories. Filmmakers intrigued by the growing body of oral histories have woven them throughout their historical films, as in *Before Stonewall* (1986) and *Forbidden Love* (1992).

The reliance on oral history for analyzing lesbian history raises questions about the veracity of such sources. Most theoreticians of oral history have come to see the practice as revealing two different, but complementary, kinds of "truth." First, oral history adds new social facts to the historical record. The urgency with which lesbians and gays went in search of their history encouraged a focus on names, dates, places, and events, and the majority of research has been of this nature. Second, being based in memory, oral history explores subjectivity—an individual's interpretation of the past. Not being born and raised in a public lesbian and gay culture, each gay and lesbian person has constructed his or her own life in oppressive contexts, a process that oral history is uniquely suited to reveal. Lesbian oral historians have learned to interpret the style of storytelling, the myths that are embedded in stories, the multiple meanings of memories, and the interaction between narrator and interviewer. In this process, they have come to understand the subjectivity and orality of their sources as a strength that keeps the experiences of individuals alive.

*Elizabeth Lapovsky Kennedy*

## Bibliography

D'Emilio, John. *Sexual Politics, Sexual Communities: The Making of a Homosexual Minority in the United States, 1940–1970*. Chicago: Chicago University Press, 1983.

Duberman, Martin. *Stonewall*. New York: Dutton, 1993.

Hall Carpenter Archives, Lesbian Oral History Group. *Inventing Ourselves: Lesbian Life Stories*. New York: Routledge, 1989.

Katz, Johnathan, ed. *Gay American History: Lesbians and Gay Men in the U.S.A.* New York: Crowell, 1976, pp. 249–250.

Kennedy, Elizabeth Lapovsky. "Telling Tales: Oral History and the Construction of Pre-Stonewall Lesbian History." *Radical History Review* 62 (1995), 58–79.

Kennedy, Elizabeth Lapovsky, and Madeline D. Davis. *Boots of Leather, Slippers of Gold: The History of a Lesbian Community*. New York: Routledge, 1996.

Newton, Esther. *Cherry Grove, Fire Island: Sixty Years in America's First Gay and Lesbian Town*. Boston: Beacon, 1993.

**See also** Diaries and Letters; History; Lesbian Herstory Archives

# P

## Pacific Islands

Grouping of linguistically and culturally diverse peoples of Melanesia, Micronesia, and Polynesia, three culture areas identified by anthropologists. None of these categories is indigenous, and each hides differences between what are today dozens of different nation-states and European and American colonies. The categories also collapse the quite different historical paths created by the peoples descending from the Austronesian speakers who began settling the Pacific islands six thousand years ago. This contemporary diversity, combined with the scarcity of published accounts of Pacific Islander forms of lesbianism, makes what follows an overview highlighting the variability of Pacific forms of lesbianism and the need for more research.

### Identity Categories

Unlike the situation in the United States and Europe, "lesbian" is not meaningful as an identity category in most Pacific societies. (The exception is the organized lesbian communities in urban areas of Aotearoa/New Zealand and the Hawai'in Islands, both sites of particularly destructive colonial interventions.) The phrase "forms of lesbianism" used in this entry foregrounds the complexity of forms through which female-female sexual relationships are socially structured and understood. The different forms of lesbianism found across the Pacific are meaningful in relation to specific cultural ideas and practices; in particular, personhood, epistemology, and cosmology, as well as kinship, gender, and exchange.

### Polynesia

In precolonial Polynesia, sexuality was "an integral force of life—indeed the cause of the life of the universe" (Hall and Kauanui 1994). This cosmological perspective was reflected in both the presence of, and the lack of interdiction against, same-sex intimacies: Sexual relationships among females have been documented in most Polynesian societies. In *Coming of Age in Samoa* (1928), for example, anthropologist Margaret Mead stated that, for Samoans, homosexual practices among adolescents were "simply *play*, neither frowned upon nor given much consideration" (emphasis in original). Seventeen of the twenty-five adolescent girls with whom Mead worked closely reported to her that they had had homosexual experiences, and several of these girls' sexual involvements with each other resulted in "really important friendships," as Mead put it.

Since colonization, missionaries and colonial powers throughout Polynesia have stigmatized forms of homosexuality in ways unprecedented among indigenous people. Yet the bases of Polynesian personhood and epistemology—particularly Polynesians' emphasis on action over ideology—give individuals significant latitude in shaping others' views of them. This may be crucial in accounting for variability found in the status of "lesbians" in the late twentieth century: The importance of individual personalities, kinship networks, family histories, and individual actions toward others may be fundamental in accounting for why some "lesbians" are relatively isolated, while others are respected members of their communities.

In some Polynesian societies, forms of lesbianism have a complex relationship to gender. In the early 1960s, for example, Levy (1973) found that "[w]omen dressing and living somewhat as men and playing western-type lesbian roles have been known in the island of Tahiti for some generations at least."

P While the Polynesians with whom Levy worked used the term *vahine pa'i'a* to refer to "female homosexuals," the prevalence of "butch-femme" relationships among females in this part of Polynesia may be historically related to the concept of the *mâhû*. The term *mâhû*, which is indigenous to the Hawai'in and Society Islands (French Polynesia), means "half-man, half-woman" and highlights the interrelationships between gender and forms of lesbianism. *Mâhû* are males or females who deploy complex combinations of masculinity and femininity (cultural signs of gender difference) and who, in many cases, are sexually active primarily with individuals of the same sex. Importantly, the lovers of *mâhû* are never other *mâhû*, but are socially categorized as either (*tane*) men or women (*vahine*). More recently, in urban Papeete in 1995, "butch" females who dressed and behaved "in the manner of men" were most consistently described, by other Polynesians, as *lesbiennes*, the French term for "lesbian." Their "femme" lovers, however, who dressed and behaved "in the manner of women," were rarely referred to as *lesbiennes*, despite their sexual intimacies with "butch" females: They were simply "women."

## Melanesia

In contrast to the scholarship on forms of lesbianism in Polynesia, for Micronesia and Melanesia the ethnographic information is extremely thin and difficult to interpret. It is probably not a form of lesbianism, for example, that is found in the ceremony performed by Solomon Islanders for a girl's first menstruation. During the ceremony, "the [adult] women all play at copulating with one another," play that includes taking "bits of ceremonial pudding and pieces of pig and rub[bing] them on to their genitals, and then on one another's mouths" (Blackwood 1935). On the other hand, in his description of the Malekula people of Vanuatu (formerly, New Hebrides), Deacon (1934) wrote that, between women, "homosexuality is common, many women being generally known as Lesbians, or in the native term *nimomogh iap nimomogh* ('woman has intercourse with woman'). It is regarded as a form of play, but, at the same time, it is clearly recognized as a definite type of sexual desire, and that the women do it because it gives them pleasure."

Anecdotal evidence of sexual relationships between females in various parts of Papua New Guinea, as well as occasional ethnographic references to forms of lesbianism elsewhere in Melane-

sia, suggests that these forms are often meaningful in reference to the same social practices as forms of heterosexuality: namely, kinship and exchange. An anthropologist who worked in Island Melanesia, for example, encountered two "lesbian couples" on two different islands (Macintyre, personal communication). In both cases, the couples divided their work like a husband and wife, adopted children, participated in village feasts, and had high statuses in their villages, in part because they were successful gardeners. While these female couples practiced a gendered division of labor that paralleled that of husbands and wives, their styles of dress and manner were "feminine" by their societies' standards. In other words, complexly gendered statuses were not part of these forms of lesbianism. However, the women were categorized into life stages at odds with their ages: Despite the fact that one couple was in their forties and the other in their fifties, the women of both couples dressed like young, unmarried girls, not adult women. This is a potentially important statement that the social criteria for adulthood were not met by their relationships, despite their apparent social and economic successes.

## Micronesia

Anthropologists have referred to Micronesia as the place where homosexuality does not exist, a statement true primarily in the sense that there are no homosexual identities. One anthropologist who worked on Chuuk suggested as an alternative that different definitions of "sex" may underlie this characterization: "Sex" is locally defined as heterosexual, making the group masturbation that takes place among males, and probably among females as well, something other than "sex" (Moral, pers. comm.). Definitions of "sex" occasionally combine with an anthropologist's own prejudices to make it difficult to interpret local understandings of sexual practices between females. In his ethnography of Ulithi, for example, Lessa (1966) wrote: "Boys sometimes indulge in mutual masturbation, as do girls, and for this they are scolded and occasionally even beaten by their parents. Women of mature age, usually because of involuntary continence, are said sometimes to resort to mutual masturbation, but only as a substitute for the normal sexual congress being denied them."

As in many other societies, gender can be one of the main vehicles through which a people understand sexual desire and intimacy—and the site of cultural work when an individual's desire is same-sex. During her fieldwork on the Micronesian island of Pohnpei, for example, anthropologist Ward (1989) describes how

> [a] young girl named Maria began exhibiting the habits of a boy as she grew into her teens. She began to go walking about at night looking for girls.... Family and neighbors held a meeting to discuss the problem. Then they held a feast where they publicly declared her a boy. Her hair was cut and she was presented with male clothing. Henceforth they announced Maria would be Mario. I heard that Mario became a responsible citizen with a wife and children.

In addition, on Chuuk, Micronesians have indigenous terms that complicate the gender dualism man/woman in ways similar to the category *mâhû*: *Wininmwáán*, for example, references "women who behave like men," although, also as with *mâhû*, this does not necessarily mean that *wininmwáán* are sexually active with other females (Moral, personal communication).

[The author wishes to extend special thanks to Evelyn Blackwood, J. Kehaulani Kauanui, Elizabeth Keating, Martha Macintyre, Mac Marshall, and Beatriz Moral for their insights and contributions to this entry.]                    *Deborah A. Elliston*

### Bibliography

Blackwood, Beatrice. *Both Sides of the Buka Passage*. Oxford: Clarendon, 1935.

Deacon, A. Bernard. *Malekula: A Vanishing People in the New Hebrides*. Ed. Camilla Wedgewood. London: Routledge, 1934.

Hall, Lisa Kahaleole Chang, and J. Kehaulani Kauanui. "Same-Sex Sexuality in Pacific Literature." *Amerasia Journal* 20:1 (1994), 75–81.

Lessa, William A. *Ulithi: A Micronesian Design for Living*. New York: Holt, Rinehart, and Winston, 1966.

Levy, Robert I. *Tahitians: Mind and Experience in the Society Islands*. Chicago: University of Chicago Press, 1973.

Ward, Martha. *Nest in the Wind Adventures in Anthropology on a Tropical Island*. Prospect Heights, Ill.: Waveland, 1989.

*See also* Anthropology; Hawai'i; Indigenous Cultures; *Mâhû*; Pacific Literature

## Pacific Literature

Lesbian writing from the Pacific Island region, from Aotearoa in the south to Hawai'i in the north. Pacific lesbian authors reflect indigenous issues in their writing, from colonization of their islands by outsiders to the struggle for island sovereignty by reclaiming the land and the spirit of the people.

Pacific Island lesbian writing tends to be inclusive rather than exclusive. Bisexuals, transsexuals, and lesbians are a natural part of island cultures, despite the work of Christian missionaries in the region to reverse this. Colonial Pacific literature reflected Pacific Islanders as objects to be studied and analyzed or as "exotic." In this canon, both Pacific Island and lesbian oral storytelling and writing were not reflected in anthologies or single-author publications. Oral storytelling, songs, and chants are still by far the greatest conveyors of knowledge throughout the Pacific Islands, and it is only since 1980 that lesbian voices have begun to emerge strongly in print.

The first Australian-Aotearoan/New Zealand lesbian anthology, *The Exploding Frangipani* (1990), edited by Susan Hawthorne and Cathie Dunsford, included indigenous Maori, Pacific Island, and Aboriginal writers. Pacific lesbian authors have featured in other lesbian feminist anthologies since, such as the New Women's Fiction series, *Subversive Acts* (1991) and *Me and Marilyn Monroe* (1993), both edited by Dunsford.

Pacific lesbian writing was generally excluded from major anthologies documenting gay and/or lesbian writing until anthologies like *The Very Inside: Asian-Pacific Lesbian Writing* (1994), edited by Sharon Lim-Hing. Northern Hemisphere readers, editors, and publishers have become more aware of the distinctive and varied lesbian literature from the Pacific region, as indicated by the inclusion of a regular Pacific lesbian column in the U.S. journal the *Lesbian Review of Books* since its inception in 1994.

Pacific lesbian writing reflects strong movements for political independence and decolonization throughout the Pacific region, as well as personal issues of sexuality, oppression, and empowerment. In some of the lesbian literature, music is vital for the bridging work between cultures; in others, *ki'i pohaku* (ancient rock drawings) may be integral to the text. The issues of Pacific lesbian writing have much in common with those of Native American lesbian writers. *Pakeha/haole/palangi* (European) lesbian authors from the Pacific have wide-ranging concerns that sometimes also include indigenous issues.

Keri Hulme, Ngai Tahu (Maori) author of the Booker Prize–winning novel *The Bone People* (1983), describes herself as "neuter," or gender neutral. This terminology suggests that, as yet, there are not categories invented to fit identities that may not easily fall into European-defined criteria. Similarly, Pacific Island lesbian authors do not always fit easy cultural stereotypes. There are many mixed-blood Pacific authors. Often their multiple identities require coming out of the closet several times over.

Postcolonial lesbian writing does not assume that colonization is over. Rather, it seeks to deal with the issues provoked by colonization and to redefine the past, present, and future based on decolonization and reclamation of land, spirit, and self. For Pacific lesbians, this means redefining the self in their own languages, songs, and rituals, as well as through new literatures in English. The influence of oral storytelling emerges in many of the styles chosen for writing and often incorporates other oral traditions, such as dance, art, music, mythology, dreams, and indigenous philosophy and psychology, that differ from European models significantly. In fighting oppression, rituals, chanting, and often great humor are used in the struggle and in the writing. There is empowerment through sharing a common vision that flames through the writing, as it often does when lesbians share common goals in their various struggles for identity, but each island nation has its own different identities and languages.

The lack of Pacific Island lesbian publishing houses has constricted the availability of more Pacific lesbian writing. However, lesbian feminist presses such as Spinifex in Australia, New Women's Press in Aotearoa/New Zealand, and, Sister Vision in Canada are leading the way in getting Pacific lesbian voices into the mainstream of global literature, as is the *Lesbian Review of Books* in reviewing the literature. In 1995, the University of Osnabruck Press published the first bilingual German-English-Maori anthology of Pacific women's writing, *Nga Uri a Papatuanuku: Descendants of the Earth Mother*, edited by Sigrid Markmann and Powhiri Rika-Heke, including contemporary Maori lesbian writers Renée, Marewa Glover, Cathie Dunsford, and Powhiri Rika-Heke.   *Cathie Dunsford*

### Bibliography

Hall, Lisa Kahaleole Chang, and J. Kehaulani Kavanui. "Same-Sex Sexuality in Pacific Literature." *Amerasia Journal* 20:1 (1994), 75–81.

Sayer, Susan. "Alive and Well: Lesbian Writing in Aotearoa/New Zealand." *Hecate's Australian Women's Book Review* 10 (1998), 24–26.

*See also* Australia; New Zealand; Pacific Islands

## Paris

Largest city and capital of France; best known for its famous lesbian salons (private artistic circles) of the 1920s. Paris has played a particular role in the construction of modern lesbian identity.

The earliest definitions of female same-sex relations in France have legal, theological, and cultural roots. In sixteenth-century Paris, church and state law condemned to death women ("tribades") engaged in mutual "lust." The law was evidently enforced, however, only insofar as a woman also cross-dressed, thereby mixing visual codes of identification and challenging patriarchal laws of sexual division.

Revolutionary politics and science in eighteenth-century France redefined the tribade. Medical language considered her an anatomical anomaly: the woman who does more than masquerade *as* a man (in men's clothing), but also acts *in place of* a man (with a malelike physical member). On the other hand, Parisian male libertines, who wrote quasi-pornographic tales featuring tribades, saw female same-sex love as either a delicious affront to middle-class moral values or, more positively, as a utopian sexual possibility.

The French Revolution in 1789 did not, however, radically reimagine sex roles. Instead, several notable women (including Marie Antoinette [1755–1793]) who had expressed a passion for women were among the casualties of the Old Regime's fall. The libertine's critique of old mores, in which the tribade might be invoked as revolutionary alternative, yielded to a critique of aristocratic decadence, in which the tribade would now function as emblem and proof.

In 1800, Napoleonic law renewed the legal sanction against female cross-dressing, now possible only with special authorization from the police, local government officials, and health officers. Although aristocratic novelist George Sand (1804–1876) cross-dressed in Paris without obtaining this official permission, self-supporting painter Rosa Bonheur (1822–1899) made multiple requests for certificates (valid for six months). Bonheur cited "professional necessity," without drawing attention to her lifelong relationship with another woman, Nathalie Micas (1824–1889).

Also in the nineteenth century, French literature discovered an almost obsessive interest in the lesbian, who was depicted in popular (and sometimes prurient) poetry and fiction published from 1835 onward by male writers such as Charles Baudelaire (1821–1867), Emile Zola (1840–1902), Honoré de Balzac (1799–1850), and Théophile Gautier (1811–1872).

By 1900, the vogue in Paris for Sappho (ca. 600 B.C.E.), the visibility of paintings and novels featuring lesbians, and the emerging modern medical writings about sexual "inversion" all created an ambience that has been called "Paris-Lesbos." Lesbian relationships were suddenly fashionable among some society women, prompting one lady of fashion to declare that all of the chic women were taking women as lovers.

Urban Paris in 1900 was a highly sexualized space. In a positive sense, the city tolerated not simply private salons where aristocratic lesbians from all over Europe gathered, but also working-class bars, such as the Palmyre in Montmartre. Lesbian theatricality experienced popularity and scandal: the cross-dressed roles of actress Sarah Bernhardt (1844–1923) or the famous veiled Egyptian mummy dance performed by writer Colette (1873–1954) with the aid of her female lover, the Marquise de Belbeuf (also Belboeuf [1863–1944]).

More negatively, the "doomed" lesbian image circulated in both high and low culture, from the canvases of Gustave Courbet (1819–1877) to the brothels of Paris, where "lesbian" and "whore" became fused images contributing to Paris's reputation as the capital of sexual sophistication. Male writers, such as poet Pierre Louÿs (1870–1925), and painters, such as Henri de Toulouse-Lautrec (1864–1901), created images of lesbian prostitutes, drawing on firsthand observation in working-class cafés. Criminal anthropologists decried the "double vice" of lesbian prostitutes, and female cross-dressing was, as novelist Colette recalls, patrolled in 1907 by a zealous prefect of police.

In this mixed climate of fascination and intolerance, two major expatriate literary figures— Natalie Barney (1876–1972) and Renée Vivien (1877–1909)—superimposed a modern lesbian aesthetic on the classic model of Sappho. Both renounced their homelands (the United States and England, respectively) for Paris, calling it the only place in which to live. Vivien crafted a lesbian erotic in delicate French verse, but history "punished" her for this by relegating her, until the 1970s, to artistic oblivion and by cloaking her short life in mystery and vague scandal.

Barney, her lover, more successfully sustained a viable lesbian image. Her famed salon from 1905 to World War II gathered dozens of talented artists, mostly women, at regular meetings. In 1927, she founded the Academy of Women (a feminist alternative to the exclusive male French Academy), which subsidized the publication of women's works, provided a private forum for reading women's writing, and offered a literary prize. By championing lesbian artists and celebrating her love and lust for women, Barney was instrumental in modeling modern lesbian identity, even if her influence extended only to a small artistic elite.

The Parisian literary salon of Gertrude Stein (1874–1946) was likewise a fixture of expatriate Paris in the 1920s. Presided over by Stein and her lover, Alice B. Toklas (1877–1967), the salon was less obviously "lesbian" than Barney's in its tone and guest list but went far in placing Stein's writing and lifestyle at the heart of modern literary history.

Between the wars, Paris hosted an impressive expatriate community of Anglo American lesbian writers, journalists, photographers, and publishers, including Djuna Barnes (1892–1982), Janet Flanner (1892–1978), Solita Solano (1888–1975), Sylvia Beach (1887–1962), and Romaine Brooks (1874–1970). Although these women enjoyed personal privacy in Paris, they infrequently risked sexual self-disclosure in their art, which continued to mask lesbian desire or present it in acceptably heterosexual form. This may, however, say less about Parisians, who were accustomed to the lesbian in literature, and more about the struggle to reveal an authentic lesbian image to an *American* audience.

Lesbian identity continued to create itself elsewhere in Paris, which had no "gay ghetto" per se in the 1920s but which nonetheless supported a definable homosexual community. Lesbian bars (the Sphinx, the Monocle, the Fetish) attracted serious cross-dressers, and nightclubs drew women from all classes.

By the 1930s, Paris's flamboyant expatriate and indigenous lesbian cultures became subdued. Paris-Lesbos 1900 recorded in Colette's *The Pure and the Impure* (1932) now seemed remote and mythic, as French society returned to conservative heterosexual models of identity, muting gay subculture and stigmatizing collective lesbian identity. This pushed the "bar scene" underground and made women re-

**P** luctant to identify with the term "lesbian," a fear that would persist until the 1970s.     *Elyse Blankley*

### Bibliography

Benstock, Shari. *Women of the Left Bank: Paris, 1900–1940*. Austin: University of Texas Press, 1986.

Blankley, Elyse. " 'Return to Mytilene': Renée Vivien and the City of Women." In *Women Writers and the City*. Ed. Susan Merrill Squier. Knoxville: University of Tennessee Press, 1984, pp. 45–67.

Bonnet, Marie-Jo. *Les Relations amoureuses entre les femmes du seizième au vingtième siècle* (Love Between Women from the Sixteenth to the Twentieth Centuries). Paris: Odile Jacob, 1995.

Harris, Bertha. "The More Profound Nationality of Their Lesbianism: Lesbian Society in Paris in the 1920's." In *Amazon Expedition: A Lesbian Feminist Anthology*. Ed. Phyllis Birkby, Bertha Harris, Jill Johnston, Esther Newton, and Jane O'Wyatt. New York: Times Change, 1973, pp. 77–88.

Jay, Karla. *The Amazon and the Page: Natalie Barney and Renée Vivien*. Bloomington: Indiana University Press, 1988.

Lesselier, Claudie. "Silenced Resistances and Conflictual Identities: Lesbians in France, 1930–1968." *Journal of Homosexuality* 25 (1993), 105–125.

*See also* Barney, Natalie; Cross-Dressing; France; Stein, Gertrude; Tribade; Vivien, Renée

## Parker-Hulme Murder Case

On June 22, 1954, in Christchurch, Aotearoa/New Zealand, Juliet Hulme and Pauline Parker killed Honora Parker, Pauline's mother. They were age fifteen and sixteen and killed Honora with a brick in a stocking after luring her to Victoria Park. The girls were arrested for the crime following the discovery of Pauline Parker's diary, which detailed plans for the "moider" and which described a sexual relationship between them. They were interviewed by the police without legal counsel and confessed to the murder. The motive was claimed to be their impending separation because Hulme was being sent to stay with an aunt in South Africa. Parker's unmarried parents refused to allow her to leave New Zealand with her friend. After the murder, various family circumstances were exposed and became part of the scandal, especially the lives of the upper-class Hulme family.

After a sensational trial, the two girls were convicted of murder and served five years "at Her Majesty's Pleasure" in top-security prisons, being carefully kept apart during this period. They were released seperately in 1959 and were given new identities by the Justice Department, Juliet Hulme becoming Anne Perry and later establishing herself as a writer of murder mysteries; Pauline Parker becoming Hilary Nathan and qualifying as a librarian. Both women left Aotearoa/New Zealand and live in Scotland and England, respectively; they have never been in contact again, nor has either re-offended.

The case attracted international attention at the time and subsequently, with the two girls depicted as either "mad" or "bad" at the trial and by the media. Extracts from Parker's diaries were reprinted through the years, adding to a story that gained mythic proportions in Aotearoa/New Zealand and that profoundly influenced attitudes toward lesbianism for many decades in the country by constructing connections between female homosexuality, insanity, and murder. The defense psychiatrist, Dr. Reginald Medlicott, had argued that the two girls were insane and had committed the murder because they suffered from *folie à deux*, or communicated insanity, of which homosexuality was a symptom. The prosecution argued that they were perfectly sane but were "dirty minded" and "bad" girls. Both views became part of public perceptions of lesbians, some of which were internalized by lesbians themselves. In 1991, lesbian writers Julie Glamuzina and Alison J. Laurie published *Parker and Hulme: A Lesbian View*, which discusses the social and political context of the murder and its aftermath and includes interviews with a number of New Zealand lesbians about the effect the case had on their lives. This book was republished in the United States in 1995 following the distribution of the movie *Heavenly Creatures* by Peter Jackson and Fran Walsh. This fictionalized filmed version of the murder shows Parker and Hulme as frenetic teenagers and can be interpreted as based on Medlicott's ideas of *folie à deux*. There also have been fictional and nonfictional accounts of the case that depict the girls either as insane or as cold-blooded killers out to remove "an obstacle" in their path. All of these consider the relationship between the girls as the motive for the murder.

Soon after the release of *Heavenly Creatures*, Anne Perry was exposed as Juliet by the media. Perry denied that the relationship was sexual and said that she can remember little of the events before or during the murder. Hilary Nathan was exposed in 1996 as Pauline and as of 1998, had refused to be interviewed by the media.

*Alison J. Laurie*

## Bibliography

Glamuzina, Julie, and Alison J. Laurie. *Parker and Hulme: A Lesbian View*. Ithaca, N.Y.: Firebrand, 1995.

Laurie, Alison J. "Lesbians Through the Decades: Women Who Love Women." In *Standing in the Sunshine: A History of New Zealand Women Since They Won the Vote*. Ed. Sandra Coney. Auckland: Viking, 1993.

**See also** Crime and Criminology; New Zealand

## Parker, Pat (1944–1989)

African American poet. Born in Houston, Texas, the youngest of four daughters, Pat Parker grew up in a family that believed the road to freedom was paved with the bricks of education. Parker began writing poetry during her marriage to Ed Bullins (1935–), a playwright, in order to carve out a literary niche that would not be associated with his work.

Parker worked on including all aspects of her "self" in her work. A poet of vision, she moved beyond the racial separatist rhetoric of Oakland, California, of the 1970s. Bringing together feminism, antiracism, and lesbianism into narrrative poetic form, she sought to reveal the weakness of separatist politics by using African American oratory traditions, predominantly found in black churches and Sunday schools. This is abundantly apparent in her first three works, *Child of Myself* (1972), *Pit Stop* (1974), and *Womanslaughter* (1978).

Criticized for her didacticism in these early works, Parker decided to bring her vision "on the road" in 1975. Her readings in cities across the United States brought the universality of her themes to a broader audience and earned her the respect and admiration that was lacking in the critical response of nonfeminist and nonlesbian publications. The response of Parker's audience also led to a recorded collaboration with the lesbian poet Judy Grahn (1940–) in 1976.

Although Parker's three earliest works went out of print, many of the poems are included in *Movement in Black* (1978). The collection is divided into four sections. The first section is entitled "Married."

*Pat Parker. Photo by Tee A. Corinne.*

The first poem, "Goat Child," is autobiographical and examines the poet's trials and tribulations as a young woman whose potential goes unrecognized by her family, the school system, and her husband. Parker's exposé of the family, marriage, and education is directly related to her vision of a society that is not divided in to classes and subclasses. This vision is elaborated in the section entitled "Liberation Fronts," in which Parker turns her discerning eye on the flaws within the political movements she traverses. The final poem in this section, "Movement in Black," is considered by many to be her signature piece. This work not only contains a chronicle of some of the black heroines of American history, but also uses the call-and-response verse that is a part of American poetics, past and present.

Parker's final work, *Jonestown and Other Madness* (1985), continues her quest for an identity that deconstructs categories and definitions. She points to the error of insisting on an identity that disallows affiliation within a global society. These poems are longer, narrative works that give agency to the ideals of unity, peace, and love.

Parker's activities in the women's health project in Oakland was born out of her activism in the Black

**P**

Panther Party of the 1960s and the Black Women's Revolutionary Council in the 1970s. She worked as a medical coordinator from 1978 to 1987 to expand the services of a single site to six clinics. Parker's work as an activist and her growth as a poet were halted by her death from cancer in 1989. She is survived by her partner, her two daughters, and her visionary work, which reminds readers of their potential as a global family.

*Stephanie Byrd*

### Bibliography

Annas, Pamela. "A Poetry of Survival: Unnaming and Renaming in the Poetry of Audre Lorde, Pat Parker, Sylvia Plath, and Adrienne Rich." *Colby Library Quarterly* 18 (March 1982), 9–25.

Beemyn, Brett. "Bibliography of Works by and about Pat Parker (1944–1989)." *Sage* 6:1 (Summer 1989), 81–82.

Folayan, Ayofemi S., and Stephanie Byrd. "Pat Parker." In *Contemporary Lesbian Writers of the United States: A Bibliographical Critical Sourcebook.* Ed. Sandra Pollack and Denise D. Knight. Westport, Conn.: Greenwood, 1993, pp. 415–419.

*See also* African American Literature; Grahn, Judy

### Parnok, Sophia (1885–1933)

Russian poet. Sophia Yakovlevna Parnok, Russia's first (and still only) openly lesbian poet, was born into a professional Jewish family in Taganrog, Russia, in 1885. The death of her mother, a physician, in 1891 left Parnok with profound feelings of orphanhood and homelessness, which were exacerbated by her father's remarriage and by difficult relations with her stepmother.

Parnok's creativity was closely linked with her lesbianism, which revealed itself in early adolescence and brought her into conflict with her father. Parnok finished the gymnasium (secondary school) in 1903, and, in 1905, left Taganrog with an actress lover and spent a year in Europe. Lack of funds forced her to return to Russia suddenly in 1906. Life in her father's house soon became intolerable, however, and in 1907 Parnok married her close friend and literary adviser, Vladimir Volkenshtein (1883–1974). Marriage had a deleterious effect on Parnok's writing, and, despite her husband's acceptance of her lesbianism, it restricted her personal life. In 1909, she left her husband and, after months of acrimonious haggling, got him to agree to a divorce.

For the next seven years, Parnok lived in Moscow, became self-supporting as a journalist, an opera librettist, and a poet, and led an, at times, frenetic personal life. Her two most important relationships of these years were with a Moscow socialite, Iraida Albrecht (n.d.), and with the then-beginning poet Marina Tsvetaeva (1892–1941). Parnok began publishing separate poems in journals in 1906, and in 1916 her first collection, *Stikhotvoreniia* (Poems), appeared in the aftermath of her breakup with Tsvetaeva. Her creative development was slowed by her chronic poor health (Graves' disease), her lack of ambition, literary connections, and money, and her long struggle against the artistic and moral norms of Russian literary culture that discouraged and hampered the straightforward expression of lesbian desire in serious poetry.

The 1917 Revolution and ensuing civil war (1918–1921) brought Parnok's burgeoning literary career to a halt. She and her partner (since 1916), Lyudmila Erarskaya (ca. 1890–1964), a Moscow actress, spent the civil war years in the eastern Crimean town of Sudak, where Parnok's mature creativity and her new faith (Russian Orthodoxy) blossomed.

In early 1922, Parnok and Erarskaya returned to Moscow, where the poet would live until her death eleven years later. Under Soviet power, Parnok found it increasingly difficult to publish her poetry, which was censored for its religious (and possibly lesbian) content and pessimistic tone. During the 1920s, she published only three collections: *Loza* (The Vine [1923]), *Muzyka* (Music [1926]), and *Vpolgolosa* (Halfvoiced [1928]). After 1928, Parnok was effectively silenced by the Soviet censorship, and her last and best lyrics, about one-third of her total output, were published only in 1979 in a Western edition. In Russia, Parnok's *Sobranie Stikhotvorenii* (Collected Poems) was finally published in 1997, by INAPRESS, in St. Petersburg.

During the last five years of her life, Parnok endured poverty, constant illness, isolation from readers, and, most painfully, the indifference to her work of her poet colleagues, who, she believed, shunned her for "daring to say out loud what people hide, even from themselves." She drew strength and spiritual sustenance, however, from her devoted women friends and lovers, especially Erarskaya; the memoirist Eugenia Gertsyk (1878–1944); the mathematician Olga Tsuberbiller (1885–1975), with whom the poet lived from 1926 until her death; and the physicist Nina Vedeneyeva (1882–1955), Parnok's last love and the inspiration for her greatest work, the lyric cycles "Bol'shaia Medveditsa" (Ursa Major) and "Nenuzhnoe dobro" (Useless Goods) (1932–1933). The Vedeneyeva cycles recount the unique and tragic story of two middle-aged lesbian lovers in Moscow during the early years of Stalin's rule. On August 26, 1933, shortly after whispering from her deathbed four half-audible lines of farewell to Vedeneyeva, Parnok died of heart failure.

*Diana L. Burgin*

## Bibliography

Burgin, Diana Lewis. "After the Ball Is Over: Sophia Parnok's Creative Relationship with Marina Tsvetaeva." *Russian Review* 47 (1988), 425–444.

———. "Laid Out in Lavender: Perceptions of Lesbian Love in Russian Literature and Criticism of the Silver Age, 1893–1917." In *Sexuality and the Body in Russian Culture*. Ed. Jane Costlow, Stephanie Sandler, and Judith Vowles. Stanford, Calif.: Stanford University Press, 1993, pp. 177–203.

———. "Sophia Parnok and the Writing of a Lesbian Poet's Life." *Slavic Review* 51:2 (Summer 1992), 214–231.

———. *Sophia Parnok: The Life and Work of Russia's Sappho*. New York: New York University Press, 1994.

See also Russia; Tsvetaeva, Marina Ivanovna

## Parra, Teresa de la (1889/90–1936)

Pseudonym of Ana Teresa de la Parra Sanojo, Venezuelan novelist and epistolary writer. Teresa de la Parra was born in Paris in 1889, into a prominent Venezuelan family. While living in Venezuela in her early twenties, she wrote her best-known work, *Ifigenia* (1924), the story of a young woman caught in the conflict between cultural tradition and modern ideas. Other works by Parra include *Las Memorias de Mama Blanca* (1929) and *Epistolario Intimo* (1953).

Salient themes in her work include death, an idyllic colonial past, and mysticism as a feminine goal. By the time *Ifigenia* was awarded a literary prize in 1924, Parra had returned to Paris, where, like other Western expatriates, she aspired to an "independent" life, and where she presided over a literary salon.

Critics and biographers have spent much energy accounting for the absence of an overt love relationship in Parra's life. Some overemphasized her femininity, one proposed that she was married to her work, while another tried to associate her with the Ecuadoran essayist Gonzalo Zaldumbide, to whom she once wrote: "In general, I am frightened of you and feel horror toward other men. Oh, if you but knew how to love me with the soul of a woman! The soul would be enough for me and I could forgo the body" (in Molly 1995).

According to Molly (1995), Parra's texts, letters, and diaries were expurgated by "friendly hands" and by Parra herself. Thus, evidence of a lesbian connection must be read between the lines. In 1924, Emilia Barrios, an older woman whom Parra considered a mentor, died. At that time, Parra is said to have suffered a "profound spiritual depression." Shortly after, Parra met Lydia Cabrera (1900–1991), a Cuban writer and ethnologist. When the latter moved to Paris in 1927, they developed a companionate relationship that continued until Parra, diagnosed with tuberculosis, died in 1936.

Letters between Parra and Cabrera include references to "sensual love without consumation." An aversion toward *vulgaridad* (vulgarity) also appears in Parra's letters, in which she seems put off by French author Colette's (1873–1954) sexual frankness but charmed by the gentility of the eighteenth-century Ladies of Llangollen, with whom she may have identified. Parra's relationship with Cabrera may have been a "romantic friendship" constrained by the mores of nineteenth-century Latin American Catholic culture and class privilege. Further interpretation must wait until Parra's diaries and letters can be fully accessed.

*Yolanda Retter*

## Bibliography

Flores, Angel, ed. *Spanish American Authors: The Twentieth Century*. New York: Wilson, 1992, pp. 655–657.

Matta-Kolster, Elba. "Ana Teresa de la Parra Sanojo." In *Latin American Writers*. Ed. Carlos A. Sole. New York: Scribner, 1989, pp. 717–720.

Molly, Sylvia. "Disappearing Acts: Reading Lesbian in Teresa de la Parra." In *Entiendes? Queer Readings, Hispanic Writings*. Ed. Emilie L. Bergmann and Paul Julian Smith. Durham, N.C.: Duke University Press, 1995, pp. 230–256.

See also Colette; Ladies of Llangollen; Latin American Literature; Paris; Romantic Friendship

## Passing Women

Colloquial term that refers to people assigned female at birth who live some part of their lives as men. The term was part of subcultural lesbian vernacular in the 1940s and 1950s and has been defined through practice over several decades. Passing women have been most often defined as "women who live as men" or "women who pretend to be men." The first definition above derives from the more complicated understandings of gender inspired by the transgender movement. "Passing women," already a complicated term, only becomes more so as understandings of genders and sexualities expand. As is common with slang, the definition of the term is porous, and it collides, on occasion, with other terms, such as cross-dressing, transvestite, transgender, transsexual, and butch.

"Passing" has long been a word used to describe the activity of those who move in the world as part of a group to which they do not belong: Race passing, for instance, is a topic extensively treated in literature, especially in narratives of black people who passed as white, often as a means to escape slavery. There is also a tradition in literature and drama of gender passing, or cross-dressing; women passing as men are often main characters, from the plays of William Shakespeare (1564–1616) to the popular film *Victor/Victoria* (1982) and beyond. "Passing women," however, is a term initially arising out of a subculture trying to put a name to real-life passing, not the stagings and fictions of passing.

### Histories: Hidden Stories

The histories of people who passed are hard to excavate, because the knowledge of such people depends upon their having been discovered at some point. The history of passing has been written most commonly in the genre of autobiography. As long as there have been men and women, there have been stories of women who passed as men, and vice versa, for a variety of reasons. The most common are the desire to fight as soldiers in times of war, to get an education, and to be able to make a living in a world that limited the means for women to do so. Passing women have, in the past, been condemned as imitation men or as traitors to the female sex; it has become more common, however, to understand passing women as expressing a feminist revolt against their everyday constraints. Some of these lives were certainly lesbian ones, perhaps for women without the language to express lesbian desire as such.

Although categorizing history's passing women by late-twentieth-century terms may do them a disservice, or be a simplification of their stories, the urge remains to hold them up as queer heroines and heroes. The most famous passing woman is probably Joan of Arc (1412–1431), the French rebel, who was called *homasse,* a derogatory term meaning "masculine woman." The very existence of such a term in this time period suggests that Joan of Arc was not the only masculine, or passing, woman. At the age of seventeen, Joan dressed in men's clothes and led a successful military campaign to liberate the French from the English. The Roman Catholic Church condemned Joan of Arc for her cross-dressing, and she was burned at the stake. Not as well known, but also dashing characters, were the swashbuckling Mary Read and Anne Bonney, who dressed as men and were convicted of piracy in 1720. Another early passing woman, Deborah Sampson (1760–1827), fought as a man in the American Revolutionary War and was the subject of a sensationalized biography entitled *The Female Review* (1797).

The self-descriptions of passing women reflect not only their times, but also their self-understandings within these times. For instance, Mary Walker (1832–1919), who lived in the mid-1800s in the United States, did not undertake to live full-time as a man, but did undertake to dress like one, and headed the National Dress Reform Association. She was a surgeon who served in the Civil War on the Union side and was awarded a congressional Medal of Honor. She wrote widely on topics ranging from suffrage to sexuality, but her own sexual orientation remains unclear. The legendary Mountain Charley, who trekked by wagon to California in 1855, was known to have been a woman. This moniker may, in fact have been adopted by more than one successfully passing woman in the Old West. The legends of Mountain Charley's exploits rival those of any mythic hero. Where she came from is unclear, but, as a teen and an adult, she cross-dressed and passed as a man, becoming a riverboat vagabond and then a train captain, miner, and saloon owner during the Gold Rush.

Other early American passing women are written about in newspaper reports or by doctors and psychiatrists who treated them, and deciphering early sensationalized news reportage and medical assessments presents another sort of challenge. Babe Bean was a passing woman in the late 1890s in California whose story was printed in the newspaper in her hometown of Stockton and was taken up by papers in San Francisco, California, and Boston, Massachusetts. Articles describing her houseboat apartment and letters debating her male attire appeared with frequency. Lucy Ann Lobdell, who was born in New York state in 1829 and lived much of her life as a man, wrote an autobiography, *Narrative of Lucy Ann Lobdell* (1855), defending her choices as economic necessity. She was also written about by psychiatrists who treated her in the later part of her life, including a Doctor Wise, whose determination of her insanity grapples with then-contemporary thinking about homosexuality; he makes such statements as "it would be more charitable and just if society would protect them from . . . ridicule" (in Katz, 1992). The doctor's logbook of Lobdell's ten years in what is now the Willard Psychiatric Center (Willard, New York) is extremely sad and stands as an incredible example of the kind of oppression faced by early queers.

## Transgendered Analysis

In addition to layering a feminist analysis onto the histories of these women, the time has also come to consider their lives within the framework of a transgendered analysis: Accompanying the exterior male presentation of the passing woman might be a variety of interior motivations ranging from expediency to male identification, which is where the term collides with transgender and transsexuality. In fact, some passing women may not be "imitation men" at all, but transgendered men, men who are expanding the very terms of the discussion of what it means to be a man or to be a woman. The collision of the terms is suggested by the most famous recent example of a passing woman's narrative, Leslie Feinberg's autobiographical novel *Stone Butch Blues* (1993).

*Stone Butch Blues* clearly shows the blurring boundaries between the terms "lesbian," "butch," and "passing woman." Feinberg's main character, Jess Goldberg, passes from life within a butch-femme community in Buffalo, New York, to living and working as a heterosexual man—one might say as a full-time passing woman—and finally moves toward a life in which a complicated transgendered-butch identity can be claimed. Many butch women are often momentarily taken to be men. The difference between such momentary butch passing and the passing ascribed to passing women is intention: A passing woman actively undertakes to live some part of life as a man. The issues become a matter of self-definition, the options for which change over time, as understandings of gender and sexuality change.

As subcultural understandings of gender and sexuality become more complex, those of the general public are thought to follow. However, public opinion is slow to change, and prejudice and fear, not to say hatred, remain. In December 1993, twenty-one-year-old Brandon Teena was raped and murdered in Humboldt, Nebraska. Teena lived as a man and was discovered to be biologically and legally female upon his arrest for check forgery. After the police released the information to the local news, Teena was assaulted and raped by two men, who later murdered Teena, after the police failed to file charges against them for the first attack. Both of Teena's assailants were found guilty of first-degree murder. Brandon Teena is only one example of the fact that many passing women's lives have ended in terrible violence.

Another famous contemporary example—one whose life did not end in violence—is Billy Tipton, a big-band musician, who, upon his death in 1989 at age seventy-four, was discovered to have been anatomically female. There are no words from Tipton himself about his gender expression or his understanding of his own sexuality. He began living as a man while in his twenties, taking on his brother's name and Social Security number. He worked with Louis Armstrong's trombone partner Jack Teagarden and formed the Billy Tipton Trio in the 1950s, playing nightclubs until shortly before his death. He was married to a woman who said she never knew his biological sex, and he has been claimed variously as a lesbian, a feminist, and a transgendered man. Tipton himself articulated none of these identities. The only clear thing is which pronoun he preferred.

Some contend that Tipton lived as a man because it was the only way he could work as a jazz musician. This may be true in part, but Tipton's desire might also have been to live as the man he always considered himself to be. In the face of modern-day conceptions of transgender and transsexuality, the term "passing women" becomes even more layered. In historical cases in which "passing women" describe their choices, it is not in the terms used today, so it is impossible to say that these people were lesbians or were transgendered men. Even without identifying these folks by late-twentieth-century terms, they can surely be understood and cherished as a part of gay, lesbian, bisexual, and transgendered history. *Rebecca Ann Rugg*

*Bibliography*

Duberman, Martin, Martha Vicinus, and George Chauncey, Jr., eds. *Hidden from History: Reclaiming the Gay and Lesbian Past*. New York: Meridian, 1990.

Ginsberg, Elaine K. *Passing and the Fictions of Identity*. Durham, N.C.: Duke University Press, 1996.

Guerin, E.J. *Moutain Charley*. Norman: University of Oklahoma Press, 1986.

Katz, Jonathan. *Gay American History: Lesbians and Gay Men in the U.S.A.* Rev. ed. New York: Penguin, 1992.

Nestle, Joan. *The Persistent Desire: A Femme-Butch Reader*. Boston: Alyson, 1992.

———, ed. *A Restricted Country*. Ithaca, N.Y.: Firebrand, 1987.

**See also** Cross-Dressing; History; Joan of Arc (Jeanne d'Arc); Transgender; Walker, Mary Edwards

## Passionlessness

Anglo American middle-class belief (ca. 1780s–1890s) that women innately lacked sexual appetites and aggressiveness. This led to claims of "natural" female virtue and superior morality. Women's "innate" morality justified their participation in public reform movements such as temperance. The belief also allowed women to develop romantic, sometimes lifelong, same-sex relationships without public censure. The love of two passionless "true women" was considered a pure, chaste love. Ironically, women's romantic relationships, like that of the eighteenth-century Ladies of Llangollen, flourished because of their supposed passsionlessness.

Historians are divided over how to interpret romantic female relationships: as passionate (albeit asexual) friendships or as sexual love relationships. Controversy stems from an argument over the definition of "lesbian." Some insist that the only true lesbian relationships were accompanied by sexual acts or conscious lesbian identity. Others believe that women who recognized each other as their primary love or partner were lesbian, regardless of their sexual expressiveness. The "female world of love and ritual" (Smith-Rosenberg 1986) had intimacy, love, and erotic passion, and some partnerships did have a sexual component.

Due to historical beliefs in passionlessness, some historians argue that same-sex nineteenth-century intimacy cannot accurately be labeled as "lesbian," but that lesbian-like behavior can be identified. Women who wrote to each other with, what seems to modern-day readers, passionate sexuality felt comfortable revealing themselves because they believed in their innate "passionless" purity. Moreover, with sexuality associated with heterosexual intercourse, women who participated in lesbian sexual acts might not necessarily consider them sexual—merely "romantic."

Interpretations vary, for example, on letters such as Emily Dickinson's (1830–1886) to Susan Gilbert in 1852: "[W]ill you . . . be my own again, and kiss me as you used to? . . . I cannot wait, feel that now I must have you—that the expectation once more to see your face again, makes me feel hot and feverish, and my heart beats so fast."

Passionlessness ended with acknowledgment of female heterosexual desire by sexologists beginning in the 1880s. Women's feelings for one another were then deemed sexual, "acted upon," and labeled deviant, "inverted," and pathological. *Susan Gonda*

*Bibliography*

Cook, Blanche Wiesen. "The Historical Denial of Lesbianism." *Radical History Review* 20 (1979), 60–65.

Cott, Nancy. "Passionlessness: An Interpretation of Victorian Sexual Ideology, 1790–1850." *Signs: Journal of Women in Culture and Society* 4 (1978), 219–236.

Rupp, Leila J. " 'Imagine My Surprise': Women's Relationships in Historical Perspective." *Frontiers: A Journal of Women Studies* 5 (1980), 61–70.

Smith-Rosenberg, Carroll. "The Female World of Love and Ritual: Relations Between Women in Nineteenth-Century America." In Smith-Rosenberg, *Disorderly Conduct: Visions of Gender in Victorian America*. New York: Knopf, 1986.

Vicinus, Martha. "Lesbian History: All Theory and No Facts or All Facts and No Theory?" *Radical History Review* 60 (1994), 57–75.

**See also** Dickinson, Emily; Ladies of Llangollen; Romantic Friendship

## Patriarchy

A wide-ranging system by which men achieve and maintain dominance over women in all spheres of social life from the family to the economy, from religious and educational institutions to ideological constructions and psychological processes. Those theorists who have been linked with the Marxist feminist theoretical tradition highlight the economic basis for male dominance, while those associated with radical feminist tradition emphasize sexual domination. Lesbian feminists, in particular, centered the ways in which patriarchal social relations presume and reinforce heterosexual norms and behaviors. The use of the term "patriarchy" to describe a broad-based system of oppression has come under criticism as a consequence of postmodern critiques of large, explanatory narratives. However, criticism of "patriarchy" as a transhistorical and cross-cultural system of male dominance has predated contemporary postmodern critique.

Patriarchy, in its earliest usage, referred to the authority of the father (*patria potestas*) over other members of his household, including his wife, children, grandchildren, servants, and slaves. This form of rule was extended to serve as the basis for social organization of economic, cultural, religious, and political institutions in numerous societal contexts. While some feminist scholars have argued that the patriarchal family resulted from men's desire to establish paternity, others, such as Mies (1986) and Leacock (1978), have identified warfare, colonization, and the development of capitalism as central to the imposition of patriarchal rule.

The process by which private control of women (by individual husbands or family heads) shifts to public control embedded in welfare and other state programs has been the subject of numerous feminist historical analyses, such as those by Lerner (1986). While many feminist theorists of the state have recognized that such a shift did offer women greater options than was possible within the patriarchal family (such as the ability to leave abusive husbands or to resist employment in demeaning and hazardous low-paid jobs), some feminists have continued to emphasize the social control aspects of state intervention.

Early materialist feminist arguments viewed women's subordinate status as a process by which the biological division of the sexes for the purposes of reproduction of the species created the grounds for male control. Some argued that psychoanalytic processes provided the mechanism by which women psychologically incorporate and, therefore, help reproduce patriarchal culture. Noting the failure of "Marxism to fully express or conceptualize sex oppression," Rubin (1975) drew upon Claude Levi-Strauss's (1908–) theory of kinship (especially the exchange of women) and Sigmund Freud's (1856–1939) theory of femininity to articulate the ways in which male control of women's sexuality was linked to cultural and economic practices through a "sex-gender system." Subsequent radical feminist analyses further argued that patriarchal domination formed the basis for other forms of domination based on class and race.

Hartmann (1981) demonstrated the ways in which capitalism developed with specific forms of male dominance already embedded in it. Joseph (1981) argued that such an analysis neglected the ways white supremacy organized systems of capitalism and patriarchy and rendered invisible the particular experiences of women of color within contemporary patriarchal capitalist societies. Moreover, despite the predominance of patriarchy as a form of social domination, not all men benefit equally from it. Men of color, working-class men, and gay men do not have the right to claim the same power over women, especially white heterosexual women, as white middle- and upper-class heterosexual men do. Other theorists cautioned that, by linking patriarchy with capitalism, different forms of male dominance occurring within other modes of economic organization would be eclipsed.

Often neglected in feminist analyses of patriarchy are the ways in which it presumes and reinforces heterosexuality. Lesbian authors such as Rich (1980) have highlighted the ways in which lesbian existence poses a fundamental threat to patriarchy, comprising "both the breaking of a taboo and the rejection of a compulsory way of life," which Rich described as "compulsory heterosexuality." Clark (1981) asserts: "Men at all levels of privilege, of all classes and colors have the potential to act out legalistically, moralistically, and violently when they cannot colonize women, when they cannot circumscribe our sexual, productive, reproductive, creative prerogatives and energies." Rape, wife beating, violence against lesbians, sexual harassment, and other forms of physical and emotional intimidation are used to maintain control over women's bodies, as well as circumscribe women's spatial mobility and economic independence. Contemporary critiques of "patriarchy" highlight how its usage often renders invisible the ways in which gender arrangements differ across time, place, cultures, and other sites of difference. However, "patriarchy" remains a powerful concept

**P** for expressing the continued hegemony of male dominance in contemporary institutions.

*Nancy A. Naples*

### Bibliography

Clark, Cheryl. "Lesbianism: An Act of Resistance." In *This Bridge Called My Back: Writings by Radical Women of Color*. Ed. Cherríe Moraga and Gloria Anzaldúa. Watertown, Mass.: Persephone, 1981, pp. 128–137.

Hartmann, Heidi. "The Unhappy Marriage of Marxism and Feminism: Toward a More Progressive Union." In *Women and Revolution*. Ed. Lydia Sargent. Boston: South End, 1981, pp. 1–41.

Joseph, Gloria. "The Incompatible Ménage à Trois: Marxism, Feminism, and Racism." In *Women and Revolution*. Ed. Lydia Sargent. Boston: South End, 1981, pp. 91–108.

Leacock, Eleanor Burke. *Myths of Male Dominance*. New York: Monthly Review Press, 1978.

Lerner, Gerda. *The Creation of Patriarchy*. New York: Oxford University Press, 1986.

Mies, Maria. *Patriarchy and Accumulation on a World Scale*. Atlantic Highlands, N.J.: Zed, 1986.

Rich, Adrienne. "Compulsory Heterosexuality and Lesbian Existence." *Signs: Journal of Women in Culture and Society* 5 (1980), 631–660.

Rubin, Gayle. "The Traffic in Women: Notes on the 'Political Economy' of Sex." In *Toward an Anthropology of Women*. Ed. Rayna R. Reiter. New York: Monthly Review Press, 1975, pp. 157–210.

*See also* Oppression

## Peace Movement

Lesbian feminists and women-identified women have shaped the women's peace movement in many significant ways through their ideas and participation during the twentieth century. In particular, they contributed vitally to the creation of women's communities and organizations as spaces to challenge and disarm patriarchy, develop women's power, freedom, and visions of a peaceful world, and actualize feminist and nonviolent principles. They believed that the warrior mentality, as well as war, led to violence against women and that the realization of women's equality and autonomy depended upon achieving a peaceful and just world. Further, joining other feminists, they revealed the interconnections between systems of domination—militarism, patriarchy, capitalism, racism, and imperialism—and the oppression of women, the poor, people of color, and nature.

## Modern Peace Movement

While lesbians may have been part of the peace movement of the nineteenth century, most research has been done on the modern U.S. women's peace movement. It developed during the Progressive Era in opposition to World War I and flourished during the 1920s and 1930s. With the antiwar and the gay and lesbian liberation movements and the beginning of the "second wave" of feminism in the 1960s, the women's peace movement revitalized and expanded. Visible and widespread lesbian participation occurred during the 1980s women's peace encampments and antinuclear actions in the United States and Europe.

Most women peace activists in the first half of the twentieth century who appear to be lesbians by modern standards did not identify themselves as such. Therefore, scholars and historians have debated whether to use the term "lesbian" in describing them. Many of the white, middle-class, and college-educated reformers of the Progressive period chose to remain single and lived with women in partnerships for many years, relationships that society apparently condoned. Others lived and worked in female institutions, such as settlement houses and women's colleges, even as U.S. women as a whole created female voluntary organizations to promote reform. This strategy of female separatism enabled women not only to enter public life, but also to develop a reform agenda to gain political power for women and to democratize and humanize industrial and urban society.

Jane Addams (1860–1935), a founder of Hull House and the Women's International League for Peace and Freedom (WILPF) and winner of the 1931 Nobel Peace Prize, is probably the most well known peace activist who was a woman-identified woman. For years, she lived at Hull House with partner Mary Rozet Smith (1868–1934) in a deeply loving and satisfying relationship. She helped create the modern women's peace movement through her leadership of the U.S. Woman's Peace Party and WILPF, which were formed to protest World War I. For Addams, peace work was building cooperative communities to meet human needs at local and international levels. Women, given their traditional maternal work, needed power to transform governments based upon nationalism and militarism to ones that fostered human life and conflict resolution based upon nonviolent methods. Further, Addams supported a woman-centered approach to peace work that incorporated consensual decision making and respect for diversity within WILPF, which still exists.

## Feminist Activists

Ideas and concerns about the war system and strategies for change expressed by Jane Addams's generation foreshadowed those of feminists active in the women's peace and antinuclear movement of the 1980s. The Greenham Common Women's Peace Encampment (1981–1990s) in England and the Women's Pentagon Actions (1980 and 1981) and the Women's Encampment for a Future of Peace and Justice in Seneca, New York (1983–1990s), were the first major women's protests against the patriarchal institutions that produced nuclear missiles, which threatened life on the planet, and promoted militarism, sexism, racism, and the exploitation of nature. The Women's Peace Encampment at Greenham served as an initial inspiration for women in Europe and the United States to establish women's sites of resistance. Hundreds of thousands of women participated, some for days or weeks, others for years, in creative acts of resistance that ranged from breaking into the base at Greenham and dancing on the missile silos, to weaving webs of yarn across doors at the Pentagon, to women linking arms and encircling military installations.

Many lesbian feminists participated in the peace camps, and, eventually, they were the majority of residents. At the camps, lesbians having diverse identities could experience freedom of expression while defying conventional notions of femininity. At Greenham, women decided that a women-only space was necessary for continuous protest against the placement of U.S. nuclear missiles there. Other peace camps followed this model. Thus, it was in these women's spaces that participants developed nonviolent, feminist methods of organizing, decision making, and direct action; in effect, they hoped to live their principles. At times, however, conflicts did arise between women over issues relating to lesbianism and racism that did not reflect their ideal of respect for difference.

While lesbians experienced new levels of freedom and creativity in the camps, lesbianism became a controversial issue between the camps and the surrounding communities. For example, during the first summer of the Seneca Women's Peace Encampment, in 1983, local residents repeatedly condemned the women for being lesbians, witches, and Communists and expressed their hostility with signs and T-shirts sporting slogans such as "Nuke the Lizzies" and "Nuke the Bitches until they glow—then shoot them in the dark." Further, an angry, screaming mob of locals blocked the path of women on a legal march, which, ironically, resulted in the arrest of more than fifty peace activists.

Barbara Deming (1917–1984), a prominent lesbian peace and feminist activist, wrote that the lesbian spirit motivating women in the women's peace movement of the 1980s revealed "a new feeling of women daring to trust ourselves to one another in an extraordinary way" (Deming 1985). In creating the women-only spaces and committing to relationships with women, they allowed for a "deeper sharing" of themselves and provided the opportunity to invent new ways of living together in community. Indeed, women-identified women and lesbians of the twentieth century have shaped the women's peace movement by fostering feminist protest against patriarchy and developing a critique of the war system, even as they "invented" alternatives that could mean real peace, justice, and security in a world of shared power.        *Anne Marie Pois*

### Bibliography

Alonso, Harriet Hyman. *Peace as a Women's Issue: A History of the U.S. Movement for World Peace and Women's Rights*. Syracuse, N.Y.: Syracuse University Press, 1993.

Deming, Barbara. *Prisons that Could Not Hold*. San Francisco: Spinsters Ink, 1985.

Harford, Barbara, and Sarah Hopkins. *Greenham Common: Women at the Wire*. London: Women's Press, 1984.

Krasniewicz, Louise. *Nuclear Summer: The Clash of Communities at the Seneca Women's Peace Encampment*. Ithaca, N.Y.: Cornell University Press, 1992.

Roseneil, Sasha. *Disarming Patriarchy: Feminism and Political Action at Greenham*. Philadelphia: Open University Press, 1995.

*See also* Addams, Jane; Deming, Barbara

## Penelope, Julia (1941–)

American linguist and philosopher. Born to Frederick William Stanley and Frances Stanley, Julia Pene-

**P** lope was raised in Miami, Florida. (She was to eliminate the patronym for feminist reasons in 1980.) An avid reader, she decided she was a homosexual when she came upon the letter *h* in the public library. At four or five years of age, she had informed her mother that she intended to marry a girl just like her. In high school, she developed her first serious lesbian relationship, one that lasted two and a half years.

A love for language led her to decide on a career in linguistics. The investigations of the Charlie Johns Investigating Committee on Communism and Homosexuality led to her dismissal from Florida State University in 1959 on the grounds of suspected lesbianism. Ironically, she was subsequently dismissed from the University of Miami in 1960 for having men in her room. Undaunted, she went on to receive a B.A. in English and linguistics from City College (New York City) in 1966 and a Ph.D. in English from the University of Texas in 1971. Despite a lengthy list of publications in linguistics, the University of Nebraska–Lincoln, where she taught for eleven years, failed to promote her to the highest rank, sometimes suggesting that her research was "narrow." Before, during, and after her academic career, she supported herself at a variety of occupations, working as a file clerk, a handwriting analyst, and a girls' basketball coach. During the 1960s, she was also a kept butch (a butch who is supported by another woman, often, but not always, a prostitute, a call girl, or the mistress of a wealthy man).

In 1982, she met Sarah Valentine, and, by 1983, they were involved in Penelope's longest relationship to date, lasting until 1995. Together, they edited two of Penelope's thirteen published books, including *Finding the Lesbians* (1990), one of the many volumes whose content and audience was explicitly lesbian. One of her best-known collections is *The Coming Out Stories* (1980), coedited with Susan J. Wolfe. Termed by another linguist "bright but fierce," Penelope was a separatist whose lesbian publications were often controversial, criticizing sadomasochism and other practices within lesbian communities. Disheartened by lesbian infighting, she eventually withdrew from lesbian writing, devoting her energies instead to editing copy for major commercial presses.                  *Susan J. Wolfe*

### Bibliography

Tomlinson, Barbara. "The Politics of Textual Vehemence, or Go to Your Room Until You Learn How to Act." *Signs: Journal of Women in Culture and Society* 22: 1 (Autumn 1996), 86–114.

*See also* Language

## Performance Art

Catchall term describing live performance that does not neatly fit into traditional categories, such as drama, dance, film, or music, but that may incorporate elements of any of these forms. Unlike more conventional theater, performance art often lacks plot, psychological characters, and any intention that others might produce the piece again. The phrase historically encompasses a vast variety of work, ranging from monologues by artists such as Jack Smith and Carolee Schneeman, to huge events like the *Storming of the Winter Palace*, the 1920 commemoration of the Russian Revolution, which involved eight thousand performers in a reenactment of the historic siege. The term includes the plotless "happenings" of the late 1950s and early 1960s and the nonlinear, deconstructive productions of theatrical artists such as Richard Foreman, Robert Wilson, the Wooster Group, and Mabou Mines. It includes the deliberately shocking shenanigans of the dadaists, who promulgated antiart and nonsense in Zurich and Paris from 1915 to 1922, and the Romantic Festivities of the Bauhaus, the architecture and design school founded in Weimar, Germany, in 1919, promoting the unification of all of the arts. Performance art is a twentieth-century phenomenon, but, in retrospect, Renaissance pageants or even medieval mystery cycles may be considered its progenitors.

Specifically lesbian performance art, then, exists within, and against, a rich tradition of formal experiment and, often, political dissent. Lesbians and gay men seized the form in the 1980s in the United States, joining together method and material that question the very means of representation and that problematize identities and desire.

In the modern era, performance art developed within conscious artistic movements, often providing the opening to the new perspectives for which artists continually searched, especially as they sought to challenge the commercial or "high"-cultural status of the artwork. By virtue of its evanescence, performance thwarted the commodification of the art object as something that could be bought or displayed in a museum. As Rosalee Goldberg has suggested in *Performance Art: From Futurism to the*

*Present* (1993): "Whenever a certain school, be it Cubism, Minimalism, or conceptual art, seemed to have reached an impasse, artists have turned to performance as a way of breaking down categories and indicating new directions." In this respect, she describes performance art as the avant avant-garde.

In European movements such as futurism, constructivism, surrealism, and dada, performance art fulfilled this function, and, in the United States, it also played a role in developing an American avant-garde of the 1930s–1950s.

## Feminism and Performance Art

But it was the rise of feminism—and, soon after, of the gay liberation movement—that translated performance art's oppositional spirit from an essentially formalistic focus toward more overt political content. Reacting to their frequent second-class treatment within even the avant-garde art world, and recognizing the power of their own bodies as canvases for works about female experience, women began creating solo performances in the 1960s that combined the formal experiments of the period with the autobiographical revelations of the consciousness-raising process and, in the case of lesbians, of the coming out process.

Though not lesbian, works of early feminist performance artists in the 1970s, many still active at the end of the 1990s, such as Rachel Rosenthal, Joan Jonas, Cindy Sherman, and Theodora Skipitares, have had profound influences on lesbian work, as these artists used their own bodies and experiences as the ground for an exploratory art that questioned women's relationship to history, ecology, and representation. Perhaps the most telling image of this explosion of new work was Carolee Schneeman's 1975 *Interior Scroll*, in which she read critical remarks about her own work from ticker tape she extracted from her vagina. Such literal embodiment of political and artistic boundary breaking was repeated in the 1990s in the self-described "queer performance" of openly gay and lesbian artists such as Tim Miller and Holly Hughes, whose explorations of the present, unruly body were denied grants by the National Endowment for the Arts in 1990 because of their "homoeroticism," which scandalized Republican United States Senator Jesse Helms of North Carolina and legions of the Religious Right.

Meanwhile, in the late 1970s, the term "performance art" came to describe a burgeoning movement of solo works, which were often autobiographical and, in any case, meant to be performed only by their authors. While this work certainly has roots in the experiments of previous decades, it was also fueled by the financial crisis in American arts that put large spectacles beyond the grasp of most young artists and theater spaces. For lesbian artists, in particular, whose viewpoint was often unwelcome in mainstream, and even sometimes in gay male, theater establishments, presenting work as a single person on a bare stage was inexpensive and, therefore, producible practically anywhere. In this period, spaces devoted to presenting performance art mushroomed across the United States, and soon throughout the United Kingdom and other parts of Europe.

In the 1990s, a high proportion of the leading artists, critics, and theorists in the field of performance art were lesbians, perhaps because, though their work differs extensively from one another, they are able to sustain the subversive impulses of the form. Many lesbian performance artists exploit the tension between their own bodily presence and their representation of a culturally constructed female body. To cite only a few examples, the butch-femme explorations in work by Peggy Shaw and Lois Weaver celebrate these categories even as they call them into question; the disjunctive word-and-movement narratives of Pamela Sneed and the comic exhortations of Carmelita Tropicana examine, among other things, the intersection of gender and sexuality with racial and ethnic construction. With her outdoor performance company Circus Amok, Jennifer Miller, who has chosen not to remove the beard that grows on her chin, presents political circus acts, juggling, eating fire, and walking on stilts to a patter of pointed, punning commentary. The geographical imagery in Holly Hughes's performances almost literally maps cultural conflict onto her own midwestern body.

Through exposure to such works—and to workshops being taught around the United States, by, among others, Hughes, Shaw, and Weaver (who also conducts "Queer School" out of the Gay Sweatshop in London)—young lesbians and gay men are discovering in performance art a useful framework for coming out, flexing their queer bodies, and articulating their selves.       *Alisa Solomon*

## Bibliography

Carr, C. *On Edge: Performance at the End of the Twentieth Century*. Hanover, N.H.: Wesleyan University Press, 1993.

Goldberg, Rosalee. *Performance Art: From Futurism to the Present*. New York: Abrams, 1988.

Phelan, Peggy. "Money Talks, Again." *The Drama Review: TDR* 35:3 (Fall 1991), 131–42.

———. "Serrano, Mapplethorpe, the NEA, and You: Money Talks." *The Drama Review: TDR* 34:1 (Spring 1990), 4–15.

Muñoz, Josòe Esteban, and Amanda Barrett, eds. "Queer Acts." *Women and Performance: A Journal of Feminist Theory* 16 (1996) (Special Issue).

*See also* Theater and Drama, Contemporary; Theater and Drama, History of

## Performativity

The notion that the appearance of having a natural gender is an effect produced by a set of repeated acts performed within a specific cultural context. This theoretical position asserts that there is no gender identity inherently belonging to bodies; rather, identity is constituted by the very expressions that are said to be the results of gender. Thus, gender is not *being* but *doing*. There is no true or natural masculinity or maleness that originates in men; nor does femininity or femaleness originate in women. On the contrary, the idea that men and women are stable identities is a fiction that disguises itself as a law of nature and culture—a law that regulates the field (gender relations) it purports to describe.

Judith Butler popularized performativity in *Gender Trouble: Feminism and the Subversion of Identity* (1990). By using the examples of butch-femme lesbianism and drag, she describes how these and other non–status quo gender relations bring into relief the constructed status of the male/female binary—a binary construction that is given the status of being "natural" when heterosexuality is assumed to be "natural." For example, when two lesbians organize their relationship around one acting out her version of masculinity and the other acting out her version of femininity, they show that masculinity and femininity are not restricted to male and female bodies, respectively; nor are they restricted to heterosexual relations. Rather than condemn butch-femme lesbianism as a mere imitation of heterosexuality, Butler asserts that butch-femme sexuality subverts the naturalization of gender because a butch lesbian redefines the performativity of masculinity and the femme lesbian redefines the performativity of femininity in a relationship that falls outside the boundary, or "law," of heterosexuality. The disjunction, or dissonance, within the expected link between gender (identity), sex (body), and desire highlights the performative quality of all genders and sexualities.

This is not to say that gender, sex, and sexuality are free floating. On the contrary, they are historically and politically dependent and become intelligible through extended repetition. Yet scholars and activists have argued that various expressions of gender, sex, and sexuality that employ performative exaggeration, discord, internal confusion, or proliferation can mobilize new possibilities over time that exceed and expand what is intelligible. While *Gender Trouble* focuses on gender, sex, and sexuality, performativity has been broadened in relation to many identities and subjectivities. Some analyses have addressed the performativity of race, ethnicity, class, and diseases such as AIDS.          *Kate Burns*

### Bibliography

Butler, Judith. *Bodies That Matter: On the Discursive Limits of "Sex."* New York: Routledge, 1993.

———. *Gender Trouble: Feminism and the Subversion of Identity*. New York: Routledge, 1990.

Sedgwick, Eve Kosofsky. "Queer Performativity: Henry James's *The Art of the Novel: A Journal of Lesbian and Gay Studies*." *GLQ* 1:1 (Spring 1993), 1–16.

*See also* Butch-Femme; Gender; Identity; Queer Theory

## Periodicals

Publications that are issued at regularly occuring intervals. A proliferation of lesbian periodicals and lesbian writing in feminist and other periodicals followed quickly from the rise of lesbian feminism, gay liberation, and women's liberation in the late 1960s and early 1970s. By 1975, more than fifty lesbian periodicals and/or feminist periodicals with significant lesbian content had been launched in the United States, providing a forum for developing lesbian feminist political ideas and creating a sense of lesbian community nationally. Around the same time, lesbian periodicals were also founded in several countries globally, with most concentrated in North America and western Europe. The number and diversity of lesbian periodicals, and the lesbian content in both feminist and cosexual lesbian-gay-bisexual periodicals, continued to increase worldwide throughout the 1980s and 1990s.

## History

The first known lesbian publication in the United States, *Vice Versa*, was published in Los Angeles, California, in 1947 by Lisa Ben (a pseudonymous anagram for "lesbian"). For nine months, Ben distributed her typed, carbon-copied magazine to her friends and to patrons of Los Angeles's popular lesbian bar, the If Club. Although the circulation of *Vice Versa* was never more than twelve copies per issue (the maximum Ben could surreptitiously produce at work), it foreshadowed the format of many lesbian and gay periodicals in the decades to come: homegrown, upbeat, and including a mix of editorials, poems, short stories, reviews, and letters.

In 1956, *The Ladder* became the second lesbian periodical launched in the United States. For sixteen years, *The Ladder* served as the mouthpiece of the Daughters of Bilitis (DOB), a lesbian homophile organization founded in San Francisco, California, in 1955. *The Ladder* included news of interest to lesbians, editorials, reports on professional attitudes toward homosexuality, book reviews, short stories, and poetry. The DOB distributed 170 copies of the first issue to lesbians and also to (presumably) heterosexual lawyers, psychologists, and other professionals.

*The Ladder* was the first place in history in which a large number of lesbians could air their views. The magazine's circulation reached a high of about seven hundred—far more than *Vice Versa* but still far fewer than gay men's publications, foreshadowing a trend that continued over the next three decades. Readership was far larger than official circulation figures, however, since copies of gay and lesbian magazines were passed around among friends. Fear of being associated with a homophile group is evident in the number of women who asked to be removed from the mailing list of *The Ladder* and in the editor's assurances to subscribers that "Your Name Is Safe" from disclosure to police and government authorities. In the late 1960s, *The Ladder* became more aligned with feminism than with the male-dominated homophile movement.

Although it fell victim in 1972 to financial difficulties and the popularity of newer, more militant publications, it had by then inspired other DOB chapters in Boston, Massachusetts; New York City; San Francisco; Los Angeles; and Philadelphia, Pennsylvania, to publish their own newsletters and magazines. For the most part, these publications belong to the activist feminist spirit of the late 1960s and 1970s rather than the assimilationist era of DOB's beginnings in the 1950s.

## The 1970s

The explosion of specifically lesbian publications around 1970 reflects many lesbians' rejection of a cosexual gay community in favor of lesbian feminism and often separatism, perhaps in no small part because of the misogyny lesbians found in some gay men's communities. Publications such as *Lavender Vision* (Boston [1970–1971]), a cosexual, gay nationalist tabloid, were the exception until the late 1980s. Lesbian periodical material is more commonly found in feminist publications, many of which have had lesbian staff members and have included articles by and about lesbians. Lesbian and feminist periodicals were vital to creating lesbian theory, culture, and community in the 1970s, especially among lesbians who lived far from cities with large, visible lesbian populations. Starting in the 1970s, periodicals from Italy to New Zealand covered topics as diverse as film, spirituality, labor unions, sports, coalition politics, sex, and the military.

Prominent among U.S. periodicals in the 1970s were *The Furies* (1972–1973), the short-lived publication of the radical lesbian feminist Furies collective; *Lesbian Tide* (1971–1980), the first all-news lesbian periodical; *Azalea*, subtitled *A Magazine by Third World Lesbians* (1977–1983), which published the work of women from Asia, Africa, and South America, as well as the United States; and *Amazon Quarterly* (1972–1975), the largest (seventy-two pages) and widest-circulating (nine thousand) lesbian publication of the mid-1970s, which focused on literature, art, and other aspects of lesbian culture. A few journal-style lesbian periodicals that began in the 1970s and early 1980s continued publish in the 1990s: *Sinister Wisdom* (1976–), *Common Lives/Lesbian Lives* (1981–), and *Lesbian Ethics* (1984–); many more feminist journals that include lesbian content were founded during the same period, including the scholarly journals *Women's Studies* (1973–), *Atlantis* (Canada [1975–]), *Feminist Studies* (1975–), *Frontiers: A Journal of Women Studies* (1975–), *Hecate* (Australia [1975–]), *Signs: Journal of Women in Culture and Society* (1975–), *Camera Obscura* (1976–), *Fireweed* (Canada [1978–]), *Feminist Review* (England [1979–]), and *Resources for Feminist Research/Documentation Sur la Recherche Féministe* (Canada [1979–]).

The homegrown publication *Lesbian Connection*, initially a mimeographed, stapled newsletter like *Vice Versa*, has published continuously since 1974. The magazine is filled with news items, letters, responses to letters, reviews, and other commentaries from virtually any lesbian who writes to the editors. Continuing to reflect the lesbian-feminist spirit of the 1970s into the 1990s, *Lesbian Connection* (affectionately referred to as Elsie) promotes lesbian-owned businesses, ships free subscriptions to low-income readers, and maintains a list of "Contact Dykes," "women on *LC*'s mailing list who volunteer to provide information to traveling lesbians or new women in town." In 1997 there were more than 1,000 contact dykes in all fifty U.S. states and in twenty-four countries.

## The 1980s

While many of the issues discussed in lesbian periodicals in the 1970s carried over to the 1980s, emphasis and attitudes shifted. Treatment of racism, women of color, bisexuality, and sex are important examples. While racism was discussed in lesbian periodicals throughout the 1970s, the work of lesbians of color was published and distributed much more widely at the end of the decade and in the 1980s, often with an emphasis on racism within lesbian communities. Some lesbian and feminist periodicals published special women-of-color issues, such as *Conditions: Five, The Black Women's Issue* (1979), and *Sinister Wisdom*'s "A Gathering of Spirit (1983)," by and about Native American women. Lesbians of color often emphasized their inability to endorse lesbian separatism because of their shared oppression and affinities with men of color, which led to cosexual enterprises such as *Black/Out* (1986–1989), the publication of the National Coalition of Black Lesbians and Gays.

During the 1970s, many lesbian feminists published their opinions that bisexual women were "sleeping with the enemy," which bisexual activists and writers in the 1980s termed "biphobic." As a national bisexual movement grew in the 1980s, the *Journal of Homosexuality* published three special issues focusing on bisexuality. By 1990, lesbian activist and writer Jan Clausen (1950–) went public in *Out/Look* magazine about "[Her] Interesting Condition: What Does It Mean When a Lesbian Falls in Love with a Man," as lesbian communities across North America argued about "lesbians who fuck men" and an emerging postmodern "queer" sensibility.

As the "sex wars" over pornography and sadomasochism raged in lesbian communities during the 1980s, notable periodicals focused on explicit sexual content with the stated aim of furthering lesbian liberation through sexual freedom. *On Our Backs* (1984–1996) thumbed its politically incorrect nose at the feminist newspaper *off our backs* (1970–) and launched the career of "lesbian sexpert" Susie Bright (1948–). Forthright sexual imagery and language, sometimes including references to butch-femme roles, bondage, or sadomasochism, were also prominent in many personal-relationship ads, which had been a mainstay of many gay men's publications since the 1970s and became a common feature of many lesbian newspapers during the 1980s.

By the late 1980s, in the face of a continuing onslaught from the Religious Right and the devastating AIDS epidemic, many more U.S. periodicals were joint lesbian-and-gay ventures than earlier in the decade or in the 1970s. *OutWeek* (1989–1991) was most famous for "outing" celebrities; *Gay Community News* (1974–), with a national circulation of sixty thousand by the end of the 1980s, delivered news from a radical leftist perspective, highlighting issues such as racism and sexism, as well as homophobia; *Out/Look* (1988–1990) published substantive, controversial, and sometimes sexually explicit material.

## The 1990s

Notable changes in lesbian periodicals in the 1990s had more to do with form than content. Two new genres emerged, the glossy magazine supported by advertising revenues and the independent 'zine. *Deneuve* (1991–), which changed its name to *Curve* after the French actress Catherine Deneuve threatened a lawsuit, set the tone for lesbian glossies, which were far outnumbered by gay men's and cosexual, profit-making glossies. The main focus of the glossies was on white, middle-class, upwardly mobile lesbians and bisexual women; contents included features, letters, advice columns, and music and book reviews. Continuing a trend from the 1980s, the 1990s glossies tended to include at least some explicit sexual content. *Girlfriends* (1994–) carried a different nude centerfold each issue. Gone from these magazines was the didactic political content that was common in many earlier lesbian periodicals.

In the late 1990s, Haworth Press announced the new *Journal of Lesbian Studies*, at the time the only scholarly journal devoted exclusively to lesbians. Journals aligned with the academic queer-theory movement tended to be cosexual, while feminist academic journals published few articles about lesbians relative to their entire contents. By the 1990s, a variety of types of lesbian periodicals were published all over the world, with most coming from Europe and North America; there were also lesbian periodicals in Australia, Japan, New Zealand, Norway, and South Africa, among other countries.

Low-budget, independently published 'zines proliferated both on paper and the Internet during the 1990s. Lesbian 'zines were often associated with the young feminist movement of so-called riot grrrls; other lesbian 'zine writing and editing were done from a "queer" perspective, which included gay men, bisexual people, and transgendered people. It is difficult to estimate the total number of lesbian 'zines because of their small circulation and typically brief life spans, but more than fifty titles were available in the late 1990s in the United States. The punk roots of 'zine publishing influenced the tone of many lesbian 'zines. *I'm So Fucking Beautiful*, *Dork Dyke*, *Fat Girl*, *Femcore*, *Girljock*, *Lezzie Smut*, *Girl Frenzy*, *Girl Luv*, and *Muffmonsters on Prozac* were among many punk-inflected titles.

*Linda Garber*

## Bibliography

Garber, Linda. "Fact or Fiction? Lesbian Identity in *The Ladder*." Unpublished.

———. *Lesbian Sources: A Bibliography of Periodical Articles, 1970–1990*. New York and London: Garland, 1993.

Martin, Del, and Phyllis Lyon. *Lesbian/Woman*. San Francisco: Glide, 1972.

Potter, Clare. *The Lesbian Periodicals Index*. Tallahassee, Fla.: Naiad, 1986.

Streitmatter, Rodger. *Unspeakable: The Rise of the Gay and Lesbian Press in America*. Boston and London: Faber and Faber, 1995.

**See also** Erotica and Pornography; Furies, The; *Ladder, The*; *Lesbian Connection*; Sadomasochism; 'zines

## Phallus

Generally defined as a symbol for the penis. The unpopularity in daily lesbian life of the phallus is matched only, perhaps, by its popularity in lesbian studies. "The phallus" comes originally from anthropological studies of myth, especially the ancient Egyptian legend whereby Isis, unable to locate the genital of her dismembered brother Osiris, builds an artificial version and establishes it as an object of worship. In feminist discourse, "phallic" has always had currency as a metaphorical—and resoundingly derogatory—description of patriarchal power, and many artists developed clitoral and vaginal imagery as alternatives. But it was as a psychoanalytic concept that "the phallus" caught the attention of feminist theory in the 1980s. Since then, lesbian theorists have found in the phallus fertile ground on which to debate the meanings of male power, masculinity and femininity, and heterosexism.

The man most responsible for having introduced the phallus onto the critical stage is undoubtedly French psychoanalyst Jacques Lacan (1901–1981). In "The Meaning of the Phallus" (1958), Lacan reinterprets Sigmund Freud's (1856–1939) concept of castration as a description of the alienated position of the subject, male or female, in language. Lacan argues, moreover, that the phallus (like Isis' statue) is a signifier, the "master" signifier of desire, and that masculine and feminine subjects are differentiated by their unique relationships to the phallus: The former seek to have it, the latter to be it.

The importance of the phallus to Lacan's theory has been called "phallocentrism" and has raised an obvious challenge for feminists—not to mention lesbians, whose sexuality in Lacan's schema appears marginalized at best. Critics of the phallus have taken three tacks: Rose (in Mitchell and Rose, 1982) and Silverman (1992) have argued that Lacan's account is a powerful description not only of the formation of heterosexual identity, but of its impossibility. It is, thus, the critic's duty to analyze and expose that impossibility in its concrete instances. Others, including Gallop (1982) and Irigaray (1985), have emphasized the difference between the phallus and the penis, arguing that phallic power is the pernicious mystification of a more innocuous, penile pleasure. Finally, some lesbian critics want simply to appropriate it, proposing, in Judith Butler's (1992) words, that the phallus's "naturalized link to masculine morphology . . . be called into question through an aggressive reterritorialization." In *The Practice of Love* (1994), Teresa DeLauretis draws her examples of the lesbian phallus from canonical texts, and other commentators, including Lamos (1995), have compared the Freudian discourse on the phallus to popular debates over the political correctness of lesbian sex toys.

*Heather Findlay*

**P**

*Bibliography*

Butler, Judith. "The Lesbian Phallus and the Morphological Imaginary." *differences: A Journal of Feminist Cultural Studies* 4:1 (Spring 1992), 133–171.

Gallop, Jane. *The Daughter's Seduction: Feminism and Psychoanalysis*. Ithaca, N.Y.: Cornell University Press, 1982.

Irigaray, Luce. *This Sex Which Is Not One*. Ithaca, N.Y.: Cornell University Press, 1985.

Lamos, Colleen. "Taking on the Phallus." In *Lesbian Erotics*. Ed. Karla Jay. New York: New York University Press, 1995.

Mitchell, Juliet, and Jacqueline Rose, eds. *Feminine Sexuality: Jacques Lacan and the École Freudienne*. New York: Norton, 1982.

Silverman, Kaja. *Male Subjectivity at the Margins*. New York: Routledge, 1992.

*See also* Clitoris; Critical Theory; Psychoanalysis; Queer Theory; Sexuality

## Philippines

Located in Southeast Asia, the Philippines is the only predominantly Christian country in Asia and the third-largest Catholic country in the world. The Philippine archipelago is composed of 7,107 islands and is inhabited by 68 million people, making it one of the most densely populated countries in the world.

The Portuguese navigator Ferdinand Magellan (ca. 1480–1521) landed on Philippine shores in 1521 in his search for the fabled Spice Islands and promptly claimed it in honor of his benefactor, King Philip of Spain. The Spanish colonization would last for more than three hundred years until the turn of the twentieth century, when the American occupation began. The "conquistadores" systematically condemned all customs and behaviors that were not in keeping with their own spiritual and moral standards. The Spanish civil code curtailed the freedom of women to engage in, and decide on, political and economic activities. Despite major changes in the 1987 Philippine constitution, ratified after the fall of President Ferdinand Marcos (1917–1989) in 1986, the Catholic Church has continued to exert a strong influence in the formulation of laws and policies in the land. Lesbianism is not a crime in the Philippines, but lesbianism or homosexuality is a ground for legal separation or annulment in the Family Code enacted into law in 1988.

Based on accounts by traders and visitors centuries before the colonial period, Filipino women were held in high social esteem. Women in tribal communities possessed numerous skills and were honored for their contribution to their community as guardians of their progeny. It was the woman's prerogative to name her children, keep her name, and freely dispose of her property by birthright even after marriage. Male and female children were also given equal value. Women could become *barangay* (basic political unit) chiefs. Women functioned as *babaylans* (native priestesses), who took charge of the important tribal rites related to the start of the seasons, healing, death, and other spiritual activities. In the absence of women, it was said that some men wore women's clothes to take the role of the *babaylan*.

The most famous of these precolonial chiefs was Princess Urduja, who was known for her skill in armed combat and her intelligence. While there is no proof that she engaged in women-identified relationships, she never had a relationship with any man either. Legend says that she once stated that she would get married only to someone who could defeat her in combat.

There are no documented records of women-identified relationships, only stories handed down from generation to generation of communities of women or spinsters living together. However, there is proof that women-to-women relationships might have existed since precolonial times.

In Mindanao, an island located in the southern part of the Philippines, there is an indigenous tribe called the Badjao; it does not have an equivalent word for lesbian but does have a word for vaginal manipulation by another woman: *agkul-lit* or *kul-lit*. In southern Luzon, in the province of Quezon, there are women-only spiritual communities that have existed along the foot of the mystical Mount Banahaw for years. While there have been no studies on whether lesbian relationships have been formed here, at the very least it is likely that women-identified friendships have been formed.

Some of the words used to describe woman-loving-women or woman-to-woman relationships were formed in relation to men. An example would be *binalake*, wherein the words *babae* (woman) and *lalaki* (man) were put together. Around the turn of the twentieth century, when exclusive girls' schools were put up by Catholic convents to educate the daughters of the upper class, the word *byuts* was coined to refer to both the relationship and the sexual identity of the women.

In the twentieth century, lesbians have been rendered invisible, except for occasional stories about cross-dressing women living with their wives or spinsters living together for years. The public understanding of lesbians has largely been limited to the tomboy stereotype.

While women-loving-women groups have existed for a long time, they are mostly social or business related and very private in nature. Only a very few lesbians have dared talk about their lives in print and media. In the mid-1980s, exclusive lesbian dance parties came into fashion. These "women's parties" were patronized by mostly middle- and upper-class lesbians who operated an informal information network. For some women, this was as "out" as they would ever get and provided the only access to lesbian culture they would ever know.

It was only in the late 1980s and the 1990s that some lesbians in the women's movement began to group together politically over issues of lesbianism and sexuality. In 1993, a small contingent of mostly lesbian feminists joined the International Women's Day March in Manila and read a statement during the program. Subsequently, a number of lesbian rights groups were formed. By the late 1990s, there were more than a dozen lesbian groups around the country, as well as many mixed gay and lesbian groups. In December 1996, three lesbian groups—the Womyn Supporting Womyn Committee (now Centre), the Group, and LesBond—initiated the First National Lesbian Rights Conference (FNLRC '96). More than two hundred lesbians participated in the entire process, which included regional and sectoral consultations. This was the first time the Filipina lesbians from all over the country were able to come together to talk about their situation and collectively address lesbian rights issues.

*Giney Villar*

### Bibliography

Marin, Malu. "Stolen Strands: The In and Out Lives of Lesbians in the Philippines." In *Amazon to Zami: Towards a Global Lesbian Feminism.* Ed. Monika Reinfelder. London: Cassell, 1996, pp. 30–55.

*See also* Asian Lesbian Network; Tomboy

## Philips, Katherine (1632–1664)

English poet and playwright, known as "The Matchless Orinda." Widely recognized for her poems of

*Katherine Philips, frontispiece to the 1667 edition of her poems. Courtesy of Harriette Andreadis.*

female friendship, Katherine Philips was the first English female poet to achieve a considerable reputation in her own time. Praised by male writers such as Abraham Cowley (1618–1667), John Dryden (1631–1700), Andrew Marvell (1621–1678), and John Keats (1795–1821), she was admired, imitated, and emulated as a model for female literary accomplishment by subsequent generations of English women writers, among whom were Aphra Behn (1640?–1689), Delariviere Manley (1671?–1724), and Jane Barker (n.d.).

Born Katherine Fowler, the daughter of a prosperous London cloth merchant, she was educated at Mrs. Salmon's school for girls. When she was sixteen she married James Philips, fifty-four, a supporter of Oliver Cromwell (1599–1658), who brought her to Cardigan Priory on the remote west coast of Wales. Katherine Philips's royalist politics, literary ambitions, and desire for London's cultural amenities led her to seek friendships and patronage for herself and preferment for her husband at court after the Restoration. Among her writings are poems to royalty and to various aristocratic women, translations from the French of two plays by Pierre

Corneille (1606–1684), and a volume of letters edited by her friend and literary executor, Sir Charles Cotterell; it is in these writings that she expresses her concerns with politics and court activities.

Philips's school friends Anne Owen (1633–1692) and Mary Aubrey (1631–?), whom she addresses in a fashionably pseudoclassical manner as Lucasia and Rosania, provided an emotional focus both for her most successful poetry and for her life; they also provided a model for later friendships, though the poems she wrote to others were less successful than those to Lucasia and Rosania, perhaps because they lacked the same impassioned impulse. Among the most admired of her poems are "To my Lucasia, in defence of declared friendship"; "To My excellent Lucasia, on our Friendship"; "Friendship in Emblem, or the Seale, to my dearest Lucasia"; and "Orinda to Lucasia parting, October 1661, at London." In these poems, and in others, Philips uses the conventions of her time—for example, the excesively mannered pastoralism of then-fashionable préciosité (a style emphasizing elegance in language and manners), the sentiments of John Donne's (1573–1631) metaphysical school platonism, and the poetic forms used by male contemporaries in addressing their female lovers to express an intensely passionate and eroticized version of platonic love in female same-sex friendship. Her letters to Sir Charles, published in 1705, also express the intensity of her attachments to women; when Anne Owen marries a man of whom Philips disapproves, she writes, bitterly: "I find too there are few Friendships in the World Marriage—proof. . . . We may generally conclude the Marriage of a Friend to be the Funeral of a Friendship."

Philips's writings and life have been read by twentieth-century readers as lesbian. How the eroticism of this experience might have been understood by contemporaries, despite its modern-seeming articulation in Philips's poems and letters, is difficult to assess. Until scholarship provides a more complete understanding of the construction of sexuality during this period, one can conclude that Philips offers the prototype of an eroticized "romantic friendship" among respectable women in early-modern England. *Harriette Andreadis*

### Bibliography

Andreadis, Harriette. "The Sapphic-Platonics of Katherine Philips, 1632–1664." *Signs: Journal of Women in Culture and Society* 15:1 (Autumn 1989), 34–60.

Souers, Philip Webster. *The Matchless Orinda*. Cambridge, Mass.: Harvard University Press, 1931.

*See also* Behn, Aphra; Romantic Friendship; Sapphic Tradition

## Philosophy

Branch of the humanities that pursues the fundamental questions of what exists, what is worthwhile, and what can be known about either. Lesbian philosophy reflects on lesbian existence, the values of lesbian lives, and what lesbians can know. It also reflects on the universe (not just the lesbians in it) from lesbian perspectives.

### Traditional Philosophy

European philosophy has four traditional core areas. They are metaphysics (on reality and the meaning of existence), epistemology (on belief, knowledge, and truth), ethics (on right and wrong, good and bad, virtue and vice), and logic (on valid and invalid, sound and unsound, reasoning). There are also special area philosophies, such as philosophy of science, philosophy of language, and political philosophy. Philosophical movements are often identified by historical period, geographical location, or culture. The most abstract questions in any academic discipline tend to be philosophical. Lesbian philosophy comprehends both philosophy in general as pursued within lesbian cultures and philosophical reflection specifically on the meanings of lesbian existence, whether within lesbian cultures or in less friendly contexts. Both kinds of lesbian philosophy have expanded the repertoire of topics, questions, and issues subject to philosophical investigation.

Philosophy's chief method of investigation is reflection on data of everyday life. Its objectives are to understand basic concepts (such as reality, freedom, value, mind, and body) and gain insight into oneself and one's surroundings. Most academically archived philosophy comes from privileged men with leisure to reflect. They tend to center their points of view, unself-consciously, ignoring points of view of less privileged people. Against this background, lesbian philosophers self-consciously center lesbian lives, proposing theories to make sense of everyday lesbian living from the perspectives of those whose experience it is. Academic lesbian philosophy has flourished mainly since the late 1960s. It was preceded by informal philosophy published in periodicals of lesbian culture by lesbians often not trained as academic philosophers (although some were). This informal tradition continues alongside academic philosophy. There is interesting communication and overlap between the traditions.

Traditional academic philosophy has given some attention to same-sex love. Some ancients affirmed it. Modern European philosophers before the twentieth century, however, did not. Even the ancients usually ignored females. And the focus everywhere is almost entirely on sex. What is distinctive about lesbian philosophy flourishing in the last third of the twentieth century is, first, that it is lesbian affirming. Second, it centers females. Third, it does not focus only on sexuality but often includes other aspects of intimate bonding among women, such as the economics of domestic partnership and the politics of bonding across ethnic and class divisions.

Traditional academic philosophy in Europe, following Aristotle, treats metaphysics as "First Philosophy." This means that it regards metaphysics as the most basic field on which others (such as ethics) are based. For lesbians, however, moral and political philosophy plays the role of "First Philosophy." Lesbian political liberation, especially in North America and Europe, has been the most salient phenomenon of twentieth century lesbian life. Thus, it is not surprising that most contemporary lesbian philosophy begins from ethical and political concerns. Yet there is also a growing body of lesbian philosophy of science, exploring meanings of hypotheses regarding sources of lesbian desire. Such inquiries often grow out of concern to criticize the idea that same-sex intimacy is unnatural, an idea historically central to ethical rejections of lesbian relationships. A related concern is to evaluate the idea that lesbianism is a choice. As a choice, lesbian lives become subject to ethical evaluation and possible defense. Whether it makes sense to consider it a choice, or whether sexual or erotic orientations can be determined only by causes beyond one's control, is an issue on which lesbian philosophers disagree. Part of the issue is whether one's feelings and desires are the sorts of things one can control, change, or modify. Questions about the values of lesbian community also lead easily to questions about meanings of "lesbian." Some such questions are: Is a lesbian a woman? a female homosexual? Must lesbian relationships be sexual? Is sex (between females) sufficient to make a relationship lesbian? Can "lesbian" be meaningfully applied in cultures (for example, of precontact Native Americans)

whose languages did not mark the same distinctions as European cultures? One philosophically sensitive gay historian avoids the terms "lesbian," "gay," and "marriage" when writing about premodern Europeans, preferring the more noncommittal "same-sex unions." When investigators lack adequate written primary source material in lesbian history, philosophical questions about what one can know and how one can know it become especially acute. Many philosophical questions mentioned above arise in attempts to evaluate the hypothesis of some social constructionists that, prior to the late nineteenth century, there were no lesbians, gays, or homosexuals (although there were same-sex erotic attractions and interactions).

Not all questions of lesbian philosophy are determined by prejudices of heterosexist culture. Many arise internally within lesbian communities and relationships. They need not presuppose a hostile background society. The nature of friendship and its relation to justice is such a topic. Whether ideal lover relationships would be sexually exclusive is another. Yet another is how the meanings of sexuality and eroticism are related and also distinguishable.

## Lesbian Philosophy

Some issues of lesbian philosophy arise because of hostilities within lesbian relationships and communities. Examples are what should count as domestic abuse, how to distinguish between abuse and legitimate self-defense, and when, if ever, violent self-defense is justifiable. Lesbian abuse of lesbians is sometimes called "horizontal," assuming the lesbians' social power is roughly equal; abuse of lesbians by others is called "vertical," assuming the others are more powerful. How horizontal abuse is related to vertical abuse raises both philosophical and empirical questions. Empirical ones are about causes, and philosophical ones are about meanings of basic concepts, such as "lesbian" and "abuse."

Most lesbian philosophy in the last third of the twentieth century is also feminist. Feminism has challenged heterosexism in patriarchal cultures. Thus, one might expect feminism to lead naturally to lesbian philosophy. Yet, historically, it has often been the other way around. The challenges of lesbian living have motivated many to engage in feminist theorizing of the most radical sorts and to challenge less radical feminists to be more inclusive and not be deterred by fear of "the lavender menace." For feminists, reproductive concerns need not be central to long-term intimate bonding or to many enactments

**P** of sexual desire. When reproduction is not in question, what counts as "sexual behavior" can become problematic. Thus, disagreements among lesbian philosophers over the centrality of sexual interaction to lesbian relationships are partly about the meaning of "sexual interaction" and do not always, or necessarily, reflect differences of value priority regarding the physical and sensual aspects of relationships.

Lesbian philosophy overlaps both gay and queer philosophy. Gay philosophy developed in the United States from the homophile movement of the 1950s. It takes as its basic data for theorizing the everyday lives of women and men in same-sex intimate relationships, aiming to pursue issues common to both sexes. But often, in fact, it has treated men's lives as paradigmatic. Its concerns have been more with legal reform than with political revolution. It tends to emphasize sexuality more than lesbian philosophy often does. And it has not always been sensitive to feminist concerns. Thus, lesbian philosophy that emphasizes feminist and revolutionary concerns and problematizes sexuality is not redundant in relation to gay philosophy. Relations of women and men to patriarchal cultures have been historically different, yielding different problems.

Queer philosophy developed in the United States from AIDS activism in the 1980s. It aims to be more inclusive than gay philosophy. It comprehends not only sexual-orientation issues defined by the sex of one's partner but also issues of transgendering, sadomasochism, and, in general, more ways of classifying sexual desire than simply by the sex or gender of one's partner. Like gay philosophy, it tends to center sexuality. But, unlike gay philosophy, it is less ready to take for granted that we all know what counts as sexual experience. It has sometimes been more receptive than gay philosophy to feminist concerns. Some lesbian philosophers also think of themselves as queer or as gay. Still, lesbian philosophy is not reducible to a branch of either gay philosophy or queer philosophy, although it shares some common concerns with each.

Feminist lesbian philosophy has been inclusive along other dimensions. It has developed through reflection on intersections of lesbian identities with race and class identities. It includes reflections on the experiences of disabled and physically challenged lesbians. There is at least as much overlap of feminist lesbian philosophy with antiracism, anticapitalism, and movements of respect for the disabled and physically challenged as there is with gay and queer philosophy. Feminist lesbian philosophers draw on many politically insurgent literatures in pondering difficulties of theorizing across differences among lesbians, integrating multiple identities in lesbian lives, and exploring meanings and fluidities of social identities, many of which arise out of contexts of oppression. Whether "lesbian" is such an identity—whether there would be the concept "lesbian" in a society free of oppression—is an issue on which lesbian philosophers disagree.

*Claudia Card*

### Bibliography

Allen, Jeffner. *Lesbian Philosophy*. Palo Alto, Calif.: Institute of Lesbian Studies, 1986.

Beauvoir, Simone de. *Le deuxieme sex* (The Second Sex). 2 vols. Paris: Gallimard, 1949, Vol. 1, pp. 481–510.

Butler, Judith. *Gender Trouble: The Subversion of Identity*. New York: Routledge, 1990.

Calhoun, Cheshire. "Separating Lesbian Theory from Feminist Theory." *Ethics* 104 (1994), 558–581.

Card, Claudia, ed. *Adventures in Lesbian Philosophy*. Bloomington: Indiana University Press, 1994.

Daly, Mary. *Pure Lust: Elemental Feminist Philosophy*. Boston: Beacon, 1984.

Frye, Marilyn. *The Politics of Reality: Essays in Feminist Theory*. Trumansburg, N.Y.: Crossing, 1983.

*See also* Beauvoir, Simone de; Ethics; Lesbian Feminism; Political Theory

## Photography

No stylistic concerns unite the work of lesbian photographers, although most have produced self-portraits and portraits of their lovers, reflecting their interest in identity and relationships. Those who worked prior to the late 1960s did so in isolation from other lesbian photographers and seemed to have no knowledge of one another. Commissioned portraits purchased by the subject were the only lesbian-themed work for which they were paid.

### History

The history of lesbian photography is one of naming artists as lesbian, reclaiming women for whom the necessity to hide their love of women was paramount. Much of that history is hidden in scrapbooks and will never be exhibited as art. Yet personal photos by les-

*Sinister Wisdom. Photo by Tee A. Corinne.*

bians famous for other activities reflect their desire to portray otherwise hidden aspects of their lives.

Writer Natalie Barney (1876–1972) made nude pictures of herself and her lovers between 1897 and 1901. Gertrude Stein (1874–1946) photographed her intimate friends smoking cigarettes together in 1903. Art collector Etta Cone (1870–1949) used a box camera to document herself and her new love reflected in a mirror in 1913. Painter Romaine Brooks (1874–1970) photographed herself with her newest love, Natalie Barney, around 1915. Images of less famous women—like those in Mabel Hampton's (1902–1989) African American friendship circle—have been saved through the work of lesbian and gay archives.

U.S.-born E. Jane Gay (1830–1919) took up photography to document the work of anthropologist Alice Fletcher (1838–1923) for whom she had an unrequited love. In a small-group photograph, Gay recorded herself preparing a meal at their campsite while Fletcher washed clothes and the Nez Perce translator carried buckets of water.

Edith Watson (1861–1943), an early photojournalist, traveled across Canada working on articles with her lover, Victoria Hayward (1876–1956). She photographed Hayward in the Bahamas lifting her long skirts away from the waves. Watson's contemporary, Alice Austen (1866–1952), lived on inherited money while documenting the upper middle class on Staten Island, immigrants on Ellis Island, and workers in Manhattan. Jessie Lillian Buckland (1878–1939) maintained a professional studio in Akaroa, New Zealand. Buckland, like Alice Austen, made self-portraits in which she dressed in male clothing.

Photographs by bisexual Margarethe Mather (ca. 1885–1952), a business partner of photographer Edward Weston (1886–1958), are elegant and spare. Another bisexual, Hannah Hoch (1889–1978), German and associated with the dada movement in art, pasted photographic reproductions together as commentaries on politics, culture, and gender in the 1920s and 1930s.

In Paris during the 1920s, American midwesterner Berenice Abbott (1898–1991) photographed expatriate lesbians and other literary figures. Gisèle Freund (1912–), German and Jewish, photographed many of the same individuals a decade later. During the 1930s, Laura Gilpin (1891–1979), famous for

P her photographs of the American Southwest, made gentle portraits of her beloved companion, Betsy Forster (1886–1972), a nurse working with the Navajo. In Paris, her French Jewish contemporary, surrealist Claude Cahun (1894–1954), constructed complex self-portraits that experimented with gender roles and styles.

Because of the ways in which lesbianism has been hidden, any history of lesbian photography has unanswered questions and lines of inquiry that result in dead ends. For instance, was Lady Clementina Hawarden (1822–1965) bisexual, as her photographs suggest? The answer remains hidden. Was the early photojournalist Frances Benjamin Johnston (1864–1952) a lesbian? The care she took to destroy her personal papers has, thus far, totally obscured her private life.

## Lesbian Publications and Exhibitions

By the 1960s, there was an international art market for photographs, but no place within it for lesbian photographers making lesbian-themed photographs. The self-conscious history of lesbian photography in the United States began with *The Ladder* (1956–1972), a small magazine published by an educational and social group, the Daughters of Bilitis. Kay Lahusen [Tobin] (1930–) photographed political events, especially those in which her lover, activist Barbara Gittings (1932–), was involved. When Gittings became editor of *The Ladder*, they worked together to publish photographs of lesbians on the magazine's cover. This was the first time images of lesbians were published outside of sensationalized tabloid articles.

In the 1970s, lesbian-themed newspapers and small magazines began to flourish, supported by a growing network of women's bookstores. With these publications as outlets for their prints, photography became the medium of choice for many artists. JEB (Joan E. Biren [1944–]) was associated first with the Furies collective and newspaper and then with the feminist newspaper *off our backs*, both published out of Washington, D.C. On the U.S. West Coast, Cathy Cade (1942–) worked with the San Francisco Bay Area paper *Plexus* and became especially known for images of lesbian-parented families. JEB and Cade self-published photographic books whose pictures came to represent the public image of activist lesbianism. Diversity of age and race, participation in cultural institutions, lesbian mothering, separatist communal life, and spirituality emerged as recurrent themes.

Although JEB and Cade are known because of their books, hundreds of photographers working through dozens of periodicals made the dream of a lesbian nation a visual reality. Senior among lesbian photographers who came out within the women's movement is Ruth Mountaingrove (1923–), whose images, often published in *WomanSpirit* magazine, were associated with the women's back-to-the-land movements. Along with Tee A. Corinne (1943–), Jan Phillips (1949–), and others, Mountaingrove founded the *Blatant Image*: *A Magazine of Feminist Photography* (1981–1983), which showcased lesbian-content imagery and published articles on lesbian aesthetics.

Sexual imagery was often contested territory in the 1970s; however, Corinne, known early for her *Sinister Wisdom* poster (1977), and Honey Lee Cottrell (1945–) developed strategies for publishing and exhibiting graphically explicit photographs. Both were associated with the U.S. West Coast populist sex-education movement and later with *On Our Backs*, a lesbian sex magazine. Morgan Gwenwald (1950–) and Joyce Culver (1947–) produced images of butch-femme romance, and Gwenwald created an early network of activist image makers through *The Lesbian Photography Directory* (1982). Later, subtle and overt sexual imagery was advanced by French-born Laurence Jaugey-Paget (1965–), who created stylish, erotic photographs.

As a counterbalance to lesbian-as-the-girl-next-door imagery supported by early feminism—itself a reaction against images of lesbians as unhealthy predators—photographers such as Della Grace (also known as Del (la) Grace Volcano) (1957–) and Catherine Opie (1961–) began publishing images of lesbian decadence, with an emphasis on drug and bar cultures, public toilet sex, and sadomasochistic activities.

Some photographers, such as Laura Aguilar (1959–), used curating—as well as publishing and exhibiting—to reach national and international audiences. Aguilar's best-known photographs include a series titled *Latina Lesbians*. Her willingness to expose her own large body and to incorporate cultural signifiers—once binding herself with the Mexican and American flags—earned respect from diverse critics.

## Global Photographers

By the mid-1980s, as a direct result of lesbian, gay, and queer studies courses, university-trained lesbian photographers produced work that reflected postmodern theoretical concerns. The images were often layered and fragmented and frequently included words or texts. Representative examples include the work of critic and photographer Deborah Bright (1950–), who inserted intellectually intriguing, butch-appearing self-portraits into Hollywood movie stills. British photographers Jean Fraser and Tessa Boffin, working within a similar intellectual framework, crafted photographs reminiscent of early-twentieth-century living-tableau performances.

Continuing in the documentary tradition established by JEB and Cathy Cade, but broadening it to include images of gay men, as well as lesbians, Nancy Andrews (1963–), a photojournalist working with a national gay and lesbian newspaper, used oral histories and photographs to explore the lives of a cross-section of ordinary lesbians and gay men. Allowing the photos alone to tell the stories, Carolyn Vaughan (1945–) intermixed images of lesbian and gay male couples with heterosexual portraits, still lifes, and landscapes. Ann Meredith (1948–), who in the early 1980s photographed lesbians with their dogs, later concentrated on images of lesbians with AIDS.

Canadian Ann Pearson (1935–) produced a popular butch-femme spoof that was published initially in *The Furies* (1972). Pearson worked in film, documentary, and art photography and published in *Fireweed* magazine. Other prominent Canadian lesbian photographers include Cyndra MacDowell (1953–), who concentrated on emotive body and sexual imagery, and Nina Levitt (1955–), who altered images appropriated from lesbian popular fiction. Early in the 1990s, Vancouver photographer Susan Steward (1952–), working collaboratively with Persimmon Blackbridge (1951–) and Lizard Jones (1961–) under the name "Kiss & Tell," produced an exhibit and book in which viewers were asked to choose where to draw the line in censoring sexual imagery.

Beginning in the 1970s in Britain, the news journal *Spare Rib* published documentarians Val Wimer (1941–), Maggie Murray (1942–), Pam Isherwood (1949–), and Brenda Prince (1950–). They later founded Format, a feminist photo agency. Jill Posener (1953–) initially photographed activist-inspired billboard graffiti but, in the 1980s, produced images of overt sexuality. In London, Rosy Martin (1946–), who often worked with the heterosexual photographer Jo Spence (1934–1992), explored identity and photography as therapy.

Ingrid Pollard (1953–), working with the complex intersections formed by being black and les-bian, portrayed vulnerability through combined text and imagery. Two of the early women of color to publish erotic imagery were Parminder Sekhon (1968–), who published in British journals like *Wickers and Bullers*, a magazine for black lesbians and gay men, and Lola Flash (1969–), an African American who worked in Britain. Flash specialized in arbitrarily colored, surrealist-appearing photographs, which received wide distribution as book-cover art.

In Australia, Bombay-born Lariane Fonseca (1951–) published color close-ups of flowers that vibrated with symbolic erotic imagery. Her contemporaries C. Moore Hardy (1955–) and Marion Moore (1958–) documented private activities and public events while also developing a line of more complex, fine art–oriented images. Fiona Arnold (1958–) and Tina Fiveash (1970–) independently developed forms of social commentary–inspired humor.

In New Zealand, the feminist magazine *Spiral* gave lesbians a public forum. Barbara McDonald (1948–) was an early documenter of women's events, and Anne Mein (1968–) produced erotic images that echoed Rodin's work in late-twentieth-century surroundings. Fiona Clark (1954–) and Jane Zusters (1951–) specialized in journalistic and portrait work.

The imagery of some Dutch lesbian photographers was published as postcards. For two years around 1980, lovers Diana Blok (1952–) and Marlo Broekmans (1953–) collaborated on evocative self-portraits with overt sexual references. Working in a journalistic style, Gon Buurman (1939–) produced psychologically moody portraits of a broad range of women, including women in nightclubs, older couples, and disabled lesbian lovers.

In the 1980s, lesbian artists of color established exhibition sites and publications, sometimes in conjunction with gay men of color. Lebanese American photographer L.A. "Happy" Hyder (1947–) championed the inclusion of work by lesbians of color in exhibitions like *The Dynamics of Color: Lesbian Artists Respond to Racism* (San Francisco, California, 1990), which featured the photographs of Julia Youngblood (1962–), Catalina Govea (1952–), and Victoria Lena Manyarrows (1956–), among others. Hyder also organized Lesbian Visual Artists, whose newsletter networked lesbian artists internationally.

Navajo/Creek/Seminole photographer Hulleah Tsinhnahjinnie (1954–) created an urban Indian icon with the image of a woman in Native garb standing beside a motorcycle, which was published

P on the cover of *Living the Spirit* (1988), an anthology. Roberta Almerez (1953–), of Puerto Rican and Filipino descent, used clarity and humor in group portraits published in *Between the Lines* (1987) and later in the journal *conmoción*. Canadian Ka Yin Fong (1968–) and American Jacquelyn Ching (1958–) reached international audiences through the groundbreaking anthology *The Very Inside* (1994), as Gaye Chan (1957–) did through *Amethyst* (1991) and *Asian American Sexualities* (1996).

Portraiture, especially of lesbian and feminist authors, provided both a service for the subjects and a way of exploring the visual identity for photographers Jean Weisinger (1954–), of African American and Native American descent, and Theresa Thadani (1960–), of Japanese and Indian descent. Of special note are Weisinger's images of writer Alice Walker (1944–) and Thadani's images of writer Chea Villanueva (1952–).

Throughout the 1990s, lesbians continued to make personal and public photographs. Although some lesbian photographers developed mainstream reputations, the most prominent among them, like their predecessors, hid their love of women. Yet, because of social changes that had occurred since the 1960s, many openly lesbian photographers published imagery that accurately reflected their lives. Gay Pride marches, "Dykes on Bikes," women in couples, sports, identity, and sexuality emerged as primary themes in their work.      *Tee A. Corinne*

### Bibliography

Ashburn, Elizabeth. *Lesbian Art: An Encounter with Power*. Roseville East, New South Wales, Australia: Craftsman House, 1996.

Boffin, Tessa, and Jean Fraser, eds. *Stolen Glances: Lesbians Take Photographs*. London: Pandora and San Francisco: HarperSanFrancisco, 1991.

Bright, Susie, and Jill Posener, eds. *Nothing but the Girl: The Blatant Lesbian Image*. London and New York: Freedom Editions/Cassell, 1996.

Fernie, Lynne, Dinah Forbes, and Joyce Mason, eds. *Sight Specific: Lesbians and Representation*. Toronto: A Space, 1988.

Gates, Beatrix, ed. *The Wild Good: Lesbian Photographs and Writing on Love*. New York: Anchor/Doubleday, 1996.

Kelley, Caffyn, ed. *Forbidden Subjects: Self-Portraits by Lesbian Artists*. North Vancouver, B.C.: Gallerie, 1992.

McPherson, Heather, Julie King, Marian Evans, and Pamela Gerrish Nunn, eds. *Spiral 7: A Collection of Lesbian Art and Writing from Aotearoa/New Zealand*. Wellington, New Zealand: Spiral, 1992.

Soares, M.G., ed. *Butch/Femme*. New York: Crown, 1995.

Weiss, Andrea. *Paris Was a Woman*. San Francisco: HarperSanFrancisco, 1995.

*See also* Art, Contemporary European; Art, Contemporary North American; Austen, Alice

## Physical Education

Profession teaching sport and physical activity skills. Physical education has been considered a haven for lesbians, both stereotypically and within lesbian lore. It is during physical education that young women are provided role models of strong, physically active women.

## History

Throughout the history of women's physical education, there has been a strong emphasis on "moderation." Although focused on a women-centered philosophy of physical education, the women educators also stressed prevention of the "masculinizing" effects of sport. These notions emanated from their attempts to gain respect within the predominantly male physical education profession of the late 1800s, when women began to enter the profession. The early physical educators also emphasized upper-class notions of femininity, which emanated from early Victorian ideals, stressing strictly defined gender roles. Since physical activity was considered masculine at that time, the female physical educators developed policies and philosophies to minimize negative perceptions. By the 1920s, female physical educators were extremely worried about the masculinization of young women in sport; thus, they condemned competitive sport activities for women, emphasizing, rather, the credo "a sport for every girl, and every girl in a sport." Strenuous competition was deemed incompatible with femininity, so it was discouraged. Sport rules were changed for girls and women—examples include restricting physical contact and shortening game time—so that competitiveness and activity were minimized.

Ironically, it was the philosophy and actions of the female physical educators of the early 1900s, focused on the concerns about the overly masculine nature of sport and its inappropriateness for young women, that led to many of the late-twentieth-century stereotypes about female physical educators and athletes. Initially, sexual concerns emanated from the belief that sport may lead young women to loosen their inhibitions toward men. Yet, by the 1930s, this concern turned toward the view of female athletic behavior as a sign of failed heterosexuality—witness the stereotypes of the "muscle moll" or "damaged mother." In the 1940s, vague and indirect concerns about lesbians in physical education emerged; in the post–World War II era, those concerns were stated overtly. By the 1950s, the stereotype of the "mannish lesbian physical educator" loomed over the profession. Those perceptions led to an even greater focus on sport and physical activities deemed appropriately feminine. Many female physical educators adopted apologetic behavior, displaying overt signs of femininity in their dress and behaviors to divert any accusation of masculine demeanor. It was not unusual for females with short hair or obvious lesbian relationships to be expelled from physical education programs.

This atmosphere in women's physical education created a climate in which homophobia and heterosexism became common. Even in the 1990s, negative stereotypes continued to be widespread, and positive images of lesbians in physical education, sport, and physical activity were rare. The stereotype that all female physical educators are lesbians creates an uneasy environment in which accusations of lesbianism may be used to threaten and harass women in the profession. Common stereotypes that directly affect lesbian physical educators include the belief that lesbians will molest or make sexual advances toward students or will attempt to recruit students to a lesbian lifestyle. These stereotypes are especially salient in physical education because lesbian physical educators often are physically close to their students, supervise locker rooms (including showers), and are in a more open environment than traditional classroom teachers. These conditions make them prime targets of homophobia. Knowing that parents, students, and colleagues may hold stereotypical beliefs, most lesbian physical educators carefully hide their lesbian identity when at school or with other people from school.

Most remain closeted and silent about being a lesbian because they assume that there will be considerable negative consequences should their lesbian identity become known. They may feel that if it were known that they are lesbians, they would lose their job or lose credibility with their colleagues and students. Fear of exposure as a lesbian is described as constant, and it influences most job-related decisions.

## Survival Strategies

Lesbian physical educators have described a variety of identity-management strategies to conceal their lesbian identities. Some women may choose to remain closeted from colleagues and students. "Passing" is a strategy in which lesbians lead others to believe that they are heterosexual. "Covering" involves censoring personal information, maintaining personal distance, and avoiding personal conversations and social settings where people commonly share personal aspects of their lives. Using passing or covering strategies leads physical educators to separate their personal and public identities—often deemed a professional survival strategy in which one can act as a lesbian in private situations but as a nonlesbian in public situations. "Implicitly out" lesbians will share personal information yet not use gendered pronouns or directly acknowledge that they are lesbians. It is assumed that the physical educator is a lesbian, although direct disclosure has not occurred. "Explicitly out" physical educators, on the other hand, directly state to others that they are lesbians, and "publicly out" lesbians are open about their sexual orientation to the entire community.

Although most physical educators who have been interviewed for research studies are not comfortable concealing their lesbian identities, they express fear of repercussions if exposed as lesbians. Constantly hiding their lesbian identity results in high levels of stress. These educators expend a tremendous amount of energy to create this public facade, and it affects their relationships with their colleagues and students. They also miss out on much needed social support when others do not know their true identity.

## Role Models

Many physical educators feel powerless to challenge homophobia when it is experienced. To do so would jeopardize exposure of their own lesbian identity and perhaps lead to much more adverse repercussions. However, continued hiding of lesbian identities further contributes to an "enforced silence" in which issues related to homophobia and lesbians in physical education are not addressed. This silence perpetuates negative stereotypes of lesbians and further oppresses lesbian physical educators. It also reduces the possibility of students having positive lesbian role models or learning positive attitudes toward lesbians. However, on a positive note, as more gay and lesbian athletes come out, they serve as role models for physical educators and their colleagues and students. Similarly, college and university professors of physical education and exercise science are coming out and educating others about lesbians in physical education and sport. As more gay and lesbian physical educators become empowered to come out, they help create a more supportive climate in physical education and can serve as positive role models for nonheterosexual and heterosexual students.

Interestingly, lesbian physical educators have become somewhat of an enigma in lesbian lore. Although they remain mostly closeted, many young girls look to their "gym teachers" as role models of strong women. The theme of young crushes on gym teachers is common among coming out stories and has been codified in feminist folksinger Meg Christian's song "Ode to a Gym Teacher" (1974). Perhaps it is because of the all-female environment of physical education, and the ability of lesbian physical educators to break down stereotypes about female sport abilities, that leads young students to admire and emulate them. As Christian's song goes: "She was a big tough woman / the first to come along / that showed me being female / meant you still could be strong."    *Victoria Krane*

### Bibliography

Cahn, Susan K. *Coming on Strong: Gender and Sexuality in Twentieth-Century Women's Sport*. New York: Free Press, 1994.

Griffin, Pat. "Identity Management Strategies Among Lesbian and Gay Educators." *Qualitative Studies in Education* 4 (1991), 189–202.

Lenskyj, Helen. "Power and Play: Gender and Sexuality Issues in Sport and Physical Activity." *International Review for Sociology of Sport* 25 (1990), 235–245.

Squires, Sarah L., and Andrew C. Sparkes. "Circles of Silence: Sexual Identity in Physical Education and Sport." *Sport, Education, and Society* 1 (1996), 77–102.

Woods, Sherry. "Describing the Experiences of Lesbian Physical Educators: A Phenomenological Study." In *Research in Physical Education and Sport: Exploring Alternate Visions*. Ed. Andrew C. Sparkes. Washington, D.C.: Falmer, 1992, pp. 90–117.

*See also* Athletics, Collegiate; Sports, Professional; Teachers

## Pirie, Jane (ca. 1784) and Woods, Marianne (ca. 1779)

Scottish schoolteachers. Marianne Woods and Jane Pirie are remembered for a libel case in which they denied accusations of of "lewd and indecent behaviour towards each other."

In 1809, Pirie and Woods opened an elite boarding school together near Edinburgh with Woods's aunt. Their dreams of success and devoted domesticity were shattered the following year when Lady Cumming Gordon withdrew her granddaughter and advised other families to do the same. The two teachers sued for libel a month later, asking £10,000 in damages.

During the long trial, Jane Cumming (ca. 1795), the illegitimate daughter of a Scottish father and an Indian mother, gave detailed but obscure accounts of nightdresses being lifted, a "wet kind of noise," heavy breathing, a shaking of the bed, and whispered exchanges such as the following (all quotes are from Faderman 1983):

Pirie: "Oh, you are in the wrong place!"
Woods: "I know."
Pirie: "Why do you do it then?"
Wood: "For fun."

Testimony was also given by other pupils and a servant, Mary Brown, who thought they were "worse than beasts and deserved to be burned if it was true" and wondered if one of them was actually a man.

The defense counsel had accused Woods and Pirie of having some kind of sex, whether with giant clitorises, "digitation" (fingers), or "tools" or "instruments" (dildos). Lord Glenlee thought the women were definitely lovers, whereas Lord Meadowbrook was convinced that, in the United Kingdom, where women did not have the overgrown genitals he thought common elsewhere, lesbian sex was as imaginary as "carnal copulation with the devil." Still he was terrified of giving this case publicity, so the case records were kept sealed. The lawmen discussed what women could do in bed (the defense counsel presented a reading list on tribadism, from Ovid to Diderot), whether penetration was necessary for orgasm, whether women would be likely to quarrel before sex or talk during it, and whether the reference to "the wrong place" could possibly mean "sodomy" (anal sex).

Racism marks parts of the trial, such as Lord Meadowbrook's argument that the "Hindoo" Jane Cumming must have based her lies on the lewd gossip she picked up from Indian maids. This figure of the evil accuser is central in Lillian Hellman's Broadway success based on the trial, *The Children's Hour* (1934), set in contemporary America. In Lillian Faderman's generically experimental *Scotch Verdict: Miss Marianne Woods and Miss Jane Pirie Against Dame Helen Cumming Gordon* (1983)—an edited version of the trial interspersed with an autobiographical narrative of researching it—although many possibilities are raised, most of the blame seems to rest on Jane Cumming.

For the judges, believing in the teachers' guilt would have meant suspecting most of the female population; as Lord Gillies put it: "Are we to say that every woman who has formed an intimate friendship and has slept in the same bed with another is guilty? Where is the innocent woman in Scotland?" Lady Cumming Gordon was found not guilty in 1811, guilty in 1812, guilty on appeal in 1819, and finally paid Woods and Pirie about £3,000. They seem to have gone their separate ways, and nothing more is known of them.

*Emma Donoghue*

### *Bibliography*

Faderman, Lillian. *Scotch Verdict: Miss Pirie and Miss Woods Against Dame Helen Cumming Gordon*. New York: William Morrow, 1983.

*Miss Marianne Woods and Miss Janie Pirie Against Dame Helen Cumming Gordon*. New York: Arno Press, 1975. Unedited version of trial transcript.

Moore, Lisa. " 'Something More Tender Still Than Friendship': Romantic Friendship in Early-Nineteenth-Century England." *Feminist Studies* 18:3 (1992), 499–520.

*See also* Boarding Schools; Clitoris; Crime and Criminology; Faderman, Lillian; Romantic Friendship

## Poetry

As a rule, poetry embodies thoughts and feelings in its imagery and in its sound patterns, rather than explaining or describing such thoughts and feelings at length. In many lyric poems, these thoughts and feelings concern the relationship of the human to the external—for example, the relationship of the lover to the beloved, the human to the other or to the world, or to God, or to nature, or to the universe. Rather than attempt to define lesbian poetry by means of information about the sexualities or lifestyles of particular poets, or through literalist categorizations of the content of particular poems, it is more useful to place the emphasis on how a lesbian reading of a poem alters traditional assumptions. These assumptions have to do with what constitutes the "human," and what constitutes the "external," as well as how the relationship between the two might be viewed. When the word "lesbian" is used as an adjective, as it is in the term "lesbian poetry," readers and listeners are faced with a difficult choice between either regarding "poetry" as an aspect of lesbian existence or regarding "lesbian" as marking a subspecies of poetry in general. Both viewpoints are valid, but each emphasis leads to different forms of commentary, and, within each, lie temptations to reduce the complexity and to obscure the understanding of poetic texts.

### Visibility and Invisibility

Ways to examine lesbian poetry are many and various, focusing sometimes on sociopolitical phenomena and sometimes on literary-cultural considerations. Within the lesbian and gay rights movements, for example, alliances based on homosexual resistance to heterosexism have resulted in lesbian and gay (male) poetry performances and publications. At the same time, solidarity and identification within feminism between lesbian and heterosexual women in resistance to patriarchy have resulted in feminist poetry performances and publications. With these parameters still pertaining, there have been further alignments and realignments of Third World, nonwhite, postcolonial, First Nation, working-class, and similarly differentiated groups, both of activists and of scholars, resulting in poetry performances and publications that either include, or entirely comprise, lesbian work. Much of this poetry is ignored by literary critics, or it is derided as ghettoized, special-interest polemic, or it is simply misread.

In addition, not all languages and cultures recognize as their own the construction of lesbian identity initiated by Western sexologists in the latter part of the nineteenth century—and further challenged, developed, and changed by Western feminism during the latter half of the twentieth century. This circumstance, together with the increasing global dominance of English-language use and publishing, means that, at the same time as the reading and the writing of lesbian poetry in English became increasingly visible (ca. 1970), the reading and the writing of lesbian poetry in minority Western languages,

**P** and in all non-Western languages, became relatively invisible or declared nonexistent. To uncover and explore texts in these language cultures demands different methods of analysis from those now familiar to students of English, French, and Spanish literatures.

Lesbian poetry is hard to find, even with the aid of dedicated scholarship, but, despite dismissal by mainstream critics and scholars, its existence is secure. Its range is prodigious, its production vigorous, its voice authentic, its temper fully human, and its quality equal to anything elsewhere admired. But it is marginalized or excluded from reading lists, publishers' promotions, print and broadcast reviews, awards and prizes, and all of the other literary and marketing showcases used to monitor and manipulate modern readerships.

## Poetic Forms and Modes

The combined effects of English-language dominance, late-twentieth-century literary theory, and the development of information technology have resulted in a greater visibility and foregrounding of twentieth-century Anglo American writers and readers of lesbian poetry than of similar work in other language cultures. Lists of cited work will include comparatively small numbers of non-English-language writers and of pre-twentieth-century writing. Standard bibliographical searches of major databases and of sites on the World Wide Web, for example, provide accessible references to lesbian poetry by and about more than forty authors. Although the list includes some geographical and historical variety, it is dominated by nineteenth- and twentieth-century white, Western women—in particular, American women.

Given this imbalance, it is important to begin by exploring poetic forms and modes, rather than biographies. The most obviously lesbian poetry can be found in love lyrics, since the love lyric, familiar to all writers and readers, has been the most commonly used poetic form from the late Middle Ages onward. Its use extends throughout the range of crafted diction, from highly wrought literary texts, to folk poetry and folk song, to the verse of greetings cards and popular songs. Lesbian voices have been present in every part of this range. Love—and, more recently, sex—between women has more often been given shape and expression in love lyrics than in any other written form, though the greater part of such texts has never been published. These poems have been regarded by their writers and recipients as private, personal, and particular, thus devoid of any wider interest or literary status. This view has been endorsed and reinforced by those who define and control literary debate in the public arena. Further, of the published literary work that is readily accessible, much in the past was coded, either through the simple device of substituting male pronouns for female ones or through complex imagistic devices of the kinds used, for example, by Gertrude Stein (1874–1946).

In addition to love lyrics, the vast, relatively unexplored body of lesbian poetry encompasses meditations, speculations, insights, affirmations, and examinations concerning every aspect of life, both of the external known world and of the inner landscapes of memory and desire. For isolated writers and readers, poetry has offered comfort, corroboration, and connection; for those who have found social, professional, or activist networks, it has offered clarity, continuity, and celebration.

The body of lesbian poetry established by the late twentieth century has both literary and extraliterary resonances. Because women as a group have less disposable income than men, and because women's work has had considerably less visibility than men's, and because recognizably lesbian work has been censored or silenced altogether, poetry has always been highly valued by lesbian writers and readers. The writing of poetry needs neither expensive equipment nor professional institutions, and, since poems are nearly always shorter than prose works, they have been easier to reproduce and circulate at minimal cost. This has meant that the development of lesbian communities, and of lesbian sensibility, has always been supported by exchanges of poetry with political energies, both celebratory and subversive. This vast body of work is hidden in newsletters, small magazines, and other marginal or short-lived publications stored in specialist archives and in collections of personal papers.

## Readers and Lesbian Poetry

More conventional—and, therefore, enduring—modes of publication are obviously easier to locate, so that commentary, which is centered for the most part in the academy, necessarily focuses on work that has found literary, rather than activist, outlets. Even from a literary standpoint, however, lesbian poetry still requires a radical repositioning of its readership if it is to be permitted the full force of its energy and clarity. How lesbian poetry is read, that is, is at least as crucial to its understanding as who wrote it, why it was written, how it has been, and will be, written, and even what it is, since its proper reading requires a major reassessment of the assumptions brought to the reading of mainstream poetry. These assumptions concern the relationship between the writer and the reader, between the writer and the speaker of the poem, and between the writer and/or speaker of the poem and the world, the whole of creation, or the "other." Lesbian poetry requires a constant questioning of the notion of the "other" and of the relationship to that other. Virginia Woolf's (1882–1941) insight in *A Room of One's Own* (1929) that "Chloe liked Olivia" and did not regard her as a member of another species is not just crucial—it is sensational. What is at stake in the reading of lesbian poetry goes beyond the foregrounding of relationships between women, though that can have striking results.

Reading poetry involves continually placing the poem in new contexts. Samuel Taylor Coleridge's unfinished poem "Christabel" (1816), for example, foregrounds woman-to-woman eroticism, but, since it sees this through male eyes, it is only "lesbian" in the mainstream pathological sense. A conventional reading of Christina Rossetti's "Goblin Market" (1862), in which the characters are read as "fallen" and "pure" women, results in difficult enigmas, whereas a reading foregrounding the primacy of their view of each other, even though they are not a lesbian pair, reveals a satisfying and coherent pattern. Again, Elizabeth Bishop's (1911–1979) refrain, in her "Invitation to Miss Marianne Moore" (1955), to "please come flying," captures the joyful calling of like to like, regardless of whether either poet might have welcomed or rejected a lesbian identity for herself.

It is the sense of "kinship," rather than the idea of an identity, that is important. What is meant by a sense of kinship is quite simply a strong sense of similarity rather than of difference. The "other" is not necessarily different from the "human." A woman addressing another woman inevitably acknowledges the similarity between them. By contrast, in a traditional, heterosexual love poem, the male lover is different from the beloved.

Male-dominated societies generate male-dominated literary traditions. This means that the human is primarily the male human, and the relationship of the human to the external refers—with all the weight of tradition behind it—to "man's" relationship to the external. "Man's" relationship to "God," to the world, to other men, to women, and to the rest of creation has varied in accordance with a particular cultural context and "his" place in it. In no known society, however, has the relationship of the male human being to God and the world been the same as that of a lesbian reader or writer to God and the world. Moreover, it is harder for a woman to idealize or demonize another woman for her own ends, because, despite differences of race and class, for example, the phrase "another woman," with all the weight of tradition behind it, necessarily indicates that they belong to the same category. Simple statements such as "You are like me" and "You are not like me" depend for their precise understanding on who is speaking to whom and in which cultural context, since the relative power, or powerlessness, attributed to the "you"—not just by the speaker, but also by the surrounding mores and conventions—is crucial to understanding what is meant.

This is not to say that lesbian poetry contains no antagonistic figures. Many appear. Men are the obvious example, though a poem like Adrienne Rich's (1929–) "Phantasia for Elvira Shatayev" (1978), which extends understanding and fellow feeling to the figure of the husband, will often reach out to the male outsider. What matters is how power and kinship are attributed, by whom they are attributed, and to whom they are attributed. What also matters is the value placed on them.

Whatever may be the agenda, the particular politics, or the individual attitudes of a poet declaring herself to be lesbian, these stances have to take place in a context that explores some of the following questions. How does she relate to other women? Does she assume, or not, that her work will be read by other women? Does she speak to a fellow "goddess"—a fellow idealized figure—since she does, after all, inherit the mainstream tradition, however ill or well it serves her? Or does she not address a "goddess"? Is she "human" in that she is separated from the rest of creation? Or is she "human" in that she is not?

Since lesbian role models have not been set up for widespread acclaim, admiration, or imitation by absolutely everyone, it follows that the problems of kinship and of relative power and powerlessness that any lesbian poet negotiates are being read—when they are read at all—within a mainstream context. This requires a readjustment of all assumptions regarding kinship and the value attached to relative power and powerlessness. A lesbian reading of poetry, in other words, is hard work. Is it, therefore, worthwhile, apart from the novelty it generates and

**P** apart from the general principle that any new way of looking at things is worth acquiring?

For many commentators, it is not only worthwhile, but absolutely essential at the end of the twentieth century. The central question of the relation of the "I" to the "other" that lesbian poets negotiate and perforce redefine is precisely the question that needs to be renegotiated by everyone, if women, men, God, the world, and the rest of creation—lesbians included—are not to destroy themselves. Lesbian poetry embodies a major and continuing contribution not only to the needs of lesbian writers and readers, but also to the civilizing of the wider culture, in that it offers the possibility of human beings seeing themselves as a part of creation, rather than at odds with it.    *Gillian Hanscombe*
                                 *Suniti Namjoshi*

### Bibliography

Bulkin, Elly, and Joan Larkin, eds. *Lesbian Poetry: An Anthology*. Watertown, Mass.: Persephone, 1981.

DeJean, Joan. *Fictions of Sappho, 1546–1937*. Chicago: University of Chicago Press, 1989.

Hanscombe, Gillian, and Suniti Namjoshi. "'Who wrongs you, Sappho?' Developing Lesbian Sensibility in the Writing of Lyric Poetry." In *Out of the Margins: Women's Studies in the Nineties*. Ed. Jane Aaron and Sylvia Walby. London: Falmer, 1991, pp. 156–167.

Kennard, Jean E. "Ourself Behind Ourself: A Theory for Lesbian Readers." In *Gender and Reading: Essays on Readers, Texts, and Contexts*. Ed. Elizabeth A. Flynn and Patrocinio P. Schweickart. Baltimore: Johns Hopkins University Press, 1986, pp. 63–80.

Munt, Sally. *New Lesbian Criticism: Literary and Cultural Readings*. Hemel Hempstead, England: Harvester Wheatsheaf, 1992.

Rich, Adrienne. *On Lies, Secrets, and Silence: Selected Prose, 1966–1978*. New York: Norton, 1979.

**See also** Bishop, Elizabeth; Literary Criticism; Rich, Adrienne; Stein, Gertrude; Woolf, Virginia

## Poland

Republic in northern Europe with a population of 39 million. Its capital and largest city is Warsaw. In 1945, following the defeat of Germany in World War II, Poland came within the sphere of influence of the Soviet Union. Communist control of Poland continued until 1989, when the Solidarity movement, which started in 1980, initiated significant and ongoing social, economic, and political transformations.

Traditional Polish upbringing mandates that Polish girls marry young, because of the belief that an unmarried woman is less valuable than a married one. Many lesbians, especially older ones, are or formerly were married and realize only late in life that heterosexual marriage is not right for them. The inability to free themselves from the trap of marriage, especially because of children, reportedly leads many women to alcoholism. Husbands may also resort to blackmail, particularly regarding custody cases. Should a woman's lesbianism be revealed during divorce proceedings, she loses parental rights.

The Catholic Church, a dominant social and political institution in Poland, plays an important role in creating and maintaining heterosexist views of homosexuals through outspoken opinions and the imposition of moral norms. Homosexuality is attacked from pulpits, on Catholic radio shows and television programs, and in the Catholic press. Moreover, by making lesbians and gay men guilty, the Church also plays a role in causing psychological problems, as well as societal discrimination.

For all of these reasons, very few lesbians and gay men publicly identify as such, making it difficult to find partners and communities. Should they become publicly identified, they may be harmed in business, professional, and social life. For example, legislation drafted in the 1990s would require candidates for positions in state administration or diplomatic service be evaluated morally—including questions about sexual preference—to determine whether they are susceptible to blackmail. Lesbians and gay men are not allowed to marry in Poland. Because of this, lesbians cannot file joint tax returns, automatically inherit property, or make decisions for their partner in case of serious illness.

The term "lesbian" itself has negative connotations in Polish society, due in part to the mass media. No film about lesbians has ever had a positive ending. The lesbian is almost always presented as an unattractive, often dishonest person. If she is sympathetically portrayed, she can expect a tragic ending. When newspaper reporters write about a crime committed by a homosexual, they always stress the perpetrator's sexual orientation, something that never happens if the criminal is heterosexual.

Lesbians in Poland lack any publication related to their lifestyle and situation. Love between women is used in books and periodicals only as a stimulus for men or is presented as a transitional stage in the development of women's sexuality. Many youth magazines present relationships between girls as a first step in sexual awakening, thus depreciating the relevance of lesbianism. If lesbian orientation turns out to be permanent, Polish society tends to assume that such women should receive psychological treatment.

Furthermore, gay publications tend to limit the number of pages in which information specific to lesbians can be published. In 1992, two women from the region of Silesia tried to publish a newspaper for lesbians. Only one issue of *Sigma* appeared. At that time, Poland had only one newspaper distributor, which rejected the publication, defining it as pornography. In Gdansk, a low-quality bulletin, *Violet Pulse*, was published by a local gay women's group, but it was poorly promoted and unknown to most women.

In 1991, the Association of Lambda Groups was registered in Poland. At first, Lambda Groups actively worked to integrate lesbians into their organization. The Lesbian Lambda Group from Krakow organized three-day sessions in different cities for women to learn about their activities. Similar meetings were organized by the Warsaw group Bilitis. During this initial period, lesbians and gay men cooperated closely and implemented many initiatives together. However, these activities were followed by a visible decline in women's participation. There are a number of reasons why Lambda groups attract mostly men. Polish society is male dominated, and women are generally socialized into passive roles. They may have a greater fear of publicly coming out, less desire to join groups to meet other women (especially if they are in stable relationships), or wish not to work with gay men. The low level of activity by lesbians does not indicate comfort with this situation but, rather, their experience of discrimination.

*Violetta Cywicka*

*See also* International Organizations

## Political Theory

Political theories are an important part of the life of lesbian comunities. Far from being simply academic, political theories structure how lesbians see the world, what questions seem to be of relevance for lesbian communities and politics, and what lesbians' desired futures might be like. They address questions about human nature, one's ability to know and change features of the world, what justice might be, and how power works in communities and how it should be used.

Although these questions might be raised in almost every society, the earliest written discussions of political theory are from European and Islamic (Middle Eastern and North African) authors. Greek tragedy highlighted questions of justice, relations between men and women and sometimes between men, but women's close relationships were generally overlooked. The "Western tradition" of political theory, represented by authors such as Aristotle (384–322 B.C.E.), St. Augustine (A.D. 354–430), Thomas Hobbes (1588–1679), John Locke (1632–1704), Jean-Jacques Rousseau (1712–1778), and Georg Hegel (1770–1831), relegated women to a "private" sphere subordinate to men and assumed that their relationships with one another were of no importance. Plato (427?–347? B.C.E.) advocated equality for an elite class of women but assumed the subordination and inferiority of most women. Karl Marx (1818–1883) challenged the division between public and private, but he never questioned heterosexuality; for him, the "division of labor" between men and women, specifically their sexual roles in intercourse, was the only "natural" division in human history.

In spite of the shortcomings of European political theory, many feminists and lesbians have appropriated its elements in advocating change. Their arguments have been based primarily on two varieties of Euro-American political theory: liberalism and Marxism.

Liberalism, which had its beginnings in the sixteenth-century Protestant Reformation and the desire for religious independence, has generally emphasized individual liberty and equality under the law. Thinkers such as Locke and John Stuart Mill (1806–1873) urged readers to resist tyranny, whether that of a ruler or of intolerant majorities. In the late eighteenth century, Mary Wollstonecraft (1759–1797) urged women's political equality based on arguments she had adapted from liberal thinkers. She suggested that women's biological differences are irrelevant to their mental capacities and, hence, their ability to participate in public affairs, own property, and govern their own lives. In the late twentieth century, liberalism remained the dominant political tradition in the United States and

Canada; the American Civil Liberties Union bases its defense of lesbian and gay equality on liberal arguments about individual freedom and equality. Liberalism is also used by opponents of equality. The liberal focus on individual freedom is often used to justify discrimination, as defenders argue that they have a right to choose whom to hire, rent to, do business with, and the like. The defense of individual liberty has been used to justify hate speech and religious intolerance, as well as feminism or racial equality.

Marxism and other socialist traditions have been more central to the political thought of countries other than the United States. Marx argued that class is the fundamental division in society and that other cleavages result from, or are structured by, this split. Marxists' analyses of oppression and emphasis on collective action have been important sources for lesbians and gay men, as well as for feminist thought. Although most feminists and lesbians reject Marxism as a complete doctrine, many find important insights into questions of equality, freedom, and community. Many debates central to lesbian political theory have terms and concepts rooted in Marxism; for example, the concept of "male-identification" to explain a lesbian's lack of feminist perspective is an adaptation of the concept of false consciousness discussed by Georg Lukacs in the early twentieth century.

Early lesbian feminists, such as the Furies collective in Washington, D.C., often came from anti-Vietnam and civil rights struggles and used the theories of the New Left to explain lesbian oppression and recommend changes. Authors such as Bunch (1987) adapted Marxism to suggest that sex, not class, was the fundamental division in society and that other divisions were modeled on sex inequality. Lesbian feminist theorists built on this base. They argued that lesbianism was not simply a sexual orientation or preference but a political stance that defies patriarchy. If sex was the primary division, then heterosexuality was the way that sexual inequality and domination were enforced. Thus, lesbian feminists developed a political theory based on the belief that "the personal is political." Lesbian feminists argued that gay men and lesbians were not allies but were fundamentally different and even opposed. Gay male culture was viewed as the epitome of maleness, male-bonding to the exclusion of women, while lesbians were the most female.

Many feminist lesbians rejected lesbian feminism. Lesbians of color especially questioned a theory that encouraged them to separate from larger communities of color. Although not all lesbian feminists are separatists, many women have thought that the division between men and women is too starkly drawn for their needs. Lesbians such as Smith (1983) have pointed out that their need to fight racial oppression is as pressing as their battle against heterosexual supremacy and that they need male allies in that fight.

The AIDS crisis of the 1980s had a powerful impact on lesbians' relation to gay men, and this led to new directions in political theory. In response to social attacks on gay men, many lesbians began to identify again with gay men and to see heterosexism, rather than patriarchy, as the enemy. Lesbian communities are now theoretically diverse, with many different positions and viewpoints competing for attention. Women such as Vaid (1996), past executive director of the National Gay and Lesbian Task Force, have argued forcefully that sexism is present in gay communities but that lesbians must work to change that rather than leave those communities.

In lesbian communities, and especially in gay communities, liberalism has become the predominant political theory of the 1990s. Liberalism is being used in court cases to argue for individual liberty and equality, and it is the theoretical framework of a spate of new books by gay men aimed at achieving acceptance by the straight majority. In these liberal presentations, lesbians and gays are treated as a minority, genetically defined and unchangeable. This is in stark contrast to both Marxism and lesbian feminism. Lesbian feminists have often argued for the idea that "any woman can be a lesbian," that sexuality is a matter of choice and moral import, and that lesbians must use their lesbianism to break down the existing heteropatriarchy. Marxist gay liberationists of the 1970s spoke of the liberatory force of homosexuality, of the need for everyone to find the erotic bonds that were repressed in capitalist societies. Liberals, on the other hand, do not argue that accepting homosexuality will change other social structures; their arguments for acceptance have hinged on the belief that, aside from who lesbians or gays sleep with, they are just like heterosexuals, and that all lesbians and gays want is to be included in existing society. These arguments have proven to be reasonably effective in gaining heterosexual tolerance, but they remain controversial within lesbian and gay communities.

Although lesbian communities have been debating political theory as long as they have existed, academic lesbian political theory really began in the

1990s. These political theorists have begun to work on questions of group identity, law, and social change in ways that both draw on, and challenge, existing scholarship. Lesbian feminists are less present in academia than in lesbian communities, so scholarship has been weighted more toward what is being called "queer theory." In political theory, queer theory has meant a challenge to the oppositions between gay and lesbian and straight and between men and women. Thus, this political theory has concentrated on empowering lesbians and gays through subversion rather than confrontation. In contrast to liberal theories, queer theory argues that the line between queer and straight is not fixed or clear; this means that "heterosexuals" may find common cause with "homosexuals" in breaking down the barriers that keep both in line. In contrast to Marxism, queer theory refuses to privilege any one ideological position as the "truth" about homosexuality or sexual oppression. Against lesbian feminism, queer theorists have argued that lesbians are not all alike, that there is no "essence" to lesbianism, and that patriarchy is but one of a number of interlocking social structures that oppress lesbians.

Although queer theory has offered impressive insights into lesbian identity and politics, it, too, cannot be the last word. Critics have charged queer theorists with being excessively abstract and burdened by jargon, thus hiding their insights from the communities that might gain from them. They have also suggested that queer theory's intellectual positions do not make for effective politics and that more is to be gained from working within existing terms and structures than from standing outside and commenting on them. These charges are part of the larger problem of the isolation of academic political theory from the communities it speaks about and for, a problem not easily resolved.    *Shane Phelan*

## Bibliography

Blasius, Mark, and Shane Phelan, eds. *We Are Everywhere: A Historical Sourcebook in Lesbian and Gay Politics*. New York: Routledge, 1997.

Bunch, Charlotte. *Passionate Politics: Feminist Theory in Action*. New York: St. Martin's, 1987.

Phelan, Shane. *Getting Specific: Postmodern Lesbian Politics*. Minneapolis: University of Minnesota Press, 1994.

———. *Identity Politics: Lesbian Feminism and the Limits of Community*. Philadelphia: Temple University Press, 1989.

———, ed. *Playing with Fire: Queer Politics, Queer Theories*. New York: Routledge, 1997.

Smith, Barbara, ed. *Home Girls: A Black Feminist Anthology*. New York: Kitchen Table: Women of Color Press, 1983.

Vaid, Urvashi. *Virtual Equality: The Mainstreaming of Gay and Lesbian Politics*. New York: Doubleday, 1996.

Wilson, Angelia, ed. *A Simple Matter of Justice?* London: Cassell, 1995.

*See also* Furies, The; Lesbian Feminism; Liberalism; New Left; Queer Theory; Socialism

## Portugal

Republic situated at the extreme western tip of Europe, next to Spain. It is a small country of about 10 million inhabitants and is popular with tourists of all nations.

The first major discussion of lesbianism in Portugal in medical terms came in 1904 with *A Vida Sexual* (Sexual Life) by Egas Moniz, a lobotomy specialist who dabbled in sexology. Moniz drew heavily on other European sexologists, such as Richard von Krafft-Ebing (1840–1902) and Havelock Ellis (1859–1939). Lesbians were inevitably portrayed as abnormal, in terms of both sexual desire and gender performance. It was common before 1932 to find lesbianism discussed in print, one example being *A Nova Sapho* (The New Sappho [1921]), a fairly sympathetic approach for the time.

The most salient fact of Portuguese life in the twentieth century was the fascist dictatorship that lasted from 1926 to 1974. Repression and censorship became the norm in every area. Discussions of lesbianism, as of so many other topics, ceased. Just as they had always done, lesbians met by word-of-mouth circuits in certain bars, cafés, and beaches, while parties in private homes were also popular as meeting places. These were frequently raided by the police, and partygoers were taken to jail for interrogation. Many marriages of convenience between gays and lesbians were made during these years. The army takeover in 1974, which eventually led to a democratic state, not only did not improve the status of same-sex relations, it actually produced, in 1975, a civil code declaring same-sex marriage "nonexistent." The reasons given were that "complementarity" cannot exist between two people of the same sex. Two directives (1989) barring gays and lesbians from the armed forces describe homosexuality as a mental illness. Homosexuality is deemed a crime when committed with minors; heterosexuality in similar situations is not branded as criminal. In 1997, as part of a constitutional review, members of the Green Party proposed several revisions that would have outlawed discrimination on the grounds of sexual orientation and included recognition of same-sex relationships. However, none of these revisions appeared in the final revised text, so the legal situation for lesbians and gay men as of the late 1990s had not improved.

With the 1974 "revolution," a short-lived Movimento de Libertação das Mulheres (MLM; women's liberation movement) appeared in Lisbon, in which lesbians were very active, for instance, in the pro-abortion struggle. There was, however, no equivalent airing of lesbian concerns. What remained of the MLM became, in 1977, a far smaller group, Identificaçã-Documentaçã-Mulheres (IDM; Identification-Documentation-Women), run predominantly by closeted lesbians in a "just don't talk about it" climate. IDM collapsed in 1985.

Lesbianism began to be discussed in the media ca. 1990, with articles in women's magazines such as *Elle*, focusing, for instance, on the English writers Virginia Woolf (1882–1941) and Vita Sackville-West (1892–1962) but never identifying Portuguese lesbians. By 1997, it had become far more common to find lesbianism mentioned in the press, although, with one or two exceptions, lesbians were not "out" in Portugal. The Portuguese media are, on the whole, antagonistic to same-sex relations, although there is a certain sympathy when reporting same-sex-related events taking place outside Portugal. It is possible to see films with lesbian content, and the very popular Brazilian soap operas have begun to include lesbian characters, albeit timidly. Television documentaries and talk shows occasionally focus on same-sex love. This has given rise to a backlash in the press, with articles routinely linking homosexuality with socially condemned behaviors, such as prostitution, substance abuse, and pedophilia. Many articles attack same-sex aspirations in terms that are severely fundamentalist, both religiously and medically.

Although lesbians are largely invisible in Portugal, twentieth-century Portuguese literature does include poetry with an openly lesbian content; examples include *Decadência* (Decadence [1923]) by Judith Teixeira and *Mulher Repetida* (Repeated Woman [1974]) and *Amor Geométrico* (Geometrical Love, [1979]) by Manuela Amaral. Given the social climate in Portugal, it is impossible to state whether any of these writers were lesbians. The first Portuguese lesbian magazine, *Organa*, published from 1990 until 1992. In 1993, a new publication, *Lilás* (Lavender), emerged; in 1998, it was still the only lesbian magazine in the country. Its aims are consciousness raising generally, but it is, as was *Organa*, available by direct mail only. *A Homossexualidade Feminina* (Female Homosexuality [1996]) by Teresa Castro d'Aire is a slim volume of interviews, in which, for the most part, interviewees use pseudonyms, as do almost all lesbians who are interviewed in Portugal.

As a result of the lack of nationwide structures and role models, many lesbians are isolated, even in the cities. In the capital, Lisbon, there are a few lesbian-friendly meeting places, but knowledge of these is carried by word of mouth, much as in earlier years. Clube Safo (Club Sappho), formed as a correspondence club in 1996, also organizes regular meetings and outings. The local branch of the International Lesbian and Gay Association, also formed in 1996, has shown little interest in lesbians. Lesbian chic, imported from the United States, has given lesbian stances a certain veneer of glamour among minority groups, but the deep-rooted attitudes of families and employers have not kept up with this trend. Despite these difficulties, it is possible to lead a happy and productive life in Portugal, and many lesbians are working actively to produce better conditions in the future.
*Maria Josefina Silva*

***See also*** International Organizations; Sackville-West, Vita; Woolf, Virginia

## Postmodernism

Term used to denote an aesthetic, philosophy, economic form, or anti-identity politics. It is best characterized as a heterogeneous mixture of critical and artistic practices that challenge modern ideas about government, art, history, and knowledge. In the critical histories that have emerged to describe postmodernism's enormous influence, three narratives of origin are central.

The first narrative, that of the aesthetic, takes shape by tracing the turn away from the canonical traditions of high modernism in the late 1950s toward art and architectural forms engaged with postclassical pastiche and the seemingly "degraded" sphere of popular culture. Here one encounters radical antiformalist architecture, street art, and the pop movement, all of which challenged aesthetic estab-

lishments and intersected with countercultural social movements by emphasizing public access and
popular forms. The second narrative, that of philosophy, imports postmodernist thought from France
through poststructuralist theorists such as Jean Bau-
drillard (1929–), Jacques Derrida (1930–), Michel
Foucault (1926–1984), Jacques Lacan (1901–1981),
and Jean-François Lyotard (1924–). Critiquing the
dominant narratives of modernity and its antithetical twin, Marxism, these writers offered new theories of language and representation to recast the
rationalist legacies of eighteenth-century Enlightenment humanism. Their antihumanism has contributed to debates on identity politics by questioning the idea of a sovereign self-knowing subject.
The third narrative, that of the economic, focuses
on historical transformations in capitalism in the
postindustrial era. In the writings of Marxist theorists such as Fredric Jameson (n.d.) and Louis Al-
thusser (1918–1990), postmodernism is theorized as
a historical period characterized by the rise of information technology and transnational modes of
production.

Taken together, these three narratives about the
emergence of postmodernism might seem to have
little bearing on the question of the lesbian whose
critical relation to the aesthetic, philosophical, or
economic has often been subordinated to issues of
heterosexuality, patriarchy, and gay civil rights. Yet
lesbian critical theory and cultural and artistic practices have been profoundly influenced by the
broader impact of postmodern thought since the
1980s, so much so that one cannot cite queer theory
in the academic realm or the butch-femme revival in
the cultural sphere, let alone the recent focus on
transsexual and transgendered issues anywhere,
without some sustained attention to their relation to
the postmodern. How, then, does one define the relationship between the lesbian and the postmodern?

In the 1993 collection titled, appropriately, *The
Lesbian Postmodern*, edited by Laura Doan, this
question is answered from a multidisciplinary critical perspective that cuts across the explanatory
frameworks for the postmodern defined above: the
aesthetic/popular, the philosophically antihumanist,
and the economic. Erica Rand, for example, asks a
postmodern lesbian question about how popular culture can be subversively refunctioned for women's
pleasure. She begins to answer this question by taking seriously girls' play with the pop icon Barbie
and lesbian appropriations of the doll as a sex toy.
Other essays in the collection likewise use popular

culture as the sphere for critical questions about the
lesbian and the postmodern. Terry Brown offers a
tour of Jodie Foster fandom; Jean Walton traces lesbian response to Sandra Bernhard's public image;
and Dana Heller investigates the connection between lesbian sexuality and law enforcement in Hollywood film narratives since the late 1980s.

While the strategies examined in many of these
essays on popular culture identify the postmodern
with the rejection of essentialist understandings of
sexuality, Judith Halberstam in her essay uses the
postmodern to question the ideals of coherent genders that underlie not only heterosexual, but also homosexual sexual scripts. By analyzing discourses
about female-to-male transexualism, Halberstam develops an understanding of the artificiality of gender
and sex, arguing for critics to think of the postmodern lesbian body as one produced by various technologies, including the cinema and medical technology. The centrality of the body as artificial and,
hence, as constructed also underlies Cathy Griggers's "Lesbian Bodies in the Age of (Post)Mechani-
cal Reproduction" in the Doan collection. Drawing
upon a well-known essay by Marxist critic Walter
Benjamin, Griggers understands the "lesbian body"
as a composite of disorganized signs that do not refer
to some kind of real or authentic being. Part of commodity capitalism, yet resisting it at the same time,
the lesbian body she tracks poses a challenge to the
future of lesbian politics, necessitating that one understands identity politics as both a problem and an
opportunity for thinking about straight culture and
the race and class hierarchies it produces.

Other critics are not as sure as Griggers that the
postmodern rejection of essentialized notions of
identity will respond adequately to race and class
differences. Emma Perez, for instance, challenges
the postmodern assault on essential identities as a
form of cultural and political suicide for marginalized groups. Sagri Dhairyam, taking a different approach, is especially concerned with the way that
postmodern discourses have authorized the professional advancement of white, middle class, First
World lesbian academics and, hence, how any academic theory works to constitute disciplinary
regimes of power, no matter how carefully such theories may question power itself.

While the essays in *The Lesbian Postmodern*
reinforce, through their difference, the postmodern
emphasis on fragmentation, multiple explanatory
narratives, popular culture and its reception, and
post-Enlightenment organizations of power and

knowledge, they all share a concern for the future of lesbian politics—or, perhaps one should say, for a politics that can use the "lesbian" without becoming fully committed to it as a universal or unitary sign. As Judith Butler writes in *Gender Trouble*: "[I]t is no longer clear that [we] ought to try to settle the questions of primary identity in order to get on with the task of politics. Instead, we ought to ask, what political possibilities are the consequence of a radical critique of the categories of identity?" Much of the force of the lesbian engagement with the postmodern takes shape here, in the concern over the historical and cultural construction of the lesbian and that subject's consequent creation within a psychosexual regime. For critics trying to think through the various definitions of the postmodern—and the postmodern's resistance to a single coherent definition—there can be no final answer to the questions posed by the lesbian postmodern. In most cases, that deferral of final coherency is taken as a good thing.

*Robyn Wiegman*

### Bibliography

Butler, Judith. *Gender Trouble: Feminism and the Subversion of Identity.* New York and London: Routledge, 1990.

Butler, Judith, and Joan Scott, eds. *Feminists Theorize the Political.* New York: Routledge, 1992.

Doan, Laura, ed. *The Lesbian Postmodern.* New York: Columbia University Press, 1993.

Docherty, Thomas, ed. *Postmodernism: A Reader.* New York: Columbia University Press, 1993.

Lyotard, Jean-Francois. *The Postmodern Condition: A Report on Knowledge.* Trans. Geoff Bennington and Brian Massumi. Minneapolis: University of Minnesota Press, 1984.

Nicholson, Linda J., ed. *Feminism/Postmodernism.* New York: Routledge, 1990.

*See also* Critical Theory; Enlightenment, European; Modernism; Philosophy; Political Theory; Queer Theory

## Prejudice

A preconceived judgment or opinion, a feeling about a person or group, with little, if any, basis in direct experience. Although prejudice need not be negative, in everyday use prejudice refers to a derogatory attitude toward members of a social group. Prejudice entails hostility and rejection, based on categorical (and, therefore, erroneous) criteria. Even when preconceived ideas have positive associations—for example, Asian students are good in math—they deny a person's individuality. The irrational hatred on which prejudice is based can be manifest in stereotypes—a set of cognitive beliefs about the characteristics of members of a social group—in social avoidance, and in overt discrimination.

### Prejudice Against Lesbians and Gay Men

Prejudice against lesbians and gay men, referred to by the generic term of "homophobia," is endemic in the contemporary United States. Some people assume that the most blatant forms of homophobia are a historical relic; such as German Nazi Heinrich Himmler's (1900–1945) proclamation that "[i]n our judgment of homosexuality—a symptom of degeneracy which could destroy our race—we must return to the guiding Nordic principle: extermination of degenerates." Yet more than forty years later, a Dallas, Texas, judge declared: "I put prostitutes and queers on the same level . . . and I'd be hard-put to give somebody life for killing a prostitute." Those who act upon same-gender desire do not have the same legal rights and protections as those who act upon cross-gender desire. The judge's suggestion was made law in the state of Colorado in 1992 (and later overturned by the United States Supreme Court): "Neither the State of Colorado, nor . . . shall adopt or enforce any statute . . . whereby homosexual, lesbian or bi-sexual orientation, practice, or relationships shall constitute the basis of any person to claim discrimination." The inclusion of bisexuals suggests that the practice of same-gender sexuality is a "master status," making invisible the simultaneous practice of opposite-gender sexuality.

Prejudice against lesbians and gay men is expressed most directly in violence. Not only are homosexuals the most frequent victims of hate violence today (U.S. Department of Justice 1997), but a New York City Anti-Violence Project reported in 1992 that 89 percent of all incidents of antilesbian and antigay violence resulted in no arrest. Chief Justice Warren Burger offered a perhaps unintentionally direct statement of this prejudice in the *Bowers v. Hardwick* decision (1986): "To hold that the act of homosexual sodomy is somehow protected as a fundamental right would be to cast aside millennia of moral teaching."

### Explaining Prejudice

Like many other intergroup relations, prejudice has often been conceived as an individual-level phenomenon. Earlier theories of prejudice focused on personality formation or cultural explanations, with concepts such as the "authoritarian personality." More recent theory and research, primarily on racial prejudice and discrimination, has focused on intergroup conflicts. Contemporary racial prejudices are marked by contradictions: A steady decline in whites' negative attitudes and feelings about racial and ethnic minorities is accompanied by whites' continued resistance to policies such as affirmative action in employment and education. Contradictions also mark the contemporary expression of homophobia, in seemingly opposite ways. On the one hand, support for civil rights for lesbians and gays has been increasing. In a 1993 Gallup poll, between 74 and 89 percent of U.S. residents endorsed equal rights for homosexuals in job opportunities. In 1988, the General Social Survey, conducted regularly by the National Opinion Research Center, showed a gradual decline in support for proposals to remove gay-positive books from public libraries, to fire lesbian and gay college teachers, and to prohibit public speaking by lesbians and gays. On the other hand, there has been no decline in moral and social sanctions against homosexuality. From 1973 through to 1995, the U.S. Gallup polls showed that between 70 and 77 percent of the respondents believed that sexual relations between two adults of the same sex are always wrong (Vaid 1995). These apparently opposite trends are consistent with political consultants' analyses. In 1994, one consultant, based on analyses of polling and focus group data, concluded that more than half of the U.S. population view homosexuality negatively, but close to 75 percent are opposed to discrimination. This rejection is pronounced among self-identified heterosexual male youth, the group most likely to commit antilesbian and antigay violence: In a 1988 survey of adolescent males, 89 percent found such behavior "disgusting." In surveys done in the 1990s, this figure declined: 50 to 66 percent of those surveyed agreed with this position.

The assumption that one's individual opinions are shared by others validates the direct expression of prejudice. Most important, it is the visible endorsement of one's prejudices by societal institutions and authorities that validates and legitimates prejudice. Statements such as those by the Dallas judge or Justice Burger, for example, or the fact that police officers are among the most common perpetrators of antilesbian and antigay violence (Herek and Berrill 1992), affirm both institutional and individual expressions of homophobia.

## Contesting Prejudice

Direct experience with the targets of one's prejudice is assumed to undermine this hostility. In a 1993 *U.S. News and World Report* poll, 73 percent of those who said they knew someone who is lesbian or gay (53 percent of the total sample) supported equal rights for lesbians and gays. Only 55 percent supported gay rights among the 46 percent of the total sample who said they did not know someone who is lesbian or gay. Research on racial prejudice, especially the effects of desegregation, suggests that the conditions under which contact occurs are vital to determining whether contact reduces, or intensifies, prejudice. Only when direct contact is sanctioned by institutional supports and when it leads to a perception of common interests and common humanity is contact between heterosexuals and lesbians and gays likely to reduce homophobic prejudice.     *Judith A. Howard*

### Bibliography

Allport, Gordon W. *The Nature of Prejudice*. Cambridge, Mass.: Addison-Wesley, 1954.

Brown, Rupert. *Prejudice: Its Social Psychology*. Oxford: Blackwell, 1995.

Herek, Gregory M., and Kevin T. Berrill. *Hate Crimes: Confronting Violence Against Lesbians and Gay Men*. Newbury Park, Calif.: Sage, 1992.

Lott, Bernice, and Diane Maluso, eds. *The Social Psychology of Interpersonal Discrimination*. New York: Guilford, 1995.

Vaid, Urvashi. *Virtual Equality: The Mainstreaming of Gay and Lesbian Liberation*. New York: Anchor, 1995.

Young-Bruehl, Elisabeth. *The Anatomy of Prejudices*. Cambridge, Mass.: Harvard University Press, 1996.

*See also* Discrimination; Homophobia; Stereotypes; Violence

## Prisons and Prisoners

In 1994, women made up 7 percent of the more than 1.5 million persons incarcerated in U.S. jails and federal and state prisons on any given day. Of those, 49.4 percent were classified as white, another 50.6 percent as black. In states with large concentrations of Latinas, such as California and New York, Latinas made up a disproportionate percentage of the women's state prison population. The overwhelming number of women were incarcerated for economic, drug-related, and nonviolent offenses.

**P** Stereotypes about women prisoners that appear in the mass media are synonymous with stereotypes about lesbians that abound in the same media. The portrayal of women prisoners as violent, sadistic, and psychotic evokes the image of the sexually obsessed and predatory lesbian.

## Prison Families

Prison families have been one of the most persistent and studied forms of prisoner organization in women's prisons. In prison families, women generally adopt, or are assigned by other prisoners, the roles of mother, father, husband, wife, brother, sister, and so forth. Prison families and the lesbian relationships with which they sometimes overlap fulfill a number of functions. While family members may be spread throughout the institution, whenever possible they socialize with one another and share resources. Prison families offer prisoners protection from staff and other prisoners, thus helping reduce prisoners' sense of isolation and fear. They provide stability and continuity, as well as multiple opportunities for close relationships. Prison families also help socialize prisoners into the institution by familiarizing them with facility regulations and prisoner codes. There are also instances when family members recruit other "kin" for reform-oriented activities, such as work stoppages or litigation efforts aimed at changing oppressive conditions. In some cases, prison family groups have fostered the creation of other informal and formal prisoner organizations and have been the most active prisoners in these groups. Moreover, in some cases, heads of households have been leading organizers of prisoner coalitions.

## Emotional/Sexual Relationships

Women participating in prison families may identify themselves as being lesbian, bisexual, or heterosexual. If one defines as lesbians those women who identify themselves as such, both staff and self-identified lesbians agree that the number of lesbians in prison fluctuates between 5 and 10 percent of the prisoner population. This is so despite the overwhelming existence of sexual relationships among prisoners.

While lesbians do often participate in prison families, many opt not to join such networks, preferring to have one or more partners while imprisoned or to remain faithful to a partner on the outside. Once two women form an intimate bond, they may opt to perform a marriage ceremony with the participation and blessing of other prisoners.

## Gender Roles and Terminology

Women prisoners and staff use a number of terms to describe the gender roles assumed by, or assigned to, prisoners. Male-identified prisoners are generally called "little boys," "stud broads," "bulldaggers," "butches," "drag butches," and "true homosexuals." Women who assume this role are usually referred to as "he" and "him."

Many women who identify as lesbians prior to imprisonment or who assume masculine roles while in prison (hereafter called "butches") generally cut their hair short and walk and talk in ways that are identified with working-class men of their own ethnic or racial background. They frequently fashion women's prison clothing into men's shorts and T-shirts. Butches are expected to be strong, independent, provide protection, and pursue other women sexually.

Many prisoners who adopt butch roles do so to give the impression that they can take care of themselves. Others adopt a butch role because they want to exert power over other prisoners or they want to "get over" by receiving goods, services, and favors from peers. Still others, because of their mannerisms and personality, may simply be assigned such roles by other prisoners.

Butches who revert to a feminine role while in prison are said to have "dropped their belts." Such a change is generally frowned upon because of the shortage of butches within women's institutions.

Prisoners assuming feminine roles (hereafter called "femmes") are expected to provide nurturing and advice, as well as fulfill a number of services associated with traditional women's roles. Such services include cooking and ironing for the butches. Feminine-identified prisoners are generally called "femmes" or "fishes."

Women involved in "situational lesbian relationships"—that is, women who engage in sexual relationships with other women solely while they are in prison—are referred to as "flippers," "wanna-be's," "players," "LUPs" (Lesbians Until Parole), or "JTOs" (Jailhouse Turnouts). The term "JTOs" sometimes also refers to women who have had their first sexual experience with another woman while in prison. Whatever label is used, these women may have male partners on the outside to whom they return once released from prison.

Women involved in lesbian relationships are said to be "playing," "crushing," "going together," "turning out," "making it," "being together," "having husbands and wives," "tying in," "bulldogging," being in "the doll racket" or "in the life," "being married," "having people," or "housekeeping."

While butch-femme relationships usually involve bartering of some kind, these types of relationships often reproduce unequal heterosexual power relationships, with the butch often enjoying privileges accorded to men. For example, while a butch may have more than one lover, femmes are rarely allowed to do the same.

On the other hand, both butches and femmes can attain top leadership positions in formal and informal prisoner groups, as well as reform-oriented coalitions.

While a great deal of violence that takes place in women's prisons is said to result from lovers' quarrels or quarrels among two women for the same partner, much of the violence women prisoners experience is the result of the day-to-day emotional, physical, and spiritual assault perpetrated on prisoners by staff and by the experience of imprisonment itself.

## Prison Staff

Reactions by prison staff to lesbian prisoners, lesbian relationships, and prison families vary from outright tolerance to severe repression. A small number of staff may show its support or tolerance for such relationships by housing lovers together, by becoming emotionally and sexually involved with prisoners, and/or by ignoring institutional rules prescribing further punishment for women caught being affectionate with each other.

Other staff members, while not condoning such relationships, may use the prison family hierarchy to try to quell tensions among prisoners or between prisoners and staff. For example, a staff member may ask the mother or the father of a family group to speak to one of their children concerning their behavior.

However, the majority of staff either openly reject lesbian relationships or feel compelled to enforce discriminatory institutional regulations. Hostility toward lesbians is evident when lesbian friends or lovers are separated when arrested together, prisoners are asked if they are "homosexual," "butch," or "femme" when first entering the institution, and lesbians are contemptuously called "dykes," "bulldaggers," and the like. At times, "obvious homosexuals" or women presumed to be lesbians are permanently separated from the general prisoner population and/or housed in units generally reserved for prisoners considered emotionally disturbed. In the latter cases, women remain locked in their cells for twenty-three hours a day unless they are given work assign-

ments. Lesbians may also be prevented from participating in programs offered by outside volunteers. In some institutions, women labeled homosexuals have been forced to wear different-colored uniforms.

Furthermore, staff often label lesbians "mentally ill." They may house lovers in separate living units and try to discourage lesbian relationships by repeatedly giving partners minor rule infractions. Women may be written up for hugging, kissing, having hickies, making love, "standing too close," or even combing each other's hair or sitting in each other's bed. The accumulation of write-ups can lead to prisoners being sent to segregation or the loss of "good time" they have accumulated. Write-ups are also placed in prisoners' files, where they are accessible to other staff and parole board members. At times, institutional personnel have informed prisoners' families on the outside when their kin was sent to segregation for homosexual activity.

Staff also frequently harass lesbian couples who are affectionate with each other in the visiting room and deny lesbian lovers participation in overnight visiting programs available to heterosexual couples.

Furthermore, it is not uncommon for both male and female staff to frisk lesbians without provocation or force a butch to watch her lover be thoroughly patted down by guards. Staff members have been known to beat up lesbians, particularly butches, solely because they are lesbians.

While staff claim that they segregate lesbians from other prisoners to protect the latter, it is more likely that lesbian relationships are feared because they create bonds among prisoners that can lead them to collectively challenge oppressive prison conditions. This is particularly so if such ties cut across racial, ethnic, and class cleavages. The fact that women prisoners continue to violate institutional regulations prohibiting them from having intimate sexual and emotional relations with each other is an indication of their continued willingness to challenge societal and institutional regulations deemed intrusive and oppressive.

[The author wishes to thank Rosalind Ruth Calvert and Darlene Desmond for helping prepare this entry.]                    *Juanita Díaz-Cotto*

### Bibliography

Bowker, Lee. *Prisoner Subcultures.* Lexington, Mass.: D.C. Heath, 1977.

Burkhart, Kathryn Watterson. *Women in Prison: Inside the Concrete Womb.* Rev. ed. Boston: Northeastern University Press, 1996.

Díaz-Cotto, Juanita. *Gender, Ethnicity, and the State: Latina and Latino Prison Politics.* Albany: State University of New York Press, 1996.

Giallombardo, Rose. *Society of Women: A Study of a Women's Prison.* New York: Wiley, 1966.

Propper, Alice M. *Prison Homosexuality: Myth and Reality.* Lexington, Mass.: D.C. Heath, 1981.

Williams, Vergil L., and Mary Fish. *Convicts, Codes, and Contraband: The Prison Life of Men and Women.* Cambridge, Mass.: Ballinger, 1974.

*See also* Butch-Femme; Crime and Criminology; Situational Lesbianism

## Privacy

Privacy is a right not afforded to lesbians *as lesbians* under the law. Privacy is not listed as a right in the Bill of Rights or the United States Constitution. Hence, any right of privacy must originate with the judicial branch of government unless Congress or individual state legislatures decide to pass an amendment to the federal Constitution or state constitutions recognizing a right of privacy for all persons. Further complicating the law for lesbians is the fact that the courts lump gay, lesbian, and bisexual people together under the heading of "homosexual." Hence, any holding aimed at gay men is viewed as precedent for cases involving lesbians. Privacy is a legal concept that has evolved over time through judicial decisions, applying to some people some of the time.

Beginning in *Griswold v. Connecticut* in 1965, the United States Supreme Court found a right to privacy in the "penumbras" (an umbrella concept created by the courts) of the First, Third, Fourth, Fifth, and Ninth amendments and held that it extended to individuals making their own decisions about private matters. In *Griswold,* the private matter was the use of birth control by married couples in the privacy of their own bedrooms. In 1967, in *Loving v. Virginia,* the Court held that a law criminalizing interracial marriage was unconstitutional. In 1971, in *Eisenstadt v. Baird,* the Court expanded its *Griswold* ruling to unmarried persons concerning access to birth control. In 1973, in *Roe v. Wade,* the Court held that the right of privacy was broad enough to include a woman's decision to terminate her pregnancy.

In 1986, the United States Supreme Court heard *Bowers v. Hardwick,* a sodomy case involving a gay man having consensual sex in the privacy of his own bedroom. In a decision with sweeping implications for gay, lesbian, and bisexual people, the Court held that the constitutional right of privacy did not extend to gay and lesbian sexual conduct occurring in the privacy of one's own home. Hence, state statutes that criminalized homosexual sexual behavior were held to be constitutional. Focusing on the subject matter rather than the legal arguments of previous privacy cases, the Court declared that it could find no connection between family, marriage, or procreation and "homosexual activity." As of mid-1998, states with sex laws that target *only* same-sex couples included Arkansas, Kansas, Maryland, Missouri, and Oklahoma; penalties range from six months' to ten years' imprisonment and fines of $1,000. In states that have more general sodomy laws, same-sex couples are usually the target for enforcement. Sodomy laws that prohibit some kinds of sex for consenting adults, both heterosexual and homosexual, still existed in mid-1998 in Alabama, Arizona, Florida, Georgia, Idaho, Louisiana, Michigan, Massachusetts, Minnesota, Mississippi, North Carolina, Rhode Island, South Carolina, Utah, and Virginia; penalties ranged up to twenty years' imprisonment.

In addition to still being considered criminal in up to twenty states, depending upon the particular sexual practices of any individual lesbian, lesbians (in addition to gay men and bisexual people) have no right to privacy in terms of having their sexual orientation made known by others. It has been held that publishing information concerning a person's sexual orientation is not an invasion of privacy because one's orientation is newsworthy if *anything* else he or she does is newsworthy. Further, one cannot claim defamation unless one is prepared to prove that the claimed gay, lesbian, or bisexual orientation is not true and the source of the false information either knew it was false or was reckless in not verifying the accuracy at the time of publication.

Given that, as of mid-1998, only eleven states granted gay, lesbian, and bisexual people equal protection under the state constitution, lacking privacy *as lesbians* subjects lesbians to the risk of loss of employment, children, the use of public accommodations, housing, and all other benefits denied them because of their lesbian status.           *Dorothy Painter*

### Bibliography

Rivera, Rhonda R. "Our Straight-Laced Judges: The Legal Position of Homosexual Persons in the

United States." *Hastings Law Journal* 30:4 (1979), 799–955.

Rubenstein, William B., ed. *Lesbians, Gay Men, and the Law*. New York: New Press, 1993.

***See also*** Crime and Criminology; Law and Legal Institutions; Rights

## Protestantism

Those denominations of Christianity formed after the sixteenth-century Reformation, including Lutheran, Calvinist or Reformed (Presbyterians, Church of Scotland), Anglican (Church of England, the Episcopal Church), and Anabaptists (including Mennonites, Amish), plus more recent divisions (including Baptists, Congregationalists, Methodists, Churches of Christ, Adventists, Holiness churches, Pentecostals). The large number of denominations means that views on lesbianism vary widely.

While the reformers uniformly rejected the Roman Catholic emphasis on celibacy and embraced marriage for clergy, they did not immediately alter theological perspectives on sexuality, marriage, or women. Women gained the role of pastor's wife but lost the autonomy, education, and spiritual esteem of the nun. Women and sexuality continued to be denigrated theologically. However, John Calvin (1509–1564) suggested that companionship was as important as procreation in defining marriage, and Puritan John Milton (1608–1674) argued that intellectual and emotional incompatibility should be grounds for divorce. These views laid the groundwork for the modern notion of marriage as a romantic union of equals, which opens the door to same-sex unions.

While instances of Protestant punishment of male homosexuals can be cited, for the most part female same-sex activity was ignored. In the eighteenth century, Catherina Margretha Linck was executed, but whether because she cross-dressed as a man, married another woman according to the rituals of at least two Protestant sects, performed as a man with a leather dildo, or espoused "heretical" beliefs is unclear. In *Scotch Verdict* (1983), Lillian Faderman, investigating the true nineteenth-century story behind Lillian Hellman's play *The Children's Hour* (1934), found that proper Anglican jurists decided that accusations of lesbian activity were "a thing unheard of . . . a thing perhaps impossible."

Until the 1970s, homosexuality was rarely mentioned in churches at all. As cultural views of women and sexuality began to change in the 1960s, the public became more aware of homosexuality. Gay people were increasingly labeled "sinners" and ostracized. For this reason, in 1968 Troy Perry, who was ordained as a Pentecostal, founded the Universal Fellowship of Metropolitan Community Churches (MCC) In belief, MCC is conventionally Christian and Protestant. In practice, it is radically inclusive, welcoming lesbian, gay, bisexual, transgendered, and heterosexual peoples from various religious traditions. Ordained clergy within the fellowship are evenly divided between gay men and lesbians.

The ordination of lesbians in other denominations followed the curve of women's ordination. Although Quakers have always allowed women to preach, Antoinette Brown Blackwell (1825–1921) was, in 1853, the first woman to be ordained a Protestant minister. Unitarians and Universalists subsequently ordained women in the nineteenth century, and some Holiness and Pentecostal churches did so in the early twentieth century. However, Methodists and Presbyterians first ordained women only in 1956, Lutherans and Episcopalians in the 1970s. Southern Baptists and many other conservative groups still oppose the practice.

While many lesbians—some open, most closeted—have been, and are being, ordained as Protestant ministers, the issue of ordaining "self-affirming, practicing" lesbian and gay candidates was being debated in the 1990s by Methodists, Episcopalians, Lutherans, American Baptists, and Presbyterians. By the late 1990s, only MCC, Unitarian-Universalists, and the United Church of Christ ordained qualified ministers who are lesbians.

Most mainline Protestant churches are ambivalent about how to view homosexuality, despite the fact that numerous denominational task forces have generally found no scriptural or theological bars to full participation and ordination. The United Methodists are typical. They affirm that homosexual persons are "individuals of sacred worth, who need the ministry and guidance of the church in their struggles for human fulfillment" and uphold "their human and civil rights." On the other hand, they "do not condone the practice of homosexuality" and consider it "incompatible with Christian teaching." The Episcopal Church has said "homosexual persons are children of God who have a full and equal claim with all other persons upon the love, acceptance, and pastoral concern and care of the church. It is not appropriate for this church to ordain a practicing homosexual." Most groups try to impose celibacy on all homosexuals, especially clergy. While the Episcopal Church still officially opposes the ordination of homosexuals, many bishops (some of whom are gay themselves) ignore the prohibition and judge each candidate on his or her own merits.

Denominational caucuses are working to gain acceptance in local congregations. The Reconciling Congregations program in the United Methodist Church is supported by Affirmation, its gay and lesbian caucus. Among Presbyterians, the program is called More Light. Its "missionary" is the Reverend Janie Spahr, supported by a Rochester, N.Y., church that wanted to hire her as pastor. Neighboring Presbyterian ministers went to church court to prohibit them from doing so. In 1998, she was still a missionary, and not on staff. Similar programs include Reconciled-in-Christ Evangelical Lutheran churches and "Open and Affirming" churches in the United Church of Christ and the Disciples of Christ.

Same-sex marriages, commitment services, or "holy unions" are also being debated. By mid-1998, only MCC and the Unitarian-Universalist Fellowship officially offered them. However, many ministers perform such ceremonies for church members and sometimes for nonparishioners. As more people digest the evidence in historian John Boswell's *Same-Sex Unions in Premodern Europe* (1994) for religious ceremonies between two men or women in the Middle Ages, the practice may gain wider acceptance.

Some more conservative Protestant churches are quite opposed to any affirmation of lesbians. Despite all scientific and psychological evidence, they insist that homosexuality is simply a sinful choice; thus, homosexuals can change and be "healed" through so-called ex-gay ministries. They cite such works as *Homosexuality: A Symbolic Confusion* (1977) by Ruth Tiffany Barnhouse and *The Healing of the Homosexual* (1984) by Leann Payne.

Substantial scholarship has been produced exploring biblical and theological issues surrounding homosexuality, including the evolution of biblical interpretations, the lesbianism of historical figures in the Protestant tradition, polemics concerning the roles of lesbians within congregations and clergy, and works on gay spirituality.    *Nancy A. Hardesty*

## Bibliography

Gifford, Carolyn de Swarte. *Writing Out My Heart: Selections from the Journal of Frances E. Willard, 1866–96.* Urbana: University of Illinois Press, 1995.

Heyward, Carter. *Our Passion for Justice.* New York: Pilgrim, 1984.

———. *Touching Our Strength: The Erotic as Power and the Love of God.* San Francisco: Harper and Row, 1989.

Mollenkott, Virginia. *Sensuous Spirituality: Out from Fundamentalism.* New York: Crossroad, 1992.

Scanzoni, Letha Dawson, and Virginia Ramey Mollenkott. *Is the Homosexual My Neighbor?* San Francisco: Harper and Row, 1978; rev. ed. 1994.

**See also** Black Church, The; Churches, Lesbian and Gay; Marriage Ceremonies; New Right

## Provincetown, Massachusetts

Small New England seacoast village with a winter population of approximately 3,500 and a summer population of more than 20,000. Rooted in a semi-isolated location at the end of a sixty-mile-long peninsula known as Cape Cod, Provincetown is a lesbian and gay summer resort that doubles as a quiet fishing village and artist's workshop during the winter. Provincetown is also famous as the landing place of the Pilgrims and the birthplace of the Provincetown Players.

As early as 1915, lesbians, or "maiden ladies," as they were sometimes called, came to Provincetown to enjoy the camaraderie of like-minded artists and "bohemians." Examples of "singular ladies" and "bohemians" visiting Provincetown in the early twentieth century include Maude Squire (1873–?), Ethel Mars (1876–?), Mabel Dodge Luhan (1879–1962), Edna St. Vincent Millay (1892–1950), Katharine Lee Bates (1859–1929), and Edna Ferber (1887–1968). These women introduced alternative relationships to Provincetown's resident population and helped shape Provincetown into a liberal artist's colony and bohemian outpost. Most "spinsters" visiting Provincetown before World War II were white, middle-upper-class college professors, artists, and writers—women, in other words, whose racial status and class privilege enabled them to live independently of men.

World War II transformed Provincetown, as it changed queer urban centers and larger towns nationwide. In the 1950s and 1960s, Provincetown witnessed an overwhelming increase in its gay and lesbian population. The 1950s mark the opening of Provincetown's first lesbian bar, the Ace of Spades, and one of Provincetown's first lesbian-run businesses, the Plain N' Fancy Restaurant. This decade also marks a unique time in Provincetown's history when local officials and clergymen attempted to discourage "undesirables" (meaning, lesbians and gay men) from visiting.

By the late 1970s and early 1980s, a group of eight women, recently empowered by the women's liberation movement, formed an organization called the Women Innkeepers to collectively promote their guest homes in Provincetown and lure more women to visit. They launched their first off-season event, Women's Weekend, in 1985. By 1993, Women's Weekend could no longer contain the numbers of women seeking freedom in Provincetown. The Women Innkeepers organized instead Women's Week, which, by 1996, attracted more than four thousand guests. The Women Innkeepers opened Provincetown's doors to women nationwide and gave them a reason to visit what was once primarily a gay male resort mecca.

Provincetown in the late 1990s still fancied itself a fishing village even though white, middle-upper-class lesbians and gay men own and patronize the majority of its guest homes, shops, bars, and restaurants. Provincetown is a dream come true for many of its lesbian residents and visitors alike, who find there a magical gay presence and a magical gay market. Indeed, visitors often describe Provincetown as a "gay Disneyland" where lesbians, gay men, straight folks, drag queens, butch dykes, transgendered people, and transvestites parade freely up and down Provincetown's main thoroughfare while enjoying the highly visible, highly energetic, and highly creative queer culture that has made this seaport village its summer home.

*Karen Christel Krahulik*

## Bibliography

Drake, Gillian. *The Complete Guide to Provincetown*. Provincetown: Shank Painter, 1992.

Vorse, Mary Heaton. *Time and the Town: A Provincetown Chronicle*. New York: Dial, 1942.

**See also** Bates, Katharine Lee; Millay, Edna St. Vincent; Small Towns and Rural Areas

## Psychiatry

The medical science that deals with the origin, diagnosis, treatment, and prevention of mental disorders. In the nineteenth century, psychiatry became an independent medical specialty, and lesbianism soon came under its purview. Initially, lesbianism was thought to be a mental illness. Religious and cultural attitudes toward lesbians both shaped and were affected by psychiatric nomenclature and treatment. In the last half of the twentieth century, scientific studies demonstrated that lesbianism is a normal variation of sexual and emotional expression.

### Lesbianism as a Mental Illness

Several thousand years of religious censure created the atmosphere in which the disease model of lesbianism developed. Richard von Krafft-Ebing (1840–1902), one of the early neuropsychiatrists, claimed in his 1886 *Psychopathia Sexualis* that lesbianism was an acquired or hereditary anomaly that was highly resistant to treatment. Sigmund Freud (1856–1939) later disavowed the concept of congenital etiology, instead preferring a developmental model. In his first detailed case study of a lesbian (1920), Freud hypothesized that mother fixation, penis envy, and maternal indifference were causative factors. Another psychoanalyst, Helene Deutsch (1884–1982), argued in 1932 that lesbianism was a "perversion" that resulted from sadistic mothering and inadequate fathering. Subsequent psychoanalytic theorists suggested that clitoral fixation, fear of men, fear of rejection, narcissism, and sexual abuse contributed to the development of lesbianism.

Homosexuality was defined as a sexual disorder under "psychopathic personality" in the 1935 *Standard Classified Nomenclature of Disease* and as a sexual deviation under "sociopathic personality disturbance" in the first edition of the *Diagnostic and Statistical Manual of Mental Disorders (DSM)*. This manual, published and updated regularly by the American Psychiatric Association (APA), has been the professional diagnostic standard in the United States since 1952.

Although Krafft-Ebing strongly opposed sentencing lesbians to "insane asylums," psychiatric treatment of lesbians in the early twentieth century was designed to change their sexual orientation. Treatment modalities ranged from psychoanalysis and hypnotherapy to involuntary hospitalization, electroshock, and lobotomy. Conversion therapy was severely damaging to the mental and physical health of lesbians who were subjected to it and consistently unsuccessful in achieving its goal.

## Lesbianism as a Normal Variation

Psychoanalytic theories about lesbianism were based on observations of lesbians who were undergoing psychiatric treatment, not on controlled studies of the general population. Rigorous scientific scrutiny in the 1960s and 1970s proved these theories unfounded and repeatedly demonstrated that lesbians are indistinguishable from heterosexual women in psychological adjustment.

Armed with data refuting the psychopathological views of homosexuality, lesbian and gay activists lobbied the APA in the early 1970s to eliminate homosexuality from the *DSM*. Conversion therapists such as Charles Socarides (1922–) objected; Socarides cited his personal observations that lesbians and gays were "perverse" and "severely handicapped" (Gartrell 1981). Because of the controversy, the diagnosis was phased out in stages. In 1973, the APA voted to remove homosexuality from the *DSM* and replace it with "sexual orientation disturbance." This diagnosis underwent one further transformation in 1980 to "ego dystonic homosexuality" before fading to the generic category of "persistent and marked distress about one's sexual orientation" (which could be applied to heterosexuals who wished to be lesbians, or vice versa) in the *DSM*'s 1987 revision.

Since all psychiatrists trained before 1973 were taught that lesbianism is a mental illness, those who wished to continue to treat lesbians were forced to adopt new psychotherapeutic approaches. The transformation in psychiatric treatment of lesbians was spearheaded largely by lesbian and gay psychiatrists. In 1975, Nanette Gartrell organized the first all-lesbian presentation on lesbianism at the APA's annual convention. Subsequently, efforts were made to include reliable research data on lesbianism and homosexuality in residency training and continuing-education curricula. Lesbian and gay psychiatrists lobbied for and won official status within the APA in 1978 through the formation of the Task Force on Gay, Lesbian, and Bisexual Issues. This task force became a permanent committee in 1981. In addition, the APA voted in 1982 to allow lesbian and gay representatives to be elected from the Caucus of Lesbian, Gay and Bisexual Psychiatrists to its governing assembly. By the 1990s, lesbian and gay psychiatrists had been largely integrated into the APA, where they became advocates for nonhomophobic research and treatment.

Investigations into the possible heritability of lesbianism were resumed in the early 1990s. Twin studies by Michael Bailey and Richard Pillard (Bailey et al. 1993) suggested that lesbianism may be familial. They found that monozygotic (genetically identical) twins had a much higher rate (48 percent) of lesbianism than dizygotic (fraternal) twins (16 percent). This research evolved out of unbiased interest in the origins of sexual orientation, and it was published in the psychiatric literature without homophobic commentary. It is likely that the twenty-first century will see a resurgence of studies on the biologic aspects of lesbianism. If so, lesbian and gay psychiatrists will need to guard against any social or political movements to repathologize homosexuality.

## Toward a Lesbian-Sensitive Practice

The late twentieth century witnessed an important transformation in psychiatrists' understanding of lesbianism. Prior to 1973, the psychiatric community refused to acknowledge that diagnoses could be socially constructed, and untold numbers of lesbians were harmed by psychotherapies purporting to "cure" them of their sexual orientation. The elimination of homosexuality from the *DSM* freed millions of lesbians from a pathological label that sanctioned discrimination. However, most lesbians work throughout their lives to overcome internalized homophobia created by a society that pathologizes them. By the close of the twentieth century, most lesbians who sought psychotherapy consulted lesbian or lesbian-sensitive psychotherapists; treatment of lesbians by heterosexual male psychiatrists had fallen into disrepute. This shift in mental-health consumerism was one of many that forced psychiatrists to be cautious about translating patriarchal, religious, and moral values into diagnostic nomenclature and treatment.

*Nanette K. Gartrell*

### Bibliography

Bailey, J. Michael, Richard C. Pillard, Michael C. Neale, and Yvonne Agyei. "Heritable Factors Influence Sexual Orientation in Women." *Archives of General Psychiatry* 50 (1993), 217–223.

Bayer, Ronald. *Homosexuality and American Psychiatry*. New York: Basic Books, 1981.

Gartrell, Nanette. "The Lesbian as a 'Single' Woman" ["Discussion" by Charles W. Socarides]. *American Journal of Psychotherapy* 35:4 (1981), 502–516.

Krajeski, James. "Homosexuality and the Mental Health Professions: A Contemporary History."

In *The Textbook of Homosexuality*. Ed. Robert P. Cabaj and Terry S. Stein. Washington, D.C.: American Psychiatric Press, 1996.

*See also* Psychoanalysis; Psychology; Psychotherapy

## Psychoanalysis

A set of clinical practices designed to alleviate such mental disorders as schizophrenia and hysteria, psychoanalysis also refers to theories about the unconscious and psychic development. Arising in the last half of the nineteenth century in the work of Pierre Janet (1859–1947), Jean-Martin Charcot (1825–1893), and Sigmund Freud (1856–1939), psychoanalysis has always been associated with issues of gender and sexuality. Sexuality, which, according to Michel Foucault (1926–1984), emerged as a distinct category in the nineteenth century, became one of the chief areas of psychoanalytical investigation. Analysts often saw repressed sexuality and sexual trauma as the cause for the symptoms of hysteria, paranoia, and neuroses.

Psychoanalysis is a very large field with a number of variations, though most twentieth-century practitioners have followed some aspect of Freud's emphasis on the sexual origins of psychological illness. The Oedipus complex, repressed homosexuality, repressed primal-scene fantasies, and repressed incidents of sexual seduction (both real and fantasy) all provide some clue to how an individual's unconscious has responded to various childhood events. The sexologist Havelock Ellis (1859–1939), whose work preceded Freud's, was more interested in sexuality itself as a phenomenon; he understood both male and female homosexualities as forms of "inversion" and narcissism, in which individuals believed that they were really the opposite gender and formed romantic and sexual attachments accordingly. In this view, lesbians were women who believed that they were men and, thus, fell in love with women. The concept of lesbianism as inversion influenced some early-twentieth-century writers, such as Radclyffe Hall (1880–1943), who explores such inversion in her novel *The Well of Loneliness* (1928).

Freud's understanding of lesbianism was more complex than that of the sexologists. In *Three Essays on the Theory of Sexuality* (1905), published early in his career, Freud theorized that homosexual desires arose naturally as a part of the process of human sexual development. Homosexualities, which he classed as "inversions," were part of what Freud saw as humanity's basic bisexual disposition and were necessary to the ultimate development of healthy heterosexuals who aligned their appropriate sexual "aim" (or desire to discharge sexual substances) with an appropriate "object" (a member of the opposite sex) in a properly reproductive relationship. Lesbians were women who never developed a proper (that is, male) object choice; hence, their sexual object is "inverted." A "pervert" would be someone who had an improper sexual "aim." All people, according to Freud, formed their sexual disposition in relation to the "oedipal scenario" modeled by the nuclear family, in which children, like the Greek tragic hero Oedipus, form intense attachments to parents of the (presumably) opposite sex.

Throughout his career, Freud offered several accounts of lesbian patients. In the early "Fragment of an Analysis of a Case of Hysteria" (the "Dora" case) (1905), Freud discerned lesbianism, or female sexual desire for other females, as the underlying cause of his patient's hysteria, although he admits that he failed to see his patient's attachment to an older woman. In the later "Psychogenesis of a Case of Homosexuality in a Woman" (1920–1922), Freud thought that his patient's homosexual attachment to another woman was the result of a frustrated love for her father; not able to win her father's interest, the girl rejected males altogether. In this case, however, Freud did not see his patient's lesbianism as an illness.

Followers of Freud, including Karen Horney (1885–1952), Helene Deutsch (1884–1982), Melanie Klein (1882–1960), and Jacques Lacan (1901–1981), all develop some version of Freud's understanding of the place and function of lesbianism, but they disagree about its causes and relative pathology. Horney believed, unlike Freud, that female sexuality was essentially different from male sexuality; however, she adapts his reading of "Psychogenesis" to develop the theory that female homosexuality is caused by an identification with the father and that lesbians live out some version of an earlier attachment to the mother. Deutsch extends the notion of lesbians as fixed on an earlier relation to the mother. She sees lesbians as attached to an infantile oral stage; still fixated on the mother, lesbians use masculinity only as a facade. Klein develops the idea of lesbians as the product of inadequate ego development. Envy of the father's penis disenables a satisfactory relation to the mother's breast, and the les-

**P** bian thus seeks a good object in another woman to replace the one she lost.

All of these analysts see lesbianism as a regression with elements of narcissism; it is seen as the desire to repair a loss in relation to the mother. In each case, lesbians suffer from an inability to differentiate themselves sufficiently; lesbianism thus becomes the expression of a lack of difference. This same sense that the lesbian denies sexual difference is also a feature of Lacan's understanding of lesbianism. Reinterpreting Freud's work in light of structural linguistics and culture, Lacan universalizes the process by which individuals become separable beings. For Lacan, castration is less a literal fear of the loss of the penis and more a metaphorical interpretation of the fact of the individual's inevitable separation from its mother. Language itself provides the model for operations of castration and desire, while the phallus becomes the signifier of desire (everyone wants it, no one has it). In this scenario, lesbians are inevitably disappointed, since instead of having the phallus, they try to become it, but in so doing they deny castration and the sexual difference castration evokes. Thus, lesbians deny sexuality itself and live out a futile "courtly" drama, in which, like the hopeless admirers of medieval great ladies, they offer an alternative brand of inspired romance.

Lesbian and feminist critics regard psychoanalysis both as a mode of institutional oppression and a possibility for understanding and empowerment. Critics from the early 1970s, such as Kate Millett (1934–) and Jane Rule (1931–), saw Freud's ideas reiterating and justifying patriarchal culture's sexism and homophobia. Criticizing Freud for his normative ideas of gender and his belief in the natural primacy of heterosexuality, these writers blame Freud and his followers for pathologizing lesbian sexuality, seeing heterosexuality as its "cure," and enabling widespread cultural bias. Since the American Psychiatric Association had listed lesbianism as a mental disorder until 1973, feminist critics certainly had a point. Psychoanalysts and psychiatrists most often treated lesbian sexuality as a disease to be cured.

In the 1980s, feminist and lesbian critics such as Jane Gallop, Jacqueline Rose, and Elizabeth Grosz began to study psychoanalysis to understand the nature of its assumptions and biases. Seeing psychoanalysis as another symptom of broader cultural conditions, feminist critics thought that by reading psychoanalysis, they could understand the nature of its sexism and, thus, either argue more efficiently against it or use psychoanalytic principles as a way of better comprehending how patriarchy works in order to change it. If, for example, sexism and homophobia are somehow features of the psyche, and if the psyche partly governs what happens in culture and politics, then how might people change culture and politics by understanding the psychic constitution of individuals or the interrelation between the psyche and culture? Or how might one be better able to treat lesbian patients by understanding their lesbian sexuality not as a disorder, but as a normal part of an individual?

Lesbian critics of the 1980s and 1990s, including Judith Butler, Teresa de Lauretis, Judith Roof, and Diana Fuss, all began to employ psychoanalytic concepts as a way of reconceiving lesbian sexuality as a positive, and even radical, kind of desire. Situating the lesbian at the center of critical investigation challenges normative notions of masculinity and femininity, as well as the constraints of the oedipal scenario. Butler (1990) uses Lacan's insights about the relation of the subject to language as a way to argue that the relation between individuals and gender is neither natural nor normative but is constantly produced through the individual's situating self as one gender or another. When both gender and sexuality are produced in discourse, neither is natural or stable, which brings into question institutions such as marriage that depend upon clear, constant categories.

De Lauretis (1994) argues that psychoanalytic understandings of sexuality depend upon homosexuality. Reading Freud carefully enables de Lauretis to demonstrate that, in his notion of sexuality, the "perversions" are normal and necessary. Centering the perverse in her own reading of lesbian desire, de Lauretis arrives at a nonpathological theory of lesbianism, in which the lesbian is a woman who, cut off from her own body image, seeks that female body image in others. Also through detailed readings of Freud, Roof and Fuss both suggest the liberatory possibilities enabled by questioning assumptions about definitive endings, stable identities, and fixed desire.

With homosexuality no longer a "mental disorder," and with the new critical tools afforded by Lacanian psychoanalysis and deconstruction, psychoanalysis has become less a monolithic, institutional guardian of normative values and more a way of exploring more open categories of gender and sexuality.

*Judith Roof*

## Bibliography

Butler, Judith. *Gender Trouble: Feminism and the Subversion of Identity*. New York: Routledge, 1990.

de Lauretis, Teresa. *The Practice of Love: Lesbian Sexuality and Perverse Desire*. Bloomington: Indiana University Press, 1994.

Freud, Sigmund. *Standard Edition of the Complete Psychological Works*. Ed. and trans. James Strachey. London: Hogarth, 1953–1974.

O'Connor, Noreen, and Joanna Ryan. *Wild Desires and Mistaken Identities: Lesbianism and Psychoanalysis*. New York: Columbia University Press, 1993.

*See also* Hall, Radclyffe; Millet, Kate; Phallus; Psychiatry; Rule, Jane Vance; Sexology; Sexuality

## Psychology

The empirical study of the behavioral and mental functioning of individuals. Until the mid-1970s, the vast majority of psychological research presented homosexuality as a form of pathology, with lesbians and gay men characterized as the sick products of disturbed upbringings. Most of these investigations were conducted on gay male samples, and the findings generalized to "include" lesbians; the overwhelming majority relied upon samples drawn from prisons, mental hospitals, and psychologists' consulting rooms. This traditional psychology provided a "scientific" justification for the continuing oppression of lesbians and gay men. Since the mid-1970s, there has been an important shift toward the creation of a "lesbian and gay psychology" that starts from the assumption that homosexuality falls within the "normal" range of human behavior and that attempts to investigate issues of concern to lesbians and gay men, such as coming out, dealing with heterosexism, lesbian parenting, and bereavement. Since the mid-1980s, lesbian and gay psychology has established itself within the mainstream of psychology in the United States.

The success of mainstream lesbian and gay psychology has been welcomed by some lesbians but criticized by others. Many lesbians (both within and beyond psychology) applaud this new lesbian psychology for its contribution to lesbian mental health, its challenge to heterosexism, and its uses in the courts and in developing social policy. Others criticize this mainstream lesbian psychology for its individualistic focus, for the way in which it reinforces notions of an "essential" lesbian inner self, and for its reliance on traditional "scientific" methods of inquiry (tests, scales, experiments), which reinforces the power of psychology as a discipline of surveillance and control. For lesbian feminists, there is the additional concern that lesbian psychology has established itself as part of the disciplinary area of "psychology of homosexuality" (male and female): Psychological studies of lesbianism are generally published in edited volumes that address the concerns of both gay men and lesbians, that draw on a body of literature relevant to homosexuals of both sexes, and that do not engage with feminist analyses. By contrast, lesbian psychology is *not* well represented within the disciplinary field of "psychology of women," which is often criticized for its heterosexist biases.

### Depathologizing Homosexuality

In 1975, after a long history of pathologizing lesbian and gay identities, the American Psychological Association (APA) adopted the official policy that homosexuality per se does not imply any kind of mental-health impairment (the American Psychiatric Association had done so in 1973). It urged mental health professionals to take the lead in removing the stigma of mental illness that had long been associated with gay male and lesbian sexual identities. Nine years later, in 1984, the APA approved the establishment of a formal division, Division 44, within the APA, to be dedicated to the psychological study of lesbian and gay issues. The only other national psychological society with a similar group (founded in 1996) is the Australian Psychological Society; proposals to form a lesbian and gay psychology section within the British Psychological Society (BPS) have repeatedly been turned down by the BPS Scientific Affairs Board and Council, and, as of the late 1990s, no attempts had been made in other countries. Consequently, lesbian psychology is very much a U.S. product.

Although antilesbian prejudice and discrimination are still apparent within some psychological theory and practice, they do not usually receive explicit support from official organizations or from acknowledged experts in the field, and it is rare to find overt reference, within Anglo American psychological writing, to lesbianism as pathology. Research on lesbian and gay issues has moved well beyond simply demonstrating the "normality" of lesbians and gay men. Key texts outlining and defining the field of lesbian and gay psychology as

**P** it developed during the 1980s and early 1990s include Garnets and Kimmel (1993), Greene and Herek (1994), and D'Augelli and Patterson (1995).

### Lesbian Psychology in the 1980s and 1990s

The key topics in lesbian psychology during the last two decades of the twentieth century are outlined below, with, in each case, some indication of the ways in which they have changed and developed over this period.

*Lesbian Identities.* With the aim of facilitating, through therapy, the development of healthy and mature lesbian identities, psychologists have explored the processes through which a woman comes to identify herself as a lesbian and the meanings that being a lesbian has for her. Stage models of lesbian identity development are well established in the literature. In the process of identifying themselves as lesbian, women are described as moving through a sequence of stages from "identity confusion" (marked by uncertainty and anxiety about one's sexual identity) through "identity tolerance," "identity acceptance," and "identity pride," finally to "identity synthesis" or "identity integration" (when lesbianism is seen as simply one aspect of the "whole person"). Psychologists focus on how individuals can be helped to reach the highest developmental stage to achieve a healthy identity as a lesbian. One important part of this process is overcoming "internalized homophobia." The intersection of "lesbian" identities with other identities based in class, ethnicity, and disability came to the fore in the 1990s, as did a new interest in bisexuality as a stable identity.

*Building Healthy Lesbian Relationships.* Psychologists argue that models of healthy relationships based on heterosexual couples are inappropriate when applied to lesbians, who confront different challenges, both socially and psychologically. Initially, research focused on comparisons among heterosexual, gay male, and lesbian couple relationships; subsequently, attention has focused on lesbian couples in their own right. Researchers have investigated the different chronological stages through which lesbian couple relationships pass, from falling in love, through the consolidation of a relationship, its changes over time, and its eventual dissolution. Another key area has been developing an understanding of the difficulties lesbians sometimes have in sustaining couple relationships; research has focused on developing new models of sexuality in the context of lesbian couples; on conceptualizing and addressing problems of excessive closeness between partners ("fusion" or "merger") and lesbian battering; and on devising methods for couple-therapy with lesbians. Psychologists tend to focus on lesbian sexual relationships, with relatively little work in the area of lesbian friendships or lesbian communities.

*Life-Span Developmental Issues.* The psychologies of adolescence, mid-life, and old age are all based on heterosexual (often, heterosexual *male*) samples. Lesbian developmental research (Patterson 1995) explores the different experiences of lesbians at various stages of the life span, including the challenges of coming out in adolescence, in mid-life, and in old age; the ways in which issues around physical health and bereavement are experienced by lesbians of different ages; and age-related changes in orientation to work, identity, relationships, and feminism.

*Homophobia and Antilesbian Discrimination.* Psychologists have asked why some people ("homophobes") react negatively to lesbians and what can be done to alter this. Early research focused on diagnosing individuals suffering from "homophobia" using a variety of tests and scales. Homophobes were described as insecure, sexually repressed people with authoritarian personalities who purportedly differed from the rest of society in being prejudiced against gay people: therapeutic and education programs were proposed to "cure" them. While neatly reversing the diagnostic label, such that it was now homophobes, rather than homosexuals, who were "sick," this work was criticized both for its narrowly individualistic focus and for failing to differentiate between prejudice against lesbians and prejudice against gay men. Later, work on "hate crimes" led to a broader understanding of lesbian oppression as a *social* phenomenon, incorporated into the fabric of society, rather than caused by the actions of homophobic individuals. Psychologists have explored the effects of antilesbianism (in the family, the workplace, and the health-care system) on lesbians—notably, in terms of the resulting stress, depression, and anxiety suffered by lesbians.

*Lesbian Parenting.* Initially, research focused on whether (and to what extent) the children of lesbians can be distinguished psychologically from the children of heterosexuals (especially in relation to their psychosocial adjustment and their conformity with traditional gender-role stereotypes). Because of its legal and policy implications, this remains an important area of research. Additionally, psychologists are increasingly carrying out research directly rooted in the concerns of lesbian mothers—for example, coming out as lesbian to one's children or managing different coparenting arrangements, such as with a woman lover, an ex-husband, or a gay male sperm-donor.

*Ethnic and Cultural Diversity among Lesbians.* Early psychological models were often drawn from research that used only white lesbian subjects, and the results were falsely generalized to all lesbians. From the mid-1980s on, psychology began to explore the interrelation of ethnicity and lesbianism. This includes research that examines the specific characteristics of lesbians who are also African American, Asian American, Native American, Jewish American, or Latina American, as well as recent U.S. immigrants. On the whole, given the U.S. basis of lesbian psychology, these explorations are limited to cultural and ethnic diversity within the United States.

*Social Constructionism vs. Essentialism.* Until the mid-1980s, lesbian psychology was almost, without exception, rooted in essentialist theories. Lesbianism was assumed to be an inner state or "essence" (whether innate or resulting from early childhood experiences) that the individual "represses" or "discovers," "denies" or "acknowledges." Drawing on theories derived from the sociology of science and the philosophy of knowledge, social constructionists (Kitzinger 1987) pointed out the extent to which the very category "lesbian" was the product of a particular historical, cultural, and political context. Such an approach challenges the whole concept of "the lesbian" (and of "the heterosexual" or "the bisexual"). It also challenges traditional psychological scientific methods. According to this perspective, the scientific method is simply a socially and historically specific faith with no particular access to "truths" or "facts" about the world. The language and practices of scientific psychology—whether explicitly "pro" or "anti" lesbian—serve to shore up the power of an oppressive institution. Debates between social constructionists and essentialists formed a central motif of 1980s lesbian psychology. These debates left neither side convinced, and research proceeds separately and in parallel within each framework. Essentialists argue (or assume)

that lesbianism is innate or acquired in very early life and that, in "coming out" as lesbian to themselves, at whatever age, women are recognizing and acknowledging their "true selves." Using the scientific method, they often compare "lesbians" with "heterosexual" women across a whole range of measures and make statements about the differences between them. Social constructionists, by contrast, reject both the concept of "true selves" or inner lesbian essences and the method of science; comparative scientific studies of lesbian and heterosexual women are not used because such studies assume the usefulness of the scientific method and take as already given the categorical existence of "the lesbian" and "the heterosexual." Social constructionists explore, instead, the ways in which women actively construct narratives about their own lesbianism, the discourses lesbians use in talking about who they are and how they came to be that way. Although social constructionism is a very important strand of contemporary lesbian psychology, essentialist theories continue to dominate the mainstream of the field.

*"Choice," Flexibility, and Flux in Sexual Identities.* With the social-constructionist questioning of the very concept of "the lesbian," psychologists have explored how individuals construct their identities over time and in relation to changing sexual activities and political commitments. Psychology started with theories that conceptualized "lesbian," "heterosexual," (and, sometimes, "bisexual") as fixed categories or models against which women matched their experiences to uncover "true identities." By the 1990s, social-constructionist psychologists were exploring the ways in which these categories are "made real" through talk. The labels an individual uses, the assumptions embodied in everyday language about sexuality and sexual identity, affect how she understands herself. In particular, in line with the new interest in the social construction of dominant identities, such as whiteness or maleness, psychologists also began to investigate the taken-for-granted category of "heterosexuality" and to explore the way in which heterosexual identities are constructed.

## Lesbian Psychology: Its Political Impact

Lesbian and gay psychology in the United States has made important critical interventions into social policy and legislation. For example, drawing on research demonstrating the normal psychosocial development of children born to, or adopted by, lesbian mothers, psychologists have testified in court on behalf of lesbian mothers in custody cases and have provided expert witness for gays and lesbians wishing to adopt or foster children. Lesbian and gay psychologists in the United States have also been involved in developing lesbian-affirmative therapies, in documenting and protesting antigay and antilesbian violence, and in providing court testimony in support of antidiscrimination legislation for lesbian and gay citizens. These achievements of lesbian psychology have clearly made an important political impact.

On the other hand, critics of mainstream lesbian psychology point to the extent to which it, like mainstream psychology in general, retains a clear focus on *individual* health and pathology. This focus on individual victims tends to obscure the role of social institutions and structures. Lesbian and gay psychology was born out of a reaction against a traditional mainstream psychology that used "science" to define homosexuality as sick. Its reaction, not surprisingly, was to present "scientific" evidence for lesbian and gay mental health—and, subsequently, to provide evidence for the pathological nature of antigay (homophobic) individuals. From its beginning, then, lesbian and gay psychology was shaped by that which it opposed, and it incorporates the individualism and the commitment to traditional (positivist empiricist) science typical of the discipline as a whole. Few lesbian psychologists have joined with social-constructionist, postmodern, and critical psychologists in their thoroughgoing critique and deconstruction of the assumptions underlying psychology as a discipline. The overwhelmingly essentialist, individualistic, and narrowly "scientific" (positivist empiricist) approach of the mainstream of lesbian psychology has severely limited its appeal in interdisciplinary (women's studies) and international (European) contexts.          *Celia Kitzinger*

### Bibliography

Bond, Lynne, and Esther Rothblum, eds. *Heterosexism and Homophobia*. Thousand Oaks, Calif.: Sage, 1996.

D'Augelli, Anthony R., and Charlotte J. Patterson, eds. *Lesbian, Gay, and Bisexual Identities over the Lifespan: Psychological Perspectives*. New York: Oxford University Press, 1995.

Garnets, L.D., and D.C. Kimmel, eds. *Psychological Perspectives on Lesbian and Gay Experiences*. New York: Columbia University Press, 1993.

Greene, Beverly, and Gregory M. Herek, eds. *Psychological Perspectives on Lesbian and Gay Issues*, vol. 1: *Lesbian and Gay Psychology: Theory, Research, and Clinical Applications*. Thousand Oaks, Calif.: Sage, 1994.

Kitzinger, Celia. *The Social Construction of Lesbianism*. London: Sage, 1987.

Kitzinger, Celia, and Rachel Perkins. *Changing Our Minds: Lesbian Feminism and Psychology*. New York: New York University Press, 1993.

Patterson, Charlotte, ed. "Sexual Identity Development." *Developmental Psychology* 31:1 (1995) (Special Issue).

*See also* Essentialism; Homophobia; Psychotherapy; Social-Construction Theory

## Psychotherapy

The practical application of behavioral and nonbehavioral techniques that are derived from a broad range of theories of human behavior and development, as well as theories of "behavior" change. The term "behavior" may include thoughts, feelings, beliefs, actions, or the absence of actions that in some way undermine the optimal functioning of an individual in a variety of spheres. Those spheres may include, but are not limited to, interpersonal relationships, cognitive, affective, work, and/or school functioning.

Psychotherapy may be divided into three general categories: supportive, reeducative, and reconstructive. In these contexts, the focus of therapy may range from targeting specific behaviors for change to focusing on the development of insight into the underlying unconscious dynamics and motivations for behavior. It may also represent various combinations of insight and behavior change. Therapy may range from brief focused interventions that may last a few weeks to long-term work that requires years of commitment on behalf of the client. The client, in this case, may be an individual, a couple, family members, or a group of unrelated individuals. Generally, psychotherapy is conducted by persons who have advanced training in the mental-health professions, including psychology, psychiatry, and social work. However, in many institutions, nurses and other practitioners may serve as psychotherapists when their training has been appropriately augmented. While psychotherapy has been traditionally applied to ease the symptoms of mental disorders, it is useful in helping individuals cope with routine, as well as catastrophic, life stressors. Hence, a person need not be mentally ill to benefit from psychotherapy. Ideally, psychotherapy should offer a safe and private environment for a client or clients to express feelings such as anger, frustration, irrational beliefs, and other difficulties without being judged, while seeking to lessen or better understand the nature of their difficulty.

Lesbians are visible and significant consumers of psychological services and often seek psychotherapy for many of the same reasons as heterosexual women. Like heterosexual women, they face the challenge of developing healthy images and roles for themselves in a culture that has a history of labeling departures from traditional female gender-role expectations as abnormal, psychologically unhealthy, or socially inappropriate. Mental-health institutions have been guilty of this behavior as well. They have frequently given legitimacy to such thinking and to the discriminatory behavior that resulted from such thinking. Women who are lesbians clearly depart from traditional female gender roles. When lesbians seek psychotherapy, unlike heterosexual women, they do so as women who face unique challenges to their optimal functioning as lesbians in a society that is heterosexist and homophobic, as well as sexist. Whatever her personal psychological resources and handicaps may be, the woman who is a lesbian negotiates the world from a position of societal discrimination and disadvantage.

Despite the fact that all lesbians share such challenges, they are not a homogeneous group. The challenges a woman faces as a lesbian are colored by her race or ethnicity, her age, her socioeconomic status, the presence of physical challenges, the geographical region in which she lives, and her own personal and familial psychological resources. Any individual lesbian has multiple identities, some of which may conflict with or complement the others.

There are specific challenges that all lesbians confront on the road to healthy psychological development that are relevant to a discussion of psychotherapy. This is because many lesbians are apt to seek psychological services when coping with certain predictable and frequently stressful events. Depending on the individual's resources and options, these stressors may exceed her capacity to cope with them in healthy ways. The conscious acknowledgment or awareness of one's same gender-attraction and self-labeling as a lesbian is referred to as "coming out." While coming out is not a static or a singular event and continues to take place across the life span, the initial realization of a lesbian sexual orientation can be a profoundly disruptive event in a woman's life. It is during this period that many women who are lesbians seek psychotherapy services, often to first determine whether their attractions to other women have any meaning. Having determined that such attractions do have meaning, they may seek psychotherapy to learn how to integrate these new or preexisting feelings (or a new awareness of them) into their life. This is complicated by the fact that lesbian sexual orientations are still stigmatized. Coming out requires restructuring one's self-concept and reorganizing one's personal sense of history, as well as altering one's relationship with family, peers, and society (Browning et al. 1991). These tasks are often understandably stressful, and many women use psychotherapy to assist them in moving through this often difficult transition.

Other difficult transitions associated with coming out involve telling other significant figures in a woman's life that she is a lesbian. Coming out to family members may trigger old family conflicts or dynamics that may be displaced on to the family member who comes out. Such scapegoating is facilitated by society's tolerance of bias toward lesbians, which gives some family members license to behave in ways that might otherwise be considered unacceptable. It is likely that, at these times, the woman who is coming out is in greatest need of her family's love and support but may be unable to obtain it. Even worse, she may instead elicit their scorn or rejection. This should not imply that all families reject lesbian members; however, the tendency for such occurrences cannot be underestimated. This affects the emotional well-being of a person, particularly when she is in need of support. Many women in these circumstances turn to psychotherapy for help.

Another circumstance in which lesbians may seek psychological services is related to their romantic relationships. Because of the societal stigma attached to being a lesbian, many lesbians hide their relationships out of realistic fears of rejection, discrimination, or even violence. The hidden nature of such relationships leaves lesbians with fewer role models for conducting relationships and, perhaps, a narrower range of visible relationships than heterosexual women. In addition, there is less support for lesbian unions than for heterosexual marriages. Painful breakups between women may be ignored by their families or even greeted with relief, rather than the emotional support that may be offered a heterosexual woman who is getting divorced or whose relationship is impaired. This absence of support or recognition for the unique strains that lesbian couples confront can intensify other problems in the relationship. For some couples, the establishment of an ongoing relationship that is visible may precipitate coming out to family members in ways that may be quite stressful for both partners, particularly if they disagree about the need to come out to family or about the way it should be done. Therapy at such junctures may be seen as an appropriate place to turn for help.

Perkins (1996) has been critical of the use of psychotherapy by lesbians, viewing it as a process that takes the place of community relationships and connections and of political organizing that is essential to combating oppression. In her view, the danger of psychotherapy is that it tells lesbians that their problems are in their minds rather than in societal oppression. Historically, it is true that many psychotherapies have been used to pathologize healthy rejecting responses to societal discrimination. Effective psychotherapy, however, should never purport to take the place of friends, family, and other relationships. It is a specific process aimed at assisting individuals in very specific ways. Rather than take the place of other relationships, it should merely take its place among them until it is no longer needed. An important ingredient in effective psychotherapy is the validation of a client's accurate perception of discrimination and other often denied experiences. It is also important to validate a client's perception of prior inappropriate treatment as well as her appropriate anger or outrage at such treatment.

There is no literature that suggests that any specific form of therapy has demonstrated greater utility with lesbian clients. Generally, the choice of theoretical framework or approach to treatment is guided by the nature of the specific problem(s) and the success of a particular approach in clinical settings. Effective psychotherapy with lesbians must contain specific elements, however. It should be free of the heterosexist, ethnocentric, racist, and sexist biases that have long plagued mental health. The process should affirm the client's choice of healthy relationships regardless of sexual orientation, recognizing lesbian sexual orientation as a healthy form of human diversity. Psychotherapy with lesbians should be conducted by therapists who clearly understand the nature and extent of the unique stres-

sors that confront lesbians as women who routinely negotiate the realities of a sexist and heterosexist society. As lesbians are not a homogeneous group, therapists must also be culturally literate and competent in understanding that many lesbians have multiple identities and may experience racial and other forms of societal oppression, as well as heterosexism. The unique interactions among these identities must be appreciated, as well as the individual's own contribution, knowingly or not to her own dilemma. Overall, effective psychotherapy with lesbian clients should assist the client in examining the conscious and unconscious methods she employs in confronting and negotiating both systemic and personal barriers while analyzing the effectiveness of her methods and goals. If need be, it should assist the client in developing a wider range of options that are consistent with her values and goals.

*Beverly Greene*

### Bibliography

Browning, Christine, Amy L. Reynolds, and Sari H. Dworkin. "Affirmative Psychotherapy for Lesbian Women." *Counseling Psychologist* 19 (1991), 2177–2196.

Espín, Oliva. "Cultural and Historical Influences on Sexuality in Hispanic/Latina Women: Implications for Psychotherapy." In *Pleasure and Danger: Exploring Female Sexuality.* Ed. Carole S. Vance. London: Routledge, 1984, pp. 149–163.

Falco, Kristine L. *Psychotherapy with Lesbian Clients.* New York: Brunner Mazel, 1991.

Glassgold, Judith, and Suzanne Iasenza, eds. *Lesbians and Psychoanalysis: Revolutions in Theory and Practice.* New York: Free Press, 1995.

Greene, Beverly. "Lesbian Women of Color." In *Women of Color: Integrating Ethnic and Gender Identities in Psychotherapy.* Ed. Lillian Comas-Diaz and Beverly Greene. New York: Guilford, 1994, pp. 389–427.

———. *Psychological Perspectives on Lesbian and Gay Issues,* vol. 3: *Ethnic and Cultural Diversity Among Lesbians and Gay Men.* Thousand Oaks, Calif.: Sage, 1994.

Laird, Joan, and Robert Jay Green, eds. *Lesbian and Gay Couples and Families: A Handbook for Therapists.* San Francisco: Jossey Bass, 1996.

Perkins, Rachel. "Rejecting Therapy: Using Our Communities." In *Preventing Heterosexism and Homophobia.* Ed. Esther D. Rothblum and Lynn Bond. Thousand Oaks, Calif.: Sage, 1996, pp. 71–83.

Rothblum, Esther D., and Lynne A. Bond, eds. *Preventing Heterosexism and Homophobia*. Thousand Oaks, Calif.: Sage, 1996.

*See also* Psychoanalysis; Psychology

## Publishing, Lesbian

A loosely organized collection of independently or collectively operated presses, publishing houses, and distribution companies, operating primarily in North America since the early 1970s, specializing in the dissemination of such lesbian cultural materials as newspapers, periodicals, and books and united, to some extent, by a shared political commitment to women's liberation and lesbian feminism.

Although women's bookstores are its most visible manifestation, the lesbian publishing enterprise is more accurately a host of activities and affiliations that both define it as a full-fledged alternative institution and anchor it as an important part of the infrastructure of North American feminism. While lesbians were certainly active in independent publishing ventures before the "second wave" of the women's movement in the 1960s–1970s, the project of lesbian publishing differed from earlier endeavors in its fervent efforts to implement the theoretical insights of women's liberation, its exclusive interest in women's words and images, and its reliance on women's labor to perform the manifold tasks of an alternative publishing enterprise. From the publishing ferment that inspired the first national Women in Print Conference near Omaha, Nebraska, in 1976; to the founding of presses as distinct from each other as Daughters and Diana, or Naiad and Kitchen Table; to the development of such specialty trade journals as *Motheroot Journal: A Women's Review of Small Presses* or *Feminist Bookstore News* or *Hot Wire*, lesbian publishers have produced a concrete, enduring, and commercial legacy of the women's and lesbian liberation movements.

Lesbian publishers can be found in the historical record before World War II, but the lesbian publishing enterprise is a specifically postwar and North American phenomenon, with identifiable "firsts" and defining moments. The first magazine for lesbians, *Vice Versa*, appeared in Southern California in 1947 at a time when obscenity laws meant that lesbian and gay male materials could not be sent to a printer or to newsstands. Lisa Ben (pseud.), a Hollywood secretary, began composing, editing, and typing *Vice Versa* at her office typewriter. Using carbon paper, she produced the magazine ten copies at a time and relied on lesbians to circulate the magazine hand to hand at bars and other meeting places.

Almost ten years later, the much longer-lived and more widely distributed magazine *The Ladder* began its career. *The Ladder* was the first national lesbian periodical, in print continuously from 1956 to 1972. Originally the newsletter of the Daughters of Bilitis, it became an independent and well-distributed monthly magazine, publishing news, fiction and poetry, book and film reviews, readers' contributions, and reports on lesbian and homosexual life made by sympathetic sociologists, lawyers, psychologists, and other professionals. By the time *The Ladder* ceased publication in 1972, it was no longer the sole voice of lesbian culture but was one of many newsletters and journals with lesbian editorial authority, lesbian content, and lesbian readers.

The rise of the women's liberation movement in the 1970s unleashed an extraordinary amount of lesbian energy, much of it channeled into publishing, the "print arm" of the movement. In the 1970s, more than 560 newsletters, journals, and women's community papers were launched, as well as several dozen publishing houses and printing presses. The decade also saw the creation of more than one hundred women's bookstores devoted to selling the materials generated by the women-in-print movement (a term coined by lesbian publisher June Arnold of Daughters, Inc., who called the first Women in Print Conference in 1976). At a time when countercultural and alternative institutions were changing the social and cultural dynamics of both rural and urban landscapes, lesbians took on the work of creating alternatives to the mass media. The feminist appropriation of the slogan "Freedom of the press belongs to those who own the press" became the rallying call for the entire women-in-print movement, encouraging women to learn how to edit manuscripts, run printing presses, paste-up copy, bind books, and operate bookstores. Lesbian collectives, partnerships, and friendship networks would often be inspired to publish a journal or a newsletter as part of the work of liberation. For example, the short-lived, but influential, journal *The Furies* was written and produced in the early 1970s by a collective of Washington, D.C., women that included Rita Mae Brown and Charlotte Bunch. Similarly, *Sinister Wisdom*, the longest-running lesbian journal in history, was founded in 1976 and first edited by the lesbian cou-

**P** ple Harriet Desmoines and Catherine Nicholson. A lesbian or feminist periodical became, for many otherwise isolated women, the mailing address of the movement, fulfilling a traditional role of the alternative press: In its pages, activists could articulate their beliefs, organize members and recruit new ones, conserve their movement's history, and make possible its future.

Such ambitious lesbian feminist periodicals as *Amazon Quarterly*, *Chrysalis*, *Feminary*, *Conditions*, *Lavender Woman*, *Feminist Bookstore News*, *Lesbian/Lesbienne*, *Sinister Wisdom*, *Azalea*, *Connexions*, *Heresies*, *Maenad*, *Open Door: Rural Lesbian Newsletter*, *Calyx*, *Fireweed*, *La Vie En Rose*, *Lesbian Tide*, *Ache*, *Hot Wire*, *Dyke*, *Rites*, and *Common Lives/Lesbian Lives* found their way into the hands of rural and urban lesbians across North America and beyond. The periodicals produced by lesbian publishers not only contributed to the formation of a widespread, though geographically dispersed, lesbian community with identifiable cultural interests, but also proved to be a nurturing milieu for author development. Lesbian periodicals provided lesbian writers with a peer cohort of editors, reviewers, and readers. They also provided, in their classified sections and announcements pages, the calls for submissions that generated material for new lesbian anthologies and single-author works.

While lesbian periodicals were introducing authors to audiences across the continent, lesbian presses were beginning to produce the steady stream of lesbian books that would come to represent, by the 1990s, 40 to 60 percent of the sales in North American women's bookstores. Lesbian publishing houses—including Naiad, Persephone, Diana, Shameless Hussy, the Women's Press Collective, Aunt Lute, Spinsters Ink, Sister Vision, Daughters, Inc., Firebrand Books, Kitchen Table, Cleis, New Victoria, Seal, Vanity, and Press Gang—provided lesbians with unparalleled opportunities and forums for their self-expression. Typically operating, at least in theory if not always in practice, as egalitarian, nonhierarchical, nonprofit, and ideologically sound enterprises—juggling feminist principles with the demands of capitalism—lesbian feminist presses and publishers actively repudiated the often elitist, discriminatory, and censorious practices of the commercial presses. Lesbian publishers can be credited with giving first publication or wider distribution to such celebrated writers of the 1970s through the 1990s as Gloria Anzaldúa, Dorothy Allison, June Arnold, Allison Bechdel, Rita Mae Brown, Cheryl Clarke, Jan Clausen, Chrystos, Judy Grahn, Audre Lorde, Joan Nestle, Minnie Bruce Pratt, Jane Rule, Sarah Schulman, and Kitty Tsui.

If lesbian literary history during the 1970s was being made and recorded primarily on the freshly drafted pages of lesbian periodicals, then, by the end of the 1970s and into the 1980s, debates about lesbian diversity, community organizing, and political activism were generating an increasing number of book-length collections. Often these anthologies were born in the pages of lesbian journals: For example, both Beth Brant's *A Gathering of the Spirit: Writing and Art by North American Indian Women* (1983, 1984) and Melanie Kaye/Kantrowitz and Irena Klepfisz's *The Tribe of Dina: A Jewish Women's Anthology* (1986, 1989) began as special issues of *Sinister Wisdom*, while Barbara Smith's *Home Girls: A Black Feminist Anthology* (1983) grew out of *Conditions Five, The Black Women's Issue* (1979).

In the 1980s, lesbian publishing would see the rise of a powerful activist tool—the multicultural anthology. An increasing preoccupation with issues of racial and ethnic identity can be seen in a critical mass of texts produced primarily by lesbians of color and ethnic lesbians, works that were ushered into print by established lesbian feminist publishers, as well as by such newer women-of-color presses as Kitchen Table: Women of Color Press and Sister Vision: Black Women and Women of Colour Press. Perhaps the most well known of these books is Gloria Anzaldúa's and Cherríe Moraga's *This Bridge Called My Back: Writings by Radical Women of Color* (1981), originally published by Persephone Press and reprinted by Kitchen Table. This landmark anthology, with its multigenre mix of short stories, diary entries, polemical essays, poems, testimonials, interviews, and oral histories, became a model for a host of others, including Evelyn Torton Beck's *Nice Jewish Girls: A Lesbian Anthology* (1982) and Makeda Silvera's *Piece of My Heart: A Lesbian of Colour Anthology* (1991).

By lining mailboxes, magazine racks, and bookshelves, lesbian publishers have kept women's ideas in print and in circulation; dispersed new theoretical insights, particularly about multiple interlocking oppressions (the basis of identity politics), to new audiences of women; and provided women with the self-help, spiritual, activist, and imaginative literatures necessary for them to sustain themselves and their political movements. *Kate Adams*
*Alisa Klinger*

## Bibliography

Adams, Kathryn Tracy. "Paper Lesbians: Alternative Publishing and the Politics of Lesbian Representation, 1950–1990." Ph.D. diss., University of Texas, 1994.

Hodges, Beth, ed. "Lesbian Writing and Publishing." *Sinister Wisdom* 13 (Spring 1980) (Special Issue).

Klinger, Alisa. "Paper Uprisings: Print Activism in the Multicultural Lesbian Movement." Ph.D. diss., University of California, Berkeley, 1995.

Streitmatter, Rodger. *Unspeakable: The Rise of the Gay and Lesbian Press in America.* Boston: Faber and Faber, 1995.

*See also* Anthologies; Anzaldúa, Gloria E.; Arnold, June; Bookstores; Brown, Rita Mae; Businesses, Lesbian; Collectives; Daughters of Bilitis; Furies, The; Grahn, Judy; Grier, Barbara; Journalism; *Ladder, The;* Lesbian Feminism; Lorde, Audre; Moraga, Cherríe; Naiad Press; Nestle, Joan; Periodicals; Pulp Paperbacks; Rule, Jane Vance; Smith, Barbara; 'zines

## Pulp Paperbacks

The 1939 paperback revolution, brought about by changes in printing and distribution, made books affordable and widely available. Sex (of any sort) made them salable. Little lesbian fiction was published in the 1940s due to an unprecedented shortage of paper (because of military requisition of cellulose for explosives), as well as selectivity in fiction publishing. However, the 1950s and early 1960s saw an upsurge in the number of works touching upon lesbianism. While most were "pulp" paperbacks (named for the inexpensive paper on which they were printed) with little redeeming value, more novels with lesbian themes were published during this period than at any other time in history.

It is not surprising that so many lesbian-themed novels were published, since, for the most part, they functioned as Radclyffe Hall (1880–1943) claimed *The Well of Loneliness* (1928) should function: as stories warning about the dangers of a lesbian life. Despite the moralizing, the prejudices, and the bad writing, lesbians voraciously devoured these novels. They were inexpensive, generally thirty-five to forty cents during the mid-1950s, and their length seldom ran more than two hundred pages. The characters in them are almost entirely white and young. The

Cover for Odd Girl Out *by Ann Bannon. Courtesy of Linnea Stenson.*

luridly designed covers, often featuring two women embracing or in various stages of undress, signaled "lesbian" to even the casual browser, and they were widely available at drugstore book racks and newspaper stands. Despite their cautionary intent, they often served to inform lesbians that there were, indeed, others like themselves out in the world.

In the novels typical of the majority of the pulp genre, "real" lesbians are portrayed as manipulative, perverse, and evil. Their victims are generally younger innocent women, unable to comprehend the destructive sexual power of the lesbian on the prowl. Ultimately, these novels have some sort of mainstream "redeeming social value": The real lesbian is killed at the end, or a rival male gets the girl, and the normal balance of life is restored. Lesbians of color are virtually nonexistent in these works. Where they do exist, they are an exoticized, super-sexualized other, the "dark" seductress who has trouble in mind for her blond, white (and innocent) victim. Gomez (1983) cites one example in which "the lone Black Lesbian character is left to be hunted by the police as the accomplice/catalyst to [a] chain reaction of destruction," including the accidental killing of a white heiress. Another example, *Puta* (1962) by Sheldon Lord, revolves around the adventures of a Latina nymphomaniac (*puta*, which translates as "whore"). These novels add the evil of miscegenation to homosexuality.

In reviewing the huge number of pulps published, it is helpful to draw some distinctions. Some pulps were reissues of earlier "literary" lesbian novels, such as Gale Wilhelm's (1908–1991) *Torchlight to Valhalla* (1938, which was republished in 1953 under the title *The Strange Path*), or Hall's *The Well of Loneliness*. Most of these paperback originals were purely exploitative. However, with all of the others, there were a number of pulp novels published that were generally "pro-lesbian." The writers of these novels strove to present a positive lesbian identity, despite the "unhappy" ending that many editors demanded be tacked on to conform to the moralistic expectations of the day.

The "pro-lesbian" pulps, representing a fraction of these paperback originals, featured lesbian characters who rebelled against the stereotypes of perversion and social prejudice. These were particularly popular among lesbian readers, although, given that one cover was as lurid as the next, discerning from the drugstore racks which of these novels might be somewhat sympathetic and which utterly full of lesbian self-hate must have been difficult. Some of the more popular books were written by Ann Bannon (1937–) and are still recognized as "classics" by aficionados of the genre. These novels, despite their generally pro-lesbian stance, are, nonetheless, characterized by the violence, alcoholism, and weird sexual situations that most other pulp novels contain. Paula Christian, another sympathetic writer of lesbian pulp novels, explained in the lesbian journal *The Ladder* the difficulty of publishing these novels, placing blame squarely on publishing houses that would not allow any theme that seemed to promote homosexuality. Other positive writers included Claire Morgan (pseud. of Patricia Highsmith [1921–1995]); Valerie Taylor (1913–1997), and Ann Aldrich (pseud. of Marijane Meaker, who also wrote under the name Vin Packer [1927–]).

Pro-lesbian novels are set apart by an empathetic narrative, coupled with characters who (for the most part) come to their lesbian identity through struggles that must have looked (and, to some degree, still might look) familiar to many of their white, middle-class readers. Perhaps most important, their romances are often allowed to continue implicitly through the novels' final scenes; if not, the ending is, nevertheless, hopeful for the protagonist (although, given the prevalence of suicides and deaths, just being alive at the close could be considered an uplifting ending).

It is deeply ironic that, at a time when social, economic, political, and cultural forces in the United States worked so strongly against homosexuals, a literary expression existed that has not been surpassed in its impact on lesbian life. Pulp novels themselves proved to be both creations and creators of lesbian cultures and, given their popularity, appear to have crossed class boundaries. While they were often distorted and filled with "expert" psychoanalytic theories and medical pathologizing, they also introduced lesbians to one another. Moreover, despite the pressures of publishing conventions, they sometimes allowed two women to remain together, or at least one woman to gain and hold onto pride in who she was. The pulps left a legacy of rebellion against assimilation. Bar dykes and other more overtly "out" characters set the stage for the novels that came into existence in the late 1960s and early 1970s. The novels of Ann Bannon, Paula Christian, Valerie Taylor, and Claire Morgan reject the sanitized mainstream and bring marginal lives to the center.

The political upheaval of the 1960s gave birth in the early 1970s to a number of lesbian feminist publishing houses, most notably Daughters Inc., the Women's Press Collective, and Diana Press. Lesbians turned their reading interests to more politically radical works that reflected the enormous social changes in their identities and lives. In the 1980s, the republication and popularity of a small number of these novels reflected a renewed interest in these works as significant sites of some lesbian lives and cultures.

*Linnea A. Stenson*

### Bibliography

Bonn, Thomas L. *UnderCover: An Illustrated History of American Mass Market Paperbacks*. New York: Penguin, 1982.

Gomez, Jewelle. "A Cultural Legacy Denied and Discovered: Black Lesbians in Fiction by Women." In *Home Girls: A Black Feminist Anthology* Ed. Barbara Smith. Kitchen Table: Women of Color Press, 1983, pp. 110–123.

Koski, Fran, and Maida Tilchen. "Some Pulp Sappho." In *Lavender Culture*. Ed. Karla Jay and

Allen Young. New York: Jove/Harcourt Brace Jovanovich, 1978, pp. 262–274.

Tilchen, Maida. "Ann Bannon: The Mystery Solved!" *Gay Community News* (January 8, 1983), 8–12.

Walters, Suzanna Danuta. "As Her Hand Crept Slowly Up Her Thigh: Ann Bannon and the Politics of Pulp." *Social Text: Theory/Culture/ Ideology* 23 (Fall/Winter 1989), 83–101.

*See also* American Literature, Twentieth Century; Bannon, Ann; Hall, Radclyffe; *Ladder, The;* Naiad Press; Publishing, Lesbian; Taylor, Valerie; Wilhelm, Gale

# Q

## Québec

Beginning in the sixteenth century, Québec territory was the heart of French colonial activity in North America, until the signing of the Treaty of Paris in 1763, which ceded these territories to England. The French-Canadians, abandoned to their fate, were forced to accept British rule, yet, at the same time, they resisted assimilationist policies. Because of a high birth rate, they managed to maintain their demographic weight and preserve their language, their Catholic religion, and their own culture, distinct from that of their French ancestors. In 1997, Québec's population reached 6.9 million people, comprising descendants of the French-Canadians and the English, as well as other immigrants of diverse origins. Those of French descent dominate the population at more that 80 percent, yet they are marginalized in Canadian culture. The colonial process and the Franco-British wars decimated the Native American population, which, in the 1990s, represented about 1 percent of the total population.

## History

Between 1900 and 1940, the control of the Catholic Church strongly affected women, the guardians of morality and tradition. Religious women's communities took charge of the education of young girls, health, and aid to the poor. Many women who refused marriage and frequent pregnancies opted for life in the convent, but there is no way of knowing if homosexual tendencies influenced their choice. Unmarried women had great difficulty maintaining financial and general independence from their families. Little is known about lesbians during this period except that they were socially almost invisible. Within the Montréal artistic milieu between 1917 and 1919, Elsa Gidlow (1898–1986) claimed it was difficult to find any. With a gay male friend, the young Gidlow discovered European homosexual literature and published a magazine in which she included a number of Sapphic poems, before moving to New York City in 1920 in the hope of ending her isolation as a lesbian.

The period between 1940 and 1967 was characterized by the modernization of Québec society and the erosion of the power of the Catholic Church. After World War II, women had easier access to education and the job market. Now increasingly visible, lesbianism was considered a vice, a crime, and an illness. The most common terms encountered were *femme aux femmes* (woman who love women), "lesbian," "butch," and "Sapphist." There were separate, distinct lesbian networks, depending on language, social class, and generation. Lesbians who had professional reputations to protect restricted their activities to private, closed circles. The most educated were inspired by references in the literature and cinema of France, which was less censored than Québec's. To identify one another, they used the term "homosexual" or euphemisms like "to be one of us" (*en être*) or "to be part of the big family" (*faire partie de la grande famille*). The only visible lesbians were working-class women who went to bars and adopted the butch-femme code. The most overt exposed themselves to social stigmatization: insults, rejection by their families and friends, economic sanctions, and police harassment. Outside of secrecy and marginality, there were few alternatives. Isolated, without role models, and at the low end of the salary scale, many lesbians married and, sometimes, attempted to maintain secret lesbian relationships at the same time.

The period between 1967 and 1982 witnessed intense social and political agitation, including the popular sovereignty movement, which struggled for Québec independence. After the Liberation for Québec Front (Front de libération du Québec) came the Women's Liberation Front (Front de Libération des Femmes), and then the Homosexual Liberation Front (Front de Libération Homosexuel) in 1971. English-speaking lesbians started the first Canadian lesbian monthly, *Long Time Coming* (1973–1975). Inspired by the American counterculture, they also launched service organizations and consciousness-raising groups and organized conferences in Montréal that brought together hundreds of Canadian and American lesbians. French-speaking lesbians were involved in independent women's groups representing the most radical tendencies of the feminist movement. Still in the minority within Anglophone groups and wishing to create their own cultural space, Francophone feminist lesbians founded the Coop-femmes (1977–1979). A group of women participated in the first lesbian contingent in a Gay Pride Parade in Montréal in 1978. During this period, exclusively lesbian bars appeared, as well as more public and semipublic meeting places, differentiated by class and language. In 1977, the Québec Human Rights Charter (La Charte Québecoise des Droits de la Personne) prohibited all discrimination based on sexual orientation.

## Contemporary Québec

Beginning in 1982, Québec saw the explosion of militant lesbianism characterized by political activism and an enormous artistic production in literature, theater, dance, and music. Literary works by Marie-Claire Blais (1929–) and Nicole Brossard (1943–) and films by Léa Pool (1950–) were distributed internationally. There was an expansion of cultural events and community meeting places. Lesbian media became increasingly diversified as well: community radio broadcasts in English and French, magazines—*Amazones d'hier*, *Lesbiennes d'aujourd'hui* (Amazons Then, Lesbians Now [1982–]); *Ça s'attrape* (It's Catching! [1982–1984]); *Treize* (Thirteen [1984–]); *L'Evidente lesbienne* (The Obvious Lesbian [1984–1988])—and newsletters. From 1982 to 1989, annual conferences, called Journées de Visibilité (Days of Visibility) and subsequently Journées d'Interactions lesbiennes (Lesbian Days of Interaction), were held. In other words, lesbians spoke up and constructed a collective identity. Even though many lesbians continued to take an active part in the struggle for women's rights, the lesbian movement affirmed its separate status from the feminist movement, which, in turn, proved reluctant to support specific lesbian demands. However, the utopian ideal of building a lesbian community ran up against the divergent political agendas of lesbian feminists, who wanted to maintain the alliance with the feminist movement, and radical lesbians, who rejected it. These political debates were fueled as much by American as French writings. The rise of conservatism, successive economic crises, the extreme politicization of lesbian spaces, and internal division severely dampened the energy of the lesbian movement.

After what might be termed a period of disorganization in the early 1990s, the movement regrouped with a larger and more diversified base, within the context of more open social attitudes toward lesbianism. By the end of the century, groups pursued practical aims focusing on specific goals, including lesbian studies, recreational activities, sports, film, violence, and entrepreneurship. Some lesbians have continued to maintain separate status, while others have managed to establish lesbian services and groups within feminist associations. Still others are involved in the gay groups struggling for legal rights. Many young English speakers identify with the queer movement. Meeting places, more often than not mixed, exist in practically every region of Québec. Though fragmented, the lesbian movement is visible and active in many spheres of social life. After more than a year of networking and negotiating, the Reseau des Lesbiennes du Québec/ Québec Lesbian Network was founded in June 1997; its goals are to promote lesbians' rights and to develop solidarity among lesbians while respecting their diversity.

*Line Chamberland*

### Bibliography

Bertrand, Luce. *Le Rapport Bertrand sur le vécu de 1000 femmes lesbiennes* (The Bertrand Report on the Lives of 1,000 Lesbians). Montréal: Primeur Opinions, 1984.

Chamberland, Line. *Memoires lesbiennes. Le lesbianisme à Montréal entre 1950 et 1972* (Lesbian Memories: Lesbianism in Montréal Between 1950 and 1972). Montréal: Editions du Remuemenage, 1996.

———. "Remembering Lesbian Bars: Montreal, 1955–1975." *Journal of Homosexuality* 25:3 (1993), 231–269.

Gidlow, Elsa. *Elsa: I Come with My Songs: The Autobiography of Elsa Gidlow*. San Francisco: Booklegger, 1986.

Roy, Carolle. *Les lesbiennes et le feminisme* (Lesbians and Feminism). Montréal: Editions Saint-Martin, 1985.

*See also* Blais, Marie-Claire; Brossard, Nicole; Canada; Gidlow, Elsa


## Queer Nation

A multicultural direct-action group dedicated to fighting homophobia, queer invisibility, and all forms of oppression. This "in your face" (audacious and confrontational) organization is best known for its rallying cry: "We're here, we're queer, get used to it." It was founded in 1990 in New York City at the Lesbian and Gay Community Services Center. Like the Gay Liberation Front in the 1970s and ACT-UP (AIDS Coalition to Unleash Power) in the 1980s, Queer Nation used similar direct-action and confrontational strategies and rejected the mainstream assimilationist strategies. The group expanded to cities across the United States, especially those with universities and colleges, as the members were typically college age. A group was also established in London, England.

Known for disruptive protests, kiss-ins, and confrontations, the group nearly caused a riot in 1992 at the Republican Convention in Houston, Texas. Unlike ACT-UP, which focuses exclusively on AIDS activism, Queer Nation expanded beyond a single-issue political agenda to include fighting homophobia, gay bashing, and murder and incorporating antiracist and antisexist strategies and policies that addressed the specific needs of lesbians and queers of color. Often the group would "reappropriate" traditionally heterosexual spaces to stage their performance-art theatrics.

In addition to fighting racism and sexism, Queer Nation attempted to address class bias by operating as a nonhierarchical organization. An example of working groups included LABIA (Lesbian and Bisexual Women in Action), which covers spaces with posters and stickers sporting provocative slogans like "Don't call me a dyke unless you're going to kiss my clit" and "Lesbian by birth, queer by choice."

The term "queer" was adopted for its inclusiveness, since it purports to incorporate lesbians, gay men, bisexuals, transgender people, and heterosex-ual allies. As the decade of the 1990s progressed, struggles over race, gender, and bisexuality began to dissipate the effectiveness of Queer Nation, and the number of its participants began to decline.

*Akilah Monifa*

### Bibliography

Blumenfeld, Warren J., and Diane Raymond. *Looking at Gay and Lesbian Life*. Boston: Beacon, 1993.

Lewis, Andrea, and Robin Stevens. "At the Crossroads: Race, Gender, and the Gay Rights Movement." *Third Force* (April 30, 1996), 22–26.

*See also* Activism; Performance Art


## Queer Theory

Interdisciplinary body of work dedicated to denaturalizing the body and its pleasures. Queer theory arises out of, and is indebted to, earlier scholarly trends within gay and lesbian studies that attempted to construct histories of gay and lesbian people and to record their presence and influences in any number of fields and discourses. Queer theory moves beyond the endeavor to fill in the gaps left by heterosexist scholarship and tries to theorize subjectivity itself in relation to nonnormative sexual practices and identities. Queer history, furthermore, does not assume a transhistorical sexual subject but examines sexual practices within their specific historical and social contexts.

The work of Judith Butler has become synonymous with queer theory in the 1990s. In her enormously influential book *Gender Trouble: Feminism and the Subversion of Identity* (1990), she argues that the category of "woman" has been reified within feminism and that, while such a reification may have been necessary to generate a powerful critique of patriarchy, "rather than a stable signifier that commands the assent of those whom it purports to describe and represent, *women*, even in the plural, has become a troublesome term, a site of contest, a cause for anxiety" (emphasis in original). Following from Wittig's (1992) work on the "mark of gender," Butler makes gender troubling as a site for the production of identity. While Wittig questioned whether lesbians are women, Butler uses her critique of the category of "woman" to destabilize the very project of Western metaphysics itself. *Gender Trouble* has received much critical attention precisely because Butler's project is so ambitious: *Gender Trouble* seems to be about the subversive effects of cross-gender identification (within butch-femme, for example) upon feminism, but, actually, as a philosophical project, it uses cross-gender models to deconstruct the binaries (particularly male/female and hetero/homo) upon which Western metaphysics depends.

"Gender performance" is the main theoretical model that has been extracted from *Gender Trouble*. Butler argues that "gender is a copy without an original" and that gender is performative rather than expressive. If one uses this model to theorize the butch lesbian, for example, one is able to claim that butchness in no way mimics maleness but that, in fact, male masculinity actually depends upon female masculinity for its power. No masculinity exists prior to its performance in both male and female bodies, and male bodies cannot be said to originate the gender effect of masculinity. In relation to the binary relation of hetero- to homosexuality, Butler writes: "In other words, for heterosexuality to remain intact as a distinct social form, it *requires* an intelligible conception of homosexuality and also requires the prohibition of that conception in rendering it culturally intelligible." The performances of gender and sexuality, according to Butler, are in no way voluntary: We do not perform gender; in a sense, it performs us. As she puts it, it is not that there is no doer behind the deed, "but that the doer is variably constructed in and through the deed." She does mark out a place for something like agency, however, and that is in relation to gender parody, in which certain gender acts reveal the absence and, indeed, the impossibility of gender authenticity: One such act could be the drag show.

Esther Newton's 1972 ethnographic study of drag queens (*Mother Camp: Female Impersonators in America*), Gayle Rubin's 1984 work on the creation of sexual moralities ("Thinking Sex: Notes for a Radical Theory of the Politics of Sexuality"), and Michel Foucault's early volumes in his *History of Sexuality* (1980) are all crucial underpinnings of the enterprise that is now called "queer theory." While Newton's work on drag queens and on early-twentieth-century lesbian forms examines the ways in which gay and lesbian identities are translated into visible communities, Rubin's work has theorized the moral strictures that hamper what she calls "erotic creativity." As early as 1984, Rubin put out a call for a "radical theory of sex," which "must identify, describe, explain, and denounce erotic injustice and

sexual oppression." In her own weighty contributions to queer theory, Rubin has identified the basic ideological obstacles to a radical theory of sex. In addition to sexual essentialism, "the idea that sex is a natural force that exists prior to social life and shapes institutions," Rubin identifies "sex negativity, the fallacy of the misplaced scale, the hierarchical valuation of sex acts, the domino theory of sexual peril, and the lack of a benign concept of sexual variation" as the mainstays of a sexual system that demonizes and severely punishes erotic variation.

As Rubin shows, erotic variation within Western culture is not synonymous with gay and lesbian sexual orientations. Indeed, the Western sexual value system defines good and healthy sex in relation to monogamy, reproduction, and noncommercial sex, and bad, or abnormal, sex tends to involve pornography, fetish objects, masturbation, public sex, promiscuity, and prostitution. While good sex tends to be equated with heterosexuality, and bad sex tends to be equated with homosexuality, these equations do not always hold. Monogamous gays and lesbians or gays and lesbians with children can easily occupy positions within the sexual hierarchy above unmarried and promiscuous heterosexuals. Because of this complex scheme of sexual privilege and oppression, "gay" and "lesbian" do not automatically line up with "transgression," nor with progressive politics, for that matter, and "heterosexual" does not guarantee either sexual "health" or status quo politics. As Foucault suggests in *The History of Sexuality*, sexuality is a particularly unreliable marker of political transgression: "We must not think that by saying yes to sex, one says no to power."

Queer theory, in many ways, represents a move beyond thinking simply in terms of identity, and beyond even the idea of sexual identity itself. This entails the recognition that what Sedgwick (1990) has called the "homo/hetero binary" does not adequately delineate the multiple possibilities for sexuality. Queerness, in other words, designates sexualities defined by more than simply the gender of object choice; it is often used to refer to sexual minorities in general: Nongay and nonlesbian sexual minorities may include transsexuals or members of what is called the "gender community" (people in various stages of transsexual transition), sadomasochists, fetishists, transgenerational lovers, transvestites, male lesbians, queer butches, drag queens/kings, sodomists, and so on. Sexual identity can broken down into acts; it can also be broken down in terms of the relation of one's fantasy life to one's sex life. In fact, sexual identity can be based upon so many different factors that it seems reductive, if not downright violent, to insist that a person choose between two options and two alone—homo or hetero. The violence of this binary is most obvious in the AIDS crisis, in which the medical establishment has consistently refused to understand that acts, not sexual preferences, are dangerous. The AIDS crisis, in fact, emphasized the need to explode the confining discourse of identity.

Sedgwick is a queer thinker whose work has been dedicated to careful and powerful delineations of the mechanisms that uphold binarized sexual thinking. Her first book, *Between Men* (1985), demonstrated that what one thinks of as Western literary culture is a complicated web of homosocial relations between men—relations that rely, implicitly or explicitly, upon erotic male bonds. This claim was important because it allowed for a distinction to be made between the kind of male bonding that creates and sustains patriarchy, on the one hand, and relationships between self-identified gay men on the other. Sedgwick calls her theory feminist and "antihomophobic." In *Epistemology of the Closet* (1990), Sedgwick takes apart the discursive structure of the closet and demonstrates that the "open secret" of homosexuality allows for an intricate system of knowledge/ignorance to be built up around a hetero/homo binary. Sedgwick (1990) suggests that "the definitional narrowing-down in this century of sexuality as a whole to a binarized calculus of homo- or heterosexuality is a weighty fact but an entirely historical one." Sedgwick deconstructs that history and untangles the intersections between gender and sexuality that have, in some ways, obscured such a history.

Some scholars have critiqued an apparent emphasis on literary and cultural criticism within queer theory, and there are arguments about whether the queer enterprise is truly interdisciplinary. There is some irony in the apparent reluctance to apply social-science methods to the study of sex because, as queer sociologists are all too quick to point out, many of the theoretical systems that are used to talk about sex, such as social constructionism, come from sociology. In a "queer" issue of *Sociological Theory,* a group of sociologists attempted to account for the strained relations between sociological theory and queer theory. Epstein (1994) points out that it was sociology that asserted that sexuality was socially constructed, adding: "Without seeking to minimize the importance of other disciplines, I would suggest that neither queer theory nor lesbian and gay studies in general could be imagined in their present forms without the contributions of sociological theory." Other essays in this issue continue Epstein's line of inquiry to build a critique of the state of queer theory. While some of these essays represent problematic dismissals of queer cultural studies, they do point to what Duggan (1995) has called a "discipline problem" within queer theory. The discipline problem concerns not only what methods are used to study sexuality, but also what institutional dynamics conspire to house queer theory in some departments but not others.

Queer theory has been critiqued for more than just disciplinary problems. Many critics find that it provides inadequate models of the mutual constructions of race and sexuality or class and sexuality. The tendency within some queer theory to privilege psychoanalytic models of sexuality and gender has indeed, led theorists to bypass critical analyses of race- and class-based studies of sexuality. As Mercer (1994) states, "[T]he discourse of white sexual politics has been impoverished in its obsession with 'self.' " A psychoanalytic study of gay masculinity, Mercer suggests, universalizes a white model of maleness: "By emphasizing masculinity at the individual level of subjective interaction, rather than focus upon men as a sociological group, the privileged attention to "sexuality" is reductionist, as well as being ethnocentric by default." The absence of a critical discourse of whiteness within queer studies and the blindness of many queer theorists to issues of race and class has led to a widely held perception of queer theory as a white and, often, male discourse. What such criticisms overlook, however, is that queer theory cannot be limited to works by white gay men writing about canonical figures; rather, it resides at least partly in the tension between mainstream, white gay and lesbian scholarship and its critique. Queer theory, in other words, is that body of work produced by theorists of color, as well as the work they critique.

It might be asked, finally, does queer theory happen outside the academy? In many ways, queer theory originates outside the academy as a theoretical and intellectual response to the AIDS crisis. It grows out of the activism of ACT-UP and out of coalitions of people affected in one way or another by the AIDS crisis. Queer theory marks a back-and-forth relation between the academic and the public spheres, and, just as some theoretical understandings of sexuality and identity inform some community organizing, some of the insights produced within political communities, bars, sex clubs, 'zines, and popular literature feed queer intellectual production. It is important to resist using "queer" as an umbrella term for sexual minorities, and instead use it to mark radical models of sexual politics.

*Judith Halberstam*

### Bibliography

Duggan, Lisa. "The Discipline Problem." *GLQ: A Journal of Lesbian and Gay Studies* 2:3 (1995), 179–192.

Epstein, Steven. "A Queer Encounter: Sociology and the Study of Sexuality." In *Sociological Theory,* 12:2 (1994), 188–202.

Foucault, Michel. *The History of Sexuality,* vol. 1: *An Introduction.* Trans. Robert Hurley. New York: Vintage, 1980.

Mercer, Kobena. *Welcome to the Jungle: New Positions in Black Cultural Studies.* London and New York: Routledge, 1994.

Newton, Esther. *Mother Camp: Female Impersonators in America.* London and Chicago: University of Chicago Press, 1972.

Rubin, Gayle. "Thinking Sex: Notes for a Radical Theory of the Politics of Sexuality." In *Pleasure and Danger: Exploring Female Sexuality.* Ed. Carole Vance. Boston and London: Routledge, 1984, pp. 267–319.

Sedgwick, Eve Kosofsky. *Epistemology of the Closet.* Berkeley and Los Angeles: University of California Press, 1990.

Wittig, Monique. *The Straight Mind and Other Essays.* Boston: Beacon, 1992.

***See also*** Critical Theory; Cultural Studies; Performativity; Postmodernism; Wittig, Monique

# R

## Race and Racism

In the eighteenth century, taxonomist Carl Linnaeus (1707–1778) coined the term *homo sapiens* and cataloged the human species into four races based on skin tone: *homo americanus* (reddish); *homo eruopaeus* (white), *homo asiaticus* (yellow), and *homo afer* (black). His categorization provided not only phenotypic markers, such as facial features, skin color, and hair texture, to classify the races, but also a brief description of the characteristics associated with each race: *homo americanus* were said to be "ruled by custom"; *homo eruopaeus*, "ruled by opinion"; *homo asiaticus*, "ruled by rites"; and *homo afer*, "ruled by caprice." Thus, Linneaus was an early advocate of pairing personality constructs with physical differences.

## Race, Ethnicity, and Culture

Although race referred to phenotypic differences associated with geographical regions at one time, in the United States race is a social construct rather than a meaningful biological or genetic determinant. For bicultural individuals, racial distinctions based on biology are not meaningful, but phenotypic traits, nevertheless, carry certain assumptions that create a hierarchy of power and privilege. Many societies reify racial differences to create "meaningful" categories to understand human behavior. The social construction of race prevails in the United States, among other societies, and plays a central role in the assumptions about one's own racial group and the racial group of others. Adherence to meaningful racial differences carries a psychosocial meaning, including the justification of bias, discrimination, stereotypes, and prejudice. Furthermore, the "relevance" of race establishes assumptions about privilege and a justification of superiority of one group over another, which remains unrecognized by the majority of the privileged group.

The terms "race" and "ethnicity" are frequently confused and used interchangeably. Ethnicity refers to shared cultural and behavioral elements of a group: Members may be of the same race or from other racial backgrounds, but they share the same cultural practices. Culture refers to shared customs, values, traditions, and worldviews of a group of people who identify with the same ethnic group, although national cultures may grow out of, and be shared by, a number of different ethnic groups within a country. Ethnicity involves socialization patterns that begin with, but are not limited to, genotypic (genetic constitution) or phenotypic descriptors. Phinney (1996) suggests that there are three components of ethnicity: one's culture, one's ethnic identity, and how one is perceived and treated by others, given their presumed ethnicity. Since American culture is resistant to letting go of the socially constructed meaning of race, race will, for the foreseeable future, play a central role in research on human behavior. In American society, race, along with gender, are the largest categories used to describe and to distinguish individuals.

## Racial and Ethnic Identity

To understand the relevance of race or ethnicity to an individual, one must appreciate that individuals differ in the relevance of race and ethnicity in their lives. Racial identity and ethnic identity refer to how individuals differ in their identification with their racial and ethnic groups, respectively. The racial and ethnic identity of an individual is a fluid, dynamic

**R** process rather than a category or a fixed stage. For people of color, Helms (1995) states, racial identity ranges from identifying with whites, to identifying only with one's own racial group, thereby denigrating whites, to being comfortable with one's own racial group as well as appreciating the positive aspects of other racial groups.

Ethnic identity is a component of self-concept that refers to the role or impact of culture in a person's life and the extent to which one identifies with one's ethnicity. Phinney describes ethnicity as an umbrella term for race and for culture and states that ethnic identity is a multifaceted, dynamic, and fluid process. She measures ethnic identity from a developmental model and addresses a person's self-identification, ethnic behavior, feelings of affirmation and belonging, achieved ethnic identity, and feelings toward other ethnic groups. Racial and ethnic identities are processes that are reexamined throughout one's life span and may be modified, given the life experiences of an individual. In essence, to appreciate the meaning of race and ethnicity in the United States, one must also be cognizant of the ramifications of race, the role of privilege and oppression in society, and the racial and ethnic identification of an individual.

## Racism

Racism is discrimination against an individual or a group based on their assumed racial inferiority by a racial group that assumes its own superiority, a policy that is imposed by social and legal sanctions. In the United States, racism exists on many levels: individual, institutional, and cultural. While individual racism is racism manifested by one individual toward another, institutional racism is implicitly or explicitly sanctioned by society through laws and social norms that ensure the superiority of whites over people of color. Institutional racism, for example, restricts the purchase of property by people of color, interferes with the procurement of loans, and denies people of color access to clubs and organizations. Cultural racism adheres to the belief that Eurocentric customs, language, values, and the like are superior to those of people of color. For example, independence is highly valued in a Eurocentric context, while interdependence is more common and highly valued in cultures of color. As a result, dissonance emerges for people of color as they engage in the process of forming their racial and ethnic identity in a culture that creates myriad boundaries that interfere with developing one's full potential.

## Race and Racism in the Lesbian Community

Like white lesbians, lesbians of color have to contend with sexism and homophobia. Racism in the lives of lesbians of color and the influence of privilege in the lives of white lesbians influence the social and political climate of the lesbian community. All women experience sexism; in the lesbian community, the experience of sexism, along with homophobia and heterosexism, becomes the bond of unity. Because the experience of homophobia is so strong, it can blind the predominantly white lesbian community to other types of oppression and the reality of the diversity within the lesbian community. Experiences with racism compound the experiences of homophobia and heterosexism for lesbians of color. When the predominantly white lesbian community subtly demands that sexual orientation prevail as one's primary identification, it denies the relevance of race in the lives of lesbians of color. The result is split loyalties and conflicts within the lesbian community as a whole.

The predominantly white lesbian community is a product of contemporary American society and, as such, is a racist community practicing individual and cultural racism. Not to recognize the relevance of race or ethnicity for lesbians of color is an overt dismissal of the importance race and ethnicity in their lives. Not only is there pressure to identify primarily as a lesbian independent of race or ethnicity, lesbians of color are also discriminated against and oppressed within the community. The predominantly white lesbian community prides itself on its acceptance of difference, and yet many within it may cringe at the visibility of lesbians of color beyond a token number of women of color at social or political events. The presence of a disproportionate number of lesbians of color is all that is required for the predominantly white community to be in touch with the racism and privilege that predominates in the lesbian community. As a result, lesbians of color frequently feel isolated and marginalized within the lesbian community. To the extent that the white lesbian community does not acknowledge the privilege that race offers it will feel comfortable describing the white lesbian experience as representative of all lesbians. However, several groups of women of color and white women have evolved to address the racism in the lesbian community. These groups have moved from a recognition of racism to a nonracist stance ("I do not practice racism") and are working on their anitracist commitment ("I will take an active role in eliminating racism in our society"). Such groups are making the lesbian community more cognizant of the diversity within and responsive to the needs and concerns of all lesbians.

Furthermore, some white women within the lesbian community may not appreciate the bond between women and men of color that is created by a racist society. Women of color express the pressure they face to "choose" an oppression, a choice lesbians of color do not need or desire to make. For lesbians of color, there is no hierarchy of oppressions.

## Lesbians of Color in Communities of Color

For many lesbians of color, communities of color have been a safe haven for racial identification and racial oppression. Juxtaposed against this haven for racial and ethnic identification is the homophobia within the community, which is more intense in communities of color. Lesbians of color may feel abandoned in their communities of color, and communities of color frequently perceive lesbians of color as abandoning the needs of their communities of color and the struggle for equality. Communities of color accuse lesbians of color of abandoning the community, not perpetuating the race, and being influenced by white culture since homosexuality is a perceived as a "white" lifestyle choice. As a result, lesbians of color may feel a greater need to remain closeted, creating an environment that is potentially detrimental to their mental health. All lesbians share the experiences of sexism and homophobia, but lesbians of color have a history of discrimination along racial lines: Coming out makes lesbians of color triply oppressed. Losing the support of communities of color, combined with their membership in three oppressed groups (women, lesbians, and people of color) and the racism within the lesbian community, creates a significant amount of stress for lesbians of color. Audre Lorde (1934–1992), a lesbian activist, challenged the African American community, in particular, to recognize the relevance of oppression and racial pride for all African Americans independent of sexual orientation. Given their own history and experiences with oppression, communities of color find it more challenging to be open to lesbians of color whom they mistakenly label as disloyal to issues and concerns of communities of color. This alienation is unnecessary and harmful, denying communities of color the talents and energies of a vital segment of their communities.      *Ruth Hall*

### Bibliography

Greene, Beverly. "Lesbian Women of Color." In *Women of Color*. Ed. Lillian Comas-Díaz and Beverly Greene. New York: Guilford, 1994, pp. 389–427.

Hall, Ruth. L., and Suzanna Rose. "Friendships Between African American and White Lesbians." In *Lesbians and Friendships: Ourselves and Each Other*. Ed. Jacqueline S. Weinstock and Esther D. Rothblum. New York: New York University Press, 1996, pp. 165–191.

Helms, Janet E. "An Update of Helms White and People of Color Racial Identity Models." In *Handbook of Multicultural Counseling*. Ed. Joseph G. Ponterotto, J. Manuel Casas, Lisa A. Suzuki, and Charlene M. Alexander. Thousand Oaks, Calif.: Sage, 1995, pp. 181–198.

Leslie, Dorian, and Lauren MacNeill. "Double Positive: Lesbians and Race." In *Racism in the Lives of Women: Testimony, Theory, and Guides to Antiracist Practice*. Ed. Jeanne Adleman and Gloria Enguidanos. New York: Hayworth, 1995, pp. 161–179.

Lorde, Audre. "I Am Your Sister: Black Women Organizing Across Sexualities." *Practice* 5:1 (1987), 83–87.

Phinney, Jean. S. "When We Talk About American Ethnic Groups, What Do We Mean?" *American Psychologist* 51 (1996), 918–927.

*See also* Discrimination; Lorde, Audre; Prejudice; Stereotype; Women of Color

## Radicalesbians

New York City–based group originally called the Lavender Menace (LM). LM formed in response to the homophobia of the women's liberation movement, especially that of the National Organization for Women (NOW), despite the fact that some of New York NOW's leaders were lesbians. Some heterosexual feminists derided lesbians for butch-femme "role playing" and for refusing to engage and transform the male oppressor. Heterosexual feminists also tended to view lesbianism as a mere lifestyle choice, as opposed to a biologically determined and oppressed gender class of women.

LM finally coalesced around two events in 1970. In a piece entitled "Sisterhood Is Powerful" in the *New York Times Magazine* (March 15, 1970), Susan Brownmiller dismissed NOW president Betty Friedan's assessment that lesbians were a "lavender menace," implying that gay women would destroy the credibility of the women's movement. Brownmiller suggested that lesbians were "a lavender her-

**R** ring perhaps, but surely no clear and present danger." The final insult came when NOW's Second Congress to Unite Women in May 1970 completely omitted lesbians from its agenda.

Lesbians from the Gay Liberation Front (GLF) Women, the Daughters of Bilitis, and Redstockings joined forces to pen a response to this rampant heterosexism. Members of the original group included Sidney Abbott, Ellen Bedoz [Ellen Shumsky], Ellen Broidy, Rita Mae Brown, Cynthia Funk, Michela Griffo, Lois Hart, Karla Jay, Arlene Kisner, Barbara Love, and Martha Shelley. Together they slowly carved out a manifesto. The chief author was March Hoffman (later Artemis March), but many members of the group contributed to its final shape. The document, entitled "The Woman-Identified Woman" (1971), avoided the loaded term "lesbian" and tried to universalize the sexual oppression of gay women by asserting that a "lesbian is the rage of all women condensed to the point of explosion." The manifesto agreed that lesbianism was a societally created category, but no more so than heterosexuality, and argued that, in a truly free society, both categories would disappear. The document also proclaimed that a "primal commitment which includes sexual love" is essential to the liberation of women.

The document was disseminated on May 1, 1970, on the first night of the Second Congress to Unite Women. Decked out in pale purple T-shirts with the words "Lavender Menace" stenciled across the front, some members of the group cut off the lights and microphone and surrounded the audience. Other protesters were planted in the audience and "spontaneously joined" the demonstration. Workshops on lesbian issues were held, and the congress adopted a pro-lesbian platform. At the close of the congress, consciousness-raising groups were set up for those interested in lesbian feminism.

After changing the groups name to Lesbian Liberation and finally to Radicalesbians (RL), the women continued to meet and discuss politcal action. RL attempted to be nonhierarchical, but some women nevertheless emerged as leaders, causing other powerful women who were not part of this group to drop out. RL advocated strict separatism, and mainstream writers such as Kate Millett were denounced as collaborators. RL divided further when some women cooperated with the police in the murder investigation of group member Lydia French. Some were dismayed by RL's hostility to gay men, bisexual women, and all heterosexuals, while others decried RL's lack of attention to issues of race and class. Barbara Love and oth-

ers revived the GLF Women's Caucus, which drew those who were disillusioned with RL politics. Finally, the creation of Lesbian Feminist Liberation, Inc., during the winter of 1971–1972 left RL with only a handful of members.

The fact that RL was the first post-Stonewall radical gay women's group has given it an importance that belies its actual size and duration. The success of the Lavender Menace action gave RL mythical stature as the group that took over the women's movement, if only for one night.          *Karla Jay*

### Bibliography

Brown, Rita Mae. "Take a Lesbian to Lunch." In *Out of the Closets: Voices of Gay Liberation.* Ed. Karla Jay and Allen Young. New York: New York University Press, 1972. Reprint. 1992, pp. 185–195.

Echols, Alice. *Daring To Be Bad: Radical Feminism in America, 1967–1975.* Minneapolis: University of Minnesota Press, 1989.

Marotta, Toby. *The Politics of Homosexuality.* Boston: Houghton Mifflin, 1981.

Radicalesbians. "The Woman Identified Woman." In *Notes from the Third Year: Women's Liberation.* Ed. Anne Koedt and Shulamith Firestone. New York: Notes from the Second Year, Inc., 1971.

Teal, Donn. *The Gay Militants.* New York: Stein and Day, 1971.

***See also*** Brown, Rita Mae; Gay Liberation Movement; Jay, Karla; Millett, Kate; National Organization for Women (NOW); Woman-Identified Woman; Women's Liberation Movement

## Radio

Programs hosted and produced by lesbians, or programs that express, reflect, and document the varied perspectives, realities, and experiences of women-loving women.

Lesbians began producing and hosting radio programs during the "second wave" of U.S. feminism. During the early 1970s, many lesbian feminists, (some "out," some not) created weekly programs on community radio stations, the most accessible of the broadcast media, in cities and rural communities throughout the world.

While many, but not all, feminist radio programs include lesbian perspectives, few programs have been lesbian "only." *Amazon Country* (WXPN-FM Philadelphia, Pennsylvania), one of the first lesbian radio programs in the United States, first came on the air in 1974. In 1997, the producer, Debra D'Alessandro, said: "The majority of programs are on lesbian issues, but some are more broadly about issues impacting all women. Every program includes . . . a calendar of events of interest to lesbians and feminists." Lesbian and feminist radio shows, which may include music, interviews, news, and talk formats, serve an important function for lesbians and feminists: documenting cultural events, forums, and demonstrations and covering local, national, and international political controversies, always asking: How does this affect women? Which women? Lesbian and feminist radio has often been the only source of media attention for lesbian and feminist musicians, writers and poets, artists and comics.

Feminists and lesbians, slotted into a few hours once a week during low-listening times such as Sunday afternoons, have constantly battled to get their shows on the air and keep them there. Airtime has often been shared collectively by volunteers, the majority of whom have been lesbian. In large communities, such as Boston, Massachusetts, and Washington, D.C., women who secured a weekly air slot supported and trained a broad range of women in the community over a period of months to produce an annual eighteen-to-twenty-four hours of women's programming, including lesbian programming, for International Women's Day, March 8.

Some radio communities created wry and funny soap operas that challenged stereotypes about women and lesbians, such as *The Liberation of Lydia* (ca. 1970), WYBC-FM, New Haven, Connecticut; *The Well of Horniness* (1980), WBAI-FM, New York City; and *As the Rumors Fly* (1980), WZRD-FM, Chicago, Illinois.

One early lesbian radio program was *The Lesbian Radio Spectacular with a Cast of Millions* (1976–1977), WBAI-FM, New York City. Producer and writer Judith Pasternak recalled:

It was my intent to say the "L" word as often, as loudly and publicly as possible in order to forcibly insert [it] into a culture that is so profoundly misogynist, and in which loving women is not perceived as a choice, the underlying notion that one can actually choose to love a woman.

Each show opened with a taped collage of women identifying themselves by their work and their sexual identity: "I am an actor and I'm a lesbian." Said Pasternak: "The idea was to let people know we are everywhere."

Few lesbian or even feminist radio programs have lasted. Journalist Laura Flanders, an "out" lesbian and feminist, for a number of years hosted *Counter Spin*, a nationally syndicated radio program heard on community stations around the country. Lesbians produce nationally and internationally distributed radio programs with gay men, and some lesbians and feminists use the Internet as a new audio outlet and avenue for sharing radio resources—a goal for many lesbian and feminist radio pioneers of the "second wave."                    *Jennifer Abod*

## Bibliography

Kelly, Janis. "Feminist Radio: Sophie's Tells All." *Off Our Backs* (February 1982), 20–21.

Rainone, Nanette. "Men and Violence: WBAI Consciousness Raising." In *Radical Feminism*. Ed. Anne Koedt, Ellen Levine, and Anita Rapone. New York: Quadrangle/New York Times Book, 1973, pp. 63–71.

*See also* Journalism

## Rainey, Gertrude "Ma" (1886–1939)

African American blues, jazz, and vaudeville singer and songwriter. As a girl, Gertrude Pridgett sang in cabaret and minstrel shows. In 1904, she married Will "Pa" Rainey, with whom she formed the Rabbit Foot Minstrels and sang the blues in tent shows throughout the South. She separated from Pa Rainey in 1917 and continued touring the South with her own group, Ma Rainey and Her Georgia Smart Set. She made her first recording in 1923 with Paramount, and by 1929 she had recorded ninety-two songs, at least one-third of which she wrote herself. Named the "Mother of the Blues," Ma Rainey had her musical roots in the from country blues style typical of the rural South. She was a sensational and powerful stage presence, and her highly visceral renditions of the blues were often described as cathartic: Her live performances mesmerized her audiences with an unprecedented depth and richness barely matched by other "classic blues" singers of her time.

Rainey's songs express themes of poverty, heartbreak, humor, cynicism, endurance, violence, prison, and sexuality, among others. Her sexual preference for women was well known both on and off stage. In her "Prove It on Me Blues" (1928)—her most famous expression of lesbian sexuality, cross-dressing, and assertiveness—she declares: "Went out last night with a crowd of my friends / They must've been women, 'cause I don't like no men." Nearly fifty years later, Teresa Trull recovered this song on *Lesbian Concentrate: A Lesbianthology of Songs and Poems* (Olivia Records, 1977). Sexual candor and lesbianism are also apparent in Rainey's "Shave 'Em Dry Blues" (1924), which suggests that some prostitutes may be lesbians. Rainey's biographer, Sandra Lieb, writes that Rainey and blues singer Bessie Smith (1894?–1937) were close friends and occasionally performed together. Sam Chatmon, a guitarist in Rainey's tent show in Jackson, Mississippi, stated in a 1975 interview with Lieb his belief that Rainey and Smith were lovers.

Lieb (1981) describes Ma Rainey's contralto voice on recordings as heavy, rough, without vibrato, and enormously energetic. Her slurred diction, Georgia accent, characteristic moan, and jug-band accompaniments marked her musical style as distinctly Southern and set her apart from New York–based "blues queens" such as Bessie Smith, Mamie Smith (1883–1946), Lucille Hegamin (1894–1970), and Edith Wilson (1896–1981).          *Martha Mockus*

### Bibliography

Davis, Angela Y. "I Used To Be Your Sweet Mama: Ideology, Sexuality, and Domesticity in the Blues of Gertrude 'Ma' Rainey and Bessie Smith." In *Sexy Bodies: The Strange Carnalities of Feminism*. Ed. Elizabeth Grosz and Elspeth Probyn. New York: Routledge, 1995, pp. 231–265.

Lieb, Sandra R. *Mother of the Blues: A Study of Ma Rainey*. Boston: University of Massachusetts Press, 1981.

*See also* African Americans; Blues Singers; Harlem; Harlem Renaissance; Smith, Bessie

### Raucourt, Françoise (1756–1815)

French actress. Born in Paris, March 3, 1756, Françoise Raucourt was among the first French women who dared to live her love of women openly, without choosing to hide behind a marriage or an impeccable reputation. She loved her freedom so much that, in their correspondence, her contemporaries called her "the priestess of Lesbos." Some even went so far as to install her as president of the "Secte Anadryne," a group that existed only in the imagination of François Mairobert, author of *The English Spy* (1777–1778). Raucourt made her debut at the Comédie Française in 1772 in the role of Dido. Her beauty, gifts, voice, and intelligent reading of the role assured her the success that would follow her throughout her career in the theater. However, if Raucourt, the actress, charmed Paris, Raucourt, the lover, soon made the news—just as frequently for acting like a grand lord as for her relationships with the singer Sophie Arnould, Mademoiselle Virginie, Jeanne Souque, and Madame de Mailly. While her status as an actress who had been excommunicated by the Catholic Church gave her a freedom that the great ladies of the aristocracy might have envied, her taste for ostentation and her generosity toward her lovers led her quickly into bankruptcy and forced her to flee to Germany in 1776 to escape her creditors. She returned secretly to France, several months later, and eventually took refuge with the Prince de Ligne. Thanks to her many powerful supporters, including Queen Marie Antoinette (1755–1793), who paid her debts, she rejoined the Comédie Française in 1779 "in the service first of the Queen and in starring roles."

Termed an "insolent sultaness" by the *Journal of Public Safety*, Françoise Raucourt lived through the French Revolution with the same panache she showed during the Ancien Régime. Although she was imprisoned in August 1793 with the other actors of the Comédie Française for having acted in a royalist play (and perhaps for her ties to the counter-revolutionary movement), she was saved by the coup d'état of 9 Thermidor. Unlike Madame de Lamballe (1749–1792), who was mutilated and assassinated in September 1792 for her "excessive" friendship with the queen, Raucourt was not harassed for her sexual mores. During the Directory (the revolutionary government in France, 1795–1799), she was named director of the Théâtre Louvois and later, in 1803, of the French Theaters in Italy. She did not retire from the stage until 1814, after having created twenty-four roles in forty years. She died the next year in Paris, where she was so well loved that the Parisians made the priest of Saint-Roch say a Mass for her burial (despite the excommunication) before they accompanied her to the Père Lachaise cemetery.          *Marie-Jo Bonnet*

### Bibliography

Blanc, Olivier. *Les Libertines: Plaisir et liberté au temps des Lumières* (The Libertines: Pleasure and Freedom in the Enlightenment). Paris: Perrin, 1997.

Bonnet, Marie-Jo. *Un choix sans équivoque* (An Unequivocal Choice). Paris: Denoël, 1981. Revised and reprinted as *Les relations amoureuses entre les femmes du XVIe au XXe siècle* (Loving Relations Between Women from the Eleventh to the Twentieth Century). Paris: Odile Jacob, 1995.

Merrick, Jeffrey. "The Marquis de Vilette and Mademoiselle Raucourt: Representations of Male and Female Sexual Deviance in the Late Eighteenth Century." In *Homosexuality in Modern France.* Ed. Jeffrey Merrick and Bryant T. Ragan. New York: Oxford University Press, 1996, pp. 30–53.

*See also* France; Marie Antoinette

## Recovery Movement

Term, believed to have first emerged from the therapy community in Minnesota in the 1970s, that encompasses a variety of groups of individuals who either identify themselves as addicted to substances or behaviors or are connected to those who are addicted. The movement peaked in the late 1980s. Despite the fact that, becuase of the anonymity of membership, there is no definitive estimate of the number of people who were active in the movement or of those that are still active, the recovery movement achieved widespread popularity in both the lesbian community and the larger society.

### Characteristics

The critical part of the recovery movement is the way it expanded the concept of addiction from addiction to a habituating substance, such as drugs or alcohol, to characterizing a variety of behaviors as addictive. These include loving someone who is addicted (codependency); shopping too much (shopping addiction); using too much makeup (makeup addiction); and, perhaps most ominously for feminists, addiction to pornography and sexual abuse (sex addiction).

A variety of support and self-help groups were (and continued in the 1990s to be) formed, most based on the twelve-step model created by Alcoholics Anonymous (AA) to encourage people to treat their addiction by embracing the AA concept of recovery. As a result, no one is ever "cured" of an addiction; rather, one is always in recovery.

### History

Alcoholics Anonymous was founded in 1935 by Bob Smith and Bill Wilson. AA emerged from an organization called the Oxford Group, a Christian revival movement, originally called the First Century Christian Fellowship. The central insight of AA is that one alcoholic talking to another is a vital source of strength and healing. AA relies heavily on the medical concept of alcoholism as a chronic and progressive disease; its members believe that if one admits powerlessness over such a disease, that is the first step to recovery. AA groups are based on a twelve-step program that is reported to have had tremendous success in addressing issues of alcoholism. The degree of this success is a source of controversy, however. Among the many positive aspects of AA are its grass-roots organization, the widespread availability of groups, the support offered in the groups, and the fact that it is basically a free program. Many of the critiques of AA have focused on its origins as a Christian group, on whether it is as successful as it claims, and on whether AA's belief that alcoholics can never drink again is an accurate assessment.

Lesbians, some social scientists argue, have historically been at tremendous risk for alcoholism. First, because of the degree to which lesbian social life revolved around bars and bar culture, lesbians are believed to be at heightened risk of alcohol abuse. Several studies of lesbians and alcoholism conducted in the 1970s, with samples drawn from different geographical locations, estimated that 35 percent of all lesbians had a serious problem with alcohol (Sandmaier, 1980). Second, as members of an oppressed and stigmatized group, many lesbians have used alcohol and drugs to dull the pain of social ostracism. For many lesbians, AA has literally saved their lives.

In the 1970s, a number of therapists began to expand the concept of addiction beyond the habitual abuse of alcohol or other drugs to characterize a variety of behaviors as addictive, resulting in later, influential books such as Beattie's (1987) and Schaef's (1987). These addictions, they argued, represented progressive diseases that could be fatal if not treated appropriately. The treatment of these addictions still relied on the twelve-step model created by AA; however, many of the groups were now led by therapists who charged fees for working with those now defined as addicts.

### Contemporary Controversies

Many lesbians, such as McDaniel (1989), have written eloquent testimonies to the efficacy of the recov-

**R** ery movement. The central argument of those who defend the movement is that addiction, in any of its forms, has been the primary stumbling block for many women in terms of not only achieving self-actualization, but also of being more effective political activists.

Critics of these movements, such as Peele (1989), Bette Tallen, and the authors in *Challenging Codependency: Feminist Critiques* (Babcock and McKay 1995), have argued that calling behaviors such as excessive consumption of food; overdependence on sex, love, or relationships; and codependency addictive disease misses the point that many of these behaviors are individual responses to oppression.

Codependency and sex addiction are concepts that are particularly troubling to such critics. Codependency (defined as being in a relationship with an addict or being raised in a dysfunctional family) encompasses such a wide variety of behaviors that many of its proponents allege that it affects 96 percent of the population. Feminist critiques of codependency object to this pathologizing of family life. They believe that this characterization misses the point that the family is a focal nexus of institutional racism, sexism, classism, and heterosexism. By stating that being raised in a dysfunctional family qualifies one for treatment, it betrays the feminist goals of the radical transformation of the nuclear family.

Sex addicts, most of whom are male, are defined in the recovery movement as those with an addiction to pornography and sexual abuse. This terminology is particularly troubling to critics who believe that terming such behaviors a manifestation of a disease allows males to evade responsibility for such acts as rape and child abuse.

Those who defend treatment for codependency and sex addiction point out that, without these programs, many would continue behaviors that are destructive to themselves and others. Without the availability of programs that destigmatize the behavior, they argue, many would not seek treatment.

While the recovery movement appeared to lose some of its popularity in the 1990s, the debate will continue in feminist and lesbian circles about whether the movement is a progressive one that saves women's lives or whether it represents a depoliticization of feminism.　　*Bette S. Tallen*

### Bibliography

Babcock, Marguerite, and Christine McKay, eds. *Challenging Codependency: Feminist Cri-*
*tiques*. Toronto: University of Toronto Press, 1995.

Beattie, Melody. *Codependent No More*. New York: Harper/Hazelden, 1987.

McDaniel, Judith. *Metamorphosis: Reflections on Recovery*. Ithaca, N.Y.: Firebrand, 1989.

Peele, Stanton. *Diseasing of America: Addiction Treatment Out of Control*. Lexington, Mass.: D.C. Heath, 1989.

Robertson, Nan. *Getting Better: Inside Alcoholics Anonymous*. New York: William Morrow, 1988.

Sandmaier, Marian. *The Invisible Alcoholics: Women and Alcohol Abuse in America*. New York: McGraw Hill, 1980.

Schaef, Anne Wilson. *When Society Becomes an Addict*. San Francisco: Harper and Row, 1987.

***See also*** Alcohol and Substance Abuse; Self-Help

## Recreation

Activities participated in primarily for their entertainment value. During the twentieth century, when recreational opportunities for women in the United States began expanding beyond the confines of home, the community-related and community-building activities of lesbians varied, depending on the general economic and political climate of the time. During more conservative eras in U.S. history, lesbian recreation tended to be more discrete and clandestine, while more liberal climates fostered open socializing. In general, though, lesbian recreational opportunities burgeoned since the Stonewall Rebellion (1969), particularly in major metropolitan areas.

### Bars, Private Clubs, and Social Groups

As early as the 1920s, there were bars in large cities nationally that catered to a gay and lesbian clientele. In most cities, the women frequenting such establishments were young working-class lesbians, although many bars in Harlem in New York City also attracted members of a sophisticated, wealthy crowd, some merely experimenting with sexuality but also women whose primary attraction was to women. Though the poor economic conditions during the 1930s Depression years reduced opportunities of all kinds for women, bars remained a recreational option in many cities. And during the 1940s, when large numbers of women identifying themselves as lesbians migrated to large urban areas, it became possible for a number of bars catering exclusively to lesbians to survive economically. While bars did not necessarily engender political consciousness, they did provide an important sense of community to women, making them feel less isolated in their love for women. The repressiveness of the 1950s, due to the anti homosexual inquiries of the United States House Un-American Activities Committee, necessitated that visits to bars be clandestine, but, for many, especially young working-class women who could not receive friends at their families' homes, bars were one of the few options for socializing as lesbians. In the 1970s and 1980s, gay and lesbian and exclusively lesbian bars flourished in cities. While particular bars might come and go, the bar as a lesbian institution remained a perennial recreational option.

Although social mores changed enough from the nineteenth to the twentieth century to make it more acceptable for working-class women to frequent saloons, the message many women still got was that nice girls did not go to bars. These women, many of whom were middle class, often relied on private clubs and social groups—such as the New York City–based Nucleus Club of the late 1930s and the Daughters of Bilitis in the 1950s (which soon turned from social to political in nature)—which typically offered meetings and dances as social opportunities. Although taboos against frequenting bars all but vanished by the 1980s and 1990s, many lesbians found social groups to be more congenial, and such groups abounded, with organizations based on ethnic and religious affiliations and on a variety of interests, such as square dancing, choral singing, fishing, and motorcycling.

## Athletics

Sports make up another enduring recreational pastime among lesbians. Historically, softball was an important community-building activity, for both players and spectators, probably since the advent of women's industrial softball teams in the 1930s and certainly since the 1940s and 1950s. While softball continued to be, in the 1980s and 1990s, one of the most popular forms of athletic recreation—especially in rural areas, where other options tend to be limited—lesbians participated in a variety of sports, both on mixed gay and straight teams and on lesbian-only teams and in individual sports. The Metropolitan Sports Association of Chicago, for instance, in 1996 offered its all-gay membership not only softball, but also bowling, tennis, volleyball, basketball, flag football, and darts, and many les-

bians in the area were involved in sports sponsored by various other organizations, including rugby, golf, soccer, karate, racquetball, bicycling, running, and swimming.

Many lesbians—athletes and not, alike—enjoyed watching sports, both women's and men's, professional and amateur. Parties and excursions were often organized around sporting events. Women's professional teams (baseball, softball, volleyball, and basketball) shied away from courting a lesbian audience but, although historically short-lived, enjoyed a substantial lesbian audience nonetheless. Professional golf and tennis operated in a similar homophobic vein until tennis great Martina Navratilova (1956–) brought lesbian sexuality into the open on the tennis circuit. Any event featuring Navratilova always drew a crowd of lesbians, and, since her coming out, she has had a faithful following among lesbians, including some who had never before followed tennis. Golf has also been known for having a substantial lesbian following, especially seen at the Dinah Shore Ladies Professional Golf Association (LPGA) tournament. Although two professional women golfers came out in the mid- to late-1990s (Muffin Spencer-Devlin and Patty Sheehan), they did not inspire the same level of idolatry that Navratilova did.

The Gay Games, a multisport festival held every four years since 1982, counted more than seven thousand participants at the Games in Vancouver in 1990, about half of whom were women.

Lesbians were also involved in the gay rodeo circuit (twenty-two such rodeos existed in the 1990s across the United States), both as spectators and participants. Participants competed against other women in everything from bull riding to calf roping and barrel racing.

## Festivals, Concerts, and Other Cultural Events

Women's music and literature, which proliferated in the 1970s, became the cornerstones of a large entertainment industry geared toward lesbians. Lesbians could, in the 1990s, choose from nearly a dozen national and regional music and culture festivals, and many major cities have had production companies that staged music and comedy concerts locally for lesbians, although such events waned somewhat following the advent of mainstream lesbian performers, such as Melissa Etheridge (1961–) and k.d. lang (1961–), in the 1980s. Bookstores and women's coffeehouses offered readings, performances, and discussion venues to their clientele. And Gay Pride events provide seasonal entertainment for lesbians, often featuring a weeklong menu of parades, dances, and rallies.

## Travel/Outdoor Activities

Since the late 1970s, lesbians have participated in a broad spectrum of activities emphasizing some combination of nature and mobility. The more rugged enjoyed wilderness excursions, ranging from canoeing, backpacking, and mountain climbing to rafting, kayaking, and dogsledding. There were numerous women's wilderness-excursion organizations around the country in the 1990s, attesting to the popularity of this pastime. A precursor of such female-oriented outings was camp counseling, which dates back to the 1930s as a recreational opportunity for women, especially lesbians.

Equally adventurous, but perhaps less hardy, lesbians could satisfy their wanderlust and recreational needs by participating in such activities as "RVing" (traveling in recreational vehicles) and women-only ocean cruises. While RVers traveled predominantly as couples, they found community not only by chance meetings on the road, but also through newsletters and Internet chat groups. In addition, enthusiasts gathered at regional RV rallies to share tips and experiences. Even more luxurious were the ocean-liner cruises sponsored by Olivia Records and Cruises since 1990. These cruises, which drew their patrons from all economic and racial groups, have been described as floating festivals. [The author wishes to thank Linda Dederman, John Jacoby, Anne Mania, Judith Niemi, and Don Nowotny for help in preparing this article.]

*Yvonne Zipter*

## Bibliography

Armstrong, Toni, Jr. "Olivia Turns Twenty: Anniversary Weekend." *Hot Wire: The Journal of Women's Music and Culture* 10 (January 1994), 24–26, 46–47, 62.

Franzen, Trisha. "Differences and Identities: Feminism and the Albuquerque Lesbian Community." *Signs: Journal of Women in Culture and Society* 18 (1993), 891–906.

Lurie, Rachel. "Martina and Me: A Trilogy." In *SportsDykes*. Ed. Susan Fox Rogers. New York: St. Martin's, 1994, pp. 120–129.

Murphy, Marilyn. *Are You Girls Traveling Alone? Adventures in Lesbianic Logic*. Los Angeles: Clothespin Fever, 1991, pp. 21–33.

Niemi, Judith. "Lesbians, Lightning, and Bears." In *Lesbian Scouts: On My Honor*. Ed. Nancy Manahan. Boston: Madwoman, 1997.

Zipter, Yvonne. *Diamonds Are a Dyke's Best Friend: Reflections, Reminiscences, and Reports from the Field on the Lesbian National Pastime*. Ithaca, N.Y.: Firebrand, 1988.

*See also* Bars; Choruses, Women's; Gay Games; Girl Scouts; lang, k.d. (Kathryn Dawn); Marches and Parades; Music Festivals; Navratilova, Martina; Olivia; Sports, Professional

## Relationship Violence

Violence, abuse, and/or battering in lesbian relationships are defined as patterns of behavior whereby a lesbian seeks to control the thoughts, beliefs, or conduct of her intimate partner or to punish her partner for resisting this control. Results of studies indicate that physical violence in same-sex relationships occurs at approximately the same rate as in heterosexual relationships, and it is clear that the exploration of violence in same-sex relationships requires an examination that reflects the prevalence of these issues while encompassing "the uniqueness of same-sex domestic violence" (Renzetti and Miley, 1996). Without taking sexual orientation into consideration, generalized conclusions could easily be reached regarding the misuse and abuse of power and control within all intimate relationships. Despite these similarities, however, it is critical that, in the process of understanding the causes and dimensions of violent and coercive behaviors within the specific context of lesbian relationships, the important differences be established. The roles of perpetrator and victim in female-to-female intimate violence cannot be defined by gender, and it has been suggested in the literature that lesbian women report physically fighting back more often than women who are battered by men. The understanding of this and other unique characteristics can contribute directly to the quality of assessment and the effectiveness of intervention.

Late-twentieth-century trends in understanding and addressing the issue of lesbian relationship violence in the United States are directly related to the discussion of the historical social response to violence against all women. Domestic violence grassroots activism and community organizing in urban areas during the mid-1970s were influenced by the civil rights and the women's movements and the corresponding cultural shifts that allowed for previously taboo personal disclosure of physical and sexual victimization. The creation of domestic-violence shelters and safe homes was a grass-roots effort by feminist-identified women (many of whom were lesbian) to provide support for battered women (initially identified only as heterosexual).

The first national hearing to address violence in the lives of women was sponsored by the United States Commission on Civil Rights and held in Washington, D.C., in 1978. The testimonies of battered women that were heard at that meeting resulted in the formation of what would become the National Coalition Against Domestic Violence (NCADV). Institutionalized homophobia, combined with concerns about loss of potential support and the need for credibility as an organization, resulted in a significant NCADV decision to focus its efforts on heterosexual violence. The issue of lesbian relationship violence was virtually tabled until a 1982 meeting, when formerly battered lesbians within NCADV organized and demanded that the caucus address lesbian battering as a priority. Dialogue began to address homophobia within the movement, and the Lesbian Task Force assumed a lead role in the 1986 NCADV publication of *Naming the Violence: Speaking Out About Lesbian Battery*, an anthology of lesbian stories of relationship violence accompanied by articles describing community-organizing strategies.

Due to the limitations of nonrandom and self-selected samples, it is difficult to measure accurately the prevalence of violence in lesbian relationships. However, as indicated by Renzetti (1992), research studies since the mid-1980s have clearly demonstrated the existence of physical, emotional, and sexual abuse in lesbian relationships. These more recent research perspectives have identified stressors specific to lesbian relationships (which generally exist within the context of homophobic and heterosexist environments) that contribute to major conflict and potential for violence. In addition to considering factors such as the complex association between the use of alcohol (and other drugs) and relationship violence and intergenerational violence, specific stressors have been identified as variables contributing to abuse in lesbian relationships. Renzetti (1992) conducted a nationwide study of violence in lesbian relationships, and has identified three primary indicators of abuse including dependency (versus autonomy), jealousy, and the balance of power between partners. It is especially important to take into consideration that the two most common characteristics of a lesbian who is abusive are her need to know and control her partner's activities and her own previous history of being abused. In addition, the pervasive problem of jealousy in lesbian relationships is due, in part, to the fragile nature of homosexual relationships (Renzetti 1992). The absence of legal ties and positive social support also contributes to feelings of isolation and fear of abandonment, which are related to increased levels of dependency and jealously, which often leads to various forms of violence between intimates.

It is understandable that, without available intervention and support services, lesbian women who are victimized by their partners have historically not defined the behavior as violence. Their minimization of the violence and their reluctance to disclose their experience may also have been based on their need to protect not only the reputation of their partner, but also the lesbian community in which they live. Many communities within the United States have begun to address the need to provide a wide range of services to lesbian victims/survivors. It is anticipated that, as awareness levels of the problem increase and as services specific to the needs of lesbian victims/survivors continue to be provided, lesbian communities will also be successful in beginning to face the challenges of responding to the needs of the lesbian perpetrator of violence—who historically has either not been held accountable for, or been shunned and ostracized as a result of, her abusive behaviors.

*Irene Anderson*

## Bibliography

Holiman, Marjorie. *From Violence Towards Love: One Therapist's Journey*. New York: Norton, 1997.

Lobel, Kerry, ed., for the National Coalition Against Domestic Violence Lesbian Task Force. *Naming the Violence: Speaking Out About Lesbian Battering*. Seattle: Seal, 1986.

McDaniel, Judith. *The Lesbian Couples' Guide: Finding the Right Woman and Creating a Life Together*. New York: HarperCollins, 1995.

Renzetti, Claire M. *Violent Betrayal: Partner Abuse in Lesbian Relationships*. Newbury Park, Calif.: Sage, 1992.

Renzetti, Claire M., and Charles Harvey Miley, eds. *Violence in Gay and Lesbian Domestic Partnerships*. New York: Harrington Park, 1996.

*See also* Couples

## Religious Communities

**R** Institutions that have historically constituted a refuge from compulsory heterosexuality by offering women the possibility of communal living in convents, *béguinages* (female religious communities with looser ties to the institutional church than convents), or sisterhoods of a religious order. Convents and *béguinages* are Catholic communities, whereas sisterhoods are Protestant ones.

Women in religious communities take vows of poverty, chastity, and obedience. In both cloistered and working orders, they lead lives of prayer and work that combine personal spirituality with practical communal endeavors. Members of cloistered orders are confined to their convents; members of working orders have more social impact and greater visibility.

Because religious communities have typically provided women with an alternative to marriage and motherhood while simultaneously fostering their advancement in a separate female space, they have inevitably aroused patriarchal anxieties. Given that religious communities ultimately abide by decisions made by the Church, however, their freedom from male intervention could only be described as relative.

### History

Central as religious vocation has been to the members of these communities, it was also to find productive occupations that women began forming and joining them. A monastery of virgins and widows founded by Marcella, a widow who was a friend of St. Jerome (ca. A.D. 347–419/420), is considered the first female religious community in the West. Only women who did not have occupations or family duties were allowed to join it, and their dedication was mainly to charitable works. Subsequently, more religious communities were formed, and, until the Council of Trent (1545–1563) imposed the rule of enclosure for nuns, most of them focused on providing material and spiritual comfort to the needy.

Intellectual pursuits, though limited, were available to the women in these early communities: The high levels of literacy among Anglo-Saxon nuns suggest that convents were, from early on, places where women had the opportunity to read and write. From the Middle Ages until the Reformation in the sixteenth century, nuns and *béguines* often wrote their *Lives* as spiritual exercises. Some, like Hildegard of Bingen (1098–1179) and Hadewych (thirteenth century), were also famous for their po-

etry and other writings. By the seventeenth century, it became harder for women in religious communities to pursue intellectual interests because the Reformation had put severe restrictions on women's active participation in religious debate; still, these communities remained spaces where a small degree of leisure and opportunity could be found for writing. Some extant manuscripts of seventeenth-century women religious from England, the Low Countries, and Latin America prove that reading and writing were regular activities for them and, as in the case of Mexican nun Sor Juana Inés de la Cruz (1648–1695), strongly influenced some in their decisions to join communities.

Until the twentieth century, religious communities allowed women the possibility of attaining independence from men and supplied a venue for talents that they would otherwise have been unable to pursue for lack of a socially acceptable outlet. Working in hospitals, schools, and in communal-property administration, women continued to have access to areas of public life that had begun to be denied to them around the seventeenth century with the professionalization, and, thus, masculinization, of many of the very tasks that had previously been theirs. As such, and to a relative degree, religious communities have historically been sites of feminist resistance. However, they have also been seen as privileged spaces for controlling women—places where, because of the patriarchal structures of the Church, women have internalized and lived out patriarchal notions of their role as relational.

### Sexuality and Resistance to Patriarchy

Conspicuous exceptions were usually punished. Sor Juana Inés de la Cruz, for example, incurred the anger of the Church fathers for writing love poetry—the most passionate of which she dedicated to the women to whom she was closest, the Vicereines Leonor Carreto and Maria Luisa Manrique de Lara y Gonzaga—and for daring to get involved in theological argumentation. The public admonition and implicit threat of persecution constituted by the 1690 letter from the bishop of Puebla led to her silence. In 1694, she signed in blood a declaration of faith, repenting and giving up secular studies. Another nun who was punished by the religious authorities was Benedetta Carlini (1590–1661), abbess of a convent in Tuscany. The notoriety caused by her mystic experiences was followed by accusations of lesbianism. These led to her imprisonement, which lasted for the last thirty-five years of her life.

Public discourse on religious communities has always betrayed their controversial nature and, more particularly, the fears of uncontrolled female sexuality they aroused. Indeed, alongside pleas such as Mary Astell's (1666–1731) *A Serious Proposal to the Ladies* (1692) in seventeenth-century England for the creation of religious communities—which she deemed essential to provide women with a dignified alternative to marriage—there were literary depictions of convents as brothels and nuns as unchaste. Jean Barrin's (ca. 1640–1718) *Venus in the Cloister* (1683) represents sex as a common practice in the convent and includes several scenes of lesbian sex. In the eighteenth century, Denis Diderot's (1713–1784) *La Religieuse* (The Nun) condemned forced vocations and represented the convent as a place threatening to the social structure because it fomented lesbianism. Scores of literary works continued to represent convents and sisterhoods in a negative light, even as nineteenth-century English feminists such as Dinah Mullock Craik (1826–1887) spoke of entering a sisterhood as potentially keeping women from the lunatic asylum.

## The Twentieth Century

Twentieth-century developments in feminist thought, together with changes in the Catholic Church's attitude brought about by Vatican II (1965), have led to dramatic reevaluations of female religious communities. During the 1960s and 1970s, the number of women leaving such communities was considerable. Members questioned their roles in both the Church and society. When outspoken demands for change and equal representation in the Church hierarchy fell on deaf ears, many chose to leave their communities. In the United States, the leaving could only be described as a virtual exodus. Those who left have become outspoken critics of the institutional Church's sexism, while continuing to stress that, at the core of women's religious communities, is the desire for true sisterhood.

Among those who have written about their experiences in the convent, lesbian ex-nuns have offered an especially candid assessment of the difficulties of reconciling their individuality as lesbians with the demands of their position as members of institutionalized religious communities. Because the status of women religious had always been represented as appealingly exemplary, and because both unconditional obedience and celibacy were expected, many women had to struggle against internalized principles that kept them from accepting their own subjec-

tivities. For many, this struggle ended in open rebellion that led to a radical break with institutionalized religion. In Rosemary Curb and Nancy Manahan's *Lesbian Nuns: Breaking the Silence* (1985), lesbian women religious describe their experiences in the convent and discuss the reasons for ultimately choosing to leave. Most found support in alternative lesbian communities that keep a strongly religious and spiritual dimension while defining themselves in opposition to the institutional Church.

While the number of women religious is still decreasing, and their struggle to attain a higher degree of independence from male influence continues, their sphere of action has widened considerably since they gained access to higher education. While the central drive of their lives remains spiritual, the scope of their participation in the social fabric is no longer substantially different from other women's.

*Manuela Mourao*

## Bibliography

Allchin, A.M. *The Silent Rebellion: Anglican Religious Communities, 1845–1900*. London: Scm, 1958.

Bernstein, Marcelle. *The Nuns*. New York: Lippincott, 1976.

Borromeo, Sister M. Charles, ed. *The New Nuns*. New York: Signet, 1968.

Curb, Rosemary, and Nancy Manahan, eds. *Lesbian Nuns: Breaking the Silence*. Tallahassee, Fla.: Naiad, 1985.

McKenna, Sister Mary L. *Women of the Church*. New York: Kennedy, 1967.

McNamara, Jo Ann Kay. *Sisters in Arms: Catholic Nuns Through Two Millennia*. Cambridge, Mass.: Harvard University Press, 1996.

*See also* Catholicism; Hildegard of Bingen, Saint; Juana Inés de la Cruz, Sor; Protestantism

## Renault, Mary (1905–1983)

English/South African novelist. Mary Renault (pseud. of Eileen Mary Challans) was born in London and, at an early age, decided to become a writer. After her graduation from college, she entered nurses' training at Radcliffe Infirmary, Oxford, where she received her degree in 1937 and met her lifelong companion, Julie Mullard. They were together forty-eight years until Renault's death in 1983.

Two of Renault's early fictional works deal with homoerotic friendships between women, *Purposes of*

*Love* (1939) (published in the United States as *Promise of Love*, [1940]) and *The Friendly Young Ladies* (1944) (published in the United States as *The Middle Mist*, [1945]). However, it is *The Charioteer* (1953) that finally focused explicitly and sympathetically on a young homosexual's coming of age. Renault modeled the young man's struggle in "straight" society on the chariot in Plato's *Phaedrus* (ca. 360 B.C.E. or later): one horse pulling the chariot toward heaven, the other toward hell. Renault's self-taught knowledge of ancient Greece led her to publish eight novels between 1956 and 1981 that all revolve around Greek heroes and philosophers, examining the conjunctions of power, social conventions, and spiritual existence. These novels feature principled characters who were often homosexuals. Due to her attention to detail and her ability to invoke atmosphere, classical scholars became some of her biggest fans.

Renault immigrated in 1948 to South Africa, where she lived the remainder of her life. There, while continuing to write, she became active in politics, in 1956 joining the Women's Defence of the Constitution League, popularly known as the Black Sash for the shoulder-band worn by its members as they protested the South African government's escalating apartheid system. Renault's failure to persuade the Black Sash to fight legal restraints on homosexuality convinced her of liberal South Africa's larger moral failing. Renault also became involved in the difficult and contentious politics of PEN International (Poets, Playwrights, Editors, Essayists, Novelists) as the president of the Cape Town center.

Renault was generally a reluctant public political figure and conflicted, to some degree, about her own lesbianism. Nonetheless, Renault's literary works brought homosexuals forward as admirable characters and gave them an acknowledged place in history.                    *Linnea A. Stenson*

### Bibliography

Sweetman, David. *Mary Renault: A Biography*. New York: Harcourt, 1993.

Wolfe, Peter. *Mary Renault*. New York: Twayne, 1969.

***See also*** English Literature, Twentieth Century; South Africa

### Rich, Adrienne (1929–)

North American poet. Born in Baltimore, Maryland, "Southern Jew . . . split at the root," raised as a

*Adrienne Rich. © Lynda Koolish.*

"white-skinned social christian / neither gentile nor Jew," Adrienne Rich began writing poetry as a child. She entered Radcliffe College, and, upon graduation in 1951, her volume of poetry titled *A Change of World* was chosen for the Yale Younger Poets Award by W.H. Auden, who wrote in the foreword that her poems were "neatly and modestly dressed, speak quietly but do not mumble, respect their elders." Accepting at first this role assigned to her, Rich excelled poetically, but at mid-life she began to break out of those boundaries: "Locked in the closet at four years old I beat the wall with my body / that act is in me still ("Tear Gas," 1969)."

*Snapshots of a Daughter-in-Law* (1963) contained poems that were no longer nice, in forms that reflected Rich's search for new visions. In this volume, she proclaimed: "A life I didn't choose / chose me." Finding the tools to create a life of her choice was a theme in several following volumes. With *The Will To Change* (1971) and *Diving into the Wreck* (1973), Rich began the search for her own tools and her own language, a new way to express a woman's experience.

Rich's first prose book, *Of Woman Born: Motherhood as Experience and Institution* (1976), explored her own experience as the mother of three sons against the backdrop of patriarchy's definition of motherhood. "As a mother," she wrote, I experienced great internal violence; yet it was as a mother that I first became politicized." Recognition of, and responses to, that violence—both internal and external—have been the subject or subtext of much of Rich's work, as in "The Burning of Paper Instead of Children" (1968) and "The Phenomenology of Anger" (1972). Images of testing bombs in the desert are juxtaposed with newly discovered tenderness in her first explicitly lesbian poems, "Twenty-One Love Poems" in *The Dream of a Common Language* (1978). Celebrating the beginning of her decades-long partnership with writer Michelle Cliff (1946–), Rich wrote in those poems: "I believe I am choosing something new," and concluded the set with her own statement of self-definition: "I choose to be a figure in that light, / . . . a woman. I choose to walk here. And to draw this circle."

The publication of "Compulsory Heterosexuality and Lesbian Existence" (1980)—later collected in *Blood, Bread, and Poetry: Selected Prose 1979–1985* (1986)—established Rich as one of the most visible lesbian feminist theorists. Written originally to "encourage heterosexual feminists to examine heterosexuality as a political institution which disempowers women," Rich's essay became a touchstone for some feminists, a lightning rod for others, sparking debate on sex and sexuality among feminists and lesbians, on pornography and censorship, on sadomasochism, on coercion and compulsion, and other topics.

Rich's awareness of the privilege of being an educated white woman was undoubtedly enhanced by her relationship with Michelle Cliff, but her empathy for ordinary, as well as extraordinary, suffering was deepened over the years by the painful rheumatoid arthritis that progressively limited her physical ability. Surgery for joint replacements on several occasions helped her mobility but only temporarily. In "The Transit" (in *A Wild Patience Has Taken Me This Far*, [1981]), she wrote for the first time about one of the differences that separated her from her younger sister, Cynthia, who walks, "free-swinging in worn boots." Privilege, whether that of the able-bodied person or the woman with white skin, allows the possessor to be "unaware" that others cannot do simply or easily those things that she takes for granted. In the two other volumes Rich published during the 1980s, *Your Native Land, Your Life* (1986) and *Time's Power* (1989), she included Puerto Rican revolutionary and poet Julia de Burgos (1914–1953), the sixteenth-century Aztec woman La Malinche, Jewish freedom fighter Hanna Senesh

(1921–1944), abolitionist John Brown (1800–1859), and others, always striving to expand her own awareness and that of her readers.

In 1973, Robert Boyers, an early reviewer of Adrienne Rich, observing her shift toward a specifically feminist politic, accused her of "the will to be contemporary," an unhappy influence on her poetry, he thought, as she was "neither a radical innovator nor the voice of an age." She is, in fact, both. No other poet's voice has spoken as clearly and pointedly to the issues raised in this historical period—issues between women and men, issues of privilege, of disempowerment, of the loss of a humane perspective. She speaks exactly as the voice of a profound and compassionate intelligence observing the world shifting around her. The epigraph from William Carlos Williams (1883–1963), which introduces and titles *What Is Found There: Notebooks on Poetry and Politics* (1993), describes her work in the five decades she has been writing and publishing poetry: "It is difficult / to get the news from poems / yet men die miserably every day / for lack / of what is found there."

*Judith McDaniel*

### Bibliography

Cooper, Jane Roberta, ed. *Reading Adrienne Rich: Reviews and ReVisions, 1951–1981.* Ann Arbor: University of Michigan Press, 1984.

Gelpi, Barbara Charlesworth, and Albert Gelpi, eds. *Adrienne Rich's Poetry and Prose.* New York: Norton, 1993.

Keyes, Claire. *The Aesthetics of Power: The Poetry of Adrienne Rich.* Athens: University of Georgia Press, 1986.

***See also*** Compulsory Heterosexuality; Lesbian Continuum

### Rights

Broad concept centering primarily on equal protection under the law. Until 1996, lesbians had no equal protection under the law at the federal level. Then, in *Romer v. Evans*, the United States Supreme Court held that an amendment to the state constitution of Colorado was unconstitutional. The amendment precluded all legislative, executive, or judicial action at any level of state or local government designed to protect the status of persons based on their "homosexual, lesbian or bisexual orientation, conduct, practices or relationships." Because the Colorado amendment, Amendment 2, infringed on the

**R** rights of gay, lesbian, and bisexual persons to participate in the political process, the Court applied the standard of strict scrutiny and held that the amendment failed under the Equal Protection Clause of the Fourteenth Amendment. Although *Romer* is the most important judicial victory for gay, lesbian, and bisexual people in the history of the United States, the consequence of *Romer* is not to confer equal protection per se, but only the ability to petition one's local or state government in an attempt to gain equal protection. Each state may decide for itself whether to grant equal protection to gay, lesbian, and bisexual persons, and, if protection is not achievable on a statewide level, thanks to *Romer* it may be sought on a local level. Supreme Court Justice Anthony Kennedy's pronouncement, "A State cannot so deem a class of persons a stranger to its laws," confers the ability only to petition one's government for rights, not necessarily to achieve them. However, in 1998, the Supreme Court refused to rule on a similar law passed in 1993 in Cincinnati, Ohio *(Equality Foundation of Greater Cincinnati, Inc., et al. v. City of Cincinnati et al.),* thus implying that, while it is unconstitutional to deny a group the right to petition the government for rights when it is done on a state level, it is permissible on a municipal level. By denying to hear the case, the Supreme Court did not set precedent, but it did signal that such local laws can be upheld.

In 1998, the only states that included sexual orientation as a protected category for equal protection, were Rhode Island, Wisconsin, Massachusetts, Connecticut, Hawai'i, California, New Jersey, Vermont, Minnesota, and New Hampshire. Equal protection was passed in Maine in 1997, but in 1998 opponents succeeded in overturning it through a general referendum. In the remaining states, gay, lesbian, and bisexual people do not enjoy equal protection and, hence, may be discriminated against in employment, housing, public accommodations, insurance, custody, adoption, loans, and other areas in which discrimination could hinder one's enjoyment of public amenities and private rights.

Although very few of the states still view gay, lesbian, or bisexual identity as automatic grounds to disqualify a parent from gaining custody of minor children, the majority of states consider sexual orientation as "one of a number of factors" that should be taken into account when determining the "best interest of the child." Any gay, lesbian, or bisexual person who wishes to seek a divorce from a heterosexual marriage to gain custody of children of the marriage needs to locate an attorney experienced not only in domestic law, but also in sexual-orientation law. Statewide legal organizations can often make referrals to a qualified attorney.

Another highly significant area in most peoples' lives, employment, can be difficult for gay, lesbian, and bisexual people. If one lives in an employment-at-will state, employment can be terminated by either party for any reason as long as federal and state employment discrimination legislation is not violated. The major U.S. employment-protection act, Title VII of the Civil Rights Act of 1964, applies only to race, color, national origin, sex, and religion. In addition, separate acts exist to protect those who are terminated or discriminated against based upon age or disability. Strikingly absent is sexual orientation. Not only may one be fired from one's job, regardless of the quality of job performance, because one is a lesbian (or gay or bisexual), one may also be fired because one is perceived to be lesbian regardless of the perception of the individual herself. As such, a woman whom coworkers believe to be a lesbian may be fired for being a lesbian even if she does not think of herself as a lesbian. In all court cases, without exception, even when courts have stated that the discrimination is "outrageous," no discrimination has occurred, and the individual has no legal recourse unless she lives in one of the minority of states in which, as of 1998, lesbians were covered by equal protection. *Dorothy Painter*

### Bibliography

Robson, Ruthann. *Lesbian (Out)Law: Survival Under the Rule of Law.* Ithaca, N.Y.: Firebrand, 1992.

Rubenstein, William, B., ed. *Lesbians, Gay Men, and the Law.* New York: New Press, 1993.

**See also** Custody Litigation; Human Rights; Law and Legal Institutions; Privacy

### Romantic Friendship

The Renaissance interest in Platonism encouraged a revival of passionate friendships between men, reflected in works such as Michel de Montaigne's (1533–1592) "On Friendship" (1572–1576, 1578–1580), Baldassare Castiglione's (1478–1529) *The Book of the Courtier* (1528), William Painter's (ca. 1540–1594) *The Palace of Pleasure* (1566), and Thomas Lodge's (ca. 1557–1625) *Euphues Shadowe* (1592). Literary examples of such relationships between women are less numerous in the Renaissance, but they may be found in work such as Lodge's *Rosalynde* (1590), and after, in the seventeenth century, in many of the poems by Katherine Philips (1632–1664). It is in the eighteenth century that such relationships, which came to be called "romantic friendships," became common. Romantic friendship between women was socially condoned, originally because it was not believed to violate the platonist ideal and later for more complex reasons. But while it is true that love between women was "in style," women's experiences of that love were no less intense or real for their social acceptability.

## The Eighteenth Century

Such passion in the eighteenth century was not believed to seriously violate any code of behaviors, even when it was taken to such extremes that women eloped with each other, as did the Ladies of Llangollen—Eleanor Butler (1739–1829) and Sarah Ponsonby (1755–1831)—in 1778. One relative observed: "[Sarah's] conduct, though it has an appearance of imprudence, is I am sure voide of serious impropriety. There were no gentlemen concerned, nor does it appear to be anything more than a scheme of Romantic Friendship."

The English, during the second half of the eighteenth century, prized sensibility, faithfulness, and devotion in a woman but forbade her significant contact with the opposite sex before she was betrothed. It was reasoned, apparently, that women could practice these sentiments on each other so that, when they were ready for marriage, they would have perfected themselves in those areas. It is doubtful that women viewed their own romantic friendships in such a way, but—if we can place any credence in eighteenth-century fiction as a true reflection of that society—men did. Because romantic friendship between women served men's self-interest, in their view, it was permitted and even socially encouraged.

The novels of the period show how women perceived these relationships and what ideals they envisioned for love between women. Those ideals generally could not be realized in life because most women did not have the wherewithal to be independent. In fiction, however, romantic friends (having achieved economic security as a part of the plot, which also furnishes them with good reasons for not having a husband around) could retire together, away from the corruption of the man-ruled "great world"; they could devote their loves to cultivating themselves and their gardens and to living generously and productively, too; they could share perfect intimacy in perfect equality. The most complete fictional blueprint for conducting romantic friendship is Sarah Scott's *A Description of Millennium Hall* (1762), a novel that went through four editions by 1778.

Even the mention of such a relationship in the title of a work must have promoted its sales—which would explain why a 1770 novel that sees friendship between women as nothing more than an epistolary device was entitled *Female Friendship*. Women readers could identify with the female characters' involvement with each other, since most of them had experienced romantic friendship in their youth at least. Mrs. Delany's (1700–1788) description of her own first love (in *The Autobiography and Correspondence of Mary Granville, Mrs. Delany* [1861]) is typical of what numerous autobiographies, diaries, letters, and novels of the period contained. As a young woman, she formed a passionate attachment to a clergyman's daughter, whom she admired for her "uncommon genius . . . intrepid spirit . . . extraordinary understanding, lively imagination, and humane disposition." They shared "secret talk" and "whispers" together; they wrote to each other every day and met in the field between their fathers' houses at every opportunity. Typical of many youthful romantic friendships, it did not last long (at the age of seventeen, Mrs. Delany was given in marriage to an old man), but it provided fuel for the imagination that idealized the possibilities of what such a relationship might be like without the impingement of cold marital reality. Because of such girlhood intimacies (which often were cut off in an untimely manner), most women would have understood when those attachments were compared with heterosexual love by the female characters in eighteenth-century novels and were considered, as Lucy says in William Hayley's (1745–1820) *The Young Widow* (1789), "infinitely more valuable." They would have had their own frame of reference when, in those novels, women adopted the David and Jonathan story, about a same-sex love that surpasses the love of man for woman, for themselves and swore that they felt for each other (again, as Lucy says) "a love passing the Love of Men" or proclaimed, as does Anne Hughes, the author of *Henry and Isabella* (1788), that such friendships are "more sweet, interesting, and to complete all, lasting, than any other which we can ever hope to possess; and were a just account of anxiety and satisfaction to be made out, would, it is possible,

**R** in the eye of rational estimation, far exceed the so-much boasted pleasure of love."

## Romantic Friendship in the United States

By the mid-eighteenth century, romantic friendship was a recognized institution in America, too. In the eyes of an observer such as Moreau de St. Mery, who had just recently left Revolutionary France for America and must have been familiar with the accusations of lesbianism lodged against Marie Antoinette (1755–1793), the women of her court, and most of the French actresses of the day, women's effusive display of affection for each other seemed sexual. St. Mery, who recorded his observations of his 1793–1798 journey, was shocked by the "unlimited liberty" that American young ladies seemed to enjoy and by their ostensible lack of passion toward men. The combination of their independence, heterosexual passionlessness, and intimacy with each other could have meant only one thing to a Frenchman in the 1790s: that "they are not at all strangers to being willing to seek unnatural pleasures with persons of their own sex." It is as doubtful that great masses of middle- and upper-class young ladies gave themselves up to homosexuality as it is that they gave themselves up to heterosexual intercourse before marriage. But the fiction of the period corroborates that St. Mery saw American women behaving openly as though they were in love with each other. Charles Brockden Brown's *Ormand* (1798), for example, suggests that American romantic friends were very much like their English counterparts.

## The Female Island

Many of the fictional works about romantic friendship were written by women, and they provide a picture of female intimacy very different from the usual depictions by men. The extreme masculine view, which is epitomized in Casanova's *Memoirs* (1826–1838), reduced female love to the genital, and, as such, it could be called "trifling." But love between women, at least as it was lived in women's fantasies, was far more consuming than the likes of Casanova could believe.

Women dreamed not of erotic escapades but of a blissful life together. In such a life, a woman would have choices; she would be in command of her own destiny; she would be an adult relating to another adult in a way that a heterosexual relationship with a virtual stranger (often an old, or at least a much older, man), arranged by a parent for considerations totally divorced from affection, would not

allow her to be. Samuel Richardson (1689–1761) permitted Miss Howe (in *Clarissa* [1747–1748]) to express the yearnings of many a frustrated romantic friend when she remarked to Clarissa: "How charmingly might you and I live together and despise them all."

## The Nineteenth Century

In America and England during the second half of the nineteenth century, as more women began to claim more of the world, the reasons for bonding together against men who wished to deny them a broader sphere became greater. Smith-Rosenberg (1975) has amply demonstrated that deeply felt friendships between women were casually accepted in American society, primarily because women saw themselves, and were seen as, kindred spirits who inhabited a world of interests and sensibilities alien to men. During the second half of the nineteenth century, when women slowly began to enter the world that men had built, their ties to each other became even more important. Particularly when they engaged in reform and betterment work, they were confirmed in their belief that women were spiritually superior to men, their moral perceptions were more highly developed, and their sensibilities were more refined. Thus, if they needed emotional understanding and support, they turned to other women. New England reform movements often were fueled by the sisterhood of kindred spirits who were righting a world men had wrong. In nineteenth-century America close bonds between women were essential both as an outlet for the individual female's sensibilities and as a crucial prop for women's work toward social and personal betterment in man's sullied and insensitive world.

What was the nature of these same-sex bonds? Margaret Fuller (1810–1850), an early feminist, saw same-sex love as far superior to heterosexuality. She wrote in her journal in the 1840s: "It is so true that a woman may be in love with a woman, and a man with a man." Such love, she says, is regulated by the same law that governs love between the sexes, "only it is purely intellectual and spiritual, unprofaned by any mixture of lower instincts, undistured by any need of consulting temporal interests."

William Alger, in *The Friendships of Women* (1868), cites one historical example after another of love between women. Typically, the women wrote each other: "I feel so deeply the happiness of being loved by you, that you can never cease to love me"; "I need to know all your thoughts, to follow all your motions, and can find no other occupation so sweet and so dear"; "My heart is so full of you, that, since we parted I have thought of nothing but writing to you"; "I see in your soul as if it were my own."

## The Twentieth Century

In 1908, it was still possible for an American children's magazine to carry a story in which a teenage girl writes a love poem in honor of her female schoolmate. In the early twentieth century, popular stories in magazines such as *Ladies Home Journal* and *Harpers* often treated the subject totally without self-consciousness or awareness that such relationships were "unhealthy" or "immoral," even for several years after French novelists and German sexologists started writing voluminously about lesbianism and were published in America.

America may have been slower than Europe to be impressed by the taboos against same-sex love, in part, because, by virtue of distance, America was not so influenced by the German medical establishment as other countries were, such as France and Italy and, to a lesser extent, England. Moreover, there was not so much clear hostility, or rather there was more ambivalence, to women's freedom in a land that, in principle, was dedicated to tolerance of individual freedom. Therefore, romantic friendship was possible in America well into the second decade of the twentieth century and, for those women who were born and raised Victorians and remained impervious to the new attitudes, even beyond it.

*Lillian Faderman*

### Bibliography

Alger, William Rounseville. *The Friendships of Women*. Boston: Roberts Brothers, 1868.

Faderman, Lillian. *Surpassing the Love of Men: Romantic Friendship and Love Between Women from the Renaissance to the Present*. New York: William Morrow, 1981.

Smith-Rosenberg, Carroll. "The Female World of Love and Ritual: Relations Between Women in Nineteenth Century America." *Signs: Journal of Women in Culture and Society* 1:1 (Autumn 1975), 1–29.

*See also* Boston Marriage; Fuller, Margaret; Ladies of Llangollen; Marie Antoinette; Philips, Katherine

## Roosevelt, Anna Eleanor (1884–1962)

American politician, author, teacher, businesswoman, social reformer, and U.N. diplomat. Her childhood marked by the early deaths of her mother, Anna Livingston Hall, and then her beloved alcoholic father, Elliott Roosevelt, Eleanor Roosevelt was raised by her maternal grandmother within the confines of a New York society whose rules she broke to become the most important woman of the twentieth century. In 1899, she enrolled in Ravenswood, a girls' school outside London; over the next three "happy" years, inspired by the affectionate companionship of the magnetic, liberal headmistress, Marie Souvestre (d. 1905), Roosevelt flourished. Returning to New York City at eighteen, she began her lifelong commitment to social reform by investigating working conditions in garment factories for the Consumers League and teaching calisthenics at a settlement house on the Lower East Side for the Junior League. On March 17, 1905, with President Theodore Roosevelt (1858—1919) giving his niece away, she married Franklin Delano Roosevelt (1882–1945), a distant cousin and her father's godson.

During the next years, while raising five children, Roosevelt developed her acumen as a politician's wife, first in Albany, New York, and then in Washington, D.C., where she coordinated the Union Station Canteen and organized Red Cross activities. But after 1918, betrayed by FDR's affair with Lucy Mercer (1891?–1948), long stifled by her possessive mother-in-law, and later challenged by FDR's crippling polio, Roosevelt, politically and privately, forged her independence while maintaining a partnership with FDR. In New York City, with Louis Howe as her political adviser, Roosevelt assumed leadership in the Women's City Club, the League of Women Voters, the Women's Trade Union League, and the Women's Committee of the State Democratic Party working with women such as Mary Dewson (1874–1962), Mary Dreier (1875–1963), and Rose Schneiderman (1884–1972). Supported by several intimate friendships within this network of politically conscious women, Roosevelt became, according to biographer Cook (1992), a "New Woman."

In the early 1920s, lawyer Elizabeth Read (1890–1983) and her life partner, Esther Lape (1881–1981), became her close friends. As first lady, Roosevelt often retreated to her rented apartment in their Greenwich Village home. After 1925, she established an independent home with the social feminists Marion Dickerman (1890–?) and Nancy Cook (1884–1962), her constant companions, at Stone Cottage, which they built at Val-Kill in Hyde

Park, New York. Their Val-Kill partnership included the *Women's Democratic News*, the Val-Kill furniture factory, and the Todhunter School in New York City, where Roosevelt taught. Meanwhile, Earl Miller (n.d.), her Albany bodyguard, also became a central figure in her life.

Upon FDR's election to the presidency in 1932, Eleanor Roosevelt established a profound intimacy with lesbian Lorena Hickok (1892–1968), a highly regarded Associated Press reporter assigned to cover the woman she called the "Reluctant First Lady." "Hick," as she was called, advised Roosevelt to hold women-only press conferences and encouraged her to write the "My Day" newspaper columns. Hickok had a bedroom in the White House. They took vacations together; when apart, they wrote daily passionate, sensual letters. After the relationship cooled, Roosevelt, for whom friendships were precious, arranged a home for Hick in Hyde Park.

After FDR's death, Eleanor Roosevelt continued her humanitarian work from Val-Kill. President Harry Truman (1884–1972) appointed her delegate to the United Nations, where, as chair of the Human Rights Commission, she framed the Universal Declaration of Human Rights (1948). During the 1950s, she canvassed for world peace, traveled extensively, campaigned for Democratic presidential candidate Adlai Stevenson (1900–1965), supported the creation of a Jewish state, and championed minority rights. A fighter for women's political independence, she accepted President John F. Kennedy's appointment to the Commission on the Status of Women. Eleanor Roosevelt died of bone-marrow tuberculosis at the New York City home of David Gurewitsch (1902–1974), her friend and physician, and is buried next to FDR at Hyde Park.

In October 1996, her statue was unveiled in New York City's Riverside Park, and Stone Cottage is now part of the Eleanor Roosevelt Center at Val-Kill. The Eleanor Roosevelt papers are collected in the Franklin Delano Roosevelt Library, Hyde Park, New York.                                   *Judith C. Kohl*

### Bibliography

Cook, Blanche Wiesen. *Eleanor Roosevelt,* vol. 1: *1884–1933*. New York: Viking Penguin, 1992.

Faber, Doris. *The Life of Lorena Hickok: E.R.'s Friend*. New York: William Morrow, 1980.

Goodwin, Doris Kearns. *No Ordinary Time: Franklin and Eleanor Roosevelt: The Home Front in World War II*. New York: Simon and Schuster, 1994.

Hickok, Lorena A. *Eleanor Roosevelt: Reluctant First Lady*. New York: Dodd, Mead, 1962.

*See also* Electoral Politics; Greenwich Village; Human Rights; Journalism; New Woman

### Routsong, Alma (1924–1996)

American novelist. Born November 26, 1924, in Traverse City, Michigan, Alma Routsong received an honors B.A. in art from Michigan State University in 1949. She interrupted studies begun in 1942 to serve two years in the United States Navy. Her marriage to Bruce Brodie lasted fifteen years, and she published two novels, *A Gradual Joy* (1953) and *Round Shape* (1959), in the 1950s.

Routsong is best known for her historical romance *Patience and Sarah*, published under the pseudonym Isabel Miller. Inspired by the relationship between Mary Ann Wilson and Miss Brundidge, who lived in the 1820s in upstate New York, the novel was completed in 1967 and published as *A Place for Us* in 1969. Routsong financed its one-thousand-copy press run herself as a Bleecker Street imprint. She sold it on Greenwich Village street corners and at meetings of the New York chapter of the Daughters of Bilitis. After the novel received the American Library Association's first Gay Book Award in 1971, McGraw-Hill released it in 1972 as *Patience and Sarah*.

The story of Patience White and Sarah Dowling, a cross-dressing farmer, may strike some readers as overly idealized, but lesbian readers were quick to celebrate Routsong's portrayal of strong lesbian characters in a positive love relationship. Mainstream readers, however, generally failed to recognize the lesbian-feminist encoding in the author's pen name. By combining an anagram for "lesbian" with her mother's birth name, Routsong created Isabel Miller, fictitious author of a novel that stands as a touchstone for affirmation of women loving-women.

*For the Love of Good Women* followed *Patience and Sarah* in 1986; *Side by Side*, in 1990. In *Side by Side*, Patience and Sarah are modernized and recast as Patricia and Sharon, artist and herbalist. Partners in a loving relationship, they belong to a lesbian group called A Place for Us. Routsong originally planned a novel-length sequel to *Patience and Sarah*, but she condensed her material into a short story titled "A Dooryard Full of Flowers" for a 1993 collection of stories by the same name.

All of Routsong's fiction explores lesbianism in a white, middle-class milieu. If her cultural horizons are limited, she sees beyond internalized homophobia to love between women as mutually supportive.

Alma Routsong died October 3, 1996, at her home in upstate New York after a long illness.

*Sonya Jones*

## Bibliography

Breen, Margaret, and Elsa A. Bruguier. "Miller, Isabel." In *The Gay and Lesbian Literary Heritage*. Ed. Claude J. Summers. New York: Henry Holt, 1995, p. 488.

Katz, Jonathan. Interview: "1962–1972: Alma Routsong, Writing and Publishing Patience and Sarah, 'I Felt I Had Found My People.'" In *Gay American History: Lesbians and Gay Men in the U.S.A.: A Documentary*. Ed. Jonathan Katz. New York: Crowell, 1976, pp. 433–443. New York: Avon (paper), 1978, pp. 652–665.

Soares, Manuella, and Sara Yager. "Interview with Alma Routsong, January 20, 1990." Videotaped for the Daughters of Bilitis Project, Lesbian Herstory Archives, New York.

*See also* American Literature, Twentieth Century

## Rukeyser, Muriel (1913–1980)

U.S. poet, novelist, and essayist. Muriel Rukeyser was born in New York, City, the daughter of Lawrence B. Rukeyser, a construction engineer, and Myra (Lyons) Rukeyser, a homemaker and bookkeeper. Rukeyser's parents had a stable and comfortable existence, but she identified more with the life of her less fortunate playmates. Because of her political ideas and class consciousness, she was finally disinherited by her father.

Rukeyser was the literary editor of the leftist *Student Review* at Vasser College. She covered the trial of the Scottsboro Boys, nine African Americans who were accused of raping a white woman. From that point on, her work was marked by commitment to social justice. Rukeyser was among the first to elucidate the kinds of concerns now taken for granted in "political" poetry. Her first book, *Theory of Flight* (1935), won the Yale Younger Poets Award.

In 1945, she moved to San Francisco and taught at the California Labor School. She married Glynn Collins, a painter, but the marriage was soon annulled. She had one child, (William) Laurie Rukeyser, in 1947. She raised the boy alone, and, in *The Gates* (1976), she wrote about how this influenced her development as an artist.

Rukeyser wrote three biographies, all portraying the lives of independent thinkers like herself. She was active in the anti–Vietnam War movement and also protested the threatened execution of South Korean poet Kim Chi-Ha by going to Seoul, the South Korean capital, to seek his release. She helped establish the Exploratorium, an interactive museum of science, in San Francisco.

Reaction to her poetry over the years has always been mixed. Many critics attacked her political viewpoints, but feminist writers claimed Rukeyser as a champion, both for her poetry and her political activism. Although she had relationships with women, like many other writers of her generation, she did not openly identify as a lesbian. However, her poetry in *The Speed of Darkness* (1968) has elements that are congruent with themes and images in overtly lesbian poetry. Rukeyser accepted an invitation to speak at the Lesbians in Literature panel of the Modern Language Association in 1978 but could not attend because of ill health. She served as a model for many lesbian writers, notably Adrienne Rich (1929–).

*Eloise Klein Healy*

## Bibliography

Brinnin, John M. "Muriel Rukeyser: The Social Poet and the Problem of Communication." *Poetry*, 61 (January 1943), 554–575.

Daniels, Kate, and Richard Jones, eds. *Poetry East* 16–17 (Spring/Summer 1985) (Special Double Issue on Muriel Rukeyser).

Kertesz, Louise. *The Poetic Vision of Muriel Rukeyser*. Foreword by Kenneth Rexroth. Baton Rouge: Louisiana State University Press, 1980.

Terris, Virginia R. "Muriel Rukeyser: A Retrospective." *American Poetry Review* 3 (May/June 1974), 10–15.

*See also* Poetry; Rich, Adrienne

## Rule, Jane Vance (1931–)

Canadian writer. Born in Plainfield, New Jersey, Jane Rule attended twenty-two schools as she grew up throughout the United States. Observing contradictory customs—both serious (racial segregation) and trivial (how to wear your socks)—she concluded that a community's values may teach you how to survive but cannot teach what is right or true.

# R

*Jane Rule. Photo by Tee A. Corinne.*

Rule has often crossed geographic and social borders. After graduating from Mills College in 1952, she studied at the University of London, lived with the first woman she loved, and wrote two "unpublishable novels." She then taught at Concord Academy in Massachusetts, where she met Helen Sonthoff. In 1956, increasingly disturbed by the homophobia and political hysteria of the McCarthy era, Rule and Sonthoff moved to Vancouver, became Canadian citizens, and taught for twenty years at the University of British Columbia before retiring to Galiano Island.

In 1961, Rule completed *Desert of the Heart*. After more than twenty rejections, the novel was finally published in 1964 by World Publishing Company in Cleveland, Ohio. Made into the film *Desert Hearts* in 1985, the novel recounts the love story of Evelyn, an English professor in Reno for a divorce, and Ann, a cartoonist who works as a change apron at a casino. The novel counters the conventions of "lesbian fiction"—heterosexual marriage and/or death at the end, guilt and self-loathing throughout. Rule's fiction resonates with the great books of Western literature, questioning or confirming ideas about meaning and literary form. Yet Rule has most often been ignored by professional critics even as she has been embraced by readers who express bonds of recognition in countless letters.

When asked how she "came out," Rule has answered that she was never "in." All of her novels (*This Is not for You* [1970]; *Against the Season* [1971]; *The Young in One Another's Arms* [1977]; *Contract with the World* [1980]; *Memory Board* [1987]; *After the Fire* [1989]) incorporate lesbian characters and themes, as do many of the short stories she has had published in "women's magazines," such as *Redbook*, and lesbian journals, such as *The Ladder*. She interrogates the meanings and politics of sexuality, the relation between sexuality and language, and the stakes of communities in individual claims on identity.

Beginning in the 1970s, Rule wrote "So's Your Grandmother," a column for the *Body Politic*, a Toronto gay liberationist newspaper, in which she engaged the defining issues of feminism and sexual liberation. Rule is far from a single-minded apologist for a political movement. Anticipating resistance to one of her novels, she wrote: "I do understand the appetite in the gay community for art which can celebrate, but too often that desire gets translated into a need for narrowly correct propaganda."

Suffering from arthritis, Rule retired from writing in 1989. Since then, her work has received increasing attention. A documentary, *Fiction and Other Truths: A Film About Jane Rule*, premiered in Toronto in 1995. Academic critics are reconsidering her work in the context of queer theory and lesbian and gay studies.

*Marilyn R. Schuster*

## Bibliography

Roof, Judith. *A Lure of Knowledge: Lesbian Sexuality and Theory.* New York: Columbia University Press, 1991.

Schuster, Marilyn. "Strategies for Survival: The Subtle Subversion of Jane Rule." *Feminist Studies* 7:3 (1981), 431–450.

Zimmerman, Bonnie. *The Safe Sea of Women: Lesbian Fiction, 1969–1989.* Boston: Beacon, 1990.

*See also* Canada; *Ladder, The*

## Rüling, Anna (dates unknown)

German feminist and author ca. 1900. Anna Rüling was one of the first women in Germany who publicly addressed the correlation between lesbian identity and feminist politics and acknowledged being homosexual herself. Her 1904 speech—"What Interest Does the Women's Movement Have in the Solution to the Homosexual Problem?"—was both influential and controversial. She gave that speech in Berlin upon an invitation from the Scientific Humanitarian Committee, the largest homosexual organization in Germany, and in the presence of several renowned women's movement activists.

Consistent with the theory of innate ("natural") homosexuality that had been formulated ca. 1900, Rüling defined the homosexual woman as talented like a man, energetic, goal oriented, and of clear mind. Using eugenic arguments, which were also used by feminist theorists at the time, she appealed to the women's movement to advocate the right of female homosexuals to remain unmarried. In her opinion, the strength of lesbian women lay in professional life, such as medicine or the legal profession. They were also particularly qualified to take leading positions in the women's movement. Considering the position of many lesbians in the front ranks of the movement, most feminist organizations had taken scandalizingly little action to publicly acknowledge lesbians and to grant the homosexual question its due place in their own politics.

To broach the subject of one's own homosexuality and, in addition, to define lesbianism as a feminist challenge, as Rüling did, clearly ran counter to the mainstream women's movement in Germany at the turn of the twentieth century. Most feminists kept silent about their own desire, as well as about contemporary sexological definitions, at least in public, and the reactions to Rüling's speech, ranging from the radical Minna Cauer (1841–1922) to the moderate Marie Stritt (1855–1928), were accordingly critical, reserved, or outraged.

Further details about Rüling's biographical background and her political involvement are not known. In 1906, she published a volume with several short stories, titled *Those of You Who Are Without Sin. . . ."* Three of the narrations deal with lesbian happiness and anguish. "Mysterious" is about the suicide of a lesbian despairing of her fate; in "Moonlight Sonata," the long-unspoken desire between two women finally reaches fulfillment; and "The Baggage Porter" tells an adventurous story with a happy ending for the young couple, the understanding parents, and all like-minded women friends.                    *Hanna Hacker*

### Bibliography

Faderman, Lillian, and Brigitte Eriksson. *Lesbians in Germany: 1890's–1920's.* Tallahassee, Fla.: Naiad, 1990.

Göttert, Margit. "Zwischen Betroffenheit, Abscheu und Sympathie. Die alte Frauenbewegung und das 'heikle Thema' Homosexualität" (Between Bewilderment, Aversion, and Sympathy: The Old Women's Movement and the "Delicate Subject" Homosexuality). *Ariadne: Almanac of the Archive of the German Women's Movement,* Kassel 29 (May 1996), 14–21.

Kokula, Ilse. *Weibliche Homosexualitat um 1900 in zeitgenössischen Dokumenten* (Female Homosexuality Around 1900 in Contemporary Documents). Munich: Women's Offensive, 1981.

*See also* Germany; Sexology

## Russia

Also known as the Russian Federation and formerly part of the Union of Soviet Socialist Republics. Russia is about 6.5 million square miles in area, with a population of more than 147.5 million. The capital is Moscow, which shares special administrative status with St. Petersburg. Although the official language is Russian, many other languages are spoken throughout its republics. Major religions include Christianity, of which the Orthodox Church is the largest denomination, Islam, and Buddhism. Although there was a large Jewish population prior to 1917, which was depleted due to war and emigration, more than 650,000 Jews reside in Russia.

As a result of centuries of expansionism, by the end of the nineteenth century the Russian Empire comprised territories in eastern Europe and regions in northern and central Asia. After the 1917 Boshevik Revolution, the Union of Soviet Socialist Republics (USSR) was formed in 1922. In the 1990s, the old USSR broke up, and the Russian Federation, or Russia, began a series of economic and constitutional reforms and political reorganization. These have had varying degrees of success and, at times, have resulted in ideological and violent confrontations that have affected both political and social stability.

### Homosexuality in the Russian Empire

For most of the last three centuries, homosexuality, both male and female, was a punishable offense in Russia. But, along with hideous oppression of sexual minorities, the country has seen brief periods of remarkable permissiveness in matters of sexuality.

Some of the foreigners who visited Russia in the seventeenth to nineteenth centuries left memoirs testifying to a liberal attitude toward sexual deviance to which Europeans were not accustomed. But, beginning in the eighteenth century, as Peter the Great (1672–1721) strove to make his country a part of the cultural and legal space inhabited by Europeans, Russia acquired its first secular laws banning homosexuality. A military statute introduced in 1706, modeled on Swedish law, prescribed burning at the stake for homosexual activity. The code applied only to members of the military, so the state's attitude toward female homosexuals was not codified. Indeed, the status of lesbians appears never to have been articulated in Russian or Soviet law, although this has not protected them from official persecution.

A penal code based on a German model was adopted in 1832. The offense of *muzhelozhestvo* (the word contains the roots *muzh*, meaning "male," and *lozh*, meaning "bed" or "lying," so literally it could be translated as "man lying with man," although it is usually translated as "sodomy") was punishable by exile to Siberia for a period of four to five years with the deprivation of all rights. A 1903 code changed the punishment to incarceration for at least three months.

The prerevolutionary Russian parliament, the Duma, deliberated a measure to repeal the sodomy law. But the law remained on the books until 1918, when the new Bolshevik government abolished all the laws of the old empire, including the prohibitions of murder and rape. There is no evidence that this legal move caused or inspired the period of relative sexual freedom that ensued.

## Cultural Activity

The 1910s and early 1920s were a time of unprecedented cultural activity in Russia. Dozens of writers, poets, actors, and other artists rose to prominence, leaving an imprint on Russian culture that would last well into the twentieth century. A number of these cultural leaders made no secret of their affections for their own sex. Male homosexuals had been visible in the higher echelons of Russian society during the nineteenth century as well; the composer Pyotr Tchaikovsky (1840–1893) and the theatrical impresario Sergei Diaghilev (1872–1929) are two examples. Prominent women who openly loved women, however, represented a new phenomenon. One possible exception is Yekaterina Dashkova, a writer and publisher who headed the Russian Academy and the Academy of Sciences between 1783 and 1796; her memoirs, first published in Russia in 1987, speak of love for Martha Wilmont, an Englishwoman who lived with her in Russia for five years.

After censorship in Russia was suspended following the uprising and reforms of 1905, several writers took the liberty of publishing work that dealt openly and often positively with same-sex love. Among the female writers were Lydia Zinovyeva-Annibal (1866–1907), whose best-known lesbian-themed work is the short novel *Thirty-Three Abominations* (1907), and the novelist Yevdokia Nagrodskaya. Sophia Parnok (1885–1933) not only wrote poems about the love of women for one another, but also made no secret of her own lesbianism. In the years 1914–1916, much of literary Moscow was privy to the ups and downs of Parnok's relationship with Marina Tsvetaeva (1892–1941), one of the best-known Russian poets of the twentieth century. The lesbian-themed parts of Tsvetaeva's literary heritage—a cycle of poems written in 1914–15 for Parnok, entitled *Podruga* (Girlfriend; also translated as Woman Friend), and a 1933 essay in the form of a letter to the American writer Natalie Barney (1876–1972), written in French—remained unavailable to Russian readers and largely unknown into the 1980s. In 1983, an American publisher of Russian writing printed a book about Tsvetaeva and Parnok's relationship by Sophia Poliakova, a Leningrad scholar who sacrificed her career to the publication of this work. Poliakova, who died in 1994, was also instrumental in compiling and publishing, in the West, the first collection of poetry by Parnok, *Sobranie Stikhotvorenii* (1979), who had been virtually forgotten in the Soviet Union. The collection was published in Russia in 1997.

Members of the artistic and literary elites were certainly not the only people in early-twentieth-century Russia who explored the definitions and permissible limits of sexual identity and behavior. But, ultimately, the period of redefinition did not become a time of sexual liberation for the society at large. For decades, a view of the Bolsheviks as sexual liberators had currency in the West. But available evidence suggests that early Bolshevik ideologues, including Alexandra Kollontai (1872–1952), saw redefining the family as part of the process of subjugating the citizens' private lives to the needs and the will of the state.

## The Bolshevik Revolution

Following the Bolshevik Revolution of 1917, the legal and social concepts of private life underwent a series of metamorphoses. Abortion was legalized in 1920. The first postrevolutionary set of family and marriage laws, adopted in 1926, recognized marriages that were not registered in any way and provided for a simple and inexpensive divorce procedure. But 1936 saw a ban on abortion and adoption of a new family and marriage code that made divorce far more difficult and declared that the family was important composite part of the communist collective. Three years earlier, another piece of legislation had already outlawed those who fell outside the family unit: Sex between men had once again become a punishable offense.

This sodomy law, which later became known as Article 121 (its number in the 1961 penal code), remained in effect in the Soviet Union and Russia until May 1993, when it was repealed by presidential decree. Throughout its sixty-year history, the law was enforced in the random way that characterized political laws used against dissidents, as legal scholar Valery Chalidze's research shows. The history of lesbians in the Soviet Union is far more difficult to trace. Some research, such as street interviews with lesbians and gay men conducted by the linguist Vladimir Kozlovsky in the 1970s, indicates that the understanding of homosexuality as a political crime was sometimes extended to apply to lesbians, even though the law did not provide for punishment for lesbianism. According to Kozlovsky's sources, lesbians accused of theft or other criminal offenses were given longer jail sentences if their sexuality was known to the investigators. More often, however, lesbians became victims of punitive psychiatric measures.

In the 1930s, Andrei Snezhensky, a founding father of Soviet psychiatry, advanced the theory of "slow-going schizophrenia," a condition that developed over a lifetime, with odd, asocial traits serving as its early signals. This diagnosis, which made it possible to deem a person mentally ill for reading banned books or failing to work at a state-assigned job—or for loving people of the same sex—became a cornerstone of Soviet psychiatry. A woman suspected of being a lesbian could be committed to a psychiatric hospital at the initiative of the police, her parents or guardians, teachers, neighbors, coworkers, and assorted others. The hospital stay would normally last a few months, but the patient would be marked for life: A stamp in her internal passport would indicate that she was mentally ill, barring her from an extensive list of occupations or from receiving a driver's license, and otherwise limiting her

rights. A person branded as mentally ill had to remain registered with an outpatient psychiatric clinic, which continued to monitor the patient. The lifelong consequences of psychiatric treatment and the wide circle of people who could initiate hospitalization made lesbianism one of the most dangerous secrets a Soviet woman might have to keep.

Though high social standing did not guarantee safety for Soviet homosexuals (for example, Sergei Paradzhanov, a well-known film director, served a sentence for sodomy), in general the fear of prosecution and persecution was less among the intellectual and cultural elite. One of the best-known actresses of the Soviet era, Faina Ranevskaya (1896–1984), was widely believed to be a lesbian, and she does not appear to have taken steps to disprove this impression. She became a symbol and a magnet for young lesbians, who flocked to Moscow in the 1970s and 1980s in the hope of meeting Ranevskaya. Some of them succeeded, and many more met during their attempts, forming the lesbian social circles that sustained them and that led to the formation, in the 1990s, of the first lesbian organization in Moscow.

## Contemporary Political Activism

The first attempt to declare a political agenda for sexual minorities—a preferred term for Russian gays and lesbians in the late 1980s and early 1990s—occurred in Moscow in February 1990, when about a dozen people gathered in a Moscow apartment for a press conference to which only foreign correspondents were invited. The only person who used her real name at that event was a woman named Yevgenia Debrianskaya, then a prominent activist of the pro-democracy movement. The organization born at that press conference, called the Moscow Union for Sexual Minorities, later renamed the Moscow Union for Gays and Lesbians, ceased to exist about a year and a half later.

Later in 1990, another lesbian, a graduate student named Olga Zhuk, formed a gay and lesbian organization in the Soviet Union's second-largest city, Leningrad. The organization, the Tchaikovsky Foundation for Cultural Initiative and the Defense of Sexual Minorities, was still in existence in 1997, although Zhuk had moved to Germany. In 1991, the first lesbian organization in the Soviet Union was formed: Moscow Lesbians in Literature and the Arts, led by Liudmila Ugolkova, an amateur filmmaker. In July-August 1991, on the eve of the failed coup that spelled the end of the Soviet Union, gays and les-

**R** bians held their first public gathering in that country, a conference and film festival in Moscow and St. Petersburg; the Moscow part of the festival was accompanied by two gay and lesbian rights demonstrations. Dozens more gay and lesbian groups and publications appeared throughout Russia in the months following the conference and the demonstrations.

A new law on psychiatric treatment, passed in July 1992, made it impossible to hospitalize a person without that individual's consent. Russian psychiatry, however, continued to consider same-sex attraction a personality disorder, making it possible for psychiatrists to attempt to "cure" lesbianism in women who sought help voluntarily or, if they were minors, were brought to their attention by guardians. In 1993, Article 121 (the sodomy law) was repealed, enabling the formation of a number of gay social clubs and similar commercial establishments, which often benefited lesbians as well. But, in the absence of any other civil rights or identity-based movement, the Russian movement for gay and lesbian rights, originally based on the U.S. model,

failed to develop. Discrimination against lesbians remained legal, and many reasons for lesbians to fear for their well-being and safety, especially outside the large cities, remained.          *Masha Gessen*

### Bibliography

Burgin, Diana. *Sophia Parnok: The Life and Work of Russia's Sappho*. New York: New York University Press, 1994.

Gessen, Masha. *The Rights of Lesbians and Gay Men in the Russian Federation*. San Francisco: International Gay and Lesbian Human Rights Commission, 1994.

Karlinsky, Simon. *Marina Tsvetaeva: The Woman, Her World, and Her Poetry*. Cambridge: Cambridge University Press, 1985.

Kon, Igor, and James Riordan, eds. *Sex and Russian Society*. Bloomington and Indianapolis: Indiana University Press, 1993.

**See also** Barney, Natalie; Parnok, Sophia; Socialism; Tsvetaeva, Marina Ivanovna

# S

## Sackville-West, Vita (1892–1962)

English poet, biographer, and novelist. Born at Knole, Kent, Vita Sackville-West was the daughter of the third baron of Sackville. In 1913, she married Harold Nicolson (1886–1968); their unorthodox union, described by their son Nigel in *Portrait of a Marriage* (1973), withstood the trials of her affairs with women and Nicolson's own homosexuality. Their marriage survived as an abiding friendship. Together in 1930 they purchased Sissinghurst Castle, where Sackville-West (with designs from Nicolson) planted the superb gardens that still exist.

Sackville-West was prolific, writing, among other works, four poetry collections, three collections of short stories, two travel books, a biography of St. Joan of Arc (1412–1431), a study of St. Teresa of Avila (1515–1582) and St. Thérèse of Lisieux (1873–1897), and twelve novels. The English countryside and its populace proved her most enduring focus. Her long pastoral poem, *The Land* (1926), brought her some measure of fame and won her the Hawthornden Prize, and *The Edwardians* (1930) was a best-seller. *All Passion Spent* (1931), considered a feminist classic, deals with a woman gaining autonomy and self-determination in her widowhood.

Sackville-West's most (in)famous affair involved Violet Trefusis (née Keppel [1894–1972]), a childhood friend. Their torrid relationship, beginning in 1918 and lasting several years, included repeated "elopements" to France and brought on a public scandal. Sackville-West's *Challenge* (1924) was written explicitly as a novel about their affair, with Trefusis the unacknowledged writing collaborator. Unwilling to write openly about lesbianism, Sackville-West made the protagonists, Julian and Eve, cousins. (Sackville-West sometimes dressed as a man when they were together and was often addressed as "Julian" by Trefusis.) Sackville-West eventually returned to Nicolson, although she continued to have affairs with women throughout her life, including Virginia Woolf (1882–1941), whom she first met in 1922.

Sackville-West's birth as a woman prevented her from inheriting her beloved Knole when her father died. Woolf restored Knole to Sackville-West in *Orlando* (1928), a fantastic "biography" that included Knole portraits and photographs of Sackville-West herself. Nigel Nicolson has called *Orlando* the "longest and most charming love-letter in literature." While their love affair lasted only a few years, their long friendship as women writers was important and sustaining. *Linnea A. Stenson*

### Bibliography

Glendinning, Victoria. *Vita: A Biography of Vita Sackville-West*. New York: William Morrow, 1985.

Nicolson, Nigel. *Portrait of a Marriage*. New York: Simon and Schuster, 1982.

Rait, Suzanne. *Vita and Virginia: The Work and Friendship of V. Sackville-West and Virginia Woolf*. New York: Oxford University Press, 1992.

*See also* English Literature, Twentieth Century; United Kingdom; Woolf, Virginia

## Sadomasochism

A sexological term for a complex of desires that some would see as pathological disorders. In psychological terms, a sadist is one who derives (an often sexualized) pleasure from inflicting pain or distress and humiliation on another person or living thing. A masochist is one who derives pleasure from experiencing pain and/or forms of humiliation. In lesbian and gay cultures, the term "sadomasochism" (often shortened to "sm" or S/M) has been adopted by those who derive pleasure from such activities. This has changed it from a classificatory and often regulatory term imposed on individuals from the outside to a self-chosen affiliation that is also, at times, constitutive of a sense of group or community identity.

In taking on this classification, lesbian and gay sadomasochists would emphasize that their sadistic and masochistic practices are based on consent: In theory, no participant should ever experience anything to which they do not consent. This is achieved by the institution of "safe" words—a word other than "no" that is agreed between participants. Once the safe word has been uttered, the activity should stop. This allows the masochist (or "bottom") to experience the fantasy of events happening against her will, since she can resist and scream "no," secure in the knowledge that her safe word will allow her to intervene if necessary. Often, sadists (or "tops") use this as evidence that the "bottom" is really in control of any scenario. Some proponents of lesbian S/M would argue that, far from duplicating the patriarchal oppression of women through sexual coercion, this sex-play can be therapeutic in that the masochist can act out an experience or fantasy of powerlessness in a safe environment. Many would dispute this analysis and would point to the possibility of nonconsensual acts taking place: Power does exist in any relationship, but talking about it does not neutralize it. While it is clear that many lesbians do enjoy S/M sex and experience it as liberating, it is also emerging that some lesbians sadists do like to act beyond or without consent.

**Controversies**

The big controversy over lesbian S/M did not arise until the mid-1980s, when S/M groups began to assert themselves as a visible lesbian subculture. This occurred most prominently in the United Kingdom and North America and was prompted by a number of events, among which could be instanced the publication of *Coming to Power* (1983) and the fierce arguments at any number of conferences and meetings until the end of the decade. These, and other events, instigated the rolling debates that have come to be known as the lesbian "sex wars." The agenda-setting book *Coming to Power* was written by the

San Francisco–based S/M group Samois and argued for a recognition of the pleasures of S/M against a lesbian feminist stance that saw S/M as oppressive to women. The storm that this book and related cultural products caused in lesbian and feminist circles cannot be underestimated. Its impact was widely felt: S/M was now a crucial issue for discussion in circles that had previously never considered it part of their worldview (except in an analysis of men's sadism in sexual violence).

Critics of S/M argued that sadomasochism reproduced patterns of oppression and exploitation and should be combated on the political stage, not embraced in the bedroom. For many, the S/M predilection for leather wear, slave/slaver imagery, army uniforms, and, in some cases, Nazi insignia was anathema. It is important to recognize that, while many of the sexual acts associated with S/M took place in private or the relatively sequestered spaces of S/M clubs and bars, S/M groupings became highly visible in general lesbian and gay spaces due to their distinctive self-presentation. For them, it was important to assert their presence, and so they would attend lesbian strength and Gay Pride marches in full regalia, often leading each other by chains and neck braces. For lesbians opposed to S/M, particularly lesbians of color or Jews, this amounted to a celebration of the very forces that had oppressed millions and had killed their families. S/M lesbians argued that the fact that their practices occurred between women, plus the code of consent, meant that the power relations of hetero-patriarchy were absent. For the opposition, it was impossible to allow that the historic meanings of symbols and events could be willed away: The argument that power between lesbians could never be coercive was simply wishful thinking.

In the so-called sex wars, those lesbians and heterosexual feminists who spoke against S/M were hindered by a feminist agenda from the 1970s that had been reticent about discussing sex and sexual pleasure. The S/M alliance successfully presented themselves as "pro-sex" and the opposition as antisex. Although feminists had been concerned with women's sexual pleasure, the urgency of fights against rape and sexual violence had led to what some saw as a withdrawal from the sexual. Thus, proponents of lesbian S/M were able to argue in favor of a recognition of women's diverse sexual desires and practices against what they saw as lesbian feminists' denial of an active female and lesbian desire. This meant that S/M lesbians were able to colonize many acts not specifically sadomasochistic and include them under their sexual-liberationist agenda. For example, the belief in some feminist circles that penetrative sex replicated forms of patriarchal oppression meant that many heterosexual and lesbian women avoided this practice. The S/M assurance that all sexual acts were acceptable, including penetration, had an impact beyond the strictly S/M community—although penetration, whether by penis, hand, or dildo, is not in itself a specifically sadomasochistic act.

## Influence

The influence of S/M grew as much by style and cultural production as it did by the spread of S/M sexual practices. Indeed, in some ways, the cultural currency of S/M far outweighs its actual demographic base in sexual practice. As S/M became a main topic for discussion and successfully presented itself as pro-sex (and, of course, discussions about sex are also often themselves an eroticized experience), it became increasingly fashionable to adopt a sometimes diluted, but nonetheless recognizable, S/M style of self-presentation. By the early 1990s, a vaguely leather-S/M style had become a predominant signifier of a lesbian identity per se in metropolitan centers. The dress codings of (black) leather jackets, caps, boots, handcuffs, neck collars, and leather wristbands that had once been so shocking were now frequently on display. It could be argued that what these accessories came to symbolize was not so much a clear affiliation to S/M practices as an identification with a far looser subcultural style that had come to signify "hot" sex. In this, S/M had won the fight against the "vanilla" opposition, who, especially to a younger generation of possibly postfeminist lesbians, seemed uptight, unfashionable, and unsexy. The presence of this generational perception gap should not hide that fact that many of the women initially associated with S/M advocacy were themselves the same generation as, if not participants in, the earlier feminist movement. But it does point to a certain coming of age of lesbian culture and politics when it has, in S/M, its own subculture whose sense of transgression is premised on a rejection of a "mother" culture of feminist and lesbian orthodoxy.

The growing acceptability of lesbian S/M has occurred in the context of a postmodern emphasis on pleasure and play (one can also think of S/M role-plays in relation to theories of sexuality as performative); the development of lesbian and gay studies in the academy (which have often embraced postmod-

ern theory); the reactivation of bisexuality and queer as politicized psychosocial identifications; the development of AIDS; and a shift in lesbian S/M politics that emphasizes the links to, rather than separation from, other sadomasochists and sexual "outlaws." AIDS has given rise to a need for safe-sex material in which S/M groups, both lesbian and gay and heterosexual, have taken a lead, since they are accustomed to talking frankly about sexual practice and to minimizing risk, not just of HIV transmission.

S/M has had a great impact on lesbian culture, not only on lesbian fashion, as has already been discussed, but also on lesbian fiction, film, theater, and performance. In fiction, this is most clearly seen in the development of lesbian erotica in the late 1980s and early 1990s. This marked a willingness to challenge a feminist disapproval of erotica as a form of pornography and a new confidence in the diversity of the lesbian market. While some fiction presented an overtly sadomasochistic narrative, others, like the fashionable takeup of a faux-S/M style, merely deployed the signs of S/M without actually describing clearly classifiable S/M relations or acts. S/M codes have also been prominent in lesbian art, photography, film, and theater and much discussed in debates about sexuality, particularly those informed by psychoanalysis and concerned with an exploration of female fetishism.

*Reina Lewis*

## Bibliography

Adams, Parveen. "Of Female Bondage." In *Between Feminism and Psychoanalysis*. Ed. Teresa Brennan. London: Routledge, 1989.

Creet, Julia. "Daughter of the Movement: The Psychodynamics of Lesbian S/M Fantasy." *differences: A Journal of Feminist Cultural Studies* 3:2 (Summer 1991), 135–159.

Lewis, Reina. "Dis-Graceful Images: Della Grace and Lesbian Sadomasochism." *Feminist Review* 46 (Spring 1994), 76–91.

Linden, Robin Ruth, Darlene R. Pagano, Diana E.H. Russell, and Susan Leigh Star, eds. *Against Sadomasochism: A Radical Feminist Analysis*. East Palo Alto, Calif.: Frog in the Wall, 1982.

Merck, Mandy. "The Feminist Ethics of Lesbian S/M." In Merck, *Perversions: Deviant Readings*. New York: Routledge 1993, pp. 236–266.

Samois, *Coming to Power*. Boston: Alyson, 1983.

**See also** Butch-Femme; Erotica and Pornography; Psychoanalysis; Safer Sex; Sex Practices; Sex Wars; Sexuality

## Safer Sex

Safer sex refers to choosing sexual practices that reduce one's chance of contracting human immunodeficiency virus (HIV) or other sexually transmitted diseases (STDs).

### History

The term "safe sex" was coined by gay men in the early 1980s in response to the growing Acquired Immune Deficiency Syndrome (AIDS) epidemic. By the late 1980s, the term "safer sex" was widely used, and the concept had expanded to include prevention of all STDs, including hepatitis, herpes, chlamydia, gonorrhea, syphilis, human papilloma virus, and trichomonas. Leadership in raising awareness about safer sex was provided by sadomasochist (S/M) lesbians. They promoted the use of latex gloves and oral-sex barriers, modeling after the "use a condom every time" message for gay men, bisexuals, and heterosexuals. This suggestion was controversial. Some lesbians discounted the latex-sex fad as a capitalist effort to profit from exaggerated levels of fear about AIDS. Other women questioned whether the lower levels of risk in lesbian sexual activities warranted any protective measures. Lesbian activists pressured the U.S. Centers for Disease Control (CDC) in Atlanta, Georgia, to do research on the possibility of woman-to-woman HIV transmission.

In the 1990s, in an attempt to shift attention to other diseases directly affecting lesbians, health advocates emphasized the forty thousand U.S. women's deaths each year from breast cancer. AIDS educators shifted their focus to methods of HIV transmission that posed the greatest risk to all women: sharing injection drug needles and unprotected intercourse.

### Research

A 1980 study of 2,345 women by Susan R. Johnson, concluded that women who exclusively engaged in homosexual sex were less likely to contract STDs such as trichomonas, gonorrhea, and cystitis than were bisexual women. Five different studies, including 995,000 subjects, published by the CDC in the years 1990–1994 concluded that woman-to-woman HIV transmission was very rare (Peterson et al. 1992) A 1994 University of Turin, Italy, six-month study (Raiteri et al. 1994) of eighteen HIV-discordant lesbian couples found no evidence of woman-to-woman transmission. Five cases of suspected woman-to-woman HIV transmission appeared in the scientific literature in the years 1986–1995, but none were considered documented cases.

### HIV Transmission

For HIV to be transmitted sexually, live virus in the blood, semen, or vaginal fluid of an infected person must get into the bloodstream of a partner. HIV dies quickly in response to drying or temperature changes. HIV can easily travel through tears in the anal or vaginal lining that occur during penetration, but it can also travel through intact mucous membranes. HIV cannot travel through healthy skin, but a few cases of HIV entering the body through breaks in the skin have been reported. Immunoglobulin A found in saliva neutralizes HIV. Cuts or sores in the mouth, skin, or genitals can facilitate disease transmission. The spermicide Nonoxynol-9 and other vaginal microbicides undergoing research in the 1990s kill HIV and other STDs.

### Implications for Lesbians

Because of the lower amount of body fluid potentially transferred, the tribadism, fingering, fisting, dildo penetration, and cunnilingus commonly practiced by lesbians are not as likely to spread HIV or other STDs as a penis ejaculating inside an anus or a vagina. Oral sex is not a likely way to spread HIV, but it can spread other STDs. Kissing does not spread HIV, but it can spread herpes, colds, and flu germs. Oral herpes, called a "cold sore" or "fever blister," occurs in more than 50 percent of the U.S. population according to the American Social Health Association. Herpes is a particular lesbian concern because it can be spread from mouths to genitals.

Regardless of the lower risk of woman-to-woman sex, many lesbian couples, especially those with one HIV-positive woman, do everything possible to make sex safer. Since her immune system is weakened and she is particularly susceptible to contracting other diseases, an HIV-positive woman may have more need for safer sex practices than an HIV-negative woman.

### Safer Sex Practices

Because a dildo or a finger might theoretically transfer enough body fluid from one woman to her partner's vagina or anus to transmit HIV or another STD, safer lesbian sex requires washing hands and sex toys well with soap and water or covering them with clean latex before moving from an anus to a vagina or from one woman to another. Filing fingernails can prevent scratching the vagina or more fragile rectum. Oral sex can spread herpes and other STDs, so it should be avoided when one woman has a herpes outbreak or another STD. Some women use dental dams or household plastic wrap to add a layer of safety to oral sex.

Safer sex for women who have sex with men includes the use of latex condoms, water-based lubricant, and spermicide such as Nonoxynol-9 to avoid HIV and other STDs. *Marcia Munson*

### Bibliography

McIlvenna, Ted. *The Complete Guide to Safer Sex*. Fort Lee, N.J.: Barricade, 1992.

O'Sullivan, Sue, and Pratibha Parmar. *Lesbians Talk Safer Sex*. London: Scarlet, 1992.

Petersen, Lyle, Lynda Doll, Carol White, and Susan Chu. "No Evidence for Female-to-Female HIV Transmission Among 960,000 Female Blood Donors." *Journal of Acquired Immune Deficiency Syndromes* 5 (1992), 853–855.

Raiteri, R., R. Fora, and A. Sinicco. "No HIV Transmission Through Lesbian Sex." *Lancet* 344 (1994), 270.

*See also* AIDS (Acquired Immune Deficiency Syndrome); Sadomasochism; Sexually Transmitted Diseases

## Saints and Mystics

Saints are persons who have been canonized by the Catholic or Orthodox churches as a result of their exceptionally holy life or martyr's death. For many centuries, canonization took place through public acclamation, but, in the latter half of the tenth century A.D., the papacy took control of the process. The hierarchy was then able to manipulate the making of saints to reflect its own concerns and ideologies. However, the Church also acknowledges that there are many more saints than it recognizes, and these are venerated during the feast of All Saints (November 1).

A mystic is a person who has a direct experience of the presence of God, often through vision. Some mystics have been canonized, but, since mysticism has at times been associated with heresy and dissent and female resistance to male control, many mystics were not canonized.

## Lesbian Responses

Within the lesbian community, there have been four responses to the saints and mystics.

*Rejection.* Daly (1979) and some other lesbian feminists find little of positive value in female hagiography (lives of the saints written by people promoting their cause), pointing out that it was largely written by men and sought to conform the lives of these women to contemporary understandings of "holiness," which largely consisted in the rejection of their embodiment, self-abasement, and obedience to male representatives of the Church—hence, their disproportionate representation in the saintly categories of virgin and martyr. Some lesbian feminist Christians also find the whole concept of sainthood incompatible with feminist visions of equality.

*Appropriation.* Some lesbian scholars have attempted to identify saints and mystics who might be labeled "lesbian." This is a difficult task not only because of the general problem of defining and labeling same-sex affection in the premodern era, but also because of the heavy editing and interpreting of a woman's life that usually occurred in the process of canonization. One of the least controversial cases is saint, mystic, and doctor of the Church Teresa of Avila (1515–1582), who was put into a convent by her parents because of intimate relationships she had with two women, one a cousin. Teresa later described this passion as a mortal sin and bitterly regretted it. Saint Joan of Arc (1412–1431) has been claimed as a dyke by some lesbian scholars, such as Grahn (1984). While acknowledging Joan's own fiercely protected chastity, Grahn has argued that Joan's assumption of male clothing, her guidance by spirit voices, and her sacrificial death place her within the ancient pre-Christian tradition of the ceremonial "bulldike." Certainly, Joan's transvestism deeply disturbed her inquisitors, and it was the most obvious sign and symbol of her subversion of all that they identified with a God-given order. She dressed in "male" clothes and assumed "male" roles; she trusted in the authority of her "voices" rather than the Church; she was a woman who mixed freely with men but was not "loose"; and she was a devout Christian who was labeled a witch. It is easy to see why so many lesbians have identified with Joan's fierce resistance to what was understood to be "natural" and God-given in her day. Joan was one of a long line of female saints who assumed male clothes, but other female transvestite saints tended to disguise themselves to escape from parents or suitors or to enter the kind of religious life barred to females. Joan did not pretend to be a man. She just refused to conform to the dominant concept of "woman."

*Critical Solidarity.* This approach recognizes the historical and cultural difficulties of claiming women of past ages as lesbians but also recognizes a "family resemblance" between some women saints and mystics and contemporary lesbians, grounded in a resistance to male control and marriage and in what Daly (1979), among others, has labeled "gyn/affection." One such woman is the mystic Hadewijch of Brabant (ca. 1200s). She was part of the *béguine* movement that arose as a reaction against the enforced enclosure of religious women. *Béguines* did not take vows, nor were they under the control of bishops, but they lived lives of prayer and charity. They were often suspected of heresy. Hadewijch's letters to a young *béguine* whom she loved survive, as do her accounts of fourteen visions. Unlike contemporary male mystics who use erotic language of the relationship between the soul and God as an allegory while continuing to hold negative attitudes to sexuality and embodiment, Hadewijch uses erotic language literally. Even more significant, though she follows male mystics in using the genre of courtly love to describe the relationship of the soul to God, she inverts the roles usually assigned to God and the soul. God is Lady Love, and the soul is the knight seeking physical consummation of his love. This "queering" of theology continues in the writings of mystics such as Hildegard of Bingen (1098–1179) and Julian of Norwich (1343–1413), who referred to Jesus as "Christ, our Mother" and completely rejected the dualistic attitude to the physical and the spiritual that tended to characterize mysticism at that time.

*Reclamation of the Process.* Some groups of lesbian and gay Christians have attempted to reclaim and subvert the process of canonization, to "queer" the ecclesiastical calendar, by proclaiming their own saints or reinterpreting the lives of those who were canonized for other reasons. The biblical characters of Ruth and her mother-in-law, Naomi, are venerated as models of same-sex devotion. Lesbian theologian Wilson (1995) has argued that Martha and Mary (Luke 10:38–42; John 11:1–46), with their "brother" Lazarus, may, in fact, represent a new type of family that flourished in the early Church based not upon blood relationship but on friendship. Other female figures venerated by queer Christians include Sor Juana Inés de la Cruz (1648–1695), the Mexican nun who joined a convent to avoid marriage and fought ecclesiastical authority, and Benedetta Carlini (1590–1661), an Italian nun who entered into a sexual relationship with another nun and was imprisoned for thirty-five years as a result. Contemporary lesbian figures, like Audre Lorde (1934–1992), are also being embraced within the queer canon. Lesbian theologian Stuart (1996) has endeavored to make theological sense out of this desire to reclaim and proclaim saints in terms of the distinctive lesbian theology of friendship. *Elizabeth Stuart*

## Bibliography

Daly, Mary. *Gyn/Ecology: The Metaethics of Radical Feminism*. Boston: Beacon and London Women's Press, 1979.

Grahn, Judy. *Another Mother Tongue: Gay Words, Gay Worlds*. Boston: Beacon, 1984.

Jantzen, Grace M. *Power, Gender, and Christian Mysticism*. Cambridge: Cambridge University Press, 1995.

Maitland, Sara, and Wendy Mulford. *Virtuous Magic: The Meanings of Women Saints*. London: Mowbray, 1997.

Stuart, Elizabeth. *Spitting at Dragons: Towards a Feminist Theology of Sainthood*. London: Mowbray, 1996.

Wilson, Nancy. *Our Tribe: Queer Folks, God, Jesus, and the Bible*. San Francisco: HarperSanFrancisco, 1995.

**See also** Catholicism; Hildegard of Bingen, Saint; Joan of Arc (Jeanne d'Arc); Juana Inés de la Cruz, Sor; Lorde, Audre; Religious Communities; Teresa of Avila

## San Francisco, California

Port city in California with a long history of lesbian and gay community life. With the California Gold Rush of 1849, San Francisco became a destination for transnational and transcontinental migrations. By the turn of the twentieth century, San Francisco had gained a reputation for licentious entertainment and sex tourism. The first-known lesbian establishment was Mona's, which opened in 1933 at the foot of Telegraph Hill near the infamous Barbary Coast, the vice district fueled by Gold Rush entertainments. Originally intended as a hangout for local bohemians, Mona's gained a reputation for its unconventionality and soon became a nightclub where lesbian waitresses cross-dressed and sang showtunes to eager tourists and each other. Some of the performers, including Kay Scott (ca. 1916–?), Beverly Shaw (active ca. 1940s), and Gladys Bentley

(1907–1960), became local favorites around whom San Francisco's lesbian bar culture took shape.

World War II (1941–1945) stimulated the expansion of San Francisco's lesbian communities, since the city served as a port of embarkation for GIs who served in the war's Pacific Theater. Servicewomen who had homosexual experiences during the war and did not want to return home afterward often chose San Francisco for their new home because of its familiarity and its reputation as a wide-open town. In the postwar years, the local police, the Armed Forces Disciplinary Control Board, and the Alcohol and Beverage Control Department coordinated their efforts to survey San Francisco's gay and lesbian nightclubs, working systematically to shut them down. It was during this time that the first lesbian-owned establishments opened in San Francisco. In the late 1940s, Tommy's 299 opened at 299 Broadway, just down the street from Mona's, and, in 1951, Charlotte Coleman (ca. 1924–) opened the Front, the first lesbian bar on San Francisco's waterfront.

In 1955, a handful of women founded the Daughters of Bilitis (DOB) so that San Francisco lesbians could socialize privately, outside bars. Through the next two years, Del Martin (1921–) and Phyllis Lyon (1924–), two of the original eight members, steered the Daughters of Bilitis toward greater public involvement. They initiated open discussion meetings focused on lesbian issues and encouraged other lesbians (whom they called "female sex variants") to join their group. In 1956, the Daughters of Bilitis began publishing a monthly newsletter, *The Ladder*, which was distributed nationally until 1972. As DOB chapters spread through the United States, the Daughters of Bilitis became a vital national organization, and, with San Francisco as its place of publication, *The Ladder* positioned San Francisco at the center of lesbian homophile organizing.

With an impressive number of lesbian bars and a national organization dedicated to lesbian emancipation, through the 1960s San Francisco transformed itself into a haven for lesbians and gay men. Homophile activists worked alongside bar owners (both gay and straight) to quell police harassment and to suspend post office regulations that threatened the distribution of homophile newsletters. In 1961, an association of gay bar owners and bartenders formed the San Francisco Tavern Guild, an organization dedicated to protecting the interests of lesbian and gay bar owners and the safety of their patrons. By the mid-1960s, the efforts of homophile activists and Tavern Guild members established limited legal protections for lesbians and gay men in San Francisco, such as the right to public assembly. As a result, lesbian bars became a center for lesbian life in the city. Maud's, near the Haight-Ashbury district, ran from 1966 to 1989, and it was never raided by the police. Instead, Maud's functioned as a community center. It stayed open 365 days a year and hosted a wealth of social and athletic events, including variety shows, poetry readings, a bowling team, and its notorious softball league.

San Francisco's lesbian communities flourished in the 1970s as cafés, bookstores, small presses, and record companies sprang up. The Full Moon Coffeehouse and Bookstore, a worker-owned collective, became a nexus for San Francisco's lesbian feminist community. The Full Moon had nightly lesbian raps, poetry readings, music, workshops, and speakers, and it maintained a women-only admission policy. Valencia Street became a corridor of lesbian life in San Francisco as the Women's Press Collective, the Old Wives' Tales bookstore, Artemis Cafe, and the Women's Building opened through the 1970s, and the Valencia Rose, a lesbian performance space, opened in the early 1980s. In nearby Oakland, Olivia Records, a small lesbian feminist collective, worked to promote women's music by sponsoring large annual music festivals. These events and social spaces shaped the emergence of lesbian feminist ideologies and separatist political action. Lesbians also continued to participate in homophile organizations such as DOB and NACHO (North American Committee of Homophile Organizations); they maintained leadership positions in feminist organizations such as NOW (National Organization for Women); and, along with a coalition of progressive movements, lesbians organized to defeat California's Proposition 6, the 1978 Brigg's Initiative, which would have expelled gay and lesbian schoolteachers from the classroom.

As the 1960s and 1970s witnessed the flowering of lesbian culture and organization building, the 1980s and 1990s witnessed the incorporation of lesbians into city politics, culminating in the 1990 election of two lesbians, Roberta Achtenberg and Carole Migden, to San Francisco's City Council. Lesbians continued to participate in direct-action politics such as ACT UP, Queer Nation, WAC (Women's Action Coalition), and the Lesbian Avengers, but, by the mid-1990s, Bay Area Career Women, a social organization with a dues-paying membership of more than one thousand, had become the largest lesbian organization in the Bay Area. Through the twentieth century, the legacy of lesbian bar cultures, homophile movements, and lesbian feminist institutions ensured lesbian visibility and secured San Francisco's importance as a locus of lesbian social life and political resistance.

*Nan Alamilla Boyd*

## Bibliography

Boyd, Nan Alamilla. *Wide Open Town: San Francisco's Lesbian and Gay History*. Berkeley: University of California Press, forthcoming.

Lyon, Phyllis, and Del Martin. *Lesbian/Woman*. New York: Bantam, 1972.

Stryker, Susan, and Jim Van Buskirk. *Gay by the Bay: A History of Queer Culture in the San Francisco Bay Area*. San Francisco: Chronicle, 1996.

*See also* Bars; Bentley, Gladys; Bookstores; Daughters of Bilitis; *Ladder, The;* Lesbian Avengers; Martin, Del, and Lyon, Phyllis

## Sand, George (1804–1876)

French writer. Born Amandine Aurore Lucie Dupin, of a working-class mother and an (illegitimate) aristocratic father, she was raised primarily by her paternal grandmother in Nohant, in the French region of Berry. She was tutored at home until the age of fourteen, when she was sent to the Convent of the English Augustinians in Paris. In 1822, she married Baron Casimir Dudevant. Her son, Maurice, was born in 1823; her daughter, Solange, in 1828. Sand's career as a writer began in 1831, when she left her husband and moved to Paris to collaborate with her lover, Jules Sandeau (1811–1883), under the pen name J. Sand. She began an independent career with the publication of the novel *Indiana* (1832) under the male pseudonym G. Sand. The novel was an immediate success, which ensured Sand's entry into the world of romantic literary bohemia. Sand was a notorious figure in her day, primarily because of the transgressiveness of her personal life: In her early career, she was known for wearing men's clothing and smoking cigars, which earned her the label of hermaphrodite in the popular press; she was also famous for her illustrious lovers, including Alfred de Musset (1810–1857), the actress Marie Dorval (1798–1849), and Frédéric Chopin (1810–1849).

Sand's early writings are marked by forceful critiques of the institution of marriage. Her third novel, *Lélia* (1833), created a scandal by raising the possibility of an incestuous lesbianism as an alternative to female sexual frustration. Following the uproar caused by this novel and the negative publicity of separation hearings from her husband in 1836, Sand shifted the focus of her writing away from sexual inequality toward class inequality. Most of her work published after 1840 is categorized as pastoral. Her autobiography, *Story of My Life* (1854–1855), is often misleadingly evasive about the scandalous aspects of her personal life and career. *Leyla Ezdinli*

## Bibliography

Barry, Joseph. *Infamous Woman: The Life of George Sand*. New York: Doubleday, 1977.

Naginski, Isabelle Hoog. *George Sand: Writing for Her Life*. New Brunswick, N.J.: Rutgers University Press, 1991.

Schor, Naomi. *George Sand and Idealism*. New York: Columbia University Press, 1993.

*See also* France

## Sapphic Tradition

The Greek lyric poet Sappho (ca. 600 B.C.E.), who lived on the island of Lesbos in the Aegean Sea, was renowned throughout the ancient world. Her preeminence in the world of letters was acknowledged by numerous tributes, not least of which was Aristotle's (384–322 B.C.E.) remark: "Everybody honors the wise. . . . and the Mytileneans honored Sappho although she was a woman." Plato (427?–347? B.C.E.) called her "the Tenth Muse," an epithet that was to become conventionally attached to her name. Her works were lost during the early Christian era, and it was not until the late nineteenth and early twentieth centuries that fragmentary remains of her poems were recovered. However, two of her poems and a number of fragments had been transmitted to Renaissance Europe through the works of others and established the basis of her reputation in Western culture. During the sixteenth and seventeenth centuries, the French and the English preserved and translated the available poems and fragments of her work so that knowledge of her was perpetuated.

It was known that both extant Sapphic odes—the *Ode to Aphrodite* and *Phainetai moi*, in which the speaker's passion for her beloved is triangulated by a man—probably addressed love between women. Sappho was reputed to have established a school for girls, to whom she taught the lyric and choric arts and with whom she was reputed to have developed pedagogical-erotic friendships. Despite the ambiguities of her sexual reputation—she was also said to have been infatuated with a much younger ferryman, Phaon, on whose account she committed suicide—Sappho's became the one name associated with female poetic excellence. She was the sole ancient model to whom early-modern women writers might compare themselves and to whom they might be compared. Madeleine de Scudéry (1607–1701) in France presented herself as a second Sappho, composing the first full-scale modern biography of Sappho. Katherine Philips (1632–1664) in England, who emulated Scudéry's literary style, was compared repeatedly to Sappho, often with a disclaimer about her sexuality. The compliment was later taken over, without the sexual disclaimer, by English women writers, who used it among themselves. Sappho's literary reputation was, thus, well established in early-modern Europe. She was also the most prominent exemplar of erotic behaviors between women, having been used repeatedly to illustrate "tribadism"—the classical term for female same-sex eroticism, from the Greek *tribein* (to rub)—in early-modern European medical accounts of the clitoris. It is this latter aspect of her reputation that was instrumental in establishing her stature in the twentieth century as a kind of lesbian foremother.

During the period between the late seventeenth and the mid-nineteenth centuries, a broad range of fictions of Sappho was produced in France, Germany, and Italy, in addition to various scholarly translations of the available—and fragmentary—corpus of Sappho's poetry. These fictions were usually motivated by the various nationalistic, political, and/or scholarly agendas operating at any particular historical moment. As a result, simultaneous, yet contradictory, traditions of Sappho (continue to be) perpetuated: A desexualized, chaste Sappho coexisted with a second, hetero- or bisexual and promiscuous Sappho, recapitulating yet again, but in a more contemporary key, the garbled tradition of "the two Sapphos" that went back to eleventh-century commentators. At the same time, in France, Germaine de Staël (1766–1817)—as had de Scudéry before her—kept invigorated, through her own identification with the classical poet, the power of Sappho as a model for women writers.

It was, however, the elaborate fiction of Sappho created by Pierre Louÿs's *Les Chansons de Bilitis* (Songs of Bilitis) (1895) that initiated the consol-idation of Sappho's role as classical exemplar of female homosexuality and her subsequent use by literary modernists as their patroness of modernity. Natalie Barney (1876–1972), a wealthy American expatriate in Paris who was the center of a well-known lesbian salon, established the basis for the twentieth-century tradition of Sappho as a kind of proto-lesbian example. Her discovery of an edition of Sappho and of Louÿs's version of Sappho's sexuality—which together provoked striking personal revelations for her, her pseudonymous publication of *Cinq petits dialogues grecs* (Five Small Grecian Dialogues) in 1902, her influence on Renée Vivien's (pseud. of Pauline Tarn [1877–1909]) spurious edition of Sappho's poems in 1903, and her integration of what she understood as Sapphic eroticism into her Paris salon, which featured classical costumes and gestures à la Sappho—inaugurated the twentieth-century's popular understanding of Sappho as lesbian poet. Barney, Vivien, and their Paris circle ignored what had been (and continue to be) the profound ambiguities in what is known about Sappho's sexuality to create a figure of erotic obsession and a model for emulation. Their movement and the cult of Sappho's person was to be called Sapho 1900 or *Sapho cent pour cent* (Sappho one hundred percent).

French dictionaries note the occurrence of *sapphisme* in the sense of "female homosexuality" as early as 1838 and *lesbienne* in the sense of "female homosexual" in 1867. In English, a similar vocabulary for female same-sex love develops later, probably inspired by French usage. By the early twentieth century, it is not unusual to find references to "sapphists" or to "a Sapph" in the writings of Virginia Woolf (1882–1941) and other members of London's sexually and socially progressive Bloomsbury group. A nomenclature derived from constructions of Sappho was, thus, replacing the language of tribadism by the mid-nineteenth century. By the end of the twentieth century, the conflation of modern lesbian identity with the sixth-century B.C.E. Greek poet and her Aegean island was complete.

It is almost certainly the very fragmentary nature of what remains to us of Sappho's life and work, rather than any enterprise of accurate historical reconstruction, that has enabled the invention of elaborate and contradictory Sapphic fictions that serve the purposes of their creators. By the end of the twentieth century, apart from continued scholarly debates among classicists about the nature of Sappho's poems and sexuality, Sappho continues popularly to be regarded as a cult figure by lesbian women, especially by the many lesbian feminists who make the pilgrimage to Lesbos to partake of the environs inhabited by their precursor so many centuries ago.                     *Harriette Andreadis*

### Bibliography

Andreadis, Harriette. "Sappho in Early Modern England: A Study in Sexual Reputation." In *Re-Reading Sappho: Reception and Transmission*. Ed. Ellen Greene. Berkeley: University of California Press, 1997, pp. 105–121.

DeJean, Joan. *Fictions of Sappho, 1546–1937*. Chicago: University of Chicago Press, 1989.

DuBois, Page. *Sappho Is Burning*. Chicago: University of Chicago Press, 1995.

Williamson, Margaret. *Sappho's Immortal Daughters*. Cambridge, Mass.: Harvard University Press, 1995.

*See also* Barney, Natalie; Philips, Katherine; Sappho; Tribade; Vivien, Renée; Woolf, Virginia

### Sappho (ca. 600 B.C.E.)

Most famous lyric poet of the ancient Greek and Roman world. Sappho lived on the island of Lesbos ca. 600 B.C.E. Unfortunately, only one of her songs survives completely intact, but it and the fragments of nearly two hundred other poems make clear that prominent themes in her songs included Aphrodite (goddess of love) and the subject of love between women. Virtually nothing is known of her life from sources dating to her own time, for the only contemporary reference to her is in a brief fragment of the poetry of Alkaios, a fellow aristocrat from the same island. Most of the later stories about her life and death belong to the realm of legend. Of these, by far the most pervasive in shaping the later image of Sappho has been *Heroides 15* by the Roman poet Ovid (43 B.C.E.–A.D. 17), in which the fictional "Sappho" writes a letter addressed to a young man (named Phaon) who has been her lover and then deserted her; at the end, she alludes to a cure for her misery, a suicide leap off the cliffs of Cape Leukas. About the real Sappho we have only the sketchiest information, of which some details (such as a daughter named Kleis) may be fictions based upon an overly literal interpretation on the part of ancient biographers of the poems of Sappho known to them.

Sappho's poetry has come down to us today through several kinds of sources. Ancient grammar-

*Attic vase showing Sappho and Alkaios, ca. 500–475 B.C.E. (Munich 2416). Staatliche Antikensammlungen und Glyptothek, Munich.*

ians and rhetoricians were sometimes struck by some phrase or unusual word or, indeed in one case, by an entire poem, which they chose to preserve in quotation. The one completely extant song, a hymn to Aphrodite, was preserved in just such a way by Dionysios of Halicarnassos (first century B.C.E.), who quoted this hymn as an example of outstanding grace and charm. Another fragment of Sappho's poetry was found scratched onto a potsherd (broken pottery was the scrap paper of antiquity), and a few other fragments have turned up on a parchment dated to the sixth century A.D. In the nineteenth and twentieth centuries, several more fragments, many of them of substantial length, have been found in papyri preserved in the dry sands of Egypt. Besides deliberate destruction of her work during medieval times, ignorance of her particular dialect of Greek (called Lesbian-Aeolic) on the part of scribes has contributed to the dearth of surviving poems.

If the one complete poem is an accurate indication, most of Sappho's songs were relatively short. The hymn to Aphrodite (fr. 1 Voigt) consists of seven four-line stanzas, in which the poet as narrator describes her past encounters with the goddess, who has come to her aid in winning over reluctant lovers. The Sappho figure concludes the song by calling upon Aphrodite once again to be her fellow-soldier. In another song, the narrator describes her sensations of overwhelming desire as she gazes upon a woman she loves (fr. 31 Voigt). One nearly complete poem (fr. 16 Voigt) examines the question of what constitutes "the most beautiful thing upon the black earth," rejecting military splendor (so prized in earlier Greek literature such as Homer's *Iliad*) in favor of "what one loves"; the point is then illustrated by two examples, namely Helen's love for the Trojan prince Paris and the narrator's love for a woman called Anaktoria. Other songs focus on the pain of separation of lovers and on the power of memory to re-create the presence of an absent beloved. Additional themes include folk motifs, mythological descriptions, and wedding songs. All of these songs were no doubt composed for live performance by a singer accompanied by the music of the lyre, but little is known of the specific circumstances of performance on the island of Lesbos.

Sappho's poetry is distinguished by the beauty of many vivid images: Eros compared to wind blasting mountain oaks; the rosy-fingered moon; a red-ripe apple on the very top of a tree, just out of reach of the apple-pickers; Aphrodite's sparrow-drawn chariot; and sleep descending from apple boughs.

Sappho's influence on later literature has been considerable despite the paucity of her surviving poems. Besides her impact on Roman, English, and French literature, perhaps her most significant influence has been on twentieth-century American women poets, particularly Amy Lowell (1874–1925), H.D. (Hilda Doolittle [1886–1961]), and Olga Broumas (1949–).                    *Jane McIntosh Snyder*

## Bibliography

DeJean, Joan. *Fictions of Sappho, 1546–1937.* Chicago: University of Chicago Press, 1989.

DuBois, Page. *Sappho Is Burning*. Chicago: University of Chicago Press, 1995.

Snyder, Jane McIntosh. *Lesbian Desire in the Lyrics of Sappho.* New York: Columbia University Press, 1997.

———. *Sappho*. New York: Chelsea House, 1995.

———. *The Woman and the Lyre.* Carbondale: Southern Illinois University Press, 1989.

Williamson, Margaret. *Sappho's Immortal Daughters.* Cambridge, Mass.: Harvard University Press, 1995.

*See also* Antiquity; Classical Literature; H.D. (Hilda Doolittle); Lesbos, Island of; Lowell, Amy Lawrence; Sapphic Tradition

## Sarton, May (1912–1996)

Novelist, poet, and New England woman of letters. "I'm proud of the fact that I came out as a lesbian in 1965, long before anyone did, but I lost two jobs because of it. It was easier for me because I had no family, but it's true that I wrote about it only after my parents' deaths," so Belgian-born May Sarton wrote, at age sixty-seven, about her lesbianism for the first time in her 1979 autobiography, *Recovering*. It is significant that her coming out coincided with her healing process after a mastectomy and radiation treatments. This honesty and openness characterize Sarton's oeuvre and offer explanation for her popularity with standing-room-only audiences. The author of seventeen novels, fourteen books of poetry, five biographical works, and short stories in the *New Yorker*, *Harper's,* and the *Atlantic Monthly*, Sarton lectured and taught at Harvard University and Radcliffe and Wellesley colleges and read her works to eager listeners at more than fifty other institutions of higher learning. In addition, she served as a Guggenheim Fellow in Poetry and a Fellow in Poetry at Bryn Mawr College.

The daughter of historian of science George Sarton and fabric designer Mabel Elwes Sarton, she came to the United States at the age of four, when her father accepted a professorship at Harvard University. Attending Shady Hill School in Cambridge, Massachusetts, the Institute Belge de Culture Française in Brussels, and Cambridge High and Latin School, from which she graduated in 1929, Sarton joined Eva LeGallienne's (1899–1991) Civil Repertory Theatre, with which she acted for several years. She founded a small company of her own, the Associated Actors' Theatre, which disbanded after its third season. Publishing her first book in 1937 (*Encounter in April*), Sarton set about her life's work of publishing in five genres: poetry, novels, memoirs, journals, and short stories.

*Mrs. Stevens Hears the Mermaids Singing* (1965) was the novel that introduced lesbianism in Sarton's work ("I suppose people were shocked because you talked about things like women falling in love with each other, took this for granted, set it in its place," asks the young woman in her interview with Mrs. Stevens). It was the publication of this book that caused Sarton the loss of several employment opportunities.

*Plant Dreaming Deep* (1968) is dedicated to Sarton's partner, Judy, with whom she lived for fifteen years, "who believed in the adventure from the start," as they made a home together in Nelson, New Hampshire. By the time *Journal of a Solitude* (1973) was written, Sarton lived alone. Both her partner, Judy—referred to in the journal simply as "X"–and her faithful gardener, Perley Cole, were "suffering from the change to a new place," nursing homes. This journal appears to be the work by Sarton that is most frequently mentioned as readers' introduction to Sarton's voluminous writings.

In 1973, Sarton moved to York, Maine, to Wild Knoll, where her second-floor study looked out upon a field mown with a walkway for her and Tamas, her beloved dog, which led to the rocky Atlantic Ocean coast. Her gardening spirit sustained her soul and her writing. In her later years, Sarton wrote with the voice of truth and clarity about her aging process and her sadness at the loss of energy to write and to be with and correspond with people. She died on July 16, 1996. Her final journal, *At Eighty-Two: A Journal* (1994), was published posthumously.              *Nancy Seale Osborne*

### Bibliography

Osborne, Nancy Seale. "May Sarton." In *Contemporary Lesbian Writers of the United States: A Bio-Bibliographical Critical Sourcebook*. Ed. Sandra Pollack and Denise D. Knight. Westport, Conn.: Greenwood, 1993.

Straw, Deborah. "Belles Letters Interview." *Belles Lettres* 6:2 (Winter 1991), 34–37.

*See also* Autobiography; Poetry

### Scholars

Lesbians who conduct scholarship pertaining to lesbian- or nonlesbian-related issues outside or inside educational institutions. Many lesbian scholars point to social change and movements as enabling and motivating their scholarship, as they seek to reshape scholarly traditions that have debased and denied lesbian existence, to represent the specificity and multiplicity of lesbians' lived experiences, and to explain and change the social order. These scholars have worked within and beyond academia to create legitimate areas and methods of study. Even lesbian scholars who do not engage in lesbian-specific scholarship frequently face professional marginalization in their fields when they are publicly lesbian.

Women's access to higher education and the emergence of women's colleges in the late nineteenth century in the United States facilitated the development of quasi-lesbian feminist scholarly communities. However, although lesbian scholars worked in universities throughout the twentieth century, there were few networks or outlets for self-consciously lesbian scholarship beyond initial work by homophile organizations, such as Daughters of Bilitis.

Lesbian scholarly work did not coalesce in significant, organized forms until after the Stonewall Rebellion (1969) in New York City. Spurred by the activism of gay liberationist groups, gay and lesbian scholars formed the Gay Academic Union (GAU) in New York City in 1973. By 1975, the organization had formed chapters in cities including Philadelphia, Pennsylvania; Ann Arbor, Michigan; Boston, Massachusetts; and Chicago, Illinois—with writers such as Kate Millet (1934–), Adrienne Rich (1929–), and Rita Mae Brown (1944–) giving readings at conferences and fund-raisers. The GAU emphasized a connection between personal liberation and social change and stressed its opposition to discrimination against women and gay people in academia, support of faculty and students coming out, and promotion and development of new approaches to gay studies in universities. However, sexism within the GAU precipitated the almost immediate formation of separate men's and women's caucuses and the eventual exodus of many women from the organization in 1976.

Early post-Stonewall scholarly work was tied to community organizing and social movements in the form of lesbian archives and history projects, including the founding of the Lesbian Herstory Archives in New York City by Joan Nestle (1940–) and Deborah Edel (1944–) in 1973. This work was instrumental in initiating a field of study that displaced models of social, medical, and psychological deviance in the study of lesbian lives. With the success of GAU members in forming gay and lesbian caucuses within disciplinary professional organizations, including the Modern Language Association in 1973 and the American Anthropological and American Sociological associations in 1974, scholarly activity shifted to the disciplines as a primary location for defining gay and lesbian scholarship.

At the same time that lesbian scholars worked with gay men, their scholarly work was enabled by the gradual institutionalization of women's studies courses and departments in universities in the 1970s and 1980s. However, despite the role of lesbians in inaugurating many women's studies programs, it was not until the early to mid-1980s that mainstream academic feminism, responding to critiques of its exclusionary practices by women of color and lesbians, began to include those it had previously excluded.

Initially, the work of lesbian scholars was shaped by their marginalization in gay and lesbian and feminist movements, as well as their desire for disciplinary and personal legitimation within the academy. Lesbian scholars defined lesbian identity and experience, constructed a visible history, literature, and culture, and identified specific forms of discrimination that they faced as a group. Feminist and gay male work in the academy developed around collective identity and experience and led to the recovery of lost history and literature and the identification of narratives of oppression and resistance. These strategies excluded lesbian concerns; nevertheless, they were appropriated by lesbians seeking to create their own area of study by defining lesbian identity and experience. Definitions of the lesbian, based on such criteria as affective ties, genital sexual experiences, and politics and resistances forged a lesbian identity and helped construct historical accounts of lesbian lives.

From the late 1970s to the early 1980s, so-called "sex radicals" challenged lesbian feminists' models of lesbian sexuality and politics while women of color challenged white lesbians' exclusionary definitions of lesbian identity and experience. These political breaks with monolithic understandings of lesbians intersected with the rise of social-construction theory, which argued for the social, historical, and discursive formation of identities rather than fixed, timeless identities. Some lesbian scholars criticized poststructural analysis, arguing that it displaces the lesbian identity and history constructed through activist scholarship with a theoretical focus on ideology, representation, and the cultural construction of identity categories. They were concerned that, by seeking legitimacy within academia, poststructuralist scholars impose orthodoxies for scholarship that undermine lesbian specificity and sever connections to social and political movements that have historically enabled their work.

Independent lesbian scholars often had little access to material or institutional support for their work. Nonetheless, they inaugurated presses, journals, and newspapers, created resources for research and teaching through history projects and community centers, and promoted lesbian cultural expressions through film, drama, and art collectives.

The gains made in validating lesbian scholars and scholarship have increasingly situated openly lesbian scholars in universities, where institutionalized homophobia may discredit them personally and professionally. Whether they engage in scholarship pertaining to lesbian issues, many lesbian academics struggle with issues of "coming out" in terms that are specific to their roles as educators. A number of lesbians write of their responsibility to come out in order to offer students role models, support, and mentoring and to use their presence in classrooms to foreground the personal and political relevance of classroom discussions. Beyond the classroom, coming out is often used to work against institutional and social discrimination, although it may diminish a scholar's credibility with colleagues, who may marginalize her scholarship as politicized and endanger her professional status, possibilities for networking, and job security. On the other hand, in the 1990s, as lesbian studies and queer theory made inroads in cultural and literary studies, some lesbian scholars faced tokenization, becoming commodities who are called upon to be representatives of "the lesbian community" or spokespersons for lesbian issues in departments and universities.

[The author wishes to thank the Lesbian Herstory Archives for making available documents pertaining to the Gay Academic Union.]

Susan Talburt

## Bibliography

Cruikshank, Margaret, ed. *Lesbian Studies: Present and Future*. Old Westbury, N.Y.: Feminist Press, 1982.

Garber, Linda, ed. *Tilting the Tower: Lesbians Teaching Queer Subjects*. New York: Routledge, 1994.

Kitzinger, Celia. "Beyond the Boundaries: Lesbians in Academe." In *Storming the Tower: Women in the Academic World*. Ed. Susanne S. Lie and Virginia E. O'Leary. New York: Kogan Page, 1990, pp. 163–177.

McNaron, Toni A.H. *Poisoned Ivy: Lesbian and Gay Academics Confronting Homophobia*. Philadelphia: Temple University Press, 1997.

Zimmerman, Bonnie, and Toni A.H. McNaron, eds. *The New Lesbian Studies: Into the Twenty-First Century*. New York: Feminist Press, 1976.

*See also* Archives and Libraries; Brown, Rita Mae; Daughters of Bilitis; Lesbian Feminism; Lesbian Herstory Archives; Lesbian Studies; Millett, Kate;

Nestle, Joan; Queer Theory; Rich, Adrienne; Social-Construction Theory; Teachers; Women's Studies

## Science

Lesbians have worked in science and technology as long as women have had access to these fields. Prior to the twentieth century, however, very little is documented about their affectionate preferences. During certain periods of time, western European medieval convents offered some women possibilities of engaging in the pursuit of knowledge in communities consisting of other women. Some, for example, read lesbian passion into the friendships of Hildegard of Bingen (1098–1171), the medieval visionary, composer, and writer of medical and philosophical texts.

## History

At the beginning of the modern era (ca. 1500), many European women had roles in their communities as healers and wise women (or witches), practicing knowledge and skills that had been developed by women over several centuries. During the so-called scientific revolution, this traditional knowledge was replaced by the emerging modern science, practiced by well-to-do men. In large-scale witch-hunts, lasting from the late Middle Ages until the eighteenth century, vast numbers of women (estimates range from 100,000 to several million) were killed.

During and after this violent era of scientific revolution, women of wealthy families still had some limited access to science and learning. However, they were isolated, particularly from communities of other women, in their roles as family members (wives, daughters, sisters, or in otherwise secretarial functions) and helpmates to the scientist, who was their father, brother, husband, or master.

By the nineteenth century, western European science and technology had become institutionalized as a profoundly male realm. Not only did the scientific establishment consist of men, but, in addition, the scientific approach that had developed in the modern era represented the point of view of the enlightened Western "man of science." He treated nature and women as objects of study and as the "other," seen as inherently inferior to the "objective" male scientist. Women's control of their bodies, now reduced to biological objects, were placed in the hands of men, and women's sexuality was reduced to a means for heterosexual procreation.

From the late nineteenth century onward, women in many industrialized countries slowly regained access to this institutionalized practice of science, but their roles as scientists were isolated and marginal. Science and technology remained male dominated in both their practices and discourses. The conventional image of a scientist was white, male, Western, and heterosexual, while the role of a woman in science stayed that of the "other" by definition.

## The Twentieth Century

The twentieth-century female scientist is thus a deviant from traditional male-controlled femininity. Her stereotype has often been that of a spinster, dedicated to her career instead of to a husband and children. This seeming asexuality could hide potential lesbian lifestories of many female scientists from sight. The main affections we know from their documented lives are their often passionate pursuit of scientific knowledge and their friendships and contacts with other women. The latter have been routinely ignored by historians of science, who have treated women scientists almost solely in their relation to male colleagues and superiors. For example, the 1996 biography of the Austrian nuclear physicist Lise Meitner (1878–1968), discoverer of nuclear fission, could be read as containing a possible lesbian subtext, instead of the usual reading of Meitner as a spinster colleague of the most eminent nuclear physicists of her time. Meitner's close friendships were with other women, but no documents about their intimate exchanges remain, as is often the case with scientists' personal correspondence.

Various lesbian feminist movements that emerged from the 1960s onward were often critical of established science. This criticism took several forms, some of which rejected science altogether. Many lesbian feminists were actively involved in practicing alternatives to science and technology, such as astrology and witchcraft, with the purpose of reclaiming the power that the scientific revolution had taken from women. These approaches became threaded into lesbian feminist culture, while offering little of interest to those lesbians working as scientists.

Since the late 1970s, Western feminist thinkers, including Merchant (1980) Evelyn Fox Keller, and Harding (1991), have vocally challenged the objectivity and rationality of science and technology. These challenges have emerged both from the feminist rethinking of knowledge and from the general development of social and cultural studies of science and technology.

There have been various approaches to the question of how science should be treated and transformed. Some 1970s feminist writers of theory and utopian fiction outlined science as a threat, unavoidably leading to violence and domination. Others suggested it had a liberating potential and could be used to transform human reproduction, thus freeing women from their biological, heterosexual destinies.

The intrinsic resistance of physical science and technology to feminist critiques has been much stronger than in the humanities and the social sciences. Because of this, there has been little change in the theory and practice of science itself, although some in the consciousness of women (and men) involved in doing it. There is no unique approach to a specific "lesbian science" but, instead, a variety of approaches. Although creating lesbian viewpoints on science and technology might not significantly alter existing scientific practices, they are well worth exploring.

Many lesbians incorporate the insights of feminist critiques of science. Some researchers have, however, attempted to outline a more explicitly lesbian approach. Sandra Harding, in *Whose Science? Whose Knowledge? Thinking from Women's Lives* (1991) asks: "Shouldn't there be a distinctive lesbian epistemological standpoint?" Harding outlines several lesbian contributions to feminist standpoints. These include seeing women in relation to other women and imagining communities consisting of women, challenging compulsory heterosexuality, and centering on female sexuality as constructed by women. A lesbian standpoint also points to a link between the oppression of women and the oppression of deviant sexualities, originating in the way science has been structured.

## Lesbian Perspectives

But what could lesbian perspectives in natural sciences be like? They could include, for example, an approach to gynecology that does not imagine female bodies as just reproductive systems. Another contribution could be to use metaphors of positive woman-to-woman relations in describing how a scientist interacts with nature. Instead of having "penetrating insight" into something unknown, a scientist could rely on interdependencies, seeing herself as a part of what is being observed, not as someone fundamentally different and dominant. Lesbians can also be placed into focus explicitly, like in lesbian sociogeography, which aims at placing lesbians concretely on the map.

Many lesbian scientists are involved in mainstream scientific research and teaching, but communities of lesbian scientists for socializing, or for furthering the practice of lesbian science, hardly existed until the early 1990s. In the last decade of the twentieth century, lesbian scientists created some loose networks—for example, LIS (Lesbians in Science), which was formed in 1991 in the United States and connects its members through an electronic mailing list. There have also been gatherings of lesbian scientists in connection with meetings for women in science and technology, in Germany and elsewhere. However, in many branches of science and in most countries and cultures, science and technology still lack lesbian viewpoints and a sense of lesbian community. Coming out, connecting with others, and providing role models for lesbian students are practical concerns for many lesbians in science around the world.

There are a few examples of how lesbianism has informed a scientist's approach to her discipline. One such testimony can be found in the writing of Rachel Carson (1907–1964), the well-known U.S. ecologist and author of *The Silent Spring* (1962). Carson fell in love with a married woman ten years her senior at age forty-five, although they could meet only during the summer at their vacation homes on an island in Maine.

In her best-selling book about seashore ecology, *The Edge of the Sea* (1955), Carson describes life forms that belong both to the wet and the dry worlds in a way that seems to reflect her own lesbian life, closeted out of necessity:

> In my thoughts of the shore . . . is a pool hidden within a cave that one can visit only rarely and briefly when the lowest of the year's low tides fall below it, and perhaps from that very fact it acquires some of its special beauty. . . . Here were creatures so exquisitely fashioned that they seemed unreal, their beauty too fragile to exist in a world of crushing force.

Lesbian scientists like Carson, with their hidden and marginal viewpoints, have stood among others (women, eco-activists, indigenous peoples) with equally marginal viewpoints, helping transgress the established borders of science and technology.

*Eva Isaksson*

## Bibliography

Freeman, Martha, ed. *Always, Rachel: The Letters of Rachel Carson and Dorothy Freeman, 1952–1964*. Boston: Beacon, 1995.

Harding, Sandra. *Whose Science? Whose Knowledge? Thinking from Women's Lives*. Ithaca, N.Y.: Cornell University Press, 1991.

Merchant, Carolyn. *The Death of Nature: Women, Ecology, and the Scientific Revolution*. San Francisco: Harper and Row, 1980.

*See also* Ecology and Ecofeminism; Hildegard of Bingen, Saint; Technology

## Science Fiction

The roots of modern science fiction (SF) can be traced back to a range of nineteenth-century literary traditions, including Gothic horror, utopian fantasy, and adventure fiction, but it was not until the early twentieth century that SF emerged as a distinctive genre. Editors such as Hugo Gernsbeck (1884–1967) and writers such as Edgar Rice Burroughs (1875–1950) forged the conventions of SF in pulp magazines and novels intended primarily for adolescent boys. Thus, it is not surprising that lesbians, on the rare occasions that they appeared in early SF at all, were portrayed as sexless man-haters or loathsome monsters. Some notable exceptions occurred in the context of the mid-twentieth-century homophile movement. Lisa Ben (pseud.) included several SF stories in *Vice Versa*, a short-lived magazine for lesbians that she edited and published in Los Angeles, California, in 1947. The Daughters of Bilitis—a small but influential group of early lesbian activists—also published SF in its national newsletter, *The Ladder*, including a three-part series about a Martian anthropologist in a lesbian bar.

Riding the "second wave" of the feminist movement, large numbers of lesbian and feminist writers entered SF for the first time in the 1970s. Utopias—visions of ideal future societies—have been a predominant feature of lesbian SF ever since. Lesbian utopias frequently rest on separatist principles, imagining future harmony in pastoral societies inhabited solely by women. Examples can be found in Joanna Russ's pioneering book *The Female Man* (1975), as well as Alice Sheldon/James Tiptree Jr.'s "Houston, Houston, Do You Read?" (1976), Sally Gearhart's *The Wanderground* (1980), Katherine Forrest's *Daughters of a Coral Dawn* (1984), Joan

Slonczewski's *A Door into Ocean* (1986), Nicola Griffith's *Ammonite* (1992), and Suzy McKee Charnas's *The Furies* (1994), the sequel to *Motherlines* (1978). Marion Zimmer Bradley (1930–), an early contributor to *The Ladder* who went on to become a popular and prolific SF writer, both depicts and critiques lesbian utopias in *The Ruins of Isis* (1978) and her Free Amazon trilogy, *The Shattered Chain* (1976), *Thendara House* (1983), and *City of Sorcery* (1984).

Despite the continuing popularity of utopias, the 1980s and 1990s saw the growth of more dystopian future visions as feminist and lesbian writers began to engage with the realities of technology, the limitations of the lesbian community, and the inescapable presence of men. SF writers of the 1990s, such as Eleanor Arnason, Lynda Lyons, Laura Mixon, Mary Rosenblum, and Melissa Scott, challenged the heterosexist and frequently misogynistic conventions of "hard" (high-tech) SF like cyberpunk by giving lesbian and bisexual women characters central roles. Feminist male writers, including Samuel Delany and John Varley, have also included sympathetic protraits of female homosexuality in their work.

The 1980s and 1990s also saw a shift in publishing trends. In the 1970s and early 1980s, small, independent, feminist and lesbian presses were largely responsible for seeing lesbian SF into print. In the United States, Naiad Press, Spinsters Ink, New Victoria Publishers, Rising Tide Press, and others have printed a variety of SF and fantasy novels. In the United Kingdom, Onlywomen Press and the Women's Press have put and kept an impressive number of lesbian SF titles in print, including Anna Livia's *Bulldozer Rising* (1988) and Lorna Mitchell's *Revolution of Saint Jone* (1988). Since the late 1980s, however, large commercial SF publishers, such as Del Rey, Daw, and Tor, have come out with an increasing number of novels with realistic lesbian characters. Simultaneously, Naiad Press, the oldest and largest independent lesbian press, gradually ceased publishing SF altogether.

Lesbian SF, like both lesbian fiction and mainstream SF more generally, continues to be written predominantly for, by, and about white, middle-class people. Jewelle Gomez (1948–) is among the few lesbians of color writing SF. Published in 1991 by independent feminist press Firebrand Books, Gomez's first novel, *The Gilda Stories*, follows the life of a black lesbian vampire from the time of slavery to a terrifying near-future world. Other women of color, including Gloria Anzaldúa and Michelle Parkerson, have produced a handful of poems and short stories that fall in the category of lesbian SF. Gomez (1993) believes that the historical and cultural legacies of racism make it impossible for women of color to escape into utopian narratives. Thus, the fact that the utopia has been at the heart of lesbian SF since the 1970s may be one of the reasons few women of color have chosen to write it.

Karen Cadora

## Bibliography

Decarnin, Camilla, Eric Garber, and Lyn Paleo, eds. *Worlds Apart: An Anthology of Lesbian and Gay Science Fiction and Fantasy*. Boston: Alyson, 1986.

Garber, Eric, and Lyn Paleo. *Uranian Worlds: A Guide to Alternative Sexuality in Science Fiction, Fantasy, and Horror*. 2nd ed. Boston: G.K. Hall, 1990.

Gomez, Jewelle. "Speculative Fiction and Black Lesbians." *Signs: Journal of Women in Culture and Society* 18:4 (1993), 948–955.

Yntema, Sharon, ed. *More Than 100 Women Science Fiction Writers: An Annotated Bibliography*. Freedom, Calif: Crossing, 1988.

***See also*** Anzaldúa, Gloria E.; Naiad Press; Utopian Literature

## Scudder, Vida Dutton (1861–1954)

American writer, teacher, and social activist. She was born in India and christened Julia Davida Dutton Scudder; after the death of her missionary father when she was less than a year old, she was raised by her mother in Auburndale and Boston, Massachusetts, where both the Scudders and Duttons, old New England families, resided. She was a member of the first class of the Boston Girls' Latin School and attended Smith College, where she got her B.A. and M.A. in English studies and published her first writing, under the pseudonym Davida Coit. In 1887, she joined the faculty of English literature at Wellesley College, where she taught until her retirement in 1928.

Not only was she a prolific writer (seventeen books and several hundred articles), Scudder also acted on her progressive social vision, which took such forms as organizing the College Settlement Association in 1887 and, during 1893, working at Denison House, Boston's first settlement; campaigning in 1900 against a gift to Wellesley from the Rockefeller family's oil fortune; joining the Socialist Party in 1912; speaking to the women of the 1912 Lawrence textile strike; helping found the Church League for Industrial Democracy in 1919; lecturing at the New School for Social Research weekly in 1931; and organizing a 1944 conference on "The Church's Responsibility Toward Racial Groups."

All of Scudder's work was situated in a female-centered world, about which she wrote extensively in her 1937 autobiography, *On Journey*. She wrote of friendship between women as the "definitive experience of reality." Scudder's friendship with Florence Converse (1871–1967), her student, a woman who "has entered the inmost region in my power to open," was lifelong, as was the closeness between Scudder and her mother. At Wellesley, she and Converse became the center of a vital community of women. In 1919, with their mothers, they established a household, about which Scudder wrote in *On Journey:* "Miss Converse had for years shared my life in all ways except living under the same roof. Now that joy was given us, and we have never been separated since."

In the plots of their fiction and in the dedications of their books is a record of their enduring and loving relationship and an exploration of what women's relationships mean. For example, in Scudder's *A Listener in Babel* (1903), the main character, a female settlement worker from a rather privileged background, decides with a group of multiethnic working-class women to do factory work while they plan a cooperative living community. In Converse's *Diana Victrix* (1897), Enid, modeled after Scudder, and Sylvia, modeled after Converse, both reject men, embracing their work and each other. Scudder dedicates her 1937 autobiography to Converse, her "Comrade and Companion."

In addition to the female-centered worlds of college and the settlement house, Scudder was also devoted to the Companionship of the Holy Cross, a sororial religious community. Scudder wrote on the life of St. Catherine of Siena (1347–1380) and on Christian social thought and became one of the leading Franciscan scholars of her day.

Nan Bauer-Maglin

## Bibliography

Balch, Emily Green. "Vida Dutton Scudder, 1861–1954." *Wellesley Alumna Magazine* (January 1955), 89–90.

**S** Corcoran, Theresa. *Vida Dutton Scudder*. Boston: Twayne, 1982.

Frederick, Peter J. "Vida Dutton Scudder: The Professor as Social Activist." *New England Quarterly* 43 (September 1970), 407–433.

Maglin, Nan Bauer. "Vida to Florence: 'Comrade and Companion.'" *Frontiers: A Journal of Women Studies* 4 (Fall 1979), 13–20.

*See also* Boston Marriage; Colleges, Women's; Female Support Networks

## Self-Defense

Skills that help individuals protect themselves. In a society that expects women to limit their freedom, to rely on male protection, and not to fight back if assaulted, self-defense classes teach women and girls mental, psychological, and physical skills and empower them to feel confident on their own. Women's self-defense is one of many examples of feminist political action led and supported disproportionately by lesbian energy. Beginning ca. 1970, feminists sought martial-arts training and organized classes to defeat female victimization, passivity, and powerlessness. In the late 1990s, community centers, religious institutions, workplaces, recreation programs, universities, Girl Scout troops, feminist organizations, and martial-arts schools hosted self-defense classes.

Anger at violence against women; the conviction that women have the right to feel safe in their homes, on the streets, and in the workplace; and the desire to challenge ingrained fears and lack of confidence motivated this movement. Feminist antiviolence politics and martial arts contribute to self-defense philosophy and practice. But while rape crisis groups, battered women's shelters, and domestic violence projects strive to mitigate the effects of violence perpetrated against women, self-defense teaches prevention and successful response to attacks. Child assault prevention programs incorporate the same philosophy of safety and empowerment for children.

Although success stories are rarely heard—the media publicize rapes, assaults, and murders—countless women have avoided, escaped, and successfully protected themselves from threatening situations. Self-defense teaches assertiveness, reliance on intuition, and knowledge of vulnerable areas on attackers' bodies. Self-defense classes are not martial-arts classes, although they freely borrow martial-arts techniques. Students practice using their minds, their voices, easily learned physical techniques, and objects at hand, rather than weapons. They learn realistic information about attacks in order to minimize media distortion and to counter pervasive advice not to resist. Sociological research has shown that resistance works; the more strategies a woman used, the more likely she was to escape from an attacker with minimal injuries. To make skills widely accessible, most feminist self-defense classes are relatively inexpensive, although a few, widely publicized businesses sell courses at prices that only affluent women can afford. Typically, self-defense classes last six to ten weeks. Some programs teach courses for women with disabilities or adapt their curriculum to disabled women's capabilities. Mixed gay and lesbian organizations have also sponsored self-defense classes, often taught by lesbians.

All women can benefit from self-defense classes, but not all continue training in a martial art. Lesbian and feminist martial artists are noteworthy for their cooperation, despite style chauvinism in the martial arts. The National Women's Martial Arts Federation and the Pacific Association of Women Martial Artists, both founded in the 1970s, hold annual training camps, as well as local and regional get-togethers, that feature self-defense classes and training for self-defense teachers. Competitors at the 1994 Gay Games in New York City included more than two hundred lesbian martial artists.

*Lois Rita Helmbold*

### Bibliography
Bart, Pauline, and Patricia O'Brien. *Stopping Rape: Successful Survival Strategies*. New York: Pergamon, 1985.

Caignon, Denise, and Gail Groves, eds. *Her Wits About Her: Self-Defense Success Stories by Women*. New York: Harper and Row, 1987.

*See also* Violence

## Self-Help

The variety of strategies by which people meet their personal needs outside professional arenas. All of these strategies focus on giving people access to the information they need to cope with personal concerns and empowering them to believe that they can do it. The terms "self-help" and "mutual aid" are sometimes used interchangeably because most forms of self-help involve helping one's self and being supportive of others with the same problem or concern.

The most commonly recognized form of self-help is the "self-help group." These small, organized groups of individuals who share a common set of concerns or characteristics have become more common in the last two decades of the twentieth century. Self-help groups usually focus their activities on supportive discussion, but many also provide material assistance to participants, plan outings, and/or educate the public about their particular concerns. Although professionals may be involved as members, self-help groups can be distinguished from "therapeutic support groups" in that they do not rely on professionally trained leaders. Some of these groups are independent, but many are linked with regional or national self-help organizations that provide information and resources.

Self-help is not limited to support groups. Another common form is self-help reading. Bookstores are full of self-help books, providing information and advice about specific concerns. Many self-help organizations publish newsletters in which members give firsthand accounts of their experiences. In the women's community and, particularly, the lesbian community, self-help has also taken other forms, such as self-defense training, co-counseling groups, and legal clinics.

Self-help has played an important role in the lesbian community and in the gay, lesbian, and bisexual movement. In the 1970s, lesbian feminists organized around the concept of self-help, establishing economic co-ops, child-care centers, health clinics, and halfway houses, in addition to more traditional support groups. Olivia Records, a successful women's music company, began as a part of this effort to establish a separate, self-sufficient "lesbian nation." In the late 1970s through the 1980s, these self-help groups branched off in many directions. They became more racially and ethnically diverse, and groups organized to represent other specific subgroups in the community. Groups such as Chicago Asian Lesbians Moving (CALM), Fat Dykes, and the San Francisco Bay Area Career Women are examples of self-help groups emerging during this time period. In the 1990s, groups organizing around specific health concerns, such as cancer, have become common.

Some feminists accuse self-help groups of encouraging women to define problems in individual terms instead of pointing out the political, economic, and cultural barriers women face. According to this perspective, women's self-help promotes a culture of "victim feminism" or a "cult of victimhood." Others view self-help groups as promoting social change while meeting individuals' needs. For example, the AIDS self-help movement has changed medical definitions of the disease, increased federal funding for research and services, and demanded protection for the rights of individuals with AIDS/HIV. Self-help, according to this perspective, has encouraged women to recognize that others share their concerns, empowered women to seek solutions, and brought the issues of specific subgroups of lesbian, gay, and bisexual women to the attention of the community as a whole.

*Marieke Van Willigen*

### Bibliography

Kaminer, Wendy. *I'm Dysfunctional, You're Dysfunctional: The Recovery Movement and Other Self-Help Fashions*. Reading, Mass.: Addison-Wesley, 1992.

Katz, Alfred. *Self-Help in America: A Social Movement Perspective*. New York: Twayne, 1993.

Simonds, Wendy. *Women and Self-Help Culture: Reading Between the Lines*. New Brunswick, N.J.: Rutgers University Press, 1992.

Wuthnow, Robert. *Sharing the Journey: Support Groups and America's New Quest for Community*. New York: Free Press, 1994.

***See also*** AIDS (Acquired Immune Deficiency Syndrome); Olivia; Psychotherapy; Recovery Movement; Self-Defense

## Separatism

Act of separating both privately and publicly from men and/or those who promote or maintain male supremacy (patriarchy). The motivation behind separatism—to remove one's self from patriarchal influence or behavior—distinguishes separatism from other gestures of all-female community, such as those embraced by women who join convents. While no exact date has been established for the origins of separatism in the United States, women have practiced it in their private lives since at least the mid-nineteenth century. During the late 1960s and early 1970s, however, separatism evolved as political activism designed to destroy patriarchal institutions. Initially, separatism was practiced by lesbians and nonlesbians alike; as it became increasingly

**S** politicized, separatism emerged as almost exclusively lesbian.

## Characteristics

Separatism adheres to several radical and lesbian feminist principles. It holds that sexism is the first oppressive division in human society upon which all other oppressions are modeled. Such a belief emanated from early radical feminist response to Marxist analyses of classism; many on the Left contended that class was the original and, thus, most pernicious division in human society. In part to assert the importance of the devastation caused by sexism, radical feminists contextualized their analyses within the accepted framework of Marxism. Most separatists view sexism as so pervasive that reformist measures will never end women's oppression; women can overcome their subjection only by dismantling and rebuilding society.

Further, the reliance on concepts of sexism as the primary, or "root," oppression in human society compels many separatist theorists to name men as the agents of most, if not all, social ills. If sexism served as the first oppression upon which all other hierarchal thought or behavior was modeled, then men, as the benefactors of sexism and the possessors of power within patriarchal societies, must be the architects and agents of that oppression. In addition, any society requires the work of most of its members to function or survive. Because separatism withdraws women's energy and labor from the patriarchy and denies male access to women, separatism theoretically should bring about the end of society in its current form. For most separatists, separatism is, thus, a political strategy and a way to affirm lesbianism through the support of women in all aspects of one's life.

Despite the cohesiveness that these characteristics imply, separatist thought has not been monolithic or even broadly unified. For example, while most separatists agree that men are the primary enemy, widespread debate over the degree of separation necessary to separatist practice occurred, particularly during the 1970s and early 1980s. Some theorists, such as Marilyn Frye in "Some Reflections on Separatism and Power" (1978), wrote that separation from men—whenever reasonably possible—is the key component of separatist practice. By 1973, other separatists began to point out that women who refused to sever their ties with men also played a role in the maintenance of patriarchal society. Separatists identified heterosexual women, in particular, as those responsible for colluding in women's oppres-

sion. Thus, debate carried out in newspapers such as *The Furies* often included calls for separation from men and heterosexual women. As the debate followed this path, other separatists began to note that even lesbians allied with the patriarchy when they refused to remove their energy from mainstream society. Such a recognition compelled separatists to issue position papers, such as one by members of the Gutter Dyke Collective that proclaimed: "[W]e have found it necessary to separate ourselves from certain lesbians. . . . For the most part, we want to withdraw ourselves from very oppressive, negative situations into more positive ones" (quoted in Hoagland and Penelope 1988). But whatever the differences in their definitions of separatism, many separatists sought out all-female living and business arrangements. Separatists often participated in the creation and maintenance of residential and/or business collectives, particularly during the 1970s.

## Criticism

Separatism has created considerable controversy within and outside lesbian communities. Because it usually names men as the agents of male supremacy, much of separatist theory insists that women should have nothing to do with men. Feminists of color such as Audre Lorde (1934–1992), Chrystos (1946–), and members of the Combahee River Collective criticized this stand for its racist and classist implications because it denies minority women's desire to ally with minority men against all oppressions in their lives. Similarly, lesbians and nonlesbians alike fault separatism for its tendency to universalize women's experience—a tendency that often occurs in conjunction with belief in sexism as the primary oppression. In other words, if all men are agents of women's oppression, then all women—by virtue of their second-class status—are at least potential allies. Such a concept worked as a strong call for women's unity: The popularity of the slogan "Sisterhood is Powerful!" is but one example of its appeal. Yet the concept of women's natural affinity or unity also worked destructively in women's communities, particularly when it allowed women to dismiss their own racism, classism, heterosexism, or other oppressive behaviors. Critics have argued that these behaviors became relatively easy to justify as bad habits learned from a patriarchal society; the justification implied that women, on their own, would not create or engage in oppressive behavior. Because such dismissals allowed women to deny ultimate responsibility for their own oppressive actions, separatist communities often became divided or destroyed over struggles with racism, classism, and heterosexism. Finally, many lesbians dismiss separatism as impractical because it requires unilateral action by most (if not all) women in order to succeed as a political agenda.

## Contemporary Status

Although much of separatist thought emanates from the United States, separatism is international in scope. France, in particular, has generated a substantial body of separatist theory; members of separatist collectives in Denmark wrote of their experiences in Joyce Cheney's *Lesbian Land* (1985). While the strength of, and interest in, separatist thought waned during the 1980s and early 1990s, lesbians have renewed calls for separatist practice in the United States, particularly through the re-creation of separatist collectives. Separatist residential collectives, in particular, continue to compel the interests of lesbians, as might be exemplified by discussions of separatism in newsjournals such as *Lesbian Connection* during 1995–1996 and subsequent calls for women's participation in the creation of new rural collectives. And while the number of business collectives decreased during the 1990s, the importance of separatist thought remains evident in the structure and practice of organizations such as the women's music industry, domestic abuse shelters, women's historical archives, rape crisis lines, and women's health-care centers.          *Dana R. Shugar*

## *Bibliography*

Cheney, Joyce, ed. *Lesbian Land*. Minneapolis: Word Weavers, 1985.

Freedman, Estelle. "Separatism as Strategy: Female Institution Building and American Feminism, 1870–1930." *Feminist Studies* 5:3 (Fall 1979), 512–529.

Hoagland, Sarah Lucia, and Julia Penelope, eds. *For Lesbians Only: A Separatist Anthology*. London: Onlywomen, 1988.

Jo, Bev, Linda Strega, and Ruston. *Dykes-Loving-Dykes: Dyke Separatist Politics for Lesbians Only*. Oakland, Calif.: Battleaxe, 1990.

Rich, Adrienne. "Notes for a Magazine: What Does Separatism Mean?" *Sinister Wisdom* 18 (Fall 1981), 83–91.

Shugar, Dana R. *Separatism and Women's Community*. Lincoln: University of Nebraska Press, 1995.

*See also* Collectives; Combahee River Collective; Community; Essentialism; Furies, The; *Lesbian Connection*; Lesbian Feminism; Lesbian Nation; Lorde, Audre; Music Festivals; Patriarchy; Penelope, Julia; Sexism; Sisterhood

## Sex Education

As defined in guidelines issued in 1991 by the National Guidelines Taskforce, comprised of groups such as the American Medical Association and the U.S. Centers for Disease Control, "a lifelong process of acquiring information and forming attitudes, beliefs, and values about identity, relationships, and intimacy." These groups suggest that all children would benefit from comprehensive sex education. Such programs would include basic information, as well as instruction about attitudes and values, relationships, and sexual responsibility.

Mainstream sexuality education has evolved over the last one hundred years. Contemporary sexuality education has its roots in the social-hygiene movements at the turn of the twentieth century. As part of initiatives to curb prostitution and venereal diseases, a diverse group of physicians, educators, and social workers proposed sex education in the public schools. Although the National Education Association endorsed sex education in 1912, schools did not integrate such programs into their curricula until much later. Activists like Margaret Sanger (1879–1966) in the 1930s and organizations like Planned Parenthood in the 1940s and 1950s supported efforts at sex education and counseling.

By the mid-1960s, many schools had implemented some type of instruction on sexuality and reproduction. One important example was the school system in Anaheim, California, whose Family Life and Sex Education program was a national model. In response to an increasingly sexually liberal society, schools began to teach more comprehensive programs rather than focus simply on anatomy and physiology. Some educators began, for example, to include lessons about homosexuality, masturbation, and sexual decision making. The Sex Information and Education Council (SIECUS), founded in 1964 by physician Mary Calderone (1904– ) and colleagues, served as an organizational resource and clearinghouse for this new educational movement.

The years 1968–1969 marked a moment of intense controversy over sex education that raged on both local and national levels. National right-wing groups, notably the Christian Crusade and the John Birch Society, discovered the enormous potential in sex education to galvanize and organize communi-

S ties, raise money, and consolidate political power, beginning with school boards. They were frequently the moving force behind the myriad local groups that sprang up to exploit parental fears and concerns, such as MOTOREDE (Movement to Restore Decency) and POSE (Parents Opposed to Sex Education). Therefore, a consistently successful oppositional tactic has been the spinning of sex-education apocryphal tales. One such story in 1969 asserted that seventeen male students had raped a twenty-five-year-old sex-education teacher after watching a film in class. The story could not be verified and, although assumed to be false, reappeared in 1979 in a Christian Defense League broadside. But in that version, twenty male students raped a twenty-four-year-old teacher during their final exam. One of the rapists was alleged to have said: "Didn't she spend the whole year telling us how to do it, when to do it, and how much fun it would be?" Other apocryphal tales consistent to both the late 1960s and the 1990s include the teacher who disrobes in class and the teacher who masturbates in class or forces her students to masturbate. Sex-education supporters may expend exhaustive efforts to convince the public that they do not force students to listen to the teacher's sexual fantasies, watch pornography, or practice putting on condoms in class.

Communities in at least thirty states were riven by sex-education controversies in 1968–1969. By the end of this period, approximately twenty states had considered or implemented legislation regulating sex education. The United States Congress debated bills to end federal funding for sex education and to launch an investigation into SIECUS. By the early 1970s, however, the intense furor over sex education had waned, and very slowly and carefully school districts began to reinstitute programs.

Yet sex education's enduring power as a condensed symbol for sexual chaos, disease, and difference was evident in the reintensification of debate a quarter-century later. In the mid-1990s, SIECUS documented controversies in one hundred communities. The actual number of such community debates was likely much higher, since, in Massachusetts alone, there were challenges to comprehensive sexuality or AIDS curricula in almost thirty towns in early 1994. Congress once again began debating bills that would regulate what schools could teach about sexuality and homosexuality. The swift escalation of these controversies suggests that sex education replaced abortion and anti-Communism as major fund-raising and organizational tools for the secular and the Religious Right.

Although embattled, the mainstream sexuality-education movement has been largely supportive of lesbian and gay rights. The guidelines from the national task force call for tolerance of sexual diversity and an end to discrimination and bigotry. In particular, they assert that curricula should include messages such as "homosexual love relationships can be as fulfilling as heterosexual relationships" and "homosexual, heterosexual, and bisexual people are alike except for their sexual attraction." Increasingly, educators are integrating positive messages about homosexuality in the schools.

School reform assumed increasing importance for the lesbian and gay movement during the 1980s and 1990s, despite formidable obstacles. The need for safety and tolerance propelled the first programs. Project 10 was the first major school-based program developed to provide education and counseling to students on sexual orientation. Its formation in Los Angeles, California, in 1985 was prompted by the harassment of an openly gay male student who eventually dropped out of school. This incident heightened faculty awareness of homophobia in the schools and eventually resulted in the implementation of Project 10. Since its inception, Project 10 has been the subject of extensive publicity and has been routinely characterized by the Religious Right as a program for seducing innocent children.

In the late 1990s, there were a range of other programs throughout the country that either taught about lesbian and gay issues or offered counseling and support to youth. Lesbian and gay content was increasingly integrated into comprehensive sexuality education, AIDS education, and multicultural education. Many public schools also established support groups, such as the increasingly common Gay/Straight Alliance.

*Janice M. Irvine*

### Bibliography

Brandt, Allan. *No Magic Bullet.* New York: Oxford University Press, 1985.

Breasted, Mary. *Oh! Sex Education!* New York: Praeger, 1970.

D'Emilio, John, and Estelle Freedman. *Intimate Matters: A History of Sexuality in America.* New York: Harper and Row, 1988.

Gordon, Linda. *Women's Body, Woman's Right: Birth Control in America.* New York: Penguin, 1974.

Sears, James, ed. *Sexuality and the Curriculum: The Politics and Practices of Sexuality Education.* New York: Teachers College, 1991.

Trudell, Bonnie. *Doing Sex Education: Gender Politics and Schooling.* New York: Routledge, 1993.

*See also* High Schools, Lesbian and Gay

## Sex Practices

Erotic activities engaged in by women who identify as lesbians. A survey of one thousand lesbians conducted in the late 1970s in the United States and Canada revealed that the most popular sexual activities among lesbians were manual stimulation of the clitoris or vagina, kissing, breast stimulation, cunnilingus, and tribadism. A late-1980s survey of more than 1,500 U.S. lesbians had similar results: Hugging, snuggling, kissing, masturbating, getting naked, holding hands, and French kissing were listed as the most popular sex acts. A 1975 lesbian sex manual described similar practices.

As lesbians moved from feminist separatism in the 1970s toward working and socializing with gay men in the 1990s, sex styles changed. A lesbian sex manual by Schramm-Evans and Jaugey-Paget (1995) described fisting, penetration, sex with men, voyeurism, fetishism, S/M (sadomasochist) gear, and anal toys, in addition to the sex acts reported as popular in the previous two decades.

Lesbian sex practices incorporate a wide range of techniques engaged in by females and males of all sexual orientations. Many of the behaviors, such as snuggling, kissing, and caressing, can be nonsexual expressions of affection. When these activities are combined to produce erotic feelings by women who consider themselves lesbians, they are called lesbian sex practices.

Sleeping together can mean sharing a bed, snuggling, and/or having sex. Spooning refers to lying close together, front to back, usually on the side with knees bent so bodies form an S-shape. Stroking and fondling of body parts, including breast stimulation, are common among lesbians.

Kissing means pressing the lips against another person's lips or body. French kissing, deep kissing, tongue kissing, and wet kissing refer to opening the mouth to allow a partner's body parts to enter or sliding the tongue out to touch a lover's tongue, ear, armpit, neck, or skin. Sucking refers to taking a finger, nipple, toe, or clitoris into the mouth. Cunnilingus is oral sex: licking the vulva or clitoris or penetrating the vagina with the tongue. Oral sex is also called eating out, going down, or eating pussy.

Analingus, also called rimming, means stimulating the anus with the mouth.

Tribadism refers to rubbing bodies together while women face each other. Examples include lying one woman on top of the other and rubbing pubic areas together for mutual clitoral stimulation, one woman rubbing her clitoris against another woman's hip bone, or sitting face-to-face with legs open and entwined to rub vulvas against each other.

Fingering of genitals, sometimes called mutual masturbation, means rubbing the clitoris and labia, or sliding fingers into the vagina. Penetration refers to putting fingers, a dildo, or other object into the vagina. Finger-fucking means sliding one, or more, fingers into the vagina, either gently or vigorously. Sliding a whole hand into the vagina or anus is called fisting. Butt-fucking refers to penetration of the anus with fingers or sex toys.

Packing means strapping on a dildo with a harness and, often, wearing these sex toys under clothing on a date or out cruising. A dildo and a harness allow a woman to penetrate her partner standing up, kneeling, or lying down, leaving her hands free for breast fondling, hugging, hair tugging, back scratching, or clitoral stimulation.

Fantasy and role playing can involve wearing costumes or acting out stories. Acting butch means wearing traditional male clothing, initiating sexual activity, being aggressive, or stimulating one's partner to orgasm. Acting femme means wearing stereotypical women's clothing and makeup, initiating emotional intimacy, being receptive, or encouraging the sexual advances of a partner. Cross-dressing can refer to a woman wearing male clothing or to a butch woman wearing feminine clothing.

Topping refers to controlling, suggesting, initiating, or acting out sexual activity. Bottoming refers to requesting, agreeing to, limiting, or receiving sexual stimulation.

Sixty-nine means lying head-to-toe so that one woman stimulates her girlfriend's vulva while her own genitals can be touched by her partner. A daisy chain is a group sex circle with one woman's genitals being stimulated by the second woman, while her breasts or clitoris are caressed by the third, while she is being stroked or sucked by the fourth, who can be kissed or fisted by the fifth . . . who is being tongued or penetrated by number one.

S/M (sadomasochism) involves pairing pain with pleasure to heighten physical sensitivity and emotional vulnerability. S/M includes activities that might be considered uncomfortable in a non-S/M setting, such as scratching, biting, pinching, spanking, whipping, cutting, humiliation, piercing, or burning. Bondage and discipline (B/D) involves physically or psychologically restraining and controlling a partner for the pleasure of both. Sex toys, fantasy, and role playing are often a part of S/M or B/D.

According to S/M lesbians, vanilla sex is anything other than S/M. To some women of color, vanilla refers to sex with a white woman.

Viewing pornography, either alone or with others, has become a more common lesbian sexual activity since the appearance of lesbian-made erotic videos in the 1980s. Cyber sex, or having erotic encounters via computer, gained popularity in the 1990s.

Self-stimulation, self-pleasuring, masturbation, and solo sex are terms for touching one's own body for sexual excitement, either while alone or in the company of a lover.

Bestiality refers to getting sexual pleasure from animals—for example, encouraging a cat or dog to lick a person's breasts or genitals.

Safer sex refers to practices that reduce the chances of spreading sexually transmitted diseases, such as refraining from kissing or oral sex when one has a cold sore (herpes) on the lips.

Group sex means three or more people having sex with each other during one sexual episode. Polyamory, polyfidelity, nonmonogamy, and open relationships are terms for being sexually involved with more than one person, but the actual sex acts are usually in couples. A triad is three lovers who simultaneously share emotional and/or sexual intimacy. Cheating, sleeping around, and stepping out are derogatory terms for sexual styles other than monogamy, which refers to having just one sex partner at a time.

Making love refers to sex as an expression of emotional closeness. Casual sex implies lack of attachment or expectations of becoming a couple.

Lover, partner, spouse, date, wife, fuck-buddy, play partner, significant other, and girlfriend are some of the words lesbians use to describe a woman with whom they have sex.

The particular array of sex practices engaged in by an individual lesbian depends on the time, the setting, her partner, her community, and her personal preferences.          *Marcia Munson*

### *Bibliography*

Jay, Karla, and Allen Young. *The Gay Report*. New York: Summit, 1977, 1979.

Kinsey, Alfred C., Wardell B. Pomeroy, Clyde E. Martin, and Paul H. Gebhard. *Sexual Behavior in the Human Female*. Philadelphia: Saunders, 1953. 6th ed. New York: Pocket Books, 1973.

Loulan, JoAnn. *Lesbian Passion*. San Francisco: Spinsters/Aunt Lute, 1987.

Munson, Marcia. "Eliminating the Barriers to Communication: Safer Sex Education for Lesbians and Bisexual Women." In *Sexualities*. Ed. Marny Hall. New York: Haworth, 1996, pp. 75–84.

Schramm-Evans, Zoe, and Laurence Jaugey-Paget. *Making Out: The Book of Lesbian Sex and Sexuality*. San Francisco: HarperCollins, 1995.

**See also** Clitoris; Erotica and Pornography; Love; Masturbation; Sadomasochism; Safer Sex; Sex Toys; Sexuality; Tribade

## Sex Toys

The least-euphemistic term available for what many nonlesbians know as "marital aids" or "personal massagers." Used primarily to induce or enhance orgasm, basic types include electric massage wands, plastic and silicone dildos for vaginal or anal use, and a variety of lubricants, body paints, and restraints.

### History

Sex toys have a long, colorful, and specifically lesbian history. Medieval courts prosecuted women for using "implements," most often handmade of leather, to penetrate their lovers. Seventeenth-century libertines and eighteenth-century criminal biographers showed particular interest in dildos, the most prominent English examples being the Earl of Rochester's (1647–1680) "Signor Dildo" and Henry Fielding's (1707–1754) *The Female Husband* (1746). Even Marie Antoinette (1755–1793) was featured in French antiroyalty pamphlets using a dildo on a female lover.

Until the eighteenth century, the punishment for using a dildo was death. In the hands of male doctors, however, vibration was considered a legitimate treatment for hysteria—which some sexologists defined as the suppression of perversion, including lesbianism—throughout the late nineteenth and early twentieth centuries. As such, early vibrators enjoyed a popular reputation for promoting "health, vigor, and beauty" of men and women. By 1981, the *New York Times* reported that the U.S. vibrator business, including personal-care products, adult novelty toys, and cottage-type manufacturers, had grown into a $15 million industry.

## Community Aspects

In the 1980s and 1990s, sex toys achieved subcultural prominence among self-identified lesbians by virtue of the advent of women-owned sex-toy stores and mail order companies. Organized around feminist and sexual liberationist principles, Eve's Garden, Toys in Babeland, and other retailers openly marketed their products as sexual, empowering, and lesbian friendly. Good Vibrations, for example, promoted Hitachi's "Magic Wand" massager as a clitoral stimulator and debuted a line of dildos shaped as goddesses. As a result of sex toys' greater availability—as well as the ideological facelift provided by the dyke magazine *On Our Backs*'s regular column "Toys Are Us," in which "sexpert" Susie Bright reviewed and defended the politics of toys and erotica—in 1995 43 percent of lesbian readers of the national gay magazine the *Advocate* reported "use of a hand-held dildo with a partner" in the last five years. Twenty-seven percent had strapped one on.

## Political Aspects

In 1998, laws in Texas and Georgia still prohibited the sale of sex toys, and many lesbians—despite Bright's (1990) insistence that "penises can only be compared to dildos in that they take up space [in the vagina or anus]"—have objected to dildos because of their reputation as a penis substitute. Radical feminist Sheila Jeffreys's *The Lesbian Heresy* (1993), for example, criticized the "avalanche of dildos" let loose on lesbians by Good Vibrations and its sister retailers. From a different perspective, *Black Lace* editor Lane (1991) compared the popularity of oversized, black dildos to the stereotype of African hypersexuality, proposing that dildos may be the "location" of both sexual and racial "terror and desire." *Heather Findlay*

## Bibliography

Bright, Susie. *Susie Sexpert's Lesbian Sex World*. Pittsburgh: Cleis, 1990.

Lane, Alycee J. "What's Race Got To Do with It?" *Black Lace* (Summer 1991), 21.

Semans, Anne, and Cathy Winks. *The Good Vibrations Guide to Sex*. Pittsburgh: Cleis, 1995.

*See also* Clitoris; Marie Antoinette; Sex Practices; Tribade

## Sex Wars

Term referring to the debates over issues such as pornography, butch-femme identities, and sadomasochism (S/M) that began in the mid-1970s. The feminist antipornography movement that gained prominence at that time provoked a reaction by lesbians and feminists, who argued for the liberatory nature of stigmatized sexual practices, particularly S/M. This community of "sex radicals" bonded through their ostracism from the self-identified antiviolence "feminist" community. The division into opposing sides in these wars challenged any coherent definition of lesbian and feminist sexuality, as well as the relationships among identity, politics, and sexuality.

These debates heated up throughout the late 1970s and into the early 1980s, culminating with The Scholar and the Feminist IX conference, "Towards a Politics of Sexuality," held at Barnard College in New York City in April 1982. The conflict exploded, in part, due to the exclusion of antipornography activists from planning and participating in the conference. The conference organizers were exclusionary because, they argued, since the antipornography side dominated the movement, their inclusion would implicitly prevent all (other) positions from being heard. Women Against Pornography (mainly, although other groups were involved) fought back, both before and during the conference. Prior to the conference, antipornography activists (or people claiming to be antipornography activists) telephoned Barnard College denouncing the organizers for inviting "antifeminist" speakers to participate. On the actual day of the conference, antipornography feminists picketed and distributed leaflets that criticized organizers for their exclusionary practices, claiming that the decision to deemphasize pornography silenced a significant feminist presence. According to conference organizer Carole Vance, the leaflet also "attacked individual women by name and accused them of unconventional sexual options, practices, and fantasies. The leaflet further blurred the boundary between thought and practice, as defenders of other feminists' right to speak were crudely transformed into advocates or practitioners of stigmatized sexual acts" (Vance 1984).

The effect of the fighting that occurred prior to and during the conference illustrates the extent to which these debates over sexuality became polarized. The controversy surrounding Barnard brought the issues of butch-femme, S/M, and pornography to the forefront, even though the organizers intended to address a much wider variety of issues, including the relationships among female sexuality and issues such as race, class, body size, and disability. Many reviews of the conference noted the way that Barnard had been misinterpreted in order to focus attention once again on S/M and pornography, although no workshops or theoretical essays focused on these issues. The oppositional structure of this debate left out a variety of political and theoretical positions.

These particular debates over sexuality reflected earlier gay-straight splits within feminism. The issue of lesbian sexuality split the feminist movement in the late 1960s and early 1970s. Consequently, some feminists reformulated lesbian sexuality as an extension of female sexuality or woman-identification, in part through opposing women's sexuality to men's. This reformulation also contributed to, and reflected, the idealization of lesbianism that, in some circles, replaced its ostracism.

The model of woman-identification became significant in the sex wars through its marginalization of some lesbians within feminism, especially those who identify as butch or femme. Much of the critique of butch-femme attacked "role-playing," generally by reasoning that butch-femme relationships replicate heterosexuality. This critique provided the basis for much of the critique of S/M as well; in fact, many anti-S/M critics conflated these issues. Hoagland (1980) wrote that the "current belief that S/M is compatible with a feminist consciousness is a hangover from patriarchal social reality and inimical to our attempts to construct a sexual identity distinct from masculinist conceptualizations of sexuality." The conflation of butch-femme and S/M exemplifies the way all of these issues and experiences became consolidated into singular positions. Furthermore, although pornography has been seen as the emblematic issue for anti-violence feminists, S/M, or representations of S/M, bore the brunt of moral condemnation.

These conflations contributed to the polarization of the two sides, largely through equating the political identity of "feminist" and the sexual identity of "lesbian" despite repeated attempts to keep them separate. The resulting identity, or subject position, of "lesbian feminist" relieved some women's anxieties over the challenge of lesbian sexualities to dominant feminism. One way in which this occurred was by separating out notions of "good" sex and "bad" sex. The idea of "good" sex implied not only satisfying sex, but also "moral" sex; in other words, sex should be nurturing, mutual, and nonhierarchical. On the other hand, "bad" or "immoral" sex is driven by unequal power relations or the relation between pain and pleasure. This connection between morality and sexuality intensified anxieties about sex within feminist and lesbian communities. For example, the self-identification as "feminist" by sex radicals frequently was the source of skirmishes in the wars. Partly, then, the sex wars were fought over who had the right to claim the term "feminist."

In the earliest defense of S/M, "Cathexis: A Preliminary Investigation into the Nature of S-M" (1975), Barbara Lipschutz (later Ruth) responded precisely to the question of how one can be both a lesbian feminist and a practitioner of S/M. Because of the power of the argument that S/M requires roles thought to be the province of heterosexuality, she began her essay by noting that she thought S/M was desirable only in lesbian relationships, since they do not involve the power relations endemic to heterosexuality under patriarchy. For her, S/M was justifiable for two main reasons: the explicit nature of the exchange of power, and the fact that it transforms pain into pleasure (hence, the title "Cathexis"). While she acknowledged that some lesbians may not enjoy S/M, she urged women to "listen to their bodies" to discover what sexual practices they might prefer. Rather than see S/M as antifeminist, then, she argued that discovering one's sexual pleasure is radical; it is having rules that govern "appropriate" sexuality that she identified as patriarchal.

The primary focus on pornography and S/M allowed other issues of structural oppression, such as race and class, to be continually subsumed into the oppositional framework of the sex wars. In an interview in *Against Sadomasochism: A Radical Feminist Analysis* (Linden 1982), Audre Lorde (1934–1992) argued that debates over S/M can serve as a displacement from other issues: "When sadomasochism gets presented on center stage as a conflict in the feminist movement, I ask, what conflicts are *not* being presented?" In particular, this critique indicates that the timing of the sex wars may have served as a bulwark against fears of acknowledging racism, classism, and fragmentation among women at a time when working-class women and women of color were effectively bringing their concerns to the center of mainstream feminist movements. These problems led later theorists to argue that the very structure of the sex wars was racist. Noted Rich (1986): "The ethnocentrism of the sexuality debates remains acute ... in terms of a sexuality constructed to exclude the experiences and perspectives of so many women of color."

Similar problems were enacted with respect to class: Working-class women's perspectives were frequently excluded from debate, and class as a category of analysis that might challenge the structure of debate or the focus on sexuality was frequently ignored. Very few of the activists from the 1970s and 1980s on either side even mentioned class or presented a detailed analysis of class in relation to sexuality, and fewer still brought together issues of race and class in relation to sexuality. Once again, later analysts, such as Nestle (1980), pointed to the ways in which debates over "sexuality" can also reproduce dominative class politics.

These oppositions continued through the end of the 1990s; Cvetkovich (1996) notes: "Too often, lesbian subcultures that focus on healing from abuse and those that encourage sexual exploration have been constructed, and have constructed themselves, as mutually exclusive, repeating anew the schism between pleasure and danger." Although the furor that followed the Barnard conference has died down, the legacy of this conference includes deep distrust, as well as a considerable amount of anxiety in talking about sex and the relationships among sexual experiences, practices, and politics.

*Juliana M. Kubala*

## Bibliography

Cvetkovich, Anne. "Sexual Trauma/Queer Memory: Incest, Lesbianism, and Therapeutic Culture." *GLQ: A Journal of Lesbian and Gay Studies* 2:4 (1996), 351–377.

Hoagland, Sarah Lucia. "Violence, Victimization, Violation." *Sinister Wisdom* 15 (1980), 70–72.

Lederer, Laura. *Take Back the Night: Women on Pornography*. New York: William Morrow, 1980.

Linden, Robin Ruth. *Against Sadomasochism: A Radical Feminist Analysis*. San Francisco: Frog in the Well, 1982.

Lipshutz, Barbara. "Cathexis: A Preliminary Investigation into the Nature of S-M." *Hera* (1975), 10.

Nestle, Joan. *The Persistent Desire: A Femme-Butch Reader*. Boston: Alyson, 1980.

Rich, B. Ruby. "Feminism and Sexuality in the 1980s." *Feminist Studies* 12 (1986), 525–563.

Samois, eds. *Coming to Power: Writings and Graphics on Lesbian S/M*. Palo Alto, Calif.: Up Press, 1981. 2nd ed. Boston: Alyson, 1987.

Snitow, Ann, Christine Stansell, and Sharon Thompson. *Powers of Desire: The Politics of Sexuality*. New York: Monthly Review Press, 1983.

Vance, Carole S. *Pleasure and Danger: Exploring Female Sexuality*. London: Pandora, 1984.

***See also*** Butch-Femme; Erotica and Pornography; Leather; Sadomasochism

## Sex Work

Term coined by prostitutes' rights activists of the 1980s as part of an effort to legitimate erotic labor. Sex work includes prostitution, pornography, exotic dancing, phone sex, and peep shows.

## History

Commercial sex, like same-sex eroticism, has existed for millennia. The meanings attached to it, however, are historically and culturally specific. Nonetheless, just as many contemporary gays and lesbians claim a strategic kinship to such honored "ancestors" as ancient Greek man/boy lovers or Sappho (ca. 600 B.C.E.), so to do some sex workers attempt to trace their genealogy back to the Sacred Prostitute or the Greek *hetairae*. Modern understandings of prostitution as a deviant identity (and not merely a practice) date to the nineteenth and early twentieth centuries when sexologists began to distinguish between "normative" and "pathological" sexuality. Sexual "deviants," such as prostitutes and lesbians, were understood to differ from "normal" women not only through their participation in nonreproductive sexuality, but also through their physiology. From this perspective, the prostitute's "appearance and her sexual identity are pre-established by heredity" (Gilman 1985). Like the "congenital invert" (the "innate" lesbian) and the African Hottentot (a favorite nineteenth-century racial "other" among whites), prostitutes were believed to have "errors in development of the labia and overdevelopment of the clitoris." The physiological differences believed to be present in the whore, the pervert, and the savage were used to distinguish them from the True Woman, whose sexuality would be expressed only through reproductive sex in the context of a monogamous, heterosexual marriage. Not only were lesbians and prostitutes believed to share certain physical anomalies, but both "perversions" were considered likely to appear in the same individual. Early sexologist Havelock Ellis (1859–1939), for example, argued that a considerable proportion of prostitutes showed signs of "a congenital condition of sexual inversion," while others "adopted

**S** homosexuality because of an acquired distaste for normal coitus due to professional intercourse with men."

Sexually "deviant" women were commonly seen as not only diseased themselves, but also potentially contaminating to others. Just as the "true invert" (the "innately" lesbian woman) might corrupt an otherwise "normal" woman through seduction, so, too, were prostitutes assumed to be "pools of contagion" threatening to infect the "general population" with venereal diseases. As a result, in both the nineteenth and the twentieth centuries, sex workers (but not clients) repeatedly were targeted for mandatory medical testing. Some of the most extreme measures taken, ostensibly to protect public health and the moral fiber of the nation, have included the 1930s German Nazi policy of identifying with black triangles "asocial" women such as prostitutes and lesbians and confining them to concentration camps.

Not all nineteenth- and twentieth-century observers accepted the notion that prostitution was a form of individual pathology; some argued, instead, for the importance of social and economic factors. In the early twentieth century, Emma Goldman (1869–1940), for example, forcefully advanced the argument that prostitution should be viewed as an occupational, rather than an erotic, choice made compelling by economic desperation. Similar arguments have been made in the late twentieth century by the prostitutes' rights organization US PROS. Other activists have insisted that prostitution cannot be fairly described as a choice at all; rather, the prostitute should be seen as a victim of violence and sexual slavery. Significantly, despite important differences among these approaches, each assumes that commercial sex is a "problem" in need of an explanation.

Beginning in the early 1970s, a historically unique perspective on prostitution was advanced by sex workers themselves. Sex worker self-advocacy groups like COYOTE (Call Off Your Old Tired Ethics) and the International Committee for Prostitutes Rights argued that the problem with prostitution wasn't the practice itself but working conditions within the trade and social attitudes toward it. From this perspective, the very attempt to explain why women are engaged in prostitution is itself as misdirected as efforts to "explain" homosexuality.

## Sex Work and Lesbianism
In addition to a shared experience of social and sexual stigmatization, sex workers and lesbians also share a history of deliberate political and erotic alliances. Erotic alliances between the two, overlapping, groups have taken the form of both commercial and intimate relationships. While the great majority of commercial sex is performed for male clients by both female and male sex workers, some small percentage of sex work is undertaken by women for women. This form of lesbian sex work remains the least documented and discussed. The San Francisco Lesbian and Gay History Project has uncovered limited references to women clients in the Barbary Coast brothels of that city in the late nineteenth century, and the Lesbian Herstory Archives in New York City has evidence of at least one Harlem brothel in the 1930s that catered exclusively to women. Accounts by contemporary sex workers suggest that lesbians continue to represent a small portion of sex workers' clientele. With the advent of lesbian "sex radicalism" in the 1980s and 1990s, there has been a dramatic increase in the availability and visibility of lesbian sexual commerce, including pornographic magazines and videos (such as *On Our Backs*, *Bad Attitude*, *Blush Productions*), strip shows, sex parties, and lesbian escort and erotic-massage services.

Intimate, noncommercial erotic alliances also always have existed between women inside and outside the sex trades. Some accounts of lesbian life of the 1950s in the United States suggest that one compelling point of connection between (femme) prostitutes and (butch) lesbians was a shared understanding of the experience of being "stone." The stone butch would not allow herself to be physically vulnerable during lovemaking with her intimate partners, while the femme prostitute exercised similar psychological control in sexual encounters with her clients. Other common experiences included those of police harassment and social marginalization.

In addition to erotic alliances (commercial and intimate) between sex workers and women outside the trade, there also exists a complicated history of political collaboration and struggle between these two groups. Contemporary feminists and former sex workers opposed to the practice of prostitution have united in abolitionist organizations like WHISPER (Women Hurt in Systems of Prostitution Engaged in Revolt) and the Coalition Against Trafficking in Women. Similarly, sex-worker rights organizations including COYOTE and US PROS, have created powerful coalitions of sex workers and feminist supporters demanding decriminalization of the trade. Prostitutes rights' advocate Gloria Lockett insists that such alliances are crucial to social change: "No single group by itself can make an impact. We need everybody: street prostitutes and call girls, lesbians and feminists, everybody. We've got to figure out how to support each other in this" (Chapkis 1997).

*Wendy Chapkis*

### Bibliography

Barry, Kathleen. *Female Sexual Slavery*. Englewood Cliffs, N.J.: Prentice-Hall, 1979.

Chapkis, Wendy. *Live Sex Acts*. New York: Routledge, 1997.

Delacoste, Frederique, and Priscilla Alexander, eds. *Sex Work*. Pittsburgh: Cleis, 1987.

Gilman, Sander. "Black Bodies, White Bodies: Toward an Iconography of Female Sexuality in Late Nineteenth-Century Art, Medicine, and Literature." *Critical Inquiry* 12:1 (Autumn 1985), 204–242.

Jenness, Valerie. *Making It Work*. New York: Aldine de Gruyter, 1993.

Pheterson, Gail, ed. *A Vindication of the Rights of Whores*. Seattle: Seal, 1989.

Roberts, Nickie. *Whores in History*. London: HarperCollins, 1992.

*See also* Economics; Goldman, Emma; Nazism

## Sexism

A system of beliefs and practices that assumes the superiority of males over females and usually results in male dominance of females. Although different groups of men and women benefit, and are disadvantaged by, sexist practices in different ways, this entry focuses on the implications of sexism for lesbians.

Sexism as an ideology often rests on the following assumptions about human nature, called "essentialism": (1) there are two and only two natural sexes, male and female; (2) the sexes are biologically "opposite" and complementary; (3) masculinity and femininity, gender, are social roles that naturally extend from the biological sexes of male and female, respectively; and (4) men and women are essentially interdependent, both biologically and socially.

Essentialist beliefs about sex and gender have implications for norms regarding sexuality, particularly lesbian sexuality. For lesbians, sexism includes not only the subordination of females to males, but the assumptions surrounding "women's sexuality." To be "feminine" or a "woman" means to be sexually complementary to a man. Sexist ideology contends that a woman's reproductive biology makes her naturally suited for nurturing and caretaking of children and that a man's biology naturally suits him for providing sustenance for his family. Lesbians, by definition, are "unfeminine" women since they do not choose sexual relationships with men.

This is what Rich (1980) elaborated in her theory of "compulsory heterosexuality," the enforcement of heterosexuality and male control over women's sexuality, which translates into male dominance of women in both public and private spheres. Although compulsory heterosexuality has implications for the social control of sexuality for all women, this aspect of sexism makes lesbians suspect as women. Therefore, sexism is inherently heterosexist, and its effects are experienced differently by heterosexual women and lesbians. Rich has argued that compulsory heterosexuality is a cornerstone of male dominance.

According to Hartmann (1984), sexism has a material base. Sexist practices are maintained by male control of female labor through the sexual division of labor in both public and private spheres and male control over female sexuality. Sexist practices manifest at the interpersonal and organizational levels of social life and are reflected in cultural representations and social institutions. Sexism operates through blatant, covert, and subtle forms of discrimination, harassment, and violence and is maintained and reproduced, like gender, in social interaction.

Sexist ideology "informs" heterosexist practices that politically, economically, and socially oppress lesbians. Sexism, as it applies to lesbians, is evident in court decisions that declare lesbians "unfit" mothers solely on the basis of their sexual orientation. Sexism is also evident in legal definitions of family in the United States, which disenfranchise lesbian couples from the privilege to marry and adopt children.

The wage gap between the sexes disadvantages women in the United States so that they earn only approximately 75 percent of what men do, which has special implications for unmarried women, including lesbians and lesbian families (with and without children). The wage gap reflects persistent [hetero]sexist beliefs about the paid labor of men and women as the "family wage"—that males ought to be the primary breadwinners in society, supporting an economically dependent wife and their children. Heterosexual marriage remains a means of upward social mobility for many women, although this is clearly not universal for all women who marry.

Sexism disadvantages lesbians and heterosexual women in different ways. Heterosexist ideology and practice logically extend from essentialist beliefs about sex and gender. Lesbians, by definition, are "unfeminine" females and face economic, political, and social consequences. Social change for sexual equality targets both the ideological underpinnings and the material consequences of the sexual division of labor and male control of female sexuality. *Christine Robinson*

### Bibliography

Benokraitis, Nicole V., and Joe R. Feagin. *Modern Sexism: Blatant, Subtle, and Covert Discrimination*. Englewood Cliffs, N.J.: Prentice-Hall, 1986.

Connell, R.W. *Gender and Power*. Cambridge, U.K.: Polity, 1987.

Hartmann, Heidi. "The Unhappy Marriage of Marxism and Feminism: Towards a More Progressive Union." In *Feminist Frameworks*, 2nd ed. Ed. Alison Jaggar and Paula Rothenberg. New York: McGraw-Hill, 1984, pp. 172–189.

Rich, Adrienne. "Compulsory Heterosexuality and Lesbian Existence." *Signs: Journal of Women in Culture and Society* 5:4 (1980), 631–660.

West, Candace, and Don Zimmerman. "Doing Gender." *Gender and Society* 1 (1987), 125–151.

*See also* Compulsory Heterosexuality; Essentialism; Gender; Heterosexism; Oppression

## Sexology

Branch of science that incorporates various disciplinary approaches in the study of human sexual behaviors and relationships. First practiced in late-nineteenth-century Europe, sexology medicalized a host of behaviors that had previously been considered criminal, immoral, or sinful. Normalizing a white, bourgeois, heterosexual family, sexologists played a large part in transforming particular sexual acts, such as masturbation and sodomy, into fixed and readily identifiable personalities, such as the onanist and the homosexual, two figures key to early sexological literature.

### Nineteenth-Century Debates

Questions concerning the physiological sources and proper channels of sexual gratification informed many nineteenth-century sexological debates. Though early sexologists drew from a variety of disciplinary approaches, most were physicians invested in medical theories such as those of Samuel Auguste Tissot (1728–1797), a Genevese physician whose *L'Onanisme* (1760) prescribed that ejaculation be limited to reproductive purposes because it weakened the body and caused insanity. Tissot was instrumental in pathologizing the onanist, a personification of a rigid, pleasureless Victorian sexual economy fixated on ensuring reproduction and regulating sexual excess.

The writings of Karl Heinrich Ulrichs (1825–1895) similarly fomented sexological discussions, particularly those concerning the etiology of the homosexual, another figure who troubled Victorian mores. Ulrichs, a Hanoverian attorney and avowed homosexual, wrote the first extended study of male same-sex desire in the West, *Forschungen über das Räthsel der mannmännlichen Liebe* (The Riddle of "Man-Manly" Love). Published pseudonymously as twelve treatises between 1863 and 1879, *Riddle* employs philosophy, law, history, literature, religion, and mythology to develop the third-sex theory of the Urning (named after Uranian love as described in Plato's *Symposium*).

The Urning, Ulrichs maintained, suffered from a female soul and psyche trapped in a biologically male body. His theory, informed by a rigid biological determinism, holds that emotions, needs, and drives are as gendered as the sexual organs themselves. Though Ulrichs had little to say about female inverts, he did propose a fourth sex, the Urningin, a biological female whose body similarly confines male desires and drives. His several reconfigurations of the third-sex theory eventually led Ulrichs to posit sixteen types of sexual intermediaries. Later, British poet Edward Carpenter (1844–1929) took up Ulrichs's theory in *The Intermediate Sex* (1908), a historical discussion of sexual intermediaries as mystics and shamans in various cultures. Expounding upon Ulrichs's model, Carpenter asserted that the third sex is superior because it balances male and female elements in one body.

Few medical sexologists, however, adopted such a model; instead, most relied upon cataloging case histories that highlighted the bizarre and pathological and documented treatments ranging from bed rest and behavioral modification to sterilization and castration. In 1869, German psychiatrist Carl von Westphal (1833–1890) published "Die conträre Sexualempfindung" (The Contrary Sexual Feeling), the case history of a young woman suffering from a hereditary, congenital neurosis and contrary, or inverted, sexual desire. This case history fueled an onslaught of similar publications, and later, in anonymous political pamphlets, Karoly Maria Kertbeny (1824–1882), a Hungarian translator, first coined the terms "homosexuality" and "heterosexuality." The term "sexology" was first coined in the writings of German dermatologist Iwan Bloch (1872–1922) as *Sexualwissenschaft* (sexual science). Bloch, who planned the unfinished collection of monographs *Das Sexualleben unserer Zeit* (The Sexual Life of Our Times), was among the first to argue that cultural and historical specificities should inform medical discussions of sex and sexual behavior.

Most early studies, though, centered on the contemporary Victorian economy of sex for reproduction. In the case histories, an innate, immutable sex differentiation was simultaneously suggested and evidenced by women's "natural" passivity and domesticity and men's "natural" activity and aggression. Often, sexological treatments sought to reimpose this "natural" balance by regulating women's bodies and desires—particularly those of prostitutes, women of color, and poor women. Sexologists proscribed women's sexuality through procedures such as clitoridectomy and ovariectomy, as well as through a host of restraining devices designed to keep these supposedly sexless beings from any erotic activity not directly related to reproduction.

Most influential in disseminating this medical ideology was Richard von Krafft-Ebing (1840–1902), a German psychiatrist and neurologist whose career began with the study of the criminally mentally disturbed. Krafft-Ebing's *Psychopathia Sexualis* (1886) provides myriad lurid case histories of murderers and sexual predators. Here, Krafft-Ebing coined the terms "sadism" and "masochism," bringing these, along with "fetishism" and "exhibitionism," into common medical usage and providing one of the earliest medical discussions of what is now known as transgenderism. Krafft-Ebing proposed causal links among masturbation, criminal deviance, and sexual inversion, a degenerative and pathological taint that "disturb[ed] the development of a well-defined and complete being." Following the lead of German sexologist Albert Moll (1862–1939), Krafft-Ebing contrasted the true invert to the "makeshift," or pseudo, homosexual, one in whom the "heterosexual instinct long remains predominant, and the impossibility to satisfy it gives pain." While the pseudohomosexual might benefit from behavior modification or hypnosis, the true invert,

Krafft-Ebing asserted, could look forward to nothing less than "a hopeless existence, a life without love, an undignified comedy before human society, and moral and psychical marasmus." Krafft-Ebing maintained that genital contact was generally less common among female inverts, attributing such behavior primarily to women in prison and prostitutes disenchanted with, or disgusted by, the unseemly demands of male clients. Among women, as among men, he argued, acquired homosexuality could become permanent, as when heterosexual women were seduced by "subtle and persevering" tribades. He urged parents to prevent pseudohomosexual tendencies by guarding children against masturbation, inappropriately gendered play, and same-sex tutors. Although toward the end of his career Krafft-Ebing recanted his position that homosexuality was necessarily a disease, *Psychopathia Sexualis* remained influential in medicine and psychology well into the twentieth century.

Most histories of sexology set up a dichotomy between Krafft-Ebing's work and that of British literary critic Henry Havelock Ellis (1859–1939), author of *Studies in the Psychology of Sex* (1896–1910), a seven-volume collection on modesty, autoerotism, sexual inversion, and other topics. Ellis, many contend, should be extolled as a sexual reformer for providing the first real challenge to Victorian prudery. While Krafft-Ebing kept a moralistic and judgmental distance from his sordid subject matter, Ellis held that the normal and the abnormal exist along a continuum. Like Ulrichs, he questioned sexual dimorphism, arguing that male and female organs and desires are potentially mutable. In his fluid formulation, the invert could conceivably live a normal, healthy life, and the aberration was the province of neither the courts nor the clinics.

Ellis delineated his theory in *Sexual Inversion*, the first volume of *Studies*, completed in collaboration with his correspondent and friend literary scholar John Addington Symonds (1840–1893). In *A Problem in Greek Ethics* (1883) and *A Problem in Modern Ethics* (1891), Symonds suggested that both the potential for sexual inversion and the propensity for pathological behavior are common to all humans; thus, his treatises challenged notions that inversion necessarily results in, or from, pathology. Symonds died before the 1896 German publication of *Sexual Inversion* as *Das Konträre Geschlechtsgefühl*. Symonds's family, who steadfastly denied his homosexuality, purchased all copies of this edition and destroyed them. Symonds's name does not appear on subsequent editions of *Sexual Inversion*.

In addition to being lauded for proposing toleration toward inverts, Ellis has been credited for being the first to theorize that a woman's body is replete with erogenous zones and that women are fully capable and deserving of sexual gratification: Some scholars joke, for instance, about his "discovery" of the clitoris. However, his theories suggest that sexual pleasure for women is contingent upon their inherent passivity and masochism. Moreover, Ellis, like most early sexologists a champion of eugenics, charged women with the goals of racial purification and selective breeding because of their greater innate inclination toward heterosexuality and child rearing.

## Sexology, Lesbians, and Feminists

Ellis's views on lesbianism, based on a handful of case histories, including that of his wife, Edith Lees Ellis (1861–1916), also relied upon the distinction between congenital inversion and pseudohomosexuality. Focusing on the habits of female inverts—for instance, a tendency toward transvestism combined with "a decided taste and toleration for cigars" and "a dislike and sometimes incapacity for needlework"—Ellis asserted that the female invert exhibits "nothing of that sexual shyness and engaging air of weakness and dependence." In addition, she often produces in an otherwise heterosexual woman the "spurious imitation" of lesbianism, one Ellis specifically linked to feminist and suffrage movements.

Numerous feminist and lesbian scholars, most notably Lillian Faderman (1940–) point to the connections among nineteenth-century sexology; the morbidification of lesbians, spinsters, and feminists; and the pathologization of women's romantic friendships. Jeffreys (1985) charges Ellis with condemning rituals and relationships common within feminist social movements that threatened the sociopolitical structures of patriarchy in the West.

Faderman (1981) indicates that the period between 1898 and 1908 witnessed increasing interest in all matters sexual: Germany alone produced more than a thousand publications on sex and sexuality in these years. In addition, in the first decades of the twentieth century, sexological literature entered the popular imagination for the first time. As the new sexual vocabulary captured the attention of the masses, increasingly more literature condemned the lonely, unstable, or suicidal female invert, ending, in Faderman's view, hundreds of years of tolerance for,

and encouragement of, romantic, often passionate, relationships between women. For years, Radclyffe Hall's (1880–1943) *The Well of Loneliness* (1928)—a novel that draws heavily from Ellis's work—epitomized this view of the tragic female invert. In addition, this period witnessed the birth of the best-selling marriage manual and sexual handbook, exemplified by the work of Marie Stopes (1880–1958), a British physician, sexologist, and birth-control advocate whose *Married Love* (1918) critiqued female same-sex desire and burgeoning feminist movements while normalizing and celebrating a female pleasure circumscribed by heterosexual marriage. "The effect of the new science of sexology," Kitzinger (1987) argues, "was to scare women back into marriage and conformity with fears of abnormality."

## Twentieth-Century Developments

Married love and heterosexuality were also promoted by the growth of psychoanalysis, the domain of Moravian neurologist and psychiatrist Sigmund Freud (1856–1939). Freud's work drew heavily from the writings of the nineteenth- and early-twentieth-century sexologists, some of whom he befriended. From Ellis, with whom Freud exchanged letters and personal photographs, Freud adopted the term "autoerotic." However, Freud parted from the sexological theory of congenital sexual inversion, positing instead a developmental model associating inversion with parental influence, childhood trauma, and stunted sexual development. His "Psychogenesis of a Case of Homosexuality in a Woman" (1920), for example, examines the "mannish" lesbian and suggests that psychotherapy may restore a female invert's fuller potential for bisexuality, though not heterosexuality. Ellis and others rejected psychoanalytic theories of the Oedipus complex and childhood sexuality, and most sexologists held that psychoanalysis could not effectively "cure" sexual inversion.

Though Freud's work captured public attention, primarily in the United States, the partial transformation of sexology from an inaccessible medical discourse to one suitable for a lay audience was largely the work of German physician, author, and reformer Magnus Hirschfeld (1868–1935). Hirschfeld, perhaps the first celebrity "sexpert," argued against the use of specialized terminology and ancient languages in sexological publications: Krafft-Ebing's *Psychopathia Sexualis*, for example, was published in Latin to avoid prosecution and censorship, as well as to maintain an aura of scientific mystique.

Like Bloch and Carpenter, Hirschfeld adopted an interdisciplinary sexology, incorporating endocrinology, psychology, evolutionary theory, ethics, and ethnology in his work. Moreover, Hirschfeld was one of first sexual scientists to use biography and autobiography, devising and applying a psychobiological inventory composed of more than 135 sets of questions on kinship and family oral history; racial, ethnic, and class background; medical history; dreams and memory; sexual behavior; hobbies; and political views. Though the questionnaire was used primarily on men, Hirschfeld was among the first to suggest that lesbianism be studied according to different theoretical paradigms than male homosexuality. Relying upon the distinction between true inversion and pseudohomosexuality posited by Ellis and others, Hirschfeld argued that harems, women's prisons, hospitals, and boarding schools were the main sites of lesbian sexuality. His 1910 study, *Die Transvestiten* (Transvestites), coined the term "transvestism" and distinguished it from sexual inversion, a category under which it had previously been subsumed. *Transvestites,* which includes an extensive section on the history of women who passed as men in various military units, presents a theory of intermediaries based on a persistent questioning of fixed realms of masculinity and femininity. Here, Hirschfeld posits the existence of more than 43 million types of sexual intermediaries, arguing that "absolute representatives of their sex are . . . only abstractions, invented extremes."

A pioneer, reformer, and early political activist, Hirschfeld campaigned extensively against the criminalization of male homosexuality. He is reported to have saved thousands of men from criminal prosecution under Germany's paragraph 175, which he campaigned to repeal. In addition, he traveled extensively, collecting sexological data and presenting his work throughout Europe and Asia. In 1897, he founded the Scientific Humanitarian Committee, an organization that aligned itself with eugenics movements to pursue tolerance for homosexuals, who, Hirschfeld assured, were ill-suited for marriage and could, therefore, not reproduce themselves. From 1899 to 1923, Hirschfeld produced and contributed to the first sexological journal, *Jahrbuech für sexuelle Zwischenstufen* (Yearbook for Intermediate Sexual Types). He also organized the first International Congress for Sexual Reform (1921) and the World League for Sexual Reform

(1928), venues that brought together sexologists from all over the world. He is perhaps best known as the founder of the Institute for Sexual Science in Berlin, a medical center, marital therapy service, university, library, and archive housing tens of thousands of publications, case histories, and photographs. The institute was one of the first organizations targeted for destruction by the Nazis in 1933, twelve years after Hirschfeld himself barely escaped death in a Nazi assault.

The rise of Nazism and the destruction brought upon Europe by World War II ravaged the burgeoning sexological industry in Germany and throughout Europe. The mid-twentieth century saw sexology move from German medical models to more quantitative models in the United States, first at the Institute for Sex Research at Indiana University, Bloomington, headed by U.S. zoologist Alfred Charles Kinsey (1894–1956). Kinsey and the institute gained fame and notoriety for the publication of *Sexual Behavior in the Human Male* (1948) and *Sexual Behavior in the Human Female* (1953), both based on thousands of lengthy interviews similar to Hirschfeld's substantive questionnaires. Though Kinsey's famous seven-point scale suggests a continuum of sexual desires and object choices influenced by Ellis, Freud, Hirschfeld, and others, Kinsey's studies differ from earlier sexological methods in its reliance on mathematical and statistical models of quantitative analysis. Widely criticized and censured for his views on homosexuality, Kinsey, as Jones (1997) contends, "attempted to stand conventional morality on its head" by insisting that the criminalization and pathologization of homosexuality run counter to humanity's mammalian evolutionary heritage. Characterizing sexual behavior as "fluid and diverse" (Jones 1997), Kinsey planned, but did not complete, an extended study of differences between the learned patterns of behavior among homosexuals and heterosexuals. Kinsey suggested that female homosexuality was "largely confined to single females who had been widowed, separated, or divorced" (Kinsey et al. 1953). He denied the existence of vaginal orgasm—the heteronormative ideal espoused by numerous contemporary sex and marital handbooks—and concluded that lesbian sexual practices "may be as effective, or even more effective than the petting or coital techniques ordinarily utilized in heterosexual contacts" (Kinsey et al. 1953).

Though sociological, literary, historical, ethnographic, and anthropological approaches occasionally accompany statistical ones, late-twentieth-century sexology remains largely the province of medicine and disaffected, scientific observation. In the United States, for instance, Kinsey's quantitative model has been inherited by the research team of dentist William H. Masters (1915–) and psychologist Virginia E. Johnson (1925–) and by pediatrician, psychiatrist, and behavioral scientist John Money (1921–). Masters and Johnson's *Human Sexual Response* (1966) relied upon clinical observations of thousands of individuals and heterosexual couples engaged in masturbation and intercourse. Their work, which focuses on the physiology and anatomy of human—primarily heterosexual—sexual activity, has been critiqued by Janice Irvine and others for suggesting that men's and women's sexual responses are fundamentally alike and, by extension, that the sexual responses of heterosexuals and homosexuals are similarly complementary. Their *Homosexuality in Perspective* (1979) provides, as Irvine (1990) suggests, a model of heterosexual/homosexual sameness that occludes cultural and social differences and power imbalances; the study excluded, for instance, noncoupled homosexuals and those who practice casual sex, various forms of anal eroticism, and sadomasochistic rituals. While Money's work also privileges heteronormativity, it calls into question models that polarize masculinity and femininity. The author of *Gay, Straight, and In-Between: The Sexology of Erotic Orientation* (1988), Money has defined more than forty paraphilias, the conditions or rituals necessarily for sexual arousal and orgasm, and completed extensive research on intersexuality in children, outlining varying types of intersexuality, including genital, as well as, chromosomal, gonadal, and endocrinological hermaphroditism.

The continuing medicalization of sex and sexuality has been loudly criticized by U.S. psychologist and sexologist Leonore Tiefer (1944–), whose collection of essays and lectures, *Sex Is not a Natural Act* (1995), urges sexologists to incorporate cultural, historical, and popular discourses of sex and sexual behavior. Furthermore, Tiefer's critique of ahistorical and apolitical sexology calls for changes in research models, increased cultural and historical specificity, and considerations of issues concerning power, gender, and ethnicity. Some late-twentieth-century conferences of the International Congress for Medical Sexology (held approximately biyearly in major world cities) do adopt more of an interdisciplinary, cross-cultural approach. Common sub-

jects of sexological debate in the 1990s included transsexual surgical procedures; new forms of contraception; sex and sexuality in relation to cancer, AIDS, paralysis, and other serious diseases; childhood sexual abuse; same-sex couples counseling; teenage pregnancy; and the more commonly discussed concerns of heterosexual genital and reproductive dysfunctions.          *Nancy San Martín*

## Bibliography

Bullough, Vern L. *Science in the Bedroom: A History of Sex Research*. New York: Basic, 1994.

Faderman, Lillian. *Surpassing the Love of Men: Romantic Love Between Women from the Renaissance to the Present*. New York: William Morrow, 1981.

Irvine, Janice M. *Disorders of Desire: Sex and Gender in Modern American Sexology*. Philadelphia: Temple University Press, 1990.

Jeffreys, Sheila. *The Spinster and Her Enemies: Feminism and Sexuality 1880–1930*. London: Pandora, 1985.

Jones, James H. *Alfred C. Kinsey: A Public/Private Life*. New York: Norton, 1997.

Kinsey, Alfred, C., et al. *Sexual Behavior in the Human Female*. Philadelphia: Saunders, 1953.

Kitzinger, Celia. *The Social Construction of Lesbianism*. London: Sage, 1987.

Rosario, Vernon A., ed. *Science and Homosexualities*. London: Routledge, 1997.

*See also* Biological Determinism; Etiology; Faderman, Lillian; Germany; Hall, Radclyffe; Heterosexuality; Homosexuality; Kinsey Institute; Nazism; Psychiatry; Psychoanalysis; Romantic Friendship; Spinsters; Suffrage Movement

## Sexual Harassment

The imposition of institutional, social, or personal power, explicitly or implicitly, in such a way as to sexually dominate or coerce an individual into giving sexual favors. Heterosexual norms may also constitute sexual harrasment to the extent that lesbians are coerced by systems of rewards and punishments into maintaining a heterosexual orientation.

Sexual harassment first became visible (in the United States), to a large degree, because of the women's movement, feminist education and small-group consciousness raising among women. The work of MacKinnon (1979) is a pivotal marker in the development of a social consciousness of sexual harassment as an abuse of power coincident with received cultural norms about gender and sexuality.

In the workplace, the separation between the private and public domains of everyday life breaks down. This allows one human being with greater power (usually male) to impose sexual and/or personal desire upon another (usually female). This may be expressed as an explicit or an implicit coercion whereby job benefits are promised for sexual favors. Rarely, however, are any job benefits actually gained by complying with sexual requests. To the degree that lesbians "pass" as heterosexual, they are subject to the same phenomenon as nonlesbians. However, like the other stressors that confront lesbians who "pass" as heterosexual, the distress of sexual harassment is compounded by the need to keep their lesbianism hidden.

While efforts to establish common rules of conduct within the workplace have helped curtail sexual harassment, these efforts do not address the underlying conditions that predispose persons toward sexually harassing behavior. Cultural norms that position male sexuality as active and female sexuality as passive construct a notion of man as taker and woman as there to be taken. Thus, some argue that sexual harassment by men against women is normative in both public and private domains. In the public domain, for example, women's relative economic disadvantage, combined with gender-segregated jobs, encourages women's tolerance of unwanted sexual and/or personal attention. Waitressing and secretarial work are prime, though not the only, examples. Conversely, heterosexual women and lesbians who work in traditionally male-segregated jobs are often subjected to especially virulent forms of sexual harassment.

For lesbians who are not "out" publicly, heterosexual norms may, in fact, constitute a "hostile environment." Such an environment is coercive in that lesbians understand that they will be rewarded for maintaining a heterosexual orientation and punished for expressing a lesbian orientation. Thus, one could argue that lesbians are sexually harassed by the cultural (and familial) effort to make them heterosexual.

In another way, publicly "out" lesbians may become targets for accusations of sexual harassment by their mere presence as lesbians. For example, lesbians and gay men are stereotyped as attempting to seduce and "convert" unwitting heterosexuals. In the particular case of the academic workplace, openly lesbian teachers who bring their lesbian-self into the classroom are, in a sense, exerting a sexual presence that—within a homophobic mindset—can be experienced as sexual harassment. There is an inherent ambiguity in the immediate and concrete experience of sexual harassment, such that, given certain contexts, virtually any behavior may be interpreted and, indeed, experienced as sexual harassment.

Hence, lesbian teachers face particular challenges promoting education in the midst of homophobic attitudes. Lesbians, like all other human beings, are capable of using sexuality as an abuse of power against other persons. Like the debates within the feminist community about sadomasochism, debates about the degree to which lesbianism might have the capacity to create an understanding of sexuality not linked to dominance are open and ongoing.

It is important to note that the veracity of the charge of sexual harassment against someone who already occupies the position of being harassed by the very norms of culture deserves a different kind of critical attention than those charges made against those who inherit positions of cultural or institutional power or authority.

One final and important point should be made about lesbians and sexual harassment: In the same way that lesbianism reveals specific features of sexual harassment concealed within a heterosexual context, so, too, does a focus on race and ethnicity reveal features of both lesbianism and sexual harassment previously concealed. Lesbians of color have revealed the coexistence and interrelationship of sexism and racism, providing an important avenue for understanding the complex interworkings of cultural power, systematic domination, and possibilities for personal and social transformation.

*Jacqueline M. Martinez*

### Bibliography

MacKinnon, Catherine A. *Sexual Harassment of Working Women*. New Haven, Conn.: Yale University Press, 1979.

Paludi, Michele A., and Richard B. Barickman. *Academic and Workplace Sexual Harassment: A Resource Manual*. New York: State University of New York Press, 1991.

Smith, Andrew R., and Jacqueline M. Martinez. "Signifying Harassment: Communication, Ambiguity, and Power." *Human Studies* 18 (1995), 63–87.

*See also* Work

## Sexual Orientation and Preference

**S** Terms used to refer to a fairly consistent pattern of sexual desire for one gender or the other. Although one may prefer or be sexually oriented toward any number of behaviors, stimuli, situations, and the like, the late-twentieth-century use of the terms refers only to the gender of one's desired partners. This limited usage both illustrates and underwrites the centrality of gender in the social organization of the modern West. It also leaves open the place of bisexuality in this scheme, and bisexual theorists and activists differ as to whether bisexuality is a sexual orientation or preference like heterosexuality and homosexuality, or whether it is the absence of any orientation or preference toward one gender over the other.

Historical and cross-cultural evidence demonstrates that the concepts—and, apparently, the experiences of self that accompany their use—are of fairly recent, Western origin. Although there is much evidence worldwide of same-sex love and sexuality, there is relatively little evidence of the now-widespread belief that individuals are distinguished from one another by an underlying trajectory of desire for one gender or the other. Cross-culturally, most relationships between women do not exclude relationships with men and do not mark the participants as different in type from women who do not love women. Where women are differentiated, as with the "manly hearted woman" in some Native American societies, it is their gender-crossing, rather than their sexuality, that distinguishes them— a distinction that does not extend to their female partners. This gender-crossing form of relationships between women does not feature the concepts of sexual orientation or sexual preference. Neither, apparently, does the romantic-friendship form, common among middle- and upper-class women in the United States and Europe in the nineteenth century.

Lesbian and gay activists in the 1980s and 1990s debated the meaning and usage of these terms, seeing them as interchangeable but not neutrally so. Over the course of the 1980s, a strong partiality to the term "orientation" emerged among most activists. It implies, they argued, an internal, unchosen, and possibly innate characteristic, as much a part of an individual's makeup as her left- or right-handedness. At the same time, antigay activists took on the term "preference," believing that it implies choice, mutability, and a focus on behavior over being. As of the late 1990s, no legal distinction between the terms existed, and antidiscrimina-tion statutes in various localities used either term, differing by the time and place of their drafting rather than by intent.

In contrast, a social-constructionist view implies that the terms refer to two different, if related, phenomena. Individuals may have underlying orientations, which may be strong or weak and which may or may not manifest in coordinating preferences. Many women who live and identify as lesbians, for example, indicate that their underlying orientation is probably bisexual and so it is their preference that is lesbian.

Lesbian feminists have sought to enlarge the understanding of lesbianism beyond a sexual preference or orientation and, as such, have downplayed distinctions between heterosexual and homosexual women. And a good body of evidence including Bell and Weinberg (1978) and Blumstein and Schwartz (1983), suggests that, indeed, women's sexual preferences and orientations are often quite fluid and flexible, particularly compared to those of men.

*Vera Whisman*

### Bibliography

Bell, Alan P., and Martin S. Weinberg. *Homosexualities: A Study of Human Diversity*. New York: Simon and Schuster, 1978.

Blumstein, Philip, and Pepper Schwartz. *American Couples: Money, Work, Sex*. New York: William Morrow, 1983.

Whisman, Vera. *Queer by Choice: Lesbians, Gay Men, and the Politics of Identity*. New York: Routledge, 1996.

Whitehead, Harriet. "The Bow and the Burden Strap: A New Look at Institutionalized Homosexuality in Native North America." In *Sexual Meanings: The Cultural Construction of Gender and Sexuality*. Ed. Sherry B. Ortner and Harriet Whitehead. New York: Cambridge University Press, 1981, pp. 80–115.

*See also* Bisexuality; Essentialism; Lesbian Feminism; Native Americans; New Right; Social-Construction Theory

### Sexuality

A much-disputed term associated with types of sexual persons and kinds of erotic attraction. Sexuality should be clearly distinguished from "sex," in the sense of a varying set of acts, practices, and behaviors that in some way or other engage the body, its pleasures, and desires. Sex has a history that goes back as far as humankind. In contrast, sexuality is a relatively new concept, gaining currency only in the 1890s and, hence, a sociohistorically specific phenomenon.

## History

Most historians of sexuality emphasize that heterosexuality and homosexuality are not the natural, unchanging categories of identity they are commonly assumed to be, at least in the Western world. Neither the idea of a sexual "essence," the belief in a fixed sexual identity grounded in biology or anatomy, nor the exclusionary distinction between homo- and heterosexuality have any historical basis. The invention of sexuality as such is usually traced back to the late nineteenth century and the emergence of modern, industrialized society. In premodern cultures, different modes of differentiation play the part of what in the twentieth century came to be regarded as a "natural" *hetero*sexual instinct, the biological link between members of two oppositionally defined sexes.

In ancient Greece, for instance, sexual relations were not structured along the binary divide between "straight" and "gay" but were, instead, organized in terms of activity and passivity. Free men—nonslave males, the only ones to enjoy full citizenship—often maintained sexual relations with both women and boys. Such same-sex relations were not considered abnormal, because the critical aspect in erotic relations was not the gender of the sexual object but the respective roles of each sexual partner in actual practice. As a free man, only the older male could legitimately take up the active role of penetrator, a role appropriate to his dominant social position. While a gender hierarchization clearly existed—in the sense that woman and boy (as not-yet-man) could function only as the passive objects of the male subject's desires—the distinction between acceptable and nonacceptable sexual behavior was not based on the assumption of a natural heterosexuality.

The Greek state is often invoked by gay male historians who seek to liberate homosexuality from its association with sickness, sin, and perversion. They do not always take into account, however, that even this "liberating" model, like all currently charted forms of Western sexuality, is rooted in phallocentrist assumptions. In line with their inferior social position, women were not considered sufficiently important for either contemporary policymakers or later (male) historians to pay them much attention. Hence, with the exception of the legendary poet Sappho (ca. 600 B.C.E.) from the Isle of Lesbos, who reputedly prepared young girls for their future roles as wives and mothers by introducing them into the realm of Eros, very little is known about the regulation of female same-sex relations in classical antiquity.

Other premodern constructions of lesbian sexuality render such phallocentrism explicit by insisting on some form of physical deformation or aberrant sexual behavior on the part of what were variously called "female sodomites," "tribades," and "fricatrices," involving elongated clitorises, dildos, and other mock penises. Historically seen, discourses of sexuality do not allow for conceptualizations of female same-sex desire outside the terms of phallocratic thought. As a result, the female body has traditionally been inevitably defined in terms of "lack," perceived to be lacking the critical instrument necessary for phallic penetration. Seen as either complementary to that of the male, or as a mere variation on the "universal" (male) model, female sexuality has rarely been treated as an object worthy of independent investigation.

Unfortunate as this may be, historical evidence clearly suggests that sexual desire and behavior are not swayed by the laws of nature. Two points, nonetheless, deserve special notice. First, prior to the creation of the modern concept of sexuality, erotic relations were officially recognized as thoroughly entwined with public interests. The separation between private and public, a distinction that centrally revolves around matters of the flesh, was installed only in the late nineteenth century. Second, all systems of sexual organization, past as well as present, critically depend on some other form of hierarchization—whether in terms of sex, class, race, or ethnicity, if not sexual orientation.

## Modern Theories

The connection between sex and sexuality has been central to all modern theories of sexuality. The first theorists to discuss same- or different-sex sexual relations in terms of (ab)normal gender behavior were the sexologists, nineteenth-century medical men who sought to appropriate human sexuality for their new profession. They furthermore began to distinguish human beings on the basis of their erotic inclinations, to define humanity in terms of sexual *identity*. In sexological discourse, any person with exclusive sexual interest in members of his or her own sex was categorized as an "invert"—that is, as a biologically distinct individual who, by fault of nature, had ended up with the sexual instinct of the opposite sex. Where sexual practices had previously seen as *acts* either legitimately or illegitimately indulged in, they henceforth functioned as the foundations of two kinds of sexual species, endowed with either "natural" or "unnatural" desires.

Although sexological theory put sexuality on the map of Western consciousness, it has been overshadowed by the ideas of Sigmund Freud (1856–1939), whose "science" of psychoanalysis continues to inform contemporary notions of sexuality. In his own way, Freud did much to reinforce the distinction between homo- and heterosexual practices in terms of (ab)normality. He did, nevertheless, succeed in separating sexual behavior from its presumed biological foundations and, instead, introduced the concept of the pleasure principle.

According to Freud, the sexual "instinct" is not fueled by the need to reproduce but, rather, by the need to satisfy (largely unconscious) desires. Presupposing that human beings are born with a bisexual disposition, he described a complex psychosexual development in which the child's early history, rather than her or his biological body, plays a decisive role. Although cultural conventions led Freud to offer the heterosexual ideal as the only successful outcome of psychosexual development, he did much to dislodge the notion of sexuality as either rightly or wrongly fixed in immutably gendered bodies. Freud's assumption that the libido is neither inborn nor natural has proved by far the most radical of his ideas.

During the 1920s, it became possible—and, all too soon, necessary—to identify oneself in terms of one's sexual behavior and feeling. For the first time in history, homosexuals and heterosexuals alike were expected, if not forced, to define their erotic preferences as vital aspects of their private and public selves. The idea that sexuality is one of the mainstays of collective, as well as individual, identities has since become almost unchallenged in Western consciousness. The construction of sexualized *persons* and, by extension, of a hierarchical system of sociosexual differentiation, is one of a number of Freudian legacies that has been put to significant, if radically different, political effects.

In the 1950s, social and economic pressures fostered a "cult of domesticity" in which the idea of healthy heterosexuality was firmly established as the only natural and mature form of sexual identity. Freud's work was used by an emerging class of practicing psychologists to convince both the general public and many a hapless individual that the only route happiness was reproductive sex. To cure otherwise doomed perverts from their pathological tendencies, a series of medical treatments was introduced to supplant the traditional, and often unsuccessful, psychoanalytical "talking cure." Homosexual men and women were routinely hospitalized and subjected to a variety of therapies, ranging from the forcible application of large doses of insulin and electroshock therapy to the more drastic measures of castration and lobotomy. From a revolutionary and potentially liberating theory of sexuality, psychoanalysis was thus, in the course of a few decades, transformed into a powerful repressive tool in the service of a highly conservative, if not reactionary, sociopolitical ethics.

Against this background, it is not surprising that, at the end of the 1960s, the rise of various countercultural movements, including feminism and gay liberation, coincided with a pervasive attack on Freudian psychoanalysis as the dominant explanation of sexuality. Despite his attempts to assign woman her own place on the map of sexuality, femininity had, after all, ultimately remained an enigma to Freud. A growing body of feminist critical work challenged prevailing theories of sexuality in which woman figured as man's "other," and "uppity" women were diagnosed with "penis envy." However, the main object of white, straight, middle-class feminist analysis was the oppressive system of patriarchal power relations. Hence, its initial focus on sexual difference—woman's difference from man—to the relative neglect of other areas of exclusion, such as race, class, ethnicity, and, somewhat surprisingly, sexuality. Indeed, when lesbian feminists occasionally brought up the question of *sexual*—as distinct from *gender*—differences as a political issue, some heterosexual feminists advised them to keep their problematical private lives to themselves, since the mere association with lesbianism might discredit the feminist cause as a whole.

Some of the most incisive critiques of patriarchal power, nonetheless, came from early feminists who, either implicitly or explicitly, dared to write from a lesbian perspective. For what, they pertinently asked, succeeded in keeping individual women in thrall to men, and women as a group subordinated to male sociopolitical power, if not the organization of both public and private relations along the lines of normative heterosexuality? Only by overhauling what Adrienne Rich (1929–) has called the system of "compulsory heterosexuality" would the aims of women's liberation be ultimately fulfilled. These radical lesbian feminist critiques, in turn, inspired some of the reconceptualizations that subsequently arose from lesbian and gay studies and theory. Such alternative sexual discourses, emerging in the Euro-Western academy only in the late 1980s, have their roots in the gay and lesbian liberation movements of previous decades.

## Identity Politics and Queer Theory

In line with the times, most lesbians and gay men in the 1970s adopted the notion of "identity politics," originally developed within black activism in the United States, to further the cause of sexual liberation. They embraced this self-definition as a sexual minority to empower themselves and end the marginalization of nonheterosexual groups. While identity politics based on a fixed and natural sexual orientation proved to be a powerful tool for effecting social change, most lesbigay theorists believed, at the same time, that sexual identities—whether gay, lesbian, bisexual, or even heterosexual—are neither innate nor Godgiven but, rather, the results of heterosexist ideologies. In other words, lesbian and gay studies have assumed contradictory positions toward their object of analysis from the start. This contradiction came newly to the fore with the birth of queer practice and theory in the late 1980s and early 1990s.

Queer theorists' primary aim is to call into question any stable notion of identity, be it in terms of gender, ethnicity, race, class, sexual orientation, age, or ability. Dislodging the traditional distinction between act and identity, they equally reject the concepts of biological essence and social construction and, instead, foreground the *performative* aspects of sexuality. Generated by a wide range of acts, thoughts, and feelings, sexuality is seen as a shifting pattern of being and behaving, as an ongoing *production*, with multiple and changing significance. The emphasis on changeability and multiplicity does not deny that individuals are variously exposed to the compulsory and compulsive demands of the dominant culture. On the contrary, the notion of the performative seeks to underscore that any meaningful act of self-identification must be continually repeated in order to *produce* the illusion of permanency and stability that is the precondition for psychosocial survival. Sexuality should, therefore, not be regarded as a freely chosen set of theatrical performances, but as the effect of a powerful system of sociopolitical regulation. Anyone who refuses to play by the rules is subject to marginalization, ostracism, and other kinds of delegitimation.

The rise of queer activism has had an empowering effect on the gay and lesbian populations of some (white, urban) communities in the United States, Canada, and several western European countries. Similarly, the renewed questioning of sexual categories and identities by self-identified queer scholars has opened up a potentially enabling space for innovative modes of thought about sexuality, gender, and other aspects of psychosocial differentiation. Still, queer practice and theory have also been met with suspicion within other segments of the lesbian and gay community, especially by those unwilling to let go of precisely such categories as gay, lesbian, bisexual, and transgender as legitimate terms of self-identity that have, as yet, barely been acknowledged as such in Western societies, let alone in other parts of the world. In view of the tenacity with which previous attempts at changing sexual norms and values have usually been resisted, and in light of the overwhelming power of the heterosexual imperative that continues to expand across many different nations, cultures, and communities, the majority of people—however sexually identified—will probably enter the twenty-first century with at least some belief in sexual identities intact.

*renée c. hoogland*

## Bibliography

Butler, Judith. *Gender Trouble: Feminism and the Subversion of Identity*. New York: Routledge, 1990.

Chauncey, George, Jr. "From Sexual Inversion to Homosexuality: Medicine and the Changing Conceptualization of Sexual Deviance." *Salmagundi* 58–59 (Fall 1982/Winter 1983), 114–146.

Feminist Review, ed. *Sexuality: A Reader*. London: Virago, 1987.

Lancaster, Roger N., and Micaela di Leonardo, eds. *The Gender/Sexuality Reader: Culture, History, Political Economy*. New York and London: Routledge, 1997.

Rubin, Gayle. "Thinking Sex: Notes for a Radical Theory of the Politics of Sexuality." In *Powers of Desire: The Politics of Sexuality*. Ed. Ann Snitow, Christine Stansell, and Sharon Thompson. London: Virago, 1984.

***See also*** Compulsory Heterosexuality; Essentialism; Heterosexuality; Homosexuality; Identity Poli-

**S**

## Sexually Transmitted Diseases

Also known as STDs; infections transmitted through sexual contact from one individual to another.

STDs are caused by viruses, bacteria, and protozoa. Viral STDs are chronic, persisting for life. They include infection with human immunodeficiency virus (HIV), which causes AIDS; herpes simplex virus (HSV), which causes genital herpes; human papillomavirus (HPV), which causes genital warts and cervical cancer; and hepatitis B. Bacterial STDs include chlamydia, gonorrhea, and syphilis; trichomonal vaginitis is the only protozoan STD.

The risks of STD transmission between lesbians are not well known. A few studies have reported a low prevalence of STDs and no risk of HIV transmission between female sex partners. However, these studies evaluated small numbers of women, did not employ newer diagnostic tests, and provided incomplete information on sexual practices. Among the 6,146 respondents to the National Lesbian and Bi Women's Health Survey (1994), many women reported contracting an STD from another woman (including herpes in 135, chlamydia in 102, genital warts in 100, gonorrhea in sixteen, hepatitis in nine, and HIV in one). However, since most lesbians (77–99 percent) have had sex with men, and many (21–30 percent) continue to have sex with men, acquisition of a chronic viral STD may occur from male partners (O'Hanlon, 1995).

Several anecdotal reports case of HIV transmission between women have been reported, but the risk of transmission for a given sexual encounter was not known by the late 1990s. Trichomoniasis and genital herpes occur among lesbians and are very likely transmitted between women (the first by exchange of infected vaginal secretions, and the second by orogenital sex). HPV infection, genital warts, and cervical cancer also occur in lesbians, including those who have never had sex with men, which strongly suggests that transmission between female sex partners occurs (probably on hands and sex toys). Marrazzo et al. (in press) suggest that lesbians receive routine Pap-smear screening less frequently than heterosexual women. Whether this stems from alienating behavior on the part of health-care providers, inability to pay for care, or low perception of risk of STDs from female partners was not known, but routine Pap-smear screening of lesbians should not differ from that for heterosexual women.

Bacterial vaginosis (BV) is a condition in which overgrowth of some vaginal organisms occurs. While it is not an STD among heterosexual couples, the prevalence of BV among lesbians has been reported to be 18–36 percent. Berger et al. (1995) found that a partner of a woman with BV was almost twenty times more likely to have BV than a partner of a woman who did not have it. Despite these data, whether BV is an STD among lesbians was not clear by the late 1990s, and further research was being conducted.

Because of the lack of any good understanding of the risks of STD transmission in a given sexual encounter, the use of protective measures, such as latex barriers (gloves, dams), or plastic kitchen wrap remained the safest approach for lesbians in the first six months of a mutually monogamous sexual relationship. In addition, the presence of oral or genital ulcers or lesions consistent with herpes should prompt caution and, at least, the use of barrier methods to prevent transmission.    *Jeanne M. Marrazzo*

### Bibliography

American Medical Association, Council on Scientific Affairs. "Health Care Needs of Gay Men and Lesbians in the United States." *Journal of the American Medical Association* 275 (1996), 1354–1359.

Berger, Barbara J., Shelley, Kolton, Jonathan M. Zenilman, Marinella C. Cummings, Joseph Feldman, and William M. McCormack. "Bacterial Vaginosis in Lesbians: A Sexually Transmitted Disease." *Clinical Infectious Diseases* 21 (1995), 1402–1405.

Lemp, George F., Melissa Jones, Timothy A. Kellogg, Giuliano N. Nieri, Laura Anderson, David Withum, and Mitchell Katz. "HIV Seroprevalence and Risk Behaviors Among Lesbians and Bisexual Women in San Francisco and Berkeley, California." *American Journal of Public Health* 85 (1995), 1549–1552.

Marrazzo, Jeanne M., Laura A. Koutsky, Kathleen Stine, Jane M. Kuypers, Thomas A. Grubert, Denise A. Galloway, Nancy B. Kiviat, and H. Hunter Handsfield. "Genital Human Papillomavirus Infection in Women Who Have Sex With Women." *Journal of Infectious Diseases,* in press.

O'Hanlan, K.A. "Lesbian Health and Homophobia." *Current Problems in Obstetrics, Gynecology, and Fertility* 18 (1995), 93–136.

*See also* AIDS (Acquired Immune Deficiency Syndrome); Health; Safer Sex; Sex Practices; Sexuality

## Shockley, Ann Allen (1927–)

Pioneering African American writer. Ann Allen Shockley's lesbian fiction explores the turbulent and formative years between 1960 and 1980, when few black lesbians were writing openly or being published. In a critical essay in Barbara Smith's (1946–) influential black feminist anthology, *Home Girls: A Black Feminist Anthology* (1983), Shockley analyzes the ideological reasons for this marginalization and documents a "trickling" of black lesbian texts newly appearing in the 1970s. Shockley's own carefully structured, classically realist fiction is central to this small, but historically significant, body of work.

*The Black and the White of It* (1980) collects ten short stories about lesbians, some written as early as the 1960s and published previously. Like her novels, Shockley's short stories are thematically innovative: They grapple with experiences rarely rendered in fiction before, exploring the consequences of racism and heterosexism while focusing on characters' creative responses and, especially, the ability to love.

Shockley's first novel, *Loving Her* (1974), is widely recognized as the first U.S. lesbian novel dealing with interracial love. Set in the 1960s, this erotic narrative avoids the racial discourses of both black nationalism and radical feminism, employing, instead, an earlier, liberal discourse of transcendence and color blindness. Still, Shockley's insights regarding racism in gay communities and the necessary conditions for nonexploitive interracial relationships fully anticipate antiracist theory of the 1990s. Shockley's characterizations of heterosexuals constitute a forceful critique of contemporary black gender relations.

Shockley's second novel, *Say Jesus and Come to Me* (1982), is more than a love story concerning two very public, closeted black women, a minister and a recording artist. It is also an ambitious political fable, with Myrtle representing the possibilities of black female leadership as she mobilizes a historic, interracial grass-roots women's movement. Myrtle finally gains the courage to come out publicly: Her last sermon boldly contradicts Saint Paul's claim, in Romans 1 that homosexuality is perverse or "unnatural."

An academic librarian at Fisk University since 1969, Shockley has produced extensive, distinguished bibliographical and critical work, including *Afro-American Women Writers, 1746–1933* (1988). Dandridge's (1987) annotated bibliography fully documents Shockley's prolific career through 1985. More recently, Bogus (1990) locates *Say Jesus* in a multigenerational, "afrofemcentric" tradition representing black lesbian musicians.     *Glynis Carr*

### Bibliography

Bogus, SDiane A. "The 'Queen B' Figure in Black Literature." In *Lesbian Texts and Contexts: Radical Revisions*. Ed. Karla Jay and Joanne Glasgow. New York: New York University Press, 1990, pp. 275–290.

Dandridge, Rita B. *Ann Allen Shockley: An Annotated Primary and Secondary Bibliography*. Westport, Conn.: Greenwood, 1987.

Smith, Barbara, ed. *Home Girls: A Black Feminist Anthology*. New York: Kitchen Table: Women of Color Press, 1983.

Wallace, Michelle. *Black Macho and the Myth of the Superwoman*. New York: Dial, 1979.

*See also* African American Literature; Smith, Barbara

## Simcox, Edith Jemima (1844–1901)

British social reformer and scholar. Edith Simcox established and managed a shirtmaking cooperative (1875–1884), supported the trade-union movement, was a representative to the International Trade Union Congress on eight occasions, was elected to the London School Board, wrote for the leading periodicals, and published three books.

As a young child, according to her journal, Simcox "liked boys best" and dreamed of some discovery that should prove her to be a boy; she and her two brothers were referred to as "the three boys." "The base of the preference was a want of sympathy with girls' games and talk—I did not care for dolls or dress or any sort of needlework." As a student, she described having an affection for a French governess "of a demonstrative, 'fondling' sort."

Simcox thoroughly enjoyed her androgyny, referred to herself as "half a man," mentioned her "young manhood," laughed at signing her name E.J. Simcox to get "mistered," and said she would be glad to serve on a government committee if women were eligible because she was "the least womanish of available women." From 1877 until 1900, she kept a private journal, *Autobiography of a Shirtmaker,* in which she attempted to deal with the painful reality that her passionate love for the British novelist George Eliot (1819–1880) was not reciprocated. She enjoyed kissing Eliot, was seldom alone with her, and strongly resented the remarks that Eliot made encouraging her to be "more charitable to men" and urging her to marry. Simcox made indignant comments such as "I have never wished to be married in the abstract and I would decidedly much rather not be married to any concrete Dick or Tom."

Simcox was herself pursued by women whose love she did not return, and she recognized the irony in causing them the same miserable pain that Eliot caused her. She often mentioned her business partner, Mary Hamilton (n.d.), being involved with other women, while Simcox cultivated relationships with the other women who loved Eliot, such as Elma Stuart (1837?–1903), Barbara Bodichon (1827–1891), and Maria Congreve (d. 1915). In *Episodes in the Lives of Men, Women, and Lovers* (1882), Simcox portrayed her secret love for Eliot in twelve fictional vignettes.                    *Constance M. Fulmer*

### Bibliography

Fulmer, Constance M., and Margaret E. Barfield, eds. *A Monument to the Memory of George Eliot: Edith J. Simcox's Autobiography of a Shirtmaker*. New York: Garland, 1998.

Haight, Gordon S. *George Eliot: A Biography*. Oxford: Oxford University Press, 1968.

McKenzie, Keith A. *Edith Simcox and George Eliot*. Oxford: Oxford University Press, 1961. Reprint. Westport, Conn.: Greenwood, 1978.

*See also* Androgyny

## Singles

A single lesbian is a woman who has a preference for female partners and who does not consider herself currently coupled. A single lesbian might be celibate by choice, uninvolved but looking for a lover, or dating one or more women but not in an exclusive relationship with anyone. A lesbian might see herself as coupled after just one date or sexual episode, while the other woman might still see herself as single. Because same-sex marriage was not legal in the United States at the end of the twentieth century, the demarcation between being single and being coupled was not uniformly defined among lesbians.

## History

Single lesbians did not exist until the late nineteenth century. Woman-to-woman sexual activity had been documented for many centuries before, but the idea of a homosexual as a distinct person was first promoted by German psychologist Carl von Westphal (1839–1890), who described a "congenital invert" in 1869. Richard von Krafft-Ebing (1840–1902) elaborated on this concept in *Psychopathia Sexualis* in 1882, and Havelock Ellis (1859–1939) published *Studies in the Psychology of Sex: Sexual Inversion* in 1897. Because homosexuality, or sexual inversion, was considered a disease in the nineteenth century, few women identified as lesbians. A woman coupled with another woman might have seen herself as homosexual; a woman alone would not have used that label because the concept of "a homosexual" as a distinct person did not exist until later.

As a result of the feminist and gay rights movements in the second half of the twentieth century, more women identified as lesbians, whether they were coupled or single.

## Finding Other Singles

Single lesbians needed a way to identify themselves to one another and the outside world so they would not be presumed to be single heterosexual women. As a result, they developed subtle and overt visual cues and social structures to proclaim their identity and sexual orientation as lesbians.

Many lesbians wore traditionally masculine clothing. Short fingernails, sensible shoes, and androgynous clothing styles were common among 1970s lesbians. Distinctly lesbian hairstyles, such as crew cuts, short on top and long in back, short with a tiny long tail, or partly shaved heads, were popular for a few years each, until these haircuts became common among heterosexuals. Pinkie rings; tattoos; rainbow flags; pink or black triangles; labyris, lambda, or double-woman symbol jewelry; and freedom rings have all offered ways for lesbians to identify themselves to one another. At some dances, single lesbians were each given a white flower to wear; at the Michigan Womyn's Music Festival, single lesbians could meet each other at a designated breakfast area each day.

Lesbian bars were a major gathering place for singles in the 1950s through 1970s, but, as alcohol consumption became less socially acceptable, other methods of meeting evolved. In the 1970s, personals ads emerged as a way for single lesbians to find partners; in the 1980s, professional dating services catering to lesbians were established; and some major cities advertised sex clubs for lesbians. Feminist organizations, women's sports teams, women's colleges, girls' camps, and the military all attracted single lesbians. A common way single lesbians met others was through introductions by friends.

## Single Lifestyles

For some lesbians, being single is a transition phase between a breakup and finding a new partner. For others, being single is a preferred lifestyle. In a 1987 survey (Munson) of 106 women at a lesbian social group in Boulder, Colorado, 40 percent described themselves as currently being part of a monogamous couple; 16 percent were in a committed, open relationship; 23 percent were single and looking for sexual involvement; 6 percent were celibate by choice; and 15 percent were dating one or more women. When asked to describe their ideal sexual involvement, 55 percent preferred to be in a monogamous couple; 31 percent would choose a committed, open relationship; 8 percent preferred multiple committed relationships; and 6 percent preferred something else. This survey revealed that about 50 percent usually became sexually involved with someone after a few dates, about 25 percent had sex after many months of getting to know each other, about 12 percent usually had sex on the first date, and the rest gave some other answer.

## Finding Community

Feminist bookstores throughout the country, many of them started by lesbians, served as de facto lesbian community centers in the 1970s through 1990s. Their bulletin boards advertising events, services, and housing for women were an especially important resource for single lesbians new in town or in transition. In many smaller cities, a feminist bookstore was the only public place a woman could go, knowing she would find lesbian-friendly women.

A single lesbian moving to a small city would likely be included in the community with invitations to potlucks, picnics, or parties organized by local lesbians. In a large urban area, choosing a particular subgroup, such as the lesbian chorus, an S/M (sadomasochism) group, a two-step or a twelve-step group, a sports team, a recreational or political club, a career women's group, or an organizing committee around issues of ethnicity or age, would offer the newcomer more opportunity for becoming part of a community, establishing friendships, and finding lovers.

As gay politics focused on securing domestic-partnership and marriage benefits for gays, lesbian couples moved toward acceptance in mainstream American culture. This inspired many single lesbians to create and support visible lesbian social institutions catering to their lifestyles. Numerous women's theater groups, coffeehouses, community centers, dances, concerts, and bookstores in the United States at the end of the twentieth century resulted from the creative and organizing efforts of coupled and single lesbians in search of friendship, lovers, and community. *Marcia Munson*

### Bibliography

Munson, Marcia. "How Do You Do It?" *On Our Backs* 4:1 (1987), 12–41.

Stevens, Robin, ed. *Girlfriend Number One: Lesbian Life in the 90s*. San Francisco: Cleis, 1994.

*See also* Bars; Bookstores; Choruses, Women's; Community Centers; Couples; Domestic Partnership; Monogamy and Nonmonogamy; Music Festivals

## Sisterhood

Term generally referring to the unity of women, particularly as that unity is connected with feminist activism. Popularized during the nineteenth-century fight for women's suffrage, the concept of sisterhood reemerged during the 1960s and 1970s. Since then, many feminist groups have utilized it, often for different reasons and with different meanings.

## Characteristics

At its reemergence during the 1960s, the concept of sisterhood was used by radical feminists (as in Robin Morgan's *Sisterhood Is Powerful* [1970]) to counter the generic usage of the term "brotherhood" by male-dominated leftist organizations. Its usage was designed to reveal the sexism pervasive in these organizations and—many women hoped—motivate the Left to address sexism as seriously as it did racism and classism. The concept illuminated the status of women as an oppressed class and illustrated the need for female solidarity. Many feminists also employed the phrase to emphasize the magnitude and power of women united in the fight against oppression. Because it challenged the Left's male supremacy and emphasized the solidarity of women,

S "sisterhood" was one of several theoretical constructs that served to validate feminism (particularly radical feminism) as an important, effective movement for change.

As its usage grew, "sisterhood" was adopted by other women's groups to differentiate their particular experience of oppression. Lesbians utilized the term to emphasize the homophobia of mainstream society and the need for women to unite in ways that affirmed lesbian existence. Similarly, women of color used the phrase to signify the need to bond against racist and ethnocentric practice.

## Criticism

These different uses and meanings of "sisterhood" revealed problems inherent in the primary definition of the term itself. Those wary of the term criticize its tendency to universalize female experience. Such a tendency emphasizes women's assumed shared experiences at the expense of the differences among them. For example, early in its history (1971), the National Organization for Women (NOW) simultaneously advocated sisterhood and instituted a purge of every known lesbian within the organization. Thus, many women were uncomfortable with feminist uses of the term, particularly when they seemed to exclude women who were not heterosexual, middle-class, or of western European descent. The use of the term within lesbian communities carried similar problems: Although it was redefined to address more specifically the oppression of lesbians, it still operated to separate and, thus, gloss over the very real problems of racism, classism, and other oppressions rooted in social-identity differences among lesbians themselves.

## Status

Despite its sometimes rough reception, sisterhood remains an important concept for lesbians and non-lesbian feminists alike. While most recognize its practical limitations, it still represents for many the power and magnitude of women's bonds with other women. In its most effective sense, sisterhood has come to mean the necessity for women to build alliances against all oppressive structures and institutions and resist the temptation to privilege one struggle over any other.          *Dana R. Shugar*

## Bibliography

Cohen, Marcia. *The Sisterhood: The True Story of the Women Who Changed the World.* New York: Simon and Schuster, 1988.

Chrystos. "Nidishenok (Sisters)." *Maenad* (Winter 1982), n.p.

Combahee River Collective. "A Black Feminist Statement." In *This Bridge Called My Back: Writings by Radical Women of Color.* Ed. Cherríe Moraga and Gloria Anzaldúa. New York: Kitchen Table Press, 1981, pp. 210–218.

Joseph, Gloria I., and Jill Lewis, eds. *Common Differences: Conflicts in Black and White Feminist Perspectives.* Boston: South End, 1986.

Phelan, Shane. *Identity Politics: Lesbian Feminism and the Limits of Community.* Philadelphia: Temple University Press, 1989.

*See also* Essentialism; Feminism; Identity Politics; National Organization for Women (NOW); Political Theory; Race and Racism; Suffrage Movement; Women's Liberation Movement

## Situational Lesbianism

Sexual contact between women that is caused by social or other circumstantial factors, rather than by the women's internal psychological or emotional characteristics. The term implies that the women would not have engaged in lesbian behavior were it not for their unusual situation and that they are, therefore, not "really" lesbians. The term "situational lesbianism" is most commonly used to refer to same-sex activity that occurs in single-sex environments, such as between women in prison or between adolescent girls in single-sex boarding schools. The concept of situational lesbianism can also be used to describe some same-sex activity among women college students and among prostitutes.

## Locations

The classic studies of women's prison culture, including sexual culture and same-sex activity, are Rose Giallombardo's *Society of Women: A Study of a Women's Prison* (1966) and David Ward and Gene Kassebaum's *Women's Prison: Sex and Social Structure* (1965). Among women who are sexually active in prison, "true homosexuals" are distinguished from "players" or "jailhouse turnouts." The latter are women who were heterosexual prior to incarceration and who are expected to be heterosexual following their release; their sexual activity with other women in prison is attributed to the single-sex environment causing them to turn their heterosexual affections toward the only potential partners available: other women. Because their female sex partners serve as surrogates for male partners, sexual contact with them arguably does not reflect attraction to another woman but is merely a distorted expression of heterosexual attractions. These women are, therefore, not considered lesbians but, rather, heterosexuals engaging in "situational lesbianism." Giallombardo estimated that 5 percent of women prisoners are lesbians before incarceration, and wardens and inmates estimate that 50 to 80 percent of all women prisoners engage in same-sex activity while incarcerated, indicating that situational lesbianism in women's prisons is common.

Most literature on "situational homosexuality" in boarding schools pertains to males. A notable exception is work by Martha Vicinus, who examines close friendships between female students and "adolescent crushes" between female students and their female teachers in turn-of-the-twentieth-century English boarding schools. These relationships might rarely have involved actual sexual contact, but Vicinus (1989) describes them as emotionally intense and replete with sexual tension. She notes that critics characterize boarding-school friendships as "emotional training" for the girls' future heterosexual relationships. Boarding-school friendships were sometimes seen as threatening the primacy of the family in girls' priorities; therefore, these friendships were the arena in which some young women fought for independence from their families.

Contemporary young women often experiment with independence from their families and find the opportunity to pursue same-sex relationships in college. Although few colleges remain single-sex, many provide access to worldly ideas, including feminist philosophy and acceptance of sexual diversity. Women who participate in lesbian relationships during college but seek male partners thereafter are sometimes called "LUGs," or "lesbians until graduation," by women who remain lesbian after graduation. Similarly, women—in or out of college—who lived lesbian lifestyles during the 1970s heyday of lesbian feminism but who later married men have been called "hasbians." The terms "LUG" and "hasbian" effectively characterize these women as situational lesbians, who engage in lesbianism under certain conducive circumstances but return to heterosexuality once they have to find employment or settle down with a permanent partner in a heterosexist society.

Ironically, for some women, heterosexual marriage provides the situation that leads to experimentation with lesbian sex. Joan Dixon studied women in couples who "swing"—that is, engage in "mate swapping." Citing other researchers' reports that 60 to 92 percent of female swingers had engaged in same-sex contact in the context of swinging, Dixon (1985) studied women whose first sexual experience with another woman occurred while swinging with their husbands. Although the experience of these women could be characterized as a form of "situational lesbianism" caused by the proximity of another woman in a sexually permissive and charged situation, Dixon herself chose to conceptualize it as an actual change in the sexual orientations of the women involved, from heterosexuality to bisexuality.

Situational lesbianism is also found among women in the sex industry. Some prostitutes and strippers, for example, exchange sex for money with men but choose women for their partners in pleasure sex. McCaghy and Skipper (1969) studied women strippers, who pointed out that strippers do not usually meet "nice guys" and that, when they do meet nice guys, they usually ask them to stop stripping, so the strippers turn to other women for intimacy. In contrast to situational lesbianism in prison, which is due to a lack of male partners, in sex work women have plenty of access to male partners but seek female partners because of the poor quality of their heterosexual experiences.

## Controversies

The term "situational lesbianism" is controversial. It assumes that same-sex activity can be neatly attributed to either internal psychological characteristics (in the case of the "true lesbian") or to external circumstances (in the case of the "situational lesbian"). But psychologists and sociologists generally believe that most human behavior is a result of the combined effects of internal and external causes; if a given situation were the sole cause of same-sex activity, then all women in that situation would be expected to engage in the activity. Much sexual behavior that is classified as "situational" might actually reflect a capacity for bisexual response that exists in some people but is expressed only in certain situations; in this view, the concept of situational homosexuality is used to deny the existence of bisexuality. Same-sex activity among allegedly heterosexual women can also be viewed as a change in sexual orientation rather than as situational lesbianism, as illustrated by Dixon's characterization of swinging women. In the eyes of critics, "situational lesbianism" is a linguistic loophole that allows some peo-

**S** ple to maintain heterosexual identity even as they engage in same-sex activity. On the other hand, the concept of situational lesbianism accurately reflects the way in which some women, who believe that they are really heterosexual despite their sexual activities with women, experience their sexuality.

*Paula C. Rust*

### Bibliography

Dixon, Joan K. "Sexuality and Relationship Changes in Married Females Following the Commencement of Bisexual Activity." In *Two Lives To Lead: Bisexual in Men and Women.* Ed. Fritz Klein and Timothy J. Wolf. New York: Harrington Park, 1985, pp. 115–133.

Giallombardo, Rose. *Society of Women: A Study of a Women's Prison.* New York: Wiley, 1966.

McCaghy, Charles H., and James K. Skipper, Jr. "Lesbian Behavior as an Adaptation to the Occupation of Stripping." *Social Problems* 17 (1969), 262–270.

Ward, David A., and Gene G. Kassebaum. *Women's Prison: Sex and Social Structure.* Chicago: Aldine, 1965.

Vicinus, Martha. "Distance and Desire: English Boarding School Friendships, 1870–1920." In *Hidden from History: Reclaiming the Gay and Lesbian Past.* Ed. Martin Duberman, Martha Vicinus, and George Chauncey, Jr. New York: Penguin, 1989, pp. 212–229.

*See also* Bisexuality; Boarding Schools; Colleges, Women's; Prison and Prisoners; Students

## Slang

The nonstandard vocabulary of a given culture or subculture. It typically consists of arbitrary, and often short-lived, coinages and figures of speech characterized by creativity, spontaneity, and raciness. The point of slang words is often to be startling, amusing, or shocking. Slang stands out against other, more ordinary lexical items. Although they must be easily understood, slang words and expressions attract attention. It is language particular to a group, its vernacular and jargon. Slang enriches day-to-day language. Sometimes it is used to replace taboo phrases or to playfully enhance them. It sets social boundaries; slang takes words already in use, imbues them with new connotations that have meaning for the speaker and a circle of like-mined or like-aged acquaintances. The ability to compe-

tently use and understand slang codes signals that one is part of a group. The newness and the fleeting nature of slang are part of the appeal, part of who is in, who is on the edge, who is doing the trendiest things, or who can pretend they are on top of the trends by knowing the vocabulary.

Slang is dynamic. It comes from using or combining existing words in a unique way. Some of the words have a short shelf life, but others become so commonplace they move into everyday usage. When slang loses its group-identifying qualities and its freshness and appeal, and when it no longer carries any social sanctions for being used, then it has moved into standard vocabulary. When particular slang is heard over and over again, it loses impact. Slang words and expressions, therefore, wear out from overuse. Popular slang is spread in much the same way as other trends, appearing in major cities and spreading to other locales.

Lesbians have their own nonstandard vocabularies or slang. It has the purpose of showing identification with one another, and it is a part of the language lesbians use among themselves for fun, social communication, and political debate. The "lesbian culture" is actually a loosely networked collection of subcultures that are, nevertheless, conscious of some important shared experiences, shared roots, and shared values. This culture has its own myths, heroes, villains, folk epics, in-jokes, taboos, and dreams. Because lesbians as a group are outsiders, they have developed a creative lexicon that self-consciously constructs themselves as on the fringe of "normal" heterosexual values and culture. Lesbian-specific use of slang demonstrates a rich and conscious tradition within a vibrant intentional culture.

The special slang vocabulary of lesbians helps hold their culture together. It helps lesbians recognize one another and places in their communities, and it expresses shared values and experiences. Not knowing the slang, or using it inappropriately, defines one as an outsider or possibly someone new to the community. Members of lesbian culture use slang, as do members of all cultures, in several ways: as a tool of communication, as a tool of inclusion, and as a tool of exclusion.

Some segments of the lesbian community love word play and are very conscious and inventive in their use of language. These women regard slang formation and use as a game to be played for conscious pleasure. Their inventions thus display an almost unique combination of enjoyment of language play and demonstration of culturally specific intelligence. Since slang functions to make speech vivid, colorful, and interesting, speakers (lesbian and otherwise) often keep up with current trends in slang for a while during their lifetimes. Veteran community members, who have found other ways to establish lesbian identity, usually find it less necessary to keep up with the most current slang.

Because lesbians have an intentional culture (one each individual must choose by action to join), it is not surprising that competency in lesbian-community talk and particular facility in use of lesbian slang can imbue individuals with popularity and personal influence within the culture. Slang has played a central role in spreading lesbian language and the culture that goes with it. For example, many persons familiar with lesbian-community talk will know that "dyke" is a slang term that means lesbian. Once vulgar and used by speakers outside the community as derogatory, it has been reclaimed in informal lesbian talk as a noun referring to members of the community. It is a normal, ordinary, and neutral word in standard lesbian talk. Similarly, even outsiders to lesbian culture and community are probably familiar with the labels "butch" and "femme," which have long ago crossed over into heterosexual lexicon, but it is unlikely that those outside the lesbian community have a full understanding of what it means to be termed "baby butch," "one of the children," or "LUG" (lesbian until graduation). Words such as "butch" and "femme" have been slang for a long time, but most slang words either make it into accepted neutral style or else die out rather quickly.

Every speech community has its own specialized informal vocabulary. Lesbians may establish a connection of more intimacy or a sense of family by shifting metaphorical registers from formal language to talk that includes slang. Both speakers and listeners take note and interpret it as a friendly gesture, even as a sign of respect or acceptance. Language between equals or near-equals tends to be less formal, so their talk will include more slang expressions. What is slang for one person, generation, or situation, however, may not be slang for another. Hence, differences in age, race, nationality, social status, and degree of outness or lesbian visibility will all affect use of, and familiarity with, slang.

*Willa Young*

### Bibliography

Allen, Irving L. *The Language of Ethnic Conflict: Social Organization and Lexical Culture.* New York: Columbia University Press, 1983.

Eble, Connie C. *Slang and Sociability: In-Group Language Among College Students.* Chapel Hill: University of North Carolina Press, 1996.

Green, Jonathon. *Slang Down the Ages: The Historical Development of Slang.* London: Kyle Cathie, 1993.

Sornig, Karl. *Lexical Innovation: A Study of Slang, Colloquialisms, and Casual Speech.* Philadelphia: J. Benjamins North America, 1981.

*See also* Community; Dyke; Language; Subculture

## Slovenia

Republic located in middle Europe adjacent to Hungary, Austria, Italy, and Croatia and containing two million citizens. Once part of Yugoslavia, Slovenia became an autonomous and independent democratic republic in January 1992. Catholicism is the predominant religion.

It is difficult to trace lesbian women or a lesbian subculture in the Slovenian past. There were some lesbian writers and artists in the twentieth century, but they rarely wrote about explicitly lesbian themes. However, lesbianism was mentioned in a police report, *Report About Prostitution and Homosexuality* (Ljubljana, April 17, 1956), although lesbianism is not prohibited by law. The report mentions the "phenomenon of lesbian love" among prostitutes, imprisoned women, and actresses.

Homosexuality and lesbianism became visible in the 1980s when movements for civil rights and peace emerged in Slovenia. Among the groups that formed in that decade were the gay group Magnus, the feminist group Lilit, and the lesbian group LL, The first gay initiative was the Magnus cultural festival in 1984 in the capital, Ljubljana. LL was formed in September 1987 as a part of Lilit. In 1988, LL became an autonomous and independent section (Sekcija) of ŠKUC (Students' Cultural Center), formed to break the silence about the lesbian lifestyle and culture in Slovenian society. It was the first lesbian group in Slovenia and the former Yugoslavia and one of the few lesbian groups in eastern Europe.

Sekcija LL took part in annual Yugoslav feminist meetings throughout the 1980s. In that decade and the 1990s, it published different newsletters (*Lesbozine* [1987–1989], *Pandora* [1990–1996], and *Lesbo* [1997–) and organized a lesbian video and film festival, lectures, dances, meetings, summer camps, discussions, and workshops.

In 1990, LL and Magnus organized the Roza Klub (Pink Club), a political organization of lesbian and gay people. The Roza Klub fought for changes in the new Slovenian constitution that would have included the term "sexual orientation" among other personal circumstances for which discrimination is prohibited. Unfortunately, the term was not explicitly written into the new document.

Since its formation, Sekcija LL had always cooperated with and occasionally fully joined gay male and feminist organizations. In 1993, when many independent groups and individuals took over an old military barracks, Metelkova, in Ljubljana, gay, women's, and lesbian groups set up their own offices and clubs. Sekcija LL sometimes shared rooms with women's groups, and sometimes with the gay men's group. In 1993, LL established a women-only pub, Monokel, within Metelkova, although it only began to operate on a regular basis in 1997. In the same year, Sekcija LL separated from Roza Klub and began an independent program, with its own office, activities, and publication, *Lesbo*. Another lesbian group, Kasandra, was formed in 1994 at the Women's Center at Metelkova. Kasandra is a lesbian feminist group, cooperating with other independent women's organizations but not with organizations of gay men. At the end of the decade, lesbians in Slovenia could take part in different group's and activities: Sekcija LL, the mixed gay and lesbian group Roza Klub, the lesbian-feminist group Kasandra, and a gay and lesbian youth organization, Legebitra (an acronym constructed from the words for lesbian, gay, bisexual, and transgender).

By the end of the 1990s, the lesbian movement in Slovenia became increasingly dispersed among multiple activities, small groups, and political orientations.

*Suzana Tratnik*

### Bibliography

Tratnik, Suzana, and Nataša S. Segan. *L: Zbornik o Lezbičnem Gibanju na Slovenskem 1984–1995* (L: An Anthology of the Lesbian Movement in Slovenia, 1984–1995). Ljubljana: ŠKUC-Lambda, 1995.

*See also* Yugoslavia, Former

### Small Towns and Rural Areas

Although lesbian life in the twentieth century has been marked by migration to urban centers, not all lesbians live in large cities. Many have stayed in the small towns and rural areas where they grew up. Moreover, when large numbers of American lesbians embraced the lesbian separatist movement during the 1970s, many of them chose to leave cities for the countryside. Lesbian separatists believed that women had suffered by giving too much of their energy to men, denying their own needs and sacrificing themselves to the needs of others, including straight women. The separatists believed that lesbians' needs had to come first. While the separatists often created communities within cities, some established communal farms. Women's science fiction novels of the 1970s created a neopastoral vision of the countryside as a refuge from the savage inequities of male-dominated industrial society. However, achieving the purist vision of rural lesbian separatist happiness proved daunting, and most rural communities died by the 1980s.

One aspect of lesbian separatism has survived and flourished in the women's music festival. The Michigan Womyn's Music Festival has been held yearly since the 1970s in a rural area near Hart, Michigan. Other women's music festivals are held not only in the Midwest (The National Women's Music Festival at Indiana University in Bloomington and the Iowa Women's Music Festival are two), but in rural areas across the country every year, from New England to the South to the West. Wanda and Brenda Henson, who, in 1993, organized Camp Sister Spirit, have been perhaps the most publicized example of lesbians living in rural areas. They have appeared on national television and in virtually every major newspaper because of the hostility they have endured from townspeople in nearby Ovett, Mississippi.

The largest lesbian-owned publishing house, Naiad Press, moved to a rural area near Tallahassee, Florida, at the beginning of the 1980s and has flourished there since. Women continue to own land in rural areas, and a network of "women's land" developed in the 1970s continued to be active in the 1990s despite the demise of many lesbian communes. Women can still travel across the continental United States, staying on women's land rather than in conventional campgrounds or motels.

Many lesbians living in rural areas are not part of a separatist community and have reported a sense of isolation. A lack of affirmative resources and fear of rejection and ostracism have led many lesbians to remain "invisible" as lesbians in their rural areas. A British woman explained her experience in a small town: "In Woking there's just no space to actually grow the way you want to. You're very pushed into one little box and if you don't fit they're going to bang you in. It's very difficult to get out to Camberley or Guildford where there are gay groups. That's a shame because there must be loads of places like Woking where people are just choosing to conform. I tried it for a long time" (King 1989). Although they may be in a satisfying relationship with a partner, many rural lesbians, especially older lesbians, say their geographic circumstances make life difficult. A woman may drive fifty to one hundred miles to attend a meeting of a lesbian or feminist organization. The lack of public transportation and other metropolitan amenities may affect lesbians more acutely, as lesbian earning power often is weaker than that of other population groups. Divorced lesbian mothers in rural areas may fear conservative judges. The impact of the Christian Religious Right is sometimes more deeply felt in rural areas. Human rights ordinances have been passed in small towns (Douglas, Michigan), but more often they are voted down (Bloomington, Illinois, and Saugatuck, Michigan) or repealed (Lewiston, Maine). In areas of rural Oregon, lesbians have organized networks and gatherings, yet rural Oregon has also seen a strong homophobic backlash resulting in violence. Reports of violence against lesbians and gay men, however, are not limited to rural areas.

Through national publications such as the *Wishing Well* (located in rural Napa, California) or *Lesbian Connection* (Lansing, Michigan) or through local chapters of women's groups such as the National Organization for Women (NOW) and, more recently, through Internet access, many rural lesbians manage to find one another and develop a sense of community. In Bloomington, Illinois, a women's bookstore operated by lesbians was founded in the 1970s and existed as an informal community center into the 1980s. And although a human rights ordinance was voted down there in 1995, the lesbian and gay community is committed to the effort. Provincetown, Massachusetts, has long been known as a gay and lesbian resort area, but lesbians in rural areas and small towns of western Massachusetts have also established a strong cultural and economic base. Many businesses in Northampton, Massachusetts, are owned and operated by lesbians, and the *Lesbian Calendar* publicizes important cultural events there. The Northampton Lesbian and Gay Business Guild lists everything from real estate agents, to dentists, to attorneys, chiropractors, restaurants, and gift shops

in its directory. Another concentration of lesbians can be found in southwestern Michigan. Several small towns near the shores of Lake Michigan have seen an influx of lesbians that began in the mid-1980. Lakeside, Union Pier, Three Oaks, Sawyer, and New Buffalo have a significant number of lesbian landowners, and real estate agents actively promote the area to lesbians. Lesbian-owned restaurants and other businesses have become popular there. Farther north, Saugatuck and Douglas, already famous as a gay vacation destination, are home to an increasing number of lesbians.

Lesbians in rural areas have perhaps gained the most from access to the Internet, where many lesbian groups and publications exist. The Pioneers in rural southwestern Wisconsin is one of many groups that help rural lesbians and gay men connect with one another for social contact and support. By establishing home pages on the Internet, these groups have become more accessible to rural lesbians. Even lesbians who cannot afford their own computers can usually use one at a nearby library and, thus, discover organizations, activities, and resources that can assist them.                    *Karen Lee Osborne*

### Bibliography

King, Sue. *Inventing Ourselves: Lesbian Life Stories.* Hall Carpenter Archives. Lesbian Oral History Group. Margot Farnham, project coordinator. London: Routledge, 1989.

Miller, Neil. *In Search of Gay America: Women and Men in a Time of Change.* New York: Harper and Row, 1990.

Rothblum, Esther D., and Ellen Cole. *Lesbianism: Affirming Nontraditional Roles.* New York: Haworth, 1989.

Sears, James T. *Growing Up Gay in the South: Race, Gender, and Journeys of the Spirit.* Binghamton, New York: Haworth, 1991.

**See also** Collectives; Computer Networks and Services; Land; *Lesbian Connection*; Music Festivals; Naiad Press; National Organization for Women (NOW); Provincetown, Massachusetts; Recreation; Science Fiction; Separatism

## Smashes, Crushes, Spoons

Words used in the nineteenth and early twentieth centuries to describe intense emotional infatuations, with or without a sexual component, between two women. Such relationships were particularly prevalent in women's colleges and boarding schools and were widely tolerated as part of school life. A crush on another woman did not carry the same societal opprobrium as a romantic entanglement with a man. Although crushes were usually confined to the women's school years, sometimes the relationships evolved into lifelong "Boston marriages" for women.

There were informal codes of behavior governing a smash. Although it could involve a student and a teacher, the most typical smash at a women's college was likely to be between a freshman and a senior or a junior, with the younger student smashed on the older one. The infatuated younger student would shower her object of adoration with small gifts, speak of her constantly, and try to attend any school dances with her. These displays of affection were not hidden and were often spoken of openly on campus. If the freshman's admiration was returned, typically the two girls would spend the bulk of their time together, and it would be a scarcely concealed secret that they were "smashed" on each other.

As Nancy Sahli points out in her important essay on crushes, "Smashing: Women's Relationships Before the Fall" (1979), such relationships between schoolgirls were typically accepted by parents, administrators, and teachers as a phase that girls would go through before reaching maturity. Crushes, however, were not without their nineteenth-century critics, who considered crushes too emotional. For instance, Alice Stone Blackwell (1857–1950) was critical of smashes and assumed they came from "massing hundreds of nervous girls together, and shutting them up from the outside world" (Sahli 1979). Views such as Blackwell's remained the exception rather than the rule in the 1800s and early 1900s, when women's romantically charged relationships with women were regarded as a sign of their having a more emotional nature than men.

Attitudes toward crushes changed in the early twentieth century, when it became far more common to label such relationships as "abnormal." The publication of sexologist Havelock Ellis's influential book *Sexual Inversion* (1897), in which he identified girls' crushes as unhealthy and possibly being of a sexual nature, made it increasingly difficult for school authorities to view girls' crushes on other girls as asexual. In addition, the spreading 1920s interest in popular psychoanalytical theory and the work of Sigmund Freud (1856–1939) made it increasingly unlikely that such relationships would be disregarded. By the 1920s and 1930s, crushes between two women were increasingly viewed as "per-

verse" and could even result in the girls being forced to leave school. Never again in the twentieth century would same-sex crushes be perceived by the general populace as other than suspect, since such relationships might be lesbian. Crushes, however, still exist, and continue to be a significant element in lesbian fiction, particularly young-adult fiction.

*Sherrie A. Inness*

### Bibliography

Inness, Sherrie A. "Mashes, Smashes, Crushes, and Raves: Woman-to-Woman Relationships in Popular Women's College Fiction, 1895–1915." *NWSA Journal* 6:1 (1994), 48–68.

Sahli, Nancy. "Smashing: Women's Relationships Before the Fall." *Chrysalis* 8 (1979), 17–27.

Smith-Rosenberg, Carroll. "The Female World of Love and Ritual: Relationships Between Women in Nineteenth-Century America." *Signs: Journal of Women in Culture and Society* 1:1 (1975), 19–27.

Vicinus, Martha. "Distance and Desire: English Boarding-School Friendships." In *The Lesbian Issue*. Ed. Estelle B. Freedman, Barbara C. Gelpi, Susan L. Johnson, and Kathleen M. Weston Chicago: University of Chicago Press, 1982, pp. 43–65.

*See also* Boarding Schools; Boston Marriage; Colleges, Women's; Fiction; Fiction, Young Adult; Students

### Smith, Barbara (1946–)

African American scholar and activist. Born in the segregated South in 1946, Barbara Smith spent most of her childhood in Cleveland, Ohio, after her family joined great masses of rural, Southern blacks who migrated to Northern cities in search of a better life.

In high school in the early 1960s, Smith became active in school desegregation efforts, attending several speeches by Martin Luther King, Jr. (1929–1968) and meeting Mississippi activist Fannie Lou Hamer (1917–1977) following a civil rights rally. In 1965, she became one of a handful of black students who desegregated Mount Holyoke College's campus and was swept up by the budding Black Power movement and antiwar activism. In 1968, she spent a year at the New School for Social Research in New York City a pivotal year in which King and Robert Kennedy (1925–1968) were assassinated and

*Barbara Smith. Photo by Tee A. Corinne.*

in which she took part in the antiwar demonstrations at the Chicago Democratic National Convention.

Moving into graduate school directly after college, Smith felt caught in the rigidity of black nationalist views of black women and wondered how she would proceed. In 1973, she went to the first eastern regional meeting of the National Black Feminist Organization (NBFO) in New York City. From her first moments at the conference, Smith "knew I was home."

Following her first NBFO gathering, Smith both defined and championed black feminism in the academy and the community, often as the sole visible lesbian of color in countless dialogues. In the early 1970s, she founded the Combahee River Collective in Boston, Massachusetts, a group of black (mostly lesbian) feminists who did progressive, antiracist organizing around a multiplicity of issues facing Boston's black community. Combahee's "Black Feminist Statement" (1977) was an early manifesto for identity politics, a practice the group forged through such work as organizing around the murders of a dozen black women in the late 1970s.

In 1974, Smith became the first black woman to be appointed to the Modern Language Association's (MLA) Commission on the Status of Women.

She immediately moved to have other women of color appointed to the commission, and, in 1975, MLA offered its first workshops on black women's literature at its annual conference. As women's studies programs began to develop on campuses, Smith traveled widely, speaking about black women's studies as a lifesaving discipline.

In 1976, Smith met poet and activist Audre Lorde (1934–1992) at a conference, embarking on an intense friendship that would profoundly impact them both. In 1980, Smith and Lorde founded Kitchen Table: Women of Color Press, which, at the end of the 1990s, remained the sole press in the United States directed by women of color and has published some of the most important lesbian feminist academics and activists of color of their time.

Smith's scholarly works include *Homegirls: A Black Feminist Anthology* (1983) and the first volume on black women's studies, *All of the Women Are White, All the Blacks Are Men, but Some of Us Are Brave* (1982), which includes her landmark essay "Toward a Black Feminist Criticism." Smith's particular contribution as a trailblazing black lesbian feminist has been to challenge heterosexual black women and men about the diversity of sexual expressions within a black context. Simultaneously, she has raised the issue of racism within the lesbian and gay movement, creating an expanded definition of lesbian and gay issues and politics.

She has won numerous awards, including the Stonewall Award for outstanding service to lesbian and gay communities and the Lambda Award for excellence in publishing.          *Jaime M. Grant*

### Bibliography

Bell-Scott, Patricia. "Reflections from a Home Girl." *Ms.* 5:4 (January–February 1995), 59–63.

Chay, Deborah G. "Rereading Barbara Smith: Black Feminist Criticism and the Category of Experience." *New Literary History* 24:3 (Summer 1993), 635–652.

***See also*** Black Feminism; Combahee River Collective; Identity Politics; Lorde, Audre; Race and Racism; Women of Color

### Smith, Bessie (1894?–1937)

African American blues and jazz singer and songwriter. Named the "Empress of the Blues," she was the most famous of the "blues queens." She performed throughout the South, as well as in Northern cities, and her first recording, "Down-Hearted Blues" (1923), written by Alberta Hunter (1895–1984), was an enormous success. She was one of the highest-paid black artists in the 1920s and went on to record two hundred songs. In 1929, she starred in the film *St. Louis Blues*, the only visual footage of her musical artistry. Smith's voice is widely admired for its power, expressivity, urban sophistication, and improvisatory flexibility. Harrison (1988) writes that "her keen sense of timing, her expressiveness, and her flawless phrasing" influenced many jazz musicians and gospel and popular music vocalists.

Smith married Jack Gee in 1923, but their relationship was volatile, marked by brutal violence and periods of separation. Smith was bisexual, and her affair with Lillian Simpson, a chorus girl, is well documented by her niece, Ruby Walker, in Albertson's (1972) biography. Walker, herself a performer in Smith's shows, also recalls an encounter in Detroit, Michigan, between Smith and a dancer named Marie: "Jack had made one of his surprise appearances and caught Marie in a compromising situation with Bessie" (Albertson 1972). Like Gertrude "Ma" Rainey (1886–1939), Smith sang about poverty, violence, independence, heartbreak, and unorthodox sexuality with great candor. In "Foolish Man Blues" (1927), she sang, with irony: "There's two things got me puzzled, there's two things I don't understand, / That's a mannish-acting woman, and a skipping, twistin' woman-acting man." In Detroit, Smith was known to frequent the buffet flats with her girlfriends, where she enjoyed the wide variety of sexualities, including lesbianism, on display.

Smith was profoundly aware of racism in American society and rarely cultivated friendships with white people. Fiercely confrontational, in July 1927 in Concord, North Carolina, she successfully cursed out a group of robed and hooded Ku Klux Klansmen who tried to collapse her show tent.

In the last years of her life, her career suffered from heavy drinking, the general decline in popularity of classic blues, and the effects of the Depression on the recording industry. However, she continued to perform, and, like her contemporaries "Ma" Rainey, Alberta Hunter, Ethel Waters (1900–1977), and Gladys Bentley (1907–1960), she sang from a woman's perspective and demanded to be heard.

*Martha Mockus*

**Bibliography**

Albertson, Chris. *Bessie*. New York: Stein and Day, 1972.

Garber, Eric. "A Spectacle in Color: The Lesbian and Gay Subculture of Jazz Age Harlem." In *Hidden From History: Reclaiming the Gay and Lesbian Past*. Ed. Martin Duberman, Martha Vicinus, and George Chauncey, Jr. New York: Penguin, 1989, pp. 318–331.

Harrison, Daphne Duval. *Black Pearls: Blues Queens of the 1920s*. New Brunswick, N.J.: Rutgers University Press, 1988.

***See also*** African Americans; Bentley, Gladys; Bisexuality; Blues Singers; Harlem Renaissance; Rainey, Gertrude "Ma"

## Smith, Lillian Eugenia (1897–1966)

American novelist, essayist, and social critic. Born and reared in an upper-class white family in Jasper, Florida, Lillian Smith saw life change abruptly immediately after her high school graduation in 1915 when bankruptcy forced the family to move to their summer home in the mountains of Clayton, Georgia. Smith attended Piedmont College, helped her parents manage a hotel, and taught in mountain schools before pursuing her chosen career in music at the Peabody Conservatory in Baltimore, Maryland. In 1925, after three years teaching music at a girls' school in China, Smith returned to direct her father's summer camp for girls near Clayton. Through Laurel Falls Camp, Smith met Paula Snelling (1899–1985), a native of Macon, Georgia, and began the lifelong relationship that encouraged and sustained her writing career.

Between 1932 and 1934, Smith wrote her first novel, about "the shadowy relationships, intense, passionate but unnamed" between white American women missionaries and Chinese girls. "No one would dare publish this book," she later recalled. "I laid it aside knowing I might never write so personal, so terribly honest a book again" (Gladney 1993).

While developing the progressive and creative camp, Smith and Snelling coedited a small literary magazine, *Pseudopodia* (later changed to *North Georgia Review* and then *South Today*), from 1936 to 1945. Through *South Today*, her best-selling novel *Strange Fruit* (1944), and her autobiographical critique of Southern culture, *Killers of the Dream* (1949), Smith established herself as the most liberal and outspoken of white Southern writers against racial injustice. Yet her attack on racial segregation was fueled by an equally bold exploration of taboo sexual relationships—specifically, same-sex and/or interracial relationships as reflections of, and challenges to, the dynamics of power in the larger social order.

While Smith never publicly acknowledged her own lesbianism, "shadowy" relationships between women appear in significant roles in her published fiction. In both *Strange Fruit* and *One Hour* (1959), her treatment of lesbian and gay male relationships sends a clear message: Society's ideas about sexual normalcy can be as destructive to the human psyche as the deeds of a lynch mob.

Margaret Rose Gladney

## Bibliography

Gladney, Margaret Rose, ed. *How Am I To Be Heard? Letters of Lillian Smith*. Chapel Hill: University of North Carolina Press, 1993.

Loveland, Anne C. *Lillian Smith: A Southerner Confronting the South*. Baton Rouge: Louisiana State University Press, 1986.

Watson, Jay. "Uncovering the Body, Discovering Ideology: Segregation and Sexual Anxiety in Lillian Smith's Killers of the Dream." *American Quarterly* 49:3 (September 1997), 470–503.

*See also* Race and Racism

## Smyth, Dame Ethel Mary (1858–1944)

English composer, conductor, and writer. Ethel Smyth's early compositions are chiefly chamber ensemble works, and her *Mass in D* (1891) for soloists, chorus, and orchestra was her first major work to win widespread recognition. Opera, however, was Smyth's greatest passion. A large, complex, and expensive art form, very few women composers have devoted themselves to opera, and Smyth composed six: *Fantasio* (1894), *Der Wald* (1901), *The Wreckers* (1904), *The Boatswain's Mate* (1914), *Fête Galante* (1923), and *Entente Cordiale* (1925). She successfully secured performances for all of her operas and occasionally conducted them herself.

Smyth's musical language was colorful and energetic, and she drew from a variety of contemporary musical styles. Elizabeth Wood, the leading Smyth scholar, hears traces of Johannes Brahms (1833–1897), Richard Wagner (1813–1883), and Edward Elgar (1857–1934) "among the hearty bugle calls and hunting horns that echo her raucous childhood, and among the English folk tunes that she remembered and renewed in her musical vocab-

ulary" (Wood 1984). Smyth's portrayals of her women characters in *The Wreckers* and *The Boatswain's Mate* are courageous, defiant, and self-assured, as was Smyth herself.

Smyth never married and was never secretive about her lesbianism. Her first major love affair was with Elisabeth (Lisl) von Herzogenberg (1847–1892), the wife of Smyth's composition teacher in Leipzig. Later lesbian attachments, some of them unrequited, were formed with Rhoda Garrett (d. 1882), Minnie Benson (1842–1918), Mary Ponsonby (1832–1916), the Princess de Polignac (1865–1943), Emmeline Pankhurst (1858–1928), Edith Somerville (1858–1949), and Virginia Woolf (1882–1941).

In the years 1910–1912, Smyth was active in the British suffrage movement; after one action, she was sentenced to a two-month jail term at Holloway Prison for throwing stones through government officials' windows. In 1911, she composed the chorus "March of the Women," dedicated to the Women's Social and Political Union. Smyth is possibly the most iconoclastic lesbian figure in classical music, and her battle to confront discrimination against women in the music professions is well documented with great candor in her letters, essays, and nine volumes of autobiography. In 1922, she was named Dame Commander of the Order of the British Empire.

Martha Mockus

## Bibliography

St. John, Christopher [Marie]. *Ethel Smyth: A Biography*. London: Longmans, Green, 1959.

Wood, Elizabeth. "The Lesbian in the Opera: Desire Unmasked in Smyth's *Fantasio* and *Fête Galante*." In *En Travesti: Women, Gender Subversion, Opera*. Ed. Corinne E. Blackmer and Patricia Juliana Smith. New York: Columbia University Press, 1995, pp. 285–305.

———. "Music into Words." In *Between Women: Biographers, Novelists, Critics, Teachers, and, Artists Write About Their Work on Women*. Ed. Carol Ascher, Louise DeSalvo, and Sara Ruddick. Boston: Beacon, 1984, pp. 68–83.

*See also* Composers; Music, Classical; Opera; Suffrage Movement; United Kingdom; Woolf, Virginia

## Social-Construction Theory

Perspective within the social sciences based upon the understanding that social reality is constructed through the process of everyday, practical delibera-

**S**tion. Social constructionism is usually contrasted with essentialism, the belief that there is a fixed essence to individuals and groups. Among the central tenets of the perspective is the understanding that social reality is created as it is lived. Facts are themselves creations of individuals who provide accounts of them. There are no experts; everyone has opinions, based on personal interpretations of community norms, social routines, and practices. "Agreement" exists where there is a taken-for-granted sense of shared social reality.

Within any social order, including lesbian social worlds, there is an understanding of an order that is "real." Competent members of a social world use community social understanding to guide everyday sense-making. "Doing" lesbian social reality and "being" lesbian are accomplished within a social context. Becoming a lesbian community member means learning to talk and act lesbian in community settings. It means learning to do recognition of other lesbian community members in straight, or heterosexual, community settings. It means conforming to lesbian social norms. Lesbian reality and existence are contingent upon community, a taken-for-granted sense of normalcy, and defining reality in a lesbian sense.

Lesbians and lesbian community exist where and when they are made accountable. The practice of lesbian reality is carried on under the auspices of those possessing skill with, knowledge of, and entitlement to the detailed work of that accomplishment. Lesbian community is constituted by those whose competence is depended upon, recognized, used, and taken for granted as they both construct and maintain distinguishing and particular features of lesbian social reality. The existence of lesbian women and lesbian communities construct a unique social reality. To be socially lesbian, a woman must pass as lesbian in lesbian-community settings. She must do lesbian reality in order to be lesbian. This understanding replaces the old model of lesbianism as a pathological affliction. That model has largely given way to a social-scientific one, which constitutes it as an alternative lifestyle, a way of loving, a sexual preference, or a source of personal fulfillment.

Under the social-construction model, lesbians constitute the conditions for their own legitimacy by way of lesbian community. Community members interact routinely, and they seem universally to become subject to taken-for-granted common rules that both restrict and enable them. When lesbians participate in organized interchange with each other, they learn and utilize a shorthand of social practices. It is the various practices and patterns of actual behavior and the routines associated with community ground rules that together constitute a "social order."

Another principle of social-construction theory is that all social realities are partial and unstable. Although community members may sense social reality as static, in actuality more than one identity is accountable. A woman perceived as lesbian may not self-identify as such. Likewise, a woman who identifies as lesbian may not fit the community norms that allow other lesbians to identify her outside lesbian settings. Bisexual women may be mistaken for lesbian or as heterosexual, depending upon which community they are in at a particular time.

The nature of social reality does not, however, entail that positions on relevant issues are discretionary, nor that the whole process is disorderly. The everyday work of practical deliberation is highly structured because it is so strictly bound by the need to come to practical actions and by the restricted range of options a culture will accommodate within a particular framework of social reality. The concrete particulars and social norms of any situation limit the number of choices available for action by community members. How lesbian women enter the deliberations furnishes the abstract principles of lesbian community with content, limits and extends application of those principles, and makes them available for practice in everyday life.

Talk is one of the most visible means of constructing an ongoing sense of social reality and community. Linguistic markers are used by some individuals or groups to keep others in "their places." On the other hand, community members utilize language to construct and maintain a sense of everyday reality that spans the larger lesbian culture as well as bridges subcommunities, each of which has its own linguistic uniqueness. The power of language is that it can be used both by lesbians and those who would oppress them. It provides a system of relationships running through the whole of society, producing incongruent and often conflicting definitions of reality. Language can be used to construct community and to construct social structures of oppression.

Late-1990s' developments in social-construction theory deconstruct altogether the assumption of group coherence based on a shared characteristic, such as gender or sexuality. This new perspective posits that identities are multiple, fragmented, and unstable. In this view, communities predicated on identity are weak, not only because the multifarious strands of identities interact in elaborate and unpredictable ways, but also because the meanings of even seemingly singular parts of our identities, such as gender or sexual identity, should not be understood as absolute social categories. With framing principles of lesbian feminist thought such as "identity" and "community" destabilized, social-construction theory contests the very foundation of knowledge as lesbian feminists had constructed it. Still, in everyday life, lesbian-community members construct their lives while maintaining a sense of identity and community as "real."

Once lesbian reality is seen as socially constructed, it doesn't make sense to suppose that one can deduce the true significance of events. Lesbian social reality will, at best, articulate and organize complexity in some settings; and it will change social reality in an ongoing manner in ways agreeable to lesbians, as well as their antagonists.                    *Willa Young*

### Bibliography

Kitzinger, Celia. *The Social Construction of Lesbianism*. Newbury Park, Calif.: Sage, 1987.

Painter, Dorothy. *A Communicative Study of Humor in a Lesbian Speech Community: Becoming a Member*. Ph.D. diss., Ohio State University, 1978.

Phelan, Shane. *Identity Politics: Lesbian-Feminism and the Limits of Community*. Philadelphia: Temple University Press, 1989.

Pollner, Melvin. *Mundane Reason: Reality in Everyday and Sociological Discourse*. New York: Cambridge University Press, 1987.

Whisman, Vera. *Queer by Choice: Lesbians, Gay Men, and the Politics of Identity*. New York: Routledge, 1996.

*See also* Community; Essentialism; Identity

## Social Work

Umbrella term that encompasses a wide range of professional activities, conducted within the social-welfare industry. Social-work intervention falls along a continuum of skills, from work with individuals, groups, and families to community organizing and advocacy, social policy analysis, and administration.

### History

Social work has its roots in the settlement movement of nineteenth-century England, although many of the attitudes about the poor derive from the punitive and judgmental English Poor Laws of the seventeenth through the eighteenth centuries. When the settlement movement crossed the Atlantic to the United States, it shared many of the characteristics of its British origins: It was principally a volunteer effort by the wealthy to ameliorate the poverty and social decay of the impoverished.

With the insurgence of Freudian theory, the social-reform attitudes of the settlement movement were replaced by a focus on individual pathology. Social work has benefited from the healthy tension between its mission to recognize and improve social conditions and maintaining a narrow focus on the individual. The person-in-environment and ecological-practice models, for example, have emphasized the importance of examining the many social, economic, and psychological factors that contribute to client well-being.

Social work has devoted a considerable portion of the twentieth century to rebuffing early claims that it lacked professional status. The inability of social work to point to a single theoretical school and method has led some to agree that it ranks among the "semiprofessions." The very strength of the profession, however, may derive from the diverse areas that it blends (such as economics, political science, psychology, and psychoanalysis) to build its knowledge, value, and practice base.

Social-work services are delivered within a variety of fields, such as health, services to the elderly, chemical dependency, child welfare, and mental health. The methods of social-work practice are equally varied and include work with individuals and families, social-service management and planning, and community organization.

### Social Work and Lesbianism

The early days of social-work practice—namely, among the settlement houses of New York City and Chicago, Illinois—can be heralded as time when intimate friendships among women social reformers were the mainstay of well-known settlements, such as Hull House in Chicago, founded by Jane Addams (1860–1935). The very fact, however, that feminist scholarship has struggled with the issue of publicly identifying the sexuality of important historical figures even in the field of social work (typically less homophobic than many other disciplines) is a sign of the level of heterosexism that flourishes even in a profession committed to social justice and diversity.

The rise of the gay and lesbian movement, beginning with the founding of the Mattachine Society in 1950 and gaining impetus in the mid-1980s as a response to the AIDS crisis, has had an impact on the provision of services to lesbians and their families. The need for greater education and awareness on the part of social work has been highlighted. It also sparked an important controversy in the social-work field. The National Association of Social Workers espouses the need for education and understanding of lesbian lifestyles. However, the Council on Social Work Education, the accrediting body for schools of social work, has been unable to support standards that would bar colleges and universities that offer social-work degrees from discriminating on the basis of sexual orientation, opting instead for a standard of respect for human diversity including sexual orientation when it revised the standard in 1997. Given the failure of the United States Congress to extend workplace protections to gay men and lesbians, this controversy is unlikely to be resolved in the near future.

Social-service needs among lesbians exist across the life span, from identity issues among young adults and others "coming out" at various times in their life cycle, to family functioning, couple relationships, issues of terminating relationships, workplace issues, and issues specific to older lesbians.

Social-work research has shifted its focus in the 1990s from the examination of lesbianism as a pathology to the examination of lesbianism as an alternative lifestyle. Since then, heterosexism (rather than lesbianism itself) has come to seen as a significant factor in the development of social problems, such as substance abuse, domestic violence, and depression, among lesbians.

Emerging feminist scholarship in social work is exploring the role of postmodern feminist theory within social-work education, research, and practice. An important contribution in this realm is the recognition of ways that existing theoretical perspectives of all types have masked the voices of women and people of color. Although not widely explored, this growing body of scholarship promises to strengthen the ability of the profession to be more responsive to the needs of a diverse population.

*Kathleen E. Nuccio*

### Bibliography

Cook, Blanche Wiesen. "Female Support Networks and Political Activism: Lillian Wald, Crystal Eastman, Emma Goldman." *Chrysalis* 3 (1977), 43–61.

Magee, Maggie. "A Response to Weille's 'Reworking Developmental Theory: A Case of Lesbian Identity.'" *Clinical Social Work Journal* 22 (1994), 113–117.

Tully, Carol T. "In Sickness and in Health: Forty Years of Research on Lesbians." In *Lesbian Social Services: Research Issues*. Ed. Carol T. Tully. New York: Haworth, 1995, pp. 1–18.

Weille, Katharine Lee H. "Reworking Developmental Theory: The Case of Lesbian Identity Formation." *Clinical Social Work Journal* 21 (1993), 151–159.

Woodman, Natalie Jane, ed. *Lesbian and Gay Lifestyles: A Guide for Counseling and Education*. New York: Irvington, 1992.

*See also* Addams, Jane; AIDS (Acquired Immune Deficiency Syndrome); Community Organizing; Economics; Female Support Networks; Gay Liberation Movement; Psychoanalysis; Psychology

## Socialism

The ownership and control of the tools of production, as well as capital, land, and large-scale property, by the entire community. This wealth is distributed to benefit the interests of all rather than to amass private profits for the few, causing poverty for the many. Karl Marx (1818–1883) and Friedrich Engels (1820–1895) are the most noted exponents of the theory of scientific socialism, which they projected as the first major step in achieving communism—a classless, stateless form of social organization.

### Origins and Methods

To explain the laws of motion in nature, history, and human thought, Marx and Engels generated a method of logic called "dialectical materialism" (dialectical meaning that continual change occurs through contradictions; materialism meaning that existence precedes consciousness). They objectively analyzed the ascent and decline of past societies, the emergence of capitalism with its vast internal contradictions, and the class struggle it inevitably engendered. The dialectical patterns of the past showed them that the profit system would be overturned by the modern working class that capitalism itself had created. Affirming the positive power of human nature and its perennial quest for evolutionary progress, they predicted how capitalism would be replaced by the global flowering of new human relations that are necessary, rational, functional, and fulfilling.

One of their basic sources was *Ancient Societies* (1877) by U.S. anthropologist Lewis H. Morgan, which revealed how patriarchy was preceded worldwide by the natural matriarchal gens, or maternal clan. There, private ownership did not exist, all basic property was vested in the community, and labor was organized for the common good and personal pleasure.

This was primitive communism, and its overthrow could be accomplished only by what Engels called the "world historic defeat of the female sex." In *The Origin of the Family, Private Property, and the State* (1884), Engels described how the bourgeois monogamous family, which was necessary to guarantee biologically correct private inheritance, and a state to enforce this startling new family form, emerged by necessity out of the changing economic level, or degree of technology, of the time. According to the social division of labor, men controlled the cattle herds, where the first significant surpluses of wealth appeared. This situation led to the shift from reckoning descent matrilineally to reckoning it along patrilineal lines, and to women and children becoming the property of men. From this original oppression ensued all subsequent exploitation and repression, including the taboo against free sexual expression in general and homosexuality in particular. Any deviation from heterosexual monogamy was a serious threat to the wealthy ruling class.

Reelevating the status of women is, thus, central to the socialism of Marx and Engels. In the *Communist Manifesto* (1848), they called for the abolition of the father-dominated family and, along with it, the role of women as mere instruments of procreation and service to males.

## The Russian Revolution
In the Russian Revolution of 1917, V.I. Lenin (1870–1924), Leon Trotsky (1879–1940), and co-thinkers such as Alexandra Kollontai (1872–1952) and Nadezhda Krupskaya (1869–1939) were faced with the opportunity to bring the ideas of Marx and Engels to life. Lenin had paved the way for the revolution's success with his pioneer insistence on the need for a vanguard party to provide global leadership for the working class and for workers to provide leadership to the new society ("the dictatorship of the proletariat" to replace the bourgeois dictatorship).

Like Marx and Engels, the early Bolsheviks understood and expressed the essential connection between the private ownership of wealth and the degraded social position of, and denial of rights to, women, national minorities, and other suppressed groups. The Soviet constitution made both divorce and abortion easily available, eliminated the legal concept of "illegitimacy," and struck down all laws prohibiting consensual sexual conduct, including gay relations. The Soviet Union recognized a multitude of freedoms for women and access to all forms of economic, political, and cultural work. In the same spirit, the Twelfth Party Congress in 1923 ratified an initiative by Lenin granting full self-determination for national minorities.

The fledgling workers state in 1917 had to contend, however, with a huge legacy of material and cultural backwardness and a protracted siege against the new Soviet Union by all major capitalist governments. A bureaucracy arose to guard and allocate scarce goods (and skim the cream for itself), and, with the accession of Joseph Stalin (1879–1953) to power after Lenin's death in 1924, the policies of the Russian Revolution were reversed. Despite a determined Left opposition led by Trotsky, Stalin introduced the notion of the "revolutionary fighting family" (a throwback to patriarchal-monogamous norms). He condemned sexual minorities, withheld self-determination from national minorities, and espoused the concept of "socialism in one country," a complete turn away from the internationalism that had previously defined the communist movement.

## Socialism and Feminism
The fall of the degenerated Soviet Union and the Eastern European workers states at the beginning of the 1990s led Western commentators to proclaim the "death of communism." Nevertheless, socialist ideas and ambitions remain alive, especially among feminists who embrace Marxism as the basis for understanding the late-twentieth-century backlash against women, sexual minorities, people of color, immigrants, national minorities, and indigenous peoples (in tandem with the poor and workers generally). These feminist intellectuals and activists have enriched socialist thought by building upon the fundamental ideas that the patriarchal family is one of the linchpins of capitalism and that women's subordination, free labor in the home, and the absence of a majority of women engaged in wage labor have resulted in discrimination and low wages.

Socialist feminists, for example, point out that the social fortunes of sexual minorities always rise and fall in direct proportion to those of women. They see that capitalism cannot abide the homosexual threat to its roots in private ownership, private property, private profit, and inheritance by legally authentic heirs any more than it can permit women's emancipation. Lesbians, in particular, are despised or made invisible because they symbolize complete independence from men. In contrast, according to feminist materialist anthropologists, the perspective on sexuality in matrilineal, communal societies was fluid and respectful of diversity.

Contemporary feminists who have connected equality for lesbians to socialism include Charlotte Bunch, who argued the importance of lesbian feminism to the socialist movement in her 1975 speech, "Not for Lesbians Only," at the Socialist Feminist Conference at Antioch College in Ohio, and Christine R. Riddiough and Hanna Frisch, who stressed the significance of lesbian and gay liberation to social and cultural change in a 1979 pamphlet, *Women Organizing: A Socialist Feminist Bulletin,* published by the Socialist Feminist Commission of the New American Movement.

Socialist feminists also view racist oppression, like sexism and heterosexism, as organically connected to capitalism. Black lesbian feminist organizers and writers of the 1970s and 1980s Pat Parker (1944–1989), Audre Lorde (1934–1992), and Barbara Smith (1946–), writing for the Combahee River Collective, put forward a credo of revolutionary feminist leadership, developed from their own experiences, that calls for a radical movement that is multi-issue and all inclusive and a socialist revolution that is both feminist and antiracist. Midnight Sun (1988), an Anishnawbe lesbian, uses Marxist theory to analyze several sex-gender systems among North American Indians. Jewish Marxist feminist Fraser (1997), founder of the explicitly feminist and Leninist Freedom Socialist Party, argues persuasively that socialist feminism offers the most logical and advanced theory and the most successful practical results in the feminist movement.

Finally, many socialist feminists in academia provide a counterweight to the postmodernist perspective that denies lesbian identities worldwide, claiming that lesbianism is solely a Western construction. Socialists, instead, offer an integrated, internationalist analysis flowing from the historical and dialectical materialist approach of Marxism.

*Merle Woo*

## Bibliography

Moraga, Cherríe, and Gloria Anzaldúa, eds. *This Bridge Called My Back: Writings by Radical Women of Color*. New York: Kitchen Table: Women of Color, 1982.

Deaderick, Sam, and Tamara Turner. *Gay Resistance: The Hidden History*. Seattle: Red Letter, 1997.

Fraser, Clara. *Socialism She Wrote*. Seattle: Red Letter, 1997.

Lenin, V.I. *The Emancipation of Women: From the Writings of V.I. Lenin*. New York: International, 1975.

Midnight Sun. "Sex/Gender Systems in Native North America." In *Living the Spirit: A Gay American Indian Anthology*. Gay American Indians, Will Roscoe, coordinating ed. New York: St. Martin's, 1988, pp. 32–47.

Trotsky, Leon. *Women and the Family*. New York: Pathfinder, 1970.

*See also* Combahee River Collective; Lorde, Audre; Parker, Pat; Political Theory; Smith, Barbara

## Sociology

The study of social organization and interaction. Sociology seeks to explain both persistent patterns of social behavior and the factors associated with social change. Research in this discipline is often categorized as either macrosociology or microsociology. Macrosociology examines entire societies or large institutions. Microsociology focuses on individuals and their face-to-face interactions in small groups. Sociological research on lesbians has typically been conducted on the micro level.

### History

Before the 1980s, sociological studies of lesbians were scarce. Sociologists had, however, opened the subject of same-sex sexuality as early as the 1940s and 1950s, when Alfred Kinsey (1894–1956) published his now-famous reports on the prevalence of same-sex erotic experiences. The research conducted in the 1960s and 1970s on same-sex sexuality typically approached the topic from an essentialist perspective—that is, it attempted to find a root cause for gay and lesbian sexual orientation. Other studies tried to uncover a universal sequence through which individuals progressed in order to discover their gay or lesbian identities. These early works were also limited because they focused on gay men. Lesbians' experiences were assumed to be equivalent to those of gay men or were left out of the discussion entirely.

The 1980s and 1990s witnessed an increase in the amount of research on same-sex sexuality and on lesbians in particular. Despite increased attention, sociology failed to undergo a "sexual revolution," according to Arlene Stein and Ken Plummer in " 'I can't even think straight': 'Queer' Theory and the Missing Sexual Revolution in Sociology," their contribution to *Queer Theory/Sociology* (1996), edited by Steven Seidman. Research on sexuality remained on the periphery of the discipline and was not well integrated into the field as a whole. The continued shortage of gay and lesbian scholarship may be due to scholars' fears of stigmatization and discrimination. A 1982 report by the American Sociological Association's Task Group on Homosexuality found that professors and graduate students were discouraged from pursuing research on topics related to gays and lesbians. The report also found that a majority of the surveyed chairs of sociology departments thought that hiring a known gay or lesbian faculty member would create problems. Ten years later, little had changed: A survey of members of the Sociologists' Gay and Lesbian Caucus found that nearly one-third had been discouraged by colleagues and mentors from conducting research on gays and lesbians (Taylor and Raeburn 1995).

## Sociological Studies of Lesbians

In spite of this resistance, sociological studies of lesbians made great advances during the 1990s. Much of this work can be classified into two areas: theoretically driven studies that explore identity and community and empirical studies that describe the everyday life experiences of lesbians.

Theoretical discussions of lesbian identity have undergone major conceptual changes. Scholars have moved away from the essentialist view that conflates the experiences of lesbians and gay men and regards identity formation as an individualistic endeavor. In the wake of a series of studies of lesbian communities conducted by anthropologists and other social scientists in the late 1970s and early 1980s, sociologists began to view lesbian identity as a collective project.

Taylor and Whittier (1992) analyze lesbian identity formation among networks of feminists. They describe how lesbian feminist communities build a culture and ideology in opposition to dominant conceptions of femininity and women's subordination. In this context, lesbianism is viewed as the ultimate subversion of patriarchy and, thus, a political identity. Taylor and Whittier also note the importance of feminist culture for providing standards of dress and language through which women can present themselves as lesbians. Through their description, the authors present a framework for understanding lesbian identity from a social-constructionist perspective.

Similarly, Arlene Stein describes lesbianism as a socially constructed identity that is continually negotiated, revised, and redefined through interaction in social-movement communities. In her book *Sex and Sensibility: Stories of a Lesbian Generation* (1997), Stein compares lesbians from two different political generations: women who came of age in the lesbian feminist communities of the 1970s and women who came of age in the 1990s. Her analysis shows how lesbians' conceptions of self have changed over time. Lesbian communities of the 1970s were consolidated by, and centered on, a feminist discourse that defined lesbian identity based on political affiliation. Lesbian communities of the 1990s, by contrast, were highly fragmented and included multiple and competing ways of defining and presenting oneself as a lesbian, which sometimes included embracing aspects of femininity and sexualized images that the earlier generation of lesbians rejected. Through this discussion, Stein points toward understanding lesbian identity as contextual, shifting, and tied to the feminist and the gay liberation movements.

The view of sexual identity as fluid and dynamic has been further explored by research on bisexual women. Paula Rust argues that sexual identity is shifting, not only on the level of the lesbian community, but also on the level of the individual. Based on surveys of 346 women who self-identified as lesbian and sixty who self-identified as bisexual, Rust (1993) reported that both groups of women experienced considerable change in how they identified themselves, with bisexual women reporting more frequent shifts in identity over their life histories. Based on these findings, Rust suggested that scholars conceptualize "coming out" as an ongoing process of describing one's social location within a changing social context.

Esterberg (1997) also discusses lesbian and bisexual women's identities and similarly describes identity as shifting and contextual. Although earlier research has commented on the sharp divide between lesbian and bisexual women, Esterberg writes

**S** that the boundary between lesbian and bisexual women is permeable and constantly renegotiated. Some bisexual women are more integrated into lesbian networks than others. Because lesbian and bisexual women have multiple and diverse identities, Esterberg concludes that scholars should not describe the lesbian community as if it were monolithic. Instead, they should conceptualize lesbian community as overlapping friendship networks with blurred boundaries.

## Queer Theory

In addition to the growth in research on lesbian identity from a social-constructionist perspective, the 1990s also witnessed the development of queer theory. This perspective is well articulated in *Queer Theory/Sociology*, edited by Seidman. As an academic movement, queer theory examines the manifestations of sexual power in the social world. Queer theorists view the conception of homosexuality and heterosexuality as separate, and opposite, categories as a central support of the system of sexual domination. As a political strategy, queer theory attempts to disrupt dichotomous categories in an effort to subvert the sexual system. Queer theorists view sexuality as ambiguous and challenge the practice of classifying individuals as homosexual versus heterosexual or feminine versus masculine. By problematizing heterosexuality and disrupting the often taken-for-granted sexual and gender categories, queer theorists incorporate the strategies of activist groups such as Queer Nation into academic writing.

Queer theory has been criticized for being too abstract, elitist, and removed from the everyday lived experiences of gay men and lesbians. Research on bisexual women lends support to the idea that queer theory may be a powerful conceptual tool but is a difficult theory to put into practice. Bisexual women, who, like queer theorists, seek to disrupt the binary heterosexual/lesbian classification, nonetheless resort to defining themselves in those terms. Also, Esterberg (1997) argues that, although queer theorists question the utility of identity politics, the act of embracing identities has been exceedingly important to the creation of lesbian communities. As a result, having multiple identities was a sign of status within many lesbian communities of the 1990s. Recognizing this tension, the work of Stein, Esterberg, and others is informed by queer theory and the possibility of deconstructing categories, but it also recognizes that people do define themselves in terms that reify categories.

## Empirical Research

Along with the growing body of literature that has developed theories of lesbian identity, a body of research that gives voice to lesbians has also emerged. This empirical work seeks to describe the actual day-to-day experiences of lesbian women. Some of the topics explored in this literature include lesbians' experiences in the workplace and responses to hate crimes, as well as lesbian health and families.

Beth Schneider's survey of 228 lesbians has revealed much about lesbians' employment conditions. Schneider (1993) describes several common patterns that emerge in the work lives of lesbian women. First, she notes lesbians' efforts to combine their employment and their social lives, meeting friends and sometimes lovers on the job. Second, she finds that lesbians, like heterosexual women, report having experienced sexual harassment by men at work. Lastly, she discusses the factors that influence lesbians' decisions to come out at work, noting that some women fear losing their jobs if their sexual identities as lesbians are exposed.

Expanding on the study of discrimination in employment, the previously mentioned 1995 study of members of the Sociologists' Gay and Lesbian Caucus by Verta Taylor and Nicole Raeburn documents the types of discrimination reported by lesbian, bisexual, and gay faculty. The career consequences of coming out professionally and writing about and teaching gay and lesbian lives include discrimination in hiring, bias in tenure and promotion, exclusion from social networks, devaluation of research on gay and lesbian topics, and harassment and intimidation.

Concerning health and health care, more has been written in the nursing field about lesbian concerns than in sociology. A notable exception to the dearth of sociological studies on lesbian health is *Women Resisting AIDS: Feminist Strategies of Empowerment* (1995), edited by Beth Schneider and Nancy Stoller. In one essay in the book, Stoller discusses lesbians' involvement in the AIDS movement; in another, Amber Hollibaugh, the director of the Lesbian AIDS Project, discusses the myth of lesbian immunity to the HIV virus. Hollibaugh states that the assumption that lesbians cannot contract HIV is based on a limited definition of lesbianism, one that excludes women who use injection drugs or who have sex with men. Her discussion argues for a more inclusive definition of lesbians to acknowledge women who are at risk of HIV infection.

Like the literature on lesbian health, the socio-logical literature on lesbian families is also sparse. Scholars in anthropology and law have discussed some of the legal issues faced by lesbian partners and mothers in the United States and the United Kingdom. Although sociologists have been slow to explore this area, some have studied the division of child care and household work among lesbian co-parents. Others have discussed how dominant images of the ideal family in the United States and Latin America facilitate the marginalization of gay and lesbian families.

## Social Movements

Studies of social movements constitute one of the most prolific bodies of research on lesbians. In addition to the numerous works mentioned above that describe the impact of social-movement ideology on lesbian identity, several scholars have examined lesbians' connections with the feminist movement and the gay and lesbian movement. Jenness and Broad (1997) analyze the grass-roots, community response to violence against gays and lesbians. They discuss how gay and lesbian antiviolence organizations have used the discourse of the gay and lesbian movement and the women's movement to frame their concerns in broader discussions of homophobia and sexual terrorism. Jenness and Broad document the formation of several of these antiviolence projects across the country and note their success in appealing to government and law-enforcement agencies, which have, as a result, begun to take gay bashing more seriously.

Taylor and Rupp (1993) add to the literature that suggests that feminist communities are important to the formation of lesbian identity by showing that the effect is reciprocal. Lesbian identity and culture have been important to sustaining the women's movement. Early lesbian organizations, such as the Daughters of Bilitis, the main lesbian organization of the 1960s homophile movement, were tied to the emergence of the modern women's movement. Moreover, lesbian identity and activism have been integral components of a variety of contemporary movements, such as the AIDS movement, the women's health movement, the homophile movement, and the gay liberation movement.

Queer theory and the social-constructionist viewpoint on lesbian identity, which dominated the 1990s literature on lesbians, provide frameworks for understanding sexual identity. These frameworks emphasize the importance of context in shaping identity and, therefore, are able to accommodate the experiences of diverse women, including lesbians of color and working-class lesbians. Despite the inclusive potential of these frameworks, however, research on lesbians has focused largely on women who are white and middle-class. Some scholars, including Kristin Esterberg, have made efforts to include women of color in their samples and discuss the intersection of race, class, and sexuality. However, the body of sociological literature on lesbians still lacks work that focuses explicitly on women of color. Although the literature is still limited in this sense, the proliferation of research on lesbians in the 1990s in the face of the continued threat of discrimination within academia is a positive indication that this research will continue to expand, accumulating increasingly more information about an increasingly diverse population of women who identify as lesbian.

*Elizabeth Kaminski*
*Verta Taylor*

## Bibliography

Esterberg, Kristin. *Lesbian and Bisexual Identities: Constructing Communities, Constructing Selves.* Philadelphia: Temple University Press, 1997.

Jenness, Valerie, and Kendal Broad. *Hate Crimes: New Social Movements and the Politics of Violence.* New York: Aldine de Gruyter, 1997.

Rust, Paula. "'Coming Out' in the Age of Social Constructionism: Sexual Identity Formation Among Lesbian and Bisexual Women." *Gender and Society* 7:1 (1993), 50–77.

Schneider, Beth E. "Peril and Promise: Lesbian Workplace Participation." In *Feminist Frontiers.* Ed. Laurel Richardson and Verta Taylor. 3rd ed. New York: Random House, 1993, pp. 223–234.

Schneider, Beth E., and Nancy Stoller, eds. *Women Resisting AIDS: Feminist Strategies of Empowerment.* Philadelphia: Temple University Press, 1995.

Seidman, Steven, ed. *Queer Theory/Sociology.* Cambridge: Blackwell, 1996.

Stein, Arlene. *Sex and Sensibility: Stories of a Lesbian Generation.* Berkeley: University of California Press, 1997.

Taylor, Verta, and Nicole Raeburn. "Identity Politics as High-Risk Activism: Career Consequences for Lesbian, Gay, and Bisexual Sociologists." *Social Problems* 42:2 (1995), 252–273.

Taylor, Verta, and Leila J. Rupp. "Women's Culture and Lesbian Feminist Activism: A Reconsider-

**S**

ation of Cultural Feminism." *Signs: Journal of Women in Culture and Society* 19:11 (1993), 32–61.

Taylor, Verta, and Nancy Whittier. "Collective Identity in Social Movement Communities: Lesbian Feminist Mobilization." In *Frontiers in Social Movement Theory*. Ed. Aldon D. Morris and Carol McClurg Mueller. New Haven, Conn.: Yale University Press, 1992, pp. 104–129.

*See also* Community; Daughters of Bilitis; Essentialism; Feminism; Gay Liberation Movement; Identity; Identity Politics; Queer Nation; Queer Theory; Social-Construction Theory; Women of Color

### Solanas, Valerie (1936–1988)

American writer. Valerie Solanas authored "The S.C.U.M. Manifesto" (1968), a vibrant, outrageous, and brilliantly contradictory treatise on relations between the genders, and the platform for the Society for Cutting Up Men. For many years, she was most famous for having shot artist Andy Warhol (1928–1987) in 1968. A peripheral member, at best, of Warhol's Factory scene in New York City, she appeared in two of Warhol's films, *I, a Man* (1967–1968) and *Bike Boy* (1967), and sent him a script, "Up Your Ass," that Warhol neither responded to nor returned to her, thinking that, because it was so obscene, it might be a police trap. When she turned herself in to the police, she explained her attempt on Warhol's life: "He had too much control over my life" (Jobey, 1996). Her original target, however, appears to have been her publisher, Maurice Girondis: She had signed over to him the rights to her manifesto and worried that she had also given him the rights to all of her future writings. She was found incompetent to stand trial, pleaded guilty of assault, and was sentenced to three years in prison.

Solanas, who described herself once as a "garbage-mouthed dyke" and supported herself through prostitution, was a reluctant and improbable postergirl for the women's movement. After her arrest, leaders of the movement like Ti-Grace Atkinson and Florynce Kennedy heralded Solanas as a heroine of and spokeswoman for the feminist movement. Though Solonas would have no part of their attempt to exploit her as an expression of their political agenda, "The S.C.U.M. Manifesto" continues to circulate at least in academic feminist circles (often unattributed) as a foundational text of radical feminism. Feminist misappropriations of Solanas in 1968 might be interpreted as an early harbinger of the struggles within the women's movement over lesbianism, sexual aggresiveness, and nonreproductive sex practices (such as prostitution).

Largely because of the inspired rhetoric of "The S.C.U.M. Manifesto," Solanas has become a "cult" heroine, a tragic but inspired figure of lesbian outrage. Born in 1936 in Atlantic City, New Jersey, she attended college at the University of Maryland and began to pursue graduate study in psychology at the University of Minnesota. She dropped out, explaining to her family that "there was nothing relevant for women, all the professorships were for men, all the research places were for men" (Jobey, 1996). As details like these emerge and she is placed in historical context, her appeal as an unapologetic and uncompromising misfit grows. In 1996, she reemerged as public figure as the subject of a film by Mary Harron, *I Shot Andy Warhol*. Little is known about Solanas's life after her release from prison except that she died in a hotel room in San Francisco, California, in 1988.     *Jennifer Doyle*

### Bibliography

Frank, Marcie. "Popping Off Warhol." In *Pop Out: Queer Warhol*. Ed. Jennifer Doyle, Jonathan Flatley, and Jose Munoz. Durham, N.C.: Duke University Press, 1996, pp. 210–223.

Harron, Mary, and Diane Minahan. *I Shot Andy Warhol*. New York: Grove, 1996.

Jobey, Liz. "Solanas and Son." *The Guardian* (Manchester, England), August 24, 1996: T10.

Smith, Howard. "Valerie Solanas Interview." *Village Voice* (July 25, 1977), 32.

———. "Valerie Solanas Replies." *Village Voice* (August 1, 1977), 28.

*See also* Women's Liberation Movement

### Sororities

Women's organizations with a long history on college campuses in the United States. Founded originally in the late 1800s, mostly in association with male fraternities, they had their first serious upsurge in membership during the 1920s as college campuses were inundated with newly arriving middle-class students. During the 1960s, memberships declined, but, as of the 1980s, they were on the upswing again.

There are two national organizations governing sororities. The National Panhellenic Conference oversees the twenty-six historically white sororities, while the National Pan-Hellenic Council oversees the four historically African American sororities (and the four historically African American fraternities). In addition to the national sororities, there are numerous local and regional sororities across the country that are unaffiliated with these national organizations. Many of these are organized around themes of ethnicity, designed to foster multiculturalism or Latina identities, for example. A few specifically incorporate diversity of sexuality into their organizational structure.

The national sororities, both historically white and historically African American, are self-consciously heterosexual, though the white organizations tend to structure the rituals of heterosexual coupling into sorority life much more rigidly than do the African American. Despite sororities' enforcement of heterosexuality, however, over the years lesbians have quietly joined sororities. Although, as of the late 1990s, there had been no published studies done of lesbians in sororities, anecdotal evidence suggests not only a historic presence, but also the logic of joining and organization so permeated by heterosexuality.

In areas where Greek life dominates college campuses and where homophobia runs particularly deep, (such as the South), few options are open to college-age lesbians. In these situations, joining a sorority may be one of the safest acts a closeted lesbian can take. To remain an "independent" opens her up to suspicion and potential ridicule. Within the sorority, however, she is protected. A sorority not only provides a cover of sorts, but also allows her networking possibilities with other women, including other lesbians who have joined for similar reasons. Anecdotal evidence suggests that some sisters come out to their sororities, while others do not. Reactions of the sororities have been mixed. Lesbians may not be invited to join a sorority if they are out before rush (the phase during which women are invited to join a sorority), but there are no grounds for removing a lesbian from the sisterhood.

Gay men have made further inroads into Greek life than have lesbians, with a national fraternity and several local fraternities at campuses around the country. In 1988, a self-defined lesbian sorority, Lambda Delta Lambda, was formed at the University of California, Los Angeles, but, despite attempts to establish chapters at a few other campuses, the experiment did not take hold. As college campuses continue to be further sensitized to issues surrounding sexuality and other forms of diversity, local chapters of new lesbian sororities may proliferate. In addition, the heterosexual stronghold of the mainstream sororities may be further challenged. Again, anecdotal evidence suggests that, at least on some campuses, sorority presidents struggle with issues around whether women are allowed to bring other women to official sorority functions as dates and whether to participate in campus events that may be associated with the lesbian and gay community.                                    *Lisa Handler*

### Bibliography
Handler, Lisa. "In the Fraternal Sisterhood: Sororities as Gender Strategy." *Gender and Society* 9:2 (April 1995), 236–255.

Risman, Barbara. "College Women and Sororities: The Social Construction and Reaffirmation of Gender Roles." In *Women and Symbolic Interaction*. Ed. Mary Jo Deegan and Michael Hill. Boston: Allen and Unwin, 1987, pp. 125–140.

*See also* Students

## South Africa
Country of 473,000 square miles, and 42 million people, located at the southernmost tip of the African continent. The early history of lesbianism in Southern Africa has yet to be fully (re)constructed, but there is evidence that a variety of homoerotic practices and queer identifications flourished among women in this region long before the first arrival of white colonists in 1652. A traditional custom of marriage between women continues in several Southern African communities, although homophobic assumptions still inform much of the Western and African scholarship on "woman marriage" in Africa as a whole; in some southern African communities, traditional women priest-prophet-healers (*sangomas*) were independent, unmarried, and often lesbians; and in Lesotho, "mummy-baby" relationships fostered sexual relations and support networks between girls.

Twentieth-century lesbian expression in South Africa has included a variety of mostly racially specific identities and cultural practices. There was a cross-dressing subculture in the Cape Malay communities in the 1950s. White upper-, middle-, and working-class lesbians socialized in professional groups, women's sports clubs, and at private parties in towns and cities in the 1950s and 1960s. Urban white lesbian and gay bars flourished in the 1970s, and lesbian feminist discussion groups were popular among white academics in the 1970s and 1980s. Lesbians participated in anti apartheid feminist organizations like the Black Sash. Specifically lesbian political and social organizations, such as Sunday's Women in Durban, the GLOW Lesbian Forum in Soweto/Johannesburg, and LILACS (Lesbians in Love and Compromising Situations) in Cape Town, were often formed because of the marginalization of women in mixed-gender gay organizations. There was a visible black lesbian and gay presence in townships in the 1980s, and the 1990s saw glossy lesbian magazines and a significant lesbian presence in black women's soccer leagues.

Although lesbianism has never been illegal in South Africa, the fear of social ostracism has ensured that many lesbians pursued the above activities clandestinely. In 1967, the South African government proposed antihomosexuality legislation that would, for the first time, criminalize lesbians, but the new legislation was not enacted, although some amendments to existing laws were, including the outlawing of dildos.

As lesbian and gay identity became increasingly articulated by activists, so racial polarization among queer South Africans also became more explicit. In 1982, the Gay Association of South Africa (GASA) was formed. The subsequent history of GASA mirrored many of the conflicts of South Africa under apartheid. GASA was male dominated and almost exclusively white. Its stated policy of remaining "apolitical" on matters of national import made its refusal to condemn apartheid complicit with a history of brutal and systemic racial oppression. In 1988, the Gay and Lesbian Organization of the Witwatersrand (GLOW), a multiracial group committed to contesting all forms of discrimination, was founded. In 1990, GLOW organized South Africa's first Lesbian and Gay Pride March (it was also the first such march on the African continent).

In 1994, formal apartheid came to an end with the election of an African National Congress (ANC) government under Nelson Mandela. At the urging of a host of new lesbian and gay organizations aligning themselves with the antiapartheid movement, South Africa became the first country in the world to constitutionally outlaw discrimination based on sexual orientation. In 1995, South Africa's leading spokesperson for lesbian rights, Palesa Beverly Ditsie, became the first open lesbian to address the United Nations when she urged the Fourth World Confer-

ence on Women to acknowledge discrimination against lesbians in its Platform for Action.

*Ian Barnard*

### Bibliography

Gay, Judith. " 'Mummies and Babies' and Friends and Lovers in Lesotho." In *Anthropology and Homosexual Behavior*. Ed. Evelyn Blackwood. New York: Haworth, 1986, pp. 97–116.

Gevisser, Mark, and Edwin Cameron, eds. *Defiant Desire: Gay and Lesbian Lives in South Africa*. Johannesburg: Ravan, 1994.

Hammer, Barbara, dir. *Out in South Africa*. Video. 51 min. U.S.: 1994.

Krouse, Matthew, ed. *The Invisible Ghetto: Lesbian and Gay Writing from South Africa*. Johannesburg: COSAW, 1993.

Maart, Rozena. "Black Feminist in South Africa." Interviewed by Carol Anne Douglas. *Off Our Backs* 19:9 (October 1989), 1–3.

*See also* Lesotho

### Spain

Country on the Iberian peninsula, almost touching northern Africa, with a population of forty million. The capital city is Madrid, at the center of the ancient kingdom of Castille. Castilian, commonly called Spanish, is the official language, but several other languages have official recognition in their respective autonomous regions. Although the Spanish constitution of 1978 replaced the old Roman Catholic statute with a secular one, there is still a deep-rooted and widespread Roman Catholic tradition.

There is little surviving documentary evidence relating to lesbian figures in Spanish history. This may be largely the result of the influence of the Roman Catholic Church, which applied strict taboos to sexuality, considering it sinful and justifiable only for purposes of procreation. Indeed, there is little historical recognition of any sexuality at all, and none whatsoever of lesbianism.

There do exist incidental records of women who did not marry and lived together, implying some form of lesbian relationship. Women who became prostitutes, thereby achieving material independence and avoiding the need to marry, remained free to have sexual and emotional relationships with people of their choice, which may have included other women. There were others who became nuns and maintained lesbian relationships within the walls of a convent. For example, elements of homoeroticism have been interpreted in the life of Saint Teresa of Avila (1515–1582). The Spanish conquistador Catalina de Erauso (ca. 1585–1650) is an example of a woman who defied gender norms and exhibited some attractions to other women.

In all territories under Spanish control, lesbians were among the groups of people, including witches and heretics, condemned by the Inquisition (fl. sixteenth century) to be burned at the stake. Historical records relate that two nuns were executed in the mid-sixteenth century for carnal intercourse using instruments. However, after the first Spanish penal code of 1822, all mention of homosexuality disappeared from the judicial system, except for the military code of justice. This position was maintained in the reforms of 1848, 1850, and 1870. During the dictatorship (1928–1932), homosexuality was again made an offense, until the Second Republic of 1932, when it was dropped once more from the law.

Legal reforms of 1944 and 1963 allowed for the punishment of homosexuality under "scandalous public behaviour." The Vagrancy Law of 1933 was further modified in 1954 to state that homosexuals be declared "a danger." This law was redrafted as the Law of Social Danger (*la Ley de Peligrosidad Social*) in 1970 to allow the decision to be taken according to the judge's discretion. During the Franco dictatorship (1938–1975), homosexuality was seen as an epidemic that had to be cured.

After the death of Franco in 1975, during Spain's transition to democracy, a series of legal reforms were achieved, including the abolition of the 1970 Law of Social Danger. During this period, lesbians within the newly emerging feminist movement began to express their identity openly, although the debate going on in society about sexuality was still defined in exclusively heterosexual terms and centred on reproduction. The 1970s also saw a flowering of explicitly lesbian literature.

During the 1980s, lesbians remained within the feminist movement, in many cases silently, and did not organize as lesbians. Debates over sexuality became more inclusive and widespread, and feminism began to diversify and gain greater social prestige, becoming accepted in mainstream institutions that took up its cause.

Outside the feminist movement, lesbians organized according to a number of different models. Some identified as separatist lesbians, organizing separately from men and heterosexual women and fighting for the abolition of patriarchal, heterosexist institutions. They tended to be opposed to the mainstreaming of the feminist movement, preferring to concentrate on the creation of alternative women's spaces, such as bookstores. Others identified as radical lesbians, who refused to identify with the category "woman." They distanced themselves from feminism, which they believed to be dominated by heterosexism, making it what they called "heterofeminism."

Since 1980, a youth group and several political and social pressure groups have appeared, using a new style of operation to fight for legal recognition. A mixed movement was born in 1990, with lesbians working together with gay men to carry out awareness campaigns, fight against AIDS, and provide social support to the gay and lesbian community. Lesbian groups within the mixed movement do not adhere to any one political or feminist ideology but are characterized by a wide range of tendencies and ideologies within a common framework. Grup Lesbia, which was formed in 1990, changing to Grup Lesbos in 1994, works within the Coordinadora Gai-Lesbiana, which arose in Barcelona in 1980. Within this federation, women may be found working in groups of gay and lesbian youth, Christians, and university students.

There are also mixed associations that carry out leisure and cultural activities in conjunction with gay men, rather than exclusively for lesbians. These mixed organizations work toward increasing and improving the opportunities available to gays and lesbians by providing services and encouraging political lobbying around legal, educational, religious, youth, feminist, and AIDS-oriented issues. Radical groups can often be found working in specific areas in common with feminist lesbians and lesbians from the mixed movement.

*Maria Angeles Ruiz Torralba*

### Bibliography

Aliaga, Juan Vicente. *Identidad y Diferencia: Sobre la Cultura Gay en España* (Identity and Difference: On Gay Culture in Spain). Barcelona: Editorial Gay y Lesbiana, 1997.

***See also*** Erauso, Catalina de; Europe, Early Modern; Spanish Literature; Teresa of Avila

## Spanish Literature

There are no literary histories of lesbian lives as represented in Spanish texts. References to intimate re-

**S** lationships between women seem either written in disappearing ink or undecipherable to a society that has suppressed nonprocreative forms of human sexual experience.

The religious tradition of the Virgin Mary cult produced an ideal of purity and an inhibition of sexual desire that became institutionalized. The permissiveness of Moslem society toward homoerotic love ceded to Christian asceticism; medieval laws and the Inquisition enforced this; and censorship under twentieth-century dictator Francisco Franco (1892–1975) continued sanctions.

In broad terms, including, but not limited to, explicit erotic relations between women, traces of lesbian identities in Spanish literature assume a variety of guises. Among them are characters that cross bounds of social or sexual propriety, women who undertake male-identified activities or don masculine attire, and figures of powerful women living independently of men. A text that questions the exclusion of women from roles other than dutiful daughter, faithful wife, obedient nun, or sacrificing mother offers an alternative vision.

**History**

Female characters in medieval literature are divided into the idealized and the condemned (for their strength or aggression toward men). Thirteenth-century epic poems contain folk motifs of Amazon warriors who have no need for the company of men except to mate. This stereotype is also found in the *serranillas* (mountain women who entrap male travelers). Such figures satirize women who refuse to be sensible, prudent, or passive.

The mystic body, exalted by sixteenth-century Carmelite nun St. Teresa of Avila (1515–1582), indicates a turn away from ascetics. Her allegorical penetration of the heart by the flame of ecstatic experience has been called a "divine jouissance," the literary expression of pleasure not traditionally accorded woman in body or spirit. Within the convent—both enclosure and space of female community—St. Teresa recovers a language of sensuality. Her writings inspired nineteenth-century poet Carolina Coronado to call Sappho (ca. 600 B.C.E.) and St. Teresa twin souls of intense spirit and novelist Jesús Fernández Santos to write *Extramuros* (Outside the Walls [1977]), exploring the confluences of mystic and lesbian desires.

The memoirs of lieutenant-nun Catalina de Erauso (ca. 1585–1650) narrate her adventures passing as a man. Basque by birth and a fortune hunter in the American Colonies, she cross-dressed and used masculine-gendered pronouns for self-reference. It is unclear whether Catalina rejected heterosexuality, the social convention of marriage, confinement to a religious order, or all of these. Episodes suggestive of liaisons with other women are elliptical and sketchy. Attracted to physical beauty, she acquiesced to one woman's caresses but rejected another as "black and ugly as the devil himself." Toward the end of her life, Catalina confesses to a bishop that she is a woman and a virgin. Her ambiguous figure serves as the model of a *virago* (a woman of "mannish" demeanor and spirit) for Golden Age writer María de Zayas, who composes a number of texts based on amorous intrigues and deceptions precipitated by confusions of identity.

Spanish drama of the Renaissance continues the formulaic character of the *mujer esquiva* (a cold, distant woman who refuses the amorous attentions of men). Based on classical sources such as Ovid, this masculine woman threatens male authority in plays by Lope de Vega (1562–1635) and Agustín Moreto (1618–1669). Their challenge to "natural" order might seem, in the twentieth century, a rejection of straight society, but it is less clear in seventeenth-century context. Scholars are debating the possible subversive undertones in the representation of mistaken sexual identities in Spanish Golden Age (sixteenth-century) drama (a confusion always corrected by the end of the play). Some reject the suggestion of lesbian motifs in these works as universalizing impositions; others seek parallels between documented phenomena of everyday life and artistic representation of sexual irregularities. Medical, legal, social, and philosophical discourses of the time may yield more information regarding correspondences between assumptions of sexual "normality" and the appearance of the character of the "masculine woman."

The same holds true for the use of the term "butch-femme" in reference to the representation of the female body by the Dulcinea/Aldonza characters of *Don Quixote* (1605). It has been suggested that the interaction between Hispanic scholarship and lesbian theory—like the relationship between the characters encoded as masculine and feminine by the society in which this work by Miguel de Cervantes (1547–1616) was produced—affords an opportunity to reinterpret literary texts and their potential for transgressing the norms of what constitutes gender identity. The idealization of the "feminine" in the character Dulcinea is juxtaposed with the traits attributed to Aldonza, who offers a performance of masculinity by a woman directed toward another woman. Their dual embodiment of women's desires may be read as counteracting the stereotypes of women or the invisibility of what is seen to fall outside societal "norms."

In the 1840s, women poets of the Romantic period found intellectual muses in Sappho of Lesbos and St. Teresa of Avila. Each inspired passionate devotion to writing, but both were read as addressing their erotic poetry to men. During the first three decades of the twentieth century, only Federico García Lorca (1898–1936) created characters (such as Bernarda Alba) whose rebellious spirits and irrepressible sensuality are socially encoded as masculine. Imbedded in rigid codes of heterosexual conduct, they are all doomed to sacrifice.

## The Post-Franco Era
With Francisco Franco's death in 1975, thirty-six years of repression came to an end. Feminism, Basque, and Catalan separatist movements and gay liberation—a conjunction of the traditionally dispossessed—exerted strong influences on the literature of the post-Franco era. Writers dealt more openly with the intersections of desire, class, and nation and explored conflicts between generations of women. Lesbian characters emerged from the shadows of earlier novels, such as Ana María Matute's *Los soldados lloran de noche* (Soldiers Cry by Night [1964, 1995]), into the foreground.

Barcelona, the capital of Catalan culture, and the Catalan language itself, were primary sites for this literary flowering. In "La búsqueda de Elizabeth" (The Search for Elizabeth [1982]), Marta Pesarrodona weaves a "coming out" tale set in 1970s London. A voyeur in Ana María Moix's "Las virtudes peligrosas" (Dangerous Virtues [1982]) uncovers the power of an erotic gaze between two women. Moix's novels explore social obstructions to female-female relationships, while suggesting their potential for psychological fulfillment. In Montserrat Roig's *La hora violeta* (The Violet Hour [1980]), a character whose intimate bonds with other women are only promises represents potential lesbian sexuality. *Te entrego, amor, la mar, como una ofrenda* (I Give You, Love, the Sea, as an Offering [1975]) by Carme Riera is composed as a letter following the suicide of a woman separated from her female lover by paternal prohibition. For María Jaén, a public bathhouse offers space for physical and emotional encounters between women in *Sauna* (1987).

As director of the Editorial Lumen in Barcelona, Esther Tusquets has actively promoted writing on the cutting edge of gender issues. The core of a trilogy of her own novels is the theme of lesbian erotics. In *El mismo mar de todos los veranos* (The Same Sea as Every Summer [1978, 1990]), *El amor es un juego solitario* (Love Is a Solitary Game [1979, 1985]), and *Varada tras el último naufragio* (Stranded [1980, 1991]), language and the lesbian body become battlefields. Through the use of images which bind them to nature and the earth, characters seek a separate, precultural space, similar to that proposed by French author Monique Wittig (1935–). Bourgeois women reveal social rituals and performances as rites of passage into the patriarchal adult world. The three novels are based on adaptations of classical myths and center on a middle-age woman caught between an empty marriage and a young woman who embodies the "natural" eroticism of the American continent.

*Claudia Schaefer*

## Bibliography
Bergmann, Emilie L., and Paul Julian Smith, eds. *¿Entiendes? Queer Readings, Hispanic Writings*. Durham, N.C.: Duke University Press, 1995.

Brown, Joan L., ed. *Women Writers of Contemporary Spain: Exiles in the Homeland*. Newark: University of Delaware Press, 1991.

Miller, Beth, ed. *Women in Hispanic Literature: Icons and Fallen Idols*. Berkeley: University of California Press, 1983.

Pérez, Janet. *Contemporary Women Writers of Spain*. Boston: G.K. Hall, 1988.

Smith, Paul Julian. *The Body Hispanic: Gender and Sexuality in Spanish and Spanish American Literature*. Oxford: Clarendon, 1989.

———. *Laws of Desire: Questions of Homosexuality in Spanish Writing and Film, 1960–1990*. Oxford: Clarendon, 1992.

*See also* Erauso, Catalina de; Saints and Mystics; Sappho; Spain; Teresa of Avila; Wittig, Monique

## Spinsters
Conventional and often derogatory term for single women. Feminists, especially lesbians, have sought to reclaim the term "spinsters" from U.S. culture's ageist and heterosexist views of older single women. Examinations of when and how the deroga-

**S** tory connotations came to be associated with this term are part of a larger analysis of both the denial and invisibility of single women and the lack of positive terms for women who do not marry. While a number of feminists have examined the origins of this word and its use in mythology, others have studied the lives of single women in the United States and the United Kingdom. While the asexual, repressed spinster has often been contrasted with the sexually predatory lesbian in popular culture and psychological literature, lesbians, from writers such as May Sarton (1912–1996), through women's businesses such as Spinsters Ink, are contributing to a reimaging of this term.

Scholars have argued that only in Western tradition has the "spinster" been defined so negatively. Within feminism, this term has taken on the meaning of a woman who chooses her own definition, and is autonomous, and without connections to husband or children. Others have uncovered powerful roles for older women as crones in pre-Christian religions and cultures.

Historians such as Chambers-Schiller (1984), Vicinus (1985), Jeffreys (1985), Meyerowitz (1988), and Franzen (1996) have studied the lives of spinsters in the United States and the United Kingdom. Chambers-Schiller's study of single women through the early part of the nineteenth century found that, for many of these women, economic factors limited their mobility and kept them assigned to family-support roles. Vicinus, Jeffreys, and Franzen discuss how these options changed with greater economic opportunities for middle-class women. Vicinus provides a full examination of the lives of middle-class British spinsters who built supportive communities while also providing leadership in the emerging professions. Jeffreys argues that these "redundant women" posed a challenge to the heterosexual order, producing a backlash in which legal, economic, and ideological constraints undermined turn-of-the-twentieth-century opportunities for women's independence.

In the United States, feminist historians early noted the role that Euro-American, middle-class, single women played in the women's movement of the nineteenth and twentieth centuries. Spinsters, from Susan B. Anthony (1820–1906) through Jane Addams (1860–1935), were disproportionately represented among the leaders of women's diverse efforts in social reform. Many of these women had women partners, and historians have argued over the appropriateness of calling these women lesbians.

Simmons (1979) argues that these women, who led women-centered public and private lives, were perceived as a threat to heterosexuality even among progressive reformers.

Spinsters/single women do not appear to have the same role among African Americans. African American Progressive Era (1890–1920) women leaders more often combined marriage and motherhood with careers and public leadership roles than did white, middle-class women. The position of single women within African American communities needs fuller exploration.

An acknowledgment of women's sexuality that contradicted the image of both the asexual celibate spinster and the sexually vulnerable working-girl victim, along with greater economic opportunities for women signaled the next turn in the fortunes of the spinster. According to many nineteenth- and early-twentieth-century sexologists, the asexual never-married woman was repressed, while the too sexual independent woman, either heterosexual or lesbian, was promiscuous or menacing. It has been against the former image that feminists have directed their rehabiliation efforts. *Trisha Franzen*

### Bibliography

Chambers-Schiller, Lee V. *Liberty: A Better Husband.* New Haven, Conn.: Yale University Press, 1984.

Franzen, Trisha. *Spinsters and Lesbians: Independent Womanhood in the U.S.* New York: New York University Press, 1996.

Jeffreys, Sheila. *The Spinster and Her Enemies: Feminism and Sexuality, 1880–1930.* London: Pandora, 1985.

Meyerowitz, Joanne M. *Women Adrift: Independent Wage Earners in Chicago, 1880–1930.* Chicago: University of Chicago Press, 1988.

Simmons, Christina. "Companionate Marriage and the Lesbian Threat." *Frontiers: A Journal of Woman Studies* 4:3 (Fall 1979), 54–59.

Vicinus, Martha. *Independent Women: Work and Community for Single Women, 1850–1920.* Chicago: University of Chicago Press, 1985.

*See also* Addams, Jane; Anthony, Susan B.; Sarton, May

## Spirituality

Term referring to human interest in, and communication with, forces ("spirits") that are believed to possess power to help or harm people. Spirituality is rooted in the human desire for support, strength, and guidance in life. "Religion" denotes an *organized* or *institutional* basis through which spiritual practices, stories, and symbols are shared. "Theology" usually refers to the *study* of historical, cultural, and other contexts and meanings of particular religions or spiritual traditions.

## Background

In Western religions, spirits such as gods, goddesses, angels, and demons have been experienced by believers as present but hidden in everyday life. Such spirits become accessible through the practice of "prayer." Other common spiritual practices in the history of Western religions have included the offering of blood sacrifices to the spirits, sharing a common meal that has been blessed by gods or goddesses, and "channeling" spiritual energy from the dead to the living.

In the last third of the twentieth century, feminist movements have generated a renewed interest in spirituality among women of different religions, races, and cultures. This woman-based spiritual renewal has shaken the foundations of dominant patriarchal Western religions, particularly Christianity and Judaism (and, to a lesser degree, Islam). In their efforts to shape spiritual resources that empower women, feminist theologians have drawn upon contemporary women's experiences, together with research into the silenced voices and outcast lives of women in patriarchal religious history. Such theologians have challenged the primacy—indeed, the existence—of "God the Father" and the authority of male-defined dogma and male-controlled religion.

Some feminist theologians have opted to work toward transforming patriarchal religions from within. Others have chosen to labor outside the traditions to build women's spiritual communities and to renew women's spiritual traditions. Many women who have left patriarchal religions have aligned themselves with the old, woman-centered, "wiccan" tradition with its roots in Celtic spirituality or with other religions that have been persecuted by Western Christianity (spiritualities, for example, that are indigenous to Native, African, or Latin American peoples).

## Lesbians and Spirituality

Because lesbians represent a foundational challenge to patriarchal spirituality, they must either deny (often even to themselves) the woman-affirming basis of their spiritual energies in order to survive in traditional, male-defined religion and society, or be "out" (at least to themselves) in search of liberating spiritualities that celebrate their love of women (including themselves). In fact, most lesbian feminists (lesbians with some political consciousness of what it means to be lesbian in heterosexist socity) live amidst the fluid dynamics of denial and consciousness. In the United States, some of the most articulate lesbian writers in the last half of the twentieth century—poets such as Adrienne Rich (1929–), Pat Parker (1944–1989), and Audre Lorde (1934–1992)—have artfully presented these dynamics of ambiguity and struggle as the spiritual "stuff" of their lives.

Since the Stonewall Rebellion of 1969 (the historical event that brought homosexuality itself "out of the closet") and the emergence of the feminist movement in the early 1970s, many "out" lesbians have helped generate, and have benefited from, at least seven spiritual movements in the United States. These movements frequently have overlapped, and many lesbians have derived benefits from all of them. Grammatical use of the plural with reference to these "spiritualities" is meant to convey a multiplicity of spiritual practices and assumptions even within movements that shared common goals and values:

*Goddess-centered Spiritualities.* Associated with such late-twentieth-century spiritual teachers, healers, and witches as Margot Adler, Starhawk, Luisah Teish, and Carol P. Christ, these diverse streams of spirituality, some of them multicultural, have provided resources for lesbians and other women who have renounced (or never belonged to) patriarchal religions. They also are important to lesbians who remain active, to some degree, in male-defined spiritual traditions, ranging from predominantly white, mainline churches, to the Black Church, to male-oriented currents of such Native and African-derived religions as Yoruba.

*"Post-Christian" Spiritualities.* Unlike Goddess spiritualities, with their roots in ancient cultures, post-Christian spiritualities are a product of the predominantly white feminist movement in the United States. They have spread, especially in Europe and other Western, Christian-based cultures, during the last quarter of the twentieth century. Originating in the early 1970s work of lesbian feminist philosopher Mary Daly (1928–), post-Christian spirituality

**S** is a radically woman-affirming (not necessarily Goddess-centered) alternative to patriarchal religion. Post-Christians do not see any value in attempting to transform Christianity.

Some post-Christian lesbians, such as Sally Gearhart, Emily Culpepper, and Nelle Morton, have become allied with Goddess spiritualities. For many lesbian and other women who are still practicing Christians or Jews, such theologians have provided important bridges between women's experiences (of, for example, their mothers or their sexualities) and Goddess spiritualities.

*Feminist, Womanist, Mujerista, and Other Woman-affirming Liberation Spiritualities.* In the United States, these theological currents have originated in the academic and congregational efforts of radical Christian and Jewish women and have been given voice by such late-twentieth-century white Christian feminists as Rosemary Radford Ruether, Beverly W. Harrison, Letty Russell, Elisabeth Schussler Fiorenza, Sharon Welch, Susan Thistlethwaite, and Sallie McFague; Jewish feminist Judith Plaskow; Christian womanists Delores Williams, Katie Cannon, and Emilie Townes; *mujerista* (a self-description used by many Latina theologians, often in place of feminist) Christians Ada Maria Isasi-Diaz and Yolanda Tarango; and Asian and Asian American Christian feminists Kwok Pui Lan, Chung Hyun Kyung, and Rita Nakashima Brock.

The distinctive, unifying, characteristic of these culturally diverse theologians is their threefold emphasis on (1) the bias of the Good Spirit(s) for poor and oppressed, outcast, and marginalized people, especially women; (2) the movement of the Spirit(s) in history through human commitment and action; and (3) the explicitly political and economic bases of spiritual movement in history. These liberation theologians vary in how much attention they give the sanctity of other-than-human creatures and the Earth and also in whether they emphasize sexual relationship, play, and pleasure as a source of empowerment and liberation in women's lives.

*"Erotically Empowering" Lesbian Christian Spiritualities.* Much of the explicitly sex-affirming spirituality in the United States has been shaped by lesbian Christians and post-Christians, perhaps largely because the church has been for so long a source of such vilification of female sexuality. Such Christian (and post-Christian) lesbians as theologians Carter Heyward, Virginia Mollenkott, Anne B. Gilson, Re-

nee Hill, Irene Monroe, and Melanie May; biblical scholar Bernadette Brooten; ethicist Mary Hunt; historians Ann Matter and Joanne Carlson Brown; and churchwomen Nancy Krody, Sandra Browders, Nancy Wilson, Sandy Robinson, Mari Castellanos, Diane Neu, Janie Spahr, and Melanie Morrison have understood women's sexual energies as a source of spiritual power for creativity and liberation.

Along with other feminist, womanist, and *mujerista* liberation spokeswomen, the presence of many erotic-celebrative lesbian Christians continues to fuel prophetic efforts within the churches to open up ordination processes and marriage to sexually active lesbians, gay men, bisexuals, and transgendered persons.

*"Recovery" Psychology and "Step" Spirituality.* Generated by widespread recognition among lesbians and other women of their addiction to alcohol or other drugs, or of their experiences of childhood sexual abuse, a psychospiritual culture of recovery emerged during the 1980s. During this period, psychotherapy became a refuge for many "survivors" of abuse and for women suffering from addiction. At the same time, many lesbians began to attend "step" programs in response to their addiction or abuse. Some of the best therapy, as well as the step programs, with origins in the twelve steps of Alcoholics Anonymous, have enabled many to live "in recovery" with a deeper sense of serenity. On the other hand, some lesbian feminists have rejected the twelve-step program of Alcoholics Anonymous, contending that its founding by evangelical Christian men in the 1930s continues to shape its spirituality. For these women, the steps simply reinforce patriarchal values of women's submission to a "higher power."

*"New Age" Spiritualities.* Evoked by the same pain and hope as the step programs, psychotherapy, and the resurgent popularity of spirituality among women toward the end of the twentieth century, New Age practices—such as Tarot readings, sitting with crystals, mutual conversations with animals, past-life memories, channeling, and astrology—have been common among lesbians. The term "New Age" refers to a deep desire, shared by many, that the old order of violence and massive social decay is giving way, mystically, to a new age of harmony and well-being for all who can see it, hear it, and believe it. Many lesbians have found certain New Age practices helpful, even though they sometimes do not subscribe to its otherworldly emphasis. What

"worldly" lesbians may find insightful in the philosophy of New Age is the assumption that all lives are connected, human and other creatures, in all times; and that human actions should reflect this radical interdependence.

*Meditation and Other Spiritual Practices Based in Buddhism, Other Eastern Religious Traditions, and/or Western Mysticism.* These ancient resources, especially the practice of meditation, have been introduced to many lesbians and other women through the teachings of such contemporary Buddhists as Joanna Macy of the United States and Thich Nhat Hahn of Vietnam. Though not necessarily feminist or lesbian, teachers and practitioners of meditation—like some therapists, step programs, and New Age practitioners—suggest paths by which individuals and groups can live in greater peace with one another and themselves. Many lesbians experience such practices as sources of personal strength, hope, and joy. When grounded in socially responsible and politically active commitments, much as Thich Nhat Hahn and Joanna Macy exemplify, these spiritualities can be wellsprings of justice-making.

In addition to the more explicitly spiritual movements, many other cultural resources—poetry, fiction, drama, music, sports, film, and philosophy—have contributed to the formation of lesbian spiritualities.                    *Carter Heyward*

### Bibliography

Daly, Mary. *Beyond God the Father: A Philosophy of Women's Liberation.* Boston: Beacon, 1973.

Heyward, Carter. *Touching Our Strength: The Erotic as Power and the Love of God.* San Francisco: Harper and Row, 1989.

Plaskow, Judith, and Carol P. Christ, eds. *Weaving the Visions: New Patterns in Feminist Spirituality.* San Francisco: Harper San Francisco, 1989.

Spretnak, Charlene, ed. *The Politics of Women's Spirituality: Essays on the Rise of Spiritual Power Within the Feminist Movement.* Garden City, N.Y.: Anchor, 1982.

**See also** Black Church, The; Catholicism; Goddess Religion; Islam; Judaism; Lorde, Audre; Parker, Pat; Protestantism; Recovery Movement; Rich, Adrienne

## Sports, Professional

The visibility of lesbians in professional women's sports has become an increasingly controversial issue for the general public. At the same time, such professionals often serve as invaluable role models for lesbians coming out. Their presence is important because the allure of sport(s) runs throughout American life. It is taught in schools, actively enjoyed by participants of all ages, enthusiastically watched by all generations and races on televisions, and discussed avidly by women and men. Sport is, in fact, a major industry amid consumer culture. It absorbs countless hours of leisure, fuels regional rivalries, provides a distinct, if limited, upward mobility for athletes of all races, and has become a source of escapist entertainment for numerous devotees.

### History: Sport and Femininity

Women's "place" in professional sports competition has been an ambivalent cultural legacy. The acceptable parameters of physicality have varied widely according to a woman's social class, region of origin, ethnicity, and race. For example, in the 1870s women's wrestling was a "titillating spectator sport performed by women in music halls and theaters" (Fox 1989). Boxing, pursued by working-class and ethnic women in the 1880s, also enjoyed a brief heyday. The editor of the popular *Police Gazette* sports magazine in the 1880s promoted female pugilists. Evidence suggests the editor/promoter never took female fighting seriously, yet "he did crown the woman champion of New York, a powerful-amazon named Alice Jennings, who had a great left hook" (Fox 1989). Other stunt types of female athleticism gained popularity at the turn of the twentieth century—most notably, Annie Oakley's (1860–1926) trick shooting. Oakley exploited narrow definitions of ideal femininity; she appeared in corseted waist, tight dark stockings, short dress, and leather boots. While these cast both a fetching and a daring image, they discredited women athletes who sought mainstream acceptance. At the professional sports level, virtually all athletes were judged and constrained by middle-class, western European ideals of appropriate femininity. Despite the rise of college athletics at all-female schools from the 1870s onward and the popular acceptance of exercises such as bicycling, ice skating, tennis, and golf from the 1890s onward, women athletes who sought professional athletic careers met with resistance and bias.

The modern Olympic Games, which served as a conduit for some athletes to enter the professional (money earning) ranks, were overwhelmingly hostile toward female athletes. This disdain was directed with particular virulence toward women who

**S** were deemed unfeminine or whose sports were, according to Pierre de Coubertin, International Olympic Committee president (ca. 1900), "against the laws of nature."

General columnists and sportswriters dichotomized women's sports into distinct categories: "beautiful sports" (golf, swimming, trapshooting) versus "manly sports" (track-and-field events and basketball). Beautiful sports were deemed by male writers, as well as some accommodationist female scribes, as ones in which women did not sweat, wore attractive costumes, and did not develop musculature. "Manly sports," conversely, were team sports, necessitated physical contact (which fueled fears of lesbianism), produced musculature, and encouraged a psychological fierceness and disregard for femininity. These terms ruled popular perceptions of women athletes in the 1920s and 1930s. Demonstrably, one commentator earnestly wrote: "Nice girls don't sweat."

### Questioning Sexual Orientation

Speculation about a female athlete's sexual orientation were rife in this cultural context. In 1933, Paul Gallico, a well-known sportswriter speculated about the sexuality of "Babe" Didrikson Zaharias (1911–1956), winner of three Olympic medals at the 1932 Games, a national basketball champion, and an excellent athlete in several other "manly sports." In *Vanity Fair,* he riddled Didrikson Zaharias with accusations of being neither male nor female and discussed, but dismissed, her lesbianism. Thus, another category was created for stellar female athletes: muscle molls, or members of a "Third Sex." Gallico, like others of his era, "wrote about her as a member of a breed of 'women who made possible deliciously frank and biological discussions in the newspapers as to whether this or that woman athlete should be addressed as Miss, Mrs., Mr. or It'" (Cayleff 1995). One historian has argued that women athletes were considered an "intermediate sex" who had "shed their primary identity as women before the world they inhabited accepted the legitimacy of androgyny." As such, they were condemned, ostracized, and legally censored.

Not surprisingly, sex testing emerged at the Olympic level. In 1936 at the Berlin Olympics, there was widespread speculation about the chromosomal and gender identity of women track-and-field athletes. A few highly touted cases fueled these suspicions. Some female athletes were male, and others were pseudo-hermaphrodites, according to the athletes' confessions and to contemporaries who relied on visual inspections. Most notable was Stella Walsh, a Polish American who captured thirty-five national championships between 1930 and 1951. Upon her death, an autopsy was performed and she *was* discovered to be biologically male.

The specter of nonfemale women athletes clung to top-level women's sports. It reached its apex in 1966 at the women's track-and-field championships in Budapest, Hungary, when athletes were required to parade nude in front of a panel of three women gynecologists. Outraged by the invasion of privacy, 234 participants complied and passed incontrovertibly. Yet several prominent Eastern European athletes failed to show up, causing speculation in *Time* and *Life* magazines about women athletes' "normalcy."

### Lesbians and Sport

In the 1940s, to compensate for the diminished content of major league baseball due to World War II, Chicago Cubs owner Philip K. Wrigley launched the All-American Girls Baseball League (AAGBL). This league, which flourished from 1943 to 1954, used the gender issue in sports to its advantage as an ingenious way to market its brand of baseball. By demanding that its players combine "masculine" athletic skill with feminine appearance, the AAGBL maintained a clear distinction between male and female roles, yet provided fans with skillfully played baseball.

Homophobia within the league was ever present. Athletes were chosen for their feminine looks, as well as their ball-handling skill. All members were made to attend company-sponsored poise and beauty classes, and uniforms were highly impractical short skirts. Players earned $40 to $85 per week in the early years of the league and up to $125 later on. The AAGBL Handbook, in the section "Femininity with Skill" noted: "The more feminine the appearance of the performer, the more dramatic the performance." It went on to say that "boyish bobs and other imitations of masculine style and habit are taboo. Masculine appearance or mannerisms produce an impression either of a masculine girl or an effeminate boy; both effects are prejudicial [to the desired image]." Management ordered players to keep their hair shoulder length or longer, to wear makeup and nail polish, and never to appear in public wearing shorts, slacks, or jeans. Those who failed to comply, Cahn argued (1994), felt "the sting of a shortened pay check." Tomboys, Amazons, and freaks—all disparaging words used to denote unfeminine athletes—were scorned at every turn.

The AAGBL barred women of color (with the exception of several Cuban Americans) and recoiled at the possibility of lesbians. While lesbian relationships existed, maintaining one's position in the league depended upon masquerading under these ideals of heterosexuality.

The 1950s continued to reflect this hostility toward lesbianism, real or imagined, in women's professional sports. Despite the women's and gay liberation movements of the 1960s, little changed for professional women athletes. The subculture of nonprofessional athletes, however, did change dramatically as a result of these liberation movements. Lesbian subculture in women's softball and the emergence of the first Gay Games in 1982 provided unprecedented opportunities for lesbian athletes to compete in nonhomophobic environments. Yet even the passage of Title IX of the Education Amendments Act of 1972, which guaranteed proportionately equal funding for women's sports at any school level, did not substantially change the tenuous lot of lesbians in sports.

Numerous examples exist that demonstrate the systematic purging some college teams pursue against lesbian college athletes. Fear and discrimination are perpetuated by homophobic male and female coaches (some of whom are themselves homosexual or lesbian) as they try to distance themselves, their sports and their own athletes from the "taint of lesbianism."

Among the professional women's sports associations things are similar, although the "coming out" of notable women athletes has done much to push (and exacerbate) the issue. Martina Navratilova's (1956–) open avowal of her lesbianism sent the tabloids into a frenzy in the early 1980s. Just as Billie Jean King's (1943–) lesbian relationship was deemed a "mistake" by her and something she strove to obscure, Navratilova's coming out focused the spotlight on lesbianism in professional sports irrevocably. The press obsessed on Navratilova's lesbianism: One *Sports Illustrated* reporter ridiculed Judy Nelson, Navratilova's partner at the time, for blowing kisses to the tennis great during a match. Criticism has also come from within the ranks of women's tennis: British champion Margaret Court (1942–) said Navratilova's homosexuality made her a very poor role model for young people. While public opinion did not dampen the amount of media coverage Navratilova received, she stated in her autobiography, *Martina* (1985), that her avowed lesbianism irrevocably damaged her endorsement opportunities. Big corporate sponsorships were inaccessible to the tennis pro and increasingly scarce for the tour as a whole. When Billie Jean King's lesbian relationship was revealed, she also reported that it cost her millions in endorsements.

Insiders also note the dismissal that often accompanies the "charge" of lesbianism. Pam Shriver (1962–) wrote in *Passing Shots* (1987) that "most of the guys on the men's [tennis] tour have stereotyped the women as a whole bunch of lesbians." Thus, athletic excellence is submerged under the "accusation" of lesbianism.

A similar trend has plagued both the Ladies Professional Bowlers Tour (LPBT) and the Ladies Professional Golf Association (LPGA). An ESPN interviewer in conversation with a top-ranked female bowler in the mid-1980s was told that the LPBT had difficulty securing corporate sponsors because "who wants to pay to see a bunch of dykes bowl anyway?" Little wonder, then, that professional bowlers continue to willingly wear skirts as a "proof" of femininity if they make "the show" (the final four of a televised match). Further, all top-money-winning bowlers are aware that public admission of lesbianism is tantamount to sacrificing endorsements. In a 1992 interview with this author, Tish Johnson, an LPBT member who had just "three-peated" as the top money winner on the tour, "came out" during the interview. She spoke of the pressures from other female bowlers (lesbian and straight) *not* to reveal her lesbianism "for the good of their sport." Her decision to come out was based on her unprecedented success as an athlete at that time, encouragement from her life partner, and a sense that her lesbianism had already cast both herself and her sport outside the realm of mainstream recognition and economic reward.

In 1992, two sponsors of the LPGA, Lucky Stores and J.M. Smucker, received anonymous letters threatening demonstrations at the stores and boycotts of the products if the corporations continued to sponsor an LPGA tournament. "The players on this professional tour," the letters alleged, "have a known reputation of being homosexual."

While neither sponsor withdrew, the sport's leadership cringed at what they perceived as the negative publicity. For lesbians within professional golf, the issue of "invisibilizing" oneself was ever present. In fact, to promote the tour's image and to silence rumors that it was *not* the Lesbian Professional Golf Association (as some observers have labeled it), in 1989 executives of the LPGA initiated a "sexy" marketing campaign that first ran in *Fairways*, the association's own publication, then reprinted in *Sports Illustrated*. Five players in skimpy and provocative swimsuits were photographed on Hawai'in beaches. As Cahn (1994): "LPGA officials admitted that they designed this marketing approach in light of the tour's 'image problem,' hoping it would "remove all the negatives" and squelch the lesbian "whisper campaign." In 1996, Muffin Spencer-Devlin willingly became the first lesbian LPGA tour member to declare her lesbianism. As of 1998, she had lost neither of her two sizable endorsements; reaction from LPGA officials and players ranged from wary ("You'll hurt the game") to pledges of support.

## Contemporary Concerns

Two other significant issues face professional women athletes. Although the buccal smear (a sample of tissue from the inside of the mouth) has revealed only one man-masquerading-as-a-woman-athlete (Hermann Ratjent in 1957 confessed that he had disguised himself as female to compete for Nazi Germany), the specter of sex testing and accusations of abnormality continue to haunt professional women athletes. Bev Francis, an Australian-born body builder, was featured in the 1980s film *Pumping Iron Two: The Women*. In this documentary of the then-fledgling women's bodybuilding tour, Francis was openly discussed by the all-male judging panel as far too masculine and *muscular* to be worthy of prize money. Questions of her genetic sex identity were discussed backstage at one meet—this, amid numerous "reassuring" photo sessions of her with her boyfriend in their hotel. Similarly, Maria Jose Martinez Patino, Spanish track-and-field athlete, was banned from international competition in 1986 because genetic testing revealed an XY chromosome. After two years of humiliation and forced competitive inactivity, she was reinstated. Yet the specter of hermaphroditism and lesbianism continued to haunt her personally and professionally. Likewise, accusations that Florence Griffith Joyner (1959–1998) was not all-female but "at least" a steroid abuser quickly followed her Olympic victories in 1988. This suspicion toward "Flo Jo" was compounded by racism. The media continuously portray her and other top African American female athletes as animal-like and needing male coaches and husbandly domination. Fre-

quently they are portrayed as either hypersexual or as "erotic aliens" (Cahn 1994).

For those professional women athletes who "pass" the feminine and heterosexual ideals scripted by culture, who are white and in elite sports, the economic rewards can be great (for example, Chris Evert [1954–], Mary Lou Retton [1968–], and Peggy Fleming [1948–]). Yet for those women *perceived* as lesbian or unfeminine, as well as for women of color and those in nonelite sports, the opportunities to earn a living or cultural apppoval are often greatly diminished. They also serve as daring role models for other lesbian athletes and the larger lesbian and gay community.          *Susan E. Cayleff*

### Bibliography

Cahn, Susan K. *Coming on Strong: Gender and Sexuality in Twentieth-Century Women's Sport*. New York: Free Press, 1994.

Cayleff, Susan E. *Babe: The Life and Legend of Babe Didrikson Zaharias*. Champaign: University of Illinois Press, 1995.

Fox, Sally. *The Sporting Woman: A Book of Days*. Bulfinch, 1989.

Garrity, John, and Amy Nutt. "No More Disguises" [re: Muffin Spencer-Devlin]. *Sports Illustrated* 84:11 (March 18, 1996), 71–73, 77.

Rogers, Susan Fox. *SportsDykes: Stories from On and Off the Field*. New York: St. Martin's, 1994.

***See also*** Athletics, Collegiate; Didrikson, Mildred Ella "Babe" (Zaharias); Gay Games; King, Billie Jean Moffitt; Navratilova, Martina

## Stein, Gertrude (1874–1946)

American biographer, essayist, librettist, novelist, playwright, and poet. Born into a prosperous Jewish family, Stein resided in Europe and Oakland, California, where she was educated privately and in public school. While at undergraduate at Harvard University, she published papers on experimental psychology.

Stein entered Johns Hopkins medical school but quit before earning her degree, mainly because her growing awareness of her lesbianism put her in conflict with her own bourgeois upbringing and medical views of the female body. Stein became involved with a group of college women who, unbeknownst to her, conducted clandestine lesbian affairs. Nevertheless, she fell in love with a student

*Portrait of Gertrude Stein (left) and Alice B. Toklas. Department of Special Collections, University Research Library, UCLA.*

named May Bookstaver. Confronted with her own naivete, moral crises, and an experienced rival for Bookstaver's affections, this relationship ultimately failed.

Stein reworked this drama in her first novel, *Q.E.D* (1903). Adele, the character based on Stein, fears "physical passion." Nevertheless, she falls in love with Helen, who is dependent on her manipulative lover, Mabel. By the time Adele has dispensed with her scruples and wants a sexual affair, Helen has become exhausted by her dithering and rejects her advances. *Q.E.D.* concludes with an anguished Adele confessing that the relationship is at a "deadlock."

Soon thereafter, Stein moved to Paris, where she became an influential collector of modernist paintings. Inspired by Paul Cezanne's (1839–1906) "democratic" method of giving equal weight to each element in a composition, Stein wrote *Three Lives* (1909). This work employs her famous style of repetition-within-variation and simple diction to great psychological effect in exploring the lives of three female outsiders. "Melanctha," one of the stories in the text, blends elements of *Q.E.D.* with African American themes and contexts. The title character has a lesbian relationship with her fellow teacher Jane Harden. Stein projects a masculinized version of herself onto Jeff Campbell, a doctor who wants his people to "live regular" and with whom Melanctha has a failed romance.

In 1909, Stein met Alice B. Toklas (1877–1967), in whom she found a lifelong lover and an artistic collaborator and audience who agreed with her assessment of her genius. The creativity of their relationship is evident in *The Autobiography of Alice B. Toklas* (1933), an engaging chronicle of artistic life in Paris that transformed Stein into a best-selling author. By assuming the voice of Toklas, Stein was able to position herself in the center of the narrative of modernism and playfully dramatize the relations between her private identity as a lesbian and her public perception by her audience.

Stein invented a genre called the "verbal portrait," which frees the subject from conventional narrative expectations and patterns of association. "Ada" (1909–1910) recapitulates the story of Toklas's separation from her family and ends on a note of domestic felicity centered on exchanging stories with "the other one," namely Stein. Her most famous portrait, "Miss Furr and Miss Skeene" (1922), was based on a lesbian couple who visited Stein and Toklas in Paris. Through strategic repetition of the verbal motifs "being gay," "regularly," and "cultivating their voices," the portrait associates, for the first time in print, the term "gay" with a homosexual couple.

*Tender Buttons* (1914), one of the outstanding achievements of modernism, is a surrealistic exploration of the mysterious "thing-ness" of common objects. Stein uses verbal encodings to create a vernacular of lesbianism that accurately reflects the richness of lived experience. Rather than use literal terms that correspond to a single referent outside the text, Stein engages in elaborate punning, so that terms hover on the boundary between paraphrasable sense and opacity. The word "pencil" not only means "writing instrument," but also connotes "phallic object" and "dildo." Similarly, "box" signifies "container" and "female genitalia" and "interiority."

Stein also wrote dialogue-style poetry in which a major theme is elaborated through the fuguelike interplay of two voices. *Lifting Belly* (1953), a tour de force of erotic literature, explores the creativity of lesbian sexuality. The poem develops the connotative meanings of the title: the "lifting up" of the female body in response to sexual arousal and the "enlarging" of the significance of lesbianism. Other erotic works are similarly ebullient. "Pink Melon Joy" (1922) celebrates oral sex, and "As a Wife Has a Cow: A Love Story" (1926) tells of a "wife" (Toklas) having a "cow" (an orgasm).

In 1942, Stein and Toklas fled the Nazi occupation of Paris. The liberation of Paris in 1944 renewed Stein's optimism and her interest in political writing. Her last work, her libretto for *The Mother of Us All* (1946), is a feminist paean to the American suffragist Susan B. Anthony (1820–1906). The evocative epilogue enshrines Anthony and Stein as monuments to which the other women pay homage, "Not to what I won but to what was done." Stein has gained overdue recognition as the leading American modernist, and her work continues to exert an important influence on lesbian literature.

*Corinne E. Blackmer*

### Bibliography

Barry, Ellen E. *Curved Thought and Textual Wandering: Gertrude Stein's Postmodernism.* Ann Arbor: University of Michigan Press, 1992.

Blackmer, Corinne E. "African Masks and the Arts of Passing in Gertrude Stein's 'Melanctha' and Nella Larsen's *Passing*." *Journal of the History of Sexuality* 4 (October 1993), 230–263.

Grahn, Judy. *Really Reading Gertrude Stein: A Selected Anthology with Essays by Judy Grahn.* Freedom, Calif.: Crossing, 1989.

Kellner, Bruce. *A Gertrude Stein Companion: Content with the Example.* New York: Greenwood, 1988.

Ruddick, Lisa. *Reading Gertrude Stein: Body, Text, Gnosis.* Ithaca, N.Y.: Cornell University Press, 1990.

*See also* Anthony, Susan B.; Modernism; Paris; Toklas, Alice B.

## Stereotypes

Abstract representations based on commonly shared assumptions about the characteristics of a type of person, situation, or thing. As symbol-using creatures, humans carry around a great deal of knowledge that is gained secondhand rather than through direct experience. This information comes in the form of abstract representations that stand in as a prototype for the "real thing." For instance, many people have never encountered a prizefighter, but, when they read or hear of one, they are able to conjure up an image in their heads. Stereotypes are associated feelings, evaluations, and prescriptions for behavior that are triggered when the stereotype is invoked. Stereotypes are necessary building blocks of cognition and social communication. They enable the processing and organizing of information quickly and without direct experience. They are also the basis of considerable social prejudice. Stereotypes act as filters that focus attention and judgment: People tend to omit information that is not consistent with the stereotype and to accentuate features that match.

### Common Stereotypes

Stereotypes about lesbians are legion. Many of the most common stereotypes are based on deviations from gender expectations. Lesbians are assumed to have been "tomboys"; inversely, it is widely assumed that "tomboys" will become lesbians. The stereotype of the lesbian as "mannish" and "butch" has persisted since the early twentieth century. A related stereotype is that lesbians possess the minds of men trapped in a woman's body; hence, the misconception of the lesbian as a "third sex." In linking mental activity with maleness and the body with the feminine, this stereotype reflects a culturally assumed gender hierarchy. Women who downplay feminine sexuality and are assertive in the classroom and the workforce are often represented as "dykes." "Dyke" is a conventionally pejorative term that evokes a stereotype of a person not fully female: someone who is aggressive and lacking in the feelings, attitudes, and sexuality appropriate to her gender. The dyke is hard and brooding and hovers at the margins of society. Other prevalent stereotypes represent the lesbian as antimale and antisex. Many people assume that a woman has become a lesbian because of unpleasant experiences with men and/or sexual abuse. Lesbians are also stereotyped as hypersexed and sexually aggressive. The contrast between these representations illustrates the point that stereotypes are often inconsistent and contradictory.

### Prejudice and Discrimination

Points of commonality between stereotypes reflect shared cultural values and ideals. General stereotypes of lesbians converge on the image of the lesbian as a sexual deviant and a gender deviant. Lesbian stereotypes are framed in reference to cultural ideals regarding the embodiment of femininity and women's nurturing role. Lesbians are typically represented as contradicting these ideals. Common stereotypes carry a valence that shadows the lesbian as having stepped out of her place and into competition with men. Much discrimination experienced by lesbians can be attributed to judgments based on stereotypes rather than careful consideration of individual characteristics. A woman is more likely to have her ideas, suggestions, and positions dismissed as "radical" and "uncooperative" if she is known to be a lesbian. Lesbians are disproportionately likely to be accused of sexual harassment. This is consistent with the stereotype that lesbians are "oversexed" and "obsessed" with straight women. The dearth of medical research on lesbian sexuality and transmission of disease can be explained in terms of the stereotype that lesbians are not sexually active. Stereotypical ideas about the relationship between fertility, female health, and lesbianism may mislead health-care practitioners when they are diagnosing and treating lesbians. The misconception that lesbians cannot parent their children reflects the stereotype of the lesbian as having abandoned appropriate gender behavior. Lesbians filing for custody of their children must fight against the court-sanctioned stereotype that they cannot be both a lesbian and a mother.

## Self-Fulfilling Stereotypes

Lesbians represent a wide range of appetites, desires, and personal and political positions. Because people cannot read each other's mind, it is necessary to let others know who one is and what one is looking for in friends and lovers. Paradoxically, an effective way to signal this information is to don attire and assume postures that manifest the desired impression. In doing so, one invokes and enacts stereotypes. In the 1950s, for instance, women traveled to large urban centers looking for "the lesbians." Without a guidebook about who to be and how to find similar others, many of these woman relied on stereotypical clues. The source of these cultural images included a genre of pulp paperback novels and similar cultural artifacts. Many of these gave the impression that lesbians were surly misfits who looked and acted "butch." Women who did not experience themselves as being particularly butch but who were attracted to other women found a place for themselves playing the stereotypical femme counterpart. The establishment of a butch-femme culture is partly a result of invoking common representations to make sense of one's own experiences and to draw the attention of others presumed to be similar. Thus, stereotypes can both shape and reflect real aggregate behavior, as well as misrepresent the experiences and behavior of the many diverse individuals who identify with a particular cultural group.

The prevalence of insider stereotypes, such as the "soft butch" and the "lipstick lesbian," convey the extent to which lesbian ideals and sensibilities are shaped by the preconceptions of a heterosexist and sexist society. A much-debated stereotype among lesbians is the "lipstick lesbian." This image reflects an ongoing and contested discourse about what it means to be a lesbian: Can a woman who embodies stereotypical representations of heterosexual femininity be a "real" lesbian? Lesbians, as well as nonlesbians, have been known to ask: Can a lesbian wear makeup and a dress? Conversely, the frequency with which women tend to describe themselves as "soft butch" suggests that an ideal among lesbians is someone who is neither too butch nor too femme. This ideal is not so much based on enlightened conceptions of gender and sexuality as it is a product of a homophobic culture: The "soft butch" can claim insider status without making herself the target of prejudice. She can pass. As much fun as it can be to enact stereotypical forms for play and pleasure, the awareness that these representations reflect stereotypical features that mark one as belonging to a stigmatized group is indicated in the prevalence of personal ads in which women seeking women frequently admonish one another to be "straight-acting."

## Reclaiming Stereotypes

One form of activism is for members of a stigmatized group to reclaim negative stereotypes and related pejorative terms. This is accomplished by highlighting some of the default assumptions implied in the stereotype and reframing them as interesting and acceptable, possibly even desirable. A new generation of lesbians are the vanguard of a progressive sexuality. By naming themselves "sex radicals" and appropriating the notion of lesbians as sexually obsessed, they have begun to manufacture ideals of female sexual awareness and pleasure. They are recasting themselves as "sex positive." Similarly, activists and artists use images such as (Del)la Grace's (1957–) "lesbian boys" to critique and reframe some of the negative gender deviations associated with lesbianism. In the 1990s, lesbianism became become "chic." Having a lesbian for a friend was a significant social accoutrement. Mainstream media portrayals cast lesbians as women with hearty professional and sexual appetites; women with just enough attitude to have an edge but not be too threatening to the men who are now their buddies. This is no less a stereotype, and it is certainly an instance of exoticizing the "other," but these contemporary images also reflect the influence of lesbians. Not only are there more lesbian roles in film and television, but these roles are often authored, played, and technically advised by lesbians. As lesbians gain more of a hand in rendering self-images, it is possible that the resulting stereotypes will reflect a wider and more representative range of lesbian experiences and sensibilities.

*Jodi O'Brien*

### Bibliography

Langer, Ellen. *Mindfulness*. Reading, Mass.: Addison-Wesley, 1989.

O'Brien, Jodi, and Peter Kollock. *The Production of Reality*. Newbury Park, Calif.: Pine Forge, 1996.

Plummer, Ken, ed. *Modern Homosexualities*. London: Routledge, 1992.

Stein, Arlene, ed. *Sisters, Sexperts and Queers: Beyond the Lesbian Nation*. London: Penguin, 1993.

**See also** Butch-Femme; Discrimination; Dyke; Prejudice; Pulp Paperbacks; Style; Tomboy

## Stigma

Physical or personal attributes and behaviors that are deemed socially undesireable, thereby discrediting the individual who possesses them. Stigma is not inherent to any attribute or behavior but, rather, is found in the culturally specific negative meanings that are attached to it.

Stigma can be based on physical characteristics that do not correspond to some standard of appearance; it can also be the result of personal behavior that is labeled as deviant. Unlike physical stigma that may be seen as misfortunes out of one's control, stigma based on behaviors or actions are typically viewed as reflecting a flaw in one's character. In addition, because Judeo-Christian beliefs underlie many of Western society's standards of appropriate conduct, instances of sexual transgression can be interpreted as abominations, moral defects, or sins. Both physical and personal stigma serve as ways to group and categorize people, perpetuating an us-them mentality. In this, stigmatizing others func-

tions to solidify one's own identity, behavior, and social position.

The need to stigmatize others, particularly large groups of people, occurs especially during times of social crisis in identity or changing standards of behavior. For example, stigmatizing and scapegoating Communists, immigrants, and homosexuals may take attention away from economic and political problems of the day, providing, instead, a moral issue over which people can locate themselves and regain some sense of security during uncertain times.

## Sexual Stigma

Many cultures regulate and monitor sexual expression and mark as deviants those alleged violators of normative heterosexual conduct. This concern over regulating sexual expression is operationalized at all levels of society: by government, churches, families, and individuals. There are varying institutional, interactional, and intrapersonal consequences to being sexually stigmatized. One can be jailed or committed, suffer economic losses, lose custody of one's children, be physically and verbally assaulted on the streets, be shunned by others, or experience debilitating levels of self-hate.

The fact that one engages in homosexual acts may or may not be apparent or visible to others. Hence, in an effort to regulate sexuality, people rely on stereotypical images of masculinity and femininity as indicators of alleged sexual nonconformity. For example, females who employ traditionally masculine characteristics or who exhibit masculine styles of dress may be seen not only as unfeminine, but also as unwomanly and, hence, lesbian. Here, the connection to stigmatized sexual status is based not on empirical or specifically sexual evidence, but on evidence that one has moved out of one's prescribed gender role and usurped that of the other.

The fear of being labeled a lesbian serves as a powerful deterrent to control women's actions and allegences. This threat affects individual women, as well as groups and organizations. For example, in the late 1960s certain factions of the women's movement actively sought to distance themselves from their lesbian members, who were seen as undermining the movement's credibility by giving it and its heterosexual members a bad name.

This is an example of stigma spillover, a process whereby people who associate with a sexually stigmatized person or group are also seen as sexually suspect. Often this happens when heterosexuals socialize with homosexuals or are sympathetic and vocal supporters of homosexual issues and concerns. Here, the pressure not to be seen as gay can make even the most openly gay-friendly people rush to declare their heterosexuality.

## Managing Sexual Stigma

There are various ways that lesbians manage a potentially discrediting (stigmatized) sexual identity, two of which are "passing" and "adopting." Passing is the ability to affect a heterosexual appearance and persona. This can be done through outward presentations of oneself as feminine and offering stereotypically heterosexual responses, interests, and demeanor. This not only entails considerable work and energy, but also often prevents one from connecting, and building community, with other lesbians. The individual who seeks to "pass" runs the risk of disassociating from her whole self. Alternatively, people who claim their stigmatized identities can form alliances based on their shared-in-common oppression—or mutual delights.

Another management strategy is to refashion the socially defined stigma by actively adopting as part of one's identity those behaviors that ironically may signify it. This "out and proud" stance can be seen in very butch women or those for whom tattooing and piercing are dominant. Another example may be seen in the push for celebrities to come out. This has little to do with concern over the improvement of the star's self-worth and psychological well-being but, rather, is directed at lending legitimacy to a problematic homosexual identity. Showing that someone successful, respected, and popular also happens to be homosexual may, indeed, minimize the extent to which gay people can be seen as "other."

## Stigma from Within

Stigma from within refers to the hierarchies among lesbians, whereby different factions look down upon or disparage other women who love women. Here, the issue is not *that* they are homosexual but *the way* that they are homosexual: sexual practices, political activism, dress, demeanor, outness. For example, some lesbians disregard bisexual females; monogamous lesbians are assumed to be better than non-monogamous lesbians; and many otherwise open-minded lesbians disapprove of women who engage in sadomasochism. Lesbians stigmatize other women who love women as a way of gaining some superior and acceptable ground in a world that deplores them. But, by judging and stigmatizing others' dress, demeanor, or, most critically, sexual practices, lesbians perpetuate versions of sexual stigma from which they are seeking relief. This is stigma in its simplist form: on an interactional level in day-to-day practices and encounters. It is at this interactional level that everyone has an opportunity to reproduce or dismantle stigma.      *Linda Van Leuven*

### Bibliography

Bornstein, Kate. *Gender Outlaw*. New York: Vintage, 1994.

Erickson, Kai T. *Wayward Puritans*. New York: Macmillan, 1966.

Goffman, Erving. *Stigma*. Englewood Cliffs, N.J.: Prentice-Hall, 1963.

Plummer, Kenneth. *Sexual Stigma*. London: Routledge, 1975.

***See also*** Discrimination; Homophobia; Prejudice; Stereotypes

## Students

Students of all sexual orientations are on college campuses seeking an education and searching for self. In a 1996 survey of first-year students conducted by the University of Michigan (UM), nearly 4 percent indicated an intention to date people of their same sex during their years at Michigan. These data verify that lesbian, gay, bisexual, and transgender students are on college campuses; some are now standing to be counted as they enter institutions of higher education.

Experiences of lesbian, bisexual, and transgender (LBT) women on campus are vast and varied. The UM Office of Lesbian, Gay, Bisexual, and Transgender (LGBT) Affairs discovered multiple terminology used by women students to identify nonheterosexual orientations. Some women identify as "homosexual," using such descriptors as "lesbian" or "gay" or "queer." Some identify as "bisexual"—or "bi"—even if they are in a monogamous relationship with another woman. They, too, might identify as "queer." Others identify as "transgender" and may or may not cross-dress or seek sex reassignment. Some describe themselves as "transfags," identifying as transgender and attracted to others like themselves who are female-to-male transgenderists. They, like the others, may also identify as "queer." There are LUGS (lesbians until graduation), who are sexual with women during

**S** their college years but marry men after graduation. Some women identify as "questioning," not yet ready to select specific terminology because they are still seeking self within a sexual-orientation context. Finally, there are women who never use specific terminology because they do not want to be labeled or categorized either by themselves or others.

The Office of LGBT Affairs at UM asked women students what it means to be LBT. Several shared feelings of difference, power, and compassion, while others spoke of invisibility:

> Sometimes I just feel different, like I know that not everyone here is like me. Sometimes I find power in that difference. It means being proud and comfortable with who you are. It means understanding how people can discriminate against you and why they do it. It means not discounting anyone because they have less experience or have been exposed to less diversity than you. Being a lesbian isn't a visible sign of difference, and I can choose to "just blend in," unlike older college students or people with physical disabilities. Sometimes it doesn't matter at all. I'm still a college student like everyone else. But I hate that feeling of not being present when I'm really there.

Students described the support received from other LBT students when each "came out" (acknowledged a homosexual, bisexual, or transgender orientation) while in college:

> Coming out, all the lesbians I met made me feel like I came home. I cried, and finally knew who I really was. One of the main reasons I can be so open is because the LBT women on campus have created such a sincere and helpful support system. I owe my sanity to these women.

LBT women students also described their general interactions with non-LGBT students:

> Not all my friends are queer and I like it that way. They're friends, neighbors, fellow-activists and always willing to gossip. They seem to be an extension of our community. My closest friends are the most

accepting because they understand it's a part of me that I hold very dear.

Leadership is a valued and integral part of campus life at most institutions. At UM, openly LGBT students hold leadership positions throughout campus. The Office of LGBT Affairs asked women what it is like to be an LBT student leader on campus. The responses were indicative of the quality of leadership found among these students:

> I feel like I'm in heterosexual-education mode all the time. When I don't speak up I go home feeling as though I betrayed not only my personal integrity but also a community that means a great deal to me. I have the opportunity to be a voice for LGBT students on campus. There's usually no one else in student government or in my sorority or in athletics who feels safe enough to offer the voice and the perspective of a lesbian; those seeds need to be planted. I know perfectly well the risks I take when I do that. If it's a choice between my popularity and my integrity, I'll choose the latter.

Students were asked what advice they would give to other LBT women who are just coming out. All spoke of seeking community and role models:

> Find the dyke community. There's no reason to feel alone. Get into a support group. Talk to other women who are gay because they'll understand you and you can feel proud of who you are. Find the role models on campus if you are lucky enough to be on a campus where there are "out" staff and faculty.

Students spoke of the impact their sexual orientations may have on their families, who are important to them and to their stability as college students. They want to come out to their families, especially when they have fallen in love—invariably at Thanksgiving, the winter holidays, or at spring break. These are the most popular times for students to go home, drop the information bomb, then return to the safety of the campus. Most parents love their children and want what they believe is best for them. Generally, nonheterosexual identities were not in the parents' game plan nor in their realm of understanding. One student explained:

When you first tell them you're homosexual, the only word that rings in their ears is "sexual." My mom probably thought I was a nineteen-year-old virgin until she found out I was "like that." Now she probably thinks I've been sexually active since I was seven, and doing quite unusual and impossible things. It will just take her time to understand that I love women with or without sex.

Whether or not they are visible, LGBT students exist on every campus. Many LGBT students have articulate, courageous voices and effective leadership skills. As with other minority students, campus services must be provided to address their needs and to acknowledge their presence and the gifts they bring to higher education.           *Ronni L. Sanlo*

## Bibliography

Cooperative Institutional Research Program (CIRP).
  1996 Entering Student Survey Addendum.
  University of Michigan, Ann Arbor, MI.

*See also* Adolescence; Athletics, Collegiate; Sororities; Teachers

## Style

Mode of self-presentation in which individuals embrace gestures, symbols, hairstyle, and clothing to convey a particular sense of self. Individuals use elements of style to claim membership in lesbian communities. Collectively, lesbian style is a form of self-expression and resistance.

The codification and eroticization of gender has been central to lesbian style. Historically, there has been a tension between those who emphasize dichotomous gender differences, or butch-femme style, and those who wish to minimize these differences, embracing a more androgynous style.

### Butch-Femme Styles

For most of the twentieth century, butch-femme roles adapted conventional gender roles to the lesbian context. Femmes appropriated elements of traditionally feminine attire, adapting it to the lesbian context. Butches adopted a more masculine style and typically wore short hair, slacks, and shirts.

Butch-femme styles were popularized in the 1950s, when sharply dichotomous gender roles were inescapable and stigma against homosexuality

most virulent. In the public at large, lesbians were generally forced to conform to feminine norms and to carefully manage their identities so as not to be found out on the job. But in the largely working-class subculture of the bars, they were able to escape from the constraints of heterosexual society.

Particularly for women who "passed as men," masculine clothes, much more than style, were also a means of survival. The writer Ann Bannon (1937–) fashioned a series of paperback novels around the character Beebo Brinker, a strapping tomboy who worked as an elevator operator and wore a man's uniform.

Butch-femme styles aided the creation of a publicly identifiable lesbian culture. They also helped potential sexual partners signal their preferences to each other. Roles eroticized differences between partners. The butch, or active partner, orchestrated the sexual interaction, but her pleasure was dependent upon pleasing her partner.

In the system of butch-femme as it was practiced in the 1950s, one's identity as butch or femme was an essential, integral part of one's being. By imposing rules and placing limits on self-expression, roles provided security in a tenuous, secretive world. They were often proud statements of lesbian resistance, but they were also the expression of an oppressed minority faced with a paucity of alternatives.

### Androgynous Styles

In the 1970s, in the context of the women's liberation movement, a very different understanding of style emerged among lesbians. Feminists attempted to erase gender differences, recodify gender and sexuality and position themselves outside of the dominant culture.

As Sidney Abbott and Barbara Love, writing in *Sappho Was a Right-on Woman* (1972), proclaimed: "[T]he lesbian . . . is not trying to be like a man, but . . . more of a human being." Gay liberationists and lesbian feminists viewed the exaggerated gender roles of butch-femme as little more than a self-hating reflection of the dominant heterosexual culture. Styles that emphasized dichotomous masculine and feminine codes were seen as vestiges of the prefeminist days and reflections of an oppressive hegemonic culture. Feminist lesbians wished to free themselves from fashion and style altogether, which they saw as synonymous with women's oppression. They wanted to free women's bodies from their possession by men, which they viewed as being syn-

**S** onymous with their sexualization. The fashion industry, they suggested, played into the objectification of women's bodies.

Lesbian feminists forged an "antistyle" that embodied ideals of authenticity and naturalness. Toward this end, feminist-influenced lesbians embraced androgynous styles of self-presentation. A study of San Francisco's lesbian community in the 1970s described lesbian feminist style as consisting of "Levis or other sturdy pants, t-shirts, and workshirts" (Wolf 1980). Simple, functional working-class clothing symbolized the wish on the part of many middle-class lesbians to be downwardly mobile, or at least to identify with the least fortunate. It also reflected their wish to replace the artifice of fashion with a naturalness, freed of gender roles and commercialized pretense.

But despite efforts to construct a "democratic" style that would submerge differences among the group, individual differences persisted. Although many feminists welcomed women of color into their circles, the dominant visual codes in lesbian and gay communities that suggested "what a lesbian looked like" often assumed whiteness.

Moreover, despite their attempt to erase gender differences and position themselves outside the dominant culture, lesbian feminists' style was ultimately dependent on the gender codes it sought to subvert. Feminists tended to privilege that which the dominant culture had historically stigmatized as lesbian—the masculine woman. But being too masculine carried the taint of butch-femme roles.

**The Revival of Butch-Femme**

In the 1980s, style, along with sexuality, became a central battleground in many lesbian communities. A younger generation of lesbians affirmed the value of individual choice of style and sexual expression. They constructed a diverse range of lesbian styles that drew upon elements of 1970s lesbian feminism, 1950s butch-femme, and other influences.

Particularly noteworthy was the resurgence of gender-dichotomous styles. The "new" butch-femme styles often self-consciously played with style and power. For some women, fashion and self-presentation, like gender and sexual identities, were little more than "performances." Clothes became transient, interchangeable. One could dress as a femme one day and a butch the next. This was partly due to the influence of punk subcultures of the 1970s and 1980s, which at times self-consciously embodied "gender-fuck" styles.

In the early 1990s, the "lipstick lesbian" became a familiar icon of urban lesbian subcultures, representing a rejection of feminist antistyle and a willingness on the part of some lesbians to publicly endorse dominant conceptions of female attractiveness. A spate of newspaper and magazine articles pronounced the arrival of "lesbian chic," playing on the apparent novelty of the "feminine" lesbian. Some companies embarked on a dual-market strategy, using advertising that coded styles and body language as lesbian without directly identifying them as such, indirectly targeting a lesbian market.

*Arlene Stein*

***Bibliography***

Clark, Danae. "Commodity Lesbianism." In *The Lesbian and Gay Studies Reader*. Ed. Henry Abelove, Michèle Aina Barale, and David M. Halperin. New York: Routledge, 1993.

Kennedy, Elizabeth Lapovsky, and Madeline Davis. *Boots of Leather, Slippers of Gold: The History of a Lesbian Community*. New York: Routledge, 1993.

Newton, Esther. "The Mythic Mannish Lesbian: Radclyffe Hall and the New Woman." *Signs: Journal of Women in Culture and Society* 9:4 (1984) 557–575.

Weston, Kath. "Do Clothes Make the Woman?: Gender, Performance Theory, and Lesbian Eroticism." *Genders* 17 (1993), 1–21.

Wolf, Deborah Goleman. *The Lesbian Community*. Berkeley: University of California, 1980.

***See also*** Androgyny; Bannon, Ann; Butch-Femme; Lesbian Feminism; Sexuality; Stereotypes

**Subculture**

Term used to describe a group of people who participate in a common identity that constitutes their shared, daily, lived experience. Membership in a subculture involves the adoption of an identity and a set of beliefs and values that are communicated to one another and to outsiders. People tend to describe their subculture with a sense of home and belonging, because it provides them with a base ("roots") from which to interpret the world around them. People in subcultures tend to focus on those aspects by which they claim membership and, by spoken and unspoken consent, assiduously police the boundaries of their subculture.

In the field of cultural studies, culture refers to "structures of feeling," a concept that developed out of the work of the British socialist critic Raymond Williams in the 1960s. Original work on subcultures was informed by the scientific approach of anthropology, although they also have been studied from the perspective of participant observation. Early studies of subcultures tended to be romanticized versions of young working-class men living in the north of England. Subculture is often used synonymously with oppositional culture, although subcultures do not necessarily transgress social norms.

Lesbian scholars have tended to argue that lesbians constitute such a subculture. For example, Elizabeth Lapovsky Kennedy and Madeline D. Davis, in *Boots of Leather, Slippers of Gold: The History of a Lesbian Community* (1993), reproduce the objectifying tendency of looking at working-class experience as "worthy of sociological attention," but they also challenge the implicit power structure of traditional academic approaches. Emma Donahue, in *Passions Between Women: British Lesbian Culture, 1668–1801* (1993), argues that a recognizable lesbian culture existed in Britain during the period 1668–1801. Perhaps the most convincing contemporary example of lesbians organizing a subculture would be the lesbian feminist movements of the 1970s, which insisted on a commitment to a specific lifestyle as an expression of explicit ideology. In the 1980s, that seeming homogeneity fractured into identity politics, as the privileging of one identity over another required to constitute a subculture ceded to a new era of postmodern complexities, in which individuals could not be so clearly "in" or "out."

Implicit within the subculture model is a notion of social hierarchies. Subcultures can breed a kind of competition, and paranoia, over identity (as can be shown in the interminable debates about whether bisexual women can participate in lesbian events). Lesbian subcultures have to reassemble with each new generation. They are constantly in the process of emergence. Allegiance to a subculture is a necessary demand for visiblity in a culture that effaces minority existence. Yet, in the rush to prioritize an identity and configure a subculture, participants must consider who are excluded and what is ignored.                    *Sally R. Munt*

## Bibliography

Donahue, Emma. *Passions Between Women: British Lesbian Culture, 1668–1801*. London: Scarlet, 1993.
Hebdige, Dick. *Subculture: The Meaning of Style*. London: Routledge, 1984.
Kennedy, Elizabeth Lapovsky, and Madeline D. Davis. *Boots of Leather, Slippers of Gold: The History of a Lesbian Community*. New York: Routledge, 1993.

*See also* Community; Cultural Studies; Identity Politics; Lesbian Feminism

## Suffrage Movement

Women's collective activism in the United States and the United Kingdom, as well as in many European countries, for the right to vote (1848–1928). Many middle-class, white suffragists maintained close loving relationships with women, which, due to social and scientific changes, were interpreted differently over time. During the last decades of the movement, the medical classification of "lesbian" as a pathology became more widely accepted. Anti-suffragists began using "lesbian" as an epithet against suffragists to discredit them—to stigmatize unmarried suffragists, stating that the desire for the vote was "mannish," unnatural, and unwomanly. Ironically, the new classification of lesbianism as a disease also allowed women to identify themselves as lesbians and become aware of others within the movement.

Many suffragists in the nineteenth century had passionate relationships with women without negative consequences. This was due to the white, middle-class assumption that women were naturally asexual and passionless. The love of two passionless women was considered a pure, chaste love. American suffragist Susan B. Anthony (1820–1906) had a passionate love with Anna Dickinson (1842–1932) that survived long distances and time. Anthony referred to this love as "motherly" or as an "elderly sister's." Yet Anthony urged Dickinson "not to marry a man," and they longed to share a bed when they were apart. Suffragists in the nineteenth century who developed "Boston marriages"—long-term, loving partnerships with women—included settlement-house founder Jane Addams (1860–1935) with Ellen Gates Starr (1859–1940), Bryn Mawr College president M. Carey Thomas (1857–1935) with Mamie Gwinn (1861–?) and Mary Garrett (1839–1915), Mount Holyoke College president Mary Woolley (1863–1947) with Jeannette Marks (1875–1964), and National American Woman's Suffrage Association leader Anna Howard Shaw (1847–1919) with Lucy Anthony (n.d.), niece of Susan B. Anthony. Similar relationships can be found

**S** among suffrage leaders in the United Kingdom and Europe.

Passionate love between women flourished in the movement, although historians are divided over how to interpret the participants: as romantic, passionate friends or as lovers. Some women's romantic partnerships did have a sexual component. But whether or not they were sexual, all close, loving relationships between women within the suffrage movement helped fuel the cohesiveness between, and motivation of, the activists. At the same time, suffragists' passionate relationships seemed to have a political component; their shared concerns for women's status intensified their relationships.

The rise of sexologists in the 1890s allowed antifeminists to attack suffragists with the authority of "science." If lesbians were "perverted," "inverted" women who preferred female companionship, then the suffrage movement seemed a lesbian hotbed. British sexologist Havelock Ellis (1859–1939), ironically a defender of male homosexuals, spread the negative definition—and fear—of lesbianism. He claimed that women's loving relationships were based in eroticism and pathological. He established that lesbians could be "mannish," working-class, and cross-dressers or feminine, genteel, educated women. He argued that lesbianism was a congenital anomaly that was especially common in highly intelligent women who influence others, either voluntarily or not. By 1913, newspapers described suffragists picketing the White House as undesirable, unwomanly, dangerous, unsexed, and pathological—all sexologist terms for lesbians.

Not all physicians fueling antisuffragists were experts. In the *New York Medical Journal* (year unknown), eye surgeon J. Herbert Claiborne described "hypertrichosis," a disease relating lesbianism to suffragism. Hypertrichosis was associated with the "invasion by woman of many forms of business, professions, trades, and heretofore recognized prerogatives of man. I refer in particular to the suffragette feminist movements." Symptoms included facial and other body hair, a deep voice, and a flat chest. Claiborne said that the "original cause" for women's political activism was "a cellular one, lying in her natural bisexuality, which in many of them is accentuated."

In England, the identification of lesbianism with suffragism prompted an attempt by Parliament to outlaw lesbianism in 1921. The bill failed because members decided lesbianism would spread if they acknowledged it. They preferred "not to notice them, not to advertise them" (Jeffries 1985).

But it was too late. Ellis's descriptions were accurate, even if his diagnosis was not, and lesbian suffragists began to bond. Antisuffragists were right to think that suffragists who were "New Women"—educated, middle-class career women who remained single or married late—would challenge traditional familial social order. Among radical suffragists of the 1910s, some New Women, such as U.S. suffrage leader Alice Paul (1885–1977), rejected the heterosocial order, remained unmarried, and had close relationships with other women without identifying as lesbian. Others lived rather openly as "gay ladies." Social groups and gathering places where lesbians could meet surfaced during this decade. Heterodoxy, a radical feminist organization formed in 1912 in Greenwich Village in New York City, was home to many lesbian suffragists. Some had lifelong relationships, such as author Katherine Anthony (1877–1965) and educator Elisabeth Irwin (1880–1942), who adopted and raised five children. Other lesbian members included Paula Jacobi, who was a Framingham (Massachusetts) Women's Prison guard in 1917 when she was arrested as a suffrage picketer; and Sara Josephine Baker (1873–1945), a medical doctor and renowned pioneer in child health and welfare.

The significant contributions of lesbians could not counteract negative "scientific" definitions of lesbianism after U.S. women received the vote in 1920 and British women in 1928. By then, sexologists' theories of women as biologically sexual yet passive—whose only "normal" outlet of sexual expression was heterosexual marriage—had spread among suffragists. Suffragist Doris Stevens (1888–1963) feared being "tinged dangerously with homoism" (Rupp 1989).

The legacy of using "lesbian" as an epithet during the suffrage movement was a repression of women's relationships with each other during the conservative 1920s and a split in the feminist movement. Many former suffragists were alienated, stereotyped as deviant, unfulfilled women. As physician John F.W. Meagher wrote in *The Urologic and Cutaneous Review* in 1929: "The driving force in many agitators and militant women who are always after their rights, is often an unsatisfied sex impulse, with a homosexual aim. Married women with a completely satisfied libido rarely take an active interest in militant movements."

The focus on lesbianism during the movement, then, was a double-edged sword: Lesbians were rejected by society but had found each other, an identity, and strength in a common cause.      *Susan Gonda*

## Bibliography

Jeffries, Sheila. *The Spinster and Her Enemies: Feminism and Sexuality, 1880–1930.* London and Boston: Pandora, 1985.

Rupp, Leila J. "'Imagine My Surprise': Women's Relationships in Historical Perspective." *Frontiers: A Journal of Woman Studies* 5 (1980), 61–70.

———. "Feminism and the Sexual Revolution in the Early Twentieth Century: The Case of Doris Stevens." *Feminist Studies* 15 (1989), 289–309.

Schwarz, Judith. *Radical Feminists of Heterodoxy: Greenwich Village, 1912–1940.* Lebanon, N.H.: [n.p.], 1982.

Smith-Rosenberg, Carroll. "The New Woman as Androgyne: Social Disorder and Gender Crisis, 1870–1936." In *Disorderly Conduct: Visions of Gender in Victorian America.* Ed. Carroll Smith-Rosenberg. New York: Oxford University Press, 1985, pp. 245–296.

Vicinus, Martha. "Lesbian History: All Theory and No Facts or All Facts and No Theory?" *Radical History Review* 60 (1994), 57–75.

*See also* Addams, Jane; Anthony, Susan B.; Boston Marriage; Greenwich Village; New Woman; Passionlessness; Spinsters; Thomas, M. Carey

## Suicide

The intentional taking of one's own life, and the third leading killer of youth in the United States, accounting for 14 percent of all deaths among teenagers in 1988 (Garland and Zigler 1993). Between 1960 and 1985, according to the National Center for Health Statistics, suicide rates rose by more than 200 percent among teenagers, compared to 17 percent in the general U.S. population.

Lesbians are less reported and less noted in the literature about suicide than are gay males. Hunter (in Remafedi 1994) reported that, in the 1980s, 30 to 35 percent of all adolescent suicides were due to questions of sexuality. These data were drawn from 500 interviews conducted in 1988–1989 with self-defined gay and lesbian adolescents; the study dealt with all forms of violence, including suicide, and extrapolated from information given by those who attempted but did not succeed. There is little data available that specifically assesses the situation for adolescent lesbians. Studies have shown that females of all ages are more likely to attempt suicide,

and that males are more likely to succeed, usually more violently, but the precipitating causes remain obscure.

It is not unreasonable to hypothesize that the still rampant homophobia in the United States is an important factor accounting for a lack of reliable figures for teen gay and lesbian suicides and that it is likely one of the major causes, if not *the* major cause, of such suicides. In the latter situation, internalized homophobia reinforces low self-esteem and self-hatred, as well as the depressing sense of isolation the suicidal person experiences, ultimately leading her or him to consider suicide as a solution. In the former instance, it is reasonable to hypothesize that there is a low and inaccurate reporting of causes of successful suicides related to sexuality because parent(s) either do not know or are too embarrassed, ashamed, or afraid to give such data to authorities. Use and abuse of alcohol and/or other drugs further compounds the problem of determining whether a death is accidental or a suicide.

The effect of puritanism (that is, sexual repressiveness) is still pervasive in the United States, irrespective of specific religions. This is evidenced by widespread traditional and conservative public values, in which neither sex nor sexuality are acceptable or comfortable topics of discussion for most adults. Hence, sex education in schools is routinely stifled, many people prohibit their children from learning about sexual information, and there is generous use of guilt and shame to effect control. Guilt and shame will exacerbate the depression a suicide planner experiences and, no doubt, interfere with honest reporting of the causes of that individual's suicide by relatives or friends.

Another cultural factor that confounds the issues of suicide, in the case of lesbians, is that female sexuality, primarily in the past, was not considered to exist or to be important, except in relationship to males. While this attitude probably allowed many lesbian relationships to go unrecognized and unchallenged in the past, it could also have contributed negatively to lesbians' sense of being acceptable human beings. The sense of unacceptableness within, and isolation from, the general society is a major contribution to depression that leads to considerations of suicide on the part of an individual.

Furthermore, alcohol and drugs have served the purpose of deadening pain for generations of lesbians and gay men. A major danger of using alcohol and other substances is their depressive action on the central nervous system, which, in turn, contributes to the likelihood of suicidal thoughts advancing to actions. The use of chemical substances to reduce the pain of being abnormal is only somewhat diminished in late-twentieth-century U.S. culture, in which a still significant portion of the population considers homosexuality a sin.

*Barbara W. Gerber*

## Bibliography

Garland, Ann F., and Edward Zigler. "Adolescent Suicide Prevention: Current Research and Social Policy Implications." *American Psychologist* 48:2 (1993), 169–182.

Remafedi, Gary, ed. *Death by Denial: Studies of Suicide in Gay and Lesbian Teenagers.* Boston: Alyson, 1994.

*See also* Adolescence; Alcohol and Substance Abuse; Homophobia

## Sweden

Country in northern Europe with eight million citizens. Until the 1960s, Swedish society was ethnically and religiously homogeneous. Swedish attitudes toward lesbianism are largely formed by the ideology of the welfare state. Swedish society is marked by tolerance toward "less fortunate" groups and social change through reform but also by a difficulty in accepting differences, a striving for consensus, and avoidance of conflict. Open expressions of antilesbianism are rare. Invisibility is the keyword.

## History

The history of lesbianism in Sweden is largely unwritten. One well-known historic person is Queen Christina (1626–1689). There has been much speculation about her sexuality, but what is undisputed is that her letters to the Countess Ebba Sparre speak of a deep and lasting affection. In 1864, a law against homosexuality, "fornication against nature," was issued. Before that time, there had been no specific law regulating same-sex relations. The law included both women and men, although only male homosexuality was of any concern for the legislators, and almost no women were prosecuted. With references to Magnus Hirschfeld's (1868–1935) theory of the great diversity of sexual types, attempts were made in the 1930s to have the law abolished, but not until 1944 were consensual relationships between adults of the same sex made legal. Lesbians were regarded as less "dangerous to society" than gay men, as

signs of lesbian affection were more tolerated, and there was no open lesbian cruising in public places that could offend the public. In the 1950s, a wave of antihomosexual sentiments swept across the country, targeting gay men mostly, but warnings against lesbian teachers were also issued.

The 1970s and 1980s brought several legal and social reforms. In 1973, the Swedish parliament declared that "cohabitation between two persons of the same sex is, in the eyes of society, a fully acceptable form of relationship." In 1978, the age of consent for same-sex relationships was lowered to fifteen years, the same as for heterosexuals. In 1979, the Swedish Board of Health abolished the classification of homosexuality as a disease. In 1987, two laws were passed. One forbids commercial organizations and public administrations to discriminate on grounds of homosexuality. The other makes it a criminal offense to make derogatory remarks about an individual's homosexuality. In 1988, same-sex couples living together were granted the same rights and obligations as unmarried heterosexual couples living together.

Beginning January 1, 1995, same-sex couples could enter "registered partnership" in an official, nonreligious ceremony, similar to the one used for nonreligious heterosexual marriages. It is conducted by a licensed "registrator" and usually held at the city hall. In daily speech, the partnership is referred to as a marriage. It has the same legal consequences as a marriage, except that same-sex partners do not have the right to adopt children together, and artificial insemination within the public-health service is given only to women in a heterosexual relationship. The law, which did not forbid hate speech against homosexuals as a group, was met with strong opposition from right-wing Christians. Since its passage, more men than women have chosen to enter registrated partnerships. In 1996, one of Sweden's most popular rock stars, Eva Dahlgren, registrated partnership with another woman.

## Organizations

Lesbians have organized both separately and together with gay men. One important place was the "female citizens' school" at the country estate, Fogelstad, founded by Elisabeth Tamm (1885–1958) and five other pioneers of the women's rights movement in 1925. Even if not openly associated with lesbianism, it provided a women-only space and many lesbians went there, both as participants in courses and as lecturers. The school closed in 1954.

The first homosexual organization in Sweden was founded in 1950 as a branch of the Danish Federation of 1948. In 1952, it became a separate organization with a separate name, the Swedish Federation for Sexual Equality (RFSL). In the beginning, very few women participated. The first lesbian group, Diana, was founded in the mid-1950s. Unlike the United States in the 1950s, Sweden had no bar culture, and the group's aim was to provide a social space for lesbians to meet. Some very big costume parties for both lesbians and gay men were privately arranged. RFSL has continued to organize both lesbians and gay men. In 1974, the first Nordic lesbian conference was held in Oslo, Norway, and, in the summer of 1975, a Nordic lesbian week was arranged at the women's camp, Femö, in Denmark.

After the third Nordic conference in Stockholm, Sweden, a group of women left RFSL in 1976 and founded the separate lesbian organization LF (Lesbian Front, later Lesbian Feminists). LF was primarily a part of the women's movement with a strong feminist and socialist agenda. Another lesbian organization, LN (Lesbian Now), was founded in 1988 out of the need to create a lesbian-only space. Two other organizations with strong lesbian influence are Kvinnohöjden (formerly Kvinnohögskolan), a year-round women-only center with courses in a multitude of subjects, such as astrology, wood-carving and lesbian sexuality, and Kvinnofolkhögskolan in Gothenburg, a women-only school for adult education that also arranges weekend courses, many of specific interest to lesbians. Lesbians have also organized together with men in such groups as EKHO (Christians), Gay Conservatives, Gay Socialists, Gay and Lesbian Jews, and youth groups.

## Culture

The first lesbian novel written in Swedish, *Charlie*, by heterosexual author Margareta Suber, was published in 1932. It gives, for its time, a positive description of a young lesbian and her love for a married woman. There is not a lot of Swedish lesbian literature, but among celebrated Swedish authors are Selma Lagerlöf (1858–1940), among whose publications is a collection of letters to Sophie Elkan (1853–1921), a Jewish woman who was also an author, and poet Karin Boye (1900–1941), who wrote many love poems to other women. In her novel *Kris* (1932), she pictures a young emotionally and religiously troubled woman who finds consolation in her feelings for another woman. In the 1990s,

several younger lesbian authors emerged. Theater and film with lesbian motifs has also been produced, mostly by independent, smaller groups.

*Karin Lindeqvist*

### Bibliography

Håkansson, Per-Arne. *Längtan och Livsform: Homosexuellas situation i ett heterosexuellt samhälle* (Longing and Lifestyle: The Situation for Homosexuals in a Heterosexual Society). Lund: Lunds universitet, 1987.

Hansson, Johan, ed. *Homosexuella och Omvarlden* (Homosexuals Around the World). Stockholm: LiberFörlag, 1982.

Parikas, Dodo. *Öppenhetens Betydelse: Homo- och bisexuella i Sverige mellan perversitet och dygdemönster* (The Importance of Being Open: Homo- and Bisexuals in Sweden Between Perversity and Paragons of Virtue). Stockholm: Carlsson Bokförlag, 1995.

***See also*** Boye, Karin; Christina of Sweden; Lagerlöf, Selma

## Switzerland

Country located in the middle of Europe that shares borders with Germany, Italy, France, and Austria. It has a population of seven million (65 percent German speakers, 18 percent French, 10 percent Italian, 1 percent Romansch, 6 percent other languages). Although Switzerland became a democratic country in 1848, women did not get the vote until 1971.

Little is known about lesbian women in the medieval or early-modern periods, but it is likely that they were sometimes persecuted as witches.

At the end of the nineteenth century, Zurich University became the first university in Europe to admit women as students, with other Swiss universities quickly following suit. Women came from all over Europe to study in Switzerland, although most were from Germany and Russia. Among them were many women who would today be identified as lesbians and who established life partnerships with other women. Many of these students published fiction, political pamphlets, or memoirs that show signs of lesbian tendencies. Examples include the Austrian philosopher and poet Helen von Druskowitz (1856–1918); the German novelists Ilse Frapan (1849–1908) and Ella Mensch (1859–1935); the historian and writer Meta von Salis (1855–1929), the first Swiss woman to receive a doctorate; the

Swiss doctor Caroline Fahrner (1842–1913); and Anna Heer (1863–1918), founder of the first Women's Hospital in Zurich.

In 1901, the Austrian Minna Adelt-Wettstein, under the pseudonym of Aimée Duc (1867–?), published the novel *Are They Women?*, which describes the milieu among students in Geneva, Switzerland, at that time and includes a discussion about the "third sex" (as homosexuals were called). At the same time, the first women's associations advocating the right of women to vote were founded in Switzerland. It took almost a hundred years for this battle to be finally won, in 1971, when an all-male electorate voted to give women the vote—quite a bit later than the rest of Europe.

The first lesbian organization was formed in 1931 after Laura Fredy Thoma (1901–1966), a clerk from Zurich, became acquainted with the lesbian ladies' club in Berlin, Germany. On her return, she published an article in Berlin's lesbian magazine *Garçonne* and an advertisement in a Zurich daily paper. Through these, she met other like-minded women, who together founded the Damenclub Amicitia (Ladies Club Amicitia). This club soon merged with the Herrenclub Excentric (Eccentric Gentlemen's Club) and, in 1932, this mixed group began to publish the magazine *Das Freundschaftsbanner* (The Friendship Banner), called from 1937 to 1940 *Das Menschenrecht* (The Human Right), and thereafter *Der Kreis* (The Circle).

Annemarie Schwarzenbach (1908–1942) from Zurich, a historian and the daughter of a millionaire, also left Switzerland in the 1930s. As a journalist and a photographer, she wrote reports and lyrical prose revealing her lesbian leanings. She was in love with actress and journalist Erika Mann (1905–1969), was loved by American novelist Carson McCullers (1917–1967), and had various affairs with other women.

After World War II, little information is available about lesbian lifestyles in Switzerland and Germany (where the Nazis had destroyed the lesbian subculture) until the early 1970s. There were a few lesbian bars in Basle and Zurich, as well as gay male bars that women also visited. The magazine *Der Kreis* had built up a readership in Zurich, and, from 1950, organized club evenings, parties, and cultural events. In 1966, the Conti-Club was founded. Lesbians were active members and met once a week for a social event.

In 1974, the Homosexuelle Frauengruppe Zürich (Homosexual Women's Group, Zurich) was formed as part of the new women's movement. It was politically active in supporting the emancipation and social equality of lesbians. Emancipatory lesbian groups were also started in Bern, Basel, and Geneva and, later, in the towns of Baden and St. Gallen. These groups were vocal in demanding rights for lesbians. The magazine *Lesbenfront* (Lesbian Front) was launched in 1975 by the Homosexuelle Frauengruppe Zürich; since 1996, it has been published, under the name *DIE* (The Feminine Gender).

Geneva, which used to have a lesbian magazine *Clit 007*, is the center for lesbians in French-speaking Switzerland, as Zurich is for lesbians in the German-speaking part. Many events connected with lesbian culture are held in Zurich. In 1993, 150 participants from Germany, Austria, and Switzerland took part in the 2. Symposium deutschsprachiger Lesbenforschung (Second Symposium for Lesbian Research in German) held in Boldern, near Zurich. An annual meeting of lesbians and gay men has been held in Boldern's Study Center since the mid-1970s. Besides issuing *DIE*, the Women's Center in Zurich also has a Lesbian Advice Center and a library for women and lesbians. Lesbians were the founders, builders, and main users of Switzerland's first women's holiday house, Villa Kassandra, in the French-speaking canton of Jura, and of the women's hotel, Monte Vuala, in Walenstadtberg.

In 1990, Lesbian Organization Switzerland (LOS) was founded with the aim of campaigning for the rights of lesbians in the whole of Switzerland. In 1994, it received favorable publicity when it participated in a widely publicized discussion on Swiss television about whether lesbians should be allowed to play women's football. While representatives of one football club presented hair-raising arguments for excluding lesbians, most journalists and a large part of the public supported the lesbians. In the end, lesbians were allowed to play on one club, but not on others.

In 1996, representatives of lesbian and gay organizations handed a petition to the Swiss government demanding equal rights for same-sex partners. At the same time, a law was drafted to ensure that lesbian and gay relationships were treated the same as heterosexual relationships but as of 1998 the government had not discussed it.      *Madeleine Marti*

### Bibliography

Kokula, Ilse. *Böhmer, Ulrike: Die Welt gehört uns doch! Zusammenschluss lesbischer Frauen in der Schweiz in der 30er Jahre* (The World Belongs to Us! Lesbian Women Organizing in the Thirties in Switzerland). Bern/Zurich: eFeF Verlag, 1991.

Marti, Madeleine. *Hinterlegte Botschaften. Die Darstellung lesbischer Frauen in der deutschsprachigen Literatur seit 1945* (Deposited Messages: The Representation of Lesbian Women in German Literature since 1945). Stuttgart: J.B. Metzler Verlag, 1992.

*See also* Berlin; McCullers, Carson; Witches, Persecution of

## Symbols

Socially rooted and supported, symbols represent the desires, histories, and identities of specific communities. As such, the more popular and pervasive a symbol, the more power it has to draw together the diverse members of a community, subsuming difference under unity. Symbols can, therefore, serve an important function for minority groups, reminding the community that, despite individual differences, the group is, nonetheless, united by common issues and experiences. The twentieth-century lesbian community has adopted a number of symbols that assert lesbians' existence, differences, and pride. Many of these symbols, such as the rainbow flag, the color lavender, the lambda, the pinkie ring, and the pink triangle, are used by both lesbian and gay communities, while others, such as the black triangle, the labrys, and the interlocking female symbols, are used specifically by lesbians.

The rainbow flag, one of the late twentieth century's most popular symbols of lesbian and gay pride, was created by Gilbert Baker and was first used in San Francisco, California's, Lesbian and Gay Freedom Day Parade in 1978. The flag's original eight stripes represented diversity, with each color symbolizing a different aspect of the lesbian and gay community: Hot pink stood for sex, red for life, orange for healing, yellow for sun, green for nature, turquoise for art, indigo for harmony, and violet for spirit. In 1979, when Baker decided to mass-produce the flag, pink and turquoise were removed, and indigo was replaced by royal blue, due to production constraints. The six-color version is widely used all over the world, symbolizing both gay pride and diversity within the lesbian and gay community.

Another color that has long been symbolically associated with lesbians and gay men is lavender.

There is no one, definitive explanation about why it is considered a lesbian and gay color, but lavender seems to have accrued homosexual connotations through multiple and repeated references pairing it with homosexuality in literary and historical documents. Some of the early references to the color, uncovered by poet and author Grahn (1984), include descriptions of the lesbian poet Sappho as violet haired. One hundred years after Sappho (ca. 600 B.C.E.), the Greek poet Anacreon used the word "purple" in a poem that is also the oldest-known text that uses the word "lesbian" to describe a woman who loves another woman. Historically, some purple flowers have also indicated homosexuality. The hyacinth is named after Hyacinthus, of whom the Greek sun god Apollo was passionately fond, while the violet was worn by men and women in England during the fourteenth century to indicate that they did not intend to marry. A more contemporary hypothesis points out that lavender consists of the combination of red and blue, gender-specific colors used in Western society to distinguish between girls and boys at birth. Thus, lavender represents the merging of the male and the female and signifies lesbian and gay resistance to traditional gender roles and identities.

Like the color lavender, the lambda is a lesbian and gay symbol with an only partly recovered history. It was popularized in the 1970s, after it was adopted by the New York Gay Activists Alliance in 1970 and then by the International Gay Rights Congress held in Edinburgh, Scotland, in 1974. However, it remains unclear why these organizations adopted the lambda as a lesbian and gay symbol. Some speculate that it was used because it is the Greek lowercase letter for liberation, while others cite the use of the lambda in physics to denote energy, claiming the lambda symbolizes the energy of the lesbian and gay community working together. Still others point to its use by the Greek Spartans, who considered it a symbol of unity. Despite the confusion surrounding its adoption, it is generally considered a symbol of lesbian and gay pride.

The pinkie ring, although somewhat obscure in the 1990s, has been used as a discreet way of indicating that one is lesbian or gay. Grahn (1984) notes that the occult sciences attributed knowledge and transformation to both the little finger and the color purple. The little finger's association with a traditionally lesbian and gay color, as well as with self-knowledge and transformation—ideas that are consonant with popular lesbian and gay identity-

**S** formation narratives—may have contributed to the pinkie ring's adoption as a lesbian and gay symbol.

The pink triangle, another popular symbol of lesbian and gay pride, has a darker history, dating back to Adolf Hitler's Nazi regime (1933–1945). Although German law prohibited homosexual acts prior to Hitler's rise to power, Hitler expanded the law to include kissing, embracing, "lewd glances," and gay fantasies as criminal offenses. Between 1937 and 1939, thousands of men convicted of homosexuality were sent to prison, then later sent to concentrations camps. Each prisoner in the camps wore a colored, inverted triangle that signified the reason for his or her incarceration. Green signified a regular criminal; red a political prisoner; two yellow overlapping triangles, forming the star of David, a Jew; pink a homosexual; and a star of David under a pink triangle a gay Jew.

Although the pink triangle was originally a symbol of shame and tragedy associated with the persecution and extermination of thousands of gay men, the 1970s gay liberation groups reclaimed it as a symbol of lesbian and gay pride, solidarity, and the fight against oppression. However, some critics have opposed the lesbian adoption of the pink triangle, believing that it conceals the specificity of lesbian experience by conflating it with that of gay men. Lesbians were never specifically targeted under paragraph 175 of German law—not because the Nazis accepted lesbianism, but because they found the idea so intolerable that they denied its existence.

Some historians have also found evidence that lesbians were included among women who were imprisoned for "antisocial behavior," violating the Nazi's construction of womanhood, which reduced women to wives and mothers. They were made to wear a black triangle, which, although far less popular than the pink triangle, is sometimes used as a symbol specifically denoting lesbian pride. Despite this attempt to differentiate between the experiences of lesbians and gay men, the use of both the pink and the black triangle as symbols of liberation has been criticized by those who believe that they cannot be extricated from their original horrific uses. Nevertheless, those who use them maintain that these symbols speak to the invisibility of gay history, recasting symbols of victimhood into a warning against complacency.

Another exclusively lesbian symbol is the labrys, a double-sided ax believed to have been used in ancient matriarchal societies as both a weapon and a harvesting tool. Ancient Greek artwork depicts the Amazons wielding labryses. The goddess of the Amazons, variously named Artemis, Gaea, Rhea, and Demeter, used the labrys as a scepter, and her priests were called "ax-bearers." The sacred rites associated with the worship of Demeter are believed to have included lesbian sex. The labrys is primarily remembered for its Amazon roots and most often appears in the form of jewelry, worn as a symbol of lesbian strength and self-sufficiency.

Finally, two interlocking female symbols are also often used to signify lesbianism. Gender symbols consist of ancient Roman astrological signs; the male is represented by the symbol of Mars, and the female is represented by the symbol of Venus, sometimes described as "the mirror of Venus." Her sign, which once represented life, love, and sexuality, is now both a botanical and zoological symbol of femaleness, as well as the astronomical symbol of the planet Venus. Lesbian and feminist communities have also adopted the symbol, using two interlocking Venus emblems to represent lesbianism or, alternatively, the sisterhood of women. *Christy Stevens*

### Bibliography

*The Alyson Almanac: A Treasury of Information for the Lesbian and Gay Community.* 2nd ed. Boston: Alyson, 1990.

Elman, Amy R. "Triangles and Tribulations: The Politics of Nazi Symbols." *Journal of Homosexuality* 30:3 (1996), 1–11.

Grahn, Judy. *Another Mother Tongue: Gay Words, Gay Worlds.* Boston: Beacon, 1984.

Plant, Richard. *The Pink Triangle: The Nazi War Against Homosexuals.* New York: Holt, 1986.

Walker, Barbara G. *The Woman's Dictionary of Symbols and Sacred Objects.* San Francisco: Harper and Row, 1988.

Yoshino, Kenji. "Suspect Symbols: The Literary Argument for Heightened Scrutiny for Gays." *Columbia Law Review* 96:7 (1996), 1753–1834.

*See also* Amazons; Nazism; Sappho

### Synagogues

Houses of worship in the Jewish religion. Gay and lesbian synagogues arose in the 1970s to meet the needs of a growing number of Jewish gay men and lesbians who wished to explore religious identity but did not feel welcome in traditional synagogues. Many gay and lesbian Jews grew up with religious affiliations but became alienated from mainstream synagogues, which were structured on heterosexuality as the norm. The negative attitudes toward same-sex love that are found in ancient Jewish texts were never scrutinized or repudiated. Gay men and lesbians could not show affection in public, seek partners, be recognized as couples entitled to family memberships, or celebrate their relationships through Jewish ritual.

In the 1970s, many Jewish gay men and lesbians sought spiritual connections in the Metropolitan Community Church, an interdenominational Protestant church founded to serve the Christian gay community. But they quickly realized that they wanted Jewish places of worship. In 1972, gay synagogues were founded in Los Angeles, California (Beth Chayim Chadashim), and New York City (Congregation Beth Simhat Torah), and, soon thereafter, in San Francisco, California (Sha'ar Zahav), Philadelphia, Pennsylvania (Beth Ahava), and Washington, D.C. (Beth Mishpaha). In 1975, these groups formed an umbrella group known as the World Congress of Gay and Lesbian Jews, which meets every other year for an educational and social conference. By the late 1990s, more than fifty gay and lesbian synagogues and groups existed in the United States and in many countries throughout the world, including Canada, Mexico, the United Kingdom, Australia, South Africa, Israel, and the Netherlands.

Many gay and lesbian synagogues have affiliated with mainstream Jewish religious organizations as well. The Reform and Reconstructionist movements have welcomed these synagogues into their national groups, the Union of American Hebrew Congregations (UAHC) and the Jewish Reconstructionist Federation (JRF), respectively. It was the UAHC that first admitted the congregation in Los Angeles, Beth Chayim Chadashim, in 1973, and helped it acquire a Torah scroll and meeting place.

The gay and lesbian synagogue movement has also met with severe opposition. When the World Congress held its meetings in Israel in 1979, rabbinic authorities tried to prevent it from meeting. And the Jewish National Fund turned down the group's gift to plant trees in Israel. In 1993, the New York City congregation, Beth Simhat Torah, was refused a place in the annual Israel Independence Day Parade.

Gay and lesbian synagogues are similar to traditional synagogues in terms of the needs they serve. They offer worship services, study groups for adults and children, and opportunities for social experiences and political action within the Jewish community. Some have formal institutional structures that include boards of directors and dues, buildings and professional staff, while others function more as informal *havurot* (small groups that gather for prayer, study, and social activities). Additionally, gay and lesbian synagogues represent Jewish interests in the gay and lesbian community.

Gay and lesbian synagogues are unique in that their members display a wide variety of religious beliefs and practices, ranging from Orthodox to Reform. This reality has necessitated compromise in the definition of communal norms. In addition, gay men and lesbians may have had different experiences with Jewish tradition that are a result of gender. Some gay synagogues have been willing to challenge traditional gender norms in Judaism, and feminism has found a supportive environment in many, but not all, of these groups. *Rebecca T. Alpert*

### Bibliography

Balka, Christie, and Andy Rose, eds. *Twice Blessed: On Being Lesbian or Gay and Jewish*. Boston: Beacon, 1989.

Brick, Barrett L. "Judaism in the Gay Community." In *Positively Gay*. Ed. Betty Berzon and Robert Leighton. Millbrae, Calif.: Celestial Arts, 1979, pp. 79–87.

Cooper, Aaron. "No Longer Invisible: Gay and Lesbian Jews Build a Movement." *Journal of Homosexuality* 18 (1989–1990), 83–94.

Shokeid, Moshe. *A Gay Synagogue in New York*. New York: Columbia University Press, 1995.

***See also*** Judaism

# T

## Taiwan

Multiethnic political entity with a complex history of successive waves of immigrants and a series of imperial, colonial, and elected administrations. The population of 21 million makes the small island (14,000 square miles) one of the most densely populated areas in the world. Politically, Taiwan was, and still is, an oddity. In the wake of his defeat in mainland China at the hands of the Communists, the general and leader of the Nationalist party (KMT), Chiang Kai-shek (1887–1975), established the Republic of China on Taiwan in 1945, vowing to reconquer mainland China in due course. Meanwhile, the People's Republic of China, which was proclaimed in 1949 also laid claim to Taiwan, considering Chiang's regime a renegade government. While never escalating hostilities to the point of war, the two Chinas have, nevertheless, been locked in a political, economic, and social rivalry. This geopolitical constellation has had a significant impact on the formation of lesbian identity in Taiwan.

In the 1950s, the autocratic KMT government promoted Confucian family-centered ideology; political allegiance to a pan-Chinese, but anti-Communist, nationalism; and capitalist development through a variety of policies. While neither female nor male homosexuality was criminalized, lesbianism, to the extent that censorship allowed for any representations whatsoever, was construed as a psychiatric disorder. Since the early decades of the twentieth century, Western sexological treatises had been accepted as a form of scientific knowledge necessary for modernization. In 1960s and 1970s Taiwan, economic modernization depended partly on women's entry into the labor force. However, female sexual access to women continued to be pathologized. Still, during this period, some women were able to eke out a lesbian existence in certain peripheral social spaces, such as local opera troupes and the entertainment sector.

Political liberalization during the 1980s paved the way for a variety of dissident social and cultural movements that challenged the status quo. Feminist organizations began to push for the reform of family laws, nondiscriminatory AIDS education, and destigmatization of divorce and female sexuality through study groups, publications, public speaking, lobbying, and demonstrations. In the wake of workers', women's, and students' activism, the first self-consciously lesbian social group was formed in Taipei in 1990. In the next few years, the coverage of lesbian and gay themes increased in both newly founded lesbian media and in mainstream venues. By 1996, female and male homosexuality had become a major media phenomenon, produced by a small number of self-identified lesbians and gays and a large number of relatively sympathetic heterosexuals. An incomplete sampling includes lesbian and gay electronic bulletin boards, radio programs aimed at a gay and lesbian audience, lesbian- and gay-themed novels, special issues of established periodicals and scholarly journals, a lesbian and gay lifestyle magazine, regular columns on gay and lesbian issues in mainstream newspapers, lesbian- and gay-related lecture series in feminist and upscale bookstores, lesbian and gay films, and lesbian- and gay-themed courses in college and university English departments. In terms of activism, 1996 also witnessed a number of firsts: the public celebration of a gay and lesbian Pride Day, the participation of a lesbian and gay political group in a feminist rally held in conjunction with International Women's

Day, and an openly gay candidate running for political office.

Lesbians confront major paradoxes. In terms of the state, in showcasing a liberal attitude toward, and financial support of, lesbian cultural activities, governmental agencies and political parties can demonstrate that Taiwan's policies compare favorably with the intolerant and repressive treatment of lesbians and gays in the People's Republic of China. In terms of the public imagination, lesbians represent a variety of positions in the question of how "modern" or "traditional," how "Western," "Chinese," or "Taiwanese" a society Taiwan wants or ought to be. For instance, if portrayed as a symptom of cultural and economic backwardness, lesbianism needs to be overcome by economic modernization, whose primary romantic reward is, supposedly, a sexually and emotionally satisfying heterosexuality. If described as an undesirably Westernized entity, the lesbian needs to be silenced in order to create a pure Taiwanese body politic. If portrayed as an emblem of a modern Taiwan—in the 1990s, the most popular media representation—lesbianism can be celebrated as the quintessential style of a hip, trendy, and modern society of an "ultra-new species" (*xinxin renlei*). The question of how comfortably one can adopt a lesbian identity without being ostracized by family, friends, and coworkers is as acute as ever. However, as public perceptions change, familial ones are likely to be transformed as well.                    *Patricia Sieber*

### Bibliography

Huang, Hans. "Be(com)ing Gay: Sexual Dissidence and Cultural Change in Contemporary Taiwan." M.A. thesis, University of Sussex, 1996.

Sang, Tze-lang D. "The Emerging Lesbian: Female Same-Sex Desire in Modern Chinese Literature and Culture." Ph.D. diss., University of California, Berkeley, 1996.

Sieber, Patricia, ed. *Red Is not the Only Color: Contemporary Chinese Writing on Love Between Women.* San Francisco: Cleis, 1998.

*See also* China; Chinese Literature

### Taylor, Valerie (1913–1997)

Author and activist. Born Velma Nacella Young, Valerie Taylor grew up in Illinois, attended Blackburn College, and taught in rural schools before marrying William J. Tate in 1939. The difficult marriage produced three sons. Taylor divorced in 1953,

*Valerie Taylor. Photo by Tee A. Corinne.*

using money earned from the sale of her first paperback novel, *Hired Girl* (1953). In the following years, she published short stories, poetry as Nacella Young, and romance novels as Francine Davenport; however, it was her writing of lesbian-themed books, using the name Valerie Taylor, that brought her lasting fame.

The market for paperback originals expanded through the 1950s and 1960s, and Taylor published three books with Fawcett—*Whisper Their Love* (1957), *The Girls in 3-B* (1959), and *Stranger on Lesbos* (1960)—and four with Midwood-Tower—*Return to Lesbos* (1963), *A World Without Men* (1963), *Unlike Others* (1963), and *Journey to Fulfillment* (1964). Her novels were praised and treasured, in part, because she wrote about ordinary, recognizable women confronting real-world dilemmas.

Taylor spent the years 1962–1975 in Chicago, where she became a founding member of Mattachine Midwest in 1965 and cofounded the Lesbian Writers Conference in 1974. In 1975, at age 62, she retired from her editing job and moved from Chicago to Upstate New York. In 1979, she moved to Tucson, Arizona.

A new phase of Taylor's career was launched in 1976 when Womanpress brought out *Two Women:*

*The Poetry of Jeannette Foster and Valerie Taylor.* Naiad Press published *Love Image* (1977), *Prism* (1981), and *Rice and Beans* (1989) and, in 1982, reprinted three earlier novels. In 1991, Banned Books published *Two Women Revisited.*

Taylor wrote poetry all of her life. She published poems and prose in *The Ladder* in the years 1961–1965 and was active in the poetry scene in Tucson. She wrote and spoke against war and poverty and for the rights of the elderly, disabled people, lesbians, and gay men. She organized a fund to help support scholar Jeannette Foster's (1895–1981) final years and wrote articles on Foster, as well as on authors May Sarton (1912–1996) and Denise Levertov (1923–1997).

Taylor received the Paul R. Goldman Award from the Chicago Chapter of One, Inc., in 1975 and was inducted into the Chicago Gay and Lesbian Hall of Fame in 1992.          *Tee A. Corinne*

### Bibliography

Brandt, Kate, ed. *Happy Endings: Lesbian Writers Talk About Their Lives and Work.* Tallahassee, Fla.: Naiad, 1993.

Corinne, Tee, and Caroline Overman. "Valerie Taylor Interview." *Common Lives/Lesbian Lives* 22 (Winter 1988), 60–72.

Kuda, Marie, and Bill Kelley. "Valerie Taylor." Chicago Gay and Lesbian Hall of Fame. Chicago: City of Chicago Commission on Human Relations, 1992.

Terkel, Studs, ed. *Coming of Age: The Story of Our Century by Those Who've Lived It.* New York: New Press, 1995.

**See also** Chicago, Illinois; Foster, Jeannette Howard; *Ladder, The*; Naiad Press; Pulp Paperbacks

## Teachers

Although quietly named within the history of women and education and, at times, submerged in histories of gay (male) teachers, lesbians have pursued educational careers. Contending with cultural and internalized constraints regarding sexuality and gender roles, lesbian teachers have often been silenced or obscured in educational narratives. They have, nonetheless, become educational leaders, respected educators, and provocative theorists. Because education—especially public primary and secondary education—historically has attracted single women and nontraditional men, significant numbers of lesbians and gay men can be found in the profession (Harbeck 1997). At least since the 1870s lesbian teachers have formed networks of personal and professional support; in the late 1970s, the Lesbian Teachers Network for public-school instructors grew out of the annual Michigan Womyn's Music Festival, and numerous lesbian or gay and lesbian caucuses organize for personal, professional, and political support within organizations.

### History

While the poet-teacher Sappho (ca. 600 B.C.E.) might be invoked as a "first" lesbian teacher, individual women have served cross-culturally as tutors or governesses and, occasionally, as teachers in small schools or select classrooms. Women as a group were recruited to teaching beginning late in the nineteenth century just as increasing numbers of women (primarily white women in the United States) graduated from women's colleges, private seminaries, and public "normal schools" specializing in educational training. As populations, as well as the need for educated industrial workers and hence schools, expanded (especially in Canada, the United Kingdom, France, and the United States), school administrators viewed a female teaching corps as "cheap labor." Simultaneously, administrators described the teaching role as a proper extension of women's duties and role: the care and nurture of children. In the United States, black women teachers—many of them graduates of Southern colleges or institutes established by black women, or specifically for black students—found work primarily in black institutions, Northern urban schools and, after 1920, segregated Southern schools. Overall, teaching for wages increased a woman's economic autonomy but did not necessarily raise her social status; for example, women teachers of all races were expected to behave primly and, in time, to choose marriage. Black women who remained single and committed to educational "uplifting" of the race were less likely than their white peers to be scorned as "spinster" teachers.

Early in the twentieth century, in Europe as in North America, the maligning of all spinster teachers rested on the work of sexologists, who disparaged such "female perversions" as lesbianism as well as independent—unmarried and wage-earning—women generally. Many "educated spinsters" remained at women's colleges as new teaching faculty, while others left to invent new careers. In either case, education—the pursuit and practice of it—

brought women together in new communities and spheres. Well-known early-twentieth-century educators who established same-sex households included Lucy Diggs Slowe, dean of women at Howard University (1922–1937), and educator Mary Birrill; and M. Carey Thomas, president of Bryn Mawr (1894–1922), and philanthropist Mary Garrett (1839–1915).

After World War I, same-sex social spheres and relationships faded as acceptable practices and ideologies; still required to be exemplars, teachers faced medical and legal, as well as religious and social consensus, regarding characteristics of proper morality that left no room for homosexual behavior or identities but required sexual and gender conformity. As local or federal government workers, lesbians at mid-century in the United States could be harassed, forced to resign, or fired from positions as teachers on the ground of "moral turpitude." In this atmosphere, lesbian teachers often chose to "pass" publicly as heterosexual by entering a "front" marriage (often with gay men) or by inventing a heterosexual social life while building lesbian social networks. Because homosexuality—or homosexual sex acts, sodomy—remained a criminal offense in most American states and many countries worldwide, school officials in the last half of the twentieth century were empowered to terminate the employment of teachers accused of criminal homosexual acts. This particularly targeted gay males arrested for committing "immoral" public sexual acts. Since the 1960s, lesbians and gay men accused of criminal homosexual activity generally retained their jobs by challenging the constitutionality of laws based on homosexual status.

## Public Policy and Teacher Organizing

In 1974, the National Education Association first included "sexual preference" in its statement of nondiscrimination; at the same time, some U.S. states, cities, and school boards began to decriminalize same-sex sex acts or include "sexual preference" in human rights provisions. Despite these legal gains, lesbian teachers still face challenges. Some human rights statutes, for example, include exemptions and limitations in the areas of education and curriculum and in hiring and leadership for youth groups and religious organizations; also, the adoption of human rights protections does not always lead to a repeal of sodomy laws. An ongoing fear that gay and lesbian teachers would teach homosexuality prompted religious and cultural conservatives to initiate campaigns to repeal various protections. In 1978, California State Senator John Briggs called for the firing of school employees who engaged in "advocating, soliciting, imposing, encouraging, or promoting of private or public homosexual activity directed at, or likely to come to the attention of, schoolchildren and/or other employees." The Briggs Initiative was defeated by California voters, but the close vote created a chilling effect for teachers across the country. In the early 1990s, voters in at least three U.S. states—Colorado, Idaho, and Oregon—considered state constitutional amendments that would have prohibited state, regional, and local governments from using public money to "promote" homosexuality, whether by enacting antidiscrimination ordinances or by hiring teachers or creating educational curricula at any grade level that might affirm homosexuals or homosexuality. Only voters in Colorado approved such a measure, but the rhetoric of gay and lesbian human rights as "special rights" spread beyond these few sites. Based on arguments posed by a coalition of educational groups and gay and lesbian organizations—that "public schools fail in their educational mission if they do not create a secure learning environment for gay and lesbian students" as well as teachers and allies ("Education Amici Curiae Brief")—the United States Supreme Court in 1996 declared the Colorado measure unconstitutional, ruling that it denied legal protections to persons based on a single trait, sexual orientation, and denied gays and lesbians equal protection.

Earlier during the 1980s, lesbian educators participated in the building of teacher organizations, campus offices, and student-centered programs intended to break silences about the subject of homosexuality, to create social and intellectual dialogues regarding sexuality in safe and supportive settings, and to engage parents, administrators, and colleagues in examining and diminishing heterosexism and homophobia. In 1984, Dr. Virginia Uribe began to invite self-identified gay and lesbian students in her Los Angeles high school to meet weekly for informal lunchtime discussions. She formalized the sessions in her own school and in the Los Angeles School District as Project 10 in 1985. Project 10 emphasizes creating places for gay and lesbian students to talk, coordinating workshops and training for administrators, and operating drop-in school sites for counseling, including peer counseling, and outreach to parents, significant others, suicide-prevention programs, and substance-abuse centers.

Across the country, lesbian educators joined in shaping schools, programs, and educational projects that brought students and teachers together. In 1985, Joyce Hunter cofounded—with the Hetrick-Martin Institute—the Harvey Milk School for sexual-minority youth in New York City. In 1994, a national coalition of gay and straight teachers, GLSTN (Gay, Lesbian, Straight Teachers Network), formed to fight homophobia through programming, networking, and offering resources to individuals and schools. Research findings indicate that teachers who participate in such organizations and who are open about their sexual orientation experience less isolation, increase interactions with students and colleagues, participate more in school change, and experience fewer negative social ramifications (Woog 1995).

## Closets, Conflicts, and Classrooms

Lesbian teachers face a dilemma in which physical safety, as well as economic and job concerns may collide with a desire to be fully present in classroom interactions. How a teacher views herself and her society often shapes decisions about coming out to colleagues and students and about how, or whether, to address sexuality-related questions and concerns in classroom discussions and curriculum design. A lesbian teacher may come out to herself, to school colleagues, and in classrooms as one who is aware of lesbian concerns, histories, and persons. Occasionally, lesbian teachers and administrators who internalize a culture's homophobic attitudes will not only closet themselves, but also work against "out" colleagues who seek equity and curricular change. Many lesbian teachers who are "out" note that the support of, contacts in, and easy access to, an established gay, lesbian, bisexual, and transgender community influence their lives as teachers. Involvement with feminist politics and theories can provide lesbian teachers with frameworks for developing a vision of the world that informs teaching choices with an analysis of how lesbian teachers are perceived within academic communities and why, and with means of understanding career and classroom choices.

Lesbian teachers of color in colleges and universities, even more than in elementary and high schools, find themselves working in an overwhelmingly white profession, in which few teachers have sufficient experience with building multicultural classrooms or mediating interpersonal differences. At the same time, lesbian teachers of color may ex-perience a mixture of discord and comfort in working with heterosexual persons of color, many of whom also have internalized various aspects of institutional homophobia and/or find it difficult to address race-, class-, gender- *and* sexuality-based concerns of students. Lesbian teachers report that being open about lesbianism does make positive differences in classrooms, whether in elementary schools, high schools, or colleges and universities. McNaron (1997) reports a burgeoning presence of gay and lesbian academic research coexisting with a determined intolerance of lesbian scholars and scholarship. Also, although gay and lesbian teachers increasingly take an educational stance, believing that their writing and teaching can change attitudes and knowledge, "coming out" remains difficult for many lesbian teachers, especially in unwelcoming environments. McNaron notes the importance of a "campus [that] has integrated its lesbian and gay faculty into the fabric of its programs and structures, not demanding silence or secrecy in exchange for acceptance or reward." Such an environment allows individual teachers to "be public in large numbers about their sexual identity, creating thereby a critical mass which makes it virtually impossible for them to be marginalized." Building on legislation, court rulings, organization building, individual scholarship, and collective curriculum building, lesbian teachers in the 1990s worked to continue improving the overall educational environment.

*Ilene D. Alexander*

## Bibliography

Harbeck, Karen. *Gay And Lesbian Educators: Personal Freedoms, Public Constraints*. Malden, Mass.: Amethyst, 1997.

Jennings, Kevin, ed. *One Teacher in 10: Gay and Lesbian Educators Tell Their Stories*. Boston: Alyson, 1994.

Khayatt, Madiha. *Lesbian Teachers: An Invisible Presence*. Albany: State University of New York Press, 1992.

Kissen, Rita. *The Last Closet: The Real Lives of Lesbian and Gay Teachers*. Portsmouth, N.H.: Hienemann, 1996.

McNaron, Toni A.H. *Poisoned Ivy: Lesbian and Gay Academics Confronting Homophobia*. Philadelphia: Temple University Press, 1997.

Parmeter, Sarah-Hope, and Irene Reti, eds. *The Lesbian in Front of the Classroom: Writings by Lesbian Teachers*. Santa Cruz, Calif.: Her-Books, 1988.

Woog, Dan. *School's Out: The Impact of Gay and Lesbian Issues on America's Schools*. Boston: Alyson, 1995.

***See also*** Boarding Schools; Colleges, Women's; High Schools, Lesbian and Gay; Lesbian Studies; Spinsters; Students; Thomas, M. Carey

## Technology

Combination of practical skills with theoretical knowledge about nature into complex craft techniques. According to late-twentieth-century feminist critiques of science, technology, as its practical application, manifests a strong inherent male bias, serving primarily the needs of those who are male, heterosexual, and wealthy. Very little of technology has been specifically developed to serve the needs and viewpoints of lesbians and other marginalized groups. Consequently, lesbian views on technology remain to be developed.

Traditional approaches to technology reduced women to a part of nature, treating them as biological and reproductive objects rather than active participants. Phallic imagery can be found in many supposedly objective traditional narratives of technology. It is particularly prominent in late-twentieth-century nuclear-weapons research and development, but also exists in metaphors used in narratives of other technological endeavors.

Many lesbians have rejected those expressions of technology, which they perceive as patriarchal, to seek women-only communities that follow ecological and low-technology principles. Some others have chosen to engage in research that respects animal rights and attempts to reintegrate humanity with the rest of the organic world.

To move beyond the struggles centered in the male/female power differentials of technology, feminist thinker Haraway (1991) has introduced the concept of "cyborg"—a metaphor that offers women and lesbians a wider position. Cyborg refers to "a creature in a post-gender world," representing a blurring of the dichotomy of nature and technology, humans and machines. It connects humans with nonhumans and allows humans to gain an approach to the possibilities of technology that could humanize it.

In Haraway's view, women need not necessarily take an antiscience stand or resort to what she calls the "demonology of technology." Instead, women can "be responsible for machines" and have the power to survive "on the basis of seizing the tools to mark the world that marked them as other."

British physicist and writer Sourbut (1991) applies these ideas to reproductive technologies from a lesbian viewpoint. Traditionally, debates about assisted reproduction have centered on the treatment of infertility. Sourbut explores how lesbian feminism might be used "to empower women as mothers and as users of technology, rather than simply as passive recipients of medical interventions." For that purpose, Sourbut adopts the concept of "gynogenesis," a term advocated by lesbian feminist scientist Edwards (1990). Gynogenesis (not to be confused with parthenogenesis, in which only one egg is present) is defined as an attempt to create an individual with two female parents, by adding the genetic material from one egg to a second egg. Currently, this is not possible because of genetic imprinting (in which both maternal and paternal contributions are needed for a successful early development of a fertilized egg). Nevertheless, Sourbut argues that gynogenesis, even if it would prove to be difficult or even impracticable to achieve by existing or future technological means, is valuable as a vision of women-controlled technology. Gynogenesis also remakes the boundaries "between science and nature, natural and unnatural," going far beyond the traditional aim of providing infertility treatment for childless heterosexual couples.

Science fiction, as a powerful tool for the technological imagination, has given a voice to lesbian technological utopias and dystopias. The cyborgs and lesbian space explorers that inhabit these stories represent the elements of an imagined lesbian future that could become reality or at least contribute to it.

Women and lesbians who are actively engaged in attempts to transform scientific and technological practices have argued that certain applications of science and technology might place a stronger emphasis on observing the complexity and interdependencies present in nature, instead of on objectifying and controlling it. These applications could include such disciplines as meteorology or oceanography or certain experimental approaches. An example of the latter is geneticist Barbara McClintock's (1902–1992) often-cited "feeling for the organism"—that is, treating her research material, maize plants, individually and watching each of them grow.     *Eva Isaksson*

### Bibliography

Edwards, Ryn. "The Choreographing of Reproductive DNA." *Lesbian Ethics* 4:1 (1990), 44–51.

Haraway, Donna J. *Simians, Cyborgs, and Women.* London: Free Association, 1991.

Sourbut, Elizabeth. "Gynogenesis: A Lesbian Appropriation of Reproductive Technologies." In *Between Monsters, Goddesses, and Cyborgs.* Ed. Nina Lykke and Rosi Braidotti. London: Zed, 1991, pp. 227–241.

*See also* Science; Science Fiction

## Television

The representation of lesbians on U.S. television, whether in prime-time network series and movies, syndicated talk shows, made-for-cable movies, traditional and tabloid news programs, public-access programs, or commercials, changed dramatically over the first fifty years of television's presence in America's living rooms. At the dawn of the Television Age in the 1950s, when television was becoming a major medium for news and entertainment, coverage of lesbian issues and portrayal of lesbian characters was nonexistent. When television news coverage of lesbian and gay issues did begin to appear on the small screen in the late 1960s and early 1970s, in response to political activism for the civil rights of lesbians and gay men, it was blatantly negative and stereotypical, fueled by homophobia and heterosexism. Throughout the 1970s and 1980s, continued political activism for gay and lesbian rights, including actions directed at television networks and other mass media, brought about a growing number of somewhat sympathetic representations.

By 1991, the prime-time TV audience was able to watch the "first lesbian kiss" on network television on NBC's *L.A. Law.* The number of nonnegative portrayals of regular lesbian TV characters in prime time proceeded to increase during the 1990s, in part due to the identification of lesbians and gay men as a target consumer market for advertisers and the media-created phenomenon of "lesbian chic." By 1997, viewers could follow the comedic antics of TV's first "out" lead lesbian character on ABC's *Ellen* and know that the actor playing the lesbian, Ellen DeGeneres (1959–), had come out along with her character, another first in TV history. Although representations of lesbians and lesbian issues had become more frequent and generally sympathetic by the late 1990s, television's view remained primarily heterosexual, meaning that depictions of lesbians had to fall well within the acceptable bounds of heteronormative behavior. The failure of *Ellen* to ob-

serve those bounds contributed to its cancellation at the end of the 1997–1998 season.

The world of the small screen is a small one, indeed. It is a world populated by mostly white, middle-to-upper-middle-class heterosexuals (primarily men) who represent idealized, sanitized social relations. Although the advent of new broadcast networks, such as Fox, Warner Brothers, and Universal Pictures Network, along with a proliferation of cable networks, such as Home Box Office, Showtime, Turner Network Television, Cable News Network, and Black Entertainment Television, has increased the diversity of characters and content of television programming, it can hardly be claimed that television even begins to represent the diversity of the social, cultural, racial, ethnic, sexual, political, or economic relations, identities, and perspectives of the U.S. population. The continued vertical integration of ownership of media production and distribution outlets, especially in television, by fewer transnational corporations during the 1990s indicates that the industry is unlikely to diversify its product unless it is profitable. These material relations and the worldview they engender are the context in which nearly all programming for television is produced. It is important, therefore, to preface any discussion of media representations by remembering the very particular filters through which television content must pass before reaching living-room screens. Only with this caveat—recognizing the tightly circumscribed symbolic world of television—does any discussion of the representations of lesbians and lesbian issues on TV make sense in relation to actual lives.

### Prime-Time Entertainment Programs

Openly homosexual nonstereotypical fictional characters first appeared on prime-time television in 1972 in an ABC Movie of the Week, *That Certain Summer.* Actor Hal Holbrook (1925–) played a father who left his family to live with his male lover and then had to tell his son he was gay. The father tells his son that he would be heterosexual if he could. The two gay men are never shown as intimate with, or loving toward, each other. Since this movie aired, more fictional lesbian and gay characters have been represented in individual episodes of programs or movies, but the number of gay men portrayed has always been greater than the number of lesbians. The groundbreaker in the portrayal of lesbians on television came six years later with ABC's broadcast of *A Question of Love* in 1978. Starring Jane Alexander (1939–) and Gena Rowlands (1934–) as a lesbian couple, the film was based on a true-life custody battle by a lesbian for her two sons. Even though, at the end, the lesbian mother loses the custody battle to her ex-husband, the film does portray the atmosphere of bigotry surrounding the couple in their lives and the case in court. *A Question of Love* was produced and aired by ABC partly in response to a challenge by lesbian media activists to networks to stop portraying lesbians negatively (after a particularly gruesome depiction of three fellow inmates in youth detention using a broomstick to rape a teenage character played by Blair Brown (1948–) in NBC's movie *Born Innocent*, aired in 1974 and 1975). Unlike *That Certain Summer*, *A Question of Love* shows the couple in an intimate and loving scene, when one dyes the other's hair. The lesbian characters, however, never express their sexuality—with even a kiss. A sprinkling of movies focusing on lesbian issues were shown by the networks during the 1980s and 1990s, with portrayals becoming more positive. *My Two Loves* (ABC), about a woman married to a man and in love with a woman, aired in 1986. In 1995, the real-life story of a lesbian colonel's fight against discharge from the United States Army, *Serving in Silence: The Margarethe Cammermeyer Story* (NBC), was broadcast. Like *A Question of Love* nearly two decades earlier, a custody battle was the basis of the 1996 TV movie *Two Mothers for Zachary* (ABC), except that, in this case, the lesbian mother is sued by her own mother for custody of her son. Made-for-TV movies paved the way for nonstereotypical representations of lesbians and gay men; afterward, lesbian and gay characters became more prevalent in TV series.

In the mid- to late 1980s, some prime-time television series, such as *Designing Women* (CBS), *Cagney and Lacey* (CBS), *L.A. Law* (NBC), and the *Golden Girls* (NBC), treated the subject of homosexuality sympathetically, despite the social backlash, and a consequent reversion to negative stereotypes, especially in news programs, occasioned by the arrival of AIDS and its early association with the gay male population.

The earliest prime-time network series with a regular (recurring) lesbian character was ABC's *Heartbeat*, a drama centered on a women's medical clinic. The series debuted in 1988, featuring a lesbian nurse-practitioner and mother as a central character. The series ran for one-and-a-half seasons, with the role of the lesbian character steadily decreasing, and was canceled for poor ratings. Hantzis and Lehr (1994) argue, based on a close reading of the show's text, that, although *Heartbeat* was impor-

tant in creating a generally positive portrayal of a lesbian on TV, the value of this inclusion was at least partly undermined by the depiction of the lesbian character as nonsexual, not independent or assertive, frequently troubled, and in feminine dress and manner but never sexy.

Representations of lesbians in TV comedy and drama programs became a bit more positive during the 1990s, but the ambiguity built in to many of the characterizations and the "acceptability" of these characters in appearance and behavior continued to neutralize, to some extent, the potential political effect. These fictional lesbians, above all, "fit in," living in heterosexual environments, rarely seen as part of a lesbian community or rallying for civil rights. The Gay and Lesbian Alliance Against Defamation (GLAAD) estimated that, in the 1996–1997 TV season, thirty gay characters were regulars on primetime series. Lesbian characters recurred as part of the ensemble of ongoing characters in *Roseanne* (ABC) and *Relativity* (ABC) (two series that also aired scenes of two women kissing), as well as *Friends* (NBC), *NYPD Blue* (ABC), and *Mad About You* (NBC). At the beginning of the May ratings sweeps in 1997, another landmark in TV history was made with the hour-long "coming out" episode of *Ellen* on ABC.

While portrayal of lesbian and gay adults on TV increased over the last two decades of the twentieth century, gay and lesbian youth were rarely portrayed. Kielwasser and Wolf (1992) note this extreme "symbolic annihilation" of lesbian and gay adolescents by network television and most mass media and concluded that it reinforced the isolation lesbian and gay youth often experienced in their daily lives. There have been few exceptions, most notably an episode in the late 1990s of CBS's *Picket Fences* that dealt with two teenage girls exploring their physical attraction to each other and the mid-1990s Fox Network's *My So-Called Life* that included a gay teenage boy who is eventually thrown out of his home.

## News Programs

The first hour-long report on lesbian and gay issues by a television network news division was *CBS Reports'* "The Homosexuals." Aired in March 1967, the show was narrated by TV news reporter Mike Wallace (1918–) and compiled many negative stereotypes of gay men, such as that they are promiscuous and incapable of long-term relationships. The program did not mention lesbians. More than a decade passed before the next network attempt at covering gay and lesbian issues. An ABC *News Closeup* on "Homosexuals," broadcast in December 1979, interviewed several lesbians, as well as gay men. Although it was the first time lesbians and gay men had been given the opportunity to speak for themselves before a nationwide TV audience, the program still focused on the most sensational aspects of gay life in the late 1970s.

The early attempts of television news at documenting the politics and lifestyles of lesbians and gay men were, indeed, biased. In April 1980, the *CBS Reports* documentary "Gay Power, Gay Politics" represented lesbian and gay communities as abnormal, characterized by promiscuity, sadomasochism, and public sex. Focusing on the 1979 San Francisco, California, mayoral race, the show also exaggerated the political influence of gay men and lesbians on the election. Because gay activists documented and filed a formal complaint of bias and inaccurate reporting against CBS with the National News Council, in October 1980 CBS aired an apology for errors it had made in the portrayal. This marked the beginning of realizing positive results from lesbian and gay activism toward television networks.

In the 1970s and 1980s, most news media, especially television, were unwilling to accord gay and lesbian political action the status of a civil rights or minority movement. Researchers reported in 1984 (see Fejes and Petrich 1994) that heavy viewers of TV, regardless of their political conservatism or liberalism, had stronger negative attitudes toward lesbians and gay men than those who watched less television, a finding that was interpreted as an indicator of the strength and prevalence of negative TV news coverage of lesbian and gay issues. But continued pressure from activists brought about less stereotypical and more balanced coverage of lesbian and gay issues from network television news. In the 1990s, for example, CNN aired activities at the April 25, 1993, National Gay, Lesbian, and Bisexual March on Washington, D.C., live and unedited, an unprecedented television news event. In the mid- to late 1990s, network nightly newscasts and newsmagazines increased and continued efforts to balance their coverage of such lesbian and gay issues as civil rights initiatives, parenting, and military service.

## Advertising

By the early 1990s, advertisers had identified lesbians and gay men as desirable niche markets representing households with greater than average disposable incomes. Some companies aired commercials aimed at these two consumer markets. For example, in a few major cities, a national chain of furniture stores ran an ad that featured two men, portrayed subtly as a couple, shopping for their home. By the late 1990s, advertisers in local, as well as regional, markets had begun using television to reach lesbians and gay men. However, on a nationwide basis, advertisers and networks still treated the representation of lesbians and gay men as taboo and refrained from using nationwide TV commercials to woo lesbian and gay consumers. ABC even refused to air an ad for Olivia, a lesbian cruise-ship line, during the 1997 "coming out" episode of *Ellen*, claiming that it was too controversial.

## Lesbian and Gay Media Activism

After controversy over a 1974 episode of *Police Woman* titled "Flowers of Evil," in which three lesbians murder patients in a nursing home, the National Gay Task Force (NGTF)—later the National Gay and Lesbian Task Force (NGLTF)—persuaded the Television Review Board of the National Association of Broadcasters to apply to homosexuals the Television Code's policy not to treat material with sexual connotations exploitatively or irresponsibly. The Gay Media Task Force was formed in the mid-1970s and monitored scripts for the networks, looking for stereotypes and making suggestions for less offensive portrayals. Throughout the 1970s and 1980s, gay activism directed toward television news and entertainment divisions was intense. The broadcast of some TV shows, such as the *CBS Evening News with Walter Cronkite* in 1973, were interrupted by "gay raiders," activists protesting negative and biased portrayals of gay men and lesbians. NGLTF activists mobilized supporters of lesbian and gay rights for phone-call and letter campaigns against the networks and sometimes protested by organizing pickets at television studios and offices. In 1985, the New York City chapter of the Gay and Lesbian Alliance Against Defamation (GLAAD) was founded to continue to mobilize action directed to mass media and to lobby television networks for more positive representations of lesbian and gay issues and characters. GLAAD has been successful in many of its efforts, including its campaign to Disney Studios, owners of ABC, to let the lead character in *Ellen* come out publicly on TV.

## Lesbian- and Gay-produced Programs

Lesbians and gay men have begun producing television programs covering lesbian and gay culture and have met with some success in getting them on the air. *Dyke TV*, a half-hour biweekly television magazine, debuted in 1993 and, by 1997, aired on public-access channels in sixty-one U.S. cities. In the 1990s, many PBS (Public Broadcasting System) affiliates carried *In the Life* and *Network Q*, two newsmagazine-style television series produced by and about lesbians and gay men. By 1997, many more TV programs with content by and about lesbians and gay men were locally produced and shown on public-access cable channels across the United States.

### Outside the United States

Much of American television programming is exported to media systems in countries throughout the world. Although little research on the representation of lesbian and gay issues and characters in these countries had been published by the late 1990s, it is possible to conclude that, to the extent that U.S. television programs are imported by other countries, at least some of the trends in U.S. television, including portrayals of lesbians, apply internationally.

Of the countries that produced most of their own television programming, only Australia, Canada, and the United Kingdom have attracted the attention of researchers studying TV representations of lesbians and gay men. British television has produced and broadcast some of the most well known miniseries involving lesbian or gay characters and themes, including *Brideshead Revisited* (1981), *The Jewel in the Crown* (1984), *Portrait of a Marriage* (1990–1991), and *Tales of the City* (1993), all of which were later broadcast by PBS in the United States. In 1989, Jeannette Winterson's novel of a lesbian's girlhood in Britain, *Oranges Are not the Only Fruit*, was filmed and broadcast in Britain (and later aired by Arts and Entertainment cable network in the United States). *Out On Tuesday* (later *Out*), a newsmagazine covering lesbian and gay issues, produced and aired by the British independent Channel 4, debuted in 1989. Throughout the 1990s, several British comedy and drama series had lesbian characters, as did a few TV shows in Australia and Canada.                              *Ruth Largay*

### Bibliography

Alwood, Edward. *Straight News: Gays, Lesbians, and the News Media*. New York: Columbia University Press, 1996.

Fejes, Fred, and Kevin Petrich. "Invisibility, Homophobia and Heterosexism: Lesbians, Gays and the Media." *Critical Studies in Mass Communication* 10 (1994), 396–422.

Gluckman, Amy, and Betsy Reed, eds. *Homo Economics: Capitalism, Community, and Lesbian and Gay Life*. New York and London: Routledge, 1997.

Hantzis, Darlene M., and Valerie Lehr. "Whose Desire? Lesbian (Non)Sexuality and Television's Perpetuation of Hetero/Sexism." In *Queer Words, Queer Images: Communication and the Construction of Homosexuality*. Ed. Jeffrey R. Ringer. New York and London: New York University Press, 1994, pp. 107–121.

Kielwasser, Alfred P., and Michelle A. Wolf. "Mainstream Television, Adolescent Homosexuality, and Significant Silence." *Critical Studies in Mass Communication* 9 (1992), 350–374.

Sanderson, Terry. *Mediawatch: The Treatment of Male and Female Homosexuality in the British Media*. London: Cassell, 1995.

Wolf, Michelle A., and Alfred P. Kielwasser, eds. *Gay People, Sex, and the Media*. New York: Haworth, 1991.

*See also* Advertising and Consumerism; Journalism; Video

### Teresa of Avila (1515–1582)

Saint, mystic, theologian, reformer, and doctor of the Church. Teresa de Cepeda Dávila y Ahumada is one of the historical figures sometimes claimed by twentieth-century lesbians to be one of their own. In her autobiography, Teresa describes a period in adolescence without fear of God, a period of mortal sin and blind passion connected to her relationship with a female cousin and another girl. Only fear of scandal and the intervention of her father, who placed her in a convent, prevented, she later believed, a complete moral calamity. There are certainly enough hints to justify the conclusion that Teresa was engaged in some kind of amorous episode with another woman. But Teresa was not positive about the incident, and, thus, her appropriation by some lesbians may be of questionable value.

A more realistic approach is to locate Teresa within the tradition of "gyn/affection" as a woman who employed a rhetorical strategy of female powerlessness to gain authority in the Church, with the specific aim of founding and maintaining female communities based upon friendship. *The Way of Perfection* (1583) centralized friendship as the hallmark of the religious life. Teresa was adamant that religious communities had to be small enough to allow all of the sisters to be friends with one another. Teresa was particularly harsh on "particular friendships" between the sisters, not because of any erotic element, but because of the factionalism they inevitably produced. However, she believed that any friendship was better than none and recognized that sometimes her sisters had to experience sentimental friendships before they could move on to the most pure friendship, which was to love the friend as God did.

Teresa's understanding of friendship as the fundamental Christian relationship was profoundly subversive in a society rigidly constructed in terms of honor and shame. Indeed, as a person of Jewish descent in a social context that was profoundly suspicious of *conversos* (converted Jews), as a mystic and a visionary at a time when the Church associated such things with dissent, and as a reforming woman, Teresa was a deeply subversive figure and, therefore, very attractive to many lesbians.

*Elizabeth Stuart*

### Bibliography

Lincoln, Victoria. *Teresa, a Woman: A Biography of Teresa of Avila*. Albany: State University of New York Press, 1984.

Williams, Rowan. *Teresa of Avila*. London: Geoffrey Chapman, 1991.

**See also** Saints and Mystics

### Thailand

Although female homoeroticism is becoming increasingly recognized in Thailand, it remains less visible and, arguably, less accepted than male homosexuality. Despite the country's large heterosexual commercial-sex industry, public discussion of all aspects of women's sexuality remains restricted, affecting the ability of lesbians to generate positive discourses of female homoeroticism and limiting their capacity to develop independent lifestyles and relationships.

Premodern references to female homoeroticism within elite circles are found in Thai law and literature and in occasional Buddhist temple murals. References in classical literature to sexual relationships between women of the court (called *len pheuan*, literally, "playing with friends") suggest tolerance mixed with humorous derision, despite the fact that medieval palace law prohibited sexual relations between women living in the inner court. Stipulated punishments ranged from fifty lashes, through disfiguring neck tattoos, to exile for subsequent offenses. While there are no records of women being punished under this law, an early-nineteenth-century temple mural from Ratchburi province appears to depict female lovers being imprisoned.

Early in the twentieth century, King Chulalongkorn (ruled 1868–1910) followed Western precedent and issued a criminal code punishing "unnatural" relations between men and between women. However, no person was ever punished under this law, which was abolished after a legal review in 1956. Since these various edicts appear not to have been enforced, practical control over female sexuality has probably been exercised through popular and religious sex/gender discourses, in which women's sexuality is consistently devalued and subordinated to male desire. For example, within the dominant religion, Theravada Buddhism, female sexuality has been portrayed historically as a tempting hindrance to the renunciate male's spiritual attainment, and, traditionally, women had to be reborn as a man before they were believed capable of attaining nirvana.

Almost nothing is known about the social history of female homoeroticism outside the court, and study of contemporary patterns of lesbianism is also very limited. Furthermore, representations of lesbians in the press and other media are much less common than those of male transvestites and gay men. It is clear, however, that, until the early 1960s, the term *kathoey* was used to describe female homosexuals as well as transgender and homosexual men. Since then, this term has been narrowed to describe males who breach sex and gender norms. While the term "lesbian" is widely known in the press and scientific discussion, it is strongly disliked within some parts of the subculture because of associations with lesbian pornography for heterosexual men. Expressions such as "women-loving women" (*ying rak ying*) are preferred amongst Thai lesbian activists.

Since the 1980s, the growing prevalence of roles similar to butch-femme roles has received public comment and occasional press headlines. Masculine women are called *tom* (from "tomboy"), and feminine lesbians are called *dee* (from "lady"). Within both popular and subcultural discourses, the *tom* is portrayed as the sexually assertive partner, having masculine dress and hairstyle, a bold personality, and an independent lifestyle. In contrast, *dee* are often considered to differ little from "ordinary" women. In some circumstances, high school *tom-dee* relationships appear to be tolerated as part of a recognized adolescent fad that is not necessarily believed to cause ongoing identity formation. However, some critics have denounced the popularity of such *tom-dee* relationships, calling for an end to single-sex schooling.

Lesbians generally lack the informal meeting places and commercial venues widely available to Thai gay men. However, some shopping malls have become known as *tom-dee* meeting spots, and a small number of Bangkok's gay venues are also lesbian friendly. Thai lesbians often argue that their ability to form relationships is constrained by parental expectations to live at home until marriage, women's general lack of financial independence, subordination in marriage, and expectations that daughters should obey and look after parents. Thai lesbians commonly maintain that they are, thus, less well situated than better-paid gay men, who are less tied by parental obligations and who, if they choose to marry for respectability, can still pursue the male-only privilege of extramarital lovers.

Anjaree (Those Following a Different Path), an activist and support group to improve the status of women-loving women by promoting women's right to choose their own lifestyle (within a human rights and feminist framework), was established in Bangkok in 1986. By the late 1990s, membership had reached about four hundred, with an estimated 40 percent of members residing outside Bangkok. Members arrange discussion meetings and social outings and produce a national (Thai-language) newsletter. A branch also operates in the northern city of Chiengmai. Anjaree members were instrumental in establishing the Asian Lesbian Network and hosted its first international meeting in Bangkok in 1990.

[This entry has been compiled with the assistance from Anjaree. The group can be contacted at: P.O. Box 322, Ratchadamnoen, Bangkok 10200, Thailand.]

*Nerida M. Cook*
*Peter Jackson*

### Bibliography

Chamsanit, Varaporn. "Women Who Love Women." *Nation Sunday Focus* (September 25, 1994). Also partly published as "Anjaree: Toward Lesbian Visibility." *Connexions* 46 (1994), 8–9.

Morris, Rosalind C. "Three Sexes and Four Sexualities: Redressing the Discourses on Gender and Sexuality in Contemporary Thailand." *Positions* 2:1 (1994), 15–43.

Otaganonta, Wipawee. "Women Who Love Women." *Bangkok Post* Outlook section (June 21, 1995).

Sinnot, Megan. "Masculinity and Tom Identity in Thailand." In *Lady Boys, Tom Boys, Rent Boys: Male and Female Homosexualities in Contemporary Thailand*. Ed. Peter A. Jackson and Gerard Sullivan. New York: Haworth, 1999.

Thongthiraj, Took-Took. "Toward a Struggle Against Invisibility: Love Between Women in Thailand." *Amerasia Journal* 20:1 (1994), 45–58.

*See also* Asian Lesbian Network

## Theater and Drama, Contemporary

Literary and performance texts in print, on audio or video records, and from oral histories of participants that represent women's erotic and affectional desire for women, relationships with each other, "coming out" stories, revisioning of powerful women of history, struggles to survive and heal from the pain and diseases of homophobia, and parodies of heterosexist culture.

### History and Documentation

Theater and drama that calls itself "lesbian" emerged as a collective movement throughout the western world in the 1970s as part of the feminist and the gay and lesbian theater movements, which had their roots in black, pacifist, socialist, and other leftist theaters. Like other political protest or performance art, it rose on the crest of a rainbow coalition of progressive liberation movements that built in force throughout the 1970s, reached a crescendo of visibility and power in the mid-1980s, and waned in the 1990s. Performances at women's and fringe theater festivals, on college campuses, and in a few surviving alternative theaters keep it alive.

Lesbian theater and drama is most accessible through books. At least four anthologies of lesbian plays have appeared in the United Kingdom and the United States since the mid-1980s. Gay anthologies usually offer a few plays by or about lesbians; women's anthologies may include one token lesbian play. Many published playscripts were originally created by solo performance artists or collectively with no expectation of publication. For a historical analysis of feminist and lesbian theater in the United Kingdom, see Michelene Wandor's *Understudies:*

*Theater and Sexual Politics* (1981); for North America, see *Women in American Theater* (1987), edited by Helen Crich Chinoy and Linda Walsh Jenkins.

## Playwrights and Theaters in North America

In the English-speaking world, Jane Chambers (1937–1983), was the first playwright to produce and publish lesbian plays in the American realist tradition. Lesbians appear as ordinary people coming out in a hostile world, finding and losing love, dying, and surviving—in contrast to the 1930s–1960s psychotic, suicidal, predatory, vampiristic, sadomasochistic stereotypes represented by popular media in films and in lesbian-hating plays.

Through the mid-1980s, sexual identity, coming out to family, and the angst of lesbian relationships took center stage in much North American lesbian drama, including that of Canadian playwrights. Later-twentieth-century lesbian performance featured camp and more complex avant-garde presentational modes that show the influence of experimental film, punk rock, and other popular music and culture.

Following Chambers, Sarah Dreher focused on coming out struggles in heteropatriarchal families and the anguish of lesbian relationships beginning, ending, or mending. Dreher's lesbian protagonists are modern heroes searching for integrity and identity amidst cruel and homophobic parents, classmates, ex-lovers, and their own internalized self-hatred.

Carolyn Gage, playwright, performer, and founding artistic director of the lesbian separatist theater No To Men (Ashland, Oregon), performed in her dramas about female oppression throughout history at numerous women's theater and music festivals. Her characters, such as Joan of Arc (in *The Second Coming of Joan of Arc* [1994]), Hrosvitha, Louisa May Alcott, Calamity Jane, and Typhoid Mary, re-create history through lesbian rage and healing. She also wrote *Take Stage! How To Produce and Direct a Lesbian Play* (1994).

In major U.S. cities and on college campuses throughout the 1980s and 1990s, lesbian playwrights with particular ethnic and cultural perspectives drew local audiences to similarly realist dramas that reflect lesbian lives. In Atlanta, Georgia, Shirlene Holmes produced fourteen mostly African American lesbian plays through the late 1990s. In Boston, Massachusetts, site of annual women's theater festivals during the 1980s, Michelle Gabow and Marty Kingsbury produced lesbian plays in a variety of styles, often from a Jewish perspective. Julia Willis wrote and performed lesbian comedy and fantasy screenplays about Provincetown, Massachusetts, lust, and alien Amazons. In Providence, Rhode Island, Shay Youngblood set her dramas in the southern African American culture. Gloria Joyce Dickler, founder and artistic director of Common Stage Theater in Woodstock, New York, wrote about urban middle-class Jewish lesbian experience. In New York City, Sisters on Stage produced the camp (stylized and parodic) Puerto Rican lesbian coming out tales of Janis Astor del Valle. In Chicago, Illinois, Claudia Allen portrayed the daily homophobia of small-town middle America, where tough survivors maintain their lesbian desire with humor and dignity from adolescence through old age. In St. Louis, Missouri, Joan Lipkin wrote and directed her own and other plays for That Uppity Theater. In San Francisco, California, Canyon Sam wrote and performed original Chinese American one-woman shows, and Cherríe Moraga (1952–) wrote Mexican American political protest drama, especially for Brava Theater. Many playwrights, notably Patricia Montley, have won awards and had productions in primarily university theaters.

Two of the most famous, award-winning lesbian playwrights resist labels. Since the 1960s, both Megan Terry (1932–) and Maria Irene Fornes (1930–), major avant-garde playwrights, have produced work that laid the foundation of contemporary U.S. experimental theater. Their plays present the matrix of oppressive forces that control and destroy the poor, women, racial and sexual minorities, and all marginalized peoples; the antirealist drama spans the gamut of settings from absurdist primeval mud to symbolic distant galaxies. Terry's more than fifty produced and published plays include pieces that expose the sadistic treatment of women in prison and focus on lesbian power and intelligence. Some of Fornes's dozens of plays feature lesbian characters in hopelessly anguished scenarios.

If Terry and Fornes resist the lesbian label, Holly Hughes flaunts it in her plays that parody classic and popular lesbian pulp paperbacks (originally produced at the WOW Café in New York City). She often foregrounds the repression and banality of heterosexual power plays with cross-dressing lesbian performers and erotic camp parodies.

From 1970 to 1990, more than one hundred feminist and gay and lesbian theaters sprang up across North America, producing hundreds of lesbian plays and performances. A few, such as the Red Dyke Theater in Atlanta, the Lavender Cellar Theater in Minneapolis, Minnesota, and Medusa's Revenge

**T**

*Shirlene Holmes, playwright. Photo by Duane Powell, 1985.*

in New York City, focused exclusively on lesbian productions. Theater Rhinoceros in San Francisco also produced many original lesbian plays.

Playwrights and directors of major feminist theaters with radically different styles featured woman-identified passion and spirituality in a variety of collectively created antirealist rituals and camp parodies of Western heterosexism. In these,

lesbian audiences can read a subtext of women-loving women in resistance to patriarchal power and of a reassertion of lesbian and women's power, creativity, healing, vengeance, and wit. Among the most notable of these are Megan Terry and Jo Ann Schmidman at Omaha (Nebraska) Magic Theater; Lisa Mayo, Gloria Miguel, and Muriel Miguel, sisters from the Kuna-Rappahannock Nation who

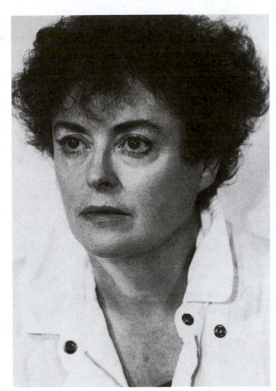

*Megan Terry. Photo © M. Terry.*

make up New York City's Spiderwoman Theater; Martha Boesing and Phyllis Jane Rose of At the Foot of the Mountain Theater in Minneapolis; Clare Coss, Sondra Segal, and Roberta Sklar of the Women's Experimental Theater in New York City; Lois Weaver, Peggy Shaw, and Deb Margolin of Split Britches in New York City; and Maureen Angelos, Babs Davy, Dominique Dibbell, Peg Healey, and Lisa Kron of the Five Lesbian Brothers, who started at New York City's WOW Café. Concurrent with, and following, the collaborative troupe productions, Boesing, Coss, Muriel Miguel, and others have also written and produced individual lesbian plays.

Some U.S. lesbian playwrights had greater acclaim abroad. Award-winning Joan Schenkar had her macabre, erotic, and chilling comedies foregrounding the horrors of history and female desire for vengeance in more than three hundred productions across North America and western Europe. Terry Baum, cofounder of San Francisco's Lilith theater, presented camp coming out stories in various theatrical styles and drew audiences, especially in western Europe, to her humorous one-lesbian performances, as well as serious drama.

Dramas by off-Broadway award-winners Paula Vogel and Susan Miller also had many productions internationally. Vogel invents absurdist comedies, while Miller features lesbian and bisexual characters at life's complicated crossroads in bittersweet comedies and dramas that explode unities of time and place.

### International Theater

Lesbian theater in the United Kingdom followed a similar rise to a crescendo of productions and publication in the mid-1980s. An overview of British lesbian theater shows slightly more emphasis on comedy and parody. In 1975, the Gay Sweatshop (London), Britain's oldest gay theater company, produced its first lesbian play, *Any Woman Can* by Jill Posener, an impassioned and angry coming out drama. The preoccupations of British lesbian theater have been comparable to those of North American lesbian theater: coming out to family, the search for identity and survival from self-hatred, celebrations of lesbian role models and historic heroes, ritual quests for an integration of ethnic culture and sexual identity. In the 1980s, British lesbian drama featured comic twists, such as Jill Fleming's *The Rug of Identity* (1986), parodying mystery thrillers through a lesbian's search her long-lost father who turns out to be another lesbian's transsexual mother; Debby Klein's *Coming Soon* (1986) mocking a lesbian nun's repentance for murdering her lover, who turns up alive and lusting in the arms of the nun's new girlfriend; *Mama's Gone A-Hunting* (1980) by Tash Fairbanks and Jane Boston, presenting a futurist intergalactic court battle for women's right to leave the planet and set up an all-woman civilization.

In Australia, scores of feminist plays, playwrights, and theaters emerged, but few that identify as lesbian. In 1981, Alison Lyssa's *Pinball* captured myriad struggles in the Australian radical lesbian community through the portrayal of a lesbian custody struggle. Sandra Shotlander has produced lesbian plays internationally since her first full-length award-winning play, *Framework* (1983), presenting snapshots of two lesbians symbolically represented by famous portraits in the Metropolitan Musuem. In 1991, Shotlander's *Is That You, Nancy?* captured daily lesbian obsessions with food, sex, and gossip, while her *Angels of Power* (also 1991) celebrated women's political alliances in resistance to new reproductive technologies. In 1990, Eva Johnson's play *What Do They Call Me?* explored, for the first time, the intersection of lesbian and Aboriginal identity, and Vitalstatistix theater presented Margaret Fischer's *The Gay Divorcee*, portraying a comic breakup from a Jewish lesbian perspective.

In Aotearoa/New Zealand, Renée wrote serious historic drama and slapstick comedy inspired by her lesbian sensibility and Maori/British ancestry. Hilary Beaton portrayed lesbian bonds among women in prison. Lorae Parry wrote and performed her *Digger and Nudger* drag shows with Carmel McGlone, foregrounding and mocking macho heterosexist attitudes toward women. Parry's plays also feature strippers and sex workers and a female television talk-show host falling in love with a prominent married socialite.

International Women Playwrights Conferences (1988 in Buffalo, New York; 1991 in Toronto, Canada; 1994 in Adelaide, Australia; 1997 in Galway, Ireland) have drawn playwrights from around the (mostly English-speaking) world, but few plays, playwrights, performances, and theaters are identified in conference programs as lesbian. Nevertheless, lesbian workshops and informal caucuses provide networks for lesbian dramatists and scholars.

## Politics of Visibility

Lesbian theater has never presented a monolithic political stance. Far more than mainstream popular entertainment, it has passionately embraced diversities and marginalities, including differences in age, race, social and economic class, ethnicity, religious practice, intellectual and artistic presupposition, modes of presentation, and, especially, political positions. In art-versus-politics struggles, most lesbian playwrights and theaters claim both. Scholars of lesbian drama and performance vehemently disagree on the political efficacy of diverse aesthetic modes. Some feminists reject realism in plays by Chambers, Dreher, Montley, Baum, and most popular playwrights named above for reinstating the heteropatriarchal norm. They prefer a postmodern lesbian subject position, as in drama by Spiderwoman, Split Britches, and Holly Hughes.

Unlike other forms of art and literature, theater must be heard and seen in public. Poems and novels can be read in solitude, film can be viewed in anonymous darkness or at home, but theater invites a communal experience. Whereas writers create their vision on paper, directors, actors, scenic artists, and other theater workers collaborate to create the spectacle of lesbian visibility. Finally, audiences complete the communal circuit by seeing the performance text and recognizing others seeing it and by

being seen seeing it, and thus become part of the spectacle themselves. Thus, lesbian theater counters the closet through a collective public coming out ceremony as no other art form can do.

*Rosemary Keefe (formerly Curb)*

### Bibliography

Allen, Claudia. *She's Always Liked the Girls the Best*. Chicago: Third Side, 1993.

Curb, Rosemary Keefe, ed. *Amazon All Stars: Thirteen Lesbian Plays*. New York: Applause, 1996.

Davis, Jill, ed. *Lesbian Plays*. London: Methuen, 1987.

———. *Lesbian Plays II*. London: Methuen, 1989.

McDermott, Kate, ed. *Places, Please! The First Anthology of Lesbian Plays*. Iowa City: Aunt Lute, 1985.

Willis, Julia. *We Oughta Be in Pictures. . . .* San Francisco: Alamo Square, 1993.

*See also* Chambers, Jane; Moraga, Cherríe; Performance Art; Theater and Drama, History of

## Theater and Drama, History of

As a generic term, lesbian theater typically refers to a modern movement, largely based in the United States and the United Kingdom and dating from the late 1960s and the 1970s, dedicated to the public performance of plays explicitly addressing the experiences and perspectives of lesbians. However, scholars are beginning to expand this definition as they uncover numerous instances of lesbian desire represented in Western theater, a ready site—according to critics as far back as Plato (427?–347? B.C.E.) and, in seventeenth-century England, the antitheatrical Puritans—for questioning the supposed stability of gender and sex. Recognizing images of female homosexuality in plays from eras before the modern concept of lesbian identity emerged, these scholars are careful to examine them within the context of the historical and cultural conditions of the images themselves. Thus, they tend to speak of representations of female-female desire.

## Origins

The earliest example, perhaps, is John Lyly's *Gallathea* (1585), in which two girls disguised as boys (and played by boys) fall in love with each other. Venus promises to turn one of them into a male as a reward for their chastity. But the question of which girl will undergo the magical sex change remains unresolved, and the play ends with the image of two betrothed girls pledging eternal devotion. In several comedies by William Shakespeare (1564–1616) and his contemporaries, intimate friendships between women offer an alternative to the antagonistic heterosexual pairings into which young women are often reluctantly placed. Such relationships between women—for instance, Helena and Hermia in *A Midsummer Night's Dream*, and Celia and Rosalind in *As You Like It*—are frequently depicted as temporary, almost as rehearsals for marriage. Yet, as scholars such as Traub (1992) are finding, these friendships are also presented as emotionally and erotically satisfying.

New scholarship is also uncovering femalefemale desire in Restoration drama, especially in the practice of female cross-dressing and, more especially, when that cross-dressing moved beyond the vogue for "breeches roles," in which women basically showed off their legs, toward travesties of the male rake, such as those played by Margaret Woffington (1714–1760), in which the disguised woman wooed other women. Scholar Straub (1992) argues that cross-dressing by women on stage in the mideighteenth century constitutes a historical possibility for pleasure in sexual and gender ambiguities.

Similar ambiguities were often evoked in works by the French playwright Pierre Marivaux (1688–1763). In *The Triumph of Love* (1732), for example, a young woman disguises herself as male to gain access to the man she loves. While disguised, she seduces both an older man and his sister. In the end, all of the confusions are resolved as she is neatly paired off with the young man she desires. But, in her wake she leaves two broken hearts and the rubble of an exploded sex-gender system. A French pornographic drama, Andréa de Nerciat's *The Spirit of Morals in the Eighteenth Century* (1789), features an unabashed sexual scene between the marquise and her beloved, Mademoiselle de Lesbosie.

There seem to have been fewer images of female-female desire on nineteenth-century stages. Two exceptions are Alphonse Daudet and Adolph Belot's *Sappho* (1895), about a Parisian prostitute who models for a statue of the poet, and Archibald Gunter's *A Florida Enchantment* (1896), in which a woman swallows a magic seed that turns her into a man, prompting her to smoke, swear, and make love to girls. Though she does so as a "man," the audience sees two actresses in passionate embrace. A contemporary *New York Times* review suggested that the play called not for criticism, but for "chloride of lime," a disinfectant.

## The Twentieth Century

By the turn of the twentieth century, especially with the growth of psychological realism as a dominant dramatic style, homosexuality became a common trope of submerged perversion and psychic disorder. Mainstream plays began to depict (and denounce) lesbian love, even if they didn't speak its name.

Broadway's first lesbian love scene appeared in 1922, when the English-language version of Sholem Asch's *God of Vengeance* moved uptown after a brief run in Greenwich Village. Written in Yiddish in 1906, the play was first produced in Germany by Max Reinhardt (1873–1943) and toured all over the Yiddish-speaking world, generally to great acclaim. But the story of the daughter of a brothel keeper who falls in love with one of the prostitutes in her father's employ was too much for puritanical guardians of the commercial New York City stage; the cast was arrested, and the producers fined, for obscenity.

Similarly, Eduard Bourdet's *The Captive* (1926) caused a sensation at its debut in Paris in the mid-1920s and then scandalized America when it premiered in English on Broadway in 1926. The heroine rebuffs a male suitor because she remains a "captive" to her female paramour (who never actually appears on stage). Broadway's Play Jury (parallel to Hollywood's Hayes Office) declared the play morally acceptable; nonetheless, it was raided by the police and declared obscene by the New York State Supreme Court. Along with Mae West's *Sex* [1926] (which she described as the "male version" of *The Captive*), Bourdet's work was grist for the Wales Padlock Bill, an anti-"obscenity" statute enacted in 1927 forbidding the presentation of salacious plays. It stood as New York State law until 1967.

Nevertheless, while male-male desire was coded on Broadway as more homosocial than homosexual, lesbians continued to appear, perhaps because they were usually presented as miserable and evil, and they typically ended up dead. One character to escape such a fate was Tony, the disgruntled butch in Thomas Dickinson's *Winter Bound* (1929). Though reviewers called the play "a study in abnormality" because it showed two women living together in a Connecticut farmhouse, Tony's lover leaves in the end to marry a man. Tony remains alone—but alive and relatively unpathologized. Not so for the woman who murders her lover's fiance in William Hulbert's *Sin of Sins* (1926); nor for the self-loathing schoolteacher in Lillian Hellman's *The Children's Hour* (1934), who kills herself after confessing to another woman that she has loved her "the way they said"; nor for the old actress in the British play *Wise Tomorrow* (1937), by Guy Bolton, who is killed off after wrecking the life (read: the heterosexuality) of the protégée she adores. The homoeroticism of the stage version of Christa Winsloe's *Mädchen in Uniform* (1931) (presented in New York City in 1932) apparently escaped the notice of local critics, who praised the girls' school tragedy as "deeply touching."

The Wales Padlock Law was invoked again in 1945 to close down a play featuring a villainous lesbian—Dorothy Baker's *Trio* (1943), in which a young man lures the young woman he loves away from an older, French woman. The two other popular plays of the decade with unconcealed lesbian characters did not rouse the authorities, probably because in Jean-Paul Sartre's *No Exit* (1944), Inez is punished with eternal damnation for driving the woman she loved to suicide, and, in Allen Kenward's *Proof Through the Night* (1942), the confused wartime nurse Steve is killed in an air raid before she comes to terms with her sexuality.

It is important to note that beyond mainstream stages, lesbians carved out venues in the early decades of the twentieth century, offering nonrepresentational alternatives to such conventional fare. The famed Paris salons of Natalie Barney (1876–1972) and others were important sites of lesbian performance. Meanwhile, lesbian desire sometimes found expression in "nonlegitimate" theatrical entertainments. Colette (1873–1954) appeared in 1907 at the Moulin Rouge in Paris in a sketch called "Le Rêve d'Egypte," playing a love scene with the Marquise de Belbeuf (also Belboeuf [1863–1944]), dressed as a man. Male impersonators in the music-hall tradition, such as Annie Hindle and Ella Wesner in the nineteenth century and Storme DeLarverie in the 1950s and 1960s, whether lesbians or not, often presented scenes that could be (and were) read homoerotically. The same could be said about Japan's all-female revues, which have attracted a devoted following of adolescent girls and women since their founding in 1914.

## Lesbian Theater

But it was not until the late 1960s, with the convergence the off-off-Broadway, women's liberation, and gay liberation movements, that women began to produce an explicit, self-named lesbian theater in the United States (paralleled in the United Kingdom by the feminist and gay wings of the fringe theater and, somewhat later, by similar strains in France, Germany, Australia, and elsewhere).

The three formative theaters of off-off-Broadway—Judson Poet's Theater, Caffe Cino, and La Mama—produced mostly works by gay men, but much of the work that was by women was by lesbians—Gertrude Stein (1874–1946), Megan Terry (1932–), and Maria Irene Fornes (1930–). Their plays may not have particularly addressed lesbian themes, but nor were their formal experiments impeded by the constraints of the closet.

By the early 1970s, gay production companies were established in the United States and the United Kingdom, but, for years, they seldom highlighted lesbian works. In the United States, Jane Chambers (1937–1983) was an exception. Her realistic dramas—among them, *A Late Snow* (1974), *The Quintessential Image* (produced posthumously in 1989), and *Last Summer at Bluefish Cove* ([1980] a commercial hit about a group of lesbians who spend the summer together on Long Island, where one falls in love with a presumably straight neighbor)—were presented all over the country.

But, for the most part, lesbian theater in the 1970s flourished within its own networks and on its own terms. While gay male performers were cavorting in froufrou and glitter, much lesbian theater was shedding the decorative role to which women had long been relegated. In the early 1970s, women's theater groups sprang up all over the United States. Reflecting the different strategies of materialist and bourgeois feminisms, some sought to use theater to change the world, while some sought to change theater so women could share an equal place in it with men. It is impossible to define many of these theaters as primarily lesbian, yet many of their members were out lesbians, and many took up lesbian issues in their frequently issue-laden plays.

This was a theater of proclamations and manifestos. One typical leaflet wheatpasted around New York City in the early 1970s urged women to join in a collective that would address their concerns in theatrical form and create "an active conscious voice in our community."

Feminist theater companies were usually organized as collectives and often grew out of consciousness-raising sessions, which were then extended into a public, dramatic enactment. The It's All Right to Be Woman Theater, founded in New York City in 1970, built plays based on personal experience through improvisation; the group included lesbians, and lesbian themes were frequently broached. Other feminist troupes included the Caravan Theater in Cambridge, Massachusetts, founded in 1965; the Omaha (Nebraska) Magic Theater founded in 1969; the Los Angeles (California) Women's Liberation Union; the New York (City) Feminist Theater; the Women's Experimental Theater (New York City); Bread and Roses Theater (Los Angeles, California); the Rhode Island Feminist Theater (Providence); and the Onyx Women's Theater (South Ozone Park, New York), an African American troupe. Spiderwoman Theater (New York City), named for the Hopi goddess of creation, was founded in 1975 by three sisters, one of whom is an out lesbian. The troupe, still functioning in the late 1990s, uses vaudevillian gags, Native American storytelling, cabaret sketches, and irreverence to layer complex experience with humor and poignancy.

The 1970s saw specifically lesbian feminist companies, too, whose stories remain to be collected, among them: the Red Dyke Theater in Atlanta, Georgia, founded in 1974 with the assertion that its purpose was to entertain lesbians, not to educate straight people about lesbians; the Actor's Sorority in Kansas City, Missouri; and the Lavender Cellar Theater, founded in Minneapolis, Minnesota, in 1973. Special short-term projects included the Lesbian Feminist Theater Workshop in Chicago, Illinois, whose purpose, an ad in a feminist newspaper stated, would be "the production of plays emphasizing a positive approach to the lesbian lifestyle," and *An Oral History of Lesbianism* (1979), at the Woman's Building in Los Angeles.

There was also a strain of celebratory feminist and lesbian theater that was often less doctrinaire and more formally experimental and sexually explicit. Perhaps the best early example was Medusa's Revenge, a multicultural theater founded in New York City in 1976. One of its well-known plays, Ana Maria Simo's *Bayou* (1977), was a raucous piece about a lesbian bar, in which, among other things, two women courting each other danced erotically across a pool table. The theater also hosted dances, benefits for women prisoners, and other events.

The WOW Café carried on this tradition when it opened in New York City's East Village in 1981, growing out of the Women's One World Festivals of 1980 and 1981, to present plays, solo performers, drag balls, and other extravaganzas. Such artists as Split Britches, Holly Hughes, the Five Lesbian Brothers, and Carmelita Tropicana cut their teeth at WOW. The theater continued to thrive in the late 1990s.

The work at WOW and at other theaters like it has inspired a new generation of lesbian theater critics and theorists, such as Sue-Ellen Case, Kate Davy, Jill Dolan, and Peggy Phelan, among others.

*Alisa Solomon*

### Bibliography

Curtin, Kaier. *"We Can Always Call Them Bulgarians": The Emergence of Lesbians and Gay Men on the American Stage*. Boston: Alyson, 1987.

Dolan, Jill. *Presence and Desire: Essays on Gender, Sexuality, Performance*. Ann Arbor: University of Michigan Press, 1993.

Ferris, Lesley, ed. *Crossing the Stage: Controversies on Cross-Dressing*. London and New York: Routledge, 1993.

Hart, Lynda, and Peggy Phelan, eds. *Acting Out: Feminist Performances*. Ann Arbor: University of Michigan Press, 1993.

Straub, Kristina. *Sexual Suspects: Eighteenth-Century Players and Sexual Ideology*. Princeton, N.J.: Princeton University Press, 1992.

Traub, Valerie. *Desire and Anxiety: Circulations of Desire in Shakespearean Drama*. London and New York: Routledge, 1992.

**See also** All-Female Revues (Japan); Barney, Natalie Clifford; Chambers, Jane; Colette; Cross-Dressing; Performance Art; Stein, Gertrude; Theater and Drama, Contemporary

### Thomas, M. Carey (1857–1935)

American educator. One of the most prominent American educators and women's activists in the early twentieth century, Martha Carey Thomas gained fame as the president of the women-only Bryn Mawr College in Pennsylvania.

Born in 1857 to a Quaker family in Baltimore, Maryland, Thomas set about developing a scholarly career, a rare dream for a Victorian girl. After obtaining a B.A. in classics from Cornell University, she studied in Germany. In 1882, with a Ph.D. in philology from the University of Zürich, Thomas returned home with the hope of a prominent role in the formation of the new Quaker women's college being planned for Bryn Mawr, Pennsylvania.

Appointed to a post at Bryn Mawr in 1883, Thomas became the first dean of an American women's college to hold a doctorate. Named president of the school in 1894, she encouraged nontraditional attitudes among the undergraduates by supporting academic and professional careers for women. *Education of Women* (1900) established Thomas's reputation as an authority on the higher education of women. Blocking some students from attending Bryn Mawr on racist, antisemitic, and elitist grounds, Thomas manifested many of the prejudices of her day, to an extent that shocked some of her peers.

While in Europe, Thomas had lived with Mamie Gwinn (1861–?), an arrangement that continued at Bryn Mawr, with the two openly sharing a home on the college campus until Gwinn married in 1904. Gertrude Stein (1874–1946) immortalized the end of their relationship in her story *Fernhurst* (1904–1905?). While involved with Gwinn, Thomas pursued a relationship with Mary Garrett (1839–1915), heiress to the Baltimore and Ohio Railroad fortune. After Gwinn and Thomas separated, Garrett and Thomas became a couple, living together at the college until Garrett's death in 1915. That Thomas was a lesbian is well established. Analyzing Thomas's reading, Horowitz (1994), her biographer, argues that the Bryn Mawr president was well aware of the possibilities for physical love between women and of the medically oriented literature on sexuality that began to appear in the late nineteenth century.

Thomas retired from the college in 1922. A forceful woman, and not always a likable one, Thomas is notable for managing to carve out a large role for women in the world of academia.

*Caryn E. Neumann*

**Bibliography**

Horowitz, Helen Lefkowitz. *The Power and Passion of M. Carey Thomas*. New York: Knopf, 1994.

*See also* Colleges, Women's; Stein, Gertrude

## Toklas, Alice B. (1877–1967)

American memoirist. Born and raised in San Francisco, California, Alice B. Toklas studied music at the University of Washington. After her mother fell ill, she returned to San Francisco, and, upon her mother's death, she began to tend house for three generations of her family's men, a task she abhorred. In 1907, Toklas left San Francisco for good, traveling to Paris with a friend who introduced her to Gertrude Stein (1874–1946).

Toklas spent her years as a tireless promoter of Stein's work, typing manuscripts, correcting grammar in Stein's periodic pieces written in French, and proofreading. Perhaps some of Toklas's greatest creative energy went into cooking for Stein, who had an appetite as prodigious as her intellect. Toklas later published many of her famous recipes, along with reminiscences of their life together, in *The Alice B. Toklas Cookbook* (1954). Her *Flavors and Aromas of Past and Present* (1958) was less successful, but her recipes and remembrances continued to be popular magazine pieces throughout the 1950s. Her memoirs of her life with Stein, *What Is Remembered* (1963), portrays their relationship and their contacts with the many literary and artistic figures who encircled their lives.

Stein wrote that Toklas "is always forethoughtful, which is what is pleasant for me" (Souhami 1991). It is to oversimplify their relationship to see Toklas in a demeaning "wife" role; indeed, Toklas generally ruled the roost. Both were in complete accord in their belief that Stein was a genius (Toklas said she heard bells ringing when they met, a certain sign she was in the presence of genius). Once they met in Paris in 1907, they were inseparable and utterly devoted to each other until Stein's death in 1946. As Toklas noted in her autobiography, *What Is Remembered* (1963), Stein had her utmost attention, "as she did for all the many years I knew her until her death, and all these empty ones since then."

Toklas's later years were financially and physically difficult. Her health declined, and provisions that Stein had arranged from her own estate were often late and insufficient. Toklas shares a single grave with Stein in Paris. Characteristically standing behind Stein even in death, Toklas directed that her name and dates be engraved on the rear of the headstone.

*Linnea A. Stenson*

**Bibliography**

Simon, Linda. *The Biography of Alice B. Toklas*. Lincoln: University of Nebraska Press, 1991.

Souhami, Diana. *Gertrude and Alice*. New York: Pandora, 1991.

*See also* Paris; Stein, Gertrude

## Tolerance

The willingness to allow a person, group, idea, or ideology to exist without interference, despite one's disliking or disapproving of the thing in question. Tolerance has long been a goal of lesbian, gay, and bisexual activists and those who advocate on their behalf. In comparison with the discrimination that lesbians, gay men, and bisexuals have suffered, being tolerated has seemed an appealing possibility. Yet tolerance has proved a goal that is both elusive and insufficient.

Pleas for tolerance toward lesbians were first voiced by sexologists in the late nineteenth and early twentieth centuries. However, even as they argued for tolerance, they depicted lesbian sexuality as a neurological malfunction, caused by a genetic flaw. Lesbians, unless they abstained from sex, were perverse and uncontrollable. This portrait, not surprisingly, undercut the sexologists' pleas for tolerance, so that the public became increasingly aware of the pathology of intimate relationships between women and increasingly intolerant of these relationships. For many years afterward, social scientists followed the sexologists in simultaneously pathologizing lesbians and pleading for tolerance of them.

The appeal of the concept of tolerance has led also to an assimilationist strategy on the part of many lesbians, gay men, and bisexuals, who argue that the best political strategy is to demonstrate how much "we" are like "them" (heterosexuals). Minimizing the difference between the two groups is seen as maximizing the likelihood of increasing heterosexuals' tolerance of those who are not heterosexual. Proponents of this strategy see a slowly increasing level of tolerance of lesbians, gay men, and bisexuals in, for example, the visibility of non-heterosexuals in the media and the appearance of sexual-orientation issues in mainstream politics. Perhaps more important, many report thinking that heterosexuals with whom they interact personally are becoming more tolerant.

One major problem with tolerance is that groups are tolerated within certain limits defined by those who are doing the tolerating. If a group member ventures beyond these limits, tolerance no longer applies. Thus, many heterosexuals argue that they tolerate lesbians and gay men so long as they are not "flaunting" their sexuality, which may consist of as little as holding the hand of one's lover in public. The absurdity of this is highlighted by the button that reverses the situation to proclaim: "I don't mind straights so long as they act gay in public." To be required to make one's lesbianism all but invisible is a high price to pay for tolerance.

Moreover, the very definition of tolerance involves a more powerful group that continues to disapprove and that can remove its limited protection at any time. Wilson (1993) argues that it was the withdrawal of tolerance that explains the assault upon lesbian and gay rights that occurred in the United Kingdom in the late 1980s. The somewhat arbitrary nature of the protection offered by tolerance is available only so long as lesbians, gay men, and bisexuals are perceived as not threatening heterosexual dominance—that is, only so long as they continue to be oppressed.

*Jodee M. McCaw*

## Bibliography

Black, Allida M. "Perverting the Diagnosis: The Lesbian and the Scientific Basis of Stigma." *Historical Reflections* 20 (1994), 201–216.

Robson, Ruthann. *Lesbian (Out)law: Survival Under the Rule of Law*. Ithaca, N.Y.: Firebrand, 1992.

Wilson, Angelia R. "Which Equality? Toleration, Difference, or Respect." In *Activating Theory: Lesbian, Gay, Bisexual Politics*. Ed. Joseph Bristow and Angelia R. Wilson. London: Lawrence and Wishart, 1993, pp. 171–189.

**See also** Discrimination; Heterosexism; Homophobia; Liberalism; Prejudice

## Tomboy

A girl who behaves in ways considered socially appropriate for boys. These may include being athletic or active, preferring "boy's" clothing or hobbies, or taking off on adventures. In fact, a "tomboyade" is a word coined in 1886 to indicate an escapade or adventure taken by girls. "Ladylike" could be considered the opposite of "tomboyish."

Since its appearance in print in 1592, according to the *Oxford English Dictionary*, "tomboy" has been connected with connotations of rudeness and impropriety: "a wild, romping girl"; "a girle or wench who leaps up and down like a boy"; "a ramping, frolicsome, rude girl." The word also has a history of sexual, even lesbian, connotations. When applied to a woman, one obsolete meaning of "tomboy" defines her as bold, wanton, or immodest. In 1888, Mrs. Humphrey Ward wrote: "As a rough tomboy of fourteen, she had shown Catherine . . . a good many uncouth signs of affection" (in Yamaguchi and Barber 1995).

The connection between tomboyism and lesbianism continued, in a more positive way, as a frequent theme in twentieth-century lesbian literature and nonfiction coming out stories. A number of lesbian novels, including Radclyffe Hall's *The Well of*

*Diane F. Germain as tomboy, ca. early 1950s. Courtesy of Diane F. Germain.*

fact that both tomboys and lesbians are "transgressing society's gender barriers ... not doing what 'normal' women do."

Barber and Yamaguchi found that commonalities in tomboy experience seemed to cut across ethnic and cultural backgrounds to a surprising degree. Contibutor Sharon Lim-Hing describes playing cowboys with a neighborhood boy in Jamaica; editor Yamaguchi, who grew up in Japan, Guam, and the United States, talks about her tomboy days catching lizards, playing army, and climbing trees. Although there are undoubtedly cultural differences, they speculate that the striking similarities among expressions of tomboyism have to do with the fact that prescriptions for gender roles "cut so broadly across cultural lines."

For many of the contributors to *Tomboys!*, what links their self-identifications as tomboys and lesbians is that both position them outside cultural and gender boundaries. As Yamamguchi and Barber put it: "As tomboys we were 'other' then; as lesbians, we are 'other' now. Though we were defined as tomboys by what we did, for many of us what we did turned out to be who we were and what we became, the behavior an expression of identity."

*Jayne Relaford Brown*

### Bibliography

Grahn, Judy. *Another Mother Tongue: Gay Words, Gay Worlds*. Boston: Beacon, 1984.

Yamaguchi, Lynne, and Karen Barber, eds. *Tomboys! Tales of Dyke Derring-Do*. Los Angeles: Alyson, 1995.

***See also*** Brown, Rita Mae; Grahn, Judy; Hall, Radclyffe

*Loneliness* (1928) and Rita Mae Brown's *Rubyfruit Jungle* (1973), emphasize their heroines' rebelliousness and boyish exploits as signs of their early separation from straight society. While Hall's 1928 novel shows her character Stephen Gordon's tomboyism as an early sign of congenital lesbianism, Brown's post-Stonewall (1969) novel presents Molly Bolt's tomboyism as a sign of her confident rebellion against traditional social mores. In *Another Mother Tongue: Gay Words, Gay Worlds* (1984), Judy Grahn characterizes being a tomboy as taking "a dyke's-eye view of myself as tough and hardy, smart, muscular, and athletic." In 1995, Alyson Press published *Tomboys! Tales of Dyke Derring-Do*, an entire anthology of poems, stories, and essays by lesbians about being tomboys.

Lynne Yamaguchi and Karen Barber, editors of *Tomboys!*, identify a strong connection for their contributors between their tomboy and lesbian identities. The prevailing social prescription is that girls should grow out of being a tomboy. However, Yamaguchi and Barber argue that "tomboyhood is much more than a phase for many lesbians"; rather, it "seems to remain part of the foundation of who we are as adults." They attribute this connection to the

## Tourism and Guidebooks

Lesbian tourism is a specific market segment of the tourism industry. It overlaps with the gay male portion of the industry but has grown from a word-of-mouth, primarily bar culture to include guest houses and cruise and tour companies catering specifically to the lesbian traveler. Guidebooks were one of the earliest and most significant offshoots of the rise of lesbian tourism.

### Guidebooks

In the 1960s and before, lesbian travelers in search of gay culture relied on recommendations from friends, knowledgeable taxi drivers, or careful conversations with people who looked like they might be gay. Even in gay meccas like New York City and San Francisco, California, much of the community was invisible. The only resource available was *Damron's Address Book*, a thirty-page guide that listed men's bars, bathhouses, and cruise areas, with a few bar or bookstore listings for women. Lesbians who traveled outside the country had no resources at all.

The first women-only guidebook was *Gaia's Guide,* which began to appear on a yearly basis in the early 1970s. The last edition—its fourteenth—appeared in 1989. *Gaia's Guide* listed itself as "the international guide for traveling women" and, by 1989, covered the United States, Canada, Europe, Israel, Australia, and New Zealand. In 1979, Marianne Ferrari created *Ferrari for Women*, which listed bars, restaurants, bookstores, organizations, and other networking information. In 1988, it expanded to cover international destinations.

*The Women's Traveler*, the only other women's guidebook in the domestic market in the 1990s, was first published in 1989 by Damron Publishing Company. Damron used a different staff for its new book and did not include the name "Damron" on the cover because of its long association with the men's community.

Fodor's became the first mainstream publishing company to address the gay and lesbian community with its 1996 release of *Gay Guide to the USA*. In 1997, it released five regional editions and in 1998, a gay guide to Amsterdam. HarperCollins also released its own guidebook under the Access imprint. Meanwhile, Ferrari and Damron have created expanded guidebooks and travel planners that focus on lodging, tour operators, and metropolitan cities.

The gay press has also entered the travel industry. *Our World* and *Out & About* are consumer travel publications covering international pleasure travel for gays and lesbians. National lesbian magazines like *Curve* (formerly *Deneuve*) and *Girlfriends* also feature travel departments. Unlike travel sections in mainstream magazines, they move beyond standard tourist attractions to include information on local gay and lesbian politics, customs, and unusual destinations with high concentrations of lesbians. Finally, by 1998, the World Wide Web had become an important source of travel information, both domestic and international.

Because of limited distribution and the difficulty of building a strong gay-identified subscriber and mail-order base, all traditional gay travel books and magazines except *Out & About* rely on advertising income to sustain their products. Publications with travel advertisers follow a code of neutrality when providing vendor information or focus only on the positive aspects of travel suppliers. Debate continues about the credibility of this uncritical approach, which is one way that traditional gay guides differ from the more widely distributed and better-funded mainstream travel books. Defenders of gay travel guides that use advertisers argue that their neutral policy is actually more reliable than mainstream rating systems, which, they argue, are not objective and reflect only one author's personal preferences and biases.

## The Tourism Industry

By the 1980s, the tourism industry had begun to offer more extensive gay-oriented travel experiences. Several men's tour companies and gay and lesbian bed and breakfasts now existed. In 1983, twenty-six travel professionals met to form the International Gay Travel Association (IGTA). The association promoted lesbian and gay travel and included primarily travel agents and members of the guest house community. IGTA soon began to include tour operators and wholesale suppliers, and, by the mid-1990s, it had more than one thousand members.

The first major lesbian tour operator was Olivia Cruises and Resorts. Judy Dlugacz had established Olivia Records in 1973; using the company's extensive mailing list, Olivia chartered its first inaugural cruise, from Miami to the Bahamas, in 1990. By 1998, it was offering five to seven international cruises and resort-oriented vacations every year.

More than one hundred companies were advertising woman-only tours by the end of the twentieth century. These packages vary from essentially "straight" tours that include only women, to "woman-focused" tours that specifically address lesbian culture. Packages for lesbians often focus on soft adventure, like hiking and backpacking, canoeing and kayaking, and active ranch, safari, or wilderness experiences. "Honeymoon" packages were also on the rise, partly due to the prominence of same-sex marriage in the national political debate. Women's travel is also often related to political, musical, and sporting events.

IGTA travel agents were writing more than $1 billion annually in travel business in the late 1990s. The electronic revolution contributed to the industry's growth in that decade, making it easier to communicate and plan travel in even the most remote parts of the world. Member agents can arrange trips to exotic destinations using exclusively gay-owned and gay-friendly businesses.

IGTA expects gay and lesbian tourism to continue growing in the twenty-first century. The market spends an estimated $17 billion a year on travel, and gay tourists are widely thought to be more affluent than mainstream travelers. While there is controversy about whether economic statistics accurately reflect the broader lesbian and gay community, any double-income household without children is generally believed to allow more discretionary income for travel.

Gay-friendly companies are one of the newest trends in the industry. In 1995, Virgin Atlantic Airways became the first airline to offer gay and lesbian deals. Despite the fear of reprisal from the Religious Right, other major airlines and established travel agencies are also offering gay tour packages. With approximately 95 percent of gay travel dollars going to mainstream wholesalers who own car rental companies, hotels, and cruise ships, gay industry professionals welcome their interest in the gay and lesbian community. Because existing gay and lesbian companies already have marketing and sales networks in place, mainstream suppliers often partner with them, rather than compete directly. In turn, gay and lesbian consumers benefit from the pricing discounts that large agencies can offer.

Growth areas for lesbian tourism include tours with children, more mixed gay and lesbian tours, and the development of the "buycott" mentality. This means that consumers actively support companies that have adopted policies against discrimination because of sexual orientation, have altered policies to consider same-sex couples, or have been the first in their industry to make such changes. As lesbian professional associations continue to form and mature, meeting and convention travel is also increasing. Associations are demographic groups that are easily definable and are considered a new marketing opportunity.

## Conclusion

As the gay and lesbian travel boom approaches the close of the century, lesbians have established themselves as a unique demographic market. Industry professionals believe that lesbians' travel needs and financial spending patterns often differ significantly from those of gay men. However, just as the gay and lesbian community became more unified, due primarily to the joint response to the AIDS crisis, the

future of gay travel and tourism will probably address both men and women jointly, with limited specialization. It will be interesting to see whether any kind of a specialized bisexual or transgendered market develops in the next wave of gay tourism.

[Primary source material for this entry came from John D'Alessandro, Judy Dlugacz, Marianne Ferrari, Heather Findlay, Gina Gatta, and Billy Kolber.]                    *Christina Allan*

### Bibliography

Ebensten, Hann. *Volleyball with the Cuna Indians and Other Gay Travel Adventures*. New York: Penguin, 1987.

Feifer, Maxine. *Tourism in History, from Imperial Rome to the Present*. New York: Stein and Day, 1985.

Gee, Chuck Y. *The Travel Industry*. Westport, Conn.: AVI, 1984.

*See also* Olivia; Recreation

## Transgender

Community-generated term coined in the early 1970s by Virginia Prince. Transgender (TG) is a concept referring to someone who lives as a woman or a man but who neither desires nor has sex-reassignment surgery. An individual who defines himself or herself in this way is referred to as a "transgenderist" or transgendered person. As with all terms, the trans-community expanded the definition of transgender, so that, in the 1990s, it was used as an inclusive term for anyone who trans-gresses, or crosses, gender boundaries, but specifically for transvestites, transsexuals, transgenderists, drag queens and drag kings, gender-benders, gender-blenders, she-males and he-shes, androgynes, and intersexed people. The commonality among these categories of people is that all of them, to one degree or another, challenge the binary of sex and/or gender. Some transsexuals object to the label of "transgender" and advocate against the use of it as an inclusive term. Nonetheless, many individuals do use the term. "Transgender" is not used in medical-psychological discourses and, as such, is not recognized as a diagnostic category.

### Definition of Terms

By clinical definition, a transvestite (TV) is a male who dresses as a woman and obtains erotic arousal while cross-dressed. Within this definition, such behavior is considered extremely rare in females. However, female transvestites do exist and can be distinguished from women who wear so-called men's clothing by their efforts to "pass" as men. Just as the clinical definition excludes females, so it excludes males who cross-dress for other reasons. More broadly defined, a transvestite is a person, regardless of sex or gender, who cross-dresses and takes on the behaviors, socially constructed as the proper domain, of the other biological sex. Many transvestites prefer the term "cross-dresser" (CD) because it more accurately describes their behavior and removes it from its sexual connotations.

By clinical definition, a transsexual (TS) is a person who has an extreme discomfort with his or her assigned sex and desires and/or pursues sex-reassignment surgery. It is commonly understood that the transsexual's goal is to have sex-reassignment surgery and to ultimately live as a "normal" woman or man. "Transsexual" is used in two ways: to describe a man who is in the process of becoming a woman, or vice versa; and, to describe someone who has completed sex-reassignment surgery. Many postoperative transsexuals no longer consider themselves transsexual and reject the term as a descriptor, preferring the term "woman" or "man." Those individuals who retain their transsexual identity refer to themselves as transsexuals or as transgendered, as well as MTF (male-to-female), transwoman, FTM (female-to-male or female toward male and/or masculine), and transman.

## Trans-Activism

The adaptation of old terminology and the development of new terms is, in part, a direct result of trans-community formation and subsequent trans-activism. In the late 1980s and the early 1990s, trans-activism focused on civil rights issues, such as employment and housing discrimination, and legal name changes. Another focus was on treatment issues, such as clinical requirements that insisted that transpeople have "textbook" biographies, that they live as their preferred gender without hormonal therapy, and that they completely change their lives by moving to a new area where no one knew of their past. The late 1990s saw a shift toward activism that challenged the medical and psychological communities' psychopathological model of transsexualism. Many transpeople object to being labeled as mentally ill and the requirement that they submit to surgeries that are supposed to "cure" them of gender dysphoria. Most members of the medical and psy-

chological communities have advocated that transpeople return to the "closet" and deny their past histories, arguing that it is necessary for a successful transition to melt into the woodwork and "pass" as "normal" women or men.

The challenge to the medical and psychological communities has arisen as a consequence of trans-community networking, in which the results of inadequate, and sometimes damaging, surgeries, as well as the sometimes harmful effects of hormones, are discussed. For some transpeople, "passing" as "normal" is impossible or nearly so, and, depending on when a person decides to transition, it may be impossible to deny a lengthy past life without suffering severe consequences, such as lost employment and loss of family. Some transpeople have come to realize that, even if they can "pass" as "normal," they are different (if only because of their histories) from men and women who have always had a gender identity that was congruent with their assigned sex. So long as transpeople were isolated from one another, these discussions could not take place. Like other minorities, transpeople felt the need to discuss these issues and others, and networks such as support groups, trans-conferences, and Internet lists developed.

Trans-activism has arisen also because of the deaths of several transpeople in the 1990s. The murders of Brandon Teena (1994), Tyra Hunter (1995), and Chanelle Pickett (1995) outraged many transpeople, and vigils, demonstrations, and leafleting were conducted during the perpetrators' trials and sentencing hearings. In part, the success of these activities led to the formation of direct-action groups, such as Transgender Nation and Transexual Menace. Along with these organizations, other groups, including ICTLEP (International Conference on Transgender Law and Employment Policy) and TOPS (Transsexual Officers Protect and Serve) have rallied, held vigils, picketed, and protested in venues as disparate as GLBT (gay, lesbian, bisexual, and transgender) and mainstream newspapers, the Michigan Womyn's Music Festival, courts of law, police and fire departments, and psychology-society meetings, and have held transgender lobby days at the United States Senate and House of Representatives in Washington, D.C.

Many transpeople have supported the work of these action groups. However, as with any community activism, there is always controversy. For example, at the 1997 American Psychiatric Association (APA) meetings, a group of protesters picketed for the elimination of the diagnostic category of gender identity disorder (GID). Many transpeople believe this diagnosis stigmatizes them with a pathological mental disorder and want it removed from the APA's *Diagnostic and Statistical Manual* (DSM). Those who object to the elimination of GID as a diagnostic category fear that not having a "disorder" will result in the loss of available services, especially reassignment surgeries. Those who are in favor of removing GID also note that it is often used for "corrective treatment" of children and adolescents who are gender variant, such as masculine-behaving girls, feminine-behaving boys, and gay, lesbian, bisexual, and transgendered youth.

## Trans-Inclusion

Another reason for the increase in trans-activism lies in the intersection between lesbian communities and trans-communities. The entry into lesbian communities by some transwomen who identify as lesbians has been met with mixed results. Some lesbians have accepted, while others have rejected, transwomen. For example, during the 1991 Michigan Womyn's Music Festival a transwoman was asked whether she was a transsexual, and, when she answered in the affirmative, she was promptly ejected from the festival. However, she did not remain silent. Along with many supporters, she organized, educated, and protested at subsequent festivals under the banner of Camp Trans until festival organizers allowed entry to transwomen in 1995. While the ejection of this transwoman brought the issue of trans-inclusion out into the open, it was just the tip of an iceberg.

One individual who was active at Camp Trans and who has tried to create a bridge between lesbian Communities and trans-communities is activist Leslie Feinberg (1949–). In the early 1980s, she wrote and published a chapbook outlining the oppression of transpeople throughout history. In 1996, she extended this historical tract into a book, which was published by Beacon Press. In part, Feinberg's activism arose from her history as a person who lived as a "passing woman" and from her personal identity as a transperson and as a lesbian. While Feinberg has been warmly received by lesbian communities, her presence is often met with consternation by some transmen, who argue that she muddies the issues concerning the differences between lesbians and transmen.

Transpeople, whether they have identified as transwomen or as transmen, have been a part of les-

bian and gay communities all along. Some transpeople identify as gay or lesbian prior to, as well as after, transitioning, regardless of the degree of their transition. Many transwomen who identified as heterosexual while living as men continue to be attracted to women and identify as lesbians. Likewise, some transmen who identified as heterosexual while living as women continue to be attracted to men and identify as gay men. Many transmen, based on their attraction to women, tried to fit in as lesbians, specifically as butch dykes or stone butches. Not all butches want to be, or identify as, men. However, some found that, although they were able to express their masculine identities within some lesbian communities, it was not enough, and they sought or found the trans-label that better expressed their identities as men. Naturally, some of these individuals leave lesbian communities. However, many transpeople remain in lesbian and gay communities and insist that they belong to, and are a part of, these communities as queer people.    *Jason Cromwell*

## Bibliography

Bolin, Anne. "Transcending and Transgendering: Male-to-Female Transsexuals, Dichotomy and Diversity." In *Third Sex, Third Gender: Beyond Sexual Dimorphism in Culture and History*. Ed. Gilbert Herdt. New York: Zone, 1994, pp. 447–485.

Bornstein, Kate. *Gender Outlaw: On Men, Women, and the Rest of Us*. New York: Routledge, 1994.

Califia, Pat. *Sex Changes: The Politics of Sex Changes*. San Francisco: Cleis, 1997.

Feinberg, Leslie. *Transgender Warriors: Making History from Joan of Arc to RuPaul*. Boston: Beacon, 1996.

Stoller, Robert. "Transvestism in Women." *Archives of Sexual Behavior* 11 (1982), 99–115.

*See also* Butch-Femme; Cross-Dressing; Music Festivals; Passing Women; Queer Theory

## Tribade

A term designating a woman who engages in erotic acts with other women or, more generally, "tribadism," designating the erotic practices of genital rubbing or penetration. "Tribade" made its way into English via the French *tribad*, which, in turn, was derived through the Latin from the Greek *tribas* τριβαζ ("to rub"). Other variants of this term are the Latin *fricatrix* and the English "fricatrice," "confricatrice," and "rubster." The English term is first recorded in Ben Jonson's (1572–1637) poem "Praeludium" (Poem X in *The Forest* [1601]) in reference to the purported activities of Venus and her Graces. In the documented sources, "tribade" is never used as a self-description; it is a term of opprobrium or, in the case of pornography, titillation.

Historically, the concept of tribadism has been mediated through beliefs about the erotic potential of the clitoris. The ancient Greeks viewed the tribade as a hypermasculine woman who penetrated either women or men with her enlarged clitoris or a dildo; later Roman authors tended to project this illicit behavior back onto the Greeks. It was not until late antiquity that the tribade was associated exclusively with same-gender eroticism. Classical definitions and attitudes, however, were only partly accessible in Europe until the sixteenth century, when newly rediscovered classical texts were translated. Through the proliferation of classical literature, anatomies, midwiferies, sexual-advice manuals, and pornography, the concept of tribadism gained wider currency.

Sixteenth-century Western authors attributed tribadism largely to non-Christian women residing in Turkey and Africa. By the mid-seventeenth century, in response to the promulgation of sensationalistic accounts, an increasing number of Western writers expressed anxiety about the existence of tribades in their own countries. Prosecutions increased, which led to further use of the term. These events gave rise to a proto-erotic identity for the tribade, who was believed to be different from other women in both her desires and her bodily anatomy. She often was believed to possess an enlarged clitoris, which she rubbed against her partner or used as an instrument of penetration; lacking this anatomical deviation, she sometimes was thought to use a dildo.

From the seventeenth through the eighteenth centuries, tribade was used inconsistently alongside hermaphrodite, female husband, virago, and, late in the period, tommy and sapphist to connote a "masculinized" woman who desired or committed sexual acts with other women. More often, however, writers avoided the term, instead euphemistically invoking "unnatural vice," "lewd behavior," "crimes against nature," "using an instrument," and "taking the part of a man." By the mid-eighteenth century, anatomical investigation led to skepticism about stories of enlarged clitorises, and anatomists and

doctors argued for a more precise distinction between clitoral hypertrophy and hermaphroditism. In part because of this distinction, tribadism came to designate primarily an erotic practice (genital rubbing) rather than an erotic type or bodily morphology—although the notion of somatic deformity reappeared in some late-nineteenth-century concepts of the invert.

Despite anatomical skepticism, "tribadism" continued to be used as a term in criminology and forensic medicine; a Netherlands judge used the term in his private annotations on a case in the late eighteenth century, and Jane Pirie (ca. 1784) and Marianne Woods (ca. 1779) defended themselves against the imputation of tribadism in a Scottish libel case in 1811. (More often, such women were prosecuted for sodomy, transvestism, or fraud.) The term had a considerable life in eighteenth- and nineteenth-century pornography (particularly of the satiric kind) and was employed in several pornographic libels against Marie Antoinette (1755–1793). By the Victorian era, tribadism tended to be constructed as a lower-class and non-Western phenomenon and often was associated with the supposed degeneration of prostitutes and criminals. By the close of the nineteenth century, "tribade" had been supplanted by the terms "sapphist," "lesbian," "invert," and "homosexual." With the movement away from physiological explanations toward notions of psychosexual causality, the specific bodily basis of the concept of the tribade became an archaism.

As a specific erotic technique, however, tribadism survives in contemporary lesbian culture, referring to the rhythmic rubbing of one partner's clitoris with the other's thigh, hip, pubic bone, buttocks, or genitals. Its equivalent slang term is "dyking."

*Valerie Traub*

### Bibliography

Brooten, Bernadette J. *Love Between Women: Early Christian Responses to Female Homoeroticism.* Chicago: University of Chicago Press, 1996.

Donoghue, Emma. *Passions Between Women: British Lesbian Culture, 1668–1801.* New York: HarperCollins, 1993.

Halberstam, Judith. *Female Masculinity.* Durham, N.C.: Duke University Press, 1998.

Park, Katharine. "The Rediscovery of the Clitoris: French Medicine and the Tribade, 1570–1620." In *The Body in Parts: Discourses and Anatomies in Early Modern Europe.* Ed. Carla

Mazzio and David Hillman. London and New York: Routledge, 1997.

Traub, Valerie. "The Psychomorphology of the Clitoris." *GLQ: A Journal of Lesbian and Gay Studies* 2 (Winter 1995), 81–113.

*See also* Clitoris; Marie Antoinette; Pirie, Jane, and Woods, Marianne; Sex Practices; Sexology

## Tsvetaeva, Marina Ivanovna (1892–1941)

Widely considered one of the four greatest twentieth-century Russian poets, Marina Tsvetaeva was born into a distinguished Moscow intelligentsia family. Her father was an art professor, and her mother a gifted pianist of Polish descent. Tsvetaeva began writing poetry at the age of six; her first volume of poems, *Vechernii al'bom* (Evening Album), was published in 1910.

Tsvetaeva revealed an attraction to her own sex from childhood and tells the story of her first love for another girl in her prose work "The House at Old Pimen" (1934). Despite her lesbian inclinations, or perhaps in an effort to neutralize the anxiety they clearly caused her, Tsvetaeva married young and immediately had a daughter. Then, in late 1914, she met and fell in love with the openly lesbian poet Sophia Parnok (1885–1933). This brief, but passionate, affair inspired Tsvetaeva's cycle *Podruga* (Girlfriend [1914–1915]), a masterpiece of lesbian love poetry that was published only in the 1970s and, as of 1998, had not been translated into English in its entirety. Tsvetaeva was traumatized by the end of her relationship with Parnok in early 1916, calling it the "first catastrophe" of her life. She nurtured vengeful feelings about Parnok for the rest of her life and constantly rewrote their love affair in her major lesbian works.

Tsvetaeva spent the 1917 Revolution and ensuing civil war in Moscow while her husband served as an officer in the white army. From 1918 to 1920, she worked with an avant-garde Moscow theater, the Third Stage, and became involved with Sonya Gollidey (1894–1934), one of the actresses. Much later, in 1936, she wrote about this love affair in *Povest' o Sonechke* (The Tale of Sonechka), which, by the late 1990s, had not been translated into English. Just after the publication of her most famous collection of poems, *Versty* (Mileposts [1922]) Tsvetaeva left the Soviet Union and was reunited with her husband in Prague. In early 1925, their son was born, and, later that year, the family moved to Paris, where Tsvetaeva lived for the next fourteen years. In the early 1930s, she was introduced to Natalie Barney (1876–1972) and gave a poetry reading at Barney's rue Jacob salon, but neither she nor her work was given an enthusiastic reception. Tsvetaeva wrote (in French) her *Lettre à l'Amazone* (Letter to an Amazon [1932, rev. 1934]), a highly encoded, autobiographical, and polemical work on lesbian love with two addressees: Barney and Tsvetaeva's former lover, Parnok. *Lettre à l'Amazone* also gives expression to Tsvetaeva's struggle with her own lesbianism: She defends lesbian relationships against the censure of society, religion, and the state, while her internalized homophobia leads her to strike out at such relationships as an offense to nature and Mother.

During the 1930s, Tsvetaeva was increasingly isolated and criticized by the Russian émigré community, in large part because of her husband's pro-Soviet political activities. At the end of the decade, she returned to Soviet Russia, where tragedy awaited her. First, her daughter was arrested in August 1939 and sent to a concentration camp; then her husband was arrested and executed as an enemy of the people. Despite her desperate situation, Tsvetaeva became involved (in 1940) with Tatyana Kvanina (1908–), the wife of a minor writer. Part of their intimate correspondence has appeared in a Russian journal. At the beginning of World War II, Tsvetaeva and her teenage son were evacuated to Yelabuga, in the Tatar Autonomous Republic. On August 31, 1941, she hanged herself from a beam in the ceiling of her quarters; she was buried in an unmarked grave in the Yelabuga cemetery.

Since the fall of the Soviet Union in the early 1990s, interest in Tsvetaeva has burgeoned; her voluminous output of lyrics, long poems, prose works, literary criticism, and letters has been published in Russian; and several biographies of her have appeared. However, despite the poet's self-acknowledged love for women, the lesbian theme that runs throughout her poetry, prose, letters, and journals continues to be ignored, or mentioned merely in passing, by most Western biographers and literary scholars. Most Russian Tsvetaeva scholars try to deny entirely the poet's lesbianism and its significance in her work.                                  *Diana L. Burgin*

### Bibliography

Burgin, Diana Lewis. "Mother Nature versus the Amazons: Marina Tsvetaeva and Female Same-Sex Love." *Journal of the History of Sexuality* 6:1 (July 1995), 62–88.

Feiler, Lily. *Marina Tsvetaeva: The Double Beat of Heaven and Hell*. Durham, N.C.: Duke University Press, 1994.

Karlinsky, Simon. *Marina Tsvetaeva: The Woman, Her World, and Her Poetry*. Cambridge: Cambridge University Press, 1985.

Taubman, Jane. *A Life Through Poetry: Marina Tsvetaeva's Lyric Diary*. Columbus: Slavica, 1989.

*See also* Barney, Natalie Clifford; Parnok, Sophia; Russia

## Two-Spirit

A term used in the late twentieth century by Native Americans who are lesbian, gay, bisexual, or transgendered (cross-dressers, transvestites, and transsexuals) to define and identify themselves. It suggests that one possesses a female and a male spirit.

Strictly speaking, being a lesbian, gay, bisexual, or transgendered person in the Western sense is not necessarily synonymous with being a two-spirit. Twentieth-century non-Native conceptions of homosexuality, bisexuality, and transgenderism do not convey the traditional meanings or roles of two-spirits within Native American societies and communities. In particular, for two-spirits one's identity is often based on spiritual and communal orientations, not sexual or affectional ones. Some American Indians, for instance, become two-spirited after experiencing one or more visions. Two-spirits have traditionally held particular social and ritual roles in many Native cultures as well. Some are asked to participate in naming a child, for example, while others have been in charge of burying the dead. It is important to note, however, that not all two-spirits are spiritual adepts or ritual leaders or are considered to be so by their communities.

Neither does two-spirited experience fit neatly into contemporary mainstream Western understandings of gender and sexuality in general. In Native American societies generally, one's physiological sex does not determine one's gender role. For instance, while a two-spirited woman may be female biologically, in every aspect of her life she lives as a man, behaving according to the male gender role appropriate to her nation. It is also not necessarily the case that a female two-spirit becomes a man. Scholarly interpretations vary as to whether, to be a two-spirit, one changes from one gender role to another (such as female to male), or is both female and male (gender-mixing), or is of an entirely separate gender. Williams (1986) points out that the Mojave, for instance, have four distinct genders: female, male, *hwame* (female two-spirit), and *alyha* (male two-spirit). Different interpretations of gender roles are due, at least in part, to variations from tribe to tribe. Similarly, the fluid nature of Native American gender and sexual roles makes the use of the categories "homosexual" and "heterosexual" problematic as well. Because many American Indian cultures have traditionally been more open and flexible in their attitudes toward sexuality, it is not necessarily the case that one will be exclusively homosexual or heterosexual throughout one's life.

The term "two-spirit" reflects more of an indigenous understanding of American Indian genders and sexualities. It has arisen, in part, because of the inaccurate and inappropriate conceptions employed by Euro-Americans in describing two-spirited people. In particular, anthropologists have regularly used the word "berdache" to refer to American Indian two-spirits, especially those who are anatomically male but engage in traditionally female gender roles. The term "berdache" stems from the Persian *bardaj*, which later developed into *bardasso* (Italian), *bardaxa* or *bardaje* (Spanish), and *bardache* (French) (Williams 1986). Regardless of the language, the meaning of the term, "boy kept for unnatural purposes" (the passive homosexual partner, especially in anal intercourse), reflects Euro-American condemnation of homosexuality. Because of the male referent implicit in berdache, the designation "female berdache," used occasionally in the literature, only compounds the inaccuracies. In its place, Williams employs the term "Amazon," in light of the Tupinamba Amazons, the female warriors of an indigenous Brazilian people.

The term "two-spirit" eliminates many of these conceptual difficulties, but it is not without its own problems. Although the word "two-spirit" is a creation of the community that it defines and describes, not all American Indian lesbian, gay, bisexual, and transgendered people use the designation. Additionally, as a generic term, it obscures the fact that each Native nation has its own understandings of two-spirited people, which are not necessarily the same as those of any other nation. These conceptions are linked to particular terms used to designate two-spirits, words that are specific to each indigenous language. The meanings embedded in these terms are not completely conveyed by the English "two-spirit" either. For this and other reasons, it is preferable to use the indigenous words to discuss two-spirits of particular Native nations, rather than the generic "two-spirit."

Because "two-spirit" is not particular to any one nation, though, its use appears to have served as a unifying force, enabling two-spirits of many nations to find common ground and make common cause. In contrast to the derogatory connotations of "berdache," "two-spirit" is generally employed in a positive way, especially by two-spirited people themselves. This use of the term reflects, in part, the positive regard many Native American peoples historically have had for two-spirits. This respect could be a response to the particular roles two-spirits play in a community, though it could also reflect recognition of the power potentially present in the two-spirit's status as a liminal being, one who intermediates between genders.

Jaimes and Halsey (1992) found that some lesbian and gay activists have romanticized two-spirits and Native community acceptance of them, inventing and appropriating an image of two-spirits to be used for legitimating homosexuality in Western societies. Not all Native nations have traditionally valued two-spirits. In some cases, a "live and let live" philosophy has been more common, although outright homophobia is not unheard of. It is not always possible to determine, however, if negative attitudes toward two-spirits are traditional in a community or are the result of the adoption of Euro-American attitudes toward homosexuality due to Christianization and colonization. Contemporary Native attitudes toward two-spirits are therefore varied, ranging from respect to toleration to rejection, and including all points in between.

*Mary C. Churchill*

## Bibliography

Blackwood, Evelyn. "Sexuality and Gender in Certain Native American Tribes: The Case of Cross-Gender Females." *Signs: Journal of Women in Culture and Society* 10:1 (Autumn 1984), 27–42.

Brown, Lester B., ed. *Two Spirit People: American Indian Lesbian Women and Gay Men.* New York: Haworth, 1997.

Jacobs, Sue-Ellen, Wesley Thomas, and Sabine Lang, eds. *Two-Spirit People: Native American Gender Identity, Sexuality, and Spirituality.* Urbana: University of Illinois Press, 1997.

Jaimes, M. Annette, and Theresa Halsey. "American Indian Women: At the Center of Indigenous Resistance in North America." In *The State of Native America: Genocide, Colonization, and Resistance.* Ed. M. Annette Jaimes. Boston: South End, 1992, pp. 311–344.

Roscoe, Will. *Changing Ones: Third and Fourth Genders in Native North America.* New York: St. Martin's, 1998.

Tafoya, Terry. "Native Gay and Lesbian Issues: The Two-Spirited." In *Positively Gay: New Approaches to Gay and Lesbian Life.* Ed. Betty Berzon. Berkeley: Celestial Arts, 1992, pp. 253–259.

Williams, Walter L. *The Spirit and the Flesh: Sexual Diversity in American Indian Culture.* Boston: Beacon, 1986.

*See also* Amazons; Gender; Native Americans; Spirituality; Transgender

# U

## United Kingdom

Political union of Great Britain (England, Wales, and Scotland) and Northern Ireland. England and Wales fall under one legal jurisdiction, Northern Ireland another, and Scotland a quite distinct third.

### The Legal Context

Lesbianism has never been illegal in any U.K. jurisdiction. Under English law, the common-law offense of sodomy has not been applied to women, and, while homosexual acts between consenting male adults in private were criminalized between 1885 and 1967, the only attempt to bring lesbian acts within the same statutory regime failed in 1921. Members of Parliament argued that the practice would be better controlled by maintaining silence than by admitting the possibility of its existence. There is no age of consent to lesbian sex, in contrast to heterosexual sex (sixteen) and male homosexual sex (eighteen).

Lesbians are not protected against discrimination in employment under the Sex Discrimination Act of 1975, though most large organizations operate equal-opportunities policies that cover sexual orientation. Lesbian mothers have historically had difficulties in custody disputes, but recent court decisions since 1990 suggest that lesbianism, which judges used to see as either perverted in itself or inevitably leading to social ostracism and embarrassment for the children, is no longer an insuperable barrier to custody.

None of the jurisdictions within the United Kingdom has a bill or charter of rights. The civil rights discourse that has been adopted by lesbians and gay men with some success in North America began to be articulated only in 1990 applications to the European Court of Justice, under its treaties and conventions, for such rights as the right to marry. Many lesbians do not support the rights movement, however, preferring to maintain a feminist critique of the institution of marriage and to continue to attack patriarchal value systems rather than seek to be included within them.

In 1988, the Conservative Party passed the Local Government Act, Section 28, which prohibits the "promotion" of homosexuality in certain state-funded venues such as schools. The campaigns against Section 28 mobilized a coalition of lesbians, gay men, and straight supporters of unprecedented size and strength, marching and demonstrating against it. Section 28 has never been tested in the courts, and legal commentators claim it is unworkable in practice, but it has had the effect of making it acceptable for homophobic people to discriminate against lesbians and gay men and gay events or enterprises.

### Lesbian History

There are still many gaps in British lesbian history before the nineteenth century. There has been some work on the witch-hunts and witch-burnings of early-modern England and on communities of nuns in pre-Reformation convents. Queen Anne (1665–1714) is an early lesbian icon, her relationship with Sarah Churchill (1660–1744) being generally recognized as lesbian despite her marriage and seventeen pregnancies.

Research into lesbian history was given impetus in the 1970s and 1980s as part of the "second wave" of feminism's search for roots. American scholars such as Lillian Faderman and Martha Vicinus, who traced the history of romantic friendships and communities of women in Victorian Britain and beyond, strongly influenced British research in this field, including the Lesbian History Group's collection *Not a Passing Phase: Reclaiming Lesbians in History, 1840–1985* (1993). This remains the classic British text on ways of doing lesbian history and the problems of definitions, methodology, and politics. The publication in 1988 of the first extracts from the diaries of Anne Lister (1791–1840), a Yorkshire gentlewoman, upset the earlier assumption, derived from Faderman's work, that women who desired other women would not have expressed their desire sexually, and would not have had a "lesbian" identity, before the naming of lesbianism by sexologists at the end of the nineteenth century. Lister, who wrote of her sexual feelings and experiences in code, clearly saw herself as a sexual outlaw. Emma Donaghue's *Passions Between Women: British Lesbian Culture, 1668–1801* (1993) offered a second rebuttal to the age-of-innocence theory. Donaghue examines a range of texts to demonstrate that images and words to indicate "lesbian" desires and identities were freely circulating in the late seventeenth and eighteenth centuries. While this provides valuable evidence of attitudes, it says little (as the author freely admits) about women's actual experiences of love and sex. The reaction against Faderman in the 1990s led to a greater focus on lesbianism as *sexual* radicalism, which, Vicinus argues, has had a limiting effect on historical research, since not only is it difficult to find evidence of lesbian sexual activity in the lives of women of past generations, but sexual activity is not an essential element in the definition of "lesbian" in history.

Much more is known about the nineteenth century. Victorian feminism provides several examples of "lesbians" among the well-to-do women who chose to direct their energies toward other women. Though few were in a position to share their lives with a woman partner, since women were expected to live with family members, even married women were permitted, even encouraged, to enjoy close relationships with other women under the ideology of "separate spheres" for men and women. Faderman is probably right in suggesting that these relationships were not, in this period, viewed as either sexual or threatening to patriarchal control because of the assumption that women were sexually passive. On the other hand, this does not mean that the relationships were *not* sexual or that the women had no consciousness of themselves as "lesbians." For example, Frances Power Cobbe (1822–1904), a member of the Anglo-Irish gentry, settled in London with a lifelong companion, Welsh artist Mary Lloyd (d. between 1894 and 1898). Cobbe had met Lloyd while visiting Charlotte Cushman (1816–1876) in Rome, on a tour that included calling on Rosa Bonheur (1822–1899) in France, suggesting that "lesbian" networks existed in the mid-nineteenth century. Cobbe's critiques of marriage and her articles in praise of spinsterhood did not prevent her from taking up the cause of women victims of domestic violence; her campaigning helped bring about the passing of the Matrimonial Causes Act of 1878, which enabled battered women to leave violent husbands and obtain financial support.

Many lesbians continued to be associated with feminism into the twentieth century. Cicely Hamilton (1872–1952), according to biographer Lis Whitelaw, wrote suffrage plays and pageants that were produced and performed by her lesbian friends; Ethel Smyth (1858–1944) composed the suffrage anthem, *Shoulder to Shoulder* (to words by Hamilton); and, in the 1920s, "equal rights" feminism was promoted by Viscountess Rhondda (1883–1958), who set up the Six-Point Group and whose fortune financed the weekly paper *Time and Tide* as a vehicle for progressive ideas. Winifred Holtby (1898–1935) was among those who wrote for it.

By the 1920s, lesbianism had been "recognized" in intellectual circles as a psychosexual problem. The successful prosecution of Radclyffe Hall's (1880–1943) novel *The Well of Loneliness* (1928) for obscenity in 1928 was the culmination of a development that had started much earlier: Clemence Dane's novel *Regiment of Women* (1919) depicts the malevolent influence of a woman teacher who preys on young women, and there was the attempt, described above, to criminalize lesbianism in 1921. By the 1930s, most lesbians had gone underground. Attempts to research the lives of this generation of women are made difficult by the absence of personal papers, destroyed by either the women themselves or their heirs, and the silence of their memoirs, where they exist, on matters of sexuality and relationships. However, biographies of some well-to-do figures like Vita Sackville-West (1892–1962) show that lesbian networks and relationships were certainly in existence in the interwar years, although there is little evidence for the same among ordinary middle- and working-class women.

Oral histories undertaken during the "second wave" of feminism, when lesbian feminists were seeking their heritage, pick up the story during World War II, when women were thrown into close association with other women, as in the days of the Victorian "separate spheres." The decade of the 1950s was a morally repressive era in Britain, with much emphasis on women's domestic role and the importance of marriage and pleasing men. In the 1960s, however, the sexual and economic bonds that tied women to husbands were loosened with the so-called sexual revolution, the increased participation of women in the paid workforce, and the rise in divorce (no-fault divorce was introduced in 1969).

In 1963, Esme Langley founded the Minorities Research Group (MRG), an organization for lesbians, which held monthly meetings in a central London pub. In 1964, the group produced Britain's first all-lesbian newsletter, *Arena 3*, with a country-wide circulation. In 1965, Kenric was founded as a social group for London lesbians, and it soon spread to the provinces; in the late 1990s, local Kenric associations continued to flourish, and Sappho, which grew out of the MRG, still existed as a London social and discussion group for lesbians.

After the legalization of gay male sex in 1967, gay men began to campaign against other aspects of gay oppression and were joined by some lesbians. Both the Gay Liberation Front (1970–1972), which was revolutionary in character, and the Campaign for Homosexual Equality (founded in 1969), which was more reformist, purported to represent the interests of both lesbians and gay men, but the sexism of the male leadership and the focus on demands to benefit men (for example, to legalize "cottaging," the practice of soliciting in public toilets) led many women to leave. Many of them found a welcome in the women's liberation movement of the 1970s and 1980s.

Lesbians were prominent in all of the main campaigns of "second wave" feminism—setting up rape crisis centers and women's refuges and campaigning against domestic violence, child sexual abuse, and pornography (though many lesbians were anticensorship rather than antipornography)—and also launched their own lesbian initiatives, such as the Lesbian Custody Project. Lesbians also continued to organize outside the women's movement; Sappho, for example, held a conference for married lesbians in the early 1970s that attracted more than one hundred women from all over England and Scotland, which led to the setting up of the Gay Wives and Mothers Group, later renamed Action for Lesbian Parents.

In the 1980s, public funding in London and other urban districts facilitated the development of feminist and lesbian enterprises, such as women's centers and gay and lesbian centers that hosted classes, clubs, associations to advise and assist lesbians (such as LESPOP, the Lesbian Policing Project), and libraries and archives. In the cities at least, lesbians became a public presence in this decade, and, while many women remained (and still remain) in the closet, others came out and stayed out. The 1980s saw the first black lesbian groups (in the United Kingdom, the term "black" encompasses people of Asian as well as Afro-Caribbean origin) and the opening of a black lesbian center in north London.

The 1990s proved, in the United Kingdom as elsewhere, to be a period of backlash and reaction, with religious fundamentalism and "family values" conservatism permitting the confident assertion of heterosexist and lesbophobic sentiments. Paradoxically, however, lesbian and gay rights gained a higher profile than ever before in British history, and young women coming out in Britain in the 1990s had an unequaled range of images, models, and access to information about lesbianism.

## Lesbian Literature

Lesbian books enjoyed a boom in the 1990s, driven largely by market forces. If Radclyffe Hall's *The Well of Loneliness*, banned upon publication in Britain though not in the United States, is still regarded as the classic text of lesbian love, many more positive representations have been produced by subsequent writers, and lesbian scholars have reclaimed some earlier literature as proto-lesbian and have given lesbian readings of a variety of genres, ranging from girls' school stories (a peculiarly British phenomenon) to detective fiction and television soap operas. It has become acceptable to write doctoral theses on lesbian romance novels or lesbian cinema, and cultural studies is perhaps the biggest growth area in lesbian studies, both in the universities and in publishing. Many major publishing houses, such as Cassell and Routledge, have extensive lesbian lists, and most bookshops in larger towns have lesbian and gay sections. Onlywomen Press in London celebrated twenty years of lesbian publishing in 1995, having maintained a radical feminist philosophy throughout its history. Other publishers present a range of feminist, queer, and postmodern critical viewpoints. black lesbian perspectives began to appear, later and more slowly than in the United States.

Several British lesbian writers, such as Maureen Duffy (1933–), enjoy critical esteem. Lesbian poetry flourishes, black Scottish poet Jackie Kay

(1961–) being considered one of the most exciting contemporary voices. Many feminist publishers, like the Women's Press and Onlywomen, publish light (but still feminist) lesbian fiction alongside their more serious lists. The London bookshop Silver Moon, Europe's largest for women, not only stocks a huge range of lesbian thrillers and romances, but also publishes them. In the 1990s, the Scot Val McDermid wrote both detective stories with a lesbian feminist heroine for the Women's Press and thrillers with a straight heroine for the mainstream publisher HarperCollins.

## Lesbians in the Media

It was in the 1970s that the British Broadcasting Commission (BBC), formerly a vigorous upholder of family values, made a few tentative forays into lesbian culture. Representatives of the lesbian organization Sappho were invited to comment on lesbian and women's issues, and, in 1975, a Radio 4 play depicting a lesbian relationship, *Now She Laughs, Now She Cries*, went out to general acclaim. In the 1980s and 1990s, the program that kept lesbians on the agenda most assiduously was *Woman's Hour*, a national institution that reaches a daily audience of 600,000. With a producer appointed to look after lesbian issues, *Woman's Hour* not only devotes space to items of specific lesbian interest, such as Section 28 and lesbian crime fiction, but also ensures a lesbian perspective on general subjects; for example, time was devoted in a 1996 documentary on interwar Member of Parliament Eleanor Rathbone to a discussion on whether she was a lesbian. The 1990s saw the introduction of programs aimed at mixed gay audiences, such as *A Sunday Outing* and *Loud and Proud* (both 1993), and regular weekly slots, such as *Gay and Lesbian London* on Greater London Radio.

The rare television appearances of lesbians before the 1980s generally took place within investigative series into "taboo" topics: for example, a *Man Alive* program in 1967 in which a number of lesbians were interviewed about their lives, including a group at the legendary Gateways Club in west London. London Weekend Television's pioneering *Gay Life* series went out at 11:30 p.m. on Sunday nights during 1980 and 1981. Gay television really arrived in 1989 with regular programs on both the BBC and commercial channels. These tend to be shared with—one might even say dominated by—gay men, and feminist approaches are conspicuous by their absence. Nevertheless, it was an *Out* program on Channel 4 that hosted the brilliant feminist documentaries about older lesbians, *Women Like Us* (1990) and *Women Like That* (1991).

Two highly successful television presentations were the dramatization of Jeannette Winterson's (1959–) *Oranges Are not the Only Fruit* (1990) and the four-part series based on *Portrait of a Marriage* (1991) by Vita Sackville-West's son Nigel Nicolson (1917–), both transmitted in 1990. By the mid-1990s most British soaps had introduced a lesbian storyline, approved by many because they brought lesbians into so many homes, criticized by others for relying on damaging negative stereotypes, such as the older teacher/younger student in one case and the suicidal lesbian in another.

The London Lesbian and Gay Film Festival premieres a small number of commercial and not-so-commercial lesbian films each year, though these are often drawn from North America and Australasia. Some proceed to open release. The most famous British lesbian film ever made is probably *The Killing of Sister George* (1968). Based on a stage play by Frank Marcus that is still often revived in Britain and abroad, it avoided censorship by refraining from mentioning the word "lesbian." In the 1970s and 1980s, lesbian and mixed gay theater companies, such as Siren and Gay Sweatshop flourished. While lesbian plays like Lillian Hellman's *The Children's Hour* (1934) occasionally appear on the West End stage, fringe theater continues to be more receptive to lesbian drama and entertainment.

Lesbian journalism made its debut with *Arena 3* in 1967. After *Sappho* folded in 1981, lesbians had to content themselves with sharing space with gay men (*Gay News* [1972–1983], followed by *Gay Times* [1983–]) or with heterosexual feminists (*Spare Rib* [1972–1993] and other shorter-lived publications). In 1988, the *Pink Paper* was launched as a free weekly for lesbians and gay men. Its bias toward male interests led to the setting up of *Lesbian London* in 1992, which survived for only three years. There are, however, specialist lesbian papers, such as *Dyke*, a magazine for walkers. Lesbian issues are increasingly aired in straight women's magazines, though rarely from a feminist standpoint: from alternative lifestyles in *Cosmopolitan*, through k.d. lang (1961–) in *Vanity Fair*, to gay parenting in *Marie-Claire*. *Diva* is a glossy devoted to "lesbian life and style" that reflects the 1990s preoccupation with lesbian chic.

## The Lesbian "Scene"

Most U.K. cities offer lesbians a range of places to go and things to do. Outside the towns, the closet doors tend to remain firmly shut, and outings are restricted to one's nearest branch of Kenric if there happens to be one.

There are places associated with famous lesbians to be visited: for example, Anne Lister's Shibden Hall in Halifax; the Ladies of Llangollen's house, Plas Newydd, in Wales; Smallhythe in Kent, home of the early-twentieth-century ménage à trois of theatrical producer Edith Craig (1869–1947), writer Christopher St. John (Christabel Marshall [d. 1960]) and artist Tony (Clare) Atwood (1866–1962); and the several London properties listed in the *Pink Plaque Guide*. Britain's Lesbian Archive is now housed in the Women's Center in Glasgow, Scotland.

*Cassell's Pink Directory* lists lesbian and gay organizations, businesses, and services in the United Kingdom and Eire. But, as listings tend to go out of date, visitors are advised to check the *Pink Paper* or local papers or to phone the Lesbian and Gay Switchboard.                    *Rosemary Auchmuty*

## Bibliography

Cant, Bob, and Susan Hemmings, eds. *Radical Records: Thirty Years of Lesbian and Gay History*. London: Routledge, 1988.

Cooper, Davina. *Sexing the City: Lesbian and Gay Politics Within the Activist State*. London: Rivers Oram, 1994.

Donaghue, Emma. *Passions Between Women: British Lesbian Culture, 1668–1801*. London: Scarlet, 1993.

Gibbs, Liz, ed. *Daring to Dissent: Lesbian Culture from Margin to Mainstream*. London: Cassell, 1994.

Griffin, Gabriele, ed. *Outwrite: Lesbianism and Popular Culture*. London: Pluto, 1993.

Harne, Lynne, and Elaine Miller, eds. *All the Rage: Reasserting Radical Lesbian Feminism*. London: Women's Press, 1996.

Lesbian History Group. *Not a Passing Phase: Reclaiming Lesbians in History, 1840–1985*. 2nd ed. London: Women's Press, 1993.

Mason-John, Valerie, and Ann Khambatta. *Lesbians Talk Making Black Waves*. London: Scarlet, 1993.

Neild, Suzanne, and Rosalind Pearson. *Women Like Us*. London: Women's Press, 1992.

*See also* Anne, Queen of England; Bonheur, Rosa; Cushman, Charlotte; Duffy, Maureen Patricia; Hall, Radclyffe; Holtby, Winifred; Ladies of Llangollen; Lister, Anne; London; Sackville-West, Vita; Smyth, Dame Ethel Mary; Suffrage Movement; Woolf, Virginia

## United States

For lesbians in the United States, the possibility of knowing any lesbian or gay history much beyond personal experience is a relatively recent development. Although discussed in sexologists' and sociologists' studies since the turn of the twentieth century, lesbians seldom were able to speak for themselves before World War II. Beginning in the late 1960s with the "second wave" of the women's movement and the gay liberation movement, lesbian activism emerged to seriously challenge both lesbian invisibility and oppression in the United States. With this activism also came the academic and grass-roots studies that have uncovered, collected, and preserved the history of lesbians and lesbian communities in the United States. This era has also seen a tremendous growth in lesbian literature, music, and culture. With only a little more than a quarter-century of work, scholars have gathered a tremendous amount of data and generated much theory, but a broad and inclusive history of lesbianism in the United States continues to be a work in progress. The newness of this field demands an acknowledgment that the parameters, the content, and the methods of this particularly hidden history are still being defined. Efforts at theory and analysis must be kept within this perspective.

### Precolonial and Colonial Times

"Sex-variant women," to use Jeannette Foster's term, have probably existed in all cultures in some form. Blackwood, in her 1984 examination of cross-gender roles for females in Native American societies, remarks on how differently sexuality was viewed in what is now the United States before the colonization by Europeans. She suggests that, while these cross-gender options, in which females took on "male" economic and familial roles, were available, and while woman-to-women sexual practices were known, they did not necessarily go together. She does not believe that there were "lesbians," as we know them today, among the indigenous people of North American. This conclusion echos the ongoing questions of definition, of the connections between sexuality and economics, and the link between the emergence of lesbian and gay identities and lesbian and gay oppression.

Moral condemnation of woman-to-woman sexual practices came to the North American continent

**U** with the Puritan settlers of New England, as documented by historians such as Jonathan Katz and J.R. Roberts. Roberts (1980) discusses the 1648 case involving "leude behauior" between two women. Her research on this case demonstrates that the Puritan community condemned this incident both as a sexual crime and as a threat to the social order. Katz's *Gay American History: Lesbians and Gay Men in the U.S.A.* (1976) also contains accounts of "passing women." These women, who dressed and lived as men and, in some cases, married women, were probably among the first Euro-American women to construct lives outside the female role prescribed by mainstream U.S. culture. These women's views on their choices or their claimed identities do not exist, and, consequently, it is not known what part their attractions to other women, their identification with the male role, their search for autonomy, or their economic need played in their decisions.

## The Nineteenth Century

During the nineteenth century, middle-class women were expected to develop close bonds with each other, and this intimacy was not seen as a threat to the heterosexual family. "Crushes" and "smashings" were accepted parts of girls' schools' culture. Hansen's (1996) finding of letters tracing the intimate relationship between two African American women shortly after the Civil War challenges the idea that these relationships were limited to white, middle-class women.

As the century progressed, middle-class women expanded their economic options through education and participation in the growth of the professions. Many such women combined the potential to be financially independent with a rejection of marriage, often choosing, instead, to live with another woman in what were called "Boston marriages." Through most of the nineteenth century, these middle-class spinsters could lead respectable lives protected by the culture's belief that, without a male partner, such partnerings must be asexual. The period from 1890 to 1920 could be termed a "golden age" for spinsters. The percentage of never-married women was higher during this time than during any other in U.S. history. Many of the most prominent women of this era were single, and many formed lifelong couples. They covered two generations, with the first including couples such as Jane Addams (1860–1935), Hull House founder, and sister Hull House resident Mary Rozet Smith (1868–1934); M. Carey Thomas (1857–1935), president of Bryn Mawr College, and

Mary Garrett (1839–1925), heir to the Baltimore and Ohio Railroad fortune; and Anna Howard Shaw (1847–1919), suffrage leader, and Lucy Anthony (1861–1944), her companion, assistant, and Susan B. Anthony's (1820–1906) niece. The next generation included Molly Dewson (1874–1962), leader of the Democratic women during the New Deal, and her companion, Polly Porter (1884–?); Martha May Eliot (1891–1978), physician and head of the Children's Bureau, and Ethel Durham (1892–1969), also a physician; and Frances Kellor (1873–1952), sociologist, and Mary Elisabeth Dreier (1875–1963) of the Women's Trade Union League. While, by the late 1990s, historians had not found any evidence that any of these women claimed lesbian identities, they lived such women-centered lives that their experiences resemble those of late-twentieth-century lesbian feminists. Critical of the institution of marriage because of the restrictions it placed on women, they constructed support networks that sustained them in both their public lives of professional responsibilities and political causes and their private lives. These circles of women overlapped across causes and geography, linking suffrage workers in California with union organizers in New York City. Additionally, a number of these couples raised children, most often the nieces or nephews of one of the partners.

As the institution building of the nineteenth century progressed and the field of sexology emerged in the United States and Europe, class and race increasingly determined how vulnerable "variant" women were to the attention, and the social-control aspects, of the medical, criminal justice, and social welfare establishments. Once the social professions accepted that women could have independent, active sexual lives, they sought to label and regulate women's sexual activities, both heterosexual and lesbian. The poor, working-class counterparts of the spinsters were the first who were targeted as dangerously deviant. Woman-to-woman sexual activities, especially within female reformatories, caught the attention of sexologists and criminologists. Women reformatory superintendents tended to be more tolerant then their male counterparts and benefactors of these sexual expressions between women, recognizing the diversity of women's sexualities and the needs of these often young women for affectionate physical relationships while incarcerated. The men among these professionals blurred the boundaries between moral judgments and legal definitions about women's sexuality, constructing the menace of the female invert.

Some female professionals, such as Katherine Bement Davis (1860–1935), tried to broaden the definition of acceptable expressions of female sexuality through scientific studies. Nevertheless, as male domination of these professions increased during the twentieth century and activist women split over such issues, the formal creation and condemnation of the modern lesbian occurred simultaneously in academia. By the 1930s, the middle-class professional woman was very much included in the lesbian label and the accompanying moral, legal, and psychiatric censure. From the founding of women's prisons through the McCarthy era of the 1950s, the middle-class professional women who managed these institutions juggled protecting their wards and protecting themselves from the myriad labels created for women who were sexually involved with other women or simple unmarried.

## The Twentieth Century

Nevertheless, while this process was taking place, women were concurrently constructing alternative definitions of lesbians. An interesting part of lesbian history in the United States involves several prominent expatriates. Both Natalie Barney (1876–1972) and Gertrude Stein (1874–1946) were among the earliest U.S. women to publicly identify as lesbians. However, neither of these women were public residents of the United States; both resided in Paris during the majority of their adult years. This was their solution to the homophobia of the United States. During these years, the era when British novelist Radclyffe Hall (1880–1943) published and was prosecuted for *The Well of Loneliness* (1928), middle-class women in the United States not only failed to publicly discuss their sexuality, but some, like novelist Willa Cather (1873–1947), destroyed, or left orders for the burning of, their private papers.

Other groups of women did claim lesbian identities in the United States during this time; a few did so quite publicly, while others did so within small closed communities. During the Harlem Renaissance of the 1920s and into the 1930s, African American women blues singers sang of lesbian love. Hazel Carby (1994) writes that Gertrude "Ma" Rainey's (1886–1939) "Prove It on Me Blues" was "an assertion and affirmation of lesbianism." What differentiated this public discourse from others on woman-to-woman loving was that the source did not disassociate herself from her material. While writers, reporters, and researchers had discussed lesbianism in print, none had spoken of lesbianism as lesbians, as Rainey and other African American women entertainers did during this era.

At the same time, working-class women of all races were increasingly establishing communities for themselves as lesbians in street bars and other marginal places in numerous urban centers. Elizabeth Lapovsky Kennedy and Madeline D. Davis's *Boots of Leather, Slippers of Gold: The History of a Lesbian Community* (1993) is the most thorough study of the emergence of such working-class lesbian communities, though numerous grass-roots history projects have been functioning since the 1970s. The largest of these efforts is the Lesbian Herstory Archives in New York City. Important aspects of these subcultures included claiming public space for lesbians in the bars; the development of their own social and sexual norms (the most visible of which were butch-femme roles), which they passed on to new members of their communities; and, eventually, a visible lesbian presence outside the bars, on the streets of their communities. From the 1930s through the 1960s, the women who risked police harassment and arrests were overwhelming the recognized lesbians of the United States.

Overlapping, to various degrees, in many regions were lesbians who chose to be more "closeted." Bullough and Bullough (1977) describe such a community in Salt Lake City, Utah, during the 1920s and 1930s. The study they inherited was done by a member of that community. While these women were white and middle-class, they differed from their heterosexual counterparts primarily on the basis that most were wage-earning women. These lesbians were well read in terms of theories of homosexuality. When *The Well of Loneliness* was published, they discussed their evaluation of its impact on public acceptance of lesbianism. For lesbians in isolated areas, any publication dealing with homosexuality, especially lesbianism, increased both self-awareness and a sense of connection with others like themselves. It was only with the emergence of middle-class homophile groups, such as the Daughters of Bilitis, during the post–World War II era that the U.S. public and U.S. professionals saw the breakdown of the barrier between respectability and a publicly claimed lesbian identity.

## Lesbian Feminism

Lesbian feminism built on these foundations, as well as the gay liberation movement, which strengthened after the Stonewall Rebellion of 1969 in New York City, and the reemergence of a women's movement

U

in the United States. The most visible component of lesbian feminism has been the growth of "wimmin's (various spellings used) culture." Lesbians supported the development of women- and lesbian-centered literature, music, and art, as well as women's businesses. Women's music festivals are held annually around the country, while women's bookstores have their own association.

Lesbians struggled for recognition within "mainstream" feminist organizations, such as the National Organization for Women (NOW) and the National Women's Political Caucus, as well as within the field of women's studies. It was within the overlap of academia and politics that women developed lesbian theory, including a strong strain on separatism. Groups such as the Furies and Radicalesbians placed lesbians at the center of feminist theory and activism, demanding that analyses and critiques of compulsory heterosexuality be integrated with feminist scholarship on race, class, and sex. With the development of such theories came arguments over definitions of lesbianism and the relationship of lesbians to the feminist movement. In a number of communities, splits developed not only between "straight" and lesbian feminists, but also among lesbians who came out within feminism, lesbians who identified with a prefeminist lesbian and gay community, lesbians who chose to live as separate from men as possible, and lesbians who continued to live and work with gay and straight men. Significant within these breaks were struggles over privilege, differences, and power based on class, race, and education.

The breadth of materials on lesbians in the United States at the end of the twentieth century was hard to capture. As lesbian visibility increases and the work to uncover and preserve lesbian history continues, lesbians are constantly challenged with new perspectives on their lesbian identities. As queer theory joins the various strains of lesbian studies as a scholarly effort to understand gender and sexuality in U.S. culture, younger generations of women challenge the identities older generations fought to have recognized. As their lesbian foremothers did before them, young lesbians define themselves, their cultures, and their communities, keeping lesbianism dynamic and responsive to new challenges and growth.          *Trisha Franzen*

### Bibliography

Blackwood, Evelyn. "Sexuality and Gender in Certain Native American Tribes: The Case of Cross-Gender Females." *Signs: Journal of Women in Culture and Society* 10:1 (Autumn 1984), 27–42.

Bullough, Vern, and Bonnie Bullough. "Lesbianism in the 1920's and 1930's: A New Found Study." *Signs: Journal of Women in Culture and Society* 2:4 (Summer 1977), 895–905.

Carby, Hazel. "It Jus Be's Dat Way Sometimes: The Sexual Politics of Women's Blues." In *Unequal Sisters: A Multicultural Reader in U.S. Women's History.* Ed. Vicki L. Ruiz and Ellen Carol DuBois. New York: Routledge, 1994, pp. 330–341.

D'Emilio, John, and Estelle B. Freedman. *Intimate Matters: A History of Sexuality in America.* New York: Harper and Row, 1988.

Faderman, Lillian. *Odd Girls and Twilight Lovers: A History of Lesbian Life in Twentieth Century America.* New York: Columbia University Press, 1991.

Hansen, Karen V. " 'No *Kisses* Is Like Youres': An Erotic Friendship Between Two African American Women During the Mid-Nineteenth Century." In *Lesbian Subjects.* Ed. Martha Vicinus. Bloomington: Indiana University Press, 1996.

Katz, Jonathan, ed. *Gay American History: Lesbians and Gay Men in the U.S.A.* New York: Thomas Crowell, 1976.

Kennedy, Elizabeth Lapovsky, and Madeline D. Davis. *Boots of Leather, Slippers of Gold: The History of a Lesbian Community.* London: Routledge, 1993.

Roberts, J.R. " 'leude behauior each with other vpon a bed': The Case of Sarah Norman and Mary Hammond." *Sinister Wisdom* 14 (1980), 57–62.

*See also* Addams, Jane; Anthony, Susan B.; Barney, Natalie; Boston Marriage; Cather, Willa; Compulsory Heterosexuality; Daughters of Bilitis; Davis, Katherine Bement; Female Support Networks; Foster, Jeannette Howard; Furies, The; Hall, Radclyffe; Harlem Renaissance; Lesbian Feminism; Lesbian Herstory Archives; Lesbian Studies; Music Festivals; National Organization for Women (NOW); Native Americans; Passing Women; Queer Theory; Radicalesbians; Rainey, Gertrude "Ma"; Separatism; Smashes, Crushes, Spoons; Spinsters; Stein, Gertrude; Thomas, M. Carey

## Utopian Literature

Depictions of an ideal society that contrasts with flaws in the author's real society. Dystopian literature portrays a very negative society. Feminists have used both forms to criticize sexism and to envision a better world for women. Like Christine de Pizan's medieval *Cité des dames* (City of Ladies [1405]), feminist utopias have often been all-female worlds. While these utopias often show loving relationships among the inhabitants, overtly sexual lesbian utopias did not appear in print until the twentieth century.

The word "utopia," based on the Greek *outopos* ("nowhere"), was invented by Thomas More (1478–1535) in the sixteenth century. While many classic utopias are set on remote parts of a contemporary Earth, most lesbian utopias are located in distant times or on other planets.

The nineteenth-century feminist movement in the United States prompted a flood of utopian fiction by women. Mary Bradley Lane's *Mizorah* (1881) and Charlotte Perkins Gilman's *Herland* (1915) both show all-female worlds, but sexuality is absent or sublimated into maternal love.

In the early twentieth century, Natalie Barney (1876–1972) and Renée Vivien (1877–1909) turned to the ancient Greek poet Sappho (ca. 600 B.C.E.) for inspiration and tried to re-create her lesbian society in their Paris salon and in their writings. Djuna Barnes's (1892–1982) *Ladies Almanack* (1928) portrays Barney and her friends in a comic utopian world. Outside France, lesbian utopian literature generally did not appear in print until feminism was revived in the late 1960s.

The first major lesbian utopian novel was Monique Wittig's (1935–) *Les Guérillères* (1969). The heros build a new society after a successful revolution against all aspects of male-dominated culture. Wittig explores how language, myths, and gender itself have enslaved women, and the struggle necessary to overcome psychological and political enslavement. Feminist males help create utopia. She later expands the utopian portion in *Le corps lesbien* (The Lesbian Body [1973]) and creates a lesbian language with coauthor Sande Zeig in *Brouillon pour un dictionnaire des amantes* (Lesbian Peoples: Materials for a Dictionary [1976]). Another important French utopian novel, Françoise d'Eaubonne's *Les Bergères de l'apocalypse* (The Shepherdesses of the Apocalypse [1977]), also depicts a revolution that founds an all-female utopia, shown in *Le Satellite de l'Amande* (The Satellite of the Almond [1975]).

Joanna Russ's *The Female Man* (1975) was the first important North American lesbian utopia. The narrator is split into four selves, each inhabiting a different possible Earth. Joanna, a contemporary feminist, is visited by Janet from the lesbian utopia Whileaway. Whileaway is not perfect, but the elimination of men (by "plague") has eradicated sexism and heterosexism. Later they meet a third self, Jael, and learn that her world's war against men was the "plague" that enabled Whileaway to evolve.

Wittig and Russ show violent revolution against patriarchy as essential to establishment of their utopias. Both see male dominance as a political structure that creates gender differences. Dominance and difference each must be eliminated. Their lesbians do not embrace femininity.

In contrast, the majority of lesbian utopias written in the period 1975–1985 view women as inherently different from men. Men are naturally violent, hierarchical, and exploitative. Technology and cities are masculine, while nature and psychological powers are feminine. In Sally Gearhart's *The Wanderground* (1979), nature has revolted against men, and men and machines become impotent outside the cities. Most women leave the dystopian cities and discover telepathy, mystical reproduction, and other powers based on an affinity with nature. Gearhart also introduces the Gentles, men who are trying to reject masculinity, a rare instance of including gay men in utopia.

Like Gearhart, several writers show a future Earth divided between a hypersexist dystopia and a separatist all-female utopia. Suzie McKee Charnas's dystopian *Walk to the End of the World* (1974) and utopian *Motherlines* (1978) show a woman's escape and her integration into the lesbian utopia. The free women have an Amazonian culture with a tribal structure.

Critics have noted that most of these utopias share similar characteristics: democratic or anarchic governments, little or no technology, affinity with nature and animals, preindustrial economies, and dedication to nonviolence except for defense. Some bisexual feminist utopias of the period, such as Marge Piercy's *Woman on the Edge of Time* (1976) and Ursula K. LeGuin's *Always Coming Home* (1985), deliberately use Native American tribal models, combined with technology. An exception, Katherine V. Forrest's lesbian *Daughters of a Coral Dawn* (1984), features a nondemocratic government and space technology.

Several lesbian utopias eliminate men through war or ecological disaster created by male-dominant societies. James Tiptree Jr. (pseud. of Alice Sheldon)

U presents such a world in the witty novella *Houston, Houston, Do You Read?* (1976). Three astronauts accidentally enter Earth's future, where an all-female culture combines technology and ecology to maintain a high quality of life. The women regretfully decide to kill them when the men exhibit violent sexist behavior. Rochelle Singer's *The Demeter Flower* (1980) also shows a lesbian postholocaust community.

Although U.S. writers produced the most utopian novels, authors in Canada, the United Kingdom, and western Europe also contributed. Louky Bersianik's *L'Eugelionne* (The Eugelionne, [1976]) satirizes the Catholicism of Québec. Norwegian writer Gerd Brantenberg's *Egalias Dotre* (Egalia's Daughters [1977]) is a comic example of role reversal.

Nearly all lesbian and feminist utopias were written by European and Euro-American authors. The works of African American writer Octavia Butler exhibit some utopian/dystopian features but do not portray a lesbian society. Her work does highlight a lack of racial diversity in many utopias. Alice Walker's *The Color Purple* (1982) and Toni Morrison's *Beloved* (1987) are examples of realistic novels containing utopian moments.

The dream of lesbian feminist transformation of society that animated the classical period of utopias from 1969 to 1985 faced an antifeminist backlash in the 1980s. Monique Wittig's *Virgile, Non* (Across the Acheron [1985]) shows heterosexual society as Hell, lesbian bars as a marginalized Limbo, and utopia as an elusive Paradise in a lesbian rewriting of Dante's *The Divine Comedy* (1308?–1321). Margaret Atwood's *The Handmaid's Tale* (1986) depicts an antifeminist fundamentalist theocracy in the United States in which women are literally enslaved. Pamela Sargent's *The Shore of Women* (1986) and Sheri Tepper's *The Gate to Women's Country* (1988) show separatist futures in which men and women occupy different spaces on Earth, but both authors reject lesbianism and aspects of feminism. Joan Slonczewski's *A Door into Ocean* (1986) portrays a feminist nonviolent utopia threatened by patriarchal invasion.

Yet lesbian utopias continue to appear. Those published in the early 1990s tend to include a strong spiritual element and often are set in the past, not the future—characteristics found in Judy Grahn's (1940–) *Mundane's World* (1988) as well. Diana Rivers's *Daughters of the Great Star* (1992) shows lesbians with magic powers in a medieval setting. Others invoke ancient Amazon myths, such as Barbara Walker's *Amazon* (1993) and Charnas's *The Furies* (1994), the delayed sequel to *Motherlines*. French author Richard Demarcy's *Angela, la guérillère soprano* (Angela, the Soprano Guerrilla [1990]) features a half-African, half-European bisexual freedom fighter whose weapon is her voice. The title and the novel allude to Wittig.

The best utopian fiction can still inspire lesbians to action in efforts to create a better world.

*Diane Griffin Crowder*

## Bibliography

Andermahr, Sonya. "The Politics of Separatism and Lesbian Utopian Fiction." In *New Lesbian Criticism: Literary and Cultural Readings*. Ed. Sally R. Munt. New York: Columbia University Press, 1992, pp. 133–152.

Bammer, Angelika. *Partial Visions: Feminism and Utopianism in the 1970s*. New York: Routledge, 1991.

Crowder, Diane Griffin. "Separatism and Feminist Utopian Fiction." In *Sexual Practice, Textual Theory: Lesbian Cultural Criticism*. Ed. Susan Wolfe and Julia Penelope. Cambridge, Mass. and Oxford, U.K.: Blackwell, 1993, pp. 237–250.

Lefanu, Sarah. *In the Chinks of the World Machine: Feminism and Science Fiction*. London: Women's Press, 1988.

Zimmerman, Bonnie. *A Safe Sea of Women: Lesbian Fiction, 1969–1989*. Boston: Beacon, 1990.

***See also*** Amazons; Barney, Natalie; Goddess Religion; Grahn, Judy; Native Americans; Sappho; Separatism; Vivien, Renée; Wittig, Monique

# V

## Vampires

In folklore, a reanimated corpse that sucks the blood of sleeping persons, or one who preys ruthlessly on others. The vampire is a tantalizing figure for lesbian writers, and it is not difficult to see why. Three elements typify vampire narratives: sadism, blood, and desire. And vampires have long been associated, though not always explicitly, with femininity, sex, and death. Although the classic vampire text, Bram Stoker's *Dracula* (1897), focuses upon a male vampire, there is evidence to suggest that Stoker fashioned Count Dracula upon a female prototype. This was Countess Elizabeth Bathory (1560–1614), who, according to legend, bathed in the blood of freshly killed girls to maintain her youthful good looks. The "Blood Countess of Transylvania," as Bathory was known, liked to dress in male attire, was a frequent visitor at the house of an aunt whose lesbianism was common knowledge, and had a predilection for torturing and killing servant girls. Although her bloodbaths are apocryphal, her cruelty is not, and her crimes, suitably embellished, have inspired many a modern depiction of the lesbian vampire.

Dracula aside, most modern vampires have been women. The earliest modern lesbian vampire novella was Irish writer Joseph Sheridan Le Fanu's *Carmilla* (1872), a popular story about a vampire who comes to visit for the express purpose of seducing and damning her innocent young niece. Though its melodramatic style blunted its impact, the basic outline *Carmilla* set was to typify the fate of the lesbian vampire for the next hundred years: Put bluntly, the monster had to die.

The vampire story, as traditionally conceived, was not just about aberrant sexuality. It was also a potent class vehicle: Vampire lesbians were typically aristocratic, feminine "ladies" who preyed on servants and peasants. This added another transgressive element to the already heady mix of the vampire's tale. Critics have outlined the workings of the vampire's dangerous allure in the way she crosses class, gender, and sexual boundaries in her relentless quest for blood. The apparently yielding, yet cruelly incisive, vampire mouth, so suggestive of cultural fears around the vagina and its emasculatory potential, the out-of-control female sexuality represented by the night-prowling, insatiable vampire, and the "queerness" of the vampire's indiscriminate choice of victims all combine to make the vampire text a story about the ultimate femme fatale. It has been especially easy to read the vampire's consummation—her messy, bloodsucking penetration—as a displacement of anxieties about oral sex. Victorians, in particular, avidly consumed vampire literature, which addressed anxieties about the new sexual emancipation of women, demonizing and then destroying the vampire figures who displayed an aberrant, aggressive sexuality.

The lesbian vampire's late-twentieth-century vogue was sparked in the first half of the 1970s, when a spate of vampire films with homosexual themes appeared, of which the most stylish (and least forgettable) was *Daughters of Darkness* (Belgium [1971]). Since then, lesbian writers have seized upon the vampire's illicit charge, using her transgressive potential to symbolize outlaw sexuality and bloody desire. No longer is this lesbian vampire a sign of unremitting evil, however, but a complex, sympathetic character whose manifestations are as various as they are compelling. Jewelle Gomez (1948–) presents, possibly for the first time, a black lesbian feminist vampire in the story of an escaped slave named Gilda (*The Gilda Stories* [1991]). Pat Califia's (1954–) memorable tale of a sadistic "top" and her femme stalker, "The Vampire" (1988), keeps the reader in the dark until the last moment about the vampire's identity. Pam Keesey's two anthologies, *Daughters of Darkness* (1993) and *Dark Angels: Lesbian Vampire Stories* (1995), offer a surfeit of such new, creatively realized lesbian vampire fiction. These writers' interpretations of the vampire are various and ingenious; they retell the original *Dracula* from a lesbian perspective, for example, or recast the vampire's legend in a science-fiction setting.          *Carellin Brooks*

### Bibliography

Case, Sue-Ellen. "Tracking the Vampire." *Differences* 3:2 (1991), 1–20.

Craft, Christopher. "Kiss Me with Those Red Lips." In *Speaking of Gender*. Ed. Elaine Showalter. New York: Routledge, 1989, pp. 216–242.

McNally, Raymond. *Dracula Was a Woman*. New York: McGraw-Hill, 1983.

Weiss, Andrea. *Vampires and Violets*. London: Jonathan Cape, 1992.

Zimmerman, Bonnie. "Daughters of Darkness: The Lesbian Vampire on Film." *Jump Cut* 24–25 (March 1981), 23–24.

*See also* Gothic; Literary Images

## Vargas, Chavela (1919–)

Latin American singer and performer. Chavela Vargas was an active proponent of the first wave of the Latin American *rescate del folclor* (rescue of folklore) movement. Born near the Costa Rican capital of San Jose, the singer, like other Latin American "personalities" of the time (often signifying "queer" in the broadest sense), moved to Mexico in the 1950s. In the wake of Vargas's nomadic travels in a career during which she recorded more than eighty albums, writers such as Nicolas Guillen (1902–1989), Miguel Angel Asturias (1899–1974), and Leon de Greiff (1895–) have praised Vargas's voice and interpretations. Her heyday in Mexico coincided with the first half of the 1960s in the "bohemian" atmosphere of clubs frequented by the patriarchs of the Mexican intelligentsia.

At the same time that Vargas was idolized for her passionate interpretations of Mexican and Latin American popular song, she cut a scandalous figure because of her out lesbianism. Anecdotes abound of her flamboyant "entrances" at clubs on motorcycles and in sports cars and her blatant flirting with women in the audience. She was ultimately blacklisted because of her so-called obscene behavior. In the early 1970s, she made her Mexican comeback in a queer-friendly venue for political theater artists in Coyoacan called El Habito, an ironic reference to nuns' habits.

In 1993, at the age of seventy-four, Vargas rode the crest of a second comeback in Spain referred to as "*El chavelazo*" (Chavela-mania), enjoying the adoration of a third generation of Spanish fans.

In addition to her outrageous public performance of lesbian identity, Vargas often appropriated the active heterosexual male subject position in songs that explicitly mark the object of desire as female, facilitating lesbian identifications within a cherished repertory of Latin American music. Furthermore, the simultaneity of Vargas as butch-desiring subject in many of her interpretations and as virtual "*estampa de Mexico*" (hallmark of Mexico) in her albums' liner notes provides a space for lesbian subjectivity within the definition of what is considered "authentically" Mexican.

*Yvonne Yarbro-Bejarano*

### Bibliography

Yarbro-Bejarano, Yvonne. "Crossing the Border with Chabela Vargas: A Chicana Femme's Tribute." In *Sex and Gender in Latin America: An Interdisciplinary Reader*. Ed. Daniel Balderston and Donna J. Guy. New York: New York University Press, 1997.

*See also* Mexico

## Vegetarianism

Form of ethical dietary separatism from patterns of male domination, a way of bringing principles of nonviolence home from the peace movement to the dinner table, from the political to the personal.

Women's culture has characteristically displayed compassion for animals. Many women in the antivivisection and the animal-welfare movements of the nineteenth century were lesbian or bisexual, and many women theorized the linkages between feminism and vegetarianism in the late twentieth century. From its beginnings in 1976, the Michigan Womyn's Music Festival has served only vegetarian food. The Bloodroot Collective, founded by radical feminist lesbians in Bridgeport, Connecticut, in

1977, supports a garden, restaurant, and bookstore, and members regularly revise their cookbook, in which they declare that "eating meat is wrong for its cruelty to creatures who can feel and experience pain, and wrong because it contributes to worldwide starvation, mostly of women and children." Founded in San Francisco, California, in 1982 by two lesbians, Feminists for Animal Rights strives to raise awareness of the connections among the objectification, exploitation, and abuse of both women and animals in patriarchal society. Lesbians involved in non-Western spiritual practices, such as Hinduism, Buddhism, and some forms of paganism and witchcraft, often adopt vegetarianism as part of their spirituality. Historically, there has been a cultural association of women's power with vegetarianism in contrast to the association of patriarchal power and meat eating.

In the context of the Vietnam War protests of the 1970s, many feminists and lesbian feminists saw a peaceful, vegetarian diet as a private counterpart to their public stance of nonviolence. Drawing on Elizabeth Gould Davis's popular work in *The First Sex* (1971), Carol Adams's "The Oedible Complex" (1975) was the first lesbian feminist essay to document a history of women's vegetarianism and to suggest a link between male violence and a meat-based diet. That link was developed more fully with Laurel Holliday's *The Violent Sex* (1978). Though not all lesbians read these foundational texts, the connection between vegetarianism and lesbian feminism became part of popular knowledge and was manifested in lesbian culture through the omnipresent potluck social. Lesbian utopian novels regularly depicted the peaceful, separatist utopia as vegetarian.

In the 1990s, many lesbian feminists and ecofeminists posited a conceptual correlation among sexism, heterosexism, racism, classism, and speciesism, in that each system justifies oppression (of women, queers, people of color, the poor and working classes, or animals) based on the subordinate group's perceived connection with nature, the body, the erotic, the emotions, or with each other. Women, for example, are conceptually associated with animals in sexist thought, just as people of color are seen as less human than whites in racist ideologies. Animal pejoratives, such as "chick," "pussy," "bitch," "dumb bunny," "shrew," or "sow," are frequently used to describe women. Lesbian vegetarians challenge the patriarchal notion that subordinated groups lack the singular characteristic of the white heterosexual male—reason—by which his superiority and rightful dominance is established and justified. Accordingly, lesbian vegetarians also reject hunting, animal experimentation, factory farming, zoos, rodeos, circuses, wearing animal skins as furs or leather, and all other forms of animal oppression. Lesbian vegetarians have contributed significantly to the development of ecofeminism, a movement linking the liberation of women, people of color, queers, animals, and nature.

*Greta Gaard*

### Bibliography

Adams, Carol J. "The Oedible Complex." In *The Lesbian Reader*. Ed. Gina Covina and Laurel Galana. Berkeley: Amazon, 1975, pp. 145–152.

———. *The Sexual Politics of Meat: A Feminist-Vegetarian Critical Theory.* New York: Continuum, 1990.

Adams, Carol J., and Josephine Donovan, eds. *Animals and Women: Feminist Theoretical Explorations.* Durham, N.C.: Duke University Press, 1995.

Collard, Andreé, and Joyce Contrucci. *Rape of the Wild: Man's Violence Against Animals and the Earth.* Bloomington: Indiana University Press, 1989.

Gaard, Greta, ed. *Ecofeminism: Women, Animals, Nature.* Philadelphia: Temple University Press, 1993.

**See also** Ecology and Ecofeminism; Ethics; Food; Peace Movement; Utopian Literature

## Video

Electronic visual medium. In the late 1960s and early 1970s, lesbian videographers began to produce realist and experimental pieces about lesbian subjects. As Martha Gever notes (in Kahn and Neumaier, 1985), this time period marked the convergence "of two important political and cultural phenomena": social change movements, including the lesbian and gay liberation movement, "and the proliferation of alternative, progressive media." One reason for the proliferation of video in particular was the late-1960s advent of "relatively low-cost portable video equipment."

Newly affordable video-production equipment and the explosion of the video-rental market enabled filmmakers and videographers to undertake

**V** financially risky projects. Whether their lesbian content or their experimental forms reduce the projects' chances of wide theatrical release, video rental creates the possibility of recouping investments. In addition, video sales and rentals make lesbian productions available in markets that may not receive independent, experimental, or lesbian-themed Hollywood releases.

"Lesbian video" refers to two distinct arenas. Video distribution makes available productions originally created on film, including Hollywood films with lesbian stories or subtexts and independent, lesbian-produced projects. "Native video" indicates productions originally created in video format. "Native video" genres include documentaries, feature-length narratives, safer-sex videos, lesbian music and comedy videos, and compilations of lesbian shorts from the festival circuit. These videos are produced with either high-end portable video cameras (Beta, 3/4", some Hi-8) or low-end personal camcorders (1/2", 8mm, some Hi-8). In the 1980s and early 1990s, lesbian artists Sadie Benning and Cecilia Dougherty each experimented with Fisher Price "pixelvision" cameras before these affordable artistic toys/tools were removed from the market.

Both production and distribution considerations lead lesbians to choose video over film. In addition to the availability of less expensive equipment and tape stock, video format lends itself to the most common distribution channels for lesbian productions: lesbian and lesbian-friendly distribution houses, such as Naiad, Women Make Movies, and Frameline; cable-access television stations; local schools or community groups; and local festivals. Since the Women's Video Festival held annually from 1972 to 1976 in New York City, cities around the world have held annual festivals that showcase lesbian videos.

A primary challenge for lesbian videographers has been to create content that accurately represents the complexity of lesbian lives. What Gever says of feminist video applies also to lesbian video: "making documentary videotapes usually proposes a redefinition of 'reality' by asserting the validity of [lesbians'] existence and experiences, by challenging accepted ideas about those experiences, or by a combination of both strategies" (in Kahn and Neumaier, 1985). A related focus of lesbian videomakers has been formal experimentation to critique dominant visual and societal conventions and also to articulate lesbians' particular perspectives on

identity and community. Experimental pieces often employ avant-garde techniques, including montage, a grainy or handmade look, ruptured narrative, visible seams, self-reflexivity, and foregrounding of the video's producers. Some such videos parody the generic conventions of MTV music videos, nightly news programs, talk shows, made-for-television dramas, soap operas, and commercials. The series *Two in Twenty* (1988) is notable for its campy lesbian revision of the latter two genres. This lesbian soap opera "deploys humor and suspense to explore the ethical and moral implications of child custody, lesbian parenting, AIDS, substance abuse, racism, and coming out." The series includes "mock commercials for fictitious products and services that blithely satirize the extravagant consumerism of daytime television" (McGavin, 1993).

Lesbians who share an interest in producing video that documents or explores a particular set of issues form collectives. In the 1970s, the Women's Video Collective in Rochester, New York, and the Women's Video Project in Los Angeles, California, created collaborative projects addressing feminist issues, including perspectives on lesbian sexuality. Airing weekly in the early and mid-1980s, Paper Tiger Television (PTTV), according to Halleck (in Kahn and Neumaier, 1985), became a paradigm of "cheap, imaginative access programming." Some lesbian (and gay) video collectives have opted to follow PTTV's example of airing their programs in a regular weekly time slot to cultivate an audience. For example, members of the grass-roots collective Dyke-TV nationwide feed locally produced pieces to their local cable-access stations and to the New York City core group for weekly distribution. However, many collectives work on a more ad hoc basis, developing and distributing projects as events and avenues arise. House of Color, a multiracial lesbian and gay collective, in New York City produces experimental videos about the interplay of race and sexuality in political alliances and personal relationships. Testing the Limits started as a grass-roots collective also in New York City, then became more stably established and produced the well-funded, four-part series on lesbian and gay politics, *The Question of Equality*, which began airing nationally on Public Broadcasting System (PBS) Stations in 1995.

Auteurs are those who earn renown for their individual contributions to the field of lesbian video. While many of these artists produce their videos through a partly collaborative process, consulting with members of their community, crew, and cast, their names have become synonymous with their cultural products. Members of this distinguished category include Cecilia Dougherty (*Grapefruit* [1989]), Pratibha Parmar (*Sari Red* [1988] and *Memory Pictures* [1989]), Ellen Spiro (*Greetings from Out Here* [1992]), and Julie Zando (*Let's Play Prisoners* [1988]). The phenomenon of lesbian-video rental and sales contributes to the cult status of particular videos and videographers because of the repeated queer viewing it enables. In their own homes, spectators have great control over the viewing experience: They can watch satisfying scenes multiple times for private pleasure and/or analyze the videos with other viewers.

Community media centers, such as Women's Access to Electronic Resources (WATER), a lesbian-led organization in Austin, Texas, serve as training and production facilities for local communities. Such centers provide lesbians with access to the means of production and with opportunities to work in nontechnocratic environments as either "collectives" or "auteurs" on videos in whatever genre and about whatever issues best suit their interests. [The author wishes to thank Amanda Johnston.]                                    *Gina M. Siesing*

### Bibliography

Gever, Martha, Pratibha Parmar, and John Greyson. *Queer Looks: Perspectives on Lesbian and Gay Film and Video*. New York: Routledge, 1993.

Kahn, Douglas, and Diane Neumaier, eds. *Cultures in Contention*. Seattle: Real Comet, 1985.

Kotz, Liz. "Anything but Idyllic: Lesbian Filmmaking in the 1980s and 1990s." In *Sisters, Sexperts, Queers: Beyond the Lesbian Nation*. Ed. Arlene Stein. New York: Penguin, 1993, pp. 67–80.

McGavin, Patrick Z. *Facets Gay and Lesbian Video Guide*. Chicago: Facets Multimedia/Academy Chicago, 1993.

Murray, Raymond. *Images in the Dark: An Encyclopedia of Gay and Lesbian Film and Video*. Philadelphia: TLA, 1994.

*See also* Documentaries; Film, Alternative; Television

## Violence

Violence in the lives of lesbians has been documented for as long as the lives of lesbians have been documented. For example, John Boswell, in *Christianity, Social Tolerance, and Homosexuality* (1980), documented violence against lesbians in western Europe from the beginning of the Christian era to the fourteenth century; Jonathan Katz, in *Gay American History: Lesbians and Gay men in the U.S.A.* (1992), documented violence against lesbians in what is now the United States as early as the sixteenth century, and the National Gay and Lesbian Task Force (1991) documented cases of violence against lesbians in the United States throughout the latter part of the twentieth century. Reports such as these reveal that violence against lesbians continues to take a variety of forms—from symbolic to fatal assaults—and to implicate a range of perpetrators—from intimates to strangers to institutions such as the state, religion, and medicine. Moreover, documented cases of violence against lesbians throughout history and across societies illustrate that physical, psychological, and symbolic violence against lesbians crosses racial, ethnic, religious, nationality, and age boundaries.

Despite an undeniable history of violence against lesbians, systematic and reliable information on the causes, manifestations, and consequences of such violence is scant. Since the late 1980s, empirical work on the epidemiology of violence against lesbians has been slowly accumulating. For example, Beatrice von Schulthess's study of antilesbian violence in San Francisco, California (in Herek and Berrill 1992), found that 57 percent of the lesbian respondents reported that they had experienced actual violence or the threat of violence because of their sexual orientation, including threats of physical violence, being chased or followed, having objects thrown at them, and being punched, hit, kicked, or beaten. Additionally, compared to gay men, lesbians report higher rates of verbal harassment by family members and a greater fear of "antigay" violence, as well as a higher rate of victimization in nongay-identified public settings and in their home and a lower rate of victimization in school and public gay-identified areas. Studies also reveal that lesbians of color are at an increased risk for violent attack because of their sexual orientation. In addition to reporting on the rate of violence against lesbians, a few studies converge to suggest that the typical perpetrator of antilesbian violence is young, white, and male and that most antilesbian violence goes unreported. In von Schulthess's study, only 15 percent of lesbians who had been victimized reported the incident to the police, with many of the respon-

**V** dents reporting that harassment is an inevitable part of life as a lesbian. At the same time, Comstock's (1991) research suggests that violence against lesbians frequently goes unreported because of fear of abuse by police, fear of public disclosure, and the perception that law-enforcement officials are antilesbian.

A defining characteristic of violence against lesbians is that it exists on a continuum, from exclusively antiwoman to exclusively antigay conduct. Lesbians who experience harassment and violence often have a difficult time distinguishing whether the violence was motivated by antiwoman or antilesbian sentiment, with many lesbians reporting a scenario in which violence begins as antiwoman and then escalates such that it is recognizable as antilesbian. Consistently, the experience of violence against lesbians as girls/women *and* as lesbians—which is defined by sexism, heterosexism, and, at times, racism, classism, antisemitism, and ageism—has most frequently been been analyzed and politicized as either "antigay" or "antiwoman," with little or no discussion of the interconnections between gender *and* sexuality/sexual orientation in antilesbian violence. Policymakers', activists', and researchers' understanding of the causes and consequences of violence experienced by lesbians is almost exclusively informed by, and subsumed under, more general discussions of "gay bashing" or "violence against women." The former is anchored in a concern for the health and well-being of gay men and explained via references to institutionalized homophobia and heterosexism, while the latter is anchored in a concern for the health and well-being of (presumed) heterosexual women and explained via references to sexism and misogyny. As a result, historically, violence against lesbians was, at best, generally treated as a second-order concern; at worst, it is more often than not rendered invisible as a category of violence in and of itself.

However, in the 1980s and 1990s, violence against lesbians began to receive public recognition as a social problem. Indeed, the 1998 murder of a young gay man, Matthew Sheppard, was immediately defined and reacted to as a hate crime by the national press as it covered the story. This framing of the story was made possible primarily because antigay and lesbian violence had already been recognized in larger campaigns to address "violence against gays" (presumed men) and "violence against women" (presumed heterosexuals). Legal reform and grass-roots activism have been the most visible venue through which violence against lesbians has increasingly been recognized as problematic. At the federal level, the Hate Crimes Statistics Act of 1990 recognized "crimes that manifest evidence of prejudice based on race, religion, sexual orientation, or ethnicity" as a new category of criminal behavior: a "hate crime." At the state level, by 1998 nineteen states had adopted "hate crime legislation" that includes provisions for "sexual orientation." Just as legal reform continues to recognize violence against gays and lesbians as a social problem, so, too, does a plethora of community-based activism. In the late 1970s, throughout the 1980s, and into the 1990s, there has been a proliferation of gay and lesbian organizations throughout the United States devoted to responding to antigay and antilesbian violence. Among other things, these antiviolence projects document the incidence and prevalence of antigay and antilesbian violence, establish crisis intervention and victim assistance programs, sponsor public education campaigns, and undertake surveillance efforts in the form of street patrols. Combined, these activities have sustained, according to the National Gay and Lesbian Task Force, an "unprecedented level of organizing against violence." As a result, violence against gays and lesbians has finally "taken its place among such societal concerns as violence against women, children, and ethnic and racial groups" (Comstock 1991).

*Kendal L. Broad*
*Valerie Jenness*

### Bibliography

Comstock, Gary. *Violence Against Lesbians and Gay Men*. New York: Columbia University Press, 1991.

Herek, Gregory M., and Kevin T. Berrill, eds. *Hate Crimes: Confronting Violence Against Lesbians and Gay Men*. Newbury Park, Calif.: Sage, 1992.

Jenness, Valerie. "Hate Crimes in the United States: The Transformation of Injured Persons into Victims and the Extension of Victim Status to Multiple Constituencies." In *Images of Issues: Typifying Contemporary Social Problems*. Ed. Joel Best. New York: Aldine, 1995, pp. 213–237.

Jenness, Valerie, and Kendal Broad. "Anti-Violence Activism and the (In)visibility of Gender in the Gay/Lesbian Movement and the Women's Movement." *Gender and Society* 8 (1994), 402–423.

National Gay and Lesbian Task Force. *Anti-Gay/Lesbian Violence, Victimization and Defama-*

*tion in 1990.* Washington, D.C.: National Gay and Lesbian Task Force, 1991.

***See also*** Community Organizing; Discrimination; Heterosexism; Homophobia; Law and Legal Institutions; Misogyny; Oppression; Race and Racism; Relationship Violence; Sexism

## Vivien, Renée (1877–1909)

British expatriate poet. Vivien was born Pauline Tarn but adopted the name Renée Vivien at the age of twenty-four when she published her first collection of poetry, *Etudes et Préludes.*

In her early twenties, Vivien moved to Paris and adopted French as the language of her published works. She is principally known as a poet of turn-of-the-century France, writing more than twenty volumes of poetry and short stories. Although she claimed the Greek poet Sappho (ca. 600 B.C.E.) as her greatest influence, her poetry is often more reminiscent of Charles Baudelaire (1821–1867) and replete with images beloved of the nineteenth-century symbolists, such as white lilies, burning candles, twisting serpents, and fragile violets. The novelist Rachilde (Marguerite Aymery Vallette [1860–1953]) dismissed Vivien's writing as "the old, decadent style, which died yesterday and is now horribly withered. . . . Too many verses! too many flowers! too many glow-worms!" (Foster 1985). Despite this adverse criticism, Vivien gained the respect and admiration of her contemporaries for the originality and power of her poetry and her mastery of complex formal verse structure. She was one of the earliest women poets to write openly, proudly, and passionately about love between women in all of its complicated and compelling emotional depths.

In her short stories, Vivien champions strong, silent, emotionally distant women over ineffectual, boasting males. With what the lesbian anthropologist Rubin (1982) has celebrated as an "insolent extremism," Vivien systematically rewrites many of the myths and legends of Western literature in a lesbian feminist setting. Her Prince Charming, for example, turns out to be a chivalrous, well-mannered young woman. Throughout her prose works, *La dame à la louve* (The Woman of the Wolf [1904]), and *Une Femme m'apparut* (A Woman Appeared to Me [1904]) there runs a recurrent image of an aloof woman turning away from man's brutish desire in distaste; lesbian love is correspondingly praised as pure, chaste, and without physical expression.

The inspiration for much of Vivien's verse was her first lover, Natalie Barney (1876–1972), with whom she conducted a stormy relationship that lasted, on and off, for four years. During this time, the couple acquired a villa on the Greek island of Lesbos, where they planned to re-create the school Sappho had held two thousand years before. Although this project was never realized, Vivien did complete a translation into French of the Greek poet's verses. When Barney's constant affairs became too much for the more single-minded Vivien, the latter found something of a safe harbor in the arms of the Baroness Hélène de Zuylen von Nyevelt, a multimillionaire. She was to coauthor several more collections of poetry with her new patron.

Vivien conducted a lifelong battle against depression, and her early death at the age of thirty-two was probably suicide caused by starvation and alcoholism. Since her unpublished letters and papers were deposited in the Bibliothèque Nationale in Paris by her friend Salomon Reinach (1858–1932) and won't be available to readers until the year 2000, many aspects of Vivien's private life remain obscure.                    *Anna Livia*

### Bibliography
Foster, Jeannette. *Sex Variant Women in Literature.* Tallahassee, Fla: Naiad, 1985.
Jay, Karla. *The Amazon and the Page.* Indianapolis: Indiana University Press, 1988.
Marks, Elaine. "'Sapho 1900': Imaginary Renée Viviens and the Rear of the Belle Époque." In "The Politics of Tradition: Placing Women in French Literature." Ed. Joan Dejean and Nancy K. Miller. *Yale French Studies* 75 (1988), 175–189 (Special issue).
Rubin, Gayle. Introduction. In *A Woman Appeared to Me.* Trans. Jeannette Foster. Tallahassee, Fla.: Naiad, 1982.

***See also*** Barney, Natalie; Colette; France; French Literature; Paris; Sappho; Sapphic Tradition

## Walker, A'Lelia (1885–1931)

One of the most important promoters of black arts in Harlem during the Roaring Twenties. Referred to as the "Mahogany Heiress" and a friend to such Harlem Renaissance luminaries as Langston Hughes (1902–1967) and Zora Neale Hurston (1891–1960), A'Lelia Walker wanted to provide a haven for Harlem's gay and lesbian artists, as well as New York City's café society. Walker herself was not an educated woman, but she understood the importance of the art and writing that abounded in Harlem.

Born to Sarah Breedlove (1867–1919) and Moses McWilliams (n.d.) in Vicksburg, Mississippi, Walker and her mother moved to St. Louis, Missouri, where her mother began to develop hair-care products that made her the first black and female American millionaire. Her mother married Charles Walker and became Madame C.J. Walker. Lelia, as she was known then, began to call herself A'Lelia. She worked with her mother to build the hair-care empire and encouraged her to purchase property on Harlem's Striver's Row and to build Villa Lewaro in upstate New York.

A'Lelia Walker was married three times, and there are no documents that positively link her to lesbianism, but she was considered a social pariah because of her fondness for lesbians and homosexuals. Certain members of Harlem's aristocracy refused to attend her parties or include her on their guest lists. Rumor and innuendo were fueled also by May Fain, Edna Thomas, and Mayme White, the beautiful women who made up part of her entourage. Anyone who expressed distaste for her entourage or her gay friends found themselves excluded from her salons and parties.

Walker's jeweled turbans, riding crop, and riding clothes were outward expressions of her own feelings about black feminine autonomy. The Madame C.J. Walker Theatre in Indianapolis, Indiana, is a monument to both women and their African heritage. The theater is an example of the Art Deco style but utilizes an Egyptian motif that celebrates black womanhood. A'Lelia Walker's influence over the architect's designs speaks clearly of her love and admiration for women. Walker died in New Jersey in 1931 while visiting friends. Mayme White, who accompanied Walker on this visit, was with her when she died.

*Stephanie Byrd*

### Bibliography

Ahmed, Siraj. "Walker, A'Lelia." In *Encyclopedia of African American Culture and History*. Ed. Jack Salzman, David Lionel Smith, and Cornel West. New York: Simon and Schuster, 1996.

Lewis, David Levering. *When Harlem Was in Vogue*. New York: Knopf, 1981.

Miles, Tiya. "Walker, A'Lelia (1885–1931)." In *Black Women in America: An Historical Encyclopedia*. Ed. Darlene Clark Hine. Brooklyn, N.Y.: Carlson, 1993.

*See also* Harlem; Harlem Renaissance

## Walker, Mary Edwards (1832–1919)

U.S. Civil War physician and author. Born near Oswego, New York, to parents who were descendants of early New England settlers, Mary Walker attended Falley Seminary in nearby Fulton, New York (1850–1852). She entered Central Medical College in Syracuse, New York, in 1853 and graduated in

1855. She was briefly married to a fellow medical school student, Albert Miller (1828–1900), and, although they practiced medicine together in Rome, New York, for several years, she never adopted his name. In 1857, Walker joined forces with women's dress reformer Lydia Sayer Hasbrouck (1829–1910), contributing to her periodical, the *Sibyl*.

During the early months of the Civil War (1861–1865), Walker traveled to Washington, D.C., unsuccessfully seeking employment as an surgeon in the Union army. The U.S. Patent Office Hospital accepted her as a volunteer, and she helped organize the Women's Relief Organization there. Earning a degree from the New York Hygeio-Therapeutic College, she then ventured entirely on her own onto the battlefields of Virginia, rendering medical assistance at tent hospitals in Warrenton and Fredericksburg, despite the complete absence of an official standing. She was finally appointed assistant surgeon in Tennessee, often passing through Confederate lines to serve civilians' medical needs. Captured by Confederates in 1864, she was taken to Richmond, Virginia, and imprisoned for several months. After being freed in a prisoner exchange, she supervised a women's prison hospital in Louisville, Kentucky, and, in 1865, received the Congressional Medal of Honor for Meritorious Service, which she wore throughout her life. It was revoked (along with 909 others) in 1917, when the criteria for awarding it was narrowed to include actual conflict only. Returned posthumously in 1977, it is on exhibit at the Oswego County Historical Society.

In the immediate postwar years, Walker was elected president of the National Dress Reform Association, and, in 1866, she traveled to England on a lecture tour. Returning to the United States in 1867, she lived for several years with Belva Lockwood, becoming active in the Central Women's Suffrage Bureau of Washington, D.C., and occasionally appearing at congressional hearings. In 1869, on a lecture tour of the Midwest, she participated in a Cincinnati suffrage convention attended by Susan B. Anthony (1820–1906), and, in 1872, she made an unsuccessful attempt to vote in Oswego. From her "home base" in the neighborhood of Bunker Hill, she continued to travel and to speak out about social and political issues of dress reform and women's suffrage. Her first book, *Hit* (1871), was autobiographical, and her second, *Unmasked; or, the Science of Immorality* (1878), openly and frankly addressed issues of women's health, such as the negative effects of wearing corsets, and women's sexual-

ity, such as a woman's right to control her body. Poverty-stricken in her later years, she attempted repeatedly to obtain her $6 a month pension from the United States government. However, the government turned her down, stating simply that she had failed to satisfy the army medical department's requirements, which may have been a reference to her sex. In the winter of 1919, Mary Edwards Walker, attired in her black frock suit, was buried in a simple ceremony in the family plot in the Oswego Town rural cemetery.

"This venturesome lady," as she was described by journalists is intriguing to contemporary lesbians largely for her courage to stand up to those who prevented her from serving on the battlefield as the physician she had been educated to be. Her knowledge about, and interest in, human sexuality, though disrespected during her lifetime, have subsequently suggested to researchers that Walker was, indeed, what is now termed "a woman-identified woman."

*Nancy Seale Osborne*

### Bibliography

Katz, Jonathan, ed. *Gay American History: Lesbians and Gay Men in the U.S.A.* New York: Crowell, 1976.

Leonard, Elizabeth D. *Yankee Women: Gender Battles in the Civil War*. New York: Norton, 1996.

Lesbian Herstory Archives. "Lesbian Fashion Through the Ages." *Archives Update* (December 1995), 1–2.

*See also* Passing Women

### Warner, Sylvia Townsend (1893–1978)

British novelist and short-story writer. Born at Harrow School, Middlesex, where her father was a schoolmaster, Sylvia Townsend Warner was educated by her father. Her first interest was a career in musicology. During the 1920s, she began to write creatively, and, within a few years, she produced several volumes of poetry and short stories (for which she was best known in her lifetime), and three novels. The most notable of these are her first novel, *Lolly Willowes* (1926), whose central character is an aging spinster who, with whimsical subversion, decides at last to pursue her much-delayed adventures, including a benign form of witchcraft; and *Mr. Fortune's Maggot* (1927), a tale of a repressed homosexual Anglican missionary in the South Seas.

At the beginning of her literary career, Warner met the poet Valentine Ackland (1906–1969). They became lovers and, despite a number of disruptions resulting from Ackland's alcoholism and occasional infidelity, remained together until Ackland's death. Their relationship is chronicled in Ackland's posthumously published *For Sylvia: An Honest Account* (1985). During the mid-1930s, both became members of the British Communist Party and actively supported the Loyalist cause in the Spanish Civil War. This interest shows in Warner's two novels of the period, *Summer Will Show* (1936) and *After the Death of Don Juan* (1938). The former, a historical novel set in the 1840s during the Paris Commune, is her most "lesbian" novel. It incorporates many of the egalitarian ideals of Communism in the love between two women, the English gentlewoman Sophia and the Jewish Minna, who, in her earlier role as the mistress of Sophia's husband, had been her rival. In this manner, as Terry Castle has demonstrated in *The Apparitional Lesbian: Female Homosexuality and Modern Culture* (1993), the novel is virtually paradigmatic in its use of erotic triangulation as a medium by which members of the same sex realize their desires for each other. A subsequent historical novel, *The Corner That Held Them* (1948), explores a subplot of female romantic friendship against the backdrop of medieval convent life.

After World War II, Warner and Ackland lived in rural Dorset, where Warner continued to write poetry and short stories until her death.

*Patricia Juliana Smith*

### Bibliography

Ackland, Valentine. *For Sylvia: An Honest Account.* New York: Norton, 1985.

Castle, Terry. *The Apparitional Lesbian: Female Homosexuality and Modern Culture.* New York: Columbia University Press, 1993.

Harman, Claire. *Sylvia Townsend Warner.* London: Chatto and Windus, 1989.

Mulford, Wendy. *This Narrow Place: Sylvia Townsend Warner and Valentine Ackland: Life, Letters, and Politics, 1930–1951.* London: Pandora, 1988.

*See also* English Literature, Twentieth Century; Romantic Friendship

## Washington, D.C.

Capital of the United States. Created by an act of Congress in 1791, the District of Columbia lies between Maryland and Virginia. While initially Washington was only one of several cities in the federal District, in 1871 the District government absorbed the smaller municipalities, creating one political unit now commonly known as Washington, D.C. Home to the federal government, Washington has been the focus of much national lesbian and gay organizing since the mid-1960s, but Washington also has its own vibrant lesbian past and present.

While little remains of a lesbian heritage from the 1800s, one of the most well documented accounts centers on the White House. Rose Cleveland (d. 1918), Grover Cleveland's "spinster" sister, assisted her brother as First Lady from 1885 until the president's marriage to Frances Folson in 1886. Though they were not together while she was in the White House, she had a passionate relationship with Evangeline Marss Simpson (Whipple) (d. 1930) for more than twenty years.

As in many other areas in the United States, the 1920s brought an increase in sexual freedom to Washington. In the 1920s and 1930s, it remained a segregated city, but several interracial bars on the U Street Corridor, known then as Washington's "Black Broadway," were welcoming to gay people (primarily men), and the noted Howard Theater hosted many well-known black gay performers. Just a few blocks away on Church Street, a private interracial club was a popular evening destination for lesbians. One patron recalls seeing Billie Holiday (1915–1959) perform at the club; during the performance, the Miss America candidate from Kentucky sensuously undressed Holiday onstage. Another notable performance occurred in 1939, when the Daughters of the American Revolution would not allow opera singer Marian Anderson (1902–1993) (rumored to be a lesbian) to sing in Constitution Hall because she was black. First Lady Eleanor Roosevelt (1884–1962) arranged for Anderson to perform on the steps of the Lincoln Memorial to a crowd of more than 75,000.

While police raids and harassment were a constant threat throughout these years, repression reached new levels in the 1950s with Senator Joseph McCarthy's (1908–1957) virulent attacks on homosexuality. After the Senate Appropriations Subcommittee concluded that sex perverts were security risks and generally unsuitable for government service, dismissal from government jobs jumped— from five people each month before 1950 to more than sixty people each month by 1952. This new antigay focus hit especially hard in Washington, D.C., a city in which the federal government was the largest employer. While much of the literature focuses on gay men, lesbians were also targeted and fired as a result of these witch-hunts. As an example, the head of the Washington Vice Squad sought increased appropriations to create a "lesbian squad" to "rout out the females." Washington's first homophile organization, a chapter of the Mattachine Society, formed in 1961 and focused on federal employment. In 1965, as part of a coalition called East Coast Homophile Organizations, society members picketed against job discrimination at the White House, the Civil Service Commission, and the Pentagon.

In the early 1970s, the Furies Collective formed in Washington. White radical lesbian separatists, the Furies promoted lesbianism as a "political choice." Including members such as Rita Mae Brown, Charlotte Bunch, and Joan Biren, the collective explored lesbian feminist ideology, heterosexual privilege, and class both in the collective and in its short-lived newspaper, *The Furies*. While splits over class and custody of children tore the collective apart by 1972, it had a lasting impact on the development of lesbian and feminist theory.

Many of the District's late-twentieth-century lesbian institutions have their roots in the feminist movement and the gay and lesbian civil rights movement. To mention just a few: In 1973, the District enacted a strong human rights law that included lesbians and gays. Two years later, the District hosted its first Gay Pride day. Black Gay Pride was established in Washington in 1991, and, in the late 1990s, it remained the only event of its kind in the nation. Lammas Women's Books and More has doubled as an unofficial community center for lesbians in Washington since 1973.

Not surprisingly, a number of major national organizations that work on lesbian and gay issues have made the nation's capital their home. The National Gay and Lesbian Task Force, the Human Rights Campaign, the National Organization for Women, the Latino/a Lesbian and Gay Organization, and the National Black Lesbian and Gay Leadership Forum are all located in the Washington area. Washington also was the site of three national marches for lesbian and gay rights—in 1979, 1987, and 1993.

Melinda R. Michels

### Bibliography

Beemyn, Brett. "A Queer Capital: Race, Class, Gender, and the Changing Social Landscape of Washington's Gay Communities, 1940–1955." In *Creating a Place for Ourselves*. Ed. Brett Beemyn. New York: Routledge, 1997, pp. 183–210.

D'Emilio, John. *Sexual Politics, Sexual Communities: The Making of a Homosexual Minority in the United States, 1940–1970*. Chicago: University of Chicago Press, 1983.

Faderman, Lillian. *Odd Girls and Twilight Lovers: A History of Lesbian Life in Twentieth Century America*. New York: Penguin, 1992.

Katz, Jonathan, ed. *Gay American History: Lesbians and Gay Men in the U.S.A: A Documentary History*. New York: Avon, 1976. Rev. ed. New York: Dutton, 1992.

Lait, Jack, and Lee Mortimer. *Washington Confidential*. New York: Crown, 1951.

Marcus, Eric. *Making History: The Struggle for Gay and Lesbian Equal Rights, 1945–1990*. New York: HarperCollins, 1992.

***See also*** Brown, Rita Mae; Furies, The; National Gay and Lesbian Task Force (NGLTF); National Organization for Women (NOW); Roosevelt, Anna Eleanor

### Weirauch, Anna Elisabet (1887–1970)

German actress and writer. Born August 7, 1887, into a distinguished immigrant family in Galati, Rumania, Anna Weirauch was only four years old when her father died and the family returned to Berlin. Due to the great success of her stage debut in 1906 in a play directed by star-actor Max Reinhardt (1873–1943), Weirauch would remain with the Deutsche Staatstheater in Berlin and, in 1917, be awarded the Gold Medal for Arts and Sciences. Following the publication of her first novella, *Die kleine Dagmar* (The Little Dagmar [1918]), Weirauch retired from the stage to pursue a career as a writer.

Although some of her earlier, unpublished, works had been staged with success as Matinees in the Staatstheater, the predominant genre of Weirauch's future literary production would be the novel. Weirauch counts among the few female authors of the Weimar Republic who would discuss gay and lesbian themes openly and without prejudice. The plot of her second novella, *Der Tag der Artemis* (Artemis's Day [1919]), centers around the homoerotic love between two teenage boys. Several lesbian relationships (and many gay characters) are portrayed in Weirauch's novel-trilogy *Der Skorpion* (1919, 1921, and 1931). All three volumes were immensely popular and sold out quickly, not only in Germany, but also in the United States, where several editions were printed in translation under the titles *The Scorpion* (1932, 1948), *Of Love Forbidden* (in a shortened version 1958, 1964), and *The Outcast* (1933, 1948). (A complete three-volume edition was reprinted as *The Scorpion* in 1964 and 1975.)

The sensitive portrayal of the protagonist's longing for other women, as well as her courageous struggle against the continual discrimination of society, make the novel an important testimony in the history of lesbian love; it also defies all common negative notions of homosexuals and homosexuality in general.

In many of her more than fifty novels, Weirauch focuses exclusively on the life of women characters, most notably in *Ruth Meyer* (1922), *Lotte* (1932), and *Frau Kern* (1936), but also in *Ein Mädchen ohne Furcht* (A Girl Without Fear [1935]), *Die Ehe der Mara Holm* (The Marriage of Mara Holm [1949]), and *Der Traum vom Glück zerbricht* (Broken Dreams of Happiness [1964]).

From 1933 to 1945, Weirauch resided with her lifelong female companion in Gastag, a small town in Bavaria. Weirauch continued writing and publishing throughout the Third Reich, although four of her novels, including *Der Skorpion*, were indexed under Paragraph 184 of the penal code and listed among the "unzüchtig verdächtige Schriften" (writings suspected of indecency) as early as 1926. While she had to enter the Reichsschrifttumskammer, the National Socialist organization for writers, she never became a member of the NSDAP (National Socialist Workers Party). After the war, Weirauch and her partner moved to Munich, but in 1961 they returned to Berlin, where Weirauch died on December 21, 1970.          *Christoph Lorey*

## Bibliography

Budke, Petra, and Jutta Schulze. *Schriftstellerinnen in Berlin, 1871 bis 1945. Ein Lexikon zu Leben und Werk* (Women Writers in Berlin, 1871 to 1945: An Encyclopedia of Their Lives and Works). Berlin: Orlanda Frauenverlag, 1995, pp. 371–374.

Schoppmann, Claudia. *"Der Skorpion": Frauenliebe in der Weimarer Republik* (The Scorpion: Female Love in the Weimar Republic). Hamburg: Frühlings Erwachen, 1985.

———. *"Ein Lesbenroman aus der Weimarer Zeit: Der Skorpion,"* *Eldorado: Homosexuelle Frauen und Männer in Berlin, 1850–1950* (A Lesbian Novel from the Weimar Years: *The Scorpion*. In *Eldorado*: Homosexual Women and Men in Berlin, 1850–1950). Berlin: Berlin Museum/Fröhlich and Kaufmann, 1984, pp. 197–199.

*See also* German Literature; Germany

## Wilhelm, Gale (1908–1991)

American novelist. Born in Eugene, Oregon, and educated in the Northwest, Gale Wilhelm published a total of six novels between 1935 and 1945, two of which deal with lesbian protagonists. Wilhelm lived for many years with Helen Hope Rudolph Page (n.d.), great grandniece of Stephen A. Douglas (1813–1861), friend of Carl Sandburg (1878–1967), and editor of the Oakdale branch of the *Stockton Herald*. Wilhelm's work, characterized by a laconic, modernist prose style, was well reviewed, and, in 1943, she received an honorary membership in the International Mark Twain Society for her outstanding contribution in the field of fiction.

*We Too Are Drifting*, first published in 1935, revolves around Jan Morale, an androgynous artist who creates woodcuts, and her attempt to disentangle herself from a destructive affair with a married woman. Jan meets and falls deeply in love with the feminine Victoria Connerly, who is engaged to a young man. Their relationship survives for a time but is eventually done in by the fact that Victoria is not a "real" lesbian. Jan is left alone at the close, watching Victoria and her fiancé depart together.

*Torchlight to Valhalla*, published in 1938, has a considerably upbeat close, perhaps reflecting Wilhelm's own life with Helen Page. Morgen, a writer in the process of grieving for her dead father, is pursued by Royal St. Gabriel, although she is unable to return his affections. However, in a fit of loneliness, Morgen mistakenly sleeps with Royal. Shortly after, she meets Toni, a childhood friend. They fall in love, and the novel closes on the promise of a long-lasting relationship for the two women.

Wilhelm lived with Page until Page's death in the mid-1950s and then disappeared from the literary world, leaving no clues to her whereabouts. In 1984, Naiad Press reprinted *We Too Are Drifting*. Barbara Grier (1933–), the publisher, included a biographical essay that ended in a plea for help locating Wilhelm. In 1985, Grier received an anonymous note that eventually led to Wilhelm's "discovery" in Berkeley, California. (Wilhelm commented: "I al-

ways knew where I was.") Aged and ill, Wilhelm was, nonetheless, delighted that her books had been reissued and provided a brief autobiographical sketch for the 1985 Naiad reissue of *Torchlight to Valhalla*.
*Linnea A. Stenson*

## Bibliography

Grier, Barbara. Introduction. In *Torchlight to Valhalla*. Tallahassee, Fla.: Naiad, 1985.

———. Introduction. In *We Too Are Drifting*. Tallahassee, Fla.: Naiad, 1984.

*See also* American Literature, Twentieth Century; Grier, Barbara; Naiad Press

*Christa Winsloe. Courtesy of Renate von Gebhardt.*

## Winsloe, Christa (1888–1944)

German writer and sculptor. Christa Winsloe was born December 23, 1888, in Darmstadt, the daughter of a Hessian cavalry captain, and raised in Berlin. After the death of her mother, she was sent to the Kaiserin-Augusta-Stift, a stifling and strictly regimented boarding school in Potsdam. In 1909, against her family's will, Winsloe entered the Kunstgewerbeschule (college for arts and crafts) in Munich to become a sculptor. Her eleven-year marriage of convenience with the Hungarian poet Baron Ladislas Hatvany (1880–1961) ended in divorce in 1924.

Winsloe's breakthrough as a writer came in 1930 with her play *Gestern und Heute* (Yesterday and Today), a semiautobiographic portrayal of the love of a shy but high-spirited student, Manuela Meinhardis, for her young teacher, Elisabeth von Bernburg, who is unable to prevent Manuela from committing suicide when her lesbian feelings become public. Although the successful staging of the drama in Berlin counts as the first truly sensitive and realistic representation of female homosexuality in German theater, it was the adaptation of the story in the 1931 film *Mädchen in Uniform*—directed by Leontine Sagan (n.d.) with an all-female cast—that brought Winsloe worldwide recognition. Winsloe's novels, *Life Begins* (London 1935; also New York 1936 under the title *Girl Alone*) and *Passeggiera* (1938), and her plays, *Der Schritt hinüber* (One Step Over [1940]) and *Aino* (1943), are less known but of equal importance for their open discussion of gay and lesbian themes.

After 1933, Winsloe, known as an "intensely feminine" (Kurth, 1990), straightforward, and outspoken woman, spent most of her time in exile from Nazi Germany. Traveling throughout Europe and the United States between 1933 and 1935, she frequently met up with American journalist Dorothy Thompson (1893–1961), with whom she had a passionate love affair that still echoes in a series of letters to her.

In October 1939, Winsloe took up residence with her lover, Simone Gentet (d. 1944), in Cagnes-sur-Mer, a French village not far from Nice on the Côte d'Azur, at times providing a home to other fugitives. To battle her profound unhappiness, caused by her increasing poverty and loneliness in exile, Winsloe kept writing tirelessly. However, the "mountains of manuscripts" (Winsloe, quoted in Schoppmann, 1995) that she produced were left behind and lost when she had to evacuate the house in Cagnes in February 1944.

On June 10, 1944, in the unrest that followed the liberation of Paris, Christa Winsloe and Simone Gentet were abducted in Cluny by a gang of mercenaries and shot in cold blood in the nearby woods of Chateau. Their executioners were acquitted of all charges four years later.
*Christoph Lorey*

## Bibliography

Dyer, Richard. "Less and More Than Women and Men: Lesbian and Gay Cinema in Weimar Germany." *New German Critique* 51 (Fall 1990), 5–62.

Kurth, Peter. *American Cassandra: The Life of Dorothy Thompson*. Boston: Little, Brown, 1990, 177–197, 342–343.

Rich, Ruby. "Mädchen in Uniform: From Repressive Tolerance to Erotic Liberation." *Jump Cut* 24–25 (March 1981), 44–50.

Schäfer, Margarete. "Theater, Theater!" *Eldorado: Homosexuelle Frauen und Männer in Berlin, 1850–1950*. (*Eldorado*: Homosexual Women and Men in Berlin, 1850–1950). Berlin: Berlin Museum/Fröhlich and Kaufmann, 1984, 180–186.

Schoppmann, Claudia, ed. *Im Fluchtgepäck die Sprache: Deutschsprachige Schriftstellerinnen im Exil* (Language of Escape: German-Speaking Women Writers in Exile). Frankfurt: Fischer, 1995.

*See also* German Literature; Germany; Nazism

## Witches, Persecution of

Hysteria, primarily European, during which unconventional women were persecuted under the conventions of demonic possession. During the European "witchcraft craze" from the mid-fifteenth to the mid-eighteenth century, Protestant and Roman Catholic Church leaders decried witchcraft as an evil to be suppressed. For more than two centuries, witches were accused of relating to the devil, often sexually. The campaign enveloped Europe, but, in general, the witchcraft craze was restricted to Scotland, France, Germany, Italy, and England. These countries, from as early as 1400 until at least the 1750s, embraced medieval Roman law that deemed sex between women a "foul wickedness" that was deserving of the death penalty.

Until almost the thirteenth century, the Catholic Church had considered witchcraft to be flights of fancy, but St. Thomas Aquinas (1225–1274) challenged that assertion, maintaining that witchcraft was, indeed, real. In 1484, Pope Innocent VIII (1432–1492) released a papal bull designed to eradicate witchcraft in Germany, incorporating folk belief in black magic and witchcraft into Church dogma. Lesbianism had already been singled out as a sin in church penitentials, having been deemed "against the order of nature, which created women's genitals for the use of men . . . and not so women could cohabit with women" (Crompton 1980–1981). As a result, the Church began identifying homosexuality with witchcraft and heresy and persecuting, among others, homosexual men and women. Fueled, in part, by an environment in which women were challenging old assumptions, the witch-hunt craze targeted unconventional women, including those considered to be lesbians.

Thousands of people were tried and convicted of witchcraft (hundreds for sexual "deviancy"), and many were executed. Birth control and abortion were seen as heinous crimes and were connected to witchcraft. The breasts and labia of women were considered models for the devil's teat. A predominantly male establishment fomented the persecution of so-called witches: 85 percent of all accused were women. Thus, the witch-hunt craze that beset premodern Europe was decidedly mysogynistic in nature. Joan of Arc (1412–1431), the female crusader, was considered a witch, in part, because she dressed and fought like a man.

Lesbianism was thought to be proof of witchcraft. Accused lesbians—or "female sodomites"—were tried, and some executed. In one case, a young French abbess was sentenced to life in a convent after engaging in sex with an assistant for several years. Another woman, of Essex, England, was hanged as a witch after a man accused her and his wife of being "lovers and familiar friendes" (Barstow 1994). In 1477, a girl was drowned in Germany "for lesbian love," and two women were tortured in France in the sixteenth century for their relationship. Both were later acquitted for "insufficient evidence." Two Spanish nuns were burned alive for using "material instruments," which historians interpreted to mean dildos (all quotations from Crompton 1980–1981).

In 1692, in Salem, Massachusetts, witch hysteria led to the hanging of nineteen accused witches and the imprisonment of others. A physician attributed unusual behavior of young village girls to demonic possession. Historians have often attributed the girl's behavior to repressed sexuality, a result of a restrictive Puritan lifestyle that permitted no outlets for female expression. "Inappropriate" sexual behavior among some of the girls is also believed to have contributed to belief in their demonic possession.   *Denise McVea*

### Bibliography

Barstow, Anne Llewellyn. *Witchcraze: A New History of the European Witch Hunts*. San Francisco: Pandora, 1994.

Bullough, Vern L. *The Subordinate Sex: A History of Attitudes Toward Women*. Athens: University of Georgia Press, 1988.

Crompton, Louis. "The Myth of Lesbian Impunity: Capital Laws from 1270 to 1791." *Journal of Homosexuality* 6:1/2 (1980–1981), 11–25.

Evans, Arthur. *Witchcraft and the Gay Counterculture: A Radical View of Western Civilization and the People It Has Tried To Destroy*. Boston: Fag Rag, 1978.

Starkey, Marion. *The Visionary Girls: Witchcraft in Salem Village*. Boston: Little, Brown, 1973.

*See also* Joan of Arc (Jeanne d'Arc)

### Wittig, Monique (1935–)

French novelist, essayist, and playwright. Born in the Haut Rhin (Alsace), Monique Wittig moved to Paris in the 1950s. Her first novel, *L'Opoponax* (The Opoponax [1964]), won the Prix Médicis and critical acclaim. Her play *L'Amant vert* (The Green Lover) was produced in Bolivia in 1969, and several short stories were published in the late 1960s.

Wittig participated in the French student/worker revolts of May 1968 and emerged a major feminist theoretician and activist. Her influential novel *Les Guérillères* (1969) portrays a global feminist revolution that vanquishes patriarchy and creates a postheterosexual society. In May 1970, Wittig and three coauthors published a manifesto for the French feminist movement. She helped organize a demonstration at the Arc de Triomphe in August 1970 that drew major media attention. She was a founding member of several radical groups, including the *Gouines rouges* (Red Dykes). In 1973, she published *Le Corps lesbien* (The Lesbian Body), a series of prose poems in which all lovers are lesbian. She rewrote, with coauthor Sande Zeig, the history of the world from a lesbian feminist perspective in *Brouillon pour un dictionnaire des amantes* (Lesbian Peoples: Material for a Dictionary [1975]).

Tensions within the movement became intense, and, in 1976, Wittig moved to the United States. She remained involved in French lesbian politics, however, and turned to theory in a series of important essays published in France and the United States, collected in *The Straight Mind* (1992).

Wittig returned to drama and fiction in the 1980s. A comic play, produced by Zeig in the United States as *The Constant Journey* (1984) and in Paris as *Le Voyage sans fin* (1985), is a reworking of *Don Quixote*, in which all major characters are lesbian. The novel *Virgile, non* (Across the Acheron [1985]) is a lesbian *Divine Comedy* set in contemporary San Francisco, California.

Wittig served as visiting artist and professor at several American universities, and, in 1986, she earned a Ph.D. in literature from the Sorbonne in Paris, France. She later became professor of French literature and Women's Studies at the University of Arizona, where she continued to teach in the late 1990s.

A materialist feminist, Wittig believes that all human culture is socially constructed and, therefore, political. Biological differences have no meaning outside a compulsory heterosexuality that creates "women" to be exploited by "men." Her goal is to abolish these unequal classes of people in order to abolish compulsory heterosexuality. Hence, she says, lesbians are not "women" because lesbians are not defined by a relation to "men." Wittig rejects feminist theories that valorize "difference" or the "feminine" as reactionary reinforcements of heterosexual dualism. In her essays, she explicitly ties language and literary work to the material oppression of women and of lesbians. While never didactic, her novels and plays are all explorations of how the world appears from the "marginalized" perspective of lesbians.

For Wittig, literature is a Trojan horse—a war machine to undermine society. By invoking and then deconstructing existing language, myths, and forms, she reveals their hidden political meanings. Like the phoenix in *Les Guérillères*, from these ashes arise visions of daring freedom and beauty.

*Diane Griffin Crowder*

### Bibliography

Crowder, Diane Griffin. "Monique Wittig." In *Fifty French Women Writers*. Ed. Eva Sartori and Dorothy Zimmerman. New York: Greenwood, 1991, pp. 524–534.

Duffy, Jean H. "Monique Wittig." In *Beyond the Nouveau Roman*. Ed. Michael Tilby. New York: Berg, 1990, pp. 201–228.

Jardine, Alice A., and Anne M. Menke, eds. *Shifting Scenes: Interviews on Women, Writing, and Politics in Post-68 France*. New York: Columbia University Press, 1991.

King, Adele. "Monique Wittig." In *French Women Novelists: Defining a Female Style*. New York: MacMillan, 1989.

Ostrovsky, Erika. *A Constant Journey: The Fiction of Monique Wittig*. Carbondale: Southern Illinois University Press, 1991.

*See also* Critical Theory; France; French Literature; Utopian Literature

## Wolff, Charlotte (1897–1986)

German psychologist and writer. Charlotte Wolff was born and raised in Germany, where she trained to be a physician. She participated in the underground lesbian community in Weimar Germany (1918–1933). When the Nazis came to power, Wolff fled to France and later to the United Kingdom. Unable to practice medicine, she became a chirologist (hand reader) and later a psychological researcher, novelist, and lesbian feminist activist.

Born in Danzig, Germany, Wolff was raised in a liberal Jewish family. Her parents were comfortable with her strong masculine identity and sexual interest in women. In her youth, she frequented the underground dance clubs that served the lesbian community of the time. After medical school, she worked as a physician in a state family-planning clinic and lived in an open lesbian relationship. When the Nazis came to power, her Christian lover deserted her. Wolff found herself obligated to leave Germany in 1933 when she both lost her job because she was a Jew and was arrested by a Gestapo agent for impersonating a man.

In France, Wolff took up a career as a chirologist. She read and interpreted the hands of many literati, including Aldous (1894–1963) and Maria (1898–1955) Huxley. The Huxleys helped her move to the United Kingdom, where she continued her hand-reading practice with leading artists and writers of the time, including Virginia Woolf (1882–1941). In the 1950s, Wolff began to publish psychological studies of the human hand, for which she became well known.

In 1969, Wolff published the first of two memoirs, *On the Way to Myself: Communications to a Friend*. In writing this volume, Wolff realized that she had never addressed the implications of her sexual interests in women in her professional work. She embarked on a series of studies of bisexuality and lesbianism that showed that lesbianism was healthy from a psychological perspective. This brought her to the attention of the nascent lesbian feminist communities in Britain and Germany and solidified her reputation as a spokesperson and resource of the lesbian feminist community.

In her later life, Wolff published her second memoir, *Hindsight* (1980), which discussed the integration of her psychological theories of lesbianism and her personal experiences. She also published poetry and novels with lesbian themes. Her final work was a biography of Magnus Hirschfeld (1868–1935), a leading sex researcher in pre-Nazi Germany.                    *Rebecca T. Alpert*

### Bibliography

Alpert, Rebecca T. *Like Bread on the Seder Plate: Jewish Lesbians and the Transformation of Tradition*. New York: Columbia University Press, 1997.

*See also* Germany; Nazism; Psychology; Woolf, Virginia

## Woman-Identified Woman

A woman whose primary political and emotional allegiances are to other women. In 1970, lesbians from a number of organizations in New York City met to write a manifesto in response to homophobia in the Women's Liberation Movement. Naming themselves Radicalesbians, they produced "The Woman Identified Woman," an essay first published in the movement pamphlet *Notes From the Third Year* (1971) and later collected in *Radical Feminism* (Koedt et al. 1973). The essay defined woman-identification and offered a new vision of lesbianism to the women's liberation movement. The Radicalesbians define male-identification as the internalization by women of a misogynist view of themselves, so that they gain self-esteem only through servile relationships with men. Woman-identification, by contrast, is a position that values women in their own right as individuals and values their relationships with each other. The woman-identified woman would appreciate what was worthy in other women and would not be afraid to give her political and emotional energy to them.

This definition implies that feminism is necessary for women's development and that homophobia is central to women's oppression. According to the Radicalesbians, women face many inequities under heterosexuality but are compensated for this by the knowledge that they have fulfilled their role as "true women." This role requires that they identify with men and against other women, which often results in homophobia toward lesbians. From a woman-identified perspective, heterosexual women's homophobia toward lesbians is a form of self-hatred, in which they value themselves and women so little that they can't imagine giving love and attention to anyone other than men.

**W** To the Radicalesbians, lesbians provide an important example for feminists of the power of woman-identification. In "The Woman Identified Woman" the lesbian is presented as a kind of feminist hero who has, through her marginality, developed insight into the relationship between women's oppression and heterosexuality. Lesbians' very strength, according to this view, is that they are not proper women: They have not developed a preoccupation with men's concerns and with men's opinions of them, and they are not isolated from other women by individual relationships with men.

Lesbians are described in this essay as "the rage of all women condensed to the point of explosion," as lifelong feminists who have always rejected the oppressive feminine role and have always been woman-identified. The Radicalesbians encourage heterosexual women to adopt this same view—to value women, to challenge men, and to examine the extent to which heterosexuality and gender roles are central to the maintenance of women's oppression. While they suggest that heterosexual women may choose to withdraw from personal relationships with men in order to strengthen their own positive view of themselves, they don't require that women do so. For the Radicalesbians, what is important is not that all women become lesbians but that all women convert from a male-identified to a woman-identified view of the world.

The idea that lesbians are inherently feminist is controversial among many lesbians. However, the image of the lesbian as an outsider whose presence challenges norms of gender and sexuality has persisted in many areas of lesbian scholarship.

'Becca Cragin

## Bibliography

Echols, Alice. *Daring To Be Bad: Radical Feminism in America, 1967–1975.* Minneapolis: University of Minnesota Press, 1989.

King, Katie. "The Situation of Lesbianism as Feminism's Magical Sign: Contests for Meaning and the U.S. Women's Movement, 1968–1972." *Communication* 9 (1986), 65–91.

Koedt, Anne. "Lesbianism and Feminism." In *Radical Feminism.* Ed. Anne Koedt, Ellen Levine, and Anita Rapone. New York: Quadrangle, 1973, pp. 246–258.

*See also* Homophobia; Lesbian Feminism; Misogyny; Radicalesbians; Women's Liberation Movement

## Womanist

Term derived from the African American women folk cultural expression "You are acting womanish." The phrase illustrates African American little girls' precociousness as they attempt to comprehend and overcome the challenges adult African American women face in their strategies for survival in an oppressive society. The term was coined by African American writer Alice Walker (1944–) in her 1983 collection of prose writings, *In Search of Our Mother's Garden.*

Walker specifically devised the term in response to literary historian Jean Humez's introductory statement in *Gifts of Power: The Writing of Rebecca Jackson, Black Visionary, Shaker Eldress* (1981). Humez suggested that Rebecca Jackson (1795–1871) and Rebecca Perot, who were part of an African American Shaker settlement in Philadelphia in the 1870s and lived with each other for more than thirty years, would had been labeled as lesbians in the late-twentieth-century climate of acknowledging female relationships. Humez supported her speculations of the Jackson-Perot relationship by pointing to the homoerotic dreams the women had of each other. Walker disputed Humez's right, as a white woman from a different cultural context, to define the intimacy between two African American women. "Womanist" was coined as a term that was both culture specific and encompassed a variety of ways that African American women support each other and relate to the world.

Walker defines a "womanist" as a black feminist who continues the legacy of "outrageous, audacious, courageous, and willful, responsible, in charge, serious" African American women as agents of social change for the wholeness and liberation of their entire people and, by extension, the rest of humanity. A womanist can be a lesbian, a heterosexual, or a bisexual woman. She celebrates and affirms African American women's culture and physical beauty.

## Christian Uses

Although the words "religion" or "Christian" do not appear in Walker's definition, there are both religious and secular usages for the term "womanist." Because Walker emphasizes African American women's love for the Spirit, African American Christian women have used "womanist" to articulate their witness to, and participation in, God's power and presence in the world. "Womanist" in the religious sense is often used by African American women who are Christian ministers and seminarians, as well as feminist scholars in the field of religion. Womanist Christian thought and practices began to flourish by the mid-1980s as a way to challenge racist, sexist, and white feminist religious practices and discourses that excluded African American women's participation and ignored their experiences in church and society.

For womanist Christian ministers and seminarians, Walker's definition serves as a springboard for their preaching style, liturgy, and pastoral ministry. For womanist Christian academicians, the definition shapes and frames their analytical and theoretical approaches. By using African American women's experiences of struggle and survival as their starting point of inquiry, these clergywomen and scholars examine the simultaneous forces of race, class, and gender oppressions in African American women's lives. A "womanist" approach also celebrates African American women's religious history and validates their theological beliefs.

Although Walker's definition includes lesbians as womanist, their voices in the womanist Christian discourse, as well as their contributions to African American women's religious histories, have been suppressed. Proponents for the exclusion of lesbians in the discourse argue that a lesbian sexual orientation is antithetical to the tenets and survival of the Black Church and the black family. As a result, many Christian lesbians in the womanist Christian discourse have responded either by engaging in the debate without disclosing their sexual identities or by opting not to engage in it at all.

## Secular Uses

The secular use of "womanist" is by African American women who either have left the Black Church because of its gender bias and/or homophobia, or do not come from the Black Church religious experience, and/or are not Christians. These women use the term to identify a culturally specific form of women-centered politics and theory. They argue that the term "feminist" is inappropriate because of its history of being identified with a predominantly white movement that has often excluded and alienated African American women. In addition, because the term "feminist" has been used to identify women as lesbians regardless of their sexual orientation, "womanist" provides a way to affirm one's identity without being associated with lesbianism. Because of this, some women have challenged the term "womanist" for its homophobic implications.

*Irene Monroe*

## Bibliography

Clarke, Cheryl, Jewelle L. Gomez, Evelynne Hammonds, Bonnie Johnson, and Linda Powell. "Conversations and Questions: Black Women on Black Women Writers." *Conditions: Nine*, III:3 (1983), 88–137.

Humez, Jean. *Gifts of Power: The Writings of Rebecca Jackson, Black Visionary, Shaker Eldress*. Amherst: University of Massachusetts Press, 1981.

Sanders, Cheryl, Katie G. Cannon, Emilie M. Townes, bell hooks, and Cheryl Townsend Gilkes "Christian Ethics and Theology in Womanist Perspective." *Journal of Feminist Studies in Religion* 5:2 (Fall 1989), 83–112.

Walker, Alice. "Gifts of Power: The Writings of Rebecca Jackson." In *In Search of Our Mother's Garden*. New York: Harcourt Brace Jovanovich, 1983, pp. 71–82.

***See also*** Black Church, The; Black Feminism; Homophobia

## Women of Color

In 1981, the National Institute for Women of Color in Washington, D.C.—which tracked the status of women of color in terms of educational attainment, earnings and employment, health, socioeconomics, and political participation—adopted the following definition:

> [T]he phrase "women of color" is a positive descriptor for women who are black, Hispanic, American Indian, Alaska Native, Asian American, Pacific Islander; this descriptor lays the foundation for new and broader alliances among women and their organizations, and focuses upon the national and global relationships among women and encourages inter-ethnic/racial group communication; moreover, the foregoing connotes a realignment of power relationships toward a status in which women of color become equal partners with women and men of all races. (Inuzaka, 1991)

Politically, the adoption of this term and definition reflected the outgrowth of the belief that the women's movement and feminism addressed only the issues of women of European descent and liter-

**W**ally excluded anyone who was not of European descent. It addressed the observations that these groups were often elitist, classist, and racist and that women of color experienced different types of oppression than white women. The concept points to the fact that commonalities exist among the types of oppression experienced by women of color and that working collectively would be more effective than having separate political groups based on specific ethnic backgrounds. Collectively, women not of European descent would have power in their larger numbers. Moreover, while individual ethnic groups might literally be in the minority, collectively they are not. In fact, 70 percent of the world is composed of nonwhite people, with 51 percent of those people being females.

The United Nations declared the 1980s the International Women's Decade. Many other women-of-color groups were formed in recognition of the fact that vast numbers of women were located outside the United States of America and select European countries. On the eve of that decade, in April 1979, after leaving a national feminist writers' organization in which they were the only Chicanas, Gloria Andalzúa (1942–) and Cherríe Moraga (1952–) wrote and sent out a letter soliciting women of color to write about, and define, feminism.

Responses to the solicitation letter resulted in the publishing of *This Bridge Called My Back: Writings by Radical Women of Color* (1981). In the Introduction, editors Moraga and Anzaldúa wrote: "What began as a reaction to the racism of white feminists soon became a positive affirmation of the commitment of women of color to our own feminism. . . . *This Bridge Called My Back* intends to reflect an uncompromised definition of feminism by women of color in the U.S." Toni Cade Bambara summarizes the political importance of women of color in the foreword of *Bridge*:

> Now that we've begun to break the silence and begun to break through the diabolically erected barriers and can hear each other and see each other, we can sit down with trust and break bread together. Rise up and break our chains as well . . . explain to white feminist would-be allies that there are other ties and visions that bind, prior allegiances and priorities that supercede their invitation to coalesce on their terms. *Akilah Monifa*

### Bibliography

Anzaldúa, Gloria. ed. *Making Face, Making Soul Haciendo Caras: Creative and Critical Perspectives by Women of Color*. San Francisco: Aunt Lute, 1990.

Inuzaka, June K. "Women of Color and Public Policy: A Case Study of the Women's Business Ownership Act." *Stanford Law Review* 43:6 (1991), 1215–1239.

Moraga, Cherríe, and Gloria Anzaldúa, eds. *This Bridge Called My Back: Writings by Radical Women of Color*. New York: Kitchen Table: Women of Color Press, 1983.

*See also* African Americans; Anzaldúa, Gloria E.; Asian Americans and Pacific Islanders; Black Feminism; Latinas; Moraga, Cherríe; Native Americans; Race and Racism

## Women's Lberation Movement

Commonly referred to as the "second wave" of feminism, with the "first wave" focusing on winning women's suffrage. The contemporary feminist movement in the United States emerged out of the generalized social discontent of the 1960s and adopted structures, ideologies, and strategies that reflect the grievances and preexisting networks of two different cohorts of women.

### History

Most scholars divide the women's movement into two wings, variously referred to as the women's rights, liberal, bureaucratic, older branch and the women's liberation, radical, collectivist, younger branch. Founders of the former were mainly older, well-educated, professional women with strong ties to state and federal governments, while the latter drew mostly from college-age women with experience in other progressive social movements. Structural facilitators of the movement included women's rising educational levels and their increased participation in the paid labor force, especially among white married women with children. The dual burden of work in and outside the home and blatant employment discrimination created, for many women, a sense of discontent and gender consciousness.

Several distinct and more immediate factors facilitated the formation of the two branches. For the liberal wing, significant facilitating events include John F. Kennedy's establishment, in 1961, of the President's Commission on the Status of Women;

the publication in 1963 of Betty Friedan's (1921–) best-selling book *The Feminine Mystique*; the passage of the Equal Pay Act of 1963; and the addition of "sex" to Title VII of the 1964 Civil Rights Act. The official birth of the liberal branch occurred in 1966 with the formation of the National Organization for Women (NOW), after participants at the Third National Conference of State Commissions on the Status of Women (Washington, D.C.) were prevented from introducing a resolution demanding that the Equal Employment Opportunity Commission begin taking sex discrimination seriously.

The radical wing grew out of the simultaneously radicalizing and alienating experience of young women involved in the male-dominated civil rights and New Left movements. African American women in the Student Nonviolent Coordinating Committee first raised the issue of sexism and gender inequality in the civil rights movement in 1964, while white women activists in the New Left also began to question traditional notions of femininity as they met strong, effective young black women in the movement. Most men reacted with hostility and claimed that women's concerns were "personal" or "apolitical." Hence, by 1965, many women began to meet separately and discuss the creation of an independent women's liberation movement. A crucial moment occurred in 1967 at the National Conference for New Politics (Chicago, Ill.), when the women's caucus followed the example of the black caucus and passed a resolution demanding that women receive committee representation and half of the convention votes. After they were ridiculed, the women met and wrote a manifesto, published in a leftist newspaper, in which they called for the organization of a women's liberation movement. Shortly thereafter, women's groups rapidly emerged in several cities and on campuses across the country, and, within a year, a mass movement for women's liberation had begun.

## Structure

The liberal branch initially adopted national-level, bureaucratically structured organizations with hierarchical leadership and democratic decision making, as exemplified in NOW. As massive numbers of women expressed interest in the movement, NOW's leadership encouraged the formation of local chapters. Many other national organizations soon formed, such as the Women's Equity Action League and the National Women's Political Caucus, which also established chapters.

The radical branch consisted of smaller, local, autonomous groups that lacked formal structure and were organized communally with an egalitarian focus. As reflections of the insight that "the personal is political" and as prefigurative attempts at structuring groups in ways that mirror feminist values and goals, these nonhierarchical, collectivist groups operated by consensus, rotated leadership and other tasks, and encouraged members to obtain multiple skills. Consciousness-raising (CR) groups, in which members taught each other to connect seemingly personal problems to larger structural inequalities, were the main source of initiation and participation for most women. CR groups fostered enormous growth in the radical branch and spread eventually to the liberal wing. Some of the most well known radical groups include Redstockings, the Feminists, and New York Radical Feminists.

From the 1970s onward, the two branches increasingly converged—as bureaucratic and collectivist organizations blended structural elements, and activists participated in both types of organizations. Although the vast majority of radical feminist groups ceased to exist in the mid-1970s, radical feminism lives on in numerous "alternative institutions" that emerged in the early 1970s and spread across the country. These counterinstitutions include feminist bookstores, newspapers, rape crisis centers, battered women's shelters, publishing and recording companies, coffeehouses, health clinics, self-help groups, and women's studies programs.

## Ideology

Liberal feminist ideology maintains that women lack power because they are denied equal opportunity in the economic and political arenas. Emphasizing individual rights, liberal feminist analysis was largely a response to the institutionalized sexism that professional women faced, yet it was readily adapted to other areas, such as education, the family, child care, and health care. Sometimes called "equal rights" feminism, liberal feminism takes an integrationist approach based on presumed similarities between the sexes.

Radical feminist ideology emphasizes women's subordination as a "sex class" and views gender as the primary form of oppression. It assumes distinct differences between women and men, attributed typically to stratification and socialization. Radical feminism conceptualizes the cause of gender inequality as the sex-class system and maintains that all institutions are structured to create and maintain that inequality. Radical feminist thinkers revealed how the sexist division of labor in the home perpetuates male advantage in the economic and political arenas. Analyses targeted patriarchal structures and practices in every societal sphere, including family, the workplace, politics, education, medicine, religion, and everyday social interactions. Among other issues, radical feminists developed influential critiques of rape, battering, and other forms of violence; compulsory heterosexuality, marriage, and motherhood; and the politics of abortion, pornography, the media, law, science, language, beauty, and culture.

The women's liberation wing also gave birth to socialist feminism, which highlights patriarchy and capitalism as interlocking systems of oppression. Socialist feminism emerged from early movement disputes between radical feminists and "politicos," the latter attributing women's oppression to capitalism. Intense movement debate in the early 1970s concerning lesbianism also contributed to the rise of lesbian feminism, which conceptualizes heterosexuality as an institution of patriarchal control and recasts lesbianism as a form of political resistance against male domination.

After the mid-1970s, the distinction between liberal and radical feminism blurred as the movement became increasingly radicalized. The movement blended ideas and goals from its various ideological strands, so that, by the late 1990s, it addressed nearly every social issue, critiquing multiple forms of domination based on gender, race, ethnicity, class, and sexuality.

## Strategy

The liberal branch primarily used institutionalized legal tactics to pursue equal rights within the existing social structure. Its main strategies were to obtain economic and legal equality through legislation, the courts, and lobbying and to gain access to elite positions in politics and the workplace. Examples include the struggles to ratify the Equal Rights Amendment and to secure abortion rights. These became mobilizing and unifying issues for both branches, leading them to work in coalition and prompting the liberal branch to begin working in the 1970s as a political interest group, which soon faced a powerful antifeminist backlash movement.

The radical branch was more apt to use disruptive tactics, such as direct, or "zap," actions and civil disobedience. Separatism was also a strategy and, for some, a goal in itself. Organizing independently

from men allowed women the space to question the status quo, build solidarity, develop crucial skills, and sustain commitment. The radical branch's first major action that received widespread media coverage was at the 1968 Miss America contest, where protesters crowned a sheep Miss America and threw bras and other items into a "freedom trash can." Although no bras were ever burned, the dismissive label "bra burners" originated from media coverage of the event. Disruptive tactics eventually spread to the liberal wing, with NOW initiating the Women's Strike for Equality on August 26, 1970, which drew participants from both branches and turned out thousands of women.

## The Impact of Lesbian Feminism

Following the emergence of the gay liberation movement in the wake of the Stonewall Rebellion (1969), lesbians in the women's movement began seeking visibility and support from their heterosexual sisters yet encountered hostility in both branches. Presaging later debates over the race- and class-bound nature of the women's movement, the "gay-straight split" emerged as a major schism in the early 1970s. Fearful that lesbians would discredit the movement, NOW founder Betty Friedan labeled lesbianism a "lavender menace" and drove many lesbians from the organization. In response, a group of lesbians with T-shirts reading "Lavender Menace" disrupted the 1970 Congress to Unite Women in New York City. Calling their group the Radicalesbians, protesters began distributing their paper, "The Woman Identified Woman," which conceptualized lesbianism as a political choice.

Other lesbian feminist groups soon emerged after the formation, in 1971, of the influential collective named the Furies, which advocated separatism, viewed lesbianism as the logical extension of "the personal as political," and characterized lesbians as the vanguard of the women's movement. Put on the defensive, some heterosexual feminists left the movement. Eventually, however, the movement began to sponsor workshops on lesbianism, incorporate lesbian feminist analyses, and fight for lesbian rights.

Scholars sometimes refer to lesbian feminism as "cultural feminism," even though the latter is but one ideological position within lesbian feminist communities. Cultural feminism entails an essentialist view of gender differences and emphasizes separatism and the building of an alternative women's culture predicated on "female values."

Critics have viewed the rise of these elements in radical feminism as a retreat from politics into "lifestyle" and have blamed radical feminism's demise on lesbian feminism. Contrary to this view, Taylor and Rupp (1993) argues that radical feminism, faced with a hostile sociopolitical environment, evolved into a different cycle of activism that is largely sustained by lesbian feminist communities. The continuing feminist resistance inherent in "women's culture" and the numerous alternative institutions of the women's community were increasingly driven by the commitment of lesbian feminists in the 1980s and 1990s. These networks encouraged women to take a variety of actions aimed at personal, cultural, and structural change. Hence, according to this view, rather than ushering in the demise of radical feminism, lesbian feminists have contributed to its survival.      *Nicole C. Raeburn*

### Bibliography

Buechler, Steven M. *Women's Movements in the United States: Woman Suffrage, Equal Rights, and Beyond*. New Brunswick, N.J.: Rutgers University Press, 1990.

Echols, Alice. *Daring To Be Bad: Radical Feminism in America, 1967–1975*. Minneapolis: University of Minnesota Press, 1989.

Evans, Sara. *Personal Politics: The Roots of Women's Liberation in the Civil Rights Movement and the New Left*. New York: Random House, 1979.

Ferree, Myra Marx, and Beth B. Hess. *Controversy and Coalition: The New Feminist Movement*. Boston: Twayne, 1985. Rev. ed. New York: Maxwell Macmillan, 1994.

Freeman, Jo. *The Politics of Women's Liberation: A Case Study of an Emerging Social Movement and Its Relation to the Policy Process*. New York: David McKay, 1975.

Ryan, Barbara. *Feminism and the Women's Movement: Dynamics of Change in Social Movement Ideology and Activism*. New York: Routledge, 1992.

Taylor, Verta, and Leila J. Rupp. "Women's Culture and Lesbian Feminist Activism: A Reconsideration of Cultural Feminism." *Signs: Journal of Women in Culture and Society* 19 (1993), 32–61.

***See also*** Consciousness Raising; Essentialism; Feminism; Furies, The; Lesbian Feminism; National Organization for Women (NOW); New Left; Radicalesbians; Separatism; Sexism; Sisterhood; Socialism; Suffrage Movement; Woman-Identified Woman

## Women's Studies

Academic discipline that seeks, through education, research, and public service, to promote the creation and dissemination of knowledge about the diversity of women's lives and experiences. As an interdisciplinary field of inquiry, women's studies examines women's participation and representation in history, culture, and society and offers new theoretical perspectives, insights, and methodologies on the relationship between sex, gender, and power. Feminist scholars working in the field of women's studies are encouraged to create new ways of viewing women and gender that accommodate the differences and similarities among women in terms of race, ethnicity, religion, social class, sexual identity, and physical ability. The women's studies curriculum generally offers courses on women writers, artists and filmmakers, the sociology of gender, the psychology of women, women's history, feminist theory and activism, women of color, lesbianism, women and work, women's health and safety, women and politics, women and religion, gender and communication, and global feminism.

### History

Sometimes characterized as the "academic arm" of the women's movement, women's studies had its origins in the social-change movements of the 1960s. Many of its pioneers believed that "women's studies was a necessary part of women's struggle for self-determination . . . and that the goal of women's studies was to understand the world in order to change it" (Boxer 1982). Women's studies began as a loose configuration of activities, courses, and resources, such as bibliographies and readings lists, newsletters, manifestos, pamphlets, conferences, schools, workshops, and campus protest actions. Many feminists who were participants in the movement to establish women's studies were veterans of the civil rights and New Left movements and, thus, provided a focus on transformation and change in the university and in society as a whole. Through their activism, women gained valuable experience in organizing, public speaking, and teaching. Participants were joined by women in government and in the professions, including higher-education administration, in articulating a new intellectual agenda for women in the academy.

The first courses in women's studies began to appear on college campuses in the late 1960s; the first integrated programs of study were established at San Diego State University and at Cornell University in the 1969–1970 academic year.

Early efforts to establish women's studies raised important questions "about the tensions between the academic and political goals of classroom teaching, the responsibility of women's studies to women's movements, and the implication of feminist organizational structure and democratic governance for impact on the university" (Boxer 1982). Furthermore, as women's studies struggled with the "double purpose to expose and redress the oppression of women," there was ambivalence about affiliating with traditional institutions of higher education. In fact, the first women's studies courses were established outside mainstream academic circles as a part of the free-school movement at the New Orleans Free School in 1966 and at the Free School of Seattle in 1965. Nonetheless, the student movements of the 1960s made it easier to challenge the curriculum taught in colleges and universities and helped create the climate on campuses for the creation of women's studies. On some campuses, women's studies became a reality only after women students, faculty, and staff, many of whom were lesbians, threatened to file class-action suits against the universities for discriminatory practices in admissions, hiring, promotion, wages, governance, and access to athletics. Proposed remedies for sex discrimination in higher education focused on affirmative action, gender equity in sports, and the inclusion of women in the curriculum through the establishment of women's studies programs.

The proliferation of specialized courses about women, gender, and sexuality gave way to the creation of coherent women's studies programs. Between 1970 and 1975, 150 such programs were established; by 1980, the number exceeded three hundred; and, by the late 1990s, there were more than nine hundred programs in the United States alone. Women's studies has been established in every region of the world, including Africa, Asia, Latin America, Europe, Canada, and Australia, and in every type of academic institution—small private liberal arts colleges, religious-affiliated schools, large public research institutions, women's colleges, and historically black institutions. With a 1988 endowment from the family of comedian Bill Cosby, Spelman College in Atlanta, Georgia, established the first chair for black women's studies.

The development and legitimation of women's studies was fueled by and, in turn, promoted, the tremendous growth in interdisciplinary scholarship on women, gender, sexuality, and sex equity. Research grants and fellowships provided by major foundations, such as Ford, Rockefeller, Mellon, and Russell Sage, and the federal government stimulated the creation of new knowledge about women. The creation of the Feminist Press in 1970 and the establishment of academic journals in women's studies facilitated the dissemination and production of this new scholarship. Increased institutionalization of women's studies has been accelerated by the explosion of feminist scholarship, so that, by the 1990s, there were more than thirty journals that published scholarship on women, dozens of feminist presses, and many women's studies series within university and commercial publishing circles.

## Lesbians Within Women's Studies

Many women's studies journals, such as *Signs: Journal of Women in Culture and Society*, *NWSA Journal*, *Gender and Society*, *differences*, and *Hypathia*, published special issues on lesbianism, sexuality, and queer theory. Many others, such as *Feminist Studies*, *Women's Studies Quarterly*, and *Women's Studies International Forum*, regularly feature articles about lesbian health, culture, philosophy, literature, and the like. Lesbian scholars within the field of women's studies have been instrumental in the critique of institutional heterosexism in society and in the academy and have helped make visible the experiences and contributions of lesbians. Lesbians of every race and nationality, along with heterosexual women of color, have historically challenged the field to honor its commitment to inclusivity and diversity in both theory and practice. The result, with much struggle, has been the development of a growing body of research that examines the intersections of race, class, nationality, gender, physical ability, and sexuality both historically and cross-culturally.

Despite the fact that lesbians have always been active in the production of knowledge about women and in the struggle for women's liberation, and were influential in the formation, growth, and development of women's studies as a field, their specific concerns as lesbians were often muted or excluded. Marilyn Frye, a philosopher and professor of women's studies at Michigan State University, is one of the most visible lesbian scholars within women's studies and a vocal critic of women's studies for its heterosexual biases and assumptions. She has argued that women's studies as a field too readily assumed that heterosexuality was pervasive, ubiquitous, and dominant throughout the world and that lesbianism was an acceptable alternative for some women. She conceptualized this assumption as heterosexualism. "In my experience with women's studies it seems common and characteristic for the women instructors to assume that widespread heterosexuality and the dominance of heterosexual conceptions have always been and will always be The Way It Is for humans on this planet, in particular, for women on this planet" (Frye 1992). As a consequence, too much of the scholarship on women's history, politics, literature, and so forth is really scholarship on heterosexual women's lives and experiences. For Frye, the more interesting and politically compelling question in women's studies is not why some women are lesbian, but why women, particularly feminists, choose heterosexuality. Advances for lesbians in women's studies grew out of these kinds of struggles over inclusivity.

Efforts to coordinate and exchange ideas across various women's studies programs at home and abroad became possible with the formation of the National Women's Studies Association in 1977 and the National Council for Research on Women in 1982 and with the United Nations International Decades for the Advancement of Women conferences held in Mexico City in 1975; in Nairobi, Kenya, in 1985; and in Beijing, China, in 1995. Some organizations, including the National Women's Studies Association, contain lesbian caucuses and forums that attempt to represent the diverse interests of lesbians in the field of women's studies. Conference meetings, resolutions, debates, speeches, and workshops have contributed to the establishment of an international network of women's studies programs and activities for women's rights, empowerment, and research. Through their work in these organizations and campaigns, lesbian scholars and activists, such as Charlotte Bunch, have brought together women's studies practitioners and supporters from every setting and region of the world. Internationally, lesbian visibility was most apparent at the Fourth World Conference on Women held in 1995 in Beijing, where lesbians won official space in the Nongovernmental Organization Forum. This allowed lesbians the opportunity to meet, to exchange ideas, and to develop an effective lobbying strategy for the conference.

## Pedagogy

Because women's studies places a premium on feminist education as a tool of liberation and empowerment, there is a well-developed body of scholarship on the changing nature of feminist pedagogy within the field. Feminist approaches to teaching and learning focus on what is taught, how it is taught, and how it is learned and includes debates and discussions about classroom dynamics, issues of authority and power, women's voices, women's ways of knowing, multiculturalism, consciousness raising, social transformation, and cultural values.

From the beginning of women's studies, participants displayed a remarkable willingness to share information, ideas, and strategies for the creation of individual women's studies courses and overall programs, as well as novel approaches for teaching the new field. *Female Studies* (Vol. 1–10), first published in 1971 by KNOW Inc. of Pittsburgh, included course listings, syllabi, bibliographies, conference proceedings, and reports of individual classes—materials that not only supported the work of educators, but also helped define the field. Feminist librarians were also instrumental in publishing and circulating resources crucial to the curricular development of the field and to the study of lesbians. Two publications, *Women's Studies Quarterly* and *Feminist Teacher*, continue to serve this function. Specialized publications and anthologies, such as *Matrices,* published at the University of Minnesota; *The New Lesbian Studies: Into the Twenty-First Century* (Zimmerman and McNaron 1996); *Tilting the Tower: Lesbians Teaching Queer Subjects* (Garber 1994); and the *Lesbian Review of Books*, focus on feminist research and pedagogical issues of interest to high school teachers and college professors who wish to incorporate lesbian experiences and issues in their courses. These resources include essays on coming out in the classroom, on teaching lesbian history and literature, and on building multicultural lesbian and gay studies programs; bibliographies and film guides on lesbians; personal accounts of lesbian teachers and professors and their encounters with homophobia on campus; lesbian periodicals indices; dissertation abstracts on lesbian topics; book reviews; and conference announcements and proceedings.

Students throughout the world can pursue women's studies courses, degrees, and certificates at both the graduate and undergraduate levels. Women's studies can prepare students to be better world citizens, to think critically and creatively

W about how the world is organized for women, and to become change agents on behalf of women internationally. The graduates of women's studies programs can be found working inside mainstream social, political, and cultural institutions, as well as in social-movement organizations at the local, national, and international levels, to meet the needs of women and to advocate for the rights of women, including their right to love other women. Women's studies enhances both individual and career development and can be beneficial in fields such as law, social work, education, the health professions, government service, business, counseling, journalism, and library science. *Mary Margaret Fonow*

### Bibliography

Boxer, Marilyn. "Review Essay: For and About Women: The Theory and Practice of Women's Studies in the United States." *Signs: Journal of Women in Culture and Society* 7:3 (1982), 661–695.

Frye, Marilyn. *Willful Virgin: Essays in Feminism, 1976–1992*. Freedom, Calif.: Crossing, 1992.

Garber, Linda. *Tilting the Tower: Lesbian Teaching/Queer Subjects*. New York: Routledge, 1994.

Guy-Sheftall, Beverly. *Women's Studies: A Retrospective: A Report to the Ford Foundation.* New York: Ford Foundation, 1995.

hooks, bell. *Teaching To Transgress: Education as the Practice of Freedom*. New York: Routledge, 1994.

Maher, Frances, and Mary Kay Thompson Tetreault. *The Feminist Classroom: An Inside Look at How Professors and Students Are Transforming Higher Education for a Diverse Society*. New York: Basic Books, 1994.

Zimmerman, Bonnie, and Toni A.H. McNaron. *The New Lesbian Studies: Into the Twenty-First Century*. New York: Feminist Press, 1996.

*See also* Activism; Associations and Organizations; Feminism; Lesbian Studies; Periodicals; Queer Theory; Scholars; Students; Teachers; Women's Liberation Movement

### Woolf, Virginia (1882–1941)

Twentieth-century English novelist. Considered one of the leading figures in the history of modernism, Virginia Woolf is the author of ten novels, several hundred essays and reviews, and six volumes of letters; she also figures prominently in the debate over definitions of lesbianism. Though married to socialist diplomat, intellectual, and diarist Leonard Woolf (1880–1969), Virginia Woolf depended upon a series of women to give her emotional and erotic stimulation. In her own words, in a letter to the lesbian composer Ethel Smyth (1858–1944): "Women alone stir my imagination."

Woolf's most significant relationships with women began with her mother, the much-lauded beauty Julia Duckworth Steven (1846–1895), and her sister, the painter Vanessa Bell (1879–1964). In her teens, she formed a deep attachment to Violet Dickinson (1865–1948), a family friend to whom she looked, at age twelve, when her mother died. The most tempestuous liaison was between her and Vita Sackville-West (1892–1962), with whom she spent as much time as their husbands and their own other interests allowed, and for whom she wrote the amazingly energetic novel *Orlando* (1928). In later life, Woolf formed a somewhat ambiguous bond with Ethel Smyth, shared literary and personal intimacies with the brilliant New Zealand short-story writer Katherine Mansfield (1988–1923), and valued her many associations with writers and activists in the burgeoning feminist movement in England.

The vexing aspect of Woolf's personality turns around her sexuality. The victim of childhood and teenage sexual abuse at the hands of her two half-brothers, George (1868–1934) and Gerald (1870–1937) Duckworth, she was able to write about her experiences in variously coded texts but never received any professional help to heal the traumatic wounds inflicted by these encounters. Not surprisingly, attempts at adult sexual relations were haunted by her unresolved but vivid memories of the insults upon her body. She and her husband were rarely sexual, though in many ways companionate, and, unlike her sister, Vanessa, Woolf did not seek sexual liaisons with any of the Bloomsbury men with whom she associated. When it came to being sexual with the women to whom she was admittedly and intimately drawn, the same anxieties and fears about physical connection obtained, making it difficult for her to express herself sexually even with Sackville-West, whom she adored.

Her letters and journal entries, however, reveal just what her intimacies with women gave her: safe venues from which to explore her passionate nature and an audience for her powerfully metaphoric and linguistic eroticism. One reason to assert Woolf's lesbian self arises from treatment of her by critics.

*Virginia Woolf. Photo by Gisèle Freund. Photo Researchers, Inc., NYC.*

Most often, she has been presented as asexual or frigid, or, more recently by feminist critics, as someone who had a brief, if important, "affair" with Sackville-West, from which both were rescued by loving husbands, to whom both gave heartfelt devotion and gratitude. Claiming her as part of lesbian history and culture not only extends to her fiction the serious regard it deserves as the site for a range of accounts of the complexity of female experience, but also provides a framework within which her more informal and personal writings make sense and take on major significance.

Readers wishing to explore markers of lesbian and/or homoerotic energy between women point to the following: the relationship between Mary Datchett and Katherine Hilbery in *Night and Day* (1919); Sally and Clarissa's youthful liaison, as well as Miss Kilman's somewhat predatory interest in Clarissa's daughter, in *Mrs. Dalloway* (1925); the intimate connections between Lily Briscoe and Mrs. Ramsey in *To the Lighthouse* (1927); Rhoda's characterization in *The Waves* (1931); the characterization of Peggy, as well as Kitty's attachment to Mrs. Fripp, in *The Years* (1937); Miss LaTrobe's representation in *Between the Acts* (1941); and short stories such as "Slater's Pins Have No Points" (1928) and "Kew Gardens" (1919).     *Toni A.H. McNaron*

### Bibliography

Bell, Quentin. *Virginia Woolf: A Biography*. New York: Harcourt Brace Jovanovich, 1972.

DeSalvo, Louise. *Virginia Woolf: The Impact of Childhood Sexual Abuse on Her Life and Work*. Boston: Beacon, 1989.

Marcus, Jane, ed. *New Feminist Essays on Virginia Woolf*. Lincoln: University of Nebraska Press, 1981.

Poole, Roger. *The Unknown Virginia Woolf*. Cambridge: Cambridge University Press, 1978.

Stape, J.H., ed. *Virginia Woolf: Interviews and Recollections*. Iowa City: University of Iowa Press, 1995.

*See also* English Literature, Twentieth Century; Mansfield, Katherine; Sackville-West, Vita; Smyth, Dame Ethel Mary

### Work

It is at work—not asleep, not interacting in relationships, not in recreation—that most people, including lesbians, spend the majority of their time. While some lesbians work at home (earning money, caring for loved ones, raising children), most work outside the home for pay.

Yet, until the 1990s, with rare exceptions, lesbians were invisible in the workplace. In the 1990s, however, increasing numbers of lesbians were willing to be open, and U.S.-based, openly lesbian individuals and groups were beginning to achieve recognition for their accomplishments from their peers and bosses, as well as in the media. In other parts of the world, lesbians were just beginning to grapple with the issues involved in coming out at work.

Although, throughout history, some self-identified lesbians have married men or been supported by their families or an inheritance, in the modern period, many lesbians have remained unmarried and have worked to support themselves and sometimes others. And, despite rampant discrimination, particularly in the past, lesbians have also been well represented among the highest-achieving working women.

### History

At the turn of the twentieth century, there was a socially sanctioned tradition for a pair of independent (middle- or upper-class) women to live together in "Boston marriages," and a number of these relationships would be called lesbian by today's definition. Many of these women worked in academia, nursing, philanthropy, or other professions open to middle-class women of the time. Some had the benefit of inherited wealth, but others were completely self-supporting. Much less is known about the lives of working-class women, although some butch women chose to pursue professions and trades otherwise restricted to men by dressing as men and living their lives as "passing women" (as did a few middle- and upper-class women).

The World War II era enabled large numbers of women to develop a lesbian identity. The all-female environment of military society, improved job training for women, the availability of jobs in urban centers, and the economic demand for the increased participation of women in the work force led to significant changes in women's life choices. For some, personal and financial independence meant that they were able to associate with other like-minded women in the service or in the cities.

After the war, lesbian communities began to thrive in urban areas. Among the working and middle classes, butch women are known to have sought work in traditional male, unionized trades, not always successfully; femme women typically obtained work in traditionally female occupations, such as waitressing, piecework, secretarial work, teaching, nursing, and social work. The economic disparity between breadwinning femmes and out-of-work or underemployed butches sometimes resulted in a reversal of the typical male-female heterosexual roles in lesbian society, not always to the mutual satisfaction of the lesbian partners.

An exclusive upper-class lesbian society also began to thrive; it included women of monied backgrounds who worked in the arts, journalism, law, and other fields that were beginning to open to women. In some cases, these privileged women were known to be lesbians by their heterosexual peers and colleagues. Academics and novelists began to show an interest in lesbian lives, and the middle-class working woman was among the objects of their scrutiny. Biographies of women like Gertrude Stein and Alice B. Toklas, or of Eleanor Roosevelt and her friendship networks, detail the overlapping social and professional circles in which they moved, while pulp novelists and semisympathetic social reporters of the period paint a far less happy picture of the lives of the more "run-of-the mill" lesbian professional. Typically, her workplace world was marked by fear of discovery, reports that are confirmed by such histories as Elizabeth Kennedy and Madeline Davis's *Boots of Leather, Slippers of Gold: The History of a Lesbian Community* (1996), and Esther Newton's *Cherry Grove, Fire Island: Sixty Years in America's First Gay and Lesbian Town* (1993).

The feminist movement of the 1960s and 1970s saw tremendous participation by middle-class lesbians, who began to organize their own political and social circles and to publish their own writing. In these circles, moneymaking was often scorned, and, as a result, downward mobility became fashionable among some middle- and upper-class lesbians. Many of these women were attracted to traditional working-class jobs in factories, farms, and the crafts, along with the newer "women's community" positions in food service, entertainment, and nonprofit work. However, particularly in the 1980s, self-identified lesbians also began to move into the professions, including teaching, law, medicine, business, and academia, alongside closeted lesbians and heterosexual women.

In the 1990s, the largest number of lesbians could be found in the pink-collar (typically female) professions, such as retail, restaurant, or secretarial work, preschool through high school education, child care, social work, mental health, allied health care, government and nonprofit agencies, library science, and residential real estate rentals and sales. As some of these fields have not lent themselves to workplace organizing of any kind, it is not surprising that few lesbians within them have become visible. However, lesbians are well represented among lesbian and gay associations in education, allied health care, and government agencies and have been among the leaders for change in these fields.

Lesbian also increasingly entered blue-collar (typically male working-class) professions as laborers, transport workers, factory workers, police officers, firefighters, and military personnel, although not to the same degree as gay men, because these fields remain so heavily male dominated.

It is in the white-collar professions that lesbians have become most visible, gaining access in large numbers to well-paying jobs in law, medicine, business, architecture and engineering, higher education, politics, and high technology. They have joined lesbian and gay and lesbian professional associations in increasing numbers, and, a number have come out in local and national media as part of their effort to gain specific workplace protections or benefits.

## The Workplace Closet and Coming Out

It was only in the 1990s that significant numbers of municipalities, states, and businesses have adopted nondiscrimination laws or policies that encompass sexual orientation. While these provisions cover the majority of American workers, they tend to be most prevalent in certain industries and geographic areas, and their enforcement is uneven. Hence, many lesbians remain afraid of coming out at work—and this fear is inadvertently reinforced by studies, produced by national and local gay organizations and publicized in the lesbian and gay and mainstream press, that highlight workplace discrimination in order to secure additional protective legislation.

For some, staying in the closet is seen as a surival issue—physical attacks in the workplace on blue-collar lesbians are not unknown. For other working-class women, who are one paycheck away from public assistence, the closet also feels safer than the possibility of being fired for being gay. Many lesbians in the newly expanded white-collar professions also feel especially fearful of coming out at work, because it was only in the 1980s that large numbers of women gained access to these better-paying jobs. However, no statistical data exist to support this fear. Rather, these white-collar positions tend to exist in industries and locations that offer the best protection against discrimination; moreover, women tend to work for companies that have among the best track records of hiring and promoting openly gay men and lesbians. In fact, the experience of lesbian professionals who are out at work shows that those who try to remain closeted or "undeclared" are more likely to experience harassment, as well as more subtle forms of discrimination (Friskopp and Silverstein 1995).

There are other benefits to being open. Since open communication about private life is often expected among co-workers, lesbians who are not out may be thought of as trying to hide something and, thus, not to be trusted. Alternatively, they may be perceived, and subsequently stereotyped, as single heterosexual women. Single heterosexual women are often thought of as unreliable (she's just going to get married, follow her husband's career, or have a baby and leave the workforce), flirtatious (she's sleeping her way to the top), or lacking social skills (why can't she get a man?).

In contrast, open lesbians ironically benefit from the typical stereotypes of lesbians—hardworking, appropriately aggressive, career minded (Friskopp and Silverstein 1995). Furthermore, open lesbians have the opportunity to allow bosses, coworkers, and subordinates to know them well, which those who are out say typically leads to closer relationships and more career benefits. Open lesbians' relationships with women may improve because they can participate in the usual forms of female workplace bonding by talking about relationships or dating. In particular, their relationships with men are improved because there is no longer any innuendo about the possibility of a sexual relationship. Schneider (1984) found that open lesbians also were less likely to report sexual harassment than were closeted lesbians. Finally, open lesbians are also more likely to find mentors among, and to provide mentoring to, other lesbians and gay men.

Another disadvantage of the staying in the closet closet is that, despite the lesbian baby boom, lesbians who intend to remain closeted at work typically avoid having children. In contrast, those who are open are more likely to feel the necessary social support for motherhood. Lesbian mothers who are open at work have reported being the recipient of social niceties, from smiles to baby showers, and corporate support, including such soft benefits as time off and such hard benefits as insurance for their partners and children (see, for example, Benkov 1994).

Finally, in contrast to the stereotype of the office romance between male boss and female employee, Schneider (1984) found that lesbians and bisexual women were more likely than heterosexual women to become involved in sexual relationships in the workplace. These were not brief affairs, but serious relationships, and typically took place between coworkers of equal status, although as women move into positions of authority, more relationships between women of unequal status may occur. Friskopp and Silverstein (1995) found a number of closeted lesbians and bisexual women who engaged in sexual harassment. This may be because lesbians see themselves as having fewer choices in meeting a suitable partner. So when a lesbian or bisexual woman meets a lesbian in her own workplace, she may be tempted to try to develop the relationship.

Closeted workplace relationships have many pitfalls, such as the need to circumvent one partner reporting to the other, to arrange simultaneous geographic transfers, or to avoid each other if the relationship ends. Lesbians who are open at work are able to secure employer support in avoiding the problems that even an acknowledged relationship may pose (Friskopp and Silverstein 1995).

The closet is a vicious circle—the fewer lesbians who are out, the more dangerous it seems to be to come out. But the reverse is also true—as more lesbians come out at work, the safer coming out seems to be, and the more obvious its advantages are. Many lesbians in the 1990s were open to some, most, or all of their workplace colleagues and bosses, but, until the 1990s they did not had the opportunity to share their positive experiences with a wider audience. Thus, while examples of discrimination are well known, success stories have been less widely reported. The reporting of these stories, however, particularly when accompanied by profiles of open lesbians who helped the storyteller achieve her goals, creates an atmosphere in which coming out is more normative.

Some of the most-reported success stories involve group action to achieve domestic-partnership health insurance benefits. The number of companies, organizations, and public employers offering these benefits is growing rapidly, although the overall numbers remain small. The typical successful effort includes some lesbian and gay employees from every part of the workplace hierarchy coming out to achieve this goal (Winfield and Spielman 1995). Other goals for such groups include pension benefits, benefits for a partner's children, corporate philanthropy to gay and lesbian causes, targeted hiring among openly gay people, marketing to gay men and lesbians, and top-management support for local or national nondiscrimination legislation.

## Networking

Virtually every large U.S. city has a lesbian and gay professional and/or business association, and a number have lesbian-only groups as well. Outside the United States, there are also lesbian or lesbian and gay professional groups and business associations. Most are in Canada, with others in western Europe. Additionally, in many U.S. cities, specific groups exist for particular professions, such as law or medicine, etc., and lesbian participation in these groups tends to be strong in most areas and growing in business-oriented groups. More than one hundred major American companies have lesbian and gay employee associations, and these groups have also seen their lesbian participation grow, particularly as they have moved from informal gatherings of friends to officially recognized organizations (Friskopp and Silverstein 1995). Their numbers include both management and hourly employees. Some unions have also developed committees and caucuses for lesbian and gay issues.

Historically, gay men have been far more likely to engage in professional networking than lesbians have been. One reason is that, in general, lesbians are disinclined to participate in social functions or organizations that are predominately male or to read media targeted primarily to gay men. Another reason is that lesbian social life tends to circle around the monogamous couple and tight friendship groups, while gay men seek a more diverse social life that encourages networking with its resultant workplace benefits. However, through the 1990s, as lesbian and gay professional associations and employee groups supplanted these informal male social groups, lesbians increasingly availed themselves of the career opportunities provided by them (Friskopp and Silverstein 1995). Additionally, the opportunities for lesbian professionals to meet each other in lesbian-only settings multiplied and continued to grow.

While previously lesbians professionals could meet others like themselves only by chance at bars or through existing friendship circles, lesbian party and vacation promoters in the 1990s identified this group as a relatively affluent marketing niche and provided golf outings, cruises, tours, and other amusements for a national and, in some cases, international clientele. The events associated with the Dinah Shore golf tournament in Palm Springs, California, every spring, for example, have become a mecca for lesbian professionals.

Some lesbians professionals are also active in national and local lesbian or lesbian and gay organizations, which provide additional opportunities for friendship and networking. The few national lesbian organizations have also captured the devotion of lesbian professionals, who make valuable social and professional contacts while fund-raising for lesbian causes.

Opportunities for lesbians who work in pink- and blue-collar fields to network include workplace venues, such as gay and lesbian employee groups and union caucuses, and social venues, such as softball teams and bars. Large numbers of lesbians also gather at women's festivals, such as the one in Michigan, which provide other formal and informal networking opportunities.

## Conclusion

As lesbians move into increasing visibility in American life—both to each other and the heterosexual mainstream—the conditions for lesbians in the workplace will continue to improve. In other countries, such changes were just beginning in the late 1990s and will no doubt take different forms, based on the unique cultural experiences and needs of the lesbians in each location. In Canada, western Europe, Australia, New Zealand, South Africa, and Israel, among other places, lesbian workplace issues were discussed among friends, on the Internet, in the press, and occasionally in organizations, and these discussions were beginning to result in tangible advances. International organizations, sporting and cultural events, parties, and Gay and Lesbian Pride celebrations thrive as the most important venues for face-to-face networking regarding workplace issues for lesbians from these countries—as of 1998, there had been no large-scale conferences devoted solely to workplace themes, as there have been in the United States. Lesbians in eastern Europe, Asia, and other places were also beginning to make their voices heard on these issues.

*Sharon Silverstein*

### Bibliography

Benkov, Laura. *Reinventing the Family: The Emerging Story of Lesbian and Gay Parents.* New York: Crown, 1994.

W

De La O, Maria. "Lesbians in Corporate America." In *Dyke Life*. Ed. Karla Jay. New York: Basic Books, 1995, pp. 265–281.

Friskopp, Annette, and Sharon Silverstein. *Straight Jobs, Gay Lives*. New York: Scribners, 1995.

Hall, Marny. "The Lesbian Corporate Experience." *Journal of Homosexuality* 12:3–4 (1986), 28–33.

Levine, Martin P., and Robin Leonard. "Discrimination Against Lesbians in the Work Force." *Signs: Journal of Women in Culture and Society* 9:4 (1984), 700–710.

Magee, Bryan. "Lesbians at Work." In *One in Twenty: A Study of Homosexuality in Men and Womem*. New York: Stein and Day, 1966.

Rast, Richard, and Lourdes Rodriguez-Nogues, eds. *Out in the Workplace*. Boston: Alyson, 1995.

Schneider, Beth E. "Peril and Promise: Lesbians' Workplace Participation." In *Women-Identified Women*. Ed. Trudi Darty and Sandee Potter. Palo Alto, Calif.: Mayfield, 1984, pp. 211–230.

Vida, Ginny, ed. *The New Our Right To Love: A Lesbian Resource Book*. New York: Touchstone, 1996.

Winfield, Liz, and Susan Spielman. *Straight Talk about Gays in the Workplace*. New York: AMACOM, 1995.

*See also* Coming Out; Discrimination; Domestic Partnership; Economics; Labor Movement: Sexual Harassment

## Wu Zao (ca. 1800s)

Chinese lesbian poet; also published as Wu Tsao. The exact date of her birth and death are unknown. Wu Tsao was a poet of the Ch'ing (Manchu) Dynasty (1644–1911). During this dynasty, the writing of poetry was considered enough of a valuable commodity to be included in a woman's dowry. Wu Zao was the daughter of a merchant, and, later, the wife of one, helping both her father and her husband in their shops, and, as such, she had more freedom of movement than most other women of her class.

Wu Zao's songs and poems were very popular and sung all over China. She was considered one of two leading women *tz'u* poets in her dynasty and highly regarded as one of the best women poets of all time. Seven of her poems have been published in translation by Rexroth and Chung (1972), although only three are titled. Unlike other Chinese women poets, she wrote about a variety of subjects and referred to other poets in her works. Her poetry reflects her unhappy marriage and also expresses an open eroticism directed toward courtesans and other women. The most explicit of these, "For the Courtesan Ch'ing Lin," evokes the other woman's "slender body" and the poet's loss of speech and memory upon seeing her smile. Wu Zao also draws upon imagery of "leaning against the bamboos," which was commonly used by male poets, specifically to refer to courtesans longing for their special lover while in their gardens.

Ca. 1837, Wu Zao went into seclusion and became a Taoist priestess. *Akilah Monifa*

### Bibliography

Rexroth, Kenneth, and Ling Chung. *Women Poets of China*. New York: New Directions, 1972. More information on Wu Zao is available on the World Wide Web at http://www.sappho.com/poetry/wu_tsao.htm

*See also* China; Chinese Literature

# Y

## Yosano Akiko (1878–1942)

Japanese poet and writer. Born Hô Shô, Yosano Akiko was a woman of extraordinary physical, intellectual, and emotional vitality. In 1900, Yosano and her close friend Yamakawa Tomiko (1879–1909) fell in love with Yosano Tekkan (Yosano Hiroshi [1893–1935]), who considered himself the leader of the new poetry movement, and he, apparently with some preference for the "softer" Yamakawa, with both of them. Yosano Akiko married him in 1901; however, Yosano Tekkan remained actively involved with both a former wife and with Yamakawa .

Yosano Akiko's first collection of poems, published the same year under the title *Midaregami* (Tangled Hair), won her instant success. Her poems were praised for the freshness of their language, the boldness of their imagery, and their passion. In 1905, *Koigoromo* (Robe of Love) was published, coauthored with Yamakawa and Chino Masako (1880–1946).

As Yosano Akiko's reputation climbed, Yosano Tekkan's fell. To help him recover his spirits and his poetic inspiration, she raised funds to send him to Europe in autumn 1911; Yosano herself followed in the spring. Back in Japan, she continued to write under the pressure of endless financial struggles. In the course of her life, she produced many collections of poetry, novels, essays, children's stories, and fairy tales. She also did several translations of classical Japanese literature into modern language, including a complete translation, of great beauty of style, of the classic *The Tale of Genji* (ca. 1020). Despite caring for her familiy of eleven children, Yosano kept her house open to new poets and writers. She died from a stroke in 1942 at the age of sixty-three.

Nonfictional sources about Yosano Akiko's life during the first few years of her marriage are scant, but fictional ones suggest that the relationship between Yosano Tekkan, Yamakawa, and herself was intense and complex. Yamakawa, who died young of tuberculosis, is considered to be the "white lily" (*shiroyuri*) referred to in many of Yosano Akiko's early poems. If so, the following example would have to be translated differently and, instead of being cited as one of her most narcisstic poems, would, rather, reveal Yosano's attraction to her friend: "Bathing in the spring, / Lapping in the warm water lay / A fair white lily — / The summer of my twentieth year / Was lovely to my gaze" (trans. E.A. Cranston). It is possible that the androgyny of the poetic speaker in *Midaregami* reflects a deeper complexity in Yosano, which did not permit her to assume any one-dimensional sexual identity, anymore than the ambiguity of poetry allows for a single interpretation. *Richmod Bollinger*

### Bibliography

Beichman, Janine. "Yosano Akiko: Return to the Female." *Japan Quarterly* 37:2 (1990), 204–228.

Larson, Phyllis Hyland. "Yosano Akiko and the Re-Creation of the Female Self: An Autogynography." *Journal of the Association of Teachers of Japanese* 25:1 (1991), 11–26 (Special Issue on Yosano Akiko).

Rodd, Laurel Rasplica. "Yosano Akiko and the Taishô Debate over the 'New Woman.'" In *Recreating Japanese Women, 1600–1945*. Ed. Gail Lee Bernstein. Berkeley: University of California Press, 1991, pp. 175–198.

Ueda Makoto. *Modern Japanese Poets and the Nature of Literature*. Stanford, Calif.: Stanford University Press, 1983.

*See also* Japan

## Yoshiya Nobuko (1896–1973)

Japanese writer. Yoshiya Nobuko is credited with developing the now pervasive genre of "shôjo fiction" (shôjo shosetsu). Shôjo does not translate easily into English: Its most rudimentary meaning is "girl," but shôjo more specifically refers to a category of problematic females between puberty and marriage that was invented in the late nineteenth century. The shôjo remains an ambiguous figure: She is at once desirable and dangerous and has long been a favorite scapegoat for social disorder. Yoshiya's shôjo fiction, which dwelled on passionate friendship and a world without dominant males, inspired the emergence of a reflexive subculture that overlapped with that of the female fans of all-female revue theaters, such as Takarazuka, whose founder collaborated with Yoshiya on several productions.

Yoshiya was born in Niigata, the only daughter in an affluent family of five children; it seems that dealing with her bureaucrat father and four brothers left Yoshiya with a jaded view of males—the title of a short story she published in Kaizô (Reconstruction), a leading, progressive journal is telling: "Dannasama muyô" (Husbands Are Useless [1931]). A self-identified lesbian—she is also recognized for her feminist politics in postwar Japan—Yoshiya met her life partner, Monma Chiyo (1907–), in 1923; their fifty-year relationship, which ended with Yoshiya's death, was referred to in the mass media as, dôseiai fûfu (same-sex-love [or homosexual] husband and wife). With her short-cropped hair, Yoshiya was also called a garçon (garusonnu [boy]) by conservative social critics, who, nevertheless, dissociated the writer's private life from her prodigious literary output and public service, including a stint as a wartime correspondent. A 1935 article on Yoshiya in the popular monthly Hanashi (Gossip) introduced her as follows: "There may be women who don't know who heads the Women's Patriotic Association, but there is not a single woman alive who doesn't know who Yoshiya Nobuko is." Given her widespread popularity and following in Japan, it is most odd that Yoshiya has been ignored by Euro-American scholars of Japanese literature, who have yet to complicate the received, androcentric, and "safe" canon.

Yoshiya's numerous essays and short stories were published throughout her career in most of the leading journals and popular magazines, and her many novels and nonfiction texts—including Tokugawa no fujintachi (Tokugawa Wives [1966]), Nyonin Heike (Heike Women [1971]), Onna no yûjô

(Female Friendship [1933–1934]), Arashi no bara (Stormy Rose [1930–1931]), Watashi no mita hito (People I Have Known [1963]), and Hana monogatari (Flower Tales [1916–1924]), perhaps her most famous book, which has been used in the past as a school text—continue to be reprinted and sold by major publishers.          Jennifer E. Robertson

### Bibliography

Robertson, Jennifer. Takarazuka: Sexual Politics and Popular Culture in Modern Japan. Berkeley: University of California Press, 1998.
Yoshitake Teruko. Nyonin Yoshiya Nobuko. Tokyo: Bunshun Bunko, 1986.

See also All-Female Revues (Japan); Japan

## Yourcenar, Marguerite (1903–1987)

French writer. Born Marguerite Cleenewerck de Crayencour of a Belgian mother, who died giving birth to her, and a French father, Marguerite Yourcenar was educated privately. In 1921, her first volume of poetry was published at her father's expense, appearing under the anagrammatic pseudonym "Marg. Yourcenar." In 1929, she produced her first major work, Alexis, a novella treating male homosexuality. In 1939, Yourcenar moved to the United States to join Grace Frick (1903–1979), with whom she lived until Frick's death. They settled in Northeast Harbor, Maine, where Frick helped revise and translate some of Yourcenar's best-known works, such as Mémoires d'Hadrien (Memoirs of Hadrian, 1951) and L'oeuvre au noir (The Abyss, 1968). In 1980, Yourcenar became the first woman elected to the Académie Française. After her death, her ashes were buried next to Frick's in Maine.

Yourcenar's attitudes toward sexuality, in life and literature, were complex. She was discreet about her personal life, choosing to leave her relationships with Frick and others in "the shadows that suit the essential things in life so well" (Yourcenar 1984). Furthermore, while almost all of her works touch on male homosexuality, references to lesbianism are rare, aside from some suggestive remarks in Quoi? L'Éternité (What? Eternity [1988]), the third volume of her autobiography, including this description of her first, adolescent experience with another girl: "[A]n instinct, a premonition of intermittent desires experienced and satisfied later in the course of my life, allowed me to find right away the posture and the movements needed by two women loving each other."

In general, Yourcenar was not so much "closeted" as impatient with modern categories of sexual identity: Throughout her writing, she insists that the modern vocabulary for sexuality is inadequate to express the infinite "plasticity of desire." The protagonist of *Alexis* asks, surely in Yourcenar's voice: "How can a scientific term explain a life?" Yourcenar herself always rejected the word "homosexuality" as "too medical," preferring to speak of "sensual choices." While disdaining public polemic about sexuality, she was not insensitive to the political ramifications of having what she called "minority tastes"; in interviews, she advocated sexual "liberty" and drew analogies between homosexuals and other victims of intolerance.　　　*Erin Carlston*

## Bibliography

Farrell, C. Frederick, Jr., and Edith R. Farrell. *Marguerite Yourcenar in Counterpoint*. Lanham, Md., and New York: University Press of America, 1983.

Howard, Joan. *From Violence to Vision: Sacrifice in the Works of Marguerite Yourcenar*. Carbondale: Southern Illinois University Press, 1992.

Savigneau, Josyane. *Marguerite Yourcenar: Inventing a Life*. Trans. Joan E. Howard. Chicago: University of Chicago Press, 1993.

Yourcenar, Marguerite, and Matthieu Galey. *With Open Eyes: Conversations with Matthieu Galey*. Trans. Arthur Goldhammer. Boston: Beacon, 1984.

*See also* French Literature


## Yugoslavia, Former

Socialist Federal Republic (SFR) located on the Balkan peninsula in southeastern Europe; formed at the end of World War II (1945). Until 1991, Yugoslavia consisted of six republics, with 22 million inhabitants, twenty-four spoken languages, and three main religions (Serbian Orthodox, Catholic, and Islamic). The six republics had their own criminal codes, so that laws against adult gay male sex differed in five of the republics and did not exist in the republic of Slovenia. Citizens had the freedom of travel, passports, and visas.

The Yugoslav state was organized as a one-party system, under the control of the Communist Party. Basic human rights were respected, including the right to social and economic security, education, and reproductive freedom. State ideology supported women's right to work; extreme poverty was eradicated by 1990; the law on abortion was one of the most radical in Europe; birth leave was eight to twelve months; and men had a right to birth and sickness leave. On the other hand, women had the classic double burden of work in the home and in the paid workforce.

Moreover, freedom of thought and speech was not permitted. Feminist organizing, which had begun by the end of 1978, was considered an activity against the system; there were no nongovernemental registered women's groups; and the right to be a lesbian almost did not exist.

On June 27, 1991—ironically, the day when lesbian and gay activists in Belgrade, for the first time, organized a public discussion for the International Gay and Lesbian Pride Day—the Serb authorities started the war in the republics of Slovenia and Croatia, signaling the end of the state of Yugoslavia. From that day until the signing of the Dayton Peace Treaty in November 1995, the war was carried on in Bosnia and Hercegovina and Croatia. As a result, five million refugees and displaced persons were produced, as well as ca. 400,000 dead and many thousands injured. Five new independent states were created: Slovenia, Croatia, Bosnia and Hercegovina, Macedonia, and the Federal Republic of Yugoslavia (made up of Serbia and Montenegro).

### Lesbian Organizing in Croatia

In the former Yugoslavia, lesbian organizing began in Ljubljana, Slovenia, when, in 1987, Suzana Tratnik initiated Lilith LL, inspiring women's groups in Belgrade (Serbia) and Zagreb (Croatia). Natasa Lalic, at that time preparing her graduate thesis on prejudices against lesbians and gay men, initiated, in 1989, the first lesbian group in Zagreb, called Lila Initiative. Some lesbians who founded this group were also active in a feminist action group, Tresnjevka, that was a charter member of the first SOS Hotline for Women and Children Victims of Violence in eastern Europe. Lila Initiative organized weekly meetings, discussions, and workshops. The group was very successful in supporting and strengthening lesbian identity, and more than hundred lesbians were, in some way, involved in the group.

In May 1990, when the Croatian pro-nationalist party won the first multiparty elections, the women's group Tresnjevka lost its meeting space, after which Lila Initiative dissolved. In 1992, LIGMA (Lesbian and Gay Men Action) was founded as a section of the Transnational Party in Zagreb. The group actively lobbied for lesbian and gay rights in public. But, as before, lesbians and gays lost their space, and their activites were reduced after that.

In 1995, lesbians from several women's groups organized women-only disco nights in the club Mobilus in Zagreb. The unexpected attention of the media caused fear among lesbians, which was substantiated when police raided the club immediately after its opening and every time there was a women-only night. After four nights, this project ended. November 1997 saw the beginning of a Lesbian Line-Kontra Project, a project that gathers activists and lawyers to support lesbians and create more social space for them in Zagreb.

### Lesbian Organizing in Serbia

In December 1990, a few women and men in Belgrade, spurred by letters from the Rosa Club in Ljubljana, began to discuss founding a Belgrade equivalent. The word spread, and the group rapidly grew in size. However, most members were gay men, with only a handful of lesbians. Shortly after, in 1991, Arkadia, the Lesbian and Gay Lobby, was formed. Its first public action was organized on June 27, 1991. After the beginning of the war, two of its founders (Lepa Mladjenovic and Dejan Nebrigic) participated in founding the women's peace group known as Women in Black and the Antiwar Center in Belgrade. Most of their time was now dedicated to antiwar activities. The war revived nationalist feelings, including among some gay men in Arkadia. Others were strongly opposed to this attitude and decided that Arkadia shall be clear about its politics on ending nationalism and all kinds of discrimination, including discrimination against women.

By 1995, more lesbians had joined Arkadia, and the decision was made to split from the men's group and form Labris (Group for Lesbian Human Rights). Lesbians started to meet in the space of the Womens Studies Center. Labris worked in two directions: empowering lesbian identity through workshop discussions and lesbian studies lectures, and lobbying for lesbian human rights in the public sphere. This is done through *Labris Bulletin*, published twice a year, and through essays on lesbian rights, translations of lesbian texts, interviews in the media, and leaflets.

In the spring of 1995, four activists from Labris were attacked by three men, with many hate words. This hate act happened while the war in Bosnia was going on and while the Serbian regime daily manufactured hatred toward Muslims, Albanians, and Croats. Lesbians of Labris were present at the 1995 United Nations–sponsored World Conference on Women in Beijing, China, and at other regional conferences and international events.

### Contemporary Issues

In the summer of 1997, the First Meeting of Lesbians of Former Yugoslavia was organized. Forty lesbians met for five days, holding workshops, video shows, poetry readings, and sporting events. After living through the pain of the war, separated by the politics of hatred and nationalism, the lesbians met together for the first time. It was a deeply emotional event that heralded reconciliation and renewal. Nevertheless, some dilemmas remained for lesbians in the former Yugoslavia. For example, what is the relationship between feminist awareness and lesbian identity? The history of lesbian activism in the states of the former Yugoslavia demonstrates that, during the Communist regime, those lesbians who started lesbian organizing came out from, and through, feminist groups. Those who joined later were less, or not at all, involved in feminist politics. Another dilemma is: To what extent can lesbian groups afford to be political and still have members? Most lesbians come to groups to socialize, and, when political ideas are introduced, many lesbians do not join. Most significant, perhaps, is the issue of nationalism, which, by the late 1990s, lesbians had yet to explore in depth within their own groups.

*Lepa Mladjenovic*

### Bibliography

Galkovic, Sanja, ed. "Lesbians in Croatia: A Critical Review of the Lesbian Question in Socialism." *The Lesbian Review of Books* 4:1 (Fall 1997), 21–22.

*See also* Slovenia

# Z

## Zimbabwe

Republic in southern Africa formerly known as Rhodesia. Zimbabwe is bordered by Mozambique and Botswana to the east and west and Zambia and South Africa to the north and south. It has a population of more than 11 million, and its largest city is Harare (formerly known as Salisbury), which is also the capital. The majority of its people, nearly 55 percent, are Christians, while most Africans maintain traditional beliefs, and Asians follow Islam or Hinduism. English, Chishona, and Sindebele are the official languages. Known as Southern Rhodesia, the territory became a British colony in 1923 when it was transferred from the British South Africa Company to the United Kingdom. After Northern Rhodesia declared independence as Zambia in 1964, Southern Rhodesia declared independence and was renamed Rhodesia in 1965. It was declared a republic in March 1970 and, after several major constitutional reforms in the 1980s, became Zimbabwe. Since the 1960s, African nationalist movements—notably, the Zimbabwe African People's Union (ZAPU) and the Zimbabwe African National Union (ZANU), among others—have played a significant role in politics. Zimbabwe is self-governing through a parliament, whose members are elected every six years, and a president, who is elected by members of the parliament for that term. The president appoints a cabinet, which is accountable to the parliament.

Gays and Lesbians of Zimbabwe (GALZ) was formed in 1989. At that time, its primary objective was to ease the isolation felt by lesbians and gay men. Much of GALZ's early work was directed toward organizing social events where lesbians and gay men could meet each other and form friend-ships. In time, it became apparent that there was a crucial need for GALZ to offer a counseling service to homosexuals and lesbians grappling with issues such as coming out, HIV/AIDS, and discrimination. GALZ's attempt, in 1993, to place a counseling advertisement in the *Herald,* a national daily newspaper was the catalyst that turned GALZ into a political organization fighting for gay and lesbian equality in Zimbabwe. The *Herald* rejected the GALZ advertizement, stating that the newspaper was a "family" paper. As of 1998 GALZ still could not advertize its counseling facility. GALZ has gone from a little-known organization in southern Africa to one that is globally recognized for having stood up to scathing attacks from the Zimbabwean government. This recognition has largely been a result of GALZ being banned from having a stand at the Zimbabwe International Book Fair in 1995. The theme of this particular event was "human rights and justice." President Robert Mugabe's opening speech, in which he said that "homosexuals have no rights at all" and were "worse than pigs and dogs," reverberated around the world, catapaulting Zimbabwe's minority gay and lesbian group into the limelight. Subsequently, GALZ managed to set up a resource/drop-in center in Harare and to secure funding from international donors who realize that GALZ has a unique contribution to make to the fledgling and beleagured human rights movement in Zimbabwe.

*Bev Clark*

### Bibliography

Desai, Gaurav. "Out in Africa." In *Sex Positives? The Cultural Politics of Dissident Sexualities* (*Genders* 25). Ed. Thomas Forster, Carol Siegel, and Ellen E. Berry. New York and

London: New York University Press, 1997, pp. 120–143.

*See also* Human Rights; International Organizations

## 'zines

Small-press publications that are known for being "homemade" or cheaply produced and often written for a very specific audience or subculture. 'zines (pronounced zeenz), sometimes referred to as zines or fanzines, take their name from the end of the word "magazine"; yet they resist conventions in the dominant magazine industry. Moreover, 'zines that define themselves as lesbian or queer usually have as conflicted a relationship with more mainstream feminist, lesbian, and gay newspapers and magazines as they do with the heterosexual establishment. Efforts to define 'zines are inevitably inadequate since they are vastly different from each other and defy fixed definitions. A significant element of the 'zine movement, if it can be called a movement, has been to reject any strategy of assimilation and embrace a politics of difference.

Some sources trace 'zine-like culture in the United States as far back as the early 1930s and 1940s, when science-fiction devotees began to copy and distribute their reviews and musings within a growing subculture of enthusiasts. The term "fanzines" is a contraction of "fan magazines" used by science-fiction fans to distinguish their publications from "prozines," or professionally produced magazines marketed for profit. 'zines have been an important form of expression and networking for particular groups and subcultures, such as those interested in punk rock, professional wrestling, comics, or queer politics. Many agree that the technological advances in photocopying and personal computing in the 1980s enabled a boom in the 'zine scene. Cheap copying and easy desktop publishing meant that access to exclusive and expensive resources was no longer required to produce and distribute information. As the editors of *The World of 'zines: A Guide to the Independent Magazine Revolution* (1992) write: "[M]ost 'zines start out with the realization that one need [not] be merely a passive consumer of media. Everyone can be a producer. . . . Generally, they're created by one person, for love rather than money." Many 'zines take this democratization of publishing further and reduce hierarchical editorial power. This is epitomized, for example, in Amateur Press Associations (APAs), in which contributors send multiple copies of their submissions to a coordinator, who collates the issue and sends it back out to all participants. Quite a few 'zines last many years, while many others come and go according to the publisher's interest, time, and resources.

Austin and Gregg (1993) locate the beginning of lesbian and queer 'zines within punk youth culture. According to them, it was lesbian and gay punks who first employed the fanzine model to add a queer slant to the straight punk scene and an outlaw sensibility to mainstream lesbian and gay publishing. They cite *J.D.s* (short for juvenile delinquents) as the first queer punk 'zine to hit the streets (Toronto, 1986). After the post-Stonewall (1969) rise in the number of newspapers and magazines geared toward a general feminist, lesbian, or gay public, 'zines emerged to address more specific audiences and subcultures within the larger population.

Many of these small alternative publications deliberately situate themselves against the big-name publications, such as the *Advocate* and *off our backs*. For example, the editors of *Bimbox* (Toronto) wrote in their summer 1990 issue that "magazines like *The Advocate* and *Out/Look* have but one mandate: to systematically render the entire international Lesbian and Gay population brain-dead." The anti-magazine position contests the notion that a unified movement or community of lesbians and gays exists at all. 'zines accomplish this in a variety of ways. *Madwoman* (Chicago, Illinois) and *Not Your Bitch* (St. Paul, Minnesota) take a separatist (women-only) stance in opposition to the dominance of gay male material in many of the slick magazines and established newspapers. *P.C. Casualties*, (Ann Arbor, Michigan), a cogender 'zine, attacks the antiporn position adopted by some lesbian feminists and demands acknowledgment of lesbian sexual diversity.

Some 'zines emerged to fill the gaps in the dominant heterosexist culture, as well as in the white, middle-class feminist, lesbian, gay, and queer mainstream. These have included the African American publications *Black Lace*, *Blk*, and *Ache*; the Asian American *Shamakami*, *Trikone*, and *Phoenix Rising*; and the Latina *Esto No Tiene Nombre* and *conmoción*. Other 'zines aim to explode the myth that all lesbians share a common sexuality. *Brat Attack* and *Up Our Butts* are only two of the many 'zines that uabashedly explore sadomasochism (S/M). *Fat Girl* caters to "Fat Dykes and the Women Who Want Them." *Girljock* presents sexy images of lesbian athletes, along with humor and commentary about dykes and sports. *Quim*, out of London, advertises itself as a 'zine "for dykes of all sexual persuasions"; similarly, the standpoint of *Taste of Latex* (San Francisco, California) is "polysexual." The proliferation of sex 'zines demonstrates that desire is much more specific and complex than a simplistic binary division between heterosexuality and homosexuality implies. Bisexual and transgender 'zines have added significantly to the variety, with contributions such as *Anything That Moves*, *Bi Girl World*, and *Boystown* for female-to-male transsexuals.

Since many lesbian, gay, feminist, and alternative bookstores have become hubs for the distribution of 'zines, fans of these specialized publications have multiplied in the last decades of the twentieth century. Electronic 'zines are increasingly available on local computer networks and the Internet. To aid in the exploration of this medium, several 'zines devote themselves solely to reviewing other 'zines. Well known in the 1980s and 1990s, *Factsheet 5* regularly includes a category of queer 'zine reviews, primarily written by San Francisco reviewer Lawrence Roberts (Larry-Bob), who also created his own bimonthly review, *queer zine explosion*.

*Kate Burns*

### Bibliography

Austin, S. Bryn, and Pam Gregg. "A Freak Among Freaks: The 'Zine Scene." In *Sisters, Sexperts, Queers: Beyond the Lesbian Nation*. Ed. Arlene Stein. New York: Penguin, 1993.

Berlant, Lauren, and Elizabeth Freeman. "Queer Nationality." *Boundary 2* 19:1 (Spring 1992), 149–180.

Gunderloy, Mike, and Cari Goldberg Janice. *The World of 'zines: A Guide to the Independent Magazine Revolution*. New York: Penguin, 1992.

Larry-Bob. *queer zine explosion* (Ongoing). Send inquiries to Box 591275, San Francisco, CA, 94159–1275, U.S.A.

Vale, V., ed. *Research: 'zines*. 2 vols. San Francisco: V/Search, 1996.

***See also*** Cartoons and Comic Books; Publishing, Lesbian

# Index

Dauthendey, Elisabeth, 329
Davis, Bette, 142
Davis, Elizabeth Gould, 793
Davis, Katharine Bement, 226–27, 787
Davis, Madeline, 141, 172, 248, 320, 741, 787, 819
Davis, Tiny, 158
Davy, Babs, 765
de Acosta, Mercedes, 239, 323
de Balzac, Honoré, 316, 475
de Beauvoir, Simone, 98, 198, 313, 318, 449
de Belbeuf, Marquise, 567, 768
de Brantôme, Pierre de Boudeilles, 309, 315, 407, 469
de Burgos, Julia, 647
de Castro, Germaine, 227
de Castro, Rosalia, 198
de Cervantes, Miguel, 724–25
de Erauso, Catalina, 723, 724
de Fougères, Etienne, 499
de Greiff, Leon, 792
*De Homo-sexueelen*, 542
de Jong, Dola, 543
*De Kruisvaarder*, 119
de la Cruz, Juana Inès, 421–22, 438–39, 494, 644, 664
de la Parra, Teresa, 147, 439
de la Peña, Terri, 442
de Lamballe, Madame, 638
de Lauretis, Teresa, 583, 614
de Lempicka, Tamara, 70
de Mailly, Madame, 638
de Maupassant, Guy, 316
De Mille, Cecil B., 303
de Montaigne, Michel, 648
de Montesquieu, Baron, 316
de Montferrand, Helene, 318
de Murat, Madame, 310
de Musset, Alfred, 271, 666
de Nerciat, Andrea, 767
de Pizan, Christine, 789
de Polignac, Princess, 516, 711
de Pougy, Liane, 94, 271, 312, 317
de Sade, Marquis, 68
de Scudéry, Madeleine, 310, 667
de St. Mery, Moreau, 650
de Stael, Germaine, 667
de Swart, Saar, 542
*De Thuiswacht*, 543
de Tyard, Pontus, 315
de Vega, Lope, 724
*De Verliezers*, 119
*De Vier doden*, 543
*Dead Heat*, 72
*Death of the Heart, The*, 127
*Death Under Duress*, 309
d'Eaubonne, Françoise, 789
Debreta's, 480
Debrianskaya, Yevgenia, 657
*Decadencia*, 602
*Deephaven*, 29, 415
*Deerslayer, The*, 28
Defoe, Daniel, 262
DeGeneres, Ellen, 177, 188, 375, 401
Deken, Aagje, 541
Dekker, Thomas, 211

Delaney, L. Joyce, 12, 190
Delaria, Lea, 185
Delarue-Mardrus, Lucie, 94, 227, 312, 317
DeLaverie, Storme, 248, 768
*Deliver Us From Evie*, 299
Demarcy, Richard, 790
Dement, Linda, 60
*Demeter Flower, The*, 790
Deming, Barbara, 119, 227–29, *228*, 577
Demography, 229–30
Demonstrations and actions, 230–32
*Deneuve*
    see Curve
Denmark, 232–34
Dennis, Sandy, 375
Densmore, Adele, 13
*Der Kreis*, 746
*Der Rosenkavalier, 557*, 558
*Der Schritt hinuber*, 804
*Der Skorpion*, 329, 802–3
*Der Tag der Artemis*, 802–3
*Der Traum von Glück zerbricht*, 803
*Description of Millenium Hall, A*, 649
*Desert of the Heart*, 33, 144, 654
*Designing Women*, 758
Desmoines, Harriet, 622
*Desolacion*, 505
d'Estrées, Gabrielle, *310*, 310
Deutsch, Helene, 611, 613
Deutscher Freundschaftsverband, 86
DeVeaux, Alexis, 11
*Development*, 134
Developmental stage theory, 4
Dewson, Mary, 651, 786
Dewson, Molly, 344
Dhairyam, Sagri, 603
Diaghilev, Sergei, 656
*Diagnostic and Statistic Manual of Mental Disorders (DSM)*, 611, 776
*Dialogues de Carmélites*, 558
*Dialogues of the Courtesans*, 48, 175
*Diana: A Strange Autobiography*, 88
Diana Press, 104, 105, 322, 621, 622, 624
*Diana Victrix*, 30, 675
Diaries and letters, 234–36
*Diary*, 425
Diaz, Jean Marie, 201
Dibbell, Dominique, 765
Dickens, Charles, 263, 264
Dickerman, Marion, 344, 651
Dickinson, Anna, 741
Dickinson, Emily, 30, 237–38, 473, 574
Dickinson, Thomas, 767
Dickinson, Violet, 816
Diderot, Denis, 68, 271, 310, 316, 645
Didrikson, Mildred Ella "Babe" (Zaharias), 108, *238*, 238–39, 730
*DIE*, 746
*Die Büchse des Pandora*, 303
*Die Ehe der Mara Holm*, 803
*Die Freundin*, 86
*Die Freundinnen*, 330
*Die Günderode*, 328